MW01074620

Resistance and Liberation

In *Resistance and Liberation*, Douglas Porch continues his epic history of France at war. Emerging from the débâcle of 1940, France faced the quandary of how to rebuild military power, protect the empire, and resuscitate its global influence. While Charles de Gaulle rejected the armistice and launched his offshore crusade to reclaim French honor within the Allied camp, defeatists at Vichy embraced cooperation with the victorious Axis. The book charts the emerging dynamics of *la France libre* and the Alliance, Vichy collaboration, and the swelling resistance to the Axis occupation. From the campaigns in Tunisia and Italy to Liberation, Douglas Porch traces how de Gaulle sought to forge a French army and prevent civil war. He captures the experiences of ordinary French men and women caught up in war and defeat, the choices they made, the trials they endured, and how this has shaped France's memory of those traumatic years.

Douglas Porch is Distinguished Professor Emeritus and former Chair of the Department of National Security Affairs at the Naval Postgraduate School in Monterey, California. His previous books include *Defeat and Division: France at War, 1939–1942*, *Counterinsurgency: Exposing the Myths of the New Way of War*, *The Path to Victory: The Mediterranean Theater in World War II* (published in the UK as *Hitler's Mediterranean Gamble*), and *The French Secret Services: From the Dreyfus Affair to the Gulf War.*

ARMIES OF THE SECOND WORLD WAR

This is a major new series of histories of the armies of the key combatants in the Second World War. The books are written by leading military historians and consider key aspects of military activity for each of the major powers, including planning, intelligence, strategy and operations. As with the parallel Armies of the Great War series, military and strategic history is considered within the broader context of foreign policy aims and allied strategic relations, national mobilisation and the war's domestic social, political and economic effects.

A full list of titles in the series can be found at: www.cambridge.org/armiesofworldwarii

Resistance and Liberation

France at War, 1942–1945

Douglas Porch

CAMBRIDGE
UNIVERSITY PRESS

Shaftesbury Road, Cambridge CB2 8EA, United Kingdom

One Liberty Plaza, 20th Floor, New York, NY 10006, USA

477 Williamstown Road, Port Melbourne, VIC 3207, Australia

314–321, 3rd Floor, Plot 3, Splendor Forum, Jasola District Centre, New Delhi – 110025, India

103 Penang Road, #05–06/07, Visioncrest Commercial, Singapore 238467

Cambridge University Press is part of Cambridge University Press & Assessment, a department of the University of Cambridge.

We share the University's mission to contribute to society through the pursuit of education, learning and research at the highest international levels of excellence.

www.cambridge.org
Information on this title: www.cambridge.org/9781009161145

DOI: 10.1017/9781009161152

First published 2024

Printed in the United Kingdom by CPI Group Ltd, Croydon CR0 4YY

A catalogue record for this publication is available from the British Library.

A Cataloging-in-Publication data record for this book is available from the Library of Congress

ISBN 978-1-009-16114-5 Hardback

Contents

Figures

Maps

All maps can be viewed at www.cambridge.org/Porch

Preface

The first volume of this study of France in the Second World War tracked the collapse of the Third Republic in a disaster which, depending on the view of contemporaries and historians since, combined strategic miscalculation with a deficit of political will and popular resilience. US Ambassador to France William Bullitt was hardly alone in attributing France's rapid downfall in 1940 to French political divisions and the "sullen apathy" of the French political class. In this spirit, France's defensive strategic posture anchored in the Maginot Line and the forward defense of the Dyle–Breda Plan was calculated to draw British forces back onto the Continent, and force Hitler to expend his military energy on the margins in Poland and the Baltic, while the German economy would rapidly asphyxiate. Unfortunately, hopes for the success of this strategy had already been undone by the Nazi–Soviet Pact of August 1939. In the Phoney War interim, rather than summon a spirit of *union sacrée* that had forged French resolve in 1914, in the view of historian and participant/observer Marc Bloch, the government had filled the winter stalemate of 1939–1940 with concrete and propaganda puffery characterized by "its irritating and crude optimism, its timidity, and above all, the inability of our rulers to give a frank definition of their war aims."[1] The precipitous German offensive of May–June 1940 had revealed a shattering deficit of mental resilience in the Allied high command that had failed to modernize its doctrine, as well as a dearth of combat motivation and preparation among Allied soldiers. As a result, the Alliance had crumbled in the face of what was in effect a sixteen-division German strategic raid. In the process, Anglo-French Phoney War strategy had been exposed as little more than "wishful strategic thinking" layered over a flawed net assessment, applied by Allied armies neither operationally, tactically, nor spiritually prepared to deal with German strategic and tactical surprise.[2] A battlefield panic of two French divisions at Bulson near Sedan had kindled a moral and positional collapse from which French arms never recovered. In this way, Hitler's Operation *Fall Gelb* exposed the breathtaking inadequacies of the French operational and tactical doctrine of *colmatage* (plugging the gap), the absence of an air–land battle concept, château generalship which straightjacketed battlefield initiative and adaptation, fragmented and unsystematic intelligence assessment and integration into operational planning, undermotorization that limited mobility, and antiquated and fragile communications and logistical systems designed for static front warfare. The inability of a disorientated French High Command to reassert control over a rapidly collapsing battlespace in the face of relentless German pressure, combined with the evacuation of British troops at Dunkirk and Saint-Nazaire, and the fall of Paris, which many French soldiers took to signal the termination of their contractual obligations to the French state, rattled morale, strained Alliance relations, and opened the door to defeatists in Bordeaux keen to exit the conflict, terminating *la Troisième* on their way out. Phillippe Pétain's 17 June 1940 announcement that he planned to seek an armistice delivered the *coup de grâce* to the morale of a French nation psychologically unprepared to deal with catastrophic military setbacks and catapulted Charles de Gaulle to London to organize an external resistance known as *la France libre*.

France's astonishing 1940 collapse reverberated globally, because it also exploded flawed calculations and Grand Strategy hypotheses in London, Washington, and Moscow upon which the security of the UK, United States, and Soviet Union had been anchored. As Michael Neiberg notes, France's fall "shattered the US assumption that they need not concern themselves with the periodic firestorms of the Old World." In this way, Washington's effective engagement in the war dated not from the December 1941 Japanese attack on Pearl Harbor, but rather from the May–June 1940 collapse of the postulation that the defense of the Western Hemisphere could be outsourced to the French army and the Royal Navy. "The France policy that the Roosevelt administration developed emerged from an atmosphere of deep fear," writes Neiberg. "Working with Vichy appeared to some of those officials like a piece of driftwood worth clinging to in stormy seas. Their reflexive dislike of Charles de Gaulle, optimism that they could manipulate successive French leaders, and suspicion of de Gaulle's links to communists and socialists caused them to hold on to this failed approach, even long after public criticism of it had become almost impossible for the administration to answer."[3]

The quandary for France emerging from the *débâcle* of 1940 had been how to rebuild French military power, protect the empire, and resuscitate France's global status and influence, which were now on life support? This task was complicated by the fact that, without agreement on what had gone wrong – whether the *débâcle* had been strategic, moral, or merely the result of an operational/tactical "military misfortune" – the formula for renewal segregated French men and women into bitterly opposing camps. While de Gaulle rejected the armistice and launched his offshore crusade to reclaim French honor within the Allied camp, defeatists at Vichy embraced cooperation – deceptively marketed as "neutrality" – with the victorious Axis as a pragmatic accommodation to Europe's historical trends. Launched at Montoire on 24 October 1940,

Vichy's sham "neutrality" also sought to gain concessions that would ease the rigors of Occupation, and allow the repatriation of roughly 1.8 million French POWs, while achieving influence within the framework of Hitler's New Order in Europe. This POW liberation effort meet with only modest success, so that, after the Germans repatriated the wounded, the sick, and those required to keep France functioning, around a million French soldiers remained incarcerated in Germany for the remainder of the war. Furthermore, as the "protecting power," Vichy failed to defend the Geneva Convention protections of French soldiers who rotted in the drudgery of *Oflags* and *Kommandos*, tormented by thoughts that their wives and girlfriends were sleeping around. In the meantime, statues of Marianne, symbols of the Republic, had been crated carefully in town hall basements and attics, in case they might be needed in future, as streets and squares named for Jean Jaurès and Émile Zola, and even Pierre Curie and Jean-Jacques Rousseau, were renamed. Civil servants who had refused to recant their Masonic, Socialist, Radical or Communist pasts had been sacked, providing a nucleus of leadership for a growing if still minuscule popular resistance. Clucking housewives clutching ration cards queued outside of shops, complaining that refugees were stealing bicycles and driving up prices, while speculating about whether unused sugar coupons would be valid next month. Meanwhile, their men, if they had managed to escape capture in 1940, were beginning to resemble tramps. Paunchy German security police combed the *quais* of railway stations in the *zone occupée*, finding fault in the most meticulously ordered "papers," in a game whose goal was to make their interlocutor miss his or her train. Communications between the "free" and "occupied" zones were strictly limited to "family matters." Vichy only feebly objected as Alsace-Moselle had been progressively annexed into the Greater Reich and roughly 120,000 of its military-age citizens conscripted into the Wehrmacht and Waffen SS. Allied bombs fell on cities. The war, some said, was going to last ten years.

As Vichy collaboration snowballed, de Gaulle sought to shift *la France libre*'s outsider position as "minor ally" toward the center of Allied politics as France's unique, legitimate political representative. To accomplish this, he had gradually to impose himself on London as a political actor, rather than a mere military auxiliary, and buck the strong headwind of FDR's strategy of Vichy engagement, while simultaneously coming to embody French hopes as the symbol of resistance to Axis occupation. His campaign had stumbled at the starting gate, with failure to rally Dakar in September 1940, followed in July 1941 by the repatriation to French North Africa (AFN), with British connivance, of most of the Vichy garrison in the Levant. These setbacks had been recouped at least spiritually by the heroic stand at Bir Hakeim in May–June 1942, which advertised that the resolve of *les Forces françaises libres* transcended their diminutive numbers and exotic recruitment. This offered a tentative step toward rehabilitating

France's martial reputation and hence political clout, symbolized in the 13 July 1942 rebranding of the Gaullist movement as *la France combattante* (Fighting France) under the *Comité national Français*, a bid to incorporate the internal resistance. At least in theory, this broadened de Gaulle's political constituency, and gave his renegade movement a degree of momentum on the eve of Operation Torch.

Nonetheless, Vichy's delusional slither toward Axis salvation had failed to cancel it diplomatically in Washington, which had sought in vain to secure an "invitation" from Vichy's *Délégué général* in AFN Maxime Weygand to preempt a potential Axis penetration of the region that replicated the infusion of Japanese troops into French Indochina. With Weygand's November 1941 recall to France at German insistence, American Minister in Algiers Robert Murphy was tasked with preparing the ground for an American invasion, which Roosevelt was determined to carry out. The result was the "group of five," which historian of AFN Christine Levisse-Touzé categorized as a metaphor for a collection of intelligence agents, saboteurs, propagandists, and civil and military conspirators who emerged after or before April 1942 to undermine cooperation with the Axis in AFN, and eventually neutralize the Vichy response to an Anglo-American invasion. While Operation Torch was "too big to fail," and the French command in AFN too muddled and understrength to respond effectively to the unanticipated Anglo-American invasion, the notion reinforced by cheerful intelligence reports that a significant "resistance" in AFN indicated that the region awaited Allied liberation quieted opposition to Roosevelt's plan in the cabinet and among US military chiefs. Unfortunately, a consequence of the hesitation and equivocation of Vichy proconsuls in AFN, in particular that of the Army commander in AFN Alphonse Juin, was a bloody and, many concluded, unnecessary Tunisia campaign, an account of which begins this volume.

At the turn of the New Year 1943, the Allies progressively gained the upper hand in the Battle of the Atlantic, Axis operations against Suez and Stalingrad folded, and the Allies secured AFN, whose allegiances and military potential nevertheless remained in doubt. On an operational level, the perfection of amphibious operations as demonstrated by Torch, combined with the Allies' command of North Africa, threatened the Axis' southern European glacis, that included a Vichy rump of bypassed, demilitarized, and progressively Nazified diehards, who nevertheless remained fully capable of inflicting pain on their own population. The effort by a divided France, amid civil war, burdened with a fractured army and scuttled navy to emerge from the conflict as anything other than a second-tier, if not third-tier, courtesy power would require de Gaulle to pursue a strategy of disruption that would rattle alliance cohesion. In this respect, Torch and the "Darlan deal," superseded by what would become Washington's politically counterproductive, even practically farcical 1943 approval of the clueless Henri Giraud to lead France's exile movement, would mark an important turning point in the war. The Anfa Conference of January 1943 would make increasingly clear that, although Washington and London had pooled their resources to defeat the Axis, Anglo-American discord over how to accommodate France as military ally and political partner threatened to rattle the alliance. In fact, a lack of consensus in Washington over the future of Europe meant that, as noted by Hilary Footitt and John Simmonds, "the Allies failed to find any way of translating their massive military power into political control." This disjuncture of inter-allied statecraft and strategy left the door ajar for Charles de Gaulle to impose his own vision for France's political future, and begin to erect the mechanisms for a new French regime to fill the void left by ill-defined Allied policy in the wake of the precipitous August–September 1944 German exit from France.[4]

De Gaulle's quest to resuscitate a French army would aim to rehabilitate France's martial reputation, prevent civil war from breaking out on liberation, and assert France's interests in post-war Europe. Torch and the subsequent Anfa Conference would launch the modernization of French conventional forces composed at this stage of the war principally of *l'armée d'Afrique*, whose coerced conversion to Gaullism would be freighted with lingering *Maréchalist* loyalties. But these soldiers had few options – their commander Alphonse Juin had concluded in November 1942 that rallying to the Allies gave France the best chance of clinging to empire, the foundation of national grandeur and *l'armée d'Afrique*'s *raison d'être*. AFN would also give de Gaulle a base of operations independent of vexatious Churchillian constraints. Even so, his quarrels with the Anglo-Americans would escalate, triggered by his apprehensions about Churchill's designs on the French empire, in particular the Levant, and amplified by FDR's obstinate refusal to recognize de Gaulle and the *Comité français de libération nationale* (CFLN), and to associate resistance in France with Allied operational planning. Picking quarrels also became a tactic to shed the image of "the squatter on the banks of the Thames," and deliver a degree of separation from his Allied sponsors, which the Prince de Condé of the era of the French Revolution – with whom de Gaulle and his exile army were sometimes inauspiciously compared – never managed to achieve. De Gaulle's embrace of the internal resistance, through his agents Jean Moulin and Pierre Brossolette, was aimed further to reinforce his democratic bona fides, as had been his public November 1942 Albert Hall pledge to restore the French Republic. This aligned *Gaullisme de guerre* with the Western Allied goal of restoring democracy. But, also, his embrace of the internal resistance defending the sacred soil of the Hexagon rebutted the charge by the "Victor of Verdun" that the external resistance had abandoned the French people.

Vichy's dogged, if naive and fruitless, attempts to strike up a cozy collaboration with the Axis allowed such figures as Fritz Todt, Fritz Sauckel, and Albert

Speer to levy more exacting demands on the French economy and manpower now that Axis occupation blanketed the entire country from November 1942. This policy of exploitation in the face of craven Vichy acquiescence was bound to produce popular backlash, in the form of a growing resistance movement, best exemplified by a spontaneous flight of young French labor conscripts into the *maquis*, in the process transforming resistance in France in 1943–1944 from a largely urban to a rural phenomenon. This emergence and expansion of an internal resistance opened opportunities for the Gaullists. Presented as a patriotic *levée en masse*, resistance in France rhetorically at least associated the French people with their own liberation, and would help to legitimize Charles de Gaulle in the eyes of the Allies as a democratic leader with a popular mandate. The Allied "interface services" – special operations branches – were poised to nurture and promote resistance in France as elsewhere in Europe, seeing it as holding the potential to furnish an extra dimension of military power and propaganda as a clandestine armed struggle. In this way, a growing popular resistance inside France promised to become a force multiplier, demonstrating a popular rejection of Vichy that would boost de Gaulle's standing in the Alliance. A mushrooming resistance also validated his demands that the CFLN, the de facto French exile government from June 1943 seated in Algiers, be included in Allied planning for the invasion of France. Finally, a growing resistance movement held out hope that resistance-occupied "cleared zones," similar to those in Greece and the Balkans, might permit the Gaullists to establish territorial authority within France independent of Anglo-American invasion forces.

However, the perils of internal resistance were also considerable, beginning with the fact that resistance in France formed a fissiparous crusade, one often captured on the local level by strong-willed leaders, some under communist influence, who nurtured their own political agendas, as the September 1943 liberation of Corsica was to reveal. This independence and willingness to ignore or reject CFLN authority was reinforced by the British Special Operations Executive (SOE) and American Office of Strategic Services (OSS) that financed, armed, and "advised" them. A second problem became how to militarize, configure, and lead a largely spontaneous tsunami of young fugitives who had collected in remote areas of the country to support a conventional invasion. Third, this resistance–special operations tandem served only to increase the divisiveness and violence of the occupation, as brutal population control methods evolved by the Germans initially for Eastern and Southeastern Europe, as well as the troops and intelligence services who applied them, were imported into France. The German occupation would be reinforced by repressive formations such as the French police, the thuggish *Milice* or the *Groupe mobile de réserve* (GMR), backed by networks of informants and "snitches," mobilized by an increasingly desperate and collaborationist-minded Vichy government. Therefore, the French reaction to a growing resistance movement was often ambiguous, when not openly hostile, because actions of resistance brought down retribution on the civilian population. At the same time, French economic collaboration had justified intensified Allied bombing of the Hexagon, whose subsequent collateral damage and high number of civilian casualties were exploited both by Vichy and by the Germans to reinforce their anti-Allied message, and caused Pétain's increasingly precarious government to double-down on collaboration, in a hollow hope of gaining concessions from a Hitler who was ever more desperate and on the defensive.

Finally, the explosion of the internal resistance would complicate the resurrection of a unified liberation army. With an eye to London and Washington, D. C., de Gaulle might tendentiously argue that French soldiers had never ceased to fight the Axis, as illustrated by the courageous defense of Bir Hakeim. But not only were the diminutive *Forces françaises libre* reliant largely on colonial subjects impressed in the few backwoods colonies that the Free French had managed to subvert, but also the liberating rhetoric of the Atlantic Charter of August 1941 promised a post-war world of generalized freedoms of the soon-to-be United Nations, which threatened France's empire. Because de Gaulle's claim to be France's legitimate leader hinged on his staunch defense of empire as a central pillar of French grandeur and influence, the Allied position potentially posed an existential threat not only to de Gaulle's base of support, but also to France's future as a global power.

Forging a French army from *les Forces françaises libres*, the overwhelmingly Muslim *armée d'Afrique*, and the internal resistance, all with different experiences, and representing often opposing political attitudes and aspirations, as well as levels of combat experience, would pose a political and institutional challenge. The Gaullist solution to the incongruity of France being liberated behind a spearhead of colonial praetorians was that, once onshore in France, sub-Saharan African levies would be switched out with a *levée en masse* of patriotic French resisters, militarized as *les Forces françaises de l'intérieur* (FFI). Not only would this "whitening" of France's army of liberation resurrect the metropolitan French army, but also *l'armée d'Afrique* could serve as a mechanism to corral and discipline very politicized "fifis." De Gaulle's objective also was to rebuild French civil–military relations, a tall task as defeat in 1940 and the exile of a small Armistice Army to the *zone libre*, followed by its dissolution in November 1942, had severed the links between the French people and their army.

Therefore, a lack of consensus among Allied leaders on the fate of post-war Europe and hence France's role in it that would on occasion find de Gaulle at loggerheads with the "Anglo-Saxons"; heavily armed resistance factions often led by “feudals” with their own political agendas, enabled in de Gaulle’s view by the Allied “interface services”; and the lack of a strong conventional army to impose order, shoo the Wehrmacht off the property, and stake out an occupation zone in Germany and Austria all raised serious questions about what war termination would hold in store for France.

Abbreviations

AAA	Anti-aircraft artillery
AC	Armistice Commission
ACC	Allied Control Commission
ACI	Advisory Council for Italy
AD	Armored Division
ADD	Amis de Darlan
AEF	French Equatorial Africa
AFAT	Auxiliaires féminines de l'armée de terre
AFHQ	Allied Forces Headquarters
AFN	Afrique française du nord/French North Africa
AMFA	Administration militaire forces armées
AMGOT	Allied Military Government of Occupied Territories
ANZAC	Australian and New Zealand Army Corps
AOF	French West Africa
AS	Armée secrète
ASDIC	Anti-submarine Detection Investigation Committee
Ast	Abwehrstellen
ASW	Anti-submarine warfare
ATS	Auxiliary Territorial Service
AWOL	Absent without leave
Bat d'Af	Bataillon d'infanterie légère d'Afrique
BBC	British Broadcasting Corporation
BCRA	Bureau central de renseignements et d'action
BCRAA	BCRA Algiers
BCRAL	BCRA London
BCRAM	BCRA Militaire
BDM	Bund Deutscher Mädel (Band of German Maidens)
BDS	Befehlshaber der Sicherheitspolizei und des SD (German Security Police)
BEF	British Expeditionary Force
BFL	Brigade française libre
BFO	Brigade française libre d'Orient

BIA	Bataillon d'infanterie aéroportée
BLM	Brigade légère mécanique
BM	Bataillon de marche/bataillon médical
BMA	Bureau des menées antinationales
BMC	Bordel militaire de campagne
CAD	Civil Affairs Division
CAF	Corps d'armée français
CCFA	Commandant en chef français en Allemagne
CCS	Combined Chiefs of Staff (US and UK)
CCZN	Comité de coordination de la zone nord
CDL	Comité départmental de libération
CDM	Camouflage du matériel
CDN	Comité de défense nationale
CEF	Corps expéditionnaire français (in Italy)
CEFEO	Corps expéditionnaire français d'Extrême-Orient
CFA	Corps franc d'Afrique
CFLN	Comité français de libération nationale
CFT	Corps féminin des transmissions
CGM	Commandment des goums marocains
CGT	Conféderation générale du travail
CIA	Central Intelligence Agency
CIGS	Chief of the Imperial General Staff
CLI	Corps léger d'intervention
CLL	Comité local de libération
CLN	Comitato di Liberazione Nazionale (Italian National Liberation Committee)
CNF	Comité national français
CNI	Commissariat national à l'Intérieur
CNO	Chief of Naval Operations
CNR	Conseil national de la résistance
COMIDAC/COMAC	Comité d'action en France
COMZ	Communication zone
COS	Chief of Staff
COSSAC	Chief of Staff to Supreme Allied Commander
CP	Command post
CPDN	Comité permanent de la Défense Nationale
CRA	Centre de ralliement et d'accueil
CRS	Compagnies républicaines de sécurité
CSAR	Comité secret d'action révolutionaire (Cagoule)
CSDN	Comité supérieur de la Défense Nationale
CSTM	Commandant supérieur des troupes du Maroc
CSTT	Commandant supérieur des troupes de Tunisie

CUAR	Comité d'Unité d'Action Révolutionnaire
CVF	Corps des volontaires françaises (female volunteers for la France libre)
DAA	Détachement de l'Armée de l'Atlantique
DAF	Détachement d'armée française
DAF	Deutsche Arbeitsfront (German Labor Front)
DAL	Deutsch-Arabische Lehrabteilung (Arab volunteers for the German Army)
DB	Division blindée (Armored Division)
DBLE	Demi-brigade de la légion étrangère
DCA	Défense contre aviation (Anti-aircraft)
DCr	Division cuirassée de réserve
DDT	Dichlorodiphenyltrichloroethane
DFL	Division française libre
DGER	Direction générale des études et recherches
DGSS	Direction générale des services spéciaux
DI	Division d'infanterie
DIA	Division d'infanterie algérienne
DIA	Division d'infanterie alpine
DIC	Division d'infanterie coloniale
DIM	Division d'infanterie du Maroc
DLM	Division légère mécanique
DMA	Division de marche d'Alger
DMC	Division de marche de Constantine
DMI	Division motorisée d'infanterie
DMI	Division de marche d'infanterie
DMM	Division de marche du Maroc
DMM	Division marocaine de montagne
DMN	Délégué militaire national
DMO	Division de marche d'Oran
DMOS	Délégué militaire pour les opérations de zone sud
DMR	Délégué militaire régional
DMZ	Délégués militaires de zone
DP	Displaced person
DSM	Direction de sécurité militaire
DSPG	Direction du service des prisonniers de guerre
DSS	Direction des services spéciaux
EAC	European Advisory Commission
ELAS	Greek People's Liberation Army
EMDN	État-major de la défense nationale
EMFFI	État-major des Forces françaises de l'intérieur
ESG	École supérieure de guerre

ETO	European Theater of Operations
FAF	French Air Force
FAFL	Forces aériennes françaises libres
FANY	First Air Nursing Yeomanry
FEC	French Expeditionary Corps
FFC	Forces françaises combattantes (Fighting France forces)
FFI or "fifis"	Forces françaises de l'intérieur
FFL	Forces françaises libres
FFO	Forces françaises de l'Ouest
FG	Feldgendarmerie
FL	La France libre
FN	Front national
FNFL	Forces navales françaises libres
FTP	Francs-Tireurs et Partisans
FTS	French Training Section
G2	Military intelligence
G3	Military operations
GCE	Groupement de commandement et d'engin
Gestapo	Geheime Staatspolizei (secret police)
GFP	Geheime Feldpolizei (Wehrmacht secret field police)
GHQ	General Headquarters
GMC	General Motors Truck Company
GMR	Groupe mobile de réserve
GPRF	Gouvernement provisoire de la république française
GQG Air	Grand Quartier Général Air
GSS	Groupe spécial de sécurité
GTL	Groupement tactique de Lorraine
GTM	Groupement de tabors marocains
HC	High command
HCM	Hôpital chirurgical mobile
HJ	Hitlerjugend (Hitler Youth)
HP	Horse-power
HQ	Headquarters
HSSPF	Höherer SS- und Polizeiführer (senior Nazi Party official in command of SS, Gestapo, or police units)
HUMINT	Human Intelligence
ID	Infantry Division
IPS	Instruction personnelle et secrète
IS	Intelligence Service
ISU	Italian Service Units (Italian POWS in Allied service)
JAG	Judge Advocate General

JCS	Joint Chiefs of Staff
JRC	Joint Rearmament Committee
KdS	Kommando der Sicherheitspolizei und des SD
KG	Kriegsgefangener (POW)
KHD	Kriegshilfsdienst (female auxiliary service)
KIA	Killed in action
LCA	Landing Craft Assault
LCP	Landing Craft Personnel
LFC	Légion française des combattants
LRDP	Long Range Desert Patrol
LSH	Landing Ship Headquarters
LST	Landing Ship, Tank
LVF	Légion des volontaires français contre le bolchévisme
MBE	Member of the British Empire
MBF	Militärbefehlshaber in Frankreich (Commander of occupation forces in France)
MEW	Ministry of Economic Warfare
MI5	Military Intelligence 5 (counterintelligence, UK)
MI6	Military Intelligence 6 (or SIS, foreign intelligence, UK)
MIA	Missing in action
MNPGD	Mouvement national des prisonnier de guerre et des déportés
MO	Maintien de l'ordre (Vichy plan)
MO	Medical orderly
MOD	Ministry of Defence (UK)
MP	Member of Parliament
MP	Milice patriotique
MP	Military Police (US)
MRP	Mouvement Républicain Populaire
MSR	Mouvement social révolutionnaire
MMLA	Mission militaire de liaisons administratives
MUR	Mouvements unis de la résistance
NAAFI	Navy, Army and Air Force Institutes
NAP	Noyautage des administrations publiques
NARA	National Archives and Records Administration
NATO	North Atlantic Treaty Organization
NCO	Non-commissioned officer
NKVD	People's Commissariat of Internal Affairs (USSR)
NS	National Socialist
NSDAP	Nazi Party

NSKK	Nationalsozialistisches Kraftfahrkorps (National Socialist Motor Corps)
OAS	Organisation armée secrète
OB West	Oberbefehlshaber West (High Commander in the West)
OCM	Organisation civile et militaire
Oflag	Offizierslager (POW camp for officers)
OG	Operational Group
OKW	Oberkommando der Wehrmacht
ORA	Organisation de résistance de l'armée
ORCG	Organe de recherche des criminels de guerre
Orpo	Ordnungspolizei (ordinary police, German)
OSS	Office of Strategic Services (US)
OVRA	Organizzazione di Vigilanzae Repressione dell'Antifascismo (Italian secret police)
PCF	Parti communiste français
PCR	Radio receiver
PCT	Poste central de tir
PDG	Prisonnier de guerre
PM	Prime Minister
PNB	Parti national breton, or Strollad Broadel Breizh
POW	Prisoner of war
PPA	Parti populaire algérien
PPF	Parti populaire français
PPSh-41	Pistolet-pulemyot Shpagina-41
PR	Propagande révolutionnaire
PR	Public relations
PT	Physical training
PTSD	Post-traumatic stress disorder
PTT	Postes, télégraphes et téléphones
PWE	Political Warfare Executive
PX	Post Exchange
Pz	Panzer
PzD	Panzer Division
Pz.Kpfw.	Panzerkampfwagen (tank)
RAA	Régiment d'artillerie d'Afrique
RAD	Reichsarbeitsdienst (Reich Labor Service)
RAF	Royal Air Force
RCA	Régiment de chasseurs d'Afrique
RCP	Régiment de chasseurs parachutistes
RCT	Regimental Combat Team
RDF	Radio Direction Finding

RI	Régiment d'infanterie
RIC	Régiment d'infanterie coloniale
RNP	Rassemblement national populaire
RP	Resistance point
RPF	Rassemblement du peuple français
RSHA	Reichssicherheitshauptamt (Reich Security Main Office)
RTA	Régiment de tirailleurs algériens
RTM	Régiment de tirailleurs marocains
RTS	Régiment de tirailleurs sénégalais
RTST	Régiment de tirailleurs sénégalais du Tchad
RTT	Régiment de tirailleurs tunisiens
SA	Sturmabteilung (Nazi party paramilitary wing)
SACMED	Supreme Allied Commander Mediterranean
SANA	Section automobile nord-africaine
SAQJ	Service algérien des questions juives
SAS	Special Air Service
SBD	Scout Bomber Douglas
SD	Sicherheitsdienst (security police)
SDPG	Service diplomatique des prisonniers de guerre
SEAC	South East Asia Command
SFHQ	Special Forces Headquarters
SFIO	Section française de l'internationale ouvrière (French Socialist Party)
SGDA	Secrétariat général de la défense aérienne
SGJ	Secrétariat général à la Jeunesse
SHAEF	Supreme Headquarters Allied Expeditionary Force
SHD	Service Historique de la Défense
SIGINT	Signals intelligence
SIM	Servizio Informazione Militari
Sipo	Sicherheitspolizei (security police)
SMERSH	Red Army Counterintelligence (from 1942)
SIS	Special Intelligence Service (MI6)
SNCF	Société nationale des chemins de fer français (French national railways)
SO	Special Operations
SOE	Special Operations Executive
SOF	Special operations forces
SOL	Service d'ordre légionnaire
SPOC	Special Project Operations Center
SR	Service de renseignement (intelligence service)
SRA	Services de renseignement et d'action

SS	Schutzstaffel (Protection Squads)
SSA	Section sanitaire automobile féminine
SSM	Service de sécurité militaire
ST	Surveillance du Territoire
STO	Service du travail obligatoire
TOE	Table of Organization and Equipment
TOE	Théâtre d'opération extérieure
TOO	Theater of Operations
TTD	Tactical target dossier
USAAF	US Army Air Force
USMC	United States Marine Corps
USN	United States Navy
VIP	Very important person
VP	Volontaire de place
WAAF	Women's Auxiliary Air Force
WAC	Women's Army Corps (US)
WAKO	Waffenstillstandskommission (German armistice commission)
WIA	Wounded in action
WRNS	Women's Royal Naval Service (UK)
WS	Winston Special (convoys around the Cape to Egypt)
ZOAN	Zone d'opérations aériennes nord
ZOF	Zone d'occupation française

1 Tunisia

"A Cascade of Contradictory Orders"

Torch's success had been eased by the surprise and magnitude of the Allied invasion that had sparked turmoil in the fragmented command structure of French North Africa (AFN), a confusion amplified by Darlan's presence in Algiers. To these factors was added what General Jean Delmas qualified as "a certain innocence, a spirit of discipline, the oath (to Pétain) led *l'armée d'armistice* into passivity and powerlessness," that sabotaged a staunch opposition to the Allied invasion in Morocco and Algeria.[1] Unfortunately for the Allies, that same "passivity and powerlessness" that had facilitated success in Morocco and Algeria helped to shuffle Tunisia out of reach. From an Allied perspective, Tunisia offered AFN's most exposed link, for several reasons. First, it was most vulnerable to Axis invasion either directly from Italy or through Italian Tripolitania, which made Tunisia's defense a challenge. Second, at the Axis control commission's insistence, Tunisia was sparsely garrisoned. But this had not especially worried the French, as Tunisia and the Constantinois were considered less likely targets of an Allied invasion. Therefore, defense measures were vague and ad hoc, despite the large concentrations of Allied planes and ships at Gibraltar noticed on 7 November.[2] Third, Tunisia contained a large Italian population favorable to the Axis. Fourth, because Torch had prioritized Morocco over Tunisia, unlike in Casablanca, Oran, or Algiers, commanders in Tunis had to react not to an Allied armada, but to an Axis assault. Finally, no resistance mobilized in Tunis that might have disputed Axis access to Bizerte, or especially to El Aouina airfield in Tunis, the initial entry point of the Axis invasion, replicating Monsabert's momentary sequestration of Blida outside of Algiers for Allied benefit, actions that might have bought enough time for an arrival of British troops.

This did not happen in part because of confusion and delay in Algiers, as Darlan and Laval attempted unsuccessfully to harness the Allied invasion to force Hitler to revise the conditions of the armistice. The result was "a succession of orders and counter-orders" that increased confusion in a way that basically "created competition among several headquarters, thus several commanders, each with a modicum of authority and all independent in the hierarchy of rank and functions in the chain of command," writes Robin Leconte.[3] Of the three main decision-makers in Tunis, two were admirals who took their rudder orders directly from Vichy, not Algiers. Meanwhile, the commander of ground forces in AFN, Alphonse Juin, complained that the *Commandant supérieur des troupes tunisiennes* (CSTT), General Georges Barré, failed to take decisive action to prevent the Axis seizure of El Aouina. In Juin's telling, Barré's "hesitation," that triggered the Tunisian "tragedy," was a direct consequence of the deliberate scrambling of the French chain of command upon Weygand's 1941 departure. Barré's primary concern was to keep his communications open with Algeria. This allowed Axis forces to occupy Bizerte and Tunis ahead of the arriving British First Army, thereby giving Rommel a new lease on life.[4] Unfortunately, blaming subordinates and systemic command muddle became a convenient alibi for Juin to obfuscate his own role in the Tunisian "tragedy." In January 1942, Juin had accurately anticipated events that would incite the Axis to invade Tunisia, and predicted almost exactly how that invasion would unfold.[5] Why, then, were the French, and Juin in particular, not better prepared to react?

Most historians have focused rightly on Darlan's nefarious role. Of course, Darlan was only playing Laval's game to protect the *zone libre* by giving permission to Hitler and Ciano at Munich to invade Tunisia. When even that huge concession failed to protect Vichy's sovereignty, Darlan reluctantly switched sides.[6] Yet, Juin's abdication of responsibility did not go unnoticed, either at the time or subsequently. Alternative explanations for Juin's hesitation highlight the fact that, as a great admirer of Rommel, and facilitator of the Paris Protocols, he nurtured a pro-Axis bias. A more benign, Allied-friendly interpretation of his behavior suggests that, aware of the ambiguous loyalties of *l'armée d'Afrique*, Juin played the clock, certain that Berlin's response to Torch would result in the invasion of Vichy's *zone libre*. Such action would implode the 1940 Armistice, expose the hollowness of Vichy "sovereignty," and tip French loyalties definitely to the Allies.[7] Juin's main concern was to maintain French control of AFN and prevent a Muslim uprising. He quickly concluded that assisting the Anglo-American invasion offered the best guarantee of continued imperial sovereignty.[8]

As in Algeria and Morocco, the tangled command structure combined with policy ambiguity and ethical uncertainty to produce "*la confusion des ordres*" in Tunisia and the Constantinois, which often whiplashed local commanders, who were either abandoned to make their own decisions or forced to decide which of their superiors' contradictory directives to obey.[9] This was compounded, in the view of Robin Leconte, by the realization that several senior French officers had conspired with the Anglo-Americans, which signaled a politically fluid situation that made commanders up and down the hierarchy reluctant to issue orders that might be countermanded by their superiors, or that their subordinates might not obey. Their decision not to act was confirmed by news from Algiers which arrived at the end of the afternoon of 8 November of a local ceasefire concluded between Darlan and American General Charles Ryder. Nevertheless, the order issued at 13:45 from XIX Corps commander General Louis Koeltz to General Édouard Welvert, commander of the *Division de Marche de Constantine* (DMC), had been to march on Algiers. When Welvert asked if that order were still in effect, he was informed at 18:45 that, "following the evolution of the situation, General Welvert has complete freedom to take all of the necessary measures." In other words, the senior command had abdicated its authority, leaving officers on their own. Tension increased on 9 November as Luftwaffe aircraft began to land at El Aouina in Tunis and Sidi Ahmed airfield at Bizerte. Welvert was besieged by subordinate commanders demanding instructions, including Barré in Tunis, who reported that Vichy's permission for Axis planes to land in El Aouina had brought French officers to the verge of mutiny. In other words, the French command was caught between the need to stop the spread of "dissidence" in the ranks and pressure to repel an Axis invasion.[10]

This confusion rippled down the chain of command to Sétif, almost 300 kilometers southeast of Algiers, where on Sunday morning, 8 November 1942, Second lieutenant Jean Lapouge, who had arrived only eight days previously in the *7e Régiment des tirailleurs algériennes* (7e RTA), was awakened by his batman with news that the Americans had invaded. Lapouge hailed from a family of infantrymen, being the son of a colonel of Zouaves and the grandson of an infantry general. A devout Catholic and former Boy Scout, an organization whose motto was "son of France and a good citizen," Lapouge's destiny since boyhood had been Saint-Cyr. Although the French military academy had been shifted by the occupation from its Paris suburb to Aix-en-Provence in the *zone libre*, Lepouge had graduated with his class, baptized "promotion Maréchal Pétain," only a few days earlier. As a native of Oran, he predictably had chosen an *armée d'Afrique* regiment upon graduation, which had assigned him to lead the machinegun platoon in one of its companies. It wasn't much of a machinegun – a gas-actuated, air-cooled Hotchkiss that sat on a tripod and weighed 25 kilos. Each company was meant to maintain an inventory of four of them, as well as two 81 mm mortars. The Hotchkiss could in theory fire 450 8-millimeter rounds per minute. In fact, its firing strips held only 24 rounds, requiring its three-man crew constantly to reload. If, that is, they had any munitions – the Axis control commissions permitted the Constantine Division, of which 7^e^ RTA was part, only 30 cartridges per rifle and 200 per machinegun for a 9-month period. The control commissions were equally parsimonious in their authorization of vehicles and petrol, which meant that the few trucks in the division's inventory were most often requisitioned civilian vehicles in precarious mechanical repair.[11] The result was a reliance on mules to transport munitions and other impedimenta. The Hotchkiss had been a state-of-the-art weapon – in 1914! But it was par for the course in the 7e RTA, whose two battalions were de-motorized and armed with Great War-vintage weaponry pulled by horse-drawn logistics. "Junk" was the verdict pronounced by American General George Patton when he had encountered French armaments at Casablanca in November. Under these circumstances, he marveled that the French fought as courageously as they did.[12]

Thinking his batman was engaged in a practical joke of the sort frequently played on new cadets at Saint-Cyr, Lapouge pulled the sheet over his head, rolled over and tried to go back to sleep. But the commotion in the corridor convinced him to rise, dress, and report to barracks, where he was confronted by his irate company commander, who reprimanded him for his tardiness. The DMC was reacting to Darlan's order sent at 07:30 that morning to resist the Allied invasion. But there was no Allied activity reported off the Constantinois and Tunisia. Rumor circulated that several senior French officers in Algiers had defected to the Anglo-Americans. The regiment collected its equipment and marched north to Kherrata, a village in the Kabylia that dominated a narrow, north–south passage between Sétif and the Gulf of Béjarïa. "Our orders were to stop the Americans!," Lapouge remembered, although why the French might think that the Allies on their way from Algiers to Tunisia might detour through Kherrata remains a mystery. The 7e RTA strung mines along the road through the narrow pass and sited their machineguns. The next day, amid rumors that American troops joined by defecting French soldiers were marching on Sétif, Alsace native and 7th Infantry Brigade commander Colonel Jacques (Jacob) Schwartz asked his DMC Commander Welvert for instruction: "Fire [on the mutineers] without hesitation," came Welvert's reply. Rather than fire on French troops, and apprised of German planes landing at El Aouina, Schwartz ordered his soldiers back to barracks.[13] At 23:00 on 10 November, word finally reached Lapogue's company that they were no longer to shoot at the Americans. On 14 November, the 7e RTA boarded a train that deposited them at Tébessa on the frontier with Tunisia. The following days melded into a fog of marches and counter-marches with heavy packs, with the fatigue of setting up camp only to break it down, and hike to a new destination.[14]

Lapouge's change of orders, from battling the Americans on 8 November to joining them only two days later, suggested an extenuated transition accompanied by hesitation, prevarication, and a muddle of orders and counter-orders – in essence, a breakdown of authority and hierarchy which caused many officers to make their own decisions. In fact, Torch followed by the Axis invasion of Tunisia forced the French military to confront an existential crisis. Unlike conventional Second World War forces, where political authority remained uncontested, soldiers in France after June 1940 were forced to choose between different concepts of legitimacy. The French army had been humiliated by its 1940 defeat. The rationale for the armistice had been poorly understood in AFN, which had required Vichy first to dispatch Weygand to shore up the loyalty of its imperial soldiers and impose an oath to the Marshal, and subsequently to scramble the chain of command to thwart a wholesale defection. This ultimately boomeranged as it fragmented the response in AFN to the simultaneous Allied and Axis invasions of November 1942.

However, Torch, and the subsequent Axis invasion of Tunisia, triggered a lengthy six-day crisis as a splintered, confused, and politically insecure command in North Africa spewed imprecise, often contradictory, frequently canceled orders that ricocheted between Algiers, Tunis, Casablanca, Vichy, and Army and Navy commands with their separate and often conflicting political agendas, service networks and personal loyalties. Lower down this multi-layered and whiplashed hierarchy, officers, with partial information and battered by rumor and confusion, were forced to choose which authority, which city, which service network, which intermediary commander, or which order or countermanded order to obey. French officers were often left to interpret the orders received in pragmatic ways. Together with time, this fluid situation multiplied misunderstandings and confusion in the military chain of command, creating space for initiative and the negotiation of individual "moral choices" within the hierarchical framework. Uncertainty and confusion generated competition between command echelons, and tensions within the rank structure between inter-dependent leaders and subordinates.[15]

Defending Tunisia

Even before the Torch planners began to consider the invasion of AFN, Tunisia was already viewed by senior French commanders as the critical node and the point most vulnerable to Axis invasion. However, one difficulty with the Vichy policy of "defense against whomever" in AFN was that it failed to define the threat and to establish clear strategic priorities for dealing with it. British advances into Cyrenaica in early 1941 had the French imagining how to reoccupy the demilitarized zone in southern Tunisia to disarm retreating Italians who might appear before the Mareth Line, a Maginot-like clutter of pill boxes and strong points built to seal the "bottleneck" between southern Tunisia and Italian Tripolitania. The arrival of Rommel in North Africa in February 1941 and the establishment of a strong Luftwaffe presence in Sicily had forced Weygand to consider the possibility of an Axis invasion of Tunisia. *Le Délégué général du government* had vehemently objected to the second Paris protocol struck between Darlan and Abetz on 27–28 May 1941, which would have allowed the Germans "in civilian clothes" to use Bizerte as a supply point for the Afrika Korps. By threatening to open fire on any German who appeared in Tunisia, he managed to scupper that part of the "protocol" at least, although the Darlan–Abetz bargain did spring Juin from his *Oflag* while eventually supplying 2,000 French trucks for the Germans.[16] On 28 September 1941, with the Mediterranean increasingly engulfed in the war, Weygand had issued a defense plan that posited the most likely threats to AFN to be German incursions either through Spain and Spanish Morocco or into Tunisia with the naval base at Bizerte as the principal target.[17]

Deprived from 19 November 1941 of Weygand's unifying vision and authority, Juin, Darlan, and de Lattre de Tassigny subsequently split over how best to defend Tunisia. At the base of this disagreement was the question of who might constitute the greater menace to AFN. With his navalist perspective and a more collaborationist construct of Vichy "neutrality," Darlan's priority was to defend against an attack by *les Anglo-Saxons*.[18] As a land-warfare professional unencumbered by Darlan's – and the French navy's – ironclad Anglophobia, Juin, like Weygand, was preoccupied with the possibility of an Axis incursion either from Sicily or through the Mareth Line. But, mindful of Weygand's fate, "prudence" initially required Juin merely to list the potential invasion routes into AFN rather than prioritize them for his subordinates. However, when, on 30 January 1941, Juin issued his *instruction personnelle et secrète* (IPS) detailing the Axis threat to Tunisia, it raised such a tsunami in the collaborationist spas of Vichy that he ordered it destroyed. Henceforth, rather like Alsace-Moselle, the defense of Tunisia against an Axis incursion became something to be thought of always, but spoken of never.[19]

In the absence of an agreed-upon external enemy, predictably the French high command declared war on each other. During his time as *Délégué général* and taking inspiration from those "hedgehogs" that had imploded on the Somme and Aisne in 1940, Weygand had envisioned taking a stand in the north by transforming Bizerte and Tunis into a French Tobruk. In November 1941, Jean de Lattre de Tassigny, commander of Tunisian ground forces (CSTT) from September 1941 until he was relieved in February 1942, and Alphonse Juin, land forces commander in AFN, had wrangled over how best to secure the Maghreb's eastern marches. That what should have been a sober staff *Kriegsspiel* quickly degenerated into an ad hominem slanging match was hardly surprising, as Juin and the temperamental de Lattre had been bitter rivals since Saint-Cyr.[20] Speaking as the resident *français d'Algérie*, and from a geopolitical optic that considers geography as destiny, Juin viewed Tunisia as "merely the prolongation towards the east of Algeria's Constantinois." Juin's mandate was to defend AFN, of which Algeria – sovereign French territory – was the keystone, with vulnerable protectorates buttressing the flanks. Judging that a forward defense of Tunisia was impractical, Juin's preference was for French forces to fall back on the Tunisian Dorsal, the eastern extension of the Saharan Atlas that slices through the frontier between

Tunisia and the Constantinois. Not surprisingly, perhaps, while Juin's early strategic withdrawal was subsequently endorsed by the French official history of the campaign, many contemporaries found it questionable.[21]

Juin dismissed de Lattre's vision for a forward defense on the Mareth Line as impractical without air cover and adequate logistics. The debate was further complicated by the fact that no one could agree whether the main threat was through Tripolitania in the east or Bizerte in the north. Juin won the argument by backchanneling Darlan, then Defense Secretary, that he too feared a British incursion through Tripolitania, and encouraged him to work Wiesbaden for the very reinforcements, armaments, logistical capabilities, and upgrades of the Mareth Line that would make de Lattre's plan feasible. It was in this context of working to secure German cooperation for the defense of southern Tunisia against the British that Juin had met with Göring and General Walter Warlimont in Berlin on 21 December 1941.[22]

But, in the opinion of one of his biographers, the actual reason for Juin's rejection of de Lattre's concentration in southern Tunisia was that it posited a scenario of Erwin Rommel in search of a Tunisian sanctuary should he be put to flight in Egypt and harried across Libya by the British. Were that to happen, Juin had no intention of resisting Rommel, Jean-Christophe Notin speculates, but rather would join forces with him to fight the British. "We'll fight the Anglo-Saxons. I guarantee it," Juin had promised Laval. This alleged declaration joined the widely accepted rumor that Juin had given his word not to take up arms against Germany as a condition for his release from Königstein, to become the ball and chain that the controversial Marshal of France dragged behind him for the remainder of his life.[23] A skeptical Costagliola counters that Juin had been made well aware, in the wake of his failed December 1941 encounter with Göring and Warlimont, that the political and military foundation for a joint Franco-Axis defense of southern Tunisia had not been laid. Furthermore, Juin feared that to make common cause with the Axis would open AFN to Anglo-American reprisals. The bottom line was that Berlin did not trust the French, fearing that, if they were allowed to rehabilitate the Mareth Line, it might be used to block Axis forces retreating across Tripolitania.[24]

But whatever the complaints about Juin's character – and they were legion – most admitted that his strategic analysis was thorough, a trait that would make him especially appreciated by the Americans. Juin's predilection to fall back into Algeria was also based on the realization that Tunisia offered a fragile redoubt for the defense of AFN. At Italian insistence, Tunisia was lightly garrisoned, with only one lean eight-battalion division of around 12,000 troops, scattered in garrisons throughout the territory.[25] Juin complained that the significant Italian population in Tunisia and eastern Algeria contained many Axis sympathizers, who compromised his ability to camouflage troops as native police, scatter supplemental soldiers in inconspicuous remote garrisons, or create secret arms caches, as had become commonplace in Morocco.[26]

If the loyalty of the European population was in doubt, the potential for indigenous defection was even greater. In August 1942, the French had incarcerated Habib Bourguiba, the leader of the Tunisian nationalist party Neo-Destour at the Fort Saint-Nicolas in Marseilles. And while Bourguiba had counseled his followers not to be seduced by Axis blandishments, Tunisian Muslims were bombarded by appeals from such pro-Axis stations as Radio Bari, Radio Berlin, Radio Roma, and, from January 1943, Radio Tunis, as well as being showered with tracts written by the propaganda office of Major Mähnert in Tunis and distributed along the front, promising favorable treatment to *tirailleurs* and Frenchmen who deserted to Axis lines. However, treachery seems not to have been widespread among the 26,000 Tunisians eventually incorporated into the French army between 1942 and 1945, in large part because it did not take a genius to realize, in the wake of El Alamein, Stalingrad, and Torch, that Axis days were numbered. Nevertheless, the food situation in AFN continued to be a critical worry for French officials, who feared that famine might shift the loyalties of Muslims in Morocco and Algeria toward the Axis. So, Juin had to calculate what percentage of his meager forces should be held back for internal security.[27]

In January 1942, de Lattre was relieved by Juin protégé Georges Barré, in a switch-out that permanently damaged relations between two of France's most senior generals. In the short term, however, the July 1942 fall of Tobruk and Rommel's subsequent surge into Egypt, that helped to precipitate the Allied decision for Torch, had seemed to render the Juin versus de Lattre strategic debate temporarily academic. By January 1943, when Rommel did appear on his Tunisian doorstep, Juin and his *armée d'Afrique* had wobbled into the Allied camp. Rommel's one-time aficionado now became his antagonist.[28] But, if de Lattre's Mareth Line defense scheme had departed with his recall to France, no agreed-upon plan to defend Tunisia (Map 1.1) had been resolved. In Weygand's view, holding Bizerte was vital. In February 1942, Darlan also had informed Juin that the retention of Bizerte in the face of a British attack was "primordial" even at the expense of other points, because it would "attract the maximum of (British) assets."[29]

Following Darlan's directive, Juin, together with Barré and Bizerte commander Vice-Admiral Edmond Derrien, wargamed the defense of Bizerte on 8–11 April 1942. Juin's conclusion was that the defense of Bizerte's harbor, arsenal, and industrial facilities would require a defense perimeter 104 kilometers long. Defending this perimeter would require the totality of French reserves in AFN and "risk the fate of North Africa and the field army on a single battle." His solution was to remove Bizerte from control of the CSTT, and hand its defense over to Derrien, who would concentrate on defending Ferryville, at

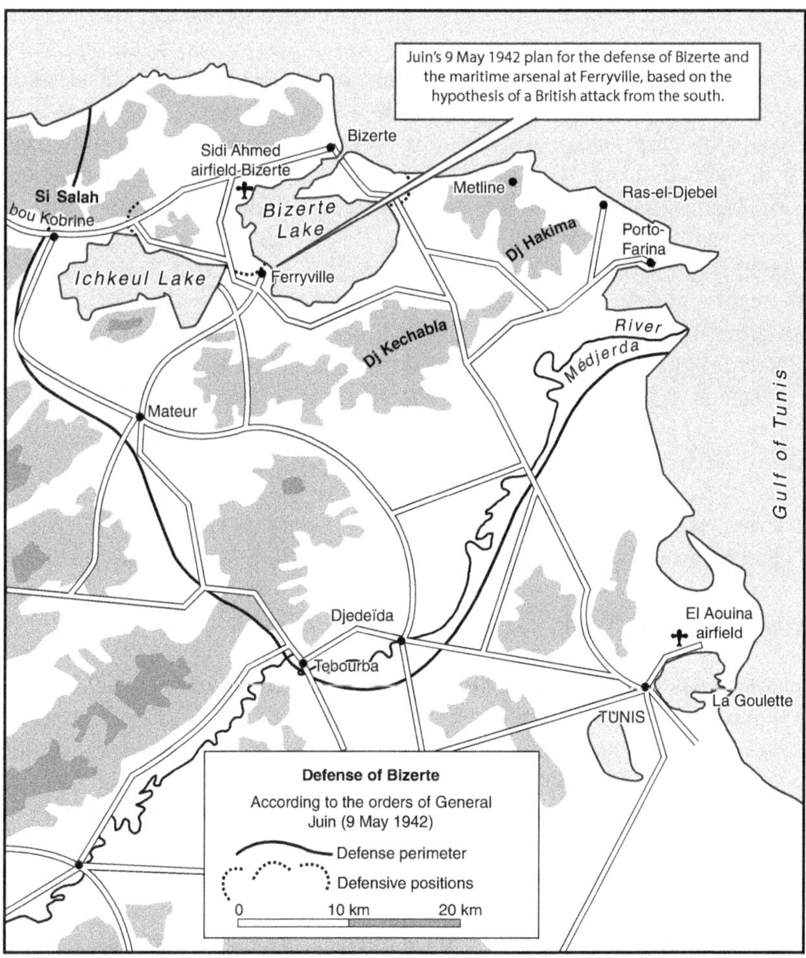

Map 1.1 Map of northern Tunisia.

the southern end of the Lac de Bizerte, which contained France's sole overseas navy yard and arsenal, and the Menzel Djemil isthmus that separates the Lac de Bizerte from the sea. In the meantime, three divisions of troops rushed from Algeria and Morocco would lift the siege of Bizerte within thirty days. Juin's plan was confirmed in a 9 May 1942 IPS, and CSTT Barré was to finalize its details by 22 August.[30]

In his memoirs, Juin insisted that his plan simply remained faithful to Weygand's vision.[31] Unfortunately for Juin, he was sent back to the drawing board by Darlan, now commander in chief of French forces, and Pierre Laval, who had been restored as premier in April 1942. "The military value of Tunisia remains in its harbors," Darlan lectured Juin on 2 May, and "The Tunis–Bizerte group must be tenaciously defended, above all Bizerte ... The defense of Bizerte against a land attack must be reevaluated; covering forces must fight tooth and nail to keep the enemy for as long as possible far from the position; the battle for the isthmuses being the final recourse." Because Darlan's corrective arrived at the last minute, Juin's 9 May IPS, which renounced the defense of Mareth, of the eastern ports of Gabès, Sousse, and Sfax, and of Tunis, remained the battle plan for the moment. But it nevertheless specified that, although abandoned, "*their harbors and airfields would be rendered unserviceable*" (italics in the original). But this admonition lacked urgency, because the calculation at Vichy was that other imperial locations were judged to be more likely Allied objectives, a strategic misstep reinforced by the 5 May 1942 British seizure of Diego-Suárez (now named Ansiranana) in Madagascar. So, it did not seem to matter much that command of Bizerte would fall to Admiral Derrien, while "the command of Tunisia" would revert to CSTT Barré, "charged with organizing the south, and the center of Tunisia, and to hold the mountainous zone to the east of Béja."[32] These remained Barré's marching orders, modified slightly by a further IPS – Juin's last before Torch – of 22 August, that laid out the "phases of maneuver" that incorporated Darlan's instructions "to insure no matter what the preservation of Bizerte." But the assumption upon which Juin's defense plan was based remained a British attack on Bizerte from the south.[33] In the event, the enemy, the direction, and the configuration of attack diverged wildly from Juin's planning assumptions.

But conflict scenarios seemed remote in AFN's somnambulant autumn of 1942, as Rommel had kicked the British into the Nile delta, Juin shuffled his troops away from the beaches and back to their winter quarters in Morocco, the Wehrmacht slouched toward Stalingrad, and the decadent Americans seemed incapable of wresting the distant island of Guadalcanal from Japanese control. Vichy's complacent planners settled on "stalemate" as the war's ascendant narrative. At least this postponed the need to reconcile conflicting threat assessments, and problems caused by a splintered chain of command and a penury of troops and matériel. But Juin at least recognized that this disorder at the top delivered mixed messages to *l'armée d'Afrique* that translated into "hesitations and contempt, because resistance to one implies for better or worse collaboration with the other."[34] This wavering at the top, accelerated from 8 November by the fact that the command in Algiers was taken hostage, first by a resistance group and subsequently by the Americans, produced a "lassitude" in the leadership, stoked fear that "dissidence" had compromised *l'armée d'Afrique*, and abandoned officers at the local level to their own devices. In these conditions, Costagliola points out that officers were freed to decide on the "relative value" of orders according to when they were issued and who or what service issued them, even as the octogenarian Marshal at Vichy squawked "You have heard my voice on the radio, it is the one you must obey."[35]

A Confused Chain of Command

Finally, and most critically, if Torch had triggered Vichy's unmasking, the slow-motion treason that played out in Tunisia further disaggregated and paralyzed an already-contorted French chain of command. Not surprisingly, while a system cross-wired to short-circuit potential pro-Allied conspiracies in AFN perhaps served the purposes of Vichy "neutrality," it hardly optimized French defense of Tunisia against invasion, especially when command consensus over the most likely threat to AFN, and how to counter it, remained undefined and in dispute.[36] Nor did it match Torch planning assumptions. In August 1942, the British Joint Intelligence Committee opined that the rapid arrival of Allied forces in Tunisia would forestall a large Axis invasion. A major premise – indeed, aspiration – of the decision to attack Casablanca had been that token French resistance would delay an Axis invasion of Tunisia long enough to permit Allied forces to leapfrog east from Algiers to Bône, and overland to Tunis. Furthermore, Allied planners had calculated that it would make no strategic sense for Berlin and Rome to commit substantial forces to a major campaign in Tunisia.[37] Unfortunately, Hitler had been taking decisions that defied military logic at least since his September 1939 attack on Poland – some might argue ever since the 1935 remilitarization of the Rhineland. And while, in November 1942, the jury was still out on Stalingrad, so far, *Der Führer*'s gambles had mostly paid off. Nor could Torch's architects factor in the likely reactions of the French high command in Tunisia, largely because they were indecipherable. But, in the event, even Allied hopes for token French resistance in Tunisia would prove illusory. In November 1942, "Defense against whomever" joined "*la comédie politique d'Alger*," the fragmentation of the French chain of command, and Juin's reflex to retreat into Algeria, leaving the door to Tunisia ajar to Axis forces.

The September 1942 command reorganization that separated AFN into "terrestrial" and "maritime" sectors, in theory, had divided military authority in Tunisia as elsewhere in AFN, into army and navy spheres. The "terrestrial" theater in Tunisia, stretching from the lower Medjerda valley to the frontier with Tripolitania, was commanded by Barré. A decorated Great War veteran, CSTT Barré had spent virtually his entire career in *l'armée d'Afrique*, commanding the 7th North African Division in 1940. A Weygand protégé, he was subsequently retained in the Armistice Army, assigned in late 1940 to oversee the demilitarization of the Mareth Line. Barré was also an acolyte of his superior in the hierarchy, Juin, who had eased his promotion to lieutenant general (*général du corps d'armée*) as a prelude to de Lattre's February 1942 reassignment under protest to lead a stripped-down Armistice Army "division" at Montpellier. Juin's little command *coup* supplanted the temperamental and ambitious de Lattre with the less able but more pliant Barré. Juin's command changeout was also meant to insure that, in the event of invasion, French troops in Tunisia would not be locked into a sacrificial defense of Bizerte and Tunis, thus opening Algeria to invasion from the east. If Juin could not win his strategic argument with Darlan and de Lattre on the merits, he would prevail through a reshuffle of personnel.

Tunisia's "maritime" sector translated into the "*arrondissement maritime de Bizerte*" that extended from the coast, down the Medjerda valley to the Algerian frontier. Its commander – a sixty-one-year-old, one-eyed veteran of the First World War, Edmond Derrien – had been slated to retire in 1941, and probably wished that he had. But as an ADD (*ami de Darlan*, friend of Darlan), he had been enticed to stay on with a promotion to vice-admiral. Many believed that Derrien had been elevated above his competence, as his nickname on the lower decks was *Der-rien-de-tout* (not up to much). His command included the "fortified camp" of Bizerte that incorporated France's sole overseas naval arsenal and shipyard as well as the harbors of Tunis, Sousse, and Sfax. A garrison of soldiers called "*le groupement de Bizerte*" defended the Bizerte naval compound.[38] For matters of naval combat and defense of harbor installations, Derrien's immediate superior was Admiral Moreau, prefect of the IVᵉ Région maritime in Algiers. However, "in the event of operations," Derrien fell under the orders of the "General commanding the Theater of operations in Tunisia for everything concerning the defense of the Bizerte sector." This should have been Barré, who held the same rank as Derrien, but who answered to "the Commander in Chief in North Africa" – namely Juin.[39] The fact that the "*groupement de Bizerte*" was commanded by Derrien and not Barré would further disarticulate the French response because it would resurrect the Darlan–Juin quarrel over the strategic value of Bizerte, set the navy against the army, and ultimately sabotage the authority of Darlan, Juin, and Moreau in Algiers in favor of Vichy and Tunisia's Resident General, Admiral Jean-Pierre Esteva.

This was because Derrien was close – physically, personally, and through service affiliation – to Esteva (Figure 1.1). German diplomat and self-styled Arab authority Rudolph Rahn described the Resident General and Dardanelles veteran as a "Gentleman of a certain age, stocky, with a large gray beard, boasting a reputation for a profound piety and a sense of almost infantile self-satisfaction." Nevertheless, he judged Esteva "incapable of making any decision."[40] Esteva answered in theory, through Vichy's foreign affairs secretariat, ultimately to Laval. But, because he was also a full admiral who had commanded both the Far East and the Mediterranean fleets, he had close personal relations with Darlan, whom he addressed in the familiar *tu* form, as

Figure 1.1 Admiral Jean-Pierre Esteva, Resident General of Tunisia, with German representative and Arab expert Dr. Rudolf Rahn, and Major Henri Curnier, commander of the *Légion des volontaires français contre le bolchévisme* in Tunisia, at the entrance of Bordj Cedria camp (Borj Cédria, Tunisia) on 15 March 1943. (Photo by Apic/Getty Images)

well as with Admiral Gabriel Auphan, who managed the Vichy admiralty.[41] The chain of command technically ran through General Georges Revers as chief of the general staff to Eugène Bridoux, the secretary of state for war, or to Auphan, who was both head of the French Admiralty and Commander in chief of Maritime Forces, who depended for their authority on Laval and ultimately Pétain. In fact, after some initial soul searching, Derrien would opt to follow the orders of Esteva and Vichy, rather than listen to Juin and Darlan.

Two Commanders, Two Choices

The reaction in Tunis to news of Torch would be complicated by command turmoil in Algiers, multiple scenarios for the defense of Tunisia, none of which seems to have received final command imprimatur, and a tortuous multi-service chain of command, with Tunis, Algiers, and Vichy all claiming precedence, and through which arrived orders, instructions, suggestions, and directives to the men on the ground. As a consequence, as elsewhere in AFN, drift, equivocation, and confusion characterized the leadership in Tunisia on 8–13 November, as communications were periodically severed, and contradictory orders arrived from various headquarters. Claims of authority from Darlan, Juin, Noguès, or Esteva, not to mention assorted figures at Vichy, as well as uncertainty that subordinate commanders would follow orders that ran counter to their individual consciences, combined to stifle command initiative. The result during those fateful hours and days, as the "orders and counter-orders" ricocheted across and around Mediterranean shores, was that Barré and Derrien shared with their superiors a culpable hesitancy and indecision, even passivity, in the face of an initially anemic Axis invasion, which filtered down to their subordinates, whose attitudes influenced their command choices.[42] By 14 November, "the passivity which had begun through indecision had . . . to be continued because of material weakness," concludes Paxton.[43]

A "menace" warning went out in the late afternoon of 6 November as reports reached Tunis of an Allied naval buildup at Gibraltar.[44] In the late morning of 7 November, troops in Constantine and Tunis were put on alert. That evening, Juin ordered Barré to deploy his defense dispositions for the harbors, beaches, and airfields in Tunisia. Moreau passed on Darlan's order to block the Bizerte shipping canal, but in a very oblique manner that left Derrien much leeway.[45] The 8 November opened at 00:25 with a warning from the Oberkommando der Wehrmacht (OKW) of the possibility of Allied landings at Bône, Philippeville, or Tunis, and the OKW offered Luftwaffe support to the French. At 01:00, American consul in Tunis Hooker Doolittle presented Esteva with a letter from President Roosevelt announcing that the invasion was, "*uniquement des Américains*," and asked that American troops be granted free passage into Tunisia, which Esteva rejected. At 01:45 on 8 November, Barré received an order from Juin "to put in place, at 08:00, the first echelon of troops designated to defend ports and beaches in the Tunis subdivision, the air bases and landing zones. Keep other subdivisions on alert." As a result, Barré subsequently issued a stand-to order condemning "Anglo-Saxon" aggression and admonishing his soldiers "to execute the orders of the Marshal."[46] At 03:50, as news of the attack on Oran arrived, Derrien sent out a "*défense totale*" order, which required the manning and arming of coastal batteries, preparations for the defense of the Bizerte arsenal, and the call up of reservists. At 05:00 the Germans offered Luftwaffe support from Sicily, followed by proposals to send Luftwaffe liaisons to Tunis to coordinate operations. At 09:45, an order from Vice-Admiral Auphan – "We are attacked. We will defend ourselves. That's my order" – was disseminated to all services. He directed that the La Goulette canal be blocked to deny entry into Tunis harbor.[47]

At 14:00, Vichy gave its permission for two Luftwaffe liaison officers to reach AFN to coordinate operations with the CSTT.[48] Barré learned in the late afternoon through the Vichy war secretariat that, "in the case that General Juin can no longer exercise command," Darlan had put him in charge of an operational theater designated as "Tunisia–Constantine," which mirrored the Morocco–Oranais command arrangement that had been imposed on Noguès. "Thus, at the end of the day on 8 November, the situation seemed clear," declares the official French naval history. "General Barré had taken command of the Eastern Theater and the defense plans were activated. The adversaries were the Americans and the British." The Axis announced that they would dispatch the *Schnellboot* (or *S-Boot*, rapid attack boat) flotilla based in Sicily to Tunisia, together with Italian troops and 88 mm dual-purpose anti-aircraft and anti-tank guns originally designated for Rommel.[49] However, a telephone conversation between Barré and his new subordinate Major General Édouard Welvert, commander of the Constantine division, concluded that there was no Allied invasion in their sector, which caused them to doubt the information they were receiving. Their main concern seemed to be the reports of the "dissidence" at Algiers that had temporarily detained Juin and Darlan, and the fear that there might be similar plots afoot in Constantine or Tunis.[50]

The problem was that the definition of "dissidence" was evolving, as the navy gradually assembled under the banner of Pétain and Esteva, while the army elected to follow the orders of Darlan, Juin, and XIX Corps commander Louis Koeltz.[51] Obeying Darlan's message, on the morning of 9 November, Barré ordered his scattered and ill-armed forces to prepare to resist the Allies as the "first aggressors," although in his memoirs he insisted that his positions were "reversible." At midnight on 8 November, the German high command had sent an "ultimatum" to the French government via the German armistice commission at Wiesbaden that the Luftwaffe must be allowed to base planes in Tunisia and the Constantinois to resist the Anglo-American invasion. This was followed by permission from Vichy at 08:45 on 9 November for Axis forces to use the air bases in Tunisia and Constantine, as well as the ports of Bizerte and Tunis. Darlan informed Barré at 07:00 on 9 November that "The Americans, having been first to invade Africa, are our adversaries and we must oppose them alone or with help."[52]

On 9 November, the commander of the Sétif subdivision, Colonel Jacques Schwartz, received a report that American and French troops had left Algiers marching toward the southeast and asked Welvert about "the attitude to adopt if it's a question of non-loyal French troops?" The Division Commander ordered him to "shoot without hesitation," which presumably resulted in Lapouge's 7e RTA being ordered to defend the Kherrata pass.[53] In the morning of 9 November, two Luftwaffe liaison officers dispatched by Kesselring arrived at El Aouina, the Tunis airport, after having first landed at Sétif in an unsuccessful attempt to contact Darlan. During their meeting with Barré and Esteva, the two officers announced that German aircraft would soon be arriving in

Tunisia, and handed the two Frenchmen "a list of requirements that constituted the basis of military collaboration." Barré ask for a postponement: "We told them that we would let them know our response after consultation with the Marshal and the Chief of the Government. Our interlocutors agreed to await this reply."[54] At 05:20 on 10 November, Barré was informed that General Bridoux at Vichy had given permission for the Germans to land at El Aouina. In a communication with Welvert, Barré expressed concern that Vichy had allowed the Germans to land before the Allies had attacked Tunisia, and that this had caused "unsettling commentaries from the majority of officers on whose loyalty I can no longer count." In other words, the command was beginning to get pushback from its subordinates over its decision to allow the Axis unfettered access to Tunisia. Perhaps this resistance was encouraged by news that arrived at 11:00 on 10 November, that Darlan had signed an armistice with the Americans, news incompatible with Barré's order to allow German planes to land at El Aouina. At 17:55 on the evening of 10 November, Welvert at Constantine received the order from Juin to "resist the Axis." But three hours later, he complained to XIX Corps commander Koeltz that Tunis was telling him the opposite. "What should I do?," he asked. Koeltz's answer: "absolute neutrality." In Leconte's view, this offered an example of how a subordinate in the French hierarchy avoided responsibility for executing orders "of doubtful origins." He did not ask for a written confirmation of Barré's order. Rather, he simply sought out someone else in AFN's fractured military hierarchy who would supply a different directive, which allowed him to take no action.[55]

The French official history insists that the German demand to use El Aouina was an ultimatum, not a request, one acquiesced to by the French representative at Wiesbaden – fifty Ju 52s, twenty-five Ju 87s, twenty-five Messerschmitt Bf 109s, two Ju 88s, and one Ju 90 appeared over Tunis at 12:30, flying so low that their black crosses and even, some claimed, the faces of the pilots were visible from the ground.[56] A detachment of the 4^e^ RCA with two squadrons of tanks under the orders of Colonel, later General, Guy Le Couteulx de Caumont took up a position on the hill overlooking the airbase. An after-action report written on 19 November 1946 placed the Luftwaffe's arrival (Figure 1.2) three hours later.

> Around 15:30 the sky was full of vibrations of the first German planes overflying Tunis before landing at El Aouina. A motorized detachment of the 4e RCA (*Régiment de chasseurs d'Afrique*) was ordered to El Aouina to oppose the arrival while a battery of the 52e RAA (*Régiment d'artillerie d'Afrique*) took up a position in the region of Notre-Dame du Belvédière overlooking the air field. The alert was given – the German landing had begun. The news spread like wildfire … The motorized detachment of the 4e Chasseurs arrived on the airfield just as the large transport planes were offloading their cargos. The armored vehicles took their position, their turrets swung round, the machinegunners with their fingers on the triggers. In a few seconds, the planes with their

Figure 1.2 German troops disembarking from a Ju 52 at El Aouina airfield in Tunis. (Photo by ullstein bild/ullstein bild via Getty Images)

black crosses would be the first objectives – emotions were taut. But the brief order rang out: "don't shoot."[57]

If this post-war report fails to mention who issued the stand-down order, it was because, far from opposing the Germans, Colonel Le Couteulx's mission, according to the 1946 after-action report, was to "assure the protection of the Axis detachments and see that they don't venture beyond El Aouina to avoid any incident at Tunis were they to go there." Barré was to prepare an order explaining the government's decision to allow Axis use of Tunisian airfields. In the meantime, French forces deployed to prevent an Allied amphibious landing. Shore batteries were armed, submarines prepared to sortie, while ships were scuttled to block the entrances to the harbors at Bizerte, La Goulette at the entrance to Tunis harbor, and Sfax.[58] When Welvert sent the 3ᵉ RCA on a reconnaissance of southeastern Tunisia, its commander, Lieutenant colonel Pierre Manceau-Demaiu, was informed by the naval command in Sfax that "at a minimum" they would assume an attitude of complete neutrality toward Axis forces. When Manceau-Demaiu urged that they adopt an aggressive posture toward the Axis, naval officers denounced him as a "dissident" and threatened forcibly to take over command of his squadron.[59] A similar "economy of force" reflex saw Air Force chief in AFN General Jean Mendigal order his pilots to evacuate their aircraft to Biskra in southern Algeria, well out of harm's way, an order which Juin never reversed after Mendigal had refused his superior's direct order on 11 November to resist Axis forces. Obviously, "defense against whomever" excluded resistance against Axis forces.[60]

Unfortunately, as Darlan prevaricated and Clark threatened in Algiers, from 9 November, Axis forces had been allowed resistance-free access to Tunisia, "courtesy of the French authorities."[61] Furthermore, by exposing the hypocrisy of "defense against whomever," Vichy had gambled on the loyalty of *l'armée d'Afrique*. "I must tell you what emotion this occupation of El Aouina by the Axis air forces has caused, and the unsettling commentaries that it has provoked among the majority of officers upon whose loyalty I can no longer rely," Barré reported to Vichy on 9 November.[62] After being notified of the landings at El Aouina and that an Axis convoy was scheduled to arrive at Bizerte, Derrien had what the Viard Commission, set up in August 1943 to investigate command behavior in Tunisia in November 1942, called "his first 'National' reaction," when he signaled the Admiralty at 16:00 on 9 November: "I must inform you that these events have produced reactions that for the moment I can control in the army, the air force and the navy at Bizerte. But I cannot answer for the consequences." In other words, Vichy was being informed by its senior commanders that the rank-and-file military was unwilling to accept collaboration with the Axis. And while Axis use of air bases such as "Sidi Ahmed (Bizerte) and El Aouina (Tunis) might probably be acceptable, a joint occupation certainly will not be." The French Admiralty replied that the Anglo-Americans had initiated the crisis, and that Vichy had no choice but to "submit" to Axis *force majeure*. "Obey Navy Commander in Algiers (Moreau)," the Admiralty urged. In a message to Esteva, Vichy's Secretariat of Foreign Affairs too laid the blame on the Anglo-Americans and pleaded that they were powerless "to prevent one or the other of the belligerents carrying the war onto our soil." At least, it pointed out, "The government has [already] requested that no Italian reinforcements be sent to Tunisia and count on this being honored."[63] Clearly, the *Maréchalisme* of the armed forces in North Africa was taxed to breaking point as Berlin and Rome exposed the duplicity of "defense against whomever."

"A new phase opened, of a particular character," the 19 November 1946 report continued. "At that point, it was a question of delaying the enemy forces without fighting them. One had to avoid engagement at all costs, but nevertheless contain the advance of the invader."[64] In fact, this 1946 report tried to portray French confusion, prevarication, and the passive posture adopted both by the Constantine division and by the CSTT in the face of Axis invasion as a clever delaying strategy against Axis forces.[65] As Leconte demonstrates, inaction was rather the response of an insecure senior command caught between pressure from their subordinates to resist the Axis and fear of issuing an order that would set the spas of Vichy boiling. On the morning of 10 November, Darlan proclaimed a ceasefire throughout AFN and "complete neutrality toward all the belligerents." These instructions were passed on to both Barré and Derrien at noon, who relayed the order to their subordinates. Moreau in Algiers also directed commanders in Bône, Philippeville, and Bougie not to resist American arrivals in those harbors. However, amid complaints that Barré was not cooperating with the Germans, and insistence from Auphan that the Bizerte channel be unblocked to allow access to the Axis flotilla, in the afternoon of 10 November, the Admiralty announced that the Germans had been given free access into Tunis and Sfax. The Secretary of State for War at Vichy, General Eugène Bridoux, forwarded the same information to Barré, with instructions to avoid contact between French and German troops while not abandoning Tunisian soil.[66] In the evening, Barré learned that Juin had been reinstated as commander in chief. At 23:00, Auphan messaged that an Axis flotilla would soon arrive at Bizerte. Consequently, the harbors at Bizerte, Tunis, and Sfax were to be unblocked, an order rescinded on the next day, 11 November.[67]

The French army's official history asserts that orders to resist neither the Americans nor the Axis placed Barré in an "ambiguous position."[68] At this moment, however, directives from Algiers and Vichy began to diverge for good. According to Notin, only on 10 November, two days after the Allied invasion had been launched, did Juin contact Barré by telephone.[69] The CSTT told Juin that Vichy had given permission for the Germans to land at El Aouina. Rather than contradict those instruction, at 19:30 on the evening of 10 November, Juin gave the following order: "Take dispositions to resist and cover communications [with] Algeria."[70] In other words, Juin preferred to defend Algeria, rather than prevent the Germans from seizing El Aouina. At 17:30 on the evening of 10 November, lumbering Bristol Beaufighters flying from Malta attacked El Aouina and left a Luftwaffe tanker, three fighters and two bombers in flames as well as two German pilots gravely wounded. This British attack caused Le Couteulx's 4e RCA, allegedly stationed as observers at El Aounia, to scatter and regroup at Pont du Fahs.[71] German air reprisals fell on Bône, Philippeville, and Bougie. On the morning of 11 November, Derrien ordered the French fighter squadron at Sidi Ahmed outside of Bizerte to withdraw to Kairouan to make room for arriving German fighters.[72] Derrien would later disingenuously complain that he could not defend Bizerte in part because he lacked air cover.

On 11 November – the critical day in Tunisia – events began with Juin informing Vichy that, as Pétain had disavowed Darlan's ceasefire order and "Given that with Admiral Darlan I am in the hands of the Americans, in my judgment I am unable to exercise command of operations and can only give complete independence to the commanders of the eastern and western theaters (Noguès and Barré)."[73] The Vichy admiralty insisted that Noguès was now in command in AFN, and that the order to resist the Anglo-Saxons remained in force. A communication from Auphan that arrived at 14:55 explained that while "my personal preference is passivity vis-à-vis all belligerents," the government's decision on the posture to adopt against the invaders would be reached on that evening. Desperate for clear orders, Derrien at Bizerte phoned Moreau, Esteva, and Barré in an attempt to cut through the confusion. "It's difficult to exercise command," Moreau told Derrien, because the Americans had cracked down on French radio communication between the Hôtel Saint-George and Bizerte. "I delegate authority to you over your military establishment. Tell the Resident General," came Moreau's pass-the-buck message to Derrien – "in other words, 'sort it out yourself,'" in the unvarnished language of the Viard Commission. That proved difficult to do when Esteva insisted that Darlan had been disavowed by the Marshal, Juin "had given a free hand to Barré–Derrien in Tunisia" (in fact, he had ordered Barré to retreat to Algeria), and, at noon, news arrived of the German invasion of the *zone libre*, that allowed Darlan to "reclaim his liberty." Barré told Derrien that he was following the order to remain "neutral" and planned that evening to begin withdrawing his troops, transport, and matériel to the west, a move that had been approved by Esteva. In these confused circumstances, the only military order that a "disconcerted" Derrien could think to issue was to prepare to scuttle.[74]

On 11 November, German forces had begun to disembark at Bizerte and La Goulette (Tunis), while the Luftwaffe airlifted more troops into El Aouina and Sidi Ahmed, the Bizerte airfield. At 08:45, Derrien informed Auphan at Vichy that "my understanding is that the arrival of German troops in Tunisia is authorized. The struggle continues against the Anglo-Saxons." Juin also told Barré by telephone that he was to observe "strict neutrality toward all belligerents." At 10:35, Barré informed Esteva that he would begin his withdrawal toward the Dorsal. Esteva raised no objections, while Juin also gave him the go ahead to depart "in the evening of 11 November." But news of the invasion of the *zone libre* caused Moreau in Algiers to signal at 15:47 that "We reclaim our freedom of action. The Marshal no longer being free to take decisions allows us to take those which are more favorable to French interests, while remaining loyal to his person." Juin, too, urged that the Axis invasion be resisted: "From the reception of this order the position of neutrality vis-à-vis the Axis ceases," read his Order 395, sent out in the afternoon of 11 November. "All attempts at intervention by Axis forces in AFN must be resisted with force. Prepare for active operations." This was followed by Order 396, which told XIX Corps (Koeltz) to put Algeria on general alert, recover camouflaged material, deny the Luftwaffe access to air bases in the Constantinois, and liaise with US forces. At roughly 17:00, Juin phoned Barré to tell him to "beat it" out of Tunis to a line running through Béja, Medjez-el-Bab, and Téboursouk. As commander of the only motorized force in Tunisia, Le Couteulx was diverted from El Aouina, where he might easily have mastered the roughly 1,500 lightly armed Axis troops there, to cover Barré's retreat. At 17:00, Barré phoned Derrien from Esteva's office to say "Everything's changed. We're fighting the Axis." Left to defend Bizerte, Derrien too informed the soldiers and sailors of the Bizerte garrison that "Our enemy is the German and the Italian ... Go for it with all your heart against the adversaries of 1940. We must avenge ourselves. Vive la France!"[75]

However, Juin quickly realized that his desire to take the fight to the Axis, still thin on the ground in Tunisia on the afternoon of 11 November, was not universally embraced by his senior subordinates. Esteva avoided contact "on a transparent pretext [a visit to the Bey] and probably to cover himself if need be." Esteva then forced Derrien to withdraw his order to resist the Axis allegedly because it opened Barré's retreating troops to attack. As Barré and his staff departed for Souk-el-Arba, Derrien received strict orders from Auphan in the Admiralty that "you must allow the Italo-German forces disembarking in Tunisia free passage without getting involved. Follow the orders of the Marshal."[76] Exercising his legendary prudence, at 20:00 on 11 November, Juin issued Order 397 that "suspended" Orders 395 and 396. He later insisted that this stand down was issued because Koeltz and air force commander Mendigal refused to act until given the green light by Noguès, whom Vichy had named to replace Darlan. Also, Barré feared that it would subject his retreating troops to Luftwaffe attack before they reached Medjez-el-Bab.[77] At this point, the Viard Commission recognized Derrien's dilemma: Barré and Juin refused to reinforce Bizerte; Esteva claimed to want no action that allegedly might jeopardize Barré's retreat, but in fact made himself unavailable for command; Vichy ordered him not to oppose the arrival of Axis forces; while Noguès' silence was deafening. At the same time, Kesselring redirected General Walter Nehring, who had been passing through Rome on his way to take command of the Afrika Korps, to take charge of the buildup in Tunisia and advance his troops toward the Algerian frontier.[78]

Juin's decision to withdraw Barré from Bizerte–Tunis opened him to criticism. On 12 November, the French still maintained an overwhelming superiority over what was estimated to be 1,000 German soldiers with a few anti-aircraft guns at El Aouina, 20 fighters at Sidi Ahmed, and 2 Italian troop transports at Bizerte, that had yet to offload their artillery and tanks, and whose destroyer escorts had already departed. Pétain ordered Barré to reverse his withdrawal and remain to defend Tunisia against the Anglo-Americans.[79] The two Admirals Esteva and Derrien had preferred to reinforce Bizerte. However, Barré believed that the occupation of the *zone libre* meant that the commencement of hostilities with the Axis was only a matter of time. It would take too long to pull his outlying garrisons into Bizerte, which, as has been seen, was considered by Juin to be an indefensible position in any case, one subject to incessant Luftwaffe attack. At this critical moment, Vichy Secretary of State for War Bridoux had authorized Barré to retreat toward the Eastern Dorsal on the pretext that he wanted to avoid any conflicts with French soldiers who might resist arriving Axis forces. "General Juin, who was commander-in-chief while avoiding behaving like one, issued suggestions," Viard subsequently opined. On the morning of 11 November, Barré had distributed order No. 2 to evacuate troops, equipment, and matériel toward concentration zones along the line Béja–Medjez-el-Bab–Téboursouk. On the night of 11–12 November, along with the troops, 800 vehicles disguised as civilian automobiles and lorries, 147 locomotives and 2,500 rail cars, odds and ends of weaponry collected from secret arms caches, as well as reserves of petrol and coal, began to travel west.[80]

Thus, according to Viard, the "tragedy of Bizerte" was shaped by multiple factors, among them "uncertainty and lack of character of the leaders," even in the wake of "the outrage of the total occupation of France." The committee attributed this hesitation to act, when every minute counted, to "the mystique of the Marshal." They also faulted French military culture. These military leaders were so "anxious to be commanded" that their "bureaucratic scruples obscured the bigger picture of national interest and the Honor of our Arms."[81] There was plenty of individual blame to spread around, beginning with Pétain, whose personal messages on several occasions stoked resistance to the Anglo-Americans. Darlan's evasion of responsibility had been particularly egregious. "Admiral Darlan refused on the 10th to issue orders for Tunisia even though the Americans asked him to, and after the 10th never gave the order to oppose the Germans at El Aouina airfield . . . Therefore, he bears part of the blame for the occupation of this airbase by the enemy." Juin had suspended Orders 395 and 396 to resist Axis forces in Tunisia. "Between the critical dates of 11 and 13 November, [Noguès] never gave an order to his subordinates who anxiously awaited them, and who until the night of 12 November remained a partisan of neutrality." Had Juin and Noguès acted more forcefully, the Axis occupation of Tunisia might have been aborted on the tarmac at El Alouina. Moreau left Derrien without guidance, while Esteva was the critical influence on Derrien's decision to surrender Bizerte to the Axis. Barré also shared responsibility, because he had failed to keep Derrien, his direct subordinate, in the picture, but instead issued contradictory orders. Derrien's error was to have executed Vichy's orders after 11 November, even in the knowledge that the government was held hostage by the Germans and even when these orders were vague.[82]

Juin's passivity and prevarication came in for special censure by Viard. From midday on 10 November, when he resumed command, his orders were vague, even "equivocal." Rather than demand El Aouina's defense, he directed Barré to "resist and cover communications [with] Algeria."[83]

"It seems that on 11 November, General Juin had reason to recommend the immediate initiation of hostilities against the Germans but made the mistake of not imposing his will by giving the order for a speedy attack on the airfield at El Aouina, where the Germans were not at that moment in a position to resist for long," Viard concluded. "As a result, as the Germans continued to reinforce, this offensive tactic became less and less viable. And it seems obvious that from the moment that the enemy occupied Tunis [14 November], General Barré's tactic of temporization imposed itself on the French command until the day it felt able to reject German requests presented in the form of an ultimatum on the night of 18–19 November, which resulted in the initiation of hostilities the following morning."[84]

Viard had probably not been aware of the pre-Torch debate over how best to defend Tunisia, that had split Juin and de Lattre, and the defense plans worked out in May. One might certainly make a case for Barré's withdrawal to preserve his force, join with the Constantine division, and shield Algeria, in keeping with a long-war strategy. However, in the commission's view, Juin's behavior simply fit a pattern for France's North African command, one in which the surprise and confusion of Torch, combined with the intentional fragmentation of authority and a paralysis of initiative caused by a slavish devotion to Pétain reinforced by the quasi-mystical "Oath to the Marshal," had pitched the French command into accountability avoidance mode. As commander in chief of French forces, Darlan's decision simply to recuse himself on 11 November by withdrawing his order to oppose the Germans who cascaded into the *zone libre* and Tunisia in clear violation of the 1940 armistice agreement, placing his precious High Seas Fleet in peril, redefined the concept of command negligence, and telegraphed spinelessness to his subordinates Koeltz and Mendigal, who pressured Juin to withdraw his 11 November Order 395 to oppose the Germans in Tunisia. Viard concluded that, "on his own initiative," Mendigal was more intent on ordering his obsolete air force in Tunisia out of harm's way, "for military reasons for which it is difficult to find a justification," than on actually directing it to defend Tunisia. Mendigal's evacuation order, opposed neither by Juin nor by Barré, "had grave consequences for which they all share responsibility." Barré initiated his retreat at a time when he might successfully have denied El Aouina to the Luftwaffe. When, on 12 November, eleven Ju 52s landed at Sidi Ahmed, and the *avant garde* of what would become an armada of Axis ships and boats sailed into Bizerte, "French guns . . . were silent," while French tugs nudged the invaders' ships toward their docks. If only Torch had been so trouble-free! Moreau phoned Derrien to whine about the "shambles" in

Algiers, but clicked off without attempting to sort out the shambles in Tunis. Auphan mumbled pious *Maréchalist* homilies into the line about "the secret path of Providence that leads our country toward its destiny." Juin asked him to send his three battalions stationed at Bizerte to Barré. Derrien refused, but it was not clear what purpose he otherwise intended for the Bizerte garrison, except to fight the Anglo-Americans or surrender them to the Germans. Noguès, the designated commander in AFN, gave no sign of having a pulse. Derrien had spent 12 November on the phone with his superiors – the Marshal, Esteva, Barré, Juin, Moreau, and Auphan – in a futile quest to divine a direction. In the end, in an act of "passive obedience," he chose Esteva, rather than his direct superior Barré, who seemed obsessed with clearing out of town as fast as possible. To be fair, Derrien had the responsibility to defend a naval base, an arsenal and shipyard, and a small flotilla of boats, none of which was easily transportable. Yet, his passivity constituted neither a military nor a patriotic reflex. In the meantime, "the fate of Bizerte had been decided," along with that of Derrien. "All of this concluded in the decision of 8 December (to surrender Bizerte to the Germans)."[85]

In Juin's defense, his directives appeared at last to have caused *l'armée d'Afrique* to shed its cocoon of "neutrality." As seen at 17:00 on 11 November, Barré had phoned Derrien to announce "Everything's changed. We're fighting the Axis."[86] However, rather than order Le Couteulx to police up the lightly armed German paratroops at El Aouina, Barré commanded Le Couteulx's force to serve as his rearguard as he sought to retreat to a viable defensive position before initiating hostilities. He asked Derrien not to fire on Axis aircraft so as not to provoke reprisals. He also rejected Juin's 12 November request that he initiate hostilities with the Germans, saying that he wanted first to regroup on better defensive positions. Barré had departed Tunis during the night of 11 November to establish his headquarters at Le Kef, 30 kilometers from the Algerian border, where the first Allied liaison officers appeared on 15 November.[87] Barré subsequently justified his tactical withdrawal toward the frontier as necessary to rendezvous with Allied forces and with Welvert's Constantine division. However, as early as September 1944, archivists noted that Barré's command log for the period 9–18 November had been considerably expunged.[88]

Like that of Moreau, Darlan's authority over French sailors also appeared tenuous. As with Laborde in Toulon, Esteva completely snubbed Darlan's 11 November invitation to rally to the Allies. This Gallic Cancan caused Eisenhower to explode. "Confronted with these high geostrategic stakes, French preoccupations seemed derisory," Notin concurs.[89] In the view of Eisenhower, the parochialism and bickering of French military leaders, and an obsession with maintaining a fig leaf of French sovereignty over a region that was clearly shifting under their feet, were seriously impeding campaign progress. This absence of a single message from a unified, resolute leadership disoriented many French officers, and led to prevarications, contradictory orders, and desertions that made the French appear to be unreliable partners.[90] As Juin's biographer notes, the combination of the political divisions at the top of the French military with the equivocations and indecision witnessed in Algiers, where everyone in a command position sought to shirk responsibility, followed by vague orders, "invitations" and "suggestions," issued in an obvious desire to avoid conflict with the Germans and accountability at Vichy, coalesced to give the impression to Allied commanders that Darlan's hesitation resulted from the fact that he was not in firm control of his subordinates. Worse, in the eyes of the Allies, these French flag officers did not even seem to be good patriots. Rather, to the Americans, they appeared as poorly rehearsed actors in frantic pursuit of the play. It did not bode well for future command cooperation, or rearmament, as France slowly and apparently with great reluctance backed into the Allied camp *faute de mieux*.[91]

"Never at any moment having issued any order to attack German forces that had set foot in Tunisia and having approved the withdrawal order issued on 11 November by General Barré, [Juin] is responsible, in his capacity of commander in chief from the 10th [November], for the fact that Axis forces could penetrate Tunisia without encountering the slightest opposition," Viard concluded. Juin's defense was that he had been fired as commander in chief by Vichy, an assertion for which Viard could find no evidence. "Juin remained commander by right and in fact and became responsible for the posture of benign neutrality toward the Axis in Tunisia." At no time did Barré cease to believe that Juin was his hierarchical superior. And at no time did Juin issue firm orders to attack the Germans. Had the French resisted, then Rommel, in full retreat from El Alamein, might have surrendered in Tripolitania or southern Tunisia three or four months earlier, Viard speculated.[92] In fact, as Robin Leconte argues, the success of Torch resulted not from a clandestine resistance, or a defection of senior officers from Vichy, but from bottom-up pressure from the lower tier of the military hierarchy:

> . . . pressure from the soldiers on the officers, the links of hierarchal subordination, the long hours of indecision that followed 8 November, the presence of Axis forces and the risks encountered by troops in Tunisia, all combined to tip AFN [into the Allied camp]. The decisive element proved to be the margin of maneuver allowed, despite themselves, to officers on the ground, left to their own devices in the middle of a confused hierarchy with intermittent contact."[93]

Juin dodged and ducked, insisting that Darlan, not he, had been in command. But Notin concluded that, "By defending Barré, he was defending himself."[94] However, in this moment that called for clear command direction, many suspected that Juin's command failures were the result of his pro-Vichy, if not pro-Axis, sentiments. A more generous interpretation might conclude that he was merely reverting to his original plan to preserve his forces – and to protect Algeria – by extricating French troops to the Dorsal. But this explanation, too, has serious weaknesses.[95] Gaullist soldiers bestowed the derisive nickname "Juin '40," a moniker lifted from a marching song ("Juin '40, la France est à terre. Présent répond les volontaires.") about rallying to defend France in June 1940, on their commander: "It required all the blood spilled by the French in North Africa and Italy and in France to whitewash this great general of the acrimony accumulated by his hours of indecision incurred during the American invasion," Georges Elgozy, who would fight through the Tunisian campaign, remarked bitterly.[96]

As the official navy history points out, on 12 November, Derrien still had two choices: defend his command against Axis encroachment, or sortie his ships and submarines, destroy anything in his arsenal that was not transportable, and, with his garrison, join Barré's bolt for the Dorsal. Derrien's fateful decision to remain in Bizerte was based on five factors. First, he believed that he did not have the means to defend Bizerte against Axis attack. Second, he considered that the abandonment of the harbor with its ships, arsenal, and shipyard, as well as what he and Esteva considered its strategic position in Tunisia, without a direct order was unlawful and tantamount to abandoning a perfectly seaworthy ship. A third factor is to be found in the confusion over who was in charge, contradictory orders, and lack of firm guidance from Algiers. Fourth, the news that the Americans had put Giraud in charge provoked a Gaullist-like reaction from Derrien that Washington had no right to dictate who was to lead French forces. Therefore, the "felonious general" (Giraud) had no legal claim to issue orders. This helped to open an inter-service divide, especially after Admiral Platon arrived in Tunis to enforce the message of "neutrality" toward the Axis. In these circumstances, Esteva, Derrien, and the navy commanders in Sfax opted to follow orders from Vichy, whose position at least had been consistent.[97]

Derrien viewed himself as a tragic figure, a victim of French command chaos in the wake of Torch. However, he took his decision neither to retreat nor to resist while fully realizing its implications. "I have seven citations and twenty-four years of service, and I'll be the admiral who handed over Bizerte to the Germans!," he lamented.[98] During the next three days, he was given every opportunity to reverse course – after all, he conceded that the Axis would occupy Bizerte one way or another. On 12 November, Juin telephoned to persuade him to join Barré's withdrawal, but could only reach Derrien's chief of staff, who informed the commander in chief that Derrien would abandon Bizerte only on Noguès' orders. In the late morning of 12 November, twenty Messerschmitts landed at Sidi Ahmed, the airfield for Tunis. Two Kriegsmarine liaison officers appeared to announce the arrival in Bizerte that afternoon of two patrol boats escorting two Italian freighters, that began to discharge troops and their cargo of artillery and tanks. On 13 November, Derrien was admonished by Barré, and ordered by Darlan to resist the arrival of Germans at Bizerte. Derrien and Esteva complained that they lacked the means to resist, although by the end of the day on 13 November only 2,000 Axis troops had arrived at Bizerte, accompanied by thirty armored vehicles and three batteries of 88 mm cannon. Another 400 to 500 Germans were at Sidi Ahmed.

"Thus, on the evening of 13 November, the military leaders in Algeria and Morocco decided to take up arms at the side of America and Great Britain to fight Germany," concluded the Viard Commission. "But in Tunisia, General Barré, Admiral Esteva and Admiral Derrien passed up the last opportunities open to them on the 12 and possibly 13 November to resist the Germans with some chance of success by taking the offensive. General Juin did not figure out how to impose on them that option which he seemed to favor, and he continued to wait impatiently for the opening of hostilities without ordering his subordinates to take the initiative."[99]

On 14 November, Giraud became overall military commander in AFN, with Juin in command of land forces. Derrien sent a staff officer to Barré carrying a letter meant for Juin, exposing his command dilemma at Bizerte. Many of his soldiers were untrained recruits. Two boatloads of German reinforcements were scheduled to arrive that day. He had no aviation. If he resisted, the Germans would take hostages in the town. And so on.

> To sum up, I'm in a fix and don't see a way out. I'm going to be the admiral who gave Bizerte to the Boches and yet, I only followed orders. My military honor is shot. I hesitate to be responsible for the massacre of hundreds of brave young men to save my reputation. I'm going to temporize: it's the only solution. I fear also that at the first shot, I'll see the arrival of transport planes here from Tunis or further afield. I'll be submerged.[100]

The staff officer was ordered to request a written order from Juin "to throw the Axis forces into the sea." But he would require reinforcements before he would be willing to execute such an order, which Barré refused to give him because he did not want to create a Tobruk-like redoubt in Bizerte.[101] However, with British forces approaching from Bône and Axis forces lacking amphibious operations capability to land outside of a harbor, the analogy with Tobruk seemed contrived.

In the meantime, Algiers and Vichy spewed contradictory directives. Juin continued to ask the retreating Barré "when are your guns going to fire?"[102] Moreau ordered the navy commanders at Tunis, Sousse and Sfax to destroy their equipment and withdraw to the west – Sousse and Sfax deferred to Tunis, while a shore battery disarmed and a minesweeper scuttled in Tunis harbor, and its captain managed to reach Barré's line at Medjez-el-Bab. Simultaneously, the ubiquitous Auphan reminded officers of their oath of loyalty to the Marshal, and ordered Derrien to tune out Algiers.[103]

On 14 November, British troops seized Bône and its airfield. The next day, 300 men from the US 509th Parachute Regiment toppled out of 33 C-47s over the airfield at Youks-les-Bains, 20 kilometers north of Tébessa on the Tunisia–Algeria border. After a few tense moments, poorly armed French troops entrenched around the field welcomed them with open arms. This would become a major base for the US Twelfth Air Force during the Tunisia campaign. British troops pushed to within a mere 56 miles of Tunis. The number of Axis troops at Bizerte on 14 November had grown to 3,500, mostly Italians, as the Germans occupied the Tunis telephone exchange. The Viard Commission's point was that, had the French leadership in Algiers and the command team in Tunis evinced more energy, focus, and moral courage early on to confront the Axis incursion at El Aouina and defend Bizerte and other Tunisian harbors, they might have spared the Allies a long and costly campaign.

Belle agrees that, in early November 1942, the Axis lacked the capacity to mount a massive break-in into Tunisia at short notice. Boats manufactured for a potential invasion of Malta had been dispersed to supply island garrisons in Greece. Hitler had shown no appetite to use paratroops as anything other than infantry following the successful but costly operation to seize airfields in Crete in late May 1941. His Ju 52s were scattered from Stalingrad to El Alamein, where they were being used to supply Rommel through Benghazi and Tobruk. The roughly 12,000 French troops in Tunisia, even with out-of-date equipment, supported by the French air force and possibly by Allied planes from Bône, Youks-les-Bains, and Malta, certainly had the capacity to prevent the Axis from gaining a foothold in Tunisia for a few critical days until Anderson's First British Army rode to the rescue. It all came down to the attitude of the French leaders in AFN. By 13 November, the Axis counted 3,000 troops and 100 planes on the ground in Tunisia. By surrendering El Aouina, and moving the French Air Force (FAF) out of range – another order that Juin had failed to contradict – the French gifted local air superiority to the Axis, which the Luftwaffe used not only to impede the Allied advance on Tunis, but also to seriously damage Allied shipping off Algiers and Bône.[104] The problem was that, of the French leaders in Algiers and Tunis, only Juin seemed prepared to join the Allies following the ceasefire of 10 November. And even he claimed to have been sidelined in the command musical chairs that played out between Vichy, Rabat, and Algiers. The other leaders began to rally to the Allies from 13 November, but this could not begin to take effect before the 14 November. In the meantime, a combination of contradictory orders from Algiers and Vichy saw Barré align with Juin, while Esteva and Derrien sided with Vichy. Meanwhile, Juin appeared more focused on defending Algeria from the Western Dorsal than on preempting the Axis incursion into Tunisia, as

Mendigal's air force hopped from airfield to airfield to avoid combat – as in 1940, the FAF's "long war" strategy appeared increasingly like a "no war" strategy. But, by then, combat avoidance had become a multi-service contagion. In this way, three lost days at Algiers and Tunis had to be redeemed at the cost of almost seven months of battle.[105] But Juin never paid the full price for his equivocal action in Tunisia: the Viard Commission was merely investigative, not a "judicial" panel. Prosecution was left up to the *Comité français de libération nationale* (CFLN), whose chief, de Gaulle, was prepared to "whitewash" the conduct of his Saint-Cyr classmate for failing to oppose the Axis incursions into Tunisia on 11 or 12 November when resistance might have succeeded, instead shifting the blame onto Noguès. Juin's help in rallying *l'armée d'Afrique* to de Gaulle, and the laurels of victory he was to earn in Italy, erased neither his Vichy taint, nor his equivocal conduct in November 1942. As a result, Juin's wartime legacy would be eclipsed by those of de Lattre and Leclerc, and even by that of Koenig. Consequently, Juin was passed over for the command of the First French Army for the liberation of France. Nor was Juin's presence requested at the surrender of Germany and Japan.[106]

The French Army Rejoins the War against the Axis

If the conduct of the French military leadership confused and exasperated the Americans, their own soldiers also found it breathtakingly bewildering. Sergeant Albert Rupert's unit had been put on alert from 8 November when news of the American attack at Casablanca was announced. They joined Barré's "repositioning" toward Pont du Fahs, one shadowed by a German reconnaissance aircraft, as Axis reinforcements occupied Tunis, and sent reconnaissance detachments toward the Algerian border. The French troops continued to retreat westward, rejecting Axis offers of cooperation, French and Germans alternately talking and stalling. On 15 November, the Germans became more insistent, presenting an order from Admiral Platon demanding that the French stand aside and allow the Germans free passage. By 16 November, French and German soldiers still mingled, but eyed each other warily. On the 17 November, the French withdrawal came to a halt at Medjez-el -Bab, a strategic crossroads at the gateway to Algeria, 67 kilometers west of Tunis. The next day – 18 November – Rupert encountered his first Americans. The French soldiers were elated, while the reaction of the GIs, not knowing exactly whose side the French were on, was more reserved. The Americans gave them chewing gum, and boasted that they would soon be in Tunis.[107]

With Allied forces closing in on Tunisia from the west, by 18 November, Nehring had concluded that he must counterattack. In the early hours of 19 November, Rahn's assistant and consul in the German embassy in Rome,

Eitel Möllhausen, handed Barré a letter from General Walter Nehring telling the CSTT to treat the Germans as allies and remove all obstacles to their advance toward Algeria, and inviting him to Tunis for an interview with the Resident General "to bring Barré back to discipline." He reminded Barré that his decision would impact 40 million French citizens under Axis occupation, and over a million POWs in German custody. When Barré respectfully declined, insisting that he must first have an order from Juin, he was informed that hostilities would begin at 17:00.[108] Rupert's description is far more prosaic. French forces, which consisted of some squadrons of *chasseurs d'afrique* and *spahis*, some Algerian and Senegalese *tirailleurs*, and a battery of 75 mm cannon, had been joined at Medjez-el-Bab by the US 175th Field Artillery Battalion, some anti-aircraft guns, and a section of British armored cars. The American anti-aircraft guns opened fire on two Messerschmitts.

> This incident irritated the Germans, and an officer came over to the French barricade at 08:45 and told the French officer: "If at 09:00 the Medjez-el-Bab garrison doesn't rally [to the Germans], it will be annihilated." The quarter-hour passed and nothing happened. But at 10:45 violent explosions occurred to the north: the bombardment had begun, precisely at the Smidia farm, our HQ [headquarters] where the day before we had received the German plenipotentiaries. Then the planes descended on Medjez, bombing and strafing. The power station was hit first. In an instant, the western part of Medjez vanished in the dust and smoke of the explosions. Few losses among our personnel, who disappeared into their holes. But the planes hammered the roads choked with vehicles, setting numerous trucks on fire. The Colonel's [Le Couteulx de Caumont] command car was traversed by a bomb that didn't explode. As soon as the planes departed, the [German] artillery opened up on the squads along the Medjerda [River].

As assault by German paratroopers across the river was turned back by French machineguns camouflaged among the cacti. Surprised by the unexpected resistance, the Germans returned in force and seemed about to overwhelm the French position when a counterattack by a company of Senegalese restored the line. The fighting continued until 15:30 when, with the aid of US anti-tank guns, the French forced a German withdrawal behind a noisy air attack. The French report admitted that Medjez-el-Bab had been a "modest skirmish" with relatively few troops engaged and the bulk of the Allied forces still far away. Nevertheless, this remote scuffle proved of monumental significance, as it signaled the reentry of the French army into the war against the Axis. While the participants in this skirmish were convinced that they had "saved Algeria," they were totally floored when, standing among their bullet-ridden vehicles turned into flambeaux by Stukas, with ten dead and fifteen wounded, Sergeant Rupert's unit received orders – it was unclear from whom – that they were to turn against the Americans. So absurd and out of date were these directives that those who had fired the opening shots of the Tunisian campaign simply ignored them.[109]

The Attack on the Bizerte Arsenal

One final indignity remained to be played out in Tunisia – the seizure of the Bizerte arsenal. This had been anticipated ever since the Toulon scuttle. At 18:00 on 7 December, Derrien and his senior staff were summoned to a meeting with Luftwaffe General Georg Neuffer and Hitler's personal emissary and long-time Rommel chief of staff General Alfred Gause. As Ju 88s circled above the camp making an ear-splitting racket, Derrien was informed that all French forces in Bizerte were to be disarmed and their equipment surrendered by agreement with Vichy. Resistance would meet the full force of German arms that promised to kill every last sailor and soldier, while sabotage would be dealt with by court martial. "Up to you to decide, Admiral," read the letter that Gause handed to Derrien. "Either you are free to return to France, or death."[110] Having concluded that he lacked the means to resist, Derrien gave in, as German torpedo boats penetrated the Lac de Bizerte and aimed their guns at the French vessels. Because of Derrien's orders, preparations for sabotage were not executed. In this way, in the early afternoon of 8 December, 300 German soldiers appeared at the Bizerte arsenal with a tank and some smaller tracked vehicles.[111] General Walter Nehring, the commander of the German contingent in Tunisia in November–December 1942, was able effortlessly to sweep up 8,300 French sailors and 3,700 soldiers, as well as a number of boats and naval stores. Most of these men were subsequently repatriated to France, although some escaped to Algeria. Nor was any attempt made to spike the shore batteries or anti-aircraft guns.[112] Historians more favorable to Vichy echo Derrien's defense at his court martial, praising him for preserving an arsenal and shipyard put to good use six months later by the Allies.[113] Not surprisingly, de Gaulle, who had softly closed the door and wept at news of Bir Hakeim, thought otherwise: "In this way, an important stronghold thus passed into the enemy's hands," the leader of Fighting France recorded. "This lamentable episode marked the end of a shameful succession of events."[114]

At his 1944 court martial that condemned him to life imprisonment, ironically in the wake of Toulon for "failure to scuttle," Derrien's defense was that he had obeyed Pétain's orders and sought to avoid the massacre of his sailors.[115] But, in a 14 November letter to Barré, Derrien argued that he had served as Darlan's scapegoat. Vichy policy had permitted Axis access to Tunisia by obeying the German ultimatum of 8 November, followed by Darlan's cascade of contradictory orders: "8 Nov., we were fighting everyone. 9 Nov., we fight the Germans. 10 Nov., we fought no one. 10 Nov. [12 h], we fight the Germans. 11 Nov. [night], we don't fight anyone," he complained. On 20 November, Admiral Jean-Marie Abrial, who had succeeded the future naval historian and Vichy apologist Auphan at the navy secretariat, ordered him to diffuse Pétain's order to "refuse to obey Darlan [and] Giraud and to oppose Anglo-American forces and don't attack Axis forces." Thus, "42 years of service and seven decorations" down the tubes, because Derrien could not make a moral decision.[116] Yet, Naval records show that Derrien cooperated closely with German requests to convince Barré to cease his opposition, and that some of Derrien's subordinates felt that their Admiral had not given clear directives on how to behave should the Germans invade the Bizerte shipyard.[117] The Germans also occupied the ports of Tunis, Sousse, Sfax, and Gabès, and took over the railways. By 11 December 1942, 50–60 German transport planes were arriving daily, each carrying around 20 soldiers and 4 drums containing 200 liters of petrol. Fifteen to eighteen ships carrying troops had also entered Bizerte harbor, whose entrance Derrien had failed to block, while special Siebel ferries brought in tanks.[118]

Esteva justified his loyalty to Vichy and his opposition to the Allies with the argument that his responsibility as High Commissioner was to maintain French "sovereignty" in Tunisia. Otherwise, the Italians would assert a claim over the protectorate. His pro-Vichy attitude was reinforced by the 15 November arrival in Tunis of Admiral Charles Platon, Secretary of State for the coordination of the armed forces, who worked closely with Nehring and Rahn to reinforce the loyalty to Vichy of French forces and to convince Barré to reverse his withdrawal toward Algeria and return to Tunis.[119] Platon messaged Barré that the Marshal's orders were to "defend the Regency against the Anglo-Saxon invader." However, Barré declined Platon's invitation to meet him in Tunis. The Germans unblocked La Goulette, the entrance to Tunis harbor, and continued to pour reinforcements into Bizerte. From the 18 November, the port of Tunis opened to the invaders. Barré's retreat continued. The Germans penetrated his lines on several occasions, while the Luftwaffe bombed his trains. But still he refused to open fire before he had made contact with the advancing Allies. Meanwhile, Platon also reported that "the entire population: postal workers, the press, the civil service" in Tunis was in "betrayal" mode. "The Germans can't count on anyone," except apparently the French navy. As "local commander" of "le groupement interarmes de Bizerte," Derrien refused to oppose the arrival of Axis forces or allow the soldiers defending the Bizerte naval base to retreat as Barré had ordered. The Viard Commission saw Platon's arrival as the pivotal occurrence that tipped Esteva, and with him Derrien, into collaboration with the Axis. On 18 November, unaware that Barré was absconding from Tunisia, Pétain congratulated both Barré and Derrien for "the faithful interpretation of my orders."[120]

Derrien had rejected the pleas of an emissary sent from Algiers during 14–20 November, who attempted to persuade him to submit to Darlan's orders. Indeed, Derrien's attitude had shifted from self-pity to active cooperation with the Axis invaders. Derrien harangued his command that their duty was to "resist Anglo-Saxon aggression," which, not surprisingly, won Kesselring's approbation. He allowed the Germans to take over some shore batteries, and, with German encouragement, agreed to organize a meeting between Barré and Rahn, who was now political advisor to the German high command in Tunisia. Even in the wake of the scuttle of the High Seas Fleet in Toulon, Derrien pledged to German Admiral Eberhard Weichold that he would continue to defend Bizerte against the Anglo-Americans and Gaullists, and would make no hostile move against the Axis, in keeping with Vichy policy.[121] After the French Navy had refused to prosecute Derrien, a May 1944 army court martial found the Vice-Admiral's defense – that he was merely applying Juin's May 1942 IPS and playing for time until the Anglo-Americans could reach Bizerte – unconvincing. He was sentenced to life behind bars for "failure to scuttle," a rather confounding verdict as the commanders of the High Seas Fleet had been condemned precisely because they did scuttle. Clearly, *la Royale* needed to clarify its scuttling protocols.[122]

"The Front Line of Europe"

If the failure to win the race to Tunis had a silver lining for the Allies, it was because the rush by the Axis leaders to invade Tunisia in the wake of Torch was poorly considered, but perfectly in character. Mussolini insisted in the wake of Torch and El Alamein that the crumbling Axis position on the Mediterranean's southern shore had transformed Tunisia into "the front line of Europe."[123] "While the Italians held Bizerta, enemy landings in Provence, on Sicily and Sardinia, in Greece and in the Aegean were 'improbable,'" according to the strategic calculation in Rome. "If it was lost the enemy might drive on Crete, the Dodecanese islands and the Balkan mainland and threaten the supplies of Romanian petrol – which were essential if the armed forces were going to be able to fight at all. The lines of communication with Tunisia were the easiest to defend because they were the shortest . . . One thing was certain: once Tunisia was lost, Italy would be exposed to the full weight of Allied air power."[124] In Hitler's mind, so long as the battle was confined to North Africa, the Mediterranean remained a peripheral theater and German involvement was the price paid to seal the so-called "Pact of Steel." After two years of maintaining the British on the defensive there, the Mediterranean's African shore had been squeezed of strategic opportunity for Berlin. The Axis leaders would have been better advised to extract Rommel's force, saving their troops, air power, and maritime assets to construct a southern European glacis. On the other hand, both dictators understood that, with North Africa entirely in Allied hands, Italy would shift into Allied gun sights. Therefore, Hitler instructed the Fifth Panzer Army's commander – the tall, severe fifty-three-year-old Prussian Guards officer Colonel General Jürgen von Arnim – to buy yet more time in North Africa in a spirit of forward defense. Publicly, however, Hitler declared that the battle for Tunisia would be "decisive," constituting "the cornerstone of our conduct of the war on the southern flank of Europe."[125]

The Axis decision to duke it out with the Allies on the Mediterranean's south shore made little strategic sense, but it was perfectly consistent with the "systematic incompetence," "structural disorder," and "strategic incoherence" of Axis decision-making, and joined a practically endless list of calamitous choices made since 1939 that had accumulated baleful consequences for Germany.[126] The British historian Simon Ball argues that the Axis leaders continued to "fantasize" that they could inflict a "stunning operational defeat" on the Allies, in either Tunisia or Sicily, in a failing – and flailing – Axis bid to maintain their grip on the central Mediterranean. "In order to survive, however," writes Ball, "the Axis had to defeat Britain and give the Americans such a bloody nose that they would withdraw their forces to the West."[127] With German defeat at Stalingrad looming, Mussolini declared the Russian war a lost cause. He proposed that Hitler seek a compromise peace with Moscow, which Foreign Minister Ribbentrop explained to the Italian Foreign Minister Galeazzo Ciano was a non-starter – a partial lie as it transpired, as the People's Commissariat of Internal Affairs (NKVD) would negotiate with Admiral Canaris' agents in Stockholm in April–June 1943, as Berlin put out peace feelers to the Western Allies through Madrid, Bern, and Ankara.[128] At the very least, the Germans might shift to a defensive strategy, to free up assets in order to "Mediterraneanize" the war. Such was *Il Duce*'s mounting desperation that he even proposed that German forces attack the Allies through Spain.[129] Admiral Émile Duplat, Vichy delegate to the Italian Control Commission in Turin, was told by Italian General Vacca Maggiolini that, while Rome was prepared to write off Algeria, "it's not finished in Tunisia," which could become a base for an Axis reconquest of Libya and Egypt.[130] In the German Mediterranean commander Albert Kesselring's post-war analysis, the failure to concentrate resources in the Mediterranean constituted the "fundamental mistake" made by the Axis. "As it was, the Axis was dismantled in the summer of 1943 in the Mediterranean," Ball continues, and "Mussolini's ouster and Italy's defection deprived German[y] of any half-credible ally, reducing it to, in Churchill's phrase, 'utter loneliness.' Even worse – and at the same time – Germany itself was reduced to the operational status of a second-class power – unable to fight a sophisticated war in three dimensions – also in the Mediterranean."[131]

The decision to make a stand in Tunisia revealed that Axis strategy had slipped into the realm of fantasy. In vain, General Giovanni Messe urged Mussolini to repatriate the Italian army from North Africa before it was too late. General Rino Corso Fougier, chief of the Regia Aeronautica Italiana (Italian Royal Air Force), warned that, even with Luftwaffe reinforcements, Axis forces would be heavily outnumbered in the air over the Strait of Sicily.

The Regia Marina (Italian Royal Navy) pointed out that it had to defend a coastline stretching from Toulon to Rhodes, and lacked the destroyers to escort merchantmen to Bizerte. Germany would need to equip the Regia Marina's ships with radar and sonar, not to mention providing air cover and supplying Romanian fuel. If Mussolini wanted to expend his naval assets to provision Tunisia, he risked having none left to supply and reinforce Sicily, Sardinia, and Corsica, let alone Greece and the Balkans.[132] Instead of heeding their advice, *Il Duce* ordered a cabinet reshuffle, replaced General Ugo Cavallero as Army chief of staff by General Vittorio Ambrosio, much to Kesselring's alarm, and named a Fascist hoodlum, Carlo Scorza, as the new party secretary with the mission of bolstering Italian popular morale. Plots to oust Mussolini were set in motion, but everyone awaited a signal from King Victor Emmanuel III to move.[133] Even as the situation turned desperate from March 1943, Hitler and Mussolini continued to feed their rapidly diminishing inventory of men, machines, ships, and planes into the maw of their Tunisian mincer.

Nevertheless, the Axis counted several advantages in what remained of their North African toehold, beginning with the fact that they had seized the central position in Tunisia that the Allies had to attack and supply from opposite directions. Axis forces would be operating close to their base, Bizerte and Tunis being only 120 nautical miles from Sicily, and 300 from Naples, along a mine-hedged route to deter British surface and submarine attacks, and ringed by Axis airfields in Sardinia, Sicily, Pantelleria, and at Tunis and Bizerte. The Ju 52 transport planes and mammoth six-engine Me323s, vital as petrol transports, offered a formidable initial logistical asset. By 10 November 1942, Fliegerkorps II counted a whopping 673 transport planes and 445 combat aircraft, including the formidable Focke-Wulf Fw 190 and the Messerschmitt Bf 109 that, especially in its later evolutions, far outperformed the British Spitfire. German pilots were also proficient in ground support operations.

But these initial Luftwaffe strengths were adulterated by the requirement to provide wrap-around service to Axis ground and naval forces: tactical ground support, air supply, long-range bombing, and maritime convoy cover and interdiction. Support for Tunisia also shrank air support for other fronts. By 30 November, Luftflotte 2 in the Mediterranean counted almost 500 more planes than did Luftflotte 4 at Stalingrad. Two *Kampfgeschwader* (attack wings) were diverted from Murmansk convoys to attack Allied ships off Algeria.[134] But it proved to be a losing effort. In the early months of 1943, Allied air and sea interdiction, combined with chaos in heavily bombed Italian ports, had reduced the spigot of Axis supplies from Naples to Bizerte to a dribble.[135] Nor could air transport make up for the shipping deficit. German fighters battled unsuccessfully to protect straggling Luftwaffe transport armadas from predatory Allied airmen.[136] By February 1943, German General

Walter Warlimont had concluded that Axis logistics in Tunisia constituted a "house of cards."[137]

Initially, these limitations were camouflaged by a stellar Axis command team made up of Albert Kesselring, Erwin Rommel, "Dieter" von Arnim, and eventually Giovanni Messe, who had led the Italian Expeditionary Corps in Russia between August 1941 and November 1942. But friction persisted between the Germans and Italians, who resented Rommel's "arrogance," and rightly saw his practice of interspersing – or "corseting" – Italian and German units as a signal of no confidence in Italian morale and fighting ability. A "prima donna" in his own right, "the calculating strategist" Messe often attempted to compete with "gambler" Rommel rather than second him in Tunisia.[138]

By the middle of February 1943, von Arnim's force numbered 110,000 troops, including 20,000 Luftwaffe personnel and 33,000 Italians, organized into the 10th Panzer Division, the Italian 1st "Superga" Division, the 334th Infantry Division (ID), the Hermann Göring Division, and an array of smaller units. Its inventory included 200 tanks, mostly Panzerkampfwagen (Pz.Kpfw.) III with either a 50 mm or a 75 mm gun and Pz.Kpfw. IV with a 75 mm gun, but among them were 11 60-ton Pz.Kpfw. VI (Tiger) tanks armed with the 88 mm gun. While Hitler assured Kesselring that the Tiger would prove decisive in Tunisia, the "furniture van," as its German crews dubbed it, was unwieldy, mechanically unreliable, a gas guzzler extraordinaire, too heavy for Tunisian roads and bridges, and too thin-skinned to deflect armor-piercing shells from the new Allied 6-pounder (57 mm) anti-tank gun with an effective range of 1,510 meters. While Alan Moorehead found the Tiger "frightening in its sheer enormity," nevertheless, "the ugliest vehicle I had ever seen on land" proved to be "a failure in Tunisia," the Australian war correspondent reported. "We even stopped them with two-pounder (40 mm) guns. They were too cumbersome, too slow, too big a target, too lightly armed to meet modern anti-tank weapons." Rommel's arrival in Tunisia at the end of January would virtually double the number of Axis tanks. More feared was the *Nebelwerfer* – literally "smoke thrower" – a wheeled launcher that fired a volley of 5.9-inch rockets that was to panic American troops at Kasserine.[139]

In contrast, those Allied commanders and troops filtering through Algeria, especially the Americans, lacked practice. Though nominally in overall command, Dwight Eisenhower remained in his distant, crowded Algiers eerie, where, according to Moorehead, "admirals were working in sculleries, and as like as not you would find a general or two weaving their plans in back bathrooms and pantries."[140] The fallout from *l'affaire Darlan* and its aftermath, the Anfa Conference, the requirement to stand up a Fifth Army under Mark Clark – a schemer in his own right – for the invasion of Italy, and, if the British are to be believed, his being too hamstrung by "amateur staff work" in his "cluttered headquarters" meant that Ike was too distracted to invigilate his subordinates at the front intently enough.[141] Eisenhower's elevation "into the stratosphere ... of Supreme Command" left operations to a British troika of General Harold Alexander, Admiral Andrew Cunningham, and Air Marshal Arthur Tedder. The US Chief of Staff (COS) George Marshall promoted Eisenhower to full general so that he would at least be the nominal equal in rank of his "subordinates." In Tunisia, however, US influence would be mitigated by the conviction among the British that Eisenhower had botched Torch, and by the flailing combat debut of US forces.[142]

The burden of battle on the Allied side would be shouldered by a neophyte First British Army commanded by the relatively inexperienced Lieutenant General Kenneth Anderson. A melancholy and deeply religious Scot, the tall, purse-lipped Anderson seemed the reincarnation of his Great War precursor Sir Douglas Haig. Obstinate, sanctimonious, and inflexible, Anderson lacked drive, imagination, and experience in handling armored divisions or grasping the possibilities offered by paratroops, for instance to seize Tunisian airfields ahead of the arriving Germans. Montgomery belittled his First Army counterpart as "a good plain cook" incapable of inventive or complex maneuvers. George Patton, who briefly served as II Corps commander in Tunisia, judged Anderson to be "earnest but dumb," a severe but mainstream opinion.[143]

German optimism about their chances in Tunisia was anchored in Allied inexperience and the superior fighting qualities of Axis forces, but above all in the significant logistical challenges that the Allies would face in Tunisia, transporting supplies landed in Casablanca, Oran, or Algiers east along a narrow-gauge railway and inadequate road system. The situation in the east was little better. Montgomery seized Tripoli on 20 January 1943. But Tripoli harbor had been so pounded by Allied bombing and Axis demolitions that it would require almost six weeks to whip it into working order. But, even then, supplies continued to be ferried around the Cape, past the Horn of Africa through the Suez Canal, before traveling the 900 miles from Alexandria to the front. Nevertheless, there was a gradual buildup of Sherman tanks, 17-pounder (76.2 mm) anti-tank guns, and 7.2-inch howitzers, not to mention the progressive attainment of air ascendency after overcoming the handicaps of flying out of hastily constructed airfields at Tébessa and Thélepte on the Algerian–Tunisian border and near Constantine in Algeria, or from Bône, 120 miles from the front. Only in March 1943 did the Allies amass enough air power, achieve coordination of the actions of the Royal Air Force (RAF) and the US Army Air Force (USAAF), and refine their tactics sufficiently both to attack Axis shipping and to support the ground campaign. Until then, Allied troops shivered in the shallow, mud-filled trenches of the Western Dorsal, the object of close attention by predatory and opportunistic Stukas, while protesting the truancy of their own pilots.[144]

"Worse Than in 1940"

The Tunisia campaign would play out in three distinct phases.[145] The first, which began on 9 November and extended until the year's end, saw the arrival in Tunisia of three German divisions, two of them panzer, and two Italian to form the Fifth Panzer Army under Nehring, and subsequently von Arnim. Von Arnim's command initially numbered 67,000 men, of whom 47,000 were Germans. These managed to seize Tunis and Bizerte, and parry a bounce of the British 78th Infantry and 6th Armoured Divisions toward Tunis between 26 November and 2 December. In January, von Arnim received another 41,000 reinforcements, of whom 30,000 were Germans. His command also included the 10th Panzer Division, with its inventory of Tiger tanks. The US Army official history argues that Eisenhower had no confidence in French forces, but only included them initially as a "political gesture."[146] In fact, he had no choice, because few other forces were available in November 1942. French forces in this period – Barré's CSTT reinforced by Mathenet's *Division de marche marocaine*, and further south Koeltz's XIX Corps – were content to form a "covering force" that sought to occupy the passes of the Eastern Dorsal from Medjez-el-Bab to the Sahara. Two divisions of the US II Corps, slowed by a lack of roads and bad weather that limited air cover, gradually occupied positions at Gafsa and Kasserine, where they joined Welvert's *Division de marche de Constantine*. With 420 aircraft stationed at El Aouina, an all-weather airfield surrendered by the French without a fight in November only 20 miles from the front, the Luftwaffe also controlled the skies in this early period. Stukas could respond to calls for help from Axis ground forces within 5 to 10 minutes. AFN's underdevelopment meant that the French had built only four all-weather airfields outside of Tunis, the closest being at Bône, 120 miles from the front. Furthermore, a combination of logistical problems, lack of ground support personnel, and the fact that the Western Desert Air Force was still supporting Montgomery and carrying out bombing missions in Sicily and Italy, meant that the RAF's successful "Libyan model" of tactical air support would not make its way west with the British Eighth Army until the New Year. These factors tipped the initial air advantage to the Luftwaffe.[147]

A second phase kicked off in the New Year with offensives by von Arnim calculated to expand the Axis bridgehead and reoccupy the passes of the Eastern Dorsal. Rommel arrived in Tunisia in late January, and wasted little time in punching through Franco-American positions at Kasserine during 14–23 February, a thrust that threatened to collapse the entire Allied defensive front. This was followed by von Arnim's offensive in northern Tunisia that continued from 26 February to 15 March. In fact, so effortless did Axis victories seem that von Arnim appeared to believe that, with the aid of a Muslim insurrection and the Axis seizure of Malta, Algiers lay within his grasp.[148] A lack of modern armaments and equipment, the inadequacies of French training and backwardness of their tactical methods, and weaknesses accentuated by Juin's decision to spread French troops in a shallow front along the Dorsals to shield Algeria caused the French to declare their situation in Tunisia to be "worse than in 1940." Nevertheless, the arrival of Allied reinforcements, combined with the squeeze on Axis logistics, gradually began to tip the military balance in Tunisia. A third and final phase began in the middle of March with Montgomery's arrival on the Mareth Line. Rommel was recalled to Europe, leaving Messe from 12 April to organize a fighting retreat to northern Tunisia. From 20 April, Allied armies jammed Axis forces on land, while naval and air elements squeezed their vulnerable supply lines to Italy, until they surrendered on 13 May 1943.[149]

Phase I: "General Ike Fights Two Wars"

Phase one[150] opened as Anderson progressively – and laboriously – occupied Bougie, Djidjelli, Philippeville, and Bône from 10–13 November, after Admiral Moreau in Algiers ordered commanders of the three harbors to prepare to receive Allied ships, despite orders from Vichy.[151] Nevertheless, delays meant that only on 25 November did Anderson launch two and a half divisions in an unsuccessful stab at Tunis and Bizerte (Map 1.2), in the process demonstrating that the British First Army lacked method and inter-arm liaison.[152] "If . . . Anderson had been willing to gamble a bit more on his logistics and had accepted an entire American armored division, as Ike had wanted him to do, then we would have had the necessary wallop to take Tunis and eventually Bizerte," recorded Eisenhower's US Navy aide Harry C. Butcher. "That means Tunisia."[153] Anderson's lumbering November 1942 advance into Tunisia also frustrated Juin and Giraud, who felt that they knew the ground and had the imagination and energy to exploit Allied advantages, but lacked the authority, troops, and weapons to do so. After Eisenhower rejected Giraud's 17 December demand that he be given command of the entire Tunisian theater,[154] Juin tried to calm his French superior. "The senior British military commanders are who they are," Juin counseled Giraud on 1 January 1943. "What we take to be incomprehension or resistance is often the result of a lack of or sluggish imagination." The place to begin in Juin's view was to clarify command arrangements.[155] Allied soldiers were scattered along a 250-mile front that intermingled the British First Army, the US II Corps under the fifty-nine-year-old Major General Lloyd Fredendall, and roughly 63,000 French troops, both *armée d'Afrique* and the "dustbin" *Corps franc d'Afrique* (CFA) – a castoff of Jews, Italians, Spanish Republicans, and other political refugees, even Muslims, who joined other unredeemable elements blacklisted from conventional French units. These scattered French forces gradually collected in

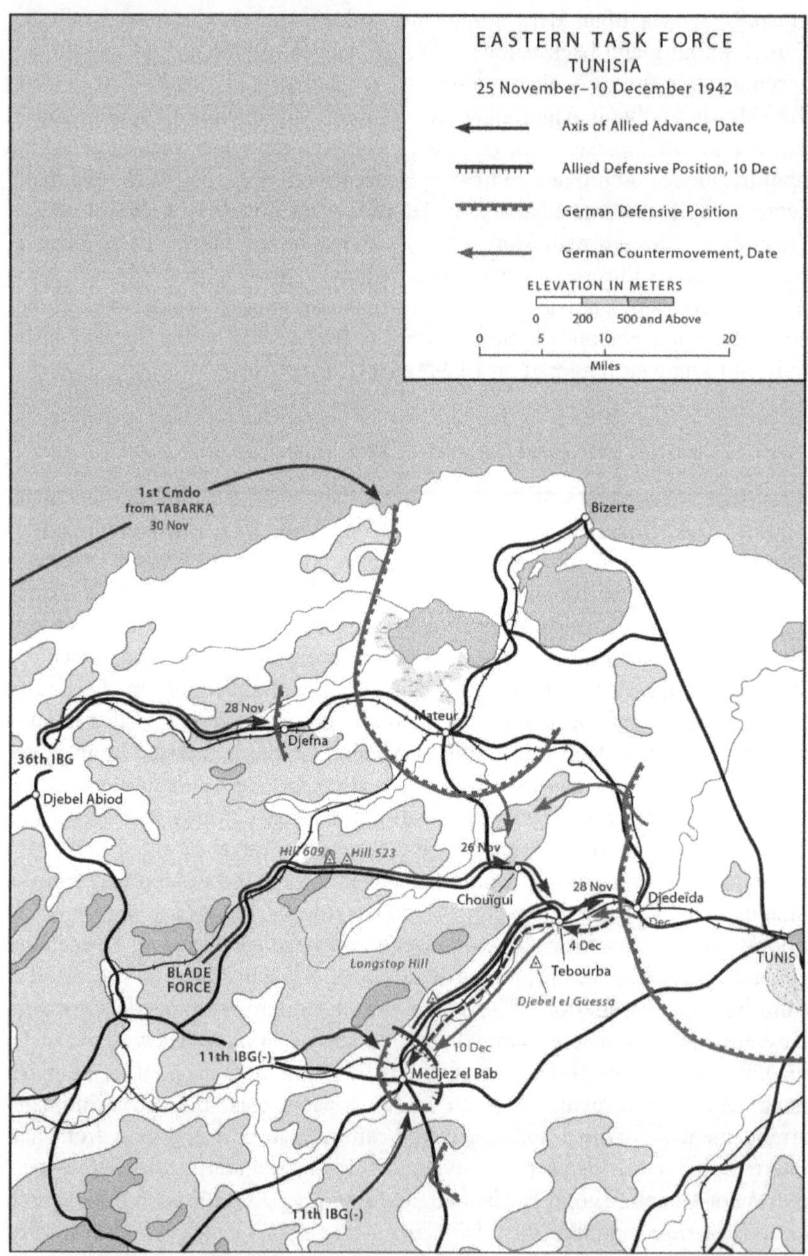

Map 1.2 The race for Tunis.

western Tunisia from early December, occupying Gafsa, Sbeïtla (nowadays called Subaytilah), and Kasserine to block Axis penetration into Algeria.[156]

Meanwhile, Giraud, eager to undertake offensive operations despite torrential rain, sought to create a staff under General René Prioux, who had commanded the French cavalry corps in Belgium in 1940, before taking charge of the First French Army on the death of Billotte, and piloting it into captivity.[157] One of Königstein's former pupils, like Juin, Prioux had been released by the Germans to repopulate the cannibalized upper ranks of *l'armée d'Afrique*. Prioux quickly organized the classic staff with bureaus 1–4 that by 14 November was sending out orders to mobilize AFN in *divisions de marche*. These were temporary, infantry-heavy agglomerations of roughly 10,000 men each that included a cavalry regiment with some diminutive D1 tanks – which US planes continued to attack in error[158] – and eventually a sprinkle of superseded Valentines released to the French as the British acquired US-made Shermans. The artillery consisted of an artillery group with mainly horse-drawn 75 mm guns and 65 mm mountain guns, which were totally useless against Tiger tanks and much else in the Axis armory, and an engineering company that had neither mines, nor mine detectors, nor anti-tank guns. The French navy contributed some trucks and 37 mm guns, and 47 mm anti-tank guns plucked from arms caches, to which Eisenhower donated "32 antiaircraft automatic guns of any type available." While the divisional transport included some aged lorries, most transport was assured by thirty-six mules allocated per company and whatever the soldiers could carry on their backs. Anti-aircraft artillery remained on the French army's wish-list unless French units were covered by British or US anti-aircraft units. Communications consisted of ER 17 radios, which had already been out of date in 1940. Motorcycle couriers proved useless on the goat tracks of the Dorsal. It is hardly surprising that Eisenhower doubted the offensive spirit of a French army whose senior ranks were populated with yesterday's Vichy loyalists, and whose armament in November 1942 would have embarrassed the *poilus* of 1914. Only gradually did three-battalion regiments become the norm, even though most infantry companies operated in isolation in the mountainous terrain. Initially, three of these *divisions de marche* were assigned to XIX Corps (Koeltz) and two to the CSTT (Barré), all grouped in theory as the *Détachement d'armée française* (DAF) commanded by Juin.[159]

The FAF Commander Mendigal collected some odds and ends from French West Africa (AOF) that, together with an infusion of American-supplied Curtis P40 Warhawks, gave him an air force of around 300 planes. On 17 November, Giraud and Juin joined Barré at Souk-el-Khemis, about 30 miles west of Medjez-el-Bab. From 18 November, American convoys began to arrive in Casablanca every twenty-five days with reinforcements. By January 1943, Oran was in full working order and jammed with shipping, but still 1,000 kilometers from the front line in Tunisia.[160] All of this answered to a distant Allied Forces Headquarters (AFHQ) in Algiers that was established on 12 November, where, as Harry Butcher noted, Eisenhower "is being careful not to interfere with Anderson, Juin, or Fredendall in any of the decisions that must be made in the field."[161] Eisenhower's detached command style simply added to the confusion and improvisation that ceded the initiative in the Tunisian campaign to the Axis.[162]

But if Darlan had concluded in the face of the Allied invasion that Algiers was well worth a mass, in the shadow of his coerced conversion to the Allied cause, the Admiral struggled to perpetuate Vichy in Algeria and Morocco *sans le Maréchal*. The fluid situation in Algiers further churned and confused the attitudes of *l'armée d'Afrique*. On 15 November, Darlan had issued a call in the name of the Marshal for unity and discipline among adherents of the Légion française des combattants (LFC) and the military. Darlan's message was that Vichy survived in AFN in a sort of Babylonian captivity, what Robert Paxton called an "inverse Vichy," where the Admiral claimed to have inherited the mantle of leadership of the "French State" with Pétain's clandestine benediction.[163] In fact, Vichy's erstwhile proconsuls in AFN had simply pivoted from German to American patronage.[164] This contradiction turned acute when, at a 16 November press conference, Roosevelt tried to defuse dissatisfaction over the Darlan deal by announcing that he had asked the Leader of France in the Maghreb to empty his internment camps of anti-fascists and political refugees and to abrogate antisemitic legislation as required under Article XI of the Darlan–Clark accords. Pressed by Eisenhower, Darlan hedged, lifting some restrictions that prohibited Jews from practicing their professions on a case-by-case basis. Meanwhile, a top priority for General Prioux, Giraud's chief of staff, was to exclude Jews from combat units because he feared that their proximity to Muslims would create a "disaster."[165]

If *la comédie politique d'Alger* delayed the Allies' arrival in Tunisia, it also disoriented and disorganized a French army that had to pivot from an Allied to an Axis enemy, rebuild its morale, mobilize seven reserve "classes," and reorient its forces, scattered along the Mediterranean littoral, toward the east. Furthermore, the arrival of Anglo-American forces had overwhelmed AFN's fragile infrastructure, and delayed the mobilization of reservists in AFN. Not enough vehicles existed in eastern Algeria to get the Constantine Division quickly to the front. Intermittent telephone service prevented XIX Corps HQ in Algiers from coordinating the mobilization of Algeria's three territorial divisions effectively. "To this, perhaps one could equally add the lack of enthusiasm shown by certain Europeans and Indigenous (Muslims) to the call to mobilize," read the 30 November report, that called for "energetic measures" to enforce mobilization and requisition orders among Europeans worried about the impact of casualties on their communities. Nationalists protested in the suburbs of Algiers, but officials reported that Muslims in the interior submitted to the call-up. However, Le Gac has discovered that recidivism remained significant, especially in the Constantinois.[166]

The one group that apparently was eager to mobilize was the Jewish population. When the classes of 1936–1939 were called up on 24 November, according to Richard Bennaïm, the Jews of Oran, "avid to return to combat against the Germans," responded enthusiastically. However, an all-day train ride crammed into cattle wagons to the Camp de Bedeau south of Sidi-bel-Abbès, where they were greeted by German Foreign Legionnaires, quickly deflated their zeal. Jews were separated out from other "recruits," and assembled in ranks, where a captain announced that they were to form a "Jewish Pioneer Corps," an *armée d'Afrique* version of solitary confinement, for "intellectuals, shopkeepers, bureaucrats who had never wielded a pickaxe in their life."[167] Bennaïm instantly recognized a *Stalag* when he saw one: 10,000 men distributed among 10-man tents called *guitournes* slept on the ground, and queued twice daily to be fed a thin soup. Although he wore his army uniform with his sergeant's stripes, he was told, "'here, you are all privates.' Having learned to translate military language, this meant: 'no Jewish non-commissioned officers here' . . . In fact, Bedeau was nothing more than a penal colony for Jews." The good news was that, unlike German *Stalags* and *Kommandos*, a stroll out of Bedeau and hitchhike to Oran proved fairly risk-free.[168] The Anfa Conference in January 1943 gave journalists the opportunity to visit several camps in Morocco where Spanish Republicans, Jews, Poles, Gaullists, and other political and "racial" prisoners were incarcerated. In the glare of Anglo-American publicity, these inmates were gradually released, beginning in February 1943, some directed toward the CFA, others absorbed in a foreign pioneer regiment created by the British. On 4 February, Juin declared that henceforth "the units of Jewish pioneers must be considered part of the regular army," and their members were therefore ineligible to enlist in the CFA.[169]

On the other hand, the "Vichyite" members of Murphy's "Group of Five" reaped their reward by being named to various positions in Darlan's High Commission.[170] On 16 November 1942, Juin brought the *Chantiers de la jeunesse* under military supervision after Van Hecke announced that he intended to "create a free corps [*corps franc*] capable of carrying out a sort of revolutionary war."[171] Juin's suspicion of the *Chantiers* appeared justified when one of its number being trained by the British at an improvised center on Cap Matifou outside of Algiers, Fernand Bonnier de la Chapelle, assassinated Darlan.[172] Convinced that Darlan's Christmas Eve 1942 murder was the prelude to a Gaullist coup, Giraud arrested medical student José Aboulker and thirteen members of the Algiers resistance of 8 November who had helped to bring him to power. After his release, Aboulker eventually made his way to

London to join the Gaullists, who parachuted him into France on various resistance missions.

But it was clear that, in the wake of the double defeats of 1940 and Torch, the French army was exhibiting symptoms of psychological strain. If the "dissidence" that had facilitated Torch fostered an atmosphere of suspicion and distrust in the officer corps, Darlan's assassination traumatized senior officers, who feared that French political divisions had turned homicidal. Giraud ordered the military magistrate Major Albert Voituriez to get to the bottom of the Darlan's death. When, however, evidence pointed to Henri d'Astier and his close associate, the economist and law professor Alfred Pose, as the *éminences grises* behind Bonnier de la Chapelle, Giraud promptly adjourned the inquiry. The prosecution dossier subsequently vanished, and charges against the two men were dropped. Meanwhile, those soldiers who had aided the invasion – such as Mast, Béthouart, Baril, and Jousse – were stripped of French nationality on 4 December, while officers who had fought the Anglo-Americans were decorated.[173] None of this reflected well on Roosevelt, with his Atlantic Charter pretensions, or on Washington's "French expert" Robert Murphy, whose "pre-landing friends . . . have been let down, in one way or another," wrote Macmillan.[174] "Murphy seems to be the main target of criticism, on the ground that he is a Vichyite and has been giving bum advice to the 'brilliant' General," Butcher concurred on 23 January 1943.[175]

Its powers ill-defined, Darlan's Vichy-lite administration proved no more successful than had been the Admiral's ideological *volte-face*. It amounted to a discredited management whose lack of accountability, aggravated by political events that had left a legacy of acrimony and tangled emotions, rendered it poorly equipped to manage AFN's and the French empire's institutionalized disorder. Rallied but recalcitrant, residents and governors general remained laws unto themselves. Although, for the moment, de Gaulle was represented in Algiers only by Air Force General François d'Astier de la Vigerie, he occupied the moral high ground and knew how to make time work for him against this Washington-enabled Vichy rump. As André Beaufre had predicted, *l'armée d'Afrique*, with its racial prejudices, conservative attitudes, and profound antisemitism provided a contentious instrument to mobilize Imperial France, let alone liberate the metropole.[176] As military commander, Giraud initially refused on principle to allow French troops to be placed under Anderson's command. "This attitude reflected a widespread Anglophobia in the French army in AFN, since Mers-el-Kébir and Syria," concludes the French official history. AFN may have been liberated, but its leaders remained shackled to out-of-date antipathies, resentments, and prejudices. The result was that, while Anderson had direct command over British and US Forces, the Anfa Conference decided that French troops were to be "coordinated with the agreement of General Juin . . . who will give all material assistance that will be necessary and possible." The result was that, in Tunisia, "French forces were deployed on the ground in a very diluted manner and with few means."[177] The immediate consequence was that Darlan reigned over – but failed to command – an aggregation of semi-independent administrative and military satrapies.[178] Meanwhile, Mark Clark complained that, while GIs were up to their knees in mud on the "front line of Europe," the French continued to wrangle among themselves.[179] This proved to be a lament that would echo – not always fairly – for the remainder of the war and beyond.

The Fight for the Dorsal

The transition to combat for Lapouge's *tirailleurs* proved as difficult as it was for Albert Rupert. After receiving contradictory orders and being whiplashed and disoriented by all sorts of rumors, on 14 November 1942, the 7ᵉ RTA entrained for Tébessa near the border with Tunisia as part of the *Division de Marche de Constantine* under Major General Édouard Welvert. At Tébessa, which Moorehead described as a "dismal town . . . where somehow the Roman ruins have been made to look more depressing and uninteresting than any I have ever seen,"[180] they were ordered to make a hellish 33-kilometer hike through the mountains to Morsott that saw many of Lapouge's *tirailleurs* collapse with exhaustion under the weight of their backpacks and other equipment. On 24 November, his unit was collected in trucks and driven 180 kilometers to Sbeïtla in central Tunisia about 15 kilometers east of Kasserine, which had been occupied by the Americans. "We contemplated the battlefield," Lapouge recounted. "Burned tanks, personal effects and Italian matériel, bandages, letters ('*fratello carissimo* . . .')." His company was ordered to hold this road junction that linked Sfax with Kairouan, with three 25 mm anti-tank guns and four 75 mm field guns. They recovered all the Italian equipment that was still serviceable, especially trucks, and put out barbed wire and anti-tank mines. Lapouge's batman dug a hole for him to sleep in, which only meant that he woke up with sand in his hair, ears, and mouth. His captain, still cross with him for arriving late to the barracks on 8 November, continued to address him in an abrupt, peremptory tone. It was too cold to sleep. He suspected that one of the sergeants was procuring wine from the locals for his *tirailleurs*. His men came to him to complain about this and that, ask for a transfer because they did not like the sergeant, and so on, which he dismissed as typical Arab exaggeration. He made his men clean their rifles and practice setting up their anti-aircraft defenses. But, otherwise, he had no way to keep them occupied without appearing fastidious and inflexible.[181]

In November–December 1942, the cautious Eisenhower preferred to build up his forces rather than rush events in Tunisia in a sprint that the Allies had already lost. On 25 November, Juin took command of the DAF made up of

Barré's CSTT, Koeltz's XIX Corps minus the Moroccan troops, and a Saharan group, all armed with whatever antique weaponry they had managed to conceal from the Axis Control Commissions. The French role would ostensibly be to hold terrain conquered by the British. But Juin planned a preemptive seizure of "strategic ground" in the Western Dorsal. The result was that the DAF became overextended in shallow, detached points that were vulnerable to German attack. When, on the night of 29–30 November, a US armored unit drove through Lapouge's position in Sbeïtla on the way to attack Sidi Bouzid, the French were left slack-jawed with envy: "Superb matériel. Open armored cars overflowing with arms: 37 mm anti-tank guns, 20 mm machineguns . . .," he noted, wondering whether the French would ever be so lavishly equipped. Two days later, in the early hours of the morning, another 100 or so US vehicles drove through on their way to attack the Faïd Pass. In fact, since the GIs set foot in AFN trussed up like "aristocrats dressed for a hunting party," the French never imagined that common soldiers could be so extravagantly outfitted.[182] For the Americans, the French with their horse-drawn artillery and mounted *Chasseurs d'Afrique* complete with rattling sabers seemed like artifacts excavated from a Franco-Prussian War battlefield.

Algiers symbolized both the contingency of AFN's break with Vichy and its transitional nature. Eisenhower's naval aide Harry Butcher recorded, on 20 December 1942, that his boss was "seeking better understanding [of the French], and the removal of 'bad eggs,'" with Noguès and Algerian Governor General Yves Châtel topping the list. But, to the Anglo-Americans, AFN seemed to offer a vast basket of "bad eggs," including "the smart pro-German staff of Noguès" and "the police chief" of Algiers, the disgruntled lapsed Gaullist Admiral Muselier, now bent on revenge.[183] In January 1943, Moorehead found Algiers to be an "unwholesome . . . French political stew." Although Algeria and Morocco had supposedly rallied to the Allied cause, Pétain's "unhappy features . . . gazed down . . . from the hoardings and the placards in every street and in every public place . . . There was a constant procession of people back and forth to Vichy by way of Spain where M. [François] Piétrie, the Vichy ambassador in Madrid, acted as a sort of official postbox." In Rabat, Noguès openly derided the Americans as "political children." Moorehead attributed the minimalist opposition to AFN's regime change to the "vast numbers of Allied troops who kept pouring off the transports with their modern arms . . . The people, moreover, were tired with the tiredness of two years of defeat."[184] Opportunism also played a role. "The Darlan–Giraud neo-Vichy regime in North Africa offered a way back to power for some Vichy outsiders," writes Paxton.[185] The "Anglo-Saxon" press denounced this Murphy-managed Vichy resuscitation on North Africa's shores as the Darlan deal redux.[186]

At the front, the Allied advance into Tunisia proved to be precipitous, piecemeal, and poorly coordinated. On 4 December, Lapouge's camp became acquainted with Stukas: "coming in low, with a thunderous noise. It's hard not to be frightened. I'm flat on my stomach on the ridge, balled up with my head behind a rock." Bullets ricocheted everywhere. When the air attack, which seemed to go on forever, finally ceased, Lapouge discovered that most of his *tirailleurs* had scattered, which meant that he spent the next few hours scouring the scrub-covered hills with a drawn pistol to force his troops back into line.[187] Nor did the GIs' fighting skills match the quality of their equipment, in Lapouge's view: "They don't know how to fight," he opined. "When enemy planes fly over, they shout, whistle, shoot their rifles in the air. It's an extraordinary waste of munitions."[188] By 5 December, the 7ᵉ RTA had moved up to the Faïd Pass, where they discovered that a plethora of weaponry did not guarantee American success. By early afternoon, ambulances were streaming back in the other direction. A rumor ran through the unit that French sailors had scuttled at Toulon. The ground was littered with bullets, grenades, tins of food, and bandages. Pools of blood were everywhere. They discovered the body of a German officer whose stomach had been blown open. Lapouge organized an impromptu burial with military honors.[189]

On 7 December, a discouraged Anderson looked to execute a tactical withdrawal, which caused Juin and Giraud to lobby Eisenhower hard to countermand it. The priority must be to hold Medjez-el-Bab and Pont du Fahs, both important road junctions that controlled access to Tunis and Tunisia's southern coastal plain. This would create a favorable strategic advantage for the Allies once Rommel spilled out of Libya through the Mareth Line.[190] Juin's rush to occupy the summits of the *petite dorsale* sent Lapouge's unit into the Faïd Pass: "a rocky promontory that overlooks the road to Sfax. No plant grows higher than 40 centimeters, except a clump of twenty palm trees around a spring. A pale green field of alfalfa lends nuance to the rocky gray terrain. Tortoises, guinea pigs, strange birds (black, ash-colored . . .). Thirty planes pass overhead." But the defensive routine, while unchallenging, became tedious: his batman woke him at 06:00 with coffee. At 07:30, he inspected his positions with the sergeant, then went to a meeting with his commander. His toilette consisted of washing in a basin. Lunch at 11:00 consisted of a piece of meat, served with either macaroni or lentils. Siesta until 15:00. Any moment might be interrupted by an alert. Another meeting in the Captain's command post. Kill time until dinner at 17:00. At 19:00 back to his dugout to try to sleep.[191]

Running low on ammunition and having encountered no Americans except a lone GI who had fallen asleep in a haystack and been left behind by his mates, Albert Rupert's unit continued to withdraw toward Algeria at the end of November. A twenty-year-old keen to fight the Germans asked to enlist, so they made him the cook. They had reason to regret it. The neophyte chef built his cooking fire in the front lines and placed his pot of boiling pasta right in the line of fire. As a consequence, the French soldiers dashed toward the simmering pot clutching their mess tins to fish out a few strands of spaghetti, before sprinting back under cover. Otherwise, they fed themselves by stealing chickens. Having reloaded their trucks in Algeria, they returned to Béja to find that the town had been bombed. Obviously, the inhabitants had been surprised, because plates of food remained on the tables. Disemboweled horses lay about the fields, while bodies of the dead had been laid out by the roadside. Oblivious to the tragedy, the soldiers promptly set about pillaging the houses. On 13 December, they left Béja driving southeast to Bou Arada. Along the way, they encountered many British troops who had been given wine by the locals, so that "the sons of Albion all stagger along in remarkable unity."[192]

In 1942, 18 December was Aïd el-Kébir, a Muslim holiday which warranted a special meal for Lapouge's tirailleurs. Everyone was bored. The rain and wind were unrelenting, which made it dangerous to move around because one often failed to hear orders and challenges from sentries. Lapouge had not changed his uniform in a month.[193] Intelligence revealed that Axis reinforcements continued to arrive at Sousse, Sfax, and Gabès, all ports which had obligingly been surrendered without a fight by the French navy, suggesting that an Axis offensive was in the offing. For the moment, French troops guarded important crossroads and passes. Juin launched the *7e Régiment de tirailleurs marocains* (RTM) toward Enfidaville on 20 December, although the attack made little progress in the pelting rain.[194] The British had only two divisions in place. Nothing was coordinated, because Giraud in his obstinacy refused to put French troops under Anderson's command. Poorly armed French reinforcements continued to trickle in, as did American soldiers from Fredendall's II Corps.[195]

Christmas dinner, which united Anderson, Eisenhower and Juin, witnessed an exchange of gifts: Anderson bestowed twenty new lorries on Juin, in return for which the grateful French commander, "pointing out that his luncheon was disgraceful because it consisted uniquely of tinned food poorly prepared by the British supply corps," promised to send Anderson a French chef. Poor Juin probably failed to realize that, for Anderson, culinary indifference advertised the values of a consummate soldier and devout Christian. Eisenhower's gift to Juin was the announcement that the US II Corps would soon take its place to the right of the French XIX Corps. This came as a relief to Juin, because the French were spread thinly in the south, as Rommel sped across Tripolitania headed in their direction. In return, Juin agreed to place French troops under Anderson's command, only to have Giraud countermand this informal agreement. As a consequence, Juin had to shift his headquarters to Constantine – his hometown – so as better to coordinate operations with the Allies, thus distancing himself from the front.[196] On 29 December, Lapouge volunteered for the paratroops. But the captain "forbade me to ask for a transfer. I gave in." Nonetheless, relations between them remained "glacial." Finally, on the night of 30–31 December, the company was relieved.[197]

Lapouge's situation seemed positively luxurious compared with that of "Captain X," who commanded the 9th company of the *Régiment de tirailleurs tunisiens* (RTT). His men were in a "detestable state" after enduring Christmas in the wind and cold rain of the Dorsal, against which their tents offered scant protection. Worn-out entrenching tools made it virtually impossible to dig defenses more than 40 centimeters deep in the concrete-like soil, despite the constant mortar fire from Germans who held the high ground to their front. He had no radio or telephone to communicate with battalion headquarters 2 kilometers away. One-third of the 110 men in his company had virtually no training. Nor, once the Luftwaffe bombed the supply depot, did food arrive on a regular basis. And when it did, it was impossible to cook it because unrelenting rain made the wood too wet to burn. So, the company was reduced to drinking coffee made from muddy water taken from the wadi and eating sodden bread. His mules had not eaten in five days. *Tirailleurs* were reduced to lubricating their weapons with vegetable oil. Fortunately, for the moment the enemy seemed content merely to keep them on edge by constantly running three tanks and two armored cars up and down the road to their front. Finally, moving into position at night, they launched a successful attack backed by 75 mm guns to take the ridge 400 meters to their front, and managed to bag two officer POWs and considerable amounts of food and equipment.[198] But this local success went unrepeated elsewhere as DAF attacks broke on strongly entrenched Germans backed by airpower.

Giraud was named High Commissioner by the Imperial Council on 26 December, a rapid reversal of fortunes for the "eternal lieutenant," who had been rejected barely a month and a half earlier as an ingrate and traitor who possessed no "mandate." Unfortunately, spooked by the Darlan assassination, Giraud saw conspiracies everywhere.[199] Despite his new political responsibilities, he persisted in meddling unhelpfully in operational decisions.[200] Juin attempted to bring his boss down to earth, explaining that his strategic vision, while perhaps brilliant, was wasted on unimaginative Anglo-Saxon generals and beyond the capacities of relatively inexperienced Allied troops. And, given French shortcomings, the DAF was obliged to submit to Allied direction.[201] At the turn of the year, Juin began to worry that, without reserves, some French sections of the front, especially around Pichon, might be in danger of collapse if the Axis mounted a serious attack. British fears focused on Gafsa.[202]

As the New Year dawned, Rupert's unit, part of the CSTT, shared his position at Bou-Arada, 70 kilometers southwest of Tunis, with zouaves, spahis, French colonial troops, and military police, and with the British. But, because they were not included in His Majesty's supply manifest, they quickly made the acquaintance of pig farmers, who invariably complained that they were unable to profit from the invasion because the Anglo-Americans ate only out of tins. However, the Tommies seemed happy enough to exchange their "compo" field rations consisting of unrecognizable foods preserved in a precooked or dehydrated non-perishable state, bouillon cubes, crackers, various drink mixes, and perhaps a pastry, nuts, or a chocolate bar for French-procured "small feisty" pigs and chickens. And while Rupert insisted that the French got on well with Brits, one had to be careful not to mention the "prickly subject" of Syria. The contrasting styles of the two contingents also were on prominent display: while the Tommies had to appear impeccable for morning parade, most of the French troops grew beards, turned out in an assortment of uniforms, and adopted a much more casual attitude to discipline and the enforcement of military courtesies.[203]

"The French Were Practically Powerless . . .": Phase II of the Tunisia Campaign, 1 January–15 March 1943

Early January 1943 found the DAF strung out along the Dorsal, the CSTT in the north with the XIX Corps in the south, with the most vulnerable point being the salient at Pont du Fahs.[204] For his part, Juin was aware that the position of French troops on the Dorsal was precarious. Responding to Juin's desperate 18 January plea for modern weapons, the Allies managed to collect 60 Valentine tanks, an assortment of useless British 2-pounder anti-tank guns, 75 mm guns, and anti-aircraft artillery, 300 General Motors Truck Company (GMC) trucks, 200 jeeps, 8 half-tracks, and other odds and ends for the French, on the understanding that all serviceable equipment would be returned at the end of the campaign. A thorough refitting of French forces must await the aftermath of Tunisia (Figure 1.3).[205]

As someone familiar with the Western Desert, where battle "was a thing of terribly fast movement that spilled in all directions," Moorehead's impression of the Tunisian front was claustrophobia, punctuated by cold and sudden death:

> . . . landmines all over the place, snipers perched in the most unlikely spots, shells and mortars dropping out of nowhere . . . This perishing cold, this all-invading mud and this lack of hot food could exhaust and kill a man just as thoroughly as bullets . . . Whoever held the high ground held the battlefield. If you won the pass then you won everything . . . all around the bush was heavy with the sweet and nauseating smell of bodies that were turning rotten in the sun after the rain.[206]

On 16 January, Lapouge's company launched a spoiling attack on the ridgeline to their front. The Germans in bunkers rained down grenades, wounding the captain and killing three platoon leaders, which by default elevated Lapouge to company command. Four days later, the chaplain climbed the hill

Figure 1.3 Oran, December 1942: US troops present arms as French troops embark for Tunisia. Relations remained tense between soldiers who only days before had fought each other.

waving a white flag to collect the bodies, only to find that the Germans had departed. Lapouge's Algerians occupied the hill, buried the dead as a corporal recited Muslim prayers, and redistributed the abandoned German equipment. Allied planes flew overhead as the Germans intermittently shelled their position. They attempted to fashion trenches and caves in the unyielding ground, before realizing that they were camped in a cemetery. Superstitious *tirailleurs* insisted that they saw ghosts along the wire. One deserted with his machinegun. Rats scurried about, as rain or sandstorms intermittently lashed their ridgeline. Lapouge's boots were worn out. On 12 February, an American captain with several NCOs arrived to relieve them.[207]

Increasing Luftwaffe activity and evidence of Axis troop concentrations suggested an impending offensive. The Americans believed Gafsa, which

Moorehead described as "a jaunty little oasis sprawling on the edge of the desert," to be "in extreme peril." In fact, the entire Allied line was threatened, as Kesselring ordered von Arnim to launch Operation *Eilbote I* (Express Messenger I), from 18 January, a spoiling operation launched southwards from Pont du Fahs that was meant to unravel Allied positions on the Eastern Dorsal and adjourn Allied plans to launch an attack via Kairouan to the coast. The initial thrust focused three divisions, including the 10th Panzer, at the junction of the British V Corps and the French XIX Corps near the Kébir dam and Pont du Fahs. While the British held their own, without anti-tank weapons or adequate artillery cover, the French folded before *Kampfgruppe* Weber – an improvised formation that contained infantry, artillery, and forty-three Pz. Kpfw. III tanks armed with 50 mm guns[208] – that scattered some Moroccan troops and hammered the Third Regiment of the French Foreign Legion with mortars and heavy artillery, before retiring from 22 January. The costs for the French proved fairly catastrophic: sixty-one officers killed in the *Division de marche du Maroc* alone. Overall, 4,880 soldiers died or were wounded, with a further 3,509 missing, plus most of their equipment, including 50 precious artillery pieces. The reasons given for the French setback offered a catalogue of rookie mistakes which recalled 1940: lack of depth of French dispositions, which were configured for offensive, not defensive, operations; surprise caused by a lack of reconnaissance aviation; a dearth of anti-tank guns or artillery more powerful than 75 mm; French artillery opened fire while the German tanks were still 2 kilometers away, which revealed their positions and allowed German counter-battery fire to neutralize them; French 81 mm mortars failed to inspire the same respect as British 25-pounder guns. Counterattacks collapsed for lack of punch; the operational commander of the CSTT, Major General Maurice Jurion, could not control the action because of a lack of communications, which had to be restored by the Derbyshire Yeomanry – the list goes on. The encouraging conclusion was that "the prudence in the exploitation [of the attack] seems to indicate an intensity inferior to that of the German forces of 1940." Axis "prudence" appears to have resulted from a shortage of assault infantry. In Juin's estimation, had von Arnim pushed his advantages as Rommel surely would have done, and had French forces not clung to "anchor points – Bou Arada, Djebel Bargou, Pichon" – the Allied line might have collapsed. Nevertheless, French units could not continue to absorb this level of punishment without serious consequences for morale, which proved to be the case on 30 January when, in *Eilbote II*, two battlegroups from the 21st Panzer pounced on French troops in the Faïd Pass. Fredendall hesitated to answer urgent French appeals for support because he did not want to disrupt his plans to attack Maknassy. Only on 31 January did American reinforcements arrive at the Faïd Pass, only to meet a bloody rebuff at German hands.[209]

At Juin's suggestion, this "close call" prompted Eisenhower to take advantage of Giraud's absence at the Anfa Conference to reorganize the front. "Whether the French approved or not, [Eisenhower] put Anderson in complete charge, directly under himself, and issued instructions to pull the French back and for the British and Americans to take parts of the French sector," Eisenhower's naval aide Harry Butcher noted.[210] This was not quite accurate. Eisenhower would now direct the Mediterranean theater. The Tunisian front would be coordinated through General Harold Alexander from the middle of February. The Northwest African Air Forces under USAAF Major General Carl A. Spaatz would report to the commander in chief of Mediterranean air forces, Air Chief Marshal Arthur Tedder. French morale remained a primary Allied concern. "The French were practically powerless to meet tanks with their inadequate weapons, and will have to be held in reserve until they can be properly equipped," Butcher recorded.[211] Giraud's "dictatorial" temperament, his "megalomania," and a prickly personality quick to take offense showed no signs of softening. At Eisenhower's behest, Lucian Truscott, one of II Corps' rising stars, prepared a 24 January report for his boss that concluded as follows: "I have the definite feeling that the French can no longer be counted on for much and that in important sectors they must be heavily supported and, to the extent possible, immediately rearmed." To be fair to the French, both Ike and Marshall expressed similar concerns about the leadership, training, discipline, and morale of American forces.[212] Officially, at least, the French welcomed this command reorganization as a vote of confidence that "marked our total ascension into the Allied ranks on the Tunisian front."[213]

For the moment, the British V corps under General Charles Allfrey anchored the northern part of the line from the coast south through Medjez-el-Bab to Bou Arada and Le Kef. On 11 February 1943, the French Chief of Staff, General René Prioux, certified that the *corps expéditionnaire* in Tunisia numbered 103,400 combat troops with 17,300 men in support.[214] Anderson's role for the CAF was to occupy the Western Dorsal. The southernmost sector was held by the US II Corps plus, for the moment, the Constantine division, under Fredendall. The American sector anchored the southern end of the line between Sbeïtla and Gafsa, "a fabulous country of stark ravines and crenellated stone ridges that were stained to the colours of pale rose and muddy brown and saffron yellow," recorded Moorehead. "A few villages struggled for wretched existence from the bare land and beyond."[215] Both the DAF and the CSTT were dissolved. Barré was tasked with organizing logistics, a step toward his forced retirement in July 1943, which many viewed as a betrayal by Juin. Among the many advantages of this new command arrangement was that the French would now benefit from Allied artillery and, they hoped, air support. A furious Giraud was confronted with this reorganization on his return from the Anfa Conference. It would not be the last time that those in the French camp would take advantage of Giraud's periodic absences to present their guileless commander in chief with a fait accompli.[216]

"We Have Taken a Severe Licking . . .":[217] Kasserine 14–24 February 1943

But this reorganization was interrupted by Rommel's Valentine's Day offensive at Kasserine (Map 1.3). February 1943 found Axis forces at the pinnacle of their strength. Hans-Jürgen von Arnim's army counted 110,000 men, with around 200 tanks, including the latest Tiger heavy tanks. This number of tanks had been doubled when, on 26 January 1943, Rommel crossed the frontier into Tunisia to take command of the Africa Army Group composed of the Fifth Panzer Army, in the north under von Arnim, and in the south the First Italian Army, the Afrika Korps, and an Italian Saharan Group, all led by Messe. Operations could be supported by Luftwaffe planes operating from all-weather airfields close to the front, while the Allies flew from improvised airstrips at Tébessa and Thélepte, or even from Constantine. Supplies arrived at Bizerte, and in smaller harbors at Sousse, Sfax, and Gabès, to outfit Rommel's forces, thus minimizing the transport problems that the German general had experienced in the Western Desert. Rommel's goal at this stage was to maintain control over Tunisia's harbors, so that he would have freedom of maneuver should he eventually be forced to retire north for an amphibious extraction. Montgomery's Eighth Army approached across Tripolitania, and would have to be blocked on the Mareth Line. But with these seeming advantages came drawbacks. The Axis command team, although experienced, often failed to cooperate, while supplies across the Mediterranean were slowly being strangled by Allied interdiction.[218] But the Allies, too, faced their own logistical challenges in Tunisia – as the main western supply base for the American II Corps and the British First Army, Algiers was almost 500 miles from the front, from which supplies must be dispatched via a rudimentary and dispersed road network and a single narrow-gauge railway that meandered out of eastern Algeria. And once supplies arrived in Tunisia, mules were required to shift them across Tunisia's challenging terrain close to frontline units.

Juin complained of Anderson's failure to respond as Rommel's troops poured across the Mareth Line into Tunisia and positioned themselves for a major offensive. To remove any threat coming out of Algeria to the north–south road that linked Tunis with Gabès and Mareth to the south, between 30 January and 12 February 1943, the 21st Panzer Division and the Italian 50th Special Brigade had pushed the overextended French out of the Faïd Pass south of Fondouk, and then defied two inept American attempts to repossess it. French 75 mm guns were simply overmatched in duels with heavy German 105 mm and 210 mm cannon, and had only a limited ability to repel tanks that enveloped their positions. German engineers opened breaches in French minefields through which infantry infiltrated, seizing 75 mm cannon that had exhausted their munitions. Finally, fifty German tanks poured through the pass as infantry surrounded French positions on the ridgelines.

Juin grumbled that on 30 January, armored elements of II Corps, 50 kilometers away at Sbeïtla, were slow to ride to the rescue of the 2nd battalion of the 2ᵉ RTA that was being leisurely carved up by Axis forces.[219] This was because Fredendall was preoccupied with his own plans to cover Maktar against a German push through the Fondouk Pass. He also schemed to seize Maknassy at the southern end of the Dorsal from the Italians. Only after the personal intervention of Giraud and eventually of Truscott, at 07:30 on the morning of 31 January, was a US counterattack launched, with insufficient air cover; and it was picked apart by German artillery. At the end of the day on 1 February, the French had lost 904 men and the Americans had abandoned any attempt to wrest the Faïd Pass from German control. In Allied eyes, French resolve seemed shaken by the fact that many soldiers had family in France – one battalion alone experienced 132 desertions. Colonel William Biddle was assigned as II Corps liaison to Juin's headquarters to avoid a repetition of the Faïd Pass débâcle.

The French autopsy blamed defeat on "insufficient numbers, inferiority of the weaponry of the infantry, the absence of artillery, lack of reserves, and the poor training of indigenous troops." The Germans proved much more complimentary of the tenacity of the French, despite their lack of supply and munitions, than of the Americans, "soldiers without experience, clumsy leadership, radio commands sent in clear, insufficient air support." A 2 February meeting at Telergma, an important forward US airbase in Algeria, between Truscott, Anderson, and Eisenhower concluded that the central front was too lightly held. Anderson began to withdraw battered French units to rest and rearm them, filling gaps in the line with Americans from II Corps. After the war, a debate broke out over who had been responsible for the faulty US dispositions – Fredendall or Anderson? At the time, received wisdom in the Allied camp held that Rommel had been so weakened by his defeat at El Alamein, followed by his retreat across Libya, that he no longer posed a significant threat. That assessment played into the hands of Rommel, who saw a chance to inflict a morale-destroying defeat on US forces whom the Desert Fox recognized were inexperienced, poorly trained, undisciplined, and thinly scattered along the Algerian border. In this way, he might turn the Allied flank, and allow his Panzers to rampage into eastern Algeria.[220]

At dawn on 14 February, the 21st Panzer Division, led by Tiger tanks supported by motorized infantry, sprang out of a sandstorm from the Maizila Pass, south of Faïd. At the same time, the 10th Panzer pitched east out of Faïd Pass headed for Sidi Bou Zid, held by units of the 1st US Armored Division

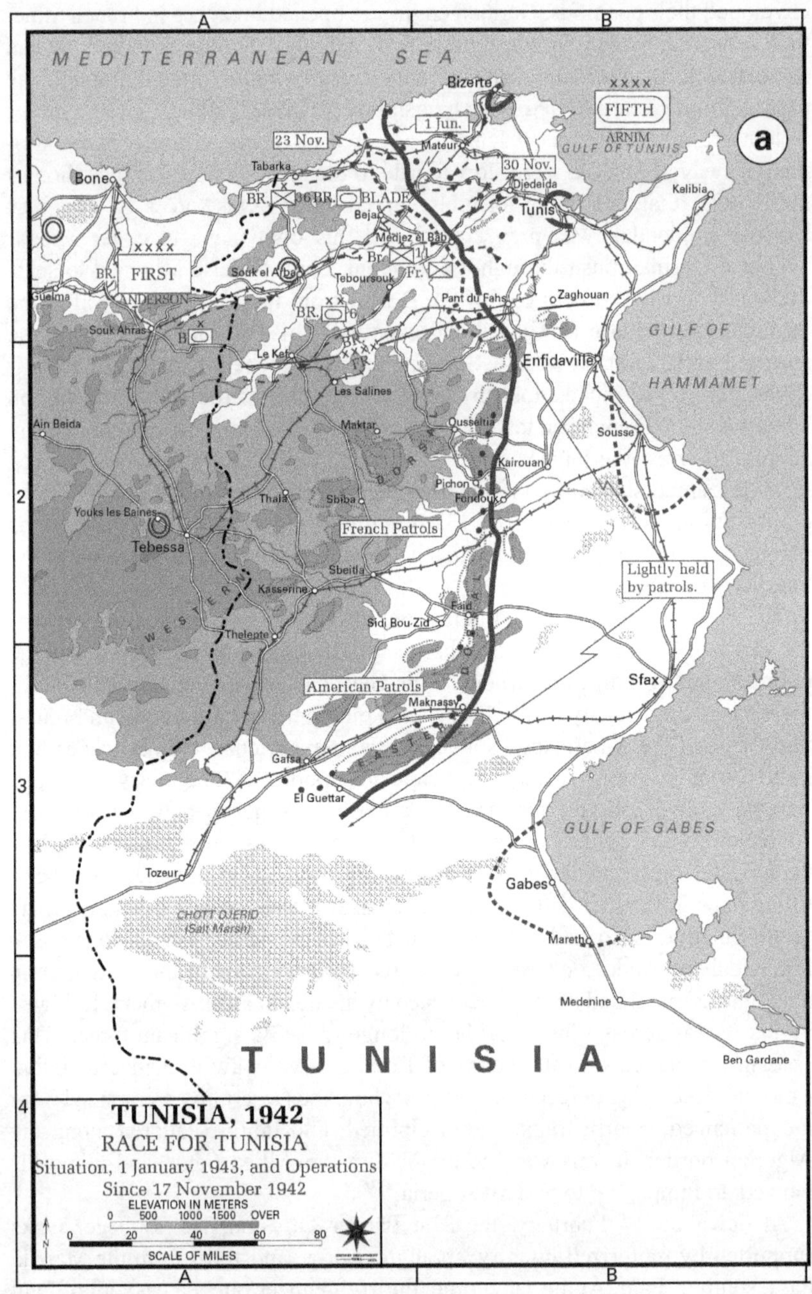

Map 1.3 Dual maps January–February 1943.

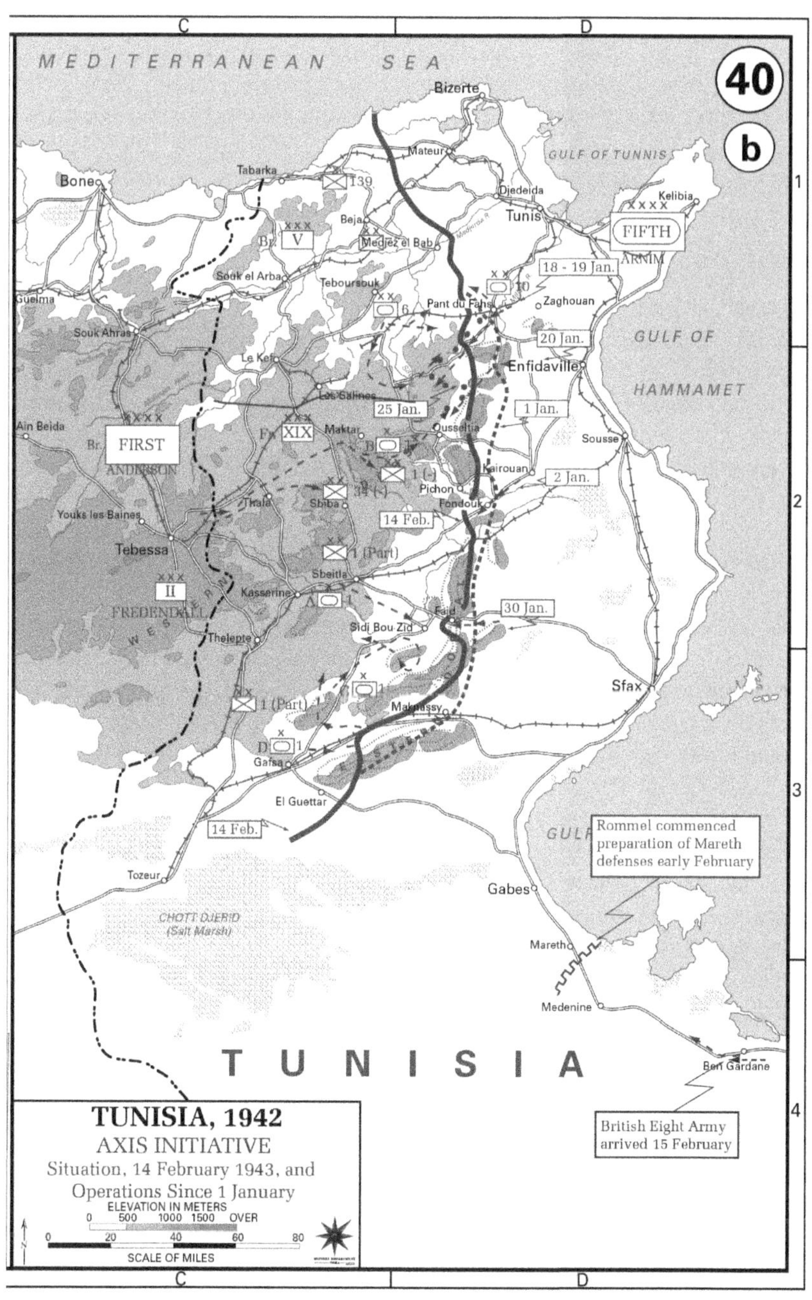
MEDITERRANEAN SEA
40
b
GULF OF TUNNIS
GULF OF
HAMMAMET
FIFTH
ARNIM
FIRST
ANDERSON
II
FREDENDALL
XIX
V
18 - 19 Jan.
20 Jan.
25 Jan.
1 Jan.
2 Jan.
14 Feb.
30 Jan.
14 Feb.
Bizerte
Mateur
Tabarka
Bone
Beja
Djedeida
Tunis
Kelibia
Medjez el Bab
Souk el Arba
Teboursouk
Pant du Fahs
Zaghouan
Guelma
Souk Ahras
Le Kef
Enfidaville
Los Salines
Ain Beida
Maktar
Ousseltia
Sousse
Kairouan
Pichon
Fondouk
Thala
Sbiba
Youks les Baines
Tebessa
Sbeitla
Kasserine
Faid
Sidi Bou Zid
Thelepte
Sfax
Maknassy
Gafsa
El Guettar
Tozeur
CHOTT DJERID
(Salt Marsh)
Gabes
Mareth
Medenine
Ben Gardane
Rommel commenced preparation of Mareth defenses early February
British Eight Army arrived 15 February
TUNISIA
TUNISIA, 1942
AXIS INITIATIVE
Situation, 14 February 1943, and Operations Since 1 January
ELEVATION IN METERS
0 500 1000 1500 OVER
0 20 40 60 80
SCALE OF MILES

Map 1.3 (cont.)

(AD). Despite Enigma warnings, the Americans were caught by surprise, in large part because Anderson insisted that the German attack would come out of Fondouk. As a consequence, the American positions were quickly overrun. But Fredendall's headquarters, believing that the situation was still in hand, refused to panic. On the next day – 15 February – they counterattacked, with Sherman tanks and tank destroyers in the lead. Unfortunately, the hapless Fredendall stumbled unaware into a classic German tank ambush as had been perfected in the Western Desert – 88 mm anti-tank guns hidden in cactus groves and buildings blasted his flanks, as Stukas lashed him from the air, for a loss of 55 tanks, 15 officers and almost 300 men missing in action. "The Americans did not seem to have much experience in open combat," Juin remarked laconically.[221]

So far, most of the damage had been inflicted by von Arnim. Eisenhower approved an order allowing II Corps to fall back on the Western Dorsal along a line running from Sbiba south to Sbeïtla, and then through Kasserine to Fériana. The Germans divided their offensive forces into two prongs, sending one to Faïd, breaking through the pass on 14 February, while the second thrust up the Gabès–Gafsa road. By 16 February, GIs had begun to filter back, while others were ordered to withdraw by radio or air-dropped messages. However, this proved almost suicidal, as the Germans caught retreating clusters of American soldiers on the plain, and either machine-gunned them or, if feeling charitable, captured them. On the night of 16–17 February, von Arnim attacked behind a barrage of rocket flares, which set off a panic flight among American soldiers that continued into the morning. Juin reluctantly ordered Welvert to evacuate Gafsa. On both flanks, the Americans began to pull back to the Western Dorsal, evacuating Gafsa and Sbeïtla. The narrow road going north-west from Gafsa was filled, "bumper to bumper, from head to tail with tanks, artillery, infantry, French Legionnaires, camels, goats, sheep, Arab and French families with crying children, jackasses and horse-drawn carts," noted one observer. An ordnance detachment following in the rear pulled tanks and vehicles out of ditches into which they had slithered in the rain and blackout.[222] In fact, the retreat was complicated by the fact that US Army engineers were blowing up everything in the path of retreat, including a railway bridge that obliged the French to abandon ten locomotives, considerable rolling stock, and six tons of precious munitions. Giraud protested not only at the loss of valuable munitions, but above all because he feared that the Allied defeat would encourage "the Arabs in the area [to] become active against us now that we have retreated from Gafsa and have taken a licking further north."[223]

On the morning of 17 February, Anderson ordered the evacuation of Sbeïtla and Fériana. At Sbeïtla, the last men to leave town were two ordnance officers who lingered to explode the ammunition dumps.[224] Rommel appeared poised to overrun the main Allied air base at Thélepte (where the Americans smashed unserviceable planes and set 60,000 gallons of aviation fuel alight), before swinging north toward Kasserine to link up with von Arnim's troops. "The loss of the airfields at Thélepte is especially hard to take," Butcher recorded on 20 February. "These were the best fields in that area."[225] Sbeïtla fell, as beaten and panicked troops streamed west from the southern flank of the Allied line. What was left of the 1st US AD retreated through the Kasserine Pass and took up positions on the high ground to the east of Tébessa and Fériana. Only half of its men and equipment still remained. Juin complained that the virtual abandonment of southern Tunisia had opened Algeria to invasion, while leaving the left flank of the XIX Corps in the air, and set off alarm bells in Algiers. Giraud sent him forward personally to reorganize the front.[226] Thélepte airfield was overrun on 18 February, as US ground crews destroyed thirty-four unserviceable aircraft on the ground. But Allied air dominance was beginning to bite, as air strikes by heavy bombers shifted away from tanks and onto troops and logistical convoys.[227] On 19 February, Rommel aimed three Panzer divisions at Kasserine Pass, a mile-wide fissure in the Grand Dorsal 30 miles east of the Algerian border, that was held by a thinly manned defense of US combat engineers and French 75 mm artillery. At first, the defenses held. But gradually confusion and localized panic set in, compromising the Allied positions. A group of Franco-American troops was constituted around General Theodore Roosevelt, son of Teddy Roosevelt and a cousin of FDR, to seize key blocking points, but without success. Intelligence predicted that Rommel would make for Thala, which Juin complained was defended by a single battalion of Algerian *tirailleurs*. "[Welvert] was literally fed up with his superior, the American Fredendall, who in his estimation had no more military knowledge than a mess hall corporal," Juin recorded. After finding an overwhelmed Fredendall preparing to abandon Tébessa and retreat into the "tormented mountainous terrain of the Ouenza," thus throwing Constantine open to the Axis, Juin vowed to defend Tébessa with French forces.[228] In a 20 February press conference, Eisenhower allocated the blame "principally to the miscalculation which 'he' had made as to the ability of the French troops, with their poor equipment, to hold the central front. When the French caved in a couple of weeks ago and their sixty-mile front had to be taken over by British and Americans, the line could only be thinly held." But the real miscalculation in Butcher's view had been made by Anderson, who had bought into a German deception operation that Rommel's attack would come further north, and so had not reinforced the threatened Kasserine front. In private, however, Butcher acknowledged the role of the poor tactical deployment of US forces and the "poor fighting quality, which reflect also on all the officers" for "one of the greatest defeats in our history."[229] For his part, Juin did not need to carry out the threat to defend Tébessa, because by 22 February, Rommel's tanks came under heavy air and artillery attack as they approached Thala. Allied planes also strafed and bombed German traffic in the Kasserine Pass. Sensing Thala to be out of reach, Rommel ordered a retreat. It may have been premature, because, when Major General Ernest Harmon was sent toward Kasserine by Eisenhower to report on the situation, he was greeted by a cascade of vehicles crammed with clearly rattled soldiers in full retreat.[230]

By 21 February, Lapouge's unit had become swept up in the Kasserine *débâcle*. Ordered to bury their munitions and withdraw in the night, his company trudged toward the rear on foot, as convoys of GIs and Tommies clinging precariously to trucks sped past them. Rain began to fall. Ten kilometers from Maktar, well to the north of Kasserine, when everyone was totally exhausted, twelve British lorries stopped to offer them a lift. Fortified with corned-beef, tea, and tinned pineapple, followed by "a remarkable 5 o'clock" of jam, butter, cheese, tea, and biscuits, they were driven to Tébessa. Lapouge was soaking wet. The British cut a towel in two, and then found him a toothbrush and a razor with blades. But they were not yet out of danger – artillery shells thudded around them, and they were again on foot, exhausted, and dispirited. Despite the pouring rain, drinking water was scarce as they trudged 18 kilometers in the mud. The night of 23 February was spent shivering in a bivouac pitched among Roman ruins, from which they might have heard the heavy bomber attacks on Rommel's retreating units. On 1 March, they climbed into large US trucks for a night convoy on twisting roads with no headlights. When one of the trucks slipped into a ditch, a crane suddenly appeared to pull it back onto the road. "Oh, if the Americans could fight as well as they can pull their trucks out of a ditch . . ." On 5 March, Lapouge's unit was sent back into line: "Half of our arms and matériel were missing. We were incapable of action . . . and we were back in line. The officers are discouraged. The *tirailleurs* hesitate a little, but they march."[231]

Le Corps Franc d'Afrique

In the wake of Torch, *l'armée d'Afrique* was besieged by what it categorized as a rush of "inopportune enlistments." The technical reasons for its reticence to enlist new recruits began with the fact that a military force "rich in generals, in senior and staff officers," was lacking in company-level cadres, as well as NCOs and specialists capable of incorporating, training, and leading them in battle. The logic of the high command was that they would receive plenty of recruits in an orderly fashion once conscription kicked in. But second, and more importantly, Darlan and other senior officers viewed the impatience of a "motley crowd" of enthusiastic patriots of 8 November to fight as a form of indiscipline, whose recruitment threatened to capsize *l'armée d'Afrique's* "imperial" concept of discipline, whose organizing principle was veneration of the commander. Furthermore, the democratic spirit of the *levée* threatened to undermine efforts to exclude Jews, "Gaullists," and other "dissidents" from the army. Not only did the presence of this class of recruit pose a threat to homogeneity and good military order, but also Algerian Jews would invariably deploy military service as leverage to reclaim French nationality.[232] And could Muslims be far behind?

Unfortunately for this military elite, momentum to broaden and democratize recruitment beyond a narrow band of largely illiterate and malleable Muslims was building from several sources. Van Hecke aspired to transform the *Chantiers* into a nucleus for military revitalization in North Africa. In this spirit, the general staff decided that 5,000 members of the *Chantiers* were to be sent to the air force, 1,000 to the paratroops, and 10,000 to the army. This allegedly left around 9,000 without an assignment. In fact, little of this redistribution of *Chantiers* manpower was realized in the post-Torch chaos when many never answered the call-up, or, eager to get into combat, enlisted on their own initiative.[233] A second motivation was Giraud's push to find a command for his partner in crime Monsabert, shunned by *l'armée d'Afrique* and excoriated by the FAF for having surrounded Blida airfield for Allied benefit on 8 November 1942. According to Monsabert, the first words out of Noguès' mouth when they had met in Algiers on 11 November 1942 were "Monsieur, you are a traitor!" Members of the Service d'ordre légionnaire (SOL) were keen to assassinate him, he insisted, and he was in such bad odor with his former colleagues that, sensing his career finished, he even contemplated enlisting as a private in the Foreign Legion.[234] Like the Gaullists, by joining the "dissidence," Monsabert had betrayed his military caste. His motives were now suspect, impure, like those of politicians or diplomats who had undermined the professional soldiers and forfeited the war. These *Maréchalists* yearned for a pure relationship that could only be found in a world they saw reflected in themselves. And Monsabert, along with Magnan, Béthouart, Mast, Toustain, Beaufre, de Gaulle, Leclerc, Koenig, Catroux, and their ilk had broken the bond of their military brotherhood.

A third impulse for the founding of the CFA was a public order requirement to control a potentially troublemaking agglomeration of Gaullists, Jews, pro-British Maltese, Spanish Republicans, those being released under Allied pressure from internment camps in the Sahara, and other "undesirables" by corralling them under military authority and dispatching them to Tunisia. There was also a desire to staunch a flight of Frenchmen, especially those connected with 8 November, into British service, where they sought protection from neo-Vichy retribution. Several from the *Chantiers*, including Bonnier de la Chapelle, had collected at what became known as "Camp Pillafort," organized on a farm on Cap Matifou outside of Algiers that belonged to a friend of Henri d'Astier and Van Hecke to be trained by British commandos. Admiral Moreau feared that Matifou had become a center designed to transform *Chantiers* inmates into an "Anglo-Gaullist" militia. Darlan concurred: "Given the danger of Anglo-Gaullist Corps Francs in the proximity of Algiers, I have asked the Commander-in-Chief of Air and Ground Forces in Africa to request that the Allied Authorities distance these irregular formations from the region of Cap Matifou."[235] For his part, Monsabert, impressed by the British training offered at Cap Matifou, saw commandos as a quick path to the "modernization" of French forces, a project that found some support in army ranks.[236] But the British, who had envisaged preparing small groups of men to carry out sabotage behind the lines in Tunisia, were overwhelmed by the numbers that had collected at "Pillafort." The French high command suspected that Matifou was a British plot to create another alternative French force like the *Forces françaises libres* (FFL). "It is true that every undesirable or unstable man who does not want to submit to French army discipline looks to enlist in the corps franc," read a French general staff assessment.[237] So Monsabert agreed to lead these men, if they could be collected in a unit sizable enough to be led by a general. In this way, on 25 November 1942, the CFA was officially stood up.[238]

Recruitment bureaus were set up in Algiers, Oran, Casablanca, Fez, and Oudja. Posters and newspaper advertisements announced that men were being sought "without distinction of race or religion," offered a 1,000 franc enlistment bonus, and pay of 10 francs a day to serve in a "*groupe de choc*." Recruiting sergeants appear to have cast a wide net to haul in those eligible for conscription, reservists from other corps, and even Foreign Legionnaires.[239] Monsabert ignored both Prioux's 12 January 1943 attempt to suspend CFA recruitment and orders from Giraud that he must not recruit in "work companies and the concentration camps," and that he should direct Jews toward the "Jewish pioneer corps."[240] Instead, on 23 December, Monsabert asked that foreigners who volunteered for the CFA would be given favorable consideration for French nationality, and that their families would not be importuned by the authorities. Unless the French enlisted these foreigners, he warned, the British would continue to recruit them.[241]

This recruitment drive produced a force that, according to Georges Elgozy, who served in the CFA, "was in effect partisan bands assembled in a kind of international brigade. They were obviously anti-Vichyite, anti-conformist, and anti- a lot of things. One could not have devised a corps more opposed to the spirit and the tradition of the sailors."[242] Indeed, the mere existence of this band of fugitives, whose unifying principle was a distrust of authority, tied *l'armée d'Afrique* in knots: screeds from Noguès protested that CFA recruitment was undermining good order and discipline in regular Moroccan units.[243] Mendigal complained on 23 January 1943 that eight irreplaceable aircraft mechanics from the Maison Blanche air base at Algiers had enlisted in the CFA, and demanded their return.[244] Monsabert's original idea of grouping his recruits in more or less ethnically, religiously, or nationally homogeneous units under

French cadres foundered on a dearth of French officers and NCOs and the sheer heterogeneity of his force. This recruiting effort eventually collected a "belle brigade" of 6,188 men, among them Jews, political refugees, foreign volunteers of 1939–1940 who had subsequently been consigned to concentration camps in gratitude for their service, Italians interned because of their nationality, *Chantiers* fugitives, and sailors who had escaped from Bizerte but been orphaned by the French navy, most of whose seaworthy craft had been scuttled in any case, or whose officers imperiously sulked in their rusting hulks in Alexandria and the Antilles refusing to fight. This CFA class of 1942 also included refugees from Alsace-Moselle, a few notorious communists, Moroccan Muslims enlisted despite Noguès' remonstrations, and some Spaniards, including a former Republican navy admiral who, according to Elgozy, "during the entire Tunisian campaign, remained resolved to understand neither French nor humor." Finally, a few unmoored SOL and *Croix de feu* alumni seeking to launder their pasts rounded out this motley muster. Historian of the FFL Jean-François Muracciole calculates that, while the ranks of the CFA contained a large number of French "dissidents," it was also 15 percent foreign and 25 percent Muslim. Furthermore, in the final phase of the campaign, with the push on Bizerte, the "très Vichyiste" battalion of marine infantry was attached to it, under the future Rear Admiral Raymond Maggiar, a Narvik veteran who had volunteered for Tunisia out of a British prisoner of war (POW) camp after his ship had been torpedoed off Madagascar. After knocking without result on several doors in Algiers, Juin instructed Maggiar to organize a regiment of marines, which would subsequently achieve celebrity as a tank destroyer unit in Leclerc's *2e Division blindée*. But that was in the future. When they arrived in the CFA for the final march on Bizerte, Maggiar's *1er Régiment des fusiliers marins* was instantly labeled the Royal-Voyou (Navy Louts).[245] To this was added a "*section féminine*" of nurses and ambulance drivers, whose "heterogeneous" equipment was upgraded by the Americans, and whose alleged sexual promiscuity or lesbian relationships became the subject of salacious speculation.[246] Nevertheless, a French doctor explained to American war correspondent A. J. Liebling that the main advantage of female nurses was that it helped wounded soldiers better to endure pain: "Since we have so little anesthesia . . . we rely upon vanity."[247]

At least three ironies hovered over the CFA's inception, beginning with the fact that command of a group of men denounced inaccurately in Muracciole's view as a "gaggle of Gaullists" would be handed to Monsabert, who by his own admission was a recovering *Maréchalist*.[248] A second irony was that no sooner had the unit been created, in part to keep the British from siphoning Frenchmen into the service of His Majesty, than it would be placed under British command. Not surprisingly, *l'armée d'Afrique* washed its hands of these "undesirables," who viewed themselves as a patriotic, international, multiracial *levée* that sought "to redeem the cowardice of many," but whom regular soldiers disdained as amateurs, and who through Matifou and Bonnier de la Chapelle became tainted by association with the assassination of Darlan. The understanding was that, while the French would supply the uniforms, the British would be responsible for arming the CFA, who would then be employed "outside the French army's combat zone."[249] Therefore, on 19 December, the first contingent of what Vichy radio denounced as "a great collection of scallywags" and "Apaches" set out in the autumn rains toward Tunisia in old railway carriages pulled behind a wheezing antique locomotive along eastern Algeria's narrow-gauge railway.[250]

The official line was that the CFA had been generously offered to Anderson on the pretext that the British lacked infantry. However, the final irony of the CFA was that the British, who in French minds were virtually kidnapping French recruits at Camp Pillafort (Matifou), became rather unnerved by the unexpected delivery of this consignment of military discards. Monsabert acknowledged that the CFA's disembarkation at First Army flabbergasted the normally reserved Anderson.[251] According to Durand, only 25 percent of the men in the two ragged CFA battalions deposited on Anderson's doorstep had any military experience. In the event, the contingent arrayed before him was heterogeneously armed, practically without munitions, largely untrained and undisciplined, contained volunteers as young as sixteen, had been outfitted seemingly out of a church rummage sale, and led by superannuated officers unable to speak either English or Arabic, many of whom had not touched a weapon since the Rif War concluded in 1925. Once they had been attached to the British 139th Brigade, on 12 January, Anderson ordered that the unit be issued British battledress, so that at least they looked like soldiers, be sent for training as a conventional force, and have its leadership upgraded.[252]

But a lack of training was only the beginning of the CFA's challenges. "For these battalions in the process of being organized there exist practically no resources," Monsabert complained on 12 January, in what would become the lament of the French army until the war's end. "So, the requirement to provide sufficient cadres for the Corps Franc is urgent." Indeed, in January 1943, a call went out in Morocco for officer and NCO volunteers from regular units for the CFA. But combat in Tunisia had transformed the pre-November 1942 shortage of cadres into a crisis, so that requests to transfer were discouraged or refused.[253] Nor is it clear that the understated Anderson immediately warmed to the effusive command style of Monsabert, who *tutoyed* everyone, addressed his soldiers as "*mes enfants*," and, clutching his swagger stick, galloped enthusiastically at the head of group trots or directed his command in collective gymnastics, "animated by perfectly irregular … usually unpredictable movements." Indeed, the combination of a flushed face beneath a thatch of snow-white hair earned Monsabert the nickname "Strawberry in Cream."[254]

Anderson must have concluded that Monsabert, with his serially evolving schemes to organize the CFA into commando groups, his intrigues to liberate Corsica with a corps of specially trained natives of that island, and other special operations-inspired caprices, had been sent by the Almighty to assay his piety.[255]

In the meantime, Anderson complained that he had to "wet nurse" the CFA,[256] to whom he assigned four British trainers, "esthetes but competent," according to Georges Elgozy, who attempted to introduced them to the fundamentals of soldiering. Regular raids by the Luftwaffe added realism to the training, as did patrols near the front lines, often integrated into British formations. Unlike regular units, the CFA had little faith in their military leadership, or even in their comrades. Platoons and sections coalesced around a primary group identity – Moroccan, Foreign Legion, Kabyle, Spanish, Jew, although Jews were a diverse lot depending on their class, education, and whether they hailed from Morocco, Algeria, or Tunisia. Elements of the CFA did well in small skirmishes with Bersaglieri on 2 and 10 February, a type of action that British paratroopers dismissed as a "Second XI Match."[257] In Durand's view, although the CFA was slow to grasp the "science" of combat, by March 1943, it had become no less efficient than were *tirailleurs* or Foreign Legionnaires, who also were led by reservists, and, in the view of the CFA at least, usually evinced less *élan*.[258]

The Axis offensive of February 1943 had also whiplashed the CFA, which entrenched alongside the British 139th Brigade near Le Kef, but, totally lacking in heavy weapons, was assaulted at 06:00 on 26 February by two battalions of the 10th Bersaglieri and as well as two German battalions reinforced by parachute engineers. The attackers infiltrated across the thalwegs behind a smokescreen, covered by a barrage of 150 mm and 88 mm artillery, as well as anti-tank guns and mortars. Tunisians had been dragooned to drive flocks of sheep before the assault wave to set off mines. While several frontline companies were cut off and submerged, a counterattack organized in the afternoon caught the Italians in a small valley and created a panic. In their first engagement, the CFA estimated that they had killed 160 Italians and captured another 380, together with 6 mortars, 8 heavy machineguns and 12 light machineguns – not a bad performance for the "Second XI." The CFA priest even captured an Italian army portable altar. CFA losses were 8 killed and 20 wounded, but 127 were missing, an indication that morale was not all that it could have been. Some Italian POWs, insisting that they were Slovenes, offered to join the CFA. Unfortunately, the British retreated in the face of an attack by German paratroops, in the process surrendering 2,000 POWs and most of the captured matériel. Magnan complained that 26 February had been very costly for the CFA, which had lost many of its most experienced cadres and equipment, and that it had no radios to control the battle or vehicles for mobility, nor raincoats and tents to protect the soldiers from the weather. As a result, the CFA had become "an inert force, unable to react." From 27 February, the CFA withdrew to the west through the mud and rain on the heels of the British, carrying their wounded as officers struggled to keep squads, platoons, and companies together. British paratroopers covered their retreat to British lines, where they were sprayed with dichlorodiphenyltrichloroethane (DDT), given tea and biscuits, and integrated into the British line on the Djebel Driss. There, they were joined by the 3rd Battalion of the CFA, which appeared to contain many former Foreign Legionnaires who in a previous life had fought for both sides in civil wars in Russia and Spain, as well as significant contingents of Jews and Muslims.[259]

A training camp was created under British supervision on the north coast at Tabarka, a bombed-out shell of a village nestled in a barren landscape, occupied by gendarmes, NCOs, nurses, and nuns, and subject to regular Luftwaffe visits. The desolation of the location was matched only by the gloom of the weather and the monotony of "English gastronomy." But, in the summer of 1943, when the soldiers of the CFA switched from British to French logistics, they mourned the absence of Player's Navy Cut cigarettes, razor blades, and the Navy, Army and Air Force Institutes (NAAFI).[260] Even British compo meals seemed superior to an *armée d'Afrique* staple of chickpeas and weevil-infested beans eaten out of a communal pot. For some members of the CFA, this reunion with the French army reminded them of the internment camps from which they had fled. As a consequence, most CFA veterans tried to make their British boots and battledress endure as long as possible into the autumn of 1943.[261]

According to the French official history, on 8 February 1943, CFA command had been transferred to Colonel Joseph Magnan, sprung from *armée d'Afrique* purdah after having made common cause with Béthouart to sequester Noguès at Rabat on 8 November. Where the ebullient Monsabert had represented the quintessential "képi bleu" (North African *tirailleurs*), Magnan, a former camel corps officer and "képi noir" (marine infantry), was deliberate, serene, austere, and meticulous. Although Magnan lacked Monsabert's panache, he understood that enthusiasm could not compensate for a lack of armaments, training, and leadership. Elgozy remarked that CFA volunteers, as a rule distrustful of professional soldiers but especially of a "'colonial' mercenary like Magnan accustomed to leading black troops," nevertheless came to respect their new commander's "cold lucidity that contrasted with the relentless exhilaration and demagogic lyricism of his predecessor." But both Monsabert and Magnan had difficulty attracting professional officers and NCOs, in part because colonial army command proved disinclined to allow professional French cadres "champing at the bit" to fight to transfer from "sovereignty forces" in Africa, "because this risks giving credence to the idea that for a colonial soldier to get into combat, he has to transfer out of his original arm."[262] In fact, everyone was competing to attract or retain scarce and much-in-demand cadres. Magnan brought with him eleven officers and twenty-one NCOs from the *Régiment d'infanterie colonial* (RIC) *de Maroc* – a unit made up of French volunteers from the mainland that was tainted in the eyes of the Giraudists by its association with the "resistance" of 8 November. On 9 April 1943, Magnan also tried to introduce more rigor into training at Tabarka. His technique, that began by reading Stalin's address delivered on the twenty-fifth anniversary of the Red Army on the virtues of discipline, must have gone down a treat at Giraud's HQ, where Magnan was already regarded as a "dissident." More volunteers appeared, but weapons for them were lacking. Many of the corporals were aged over fifty. Everyone shaved their heads to protect against head wound infections.[263]

"As Diabolical in Retreat as in Attack": Post-Kasserine Tunisia

Kasserine proved to be a destructive and humiliating defeat for the Americans, one that cost Fredendall his job after over 20 percent of II Corps had been destroyed, and 4,000 GIs taken prisoner.[264] George Patton briefly took command, before handing over to Omar Bradley for the remainder of the campaign. Likewise, Juin had been dissatisfied with Welvert's performance at the command of the Constantine Division.[265] Juin's threat to defend Tébessa with or without orders from the Allied command revealed that the French were prepared to deploy their army to prioritize their political goals. Yet, this relationship was one of mutual dependence: the Anglo-Americans required French cooperation in AFN and eventually France, while France needed the Allies to liberate their country, while upgrading and modernizing their forces.

In a flash, "Rommel disappeared from the battlefield leaving behind him a terrain difficult to cross, one sown with minefields and ruins," Juin remembered. "One realized that he was as diabolical in retreat as in the attack."[266] An 8 March circular was very critical of Allied operations in the Kasserine–Thala sector. The Luftwaffe wrought havoc on supply columns. Key blocking positions on the roads must be created quickly in mobile warfare situations because time wasted cost casualties. The first act must be to set out minefields to discourage tank attacks while preparing defenses. French defensive positions were poorly sited, not mutually supporting, easily outflanked, not covered by minefields, and not defended with tenacity. Above all, the report concluded, "the question of capitulation must be clearly understood ... No able-bodied man who is armed and equipped to continue combat should surrender to the enemy. Even those who seem to be encircled must continue to resist and organize defensive positions. By acting with tenacity, they continue to impede the enemy. The situation might seem desperate, but it is never lost so long as men have heart, high morale, and arms to fight."[267] The problem is that this report might have been written in June 1940, not March 1943. An undated American report made many of the same points.[268] On 10 March, in the wake of the Kasserine débâcle and drawing on lessons from Guadalcanal, Eisenhower ordered an intensification of training, prioritizing live fire scenarios, aggressive patrolling, and night operations.[269]

Fortunately for the Allies, Kasserine proved to be the high-water mark of the Axis performance in Tunisia (Map 1.4). Rommel's attacks were running out of steam as his supply situation worsened, there were no worthwhile strategic objectives within reach in Algeria, and, finally, the approach of Montgomery and the British Eighth Army to the Mareth Line required Rommel's attention. By 23 February, Rommel had ordered a withdrawal from Kasserine. But his *tour de force* at Kasserine, however fleeting, had revealed Allied shortcomings on the command, operational, and tactical levels. In a belated effort to impose command unity, Eisenhower tapped British General Harold Alexander to act as his deputy and commander of the 18th Army Group, which would include the British First and Eighth Armies, and their attached American and French corps. Alexander's first job was to define a coordinated plan to terminate the Tunisia campaign by the 15 May deadline fixed at Anfa.[270]

American General Lucian Truscott feared that a combination of casualties and poor armaments would soon render French forces combat-ineffective. By early March, "Command Post Kléber" complained that French troops were exhausted, that their weapons were "worn out," and that morale hovered near rock bottom. Reinforcements requested since 15 February had failed to materialize, which left "five almost useless battalions ... I'm obliged to take this into account in my tactical dispositions."[271] In a 20 March report, Colonel and future General Henri Lorber laid out the problems faced by his 3ᵉ RTA in the hills to the north of Medjez-el-Bab. A lack of munitions had prevented his regiment from engaging in realistic training since June 1940. They lacked the numbers to cover their assigned sector, let alone constitute a reserve to conduct an "active defense." Nor had they been in place long enough to work out a defensive fire plan. The 3ᵉ RTA lacked radios, reconnaissance, and close air support – even munitions and lubrication oil for its mortars and machineguns. For these reasons, his *tirailleurs* found it difficult to counter the "ceaseless infiltration and flanking" tactics of the Germans, who used electric torches and flairs to mark their phase lines, employed tracer bullets to adjust fire, and advanced behind artillery barrages. At least so far, the Germans had not brought up tanks. Nor, "surprisingly," had they sought to exploit their superiority to make a breakthrough.[272]

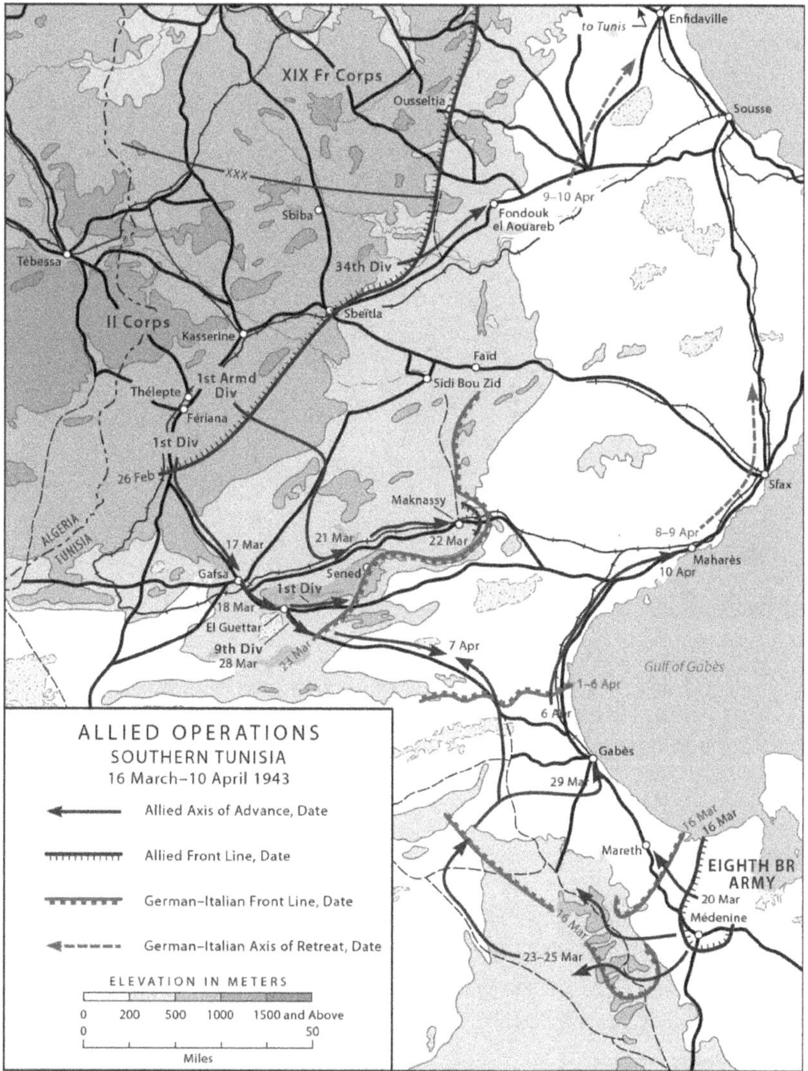

Map 1.4 Map of southern Tunisia.

Monty arrive!

Montgomery had formed a low opinion of Free French forces at El Alamein, declaring them "no good; I have had them once in battle and never want them again. I use them to guard aerodromes; they have no other value. Alex is very

Figure 1.4 Montgomery and Leclerc meet in Tripoli in January 1943. So expended was Leclerc's "Force L" after crossing the Sahara that they had to be completely reequipped by the British. (Photo by Keystone-France/Gamma-Rapho via Getty Images)

good about it and keeps them away from me."[273] This made his cautious embrace of Philippe Leclerc's "Chad Column," when he encountered it in Tripoli on 26 January 1943 (Figure 1.4), somewhat out of character. All the more so because Leclerc's tatterdemalion band of roughly 2,300 men had straggled across the Libyan desert in 543 barely serviceable vehicles. Along the way, Leclerc had filched a few oases from isolated and demoralized Italian garrisons, so that de Gaulle might use these outposts as bargaining chips to stake a claim on the Italian territory.

The meeting of Montgomery and Leclerc was hardly fortuitous, but had been networked through Cairo and General Harold Alexander. Leclerc's pitch to Montgomery was that *les forces français libres* sought a presence in the Tunisia campaign. Montgomery complained to his boss, Chief of the Imperial General Staff (CIGS) General Alan Brooke, that he was being pressured to employ the French in some role. Leclerc's Chad column clearly constituted a charity case, but its small size made an upgrade feasible. Montgomery ordered them kitted out in British uniforms, had new motors installed in thirty of their trucks, and ordered that they be issued sixteen anti-tank guns. Leclerc was given a command car, and Montgomery agreed to keep Leclerc supplied in petrol, food, and spare parts. Eighty sappers expert in mine clearing, an air liaison officer, and some jeep-mounted "Free Greeks" who called themselves the "Sacred Squadron," commanded by a former Foreign Legionnaire under indictment for treason in Athens, were attached. From 12 February, the Gaullist banner in the Eighth Army would be carried by this 4,000 strong Force L (for Leclerc), although the British referred to it as the French Flying Column.[274]

In February, Force L had advanced to Ksar Rhilane (Ghilane) in Tunisia, an important crossroads that controlled the Ksar el-Hallouf Pass through the Matmata mountains and which Montgomery planned to use as a logistical base to attack the Mareth Line. On 9 March, the Eighth Army Chief offered to allow Leclerc to turn over the defense of Ksar Rhilane to a British unit, but the Frenchman insisted that, with air support, Force L could hold its own. On 10 March, beginning at 06:30, Leclerc's men were attacked by around forty wheeled vehicles of reconnaissance units of the 15th and 21st Panzer Divisions backed by Stukas. Advanced French units gradually fell back on Ksar Rhilane, where, at 08:15, thirty RAF planes attacked the Germans as they halted to deploy their artillery. For the remainder of the day, the Germans attempted to turn the French flanks, but were repeatedly balked by the RAF. Alexander compared Ksar Rhilane to Bir Hakeim, where discipline, the use of maneuver by defending forces, and pre-registered artillery fire had combined with air support, all beautifully coordinated by radio communications, to frustrate the German attack. Leclerc even received a "Well done!" from Montgomery.[275]

"We Entered Tunis on the Tail of an Avalanche":[276] Phase III: 15 March–8 May

From an Allied perspective, the Tunisia campaign had been a costly and perfectly avoidable event. Yet, while it may be argued that the Allied effort had been poorly managed and protracted, ultimately the decision to fight at the end of a tenuous supply line proved a devastating one for the Axis. Despite the best efforts of Esteva and Rahn, German propaganda found little resonance among Tunisian Arabs, while attempts to mobilize Tunisia's colonists resulted in humiliating failure.[277] Berlin could not support both Stalingrad and "Tunisgrad," while interdicting convoys on the Murmansk route. "If the forces committed, and lost, in Tunisia had been held back to defend Sicily," Alan J. Levine speculates, "the enemy would have had a good chance of throwing back the Allied attack on the island." Nevertheless, Axis reinforcements continued to trickle through cordons of Allied submarines and motor torpedo boats thrown around Italian ports. Tunisia drove the penultimate nail into Mussolini's coffin, and formed the prologue to the break-up of the Axis. But no one on the Axis side, least of all von Arnim, could muster the courage to tell the two Axis leaders that a defense of Tunisia was a profligate waste of resources for an elusive strategic gain.[278]

On 14 March, after having been tirelessly lectured by Jean Monnet, Giraud announced that "constitutional acts, laws, and decrees passed after 22 June 1940, are declared null and void," while henceforth "Executive acts" would be promulgated by the "French Republic," and "in the name of the French people." Unfortunately, finding busts of Marianne to replace Pétain's portraits proved more challenging, as did the restoration of Crémieux guaranteeing Jewish citizenship.[279] Meanwhile, not surprisingly, the situation in Tunis was moving in the opposite direction, with rampant inflation, a diminishing food supply, forced labor drafts, and Allied bombardments. As the war increasingly tilted against the Axis in Russia and Tunisia, any initial Muslim nationalist hopes invested in the possibility of Axis-led liberation evaporated.[280]

March also found the *Corps d'Armée Français* sandwiched between the British V Corps and the US II Corps to cover a sector that Koeltz protested lacked both sufficient troops and adequate armaments. French forces at the front numbered 72,802 according to Belkacem Recham, 50,601 of whom were North African Muslims.[281] On 5 March, Lapouge's unit, which, like most *tirailleur* regiments, was 90 percent Muslim before being "modernized" to US standards, was sent back into the line, despite that the fact that "half of our arms and matériel have been lost." But the Allied effort was gaining momentum: day and night, innumerable jeeps, trucks, and half-tracks, "bristling with anti-tank arms and radio antennae pointing toward the sky, full of pompous and colorful English, unkempt, laughing Americans, French, Senegalese, etc." drove at top speed along roads lined with munitions dumps, hospitals, tank parks, airfields, and motor pools, directed by "lighted road signs in all the Allied languages, [and] military policemen with immense white sleeves."[282] On 9 March, Rommel was recalled to Europe, bequeathing to von Arnim the honor of closing out a doomed campaign. Patton attempted to take advantage of the Battle of Mareth, launched by Montgomery on 20 March, to deploy his II Corps to reoccupy Gafsa on 17 March as a base to seize some of the passes on the Eastern Dorsal. An offensive launched on 27 March by the French XIX Corps backed by the 34th US ID toward Kairouan via Pichon and Fondouk slowly gained momentum, despite fierce Axis attempts to keep their north–south corridor open. The CFA found itself in the line next to General Manton Eddy's 9th US ID set to attack the 21st Panzer. Eddy took pity on them, and issued sub-machineguns to the NCOs and M1 carbines for officers, as well as some radios, jeeps, GMC trucks, and bazookas. He also attached two sections of tank destroyers, M7 tracked 105 mm artillery pieces, and a company of engineers to the CFA.[283]

While Leclerc experimented with the formation of inter-arms combinations, Force L remained too undergunned to be of much use in main encounters. Therefore, on 19 March 1943, Montgomery attached them as flank guards to the New Zealand Division. Operation Pugilist, launched from 20 March, aimed to break through the Mareth Line, ironically built to keep out the Axis but now garrisoned by them, which the Germans had strengthened with additional minefields and a forward band of defensive posts.[284] Only after a nine-day assault combined with a flanking movement by the New Zealand Division reinforced by an armored brigade and the King's Dragoon Guards, and Force L, did Messe withdraw from the Mareth Line on 28 March, to a blocking position on the Wadi Akarit. Alexander was keen to sever Messe's line of retreat. Leclerc's small unit continued to follow the British X Corps as it advanced through Gabès on 29 March.[285]

During 8–15 April, French and British troops, together with the 34th US ID, seized passes in the Eastern Dorsal. However, they failed to block the retreat of Axis troops under Messe who, pushed out of the Wadi Akrit, fled north through Enfidaville. As a consequence, the Franco-American attack ran into the flank of Montgomery's Eighth Army, which took Sousse on 12 April. The Fifth Panzer Army was down to three infantry divisions, each of only four or five battalions. Messe had at his disposal six infantry divisions, all bled white by previous combats, plus the 15th Panzer, which had practically no tanks, and the three-division Afrika Korps under General der Panzertruppe Hans Cramer.[286] Von Arnim issued orders condemning "rumor-mongering" and "defeatist opinions," an indication of teetering Axis morale. Arabs did a brisk business selling safe conduct leaflets dropped by the Allied Psychological Warfare Bureau to Italian soldiers, who would sheepishly hand them over to Allied guards as they entered POW cages in the middle of May.[287]

While this Axis agglomeration was significantly reduced in firepower, von Arnim's roughly 250,000 soldiers nevertheless occupied a formidable position in Tunisia's hilly headland along a 130-mile perimeter running between the Mediterranean in the north to the Gulf of Hammamet in the east, along a line from the north coast west of Mathur – Jebel Fkirine – to a position north of Enfidaville. On the left, at Eisenhower's insistence that all four American divisions be given a role in the final push, II Corps, which had quietly been transferred from Patton to Omar Bradley's command, shifted north. With the CFA, it would strike through the difficult country around Mateur toward Bizerte.[288] The First Army would punch up the Medjerda Valley, Koeltz's XIX Corps made up of Conne's *Division de marche d'Alger*, Boissau's from Oran, and Mathenet's *Division de marche du Maroc*, plus Le Couteulx's armored group with their Valentine tanks and US-supplied vehicles would

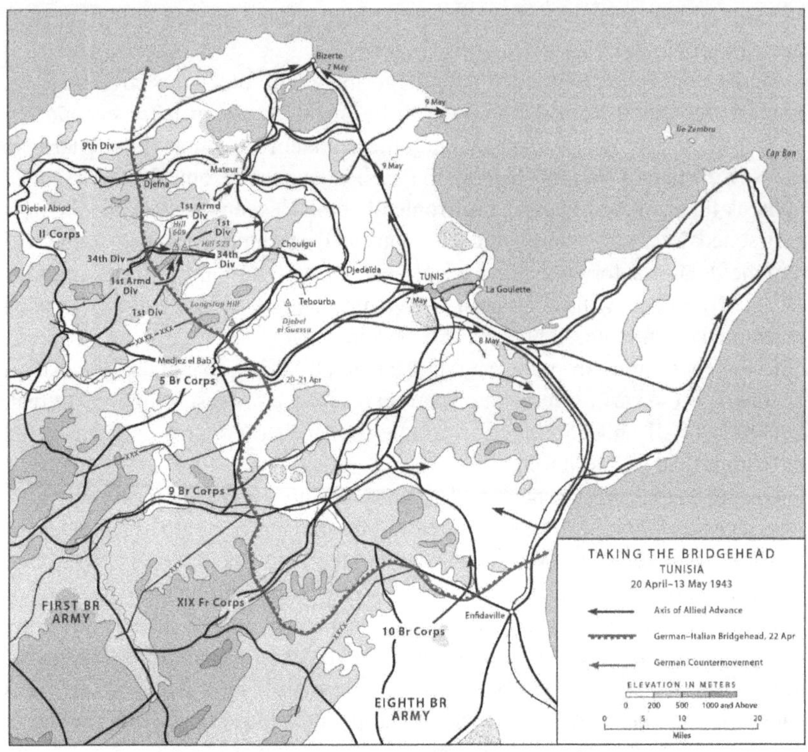

Map 1.5 The end of the Tunisia campaign.

apply pressure from Pont du Fahs, while the Eighth Army would tackle the hilly terrain north of Enfidaville (Map 1.5). The Allies had amassed overwhelming air superiority. Front lines reported a growing number of duds – as high as 60 percent – among incoming German artillery rounds.[289] Nevertheless, in Juin's view, the terrain offered only narrow corridors of attack that discouraged concerted armored thrusts.[290] Speculation swirled about how well the Eighth Army, accustomed to open armored maneuvers in the desert, would perform in the broken terrain of northern Tunisia.[291] Secretly, many hoped that the "noisy and over-confident" desert soldiers, who treated their First Army comrades "as a parade-ground army, beautifully equipped but not much good at fighting," and Monty, who descended upon Tunisia like the Second Coming, might embarrass themselves.[292]

The offensive against the final Axis stronghold kicked off on 19 April. Anderson's objective was to pressure von Arnim to throw in his reserves.

Fighter swarms guided by radio direction finding and ground control intercepts found, illuminated, and attacked Axis vehicle convoys, bombed and strafed airfields, and shot down any Axis fighters that dared contest them. Axis supplies dwindled rapidly as Allied bombers equipped with air-to-surface radar picked even the smallest ships off the surface. Incredibly, Axis troops continued to arrive to support a losing enterprise – 30,000 men, 1,861 tons of fuel, and 1,114 vehicles in March alone. But round-the-clock air attacks inflicted considerable damage, as did attacks on Luftwaffe bases in Sicily. Planes could no longer be repaired in Tunisia. Operation Flax, guided by Y Service tactical radio intercepts, which tracked routes and flight times, resulted in what Robert Ehlers calls "an aerial massacre," in which 432 Axis planes, mostly transports, were shot out of the sky in exchange for 35 Allied fighters. "Along with Stalingrad, this broke the back of the German air transport force for the rest of the war," concludes Ehlers.[293]

The CFA was assigned to cover the left flank of Omar Bradley's II Corps, whose role was meant to be a diversionary one in an attack on a 15–20-mile front on the scrub-covered hills and escarpments that dominated the way to Matheur, and Bizerte beyond. The three battalions of Magnan's CFA and the 4th and 6th Tabors of Moroccan *goumiers*, or goums, were to open *piste* 11 along the Sedjenane River, which was blocked by the 10th Bersaglieri and the German 962nd *Afrika* Rifle Regiment, a disciplinary unit. *Goumiers* fanned out over the hills to prevent surprises. Attacks went ahead on II Corps' front from 23 April, with the French and Americans from the 9th US ID's 60th Regimental Combat Team (RCT), shooting blindly into foliage still thick from the winter rains. German anti-tank guns took out three tank destroyers, while engineers struggled to defuse the tangle of mines that made roads impassable. Valleys that were heavily mined and easily defensible from the hillsides had to be avoided, while seizing hills and ridgelines proved to be fastidious, deadly work. Mules kept the advancing soldiers supplied. The CFA counted 20 killed and 100 wounded. American casualties from mines and mortars were also high.[294]

By 25 April, just when it looked as if the attacks had stalled, it became clear that the enemy was abandoning its positions. "What euphoria to capture ground, to reconquer territory so recently lost!," Elgozy enthused. "The enemy abandoned a huge amount of matériel. One finds everything: machine-guns and condoms, staff plans and pornographic photographs, Bank of Tunisia bank notes and grenades, suppositories against hemorrhoids and tins of sauerkraut."[295] But the fighting was hardly finished. The French continued to push forward up the Wadi Sedjenane with the 9th US ID. Intense artillery fire had ignited fires that burned the underbrush, thereby exposing mines to be more easily defused by British and US sappers. Mines seemed to be the only thing that struck fear into the *goumiers*. The advance continued, but with heavy losses, which reduced the CFA to two battalions. On 30 April, as Foreign

Legionnaires celebrated Camerone, the CFA advanced 15 kilometers. On that day, Mussolini sent a desperate plea to Hitler that unless the Tunisian redoubt could be bolstered, their fate would be sealed. Even as late as 4 May, *Il Duce* and Kesselring were still making plans to reinforce the Tunisian bridgehead.[296] While the British had expected little out of the II Corps front, it was II Corps with the CFA that had made the most progress. By 1 May, Axis counterattacks had been bloodily repulsed, and their control of Matheur hung by a thread. Bradley considered making a rush on Bizerte, but feared that von Arnim might pinch it off by concentrating reserves from the stalled First and Eighth Army fronts. Bersaglieri had begun to surrender in droves, often when they saw that they had been surrounded by *goumiers*. "Nothing is more pathetic than these Italian reunions between Italian POWs and Italians in the CFA," remembered Georges Elgozy. "No animosity on anyone's part, just a profound shared sadness, almost always cordial." In contrast, German POWs "overflowed with disdain and hostility," unless they were Poles or Czechs, who invariably claimed to have been dragooned into the Wehrmacht.[297]

On 26 April, Montgomery complained that Anderson's final offensive boiled down to a "dog's breakfast" of piecemeal attacks, and urged him to pick up the pace.[298] But, by 1 May, Axis forces were down to seventy tanks, only four of which were Tigers. Munitions were in short supply, when not totally exhausted, as was petrol. In the final offensive, the CFA was to mount a diversion to persuade the Axis to commit their remaining reserves. A follow-up attack on 3 May advanced behind bulldozers, air attacks, and rolling artillery barrages that leapt forward 100 meters every 3 minutes. But the exercise was hardly casualty-free – for instance, the second battalion of the 3rd Foreign Legion Infantry Regiment registered 170 casualties on 4 May, mainly due to efficient Axis artillery fire, which the French lacked the guns and air spotters to counter. In fact, until the end, the fighting continued to be difficult, and minefields posed a constant threat. At 03:00, the British kicked off Operation Strike, which moved along the Medjez-el-Bab–Tunis road behind a barrage of 442 guns and a significant tactical air input, which caught von Arnim by surprise, and opened the road to Tunis for the British 7th Armoured Division. The next day, the 47th US ID cleared the road into Bizerte. Allied pilots reported the skies empty of Axis planes. Von Arnim ordered his remaining troops to retreat to the Cape Bon peninsula. The CFA, having taken 345 casualties since 23 April, including 131 killed in action (KIA), were given the honor to be the first into the city, raising their flag over the Fort d'Espagne on the north edge of the harbor at 07:00 on 8 May. "No town I had ever seen in the war had ever been knocked flat," wrote Moorehead. "But Bizerta [sic] was the nearest thing to it. Some buildings were turned upside down. The roofs had fallen to the floors and the floors had been blasted up against the walls. Fire had done the rest."[299] Arab looters in Tunis ignored German cannon and sniper fire that continued from the rubble, until silenced on 9 May by US tanks. The 1st Battalion of the CFA was subsequently lauded by Giraud in army orders as a "magnificent unit of energy and undisputable warrior courage. It was barely organized before being engaged, and gave proof from the beginning of its splendid qualities."[300] While most of the CFA were proud of their unit's performance, Magnan complained that it had lacked audacity. Nevertheless, Axis troops continued to resist the French forces south of Tunis around Pont du Fahs and Zaghouan. On 9 May, the last Ju 52 lifted off the runway at El Aouina, with mechanics wedged into the fuselage behind the pilot's seat, and paratroops lashed to the undercarriage.[301] The airfield that had offered Axis access into Tunisia in November 1942 had been transformed into a scrapyard of smashed aircraft. Even the runways were deserted, the Germans having concealed their surviving aircraft under the trees. The remnants of the Fifth Panzer Army – about 40,000 men – surrendered. On 11 May, orders came for troops to contact German and Italian units that were still resisting. But the subsequent ceasefire came too late for Caleb Milne, who was wounded by a mortar round near Enfidaville as he tended one of Leclerc's wounded legionnaires. He was lifted by three Spanish Civil War veterans to the dressing station where he died that afternoon.[302] Kampfgruppe Pfeiffer of the Deutsche Afrika Korps entrenched at Zaghouan asked specifically that no reprisals be taken against French who had fought for the Axis. While even the French acknowledged the pro-Axis sentiments of Tunisia's Muslims, few had proved keen to enlist. At campaign's end, 43 Frenchmen from the *Légion tricolore*, including 2 officers fighting in German uniform, and 221 Muslims from the *Phalange africaine* or the Arabian Legion, who seem to have been recruits from the Levant, were captured. French reports concluded that most of the Muslims were unemployed men who had been impressed by the Germans or by French police as labor troops. As punishment at the end of the campaign, most were subsequently enlisted into *tirailleur* units and sent to Italy.[303] Von Arnim destroyed his communications center and surrendered to the British V Corps at 07:30 on 12 May. On 13 May at 13:32, the last German radio station in Tunisia went off the air, marking the eclipse of the era of German mobile warfare. Messe evaded capture by the third battalion of the 1re RTA, preferring to surrender to the British.[304]

By 9 May, Tunis was in full celebration. "The French soldiers who came in were nearly smothered in kisses," wrote Moorehead. "Staid old French dowagers leaned over the balconies and screamed 'Vive de Gaulle!' – they had not yet heard about General Giraud, and our propaganda units were busy plastering the town with coloured posters showing Giraud's features. The V sign, enclosing the Fighting French Cross of Lorraine, was being chalked up everywhere ... Tunis still had food and liquor of a sort and the troops made pretty free with it." This was presumably an oblique reference to the soldiers of the 1st US ID who, in Omar Bradley's estimation encouraged by their unmanageable division commander Terry Allen, "had left a trail of looted wine shops and outraged mayors" in Tunisia. Italian troops changed into civilian clothes, or proffered their safe conduct leaflets as they entered POW cages. Many German troops, surprised by this unexpected break-in of Allied troops, watched the spectacle from cafes, or stood around in groups with rifles slung, mingling with liberated British POWs, providentially rescued from shipment to *Stalags* and *Oflags* in Europe. On the outskirts, engineers hastily erected barbed wire pens to contain tens of thousands of Axis prisoners. France's share of this human booty was 16,040 Germans and 41,837 Italians, modest compensation for the million or so French POWs still held in Germany. In fact, they proved to be just more useless mouths to feed, and bodies to clothe. A search for POWs from Alsace-Moselle began, but some had already been shipped off to the United States. Axis POWs found a modest amount of consolation in the fact that they nevertheless had outfought the Allies and had been overwhelmed by Allied matériel superiority.[305]

Giraud congratulated Eisenhower on his victory in Tunisia, but was especially appreciative to the Allied commander "for publicly recognizing the fighting qualities of the French Army in Africa. (Same is true privately)," noted Butcher. On 29 May in Algiers, Giraud bestowed a *Légion d'honneur* on Eisenhower in a "sentimental" ceremony, a decoration which Eisenhower vowed he would not wear until "the two men met again in Metz."[306] This declaration would come back to haunt him when Eisenhower clashed with de Gaulle and Leclerc over Ike's order to abandon Strasbourg in December 1944. Initial contacts were made between Giraud and Catroux to establish a committee to coordinate the French war effort.[307]

One thing that Tunisia had accomplished was the reintegration of the rebels of 8 November into the fold of *l'armée d'Afrique*. Mast was initially named as Tunisia's new resident general. However, because he was "indisposed," Juin accepted Mast's job. Magnan was promoted to general and named to command Bizerte, and eventually to organize the 9th Colonial Infantry Division (9e DIC), much to the chagrin of Monsabert, who had coveted that job.[308] With considerable difficulty, on 4 February 1943, Giraud had persuaded Koeltz, who had told Monsabert to his face that he had "destroyed the bonds of goodwill" in the army, to give Monsabert command of a couple of tired battalions. These would eventually be upgraded into an American-refitted *3e Division d'infanterie algérienne* (3e DIA), a stellar *armée d'Afrique* division that was a long way from the improvised CFA. "It's a magnificent command!," Monsabert enthused. "It's the beginning of a grand dream."[309] Monsabert would lead this division in the breakthrough at Monte Cassino in May 1944, where he would earn the nickname of "the Butcher of the Rapido (River)."[310]

Retribution

Louis Xueref, a lycée student in Tunis in November 1942, recorded that Italian troops had been welcomed with open arms by Tunisia's large Italian population, to the point that "Lots of young Sicilian girls wore red skirts that they fashioned out of the waistbands taken from the Senegalese barracks at la Goulette. Compared with the Germans, the Italians looked like soldiers out of an operetta, and we readily denounced their cowardice."[311] But, by 2 April 1943, Barré reported that the initial arrogance of Tunisia's Italians was on the wane.[312] Nevertheless, Axis POWs marched through Tunis in May 1943 were given food and cigarettes by a sympathetic population. The campaign's aftermath would also witness a bitter if relatively brief settling of scores between French and Italian settlers – an estimated 500 shot and 5,000 imprisonments. Rahn had evacuated French and Muslims most compromised in collaboration in April, especially those who had made radio broadcasts. Fearing that he might become a new Giraud, on 7 May, on von Arnim's orders, Esteva was evacuated under protest from El Aouina to the Ritz Hotel in Rome.[313] He was captured in Paris after the liberation. Esteva's March 1945 court martial charged the former Resident General with aiding the enemy, including employing the SOL to reinforce the gendarmerie to maintain internal order and dismantle Allied intelligence networks. Like Derrien, Esteva's "double game" defense failed to impress the court. He was stripped of his rank and condemned to life imprisonment at hard labor.[314]

"If Esteva wasn't a traitor, then traitors don't exist," declared prominent communist writer Claude Lecompte, who wrote under the name Claude Morgan.[315] But there was considerable sympathy after the war in the French old-boy network for high Vichy officials like Esteva who, in de Gaulle's exculpatory view, were "led astray by a false discipline, found themselves complicit, then a victim, of a harmful enterprise."[316] The notion that Esteva, like Derrien, had been a "victim" of Vichy, rather than a facilitator of collaboration and perpetrator of its racialized dogmas, provided the rationalization for Esteva's 1950 amnesty, which preceded his death by only a few months. The problem for France's colonial proconsuls like Esteva was that both the Axis and the Americans through the Atlantic Charter deployed ideology to radicalize imperial populations and expand war aims. In the view of Notin, Juin's defense of Esteva can be explained by the fact that the French commander's primary concern, as a *français d'Algérie*, was that any sign of hesitation or weakness in the French leadership "would have meant the immediate collapse of the French administration, anarchy, the pillage of our compatriots and probably the confinement in concentration camps of the families of soldiers and administrators."[317] According to this reasoning, by collaborating with the Axis, like Admiral Decoux in Indochina, Esteva had sought to preserve the empire. With the exceptions of Catroux, Eboué, and a handful of others who were economically dependent on the British Empire or vulnerable to Japanese encroachment, the fragility of the French imperial mandate no doubt caused French officials to seek security in Vichy continuity and "the wisdom of the Marshal." It also explains the reluctance of the invading Allies to apply the Atlantic Charter mandate to sweep up the collaborationist French administration.[318]

Conclusion

One of the arguments of post-war pro-Vichy revisionists was that the 1940 armistice ultimately had benefited the Allies, because it had kept North Africa free of Axis control, and preserved *l'armée d'Afrique* and the empire which would constitute France's main wartime contribution to Allied victory. This made Torch, not Stalingrad, the major turning point of the war.[319] Of course, this ignored Vichy's open door to the Axis in Syria in 1941, the Paris Protocols, and the fact that, when "invited" by Darlan to rally to the Allies, Vichy's fleet elected instead to scuttle. Tunisia also demonstrated that "defense against whomever" targeted the Allies, not the Axis.

Tunisia had always been Torch's wild card. The Allies had bet that they could reach Tunis ahead of Axis forces. However, distance, combined with Darlan-instigated delays in Algiers that sought to wring concessions out of Hitler to lighten the burden of occupation, further muddled an intentionally confused French command structure. Confronted not with an Allied invasion, but with an Axis riposte, commanders in Tunis and the Constantinois found that orders failed to arrive, or were by intention vague, confusing, contradictory, and constantly churning because they were issued by a timorous command whose goal was to avoid responsibility and blame. While Juin dissembled, Mendigal withdrew his planes to southern Algeria, and the navy predictably opted to follow the directives of the Marshal. Hesitancy and delay at the top communicated confusion to subordinates, who were left largely on their own to take decisions. In a situation that combined uncertainty with pusillanimity, Axis forces were allowed to gain control of El Aouina airfield and the port of Bizerte, which even a moderate demonstration of resolution by French arms could and should have protected long enough until the arrival of Allied forces. So much for the "double game." The result was that the Anglo-Americans lost the race to Tunis, and were forced to fight a campaign in Tunisia that they had hoped to avoid.

Without a doubt, the decision by the Axis leaders to defend Europe from North Africa had proven a serious miscalculation. "Tunisgrad" cost the Axis 238,000 "unwounded" POWs – 18th Army Group claimed 244,500 – as well as "vast quantities of war materials of all kinds," wrote Butcher, "including 1200 guns of all types, with at least 150 88-mm, not to mention 200 tanks, mostly

German, and aircraft in serviceable condition. In the II Corps area there were huge dumps of ammunition, as well as a million rations of food."[320] Between 8 November 1942 and 7 May 1943, 1,696 Axis planes had been lost in combat and another 633 had been captured on the ground, largely because the Axis lacked spare parts, vehicles, or petrol to fly them home. The German POWs taken in Tunisia included a significant number of skilled Luftwaffe mechanics and technicians. The Luftwaffe had committed 40 percent of new aircraft production to the Mediterranean. The grand total for Tunisia was of 2,329 Axis losses against 657 Allied planes. The Italian navy and merchant marine had suffered catastrophic losses in their attempt to supply the Tunisian bridgehead. In the process, the Allied air forces had worked out a ground support system that they would carry into Sicily, Italy, and France.[321]

In many important political respects, "Tunisgrad" proved more consequential for the Axis than was Stalingrad – Hitler forfeited a continent, while guiding Mussolini's regime to the cusp of collapse. Both contributed to the slow-motion disaster rolling toward Berlin: by May 1943, the Luftwaffe had been destroyed as an effective force, while the U-Boot challenge had been broken in the Atlantic, allowing a virtually unimpeded flow of US troops and material into the UK and the Mediterranean. Allied bomber forces were achieving the mass and geographical position that would allow them to attack almost unimpeded. There is some indication that, by March 1943, Hitler had begun to understand that his ally's future was at stake in Tunisia, which is why he continued to reinforce his shrinking African bridgehead. More surprising, however, was that, having lost a major support base and Vichy's *raison d'être* in AFN and AOF, as well as sacrificed their fleet, Laval and other collaborators at Vichy doubled down on their "Fortress Europe" bet, even as Hitler no longer had any reason to appease Vichy, and the Allies had proven that they could target amphibious operations to strategic effect.[322]

Despite a slow start, the costs of Tunisia to the Allies were comparatively light: American losses in Tunisia were 2,715 killed and 9,000 wounded, while the British First Army alone cited 4,439 killed and 12,500 wounded. But this does not include 21,363 missing, part of the 70,341 total Allied casualties according to Rolf.[323] Axis forces later calculated 8,563 German and 3,727 Italian dead. But there were many missing or evacuated as wounded before the collapse. The French announced their losses in Tunisia as 1,105 killed, 8,077 wounded, and 6,982 missing, figures that the French official history rejects as a significant underestimate. The high number of missing in action (MIA) suggests a considerable – and continuing – morale crisis in French forces.[324] According to one post-war calculation, it seems that French forces suffered 9,600 casualties, or 24 percent of the force of the estimated 40,000 French soldiers actually committed to combat. These high casualties were blamed in the main on the inadequacy of French training, arms, and equipment.[325] The greatest losses had occurred in the December–January fight for the Dorsal, and at Kasserine during 14–26 February.[326]

While Juin conceded that the British captured the honors of the Tunisia campaign, he also argued that the French contributions were nevertheless considerable, especially given their scant resources and the immense fronts that they were forced to defend. They had provided the initial "cover" on the Dorsal, under conditions of considerable hardship, that allowed the gradual Allied buildup. They had also actively participated in the fighting, the XIX Corps alone capturing 37,000 Axis POWs despite the fact that it constituted only a sixth of the Allied forces. This victory, in Juin's estimation, "erased the memory of Dunkirk."[327] But the Tunis victory parade would showcase that the French still had a long way to go to recoup their status in the eyes of the Allies, the enemy, and their colonial subjects.

2 "A Sort of Resurrection of France"

The Tunis Victory Parade

The Tunis victory parade held on 20 May 1943 proved symbolic, and everyone took away their own particular interpretation of it. "Every street was packed," remembered Harold Macmillan, "every window in every house was packed; every roof was packed ... Troops presenting arms, people cheering ... The audience consisted of *all* the civil population [including Italians] and all the remaining troops. The atmosphere was extremely cheerful – like a jolly football crowd."[1] For his part, according to Butcher, Eisenhower had resisted the whole idea of a "Victory Parade," preferring a ceremony to honor the dead.[2] However, for its participants, the Tunisia victory was too redolent with symbolism and conducive to messaging both status and strategic priorities merely to commemorate in a style more appropriate for a First World War "memory of the fallen."

On a strategic level, the victory over Rommel at El Alamein, the capture of considerable numbers of Axis prisoners of war (POWs), the destruction of much of the Luftwaffe and the Italian merchant marine, and the laying bare of the Axis' southern flank advertised to Stalin and to Roosevelt's critics that the Mediterranean constituted a true Second Front, and that the decision to engage there had failed to bear out Eisenhower's "blackest day in American history" prophesy.[3] The American contingent was limited to two regiments of the 34th US Infantry Division (ID) representing II Corps, a participation so diminutive that Patton declared the parade "a goddamned waste of time."[4] This did not stop the patrician Macmillan from observing with no apparent sense of irony that the GIs appeared "almost indecently rich," equipped with, "lovely brown leather shoes with rubber soles . . . a wonderful kind of golfing jacket, a splendid helmet, lots of gadgets hung round, and is altogether a very expensive fellow who has cost his national treasury a lot of money . . . And they nearly all wear spectacles, of the most expensive kind!" . . . [and] a pair of leather gloves that would cost me a fiver in England."[5] Yet, although relatively small, by its appearance, this American contingent offered a none-too-subtle hint that Washington intended to mobilize its considerable resources to fight a rich man's war, and reduce the British and French to tributaries of American policy.

Like Patton, Montgomery boycotted the parade because, apart from a contingent of Derbyshire Yeomanry, a few Hussars, and a smattering of Gurkhas, "it was a First Army affair." In his somber piety, Anderson was also eager to fête Tunisia as payback for Dunkirk. Macmillan insisted that the British stole the show – sunburned soldiers in berets, shorts and shirts, led by bagpipers, marching impeccably in step, even counter-marching as the band played from a stationary position beside the reviewing stand.[6] So, in an oblique way, the 20 May parade also offered a celebration of Britain's desert warriors and the last victory that the British army would win largely on its own.

For the French, the parade was symbolic for multiple reasons. As for Anderson, "Tunisgrad" offered revenge for 1940, as well as retribution against the Italians who had dared declare war on France in June 1940, and whose armistice commission had for two years missed no opportunity to superintend, regulate, and humiliate *l'armée d'Afrique*. Considerable stamina was required of Eisenhower and Giraud, who took the honors at attention. According to Butcher, this was because the "Giraudist French wished to impress both the Arabs and the Tunisian population with their strength," by exceeding their allotment of troops and so considerably lengthening the parade.[7] Bradley, too, had been in Tunisia long enough to realize that the celebration offered the French an opportunity to intimidate a crowd of "impassive Arabs and chastened Italians," while pumping the morale of "120,000 jubilant French" (Figure 2.1).[8] But the message was a mixed one. According to Butcher, "the Goums, those stealthy, throat-slitting Moroccan mountaineers, who had become legendary, attracted the most applause," but, apart from them, the French forces conveyed a particularly penurious appearance with their antiquated weaponry, torn uniforms, and undersized physiques.[9] Macmillan shared Butcher's verdict: "The great majority of the French were of course natives. The men are splendid – many with great beards and whiskers. But their equipment and clothing were pitiful – antiquated rifles, torn cloaks, slippers or bare feet ... I did not think much of most of the French officers. The few purely French battalions were also poor, in physique and general appearance." Nevertheless, "one felt [that the parade amounted to] a sort of resurrection of France, and because one realized what a brave show they had put up during all these months with such poor equipment and material."[10]

For French soldiers equipped in Great War surplus uniforms and weapons, richly equipped GIs reinforced the same sense of backwardness and military inferiority that had engulfed them in 1940 at the appearance of the Wehrmacht. Disembarking in Casablanca from Dakar for the final stage of the Tunisia campaign, Hungarian Jew and Foreign Legion Sergeant Erwin Fuchs had spent the last two years perspiring in his wool uniform and fighting tropical diseases in the Niger Delta:

> ... I lay my eyes the first time on an American G.I. who happens to be a young strapping M.P. (Military Police) wearing a practical, wellcut uniform and gear, making

Figure 2.1 The 20 May 1943 Tunis victory parade was staged to intimidate a crowd of "impassive Arabs and chastened Italians," while pumping the morale of "120,000 jubilant French." (Photo by Universal History Archive/ Universal Images Group via Getty Images)

the impression of a PROFESSIONAL SOLDIER, and he is smiling too, probably at the archaic gear and uniform this Travelling Circus is wearing. It starts raining and he pulls out a little packet from his uniform extracting from it a RAINCOAT! How 'bout THAT? His ammo pouches and canteen are all attached to his "web belt" with hooks. Everything is well designed and practical. While I'm eyeballing what a MODERN soldier ready to fight a MODERN war should look like, an ambulance is turning the corner and can I believe my eyes? A beautiful gal in uniform is sitting behind the wheel! She is groomed with lovely dark hair down to her shoulders, lipstick and nail polish expertly matched. I realize it is the first time that I'm confronted with the fact that there is a WAR going on. Some of the Legionnaires are running over to this 'apparition' driving an ambulance looking like a 'movie star' . . . gesticulating like a bunch of maniacs. She is smiling demurely and drives on. – We get our order: *Materielle à la main! En Avant – MARCHE!* We take off for the train station loaded down like pack animals. We board our usual cattle Pullman which does not even have straw to lay down on, and we're again crammed together like sardines to make us feel at home, I guess. They are distributing out "meal": two eggs and a piece of bread but most of the guys are too tired to stand in line for this royal repast . . . We're supposed to go to Fez but nobody knows for sure.[11]

Although Giraud sought to use the Tunis celebration to showcase the return of a reunified and revivified France to the war, for Durand, the Tunis parade itself offered a symbol of French backwardness and simmering discord. Despite their remarkable combat performance, the *Corps franc d'Afrique* (CFA) was allocated last rank among the French troops. They chose to demonstrate their defiance by marching in their British uniforms carrying submachineguns. For Giraud, the CFA continued to emit a whiff of the *Chantiers*, Special Operations Executive (SOE) trainees at Cape Matifou symbolized by Bonnier de la Chapelle, while the Gaullists dismissed them unfairly as "a Giraudist militia."[12] The parade also offered *l'armée d'Afrique* an opportunity to outnumber and so diminish their Gaullist rivals. While Giraud conceded that those who initially had joined the *Forces françaises libres* (FFL) had done so for patriotic reasons, he condescendingly noted that the FFL had played a fairly minor role in the Tunisia campaign, with Koenig's "division" intervening only at the end at Enfidaville. While acknowledging Leclerc's contribution in bypassing the Mareth Line and at Gabès, Force L numbered barely 3,000 men, paltry compared with the 300,000 men according to inflated estimates in *armée d'Afrique* ranks, plus the French navy and air force. The FFL had been offered only a minimalist presence in the parade by the French authorities, while the FFL "generals" were consigned to ancillary reviewing stands, from which they could observe the arrival of "tired and dyspeptic" Giraud surrounded by his entourage of "glabrous and constipated figures, fearful of responsibility."[13] The cantankerous Larminat declined to be impressed by 10,000 Giraudist troops armed with 1886 Lebel rifles and "fishing pole" bayonets, uniformed as if cast in some nineteenth-century imperial epic. Like the CFA, Leclerc elected to muster with the British, a modern force that incorporated an FFL drive past in two dozen vehicles, in part because he did not want "to drown his few troops, who never ceased to fight, among a mass of North African units who only took up their weapons to shoot at the Allies." The decision to parade with the British was also a protest against de Gaulle's exclusion from Algiers, although this had been at Catroux's instigation, not the Giraudists'.[14] Leclerc also declined an invitation to the post-parade official luncheon, which Juin hosted as Tunisia's latest Resident General. This boycott left the Giraudists feeling that they had been snubbed and their honor and patriotism impugned by an upstart Gaullist "general." This "farce" of a parade from a French perspective allowed Juin to denounce Leclerc for exhibiting the typically Gaullist "émigré mentality," a verdict that had become a cliché among Giraudists.[15]

For Eisenhower at least, Tunisia had confirmed French loyalties to the Allies, although dissenters abounded: "In a sense, the Tunisian campaign proved to be the testing ground for French loyalty and French determination to fight," concluded a US official history. "Engaged in battle on greatly unequal terms,

French troops achieved only limited military objectives. But they succeeded in winning American confidence, in overcoming British skepticism, and in restoring faith in themselves. These intangible gains, more than actual victories, amply justified the large investments in materiel and effort then being made on their behalf by the United States."[16] Historian Robert Belot agrees: "But for all the refugees, with Gaullist or Giraudist sympathies, or simply patriots, Tunisia was the beginning of *la revanche*, the inaugural act of hope, of rediscovered honor."[17] However, Tunisia was a stage in a process that simply teed up the next round of French discord and infighting.

Unfortunately, if, from a French perspective, the "victory parade" was meant to impress, it failed, because Tunisia disintegrated into chaos and retribution at the end of the campaign. Politically, Tunisia simply confirmed the trending twilight of France's dominion in French North Africa (AFN). The French moved rapidly to scour the battlefields lest arms and ammunition fall into the hands of Muslim nationalists. Members of the *Service d'ordre légionnaire* (SOL), the leadership of the *Chantiers* and the *Compagnons de France*, and members of the *Phalange africaine* and the Arabian legion were arrested and confined to camps in the Sahara. A court martial convened in Algiers in October to judge the most culpable collaborationists who had failed to depart with the retreating Axis. A replacement for the pro-Axis Bey of Tunis was immediately labeled "the French Bey," while the deposed predecessor was hailed as a martyr and swathed in the mantle of Tunisian nationalism. As interim resident general, Juin proceeded to cleanse the Tunisian civil service in what resembled "a policy of colonial reconquest" – US consul in Tunis Hooker Doolittle labeled Juin's crackdown a "reign of terror." Neo-Destour leader Bourguiba found this "victory of democracy" and Atlantic Charter triumph in Tunisia both vindictive and ironic. Nevertheless, despite popular demand among Tunisians, de Gaulle would later refuse to rescind the statute of the protectorate, because to do so would open him to Vichy attack as the man willing to forfeit France's empire.[18] Churchill's ennoblement of Harold Alexander as "1st Viscount of Tunis" offered a final indignity for de Gaulle, who objected not only to Churchill's impertinence shown by incorporating a French possession into Alexander's title, but also to the anachronism, as no Muslim country had hosted a viscountcy since the Crusades.[19]

On the military level, the Tunisia campaign was judged a preventable and poorly managed affair redolent with missed opportunities. There was plenty of blame to share: Torch planning had been too conservative, too focused on Casablanca and holding harbors, when planners should have prioritized Tunis as the British originally had argued. Delays in Algiers that culminated in the controversial Darlan deal showcased US inexperience on the world stage, that "tarnished and tainted … a brilliant military episode," missteps that would have been avoided "had a British general commanded Torch instead of an

American," the Foreign Office insisted.[20] Unfortunately, the credibility of that hypothetical conjecture was rather belied by the plodding performance of General Sir Kenneth Anderson, whose cautious advance on Tunis masked an absence of imagination and deficit of *métier*. Inexperienced in the use of armored forces and paratroops, overly concerned about logistics, with air and land power poorly coordinated, the British commander had let slip an opportunity to seize Tunis and Bizerte ahead of the arriving Axis from 10 November. But a monumental reason for failure lay with French leadership: precious time was squandered by Darlan's vacillation, intrigues, scheming, and contradictory orders, matched only by the failure of Juin, Esteva, Derrien, and Barré to defend Tunisia against the arrival of German forces while they still held the upper hand. This exposed the duplicity and bankruptcy of Vichy's doctrine of "defense against whomever" that failed to define a threat; the confusion of a splintered chain of command, focused on the internal threat and fearful that subordinates might not follow orders; toxic inter-service rivalry; and a military leadership deficient in civic courage, patriotism, and strategic sentience. Tactically and operationally, Tunisia had been a steep learning curve for all of the Allied forces, especially II Corps that had hit its stride only in April–May. Looking back, the Western Allies were left to speculate that, "if only" Montgomery had cut off and destroyed Rommel at El Alamein, and Anderson had won the race to Tunis, then the Allies might have spent the winter of 1943–1944 camped in the Po Valley. Instead, Anglo-American armies seemed dead-ended in a Mediterranean cul-de-sac with no obvious center of gravity, whose apparent only short-term advantage was that they had sort of brought the French back into the war. The next two-and-a-half years would give them the leisure to debate whether it had been worth it. In the meantime, II Corps was disbanded at Mostaganem in Algeria, as was Anderson's First Army.[21] A charity case if there ever was one, *l'armée d'Afrique* was to be reorganized, rearmed, and "fused" with the FFL. What already had been a long war for the French would become protracted with the invasion of Italy and Northern Europe. And the Germans would not always constitute the principal enemy. Questions about the depth of French unity and loyalty to the Allied cause would sharpen discussions over French rearmament at Anfa in January 1943.

Anfa

Anfa, a fashionable seaside suburb of Casablanca, hosted a conference of the two Western Allied leaders during 14–24 January 1943, codenamed Symbol, to plan for the war's follow-up phase. Stalin declined to join them, citing ongoing operations at Stalingrad, which was only partially true.[22] At least four agenda items directly concerned France and the French: three of them were the timing of the cross-Channel invasion; the issue of unconditional surrender; and French rearmament. Arguably, the coordination of the Allied air campaign against Germany also impacted France as it resulted in the Casablanca Directive of 21 January. Among other things, this prioritized attacks against German bases supporting the U-boat war on the Bay of Biscay. French industries working for the Germans would also become targets, as would POWs and French workers conscripted to work in German industries. To protect French targets from Allied air attacks, Vichy organized the rump of the armistice air force into anti-aircraft batteries.

These issues were intertwined in ways that de Gaulle, at least, was acutely aware of. Civilian casualties from raids by Allied bombers were exploited by Vichy and German propaganda to reinforce a narrative that the Allies sought to diminish France, not "liberate" it. However, the most important development to come out of Anfa for the French was the American proposal to rearm eleven French divisions. This took place in the context of Washington's January 1943 decision to scrap its blueprint for a 200-division US army in favor of a target strength of 100 divisions. This resulted from the realization that Washington could leverage its enormous industrial capacity, as well as its burgeoning sea and airpower, without having to mobilize a massive ground force that, in the minds of Roosevelt and his Chief of Staff Admiral William Leahy, "would inevitably lead to high and unnecessary casualties." In their minds, "mass armies belonged to the past, and America needed to win an air–sea war based on machinery over human sacrifice."[23] This put Roosevelt on the defensive with Stalin, who continued to needle the American President that the Western Allies were only fighting on the margins and must launch a serious "second front," a charge that was at best inaccurate, at worst duplicitous.[24]

Roosevelt had also calculated that US production would give Washington political and strategic influence, especially with a French elite represented by men like Jean Monnet, who were acutely aware that only Washington could restore French power. "Given the sharp clashes that continued to mark Franco-American relations to the end of the war and beyond, this may seem to be an exaggerated claim," Andrew Buchanan asserts. "But with its path smoothed by the provision of trade and military aid, Washington shifted its relations from Pétain, to Darlan, to Giraud, and finally de Gaulle without crippling break-downs and disjuncture ... The result was a reciprocal relationship that, if plagued by personality clashes, nevertheless laid the basis for the postwar re-establishment of French power and for a revived France capable of playing a key role in the new, U.S.-sponsored, world order." The tradeoff was that, despite the promise of the Atlantic Charter that "all people had a right to self-determination," Washington would do nothing to rattle French colonial rule in North Africa, nor, initially at least, challenge Vichy's antisemitic legislation, which endured long into the "liberation" of AFN. And, in fact, to have done so would have been at odds with a policy of French rearmament, whose manpower depended on imperial levies.[25] "This shared Franco-American desire to contain Arab nationalism played a much greater role in setting American policy than the more famous disputes with the prickly personalities of de Gaulle and Giraud," concludes Michael S. Neiberg.[26]

Despite promises of rearmament made at Anfa, significant impediments remained, among them confusion over the actual scope of the rearmament agreement; the low education level of French imperial subjects; the lack of industrial infrastructure in AFN; a shipping shortage; disputes between the Americans and the French over the proper balance between support and combat forces; and language barriers. All of these factors combined to limit the rearmament's scope and consequently the impact of French forces on the war effort. Nor were the Anglo-Americans in complete agreement with the logic of French rearmament. For one, British Chief of Staff (COS) Lieutenant General Sir Alan Brooke, whose experience in command of the British II Corps in Flanders in 1940 had left an unfavorable impression of French discipline and military skill, argued that rearmament of a force capable only of "garrison work" would prove a titanic dissipation of resources. Nor, in his view, should an army – and, more importantly, a French navy – that had aligned itself against the British at Dakar and in Syria, and against the Anglo-Americans during Torch, which had scuttled in Toulon, and that retained a residual yet stubborn allegiance to a defeatist, even collaborationist Marshal, be pronounced politically redeemed. The door held ajar so that Axis forces might enter Tunisia had been particularly galling and costly. Crémieux-Brilhac called the "schism between *maréchalisme* and Gaullism" the most profound split in the army since the Dreyfus affair, although, like the Dreyfus affair, Vichy fidelity did more to unite the army against the Republic than divide it.[27] Rumors of assassination plots against de Gaulle or of a military putsch carried out by disgruntled Pétainists that persisted to the end of 1943 in AFN hardly served to convince the Allies that *l'armée d'Afrique*, to paraphrase Eisenhower, had fully decided on which side its bread was buttered. Indeed, as late as February 1944, de Lattre disbanded the *2e regiment de spahis algériens*, citing stubborn *maréchalist* loyalties.[28] While Eisenhower initially shared Brooke's reservations, nevertheless, he concluded that raising French divisions would economize on American manpower, as well as provide "a political gesture" to win French cooperation, which was critical in early 1943 as the Tunisian front at this stage of the battle relied largely on the poorly armed French to hold the line on the Dorsal. But the bigger picture of a post-war European order was also imbedded in the Anfa rearmament program: "Only a large-scale re-entry of the French into the common struggle, as took place in mid-November 1942, could regain for them the esteem of the Allies and a place among the democratic nations of the world," declares the US Army official history.[29]

France's "place among the democratic nations of the world" pointed to a fifth agenda item at Anfa – cajoling the French exile movements of de Gaulle and Giraud to cooperate. Allied policy was "to win campaigns in the field while allowing the French to work out their own internal problems, unhampered and unaided," an approach that Neiberg correctly labels as "both politically naïve and strategically misguided." It was also inaccurate, as both London and Washington had intervened directly to influence French policy. British leaders interpreted the Darlan deal not as some pragmatic operational decision taken in the heat of the action by Eisenhower, but as a deliberate ploy to cut London out of post-war planning for France and its empire. "The distasteful American decision to back Darlan and then Giraud forced the British to rely almost exclusively on de Gaulle," and stored up problems for French policy going forward, to the point that Eden believed that Washington's backing of Giraud actually placed the Anglo-American alliance in jeopardy.[30]

In the aftermath of Torch, especially given the fallout over the "Darlan deal," Roosevelt might have reminded himself of Aesop's adage: "be careful what you wish for." In one respect, Giraud offered a greater threat to de Gaulle and Gaullism than had Darlan, because he was untarnished by collaboration, and too guileless to realize that he was being exploited as Roosevelt's pawn to promote Washington's agenda of creating a compliant France "capable of playing a key role in the new, U.S.-sponsored, world order."[31] While Roosevelt and Churchill dismissed de Gaulle's attitudes and posturing as childish and contrived, his defense of French interests against the Allied juggernaut increasingly came to be perceived as noble and courageous, as well as skillful. A senior general with no Vichy past, a man of distinguished bearing and apparent integrity, albeit resolutely reactionary, Giraud seemed to Washington to be an obvious, if imperfect, choice to steer France's North African resurrection. Indeed, Jean Monnet, tasked by presidential advisor Harry Hopkins to conjure a more democratic image for Giraud, remarked that his new apprentice was "inclined to simplify things."[32] Darlan's erstwhile supporters had fallen into line when, on 26 December, Giraud had proclaimed himself "Civilian and Military Commander-in-Chief in North Africa," in large part because he promptly proceeded to arrest many of those who had aided the Anglo-American invasion, while retaining antisemitic legislation and reaffirming the mandates of Vichy's imperial proconsuls. The battle for Tunisia was not going well in the New Year, and the Allies both needed a stable political base in AFN and required the outgunned *armée d'Afrique* to hold the line until sufficient Anglo-American manpower and resources could reach Tunisia. The result was that, "Under the patronage of the American army, the Vichy regime, headed by Giraud, had in effect reconstituted itself in Algeria," concludes Julian Jackson. And while this might be perfectly acceptable to the officer corps of *l'armée d'Afrique* and the settler population, the internal resistance in

France, whose ranks swelled as their war against Vichy and the occupation intensified, would not tolerate it.[33]

In the immediate aftermath of Darlan's assassination, de Gaulle had published a communiqué suggesting that the two men meet to discuss creating a "'central political power' respecting the 'laws of the Republic.'"[34] At Anfa, Roosevelt sought to transform what he called these two "prima donnas" into "trustees" of AFN until more democratic options emerged. While it might be argued that Roosevelt's "trustee" formula was to find success in Italy with the eventual transition from King Victor Emmanuel and Marshal Pietro Badoglio to more democratic leadership following the fall of Rome in June 1944, de Gaulle was determined to seize control of events early on. While some historians have attempted to rehabilitate Giraud as at least politically aware, Murphy noted, even at the time, that, by selecting as French leader a man who could not pass a mirror without stopping to gaze at himself, Washington had opted for a policy of last resort. The President "referred to Giraud as a rather simple-minded soldier and commented jocularly on my judgment – or lack of judgment – in having picked him ... Giraud's attention wandered whenever Roosevelt raised political questions, and he turned back the conversation as quickly as possible to pleas for more American equipment for French troops. Clearly, this fighting general was willing to accept any political arrangement which respected French sovereignty over its empire and left Giraud in command of the French forces."[35] That was precisely de Gaulle's point.

By promoting the shallow and narcissistic Giraud, the Americans had only increased "*la confusion intérieure*" in AFN, and virtually guaranteed that Algiers must succumb sooner or later to de Gaulle. Already, and in reaction to the Darlan deal, the Gaullist propaganda machine had cranked up the theme that French unity must be anchored in republican principles, not in fealty to the Marshal.[36] After considerable hesitation, de Gaulle reluctantly accepted Churchill's invitation to join the two Allied leaders and Giraud at Anfa, where Roosevelt had planned "a shotgun wedding," which de Gaulle preferred to compare to an Allied choreographed Munich in the Maghreb, with Roosevelt acting as Chamberlain's stand-in.[37] However, Roosevelt had not entirely reckoned with Charles de Gaulle, the black cat of the Western Alliance, whose posture of permanent revile and obstinate outrage incited an antagonism in others that obscured the fact that he was by far the most politically astute player in January 1943 Casablanca, and arguably in the war. De Gaulle understood that Giraud was Roosevelt's straw man, who must be either suborned or eliminated. His invitation to Giraud to join in a common effort for French unity had been answered by the incarceration of many Gaullists in AFN.[38] Convincing de Gaulle actually to appear at Anfa had been a chore that sent Churchill – squeezed between Roosevelt's refusal to recognize *la France combattante* and de Gaulle's imperious ingratitude – into paroxysms of rage and frustration. But the Prime Minister's rubber stamp of the Darlan deal had transformed much of the British press, public opinion, and a majority of MPs into Gaullist partisans. De Gaulle at first refused the invitation to Anfa, and then only materialized on 22 January toward the close of the conference. No sooner had he landed in Casablanca than this American show "on sovereign French territory struck me as a kind of insult," de Gaulle recorded. "If I had known that it would have been necessary to surround me, on French territory, with American bayonets," he would have remained in London, de Gaulle informed Churchill. Giraud merely greeted him with a limp handshake accompanied by a curt, "Bonjour, Gaulle." At lunch, where Giraud predictably offered a well-rehearsed account of his Königstein escape,[39] de Gaulle maliciously asked for an equally detailed narrative of his less than dignified June 1940 capture by a German mess squad.[40] The two Western Allied leaders smiled approvingly as the French rivals briefly shook hands in a show of glacial comity, behind a blitz of Anglo-American press photographer flashbulbs – the French press had not been summoned.[41] Alan Moorehead compared the famous handshake to "an amateur play," especially because the two men had to repeat it for the benefit of the press. "It was not a very successful little act. It lacked conviction. It certainly lack[ed] showmanship."[42]

Nor were relations off-camera any better – the dinner which Giraud hosted for de Gaulle was "frankly disagreeable," according to André Beaufre. De Gaulle tiresomely complained about the American presence in Casablanca. Thierry d'Argenlieu, a member of de Gaulle's entourage, in particular, was "immediately sectarian and violent," while the two pretenders began to quarrel.[43] But de Gaulle's last-minute appearance at Anfa was not meant to showcase diplomatic comity, but rather to drive home three points: first, to demonstrate that he was not Churchill's poodle; second, to upstage Giraud, who had consistently rebuffed de Gaulle's calls for French unity under a central Republican authority; and, finally, to notify the "Anglo-Saxon" leaders that they were unwelcome referees to French political disputes. The leader of Fighting France recognized that his performance served merely to showcase French factiousness – indeed, in Murphy's telling, de Gaulle's boorish behavior confirmed Roosevelt in his belief that engagement with Vichy had been the correct policy all along. And, of course, the Allies did have a serious stake in the outcome of French political battles. "The President still deplored what he called de Gaulle's readiness, almost eagerness, to start civil wars, and he told me that it was as important as ever to prevent any disputes between Frenchmen which might interfere with military operations," because success in Tunisia, and eventually in France, required French cooperation. Nevertheless, Roosevelt was persuaded that he had "managed" de Gaulle at Casablanca, when, in fact, US policy toward France appeared improvised, misguided, hypocritical, and clearly steaming toward the rocks.[44]

Nor did Roosevelt's declaration of the requirement for "unconditional surrender" at Casablanca ease concerns. There are at least four myths about Roosevelt's "unconditional surrender" declaration, beginning with the fact that it was an impulsive reaction to an almost universal condemnation of the Darlan deal in Britain and the United States. The "Darlan deal" had been marketed by the White House as a spur-of-the-moment tactic to end French resistance in Algeria and Morocco. While it is true that Roosevelt was surprised and deeply wounded by the adverse reaction to the Darlan agreement, in fact, the "Darlan deal" was no example of a mid-level operational requirement driving policy and strategy. Rather, the pact with Darlan may be viewed as a third reiteration of Washington's "Vichy gamble," in that, having failed to strike a "Pétain deal" at Vichy or a "Weygand deal" in AFN in 1941–1942, Eisenhower finally applied *force majeure* to coerce a covenant from a cornered French admiral. Furthermore, the origins of the demand for unconditional surrender lay in the American President's view that the Central Powers had been let off the hook in 1918 and subsequently at Versailles, which had led to the "unjust peace" narrative that was not only exploited by Hitler, but also held the high ground in the diplomatic establishment.

A second myth was that Roosevelt's declaration of the requirement for unconditional surrender had blindsided Churchill, as the British Prime Minister subsequently claimed. But, according to American diplomatic historian Robert Dallek, this seems to have been an attempt by Churchill to distance himself from a decision that was subsequently criticized for having extended the war by hardening German and Japanese resolve and knocking the props from beneath the anti-Hitler resistance in Germany, a third myth associated with the demand for unconditional surrender.[45] In fact, the unconditional surrender declaration had been discussed in a meeting between Roosevelt, Churchill, and the Combined Chiefs of Staff on 18 January. It was Churchill who had urged that the conference should "release a statement to the effect that the United Nations had resolved to pursue the war to the bitter end, neither party relaxing in its efforts until the unconditional surrender of Germany and Japan had been achieved." The statement was run by the British cabinet, which suggested that Italy be included, lest the announcement "create misgivings in Turkey and the Balkans and [be] unlikely to help [by virtue of] discouraging the Italian resistance." As for prolonging the war, this "was determined largely by other factors, including the Allies' objective of total victory and Hitler's . . . refusal to admit the possibility of any kind of surrender."[46]

A fourth myth was that unconditional surrender was meant to reassure Stalin that the Western Allies would not cut a deal to end the war with one of Hitler's henchmen. In fact, at the Tehran Conference (28 November–1 December 1943), Stalin condemned the Anfa declaration requiring unconditional surrender as a "terrible idea" that would "unite the German people" against the Allies.

However, eleven months earlier he had dismissed it for what it was: a "political and psychological substitute for a second front," according to Sean McMeekin. In fact, he notes the irony of Roosevelt working so hard to impress Stalin with Western resolve to take the war to total victory, even as "Stalin was approaching Hitler for an armistice, however tenuously," in Stockholm in April–June 1943, in secret talks that were terminated by Hitler, not Stalin.[47] Nor could "unconditional surrender" waylay concerns raised by the Darlan deal, and subsequent US support for Giraud. As Harold Macmillan and others feared at the time, by promoting Giraud, it was Roosevelt, not de Gaulle, who flirted with a potential French civil war, which in light of the ongoing turbulence in AFN, and the weaponization of a swelling internal resistance promoted by the "interface services" of the SOE, Office of Strategic Services (OSS), and Bureau central de renseignements et d'action (BCRA), he feared might ignite on liberation. Hence, planning for an Allied Military Government of Occupied Territories (AMGOT) continued, but only as a last resort.[48] In November 1942, Washington had rationalized the recourse to Darlan as a way of "destroying the powers of a Vichy incarnated at the time by Laval," although striking a bargain with the "Quisling" Darlan had "proved a step too far even for the hardhearted Henry Stimson."[49] Suspicions lingered well into 1943 that Secretary of State Cordell Hull, through Leahy, maintained backchannel contacts with Vichy via Madrid.[50]

In de Gaulle's view, the fault for the miscalculations of US policy toward France lay with Murphy's perverse counsel, and the fact that, in coordination with the American embassy in London, where anti-Gaullism amounted to a "phobia," the American Minister sought to transform Algiers into an anti-Gaullist "honeypot" to draw in apostates like Admiral Muselier. And while Roosevelt, who, in de Gaulle's view "certainly did not want a true French government," was quick to dismiss de Gaulle as an authoritarian pretender, Giraud's dazzling inadequacies passed without comment, a situation that threatened the comity of the Anglo-American alliance and possibly the stability of post-Liberation Europe.[51] Instead, de Gaulle perceptively recognized that the President's purpose was to impose a refurbished Wilsonian "American peace" on Europe, and he was having none of it.[52] For de Gaulle, France's role in Europe was that played by Athens in classical antiquity – exceptional, essential, the only thing that counted.[53] De Gaulle's objective at Anfa, therefore, was not to please the Allies, but to make his point that Giraud was a counterfeit representative of French sovereignty, who ruled AFN by virtue of an illegitimate and circuitous transference of authority from Pétain via Darlan through Washington. By general consent, de Gaulle "stole the show" at Anfa with a clear vision for France guided by republican principles, and by exuding a sense of determination that forced those in attendance to look beyond his sandpaper personality. Meanwhile, Giraud struck poses like a showroom mannequin, his "inane vanities" on prominent display. Even Murphy conceded that de Gaulle's political calculations were "two jumps ahead of everyone else's." De Gaulle's tactic would be continually to outmaneuver Giraud, and force the Americans to step in to rescue their clueless client, further showcasing his illegitimacy.[54]

Although, after Anfa, de Gaulle resumed his London exile, smart money from then on had to be on "the Squatter on the shores of the Thames."[55] The enthronement of Giraud simply offered the latest reiteration of Roosevelt's "Vichy gamble," a strategy of reckless extemporization, facilitated by Leahy and Murphy, who had guided Washington's French policy into bankruptcy. This should have become apparent from the moment that Leahy had reported Vichy's view that, while the United States might prevent a UK defeat, Washington and London combined could not be secure an Allied victory. Vichy had assumed that the United States' motives in helping London were economic rather than geostrategic. The result would be a stalemated war, that might open the door to a Vichy-mediated settlement between Germany and the UK that would refurbish France's tarnished status and secure Vichy's longevity.[56] Washington had doggedly pursued a series of dead-end policy initiatives, doubling down after Pétain had declined Leahy's invitation to return France to belligerency and Weygand's "invitation" to invade AFN had failed to materialize, despite Murphy's obsequious courtship. That the "Darlan deal" had survived a bare six weeks and that the Admiral's assassination had been greeted with immense relief offered another policy fiasco. The High Seas Fleet had scuttled rather than join the Allies. Axis forces gained friction-free entry into Tunisia. "Defense against whomever" had proven hollow. Despite repeated failure, the "Anfa memorandum" of 24 January 1943 basically reaffirmed the Murphy–Giraud arrangement of 2 November 1942, whereby Giraud was recognized as the "trustee" of French military, economic, and financial interests, "until the day when the French people could freely choose a regular government."[57] De Gaulle knew full well that France's growing internal resistance would never accept this "ghost from 1939."[58]

In retrospect, de Gaulle's triumph in the shadow of Washington's ineptitude appeared practically foreordained, and offers a seminar in political warfare. From early on, he evinced an unmatched level of political skill in defining a strategic vision, without which his embryonic movement would have been relegated to an obscure footnote in the history of wartime France. He assigned tasks to its adherents to achieve his goals, while rapidly consolidating power over *la France libre.* Of course, that he was on the right side of history proved to be a huge plus. But that, too, had been a strategic calculation, at a time when most Frenchmen considered exile on a beleaguered island an ill-advised, if not illegal, criminal, and even treasonous choice. Even those who knew him – especially those who knew him – could explain his actions only as a manifestation of de

Gaulle's legendary idiosyncrasy and condescending cantankerousness. Once he had arrived in Algiers in the summer of 1943, however, a Gulliver among Lilliputians, de Gaulle's political sagacity was on public display, as he outflanked, outmaneuvered, marginalized, and then decapitated his principal rivals, and inserted his loyalists into key positions in his government, with himself at the summit.

Like most French statistics for this period, exact numbers for the FFL are difficult to establish at the time of the 31 July 1943 amalgamation of *l'armée d'Afrique*, *l'armée colonial*, and the FFL. One estimate is that the FFL numbered 50,878 in the summer of 1943 – 45,500 in the army, 5,100 in the *Forces navales françaises libres* (FNFL), while 3,500 (6.4 percent) were in the *Forces aériennes françaises libres* (FAFL). Of these, 35,700 (66 percent) were colonials, 8,000 (16 percent) were Foreign Legionnaires, and only 9,700 (18 percent) were *Français de souche* (native French). But it is very difficult to assess with accuracy the size and status of a composite force that included militarized sovereignty units such as the *troupes spéciales du Levant*, *goums*, and the 5,000-strong *gendarmerie syrienne*, which were technically police and not soldiers. Some of the "Senegalese" *tirailleurs* might not have signed enlistment contracts, but were simply enrolled as soldiers paid by the day. Between "desertions" and a trickle of refugees who escaped to North Africa through the Iberian Peninsula, perhaps the FFL added as many as 10,000 more men in the spring and early summer of 1943. But, as will be seen, whether refugees arriving in North Africa in 1943 ended in a Gaullist or *armée d'Afrique* unit was often a question of circumstance, vacancies, or bureaucratic bias rather than political preference. Composed of Africans, Levantines and other colonial subjects, refugee Europeans of sundry nationalities, kitted out in inherited French colonial uniforms and weapons, or Eighth Army hand-me-downs, the FFL looked more like a deracinated international brigade or a gathering of partisans than an expeditionary French army.[59] Resistance networks run by the BCRA numbered around 5,700, with a further 3,000 at least serving in Free France committees by the summer of 1943, which would push up the numbers of *français de souche* and perhaps increase overall FFL numbers to around 70,000. British figures put FFL ration strength at 80,000 on 3 May 1943, of whom 70,000 were in the army. But this was a very general and probably inflated estimation based on notional numbers.[60]

On 1 June 1943, Giraud appeared to hold all the cards: the victor of Tunisia, he commanded roughly 130,000 soldiers – by his estimation 300,000 when reservists and "sovereignty troops" were added – while de Gaulle mustered only a few thousand romantics and "unfortunates" in AFN, whose only bond was a narrative of purpose and redemption spun by their aloof and autocratic leader.[61] Giraud had negotiated French rearmament at Anfa. He controlled the police, the judicial system, an intelligence service – the *Direction des services spéciaux* (DSS) – and media in North and West Africa, and had Washington in his pocket. He was armored by an entourage of committed anti-Gaullists led by Lemaigre-Dubreuil, Prioux, Labarthe, Georges, and Muselier. In September 1943, Giraud would add another feather to his cap when he directed the liberation of Corsica.[62] Nor were those chary of de Gaulle's purposes all reactionaries by any means.[63] Even Macmillan conceded that, although official American antipathy to de Gaulle "amounted in some cases to a phobia ... this strange – attractive and yet impossible – character" had brought much of the distrust upon himself, "by neglecting and even scorning to earn the confidence of the President and the PM ... It is very difficult to know how to handle him ... I'm afraid that he will always be impossible to work with. He is by nature an autocrat. Just like Louis XIV or Napoleon. He thinks in his heart that he should command and all others obey him. It is not exactly 'Fascist' (an overworked word); it is authoritarian."[64] Given his inherent military weakness, de Gaulle's improbable ascendency over the American-supported Giraud resulted from four factors, according to Muracciole: de Gaulle's "extraordinary genius"; the "boundless devotion of resistance leader Jean Moulin"; Giraud's total "absence of political sense"; and the support of British Foreign Secretary Anthony Eden. "The political certainly rescued the military," Muracciole concludes.[65]

The contours of de Gaulle's outflanking Giraud to assume the presidency of the *Comité français de libération nationale* (CFLN) and later of the provisional government are well known. If Beaufre had believed that AFN offered unpropitious territory for resistance in general, and the Gaullists in particular, a combination of factors would soon facilitate Gaullist infiltration into Algiers. The Darlan deal gave total credibility to de Gaulle's consistent message that, unless the French gripped their destiny, "les Anglo-Saxons" would hijack their future. A second factor was an intelligence services turf battle ignited by the Darlan assassination, which the OSS credibly attributed in part to SOE machinations in AFN. As a result, the SOE was forced to assume a low profile in Algiers. But many French dissidents preferred to work through the British, who were seen as more favorable to the Gaullists, rather than with the Americans. A third factor was the realization by *la France combattante* that AFN offered a better platform than did London from which to launch operations in Corsica and the former *zone libre*, where, for a number of reasons – geography, relative shortage of repressive forces, and traditions of political dissidence – resistance groups found firmer footing. On 9 November 1942, "Colonel Passy's" (André Dewavrin's) request to send a BCRA "technical mission" to Algiers not surprisingly met with an OSS veto. Darlan's assassination temporarily put paid to other tentative Gaullist efforts to create networks of followers in Algiers.[66]

According to American sources, at Anfa de Gaulle and Giraud "agreed in principle that a union of their respective followers and armed forces was highly desirable."[67] The decision to rearm up to eleven French divisions taken at Anfa also created pressure for amalgamation of the two factions. The British were keen that the FFL be included in the rearmament program, while Eisenhower concurred that the French army should be equipped to US standards. British Foreign Minister Anthony Eden recommended that Georges Catroux lead an "exploratory mission" to lay the groundwork for a rapprochement between de Gaulle and Giraud, an assignment that the normally diplomatic Catroux complained had entrapped him "between a madman and an ass,"[68] leaving his interlocutors to divine which was which. To work toward reconciliation, and no doubt in response to American pressure, on 14 March, guided by Jean Monnet, Giraud repealed sixty-three Vichy-era laws, which provoked the resignations in protest of Rigault and Lemaigre-Dubreuil, a good first start. However, for the moment, the 1870 Crémieux Decree, which had bestowed French citizenship upon Algerian Jews, remained in abeyance, with the support of the egregious Murphy, who parroted the standard antisemitic codswallop that the Crémieux decree's reinstatement would alienate Muslims.[69] But Giraud's policies appeared increasingly opportunistic, while his entourage of former Vichy loyalists, together with his pronouncements that liberated France would require a (further) period of military dictatorship, seemingly torpedoed any republican aspirations. In private, Giraud vowed that he would never accept the leadership of de Gaulle, who was his junior and not even a real general.

Taking up residence in Algiers on 25 March 1943, Catroux quickly concluded that the Gaullists commanded the loyalties of only a small sliver of the population of *français d'Algérie*, which obliged them to court Giraud's cooperation. But Catroux's predictably cautious reading of Algerine opinion was disputed by André Pélabon, a graduate of the *École polytechnique* and BCRA hardliner who was listed as a deputy in the "naval section" of the Gaullist mission. In Pélabon's estimation, widespread Gaullist sympathies were silenced and intimidated by AFN's Vichy-legacy security apparatus. Like Darlan, Giraud had no personal following in AFN, but was propped up by the "Pétainists," who were relatively scarce in the civilian population, but more numerous than he had expected in the army, and who "seem to make up the totality of naval officers."[70]

Pélabon's orders from de Gaulle were "thoroughly to prepare public opinion" in AFN through "direct, semi-clandestine" action to provoke "unrest," that aimed to "open the eyes of the American High Command in North Africa," and so undermine the main prop of Giraud's power base. The BCRA's non-military (NM) section worked out a campaign plan whose themes would emphasize "reestablishing the laws of the Republic"; calling for sanctions against collaborators, and criticizing Giraud for not according amnesties "for services to the Allies" during Torch; and a demand that AFN be brought under the banner of Fighting France. Radio Brazzaville and Radio Londres were mobilized to spread this message, as were tracts, newspaper articles, public demonstrations against Vichy, "and individual attacks against torturers in the police and the members of the *service d'ordre légionnaire* and the PPF [Parti populaire français]." A petition soon circulated in Algiers, backed by Combat's newspaper, demanding that de Gaulle be made head of the provisional government. As the Tunisia campaign drew to a conclusion, and French soldiers began to "desert" *l'armée d'Afrique* for Gaullist units, Giraud and Catroux together appealed to Macmillan to expel Pélabon. Although de Gaulle smothered Pélabon in praise, on 15 May, the Gaullist agitator was deported to Gibraltar.[71]

But it was already too late. Because the foundation for de Gaulle's ultimate triumph had been laid by the BCRA, which Giraud, with his narrow military view of intelligence, complained appeared "much more civilian than military, essentially political," which, of course, was the point.[72] On 27 April, Catroux had negotiated an agreement for Giraud to share the co-presidency of a "National Committee" with de Gaulle. Murphy, Macmillan, and Monnet signed off on the arrangement. To waylay another "Darlan deal" at liberation, on 8 May Jean Moulin had pried a declaration from the leaders of the internal resistance that only de Gaulle could restore the Republic and initiate France's renewal. On the night of 14 May, Moulin messaged the BCRA that the "*Conseil de la Résistance*" composed of leaders from several resistance groups had called for the creation of a "Fourth Republic that will not be modeled on the Third." A second message reiterated that the Council would never accept the subordination of de Gaulle to Giraud, that a provisional French government should be installed under de Gaulle in Algiers, and that "de Gaulle continues for everyone to be the only chief of the French Resistance." The next day, the Gaullists issued a press release, picked up by the *Times* of both London and New York and broadcast on Radio Brazzaville, that "a Council of the French resistance" speaking in the name of "movements, political parties, and clandestine unions" had affirmed its faith in de Gaulle's leadership.[73]

On 17 May, in his capacity as head of the *Comité national français*, Giraud invited de Gaulle to Algiers to realize the fusion of the French effort agreed to in principle at Anfa. The BCRA attributed this surprise to Moulin's dispatch from occupied France.[74] However, although the resistance declaration, which was reaffirmed at the end of the month, expanded and legitimized de Gaulle's political base, the invitation from Giraud had been assiduously worked by Macmillan and Monnet in Algiers, who actually feared that Moulin's dispatch from occupied France might jeopardize an agreement. During his May 1943 Washington visit, Churchill again resisted strong pressure from Roosevelt and Hull to jettison de Gaulle, precisely because he had been made to understand that there was no support in the Foreign Office, much less in his cabinet, to file for divorce from *la France combattante*, their companions since the early trials of the war. Meanwhile, Roosevelt's sequence of French initiatives to sideline de Gaulle worked through Leahy and Murphy had merely produced a diplomatic debris trail. Eden added his own warning that it would be imprudent to disavow a movement that "numbered 80,000 men, commanded forty-seven warships and an efficient air force," not to mention a resistance that the SOE and the BCRA were organizing into a serious military force. An Anglo-American repudiation of *la France combattante* at this stage of the war would undermine the foundation for reconciliation laid at Anfa and by Macmillan in Algiers. This offered a refrain that would increasingly be advanced by the British to counter US policy – that France must not be belittled for its wartime weakness, but cultivated because its influence would be required in post-war Europe. As Macmillan noted in his diary, Washington's snub had only served to increase de Gaulle's popularity, and allowed him to play the "French sovereignty" card against Roosevelt.[75] The resistance declaration gave de Gaulle a "legitimate mandate." Disowning de Gaulle would provoke an eruption of accusations of illicit "Anglo-Saxon" meddling in French affairs that, in the wake of the "Darlan deal," would only transform the French leader into "a national martyr." Thus, disarmed by his own team, Churchill was left to remind Roosevelt that, for better or worse, de Gaulle had now become the symbol of French resistance. Instead, the two rival French leaders must be made to collaborate in the context of a National Liberation Committee, a collective body whose configuration would be worked out by Catroux, Monnet, and Macmillan in Algiers to guide France's liberation.[76]

The "Desertion Crisis"

Although angered by the fact that the Western Allies had excluded him from the secret of Torch, de Gaulle realized that the Allied invasion of North Africa offered a golden opportunity to transition *la France combattante* from a minority sect into a functioning state, with a significant military, and a secret service capable of exerting influence over a burgeoning resistance movement on the mainland. Giraud's most solid assets were first, US backing, which de Gaulle would transform into a liability; and, second, the allegiance of *l'armée d'Afrique*, whose stubborn devotion to Vichy was attested by portraits of Pétain that continued to decorate official buildings, barracks, and officers' messes at least until the end of 1943.[77] While the "moral unity" of French forces was deemed desirable in theory, *l'armée d'Afrique* complained that the FFL displayed a "partisan spirit," while Diego Brosset countered that *armée d'Afrique* resentment toward the FFL was rooted in "shame and jealousy, shame at having transgressed military honor, [and] jealousy of our pride and our promotion."[78]

However, the fusion between the two forces decided at Anfa would prove a fraught process, as resentment and competition would continue to simmer. The once self-contained imperial force would face rearmament and reorganization that would require it to incorporate new categories of recruit, and to "fuse" with FFL and eventually *Forces françaises de l'intérieur* (FFI) volunteers in France, who were defined by their contempt for Vichy and Pétain. The bitterness of 1940, of Mers-el-Kébir, Dakar, and Syria, followed by the Giraud–de Gaulle power scuffle that would define 1943, coarsened factional rivalry. As has been seen, an unpacking of the Tunis victory parade of May 1943 revealed the French army to be a jerry-rigged confederacy of antiquated units profoundly divided along racial, religious, political, and military lines. These fault lines persisted deep into the autumn and winter as *l'armée d'Afrique* struggled to retain control of the military command against an increasingly assertive CFLN and the Provisional Consultative Assembly. The end of the Tunisia campaign signaled the onset of the de Gaulle–Giraud struggle for ascendency in the CFLN, one punctuated by a wave of "desertions" to the FFL, a phenomenon that was to enflame intra-French and Franco-Allied relations. While official – as opposed to actual – American policy was "not to intervene in squabbles between the Free French and the Giraud French," both governments recognized that "a French Army to be strong not only had to be well armed but well disciplined. Political factionalism threatened discipline. The two major Allies could not permit themselves to fall completely into a situation in which each had its own protégé."[79]

The first indications of the so-called "desertion crisis" came in February 1943, when Secretary of the Navy James Forrestal had alerted Secretary of State Cordell Hull that "mass desertions from Giraudist to Gaullist vessels docked in New York Harbor threatened to cripple the battleship *Richelieu* and other North African naval units." But the *Richelieu*'s problems proved merely a nautical curtain raiser, when the end of the Tunisia campaign in May witnessed "numerous desertions of individuals, even units, of one faction to the forces of the other, as well as by the reported undisciplined behavior of troops currently assigned to guard duty." Hull correctly feared the "desertions" would not only compromise the overhaul of the French navy, but also offered testimony to the growing ascendency of the Gaullists in the CFLN, which was precisely the message that "desertion" was meant to send.[80]

One of de Gaulle's objectives had been to build FFL forces into a two-division presence in the Eighth Army. No sooner had Sfax been liberated than Leclerc, who had arrived with the Eighth Army in March, opened an FFL recruiting bureau.[81] On 1 May, Giraud had officially complained to Catroux that the Gaullists had persuaded a truckload of Senegalese to defect. The next day, he blistered Leclerc, whose FFL "mercenaries" were "kidnapping" *armée d'Afrique* soldiers. Leclerc's biographer André Martel concedes that Leclerc was particularly guilty of this practice because the FFL in North Africa numbered only 16,019 men in June 1943. But also, de Gaulle invoked desertions to undermine Giraud's assertion that he did not need the FFL to mobilize

AFN, and to support his claims to Macmillan that 25,000 soldiers from *l'armée d'Afrique* stood poised to defect to *la France combattante*. What the Gaullists referred to as "spontaneous transfers" were also mobilized as a means to advertise Giraud's fragile political legitimacy and his crumbling popular support to Roosevelt and Eisenhower.[82] No sooner had Axis troops in Tunisia laid down their weapons than, on 8 May, Leclerc requisitioned a prominent Italian villa in Tunis, festooned it with "Vive de Gaulle!" banners and Cross of Lorraine tricolors, and welcomed walk-ins. Lorries crisscrossed the town, while FFL recruiters scoured bars and brothels looking to entice *armée d'Afrique* soldiers willing to switch units with promises of promotion and women. Leclerc handed out generous leave to his soldiers in Tunisia, with the proviso that they return from as far away as Morocco with recruits.[83]

Giraud vociferously complained about Gaullist-incited "desertions" from *l'armée d'Afrique*. In a 15 June 1943 circular, an unapologetic Larminat insisted that the Gaullists, who had refused to accept the 1940 armistice, saw it as their duty to gather all available forces in the most efficacious manner, and breathe the spirit of resistance into the nation so that it could be "reconstructed in a purified atmosphere." "We are well aware how the French have been lied to, abused, and misled, how they have been placed in the material impossibility to react against what they oppose." For this reason, their attitude toward those who had collaborated was "intransigent." Those who had rallied to the FFL had done so voluntarily. Officers who opposed returning to the war out of opposition to *la France combattante* or the Allies must be eliminated. "The vast majority of the nation wants an army that will fight the external enemy, and not one that reinforces a dictatorship." However, the FFL were willing to entertain a "cordial union" with the Giraudists. While they understood that some officers remained faithful to the Marshal out of "noble and respectable sentiments," the best way to resolve the issue would be to remove all visible signs of fidelity, avoid discussions, and to concentrate on making the army "more efficient than the army of 1938." And those who feared that the FFL planned to take their places should rest assured that "we only have enough cadres for our own units."[84]

For their part, the Allies were at the end of their patience with French intramural bickering and indiscipline, and alarmed by Giraud's claims that the Gaullists were preparing a coup, lingering buzz since the Darlan assassination that stoked more general Allied fears of a brewing French civil war.[85] Martel suggests that coup rumors were based on loose talk by the headstrong Larminat, commander of the *1ère Division française libre* (1ère DFL), about the need to "clean out the high command in Algiers," a scheme that de Gaulle and Catroux had quashed.[86] On 26 May, the Americans exiled the FFL contingents – Leclerc's Force L, which had been renamed the 2e DFL, and Larminat's 1ère DFL – to Sabratha, a flyblown camp on the Libyan coast, to spend the summer simmering under canvas. By August, the commander of the British XX Corps complained that the FFL had become a menace to the local population, and demanded that they be expelled from Tripolitania.[87]

In fact, the "desertion crisis" proved little more than Gaullist public relations spin amidst a general military reorganization. The aftermath of the Tunisia campaign left the region fumbling to create a stable, legitimate authority. Tunisia, especially, was in chaos, while war refugees crowded into the Constantinois. The future of the French forces remained uncertain. Rumors of army reorganization abounded; enlistment procedures during the Tunisia campaign had been perfunctory, training minimal, and discipline informal; and soldiers had not been together long enough to establish firm bonds with their superiors or comrades. Although, in June 1943, the CFLN demanded a halt to "irregular enlistments" and "clandestine recruitment," enforcing that edict was another matter.

At the end of the Tunisian campaign, the North African recruiting grounds abounded with game – young *pieds noirs* grown impatient with "*attentisme*"; those on the left offended by Vichy and its Giraudist succession; Jews excluded from the *levée*; Spanish Republicans and other foreign refugees looking for a home after the dissolution of the CFA. Those in search of elite military status and a fast-track route into combat might be drawn to the paratroops or Major Fernand Gambiez's *Bataillon de choc*, which had been created from the end of May, as was a *Groupe de commandos d'Afrique*. When soldiers of the CFA learned that their unit was officially to be disbanded on 29 July 1943,[88] two days before the "fusion" of the FFL and *l'armée d'Afrique* was officially decreed, platoons and companies that incorporated its estimated 4,200 soldiers voted on collective destinations.[89] Some soldiers had already made their choices, as battalions recorded from 14–50 percent of their soldiers absent without leave (AWOL), some departing with vehicles and weapons for unknown destinations. Governments in exile, such as that of the King of Yugoslavia, demanded that their nationals be handed over. Some eager to get into combat signed up to join their old commander Joseph de Monsabert, who had been designated commander in chief of the *3e Division d'infanterie algérienne* (3e DIA) destined for Italy. Gambiez netted around 500 recruits for his commandos.[90]

Politics aside, the FFL's draw was anchored in their status as an elite, who combined "*la belle allure*" of Eighth Army insouciance and combat laurels gained at Bir Hakeim. Their units had panache, were in the newsreels, and were modern. Young men liked their British issued shorts and shirts, especially when matched against the "derisory" *armée d'Afrique* greatcoats, puttees, and Lebel rifles topped with fishing pole bayonets. "[*Armée d'Afrique*] soldiers in their old-fashioned uniforms try to adopt an attitude, but cannot hide their feeling of defeat," Brosset noted in Sfax on 30 April 1943. "One understands why the soldiers want to leave Giraud to join us, because we have powerful automobiles, modern arms, abundant rations, more flattering than their pre-war gabardines." The next day, he insisted that, among *armée d'Afrique* soldiers, "the bulk are profoundly Gaullists, the divorce from their cadres is growing." A number of *spahis* defected, including an officer with his staff.[91] Both Larminat and Leclerc claimed to be overwhelmed with recruits. The heavily Spanish 9th Company of the CFA integrated into Leclerc's *2e Division blindée* (2e DB), where they became celebrated as *la nueve*.[92]

Yet, joining Gaullist ranks was not always friction-free. Potential enlistees might be told to turn up at a café at a certain hour, where a truck would collect them. Yet, when Sergent-chef (Staff Sergeant) Pierre Croissant left the CFA to enlist with the Gaullists in June 1943, he was arrested as a deserter.[93] Above all, the Gaullists were favored by many, especially Jews, precisely because they were not *l'armée d'Afrique* – Jean Ghenaissia appeared at an anticipated rendezvous with Gaullist recruiters in an Algiers suburb, to find himself among "*une vraie synagogue*" of 200 other young Jews looking to enlist under the Cross of Lorraine. Unfortunately, *gardes mobiles* delivered these Gaullist hopefuls to a Giraudist unit, where, unsurprisingly, the colonel refused to enlist them. Soldiers from the *7e chasseurs d'Afrique* and the *4e spahis*, that had incorporated significant contingents from Van Hecke's former *Chantiers*, seemed particularly receptive to the Gaullist recruitment pitch. One hundred and ten Foreign Legionnaires, a unit whose members were always up for a change of scenery, switched allegiance to the Gaullist *13e Demi-brigade de la légion étrangère* (13e DBLE). But the Gaullists also had a reputation as a tight fraternity that did not invariably welcome converts and novices with open arms. Instead, recruits were submitted to an extensive cross-examination that might end in rejection. Even if enlisted, they quickly discovered that those who had not burnished the legend by fighting at Kub Kub or Keren, crossed the desert – both literally and metaphorically – with Leclerc, or battled at Bir Hakeim or El Himeimat were never fully embraced, whatever their rank.[94]

However, in the context of the political struggles for control of the CFLN, defection to the FFL was interpreted as a rejection of *armée d'Afrique* routine, "formalism," and outdated rules, being instead an expression of a spirit of equality, mutual respect, democratic discipline, and a desire for a renewal and revitalization of an antiquated and discredited French military.[95] The ever-cautious Catroux decried what he judged to be an unseemly scramble for recruits as a provocation, and de Gaulle eventually ordered his subordinates to knock it off. However, from Carlton Gardens the BCRA deployed desertion as a tactic to force Giraud to fuse French forces on terms that would leave the two Gaullist "divisions" intact. Muracciole categorizes these desertions as "more spectacular than profound," testimony to the bad blood and competition between Giraudists and Gaullists rather than signaling a significant transfer of personnel. According to Crémieux-Brilhac, these aggressive methods delivered only about 3,500 soldiers to the FFL. Other estimates place "desertions" at half that number.[96] "Desertions" might also go the other way, with Gaullist legionnaires breaking ranks to enlist in the British or Free Polish forces, and being replaced in part by 200 Muslims who had fought for the Wehrmacht in the *Phalange africaine* and were allowed into the Legion as penance. Muracciole estimates that, of the 7,600 men who joined Gaullist units in 1943, 3,900 came from the old Armistice Army, 3,800 were *évadés de France* who had escaped through Spain, 900 came from the CFA, and around 600 were Muslims, who joined the 1,500–2,400 "deserters." What he calls *la France libre*'s "second generation" was built around a strong nucleus of *français d'Algérie*, girdled by a fairly eclectic membership.[97]

Brosset acknowledged that this carousel of reorganization and personnel transfers made it difficult to create stability and command continuity in units: he complained about officers being constantly diverted for "training," or tempted by BCRA offers of missions to France. *L'armée d'Afrique* triaged *évadés de France* at Casablanca, which had also starved Gaullist units of recruits.[98] Leclerc sent his adjutant to "sift" the CFA for suitable European recruits for what would become the 2e DB, and later would replicate his "kidnapping" of *évadés* in Morocco. Nor were the Gaullists the only group trolling for soldiers. Gambiez sent a captain to the *chasseurs d'Afrique* to enlist volunteers for his *Bataillon de choc*, which so annoyed the Colonel of the *6e Régiment de chasseurs d'Afrique* that he admonished his officers after two of them allowed a certain Lieutenant Vincent entry into the barracks at Meknès to recruit for the commandos:

> Without question, this sort of propaganda has a great chance of success in a regiment like the 6e RCA, composed in the majority of volunteers from France, and especially from the "occupied zone" where all the officers, NCOs [non-commissioned officers] and chasseurs only think of one thing: be equipped as rapidly as possible to fight against Germany to liberate France. But the matériel isn't yet available, and everyone is impatient.[99]

In July 1943, Monsabert even had the gall to appear in his old CFA command, which he had "deserted" in their view, and which he had urged Giraud to disband, to recruit for his new up-gunned 3e DIA. This competition for recruits pitted Magnan's sub-Saharan *armée coloniale* (marines) against Monsabert's North African *armée d'Afrique*: Magnan complained to Juin and forbade Monsabert or his officers from entering CFA camps. The end of the Tunisian campaign also saw significant desertions full stop – up to 50 percent in some CFA battalions according to Durand. As Muracciole notes for the FFL, enlistment was more often a spontaneous than a political act.[100] Some soldiers simply wanted a change – the grass is always greener! Some officers were expelled by Magnan, either for being too Giraudist or for lacking requisite professional qualities, which sent them in search of units that would foster them.

With the French army in complete flux in the summer of 1943, rumors abounded. Magnan apparently announced that the CFA would become a regiment in the "Division Leclerc" with "*musique et drapeau*."[101] On the other hand, he did not help the CFA's case when he confessed to Giraud on 20 May that, while many French and foreigner recruits had joined to serve a cause, the Jews and "natives" had merely enlisted for the pay. "This anti-Vichyite spirit persisted and was even reinforced as the men and cadres watched Laval become subservient to Hitler. While the men fought bravely in the conquest of Bizerte" at the side of the Americans, synergy between the mongrel CFA and *l'armée d'Afrique* had failed to develop. On the contrary, 250 men and a few officers and doctors deserted to Leclerc, demonstrating, in Monsabert's view, that the *Corps franc* was in the throes of a profound morale crisis which would take a minimum of eight to ten weeks to repair. Clearly, Monsabert had higher professional aspirations, sought to mend fences with his former colleagues, needed to find cadres for his new command, and was willing to throw the CFA under a Giraudist bus. With the CFA disbanded, its former soldiers had no choice but to search for new homes.[102]

Some might follow a popular officer. Others stuck with their "primary group" comrades. The CFA also peopled the commandos and "shock" battalions.[103] Many Tunisia veterans chose "Giraudist" units, because *français d'Algérie* had *armée d'Afrique* links, and because the CFA had included a sprinkle of followers of Doriot, SOL, Boy Scouts, *jeunesses Catholique*, *Compagnons de France*, and *Chantiers* inmates, who, in the view of Gaullists, were simply "camouflaged PPF." Some foreigners saw service in a Giraudist unit as a pathway to French nationality. Professional soldiers and those looking for combat assignments feared that, if they did not transfer to a fighting unit, they might be left to molder among "sovereignty forces," or assigned to service and support formations.[104] To the many who had escaped from France to AFN at great risk and peril, "and to most white elements already in North Africa, the idea of serving in administrative, labor, maintenance, or other service units was repugnant," reads the US official history. "Their reluctance to pick up the shovel instead of the rifle greatly hampered the organizing of service troops ... The native element, although numerous, in general made poor technical personnel."[105] When *évadé de France* and avowed "Gaullard" Louis Bacquier attempted to enlist in a Gaullist unit in Casablanca in 1943, he was simply told that the only openings were in the six regiments of *tirailleurs marocaines*. He chose the *2e Régiment de tirailleurs marocains* (2e RTM) because it was garrisoned in Marrakech, and counted himself lucky that he had not been directed into the anti-aircraft artillery as were many of his comrades.[106] Algerian Jews, and even women, suddenly found themselves courted by units that required literate staff, supply staff, drivers, nurses, and communications troops, categories for which a low education level disqualified most indigenous Muslims.

Desertion also exposed differences in organizational culture between the FFL and *l'armée d'Afrique*. While its leader and subsequent historiography often portrays *la France libre* as a quasi-religious cult, for Muracciole these incidents defined the frontiers of the Free French mystique, and the apolitical character of the "overwhelming majority" of the FFL, many of whom were foreigners or colonial subjects uninitiated into de Gaulle's freemasonry of French grandeur. While de Gaulle was obsessed with winning over French public opinion, he paid no attention to the political education of his soldiers, in part in keeping with the "apolitical" traditions of the French army. Many of those bona fide Frenchmen were young, from Brittany and the conservative west of France, who had Catholic educations and had never belonged to a political party. Those who had been interned in France and North Africa, or who had been forced into the Foreign Legion, remained wary of the volatility of French politics, and joined the FFL in search of security and stability.[107] They remained largely indifferent to and ignorant of the political events that roiled Algiers in the summer and autumn of 1943, in part because they were often parked in remote areas and were out of touch with their families. But while Jews and Protestants might be over-represented in *France libre*'s headquarters in Carlton Gardens, the movement's political center of gravity was to the right of French public opinion of the 1930s, while some of its senior leadership, beginning with de Gaulle, was defined by a nationalist Maurrassian outlook, at once pessimistic, inward-looking, and freighted with *vieille France* nostalgia. So, little separated the elite of the two French military factions ideologically or philosophically. "What gives right-wing anti-Gaullism its visceral, but also poignant, quality was the fact that its spokesmen recognised their adversary as one of their own: two visions of nationalism were in conflict," writes Julian Jackson. "There was a sense of a brother who had gone astray, a fellow-believer who had lapsed: 'How could de Gaulle, pupil of the Jesuits, protégé of the liberal Paul Reynaud have done all this." The answer in their view was to be found in de Gaulle's partisanship, sectarianism, and utter cantankerousness.[108]

And, once they had landed in France, Gaullist soldiers were quick to criticize the resistance as being far too political. Indeed, in 1943 one of Brosset's chief concerns about the consequences of the de Gaulle–Giraud feud within the army was that the military would need to present a united front to control a communist-led resistance upon liberation.[109] Furthermore, judged by the relatively low numbers, the uproar over the Gaullist "kidnappings" seemed on the surface to have been a tempest in a teapot. But, while in absolute numbers, these "desertions" were militarily marginal, they offered symbolic evidence of profound differences in military culture, and a maturing FFL moral ascendancy over *l'armée d'Afrique*.[110]

So, while the rank-and-file FFL members were not political in a formal sense, neither were its soldiers apolitical. Unlike the Allies and the Germans, many of the French lacked confidence in their military leadership. The catastrophe of 1940 had overturned habits of military discipline that dated from the early twentieth century. Many volunteers were reluctant to follow officers who, in their eyes, had failed in their military duties and civic responsibilities.[111] The virtuosity of the FFL leaders, according to Muracciole, was their ability to fashion a fighting force out of disparate elements that ran the gamut from *la petite noblesse Catholique*, like Leclerc and de Gaulle, to Spanish Reds, with sub-Saharan Africans and Levantines in between. While most FFL soldiers would have been hard pressed to articulate the political differences between de Gaulle and Giraud, both of whom held deeply conservative political views, they strongly identified with their leader, and built an *esprit de corps* around being "Gaullists." *La France libre*'s identity was defined by exile, by a profound sense of exclusion, solitude, and struggle, and above all by a refusal to accept defeat. The FFL was a fighting unit that practiced an informal field discipline – which the English complained translated into a conspicuous contempt for regulations. Even Brosset conceded that the FFL's concept of "democratic discipline" might require a few courts martial and even firing squads to rectify.[112] However, he had to recognize that the very act of enlistment singled out the FFL as non-conformists, few of whom nurtured an innate affinity for military life. Less than one-third of the officers and only 8.7 percent of the NCOs were professional soldiers. "The Free French soldier is truly a free man," Larminat told the *Echo d'Oran* in June 1943, whose discipline flows from a sense of equality and mutual respect, rather than the "formalism" that characterized *l'armée d'Afrique*. The voluntary emigration, moral intransigence, and disinterested military spirit of *la France libre* assimilated them to the aristocratic *émigrés* of the French Revolution. They differed in mentality, outlook, and lifestyle from the rigidly reactionary *armée d'Afrique*, as much as they did from the peasant soldiers at Verdun in 1916.[113] Their rejection of Vichy and Giraud was tribal as much as ideological.

In February 1943, Free French officer cadets in Great Britain had expressed their concern at being "fused" with their *armée d'Afrique* contemporaries: "We don't want to be faithful dogs … or mercenaries who fight without thinking. We fight for Free France and for honor, nothing but for honor." Indeed, a Saint-

Cyr instructor who had rallied to *la France libre* commented that, beyond the uniforms and perfunctory drill, their six-month training period at a military college in England resembled a *lycée* rather than the formalized two-year slog at Saint-Cyr. "For *la France libre*, the questions of obedience and discipline weren't essential [in the officer cadet curriculum]," concludes Morgane Barey. This was in contrast to Saint-Cyr, which had been displaced to Aix-en-Provence in 1940 and subsequently reimagined as the "school for student cadets" by Giraud at Cherchell in Algeria from 1943, where rebuilding "moral values" to counteract the "decadence" that had capsized France in 1940 was regarded as the central mission.[114] Cadets at this so-called "African Saint-Cyr" objected when the local population in Cherchell displayed tricolors bearing the cross of Lorrain. "*Maréchal, nous voilà!* " remained the anthem of choice among a student body plucked initially from the *Chantiers* and which consisted overwhelmingly of *français d'Algérie*. The arrival of *France libre* cadets or *évadés de France* barely dented Cherchell's Pétainist ambience. When the first graduating class chose the name "Weygand" as its moniker, the BCRA complained that Cherchell was merely a conveyer belt of incorrigible Vichyites.[115]

In contrast to the Gaullists, *l'armée d'Afrique* was composed of professional soldiers who operated according to a strict code of conduct, who fought out of a sense of discipline and duty. It claimed to be "apolitical," especially when compared with its intensely partisan Gaullist rival. However, together with an overlay of racial stratification, its culture refracted and magnified its sense of victimhood at the hands of a hostile republic, with roots deep into the nineteenth century. Central to the modern catechism of what Pétain called "our admirable army" was the certainty that in 1940 they had been overwhelmed by a more numerous and better armed foe, and betrayed by the "stab in the back" delivered by a decadent and defeatist French population in the thrall of a debased political system. Only Vichy's National Revolution could rehabilitate a French population deficient in morals and patriotism. Absolute loyalty to Pétain was the *sine qua non* because it shielded the army from popular criticism while precluding any requirement for self-reflection. The Gaullists' rejoinder was that *l'armée d'Afrique* suffered from an inferiority complex rooted in a deep sense of guilt over defeat and surrender in 1940, and their professional inadequacies that had been exposed by Torch and Tunisia.[116]

The "Fusion" of French Forces

De Gaulle sought to gain control of a significant military force through "fusion" of the FFL with *l'armée d'Afrique*. But, since the relatively diminutive émigré FFL could never impose its command and culture on the far larger and more established *armée d'Afrique*, the process of integration had to be political and

Figure 2.2 Henri Giraud greets de Gaulle on his 30 May 1943 arrival in Algiers. The two exile French leaders assumed joint presidency of the CFLN, until Washington-backed Giraud was ousted on 2 October 1943 following the liberation of Corsica. (War Office Second World War Official Collection)

top-down. When the leader of Fighting France landed at Boufarik airfield in Algiers on 30 May 1943 (Figure 2.2), he rediscovered what Macmillan described as "a great hot town, crowded into the bay and sprawling up the hill; with large apartment houses, villas, etc., all jostling together; a political and now a sort of fashionable French society, over- and under-dressed women, politicians, journalists, businessmen, concession-hunters, hangers-on of all kinds and sexes, Tapers and Tadpoles and all the normal appurtenances of a capital."[117] Accommodation even for the well-connected was rudimentary, the food was bland and expensive, electrical power was intermittent, and anything not nailed down – and many things that were nailed down – risked being pinched.[118] Armed with his new, resistance-bestowed democratic legitimacy, de Gaulle was greeted by a large and enthusiastic crowd mustered by Combat at the behest of the "politicized" BCRA.[119] Despite Giraud's apparently unassailable position in AFN, de Gaulle's ascendency would prove stunningly swift.

After six months of stand-off and negotiations, on 3 June, as rumors of a Giraudist coup against de Gaulle swirled, the CFLN was formed under the co-chairmanship of de Gaulle and Giraud as "the central French government," whose mission was "to lead the French effort in the war ... exercise French sovereignty over all the territories outside enemy control ... insure the administration and the defense of all French interests in the world." The scenario called for the CFLN in due course to surrender power to a provisional government, "established in conformity with the laws of the Republic," upon liberation of metropolitan France.[120] On 9 June, de Gaulle insisted that France's new governing body enforce the republican principle of civilian control of the military. This meant that Giraud could not act simultaneously as co-president of the government, commissar of defense, and commander in chief of the French forces. When this failed to happen immediately, largely because the three new Gaullist members of the CFLN had not yet arrived from London, de Gaulle stormed out of the room, vowing not to return until the matter was resolved. However, these attempts to oust Giraud as commander in chief gained a quick veto from Roosevelt, who threatened to curtail French rearmament. Eisenhower counseled Roosevelt that the United States should stay out of French affairs. Churchill added to the pressure on de Gaulle by blocking all funds to the *Comité national français* and the BCRA after 30 June.[121]

The early rounds went to de Gaulle, who gained approval to decapitate the proconsular corps, which meant the dismissal of Noguès in Morocco, Boisson in Dakar, and Peyrouton in Algiers, as well as the senior military leadership in AFN, over the protests of Giraud and Georges. Two days later, amid continuing rumors of a coup, the CFLN was enlarged from seven to fourteen "commissars," each with assigned ministerial portfolios. Not only did the Gaullists retain a one-vote majority in the CFLN, but also, with René Massigli in charge of foreign affairs, René Pleven holding the colonial portfolio, and André Philip in charge of the Interior Ministry, they held sway over the empire and the resistance as well. Catroux replaced Peyrouton as Governor General of Algeria, and also served as a "commissaire d'état" in the CFLN.[122] Nevertheless, Jews discovered that de Gaulle's full embrace of Republican values translated into a "dilatory" Gaullist campaign to restore the Crémieux decree, which came to fruition only on 22 October 1943, almost a full year after Torch.[123]

Against a backdrop of CFLN deadlock, on 19 June, Eisenhower summoned the competing French leaders to his office to "reconcile the points of view as to France's participation in the war." The American Commander insisted, with all the tact that he could muster, that each French leader must remain in control of his own force. Existing agreements giving the Allies access to harbors and railways must be respected. Otherwise, US aid would cease. De Gaulle protested "the interference of a foreign power in French affairs." He was correct, of course. But Macmillan justified Eisenhower's intervention on the grounds that the Allies too had a huge stake in AFN, and in the war.[124] According to his memoirs, de Gaulle insisted to Eisenhower that France's three armies – the FFL, *l'armée d'Afrique*, and "that which is forming on the mainland" – must be "fused" under a single command. Eisenhower replied that he had no intention of interfering in the internal workings of the CFLN, but was merely carrying out his responsibilities as military commander. Fusion carried the considerable risk that the diminutive FFL of around 50,000 men might be swallowed whole by Giraud's much larger force. Giraud insisted that the "small" *armée d'Afrique* could only function under Allied command. De Gaulle then resorted to his favorite tactic of slamming the door on his way out of the room.[125]

De Gaulle's complaint was that, although the Allied governments purported to respect French sovereignty, in practice they regularly violated it. As Macmillan noted, the avowedly anti-colonialist Roosevelt seemed to consider AFN to be "an occupied country in which his representative, General Eisenhower, had something of the position of a Viceroy."[126] The meeting with Eisenhower had proved critical to the evolution of the political situation, because the fact that the assertion of Giraud's authority obviously required Eisenhower's intervention worked further to isolate Washington's chosen leader within the CFLN.[127] In contrast, de Gaulle's resistance to American interference in French sovereign matters during the "June crisis" won over former Giraudists in the CFLN, including Monnet, René Mayer, and Couve de Murville. His fingers burned, Eisenhower realized that his attempts to sideline de Gaulle had backfired among French moderates, who had concluded that only de Gaulle could thwart a communist takeover of their country – a somewhat ironic conclusion, as US intelligence predicted that de Gaulle would open France to Soviet influence.[128] At Eden's request, the British cabinet accorded limited diplomatic recognition to the CFLN, with the goal of facilitating French military reorganization and rearmament. In the wake of the showdown with Eisenhower, the CFLN struck a compromise, eliminating the rotating presidencies in favor of a system in which Giraud would be responsible for military affairs and de Gaulle for the rest. Giraud appeared pleased that the military's position had been strengthened. However, on 22 June, the CFLN issued a Decree on the Organization of the Armed Forces that established a Permanent Military Committee. Co-chaired by Generals Juin and Larminat, this committee was tasked with engineering the fusion of the FFL and *l'armée d'Afrique*. But, until the amalgamation was complete, each co-president was to control his own forces. Eisenhower batted down Larminat's proposal that the FFL establish its own rearmament office in Allied Forces Headquarters (AFHQ) and appoint a representative to the Joint Rearmament Committee (JRC), insisting that FFL requests for rearmament must go through existing structures.[129]

On 2 July, without coordinating with the CFLN, Giraud departed for Washington in an attempt to "gain him such material and moral advantages as to strengthen his own authority."[130] Giraud's absence cleared the field for de Gaulle's "well-oiled" propaganda machine to discredit Giraud's Washington journey as yet another example of Roosevelt's bypassing the CFLN to deal directly with a French general who was not empowered "to speak for France."[131] Giraud virtually disappeared from the press and newsreels in AFN, to the point that Eisenhower's naval aide Harry Butcher recorded "de Gaulle overshadowing Giraud in all the news shorts. De Gaulle even took credit for the Tunisian victory by the film's emphasis of Le Clerc's [sic] Fighting French and by his own presence in the film and by the absence of Giraud."[132] In the opinion of Robert Belot, it was part of a campaign of, "crude de-Giraudization for the benefit of a one-dimensional Gaullist redefinition of the history of the liberation of France."[133] Its success relied on a narrative that emphasized the dishonorable display of hesitation, indecision, and moral cowardice of the North African command during Torch. The clear message was that the Giraudists were close to Vichy in spirit, men who venerated hierarchy above patriotism and moral courage.[134]

Hardly had Giraud's plane disappeared over the western horizon than de Gaulle set out to erect what Julian Jackson calls his "state in exile."[135] However, rebuilding "France" required a pragmatic approach, because the Gaullists were simply too scarce to populate the military, the diplomatic corps, and the administration without recourse to Pétainist converts, even reluctant ones. Many officers of *l'armée d'Afrique* still loathed de Gaulle as a figure of division and the reincarnation of the despised Third Republic. He had catapulted undeserving and opportunist company and field-grade officers such as Leclerc, Larminat, and Koenig to flag rank. Never mind that real republicans like André Philip fretted at de Gaulle's tendency to keep his own counsel, his "distance . . . from the spirit of democracy," his "profound contempt for human nature" that translated into a lack of charity, even brutality, toward his collaborators, his "authoritarian attitude," and reluctance to consult before taking important decisions. But, like Monnet and Couve de Murville, the leadership of *l'armée d'Afrique* was forced to recognize that, despite his inflexible Olympian severity – or perhaps because of it – de Gaulle had become inevitable.[136]

On 6 July, the CFLN dissolved the proto-fascist PPF, which numbered 1,500 members in Algiers and had helped to recruit the 40 officers and 80 NCOs who had volunteered for the *Légion tricolore*.[137] Portraits of Pétain began to be swapped out for those of de Gaulle in public spaces, although the former continued to be accorded pride of place in *armée d'Afrique* messes and barracks and navy wardrooms for a few months more.[138] The trajectory of history was confirmed when *la France libre*'s leader starred in the first public 14 July celebrations in AFN since 1939, which solemnized the return of Republican rule to Algeria, and to the French West Indies, where French Ambassador to Washington Henri Hoppenot arrived to displace Admiral Robert, who was subsequently accorded a heroic homecoming at Vichy. The next month, the Alexandria squadron ended its armistice-imposed neutrality.[139] In contrast, New York's 14 July celebration, over which Giraud presided, garnered general public indifference – and that was the good news. Giraud's glaring limitations, heretofore revealed only to the American President's intimate circle at Casablanca, were on public display during his June–July North American tour – for instance, his insistence during a visit to Ottawa that the Nazis had accomplished much good for Germany before the war. To camouflage his stunning gaffes, the White House emphasized the military dimensions of Giraud's visit and attempted to censor the Frenchman's statements. But even American generals found Giraud's lectures on strategy nearly as tiresome as his recurring Königstein escape saga. Giraud's American tour represented a "political fiasco" in the opinion of Lacouture, although typically the General remained totally oblivious to that fact.[140]

De Gaulle's soaring prestige also benefited from a wave of popular disenchantment with 250,000 boisterous and entitled GIs who, impatient with French routines and conventions, did not exactly win the affections of North African populations by behaving as if in conquered territory. Torch had transformed Algiers, the once sleepy provincial capital where an automobile had been a relative rarity, into "the nerve centre of the North Africa campaign," that "fairly bulged with the crowds who pressed along the streets . . . Now the traffic was overwhelming." The presence of so many newcomers placed a serious strain on the food supply, while the exchange rate set at 75 francs to the dollar drove prices so high that even the black market struggled to supply the growing demand. "The scent and the champagne disappeared. Prices rocketed. Things like leather goods were unobtainable. Eggs, once sold for a penny a dozen, reached sixpence each. Prostitutes hovering around the bar at the Aletti Hotel – the place where officers went to relax in the evening – were asking their clients for £10 and £20 and getting it. Apartments became unobtainable, and you had to go twenty miles out of the city into the hills or along the coast to find an unoccupied villa." At the Maison Blanche airfield, planes of every description stood wing-tip-to-wing-tip among the destroyed hangers. Airborne hitchhikers might catch a bomber or transport plane to just about any destination that was not Axis-occupied. At night, the blazes of anti-aircraft batteries lit up the surrounding hills. Suzanne Lefort-Rouquette found navigating senior officers through "the mechanical tide" of Algiers at least as harrowing as anything she had experienced while behind the wheel of ambulances in Tunisia – a slalom between trolleys, trucks, taxi drivers apparently bent on murder–suicide, donkeys, and men straining at the shafts of heavily laden carts, as her passengers sat white-knuckled in the rear seat.[141] Although Algiers was far from boring, everyone hated the place, according to Moorehead. The dreary weather, "depressing tenth rate" accommodation, oppressive crowds, monotonous bulk rations, and acidic, stomach-churning wine all played their part. But above all, discontent with Algiers flowed from "the overriding atmosphere of suspicion and bickering argument . . . the feeling that the intrigues were a mean and petty betrayal of the men at the front who were fighting for something quite different."[142]

The future General and 1961 *putschist* Raoul Salan concurred that Algiers offered "a free-for-all with so many interests in competition. The town is full of soldiers of every arm and every uniform, a real image of the French army. The Allies command the pavement, and dominate with their cash. The question of 'restaurants' is a delicate one." He preferred to wander down to the harbor, buy some bread and sardines, and spread a handkerchief over zinc-covered boards laid over sawhorses.[143] "*Les français d'Algérie*" saw the Americans as a threat to social stability, as well as economic competition, because US bases paid top dollar and drew Muslims away from their day jobs. "Liberation" had given way to humiliation – persistent, daily, and ubiquitous. The GIs were competition not only for restaurant tables, but also for the women.[144] In this burgeoning Allied presence, the truncheon-wielding hillbillies recruited as Military Police were particularly detested by French soldiers. The feelings of antipathy were mutual. While all Allied forces experienced morale problems at the end of the Tunisia campaign, American troops especially were livid that many German POWs were being shipped off to the United States, while they crawled under canvas in dreary camps for more training. Many British troops who had been in the Western Desert for two years had looked forward to becoming reacquainted with Blighty. While relatively undestroyed by the fighting, liberated Tunis offered few distractions for soldiers on leave beyond cheap wine and initiating brawls between British and Americans, or between soldiers of the competitive British First and Eighth Armies. So appalling was the conduct of GIs in the wake of the liberation of Tunis in May 1943, importuning women in the streets and banging on doors demanding "Vino! Vino!," that Louis Xueref wondered whether the United States had emptied its prison population straight into the US Army. But, because many GIs seemed to be of Italian origin, the Italian population of Tunisia showered them with the same warm hospitality that they had demonstrated toward Mussolini's men.[145] In Oran, soldiers of the 1st US ID became particularly infamous as a unit of brawlers.[146]

Having invaded AFN without a "preventative medicine plan," the US military proved ill-equipped to deal with the region's many sanitary challenges, which included mosquitoes, prostitutes, polluted water, open sewers, garbage, and dead animals simply left to decompose in the streets. "Low moral standards, combined with the unsanitary surroundings, presented a serious threat to the health of the American troops," complained the official US medical history of the campaign, although whose "low moral standards" the history condemns is unclear. Diarrhea and dysentery soon swept the ranks, along with venereal disease. Even hepatitis and malaria made an appearance. But the Allied command complained that French officials, led by the mayor of Oran, "had been generally indifferent to public health problems." Oran's restaurants "were particularly filthy."[147]

In this way, poor Franco-American relations helped to erode Roosevelt's anti-Gaullist policy from below, as the French failed to embrace his hand-picked leader, his economic policies increased wartime shortages, and his soldiers quickly wore out their welcome, as they were later to do in France. Despite his new fame, even Leclerc was not spared the indignity of being forced on two hours' notice to surrender his harbor view room in the Hotel Aletti to an American major. The Allies had definitely overstayed their welcome. People faulted the Clark–Giraud accords, engineered by Murphy, the "American Abetz," that had placed AFN under virtual Allied military occupation. They chaffed at American censorship, wearied of plagues of inebriated and belligerent GIs, jeeps driven at top speed through narrow, pedestrian-clogged streets, and inflated prices. French troops had not been invited to join the 10 July invasion of Sicily on the pretext that they required rearmament and training. In September, fatigue turned to indignation with news that France had been cut out of secret Armistice negotiations with Italy – so much for "unconditional surrender!"[148] De Gaulle feared that the Badoglio deal might be a dress rehearsal for a Laval deal on France's liberation, which spurred him to complete the "fusion" of the FFL and *l'armée d'Afrique* so that French boots on the ground might give him a veto on any such arrangement.[149] Suddenly, de Gaulle's diatribes against "les Anglo-Saxons" in defense of French sovereignty became more broadly understood. In the process, Giraud, Georges, and the cast of elderly generals who crowded *l'armée d'Afrique*'s pinnicle transitioned in the public mind into yesterday's men, artifacts of defeat and of Vichy accommodation with the Axis occupier. Worse, more prescient observers such as Couve de Murville explained to Churchill's personal assistant Desmond Morton that, by supporting this claque of superannuated senior officers, Roosevelt risked installing "a sort of post-war communism in France, against which Couve de Murville by no means gladly regards de Gaulle as the sole visible barrier."[150]

On 30 July, the Combined Chiefs of Staff recommended that FFL units be included in the Anfa rearmament program. This happened in part because many in the US military, led by Eisenhower, had concluded that the Gaullists were more likely to impel the modernization of the French military than was "old school" Giraud.[151] In fact, on the issue that was to roil Franco-American deliberations on military modernization – a requirement for support and service troops – the Gaullists backed the Americans, for several reasons: because it allowed them to stigmatize Giraud and *l'armée d'Afrique* as a geriatric old guard locked in a passé war-fighting style; it strengthened their calls for a renewal of French senior leadership; it allowed them to needle "les Anglo-Saxons" led by

Murphy for installing a reactionary claque at the helm in AFN; and, finally, it might move Gaullist units up the priority list for upgrades.[152]

On 31 July and 2 August, the CFLN promulgated two decrees, one that virtually confined Giraud to military matters, while the other amalgamated the general staffs of France's three services, with Giraud as commander in chief, under a CFLN that "*assure la direction générale de la guerre*." In an arrangement lifted from Third Republic practice, Giraud would be assisted by a deputy commissioner of defense appointed by the CFLN, seconded by the Permanent Military Committee to be chaired by de Gaulle that had been created on 22 June.[153] In this way, by early August, the total takeover of the CFLN by de Gaulle assisted by his acolytes was already within reach. They decreed that a "Consultative Assembly" would convene from November. The National Defense Committee moved forward with the fusion of French forces, laboriously rearming with US assistance. Other members of the CFLN were offered no grounds to challenge de Gaulle's moves, because they had been based on republican practice and as such constituted steps in the resuscitation of republican legitimacy and civilian control. In August 1943, Eisenhower recommended that Washington accord full diplomatic recognition to the CFLN. But Roosevelt and Hull opted merely to acknowledged the CFLN's authority in the empire, while awaiting the moment when "the French people freely choose their government." For its part, London recognized the CFLN as "competent to insure the defense of French interests," and, on 26 August 1943, Moscow accorded full diplomatic recognition to the CFLN as "representing the governmental interests of the French republic." "Thus was constituted, from the summer of 1943, the beginnings of what can already call the 'Gaullist State'" concludes Lacouture, although on a provisional basis and with limited recognition by the Western Allies.[154]

"With all the President's immense virtues, he has a curious blind spot about France and especially about de Gaulle," Macmillan recorded. "This is the old story of the American recognition of Vichy – the evil influence of Admiral Leahy – and the series of gradual defeats which Americans have suffered in their French policy. Now their favourite Giraud meets his final decline." He predicted that Roosevelt "will gradually yield to realities." In the meantime, de Gaulle's growing ascendency over his political rival had altered his disposition: "He improves all the time," the British representative in AFN recorded on 24 October 1943. "As he obtains power, so his sense of responsibility increases. He is still shy, sensitive, and very prone to take offense. But he *has* a sense of humour (rather puckish) and he can relax in company where he is at ease." He even carried off a meeting with the "thin-skinned, stubborn and sensitive to perceived slights" Secretary of State Hull without exploding: "He did not speak so bitterly about the Americans as he generally tries to do – unless one stops him."[155] Brosset agreed that de Gaulle's improved demeanor evolved with the realization that, having bested his rivals, he must now behave with more calm and moderation.[156]

Brosset, who replaced Larminat at the head of the 1re DFL in August 1943, complained that there was no true "fusion" of the two forces, merely a mix and match transfer of intact units from one force into that of the other, where the new arrivals were greeted like malignancies, surrounded by distrust and hostility. "We resume our place in the French army," Brosset acknowledged in the autumn of 1943, "set in its ways, with its pettiness, self-importance, and its old generals." For this reason, army modernization had to tack against strong reactionary headwinds.[157]

Mobilizing France's Hinterland: "The Improbable Becomes Possible"

Despite the unsettled French political situation, arming the French was imperative, Eisenhower had told the Combined Chiefs of Staff (CCS) on 15 January 1943, from both a manpower and a political perspective. A potential collapse of their antiquated forces on the Dorsal in the early weeks of the Tunisia campaign would have threatened to crumple the Allied front. And, if French forces were to be upgraded in the short term, the Allies must also formulate a plan for their future deployment. However, in Washington's view, a precondition was that French ground forces, as well as a French Air Force (FAF) that Anfa ordered into being, must conform to a US operational, tactical, and logistical model. This insistence on the part of the Americans set off a running dispute that would churn until the end of the war.

L'armée d'Afrique's capacity to adapt to the Second World War's industrialized format and an American managerial model remained an open question at the end of the Tunisia campaign. The 1940 campaign had found the French military on the trailing edge in practically every modern dimension of warfare. It was useless to argue that so had been almost everyone else, a situation that had allowed Hitler to choreograph a series of operational and tactical triumphs in 1939–1942. By 1943, as the French had spectated from the touchline, the learning curve on a rapidly evolving three-dimensional battlefield had spiked. As professionals, *l'armée d'Afrique* believed that, supplied with adequate weaponry that in their minds had been denied by the Popular Front, it would prove its true worth. This it was largely to do in Italy, albeit on a small scale and in mountain warfare conditions that devalued technology and played to its incontestable homespun strengths. However, how France's renaissance as a great power could be improvised from AFN, a provisional filament of coastal settlements buffered by frontier stockades and internment camps on the lip of the Sahara, around which simmered a sullen, walnut-tanned population, remained an open question. Yet, upon an indoctrinated resentment of republican betrayal was grafted *l'armée d'Afrique*'s historical imagining of AFN as France's imperial glacis, where a Spartan military spirit engendered in a stolid settler population, combined with the requirement to dominate AFN's indigenous inhabitants, had nurtured an innate resilience, alloyed with a robust reservoir of patriotism. However, *l'armée d'Afrique*'s ability to adapt to a modern battlefield by drawing on AFN's narrow settler base for leadership and a largely illiterate and recalcitrant Moslem population for manpower saw it struggle to meet Anfa-imposed US personnel and support requirements and norms. Once in France, a cultural collision with a largely left-leaning resistance wary of *l'armée d'Afrique* as a coterie of colonial mercenaries and unreconstructed *Maréchalists* would complicate France's military revival.[158] Nevertheless, the urgency of the reorganization and modernization of French forces had been driven home by the high casualties suffered in Tunisia, which were blamed in the main on antiquated French arms and equipment, a paucity of medical services, and other French military inadequacies.[159]

Modernization and expansion also hit the army at a bad time. Most of the officer corps remained incarcerated in *Oflags* while NCOs labored in *Kommandos* in the Reich. Those who had replaced them in North Africa might be professionally inadequate – for instance, the Legion company to which Sergeant Erwin Fuchs was assigned for the Tunisia campaign was commanded by a pot-bellied antisemitic pen-pusher with an aristocratic surname, who had miraculously escaped capture in 1940, probably because the Germans had failed to search under his desk. "Not the type who should be in the Legion and would have never gotten here in the Old Times for sure," Fuchs opined. He almost caused a friendly-fire massacre when he ordered Fuchs to fire his mortar into a headwind, which pushed the projectile back to explode on their own position.[160] Only a trickle of professional officers and NCOs would make it over the Pyrenees through Spain to AFN. Mobilization in an imperial setting would prove a challenge on several levels. Politically, de Gaulle's legitimacy hinged on his ability to maintain the integrity of the empire. French prestige and military dominance were seen as "the foundation of colonial equilibrium" in the face of increasingly restive indigenous populations, in particular in AFN. Furthermore, any show of weakness or concessions in the face of Allied demands would open de Gaulle to attack by Giraud and Vichy, which helps to explain the violence of his reactions whenever Eisenhower's invocation of "military considerations" infringed French sovereignty.[161] But his options were limited while AFN was occupied by Allied soldiers, its economy as well as the rearmament of French forces was hostage to Washington, and Giraud had not imposed political conditions in exchange for France's participation in the war.

A second problem, following from the first, was the question of which forces exactly were to be upgraded by the Anfa agreement. In November 1943, the

French complained that an agreement "between high personages" to arm up to eleven French divisions concluded ten months earlier was "not followed by staff accords that made precise the Services and above all the equipping of territorial units in North Africa, that the French see as essential, but whose importance the Americans have totally ignored and underestimate ... Territorial divisions, logistical centers, sovereignty forces represent for them a separate and second army that we seek to arm to ill-defined purposes at the expense of an Expeditionary Corps."[162] In short, it became apparent from the beginning that French and US priorities diverged, and would continue to do so until the war's end. While the Americans envisaged eleven hard-hitting French combat divisions with requisite support and logistical services to grind down the Wehrmacht and allow US manpower allocation to favor sea and air forces, de Gaulle understood that the Allies were going to win the war with or without the French. Therefore, his priorities became the preservation of the empire; restoration of public order and the State upon liberation; and insuring France's postwar interests in Germany and influence in Europe.

The truth was that the French lacked the human resources and infrastructure in Africa to replicate the industrialized US paradigm imposed at Anfa, to transform an imperial constabulary into a modern combat force. As those who had supported the 1940 armistice had argued, the social and economic underdevelopment of Francophone Africa, combined with its ethnic, racial, religious, geographical, linguistic, and political fault lines, made the empire a precarious foundation for a French *levée*. Furthermore, the empire was peripheral to the French concept of the "hexagon." Rather, it formed a "backdrop" whose soldiers, the vast majority of whom remained in colonial garrisons, served merely as "extras in an epic film of European warfare," not as a *levée* proxy.[163]

For these reasons, Giraud's proposal at Anfa to raise thirteen French divisions in AFN, as well as assemble a 1,000-plane air force, had encountered skepticism, when not disbelief, from US observers.[164] In the end, FDR had agreed to rearm and reorganize eight infantry and three armored divisions, as well as to reestablish "a first line air force consisting of five hundred fighters, three hundred bombers and two hundred transport planes," plus 400 trucks, equipment for two armored regiments, three reconnaissance battalions, three battalions of tank destroyers, and three motorized divisions, and "such of the aviation equipment as can come by air."[165] A program of repairs and upgrades for the remnants of the sadly depleted French navy was also formulated, although separate from Anfa. It also made perfect sense.[166] For Eisenhower, the early weeks of fighting in Tunisia had ticked the box of French loyalty. And, looking forward, he knew that he would need French cooperation on D-Day in 1944, and so began gently to nudge Roosevelt toward an acknowledgement of de Gaulle's growing ascendency. As the health of the American President deteriorated, many policy decisions defaulted to Chairman of the Joint Chiefs of Staff (JCS) Admiral William Leahy – ironically it was the former American ambassador to Vichy, an avowed de Gaulle skeptic, who was to approve Eisenhower's request to turn over civil administration in France to the Gaullist-directed CFLN after D-Day.[167] But, while the American military leadership appeared willing to turn the page, this was not so for the British, who "seemed hesitant to rely on an army which until recent weeks had remained obstinately loyal to Marshal Pétain's government, in their eyes a defeatist, even pro-German regime."[168] In the short term, however, Churchill was concerned lest the FFL be excluded from Anfa rearmament.

Deciding at Anfa on the principle of French rearmament was one thing. Actually getting arms to North Africa, and training the French to use them, was another. Among the technical details, the one that loomed immediately as most critical was a dearth of shipping. While perception of France's naval débâcle of November 1942, followed by the German seizure of the naval base at Bizerte in December 1942, had focused on lost warships, now it appeared that the forfeiture of cargo ships had also been costly. When Giraud complained about the slow pace of rearmament, Roosevelt told Murphy that the French must "stop acting like children." At Anfa, the American President had agreed to the "principle of rearmament," not to draw up a supply schedule.[169]

Quite apart from a shipping shortage, a second but equally pressing problem was what to do with the supplies and equipment once they reached North Africa. The Allies had taken over most of the main North African harbors, including their docks, dry-docks for repairs, and warehouses. Furthermore, the French lacked the personnel – even the typewriters – required to receive, inventory, stock, and dispatch equipment to the front. Giraud and his staff of colonial soldiers were largely clueless about how to set up and manage a complex reception and distribution service.[170]

Of necessity, resupply fell back on "*le système D*," embraced by French military culture as evidence of resourcefulness and a compensatory ability, in the absence of method, to adapt on the fly.[171] At the end of April 1943, when the first shipment of equipment had reached AFN, the US Mediterranean Base Section created an assembly line with American-supplied plant on the Algiers docks, where 75 French officers and 2,300 workers, mostly conscripted from the *Chantiers*, uncrated and assembled 7,000 vehicles in less than a month. However, this exceptional effort could not be repeated, especially for tanks, artillery, and larger trucks, because assembly was more complex and parts arrived via separate shipments, often weeks apart. On 8 May, the day that Tunis fell, a ceremony took place in Algiers to mark the symbolic hand over of US matériel, which featured a parade of horse cavalry reequipped as an armored unit, complete with tanks, jeeps, and trucks to demonstrate the transformation. By early May, the *2e Division d'infanterie du Maroc* (2e DIM) had been rearmed, while Monsabert's *3e Division d'infanterie algérienne* (3e DIA) and a division that would later become the *4e Division marocaine de montagne* (4e DMM) were in the process of rearming. But, in US opinion, these divisions still lacked sufficient ordnance, signals, engineer, and medical components. They had yet to be trained in the use of their weaponry, although an instruction program had been created in April. Nor had technical manuals been translated into French. Furthermore, with North African ports crammed with shipping to support Operation Husky – the July invasion of Sicily – new shipments for French rearmament became delayed and piecemeal. "French rearmament had become a 'hand-to-mouth' procedure in which the basic directive was vague and its execution unmanaged," the official US history understates.[172]

The problem of inadequate French logistical arrangements was brought to a head at the end of September, when a convoy bringing mostly maintenance equipment and spare parts arrived at Casablanca. The French proved totally unprepared to deal with it, in part because of a lack of warehouses and dock space. In October 1943, Fuchs' legionnaires mustered at Ain Diab, a Casablanca suburb, to uncrate and assemble their trucks, "without having been given any kind of explanation or instruction about it. *Débrouillez vous!* . . . Not surprisingly, most of the work was done backassward . . . I wonder who was the poor shithead who decided to give us this kind of work for which by no stretch of the imagination are we qualified?"[173] This fiasco, which left the Americans indignant, drove home the point that the French lacked the organization and personnel to sort, inventory, and assemble the avalanche of spare parts and equipment. As a result, the Americans separated out the equipment destined to equip those French units designated for Italy, and attached 385 maintenance instructors to the French Training Section.[174] But the problems caused by the inadequacy of French support services continued. Nor were they resolved – Brosset noted in December 1943 that the English were constantly complaining to him about the chronic disorganization of the French "*service du matériel*."[175] And the French were to pay the price for their neglect of support services in Italy in 1943–1944. Upon arrival in the Peninsula, they had hastily to improvise hospitals, messes, and rest centers behind the lines. French hospitals were described as "Spartan," and their medical services had to beg penicillin from the Americans, who also found themselves on the hook for cigarettes, toothpaste, shaving cream, sweets, and so on for French soldiers. Despite repeated warnings, the French continued to dispatch reinforcements into Italy with inadequate winter clothing, which led to many cases of frozen feet. GIs had to service French artillery pieces, and eventually take over the feeding of French troops in Italy. Indeed, the food situation in Italy eventually led to a minor crisis when many Muslim soldiers were found to be malnourished.[176] One result became that the Americans were quick to blame French ill will or incompetence when things did not go smoothly, while the French complained that Washington failed to acknowledge the constraints under which they labored.

"The American view of us varied," read a 23 November 1943 report. "Most believed us totally incapable of equipping our services. Some, and not the least influential, even believed it was intentional, and a number of apparently superficial acts helped to create that impression. For those who lived with [the Americans], it was easy to see. At the moment, another viewpoint is emerging: their inspections are showing that we have made a considerable effort with limited resources and personnel. They can see first-hand our problems and our results, while a month ago they could see the results without knowledge of our difficulties."[177]

Personnel

The French empire offered a vast potential reservoir of soldiers. But to lead, train, organize, and supply them, not to mention find men for the navy and FAF, required an imperial *levée*, that for the first time would include women. Enthusiasm for a *union sacrée* with France was on the decline in a settler population freighted with sub-national identities, and that felt only a remote attachment to a mainland that many had never visited. Memories of Great War sacrifices certainly played a part in this estrangement, followed by the 1940 defeat that helped to weaken bonds with the Metropole. In these conditions, *l'armée d'Afrique*'s place in a racially and religiously riven, highly politicized, and self-absorbed North African society no longer seemed secure.[178]

"*La comédie politique d'Alger*," which foreshadowed infighting between Giraud and de Gaulle for control of the CFLN, combined with lingering loyalties to the Marshal to produce what Julie Le Gac calls "a morale crisis" in a *pied noir* population that had folded in on itself. For them, the takeaways of Torch had been inflation compounded by increased taxes to support the war, the severe disruption of the economy due to premature mobilization before the arrival of US arms and equipment that recalled Phoney War immobility and idleness, the ubiquity of Allied troops, and confused and shifting mobilization edicts that included recruitment of women of European extraction. If irrational prejudice excluded a relatively well-educated population of Algerian Jews from military service, female mobilization was viewed as a shocking invitation to promiscuity that transgressed Mediterranean social mores and gender relationships. In the thrall of antisemitism and anti-Masonic complexes, not keen to enlist in an *armée d'Afrique* that seemed antiquated, inept, brutal, and incapable of delivering victory, the *français d'Algérie* was viewed on the mainland as "a resentful person, afflicted with a class complex vis-à-vis the homeland," content in his egotism to win the war so long as someone else did the fighting.[179]

In these circumstances, Giraud's slogan "one goal, victory" pleased the Americans because it suggested that French national goals would be subordinated to an Allied strategic agenda. However, it failed to rally the population, communicate any political or ideological program, or sequence priorities. What "victory" would look like was also unclear – many *pieds noirs* imagined that the goal of the "liberation" of the mainland was to free the Marshal, and indeed it was often advertised as that in *l'armée d'Afrique*. High losses in Tunisia cooled enthusiasm for combat service, and instead multiplied the numbers of aspiring "*planqués*" – "shirkers." Numerous Jews, Spanish Republicans, and other political refugees, most of whom had enlisted in the Foreign Legion in 1939, were due to collect their "straw hat" in 1944 as their enlistment contracts expired. Instead of fighting fascism, most had spent five years in remote colonial garrisons, where they were left to wonder whether starvation or tropical disease would claim them, all the while "being treated like dirt," denounced as a "Bande de Bolcheviques" by their officers, or invited to depart for Palestine, while the French made up their minds whose side they were on. When the blandishments of the recruiting sergeants who encouraged legionnaires to reenlist "*pour cinq piges*" (for five years), speeches of commanding officers insisting that "there are big jobs ahead for the Legion," and large posters that proclaimed "À l'Empire il manque l'Indochine!" ("The Empire lacks Indochina!") failed to work, "they use every dirty trick in the book," like intercepting mail to one's consul, or losing a legionnaire's papers, thus denying him a residence permit and forcing him into an internment camp at Colomb Bechar, "the Gateway to the Sahara!" Interned, they were hired out as contract labor to companies for 0.90 francs a day, which, after deductions for food, lodging and clothing, left 0.25 francs for "wine and women!" "Fat chance! It made us only even more disgusted. Hardly anybody re-enlisted," Fuchs claimed. He eventually joined the British Pioneer Corps.[180] The call-up in Tunisia, where mobilization centers had been abandoned and archives destroyed during the Axis occupation, had yielded barely half of the expected recruits. Fully a quarter of conscripts remained unaccounted for or had been rejected on medical grounds. Despite these problems, by 1 November 1944, 176,500 French North Africans were more or less in uniform, or 16.4 percent of the settler population in AFN, together with 19,000 *évadés de France*.[181]

In contrast to the settler community, the French counted more indigenous recruits than they could profitably muster. Conscription had been established for Algerian Muslims since 1912. In 1939, 170,000 Algerians, 80,000 soldiers each from Morocco and Tunisia, and 180,000 "Senegalese" had been mobilized.[182] Of these, between 90,000 and 100,000 had been taken prisoner in 1940.[183] However, after Torch, Muslims in Algeria initially had not been mobilized, because it would have resulted in an excess of infantrymen, and the

French lacked the cadres for them in any case. Instead, the general staff sent quotas to each "administrative circle," instructing them to call up the youngest veterans first. While this method had placed 12,800 Algerian Muslims in uniform by December 1942, devolving conscription to local authorities produced "mediocre" soldiers while leaving locals disgruntled over the "inequality" of a process vulnerable to local favoritism and corruption.[184] During the course of the Tunisia campaign, the troop strength of the XIX Corps had virtually doubled, from 28,972 in November 1942 to 53,693 by April 1943, of whom 30,167 (roughly 56 percent) were Muslim. Of 72,802 French soldiers in Tunisia on 15 March 1943, 50,651 (69 percent) were North African Muslims, although Muslims were desperately underrepresented in the officer and NCO corps, and in the technical arms.[185] To be fair, barriers to "colored" leadership were hardly a French monopoly.[186]

Algerian nationalists sought to employ Muslim participation in the war to demand more participation in government and the opening of the civil service to Muslims. On 10 June 1943, Ferhat Abbas, a pharmacist from Sétif and Algerian nationalist leader, delivered to Allied principals copies of the *Manifeste du peuple algérienne*, which documented a long history of Algerian Muslims being "maintained in a state of defeat and subjugated" by the French.[187] While the CFLN organized a reform committee to look into the nationalist complaints, the local view was that the Allies were stirring up trouble with their Atlantic Charter, tanking the prestige of the French army and administration, and creating divisions in the French leadership that Ferhat Abbas, Messali Hadj, and other Muslim nationalists sought to exploit. On 12 December 1943, de Gaulle announced limited reforms, followed by a 7 March 1944 ordinance that expanded access to citizenship for a restricted category of Muslims, and that ended *le code de l'indigénat*, which imposed indigenous forced labor. Nevertheless, French authorities worried that weaponry might be diverted into the hands of nationalists.[188]

Once the promise of US arms had been secured, the conscript classes of 1941 and 1942 were mobilized in Algeria, with a few exemptions for agricultural workers. This produced a huge recidivism rate of between 40 and 84 percent, depending on the region. But Le Gac points out that this did not necessarily indicate a political boycott, but might have resulted from outdated conscription lists, or from the fact that many Muslims were migrant workers, or transhumant pastoralists, or might even be already in uniform unbeknown to local authorities. Nevertheless, a polarization between the European and Muslim communities had been growing, especially in the Constantinois, since 1918.[189] Muslim Algerians on the whole did not honor service in an army that had conquered and subjugated them. To alleviate this situation, pay was equaled for Algerian *tirailleurs* in August 1943. But tracts calling for revolt, and strikes in the historically nationalist Constantine and Sétif, meant that the gulf between the

Muslim and European communities yawned widely during the war.[190] In fact, a combination of economic misery, the appeal of Muslim nationalists, public divisions and purges in the French administration and *l'armée d'Afrique*, and the stark material differences between Allied and French soldiers did much to erode French authority in AFN. In practical terms, this meant that the French had to maintain more sovereignty troops in the countryside, rather than deploy them to fight the Germans.[191] For all these reasons, although from 1942 indigenous mobilization was the subject of contention between Muslim nationalists and French officials, and mobilization produced growing conscript absenteeism, not until 8 May 1945 did outright rebellion erupt at Sétif and Guelma.[192]

In Morocco, *l'armée d'Afrique* relied on volunteers, and from early 1943, individual regiments dispatched recruitment parties to bulk up their units prior to rearmament. Officers enthused that an attachment to France and an ingrained warrior ethic of loyalty and honor that bonded soldiers with their officers combined to make Morocco especially prime recruiting ground. This was true to a point. Morocco was heavily garrisoned, and military service with the French carried the imprimatur of serving the Sultan. Pay, the enlistment bonus, and a family indemnity, together with two meals a day, also served as incentives.[193] Initially, French military units sought out volunteers in areas that reflected their martial race preferences – the Atlas Mountains and the Tafilalet, Berber Marrakech at a pinch, but not Arabized Meknès and Fez, and certainly not detribalized, uprooted, and urbanized Casablancans. Thus, 82 percent of Moroccan recruits hailed from rural areas, while roughly 58 percent were Amazigh (Berber) speakers. Unit-based recruiting parties raised complaints, however, that their enlistment bonuses attracted men in debt, and siphoned off workers vital to the local economy. So, from March 1943, recruitment was centralized under Muslim Affairs. This meant basically that it was thrown into the hands of the *Chiocks* (notables) and the *Caïds* of the douar whose job was to "hunt up" recruits in their bailiwicks, assuring them that the community would take care of their animals and family. This sort of local pressure made it difficult for "volunteers" in Morocco to evade service. In Algeria, where Muslims were subject to conscription, gendarmes instituted "*rafles*" or raids by surrounding a neighborhood and carrying out a "*contrôle d'identité*." These methods netted 6,573 deserters or "*insoumises*" (refractory soldiers) between November 1943 and November 1944. But this was only a small percentage of those serving.[194] For *pieds noirs*, the preference was to find a soft job or at least a unit "less exposed than the 4e RTM." By 1944, Bacquier's platoon, with a theoretical strength of thirty-five but which seldom exceeded twenty, combined Amazigh from southern Morocco with *pieds noirs* and a sprinkle of metropolitan Frenchmen.[195]

Accurate statistics are elusive, but this mobilization in AFN would deliver a strength of between 230,000 and 250,000 Muslims, although how they were distributed over Tunisia, Algeria, and Morocco is unclear. Juin reckoned that, while 16 percent of Frenchmen in North Africa were mobilized, only 1.6 percent of Muslims had been called up by 1 November 1944, most of them from Algeria, where the French exercised a tighter administrative control over the indigenous population.[196] A US-imposed requirement for technicians and specialists, combined with memories of 1916, when conscription had sparked a rebellion in the Aurès mountains, made the French authorities reluctant to impose conscription in a draconian manner in Algeria. One result was that the manpower contribution of Algeria to the war effort between 1943 and 1945 was one-third inferior to that of the First World War.[197] Most Muslims were directed into the infantry, or to anti-aircraft units, whose personnel was roughly one-quarter Muslim. Reorganization and the call-up of *pieds noirs* and eventually Jews decreased the percentage of Muslims in *tirailleur* regiments from 90 to 66 percent. Muslims were largely absent from armored divisions and from artillery, signals, and engineer units. In *armée d'Afrique* infantry units, where "the subtle poison of prejudice could work its mischief," Europeans made up three out of four NCOs, half of the corporals, and only one out of seven riflemen.[198]

The four combat divisions that would eventually make up the *Corps expéditionnaire français* (CEF) in Italy counted only twenty-six Muslim officers, fifteen of whom were in the 3e DIA. The 1,419 Muslim NCOs represented 22 percent of all NCOs in combat units, in which over 60 percent of the soldiers were Muslim. The two Moroccan divisions in the CEF – the 2e DIM and 4e DMM – which together numbered 18,000 infantrymen, contained many French-speaking Algerian NCOs, of whom Ahmed Ben Bella was one. But, if the French were going to expand their army from a colonial, mainly North African, foundation, they were going to need "natives." By June 1944, even the 1re DFL contained 41 percent "natives."[199] The infantry reserve was essentially Moroccan, while Algerians, who had had a longer exposure to the French, were pooled as a reserve for the cavalry and artillery. Of the troops who were to participate in Operation Dragoon, the 15 August 1944 invasion of southern France, 50 percent, or 130,000 of 267,654 men in the First French Army, were North African Muslims. If one adds "colonial troops" (*képi noir* marine infantry) from outside AFN, estimated at between 60 to 80,000, roughly 55 percent of French troops counted as "indigenous" between 1942 and 1945, though they were led overwhelmingly by French cadres.[200]

The Anfa agreement stipulated that a generic infantry division number 15,000 men and 2,300 vehicles, while an armored division would count 11,000 men and 3,000 vehicles, which required a significant logistical tail. Unfortunately, the French lacked "even semi-technicians, necessary to organize all the service troops required for a modern eleven-division army."[201] Muslims were virtually absent from motorized infantry or armored divisions because *l'armée d'Afrique* had failed in the inter-war years to train Muslims in technical and logistical specialties, principally because of racism, but also because the French education system had largely neglected them, and out of fears of facilitating indigenous unrest. In this way, the expansion and modernization of *l'armée d'Afrique* fell hostage to a dearth of "European" cadres.[202]

French pushback against US logistical requirements asserted that French and Muslim soldiers could rely on local resources and did not require the lavish support apparatus that supplied C-rations, chewing gum, Hershey bars, and individual toilet paper packets to coddled GIs. The Americans, led by Eisenhower, recognized that the French sought to maximize the number of fighting divisions for political reasons, and that they lacked enough educated manpower to assign to support organizations. However, the Americans were also quick to conclude that "pampered GI" arguments masked the cluelessness of Giraud and his staff about the technical and logistical requirements of modern warfare. Nor did the Americans want to be on the hook for providing support services for the French, although that is precisely what would transpire.[203]

Armaments

The American-imposed requirement for service troops ultimately eroded the Anfa promise to equip eight infantry and three armored divisions for the French. Like de Gaulle, the Americans complained that, conceptually, Giraud and his entourage "had not progressed beyond the pre-war concept. They suffered from the same incomprehension that had been one of the causes of the French Army's downfall in 1940. The JRC could point to the fact that, whenever the French General Staff submitted requisitions, they invariably gave last priority to the equipping of service units.[204] De Gaulle complained incessantly in 1943 that the Americans had pressed upon him generals like Giraud and Georges who were "not modern." However, things hardly improved in 1944–1945, when his hand-picked Jean de Lattre de Tassigny took command of the First French Army in France, where he clashed repeatedly with his Gaullist subordinates Larminat and Leclerc. While these strong personalities found it difficult to evolve a team spirit, Larminat and Leclerc, whose combat experience since 1940 had been principally with British and US forces, complained that de Lattre's command style was hesitant, and he failed to deploy armored forces for maximum effect, while the Americans repeatedly had to bail him out logistically.

The decision to resurrect a French air force virtually from scratch, and revive a moribund French navy, triggered a competition with the army for experienced cadres, technicians, and mechanics, one intensified by political rivalries and racial and religious prejudice. Eisenhower vetoed attaching "excellent [French] fighting troops" to a US logistical tail, probably because he knew that Roosevelt would never accept it. But, in practice, the Americans assumed much of the burden of French support in Italy and France. For, once they realized how well the French were fighting in Italy, they were hardly going to let them starve, allow them to exhaust their munitions, or deprive them of artillery and air support. Giraud's request that the Americans rearm twelve divisions further undermined his credibility in Washington. In the end, it was the French who paid, when Eisenhower recommended that the original eleven divisions agreed upon at Anfa be reduced to eight – five infantry and three armored. In that way, the French could "free qualified troops for the organization of a balanced army adequately supported by the necessary troops and base units." These debates were still ongoing when, on 8 December 1943, advanced elements of the CEF arrived in Italy. The subsequent brilliant success of French-led troops in Italy offered "a record that those responsible for French rearmament could well be proud of," concluded the US Army's official history. But the process of getting those troops into combat had been a fraught and sometimes acrimonious one.[205]

The French calculated that they would require 40,000 men for logistical and support functions for an expeditionary force numbering 250,000 to 260,000 men with their staffs. But as what was to become the French First Army was poised to invade southern France in July 1944, they had yet to raise half that number. US estimates were even higher – the French would need at least 100,000 men to run headquarters, training centers, schools, ports, bases, hospitals, motor pools, depots, and so on. On top of the rearmed combat divisions, the French also required 103,000 sovereignty forces to police their empire, plus 8,000 French soldiers employed by the US military to guard POWs captured in Tunisia. In fact, French mistreatment of 5,000 German and 41,000 Italian POWs in French custody by 1943 brought a formal protest from Berlin via the Swiss authorities to Eisenhower. The lack of French manpower and resources to guard an increasing number of German POWs who fell into their hands became another increasingly contentious issue that divided the Allies, who feared German retaliation against Anglo-American POWs as a result of French neglect or abuse of German captives. This problem was also complicated by the Anglo-American refusal officially to recognize the CFLN.[206]

Torch had found the French air forces in parlous condition. The FAFL counted five RAF-equipped squadrons under General Martial Valin – two stationed in the UK, one in the Middle East, and one in Africa to support Leclerc. In October 1942, one squadron left the United Kingdom for the USSR, where it was reequipped with Soviet matériel. In November 1942, the French air force in North Africa under Jean Mendigal had numbered twenty squadrons of all types, with ten more in French West Africa (AOF) – in all 12,000 to 15,000 men including 1,500 trained pilots, most of whom had seen action in 1940, and corresponding crews. However, roughly two-thirds of an outdated air inventory had failed to survive the Allied invasion. In January 1943, two squadrons were moved to the UK to be equipped with British Halifax bombers. Despite the fact that what was left was "in various degrees of air worthiness," American General Carl Spaatz had been impressed by the quality of French pilots, to the point that he had integrated three French squadrons into his Northwest African Air Force in Tunisia from March. By the end of April, the French had received 100 US planes, mainly at the initiative of the US Army Air Force (USAAF), including P-47 Thunderbolts for the Lafayette Squadron.[207]

Béthouart drew up a plan for rearming of the FAF for USAAF Chief General Henry Arnold, which called for Gaullist and "Giraudist" elements to be "fused" as in the army and navy from July 1943. But, despite requests by Eisenhower, Giraud, and de Gaulle to accelerate the process, FAF rehabilitation was slowed because decisions snagged in the CCS, because of training, maintenance, and standardization issues, and because the US and UK air forces had priority. Plan VII, drawn up at the end of September 1943, sought to create a balanced FAF, which operated in Sicily, southern Italy, and Corsica. But, as with the French army, the supply and support situation remained unsatisfactory. By the end of 1943, the FAF numbered twenty-two squadrons – a mix of sixteen fighter, bomber, and transport squadrons in North Africa and three fighter and three bomber squadrons in the UK, with eleven more scheduled to come on line by July 1944. French planes based in the UK participated in the Normandy invasion, while those in the Mediterranean continued to operate in Italy and supported the Dragoon invasion of southern France, although they were maintained by 450 USAAF mechanics.[208]

The French navy would also prove a significant consumer of scarce manpower. With the amalgamation of the two navies and the end of the war boycott by the West Indies and Alexandria squadrons, the French navy numbered eighty ships: three battleships, one "carrier," nine cruisers, twenty-one destroyers, twenty-two submarines, plus twenty smaller vessels and sixty auxiliary craft. It had a combined total of 45,000 naval personnel. But in the middle of February 1944, as the CEF struggled to replace heavy losses in Italy, fully 10,000 French naval personnel remained unemployed, which caused the British and Americans at Giraud's request to give them more ships, as well as refloated French craft or requisitioned Italian ships, to raise the French naval inventory to 240 vessels. French naval personnel had to be trained in air defense, ASDIC (a form of sonar named after the Anti-submarine Detection Investigation Committee), radar, and gunnery. The French navy participated in the Normandy and especially the Dragoon operations, and also performed convoy duty. And, of course, as many of its bases were for the moment occupied by the Allies or the Germans, much of the rebuilding project was done with an eye to the revival of post-war French power and support for the empire, especially the reoccupation of Indochina. However, one wonders whether, given the dearth of cadres and support forces in AFN, the rebuilding of the French navy, especially the refitting of the battleship *Richelieu*, whose crew of 1,569 contained large numbers of machinists, gunners, and other specialists, was a prestige project that absorbed too much of France's limited skilled manpower.[209]

Training

"As far as the Legion is concerned," opined Erwin Fuchs, "our biggest problem is that we were never anything like a 'modern army,' trained to fight with modern weapons."[210] To prepare the French to utilize American weapons and integrate them into an Allied operational system, in May 1943 a "French Training Section" (FTS) was stood up, initially to oversee the instruction of French divisions assigned to Mark Clark's Fifth Army in Italy. While the French were responsible for the basic and company-level training of their own troops, under Brigadier General Alan Kingman, personnel from seven French divisions were trained on the maintenance and repair of US matériel, as drivers of US vehicles, in signals, and as radar operators, as well as in small-unit infantry tactics and amphibious landings. Most of this instruction was organized in training sites in Morocco, after which an inspection team consisting of a French officer and a US officer from Kingman's FTS would certify French units as combat ready. However, the process was initially slowed by the Tunisia campaign, by the delayed, piecemeal arrival – even loss – of equipment and vehicles, and by the dearth of American instructors. So, in the summer of 1943, the process was accelerated by creating schools to train French personnel in AFN, rather than dispatching US instructors individually to French units. French officers were also sent for training in the United States, while US and French service units were often paired to standardize techniques and procedures. Pilot trainees were also dispatched to the United States for flight training. An Ordnance school was created at Meknès and an air force mechanics course at Larbaa, near Blida.[211]

Named in July 1943 to command what was to become the CEF, headquartered for the moment at Trouville, a western suburb of Oran, Juin supervised the rearmament and training of roughly 70,000 troops. Under FTS direction, French soldiers were introduced to US (Figure 2.3) weapons and kitted out in American uniforms, although some officers stubbornly continued to turn out in French gear. From the end of August, Kingman's Franco-American teams of inspectors began to evaluate the French army's mastery of their new weaponry and training. On the whole, the French were impressed by the power and

Figure 2.3 A GI demonstrates how to operate a .50 caliber machinegun to French soldiers in Algiers in 1943, part of a shipment of war equipment sent from the US under Lend–Lease. (Photo by Keystone/Getty Images)

practicality of the US equipment, and by the tact and professionalism of their instructors. Nevertheless, American-directed inspections during which French officers might be corrected by a gruff staff sergeant from New Jersey or rural Georgia offered a humiliating reminder of France's tributary status. "One had to acknowledge the role played by the American inspectors, graders and trainers," Goislard de Monsabert wrote on 27 September 1943 as his 3e DIA prepared to embark for Italy: "they were not always diplomatic. Many junior cadres, unfamiliar with the 'direct' American approach, were offended by the offensive comments made during inspections and the manner in which they were made." But this would fade away as bonds were established in combat.[212] In the meantime, unit exchanges, combined training sessions, and receptions were organized that aimed to build confidence and comradeship between French and American soldiers. But the often negligent French maintenance of US equipment, adhesion to the Mediterranean tradition of the midday siesta, and a reluctance to work at weekends combined to project a negative impression of the French work ethic. Fuchs' account of the inspection of his unit by FTS officers in October 1943 was practically farcical. When an American colonel asked a Legion sergeant to explain how an anti-tank gun worked, the sergeant replied that he had no idea. He was there only to "escort" the weapon, not fire it. "The Legion colonel, who was standing close by, didn't know on which foot to stand, poor guy." A second US colonel discovered that "our poor morons" had covered their halftrack with a thin layer of engine oil, calculating that a gleaming vehicle would impress the inspectors. Mumbling to himself, the officer "proceeded to flip up the hood of the halftrack, took off his jacket, rolled up his shirtsleeve, took off the top of the oil filter and plunged in his hand, pulling it out with the palm of his hand full of black sludge and all kinds of crap. Looking more bewildered than angry, he says: 'are you people using the oil filters as a shithouse?' Deafening silence, while the American is shaking his head in disbelief and walks away disgusted."[213] In fact, the entire process and demeanor of the Americans suggested that the Allies retained scant faith in French combat qualities, concludes Le Gac.[214]

The French insisted that armaments, not tactics, had proved deficient in 1940. Juin, for one, remained convinced that the Americans had nothing to teach the French in the domain of tactics and inter-arm cooperation.[215] Nevertheless, "training notes" were passed on from AFHQ to acquaint the French with the lessons of the campaigns so far and the latest inter-Allied techniques and procedures, so that everyone would operate on the same page. The French also produced in April 1943, in the midst of the Tunisia campaign, a tactical update to Georges' 1936 *Instruction sur l'emploi tactique des grandes unités*, expanded to include combined arms and air power, and the concept of "total war," and to brand offensive operations as "the normal mode of action," compatible with the allegedly aggressive temperament of Muslim troops. By applying these methods, France's diminutive army might magnify its impact and leave its mark on the war.

For the French, the takeaways from Tunisia and Sicily were that the infantryman still required "physical endurance," an ability to support hardship and to "live rough," concepts that would be reinforced in Italy and Alsace in conditions that few could have imagined. Following Eisenhower's March 1943 instruction, training was meant to replicate a combat environment as nearly as possible, with long, cross-country marches, live demining, and night exercises, which, combined with sleep, food, and water deprivation, resulted in 1,858 training deaths in the 7 months following the end of the Tunisia campaign. Hard training and patriotic lectures that emphasized the need to redeem the shame of 1940, and realize the goal of Liberation, were also meant to avoid an erosion of morale that many officers had observed during the Phoney War. In any case, given the colonial nature of its recruitment, especially of Guillaume's Moroccan *goumiers*, the CEF's fighting style would remain rustic, anchored in tactical maneuver rather than technology, but well adapted to the mountains of central Italy.[216]

Juin declared US training methods to be "ingenious."[217] French troops threw themselves with enthusiasm into training, especially as they realized the power and efficiency of their new US-supplied weaponry. André Lanquetot confirmed that the soldiers of his 8e RTM were "euphoric" when they took delivery of 200 jeeps, Dodge and General Motors Truck Company (GMC) trucks, command cars, trailers with radios, mortars, and 57 mm anti-tank guns. "It was exhilaration. We loved and polished this equipment. . . . We were no longer poor." Several officers were sent for courses in Port-Lyautey from December 1942, and returned to instruct others on the mechanics of their new equipment. Otherwise, they trained in the "Fifth Army Invasion Training Center" on fire support, maneuvers with and against tanks, operations with engineers, and eventually amphibious training and operations with parachutists. The training process was hampered by language difficulties, by delays in translating training and technical manuals, and by a lack of spare parts and munitions. The Americans complained about a lack of initiative and support from the French military leadership. US inspection teams fanned out to evaluate the fitness of French units for combat. In September, the Americans pronounced the 2e DIM to be combat ready. However, it was noted that their use of radios was deficient. On 4–5 November, the 2e DIM carried out a divisional maneuver in preparation for their embarkation for Italy. Like Juin, Lanquetot noted that the Americans were impressed by how quickly the French caught on.[218] Although he had not witnessed the allegedly "lamentable" performance of US troops in Tunisia, Bacquier believed it took some "cheek" for an American team to assess the combat readiness of the 2e RTM. "In fact, the problem was simple: they were rich, and we were poor." The second lieutenants received a severe warning from their training officer that the first one to "do something stupid" in front of the visiting Americans would be transferred immediately to the military police, "which sent a shudder of horror through the assembly." In fact, the inspection came off well. At first, the group of five US officers led by a colonel was "a little stiff." None of them spoke French. However, after some impeccable demonstrations, followed by "banana gins," lunch, and a songfest in the mess, that included a lusty if accented version of "The Star-Spangled Banner" with all the French officers standing to attention, the American colonel professed to be "moved." Nevertheless, Bacquier recorded that relations between French and American troops remained "complex," by which he meant that, during operations, French soldiers would make up for their logistical shortcomings by stealing from American stocks. This was a compromise worked out among officers, which avoided unwelcomed paperwork and confrontations so long as the Moroccans did not touch personal effects and their larcenies remained within the limits of what the Americans could write off as "wastage."[219] By October 1943, Kingman pronounced the technical training of French forces to be satisfactory.[220]

Évadés de France

In these conditions where every semi-educated person able to assume a leadership role or fill a technical or administrative specialty counted, a category of refugee known as "*évadés de France*" (escaped from France) assumed an importance for French mobilization beyond their limited numbers. The trickle of refugees across the Pyrenees into the Iberian Peninsula had initiated by 1940, but was transformed into a gush by news of Torch, followed by the February 1943 announcement that the conscript classes of 1940–1942 were to be mobilized for forced labor, *Service du travail obligatoire* (STO), in Germany.[221] Torch also had announced that the balance of forces in the Mediterranean had shifted to favor the Allies, a trend confirmed by the Axis surrender of Tunis, which accelerated the refugee flow.

Various forces impelled men over the Pyrenees despite the risks. In the autumn of 1942, at the beginning of his second year at *l'École normale supérieur* on Paris' rue d'Ulm, Louis Bacquier's academic career was stuck in neutral. It was difficult to focus on his classical studies with the Wehrmacht at the gates of Moscow. Food was scarce. He witnessed daily the drama of Jewish refugees from Eastern Europe, wearing their yellow stars and clutching formless packages wrapped in paper and poorly secured with string, huddled in the gray winter dawn at bus stops. Hoping to visit relatives, they were instead scooped up in police roundups and trucked to the Drancy internment camp north of Paris. A stroll down the Boulevard Saint-Michel invariably provoked a frisk by "Bousquet's goons, who were 'doing their shopping.' Night after night, the same scenario repeated itself: the armpits, the belt, between your legs . . ." all to please the Gestapo, snag a resister, secure a bonus, extra rations, or a promotion. The elastic march of squads of tall, well-armed Germans provoked rage and humiliation.[222]

But why risk the perilous escape across the Pyrenees and through Spain to join Gaulle? "My communist friends considered joining Gaullist forces as treason . . . [The internal resistance] was the place for responsible patriots: in France, in the heart of the people; not in the emigration. But I held firm. I needed to fight in daylight, to breathe free air after three years of asphyxiation. It was a clean break, even if the word was never used. Besides, with my friend Bigot, whom I brought into my confidence, we quickly understood that to leave France, in the conditions of the time, constituted an athletic exploit." They broke into the town hall of the 5th arrondissement to steal some ration coupons and the Marshal's vitamin-enriched biscuits, and fled la rue d'Ulm, "without saying goodbye." Bacquier stopped at Ceyrat, near Clermont-Ferrand, to announce his decision to his parents. Expecting pushback, he was amazed when his father's only advice proved to be: "Whatever happens, never, NEVER allow yourself to be captured." And when his mother heard *la*

France libre, she immediately thought London: "Above all," she admonished, "don't bring back an English girl! They are tow-haired, have teeth like piano keys, and are worthless in the kitchen."[223] Fortunately for Mom, English girls proved to be rather scarce in Marrakech.

Bacquier makes no mention of crossing the demarcation line, which until 1 March 1943 separated the occupied from the by then former non-occupied zone, perhaps because French memory relegates it to one of the minor inconveniences of occupation. The demarcation line remained fairly porous, for the simple reason that the Germans did not have the manpower to seal a 1,200-kilometer frontier that meandered through 13 departments. From its foundation, the line spawned an industry of counterfeiters of false papers, often teachers or municipal employees, but above all of "*passeurs*" (smugglers) – mainly physically fit, unemployed young men in their twenties, often but not invariably peasants who knew the land and could cultivate contacts both in the occupied zone and in the "free" zone. *Passeurs* were also entrepreneurs who cultivated their client lists – Vichy paid them to spirit escaped POWs into the *zone libre*, usually through the Jura, although they drew the line at smuggling Gaullists, Jews, or deserters, for whom the price of passage was a steep several thousand francs. The *passeurs* also suborned the Germans by engaging them in the black market. Women were involved in keeping the safe houses where fugitives staged before they were spirited across the line. So, because the *passeurs* made the demarcation line function, everyone – resistance, Vichy officials, the Armistice Army, the Germans – maintained a preferred *passeur* list.[224]

With the dissolution of the separate zones in November 1942, the Pyrenees became France's most guarded frontier – 3,170 agents of the Abwehr, Sicherheitsdienst (SD), and Sicherheitspolizei (Sipo) were stationed at 13 bases along the Franco-Spanish frontier, focused on breaking up escape networks. Those caught in flight risked internment in France, or if Jews or STO dodgers, deportation straight to Germany, as an unknown number undoubtedly were. The Germans complained of apathetic cooperation from French police and customs officers, and of French railway workers who conspired to violate the prohibited zone created along the frontier.[225] But, in the autumn of 1942, Bacquier found crossing the Pyrenees a challenge. Escape routes were continually being closed down by the Gestapo. Railway workers, key to getting potential escapees close to the frontier, might transport them in half-filled tanker cars and release them in the tunnel de Cerbère on the Spanish border, where they might meet their Pyrenean *passeur*. Police reports refer to these men as "*rabatteurs*" or "beaters," suggesting that they were involved in the hunting industry. But it seems to have been a euphemism for those considered delinquent, who ran the gamut from mountain guides, smugglers, and shepherds, to hotel owners who took as their clients escaped

POWs, downed pilots, or important agents with their information out of the country, without necessarily being resisters themselves.[226]

Despite considerable effort on the part of the occupier, an estimated 23,000 to 26,000 people, roughly 62 percent of them young men between the ages of 15 and 23, managed to reach Spain by crossing the Pyrenees. However, men with military experience appear to have made up only about a quarter of this number.[227] Once across the Pyrenees, like Bacquier and his party, most illegal immigrants were swept up by frequently brutal Spanish carabineers and escorted to a succession of jails, hotels, or camps, where they might be booked under false names, or declare false nationalities – claiming to be American or Canadian was often recommended by *rabatteurs* as a parting word of advice.

"In the open space of the prison, five hundred prisoners are assembled," remembered Baquier. "On one side the 'French,' a colorful crowd of volunteers from all corners of Nazi Europe to join the Allied armies: Poles escaped in 1939 via Romania and Turkey, regrouped in France and incarcerated by the Vichy flunkeys; blonde, pink Dutch who had crossed the two demarcation lines; Czechs escaped from arms factories; Alsatians deserted from the Wehrmacht; anti-fascist Italians; legionnaires captured in Libya and rejoining their units via Italy, the south of France, and Spain; Allied aviators shot down over Belgium or France; and finally French – workers, students, bureaucrats, even some peasants, off to fight, or flee the Gestapo, *la Milice*, or simply to do something, to escape Vichy's sophism and the moralizing senility of '*Maréchal, nous voilà!* . . . with a flower in our caps.'"[228]

Spanish internment was a particularly unpleasant experience: Bacquier and his fellow *évadés* were thrust into an unfurnished communal cell with ten other "French" escapees in a stifling prison already overflowing with the defeated remnants of the Spanish Republic and other regime adversaries. On important religious or official holidays, a dollop of these political inmates might be amnestied to stimulate the feeble hopes of those who remained. Soon, the prison routine took over – twenty-two hours a day sitting or lying on the concrete floor of a stifling cell, with two hours on the "patio," at the end of which all of the prisoners had to stand at attention and shout in unison: "Franco! Franco! Franco!" – although they concocted obscene French variants of this abbreviated paean to *El Caudillo* that the guards never twigged.

It was here that one's declaration of nationality proved important. Internees were required to survive on an inadequate diet of thin soup and stale bread.[229] Those with money had access to the "*Economato*," where they could buy extra food or supplies, beyond those distributed by the Red Cross, which, according to Bacquier, consisted of a tin of American pork and beans or paté, a teaspoon of margarine, and a very small tin of condensed milk. Those who had declared French nationality were given 25 pesetas weekly through the Algiers Red Cross, which in the *Economato* translated into four kilos of over-ripe bananas, or two kilos of dried bread. However, Catalans from France "were considered a little like family" by the Spanish, and found fairly easy access to black market goods. The second-largest group was allegedly made up of Canadian aviators shot down over France, although few of these courageous airmen could distinguish a propeller from their landing gear. They might also list their address as Illinois, which seemed not to faze the Spanish in the least, any more than did their East Montreal accent, which sounded suspiciously similar to that of Bezier. A group of about fifteen North Africans, who had escaped from Todt Organization projects in France, were regarded as "violent and con artists" and kept in segregated cells. The "aristocracy of the prison" was undoubtedly the "English" registered under names like Errol Flynn, Clark Gable, and John Watercloset, who, once anointed as such by the British consul, irrespective of whether or not they actually spoke English, received 135 pesetas a week, which earned them the fawning solicitude of the guards. The rest were a sprinkling of Jews and refugees from all over Europe, including "tall, blond and violent Poles, who had had some incredible Odysseys. The Spanish treated them well because Poland was a Catholic nation."[230]

From May 1943, in the shadow of "Tunisgrad," the Franco regime began to empty its jails of these refugees as part of a recalibration of Spanish policy from "non-belligerence" to "neutrality," helped by the fact that the CFLN in Algiers agreed to pay the costs of transporting refugees from Algeciras to Casablanca.[231] "*Évadés*" were regrouped in Malaga, Algeciras, Gibraltar, and Setúbal, in Portugal, and paraded before a "mixed committee" of Gaullist and Giraudist officers to ascertain their preferences, before being dispatched to the UK or to Casablanca. On 19 May, Giraud's representative in Gibraltar, Rear Admiral Delahaye, rejoiced that, in the "legal convoy" that arrived in Gibraltar from Portugal, only 150 of the 800 *évadés* had declared for de Gaulle.[232] Around 9 percent of *évadés* were Muslims, women, foreigners, or men who had been so debilitated by internment that they were declared unfit for military service. Muracciole estimates that only 19,000 to 20,000 *évadés* actually joined military units in AFN, although army estimates, probably from October 1943, put the number of incorporated *évadés* even lower, at only 12,000.[233] Nevertheless, this was a welcomed supplement for a military desperate for cadres and support personnel. According to Robert Belot, about 18 percent of *évadés* who arrived in AFN in 1943–1944 were veterans of the disbanded Armistice Army, or about 1,500 officers whose allegiance to Pétain had been undermined by Torch and the Axis occupation of the *zone libre*.[234]

Judging by the admittedly random and incomplete lists of *évadés*, among this unfortunate flotsam of Eastern European Jews, escaped North African POWs, pseudo-"Canadians," and women lurked a considerable number of Frenchmen with prior military service. For instance, on 26 April 1943, Admiral Delahaye reported 69 regular and 61 reserve officers, 27 NCOs and 20 soldiers among the

333 refugees embarked on the *Sidi Brahim* for North Africa. Barely a week later, he announced that of 810 *évadés* who had arrived on two ferries from Setúbal, 106 were regular army officers, 85 were reserve officers, and 114 were professional NCOs or soldiers. A Delahaye letter of 24 August 1943 lists six officers, including a cadet from *l'École navale*, and seventeen NCOs, soldiers, and volunteers. "Finally, I must tell you how much I was struck by the high morale of these men, who are motivated by a remarkably combative spirit and an ardent faith in the destiny of our fatherland," Delahaye concluded on 26 April.[235]

April 1943 saw the arrival of 1,500 *évadés* in Casablanca. This first group of *évadés* to arrive before being sent on to Marrakech encountered "a miserable reception and over the top disorder." From May, 600 to 700 *évadés* were arriving every 3 weeks. From September, 1,500 arrived every 13 days. Out of 818 *évadés* who had arrived in Casablanca on 6 May, 300, including 100 regular army officers, chose to enlist with the Gaullists. Air Force General Mendigal complained that this was because the *évadés* had been indifferently received and housed. Nor had the air force officer *évadés* been treated with proper respect. In these conditions, everyone had been subjected to "an intense propaganda in favor of the Free French Forces," during which it was stated that the air force would not be rearmed by the Americans. "Some officers here who have waited a long time for the arrival of matériel, so that they can fight, imagine that, under General de Gaulle, that will go better and shoot off their mouths in front of excitable people," reserve Lieutenant Jacques Berger complained on 22 May 1943.[236]

Most *évadés* did not begin to reach Casablanca until July 1943, where an upgraded ceremony in the Gare Maritime now featured speeches by civilian and military officials, a guard of honor, and a band that played the "Marseillaise" and the "Marche Lorraine." After a "*lunch d'honneur*" that included a distribution of sweets and cigarettes, they were loaded onto trucks and taken to one of two camps, that reminded most *évadés* of their Spanish internment, to be vaccinated, interviewed by military police and intelligence, and given provisional identity papers. Volunteers or those deemed eligible for conscription were separated out and sent on to Marrakech for military induction.[237] Bacquier arrived in a convoy from Malaga to be "vomited" onto the quay at Casablanca with 2,000 other *évadés*. "[We] listened to the *Marseillaise* and welcoming speeches which at times sounded like apologies. And then we were locked into a camp [at Médiouna, a Casablanca suburb] surrounded by barbed wire guarded by Senegalese with bayonets on their rifles. For our own security! But they could at least have given us a blanket and two meals a day. For three weeks, I slept with an empty stomach between two mattresses." Bacquier continues:

> At night, the trucks of the 2ème DB, at the time organizing at Témara next to the ocean, waited in a depression for volunteers who, rightly disappointed by the official welcome, held onto their dream of *France libre*. I could easily have joined them: a hole in the barbed wire, crawl for 100 meters between two unmotivated sentries, leap over the ridge and done. Like all the volunteers from France, I was faithful to the cross of Lorraine. But *l'armée d'Afrique* was fighting in a very satisfactory manner in Italy, and that seemed probably the fastest way into combat, which is why we had left [France]. In short, I didn't join the 2ème DB. Second missed opportunity.

The primary purpose of Médiouna, a North African knockoff of London's Patriotic School, was to discover the identity of the person behind the invariably fabricated papers. Bacquier's "confession" was conducted before an overweight major whose breath smelled of absinth, but who, when he learned that Bacquier was a *normalien* whose father was a major of artillery, retained the presence of mind to ask: "What are you doing in this shithole?"[238]

Many of the less politicized *évadés* were stunned by the factionalism, backbiting, and lingering loyalty to "our God" Pétain they encountered at Médiouna, where the *évadés* were triaged.[239] It also offered proof that, despite the August 1943 "fusion" of Gaullist and Giraudist units, in practice clannish competitiveness lingered into the winter of 1943 and beyond. Some of this political hostility was imported by the *évadés* themselves. In a June 1943 letter, the French army liaison in Gibraltar reported that, among the latest group of *évadés*, that included twenty-two officers, "the attitude toward the regular French army stationed in North Africa is openly hostile, the product of ignorance and blind fanaticism."[240] Because the Gaullists and *l'armée d'Afrique* approached enlistment choices as a sort of plebiscite, like the "desertion crisis" that coincided with the closeout of the Tunisia campaign, the competition for relatively limited numbers of *évadés* assumed an exaggerated importance. In the view of Belot, more important for these young *évadés*, who had at enormous personal risk and hardship embarked upon the perilous trip through Spain and who were burning to fight, was to find a unit that would move them rapidly to the battlefield. As volunteers rather than conscripts, in theory *évadés* were allowed to choose their own unit. However, this option was abolished in September 1943. Former soldiers were assigned to their original service branch, while civilians were allowed to choose their arm: 40 percent chose the air force, 25 percent the navy, and only 15 percent the army. These were placed at the disposition of the General Staff for assignment, which produced serious discontentment among young *évadés*, "who make up 35% of the convoys" arriving at Casablanca via Spain and Portugal.[241] Bacquier's options of the air force or navy were eliminated by his poor eyesight. His seemingly irrefutable argument that, if he were to jump out of a plane, he would most probably find his way to earth with or without glasses, failed to persuade the recruiter for the paratroops – which was probably just as well, as French paratroops spent much of the war idling at airfields due to a lack of aircraft. The artillery would have pleased his father, but "it was rotten with Polytechnicians." The cavalry offered an assembly of equestrian snobs. "The engineers struck me as just a cushy job. I was unaware that they were organizing combat engineers." He was told that the Gaullist units – the Brigade de Tchad, the 1re DFL, and the 2e DB – were no longer accepting volunteers. So, by a process of elimination, *la biffe* (infantry) – in this instance, the 2e RTM at Marrakech – remained his only option. At least he was not assigned to an anti-aircraft unit, as were many *évadés* who had the temerity to express a preference for a Gaullist unit. "That was the way that the Vichy army punished the troublemakers who had pretentions to join *les Forces Françaises Libres*. There were incidents. I was told of an officer who slapped a volunteer who had a cross of Lorraine pined to his jacket." According to Bacquier, it almost came to a mutiny, that was defused only by de Lattre, himself an *évadé* of sorts, and the awarding of a special medal to the *évadés*. And, even though he was in an *armée d'Afrique* regiment, he insisted on wearing his lieutenant's stripes on his shoulder *à l'anglaise* in the Gaullist manner, rather than on his sleeve as was the practice in *l'armée d'Afrique*. "[The tailor] let out a sigh. But after all, it was *my* funeral!" As a result, his welcome in the mess was rather subdued.[242]

Bacquier was at least satisfied that he had been assigned to a prestigious combat regiment. At Casablanca, Michel Brousse and twenty *évadé* comrades had collectively volunteered for the paratroopers, or what at the time was called the "air infantry." Sent to an *armée d'Afrique* barracks at Blida, he found himself surrounded by "a gaggle of clapped-out officers and alcoholic sergeants." When the new arrivals expressed impatience to begin training, the sergeant major sermonized: "in the army you must never be overzealous, never ask questions, never try to understand. He explained to us that we would remain in barracks for a while, 'to recover from our time in the Spanish prison.' . . . In reality, we arrived in Blida like dogs in a game of bowls and we disturbed the peace of these gentlemen . . . [whose] only concern was to keep their spot in an inglorious barracks . . . We'd disturbed the army routine. We hadn't crossed Spain to molder in a barracks." The next day, together with a dozen new arrivals, Brousse deserted and made his way into Algiers along a highway hedged with anti-aircraft artillery (AAA) batteries, past "impressive American and British messes along the route, and fields stacked with munitions as far as the eye could see." Along the way, they met a commando who had just returned from Corsica. On 9 November, they all enlisted with Gambiez.[243] "The arrival in North Africa of the Free French forces and the *évadés* through Spain made the break with the French State [Vichy] unavoidable and formalized the union of all French forces," concludes Le Gac.[244]

The Feminization of *l'armée d'Afrique*

A dearth of specialists, even literate personnel, also forced the CFLN to contemplate female mobilization, thereby creating a third category of interloper that would ruffle *l'armée d'Afrique*'s traditions and outlook. Needless to say, female recruitment constituted an act of desperation rather than an initiative undertaken in a spirit of patriotism and gender equality. While the process of bringing females into the uniformed ranks of the armed forces would rattle the military customs of all belligerent nations, it was particularly culture-bending for imperial France. Indeed, the idea of the *levée en masse* had been to infuse the nation with a masculine identity through the citizen-soldier. With the French Revolution and its aftermath, military service became a rite of manhood, and the regiment a place where men merged their identity with that of the group to become warriors. As Joanna Bourke argues, combat offered a gender divide, the male equivalent of childbirth, a manifestation of virility to which women became mere spectators.[245] But this was a contemporary concept. Until the nineteenth century, women had played an integral role in warfare, as armies were essentially cities on the march, with women performing a myriad of roles short of actual fighting. Gender exempted one neither from the dangers of the battlefield, nor from the consequences of defeat.[246] However, in the wake of the Napoleonic era, increasingly the association of women with violence in the public arena came to be viewed as something perverse, even unnatural. The image of females in war recalled Amazons, prostitutes, transvestites, the fictitious *pétroleuses* of the Paris Commune, or the androgynous *cantinières*, who were phased out in the French army in 1914. The idealized image of the post-1918 woman was that of the war widow faithful until death, or the grieving mother who had sacrificed her sons so that the nation might survive.[247] Popular myth held that only men could be empowered by war. Through combat, men forge brotherly bonds inaccessible to civilians, and denied to women. The woman's traditional role was to unify the family, while the men secured the nation's independence and established a reputation for virile tenacity on the battlefield. Women in uniform seemed to pose yet another obstacle to France's campaign to reclaim the national self-respect which had been forfeited in 1940, and reestablish a narrative of French heroism and masculine identity, in the wake of national defeat, occupation, and the incarceration of a significant POW population. The feminization of war was a step toward "modernization" and equality in society that blurred the lines between soldier and civilian, between male and female, and disrupted the social order. The very act of putting women in uniform constituted an infringement on the idea of war as an exclusively male dominion.[248]

However, the idea of women in uniform was hardly unprecedented in France. The feminization of military service offered a vehicle through which women might subvert a paternalistic political system that locked them into a status of social and legal adolescence. Before 1914, French feminists had debated whether female conscription should serve as a prerequisite for suffrage. A widespread perception, especially on the left, that women were instinctively pacifists caused many to regard females in uniform as undesirable, even subversive and destabilizing for the *levée*. For these reasons, the acceptance of female recruitment required a transformation of public attitudes toward women in war. In 1914, French women had been catapulted to the center of the war effort. In all, 686,000 French women had been employed as auxiliaries in the First World War. By the war's end, 1,400 military hospitals were being run largely by women. Women replaced mobilized men as teachers and in the *Postes, télégraphes et téléphones* (PTT). However, apart from a few women such as Louise de Bettignies, who entered public consciousness as intelligence agents or activists in escape and evasion networks, women in war were still confined to traditional female roles like nurses, or to support functions in rear areas.[249] Of course, Mata Hari represented the reverse side of the coin, a Biblical update of woman as seductress and traitor.

The legal impediments to the incorporation of women into the French military had been partially cleared by the Joseph Paul-Boncour law of July 1938, which allowed a mobilization of the population "*sans distinction d'âge ni de sexe*." The law created a category called "*auxiliaires féminins des formations militaires*." From 31 January 1940, units of female drivers, first-aid workers, and nurses appeared, some organized through private initiatives like the Hadfield–Spears Ambulance Unit or the Red Cross. For instance, after a three-month-long preparatory course in Poitiers, volunteers for the Red Cross-supervised "*sections sanitaires automobiles*" (SSAs), which included Susan Travers, were organized for the planned intervention in Finland in February and March 1940, although they were repatriated by May and basically cut loose from any obligation.[250] From 21 April 1940, women could serve in the army administration, but the French created no equivalent of Britain's Auxiliary Territorial Service (ATS), which in 1939 already had enlisted 17,000 volunteers.[251] At the time of the Fall of France, the *Service de santé des armées* grouped 6,600 female volunteers as nurses and ambulance staff.[252] With the permission of their husbands – indeed, married women required their husbands' permission for most legal or administrative actions in France – women might also enlist as air raid wardens.[253] A 17 June decree even allowed the recruitment of female pilots. Although France's quick collapse had minimized the potential impact of this breakthrough, it demonstrated nevertheless that, unlike during the 1914–1918 conflict, the public was willing to envisage women in combat zones. Of course, the fear that military violence had jumped a firebreak to engulf the civilian population had become obvious with the realization of Total War, symbolized by the bombing of civilians in China and in the Spanish Civil War. Anxiety that defeat portended political collapse as a prelude to popular violence had offered appeasers their clinching argument in the chaos of June 1940.[254]

Vichy sought to reverse Republican-induced "decadence" through a remasculinization of French society, expressed through the *Chantiers*, sports events, leadership schools (*écoles des cadres*), and other feverishly virile projects. This would prove an uphill struggle for a government that had signed an armistice that allowed over a million and a half of its "vanquished" soldiers to toil in German factories, fields, and mines beneath a rising storm of Allied bombs, while their wellbeing was ineffectually defended by the Scapini mission. Women were to return to their traditional domestic roles. An April 1941 law made divorce more difficult to obtain, in part to ensure that wives of POWs and eventually those conscripted for STO remained faithful to their absent husbands.[255] An estimated 800,000 wives of POWs, many of whom were members of the *Fédération des femmes des prisonniers*, were meant to knit socks, write letters, and dispatch food parcels, while faithfully awaiting the return of their POW husbands. Vichy's scheme met only modest success. Despite Vichy opposition, 70,000 French women volunteered to work in Germany during the war, some of whom enlisted with the German Red Cross. A significant number of young women from Alsace-Moselle were conscripted by the Germans for war work. Others worked for the Wehrmacht or Abwehr in France or, according to some calculations, formed 15 percent of *la Milice*, admittedly a sprawling organization whose membership evinced an uneven level of commitment. At the same time, women are also calculated to have made up between 10 and 20 percent of the membership of resistance networks in France.[256]

The idea of women in uniform proved a hard sell in a country that hardly ranked in the feminist vanguard. De Gaulle had reluctantly acquiesced to the creation of a "*Corps féminin des Volontaires Françaises*," often referred to as the "*Corps féminin des FFL*" or "*corps des volontaires françaises*" (CVF) in November 1940, lest Frenchwomen in London simply disappear into the ATS or one of the other British female service branches. Its purpose was to liberate men for combat by standing up a militarized corps of women subject to most of the same disciplinary regulations as were men, to occupy at least fifteen support, administrative, and medical specialties.[257] However, for many, enlistment in a military force did not feel like emancipation. Enrolment was a particularly courageous act for French women in 1940–1943 because it violated at least two proscriptions – to flirt with danger by volunteering to enter war zones, and to engage with pariah organizations like *la France libre* or the CFA.[258] A third consequence for many middle-class women such as Susan Travers was that enlistment in a specialty other than nursing, or as a doctor or dentist, which was allowed but rare, mandated a sort of "*déclassement sociale*" as they were invariably assigned subordinate tasks. Despite being the daughter of a British naval captain, as a driver Travers was assimilated into the ranks of common soldiers, men who often resented her as an interloper and competitor. She eventually entered into an unhappy marriage with a sergeant, quite a demotion after having been regularly bedded by a future Marshal of France, as well as a legendary hero of the French Foreign Legion. As in the civilian sector, women did the same work as men but were paid less, so that cheap female labor suppressed wages. Females also occupied some of the safer, softer, rear-echelon "shirker" jobs coveted by some combat-shy men, who might express their antipathy through resentment, disloyalty, or spreading malicious gossip that was readily believed of women whose presence was at the very least an unwelcome trespass on male terrain, and even viewed as sabotage of French virility.

What eventually grew to around 2,500 CVF – others estimate more like 1,800 – women enlisted for the duration of the war plus three months, wore ATS-issued uniforms with an FFL insignia on the pocket, and, from November 1940, followed a three-week ATS training regimen of living in barracks, moving on the double, target practice, gymnastics, marching, military courtesies, etc. French drill was taught separately. Included was a course on military correspondence, bookkeeping, and first aid. Subsequent groups of female volunteers, raised mainly from a limited pool of French women living in London or married to British subjects, were trained in typing and stenography in both English and French, driving, mechanics, and cartography. Eventually, some females selected by the BCRA were sent to the paratroop school at Ringway to be trained in techniques of counterespionage, Morse, and radio operation. CVF recruits were eventually dispersed to various FFL units.[259]

But the process of creating female units was only gradually cobbled together, and contractual obligations at this stage appear to have been rather informal. On her return from Finland in May 1940, Travers had signed on as a "nurse" with what was to become *la France libre* at the rank of "sergeant with two-thirds a sergeant's pay," she remembered. Following the failure of the Dakar expedition, she and two other British female volunteers found themselves marooned in Brazzaville, "a seedy colonial town far from any action. As we were not real nurses, we weren't much use at serving the local population." Her two fellow "nurses" found jobs as typists at the local British consulate. Travers might have done the same, except that she did not know how to type, broke up with her British officer boyfriend, and in the meantime had developed an intense sexual attraction to Dimitri Amilakvari, a Georgian battalion commander in the Foreign Legion. So, in the tradition of Marlene Dietrich in pursuit of Gary Cooper in *Morocco*, Travers boarded a filthy troopship carrying Amilakvari and the 13ᵉ DBLE to the Horn of Africa via the Cape.[260]

The idea of women in uniform was transferred to AFN in the baggage trains of the Allies, although it was initially welcomed neither in *l'armée d'Afrique* nor in AFN's European community. As in France in 1939–1940, initial efforts to mobilize women were individual initiatives. From as early as 20 November 1942, Colonel, later General, Lucian Merlin created a *Corps féminin des transmissions* (CFT), in a belated and partial attempt to repair a particularly egregious signals inadequacy in French forces. Trained in their school at Douéra, an outlying Algiers suburb, on the latest American-supplied equipment as telephone and teletype operators, radio mechanics, translators, and "analytical secretaries," in the view of many, the CFT came to be seen as the most professional of the female military organizations, under the command of male officers. The CFT numbered 377 women in North Africa by April 1944, with 700 more in the field. Thirty "Merlinettes" recruited by the *Deuxième Bureau* were parachuted into occupied France, of whom seven were captured and executed by the Germans.[261]

In the United States, the heiress Florence Conrad formed the "Groupe Rochambeau," an ambulance corps eventually attached to Leclerc's 2e DB in 1944–1945 as the 1st Medical Company of the 13th Medical Battalion. Small sections of female auxiliaries were formed for the navy and air force. These groups quickly became known by their diminutives – *Merlinettes*, *Rochambelles*, *Marinettes*, *chaufferettes*, *filles de l'Air*, and so on. While these nicknames seemed to convey affection and even respect, in reality they sought to infantilize or diminish female contributions to the war effort. They also served to demonstrate how uncomfortable most men were with this female encroachment into a traditionally male space. Although, in January 1944, Commissioner for War André Le Troquer warned male personnel that "any inappropriate gesture, familiarity, harmful or ironic comment" toward their female subordinates and colleagues would be met with harsh punishment, diminutives might substitute for less flattering epithets soldiers applied to females in the ranks, among them "*bousilleuses*" (screw-ups), "*chaufferettes*" (a pun on female chauffeurs and warming pads), or "*pépées*" (babes). Superiors were addressed as "Madame," and other ranks as "Mademoiselle." Many treated this phenomenon of women in the military as a bureaucratic prank, while others decried the anomaly of enlisting females when so many male "shirkers" already crowded rear areas.[262]

Nevertheless, French mobilization required citizens capable of filling "*services civils auxiliaires*."[263] So a lack of female volunteers, like a scarcity of European cadres and even basic equipment like typewriters, presented severe impediments to rearmament. On 25 July 1943, the CFLN had ordered a preliminary census of French women potentially eligible to serve. Six weeks later, on 3 September 1943, that body discussed the possibility of military service for French women. Sensing a market, the *Chantiers* suggested creating a course for "Feminine Leaders" at Fort-de-l'Eau (Bordj el Kiffan) a western suburb of Algiers.[264] A 22 October 1943 ordinance signed by Le Troquer allowed for the mobilization of women, either as military volunteers or as "civil conscripts." The results of a census had shown that there were 48,000 European women in AFN born between 1899 and 1925 who did not yet occupy a military or civilian position, out of which the army wished to enlist 5,500 who had no children.[265] On 11 January 1944, the CFLN declared themselves in favor of universal conscription for women. However, the measure was applied on an individual rather than collective basis. Mothers, nuns, and *femmes de mauvaise vie*, including women who had served more than fifteen days' jail time, were excluded from volunteering, although some mothers clearly did enlist.[266] Female conscripts had to undergo a "discrete investigation into their morality and social milieu" in their first month of service. For this reason, while by some high estimates 20,500 women eventually served in some capacity with French forces, they did so as volunteers, unlike in Great Britain, where women became eligible for conscription with the second National Service Act of 1941, which extended conscription to British unmarried women and widows without children between the ages of twenty and thirty. British females were considered auxiliaries and were not issued weapons unless they requested them. The SOE began to recruit women from 1942, some of whom, like Odette Samson, Violette Szabo and Yvonne Cormeau, became legendary agents. In the view of the head of SOE's F (French) Section, Maurice Buckmaster, women could move more easily around occupied France, where military-age Frenchmen not in Germany as POWs or STO conscripts raised suspicion.[267]

In France, female volunteers were usually older than were men – average age 31.2 as opposed to 25.4 for men – and of a higher social background. Furthermore, 29 percent of female volunteers were married when enlisted, and 11 percent had children.[268] One problem with assessing the impact of women in the French military is that females could not legally become full members of a military service until 1951. The haphazard and piecemeal recruitment of women, often on the basis of individual or institutional initiatives like those of the Red Cross or outreach by particular branches of service such as signals, transportation, or the medical services, not to mention differing approaches by *la France libre* and *l'armée d'Afrique*, had created a tangle of status and contracts for women service members. On 26 April 1944, the *auxiliaires féminines de l'armée de terre* (AFAT, Figure 2.4) was created to merge the Gaullist CVF, those recruited in AFN, and women who had been incorporated into the *Forces françaises de l'intérieur* (FFI), the name officially given to the internal resistance in April 1944 to bring it under military jurisdiction. On 3 July, *les Formations féminines de l'air* came into being.[269]

Those associated with the regular forces had to sign enlistment contracts, wear uniforms, albeit without insignia of rank, and live in barracks. They were

Figure 2.4 AFAT in Brittany, 1944, with grenades attached to their belts. Uniforms were empowering, projecting a taboo image of sexual women living on the edge of danger, but having fun, that challenged conventional prejudice against women who trespassed on male territory. (Photo by Keystone-France /Gamma-Keystone via Getty Images)

required to salute officers, were subject to military discipline, and could even be sent into combat zones. They were also obliged to adhere to the idiosyncratic dress codes laid down by the "General Inspector of Feminine Personnel," Madame Marguerite Catroux, like wearing hairnets or a prohibition on wearing trousers in town, at dances, or in the mess. Lipstick was authorized so long as it was applied "in a very discreet manner."[270] Theoretically, women were not allowed to bear arms, although some formations were trained in target shooting. By some quirk of Cartesian logic, female volunteers were declared ineligible for the "*médaille des engagés volontaires*." However, unlike in Britain, where meritorious military service in the SOE might be rewarded with a civilian honor such as an MBE, in France women were authorized a gamut of military decorations. As a result, women made up 6–10 percent of French personnel decorated in the Second World War.[271]

Military rank became a more difficult issue than decorations. Technically, women remained female "auxiliaries" or "volunteers," not soldiers, demarcated by "*classe*" rather than by military rank, which potentially would in some circumstances have bestowed authority over their male counterparts.[272] As *la France libre*'s official *dompteuse*, the "active and authoritarian" Madame Catroux famously wore a star on her shoulder, the sign of a brigadier general in the American forces, but meaningless in the French military hierarchy. Her authority emanated from the prominent position occupied by her husband in Gaullist ranks, reinforced by her imperious pretense. Yet, regarded as a well-networked harridan, Madame Catroux was someone provoked at one's peril. The American founder of the ambulance detachment "Rochambelles," Florence Conrad, assigned herself the rank of "major," which upset many male soldiers. Undeterred, she proceeded to allocate military ranks in her unit, with the strict stipulation that her ladies were not to fraternize with any male of senior rank, an order that was assiduously ignored.[273] And, while not always rising to the level of the "mobile field wives" allegedly common in the Red Army, quite apart from romantic interests, women might seek protection or other advantages by becoming a senior officer's protégée. But all penalties flowing from this blossoming of emancipation were females' alone to suffer.

In February 1944, Personnel Director General Maurice Jurion reported that he simply lacked enough female personnel to meet an exploding demand for the sort of administrative, support, and medical services which women volunteers were eligible to fill.[274] General Merlin vigorously opposed the army's 26 May 1944 instruction to transform female auxiliaries into an autonomous, independent service for three reasons. The first was because the army had not authorized enough major equivalent ranks properly to supervise his burgeoning female signals service. Second, women lacked experience in exercising command in a military environment with which they were unfamiliar. A third reason was probably that Merlin wanted to control his own "auxillaries" rather than go to war with Madame Catroux over personnel assignments. In Merlin's view, women should be commanded by male officers of those units to which they had been assigned.[275] Complaints continued into 1944 that different offices were sharing a single typewriter, while officers themselves were typing out requisitions, manifests, correspondence, and so on because of a dearth of secretarial personnel, or because the army was unwilling or unable to recruit them.[276]

The more extensive recruitment of women into resistance networks benefited from several factors, among them an absence of institutional constraints and formalities; interpersonal relationships as a recruitment factor; the fact that war, occupation, and the large-scale export of Frenchmen to Germany as POWs or STO laborers had cast many women into male roles; the stigmatization of French "virility" in the wake of defeat through disarmament and relationships between German soldiers and French women; and a need for women as a cover for clandestine activities – for instance, according to Muracciole, women made up 18 percent of "*passeur*" networks on the demarcation line.[277] The concept of what contemporary feminists might call *la femme fondue* – that is, females who melted seamlessly into the anonymity of everyday life – was particularly valued in the internal resistance, where female operatives were less likely to be stopped and searched than were men. Unlike in AFN, women in metropolitan France could join the resistance without "detaching from society," an act much easier for men. Women also formed the bedrock of "*Résistance-mouvement*" – that is, a milieu of popular support that enabled resistance acts. Women defying the Occupation in the Metropole, even if merely placing flowers on *monuments aux morts* on 14 July or 11 November, were acclaimed as heroes. While, after the war, the *maquis* came to be lionized as part of a French resistance, at the time they were seen as a separate phenomenon, a burden on the social order that put many ordinary French men and women in the vicinity of *maquis* agglomerations at risk of ferocious Vichy and German reprisals. To join the *maquis* was to abandon security, to challenge the social order, and hence, for women, to forsake respectability, although some did serve the *maquis* as liaisons and nurses.[278]

In contrast, those volunteering to put on a uniform, to convoy wounded soldiers, to provide vital communication between and among military units, often at great danger to their lives, risked being shunned as harlots, lesbians, and women of dubious morals in search of sexual adventure. "In AFN in 1942, to put women in a uniform, submit them to a life and the military discipline of the barracks, camps, even combat zones, frightened families. 'My daughter, don't even consider it! What about her reputation!,'" Élodie Jauneau quotes a woman as saying.[279] And this parent was by no means an exception – in November 1943, the President of the Red Cross in Algiers protested the June decision to bring Red Cross nurses under direct medical service corps supervision, after parents complained that they had allowed their daughters to become Red Cross volunteers, not enlist in the army.[280] Because it was associated by *le gratin Algérois* with voluntary charity work, the Red Cross made enlistment acceptable for respectable, patriotic young women. But, since the abolition of *les cantinières* in the Great War, the only women under contract to support *l'armée d'Afrique* were those, mainly Muslim, in the *Bordel militaire de campagne* (BMC). Some parents feared that their daughters would be seduced by lesbians or taken advantage of by their superiors.[281]

However, attitudes began to change in Italy. "The integration of women in the medical battalions was a source of much criticism," wrote André Lanquetot. "Often we passed the ambulances. Girls drove them, our medical auxiliaries. At the beginning, we called them '*les chaufferettes*.' No longer. Everywhere, no matter the weather, they shuttled between the front and field hospitals.

Furthermore, often with a smile on their gaunt features. I take my hat off to them. They are real men!"[282] Jacques Schmitt, serving with the 7e RTA in Italy in 1943–1944, decried the "moralists" who complained about the "*chauffer-ettes*," who, in Schmitt's view, were "simply smashing: indefatigable, always smiling, they don't stop from morning till night."[283]

However, the incorporation of women into a militarized status was not linked to a push for female equality, but arose from the need for men-at-arms, competition from Allied armies, which were enlisting or at least employing French women in vital administrative roles in AFN, a military requirement for certain skills, and demands from women to serve.[284] For most female volunteers, patriotism provided the main motivation for enlistment. Also, at the end of the war, women wanted to have done something, to have made a contribution, and not to have been mere spectators to what was certainly the greatest event in a generation, perhaps ever. Enlistment offered a chance to remain within a social structure, while evading the constraints and social limitations imposed upon French women in AFN, perhaps escape an unhappy marriage, meet men, or maybe women, and travel. Some divorced women, or those whose husbands might be POWs, simply needed the work. The military offered a viable option, a "semi-unknown," where female volunteers would have food, shelter, a modest paycheck, and a basic safety net, while remaining within the boundaries of patriotic propriety. They would become feminists through their actions. In the military, they could participate in an adventure, flirting with danger, while having some sex along the way – "Up with the lark, in bed with the WRNS," became a *cliché* in the ATS, although being found "Pregnant Without Permission" merited immediate expulsion. One WAAF driver for Polish officers in London recounted "I have to say 'Yes, sir' all day and 'No, sir,' all night."[285] Suzanne Lefort-Rouquette's group of ambulance drivers in Tunisia even embraced the taboo of the fallen woman, adapting the marching song of the *Bats d'Af*, *l'armée d'Afrique*'s disciplinary battalions: "They call us warming pads/We have a bad reputation/But we don't care/they like us in the battalion."[286]

Women faced many impediments to enlistment. As with men, the recruitment of women in AFN in the autumn of 1943 was bedeviled by the Giraud–de Gaulle feud. Upon her arrival in AFN in September 1943, many *pied noir* women contacted Suzanne Torrès about the possibility of enlisting in the Groupe Rochambeau. However, once it was discovered in strongly Giraudist AFN that they had been assigned to Leclerc's 2e DB, the Rochambelles became the object of "a sort of animosity, distrust, jealousy" that dried up recruitment.[287] Despite the notion that AFN was devotedly Maréchalist, so strong was the demand among women in Casablanca to enlist in January 1943 that "it was decided to create a recruitment bureau next to each transportation corps squadron, staffed by a volunteer, preference being given to officers' wives, daughters, or widows. These bureaus were tasked with enlistment, taking information on candidates, and compiling dossiers under the orders and supervision of the transportation corps commander. Management of these bureaus was confided to a Madame Mahuzies."[288] Solange Cuvillier, who lived with her divorced mother, was studying for her baccalaureate exam in Casablanca when the Americans invaded. Because her dream was "to serve like a man," she, together with several other *lycée* students, including two daughters of generals, and perhaps Professeur Rolland's daughter as well, volunteered for classes at the Ambulance First Aid School, which had been set up in a requisitioned Catholic school. "The classes were tough, very tough: awakened by a bugle at six, the forty beds in the two dormitories had to be quickly tucked with hospital corners, obligatory gymnastics – no one exempted – driving classes, mechanics, motor maintenance, unannounced twenty-kilometer night marches in gas masks, navigation by the stars." A nurse provided basic first-aid lessons. Everyone took their turn peeling potatoes. And while an inspection found the food in the mess "very good and abundant," Cuvillier describes the menu as "rata" ("slop"). The final exam was to camouflage her ambulance while under machinegun fire. The ten top graduates were sent as instructors to Meknès. At the end of her course, Cuvillier signed a contract with the Navy transportation corps. At Mostaganem in Algeria, their unit, the *9e Bataillon médical*, which was attached to the 2e DIM, was equipped with new US ambulances. On 20 November 1943, they shipped out of Bizerte on a Landing Ship, Tank (LST) bound for Naples.[289]

However, after an initial wave of enlistment enthusiasm, by May 1943, recruitment in Casablanca was in precipitous decline.[290] Why is unclear. Certainly, there was not a deep reservoir of European women between the ages of eighteen and forty-five in Casablanca willing to volunteer. Nor, as Cuvillier suggests, was the course a pushover. The washout rate at the Ambulance School seems to have been high – on 10 May 1943, officials reported that, of twenty recent enlistees, seven had failed, four had resigned, and two more had announced their imminent departure, leaving a graduating class of seven. Serious accidents had become so problematic that women drivers had been limited to a 100-kilometer range. Nor did the army have enough ambulances for them to drive.[291] However, those who stuck with the course seemed to take great pride in their achievement, because "the recruitment of ambulance drivers in Morocco took the country's best feminine elements largely because of the reputation of SANA [the *Section automobile nord-africaine*]. This name was adopted in the different transportation squadrons for ambulance drivers. Transportation officers were very conscious of differentiating ambulance from HV [heavy vehicles] drivers and hoped that a special sky-blue crest would be approved quickly." Madame Catroux agreed that the ambulance corps should not be assimilated into transportation corps drivers, "whose moral conduct is grandly deficient."[292]

Nevertheless, even if women like Susan Torrès found the term "auxiliary" insulting, military uniforms were empowering. Weeklies such as *Life* or *Yank* published picture spreads on female soldiers that depicted them much like fashion models in elegant uniforms and shoulder bags, posing beneath palm trees in exotic Algiers, surrounded by dashing male officers. This was an image of glamour that Madame Catroux was eager to promote. In September 1943, Torrès was kept waiting for three hours in "la Reine Margot's" outer office in Algiers. But the no doubt intentional delay gave her time to admire "the numerous very elegant and busy young women in uniform."[293] However, the reality behind the magazine picture spreads and "Mad Cat's" coiffed and stylishly uniformed receptionists was somewhat different. On the basis of projections of 11,000 women incorporated into the French forces, the US Army had dispatched 11,500 sets of Women's Army Corps (WAC) and superseded blue Army Nurse Corps uniforms to AFN. Unfortunately, the Americans failed to supply female underwear, scarce items in AFN by 1943. So, women either supplied their own underwear, or made do with male undergarments.[294] Nor was this simply a French problem – at Bir Hakeim, for instance, Travers messed with the men, and slept alone in her car wrapped in a sheepskin coat. But it took a special dedication to fight the entire Western Desert campaign without a brassiere, while piloting a mechanically temperamental, requisitioned British civilian vehicle over a treacherous, uneven desert terrain.[295]

A second problem with US-supplied clothing and footwear was that French men and women were simply smaller on average than North Americans, so that fully a quarter of the items supplied could not be used, at least by the French. For instance, at the end of her course, Cuvillier and her classmates were issued WAC uniforms, together with men's boxer shorts and undershirts – "we were swimming in our masculine equipment: the boxer shorts reached up to our neck, the undershirt . . . went down to our calves . . . the most appreciated part was without a doubt the beddingroll, a practical, deep, waterproof sleeping bag. Throughout the war, it became the secure, soft nest into which we slid often with all our clothes on for a brief respite . . . A part of the US WAC kitbag included a fur-lined jacket, battledress, and boots, and French army leggings. *Adieu féminité*!"[296] Madame Catroux complained of the need for a "central service for women's clothing" because women were forced to modify their US-issued uniforms. They should also be given an allowance for underwear, which they had to purchase themselves, or it could be provided through the local "Assistance Service for the Mobilized." Although the women of Algiers had been unstinting in donating their surplus underwear, she described the lack of generosity in the more *Maréchalist* Oran as "criminally negligent." A special shop had been organized for the CEF, where female auxiliaries could purchase needed clothing items, and, during their passage through Britain prior to D-Day, Conrad managed to equip her ladies with underwear purchased through the NAAFI, even though they still wore men's trousers and overalls.[297] "The question of tailored uniforms is of great importance, because badly dressed women wear out their uniforms, don't take care of them, and feel demeaned," Madame Catroux insisted. In the field especially, it was simply not "decent" to send young women into military camps indifferently clothed.[298] It may be that men were attracted to women who projected sexuality and strength through masculine uniforms of pants, oversized shirts, and boots. Nevertheless, there were limitations – Torrès overheard a doctor on the phone issuing invitations for a party: "There will be some Rochambelles, but also some real women!"[299]

Officers' wives found these women in uniform threatening, often with good reason. Women in the ranks were also a source of friction because men competed for their attentions. Diego Brosset, who commanded the 1re DFL in Italy, complained to his superior Larminat that the presence of women had created jealousies and discord in his division.[300] Juin agreed, decrying the fact that nineteen officers in his CEF also had wives who were volunteer female auxiliaries in Italy. In his view, not only did this create a privileged category of personnel, but also it might distract them from their jobs. Furthermore, in the General's view, there was far too much fraternization when officers and NCOs regularly invited female personnel to dine in the mess. They also sparked ridicule when, to be gallant, officers lent a hand to unload trucks or helped female personnel to pitch their tents. "These practices must cease," he ordered, "if only to preserve the prestige and dignity of the officer's position in the eyes of the soldiers."[301] In fact, if Juin had complaints about women in the Italian Theater of Operations, he might have started with the Commander of the 2nd Moroccan ID (2e DIM), whose daughter, "Mademoiselle Dody," had also volunteered for service in Italy. What the soldiers saw was a group of women who might be quietly kitting while sitting on the running boards of their ambulances, but, when on alert, they went in under fire to recover the wounded, who were often caked with mud and feces, infested with vermin, and had had half their face blown off. And then they drove them through the night over broken roads, bypassing bridges knocked out by the fighting, to French field hospital 425, or, if that were overcrowded, to the American hospital at Bagnoli, which at least had antibiotics.[302]

One problem was that, by treating women as auxiliaries rather than proper soldiers, it was not clear to whom they reported in the military hierarchy, especially in the wake of Le Troquer's 26 May 1944 instruction that declared feminine personnel part of "autonomous units rigorously independent of all masculine authority."[303] While Merlin kept his female operators under the iron thumb of the Signals Corps, it was unclear whether drivers answered to the Red Cross, the *Inspectrice du personnel féminin* Madame Catroux, or the corps to which they were assigned – transportation, medical, corps of translators, signals, AFAT, and so on. In November 1943, "Mad Cat" complained all the way to the Commissar of Defense about one of her nurses who had failed to report to her assignment in Blida. "For the last three months, this nurse has refused to work," Catroux seethed, complaining that her conduct might prove contagious.[304] "It has been pointed out by several transportation corps officers that, once assigned [to a unit], these drivers become so jealously reliant on the commanding officer of their unit that it becomes impossible for their former commanders to punish them if warranted," read a complaint from Morocco.[305] No fool, Susan Travers' trysts with *la crème de la France libre* kept even the formidable Madame Catroux at bay – despite her best efforts to bring Travers to heel, in 1942, "Mad Cat" was reduced to alerting Madame Koenig, then living in Marrakech, that she should settle into Cairo's Shepard's Hotel to keep an eye on her philandering husband. In July 1943, Brosset complained that "Queen Margot," whom even the diplomatic Harold Macmillan had pronounced "*une mauvaise langue*," was again retailing rumor that the smoldering affair between Koenig and "Miss Travers" had reignited at the conclusion of the Tunisia campaign.[306] While her purpose was unclear, it was probably connected to one of her serial schemes to promote her husband's ambitions. In any case, a sex scandal was the last thing that Fighting France needed in the middle of the "fusion" of the two French forces, the rearmament of the unified French army, and the Giraud–de Gaulle fisticuffs within the CFLN.

In Algiers, Suzanne Lefort-Rouquette had been reeled in by a poster urging "French women, enlist. You will free up a combatant." She was assigned to the 27th Transportation Company. Socially, the thirty women in her section were a mixed bag that included daughters of senior officers and a police commissioner, but also an ironing woman, a stock clerk, two eighteen-year-old girls, and a "grandmother" of forty. About one-third were married and the average age was twenty-two. They departed for El Kef in Tunisia in a third-class carriage under a female "lieutenant" who forbade them to play cards or fraternize with the men, even when invited to dine in the officers' mess. In Tunisia, they were put in trucks and taken to their destination along rutted roads past burned-out tanks. Their reception at the Division Welvert (Constantine Division) rated somewhere between indifference and overt hostility. Because their arrival was a surprise, they unpacked their kit and pitched their tents for the night, with no offers of male assistance. The next day, male ambulance drivers, obviously upset because they had been "freed up" for combat, grudgingly surrendered their vehicles. In fact, the women discovered that some of these drivers had sabotaged the engines by slipping cigarette paper into the contact breakers – "What a bunch of feminists our Frenchmen!" "Behind the wheel of these scrap heap survivors, with our overly large overcoats, squaddy caps and *clochard* boots, we were the very picture of the poverty of *l'armée d'Afrique* at the time." Vehicles were inspected each morning to make sure they were clean, while drivers had "to keep their hair covered and their discrete charms out of sight." Free time was gobbled up by obligatory gymnastics, courses in mechanics, and "applied topography."[307]

Upon arrival in a combat zone, what had heretofore been merely an uncomfortable adventure turned deadly serious. Just because they worked "behind the lines" did not mean that female volunteers did not require nerves of steel. Travers' combat experiences at Bir Hakeim were perhaps exceptional. But going astray in the featureless and vast Western Desert became a common and unsettling experience for drivers, especially as, given an absence of "front lines," one might easily blunder into a caravan of Axis soldiers over the next rise. Driving at night without headlights could be particularly terrifying, especially as a wrong turn might pitch one headlong into a minefield. At night, this often required that a soldier walk in front of the vehicle with a white handkerchief to navigate between the tapes that marked cleared passages. In Italy, the wounded in the back of an ambulance driving in blackout conditions along washboard roads might suddenly be jolted by a violent slamming on of the brakes, followed by a conversation between the driver and the nurse in thick *pied noir* accents. "Oh, Guite … Look, I'd say the bridge is gone." The passengers would hear a door open as Marguerite went to inspect. "Oh yeah. You were smart to stop. There's a big hole six meters in front." Then the passengers lying on their stretchers in the back, more traumatized than the two women, began to offer suggestions for alternative routes.[308] Even on tiny Elba in June 1944, Lefort-Rouquette became so disoriented that one of her wounded German passengers had to direct her back to her own lines.[309]

The employment of French women by US forces in AFN as translators and secretaries had absorbed many potential volunteers for French forces. Because these women were vital both administratively and as linguistic and cultural interpreters, US forces were reluctant to surrender them to *l'armée d'Afrique*. French women serving with the Americans were handed significant power as administrative advisors and cultural mentors, were probably rewarded with more respect in the office, enhanced pay, and better food in the mess, and above all were spared "Queen Margot's" eccentric and hectoring directives. As a result, the French command listed these French women in US service in the category of "special assignment."[310] Because the enlistment process for women both in London and in AFN had been ad hoc and piecemeal, in December 1943, a *Direction des personnel du corps féminin* was created to regularize conditions of service and pay rates. By that time, 3,100 French women were already in uniform and 1,700 more were in the process of induction as nurses, interpreters, signals operatives, drivers, and secretaries.

While *pied noir* traditionalism and Mediterranean mores were blamed for the fact that relatively few women had been recruited in AFN, at the

Liberation, the mainland proved equally resistant. While resistance networks incorporated an estimated 10–20 percent females, few FFI groups included their female members with them when they "amalgamated" into Jean de Lattre de Tassigny's *1ère armée* in the autumn and winter of 1944–1945, in part because the army had no positions for them or did not care to create any. Nor was the Gouvernement provisoire de la république française (GPRF) eager to mobilize women, despite the desperate requirements for nurses, drivers, radio operators, clerical staff, and other logistical positions. The 4,000 women in French uniform in October 1944 doubled to 8,000 by January 1945. As with men, many women volunteered for service without having been a member of a resistance network or a *maquis*.

In the middle of December 1944, the GPRF standardized enlistment "*pour la durée de la guerre*" in the AFAT as in the regular army. On 20 January 1944, Le Troquer announced that, as equal members of French society, women were henceforth obliged to perform military service. Although female conscription was never enforced on the mainland, its theoretical possibility required the services to acquire an organization, a command structure, schools, and an inspectorate that more closely assimilated female personnel into regular army institutions and practices, which had been the purpose of AFAT.[311] The First French Army, desperate for nurses and other support staff, complained of the Himalayan bureaucratic barriers to female enlistment, beginning with the requirement to produce a "*certificate de bonne vie et mœurs*." In the chaos of the Liberation, with prefectoral administrations in turmoil, public transportation virtually non-existent, and FFI vigilantes shaving the heads of "horizontal collaborators," it was unclear – exactly – who was qualified to vouch for female virtue.[312] Having a full head of hair offered a good first start.

Comparing female participation in the war is a somewhat artificial exercise, as different countries came into the war at different times, had military services of varying dimensions, with different requirements, and in some cases had larger populations to draw on than did France. Also, while the experience of war served to unite the populations of most of the major belligerents, war, defeat, occupation, a large POW population, Vichy's policy of collaboration, the de Gaulle–Giraud dispute, the dangers of arrest and deportation attached to resistance activities, and the more restricted status both socially and legally of females in France served to divide the French and encourage a passivity that resulted in "attentisme" in much of the population, even in North Africa. In the United States, mobilization did not hit its pace until 1943. Nor did the United States require large numbers of anti-aircraft batteries for home defense that employed women, as did Britain and Germany. Many Soviet women rushed recruitment stations in the wake of Barbarossa in June 1941, only to be turned away initially. However, by the spring of 1942, women began to be conscripted *en masse* into the Red Army, numbers rising to 900,000.[313] As with

Frenchmen, until the Liberation, it became virtually impossible for French women to enlist in the uniformed French services unless they were already outside the Hexagon. Nevertheless, French women made up an estimated 2–3 percent of the uniformed French armed forces, although the percentages were higher in the internal resistance.[314] And, while this percentage fell within the norms of female participation in the armed forces of some other belligerent countries, in absolute terms, the numbers of French women in uniform were far smaller.[315]

Conclusion

The Tunis victory parade, followed by the "fusion" of the Free French and *l'armée d'Afrique*, symbolized a transition between the old and the new French army, an upgrade made possible by the January 1943 Anfa Conference. Anfa had several purposes, one of which was to lay the foundation for a modern French military, so that French troops might take part in the liberation of their country, and France could assume its "place among the democratic nations of the world." But, for this to happen, the French exile movements of de Gaulle and Giraud needed to cooperate. With Vichy's armistice army disbanded and its fleet scuttled, at the end of the Tunisia campaign, France in effect fielded three "armies" – two in AFN, while a third resistance army was mobilizing within the Hexagon. How to coordinate, "fuse," and "amalgamate" these three forces would preoccupy French leaders, especially de Gaulle, who sought a military force to impose order and waylay any Allied attempt to impose a political solution on liberated France, as they had done in AFN and subsequently Italy. Rather than a clean break with the past and the resurrection of a French union, the Tunis victory parade instead had showcased the gulf in spirit and outlook – indeed, the bad blood – that divided the FFL and *l'armée d'Afrique*.

A second problem that Anfa posed for France's military renaissance was that, although AFN had a fairly significant manpower pool, it lacked an infrastructure and a large educated settler population able to serve as cadres and as technical specialists for a largely indigenous army. This created a dilemma, because the rebuilding French military was forced to rely on hitherto marginal, even spurned sources of recruitment – Jews, *évadés de France*, and women – or further compromise France's effort to reclaim its great power status. While a Gaullist manufactured "desertion crisis" at the end of the Tunisia campaign was more provocative than substantive, voluntary troop transfers from *l'armée d'Afrique* to FFL units were meant to advertise the Gaullists' moral ascendency over their Giraudist rivals. A similar competition ensued for the trickle of *évadés de France* to Casablanca via Spain. While the numbers involved were relatively small, and the enlistment decision of most recruits usually turned more on circumstance than on politics, it showcased two things. First, there was a rivalry, tinged with rancor, between the two factions of the French army that would linger until the war's end, and become even more complex when the FFI were added to the mix. Second, these minor "crises" highlighted just how diminutive French forces actually were in the larger context of the war, and how desperate they were for literate cadres.

De Gaulle's 30 May 1943 appearance in Algiers launched his struggle with Giraud for control of the CFLN, which would give him the whip hand in rearming and expanding the French military to enhance France's status among the Allies, and a better position from which to steer France's destiny on liberation. With de Gaulle's ascendency, it quickly became apparent that French and Allied priorities would diverge. While the Americans envisaged eleven hard-hitting French combat divisions with requisite support and logistical services to grind down the Wehrmacht and allow US manpower allocation to favor sea and air forces, de Gaulle understood that the Allies were going to win the war with or without the French. Therefore, his goals became the preservation of the empire; restoration of order and the State upon liberation; and insuring France's post-war interests in Germany.

3 Triumph and Dishonor in Italy

As George Marshall and other military chiefs had feared, the commitment at Anfa to pursue Mediterranean operations acquired its own momentum and spun off its unique sets of problems. The Mediterranean was viewed as a supremely "political" theater, where deals had to be cut with unscrupulous and opportunistic characters like Darlan and Italian Prime Minister General Pietro Badoglio, where pretentious upstarts like de Gaulle had to be coddled and appeased, where a fissiparous French empire, with its racial and religious rifts, and economic underdevelopment, had to be buttressed. Roosevelt's promise to rearm and rehabilitate a factionalized and querulous French military, which was seemingly capable only of defeat or scuttle, seemed especially incomprehensible. However, rather than gratitude for American generosity, the echo in Washington reverberated with de Gaulle's tedious grievances about US violations of French sovereignty, lack of consultation on Alliance policy issues, secrecy, exclusion from operational planning, and so on. From an Alliance perspective, the French seemed parochial, mercurial, suspicious, technologically and doctrinally backward, and insufficiently committed to the West's democratic crusade. Instead of getting on with the defeat of the Axis, de Gaulle prioritized imperial restoration, the liberation of France, and the security of France's position in Europe. Juin's hopes that rearmed French troops might be included in Patton's Seventh Army for Operation Husky, the 9 July 1943 invasion of Sicily, were scuttled for "logistical" reasons. In the event, only a few *tabors* of Moroccan *goums*, who had impressed Patton in Tunisia, saw action in Sicily. Nor had the French as yet completed amphibious training, which was the excuse advanced by Allied Forces Headquarters (AFHQ) for excluding them from Avalanche, an operation that Juin confessed had caught him by surprise.[1]

One of the strategic opportunities that yawned at the end of the Tunisia campaign was the possibility of knocking Italy out of the war. Even before "Tunisgrad," followed by the loss of Sicily, had cascaded Italy toward certain defeat, King Victor Emmanuel and senior fascist officials had begun to grope for an exit from the war. Churchill deplored the Italians as rank opportunists, and brushed aside these tentative exploratory advances. But, with Torch, opposition to Mussolini gained momentum. By the end of the Tunisian campaign, an estimated 400,000 Italian soldiers serving in North Africa had become prisoners of war (POWs). The Italian merchant marine had lost 955,644 tons of shipping. What was left of the Regia Aeronautica struggled to prevent US Army Air Force (USAAF) bombing attacks. On 24 July, Mussolini was arrested and incarcerated as he exited a meeting of the Fascist Grand Council. A new government was formed under Badoglio, the former Chief of Staff sacked following the poor performance of Italian troops in the war against Greece in 1939–1940. Badoglio proceeded to disband the fascist party, and deployed the army against an explosion of strikes and demonstrations that erupted in the wake of Mussolini's ouster. On Sicily, entire battalions had surrendered to Anglo-American forces, often with their commanders at their head, while the population had greeted the Anglo-Americans as liberators. Convinced that the removal of Mussolini meant that peace was only a matter of days away, soldiers rebelled against their officers, which caused the Italian elite to fear that they might join with striking workers to foment revolution.[2] Concerned that "chaos, bolshevization or civil war" might engulf Italy, the two Western Allied leaders ordered the Allied bombing of Milan, Genoa, and Turin to quell worker unrest and bolster the authority of the Badoglio government, with which they had initiated secret armistice negotiations. Hoping to avoid a repeat of the Darlan fiasco, Roosevelt's foreign policy advisor Sumner Wells laid down the Italian government's post-surrender scenario. Anti-fascist exiles such as Count Carlo Sforza were thought to lack the experience and national following immediately to assume the reins of government. The Italian people were not to be consulted, in part out of fear that chaos – even revolution – might ensue should democracy suddenly descend upon a country long gripped in fascism's steel talons. Instead, the decision was to opt for continuity by retaining monarchical principles and the framework of government, which could then gradually be cleansed of its fascist features.[3]

Hitler denounced Mussolini's removal as a "betrayal," and Badoglio's assurances that Italy would continue to fight at Germany's side as "untruthful nonsense." Sniffing treachery, Berlin began to prepare Operation Alaric, a plan to take control of northern Italy. The sixteen German divisions rushed into Italy caused the Allies rapidly to curtail talks with the Italians and accelerate invasion plans before German commander Albert Kesselring could complete his defenses. On 3 September, as Montgomery's Eighth Army crossed the Strait of Messina to descend upon Calabria, the Italian government agreed to an abbreviated "short terms" armistice document. Badoglio insisted that the armistice be kept secret, ostensibly to give his government time to prepare to defend Rome with a reinforcement of US paratroops. Instead, Badoglio spent his time organizing his own flight to safety. True to form, when Eisenhower announced the armistice on 8 September prior to

Avalanche – the Anglo-American landing at Salerno just south of Naples – the Italian Prime Minister, the king, several military ministers and the Italian chief of staff bolted for Brindisi, leaving their military forces leaderless and without orders, most to be disarmed and shipped to Germany as POWs *sans* Geneva protections.[4]

The French *Comité français de libération nationale* (CFLN) seemed alert to an endgame being played out on the peninsula. News of Mussolini's overthrow had triggered a 2 August demand by de Gaulle that the CFLN be associated with any Allied armistice negotiations, so that France might seek "preliminary and legitimate reparations" for what its government in exile regarded as Italy's stab in the back of 10 June 1940. For this reason, the surprise 8 September 1943 announcement by Eisenhower of the Italian surrender stoked anger in Algiers, where it was seen as yet another Allied-induced "humiliation" for France. A 14 September CFLN request that France be consulted in any subsequent negotiations about "political, economic or financial" conditions imposed on Italy was also ignored when, on 29 September, at the insistence of London and Moscow, the Badoglio government was forced to sign in Malta a more punitive "long terms" of surrender. These were also kept secret from CFLN commissar for foreign affairs René Massigli. Roosevelt's policy of "unconditional surrender" announced at Anfa had lasted barely eight months, so that Eisenhower continued to refer to the "long terms" as "additional conditions" added to the Cassibile document, rather than "terms of surrender." The CFLN was further distressed when, on 13 October, the Allies accorded Italy "co-belligerent" status in the wake of Badoglio's declaration of war on Germany. Not only did this "erase the frontier between vanquished and victor" in French eyes, it also threw into question the status of 1,800 Italian officers and 42,000 enlisted men held as POWs in French custody that the CFLN refused to release to Badoglio's royal army, even after its soldiers were attached to Mark Clark's Fifth US Army from December 1943, where they were employed mainly in police and support roles. Although France was given a seat on the Advisory Council for Italy, which was formed to coordinate Allied policy on military issues, the CFLN persisted in its refusal to recognize the new Italian government until it renounced fascism and disavowed the invasion of 1940.[5]

The Liberation of Corsica

Although Corsica barely merits a footnote in the history of the Mediterrean war, its liberation was important in the French context for at least three reasons. First, Corsica exposed the French military's ongoing operational limitations at this stage of the war before the Anfa reforms kicked in, and the dangers of unilateral action in the absence of robust Allied – especially American – operational and tactical support. That "Operation Vesuvius," the codename for the invasion, did not propel the French into disaster was due to two factors. First, the Germans had no intention of defending Corsica, but instead used *l'Île de la beauté* as a lilly pad across which to hop its Sardinia garrison to bolster the defense of the Italian mainland. Second, ironically the French were given critical assistance by the defection of Corsica's Italian garrison, that upgraded a diminuative invasion force with critical manpower and artillery support.

A second reason for Corsica's importance was that it demonstrated both the military limitations and the political risks of a strategy that harnessed popular resistance as a force multiplier beyond Murphy's limited "Group of Five" conspiracy for Torch. Corsica offered a dry run for a much more expansive campaign by the "interface services" of the Special Operations Executive (SOE), Office of Strategic Services (OSS), and Bureau central de renseignements et d'action (BCRA) to organize and militarize growing popular resistance in France, and to incorporate resisters into planning for Operations Overlord and Dragoon to be executed in the summer of 1944. Unfortunately, armed civilian resistance in Corsica failed to supply the critical tactical and operational benefits that French decision-makers in Algiers had hoped it would. However, this lesson was ignored for several reasons. First of all, popular resistance continued to balloon on the French mainland in 1943–1944, as did political pressure from diplomatic, intelligence, and special operations organizations, not to mention Churchill, to fold resistance in France into operational planning for the liberation. To this was added the fact that de Gaulle required a robust resistance myth as evidence of his popular support in order further to undermine Vichy's legitimacy, to bolster France's political standing with the Allies, and to associate the French people with their own liberation. He also aspired to assemble a muster of battle-tested maquisards – even the concept was Corsican! – to reinforce and expand the ranks of the regular French army once it splashed ashore to liberate the Hexagon and carry the fight across the Rhine. On the model of Tito's Yugoslavia, a further aspiration was to create resistance "cleared zones" that might allow the CFLN to establish a political presence in France independently of Allied operations. However, Corsica revealed the potential risks of arming and empowering local actors whose independent political agendas might complicate the restoration of the French State, which was de Gaulle's primary goal. Therefore, the activities of the Anglo-American "interface services," who monopolized communications and funneled cash, arms, and military advice to networks of leaders and resistance groups, would become yet another source of strain between de Gaulle and the Allies. Finally, a third consequence of Vesuvius was that it provided the pretext to allow de Gaulle to exile Giraud from the CFLN's decision-making apparatus, thus consolidating his hold over France's exile regime.

In the wake of Torch, and in the midst of the Tunisia campaign, French planners began to consider how, and in what circumstances, to accomplish the liberation of Corsica, that, along with Sardinia and Sicily, Churchill had identified as a prime target at Anfa.[6] Until this point, the Italians had followed their usual incremental strategy to increase the number of Italian Control Commission inspectors beyond the agreed limit, from thirty-seven in September 1940 to fifty-one by April 1941.[7] However, Torch and the subsequent Axis occupation of the *zone libre* had triggered a military invasion of Corsica that eventually swelled to four Italian divisions numbering 80,000 soldiers. The Italian administration of Corsica had defined three priorities: advance irredentism, silence pro-French Corsicans, and fortify the island to resist an Allied invasion. In the short term, Rome preferred to enlist pro-Italian Corsicans as sources of support and intelligence, rather than to devise an energetic propaganda campaign in favor of integration with Italy. Well informed by long observation of island politics, from January 1943, the Italian secret police, the *Organizzazione per la Vigilanza e la Repressione dell'Antifascismo* (OVRA), worked in conjunction with Italian military counterintelligence, the *Servizio Informazione Militari* (SIM), to prepare for integration with Italy by eliminating irredentism's most prominent opponents, including members of resistance networks, through arrests, trials, internments (often on Elba), and deportations to the mainland.[8]

This Italian occupation infused new energy into a resistance which, largely cut off from groups on the French mainland, heretofore had engaged in propaganda or thwarting the activities of the Turin armistice commission. Corsican subsidiaries of French resistance groups on the mainland – Combat, Franc-tireur, and Libération – all lost members to this Italian crackdown. Resisters who avoided capture limited their activities to intelligence collection. The exception was the small but active Front national (FN), the grass-roots movement of the Parti communiste français (PCF). Unified under a communist schoolteacher, Arthur Giovoni, the FN's leadership survived because it respected the security requirements of a clandestine existence. Broken into five-man cells, communists secured FN leadership positions, while non-communists were assigned local and logistical responsibilities. Centered on Bastia, the FN managed to preserve its structure and even grow its membership through its youth organization, the *Front patriotique des jeunesses communistes*, not simply in the larger towns but also down to the village level, by emphasizing a program of the struggle of all patriots against the invader, and the destruction of Vichy. The FN's main activity was to sabotage Italian communications. But it gradually drew its members, including significant numbers of women, into increasingly dangerous activities, such as collecting and securing weapons shipped by the Allies to the island.[9]

Torch triggered an interest in Corsica, as well as Crete and Sardinia, viewed as potentially logical next steps in a reconquest of the central Mediterranean. However, the Quadrant (Quebec) Conference of 11–24 August 1943 focused on Italy and the timing of Overlord. Because Corsica offered both a strategic base to pursue the war in the Mediterranean and a stepping stone to the liberation of the mainland, the Giraudist *Service de renseignements* (SR) and Gaullist BCRA competed to create resistance networks on the island to assist in what would become a "precocious" liberation in September–October 1943. Algiers collected intelligence on Italian dispositions on the island, but also sought to carry out sabotage, and to organize the reception and distribution of arms delivered via parachute or submarine. In December 1942, the SR dispatched a mission coded Pearl Harbor under Major Roger de Saule, a Belgian whose real name was Robert de Schrevel, that included three Corsicans, as well as an American radio operator supplied by the OSS. Pearl Harbor was able to relay information supplied by a contact in the Corsican police, until the radio operator was denounced and arrested in June 1943.[10]

The BCRA mission, named Sea Urchin, under the command of Ajaccio native François (Fred) Scamaroni, was landed on 7 January 1943 from the submarine *HMS Tribune*. Scamaroni soon complained to Algiers that "de Saule" was working closely with the FN to marginalize his Gaullist mission. Both Scamaroni and his radio operator were arrested in the middle of March. One version holds that Scamaroni was drawn into a trap when a Blackshirt colonel offered to sell him the defense plans of the island. Another was that his radio operator, invariably the weak link in all resistance networks, was insufficiently security-conscious. Whatever the reason, the result was that, after being horribly tortured, Scamaroni committed suicide in his Ajaccio prison, leaving the Giraudist SR's Pearl Harbor as the sole mission on the island. The BCRA's unfounded conclusion was that the SR, in cooperation with the FN, planned to implant a Giraudist regime in the wake of the island's liberation.[11]

In April 1943, "de Saule" was replaced by Gendarme Major and Corsica native Paulin Colonna d'Istria. Colonna d'Istria felt that he had no choice but to strike an agreement with the FN for "cooperation without subordination." In this way, the minority communists were able to unify a resistance movement around a strategy of "national insurrection," as well as acquire significant armaments from the SOE through Pearl Harbor. For the Giraudists, a popular uprising would serve the tactical purpose of disorganizing the defense to facilitate an invasion by conventional forces. In fact, some in the FN leadership calculated naively that a "national insurrection" carried out independently of an Allied invasion would deliver political control of the island to the communists, that they could maintain at least until the liberation of the mainland and the return of a French administration.[12] Giraud kept the information about Colonna d'Istria's work secret from the CFLN, although de Gaulle may have been made aware through Scamaroni that the Giraudist SR was active in Corsica. In July and August 1943, without informing either de Gaulle or the CFLN, Giraud's secret service had been busy arming the FN with radios and 8,000 Sten guns,

1,000 carbines, 150 *mitrailleuses*, 98 Bren guns, and "between 12 and 36 mortars," which were infiltrated into the island either by parachute or via the submarine *Casabianca*, a survivor of the High Seas Fleet's collective Toulon suicide.[13]

Algiers planners conceptualized the invasion from an operational perspective. Their working assumption was that Axis forces would defend the island, supported by air and sea from Italy. Therefore, Ajaccio offered a vital campaign priority in their eyes because it was leeward from Italy and its harbor was essential to supply a phased campaign to conquer an island cluster of sea cliffs, rugged escarpments, and precipitous valleys, 180 kilometers long and 80 kilometers wide. On 11 September, Giraud ordered Colonna to prepare anti-tank defenses around Ajaccio to protect a French disembarkation. And, until 22 September, Algiers continued to poor arms into Ajaccio, thinking that the Germans would try to seize it in the wake of the Allied armistice with Italy. In fact, the Germans planned to use Corsica's flat eastern coastal plain as a corridor to transition their forces on Sardinia back to the Italian mainland. Hence, only gradually did the strategic importance of Bastia, which would become the Germans' Corsican Dunkirk on the northeast tip of the island, began to dawn on Algiers.[14]

A third requirement for operational success would be the "enthusiasm of the population," who would be expected to aid paratroopers and commandos to seize harbors, establish roadblocks, disrupt enemy communications, and provide guerrilla detachments to mop up behind an expeditionary force of three divisions, with some tanks, and lashings of anti-aircraft artillery (AAA) to fend off an expected Axis air assault from Italy. It would prove to be an optimistic net assessment, and a tall order for untrained, under-armed and combat-shy civilians. Barely had the Tunisia campaign ended than, on 4 June, Giraud designated a mountain division, the *Corps franc d'Afrique* (CFA), some *goums*, and service and support troops commanded by Juin to prepare an operation that would "count on an appreciable assistance furnished by the secret Corsican organizations . . . Attention is drawn to the extreme importance of maintaining the strictest secrecy for the preparation of this operation."[15]

As "chief of resistance organizations on Corsica," on 20 June, Colonna d'Istria assured Algiers that, despite the great diversity of political opinion on the island, an invasion could count on the support of 9,000 men organized by the FN. "The party that has survived, and shown the greatest dynamism, is the communist party," he announced, which had been able to surmount the island's fabled clannishness. Furthermore, "95 percent of Corsicans are militants. They are unified around General Giraud," according to his optimistic assessment. Resistance on the island was nevertheless lacking in arms and radios, and under "the strictest surveillance." The resistance had established a target list that prioritized disrupting enemy command and communication, blocking reinforcements, and preventing demolitions, especially of bridges and harbors, that would impede Allied access to the island.[16] Despite the presence of an SS brigade that took up positions south of Corte, the *Casabianca* delivered arms at an accelerated rate, which were offloaded onto the beach from a chain of inflatable dinghies, and from there distributed across the island on mule back along sinuous mountain paths. The few island sites suitable for parachuted agents or arms containers were frequently under Italian surveillance. But arms drops quickened in August nonetheless, with women, who made up over half of the resistance in Corsica, often acting as receptionists. From 28 July, three days after Mussolini's fall had boosted popular expectations that the Italians were about to fold, Algiers broadcast regularly to "the captive island."

The Italian occupiers faced multiple problems in dealing with the increasingly active FN resistance. First, they had arrived relatively late on a notoriously factionalized island. Second, their collaborators were limited to a tiny minority of "irredentists." And third, the launch of Husky – the 9 July invasion of Sicily – suggested that Italy's days as an Axis partner were numbered. *La Milice*, introduced into Corsica in February 1943, had originally attracted only 123 recruits, mainly from the *Service d'ordre légionnaire* (SOL) and Parti populaire français (PPF), a "breeding tank" of collaborators. Some PPF members served as carabinieri snitches in exchange for a monthly stipend, a laissez-passer, and a permit to carry a weapon. But *Milice* membership had dropped to a mere forty by August, not a promising demographic for collaboration. The disdained Italians complained that they could no longer count even on cooperation from the Légion française des combattants (LFC).[17] However, among the irredentists was Marta Renucci – a former "Miss Corse," fascist journalist, and wife of Colonel Pierre Cristofini, who had organized the *Phalange Africaine* in Tunisia. Renucci provided the OVRA with a list of sixty-two names from Île-Rousse, whom she claimed were Gaullists and Allied spies. Allegedly, the Italians had promised that, in return, her husband would be named governor of the island. Unfortunately for them, both husband and wife were arrested by resisters on 8 September and shipped to face judgment in Algiers, where Cristofini was court martialed and shot. The prize for "Miss Corse" became five years in jail with confiscation of property, which, one assumes, included her tiara. The pro-Vichy *Bastia-Journal* and *La Dépêche corse* achieved only a small circulation, and, in their post-war trials, their editors escaped punishment by blaming their collaboration on censorship and coercion. The most bountiful sources of intelligence for the Italians came from a significant population of Italian and Spanish workers on the island, some in small trades, but many working in forestry, who disdained Corsicans as "arrogant and lazy" and were quick to report suspicious activities. So deep were their divisions, however, that Corsicans appeared more eager to settle scores among themselves, even than to denounce Jewish refugees. That said, the break-up of

Sea Urchin had given the Italians important intelligence on the configuration of resistance networks and topographical reports and photos of likely invasion spots ordered by the BCRA in Algiers.

Until June, the Germans had been content to leave Corsica's defense to the Italians. However, with the end of the Tunisia campaign in May, they looked to insure that Corsica remained available to bounce their troops from Sardinia, to Elba and the mainland. From June, Kriegsmarine and Luftwaffe observers appeared in Corsica, along with a 4,400-man SS brigade, artillery and AAA units, and the inevitable Sicherheitspolizei (Sipo). Historian of Corsica Hélène Chaubin speculates that the Germans, unburdened by an Italian "irredentist" policy, might have enjoyed greater success in recruiting Vichy collaborators, as was the case in the Alpes Maritimes. But the Sipo arrived late, with the primarily tactical mission of deploying radio operators, who had been recruited from the PPF and trained in Paris, around likely invasion spots. Thus, unlike French North Africa (AFN) on the eve of Torch, the population of Corsica seemed on the whole to have jettisoned any residual nostalgia for the Marshal, and in the summer of 1943 lived in the optimistic expectancy of liberation.[18]

And this optimism seemed entirely justified. Corsicans closely followed the campaign on Sicily, where Palermo fell to the Allies on 22 July, and Mussolini was toppled from power three days later. Even though these events seemed to shake the morale of the Italian garrison, the occupation authority declared a "state of alert," evacuated some of the inhabitants along the eastern coast, and mined the harbor in Ajaccio. Mussolini's fall triggered debates among the leaders of the FN over whether to call for an "*insurrection nationale*." After consulting Algiers, on 5 August, the order came from Giraud to forego a premature uprising.[19] This was probably because, on 29 July, four days after Mussolini's removal from power, Eisenhower's Chief of Staff (COS) Bedell Smith had instructed Juin that planning for Corsica should be "temporarily suspended," an order repeated on 15 August: "When it appears that operations against Sardinia and Corsica are likely to be possible, we shall have to go into the whole matter afresh."[20] Yet, the leaders of the FN, realizing that an armistice between the Allies and Italy was imminent, laid plans to seize local centers of power – prefectures and town halls – and prepared tracts to distribute to Italian troops. A member of Colonna d'Istria's team made contact with the occupying Blackshirt detachment to urge them to make common cause with the Resistance. In the end, the FN leaders, tired of Giraud's "*attentisme*," inspired by the examples of Soviet, Yugoslav, and Greek partisans, upset by counter-partisan campaigns that included setting the *maquis* (dense scrub vegetation) alight to smoke them out, and fearing that their arms caches would be discovered and their movement decapitated by the occupying forces, opted to reject the authority of the "defunct IIIrd Republic" in Algiers. They would go for self-liberation, legitimated by a declaration of the "Estates

General of Corsica." The *Casabianca* embarked Giovoni for Algiers on 6 September to announce the decision for a popular uprising, but he arrived only during the morning of 8 September, mere hours ahead of the 18:30 announcement of the armistice with Italy.[21]

Article 6 of the armistice required the "immediate restitution" of Corsica to the Allies. However, the ability of the Italians to do that was complicated by the fact that, in line with Unternehmen Achse (Operation Axis) – the German takeover of Italy originally called Alaric – German troops in the Mediterranean were ordered to disarm their former Italian partners, who were to be dispatched to Germany as POWs. In Bastia, fighting broke out when the relatively small German garrison tried to disarm the numerically superior Italian troops, a metastasizing fracas joined by resistance fighters. Driven out of Bastia, German troops made for Bonifacio to assist the arrival of the 90th Panzergrenadier Division from Sardinia. Control of Bastia was critical to General Fridolin von Senger und Utterlin, a veteran of the Eastern Front and Sicily and commander of the 90th Panzergrenadier Division, the remnants of which had been evacuated from Tunisia to Sardinia, to secure a passage for the evacuation of the German garrison on Sardinia through Corsica. As the island descended into chaos, von Senger's 32,000 Panzergrenadiers and assorted support units disembarked at Bonifacio, with the goal of moving rapidly up the relatively flat eastern coast of the island to Bastia. Only on 13 September did German forces backed by tanks and Stukas manage to secure Bastia from the Italians and the resistance, and enlarged their perimeter to the north and west.[22] Meanwhile, on the western side of the island, Ajaccio descended into chaos, as the FN moved to replace the municipal council and departmental delegates, and the streets filled with people shouting "Vive de Gaulle!" (Map 3.1).[23]

On 9 September, Colonna d'Istria radioed Giraud that the resistance in Corsica had seized control of Ajaccio. The 80,000 Italian soldiers on the island were making no effort to subdue them, but, on the contrary, often joined the resistance fighters. In towns and villages, the FN was "elected" by popular assemblies gathered on village squares, that declared the municipal governments defunct and replaced by patriots whose names they read out. In this way, 200 Corsican municipalities, where 27,000 of the island's 220,000 inhabitants lived, were taken over by the Communists, who also installed a "*conseil de préfecture*" as the Vichy prefect stepped down. Colonna d'Istria requested that French forces intervene. At this point, Giraud informed de Gaulle of the situation. For de Gaulle, this was a worrying precedent for at least two reasons. First, without the authority of the CFLN and de Gaulle, Giraud and the SOE had armed the Corsican resistance, without insisting upon political control in return. Indeed, Giraud seemed happy enough to allow the communists to take power in return for intelligence on southern France.[24] Second, the Corsican

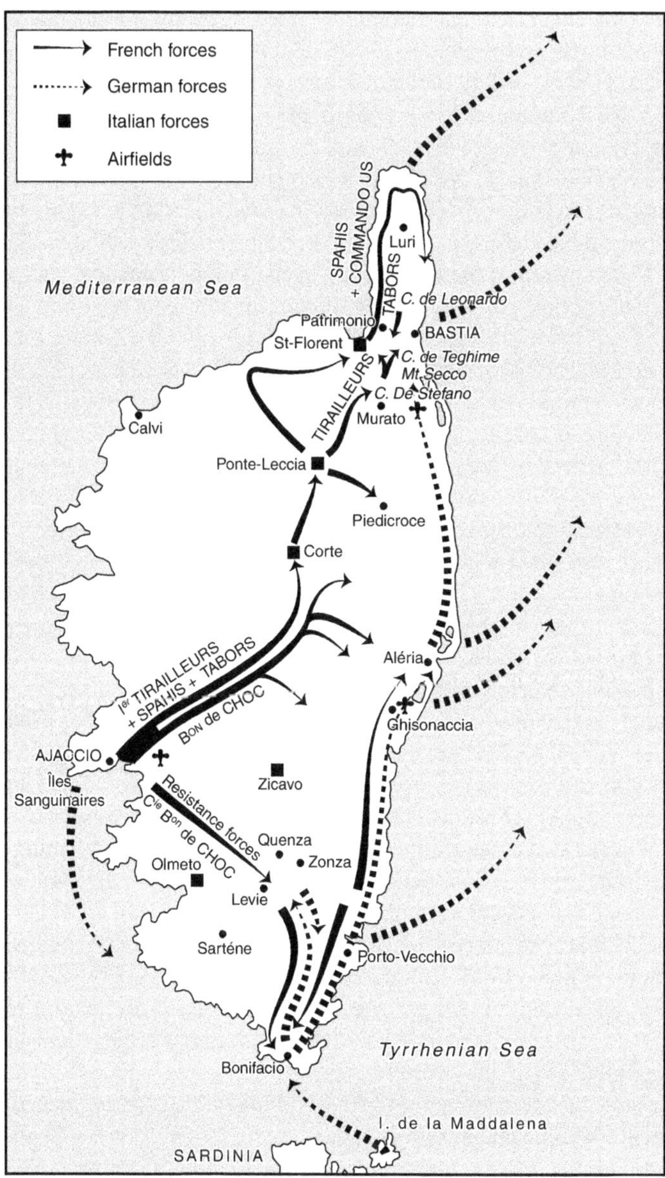

Map 3.1 The liberation of Corsica, September 1943.

insurrection suggested that a communist-led resistance on the mainland, with its own political and strategic agenda, might act independently of a main force invasion, or even seek to precipitate one, as seemed to be the case in Corsica. Indeed, the communist press praised the Corsica uprising, comparing it to Yugoslavia, part of Soviet-orchestrated pressure on the Western Allies to open a Second Front.[25] When, on 9 September, Giraud confessed his role in creating and arming resistance on Corsica to de Gaulle, de Gaulle reproached his co-president. He subsequently claimed that Giraud's secrecy suggested that he had been aware of the imminence of the Italian armistice, and plotted the Corsica uprising to coincide with its announcement. This became a useful myth that de Gaulle would weaponize to eliminate his rival. De Gaulle was probably annoyed also because it showed that, for once, Giraud and his secret service had outmaneuvered his BCRA. Indeed, the explosion of Corsica came in the midst of an attempt to "orient and control" the Gaullist BCRA and Giraud's SR which had been ordered by the CFLN on 3 September. Corsica and Giraud's cooperation with the SOE to arm the communist-dominated resistance revealed how important the battle for secret service control was to become for de Gaulle. But also, Giraud seemed to have taken a huge risk, because the Allies, in the process of landing Mark Clark's Fifth Army at Salerno from 9 September, had no ships, planes, or troops to spare for Corsica.[26] But, while Giraud and his SR had indeed armed the resistance, they had not precipitated events on the island. They had only reacted to them.

Under the circumstances, the two French leaders agreed that French troops must hasten to the island, on the assumption that the Germans would attempt to fortify it to anchor their defense of Italy. At Giraud's request, Juin had prepared an intervention force whose initial task would be to secure Ajaccio against an imminent German assault. But Juin acknowledged that his plan must be hastily improvised. One scenario was that the resistance would master the occupation forces, and that he could simply dispatch a French force, which he could gradually rearm in place.[27] The French plan further miscalculated German intentions, which, from 12 September, on Hitler's orders, were to transit Corsica, not occupy it. As a consequence, the French focused on reinforcing Ajaccio to withstand an anticipated German attack, rather than cutting the escape route along the western side of the island and occupying Bastia, which was the true German objective.[28] Finally, the French lacked transport for such a significant invasion/occupation force. Only on 11 September did Giraud give the order to prepare forces for Corsica: Gambiez's *Bataillon de choc*, the *4ᵉ Division marocaine de montagne* (DMM), the *2ᵉ Groupe de Tabors marocains*, an anti-aircraft group, an artillery battery, and a pioneer battalion. When, at one o'clock in the morning of 13 September, the *Casabianca* landed an *avant garde* of 109 commandos as the opening act of Operation Vesuvius, under the command of General Henry Martin, they were greeted by a large number of Ajacciens, who crowded the harbor. The rest of the battalion followed on board the destroyer *Fantasque*, which also transported General Amédée Mollard, the pre-war military governor of the island, who had escaped from Corsica to Algeria in August, as well as the CFLN-appointed Prefect Charles Luizet to establish CFLN control. The Giraudists were eager to court Allied buy-in for their initiative. Unfortunately, the announcement of the armistice with Italy on 8 September was followed on 9 and 12 September by reminders to Giraud that the Allies – at the time locked in a tense battle to secure a beachhead at Salerno – could not undertake operations in Sardinia and Corsica "until the situation in central Italy is in hand." "But since then, events have moved on," Lieutenant colonel R. Baillif, a member of Giraud's staff, insisted to Brigadier Cecil Sugden. "General Giraud believes it impossible to leave the patriotic Corsicans without support. Besides, the opportunity was too good to pass up. The accord between the Italians and the Corsicans hands us the port of Ajaccio. Therefore, we have to do everything to preserve it . . . not only from the perspective of French morale, but also to improve the general situation in the Mediterranean." The Allies must supply to the French the means to act. "How long will this 'opportunity' last?," Baillif asked Sugden.[29]

After landing at Ajacio, Gambiez's commandos contacted General Giovanni Magli, commander of the Italian occupation forces, headquartered at Corte in the island's interior, who informed them that the Germans had seized Bastia and Cap Corse. Only on 12 September did Magli receive formal orders to attack his former Axis partners, but he lacked aircraft and tanks, while he insisted that he could not count on the attitude of his troops in such confused circumstances. As the German rearguard moved north, it blew up bridges and a tunnel to discourage pursuit.[30]

On 21 September, Giraud arrived in Corsica. Magli, who proved eager to help, promised to lend him artillery, engineers, and transportation to assist the French advance, but continued to fear German armor. However, several factors allowed the Germans to escape: the piecemeal arrival of the 4^{e} DMM in Ajaccio; the fact that the Germans had blocked the mountain passes in the center of the island; and a lack of motorized transport.[31] At the end of the day on 30 September, French intelligence estimated that a rearguard of 5,000 German troops remained to be evacuated. Over the final days, the Germans contested every mountain pass to buy time for evacuation. On the night of 3 October, patrols sent out by *goums* reported no contact with Germans. By 09:45 on 4 October, when French and Italian troops entered Bastia, the Germans had sailed, although in the process abandoning significant amounts of equipment, munitions, and stores. A Luftwaffe raid on Bastia the next day augmented the destruction of an already-battered city.[32]

François Coulet, named by de Gaulle to take control of the Corsican police, assured his boss that "Corsica is Gaullist," and the FN had tricked the population into following them by "liberally hand[ing] out [machineguns] to twelve-year-old children."[33] Although, ironically, it had been the Italians who had provided the heft to liberate the island, Corsica offered a political victory for de Gaulle. On a military level, for French officers, Corsica's liberation evoked all the deficiencies of the Tunisia campaign, since it too was characterized by an absence of air support, anti-tank guns, and mobility.[34]

The "liberation" of Corsica left a confused situation. Bastia was shattered, as were many of the roads leading across the island. In retreat, the Germans had sewn forests of mines. American historian Arthur Layton Funk cited Corsica's special place in the history of the war as "the first French territory to be liberated solely by the French army." But, in the event, it had been the 20th Friuli and 44th Cremona Infantry Divisions who saw their erstwhile Axis allies off the island, and who were upset that the French failed to treat them as Allies.[35] According to French reports, once the liberation of Corsica was complete, Italian morale cratered. "They have all they need to fight, except a combative spirit," the French *Deuxième Bureau* reported. "They have only one desire, '*la casa*,' and the return roads toward Sardinia are full of convoys of men content with their fate." Among the local population, "The communist party is extremely active, and attempting to confiscate the unique credit for the victory." It also predicted that "the disarmament of the patriots will not be accomplished without difficulties. In sum, it's the peaceable people who were the first to turn in their weapons. As for the others, one will have to use other methods of persuasion."[36] On 8 October, de Gaulle appeared at Ajaccio to be acclaimed by the population. Having been "liberated," Corsica now joined the war on the Allied side. Among the USAAF bomber crews hosted by the "USS Corsica" was Joseph Heller, inspired perhaps by the incongruous juxtaposition of *l'Île de la beauté* and the more blatant absurdities of military life to write *Catch-22*. The liberation paved the way for the mobilization of 12,000 young Corsicans for the army, some of whom would participate in the liberation of Rome.

The closeout of the two September 1943 events – the surrender of Italy and the liberation of Corsica – speeded Giraud's eclipse. When, in the wake of Eisenhower's 8 September announcement of the armistice with Italy, CFLN *commissaire* for Foreign Affairs René Massigli expressed surprise and dismay that France had been neither consulted in the negotiations nor mentioned in the communiqué, he was informed that Giraud had been kept abreast of the progress of negotiations by AFHQ. Although this statement proved false, it allowed de Gaulle to sideline Giraud. "Our Allies invoked, if not employed, the absurd dualism of our government as an alibi to mask their neglect," de Gaulle fumed. "Now, again, almost immediately, this same dualism demonstrated its malfeasance in an important national and military operation: the liberation of Corsica."[37] This was, of course, both absurd and disingenuous. While the

Allies kept neither Giraud nor de Gaulle abreast of their negotiations with the Italians at Cassibile, as Chaubin makes clear, every Corsican peasant, as well as Berlin, suspected that from the moment of Mussolini's eclipse, if not before, an armistice between the Allies and Italy was only a matter of time.

In the thrall of his own "inane vanities," Giraud had sensed an opportunity to boost his standing by launching an operation that he imagined would terminate in his presiding over a dramatic surrender of Italian and German forces on the island, allowing him to claim credit for the liberation of the first "metropolitan department." But he had overplayed his hand in Corsica: while de Gaulle lauded Giraud's initiative in Operation Vesuvius, he faulted his failure to keep the CFLN informed of his actions. In fact, had the Germans elected to fight rather than flee, and if Italian troops had not dramatically switched sides, Giraud's decision to land a handful of French commandos and infantry in Ajaccio, largely unsupported by airpower, armor, and artillery, would have been a downright foolhardy risk. During the invasion of the Italian mainland, the Anglo-Americans had no spare assets to rescue what, in the face of Axis resistance, might have been mistaken for a reenactment of the Dieppe "Raid." "By nature and by habit, but also by utilizing a sort of tactic, [Giraud] locked his mind into a military sphere, refusing to consider human and national reality, rejecting what belonged to the political dimension," de Gaulle recorded. He had failed to foresee the communist power grab on the island. But even if one remained confined to the "military sphere," the decision to invade Corsica confirmed the general view that Giraud was little more than an empty uniform, whose single *fait d'armes* consisted of a dramatic escape from Königstein. De Gaulle made the rounds of Corsica delivering public addresses from 8 October. In his memoirs, he denounced his co-president both as a tool of the Americans and as a conduit for the "sustained resentment" of anti-Gaullist Frenchmen. "We needed to put an end to this false situation. Henceforth, I was resolved to force General Giraud out of the government."[38]

In de Gaulle's mind, the attempt by the FN to seize power further underlined the need to end the clumsy compromise of a CFLN co-presidency. De Gaulle's dilemma was that, as a man without much of a regular army, he required popular participation in France's national liberation, with the resistance in the lead, both to enhance his political standing with the Allies and as a force multiplier. Yet, Corsica demonstrated the perils of mobilizing the resistance in the absence of strong CFLN direction. De Gaulle was no doubt upset that the demise of Sea Urchin had cleared the field for Pearl Harbor and Colonna d'Istria's flirtation with the FN. But, as Julian Jackson points out, if de Gaulle had been surprised by the robustness of the communist resistance on Corsica, it was because, focused on his dispute with Giraud, he had not taken communist plans for "national insurrection" seriously enough.[39] Corsica alerted de Gaulle to the dangers of a communist manipulation of the *maquis* for political ends on

Liberation, to the point of possibly provoking a civil war.[40] Through naiveté or pursuit of institutional interests, Giraud, his *Direction des services spéciaux* (DSS), and the SOE had armed the communist FN and facilitated its takeover of many municipalities on the island. Its militants then proceeded to hold assemblies in many Corsican towns and villages that put communist officials in power by a show of hands. "In no case did the ministers [of the CFLN] want to see this precedent repeated tomorrow in France," de Gaulle concluded. "That pressed me to realize the structural changes that would put the government beyond similar surprises. I shared their concerns."[41] For all parties, the Corsica campaign held a lesson: for the French communists, it pushed the dogma of "National Insurrection" to the forefront of their strategic and political agenda. For the Allies, it presented the challenge of integrating civilian resistance into operational planning without allowing it to disrupt or drive the conduct of regular operations. For all parties, it launched a debate over what "National Insurrection" actually meant in practice, as well as one over the advisability of arming a resistance that might use those weapons to pursue its own political ends.[42]

To waylay that possibility, the immediate priority of the CFLN became to adjust their administrative structure to the challenges of asserting government control over what promised to be resistance movements with their own activist leadership, political agendas, "feudal" tendencies, and potentially disruptive tactics that invited a civilian bloodbath on Liberation. This adjustment began with de Gaulle's 19 September proposition that the CFLN abolish the co-presidency. Initially the governing council balked at such a radical proposal, despite de Gaulle's threats that they would have to choose between "Giraud or me." Instead, they temporized, suggesting that the creation of a defense commissioner would avoid a rupture between the two leaders while circumscribing Giraud's power. It was Giraud's turn to object. But, after sulking for a week, he accepted, although this new arrangement in effect left de Gaulle in charge of the government, with Giraud's power reduced to co-signing legislation.[43]

With the possible exception of Georges, Giraud's Corsica initiative succeeded in alienating his final partisans in the CFLN. Even Cordell Hull realized that it was time to bring down the curtain on Giraud's "clumsy attempt to gain a leg up on de Gaulle."[44] In October, the *Comité de libération* decreed that henceforth the CFLN would have only one president. Giraud approved the ordinance, expecting that, in return, he would be given command of French forces slated for combat in Italy. Instead, he was forced to resign in November. When the new Consultative Assembly convened in Algiers, it did so under a single president. While AFHQ insisted that it would continue to deal directly with Giraud, and Marshall threatened to curtail Phase III of the Anfa plan, it only served to strengthen de Gaulle's argument that Giraud was an American puppet. In effect, Giraud had become a political orphan; his days as commander in chief were numbered. De Gaulle was now the master in AFN.[45]

On 16 December 1943, the CFLN transferred much of the power hitherto vested in the commander in chief to the *Comité de défense nationale* (CDN) to make decisions on the employment and distribution of French forces. With French forces in Italy under Allied command, while those in AFN answered to the Commissioners of War, Air, and the Navy, Giraud really had no role. Too senior for a field command, on 8 April 1944, he was offered the post of Inspector General of French Forces, a sinecure which he refused. On 12 April 1944, Béthouart became COS of National Defense, in effect supplanting Giraud. Two days later, the CFLN relieved Giraud of his role and assigned him to the reserve forces. On 13 April, Giraud gave "a pathetic farewell to the French forces," taking credit for rearmament at Anfa and the liberation of Corsica.[46] Many regarded de Gaulle's elimination of Giraud as gratuitously ruthless and coldblooded. But there was a war on, and, in de Gaulle's view, Giraud had become an impediment to the restoration of French power.[47]

A second problem was that Algiers' de Gaulle–Giraud dispute had been exported to Corsica, and reframed as a fight for civilian control between a Gaullist prefect and a Giraudist military governor.[48] One result was that the *Commissariat à l'Intérieur* concluded that, to keep political control of the liberation of the mainland, it must set up in advance a system of administrative organization. This included both regional and departmental prefects, and *Commissaires de la République*, assisted by "military delegates" in "forward zones" armed with a series of powers, decrees, and instructions emanating from the CFLN that set out and regulated the exercise of civilian and military powers which were to be communicated to local officials in advance. *Commissaires de la République* were to be advised by *Comités départementaux de libération* (Departmental Liberation Committees) made up of members of the local resistance, "which should be a faithful reflection of the character of the department" – that is, not dominated by communists. These were to be place holders, insuring order, liaising with the Allied High Command, and relaunching economic activity, until CFLN-appointed officials arrived to take power directly. Given the nature of the task, professional administrators were heavily represented among the *Commissaires de la République*.[49]

A third consequence of Corsica was that it raised the issue of the military contribution of the resistance to the liberation of the island, and how far those lessons might transfer to coming operations on the mainland. The internal resistance was important to de Gaulle, because it legitimized his status with the Allies, and because, through the resistance, he sought to enlist the French in their own liberation, rather than outsource operations completely to Anglo-American forces. However, questions remained about the CFLN's ability to control the resistance politically, as well as about its military role and capabilities. Both politically and militarily, Giraud's quickly improvised operation had secured Corsica for the CFLN. Otherwise, von Senger's withdrawal might have left the island divided between an armed population, led by an aggressive FN, and an Italian garrison of 80,000 men, "well armed and equipped, with luxurious means of transportation," as the *Deuxième Bureau* speculated.[50] Civil war in a liberation setting in which political power was contested definitely loomed as a possibility, as was to occur in Greece and Yugoslavia. This caused many in the BCRA in particular to become wary about parachuting arms to the Francs-Tireurs et Partisans (FTP) and FN in France.[51] On 4 October, a *Comité d'action en France* (COMIDAC), presided over by de Gaulle, was created to oversee resistance in France. The *Services de renseignement et d'action* (SRA), also under COMIDAC, was to assure liaison between the mainland and the CFLN, with oversight and direction of the intelligence services in London and Algiers.[52] However, de Gaulle's ability to control the internal resistance would be complicated further by the expanding activity of the "interface services" of the SOE and OSS, whose *raison d'être* by late 1943 became to arm and operationalize a growing French *maquis* – a name actually bootlegged into France from its Corsican precursor – in invasion planning. This competition would allow resistance groups to play off the Anglo-Americans against the BCRA and CFLN in a bid for independence, maneuvers that would particularly infuriate de Gaulle.

Lost in the bureaucratic infighting and planning was a clear evaluation of the actual contribution of the resistance to the liberation of Corsica. A 24 September report claimed that Corsican partisans had killed 1,000 Germans, taken 250 POWs, and destroyed a significant amount of matériel. Gambiez also filed impressive figures of enemy troops killed and wounded, although only 200 German graves were ever identified on the island. However, an Allied report insisted that it was the resistance that had inflicted the greatest number of casualties on the enemy, a feat which they attributed to the murderous traditions of the Corsican vendetta.[53] Colonna d'Istria proved less enthusiastic. After all the effort to arm partisans on the island, in his view their munitions were quickly exhausted, and their value as fighters was limited. While he acknowledged that they had kept the French forces informed of German movements, a subsequent *Deuxième Bureau* report complained that, while partisans at times had proven useful as guides, partisan-supplied intelligence arrived late and was often inaccurate.[54] Gambiez's commandos had managed to form a reserve company from partisan recruits, staffed by regular officers and NCOs, which, "after brief training, proved satisfactory." However, noted Colonna d'Istria,

> from 20 September, the French command, having taken the offensive, called on the reserves of armed patriots living in areas away from combat zones. These patriots were

organized in groups and sections and led toward the lines of fire far from their regions of origin. This proved a failed initiative. Far from their villages, in island regions with which they were unfamiliar, the patriots performed poorly. With no cohesion, badly equipped, supplied with food and munitions on a haphazard basis, they were destined to fail the command. During this period, only their use as security patrols proved satisfactory. Conclusion: the patriot is not a soldier, and even less a modern soldier. He can survive and fight only in his home region that he knows well.[55]

Indeed, Chaubin lists only forty-eight partisans killed as the result of combat, executions by Germans or Blackshirts, or by mines during the liberation of Corsica.[56] Nevertheless, the Allies were in need of good news. The *Daily Telegraph* correspondent in Algiers filed a story comparing the "Corsican uprising" with that of Tito's Yugoslav Partisans, viewed as the gold standard of resistance movements. Predictably, Churchill, who had never recovered from an infection of resistance romanticism acquired as a correspondent covering the Second Anglo-Boer War (1899–1902), embraced this theme when, on 29 September 1943, he enthused to CFLN ambassador to London Pierre Viénot that

the French should be inspired by the Yugoslavs and concentrate on igniting the mountainous regions in the southwest of France, from Nice to the Swiss frontier. We hold Corsica and could soon seize the boot of Italy. From these positions, arms and equipment could be convoyed to the guerrillas in France by air.

Viénot would not be the last Frenchman to point out to the British Prime Minister the geographical, strategic, and operational differences between southeastern France and Yugoslavia. Furthermore, more recent research has argued that Churchill's high opinion of Tito's partisans was based on unverified claims for their operational success that had been passed on uncritically through Cairo, and by the Prime Minister's desire to curry favor with Stalin, which caused him in September 1943 inexplicably to drop support for Draža Mihailović's Chetniks.[57] Churchill's infatuation with irregular warfare was further stoked by SOE reports that highlighted the important role played by the Corsican resistance in the island's liberation, a theme magnified by the British press and the British Broadcasting Corporation (BBC). By the time that a March 1944 OSS report offered a more nuanced, but nonetheless favorable, evaluation that suggested that resistance shortcomings in Corsica could be overcome by better training and weaponry, the narrative of resistance heroism and efficiency, joined with hyped claims for the military success of Tito's partisans, was anchored in stone. In this way, the myth of the Corsican resistance, promoted by Allied "interface services," amplified by Churchillian resistance romanticism, and sustained by French pride, the tradition of the *levée en masse*, and the realization that the participation of regular French forces in the invasion of France could only be "symbolic" had catapulted civilian resistance into the mix of Allied planning for the invasion of France. Behind this celebration of resistance in Corsica, however, lurked the dread that arming politicized civilians to spark a "national insurrection" had flung open the door to civil war.[58]

The CEF in Italy

In retrospect, with the possible exception of Elba, Corsica did not offer a stepping stone to anywhere, least of all Italy. The Allies' decision to invade the peninsula, which had been based on wishful thinking and best-case scenarios, had drawn them into a campaign without clear strategic objectives beyond a vague desire to capture Rome and tie down German divisions. Nevertheless, while Stalin continued to complain about the lack of a "Second Front," by the summer of 1943, 30 percent of German forces were deployed elsewhere than the Eastern Front, "a share soon augmented dramatically by the German redeployment after the Allies invaded Sicily and Italy," writes Sean McMeekin.[59] But, in December 1943, with Italy surrendered and Overlord imminent, the strategic significance of Rome and the Mediterranean theater was slipping from the attention of a public aware that the war would be decided on other fronts.[60] Furthermore, the requirement to pin down German divisions obliged the Allies to execute offensive operations across a tortuous Italian landscape. The degree of difficulty spiked considerably once German commander Albert Kesselring had completed a series of defense-in-depth barriers across central Italy, the most formidable of which was the Gustav Line which ran from the Adriatic to the Tyrrhenian Sea, anchored by the medieval Benedictine monastery of Monte Cassino. Perched atop the 1,706-foot Monastery Hill at the confluence of the Rapido, Gargliano, and Liri river valleys, Cassino dominated Route 6, the critical axis that followed the Liri Valley north to Rome. Cassino came to epitomize the mind-numbing, blood-spattered slogging march up the peninsula's spiny boot, which replicated in its strategic futility and tactical frustrations the full measure of command uncertainty and mud-soaked mayhem that had typified trench warfare in 1914–1918. In Italy, heroism became devalued, commoditized, and expendable.

Because the German collapse on the peninsula coincided with the downfall of the Reich in May 1945, Italy might have proven even more humiliating for the Allies had it not been for the vital contribution of the French. By May 1944, Juin's CEF counted four divisions of French-led, predominately North African troops, comprising roughly 115,000 men. It was the CEF that intervened in the winter of 1943–1944 to break what Churchill christened the "scandalous" stalemate at Monte Cassino. "Sons of bitches!," US general and Fifth Army commander Mark Clark raged when news of the Normandy invasion arrived barely two days after the Liberation of Rome on 4 June 1944. "They didn't even let us have the newspaper headlines for the fall of Rome for one day."[61] But the simple truth was that, without the CEF, Clark (assuming he had retained his command) might have signed the German surrender on 2 May 1945 south of Rome, rather than in the Po Valley. And even then, by virtue of his stubborn twenty-month defense of the Italian peninsula, Kesselring could claim something of a moral victory in Italy. In the event, Juin's CEF supplied the critical margin of success at Monte Cassino in May 1944, as Clark conceded: "General Juin's entire force showed an aggressiveness hour after hour that the Germans could not withstand," he wrote. "[It was] one of the most brilliant and daring advances of the war in Italy."[62] Juin broke the Gustav Line by convincing Clark to substitute his predictable, futile, and bloody frontal assaults on Monte Cassino with a combination of surprise, maneuver, and infiltration as the key to success in mountain warfare. Furthermore, Juin's French-led Muslim troops, especially the *goums*, proved particularly adept at mountain warfare. They not only almost single-handedly cracked the German front on the second day of the May 1944 battle, but also, through a rapid exploitation of the breakthrough, thwarted Kesselring's attempt to reconstitute his defense on his reserve Hitler Line. In this way, Juin and the CEF enabled the Allied vault up the peninsula that brought them to the Gothic Line, a defensive backstop north of Florence that stretched across the Apennines of northern Italy.

The stunning success of the CEF was all the more remarkable for several reasons, beginning with the fact that the French had first to implement a mobilization that for the first time included women across an increasingly restless imperium. Second, they had to satisfy stringent US conditions for rearmament.[63] Nevertheless, American largesse had been encouraged by what US soldiers viewed as a game French performance in Tunisia despite a serious deficit of armaments. In the process, the French were expected to become acquainted with the tactics, techniques, and procedures of modern warfare. One of the ironies was that the rusticity of *l'armée d'Afrique*, its familiarity with mountain warfare, and its iron discipline anchored in a race-based hierarchy alien to the freely accepted discipline of the citizen *levée* would actually prove an advantage in Italy. Nevertheless, this was not apparent to Allied service chiefs, who initially had no role for French forces in Italy. The CFLN also lobbied to preserve its army for the liberation of the metropole, rather than squander it in what they saw as a marginal campaign. But French forces were needed to replace the seven Allied divisions pulled out of the Mediterranean at the end of the Sicily campaign to prepare for Overlord. Yet, the French would embark for the Italian campaign seriously undermanned in service and medical personnel, and with inadequate communications and artillery support, in part because Giraud sought to obfuscate his problems rather than create a balanced force structure that would have required the enlistment of Jews and foreigners and reequipping the 1ère DFL to US standards. This forced the CEF to rely heavily on US support in Italy.[64]

The problems of rearmament almost paled beside a final challenge – combining a mulishly *Maréchalist armée d'Afrique*, with its panoply of reactionary and racist dogmas, with the *Forces françaises libres* (FFL). "Giraudist propaganda portrayed the *attentisme* of *l'armée d'Afrique* as a praiseworthy sacrifice," notes French historian of the CEF Julie Le Gac, a theme that sought to create a patriotic equivalence between the two forces, elevate the moral standing of *l'armée d'Afrique* in Allied eyes, and therefore facilitate amalgamation. "While General de Gaulle maintained the French flag in battle, French Africa prepared the liberation of the Fatherland," declared the patriotic North African newspaper *TAM*.[65] In fact, the two French camps coexisted in barely veiled hostility, the former FFL continuing to wear their Cross of Lorraine insignia, while the "Giraudists" denounced the "émigré mentality" and "attitude of disdain" of their former rivals, who continued to maintain their separate messes and even leave centers into 1944. *L'armée d'Afrique* took revenge by monopolizing senior positions in the CEF, initially prioritizing for rearmament the *2e Division d'infanterie marocaine* (2e DIM) under André Dody, Joseph de Monsabert's *3e Division d'infanterie algérienne* (3e DIA), and the Moroccan *goums* commanded by Noguès' former director of political affairs, General Augustine Guillaume. Over Larminat's protests, Giraud deliberately excluded Brosset's battle-experienced 1ère DFL, officially renamed the *1ère Division motorisée d'infanterie* (DMI), from the Anfa program, and initially refused to assign the *9e Division d'infanterie coloniale* (9e DIC) to Joseph Magnan, who had unsuccessfully attempted to sequester Noguès on 8–9 November 1942.[66] Animosity was running so high that, toward the end of 1943, as Giraud was being eased toward retirement, many in the Provisional Assembly feared a brewing military coup. Under the guise of rejuvenating the high command, the CFLN sought to impose civilian control by holding hearings on collaboration, but also by cleansing the high command of some of its more pro-Vichy elements by enforcing statutory age limits: fifty-six years for a major general, fifty-three for colonels, and forty-nine for captains.[67] Given Algiers' political volatility, busying *l'armée d'Afrique* with rearmament, and dispatching its vanguard divisions to Italy under American command, no doubt served de Gaulle's interests – if France's colonial soldiers were so keen "to restore France's honor," they could do it in Italy, not in Algiers, as they were to attempt fifteen years later.

The CEF had to be fashioned from the limited and extremely diverse, if not mutually antagonistic, manpower resources available in AFN. As noted earlier, Algeria and eventually Tunisia relied on conscription, while Morocco called for "volunteers," who were reeled in initially by recruiting parties dispatched by individual units, which produced a disproportionate number of Imazighen.[68] Twenty-five-year-old reserve Sergeant Ahmed Ben Bella was recalled in the summer of 1943 and assigned to the 6e RTA at Tlemcen. The contrast between this *armée d'Afrique* unit and the *141e Régiment d'infanterie*, in which he had served in 1939–1940, shocked him: "The inequality between the Algerian and French NCOs was flagrant," he wrote. Muslim officers and NCOs dined in a separate mess: "I'll forgo a description of the awkwardness and humiliation that ensued from this segregation." However, when he tried to organize his fellow Muslims to protest, he was promptly transferred to the *5e Régiment de tirailleurs marocains* (5e RTM).[69]

The Muslim–French friction that Ben Bella believed characterized command relationships in Algerian units was less evident in Moroccan regiments. For starters, André Lanquetot, who served with the 8e RTM in Italy, noted that his overwhelmingly Imazighen soldiers were not "volunteers" at all, but had been "designated" by tribal elders at the behest of the French for a four-year enlistment. Rustic and illiterate, many were often too young to sprout the obligatory moustache. However, a system of "tough paternalism" ("*dure caïdat*"), applied by native corporals who did not hesitate to employ brutality, whipped them into soldiers. As everyone was named Mohammed or Ahmed, they were called by their number, even among themselves, or given a nickname based on a physical attribute – the bald, the tall, the educated, the bearded, the Saharan if he had dark skin, the Casablancan, the old, and so on. The major was called Bou Arba (the father), the Captain "Si al Coptan," and the Lieutenant was "al Ficiann." Commands cascaded in a mixture of pidgin Arabic and French. Officers and men shared "a sort of vigorous camaraderie, tacit, smiling, because we knew how to joke and communicate," Lanquetot insisted.[70]

Ben Bella, too, found his "punishment" of the 5^{e} RTM, whose recruitment base was in northeast Morocco on the Algerian frontier, much to his liking. "An Algerian among the Moroccans, I found myself in the middle of old soldiers, innocent of all ideology, and as if married to their regiment. And so should they be, because they were well treated. In the 5th Moroccan, I discovered a spirit very different from that which had reigned in the 6th [Algerian] *tirailleurs* . . . At first, the Moroccans struck me as a little distrustful, unforthcoming, but they opened up quickly, and I found them very endearing." The soldiers seemed to have a real affection for each other, which gave the unit "a quasi-familial cohesion." For starters, most of the officers were from France, and so had not been tainted by Algerian *pied noir* racism. But Ben Bella's reputation as an Algerian nationalist had preceded him. This precipitated a heart-to-heart chat with his company commander, who explained that, while Ben Bella was entitled to his political opinions, "one was going to fight. He knew that I was anti-fascist . . . Can't we forget our differences in the fight against the common enemy? This language struck me as reasonable, and I promised Captain de Villaucours that I would not create unrest among the troops." In any case, Ben

Bella recognized that "I would be wasting my time seeking to propagandize among these Moroccans," few of whom fasted at Ramadan, and seemed surprised that he did, because, as a French speaker, they assumed that he had been totally Westernized. "They were used to very strict discipline, but accepted it, because it was clear and simple. They were totally devoted to their officer, whose affection and desire for justice they recognized."[71] The revival of conscription and the recall of reservists in Algeria from December 1942 also reeled in 175,000 *français d'Algérie* and eventually Jews, many destined for the artillery, or to serve as cadres, technical specialists, and in support units.[72] Also, many among the 20,000 or so *évadés de France* were also gradually filtered to the units.

The reconstruction of the French army was also hindered by an Allied attitude of condescension toward the quarrelsome French. Indeed, presumably without the slightest trace of irony, Juin accused the Allies of treating the French forces as "colonial auxiliaries."[73] A Fifth Army Liaison Mission had been created in Mostaganem east of Oran in early September 1943. French troops began training for Italy at Porte-aux-Poules (Mers El Hadjadj, an Oran suburb), while, during October, French liaison officers began to establish contact with Fifth Army sections, to take over a base for arriving troops at Caivano, a northern suburb of Naples, and "to study American field procedure in regard to hospitals, air tactics, evacuation of wounded, and other techniques."[74]

While, to his credit, Clark was more open-minded (or more desperate), even as the first units of the CEF began to disembark in Naples in November 1943 and take their places in the line along the Garigliano River, his subordinate commanders remained skeptical that the French might contribute significantly to the Allied effort. And well they might, as 54 percent of the CEF was largely illiterate North African Muslims, 40 percent "French," and 6 percent odds and ends of overseas subjects.[75] It was also desperately short of technical and support troops for ordnance, signal, engineer, and medical units that placed an additional logistical and support burden on the Fifth Army. The CEF had also acquired 3,000 female secretaries, radio operators, drivers, and nurses, an unwelcome but necessary addition. Clark's original intent was to divvy up the French troops among US corps commanders. However, Juin insisted that the CEF be assigned its own sector.[76]

Delays in reequipment meant that initially only the 2^{e} DIM and 3^{e} DIA were available for operations. Each division had been assigned a *tabor* or battalion composed of 4 *goums* or companies of 175 officers and men divided into 3 platoons. "Goums are companies of irregular light mountain infantry which are recruited almost exclusively from the Berber tribes," read an undated Seventh US Army report. Each *goum* is commanded by "four commissioned and six non-commissioned officers [, who] are white Frenchmen. It is essential that they speak Berber fluently."[77] Lean, bronzed men recruited largely in the Atlas Mountains of Morocco, their American-supplied uniforms were camouflaged under striped woolen North African *djellabas* or robes. Armed with First World War-vintage bolt-action Springfield and Enfield rifles and wearing Great War-style French helmets whose central ridge was obscured beneath camouflage netting, this vanguard of the CEF appeared as a study in anachronism. Edward Bimberg, who first encountered a procession of *goums* – whom GIs persisted in calling "goons" – in Corsica, thought this "bizarre caravan" of "bearded and steely eyed" men a vision straight out of the *Arabian Nights*. Some were leading mules that carried machineguns, mortars, and other accouterments, preceded by a mounted French officer with a sky-blue kepi, his uniform swathed in the inevitable striped *djellaba*. "You saw no saluting," Bimberg remembered. "*Goumiers* and officers greeted each other with Muslim gesture of hand to lips and heart." Such was their reputation earned in Tunisia and Sicily for rusticity, adaptability, physical endurance, raiding, and night operations, that, in October 1943, Clark insisted that Juin include *goums* in his CEF. While American reports acknowledged that the discipline of the *goums* was "less strict" than in the regular army, none hint at the predatory conduct toward non-combatants that would stain the CEF's, and by association the Allies', reputation in Italy.[78] GIs found *goumiers* to be colorful and exotic, but were intimidated by their "appearance of slyness and cunning," and repelled by their reputation for brutality. Rumors that they cut off the ears of dead enemy soldiers caused GIs to view them as "savages" and "mercenary degenerates," who reflected poorly on France and gave the Allies a bad name. The battlefield practices of the *goumiers* were casual at best – they roasted goats at night, which drew artillery fire, and ignored signs indicating minefields, which cost some of them essential appendages. The fact that the French tossed them into battle after minimal training, indifferently equipped and armed with vintage weaponry and long knives, caused indignation among some GIs.[79]

Alphonse Juin

De Gaulle was more concerned about the proficiency of his army than by its politics. For reasons of competence, because he had the support of the Allies, and to ease the fusion of the two forces, de Gaulle favored the retention of his Saint-Cyr classmate Alphonse Juin as CEF commander. Given that Juin's conduct at the time of the Axis invasion of Tunisia was the subject of an official enquiry in Algiers, it was either a courageous or a foolish choice. Juin remained unpopular in the internal resistance, and among the FFL rank and file, who nicknamed him "Juin '40."[80] But, quite apart from the personal bonds between the two men, Juin's loyalty to de Gaulle was further reinforced by his contempt for Giraud, whom, according to irascible Larminat, "he

Figure 3.1 General Alphonse-Pierre Juin, commander of the French Expeditionary Force (CEF) in Italy, March 1944. (Photo by Keystone/Getty Images)

detests and despises . . . [Juin] is [*l'armée d'Afrique*'s] only soldier of quality, the only one who commands respect among those who have decided to fight with all their heart." Juin was a general who could win battles and win over the Allies, especially the Americans, with his straight talk and professionalism. A principal political payoff for de Gaulle was that Juin allowed the CEF's overwhelmingly anti-Gaullist command to focus their loyalties on their corps commander and get on with fighting the war.[81]

De Gaulle's decision to name Juin to lead the CEF had proven controversial, especially among former members of the FFL. If Italy were to witness the redemption of the French army, so too would it salvage the reputation of the CEF's commander. A soldier's soldier who enjoyed the rough humor of the barracks, Juin's bearing was collected, reserved, and understated. De Gaulle conceded that Juin's authority sprang from his competence rather than any obvious charisma or martial bearing.[82] His signature left-handed salute became authorized after his right arm was badly wounded in the Champagne offensive of 1915. With his beret pulled down to his ears, the inevitable cigarette dangling beneath a full mustache, a contorted smile that displayed a mouthful of crooked teeth, and a thick *pied noir* accent, Juin (Figure 3.1) might easily have been mistaken for a Mediterranean peasant who had wandered onto the battlefield, were it not for his insignia of rank.

But those inclined to underestimate him soon discovered a man who succeeded through an intuition for the right answer, and more than a touch of cunning.

In the aftermath of Torch, the newly reunified French army required a commander, and the alternatives were either too old or, like the rising stars of Free France, too junior and inexperienced. His now bitter rival – Jean de Lattre de Tassigny – had not yet reached North Africa. Despite Juin's close association with Vichy, de Gaulle nevertheless regarded his Saint-Cyr contemporary as the best soldier of his generation. For better or worse, in the autumn of 1943, Juin could silence the sizable chorus of sceptics only by demonstrating his leadership in combat.[83]

Allied commanders in Italy quickly came to realize that Juin's political astuteness was matched only by his operational finesse. His reconciliation with de Gaulle, who, for both political and operational reasons, required a general of Juin's stature, assured his position in the newly aggregating French forces. Juin's strengths resided in his understanding of the capacities and limitations of the North African troops who formed the backbone of his command, and in his straightforward but robust battle planning. Juin's experience of mountain combat gained during the French phase of the Rif War in 1924–1925 was to prove ultimately decisive in shattering the Gustav Line in May 1944. Critics found Juin workmanlike rather than brilliant, methodical rather than inspired. But spontaneity and opportunism were seldom options in Italy. Rugged terrain, the steel band of German defenses that had to be attacked head on, and the diminutive size and fragile composition of his force imposed meticulous planning and tight operational constraints that discouraged flights of fancy and innovations on the fly.

The situation Juin encountered in Italy was hardly brilliant from an Allied perspective. By late November, the Anglo-American advance had stalled along a seamless and near-impregnable string of fortifications that ran from the Tyrrhenian Sea, along the jagged ridges and peaks of the Aurunci Mountains, which followed the Garigliano, to the confluence of the Gari (an extension of the Rapido) and Liri Rivers about a mile and a half south of Monte Cassino (Map 3.2). Route 6 wound southwest through the town of Cassino, round the foot of what the British called Monastery Hill, which was crowned by the majestic medieval mother abbey of the Benedictine order, before it turned in a northwesterly direction toward Rome. Unfortunately, to exploit this most practical route toward the Italian capital, the Allies would have to cross the Rapido and charge up the funnel of the Liri Valley. To do so would expose their flanks to German troops entrenched to the south on the Aurunci Mountains and, to the north, at Monte Cassino, a shoulder of rock that stretched southeast from the 5,000-foot pinnacle of Monte Cairo. Recognizing that Monte Cassino and the Liri Valley offered the most obvious passage to Rome, Kesselring took care

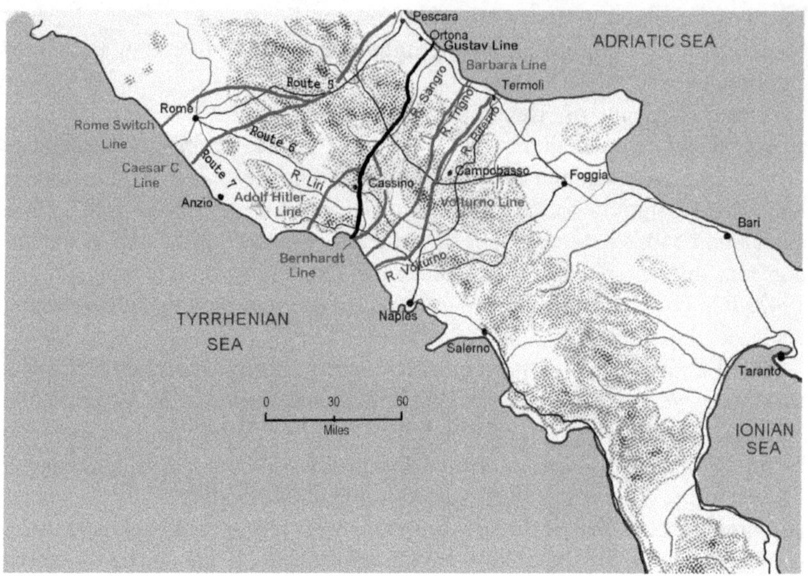

Map 3.2 The Allied advance to Monte Cassino and the Gustav Line, autumn 1943.

to concentrate his strongest defenses there. To the northeast, the Gustav Line curved through a series of spurs and ridges dominated by Monte San Croce and Monte Belvedere before it joined the Sangro River as it dropped out of the mountains to the Adriatic. This chaotic landscape enfolded 60,000 German defenders, protected behind ridges, outcroppings, crags, and ravines. "Discontinuity, depth, fluidity and flexibility are the characteristics of the enemy defensive organization," concluded the Americans. While the Germans did not offer an unbroken front, ridgelines that appeared from a distance to offer smooth routes of advance were, in fact, shattered into irregular knolls and outcroppings transformed by the defenders into strongpoints reinforced with concrete and railway tracks and ties, protected by kilometers of barbed wire and mines, and watched over by well-camouflaged observers and snipers.

The access to these strongpoints is covered by minefields and booby traps, placed in all of the ravines that seem at first view to offer infiltration points on the flanks and rear. A permanent daytime garrison occupies these strongpoints: a well-protected reserve is on the reverse slope, ready to counterattack with grenades and mortars an enemy deprived of artillery support. The strong defense in depth [12 kilometers deep in the organized zone] presents its maximum density in its field fortifications, as well as in its local reserves and artillery positions on the axes of approach toward the northeast.[84]

For these reasons, Allied attacks launched in the wake of truly awe-inspiring artillery barrages – which GIs called "stonks" – were met by the fire of mobile artillery batteries alternating among narrow valleys on the rear slopes guided to their targets by forward observers sited on mountain crests. Attackers were often deliberately allowed to progress for up to 300 yards, so that company and battalion-sized counterattacks, launched preferably at dusk or dawn and aimed at the flanks of the advancing infantry, could advance behind a curtain of artillery and mortar fire, where possible reinforced by armored vehicles and Pz.Kpfw. IV tanks. At night, German patrols were supplemented by artillery that kept up an incessant, if random, harassing fire on all approach routes. "The aggressive tactics of the enemy, the discontinuity of the fronts, and the broken nature of the terrain require constant viligance on the flanks and rear."[85] The German position in Italy had two weaknesses: the German defenses could be outflanked by sea, while the massive extension of the front caused by the sheer size of the mountains meant that the Germans could not be strong everywhere. It was the latter deficiency that Juin and the CEF would exploit.

Juin and Clark met at Clark's sprawling headquarters (HQ) in the eighteenth-century Palace of Caserta 16 miles north of Naples on 26 November. Of course, the two men were hardly strangers. Quite apart from their confrontation during the tense Algiers barney in November 1942, the two generals had also corresponded in early October 1943, Juin insisting on the need for mule companies, while Clark expressed a strong desire to see *tabors* of *goumiers* included in the CEF.[86] As they studied a map of Kesselring's Winter Line, of which the Gustav Line was the most important part, Clark proved evasive on how he would deploy the CEF. This upset Juin, as it not only proved that Clark had failed to plan for the deployment of French forces, but also suggested that he did not hold the CEF in high esteem. Rumor held that the Fifth Army Commander planned to disburse divvies of French-led "combat teams" to those US corps commanders who requested them, while Juin would serve as Clark's deputy. This, of course, would have been totally unacceptable to de Gaulle, let alone to Juin, who protested to Giraud, and then lobbied for his own sector where French troops would fight under the tricolor. In his memoirs, Juin modestly reminds us *en passant* that as a *général d'armée* – the American equivalent of a four-star flag officer – he actually outranked Clark, a mere temporary Lieutenant General. But Juin would have been on shaky ground, not to mention appearing ungrateful, had he attempted to assert seniority. Despite Juin's protestations that "politics isn't my thing," he proved remarkably politic, determined to win over Clark, seven years his junior, and the Americans, who, in Juin's view, were simultaneously powerful and desperately insecure, through humility, charm, and tactical sagacity. For this reason, Juin chose to call what eventually became a 4-division contingent, that by June 1944 would number slightly over 100,000 men or 26 percent of the Fifth Army's strength, a French "expeditionary corps" rather than the First French Army. In the short term, however, there was a price to pay for assuming a subordinate position: Juin was forbidden to correspond directly with Algiers, but had to send all correspondence only through Fifth Army headquarters. This was done for security reasons, but it also inhibited any political conspiracies. Nor did he initially visit French troops or their American corps commanders lest he give the impression that he was seeking to meddle in their command relationships.[87]

The 15,000 man 2e DIM commanded by André Dody officially entered the line on 11 December to relieve the US 34th Infantry Division (ID), and to serve as the link between the US Fifth Army and the British Eighth Army in a rock-strewn, mine-infested, snow-whipped confusion of stark 6,000-foot peaks and ridges that towered over deep river valleys. They would be followed later that month by Monsabert's 3^e^ DIA. The CEF rapidly realized that they had to leave most of their American equipment at the foot of the mountains; that the mule, not the jeep, reigned in Italy.[88] They also recognized that they had a lot to learn about mountain warfare. In some respects, Italy replicated First World War trench warfare on the Western Front, where the battle line was confined to a narrow strip of mayhem.[89] But, in Italy, the terrain was chaotic. Behind a low range of foothills rose a rugged wall of peaks, beginning with the 1,478-meter Mainarde in the west, rising to the 1,770-meter Marrone, and finally to the 2,021-meter Mont Mare. To reach Rome, roughly 150 kilometers to the north-west, the Allies would have to cut a swath through a diabolical tangle of trenches, bunkers, minefields, barbed wire, and observation points that the Germans had burrowed into their slopes. Two highways led there – the via Appia, along the Tyrrhenian Sea, and the via Casilina or Route 6 – that ran up the Liri Valley through a narrow chokepoint in the shadow of the Monastery at Cassino. Otherwise, one could go by sea. The few roads were hardly more than tracks that snaked between remote mountain villages nestled at the foot of escarpments or perched on limestone crags, through a lacerated landscape of boulders, promontories, ridgelines, and stream-swollen canyons. From behind this wall, and guided by unseen observers on the slopes, German 105 mm and 150 mm guns, mortars, and *Nebelwerfers* routinely spat up to 300 shells a day at the French lines. But "12 to 20% missed," Lanquetot noted laconically.[90]

Hardly had the French arrived than mines began to kill and maim incautious soldiers "and reinforced our fear of mines."[91] Two lieutenants and three *tirailleurs* killed by mines inaugurated the French cemetery at Roccaravindola. Alas, grave sites soon spread faster than the pox in Naples. The enemy knew the sector well, was backed by artillery and mortars, and was always shifting his position out of view. Officers had to prevent *tirailleurs* from lighting fires against a cold so bitter that the mechanisms of rifles froze, from shooting in the air when they took up a new position, and from assassinating German POWs – at least before they had been debriefed. Because of imposed radio silence, messages had to be passed by runners, who frequently became lost.[92] Allied attacks, especially successful attacks, could not be sustained because they could not be supplied – even when mules were assembled, the pack saddles were poorly adapted to transporting military equipment, much less the wounded. Mule skinners often became lost in the labyrinth of mountain trails and passes. This meant that heavy weapons were often left behind in favor of ammunition.[93] American uniforms were too light for the frigid mountain winter, while US rubber-soled boots slipped treacherously in the ubiquitous mud. However, early remedies such as stripping dead Germans for their warm jackets and more adaptable boots had to be discouraged after incidents of fratricide.

On 1 December, the 34th US ID's attack to take the heights east of Cassino had come to a halt at the foot of the Pantano mountain, "a sort of platform with four peaks that barred the approach to Monna Casale," after having suffered 800 casualties in barely 2 days.[94] Juin knew that he was taking a risk in throwing the untested 2ᵉ DIM into the front lines to relieve the battered 34th US ID, with the British to its right, and the 45th US ID on its left. He armed his soldiers with US campaign assessments, noting, among other things, that the enemy tended to leave the summits of mountains unoccupied. The US strictures cautioned against unnecessary movement, while stressing the importance of camouflage, the need for aggressive reconnaissance, the requirement to limit radio communications, that combat engineers must be in the vanguard of attacks to remove mines and booby traps, and understanding the capabilities and limitations of artillery support. "Watch where you step and don't be curious," the Americans warned. "Use a 50-meter wire to pull the mines," that could be placed under pavements, in trees, or in wood-burning stoves. "It's easy to reduce casualties if you avoid curiosity."[95] Hardly were they in place than the French dispatched patrols to collect German POWs, who were totally unaware that the French had switched out with the Americans.[96]

The attack began at nightfall on 14 December, but soon came to a halt against solid German resistance. The German defenses were sited so as to have interlocking fields of fire, which meant that a platoon attacking one bunker might come under fire from another, unanticipated direction. The following day, the 5ᵉ RTM reached the crest of the Pantano, only to be pushed off by a fierce German counterattack. But at 06:30 on 16 December, the 2ᵉ DIM launched itself up a mountainside still littered with GI corpses behind a thirty-minute artillery barrage.[97] In two days of often fierce hand-to-hand fighting amongst a line of blockhouses sited along narrow ridges well covered by German artillery, the 2ᵉ DIM became the master of the Pantano. French troops pushed forward to occupy Mount Cerasuolo and pressed toward Mount Monna

Casale and Mainarde Ridge, where German resistance firmed up. "Our allies saw us as the defeated of '40," remarked Lanquetot. "After these initial engagements [on the Pantano], we were accepted as companions in arms." Maybe that was so, but, in their eagerness to impress the Allies, the French had taken too many risks: set overly ambitious objectives, launched their offensives before thoroughly reconnoitering their sector, packed too many men in the attack echelon, and forced their attacks with understrength and underequipped units, for which they had paid dearly – 103 killed in action (KIA) or missing in action (MIA), and 701 evacuated with wounds or frozen feet. The limitations of mountain warfare had also been made apparent. For instance, mules might prove vital to supply on the slopes, but their hooves cut telephone wires, which impeded communication. The accuracy of German mortar fire had surprised and unsettled *tirailleurs* in their debut combat, as had the *excès de zèle* of French cadres, who seemed to believe that élan rather than meticulous planning and preparation offered the keys to success.[98]

During a glacial and joyless Christmas, the French attempted to assimilate the lessons of the Pantano engagement: the difficulties of night operations; the requirement to carry out their own reconnaissance rather than rely solely on US intelligence reports, which they found to be fragmentary, infrequent, and imprecise; the need for operational security; not to precipitate attacks prematurely under US pressure; the requirement to lighten the load carried by the soldiers; and the needs for better coordination among battalions and better infantry–artillery liaison. "We took too long to learn that one had to commit enough men to 'saturate' very dispersed defenses," Lanquetot wrote.[99] This turned out to be crucial, as IV Corps commander John P. Lucas was eager to seize a troika of peaks collectively called the Catenella delle Mainarde, which US reports translated as Mainarde Ridge, before the Germans could reinforce them. The first attack, launched on the 26 December, was unsuccessful, in part because low visibility precluded close air and artillery support, and because US engineers working on the road inadvertently cut the telephone wires, which prevented coordination of the attack. The only success was that the *goums* had gained a foothold on the Mainarde Ridge, but at significant costs in a role for which they were not configured.[100]

On 27 December, a renewed attack was announced by a "short, but powerful and furious" artillery barrage on the 800-meter-long Mainarde Ridge and at pill boxes on adjoining heights. Three battalions of the 8ᵉ RTM, each man's pack reduced to a blanket, a shovel, a tin of rations, and as much ammunition as they could carry, surged forward shoulder to shoulder at 08:45. The 5ᵉ RTM followed at 10:30. The chaotic nature of the terrain shattered the attack into a constellation of individual duels, as sections duked it out with grenades and bursts from Thompson sub-machineguns against pockets of German resistance. Because German defenses were sited on the reverse slope, *tirailleurs* on neighboring heights often had a better view of the defenses than did those directly engaged, and so hit them from the flanks with mortars and machineguns. On the other hand, the French would seize a ridgeline only to find themselves fired upon by Germans dug in on a higher elevation, or on a flanking hill. Mines and German artillery took a heavy toll, while units moving to bypass strongpoints had to be wary of friendly fire. German POWs were assembled and ordered to carry the wounded down the slopes, as survivors counted their ammunition and braced themselves for the inevitable German counterattack. "Whether you survived was just luck and guts," Lanquetot remembered. "A dead angle saved you. The owner of a submachine gun stood up, fired a burst and leapt forward. Move to the left. Throw a couple of grenades in a blockhouse," and climb the slope. The fog allowed some sections to take the defenses from the rear, where they hurriedly collected all the valued German stick grenades they could find. Acrid chemicals projected by exploding munitions singed nostrils and scalded throats. As night fell, the battlefield was swept by a violent snowstorm, which shrouded corpses as it froze the feet and rifles of the living. *Tirailleurs* sucked on snow for moisture, stripped the German dead of their clothing, and struggled to scrape a hole for the night over which they rolled their tent half. Walking wounded stumbled painfully down the rocky, frozen mountainside. Stretcher bearers falling every 4 to 6 meters took six hours to transport a wounded man back to the start line. Soon no stretchers were left as none returned. Through the night, mule convoys loaded with munitions toiled up the hill, while men hauled .50 caliber machineguns on their backs. On the return trip, badly wounded men and corpses were wrapped in tent halves and lashed onto mule back. On 28 December, the Germans contented themselves with bombardments of the French positions, which nevertheless caused significant casualties. By the end of the month, the 2^{e} DIA was short 45 officers and 944 men.[101]

"The Americans were stunned," Juin remembered, because they had been unable to make any progress for two weeks. The 27 December success of the 2^{e} DIM on the Catenella delle Mainarde against hardened Wehrmacht veterans dug in on the heights was all the more remarkable given that it was the division's combat debut. But the cost had been significant – 16 officers, 46 NCOs, and 235 *tirailleurs* had fallen.[102] Furthermore, the French-led Muslim troops had paid a heavy price for French neglect of logistics – inadequate radios; lack of warm clothing and proper footwear; absence of replacement parts, equipment, and weapons. Nor, despite warnings from the US supply corps, had the "intendance" bothered properly to equip 600 replacements for the 2^{e} DIM, who arrived virtually with their hands in their pockets on 6 January 1944. Complaints from the JRC about the apparent inability of the French to inventory, stock, and deliver supplies and equipment had become practically routine. Juin, too, berated the General Staff in Algiers, asking whether they expected him to strip the dead of their uniforms and arms to give to replacements. Clark was almost moved by the plight of the soldiers of the 2^{e} DIM and urged AFHQ to supply more winter uniforms and blankets. AFHQ responded with a 16 January 1944 circular that stipulated that, henceforth, French troops must arrive in Italy entirely equipped. The Fifth Army would supply the troops with tinned rations, which the French would supplement with "products suitable to the dietary habits of its combatants" from North Africa, such as flour, cooking oil, fresh meat, vegetables, tea, and sugar. However, the French proved unable to organize and supply these items from North Africa, while their purchase on Italian markets contravened Allied Military Government of Occupied Territories (AMGOT) policy of protecting the fragile food supplies of an Italian population that already subsisted on the margins of famine. The result was that not only did France expect its Muslim soldiers in Italy to fight "a war on the cheap," but also they had to do it while suffering from malnutrition. The general verdict of the French was that US rations were both monotonous and bland. At the front, they had to be eaten cold because heating them drew German fire. Ben Bella found US rations to be so insipid that he carried two canteens, one full of water, the other of honey, which he poured on bread.[103] Jean Lapouge grew tired of "the hideous *meat and beans* [in English in his text] of K and C rations," which meant that "we don't even take a small pleasure in eating."[104] But it was a question of taste – Lanquetot found K rations were monotonous, but C rations consisting of a box of six cans containing meat, vegetables, chocolate, and coffee were much appreciated. A mix and match of C, K, and B rations could produce an acceptable *ragoût*. And, if all else failed, there was an abundant supply of cigarettes.[105]

However, if the Gustav Line had crashed the Allied dream of a mechanized war of maneuver, the French were gradually mastering the art of mountain warfare – more effective counterbattery fire aided by microphones on US sound trucks that allowed the US artillery supporting the French to pinpoint the position of German artillery; placing mine-lifting engineers in the attack vanguard; more mules to convey ammunition to the front and casualties to the rear; more radios in order better to coordinate attacks; and enlisting fog, rain, and snow storms – of which there was no shortage in January – to turn and seize lines of resistance from the rear. Four-man "stiff patrols" were dispatched to collect the dead, and strip any German corpses of their warmer boots and jackets, which soon made the two armies indistinguishable at a distance. The days were spent digging, and digging more. One day a bomber overhead was hit by flak, disgorging three parachutes, one of which landed among the machinegun section. "The aviator detached himself from his shroud, straightened up, tall, thin, elegant among us. He must have had the impression that he had landed among savages. Calm, he didn't bother to raise his hands. His first gesture was to pull out a cigarette and light it. Then ask: 'German? American?' 'No, French'. The guy was rather surprised," especially when the *tirailleurs* immediately began to cut up his parachute to send pieces home to their wives.[106] Some units had taken a crushing 70 percent casualty rate, often because they ran out of ammunition and fell victim to German counterattacks. How many more peaks remained to assault in Italy?

Detoxifying *l'armée d'Afrique*

Many of the casualties at the top of the CEF were of a political rather than a combat nature. While the CEF brawled and perished in the icy mountains of central Italy in a heroic attempt to recuperate French prestige and validate France's commitment to the Allied cause, Juin complained disingenuously that "the climate of hostility" stoked by the Gaullists threatened the cohesion of the army. While he had naively hoped that the army would be exempted from the political wrangling, unscrupulous politicians and "false resisters" launched a bout of score settling in Algiers.[107] In fact, in the view of the newly ascendant Gaullists, *l'armée d'Afrique* was "malade," "intoxiquée," and "empoisonnée" with "hyper-Pétainism." De Gaulle prioritized the cleansing of AFN of pro-Vichy functionaries and organizations, establishing his control over his military forces and the civil administration, and reinforcing the legitimacy of the CFLN on the international stage. For the Americans, worried that Darlan's assassination might portend civil war, the French ship of state in AFN looked increasingly like "The Raft of the Medusa." On 15 August, the "Special Investigative Commission for Tunisia," familiarly known as the Viard Commission after its chairman Paul-Émile Viard, Dean of the University of Algiers law faculty, had convened to examine the events of November 1942 in Tunisia. Three days later, the CFLN passed an ordinance establishing a "purge committee" whose mandate was to ferret out "all those, leaders or administrators, who by their acts, writings, or behavior encouraged enemy action." Convened in the middle of September 1943, this committee of five members was armed with investigatory powers to recommend prosecutions of "elected officials, civil servants, and public agents" to the commissariat of justice. "Abdication of national sovereignty," clearly aimed at Pétain, was declared a crime. Those found guilty risked suffering "national indignity" at a minimum. This was followed by the creation of a "military tribunal with special powers" on 2 October 1943, to investigate infractions that had occurred since September 1939, with a focus on the empire. Similar "purge committees" were replicated in the diplomatic corps, public education, the prefectures, and even governor and resident general offices. But the de-Vichyfication of the civil service in AFN registered few victories at this stage. By the end of 1943, 352 French citizens, including members of "collaborationist organizations," and 233 "natives" had been incarcerated in AFN. Meant to serve as evidence of the restoration of Republican legality, trials in the New Year targeted administrators and guards in internment camps. In this way, "Algeria served as the crucible of the purges in the metropole, with on one hand the elaboration of a legislative arsenal that would permit the cleansing of the country following the liberation, and on the other the executions like those of Pucheu and Cristofini," conclude Rouquet and Virgili. However, "Republican legality" was a courtesy seldom extended to "natives" accused of collaboration, such as the 3,000 non-French interned on the island of Djerba at the end of the Tunisia campaign, many of whom allegedly were tortured or summarily executed.[108]

Called into session from 3 November 1943, the Consultative Assembly prioritized the creation of a republican *levée* to liberate the mainland, and perhaps also to preempt an incipient military coup, rumors of which had swirled since Torch. This effort was spearheaded by the commissar for war André Le Troquer, a socialist activist in the Section française de l'internationale ouvrière (SFIO), who in 1940 had numbered among the twenty-seven deputies refusing the armistice who had boarded the *Massilia* at Bordeaux with the intention of fighting on from North Africa, a plan balked by Noguès allegedly at Darlan's orders. But Le Troquer's real sin in the eyes of the *Maréchalists* was successfully to have defended Léon Blum at Riom, which had helped to abort the trial, and which also sent Le Troquer into hiding. Despite, or perhaps because of, his Great War *croix de guerre*, Le Troquer remained a doctrinaire anti-militarist whose foundational virtue in the eyes of the Gaullist Brosset was that he cultivated a particular animus for Juin and *l'armée d'Afrique*.[109] The immediate goal of Le Troquer and the purge committee was to deny to veterans of the PPF, the SOL, the LFC, the *Légion tricolore*, and the *Phalange africaine*, the most compromised Vichy officials, and other collaborators redemption by fire in Italy. He had his work cut out for him, as the "hyper-Pétainisme" of *l'armée d'Afrique* had been exported to Italy in a particularly distilled form, led by the "convinced Maréchalist" André Dody who, before he took command of the 2e DIM, had become infamous for harassing Gaullists and republicans in Meknès, where he had been in command when Torch crashed onto Moroccan shores. Despite the fact that 3e DIA commander Joseph de Monsabert had aided the Allied invasion in November 1942, his particularly reactionary brand of Catholicism and loyalty to Giraud had caused him to refuse to meet with de Gaulle before his unit's departure for Italy. Prior to commanding the *goums* in Italy, General Augustin Guillaume had served as Noguès' enforcer in Morocco. Each cocooned himself with compatible staffs, so that the political ambience in the CEF remained stubbornly Giraudist. But, as Giraud was gradually eclipsed, they dexterously transferred their allegiances, so that the CEF became "Juin's army."[110]

Lamentations from the CEF in Italy that this panoply of "purge committees," boards of inquiry, courts martial, and the like offered venues where Jews, Freemasons, and Gaullists pursued political retribution and personal vendettas echoed as far as Algiers. Officers grumbled that the ascendant Gaullists had shipped them to Italy to be stigmatized, forsaken, and sacrificed. The irony that their combat pay in Italy was lower than their overseas pay in AFN, and would take another cut when they invaded France, on the logic that they were now "home," intensified their sense of grievance. Comrades who remained in AFN and were assigned to de Lattre's *Armée B*, to prepare for the invasion of southern France, were alleged to be promoted at faster rates than those risking their lives in Italy. Juin complained that the purge committees were exporting the political turmoil of AFN to Italy, especially when officers were summoned back to Algiers to be interrogated and possibly charged, or news arrived that friends or relatives had been arrested or sanctioned. This was interpreted as a lack of respect for the CEF, a feeling reinforced in late January 1944 when Le Troquer and Georges publicly clashed over the army's blame for 1940, a civil–military wound that continued to fester. "The visceral denunciation of the political activity of Algiers, in particular the purges, expressed the lingering traumatism of an officer corps that rejected any criticism," concludes Le Gac. *Armée d'Afrique* sensitivities were raw with fears that rifts in the French community might loosen the loyalty of their Muslim soldiers. However, nationalist propaganda does not seem to have impacted Algerian units. Nor did the nationalist demonstrations that rocked Morocco in January 1944 find an echo among the 3ᵉ DIM's largely Amazigh rank-and-file soldiers. Nevertheless, as a precaution, Juin reinforced postal censorship in the CEF, as did the Residency in Rabat. Nor did German propaganda that sought to convince Muslim troops that they were being deployed as cannon fodder to save American and British lives appear to have had an effect. Attempts were made to reinforce internal solidarity by having *pieds noirs* write letters for illiterate Muslim soldiers, and read to them letters that they received. The CEF was careful to respect Muslim holidays, even though, in his memoires, Ben Bella complained that each European soldier received a US Christmas package for himself, while Muslims shared a package among three soldiers. But, like any colonial system, that of France was anchored in a concept of racial privilege and superiority.[111]

In fact, despite the lamentations of the CEF and the fierce bark of Le Troquer and the *commission d'épuration*, its bite was tempered by realism, as ultimately only 31 officers were struck from the army's rolls and 4 demobilized as a result of their efforts, although a further 1,436 "disciplinary measures" of varying severity were pronounced by Le Troquer. Meanwhile, the French navy had basically scuttled itself out of a job, an own goal that allowed the CFLN's *commissaire de la marine* to eliminate half the serving admirals simply by enforcing the upper age limit on command, and retire 1,300 officers in 3 months. And while, by 1950, an estimated 7,833 officers and NCOs of all services had been "sanctioned" for their conduct under Vichy, as Julie Le Gac notes, for an army that eventually grew to 350,000 men, 176,500 of whom were French, this barely represented a slap on the wrist. Why this was so can be traced in part to de Gaulle's pragmatism. But also, as the liberation loomed, de Gaulle realized that he must begin to alter his image from avenger to healer, to reconcile a people traumatized and polarized by defeat and occupation. The French leader attempted to moderate the rhetoric, shift the horizon away from 1940, collaboration, and *attentisme*, and excuse officers who, misguided by Vichy's twisted concept of discipline packaged in the Weygand-imposed "oath to the Marshal," had made "bad choices." In this ecumenical spirit, the purgatory of "administrative sanctions" substituted for excommunication from the national community. Emphasis on "*la rassemblement nationale*," the "amalgamation" of the external and internal resistance, the restoration of the state, and *la grandeur de la France* increasingly shifted the theme of Liberation from retaliation to reconciliation and renewal, even as the recriminations that flowed from defeat and occupation stubbornly lingered.

However, Vichy's high-placed enablers were not to be spared. Allied pushback following the conviction and 20 March 1944 execution of Darlan's former Secretary of the Interior Pierre Pucheu also played a role. For those with a ringside seat to the trials, like Macmillan, it was time for the French to put the misunderstandings of Torch behind them, rehabilitate the French army, and get on with the war.[112] One consequence of Pucheu's execution was that popular sentiment concluded that the action of the *commission d'épuration* represented a "disorganized and blind" retaliation imposed by "metropolitans" on the *pied noir* community and its venerated *armée d'Afrique* paladins. While the goal was to eliminate Vichyism from the forces prior to the liberation, to dispel the popular sentiment of betrayal by France's political leadership, to facilitate the "amalgamation" of the civilian resistance with the regular army, and to rebuild civil–military relations, as a practical matter, even the communists conceded that it was counterproductive in the middle of a war to court martial professional soldiers in a force already starved of cadres. The Allies looked upon the recall of professional officers from Italy to appear before Algiers tribunals as yet another example of French infighting and political agendas taking priority over the Allied goal of winning the war. Not surprisingly, Gaullists and some members of the internal resistance complained that *épuration* did not go far enough, and that the CEF had become a refuge for erstwhile Pétainists on a quest "to regain their virginity" through combat.[113]

The First Battle of Cassino

Second lieutenant Jean Lapouge was delighted to exchange "AFN's rotten atmosphere" for the virile adversities of Italy, "because each drop of French blood that flows wherever in the world contributes to national grandeur. And then, combat is the domain of the strong." Gripped by a sort of death cult born of national humiliation, Lapouge sermonized that young Frenchmen must "wash away the humiliation with their blood, to show the world that it's still us who know best how to die. The regular army, above all we *tirailleurs*, who constitute a professional army, seem destined for that."[114] The French assault of the Pantano had offered a mere warm-up for what is sometimes called the First Battle of Cassino. Under pressure from Churchill, who declared the stalemate in Italy to be "scandalous," Clark's plan called for a rolling attack on the Gustav Line launched by the three divisions of McCreery's X corps from the Tyrrhenian Sea north across the Garigliano River, designed to draw off General Fridolin von Senger und Etterlin's panzers. This would allow Fred Walker's 36th ID, part of the US II Corps, to vault the Rapido River, just northeast of its confluence with the Liri to form the Garigliano, that would open a path for Ernest Harmon's 1st AD to charge up Route 6 that bisected the Liri Valley toward Rome. To protect Harmon's right flank, the 34th ID would also cross the Rapido to assault the abbey and Monte Cassino town from the north. They were to have the support of Juin's two divisions, directed to seize the Belvedere almost 4 miles north of Cassino to outflank German positions at the mouth of the Liri Valley. This assault on the Gustav Line would be assisted by an amphibious flanking movement code-named "Shingle" to seize Anzio, a seaside town 35 miles south of Rome. The theory of victory was that, outflanked in the Liri Valley, and with his communications threaten by the landing of Allied troops at Anzio, Kesselring must weaken the Gustav Line to deal with the Anzio landing. If he did not, troops at Anzio could seize Rome and threaten Kesselring's line of retreat. In that case, he would have no choice but to abandon the Gustav Line and withdraw north, flinging open the road to Rome (Map 3.3). Unfortunately, this victory scenario flipped when Clark became the commander forced to shift troops from Cassino to rescue the Anzio beachhead.[115]

Clark's plan encountered little enthusiasm on the ground. In the first place, it had been prepared by staff officers at Caserta with minimal input from local commanders, who found its assumptions optimistic and beyond the capacities of their troops. Second, senior British army officers in particular were in despair over a lack of aggression in their units that recalled Singapore. The swagger that had characterized the Eighth Army in North Africa under Montgomery had ebbed away in Italy, as British manpower reserves peaked, and the experienced company-grade officers and NCOs so important in pushing attacks on the ground and so difficult to replace were rendered *hors de combat*.[116] Desertions skyrocketed, as what were dubbed the "Free English" hid in the mountains or skulked in Naples' dark alleys. In comparison, the CEF appeared to offer a model of cohesion and discipline, although, to be fair, the Eighth Army had been fighting for a long time with no end in sight. The

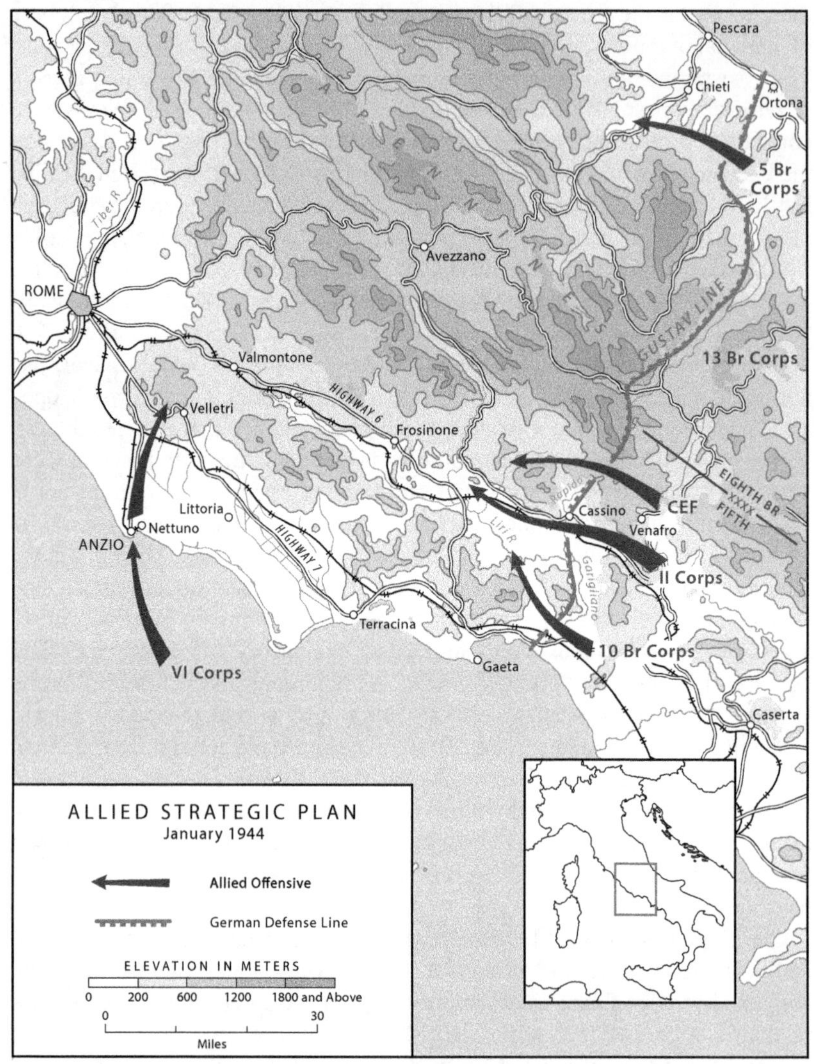

Map 3.3 The Allied plan to break the Cassino Line 1943–1944.

propensity of Tommies to desert was such that at Monte Cassino officers patrolled the front with drawn pistols to discourage their men from scuttling to the rear.[117]

Shingle – the assault on Anzio – also boasted a dubious provenance. The success of Torch, followed by Husky and Avalanche, had transformed amphibious operations from a tactic for relatively small-scale raids into a strategic game-changer for the Allies. A combination of Eisenhower's desire to speed up the advance in Italy and Churchill's hectoring had caused Clark to send "Iron Mike" O'Daniel to search out a likely landing spot within air range. O'Daniel proposed Anzio, a tiny harbor on the sandy, pine-sheltered coast 70 miles north of the Cassino front. The idea was staffed, debated, modified, vetoed, and resuscitated in the shadow of Churchill's impatience and Clark's desperation, and handed off in late December to fifty-four-year-old Major General John P. Lucas. The rehearsal for Shingle did not go well. Convinced that the assault was underresourced, Lucas seemed dispirited and fatalistic, hardly emboldened by Patton's prediction that his friend would never "get out of this alive."[118]

Shingle also increased the profile of the CEF, as Dody's 3ᵉ DIA was slotted in to replace the 45th US ID, which had been selected for the amphibious operation, on the Cassino front. This gave Juin a two-division sector early in the New Year. In Juin's opinion, Clark's plan offered a chain reaction of inchoate and poorly supported attacks without adequate reserves to exploit opportunities should they arise. Clark needed ten more divisions than he actually commanded to enjoy any chance of success. Nor were armored and motorized Allied divisions configured to fight an infantry war in the mountains. Juin's earlier warnings that mules would be the foundation of logistics in Italy were finally heeded at the end of November 1943.[119] This triggered Herculean efforts to purchase 15,000 mules from throughout the Mediterranean, and to integrate 6 Italian, 7 Indian, 5 Cypriot, and 8 French North African mule transport companies into the Allied order of battle. "No mules, no maneuver," Juin was fond of repeating.[120] Indeed, so vital did mules become to Allied operations around Cassino, to transport weapons and munitions and evacuate the wounded, that German artillery prioritized mule parks.[121] Nevertheless, there were never enough mules, while relying on animal logistics posed many of the same problems in Italy as it had in France in 1940.[122]

Tactically, Juin had been unhappy with the role Mark Clark had allotted him even as the combat raged. He felt that the strengths of his troops – mobility, fluidity, the ability to maneuver and infiltrate – were mismatched against the tightly constructed German defensive system. What Kesselring called his "string of pearls" across the Italian boot looked, to those forced to attack it, increasingly more like a garotte.[123] The Gustav Line as it had taken shape from October 1943 handed considerable advantages to the defenders: unobstructed observation from summits; camouflage; inaccessibility for the attackers, who must first traverse a river swollen with winter rains and whose banks as well as the mountain slopes were laced with belts of 23,000 anti-personnel mines, many of them with non-metallic casing, and hence virtually undetectable, including foot-shattering *Schützenminen* (or *Schü-Minen*, riflemen's mines).

Springminen (or *S-Minen*, bounding mines), called "Bouncing Betty" by the Americans, were the most dreaded – small cylinders that leapt 3 feet into the air when triggered by a trip wire or detonator to release a spray of ball bearings. The goal of these mines was to wound rather than kill, thereby further thinning the ranks of attackers by requiring stretcher bearers to carry the injured men to the rear.

A reinforced line of blockhouses located 10 meters behind the crest on the reverse slope, so as to be out of sight of Allied artillery observation, was garrisoned by squads of four or five men, each squad armed with a light and a heavy machinegun. The bulk of the garrison huddled in shelters 150 meters behind the crest, where they were safe from Allied artillery barrages. The German tactic was to launch sudden counterattacks from their strongpoints behind a barrage of mortars against attackers exhausted by the ascent, whose ranks were thinned by mines, who had probably run short of munitions, and who would be too surprised by the sudden violence to react effectively. Artillery concentrated on the reserves. The operational genius of this defense system was that it economized on manpower, while also neutralizing the Allied technical advantage of armor, massive artillery superiority, and airpower. In this way, war on the Gustav Line became an infantry siege. Meanwhile, German artillery could register on the most obvious approaches, which quickly became "death routes." Surprise was virtually impossible to achieve, despite later use of camouflage screens and smoke rounds fired from mortars to hide movement.

Once they had arrived in position, the French sent out night patrols to map German minefields, blockhouses, and machinegun nests and locate approach routes. The attackers attempted to dig in for protection from artillery and mortars, which was often impossible in the stone-hard mountains, and then creep forward at night to toss a grenade into a machinegun embrasure as a prelude to seizing a small strongpoint. They would then stand by for the inevitable German counterattack behind a storm of *Nebelwerfer* (literally "smoke projector," multiple-barrel rocket artillery) fire. It was slow, patient, lethal work, made more difficult by extreme weather conditions in which temperatures might drop to −30 °C, and by sleep deprivation.[124] Ben Bella's unit landed in Naples in December 1943, and relieved the Americans before Montano. The slopes were so steep that his soldiers had to hoist up food and munitions by rope. The American Garand rifles were so heavy and cumbersome that he preferred simply to use a pistol. Cadavers of US soldiers were scattered over no man's land. Snow, glacial wind, and German night patrols that would shout taunts in English because they believed the Americans were still there, and throw grenades to gain a psychological advantage, made sleep impossible. Mines, including explosives encased in concrete and surrounded by shrapnel, made it difficult for Ben Bella's Moroccans to reciprocate in kind.

When one of his soldiers was killed by a mine 30 meters to the front, it took two hours walking gingerly on stones to retrieve the body. German artillery barrages were both random and precise, when a shell would land every two to three minutes on obligatory approach routes. In any case, the constant shelling was psychologically exhausting. Between bombardment, wounds, frostbite, and pneumonia, the company was soon reduced by two-thirds. Because replacements were disoriented and virtually untrained, Sergeant Ben Bella had to take them in hand, select their firing positions, and explain their duties.[125] Lapouge had the same complaint about a draft of replacements who arrived in February 1944: "They are poorly trained, poorly equipped, physically unfit." While he had been ordered to haul eight machineguns up the mountain, he had crews to man only six of them. Many of his *tirailleurs* had not even been taught how to pull the pin out of a grenade. According to Lapouge, Monsabert kept quiet about French deficiencies so as not to give the Americans an excuse to withdraw French troops from the front lines.[126]

"At night, the landscape comes alive, the round of patrols begins, because it is necessary to learn whether the enemy has moved on," noted a December 1943 description of the front. "But, in general, [the German] plays the reverse game, reinforcing at night the essential points weakly held if at all during the day. Flares, bombardments, true illuminations of the rear caused by friendly artillery firing massive barrages. Harassing fire of German artillery on divisional CPs [command posts] and the roads around them intensifies at fixed times: dusk – midnight – dawn. The precision of this shelling is remarkable: the Germans have excellent ground observers. The rear is not secure. One encounters Jerry patrols in villages that we occupy. Audacious detachments that seek to blow roads and bridges operate behind division CPs."[127]

Clark's problem, as Kesselring realized, was that attacks had to follow the flanks of the mountains. This meant that even large-scale offensives shattered into a constellation of independent assaults funneled into narrow corridors and passes through the mountains. This allowed the Germans, who commanded both the high ground and interior lines, to shunt reserves more easily among threatened sectors, and to concentrate defenses on obvious lines of approach.[128] Ballistic challenges and lack of observation in poor weather largely negated the allied advantage in firepower, because it was very difficult to calculate artillery or even bombing precision in mountainous terrain where abrupt variations in elevation and air pressure affected artillery and mortar trajectories. Attacks required a level of discipline, coordination, and organization which the Allies struggled to master in January 1944. Ascent was usually in a single file along narrow tracks – the more remote the better – at first through mud, and then in snow and ice at higher elevations. "The trails are impossible," remembered Lapouge, "melted snow, rocks, underbrush to cross." A soldier's kit weighted

16 kilos, plus grenades, and above all ammunition because resupply was so precarious for an ascent lasting several hours.[129]

With orders from Clark to conquer the heights of the Rapido by 20 January, on 12 January the CEF's Commander launched his two divisions at the 1,395-meter Monna Casale, which he considered the key to the German positions, behind a hurricane barrage of 15 minutes, that Lapouge observed made the mountain explode like an erupting volcano. One could see the *tirailleurs* advancing like black specks through the snow, throwing grenades, outflanking positions, "following the classic schema, as in a training exercise," while a tank destroyer on the road below fired at German positions. By 15 January, the French had seized three peaks and advanced 6 kilometers, and on 16 January the Americans topped Mount Trocchio. Hoping to turn the Cassino position from the northeast, Clark directed Juin to outflank the German defenses by seizing the ridgelines northwest of the Rapido. Juin renewed his offensive on 21 January, his agile Moors scaling the most difficult routes in the hope that these would be the least well defended. "Our casualties were light," concluded the CEF's after-action report, "because our attempt on Mount San Croce had been conducted mainly by means of infiltration and maneuvering tactics."[130] On 23 January, Clark had asked him to shift his attack to German lines just north of Cassino (that is, on the left side of the French line) to support the attack of the 34th US ID, which required shifting all his artillery over mountain roads under the German harassing fire. On the night of 25 January, the 3ᵉ DIA took Hill 470 by surprise, and then bounced to seize the three peaks collectively called the Belvedere. But, as the Belvedere constituted one of the main strongpoints of the Gustav Line and blocked the way to the Colle Abate, the Germans were not to be fooled twice. "General Juin was employing his forces in attack by infiltration and maneuver [especially tactics involving flanking movements], a method which allowed him to gain ground quickly with few losses but which was difficult to adapt to the defensive," reads the US after-action report. This also meant that the rushes forward left many German troops in his rear areas, which required "mopping up" operations.[131]

On 29 January, the US 142nd Infantry Regiment was thrown into the fight for Colle Abate, which was seized on 30 January in bitter fighting – squads of French-led troops infiltrating over the most treacherous and hence least well-defended terrain cautiously approached German bunkers from the flanks, to push grenades through the embrasures, and machinegun defenders fleeing out the back door. Peaks and ridges were taken, surrendered, and retaken as men fought for days without food, their weapons often frozen in their hands, depending on captured German munitions to continue the struggle. In these conditions, gaining a psychological advantage over the enemy was crucial. "I don't know how to explain this phenomenon," Ben Bella remembered, "if not that, in a war of position, when two armies face off for a long time, one ends up by its tenacity and enterprising spirit gaining an irresistible ascendency. One becomes well aware of the moment when the adversary suddenly gives up, not because we hit harder, but because he feels dominated." Ben Bella speculated that the enemy in front began to melt away because they were Panzergrenadiers (mechanized infantry) without tanks. "Their breakdown was only momentary." Unfortunately, his company commander Captain Villaucourt was wounded during the 20 January attack at Santa Croce and replaced by an Alsatian aspirant he calls "Z," apt to vanish during firefights, only miraculously to materialize once the position had been secured.[132] Only two of the eighty mules sent to resupply the French defenders reached the summit. The French advance placed the defenders in crisis mode. Kesselring milked his divisions for reserves.[133]

By the first week in February, the German defenses around Monte Cassino had hardened, while lashing rain, logistical problems, and sheer exhaustion had stalled the Allied advance. The costs for the 3ᵉ DIA had been high – 2,091 soldiers *hors de combat*, including 64 officers. The 2ᵉ DIM announced 678 killed and 229 wounded. Loss rates for the Germans were unclear, but included 450 POWs.[134] Lapouge noted that, while the carnage among French officers was significant, they seldom came across the bodies of German officers.[135] However, this huge effort had barely made a dent in the Gustav Line. Nor had the attack facilitated a success for Shingle, launched on 22 January, an event that many troops around Cassino prayed would soon liberate them from the accursed mountains.[136] Unfortunately for them, by pulling in reserves from as far away as France and the Balkans, Kesselring managed to import 90,000 men to seal off Lucas' beachhead, and even launch punishing counterattacks by 3 February. Ungraciously, Churchill blamed Anzio's failure on the "lack of audacity" of American generals.[137] Nevertheless, the French congratulated themselves for what was "in every respect ... a remarkably well-conducted affair" east of Monte Cassino, not least because of the nature of the terrain, the fact that the attack had to be supported along a single mountain road under constant German bombardment, and because "it required of the artillery that it should alter its whole disposition, to be able to give effective support to the attack." Monsabert proudly quoted a German POW: "I have just discovered that the French army is not dead yet."[138]

The French success raised Juin's stature in the Alliance and gave him a greater voice in Allied decision-making. It also lifted the prestige of de Gaulle and the CFLN, and sealed their association with the success of the Allied endeavor. But the cost had been high – 15,864 casualties, of whom 3,305 were French. Despite the congratulations showered on the French, Juin feared that the morale of his North Africans might crack as their cadres were decimated and their casualty rates skyrocketed.[139] While Kesselring praised the "excellent troops of the French Expeditionary Corps," he concluded that the

Allies could not continue such a "reckless" expenditure of men indefinitely.[140] "What a massacre!," recorded Lapogue of the mid-January attacks. "This morning we crossed these conquered rocks. Until now, I never understood the expression 'a carpet of cadavers.' And these are French in every posture, hands stretched toward the sky, contorted in their regulation half-leather, half-wool gloves, craniums split, *tirailleurs* cut in half, disemboweled." By the first week in February, companies were down to thirty men. Lapouge and the captain were the only two officers left in his company, while the 2nd Company was commanded by a sergeant.[141] The first nurse casualty, Marie Loretti, had been killed by shrapnel as she evacuated the wounded. At her funeral, Juin awarded her a posthumous *médaille militaire*; she was the first of 3,000 females in the CEF so honored in Italy.[142]

The French success was all the more impressive as it contrasted with the relative failure of British and American endeavors, which many attributed to Clark's underresourced attacks and poor battle management. Instead, Clark attributed the failure of the British attack to the "lack of strong aggressive leadership at the divisional level."[143] In fact, the British had taken over 4,000 casualties and had been stymied by repeated German counterattacks. Meanwhile, he required Fred Walker's 36th US ID to attack across a rain-swollen Rapido River into the teeth of formidable defenses manned by the 15th Panzergrenadier Division. This American attack failed at the cost of 1,681 casualties. As usual, rather than accept responsibility for what was denounced as "Bloody River," Clark unleashed a search for scapegoats.[144].

The 34th US ID and the CEF had snatched the honors of this first attempt to crack Monte Cassino.[145] Juin reported that the Germans had required seventeen battalions to halt the CEF, or 44 percent of their forces. "One can say that the French army has recovered its reputation," he reported triumphantly. The British were especially impressed by the ferocity of the Moroccans, who "regarded the killing of enemies as an honourable and agreeable duty to be undertaken with zest." Indeed, "gouming it" entered the British military vocabulary to describe an especially audacious attack. German General Julius Ringel reported that the Moroccans had inflicted 80 percent casualties on his troops who had opposed them.[146] Nevertheless, losses for the 3ᵉ DIA alone between 25 and 31 January had been 103 killed, 913 wounded, and 25 missing, and its supply line was precarious. Two US infantry battalions had to be rushed in to secure the French foothold on the Belvedere.[147]

The Aftermath of the First Battle of Cassino

Clark had been obliged to persist in his futile offensive in order to prevent the Germans from reacting to the Anzio invasion. In the end, it had not mattered – the Anzio incursion had been too diminutive, and Lucas' options too limited, to pose a real threat to Kesselring, who quickly assembled 88 mm guns to seal off the Anzio beachhead until he could muster a sufficiently large blocking force. By February, the overmatched Lucas had been relieved by Lucian Truscott. As early as 1 February 1944, even Giraud complained that Allied thrusts to date – at Monte Cassino, at Anzio, and on the Adriatic – lacked the concentration and muscle to force a breakthrough, and mustered insufficient strength to seize Rome. From a French perspective, this was catastrophic, because, until Rome was secure, the Allies could not prepare for the invasion of southern France, whose success Giraud believed was critical for the cross-Channel invasion from Great Britain. "It's a compromise peace on the horizon, with all of its consequences," he feared.[148]

With the failure of the January offensives, the baton for the Second and Third "Battles of Cassino" was passed to the Eighth Army, with the CEF poised to attack as soon as British forces made a breakthrough. "New dispositions were necessary and the keynote was constant alertness," read the Fifth Army's report. "However, the Cassino battle was to continue on well into March with the result that the French Forces were unable to take up their advance for the remainder of their stay in the sector. Instead the period is filled with planning, reliefs, repositioning, and the maintenance of contact with the enemy. The excitement of successful attack did not come again to the troops on the Belvedere Bridgehead."[149]

The First Battle of Cassino had been a remarkable but unsustainable show by the French, as casualties were running at 2–4 percent of strength *per day*. While mines were most feared by the soldiers, artillery proved by far the biggest killer, which was why soldiers were constantly engaged in the exhausting work of digging holes.[150] By February 1944, the French commanders recognized that their troops had reached the limit of their physical and psychological resilience, a situation acknowledged by Juin the following month.[151] "In the mountains, at night, sounds reverberate," testified Sergeant Guy Martinet of the 4^{e} RTM. "Silence is difficult to achieve [the men must march with canes so as not to fall, or unloosen stones]. Also, at night, one gets lost. Several reliefs have realized the advantages of sending men to reconnoiter the itinerary *after dark* [italics in the original]. The relieved sections are in too much of a hurry. The heavy weapons have already been withdrawn. Information is too quickly exchanged. The relieved unit needs absolutely to leave behind an NCO for 24 or 28 hours to pass on information impossible to give at night or the next day [even if it's just to indicate the enemy positions]. Preferably in written form [especially to the heavy weapons section.]"[152] Soldiers were losing their concentration, often just firing without aiming, sometimes into the air. Loneliness, a feature of all combat, was particularly acute in the mountains, where one must always stay vigilant. As Ben Bella testified, being surrounded by cadavers was particularly shocking and demoralizing to Muslim troops. Collective panics *à la* Bulson or

Kasserine were rare. But, if someone abandoned his post, the example might prove contagious, although this seems to have seldom happened, or at least was seldom punished. The sense of powerlessness was overwhelming. Ben Bella complained that living in mud and snow, under persistent shelling, and being unable to move in daylight was especially taxing. Soon, only one-third of his original company remained, the rest dead, wounded, or evacuated with frozen feet or pneumonia. Their poorly trained replacements quickly became disoriented, and so had to be taken firmly in hand.[153] Lapouge found that combat conditions in Italy were far worse than in Tunisia. "Nothing is more demoralizing than this system of reinforcements that gives the impression to the veterans that they will fight until everyone is dead," noted Lapouge. Yet, at this low point, his Saint-Cyr indoctrination kicked in: "But we continue. It's a question of making the world understand that our race still has the courage to be worthy of its high destiny."[154] Incidents of suicide and self-mutilation among *tirailleurs* increased, as high losses and a paucity of reserves meant that the soldiers of the CEF had little rest, even during brief periods out of the line.[155]

While the Anglo-American armies attempted to medicalize trauma as a symptom of psychological stress, the CEF politicized it as a threat to the survival of the military institution, the bedrock of French imperialism, and to France's potential impact on the war. This was a natural reflex for an allegedly "apolitical" force that nonetheless had embraced *le culte du Maréchal* and the exclusion of certain "racial" categories – notably Jews. Larminat for one decried the hypocrisy of *l'armée d'Afrique* that professed to be apolitical, but in fact censored only those opinions to which its leadership objected.[156] The army's sense of isolation from French society and its republican traditions was particularly acute in North Africa, where officers perceived their imperial mission as being undervalued, while besieged by Muslim nationalists who sought to undermine the loyalty of indigenous troops. The events of 1940 followed by Torch had disoriented *l'armée d'Afrique*. The presence of large numbers of well-armed and professionally uniformed and equipped Allied soldiers in North Africa revived the humiliation of 1940, and caused the French to lose face with the Muslims. The sense of marginalization was further reinforced as instructions and decrees forbade communication with Vichy and ordered the removal of Pétain's portraits, as political parties began to reorganize within the CFLN, repeal discriminatory laws against Jews and Freemasons, and launch investigations of officers' collaboration followed by purges. This impelled the CEF to double down on "traditions" anchored in colonialist paternalism, a rejection of materialism, and a sense of French racial superiority that legitimated their authority and status. French officers justified their visceral antisemitism with spurious arguments that Jews made indifferent soldiers whose presence in the ranks would offend Muslims. Their loyalty to Pétain, the man who had offloaded responsibility for 1940 onto politicians and popular pacifism and hence had restored their "honor," had been severed by outside intervention, not through spiritual conversion, so that the full panoply of Vichy pathologies endured in the mess.[157]

One of Juin's goals in Italy was to win victories that would restore the army's prestige, strengthen unity, and create an image of military strength to impress foreigners and Muslims. He feared that the high losses among junior officers and NCOs, combined with combat stress, might threaten the CEF's cohesion and combat effectiveness. Army orders emphasized "bravery," "abnegation," and "the qualities of the leader" as a means to stimulate individual heroism within a collective service. The idea was to encourage pride in belonging to an elite. If a soldier failed, he let down his comrades and sullied the reputation of his unit. The standard argument for limiting the numbers of Muslims in the officer and NCO corps was that, in the French view, they possessed "neither the spirit of sacrifice, nor the professional conscientiousness of French cadres." For this reason, Muslim soldiers naturally looked to their French leaders, who had to guide them as if they were children who, if treated fairly but firmly, would respond. The fear was that, if French leadership were decimated in combat, the cohesion of North African units might dissolve. The problem was that there were not enough Europeans in North Africa to provide cadres for a mobilized indigenous population.[158]

Furthermore, the medicalization of trauma was a luxury the CEF could ill afford. French medical services were so inadequate, doctors and medical staff particularly sparse, and field hospitals so Spartan and lacking in beds, medicines, and surge capacity during periods of high operational tempo that the wounded were increasingly diverted to Fifth Army field hospitals, where, among other things, "combat exhaustion" – a significant problem, especially in infantry units in Italy during offensive operations – had a better chance of being identified and treated than in French medical facilities. Psychological casualties had been categorized in French trench medicine of the First World War as "*obusite*" (shell shock) or "commotion." But a combination of a loss of interest in the subject after 1919 and a desperately overstretched French medical corps after 1942, with no spare capacity to carry out observation and research, meant that French military medicine had been disarmed when confronted by the phenomenon. Furthermore, the idea of psychological or psychoneurological casualties challenged racial stereotypes about "Arabs."[159]

While *l'armée d'Afrique* was hardly the only Second World War military organization to cultivate a "psychologically coercive culture," it treated battle fatigue as a racial manifestation that presaged a political threat. North African Muslims were viewed as physically resilient but psychologically brittle primitives suffering from "great intellectual impoverishment," under the influence of "oriental fatalism ... the habitual indolence of the Arabs," ever on the lookout for any pretext to shirk their duty. The logic of this diagnosis held that "hysteria" was a scourge of the weak that manifested itself as a racial trait. For their part, North African infantrymen interpreted psychological stress to mean that they were possessed by *djnouns* (spirits), whose influence might be warded off by a prolific use of amulets. While French officers derided this phenomenon as yet another sign of the primitive mentality of their Muslim soldiers, in fact, charms offered a very logical way to "purify" the soul, thereby functioning as aids to surmount trauma and permit the spiritually afflicted to rejoin the community. So, while officers disparaged African "charms," European soldiers grasping rosaries for spiritual comfort, and the ritual superstitions of American bomber crews or submariners, were seen as perfectly normal behavior of men who had lost control over their circumstances, and who as a consequence entrusted their fates to a higher power. "In a world where the most consequential things happen by chance, or from unfathomable causes, you don't look to reason for help," writes Vietnam combat veteran Tobias Wolf. "You consort with mysteries. You encourage yourself with charms, omens, rites of propitiation."[160]

The irrationality lay with the military. In fact, the medicalization of combat trauma offered the military a means to escape the "binary trap" of judging a soldier's conduct in a particular instance as courageous or cowardly, but contingent on circumstance, or time at the front, or even as episodic. "Showy" actions "inevitably brought retribution," remembered US Second Lieutenant Paul Fussell in Alsace in 1944–1945, so that, "in the absence of orders to the contrary, the best policy was to leave well enough alone … We came to understand … that normally each man begins with a certain full reservoir, or bank account of bravery, but that each time it's called upon, some is expended never to be regained. After several months it has all been expended, and it's time for your breakdown."[161] The problem, as illustrated by Patton's infamous slapping of shell-shocked GIs in two field hospitals in Sicily, is that traditional soldiers might view "shell shock" as a sign of cowardice, or as an expedient like self-mutilation to avoid combat. However, rather than attempt to understand "combat fatigue" as a medical or morale problem, *l'armée d'Afrique* racialized it, categorizing soldiers suffering from psychological disorders as "good for nothing," whose medical diagnosis might be "crazy," "diabolical possession," "fatigue," "precocious senility," "worn out," or "asthenia." "Because of the shortcomings of the CEF's medical services, treatment of psychiatric casualties, seen as marginal, was not assigned priority," concludes Le Gac. Rather, they were stigmatized by grouping them with evacuees infected with venereal and other contagious diseases, and POWs whatever their malady. The imperative for the medical orderly (MO) was to return the soldier to combat as expeditiously as possible. French doctors were surprised to find a category of "neuropsychiatric" casualties in US and British military hospitals, possibly as high as 26 percent in Fifth Army infantry units during offensive pushes, which they disingenuously attributed to the fact that French-led soldiers simply had higher morale than did those of the Allies. Only during the harsh winter campaign of 1944–1945 in the Vosges did French military medicine begin to acknowledge battle fatigue, mainly among members of the *Forces françaises de l'intérieur* (FFI), which they attributed to the poor socialization of civilian resisters into a military milieu.[162]

That said, the CEF made few efforts to improve the morale of its soldiers. While the command remained attentive to Muslim holidays and tried to stop card playing and other gambling because it piled up debt and created ill feelings and resentment that undermined morale, time out of the line proved short, and distractions few. In early February 1944, Lapouge's unit was withdrawn to the village of Portella to the northeast of Cassino, which he described as "an outrageous caravanserai," within artillery range of the front, crowded with Italian refugees, gum-smacking GIs who huddled around fires for warmth, and French soldiers who dossed down in surrounding farms, which were usually filthy, where they were also expected to clean and replace weapons, and train. The good news was that most were adopted by a family, who would transform their insipid American rations into something edible and warm.[163] A *foyer du soldat* (soldiers' center) with chairs, rugs, and ping pong tables was established in Naples in January 1944, while officers might dance and more with feminine personnel at the Arizona Bar. The Red Cross ran five cinemas that showed American films. AFHQ organized military tourism of Naples and surrounding sites, like Pompei, Capri, and Salerno. And while Naples could prove endlessly fascinating – it was the only oriental city without a resident European quarter, according to popular lore – much of it lay in ruins, while its population seemed composed in the main of thieves, prostitutes, and swarms of destitute children known as *scugnizzi*, who relied on robbery, pimping for their "sisters," and the black market for survival. Some enterprising soldiers like Lapouge acquired a "girlfriend," who provided a *pied-à-terre* and other domestic comforts in Naples, although she had to take care not to double book.[164] CEF chief of staff General Marcel Carpentier complained of the "*laisser-aller*" of French troops on leave in Naples, who were allowed to go to areas "off limits" to GIs, but whose conduct and appearance he feared diminished the reputation of the CEF. A belief that the excessive libido of North African males was responsible for the spread of venereal disease, which already by December 1943 threatened to undermine operational effectiveness, a desire to prevent incidents of homosexuality, which was supposedly "already frequent with them in normal times," and the need to curtail sex crimes against the local Italian population caused the CEF greatly to expand *bordels militaires de campagne* (BMC), military brothels, which in Italy originally had been restricted to the *goumiers*. Juin created three BMCs in each of his two divisions, and one for the rest center at Bagnoli, although the army, reluctant to stock brothels with locally recruited talent so as not to subvert the racial hierarchy, was continually challenged to recruit females in AFN and transport them to Italy.[165] While Solange Cuvillier conceded that the sex workers of the BMC "must be strong as horses" to service an endless flow of clients, the nurses and ambulance drivers of her medical battalion serving with Dody's 2^{e} DIM protested to the divisional chief of staff that many prostitutes wore uniforms, which seemed to confer an auxiliary military status equivalent to that of the division's nurses. Furthermore, the sign "BM" indicating the "*bordel militaire*" where a soldier might contract venereal disease was frequently confused with that of the "*bataillon médicale*," where this malady was treated. A final shortcoming of the BMC was that it neither curtailed venereal disease nor prevented the infamous rapes carried out by French-led soldiers in May–June 1944, "that cast a pall over our victory."[166]

Stalemate

Lack of progress at the front stoked tensions among the Allies, and kindled smoldering rivalries within the French camp. Already, de Gaulle and the CFLN had protested when the French were excluded from the formulation of Italian policy. While Macmillan complained of the CFLN's petulance in its refusal to recognize the Badoglio government, Algiers was not prepared so easily to allow Italy off the hook for the "stab in the back" of 10 June 1940, subsequent indignities imposed by the Armistice Commission in Turin, and depredations caused during the Italian occupation of Corsica and southeastern France between November 1942 and September 1943.[167] But French resistance to Italian rehabilitation ran counter to Roosevelt's Italian policy, which was to scrape away the "stucco surface" of Italian fascism and retain Italy's administrative structure.[168]

In the event, French resistance to Italian co-belligerence crumbled as the result of Italian participation in the liberation of Corsica and the fact that ships of the Italian navy helped to convoy French troops from North Africa to Italy, and because, on 3 February 1944, the "Italian Liberation Corps" was placed under Juin's orders. Even though this "Corps" was useful only in police and support roles, its availability at least allowed the French commander to rotate some of his North Africans out of line. But the French found it more difficult to penetrate the inner sanctum of Allied decision-making. Although the CFLN was represented on the consultative Advisory Council for Italy (ACI) that sat in Algiers, so were Yugoslavia and Greece. When the CFLN's commissaire for foreign affairs René Massigli threatened to boycott the ACI, the Foreign Office counseled patience, and the Anglophile Massigli decided to bide his time, and count his victories one by one, confident that no Allied policy for post-war Europe could succeed without France's participation.

From an Allied perspective, governing Italy would be difficult enough without inviting vengeful French leaders to shape Italian policy. Only from 13 February 1944 was a French representative permitted to join the Allied Control Commission (ACC), which was created on 10 November 1943 during the Moscow conference, to oversee the governance of Italy. But he lacked a defined role, was marginalized by the Americans, and basically merely reported on ACC consultations to the CFLN. As Andrew Buchanan recognizes, a combination of Washington's refusal to recognize de Gaulle and the CFLN while simultaneously collaborating militarily with France effectively sealed France's dependent – Juin would argue "colonial" – status. If France aspired to earn equality in the Allied camp, it would have to be on the battlefield.[169]

But that seemed unlikely, as Allied assaults continued to sputter before Monte Cassino. A Second Battle of Cassino, launched on 17 February 1944 by British, Indian, and New Zealand troops to distract German forces from attacking the vulnerable Anzio beachhead, managed to transform the sixth-century Benedictine abbey to rubble without putting a divot in the Gustav Line. A mid-March assault enjoyed more success. But, after giving ground under massive air and artillery bombardment, German resistance stiffened. On 23 March, after New Zealand and Indian forces had taken casualties that "without being enormous, are severe," Alexander had run out of reserves, and so shut down the Third Battle of Cassino. Morale in the Allied camp crashed – "This stubborn, and it seems unexpected, resistance unsettles the Allied high command," Juin reported on 23 March 1944, because it had "dangerously compromised" the "grand spring offensive." "In these conditions, the question is the following: should one continue whatever the cost or, on the contrary, would it not be wiser to stop the current attacks?" Although the failure in this instance had been a British one, "[Clark] remains for everyone the man who can't take Cassino. He's torn. What's more, prestige is on the line. One made such a ballyhoo over massive preliminary bombardments that advertised the operation as a new concept in grand style, that one would rather that it not run aground. In other words, we're sprinting after the communiqué." Rather than continue to batter Cassino, Juin once again laid out his grand vision for an enveloping movement to outflank "tough obstacles like Cassino. I get the impression that, deep down, General Clark shares this view."[170]

The winter stall-out in central Italy, which had shattered the Allied strategic optimism of the previous summer, also sharpened rivalries in the coalition. The stumble before Cassino combined with the disappointment of Anzio to cast British and American generals into mutual reproach for operational failure and high casualties – by the close of the Third Battle of Cassino in March 1944, the Allies counted 8,000 dead, 30,000 wounded, and 12,000 missing, as well as considerable numbers of psychiatric casualties.[171] Above all, stalemate in central Italy called into question the Allies' strategy of Mediterranean engagement, because it seemed to throw the success of Overlord into question. Hardly had he closed down the Third Battle of Cassino than Alexander urged Mediterranean Commander Maitland Wilson to propose the abandonment of Anvil, which signaled the beginning of a campaign by Churchill to keep the focus on Italy.[172]

Despite Stalin's demands that the Western Allies open a "second front," by the end of 1943, 40 percent of the Wehrmacht's strength was either fighting the Allies in Italy, or deployed to defend against an anticipated Allied invasion in Western Europe, or Greece and the Balkans. By 6 June 1944, German deployments on the Eastern and Western fronts had reached near parity.[173] Therefore, an argument could be made that, by the time their strategic momentum stalled at Cassino, the Allies had attained their fundamental goals in the Mediterranean. But Eisenhower and Marshall pushed back for several reasons: because, at Tehran in November–December 1943, Stalin had advocated simultaneous attacks in northern and southern France, a strategy to divert the Western Allies from the Balkans and lay the groundwork for a Soviet advance in Eastern Europe; because the Allies had positioned troops in AFN, including de Lattre's *Armée B*, to carry out an invasion of the Côte d'Azure; because, without Anvil, Overlord might prove too small to succeed; and because Eisenhower needed the ports of Marseilles and Toulon and French railways to sustain post-D-Day operations in Northern Europe. While, at Tehran, "disparaging de Gaulle and the French was the one thing all of the Big Three could agree on,"[174] a decision to abandon Anvil would nevertheless have complicated relations with the CFLN, that had committed troops to Italy only under protest. Shipping shortages meant that the only efficient way to transfer significant numbers of French troops into France was via the Mediterranean. Roosevelt's vision for a reconstituted Europe required both the liberation of Rome and the creation of a democratic Italian government, as well as an effective French army to fill manpower gaps caused by Washington's decision to limit US ground forces to 100 divisions. He also required "the re-establishment of the armed power of the French ruling class on its native soil," at the head of a strong state able to disarm partisan fighters, and neutralize potential rival centers of political power under Washington's supervision. Nevertheless, given the stalemate in Italy, at the end of March, Eisenhower agreed to uncouple Anvil from Overlord.[175]

This debate over Anvil also had an intramural dimension, as it also stoked the simmering Juin–de Lattre enmity. On 7 January 1944, the CFLN reorganized its expeditionary forces into two armies: *Armée A*, which became the CEF, commanded by Juin, and *Armée B*, which was to become the *1ère Armée française* led by de Lattre, to incorporate those units still organizing in AFN, which for the moment included both the 9e DIC and the 1ère DFL. Juin insisted that he needed more troops to crack the Gustav Line. Not surprisingly, de Lattre deduced a power play by his old rival to embezzle his troops and resources and leave him in command of a phantom army. The 4e DMM had already been assigned to join the 2e DIM and the 3e DIA in Italy as transport became available in the spring.[176] On 15 March 1944, while stressing that his priority was the liberation of France, de Gaulle offered Wilson either the 1ère DFL or the 9e DIC, which, he warned, had "little combat experience." Much to the chagrin of its commander Diego Brosset, who viewed Italy as a "dead end," Wilson selected the 1ère DFL.[177]

In fact, Brosset could hardly be surprised by the choice. The Allies had clamored for a fourth division to be added to the CEF since December 1943. While de Gaulle had sought to preserve French forces for Anvil, he was bound by the Anfa agreement to put his troops at the disposition of the Allied command. Furthermore, the CFLN's President was not averse to dispatching a division with an impeccable Gaullist pedigree to crack *l'armée d'Afrique*'s stranglehold on the CEF, and so informed Eisenhower that the 9e DIC was unavailable.[178] The problem with the choice was that the 1ère DFL had already been rejected by AFHQ in December 1943 because it was British-armed and -equipped, and so would be incompatible with the Fifth Army's organization and logistics.[179] For these reasons, before it could sail for Italy, the 1ère DFL must be kitted out according to the US ID Table of Organization and Equipment (TOE). The DFL had spent the winter reequipping, and engaged in courses, exercises, divisional maneuvers, and what the British called "fire inoculation." Units were topped up with *pieds noirs*, *évadés de France*, and Corsicans, who mingled with veterans from Tahiti and New Caledonia. Senegalese were switched out for Chadians. Replacements for the two battalions of the 13e DBLE were scarce, so that the Legion, while preserved in the hope that it might be topped up in France, remained understrength. The division artillery, formed in Eritrea, offered a constellation of colonial subjects. All these accretions of over three years of tramping through Africa and the Near East had to be hammered into a US TOE. The DFL's Achilles heel, like that of the rest of the CEF, was a lack of technical specialists.[180] "Fusion" obliged the 1ère DFL to accept a battalion of marines, who insisted on using nautical lingo and remained suspect because of their Giraudist sympathies. Only the medical service retained its British prototype – all the doctors were French, and the ambulances remained those from Africa, driven by Quakers and served by English "Spearettes." Once the barnacle of Admiral Robert had been pried out of the French Antilles, a contingent of 100 Caribbean soldiers trained at Fort Dix, New Jersey, could be integrated into the DFL in January 1944. By the end of March 1944, the DFL numbered 18,000 men. They were organized into three infantry brigades, with a complement of support and service units.

While all military units develop their own personalities and even cultivate eccentricities as a component of unit pride, the 1ère DFL topped the charts. While it contained a solid core of veterans, most recruits had never heard a shot fired in anger. Nor did the heterogeneity of recruitment, or the babble of languages and accents, favor assimilation into a common esprit de corps. However, the central element around which the division's identity congealed would be the fact that the DFL would serve as the outlier FFL division in a Giraudist CEF. Its sense of uniqueness had been shaped by years spent as the "French" unit in the British forces in Africa. DFL veterans nurtured a nostalgia for the Eighth Army down to their colored forage caps, their British shorts, brown boots, argyle sweaters, and their rank displayed on the shoulder rather than the cuff in the French manner. Above all, they rejected their official designation as the 1ère DMI, and refused to exchange the Cross of Lorraine for the CEF's "cockerel against a rising sun" shoulder patch, which they derided as "Giraud's chicken." In Italy, they clung to their British "plate with a beard" helmet. Veterans took a perverse pride in their Bren guns, refusing to exchange them for more dependable US light machineguns. But, while to outsiders the 1ère DFL's cosmopolitanism appeared its defining characteristic, its internal cohesion was precarious. The division offered a layered hierarchy, topped by a nobility of "Gaullists of the first hour," augmented by a knighthood of those who had "fought in the desert." "Resisters" and "*évadés de France*" were more or less tolerated. But, at its core, the DFL presented a freemasonry of Gaullist fanatics, who disdained those who joined after the 1 August 1943 "fusion" as "converted heretics," who were denied the privilege of wearing the FFL insignia. This did not prevent new recruits, in an effort to fit in, from affecting an FFL mentality that was notable for three characteristics: first, an "insolent pride" of those who defied traditional notions of discipline to claim the honor of fighting in the first ranks; second, a passionate patriotism characterized by a refusal to associate France with the débâcle of 1940, and the certainty that they had followed the honorable choice; and, finally, the secret satisfaction of belonging to a division like no other, "the first among the first," as de Lattre called them.[181]

Diadem

Juin understood that he required more firepower and heavier units if the French were to participate fully in the battle to crack the Gustav Line. The arrival of Brosset's 1ère DFL in Italy, where they joined Dody's 2e DIM, Monsabert's 3e DIA, Guillaume's *Groupement de tabors marocaines*, and Juin protégé François Sevez's 4e DMM, brought the CEF to a balanced four-division corps, reinforced by goums, as well as supply, medical, and especially artillery units, that made it the largest corps command in Italy. This advanced Juin's ultimate goal – to demonstrate the worth of the CEF in the spring offensive.[182] Unfortunately, the CEF also appeared to be in the throes of a morale crisis. Without any real home front, it felt neglected, undervalued, and besieged. Conditions in Italy were difficult, and casualties high. Despite some local successes in the "First Battle of Cassino," the Allies did not yet take the CEF seriously as soldiers or accept them as full partners. Seen from the perspective of Italy, Algiers was a cauldron of Gaullist intrigue, Muslim nationalism, and German propaganda that targeted the loyalties of the troops. While as yet no overt demonstrations of political discontent were evident in the CEF, Muslim soldiers increasingly appeared unwilling to tolerate inequities.[183]

The arrival of the 1ère DFL lifted the Allied forces on the Cassino line to 615,000 men: 265,000 for the Eighth Army and 350,000 for the Fifth Army, which included the 100,000-man CEF, for the first time with enough combat engineers, but which still relied on the US army for artillery and armor support. For logistical reasons, the CEF had been grouped with Clark's Fifth Army and shared with Keyes' II Corps a 19-kilometer front that ran from the Tyrrhenian Sea to the confluence of the Liri and Minturno Rivers. In this way, the CEF replaced the British XIII Corps at a portion of the line that paralleled the Garigliano River between Cassino and Gaeta.[184] Across the river and looking down on them from the Aurunci Mountains opposite that ranged from 900 to 1,500 meters in altitude was the 14th Panzer Group, consisting of two infantry divisions and one panzer division under General Fridolin von Senger und Etterlin, part of the 412,000 German troops arranged in four successive defensive lines across central Italy south of Rome. Quite apart from their numerical advantage, the Allies held a massive superiority in artillery. Command of the air, from which Operation Strangle sought to sever the rail lines north of Cassino, also allowed the Allies to pinpoint German artillery batteries for destruction. French and American troops would face off against the XIV German Army Corps.[185]

Juin's immediate task was to convince Mark Clark that the path to Rome lay over the mountains, not along Route 6.[186] At first glance, this sector, dominated by the 3,000-foot Monte Majo appeared too formidable even for Juin's North Africans to master.[187] Rivers slashing through narrow valleys had molded a bewildering maze of cliffs, crags, and stark hillsides studded with pale, primeval boulders and dwarf oaks. True to form, the Germans had improved on nature with a solid belt of well-sited bunkers and machinegun nests, supported by artillery well out of Allied view. But 5th Army intelligence told Juin that:

> The 44th [German] ID had only recently arrived and appeared to be weary and badly depleted. The enemy regarded a breakthrough on this part of the Gustav Line as unlikely because of the intensity of the mountain masses to the west and the scarcity of roads and

trails through the region which seemed to eliminate the possible use of armor and involve very difficult supply problems. The terrain to the west and north of the German Gustav Line was considered too formidable by the enemy to become the object of an attempted breakthrough by the allies. Close scouting shows what the enemy was relying on and the weakness of this theory.[188]

In February 1944, 15th Army Group commander General Harold Alexander had sketched a concept of operations for Diadem that prioritized the destruction of German forces rather than the seizure of Rome. For the most part, it offered a reprise of the failed winter offensives, with the monastery designated as the *Schwerpunkt* to be seized by Oliver Leese's Eighth Army, that would then surge up the Liri Valley and Route 6 to break into the reserve Hitler Line, 10 kilometers behind the Gustav Line. Alexander then left British and American planners to work out the details on their respective fronts. When, on 1 April 1944, Fifth Army Assistant Chief of Staff for Operations Brigadier General Donald Brann unveiled the Fifth Army's plan to envelop the left flank of the Gustav Line, he provoked "a general outcry," according to Juin.[189] Not only had everyone, including Kesselring, seen this movie before. But, also, it was clear that the Franco-Americans were meant to hold the flank while the British seized Rome. Already on 22 March, Juin had sought to convince Mark Clark that a firepower-intensive, battering-ram approach at Cassino was unimaginative, predictable, and unlikely to succeed. The key to warfare in the mountains was surprise and a seamless advance that denied the enemy the leisure to react. In the wake of Brann's briefing, Juin uncharacteristically protested by pounding his usable left arm on the map laid out on the table.[190]

Because the defenders would be forced to spread their reserves to cover the obvious lines of approach along the road networks and passes, Juin's staff set to work on a plan to scramble over the lightly held mountain peaks to maneuver against the rear of the German Tenth Army, with the goal of blocking the roads over which they would rush in reinforcements. Although what became known as Juin's "Memorandum of 4 April," a scheme to launch two divisions numbering 35,000 men supported by 7,000 mules along a goat track that ran for 45 miles into the German rear, appeared "bold," Juin got the backing of both de Gaulle and the US 36th ID's commander, Fred L. Walker. Even some generous historians of the Cassino battle have dubbed Juin's scheme "somewhat over-optimistic," in large part because the terrain, a largely roadless chaos of steep slopes and depressions dominated by the 940-meter Monte Majo, combined with the German defenses, was simply too formidable for the limited firepower that Juin could muster.

"Thus, the entire region from the Garigliano to the Itri–Pico gap affords few possibilities for passage, almost none for vehicles except around its margin," agreed the Americans. "From the defensive viewpoint, the enemy held all the dominant positions and the controlling gaps to the watersheds in the Monte Majo–Asonia area. In the Mount Petrella area the enemy held the crests of Mounts Famera and Petrella with the fair supply route . . . The general enemy plan for the defense of the east–west area from the Garigliano to the Itri–Pico road consisted of two main lines of defense on the boundary areas with scattered 'recover' and delaying positions along the axis Pontecorvo–Ausonia–Formia."[191] But, if Juin wanted to crucify the CEF on Monte Majo, that was his problem, so long as he made no preparations that would alert the Germans. His attack, therefore, would be launched from a standing start.[192]

The front selected for attack assembled all the usual German impediments: the defenses, sited on the lower slopes about 200 meters from the river, consisted of mines and a continuous belt of barbed wire 2 meters deep, backed by bunkers, dugouts, and unsheltered gun pits. On the reverse slope, larger dugouts shielded troops poised to launch counterattacks. But the most formidable characteristic of the German defenses was the rugged terrain, which allowed most of the defending forces to remain under cover, depending on single-man observation posts to warn of attack. The Gustav Line was backed by the "Adolph Hitler Line," which stretched across the Liri Valley and was anchored on Aquino and Pontecorvo. But all indications were that the German forces, two divisions strong on the Garigliano front, had invested their faith in the inviolability of the Gustav Line and the impenetrability of the terrain. And, given the lack of success of three Allied offensives to date, it seemed a good bet. Still, although the German artillery could not cover all approach routes, German confidence was such that they barely bothered to camouflage their troop rotations, which the French could follow in detail. In the middle of April, the Germans were found to be floating remote-controlled mines down the Garigliano to destroy pontoon bridges over the river. The French threw a naval mine net across the river to collect them, without alerting the Germans. The fact that the Germans were still firing propaganda leaflets in English at the bridgehead indicated that they remained unaware of the French presence. From a German perspective, "the entire region had been organized for the best defense possible with a minimum force." Despite aggressive spoiling attacks covered by heavy artillery and mortar barrages throughout April, 5th Army intelligence concluded "that the eneny had not strengthened his troop disposition in the sector and was no better prepared for the impending onslaught than he would have been had he had no suspicion at all of our offensive."[193]

These tactical preparations were ignored in Allied capitals, where, in any case, people had all but given up on the Italian front, while in Washington, Clark's job appeared to be on the line.[194] In early April, before the launch of the Fourth Battle of Cassino, Clark was recalled to Washington in secret to meet with Roosevelt and Marshall.[195] What actually transpired at this meeting is unknown. But it is probable that Clark was made to understand that, if he did not take Rome, he would spend the rest of the war pushing the tea trolley around the corridors of the Pentagon. Andrew Buchanan speculates that, in the context of Roosevelt's larger political agenda, "it is entirely possible that the President stressed the political importance of having *American* troops capture Rome." As a result, for Clark, Alexander's "orders" subsequently became "mere suggestions." This might help to explain why the trap laid by Alexander, which envisioned Truscott attacking northeast out of Anzio to cut off the retreat of the German army fleeing the Gustav Line, never snapped shut, because Clark ordered Truscott instead to take Rome.[196]

Because he was staring personal and professional oblivion in the face, and because no one, least of all the British, seemed to have any better ideas, Clark proved extremely amenable to Juin's operational vision on his return from Washington in the middle of April. "There was perfect understanding between Clark and Juin," insisted Juin's chief of staff Marcel Carpentier. "Never any disagreement." Clark agreed to provide air support for the CEF, and ninety replacements a day.[197] Lapouge recorded that Monsabert made his division train hard: practicing patrols beneath olive trees, digging foxholes, above all firing machineguns, mortars, and anti-tank guns above the heads of soldiers as they advanced. While everyone complained, Lapouge insisted that Monsabert had been correct: "The reinforcements had turned the battalion into a herd," he wrote. Under Monsabert's direction, however, "It's become a magnificent tool of combat: its uniforms are neat, discipline total, salutes snappy. In short, sleeves rolled up, arms and legs tanned, our *tirailleurs* look great, morally and physically. They're ready." *Tirailleurs* switched out the Garand rifles for carbines and sub-machineguns to lighten their load and boost their firepower. Monsabert also organized motorized "cadres maneuvers," where officers practiced "fast pursuit" and the swift transmission of orders.[198] Juin, of course, attributed Clark's receptiveness to his plan to "the high esteem in which the French were held by the Fifth Army command since they had seen them at work during the winter campaign."[199] But, had the Little Sisters of the Poor come forward with a plausible plan of attack, Clark probably would have leapt at it.

Fortunately for the Fifth Army's commander, the Frenchman offered a sound operational construct, not merely a roll of the tactical dice *faute de mieux*. Kesselring had assembled 412,000 men to occupy strongly fortified positions on the high ground of Italy's central mountain range running from the Adriatic to the Tyrrhenian Sea, plus six divisions, including two Panzer divisions, to seal off Lucian Truscott's seven divisions at Anzio. In Juin's view, the German commander's problem would be how to rush reinforcements to critically threatened portions of his front. On the Garigliano, the key was to seize Monte Majo, block the bypass north of Ausonia, and then enlarge the breech to Pico to open the Esperia–Pico road. Keyes' II Corps was to seize Mount

Damiano, then move along the south ridge to sever the road through the valley.[200] But strategic vision is worthless unless it can be supported tactically and operationally. In a remarkable 15 April 1944 memo issued by the CEF operations bureau, Juin laid out his concept of mountain warfare, beginning with the seemingly obvious observation that success begins with capturing those mountain peaks which give "the best observation and fields of fire" as well as the possibility for flanking movements. Commanders must begin with a thorough reconnaissance to understand which terrain features were the most important ones to seize, as well as study the combat methods of the enemy. Overwhelming force was a liability in mountain warfare, where infiltration tactics offered far more promise. Large numbers of infantry became impediments in a constricted battle space. Small groups of men acting against "islands of enemy defense" can produce "great results" in breakthrough operations. The infantry must be organized in what Juin called "torrents," so that fresh elements are always available to seize a ridge, execute a flanking movement, or press forward as soon as the objective is occupied. In the 2ᵉ DIM, companies were organized into attack and "clean-up" echelons, so that troops could "drive at all speed across the mountain, where the enemy cannot hold in force – to reach the rear of the adversary as quickly as possible, cut the routes that supply the defense and open the way for frontal assaults." Allied air forces were to suppress German artillery fire and saturate choke points. In this way, the offensive could sustain an unrelenting momentum.[201]

Surprise and speed were vital, both in the timing of the attack and in the selection of unexpected approach routes. Alexander's chief of staff, General and future Field Marshal Alan Harding, dispatched the 36th US ID on amphibious training to send the message that the Allies were preparing another amphibious end run on the Tyrrhenian coast. The preparations of French troops, who wore British helmets to give the impression that McCreery's X Corps still occupied the sector, were obscured behind large canvas screens and bags of smoke. Allied patrols, air reconnaissance, and artillery range finding remained within the bounds of routine. The subterfuge must have worked, because, when the attack was launched at 23:00 on 11 May, several senior German officers, including the Tenth Army's commander Heinrich von Vietinghoff, had been recalled to Berlin to receive decorations from Hitler and did not return to the front until 17 May. Juin's memo stressed the importance of infiltration, decentralization of command, flexibility to adjust to rapidly evolving circumstances, avoiding "hard" positions, selecting angles to attack the defenses, the need for converging and mutually supporting advances, and the liberal use of smoke screens. Seizing choke points – passes, valleys, and road junctions – would keep the enemy from reinforcing threatened sectors, or transforming them into "centers of resistance." In the almost total absence of tanks, and given the imprecision of air support on the slopes, corps-level concentrations of artillery and mortars must suppress

Figure 3.2 Prior to the launch of Operation Diadem, three Moroccan soldiers, wearing British helmets, allegedly so as not to tip off German observers that the CEF had replaced British troops on the Garigliano front, fire mortar shells against German posts, April 1944. (Photo by Mondadori via Getty Images)

enemy defensive fire so that the infantry could close on fortifications before revealing themselves (Figure 3.2). The artillery must also organize mobile elements capable of following the advance. Engineers progressed with the infantry to demine and rapidly open roads and trails so that mules could reinforce the offensive momentum. But main centers of resistance were not located on ridges, but often found on reverse slopes, or on flanking peaks. Finally, Italy was scoured for mules, without which no breakthrough could be sustained.[202]

On 8 May 1944, Brosset received orders for his 1ère DFL to attack on the right of Dody's 2e DIM between the Monte Majo–Cantalujo ridge and the bend in the Girofano toward San Giorgio and then reach the Hitler Line at Pontecorvo. "The difficulty of this operation lies in the requirement to introduce heavy attack elements into a narrow bridgehead that we possess on the right bank of the Girofano … The affair is well set up, the German is well entrenched, well organized, but not numerous. The terrain favors them, steep slopes, our people are ready, matériel is abundant, our aviation completely dominates the sky. *Good luck.*" Before the attack, Marlene Dietrich was brought into the DFL mess by French actor Jean-Pierre Aumont.[203] After having sought refuge in Hollywood in 1940 because of his Jewish origins, Aumont had enlisted in the FFL in

June 1943, where he subsequently became Brosset's aide-de-camp, and ended the war with two wounds and a *Légion d'honneur.*

"A Nightmare of Hell"

The genesis of what would be called the Battle of the Garigliano, a sub-section of Operation Diadem, launched at 23:00 on the night 11 May. As darkness fell, silent crocodiles of colonial troops freighted with arms and supplies and escorted by mules snaked down trails and roads leading toward the river, where engineers had silently begun to assemble pontoon bridges. At 23:00, the night exploded in a hurricane barrage of 2,000 guns firing 284,000 shells in 4 hours against "gun emplacements, fortified localities, dumps and fixed defenses," recorded Clark. "In this way the infantry was able to advance almost simultaneously with the opening of artillery fire . . . producing a nightmare of hell in the German's battery positions along the forward wall." Keyes' II Corps and the CEF attacked abreast.[204] The 2e DIM in the lead, flanked by the 1ère DFL and the 4e DMM, rushed the German defenses as tracer bullets and parachute flares lit up the sky. Barely had the attack begun than the radios crackled with calls for ambulances. Pre-arranged artillery targeting had failed to silence the German batteries. "Characteristic of the early fighting were many instances of strongpoints being won only when they had been completely isolated, outfought and overrun, and subsequent fierce counterattacks had been repulsed by our troops," recorded Clark."[205] The three attacking French divisions became entangled in minefields, subjected to heavy bombardment and counterattacks, and often suffered horrible casualties. Brosset recorded that his division had "hit a bone." It was tough everywhere. "Not a disaster but must rethink the attack." Quite apart from the steep slopes and the ferocity of the resistance, there was "often inertia. We're a little too easily showoffs in France. One often hesitates to take objectives straight on, reacts badly to setbacks. One thinks he is precious and is surprised to have to sacrifice his life, or even a foot."[206]

Having decided to take personal control of the battle, on the morning of 13 May, Juin jumped into his jeep, crossed the Garigliano, and picked his way forward through a carnage of dead mules and mutilated men to assess the situation. Armored forces had broken into Castelforte, opening the way for 4,200 *goumiers* and 1,200 mules, who in the night "were off on their dangerous bid to reach the Petrella massif." Calculating that the German defenses must be stretched to the limit, Juin took the risk of renewing the attack with his single remaining reserve division on 13 May, this time behind a "stonk" that disoriented the defenders, who began to surrender in large numbers. French units were mixed and matched into battle groups to conform to new tactical challenges. Clark shifted his artillery to support a promising French initiative, just in time to catch two German counterattacks in the open and stop them cold. By the afternoon of 13 May, Monte Majo had fallen to Dody's 2^{e} DIM, who had more trouble scaling the steep mountainsides than overcoming the resistance at the summit, signaling the rupture of the Gustav Line through which the entire CEF surged, "the first to break through the enemy line," declared the US Army official history (Map 3.4).[207] "A sense of futility seemed to have entered the German forces, and, though their mortars and artillery reacted as strongly as on 12 May, the infantry did not fight as stubbornly," read the after-action report. "Over a hundred prisoners were taken on Mount Girofano alone, a testimony to the change in the German spirit as well as to the fierce onslaught of the French troops and their excellent support"[208] The ground was littered with cadavers and destroyed German equipment, much of it caused by the 185,000 artillery rounds fired on 11–12 May by batteries supporting the French alone. The air smelled of burning flesh. Kesselring, his attention riveted on the British Eighth Army's thrust at Cassino, was reluctant to commit his reserves against the advancing French. "The fall of Mounts Feuci and Girofano signaled the 'breakthrough' which was essential to the success of the plan to turn the enemy's right flank. The 71st Infantry Division and the Kampfgruppe Nagel were collapsing."[209] Brosset recorded that his casualties decreased as German resistance waned: Sant'Andrea del Garigliano fell at the end of the day on 13 May; 14 May saw the capture of Sant'Apollinare. The French advance was all the more remarkable given that, on their left flank, Keyes' II Corps had advanced barely 2.5 kilometers, while to their right Monte Cassino, where German paratroopers had inflicted 50 percent casualties on the attacking Poles, continued to defy conquest.

Amidst this carnage (Figure 3.3), Solange Cuvillier's triage company was working round the clock: "The spectacle brought tears to our eyes: shelters ripped open, twisted metal, exploded mules, this insufferable odor of grilled flesh that enveloped the front . . . as we were loading in total darkness we didn't notice that one of the bodies was decapitated." Cuvillier's team prioritized stomach wounds and open fractures. "Head wounds could wait."[210] Ambulances were packed with a volatile mix of *goums*, zouaves, legionnaires, *tirailleurs*, and Germans, who required some serious supervision. At best, the nurse might have to console the wounded. Muslim troops were on the whole respectful, addressing the drivers as "Madame Croix-Rouge." However, things might get out of hand, especially when wounded Germans and Muslims were loaded into the same vehicle: "The Arab insults came thick and fast: *nalbouk, nanoualdik, halouf* . . . ('May God curse your father! May God curse your parents! Pig!')," remembered Cuvillier. "To satisfy his vengeance, [the Arab] didn't hesitate to urinate on the Fritz placed beneath him. Our protests were ignored. The hatred was too great." However, when the knives came out, Cuvillier swerved into a traffic control point to allow the military police (MPs) to sort it out. Attitudes toward wounded enemy soldiers were understandably complex. When, during the liberation of France, Cuvillier explained

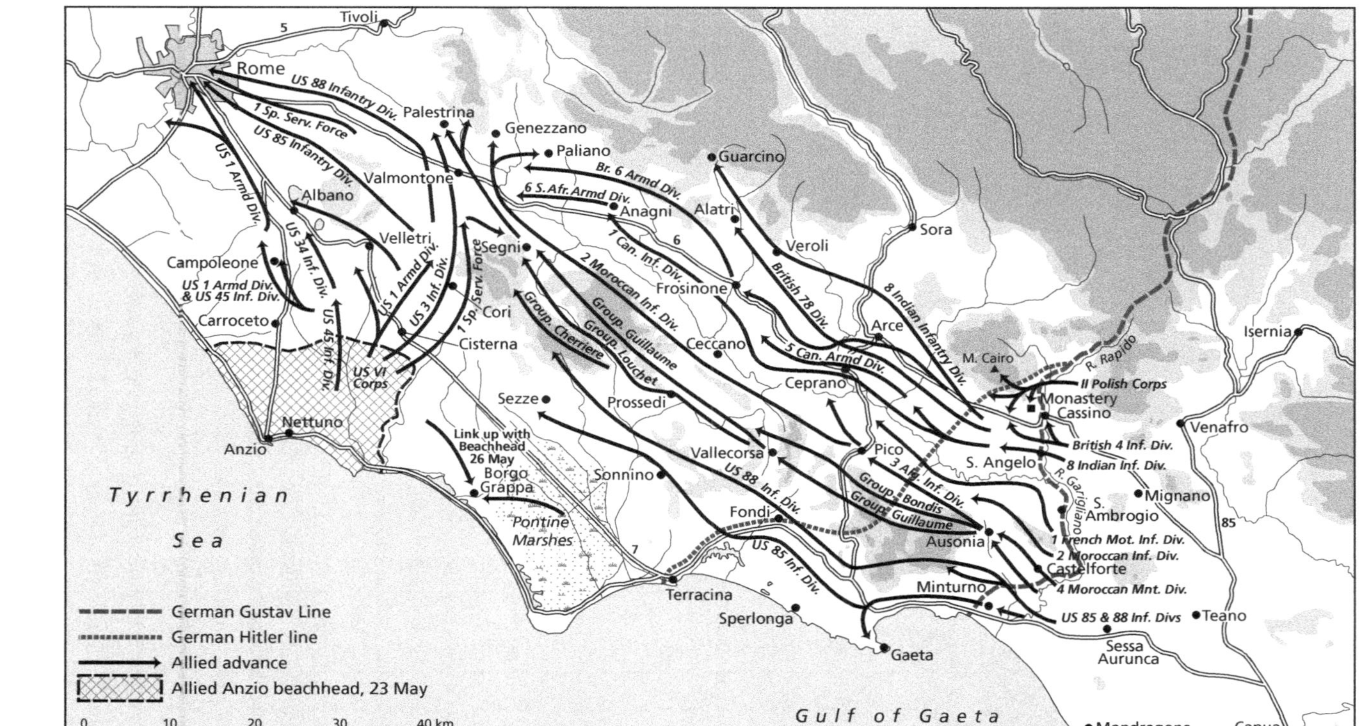

Map 3.4 The Allied breakout at Monte Cassino, May–June 1944.

Figure 3.3 French infantrymen stand near a soldier and his mule killed by a German shell after the breakthrough at Cassino in the summer of 1944. (Photo by Hulton-Deutsch/Hulton-Deutsch Collection/Corbis via Getty Images)

that her wartime job was to save all combatants, the common reaction was: "Why transport and treat those bastards – let them croak . . . better . . . waste them."[211] Given these attitudes, it was not surprising that Lefort-Rouquette had to separate one of her Senegalese stretcher bearers from his *coupe coupe* (machete), because he seemed more intent on taking German ears as souvenirs than on tending to his patients.[212]

Running bumper-to-bumper in full blackout, with an ambulance full of seriously wounded soldiers, "our obsessive fear was dysentery," recounted Cuvillier. One simply could not just pull over, because, even though the roads had been demined, the roadside remained strewn with explosives. "Women's latrines" existed. But, before entering, one had to be sprayed with dichlorodiphenyltrichloroethane (DDT) out of a long tube, not necessarily a delay to endure when in a distressed state. When once, in desperation, Cuvillier darted into a "women's latrine," the blue light in the interior exposed a long row of wooden seats, occupied by women hunched in a "collective evacuation." "Come in my dear," was an invitation issued by a middle-aged

American woman. In the event, Cuvillier preferred to take her chances with the mines.[213] And yet, despite all of these indignities endured by female volunteers who shared all the hardships of the men, Cuvillier's commander resented female drivers, "and constantly made us make detours to look for hospitals located twenty, thirty, sometimes forty kilometers distant in full black-out."[214]

Eager to prevent the Germans from retreating to the reserve Hitler Line, on 14 May, Juin fashioned a 12,000-man corps out of the 4e DMM and the *goums* supported by 4,000 mules. Reorganized into three mixed "task forces" of *goumiers* and *tirailleurs*, they were ordered to push through the mountains. Divisional artillery and tanks crossed the river on the night of 13–14 May to be deployed along the Sant'Andrea del Garigliano–Sant'Apollinare road. Ridge after mountain fell before the Germans could organize a defense. By 18 May, the French had seized the Aurunci massif and blocked the Itri–Pico road to prevent the Germans from shifting reinforcements. The 3e DIA and 1ère DFL coordinated by Larminat seized towns and road junctions. "In this entire area the enemy was completely surprised by the sudden appearances of our troops many miles from what he thought was still the front lines. Little resistance was offered and many prisoners were taken before they recovered from their surprise and could assume battle positions ... The enemy had been broken through and was running for the 'Hitler' line, but General Guillaume was determined to bring the full weight of his force against the rear of Pico in order to destroy the effectiveness of that line before it could be manned."[215] In the process, they had outstripped the British Eighth Army, which nevertheless had entered the Liri Valley and forced the German paratroopers to abandon Monte Cassino by the end of the day on 17 May. By the time de Gaulle dropped in for a visit, the 1ère DFL had advanced 30 kilometers over very rough terrain.[216]

In what must be considered the high point of French arms in the Second World War, Juin pushed his troops mercilessly forward to break into the "Hitler Line" before Kesselring could regroup to defend it. "Ability to cross country is especially notable among French and Moroccan troops," Kesselring reported. "They have quickly surmounted terrain considered impassable, using pack-animals to transport their heavy weapons, and have on many occasions tried to turn our own positions (sometimes in wide encircling movements) in order to break them open from the rear."[217] By 17 May, the CEF had outdistanced its mules, and hence its ammunition. Boston bombers of the Twelfth Air Force's Tactical Air Command dropped water, ammunition, and food to the lead French units. Though his men were exhausted, Juin realized that they had to pursue the remnants of the retreating German forces, infiltrating their positions, turning their flanks, focusing resources on weak points, ambushing unsuspecting units, giving them no time to recover. On 18 May, the Monastery, which had haunted the Allies all winter long, fell. With the Gustav Line smashed and the right flank of the Hitler Line threatened, at 18:00 on 19 May, Kesselring ordered all troops south of the Liri and east of Pico to fall back on the line Pico–Pontecorvo. But, with five divisions and two *Kampfgruppen* (battle groups) destroyed or scattered, and a sixth division seriously chewed up, the German commander's best bet was to try to organize a defense south of Rome along a line running between Valletri and Valmontone. Juin organized three divisions into two columns and aimed them at Pico, "the hinge and vital connecting link between the sector of the Hitler Line that lay across the Liri valley and that still blocked the way to the II Corps' junction with the Anzio beachhead." The plan was to drop off groups for clean-up operations without halting the forward movement. Clark lent Juin some tanks and tank destroyers. Despite their losses, the Germans fought hard to retain Pico, which fell only after a three-day battle. But, in the process, the Germans had redeployed the 15th and 90th Panzergrenadier Divisions from the Liri Valley that might have been more profitably deployed against the Eighth Army or Key's II Corps. By 22 May, the CEF and II Corps had pierced the Hitler Line and closed in on the Liri Valley from the south, facilitating the advance of the Canadians. His line breached, the German commander had no choice but to scamper north with those troops he could salvage.[218]

On 23 May, Truscott launched his breakout from Anzio. However, rather than follow Alexander's campaign plan to cut off the retreat of the German Tenth Army, Clark instead ordered Truscott to enter Rome. This was viewed at the time and since as an egotistical reaction by Clark that permanently tarnished his reputation. However, as discussed above, while no one can be certain, Buchanan speculates that Clark was most probably ordered by Roosevelt to seize Rome ahead of the British. This allowed the Italian CLN to arrive in Rome on 8 June, push aside Badoglio and impose the government of Ivanoe Bonomi, much to Churchill's fury. And, although the British Prime Minister denounced the Bonomi government as an "untrustworthy band of non-elected political come-backs," it was immediately recognized by Washington.[219]

In the short run, for French soldiers, the breakout from Anzio absorbed most of the Allied air support, requiring a reorganization of the artillery into mixed mobile groups of 105 mm and 155 mm howitzers to trail the French forces as they moved out of Pico to preempt the Germans from settling into the Hitler Line. But, having taken Pico, the French found that the Germans had blocked all the exits from the town.

It was in this phase that the *goums* once again proved their worth, slipping behind German positions on the high ground and taking them from the rear.[220] "It was the Goums who caused real havoc behind the German positions," read a Fifth Army after-action report. "By infiltrating through the enemy lines at night in groups of two or four these troops attacked sentry posts, isolated rest bunkers, and in general succeeded in keeping the rearmost Germans on the line in constant fear of being isolated. By these means the enemy was given many false indications of attack. The result was that the German was under a constant nerve strain which contributed to tiring out the enemy forces."[221] This report appears understated – the Germans were not "tired out." Rather, they were terrorized by the Moroccans, who took no prisoners, and even reportedly seized POWs from GIs and murdered them. So eager were some German units to clear out that they threw down their weapons and neglected to plant mines, which further facilitated Juin's dogged pursuit. The élan of the Moroccans faciliated the more methodical – when not plodding – Anglo-American advance.[222]

The breakthrough at Cassino followed by the liberation of Rome offered a vindication on multiple levels. In the minds of French officers, victory over the Germans erased the shame of 1940. Cassino also appeared at last to have prompted the Anglo-Americans to accept the French as equals. Clark praised the "courage, determination, and skill" of the CEF, while Eisenhower congratulated de Gaulle on the "valorous performance of the French Expeditionary Corps in Italy." In Washington, George Marshall hailed the "rebirth of the French army, that of Verdun and the Marne." The Eighth Army's general staff sought to send a delegation of staff officers to study Juin's methods. Even the Consultative Assembly in Algiers, which hitherto had seemed obsessed with bringing several of the CEF's senior commanders to justice, claimed to be "moved" by the victory. Guillaume rejoiced that the same politicians who literally days before were howling for Juin's scalp now, "with their arms upraised, implore your pardon. What a revenge!" Churchill informed Roosevelt that the breakthrough at Cassino had unleashed a wave of sympathy for France. But while the feat of the CEF had advanced Roosevelt's agenda in Italy and allowed Anvil to go forward, it failed to benefit de Gaulle in Washington's eyes, insofar as de Gaulle's counsel was not solicited for the invasion of France. The CEF made itself at home in the historic French landmarks in the Eternal City – the embassy in the Piazza Farnese, the Villa Medicis, which housed the French Academy in Rome, and the Church of Saint-Louis-des-Français, while it requisitioned the Plaza Hotel near the Spanish Steps. On 9 June, after a mass in Saint Peters, the Pope held an audience for a large delegation of French officers that lasted two hours. A 17 June victory parade through Rome was especially savored as revenge for Mussolini's "knife in the back" of June 1940.[223]

The Aftermath of Victory

But the Rome victory celebrations were short-lived, for several reasons, beginning with the fact that news of Overlord rapidly pushed the capture of Rome out of the headlines. Second, historians endlessly debate whether Truscott might have been able with his seven divisions at Anzio to sever the retreat route of

Kesselring's Tenth and Fourteenth Armies, had not Clark ordered him instead to prioritize the capture of Rome, possibly at Roosevelt's direction. But, with the Germans fleeing northward, the Allies gave chase, with the Fifth Army ordered to sprint up the coast to Pisa, while the Eighth Army raced for Florence. The heat was especially on Clark, who was notified that he would soon lose Truscott, with three US divisions and the CEF, to Anvil. On Clark's right flank, Juin organized a pursuit column made up of the 1ère DFL and the 3e DIA, reinforced by US armor and *goums*, under the command of his COS Larminat, and told his troops to make haste for Siena. Juin complained that the Allied pursuit had been hastily cobbled together, with no discernable scheme of maneuver, and that its major purpose seemed to be to allow the Eighth Army to take Florence in compensation for Clark having filched from them the glory of Rome's liberation.

With four French and three US divisions, plus three *groupes* (regiments) *de tabors* of *goums*, scheduled to be shipped out of Italy in June and July, Larminat's column received no reinforcements. Alexander's pursuit also slowed, allowing Kesselring to catch his breath. Juin protested the rollback of the French contribution to the Italy campaign to de Gaulle and to the Algiers general staff, while Clark, who would soon replace Alexander as Fifteenth Army Group commander, also decried the dissolution of the CEF. In the summer heat, losses in Larminat's pursuit column mounted, as did desertions among soldiers who realized that Italy was no longer an Allied priority. On 14 July 1944, in the main square of Siena, which was bedecked with tricolored flags, Alexander, Clark, Murphy, Soviet representative Bogolomov, and Couve de Murville mustered to bid adieu to Juin and the CEF. De Gaulle and the CFLN had two goals: introduce as large an army as possible as part of the Allied invasion of France; and utilize it to gain status as an equal partner in the coalition and diplomatic recognition of the CFLN's sovereignty in France. The CEF had been an important step in that process. Furthermore, the Allies realized that maintaining French forces in Italy indefinitely would be well-nigh impossible. Besides, in Eisenhower's view, the whole point of rearming the French was to have French forces participate in the liberation of France. What remained to be settled was France's status, especially since Roosevelt refused, much to Eisenhower's exasperation, officially to recognize de Gaulle and the CFLN.[224]

But de Lattre de Tassigny would command French troops in Anvil, not Juin, a relegation that Clark denounced as "scandalous," while the Anglo-American commanders petitioned de Gaulle to retain Juin, "the most capable and the most determined of French leaders, the only one capable of carrying out that role." Even the Gaullist hardliners like Larminat had become reconciled to Juin as even-handed and competent. In contrast, they pronounced their future commander Jean de Lattre de Tassigny as "excitable and too political." While de Gaulle acknowledged Juin's incontestable battlefield *coup d'œil*, his Saint-Cyr contemporary carried more baggage than a Moroccan mule. While Juin's close association with Vichy policies in AFN had made him a hero in the eyes of *l'armée d'Afrique*, a wartime record that included an unexplained release from a German *Oflag*, a meeting with Göring, the execution of the Paris Protocols on his watch in AFN, and questions still hanging over his conduct during Torch and the Axis invasion of Tunisia made him a problematic command choice. The French Leader stressed to Juin that his future mission as Chief of the General Staff of National Defense was essential to the successful reorganization of French forces and their maintenance in the field. For his part, Juin blamed Giraud, not de Gaulle, for creating "two armies and two general staffs when we could hardly pull together the resources for the semblance of one small army."[225]

But not everyone was sorry to see Juin's exile from active command, because his legacy in Italy, as it had been in North Africa, was a mixed one. While French élan had rescued what was otherwise a fairly plodding plan to break the Gustav Line, the initial euphoria over the French breakthrough began to diminish as it gradually became clear that Diadem's success had come at the significant cost of 7,771 Allied KIAs between 1 April and 4 June 1944. As the casualty figures began to be tabulated, rather than being praised for his operational *finesse*, Juin instead was critiqued for a casualty rate that threatened seriously to undermine the combat efficiency of mobilizing French forces. Estimates of battle casualties vary. But, between November 1943 and August 1944, the CEF lost over 6,500 officers and men killed, around 23,500 wounded, and 2,000 missing out of a corps of around 112,000 men. Some Moroccan units lost half of their strength. Eleven percent of French officers were killed, and 23 percent were wounded; 5.2 percent of NCOs and soldiers died, and another 23 percent had been wounded.[226] During Diadem, the CEF shed 13.5 percent of its strength, which proportionally made it by far the hardest hit of the Allied armies.[227] Kesselring had been correct – French losses were unsustainable, especially given their narrow recruitment base in AFN. The great bulk of the French losses in Diadem were taken on 12–13 May, and were especially heavy among junior officers and NCOs. De Lattre's COS General Marcel Carpentier complained that commanders in indigenous units placed junior officers in the vanguard of attacks to lead by example, which helped to account for the high casualty rate of irreplaceable cadres.[228] For Sergeant Guy Martinet of the 4e RTM, high casualties were the price that the French paid for the courage and resolve of the *évadés*: "The French coming from France, or through Spain, are extremely committed to the fight," he insisted. "At San-Michel on 15 December, when the *tirailleurs* ran away, only the French [with a few native NCOs] fixed bayonets and charged. The proportion of French killed [NCOs, officers, squad leaders or corporals] is enormous, almost equal to that of the natives who are five times more numerous."[229]

Another explanation lay with the fact that the CEF had a higher ratio of combat to support troops. Aware that he faced criticism in AFN for this high casualty figure, especially among North African Muslims whose lives might be considered more expendable than those of white Frenchmen, Juin dispatched Major Paul Gandoët, a battalion commander in the *Tirailleurs tunisiens* who had been wounded in the January battle for the Belvedere, with a personal message for de Lattre: "Tell him that none of my *tirailleurs*, my NCOs, or my officers think that I am profligate with their lives, or that I bathe in their blood to clear my name." Having received this message, de Lattre, without looking up, replied as follows: "Nevertheless, he fired on the Americans, and not on the Germans, and now he cleanses that with the blood of his soldiers." De Lattre's comments boomeranged, because, as commander of the First French Army during the liberation of Alsace in 1944–1945, he too acquired a reputation as "a killer of men," which reportedly meant that many officers were reluctant to follow him to Indochina in 1950 when he became commander in chief there.[230] The only positive thing that could be said about the high CEF losses in Italy was that at least they were below the 20 percent casualty figure in Tunisia.[231] But the impact of losses is cumulative, as is the erosion of morale.

The Germans were too disorganized to evolve an accurate casualty figure. But post-war calculations put German losses at 51,574, which included 25,000 POWs and 5,820 KIAs – not equal to Stalingrad or "Tunisgrad," certainly, but significant losses nonetheless, that required Hitler to pull four divisions out of other fronts to reinforce Italy. Nevertheless, in part because of Clark's controversial order – for reasons of politics or prestige – to seize Rome rather than attempt to cut off the retreat of the Tenth Army, Kesselring's force endured to fight on until the war's end.[232]

"Under the Eyes of the Madonna": CEF War Crimes in Italy

A final stain on Juin's and the CEF's triumph at Cassino began to emerge as reports arrived from both British and American soldiers as well as Italians, and even gendarmes attached to the CEF, of serious misconduct and indiscipline among French troops. The first reports of indiscipline came in on 15 May as *goumiers* reached Pollega and the region of Esperia, where many Italian civilians had taken refuge from the fighting. From 19 May, Fifth Army's military intelligence (G2) warned the ACC that numerous civilians arriving in refugee camps were recounting that Muslim soldiers, especially the *goumiers*, were raping women, abusing POWs or even selling them to the Americans, ransacking houses, stealing or killing livestock, and committing armed hold-ups of Italian civilians. By 19 May, General Dody had ordered his officers to crack down on incidents "that stain the good name of the French army." When a village was taken by a unit in his 2e DIM, the population was to be assembled in a separate, guarded area. Military police might also be assigned to guard women or keep an eye out for brutality against the population. But, in the fluid situation of May–July 1944, and given the high casualty rate for cadres, there were not enough men both to keep order and to pursue the retreating Germans. On 24 May, Juin also belatedly reacted, fully eleven days after the first reports of widespread rape had begun to reach his HQ.[233]

It usually fell to GIs, if anyone, to protect the Italian population. On 23 May, the US 313th Engineer Battalion reported that French colonial troops were raping civilians near Fondi. "We were repeatedly confronted with cases of rape, the massacre of cattle and other barbarous acts perpetrated by *goums* in our zone of occupation," reported the chaplain of the US 17th Artillery Group on 29 May. "In the region situated between Vallecorsa and Terracina, the 26 May, 1944, the situation is intolerable. All day, our men watched as they searched the area looking for women, [and] killing all the cattle." The fall of the Hitler Line triggered a renewed wave of rapes and violence, "above all by troops of color." Indeed, violence against civilians so shocked the men of the American 13th Artillery Brigade assigned to support the CEF that they requested transfer to a US division, avowing that they would rather fire on the French than on the Germans. US infantry units in proximity to the French expressed disgust that the behavior of French colonial troops dishonored the Allied cause. On 15 July, the Bishop of Siena reported that twenty-four children aged from twelve to fourteen had been admitted to hospital after having been raped by *marocchini*.[234]

"Unfortunately, the rapes carried out by some North African soldiers cast a pall over our victories," Solange Cuvillier remembered. "At Spigno, a sort of mountainous eagle's nest full of mines taped off by the Engineers, over the noise of the fighting we could hear the screams of women that cast us into the depths of despair." Although she insisted that the command executed some guilty soldiers on the spot, "I had to evacuate a woman in her thirties who was put in a straitjacket. A medic had to keep an eye on her as we wandered through the night looking for an Italian asylum that would accept her. This episode remains the only shameful moment of my war."[235]

By 24 May, the Badgolio government protested to the ACC, demanding that Alexander urge Juin to control his troops. Because these events occurred behind the line of advance, the French would invariably cast blame on service and support troops. And surprisingly, after all the fuss about the *goums*, only one *goumier* was found guilty of sexual assault. The vast majority of those held accountable were from the combat arms, and 56 percent of them were from Morocco.[236] It was certainly true that, as units advanced, and split into groups to clean out remote villages or mountainous regions where the Italian population sought refuge from the fighting, they became increasingly difficult to supervise or control, especially as particularly heavy losses among their French cadres meant that "30 percent of units were today commanded by Moroccan NCOs." But, while some officers argued that *goumiers* were merely obeying a cultural dictate of "the holy razzia," or looking for a just recompense for their low pay, and rewards for their sacrifices in combat, *l'armée d'Afrique* could never concede that their *goumiers* were beyond control. The excuse that the *goums* got out of hand because "too few [French] cadres insufficiently trained were overwhelmed by the situation" offers only a partial explanation for the rapes and disorder, Le Gac concludes. The truth was that "Others, out of a desire for revenge against the Italians, gave their men free reign," as Juin conceded to ACC Chief Mason-MacFarlane.[237]

Complaints about the behavior of French troops soon reached Cordell Hull in Washington. To nip the possibility of a political enquiry in the bud, COS to the Commander in Chief William Leahy and Maitland Wilson admonished Clark to keep the burgeoning scandal *entre militaires*. Juin got the word, but not the spirit, of the Allied request: "However harsh our sentiments toward a nation that treacherously attacked France, it is important to maintain our dignity," he announced to his troops on 24 June. "The French army has earned the respect of everyone on the battlefield of Italy. It is easy for us to add to this reputation by adopting an appropriate attitude, in a conquered country, *vis-à-vis* a population that is experiencing the most terrible evils of war and whose situation is pitiable in the eyes of our Allies who are administratively responsible for them."[238] The Italians took exception to Juin's reference to Italy, now an Allied co-belligerent, as "a conquered country" whose people were in a "pitiable situation." Clark's COS, Alfred Gruenther, reminded Juin that the conduct of his soldiers simply gifted to the Axis, busily retailing reports of French indiscipline, a propaganda triumph as their military front crumbled. In a 27 May redo, Juin ordered his subordinates to impose the most severe disciplinary measures against rapists. One of Juin's biographers, Jean-Christophe Notin, argues that, from 20 June, Juin had ordered his commanders to reinforce discipline, which produced a spate of courts martial as well as drumhead justice that incorporated a range of measures that ran from shaming, to taking the bolt out of the miscreant's rifle before sending him back into combat, to summary executions.[239]

While Clark denounced the incidents as "intolerable," so indebted was he to Juin for rescuing the Italian campaign, and his career, that he was willing to categorize the incidents as "comprehensible given the history of the troops implicated and the past political relations between France and Italy." By the end of the month, the ACC had condemned the "atrocities" and "abominable acts" carried out by French troops as they continued to pursue Kesselring northward – on 2 July, Alexander personally intervened with Larminat to demand that he control the behavior of the troops in his pursuit column.[240] The extracurricular activities of the CEF tarnished the Allies' "liberation" narrative, a fact gleefully retailed by German radio. Despite the Allied attempt to contain the situation on the military level, soon the Italian Ministry of Foreign Affairs and the Vatican, acting on reports from local priests, weighed in to protest the continuing depredations of the CEF. Civil Affairs officers reported that women were refusing to leave their homes when French troops were present, which delayed reestablishing normal activity. The ACC feared that this French action would turn the Italian population against the Allies, or that fratricide between French colonial troops and GIs who intervened to prevent atrocities might result. The Rome press was soon full of stories of rapes by *marocchini* – an Italian term that might mean "Moroccan" or more generally "Maghrebian" – to the point that *marocchinate* entered the Italian lexicon to categorize the wave of rapes. The Pope reproached de Gaulle about the depredations of Muslim soldiers when the two met in Rome on 30 June, a fact that de Gaulle fails to record in his memoirs. The new Italian Prime Minister Ivanoe Bonomi protested the "shameful conduct" of French troops who were "terrorizing" the Italian population by committing "war crimes." In the Italian mind, the fact that the Allies had imported troops of color into Italy was an affront to European civilization, which sought to racialize the violence by associating it with men of an inferior race. Not only did rape desecrate a woman's purity and honor, it also brought "shame" upon their fathers, husbands, and families – which, of course, was one of its goals, as a strategy to demonstrate the domination over the enemy community. Rape, especially by *marocchini,* became a degrading reminder of defeat, a metaphor for national humiliation, Italy's diminished political status, and its fall from Hitler's proud "Pact of Steel" partner to a country without a future. It also represented payback for the colonial violence that the Italians had inflicted in Abyssinia, and which French imperial troops considered customary on the basis of their own experience in North Africa. Indeed, the Italians rationalized the withdrawal of the CEF for Anvil as the only way the Allies could curtail the crimes of its soldiers. These complaints may have had an impact, because de Gaulle initially forbade the use of *goumiers* in the invasion of France, although de Lattre later convinced the French leader to reverse the decision, with the argument that *goumiers* were vital for operational success.[241]

Fearing an Allied enquiry that might reach a political level, Juin sought to show that he had taken strong action to restore discipline in the CEF, while simultaneously deflecting criticism onto Allied troops. CEF lore holds that twenty-eight soldiers caught in the act of rape or armed hold-up had been summarily executed on the spot or after a drumhead court martial. But Le Gac could locate no archival evidence to support this oft-repeated assertion, or identify units which claimed to have carried out summary justice. And, in the end, only sixty French soldiers were ever punished for rape in Italy.[242] While rapes were put down to the savagery of the *goumiers*, in fact, as noted above, only one *goumier* was convicted of rape and few of pillage or other crimes. This might have been because they were difficult to identify individually – most had no surname, were known in their *tabors* only by a number, and wore the identical striped burnoose, or cloak. Nevertheless, 91 percent of those CEF soldiers who were convicted of crimes of sexual violence were North African Muslims.[243] White French soldiers who had also participated might be pardoned or let off with a lesser sentence because "they followed the lead of their indigenous comrades without realizing the gravity of the crime."[244] Juin insisted that relations between French soldiers and the Italian population were generally cordial, and that accusations of misconduct had been grossly and deliberately "exaggerated" by the Italians to discredit the French.[245] He blamed Italian women for inviting rape through overly familiar behavior toward French soldiers and even of exhibiting "a morbid desire for sexual experiences of an exotic character."[246] As Richard Overy notes, while rape was generally "opportunistic," the degree to which the military establishment considered it a crime was influenced by the fact that many women in war zones, including Italy, "resorted to temporary prostitution to alleviate hardship and hunger, stretching the idea of consensual sex to its limits." Furthermore, in a conflict in which enemy civilians were regularly the targets of military violence by both sides, where looting and seizing "sexual booty" were "regarded as a male perquisite of war" and "compensation" for "frustrated and tense soldiers . . . any legal or ethical judgement on the failure to respect civilian immunity . . . remained a contentious issue."[247]

Unfortunately, official complaints, Juin's alleged crackdown, press publicity, and Papal intervention failed to solve the problem of indiscipline in the CEF, as the reputation for rape and other crimes against the civilian population pursued the CEF as Larminat's column advanced up the peninsula to Siena, and French troops eventually invaded Elba and Germany. In the post-war period, the rapes became a source of contention in Italian–French relations, although the scope of the rapes will never be known.[248] The French accepted responsibility for 60 percent of damage claims, and acknowledged 80 percent of the claims of rape. "Given the classic phenomenon of underreporting, sexual violence can be estimated at several thousand, while the damage certainly exceeded tens of thousands," concludes Julie Le Gac.[249] The French reparations commission tried to shift the blame for acts of violence attributed to French soldiers onto Black GIs and Indian troops in the Eighth Army, believing Italian accusations to be the product of an exaggerated and orchestrated campaign hatched among fascists still in the government to discredit the French army. But even initially skeptical French personnel attached to the "*services des réparations civiles*" were persuaded by a mountain of irrefutable evidence.[250]

How does one account for the CEF's violence against the Italian population? "The fate reserved for the women of the enemy and their bodies probably speaks volumes about the vision of the enemy," French historian Claire Miot perceptively insists.[251] Therefore, the first explanation, and one that partially exonerated *l'armée d'Afrique*, was that rape was simply a byproduct of the violence of war. It is "what soldiers do" in the formulation of Mary Louise Roberts.[252] However, when wartime sexual violence occurred on a large scale, it was not only tolerated, but even tacitly encouraged by the hierarchy, for several reasons, beginning with a desire for political retribution.[253] At the very least, the message sent by the CEF's command was an ambiguous one. While French officers may have publicly condemned violence toward civilians, they viewed the Italians, and subsequently those German women who were to experience a similar ordeal at French hands, as "hypocrites" who deserved no pity. A desire for revenge to surmount the shame of defeat and occupation, to assert French virility by humiliating Italian women, underpinned the complicity of the French command in violence against civilians.[254] While he never mentions rape, as his Muslim *tirailleurs* pillaged houses and terrified no doubt pious Italian women, Lapouge confessed that "it's with a certain pleasure that I see these people tremble before the French conquerors."[255] Because civilians often huddled in abandoned or partially destroyed buildings or churches, they became particularly vulnerable targets to soldiers operating in groups, taking turns raping a victim while others held off her family at gunpoint. Anyone who tried to intervene to save their wife, sister, or child risked assassination. Rapists might tie the victim to a tree, or even shoot her in the leg to prevent flight, as the ACC reported.[256]

Le Gac identified a "culpable permissiveness" among some French cadres toward the behavior of their troops.[257] Most rapes occurred in waves during lulls in the fighting, after the troops had taken an objective. The fact that Juin and his officers seemed in no hurry to bring their troops under control seemed to suggest that this so-called "50-hour rule" of allowing their soldiers *carte blanche* to let off steam was informally accepted procedure. The lack of punishment for increasingly egregious acts of indiscipline sent a strong message that such conduct was tolerated by the command, especially by Juin, who reacted only under Allied pressure, and, when cornered, looked to offload blame.[258] As will be seen below, a similar pattern was to occur in Germany in 1945 under Juin's successor de Lattre. In other words, rapes in Italy carried out by soldiers of the CEF, and later rapes in Germany by de Lattre's First French Army, were hardly an unfortunate byproduct of indigenous indiscipline, opportunity, and sexual desire. Rather, it is certainly reasonable to hypothesize that contempt for and resentment of the enemy in a French high command humiliated by 1940 and the indignities of occupation communicated itself downward.

Contempt for Italians might have been reinforced also by the direct experiences of the soldiers. Italian troops in Tunisia had distinguished themselves by surrendering often in practically unmanageable numbers. In 1943–1944, Naples was an impoverished, squalid, partially destroyed city, whose primitive living conditions reminded one of North Africa. To survive, many women slipped into prostitution, or at least looked for a protector among the occupiers, for whom Naples seemed to be hardly more than a teaming brothel. Trading food or money for sex taught Allied soldiers to expect subservience from the population, to view women as sexual targets, and blurred the lines of consent.[259] "The people leave a painful impression of misery and a lack of dignity," Lapouge recounted as his regiment marched through Naples on their arrival in December 1943. "Men, kids, dirty girls, disheveled and provocative run alongside our column, mingle with our soldiers to beg for money, cigarettes, or food." While Italian villages were often picturesque, they were "stunningly filthy and disordered." Even a common Catholic heritage failed to elicit sympathy from the devout Lapouge, who attended mass only to discover the same level of disorder as on the street, as some worshippers sang, prayed, or "prostrated themselves with no apparent reason," while children played marbles on the floor of the church.[260]

Italians were despised by North African soldiers as dirty, with low morals, "peddlers of goat milk," whom they could abuse by right of conquest "because they were enemies."[261] Rapes might also be excused as a primitive, if customary, Muslim cultural response. Guillaume and other officers excused the thefts and even rapes committed by their *goumiers* as consistent with the North African tradition of "*une belle razzia* [raid]," one not only tolerated, but also reinforced by the French conquest. Guillaume insisted that the "love of the fight" that characterized his *goumiers* was matched only by "a spirit of pillage . . . Theft, when it involves a degree of danger, does not disgrace its author. On the contrary, it becomes an exploit."[262] Pillage and rape were explained by French officers as a North African cultural response that was transferred together with indigenous troops, especially *goumiers*, from North Africa to Italy, and later to Germany. The French command was well aware of the reputation of the *goumiers* for violence against civilians, because a September 1943 report had recommended that *tabors* be deployed in the liberation of France "only with prudence."[263] But this offers only partial exoneration, because historically the French had enlisted indigenous forces in Africa by dangling the prospect of pillage and rape as part of the compensation package, and then shirked responsibility for war crimes that they had tacitly encouraged, by insisting they were endemic to indigenous culture. Therefore, refusing to make a distinction between combatants and non-combatants, and deploying violence against populations in what evolved as a ritual, had a long tradition in colonial warfare in general, and North Africa in particular. To this was added the violence of twentieth-century total war, which made few distinctions between combatant and civilian. And, of course, because of *l'armée d'Afrique*'s reverential status in AFN, no officer was ever expected to be held accountable for what in effect were war crimes, because he could always attribute regrettable excesses to the savage character and barbaric customs of the native populations which had shaped tribal warfare and subsequently underpinned the combat performance of indigenous troops.[264] So, in the minds of France's military leadership, "The tolerance of rape as war booty attenuated its moral interdiction," concludes Le Gac.[265] Guillaume conceded that his North African troops carried out rapes in Germany, "but no more than was normal for primitive troops."[266] Because *goumiers* were hypersexualized, lacking civilized restraints, and paid less than *tirailleurs*, rape and pillage came to be interpreted as "normal" – even predictable – behavior for indigenous soldiers. The more stout the enemy's resistance, the more severe the retribution that followed. After Tunisia, where Italian soldiers often surrendered after desultory resistance, the difficulty of the extremely hard fighting in Italy had not only come as a shock, but also created an accumulation of frustrations, unleashed by the breakthrough on the Garigliano. The fact that it was Italian women and their families who paid the price could be shrugged off as "*c'est la guerre*."

Blaming Muslim avarice and uncontrolled sexual impulses, as well as the predatory culture of North Africa, for post-Cassino indiscipline also camouflaged the possibility that a large number of the rapes, perhaps even the majority, were carried out by French, not Muslim troops.[267] In April 1944, the *Deuxième Bureau* had warned that the flip side of the *goumiers*' reputation for ferocity was that, "each time there is a theft or act of indiscipline," blame would inevitably fall on them.[268] The pillage of churches, violence against priests, rapes of nuns, and lack of respect for sanctuaries where a refugee population congregated "under the eyes of the Madonna" were viewed as Barbary payback for the desecration of Muslim religion and culture by European imperialists. The Rabat Residency soon complained that up to 5,000 packages a month containing stolen goods, including sacred items pillaged from churches and even medieval manuscripts, were being posted back to the Sultanate by indigenous soldiers in Italy. For their part, Italians viewed acts of vandalism and assault by *marocchini* as not only criminal, but also blasphemous, a theme exploited in the 1957 Alberto Moravia novel *La ciociara* (published in English translation as *Two Women*), which was adapted by Vittorio de Sica in a 1960 film with the same title. And by introducing Moorish soldiers, the French had imported a race and religious war into Italy. While one must be careful not to see Muslim indiscipline as a precursor of rebellion against the colonial order, crimes committed by all liberating armies expressed in some degree a contempt for the liberated.[269] By insisting that rape was a problem to do with "*marocchini*," rather than a French problem, the *pied noir* Juin was able to incriminate the very troops who had given him his victory, and deflect criticism of the French command onto Muslim character and culture. And, given their prejudices against North Africans, the Italians became willing co-conspirators in this explanation.

Among contemporary historians, Jean-Christophe Notin supports Juin's contention that the accusations of violence against the CEF were exaggerated, especially by the Italian press. Reports often dribbled in a month after an alleged crime and constituted a form of political and financial blackmail.[270] Unfortunately, these exonerations do not stand close scrutiny. Italian historian Tomaso Barris concedes that some of the accusations were collected up to twenty years after the event by a war victims' group with some political support in the Italian parliament whose purpose was to collect reparations from the French government. This campaign may have even stimulated a collective memory of the CEF's indiscipline that exceeded in some cases the amplitude of the actual events while attributing to the perpetrators motivations which were simply not present. The problem with dismissing the claims as exaggerated and late, however, was that even at the time the brutality and indiscipline of French soldiers in Italy was chronicled and became a source of concern for Juin and in the Allied command more generally, because these actions were viewed as undermining the liberation narrative and the honor of Allied forces, while suggesting that the Allied commanders could not control their undisciplined troops.[271] Many women were no doubt reluctant to report that they had been raped, especially by North Africans, because it brought shame on them and their families. Unfortunately, French soldiers would return for an encore on Elba and in Germany in 1945 that would earn them the nickname "The Russians of the West."[272]

Conclusion

The January 1943 Anfa conference had set the parameters of French rearmament at eleven army divisions, as well as a French air force to be stood up virtually from scratch. The remnants of a scuttled and sidelined French navy were also to be refurbished. Recreating a modern French army would prove more problematic. While AFN's manpower pool bulged with potential indigenous infantrymen, it lacked European cadres and specialists, not to mention the infrastructure required to build and train a modern, mechanized force with a significant logistical tail on an American model. If the empire quickly revealed its manpower and logistical limitations, many anticipated that a growing resistance on the French mainland might act as a force multiplier to bolster French clout in the alliance. This concept received a trial run when Giraud launched the liberation of Corsica in September 1943. While Arthur

Layton Funk cited Corsica as "the first French territory to be liberated solely by the French army," in fact, launched on a shoestrine, Operation Vesuvius succeeded only because the Germans had no intention of defending the island, and because Italian occupation forces provided the heft for Corsica's liberation in the wake of Badoglio's defection from the Axis. Furthermore, the minimal military effectiveness of civilian resistance in Corsica was overlooked because it ran counter to the requirements of Gaullist political influence, as well as the aspirations of the Allied interface services to carve out an operational niche for themselves in the liberation of France and Europe. What did ring alarm bells in Algiers and London, however, was communist attempts to manipulate their control of many of resistance cells to seize political power on the island. With de Gaulle now firmly dominating France's exile movement after brandishing Vesuvius' shortcomings to oust Henri Giraud from his "co-presidency," the CFLN began to create a shadow government structure to be transferred onto the mainland upon liberation.

While at the time the Italian campaign was decried as a distraction forced on France by Anfa, in fact it brought at least two benefits for France. First, unlike a decade and a half later when the French army's North African praetorians would capsize French democracy, the removal of much of *l'armée d'Afrique* from the very politicized wartime environment of AFN, and its placement under US command, which forbade direct communications with Algiers, was critical in keeping the French army focused on its professional mission. And this came at a delicate transitional moment when de Gaulle was both consolidating his power in the CFLN and initiating a purge of former Vichy elements in AFN, including in the French military. Second, participation in a very arduous Italian campaign allowed the French army to showcase its most gifted operational commander, and recoup the combat laurels which it had forfeited in 1940. Historians generally concur that the Juin-orchestrated May 1944 breakthrough at Monte Cassino offered "one of the most remarkable feats of a war more remarkable for bloody attrition than skill." It was perhaps ironic that the momentum of the Roosevelt–Leahy vision of a US-empresarioed aeromaritime war to reestablish European democracy hinged on the rusticity, endurance, and tactical skill of an undemocratic force composed of largely illiterate imperial levies. This combined with the operational vision of Alphonse Juin to make the CEF the pivotal military force in Italy in 1944. And, while the triumph at Cassino is sometimes hailed as the renaissance of the French army, Le Gac reminds us that, in a French imperial context, the breakthrough on the Garigliano rather marked the end of an era, being "the last avatar of the fraternity of arms between Europeans and (North African) natives."[273] Cassino showcased the triumph of France's imperial subjects, men who heretofore had served as a mere parenthesis, protagonists of "skirmishes on picturesque and far-flung fronts" that were of marginal military importance.

Without the breakthrough at Cassino, the August 1944 invasion of southern France – Operation Dragoon – could not have proceeded, most likely leaving Jean de Lattre de Tassigny's *Armée B* stranded in AFN and further diminishing France's contribution to the liberation.

The Italian campaign also offered a major step in realizing Roosevelt's agenda of the post-war democratization of Europe. On 23 May 1944, the Badoglio government repudiated Fascist foreign policy, including the 1940 declaration of war on France and Rome's claims to Tunisia. On 5 June 1944, the day following the capture of Rome, the Italian cabinet abrogated the 24 June 1940 armistice signed between representatives of Pétain and Mussolini.[274] However, Franco-Italian political reconciliation as well as the military laurels won by the French army in Italy were tarnished by rapes carried out by some members of the CEF following the breakthrough on the Garigliano. French indiscipline called into question the command climate and tacit complicity of the CEF hierarchy in war crimes against the Italian population. Juin's attempts to shift the blame for the rapes carried out under his leadership, when combined with his equivocal behavior during Torch and the Axis invasion of Tunisia, also suggested that his strength of character failed to match his demonstrated military talents. The wartime rapes continued to be an unresolved political issue between Rome and Paris into the post-war era. Italian civilians who had been victims of the *marocchinate* failed to receive justice. While the Italian government continued to denounce the barbarous conduct of the CEF, nevertheless the 10 February 1947 peace treaty between France and Italy acknowledged Rome's responsibility for the war. As a consequence, Article 76 of that treaty required Italy to renounce any claims for indemnities that resulted directly from the war. While the Italian Communist Party in particular, and various victims' associations, on occasion raised the issue of reparations for the *marocchinate*, the priority for the Italian government was clearly to turn the page and get on with reconstructing Europe.

4 Resistance on the Eve of D-Day

In the wake of Torch, Tunisia, and Anfa, it was clear that the French army had condensed to a "one shot" force puttering on the margins of the world war. Indeed, when Louis Bacquier attempted to speak of "my warrior exploits," his father

> listened to me with indulgence. For Major Bacquier, the French army died in '40, on the Aisne, like the Guard at Waterloo. The skirmishes that followed on picturesque and far-flung fronts were not devoid of interest for their handful of participants, but were militarily unimportant. The sons of the soldiers of Verdun had become auxiliaries in the Anglo-American armies. Of course, basically he was correct, but it was unpleasant to hear, and I felt not a little idiotic in my blue (North African *tirailleur*) *képi* of which I was so proud.[1]

France had faced dark days in its long and glorious history. It simply needed to regenerate. But a strategic landscape in which a million French soldiers remained incarcerated as prisoners of war (POWs), with Vichy's illusions of military revival through the armistice army, the High Seas Fleet, and the empire shattered, and the Hexagon in the vice grip of German occupation buttressed by Vichy collaboration left little space for France's "greatest generation" myth to evolve. In this context, the *levée*'s revival as resurrection from within in the form of "the French Resistance" would owe more to morale-boosting myths of French opposition to the German occupation and to political expediency, as a bid to enhance France's role in its own Liberation, than to the broad popular participation and significant military utility that sustained the memory of earlier *levées*. The "national insurrection" of 1941–1944, followed by "*l'amalgame*" of the Forces françaises de l'intérieur (FFI) and the regular army, would constitute a successful Gaullist Information Operations stratagem to force the Allies to recognize French sovereignty at the Liberation and treat France as an equal member of the Alliance.[2]

While historians have come to view resistance to Axis occupation and fascism as a global phenomenon, it nevertheless assumed national characteristics shaped by history, circumstance, geography, and personalities. France's resistance myth resonated because it tapped into images and legends dating from the French Revolution to make an emotional connection with the righteous fury of the people mobilized in mystical communion to topple tyranny. The 1789 stormers of the Bastille transformed into the *levée en masse* of 1793. In this way, the myth of the French Resistance traced a familiar historical trajectory to recast a narrative of defeat and national humiliation into a crusade of moral purpose behind a self-sacrificing leader to export French grandeur beyond the boundaries of the Hexagon. But subordinating history to *faux* and contrived patriotic analogies perpetrated a collective delusion, one that devalued the contribution of the professional soldiers and colonial subjects of the FFL and *l'armée d'Afrique* – not to mention the Allies – to France's resurrection, in favor of a spontaneous assembly of military amateurs. "The North African army which was France's contribution to Allied victory, was the army which the Armistice allowed France to preserve; it was infinitely more important than the Resistance," ran the argument of what Julian Jackson labels "the right-wing anti-Gaullists."[3]

And they had a point. The truth was that resistance in France remained a minority, even an elite phenomenon. Outside estimates put "authentic" resisters – those who engaged in "some degree of illegal action" out of patriotism and not for profit – at between 300,000 and half a million, or between 0.75 and 1.25 percent of the population.[4] This hardly achieved in scope the participation, intensity of action, or robustness found in Yugoslavia, where resistance drew in an estimated 6 percent of the population, or Poland, where 4–5 percent of the population are reckoned to have been active, not to mention insurgency behind the lines on the Eastern Front, which eventually became highly militarized and coordinated by Soviet military intelligence.[5] When the Anglo-American armies splashed ashore in Normandy on 6 June 1944, France counted "probably 100,000 badly armed *maquisards*," a number which quadrupled over the summer. On the other hand, such comparisons have their limits. The real question, Jean-François Muracciole insists, is not what percentage of the population participated, but "was it effective on the military level?"[6] Mass resistance would have been difficult to organize and sustain in France, which was both a major theater and lacked the vast ungoverned spaces of the Balkans and the Eastern Front. Also, there was no way that resistance groups in France could amass the resources to accommodate a significant influx of recruits, as those in flight from *Service du travail obligatoire* (STO) from early 1943 discovered, much less have found productive military tasks for them. Furthermore, Axis counterinsurgency operations in Eastern and Southeastern Europe were intermittent and unsustained, especially in the Balkans after September 1943, when Italy opted out of the Axis. As will be seen below, even a modest attempt in France to hold territory in the manner of Tito's Partisans invited massacre and dispersion. For this reason, French historian of the resistance Olivier Wieviorka rejects such comparisons with less developed areas or census taking as a mechanism of resistance legitimization. Rather he distinguishes between "*Résistance-organisation*" – that is, formally structured resistance groups – and "*Résistance-mouvement*," which is resistance as a sociological and political phenomenon, representative of a popular rejection of occupation and collaboration which was unquantifiable but significant. Popular hostility to Vichy and the occupation conditioned, shaped, and guaranteed the survival of the *Résistance-organisation*.[7] The danger is that, because the scope and reach of "*Résistance-mouvement*" is impossible to measure, an effort to evaluate its scope and importance risks toggling into faith-based scholarship.

Furthermore, if survival required "*Résistance-organisation*" to remain small and clandestine, while "*Résistance-mouvement*" merely reflected a groundswell aspiration for Allied deliverance, then, returning to Muracciole's question, what was its military value? Some resistance and *maquis* chiefs, joined by operatives of the "interface services" – that is, the Special Operations Executive (SOE), Office of Strategic Services (OSS), and Bureau central de renseignements et d'action (BCRA) – attempted to puff the military contributions of resistance to the Liberation, and deflate accusations of "*attentisme*" – that, apart from a handful of resistance heroes, the vast majority of French men and women passively awaited liberation from abroad. But the obligation to operate clandestinely and to rely on volunteers, the presence in France of the Gestapo and other German and French security organizations – police, the Groupe mobile de réserve (GMR), *la Milice* – which regularly infiltrated and shattered resistance networks, imposed discretion and dispersion. Because a collective movement organized around a centralized structure would have invited penetration and dissolution, resistance inside France remained "feudal, malleable and polycentric."[8]

Eventually, in May 1943, guided by Jean Moulin, the internal and external resistance nominally fused under de Gaulle's leadership. But it proved to be a tense, turbulent, even brittle collaboration, because resistance incorporated people from across the political spectrum whose goals and strategies were not only different, but also often at cross purposes. For de Gaulle, the integrity of resistance became a personal crusade. His challenge, both in North Africa and in France from 1943, was how to preserve the unity and strategic direction of resistance as it ballooned to incorporate communists, socialists, and conservative republicans, as well as "Maréchalist" converts who incubated most of their Vichy-endorsed prejudices, headlined by antisemitism. This made for a very uncomfortable transition for Armistice Army and *armée d'Afrique* officers from "neutrality" to reconnection with the Allies from November 1942, and subsequently from June 1943 the Comité français de libération nationale (CFLN) under de Gaulle's presidency. Many then and since refused to accept these "*Vichysto-résistants*" as bona fide resisters because, although they were anti-German, the restoration of democratic governance in France did not fit their agenda. The counter, of course, is that resistance shared a common goal of ending the occupation. The fact that legend and memory ascribe a redemptive Republican mission to the resistance *levée* demonstrates its synthetic, even contrived quality.[9]

From "*Résistance-mouvement*" to "*Résistance-organisation*"

The year 1943 would prove a pivot, when "*résistance-mouvement*" increasingly transitioned into organized opposition to Vichy and the Occupation. This evolution had two sources. The first was a requirement to unify the various resistance movements in France behind Charles de Gaulle in order to give the leader of *la France combattante* the political clout and democratic legitimacy he required to negotiate with the Allies and overcome the leadership challenge posed by Henri Giraud. A second trigger was the STO crisis. Vichy's 16 February 1943 call-up of French laborers for Germany signaled the moment when Vichy entered its most extreme phase of collaboration, one that impacted every French family. STO triggered "a vast movement of refusal . . . a spreading phenomenon of disobedience," which overwhelmed Vichy's *forces de l'ordre*, as tens of thousands of young men absconded into the countryside rather than acquiesce to labor conscription in Germany.[10] This spontaneous flight gave rise to a phenomenon referred to as the *maquis*, which commingled a humanitarian crisis with military opportunity. In each case, the interface services sought to transform popular resistance into an organized force with a viable military mission.

This evolution from symbolic gestures to clandestine warfare was often a confused, at times acrimonious, one that encountered many setbacks, even tragedies, along the way. Not only did this "resistance" struggle to find a purpose, but also it reflected the sharp political differences within the resistance leadership. Gaullist networks answered to the BCRA, while others were supplied by the British SOE. In one famous incident called "*l'affaire Suisse*," in early 1943, Henri Frenay, the leader of the resistance group *Combat*, successfully appealed to OSS representative in Switzerland and future Central Intelligence Agency (CIA) chief Alan Dulles for funds, an act which Jean Moulin denounced as "treason" because it inferred a disloyalty to de Gaulle, who was at that moment in the thick of his struggle with Giraud.[11] Not surprisingly, the communist leadership in the *Front National* (FN) and the *Francs-Tireurs et Partisans* (FTP) conspired to seize power on the Liberation, as showcased in Corsica. While their clandestine reflex and tight discipline made the communist resistance particularly effective on the operational level, its leaders also proved excessively ideological, uncooperative, indifferent to the loss of human life, and dedicated to their own maximalist interpretation of "National Insurrection." Conservatives, some pro-Pétain but anti-German, might congregate in Frenay's *Combat*, *l'Organisation Civile et Militaire* (OCM), or *l'Organisation de résistance de l'Armée* (ORA) which attracted former military officers. Non-compliant STO conscripts, some of whom began to collect in camps in France's more remote regions from early 1943 onward, were too inchoate to have a political agenda beyond a rejection of forced labor and an end to the occupation. All groups were meant to participate in *l'Armée secrète* (AS), Moulin's umbrella project to create "a virtual army of men who for the moment went about their daily lives and jobs but for whom weapons would be parachuted in and stockpiled and leadership provided, and who would be ready on D-Day to support Allied forces landing on French soil." This force was expected to be under direct Allied command, independent of the egos and political agendas of the various leaders of individual groups.[12]

Relations between internal and external resistance were also complex and constantly evolving. De Gaulle's purpose was to reestablish the French state, short-circuit a communist power-grab as per Corsica, circumvent civil war, and restore France as an equal among the Allied powers. Therefore, Moulin's role had been to create a consensus around the leadership of *la France combattante* and, together with political parties and the British Broadcasting Corporation (BBC), market the French Resistance as a democratic *levée* to legitimate de Gaulle's self-proclaimed mandate. But, by 1943, the strategic context for the resistance had shifted, from assembling and facilitating a clandestine opposition to the Occupation and those who collaborated with it, to preparing to support an Allied invasion. In terms of functional specialties, by 1943 resistance in France had divided into three main groups. *Combat*, *Libération*, and *Défense de France* sought to mobilize civilian opinion and provide military training for some. A second category of networks, led by *Alliance Réseau*, specialized in intelligence collection, sabotage, and escape and evasion networks for Allied POWs and downed pilots, tasks in which women often took the lead. A third category was the *maquis* – *ad hoc*, largely leaderless aggregations of young men scattered in France's more remote regions. Given their burgeoning importance as intermediaries with the Allies, spokesmen for the occupied French population, and actors in the upcoming invasion, resistance leaders expected to be treated as equals, and demanded a prominent role in deciding France's future.

The Political Dimensions of Intelligence

Only gradually had "the French Resistance" assumed a political importance, much less a military one, either with de Gaulle or for the Allies. Like de Gaulle, the resistance leaders were men without antecedents, who had emerged from outside the framework of the pre-war institutions, and remained independent-minded. No one knew whom, or how many people, they represented.[13] Resistance would become a new battlefield for control among the three interface agencies, and the Parti communiste français (PCF), which, unlike the other French political parties, was accustomed to a clandestine existence, was gifted with dedicated and disciplined cadres, and promoted a strategy called "national insurrection," whose actual meaning was fluid.[14]

The task of federating and coordinating this burgeoning and largely spontaneous resistance movement, and transforming it into a Gaullist power base, ostensibly fell to the BCRA, which became the indispensable intermediary between London and occupied France. It was to prove a delicate task for many reasons, beginning with the fact that Gaullist intelligence had to compete with the British intelligence services – the Special Intelligence Service (SIS) or Military Intelligence 6 (MI6) and SOE – both of which maintained their own French sections, for recruits and missions, while nevertheless remaining on good terms with their British colleagues upon whom the BCRA was totally dependent for resources – recruits, cash, air liaison, radios, training, and eventually arms and explosives. In return, the BCRA could supply intelligence, and became proficient at acquiring it to the point that, by D-Day, even OSS chief William Donovan credited the BCRA with providing 80 percent of Allied intelligence on France. In de Gaulle's initial military vision for *la France libre*, the BCRA played the role of a classic military *Deuxième Bureau*. However, from the summer of 1941, the leader of *la France libre* realized that a "spirit of resistance" was growing in France, a trend confirmed in early 1942 when Jean Moulin returned from his first mission there. BCRA chief André Dewavrin (Passy) came to realize that harnessing fissiparous and independent-minded resistance groups to the goal of imposing a Gaullist state on liberation required the BCRA to assume a more political posture. Otherwise, liberation might be defined by chaos and civil war sparked between Vichy reactionaries and communists.

This message was reinforced by the 28 April 1942 arrival in London of thirty-nine-year-old Pierre Brossolette. Normalien, journalist, Section française de l'internationale ouvrière (SFIO) activist and brilliant pre-war protégé of Leon Blum, Brossolette joined what was then known as the BCRAM (BCRA Militaire) as chief of resistance operations.[15] Brossolette's views mirrored closely those of de Gaulle, that France was "sick" and leaderless. The French people needed a "myth of de Gaulle," not simply of de Gaulle as a military leader, but a "total myth" based on the restoration of democratic stability to a liberated France. Heretofore, de Gaulle had insisted that *la France libre* was an apolitical organization, open to all, a position that had suited the British. However, since the summer of 1941, pressure had been building for *la France libre* to define a political agenda or face the possibility that, for lack of direction, emerging resistance groups would "fall into a void." By assuming an Olympian political neutrality, *la France libre* telegraphed a detachment from – even disinterest in – events in France, which encouraged a chaos of competing groups in search of operational guidance and a political center of gravity. De Gaulle needed to federate resistance groups around *la France libre* to spark France's political renaissance and boost his bona fides with the Giraudists and the Allies.[16]

Brossolette became the General's ardent, although far from uncritical, disciple, whose goal was to coordinate the political and military dimensions of resistance and prepare for Liberation. The success of his campaign became apparent when, in August 1942, the BCRAM dropped the last letter "M," after Brossolette convinced de Gaulle that compartmentalization of military and political intelligence was nonsense.[17] By the middle of 1942, the time had come for *La France combattante* to go beyond mere patriotic appeals and scoring symbolic military triumphs like Bir Hakeim, and seriously strategize for a favorable political outcome, a role in which an intelligence service that was more than a mere *Deuxième Bureau* could play an important part. Resistance was mobilizing but rudderless, living its own clandestine version of Phoney War. The post-Liberation future could not be entrusted to French political parties, which were too debilitated, too "sick," too disoriented, or too pacifist to battle for a democratic post-war France. Nor could one depend on the goodwill of the Allies – if the Americans had imposed Darlan on AFN, why not Laval on the mainland? Resistance groups needed to be gripped by London, rallied around a political message of Republican revival, and given a strategy. Contradicting Moulin, Brossolette argued that the various political factions in the Conseil national de la résistance (CNR) should merge into a "resistance party" under de Gaulle. This would place the democratic mandate at the center of the resistance mission, avoid a recurrence of Third Republic factionalism and gridlock, stifle any chance of Vichy's survival, confirm with the Allies *la France combattante*'s democratic bona fides, and isolate Giraud, while also providing a mechanism to keep the communists from power.[18] In his memoirs, de Gaulle praised Brossolette as "a prodigy of ideas, elevating our political thinking to the highest levels, measuring in all its profundity the chasm where France panted waiting for nothing but the resurrection of 'Gaullism,' for which he baptized the doctrine."[19]

Passy continued to insist on the BCRA's "technical" role to act as a liaison and source of logistics between London and the internal resistance. But this proved unconvincing both with the resistance and inside of *la France combattante*, where the BCRA and Passy actively lobbied to influence questions of politics, strategy, and the defense of French sovereignty, and sought to establish itself as the interlocutor between the Allies and the resistance. In this process, Passy and his close associates came to be viewed as Gaullist zealots, willing to achieve their goals through subterfuge and dirty tricks. For their part, the BCRA believed that, because they were directly in touch with French opinion, they were best placed to define and optimize Gaullist interests. And, while de Gaulle had an instinctive distrust of intelligence service intrigues in general, and remained a skeptic regarding paramilitary "action," he allowed Passy great latitude because he realized that he needed the BCRA, both to fend off internal challenges from Giraudist intelligence operatives, who had been "fused" in November 1943 into the *Direction Générale des services spéciaux* (DGSS), and from the British, and also to impose Gaullist authority in France through control of the resistance.[20]

By early 1943, Moulin and Brossolette had established contact with a portion of the political parties and resistance groups in France. But *la France combattante* was poorly structured to corral and steer a growing "dissidence" in France into a clandestine state. While, in Crémieux-Brilhac's opinion, the intelligence service was "the most impressive technical success of Free France," intrigue, indiscretions real and imagined, and scandals had blackened the BCRA's reputation since Dakar. Rumor, which Crémieux-Brilhac attributed to André Labarthe, a former protégé of Pierre Cot and editor of *La France Libre,* held that the BCRAM was peopled by Cagoulards and fascists, led by Passy, in the service of a reactionary soldier. In fact, the "non-military" section of the BCRA was operated largely by socialists. With a staff of only fifty-three civilians and soldiers in 1942, the BCRA's capacity to plan and coordinate "action" in France was tenuous. The intelligence organization swelled rapidly with the "fusion" of November 1943 into the DGSS, so that, by the end of 1943, it counted 157 soldiers and 193 civilians in London under André Manuel, as well as a branch office in Algiers under André Pélabon. But, as with Fighting France generally, a small manpower pool made quality recruitment a challenge. Until the amalgamation of the two French intelligence services in November 1943, the Giraudist Service de renseignements (SR) scoffed at the BCRA's amateurism, exemplified by the fact that the Gaullists lacked a counterintelligence section as well as an internal security apparatus. But the real vulnerability of the BCRA was Resistance leaders who complained that they were underfunded and inadequately resourced by Duke Street, which since Corsica had become leery of arming a "red" resistance. Nor had the Allied leaders, or even resistance leaders, coalesced around a strategy to utilize a constantly evolving resistance in France, about which information was fragmentary. Nevertheless, resistance groups continued to organize in 1943, and managed to penetrate important institutions such as the police and gendarmerie, the administration, and the Postes, télégraphes et téléphones (PTT), which was important because it controlled communications in France, while, in *la France profonde*, musters of STO refugees congregated in ever larger numbers. Only in February 1944, at Churchill's insistence, did the British begin to arm the resistance and integrate its capabilities into planning for D-Day.[21]

So far, the BCRAM had concentrated mostly on intelligence collection and the military dimensions of resistance. Passy sought to increase the number of resistance networks and professionalize their intelligence product. But he faced several obstacles, the principal one being that he was largely beholden for most of his resources and liaison to Hugh Dalton, head of the British SOE, who sought to confine the Gaullists to a purely military role. The BCRA lacked personnel to implement many of Passy's ambitious plans. For instance, it proved difficult to centralize operations and intelligence in London without adequate numbers of radios and trained operators to send to France. Finally, resistance networks were vulnerable to penetration and arrest, which hurt Passy's ability to collect intelligence, and hence elevate his standing with the Allies.[22]

In February 1942, de Gaulle had put the *Commissariat national à l'Intérieur* (CNI) in charge of political action, over the objections of Passy, who argued that it was impossible to separate political and military action in occupied France. The CNI was not even a secret service, but a ministry-in-waiting, incapable of structuring and executing a coherent political action initiative in France. The two organizations now fell into a competition for agents, missions, and influence with Dalton's SOE.[23] Brossolette's solution to the administrative overlap was that the CNI would translate de Gaulle's thoughts into directives, that the BCRA would then operationalize. Separate political and military sections received directives respectively through de Gaulle and his chief of staff. Although this compartmentalization was not always respected, in this way, the BCRAM – which shed its "M" on 1 July 1942 – became the only Gaullist intelligence service active on the mainland.[24] However, the combination of Passy's bureaucratic savvy and contacts with Hugh Dalton in the Ministry of Economic Warfare, which oversaw the SOE, and Brossolette's dynamism, intelligence, knowledge and appreciation of French politics and psychology, strategic insights, and organizational vision rapidly made him one of *la France combattante*'s key players, and helped to isolate and sideline the CNI. For his contribution, Brossolette was decorated with the *croix de guerre* and promoted to major.[25]

Yet, there were limits on the BCRA's productivity that even talented administrators and visionaries like Passy and Brossolette were powerless to rectify. Potential recruits arriving in Great Britain had first to be processed through the Patriotic School clearing house, before being handed off to the CNI-supervised *Centre de ralliement et d'accueil* (CRA), which gave the CNI first crack at the most promising recruits such as Moulin, Conféderation générale du travail (CGT) syndicalist and member of *Libération-nord* Christian Pineau, and Philippe Roques, a former associate of Georges Mandel who in 1943 would perish in Gestapo custody. Most volunteers for the Gaullist resistance wanted to take up regular combat roles, not enlist as a "solitary and anonymous volunteer" in covert espionage activities, which often ended in murder. In any case, in 1942, only two in five volunteers were judged suitable for clandestine work.

A list of candidates was sent to de Gaulle's personal chief of staff for assignment. The real Achilles heel of clandestine operations was the vulnerability of radio operators, who were increasingly placed in danger by improving German detection techniques. The clandestine services also had to compete with the armed forces, especially the navy, to recruit and train signals technicians and pilots. Albertelli reckons that, by D-Day, the BCRA was dispatching around ten agents per month to France. Forced to outsource agent training to the British, they also lacked the personnel to monitor agents' activities in France, and could not debrief them when they cycled through London or Algiers. This sent a strong signal to resistance groups, who lived in constant danger of detection, arrest, torture, and death, that the BCRA was simply not interested in their information or their work in France.[26]

Mobilizing Resistance

Restructuring operations in London was only a first step, however. A second problem to overcome was that many resistance leaders remained suspicious of de Gaulle and his *émigré* movement. Some, like Henri Frenay, whose *Combat* was the most important movement in the *zone libre*, remained convinced for some time that Vichy was resisting German demands with vigor. Like so many others from a Catholic and military background, Frenay initially placed his faith in the patriotism of the Marshal and the cadres of the Armistice Army. But, beginning with Emmanuel d'Astier's *Libération-sud* in January 1942, the resistance gradually came to acknowledge de Gaulle's leadership, largely because resistance leaders had begun to realize that, as the only name familiar to the French public, de Gaulle was coming to personify resistance. "The people have the need to fix their hope and faith in a man," wrote Frenay, who, like d'Astier and William Leahy, conceded that, after Laval had been named chief minister in April 1942, Pétain had ceased to be that man.

Thus, from early 1942, a parade of resistance leaders arrived through the air, by stealth, and at night, lifted to London via Lysander to meet that myth. A high-wing monoplane, the stout Westland Lysander (Figure 4.1) became the fragile link between the internal and external resistance. Designed as a very maneuverable artillery spotting platform for the Royal Air Force (RAF), the "virtually unbreakable" "Lizzie" could glide onto rough fields and jolt to a halt in less than 20 yards. From October 1940, the British had begun to adapt a Mark III Lysander with an 870 horse-power (HP) Bristol Mercury engine for "pick-up operations" by stripping out its meager armament and adding a ladder to access the machinegunner's cockpit, which was transformed into a snug passenger compartment with two rear-facing wooden chairs – at a pinch, a third passenger might hunker uncomfortably on the floor. A torpedo-shaped drop tank for 150 gallons of aviation fuel attached to the undercarriage considerably

Figure 4.1 The robust Westland Lysander, photographed in 1941, was adapted from its role as an artillery spotter. Fitted with an auxiliary fuel tank, its machinegunner's cockpit transformed into a snug passenger compartment, with a ladder fixed for access, it became a fragile link between London and resistance in France. (Country Life Ltd, London, 1941. Artist Unknown. Photo by The Print Collector via Getty Images)

increased the Lysander's flying radius at maximum cruising speed of 164 mph to 1,150 miles. Throttling back to 120 mph, the pilot might squeeze out an extra 500 miles. Part of the training for agents – called "Joes" – was to identify suitable fields, draft descriptions for wireless messages to Britain, and align a short "flare path" of lanterns in an inverted L so that the Lysander could land into the wind. Pilots had to be alert for abnormalities, lest their landing site had been betrayed and so occupied by the Gestapo or Sicherheitspolizei (Sipo)/ Sicherheitsdienst (SD). Most Lysanders departed RAF Tangmere on the south coast near Chichester, but some also left from airfields near Newmarket and Cambridge, at dusk. Although flight paths sought to avoid heavily defended ports such as Le Havre and flak corridors, whose locations were constantly updated, invariably passengers could nervously observe tracers arching toward them as they crossed the dark outline of the French coast. Navigation was by ground observation aided by a compass and a Michelin map torn into strips for each phase of the trip so that it could be held in one hand. But, in bad weather, the pilot had to guess his location by "dead reckoning," based on compass and air speed. Pilots wore their RAF tunic over civilian clothes without laundry marks. Every plane was equipped with a small locker containing an escape kit: a beret, a "wad of French money," a compass, a map of France printed on a silk scarf, concentrated food tablets, a fishing line and hooks, and identity photos suitable for forged documents.[27]

From November 1942, the twin-engine Lockheed Hudson was pressed into service by No. 161 (Special Duties) Squadron for trips to France. A small airliner christened the A-24, transformed into a "reconnaissance bomber" for use against U-boats by Coastal Command, the Hudson's advantages were its maneuverability and the fact that, stripped of its seats, it could accommodate eight to ten passengers and their luggage, or deliver consignments of "freight," including radios, arms and explosives, and large sums of French currency. Assisted by a navigator and combination gunner/radio operator, Hudson pilots found it easier to locate landing fields on night runs. The downside was that the Hudson required a clear 1,000 meters to land, and was heavier and less robust than the Lysander, while the plane's revving engines made so much noise that their preliminary pass and turn might wake up Göring in Berlin, or at least alert the local *Feldgendarmerie*, who, if they failed to reach the landing site before the turnaround, at the very least would plow the field to end its further usefulness.[28]

Unfortunately, many of the "Joes" airlifted to meet de Gaulle in the early days came away unimpressed. The leader of *la France libre* was tall, but with a small head, his hands were white and "rather feminine," and his movements mechanical, almost choreographed. While appreciating his messianic vision for France and the fact that he had assumed the burden of sorting out the blindside of 1940, many found him to be self-absorbed – even self-pitying about the burden he had assumed – and utterly clueless about conditions in France. Indeed, some, like Brossolette, judged de Gaulle's authoritarian personality, his military reflex to issue orders rather than allow debate, and stoic indifference to the fate of his countrymen seriously to limit his ability to inspire and direct a swelling but extremely diverse resistance. Disturbed by the poor quality of the staffing at Carleton Gardens when he arrived in April 1942, in a frank 2 November 1942 note, the iconoclastic Brossolette warned his boss that his refusal to allow discussion on certain subjects in which de Gaulle had an "emotional" investment had discouraged his most talented advisors from interacting with him, leaving only the "toadies" and "flatterers" to offer opinions. It would not be the last time that de Gaulle would be admonished for his "glacial" indifference to constructive criticism, and even for the "savage cruelty" with which he treated some of his most loyal advisors. Nor were resistance leaders quite sure exactly what de Gaulle stood for, especially as Gaullist "ultras" such as Brossolette talked openly of melding political parties in post-Liberation France into a "political Gaullism," which in the minds of some like Raymond Aron evoked Bonapartism.[29]

For these reasons, however, as much as they required the symbol of de Gaulle to legitimize their action and build their movements, resistance subservience to London was hardly unconditional. The two Gaullist "zealots" Moulin and Brossolette, dispatched by London in 1943 to consolidate and restructure resistance groups in the formerly "free" and "occupied" zones, respectively, discovered that, to a man, resistance leaders wanted decisions taken in France, not London or Algiers. Even though he had formerly been a military man, Frenay insisted that the internal resistance was equal in authority to London, and refused to be slotted into a "chain-of-command" topped by de Gaulle. Resistance leaders also resented the fact that the AS – the September 1942 union of the paramilitary formations of the three largest resistance groups in the *zone libre* (*Combat*, *Libération-Sud*, and *Franc-Tireur*) under General Charles Delestraint – answered to London and not to them. In their view, resistance groups were under attack from two directions: de Gaulle sought to transform the internal resistance into a military organization whose missions would be ordered from abroad, while German and Vichy arrests forced resistance groups constantly to reorganize and recalibrate. This fear meant that the CNR outsourced its decision-making to a five-man executive committee renamed COMAC (formerly known as COMIDAC, both denoting Comité d'action en France) in May 1944, in which the communists came to exercise a disproportionate influence. COMAC claimed to be the general staff that would control the FFI on liberation, which set it on a collision course with de Gaulle in Algiers and Allied headquarters (HQ).[30]

It fell to Moulin to coordinate the resistance groups in the *zone libre*, convince them to recognize the authority of *la France combattante*, and foster cooperation through a division of roles and missions. The stubbornly independent attitudes of resistance leaders, their competing visions of the political role that resistance should play on Liberation, and the attitude of de Gaulle, who sought to forge the resistance to assume military tasks, made the unification and coordination of the internal and external resistance problematic. However, *délégué général* Moulin pulled it off when the CNR met clandestinely for the first time in Paris on 27 May 1943. In an Assembly of representatives from eight resistance groups, two trade unions, and six of the Third Republic's main parties, representing the political spectrum from the PCF to conservatives, the seventeen delegates voted unanimously to recognize a provisional government led by de Gaulle.[31]

The January–April 1943 Arquebuse–Brumaire mission formed the counterpart to Moulin's more celebrated triumph in the *zone libre*. The message of federation of resistance groups *and* political parties around de Gaulle to resurrect the French state, to focus and centralize action, and to coordinate with Allied strategy proved a hard sell among stubbornly independent-minded resistance leaders. Despite these difficulties, Arquebuse–Brumaire seemed a great success in that it created a structure for cooperation between the resistance and the Allies in the *zone nord*. While this triumph elevated Brossolette into the pantheon of *La France combattante*, it failed to enhance his popularity, either in London and Algiers or with the resistance.[32]

It is often asserted that de Gaulle lost interest in resistance in France after the 27 May 1943 meeting of the CNR because he had extracted the political payoff organized by Moulin. Nor, as a conventional soldier, did he invest much faith in paramilitary activity. However, the real problem was that he lost control of it. On 21 June, barely three weeks after the historic meeting, Jean Moulin and seven members of the resistance hierarchy were arrested at Caluire, a suburb of Lyon, by the local Gestapo chief Klaus Barbie, tipped off, it has been speculated, by fellow resister René Hardy, although Hardy was twice tried and acquitted of the charge. After being tortured, Moulin committed suicide. As *délégué général*, chief of the CNR, and member of the leadership committee of Mouvements unis de la résistance (MUR), combined with a strong personality that allowed him to impose his will on the independent-minded resistance chiefs, Moulin would prove irreplaceable. Barbie had also captured Delestraint in Paris on 9 June, thus decapitating the AS as well. On a subsequent trip to France, Brossolette was arrested and committed suicide while in Gestapo custody on 22 March 1944. None of their successors possessed their political sagacity, gravitas, or de Gaulle's unconditional support. Nor did the administrative structures erected by Moulin and Brossolette long survive their demise, as the internal resistance reasserted its independence from London and Algiers.[33] So, while resistance endorsement had helped de Gaulle to solidify power in Algiers in 1943, and to authenticate his democratic credentials with the Allies, resistance factionalism, autonomy, and competing political visions and strategic agendas also posed a challenge to the consolidation of his power in France, and would oblige de Gaulle to act *manu militari* upon Liberation.

Even without the loss of Moulin and Brossolette, and the decapitation of both the AS and the CNR in June 1943, maintaining resistance unity and adherence to a common strategic vision would have proven problematic.[34] Resistance leaders were keen to maintain control of their groups, activities, and territory, and to have a say in strategy development over which they frequently and bitterly clashed. Their sense of independence would be emboldened by the interface services that, keen to militarize and operationalize resistance in France, showered arms and cash on local resistance satraps. For their part, politicians and trade union leaders, who by 1942 had begun to recover their stature, looked to reclaim their pre-war ascendency and independence, a move opposed by this new resistance elite that had emerged from the shambles of defeat and collaboration, to be armed and empowered by the interface services. Also, de Gaulle required the endorsement of political parties to legitimize his crusade against "Vichy under American protection" Giraud. A CNR motion to recognize de Gaulle as the leader of the French government and the "soul of resistance," passed unanimously on 27 May 1943, had forced Giraud to invite de Gaulle to Algiers.[35] A second goal of coaxing resistance unity was to avert a shattering of the resistance into warring factions before or after Liberation, a phenomenon that was to catapult Greece and Yugoslavia into civil war. Third, by including political parties, unions, and resistance groups, the CNR laid the foundation for the creation of an *Assemblée consultative* (Consultative Assembly) in Algiers. One of the pillars of the provisional government, the Consultative Assembly at the same time circumscribed the influence of the political parties, whose support in the short term contributed to de Gaulle's legitimacy, but which would reassert their independence at the Liberation.[36]

Devising a Resistance Strategy

As 1943 progressed, three fundamental issues split the Allies, the BCRA, and resistance groups. The first was the extent to which resistance movements were to be brought under a centralized direction, and how much autonomy local resistance leaders should be allowed to act on the basis of their estimates of the operational and tactical opportunities and the capabilities of their forces. The decentralization of decision-making also impacted a second issue – whether resistance groups should launch immediate action, or wait until D-Day, when the Germans would be preoccupied with invading Allied forces. Finally, were resistance forces to act in classic synergy between "guerrillas" and conventional forces? Or was the resistance to spark a "National Insurrection" upon liberation, as the communists and others imagined to be the case in Yugoslavia and Greece? In fact, defining "National Insurrection" as a strategy or a tactic sparked an active and frequently acrimonious debate between Gaullists and communists.

Given their desire to augment their forces and hence their clout in the Alliance, coordinate and optimize the military impact of resistance groups, impose a Gaullist-led government on the mainland upon Liberation, and avoid a potential communist power grab as had occurred in Corsica, the BCRA argued for a tight centralization of resistance organizations in France. Unfortunately, the arrest of Moulin, followed by that of Delestraint in June 1943, stalled their ground game. Nor did this BCRA position find support among the Anglo-American interface services, who preferred to deal directly with resistance leaders. Also, in part because of experience with the infiltration and break-up of SOE networks in France and Holland, decentralization and compartmentalization of groups and tasks had become a requirement of operational security. Above all, however, independent-minded resistance leaders like Frenay saw centralization as a Gaullist prioritization of political control that not only impeded initiative and hence military opportunities, but also rendered resistance networks more vulnerable. In the end, however, a compromise was worked out largely on the basis of the recommendations of SOE agent Edward Yeo-Thomas, who devised a system of twelve *Délégués militaires régionaux* (DMRs). Equiped with radios, the DMRs could liaise with

London to coordinate resistance action on the local level. The BCRA protested that this severed the "French Resistance" from French control, while some resistance chiefs refused to recognize the DMRs' authority. Nevertheless, on 7 November 1943, COMIDAC ordered the decentralization of resistance command to begin.[37]

This devolution of command decision-making to the regional and local level helped to resolve a second issue that roiled intra-resistance relations – immediate engagement, versus deferring action until D-Day. Not surprisingly, at its extremes, this debate pitted the communist FTP, which since the summer of 1941 had taken the fight straight to the enemy, against the more "attentiste," soldier-dominated ORA. Backed by de Gaulle, Delestraint, and the BCRA, the ORA, and other groups who shared their strategic perspective, argued that "terrorism" violated the laws of war, threatened the premature destruction of poorly armed resistance groups, and merely served to provoke reprisals against a defenseless civilian population. Also, guerrilla tactics worked best in combination with conventional operations, not as a stand-alone. Above all, London did not want the communists to seize the moral high ground by taking credit for resistance acts that were more dramatic than useful, and which might only alert the Germans to their vulnerabilities.

Distrust toward the ORA by other resistance groups weakened it along with the Giraudist cause in Algiers, and helped further to marginalize a potential military component of resistance leadership, especially after Giraud's ouster by de Gaulle. But "immediate action" faced the insurmountable hurdle that, in June 1943, only one-quarter of these resisters were armed, while the ORA had at its disposal only twenty radio transmitters. Because they were frequently men and women of the left, civilian resisters led by the communists distrusted the former *Vichysto-résistants* in the ORA and AS as Giraudists, if not closet *Maréchalists*. But desperate times required desperate measures. On the whole, soldiers were welcomed into the resistance, although the FTP's class bias favored former non-commissioned officers (NCOs).[38] Furthermore, they would be forced to serve under civilian leaders whose ignorance of military tactics did not prevent them from self-promoting to senior military rank, which, to be fair, simply replicated the behavior of the early FFL leadership. The result was a crisis of morale that gripped the AS from top to bottom, caused by lack of funds, lack of a clear mission, lack of leadership, and lack of a realistic plan about what, actually, their role in the Liberation was supposed to be.[39]

"L'Insurrection nationale"

The third issue for the resistance revolved around the "national insurrection." Drawing inspiration from Stalin's speech of 6 November 1943, in which he called on the resistance movements to become a second front to relieve pressure on the Red Army, in December the PCF's Central Committee insisted that "It is necessary to unmask these theories of degenerate nations and make the armed struggle a struggle of the masses . . . It is indispensable to bring all the people into the armed struggle."[40] Initially, both the British and de Gaulle had called for a "national insurrection," but they increasingly nuanced their view of how occupied populations might directly contribute to their own liberation, either independently or in conjunction with conventional forces, lest "national insurrection" slip from their control. While the Second World War witnessed the expansion in use of paratroops and commandos, Western military doctrine for the use of clandestine forces in 1943 was at best experimental. In the autumn of 1943, Greece and the Balkans, where the British had been active in supporting guerrilla bands since 1941, seemed to serve as the model for what a "National Insurrection" in France might aspire to become. Seemed to, because, according to Sean McMeekin, Churchill's friend Brigadier Fitzroy Maclean's "wildly inaccurate report on Tito's partisans" circulated in Cairo and London in November 1943, which vastly inflated the numbers of armed partisans while claiming that communist insurgents were inflicting devastating losses on the Wehrmacht, when, in fact, the opposite was the case.[41] Nevertheless, on the basis of this fantasy Yugoslav model, the goal of the SOE became to transform resistance in France from a clandestine conspiracy into an insurrection aimed at delegitimizing Vichy and diverting German troops from coastal defense into internal security missions. But how this transition was to be realized was never clear. "National insurrection was therefore a complex and evolving concept that referred to diverse political and military cultures, specifically for the period of Second World War France," concludes Raphaële Balu.[42]

Nevertheless, from the perspective both of Allied strategy and of French politics, how one interpreted "national insurrection" impacted plans for the mobilization of the resistance on D-Day. Even as they accorded the resistance an ever-greater role in operations, DGSS planners worried about the potential for a premature resistance uprising.[43] For conventional soldiers, the role of the resistance was to infiltrate, observe, inform, strike, and withdraw back into concealment. On the left, "insurrection" and popular uprising had been encoded in French memory since the Revolution as a "just revolt" against oppressors and tyrants in the name of liberty and equality. "*Le mythe de l'insurrection*" became a means to restore the national communion, preserve social cohesion, and salvage self-respect in a France whose contribution to the war so far had combined military obsolescence and defeat with political confusion and *attentisme*, when not treachery. To revolt is to cleanse, to rehabilitate, to redeem. "National Insurrection" therefore promised a national baptism, to reconstruct French society around a heroic memory of popular revolt against occupation, restore audacity to the national narrative, and populate a pantheon of glorious leaders, while relegating collaborators to the status of criminals and traitors. For the right, including many army officers who joined the resistance, the historical precedent of the Vendée insurrection against the French Revolution had been supplanted by the anarchy of *francs-tireurs* and the Paris Commune of 1871. As a consequence, they updated "national insurrection" as a *levée en masse* contained within a conventional military framework. Furthermore, calling for a "national insurrection," or, for that matter, even a "mobilization" which lacked weapons and coordination with conventional operations, was to invite massacre. Above all, soldiers led by de Gaulle were dedicated to reestablishing a legal state. They interpreted the "national insurrection" as a criminal conspiracy designed to catapult the PCF to power in a chaos of slaughter and bogus electoral maneuvers as previewed in Corsica.[44]

If "National Insurrection" provided the liberation strategy for the left, "immediate action" became the tactic. Reflecting the glow of rising Red Army prestige, the PCF had capitalized on the burgeoning STO crisis of 1943 to strengthen its position in the CNR by calling for immediate action, and a "National Insurrection" on D-Day. For the PCF, as well as for Emmanuel d'Astier, CNI director from November 1943, "National Insurrection" had a romanticized historical resonance which coupled Liberation with a Revolutionary *levée en masse*. De Gaulle had inadvertently endorsed the concept when, on 28 April 1942, he had stated that "national liberation cannot be separated from the national insurrection." But that was before Corsica, and before planners in London had begun to operationalize "national insurrection" in the form of military teams under the firm guidance of the Allied military command, directing discrete resistance networks to carry out targeted acts of sabotage to assist an invasion of conventional forces. While they saw the obvious benefits of guerrilla operations behind German lines, the Allies were reluctant to endorse spontaneous popular action that would only provoke a bloodbath that would complicate rather than assist invasion.[45]

Immediate action furthered the communist political goal of provoking retaliation to accelerate the alienation between the population, on the one hand, and Vichy and occupation forces, on the other, dissipate "*attentisme*," radicalize and mobilize the French population, and tie down German forces which might otherwise be shifted to the Eastern Front. Many in the intelligence community and the AS argued for immediate action as a way to blood resistance forces and initiate the population into combat prior to D-Day.[46] By the end of 1943, "immediate action" had gained the support of Frenay and Emmanuel d'Astier, who argued that the resistance was under attack and had no choice other than to respond. But the argument was largely a theoretical one, because the resistance had few arms. Under pressure, in March 1943, de Gaulle had requested weapons to arm 50,000 men, a request refused by Churchill – one imagines much to de Gaulle's relief – because arms would only bolster the communists and encourage "premature action." Some resistance leaders charged de Gaulle with intentionally starving them of funds and arms to force compliance with CFLN directives.[47] Moulin, Brossolette, and Passy acquiesced to "targeted immediate action" carried out by specialized teams because they realized that they were virtually powerless to influence the FTP's tactics in any case. For de Gaulle, the important thing was to have the resistance movements accede to the CFLN's direction rather than to quibble about tactics. So, he had instructed Delestraint on 21 May 1943 to allow resistance leaders more leeway to move toward "immediate action." That said, in London's orders, one noted "the progressive disappearance or at least redefinition of the national insurrection," concludes Raphaële Balu.[48]

But, because they were largely unarmed, resistance leaders turned to sabotage missions, which they argued might substitute for Allied bombing, which caused immense collateral damage that bolstered Vichy's justification for collaboration. Sabotage received the blessing of the SOE, so that most of the parachute drops to the resistance in 1943 delivered explosives. From 1943, discrete groups of saboteurs, graduates of an intensive three- or four-month SOE course, began to blow up dams and canal locks to disrupt fluvial traffic, as well as rail lines, electrical sub-stations, and pylons, and mount attacks on French companies working for the Germans. In the second half of 1943, the east-central canal was put out of operation, and in the middle of December Henri Romans-Petit's Maquis de l'Ain dispatched a fifteen-man team to Le Creusot to cripple a power station that miraculously had survived an Allied bombing that had devastated virtually everything else in the neighborhood and killed many French civilians. Emboldened by the prospect of imminent liberation, resistance teams also assassinated a handful of German officials and French collaborators. Attacks that aimed to destroy files on those called up for STO and to steal cash or ration tickets gave the impression that France was under siege by armed bands. Most active were the communists, keen to rebuild their revolutionary identity in the shadow of the Nazi–Soviet Pact, who organized strikes in preparation for the "national insurrection" planned for D-Day.[49]

The STO Crisis

The strategic debate over national insurrection was given special cogency by the STO crisis, which communists hoped would become the catalyst to mobilize a popular uprising. By 1942, Germany had begun to turn the screws on occupied populations, further reducing French food rations in July. The consequences of Torch had struck a blow at Vichy's credibility: occupation costs had been raised from 300 to 500 million Reichsmarks a day, the Italians had occupied the left bank of the Rhône and Corsica, and Berlin declared the former *zone libre* a "zone of operations" under Oberbefehlshaber West, commanded from Lyon by Gerd von Rundstedt, with his representative General Alexander von Neubronn installed at Vichy to monitor compliance. Beneath Vichy's phantom sovereignty, Berlin's grip on every sector tightened, forcing all but hardened collaborators to concede that France was no better off than had it refused the armistice, abandoned the Hexagon, and fought on from the colonies. Under a very confused, even chaotic, Axis occupation, France had become a vast *Stalag*.[50] Writing in the newspaper *La France libre* on 15 March 1944, Raymond Aron identified the three principal weapons of German control as "hunger, deportation, and civil war."[51]

It became increasingly clear in the course of 1943 that, if Vichy could not control its own territory in the face of mounting resistance to its channeling of German occupation demands onto the backs of the French population, it would forfeit the meager residue of Hitler's confidence. So, the corollary of Vichy collaboration became the repression of a growing resistance threat, a major Vichy contribution to Hitler's "New Europe," as well as a goal compatible with its ideological agenda.[52] "Along with the Gestapo, it was an anonymous French bureaucracy that inflicted the most serious violence," wrote Jean Estèbe. Repression began with the prefects, granted quasi-dictatorial powers at the top of an administration that commanded the police, the 6,600-strong GMR (other figures place the GMR's strength at almost twice that number) created in April 1941 by René Bosquet, a 37,000-man gendarmerie, a 6,000-man *Garde mobile*, and *la Milice*, which nominally numbered 30,000, but whose "elite" *Franc-Garde* was not armed until January 1944, backstopped by jails and internment camps. Prefects obeyed orders from Vichy with the same zeal, spirit of routine, and dearth of moral conscience with which they had served – and then abandoned – the Republic. The result was that hostility to collaboration morphed into Gaullism as the space between Vichy and its German overseers shrank, while the institutional mechanisms of repression were sharpened. But this evolution was a gradual process, in part because people were slow to realize that, rather like the French army in 1940, Pétain had become just another broken shield.[53]

To gain a modicum of freedom of maneuver and in keeping with his policy of collaboration, Laval desperately proffered concessions to his German overseers, for example "transforming" French POWs into civilian workers.[54] With roughly 9.5 million men serving in the German ground forces alone by 1943, Berlin began to pillage occupied Europe for manpower to sustain its war effort.[55] Fritz Sauckel, Berlin's General Plenipotentiary for Labor Deployment, better known as "the slave master of Europe," demanded that France supply 350,000 laborers, of whom 150,000 were to be skilled, 30,000 railway carriages, and 1,000 locomotives. As a result, on 22 June 1942, the Vichy Premier instituted *la relève* – meaning "relief" or "substitution" –

whereby allegedly a POW would be released for every three civilian volunteers supplied by France. A subsequent 4 September 1942 law laid a legal foundation for the mobilization of men between eighteen and fifty years of age, and unmarried women aged twenty-one to thirty-five, who would be "subject to any work the government deems necessary." However, no mention was made of dispatching labor conscripts to Germany, nor was female conscription ever applied, although some women were recruited as volunteers for the Red Cross or as voluntary guest workers, both of which offered a front for prostitution, did travel to Germany. But this law served as the legal basis to dispatch 300,000 Frenchmen, roughly half of the French labor contingent that eventually reached Germany.[56]

When *la relève* failed to deliver adequate numbers of volunteers, in January 1943, Sauckel demanded that 250,000 French workers be sent to Germany before the middle of March. In response, on 16 February 1943, Laval passed a law requiring young men of the conscript classes 1920–1922 to register for STO. This delivered a shock that amplified swelling dissatisfaction as Vichy collaboration entered a new and more intense phase that impacted practically every French family. At least *la relève* had suggested reciprocity, almost an altruistic liberation of POWs about whom the French guarded a guilty conscience. But, while the Vichy press and radio called on the French to accept STO in a spirit of "duty," "sacrifice," and "discipline," the BBC and the clandestine press denounced it as a cover for deportation, a logical and inevitable consequence of the "human pillage" of the occupation. Popular opinion was indignant. Unlike conscription, initially at least STO admitted no professional exclusions.[57] Unlike conscription, when "you are drafted you go . . . with a crowd and you are all together," wrote Gertrude Stein, who witnessed this phenomenon while hiding out in the village of Culoz near Annecy, "it is sad when at nineteen and twenty you have to decide for yourself, shall you betake yourself to the mountains, shall you stay at home and risk it, shall you go to Germany and hate it and perhaps be bombed working for your country's enemies . . . it is hard at eighteen or nineteen to have to decide all these things for yourself."[58]

Rumor spread that STO workers would be used on the Eastern Front, perhaps even as combatants. Repatriated workers from *la relève* retailed horror stories of the firebombing of Hamburg in the last week of July 1943 that killed 42,000 and which many claimed to have witnessed. Doctors were besieged by young men in search of medical exemptions. Berlin had outsourced the execution of its burgeoning demands onto Vichy. Collaboration, until then largely veiled, emerged from the shadows, as French police began to deliver requisition notices and apprehend evaders, which made them very unpopular. Caught between German ultimatums transmitted through Vichy and community opposition, mayors, even prefects, who failed to fill their STO quotas were removed at German behest. Resistance took the form of demonstrations, often animated by mothers, wives, and sisters, that temporarily blocked trains carrying conscripted workers to Germany, during which women pelted Vichy officials and police with rotten fruit and vegetables. But Wieviorka warns that the scope of resistance to STO must not be exaggerated. Apathy, especially in the working class, was widespread, while tight surveillance in the workplace, followed by swift and brutal reprisal for infractions, discouraged sabotage. Indeed, whatever the German views of the French as soldiers, they were prized as the most productive contingent of forced laborers.[59] The September 1943 Speer–Bichelonne agreement, exempting the work force in designated French factories from STO, helped to defuse discontent somewhat. Most young Frenchmen were forced to submit to STO because they found little support in the population for evasion. To resist in any form frightened and stressed people who rightly feared retaliation.[60]

While some seeking to avoid STO might flee into the resistance, for those whose priority was personal survival, a resistance group or *maquis* might not offer the best option. While the French desired liberation, according to reports from postal control, popular support for the resistance never exceeded 20 percent, because many feared a civil war sparked by clashes between Vichy *forces de l'ordre* and resisters.[61] Even for those who sought to join the resistance, there were many impediments to becoming an outlaw, that included the support of the episcopacy for the hierarchical values represented by Vichy, as well as for Hitler's anti-communism. The French right backed the export of French workers as a tactic to weaken the communists, as well as a chance to Nazify a captive STO congregation.[62] In fact, the roughly 600,000 to 650,000 French workers mobilized to work in Germany had few choices but to comply, especially if they had families whom they could not simply leave without resources and possibly vulnerable to state reprisals.[63] Or, when German officers descended on a French factory to demand a certain number of workers, a young unmarried man might substitute for an older, married-with-children co-worker out of a sense of comradery. Or, at best, try to get assigned to a Todt Organization project in France or a French factory designated as *sperrbetrieben* – that is, made off limits for Sauckel's recruiters by the Speer–Bichelonne agreement. Some even enlisted in the police, the GMR, or *la Milice* to avoid STO.[64]

Even then, it took six months to round up 240,000 workers, mainly from the *zone occupée*, because of a lack of cooperation. But so encouraged was Sauckel by the success of STO, and so bereft was the German economy of workers after Hitler transferred another 300,000 German workers from factories into the maw of the Wehrmacht, that Sauckel demanded that 250,000 more French workers be assembled by the end of June 1943. By autumn, the German authorities estimated that 665,000 French civilians were working in the Reich, part of an estimated 1.66 million French citizens in Germany in 1944. France contributed the third-largest contingent of workers in Germany, after the Poles and Soviets. Eventually 3.3 percent of French workers were shipped to Germany. That the number was not larger was thanks to flight and the Bichelonne–Speer agreement, rather than to any Vichy "shield."[65] Despite Laval's attempts to rebrand "collaboration" as "the politics of entente" and whisper that it had been forced upon him, this helped to discredit Vichy definitively. At the end of the war, an estimated 895,000 POWs, 605,000 STO laborers, 35,000 deportees, and 100,000 conscripts from Alsace-Moselle were repatriated to France from Germany. And these were merely the survivors.[66]

The *maquis*

Those who decided to opt out of STO had to consider their options – the proximity to a place of refuge; the presence of other fugitives who might offer comradery and a degree of security; and how they would survive without ration coupons. City and town dwellers might vanish into the bocage and exchange work for food on isolated farms of relatives or acquaintances. For those without such contacts, evasion might translate into raiding shops, farms, or even *Chantiers de la jeunesse* to steal food, *tabacs* for cigarettes, town halls and prefectures for ration tickets, and post offices for cash.[67] "Around here it is getting to be like Robin Hood," recorded Gertrude Stein in January 1944, as "the young men in the mountains ... took two tons of butter from a dairy and ... to the delight of everybody ... a pig weighing one hundred and fifty kilos ... from a local aristocrat who had been highly unpopular because of his political opinions ... They also took 800 liters of eau de vie ... everybody takes it to mean that it is the beginning of the end of course all except the collabo who say they are gangsters and what will happen after the war."[68] Parts of Brittany became a "wild west" of gangs holding up shops and farms and raiding town halls for ration tickets.[69] Vichy propaganda used this breakdown of order to discredit the resistance to STO as collections of "bandits" and "terrorists," and stoke popular fear that "liberation" would spark social collapse and civil war.

By the summer of 1943, opposition to STO had translated into a growing *maquis*, a word lifted from the Corsican *machja*, or Italian *macchia*, a reference to Mediterranean scrubland which historically had served as a refuge for bandits and other social fugitives. In this way, the flight of STO fugitives evoked an image familiar in France, through the novels set in Corsica of nineteenth-century writer Prosper Merimée, or Alfonse Daudet's descriptions of that island in his *Lettres de mon Moulin*. *Maquis* had also taken on a figurative meaning in French as a "*maquis*" (thicket) of legal or administrative complications. In the course of 1943, "'*Prendre le maquis*,' '*le maquis*,' and '*le maquisard*' entered the history and language of Resistance with an effect that is difficult to exaggerate," writes H. R. Kedward, in part because these terms fed into a mythologized lore of rural revolt in France, a replication of the "Great Fear" of 1789 that had transitioned into an earlier "national insurrection," but also because, as a collective noun, *maquis* "could indicate both the bands of fighters and their rural location" in a way that the omnibus designation of "resistance" could not.[70] Although the term "*maquis*" had begun to appear in Allied documents by June 1943, they were not distinguished from other resisters in OSS and SOE reports.

The small groups of young men who had begun to collect in remote regions to avoid *la relève* swelled in the New Year, as young men faded into a clandestine existence rather than answer their STO summons. As early as 18 March 1943, alerted by reports in the Swiss press of growing numbers of Frenchmen congregating in the mountains just south of Geneva, Fighting France's BBC mouthpiece Maurice Schumann had broadcast praise for France's "Mountain Legion" mobilizing in the Haute-Savoie. But, for the moment, the British proved reluctant to support them so long as no date had been finalized for D-Day; the date was not set until the Tehran Conference (28 November–1 December 1943). A belief that the September 1943 liberation of Corsica portended a timely arrival of Allied forces on the mainland also stimulated flight into the *maquis*. Of an estimated 200,000 to 350,000 STO dodgers, only about a quarter actually joined a *maquis*.[71] Regional traditions of rebellion, patriotism outraged by the brief November 1942–September 1943 Italian occupation east of the Rhône, communist affiliation, and the evolution of the war were factors that might trigger rejection of an STO summons. The emergence of internal resistance indicated that the war within France had transformed into an ideological clash, even if those who fled into the mountains were not self-consciously political.[72] The *maquis* phenomenon overwhelmed local police and gendarmes, especially in areas where a *maquis* was active – by late 1943, if not before, police reported that the situation in the Haute-Vienne, Corrèze, Dordogne, l'Ain, and Haute-Savoie "should be considered a war situation," one that would only worsen after D-Day.[73] Nevertheless, the maquis phenomenon was also highly localized: "Resistance networks developed among figures in key positions, and STO *réfractaires* organized Maquis here and there," Gildea writes of the Loire Valley. "These groups, of course, remained small minorities in an environment shaped by fear of anarchy and of reprisals. Most French people simply kept their heads down and waited for liberation to come from the only likely source: an Allied invasion."[74]

But evolving public opinion, which from 1942 increasingly bought into "*résistance-mouvement*" helped to sustain this illegal flight. The ballooning of the *maquis* was transformative for resistance in France, and, when combined with a groundswell of resistance to fascism in Europe, for military doctrine as well. Where 1943 would witness the integration of the *maquis* into the resistance, and the integration of the resistance into *la France combattante*, the STO crisis shook resistance out of its "Phoney War" lethargy. The emergence of the *maquis* forced the Allies to gauge the scope and seek to operationalize the military potential of resistance in France. The STO crisis also shifted the resistance's center of gravity – what had been characterized as clandestine conspiracies of ideologically committed city dwellers in 1942 had by September 1943 swelled into an estimated 11,500 to 13,000 youths flooding the countryside, with more on the way. "The time of nuclei of resistance veterans was over," concludes Balu. From a marketing perspective, victimized French youth fleeing into rural asylum associated resistance with a bucolic ideal, flipping the Vichy narrative that "the land doesn't lie" and that "resistance" was an externally generated phenomenon subsidized by the Allies and sustained by communists. This rural migration also offered a constituency that the interface services might muster to appeal to Churchill's romantic fascination with insurgency, to appeal for resources, even shape the strategic debate, all to bolster their standing within Supreme Headquarters Allied Expeditionary Force (SHAEF). In the process, the *maquis* became another source of contention between the interface services, which sought to maximize its military potential, and Charles de Gaulle, who saw the resistance in general backed by its interface service enablers as a potential threat to France's post-Liberation stability.

In the short term, this mass evasion of STO refugees caught resistance leaders and the interface services by surprise. While some resistance groups might hand out false papers to STO dodgers, resistance-coordinated attempts to protest or disrupt STO departures met scant success. Furthermore, in 1943, organized resistance groups lacked arms, were devoid of an organization with a coordinated strategy, and were as yet unstructured for large-scale operations to absorb this tsunami of potential recruits. Realizing that few resistance organizations had the presence or the resources to offer sanctuary, some STO refugees hid out on isolated farms, or sheepishly slinked home. But, by the summer of 1943, encouraged by the "myth of the *maquis*," STO evaders might be joined by Jews, Spanish Republicans, deserters from the Italian and German forces, North Africans or "Senegalese" fed up with *Frontstalags*, that is, camps in France for French colonial POWs whom the Germans did not want to bring to Germany, and other refugees. In this way, it is reckoned that foreigners made up around 10 percent of fugitive bands in France's less populated regions such as the Alpes, the Massif Central, the Dordogne, the Jura, and the Pyrenees.[75]

Internal resistance organizations scrambled to evaluate the scope of the influx, organize camps, and find leaders, not to mention food and clothing. From a practical perspective, urban flight meant that city-based resistance leaders must now court cooperation in rural milieus with which they had little familiarity. This was not invariably easy, because the proximity of a *maquis* band invited stopovers by *la Milice*, the GMR, or increasingly the Germans, which were hardly courtesy calls. Locals also had to be alert for Gestapo-organized "*faux maquis*," as well as "*maquis noirs*" – basically bandits, whose robberies and worse were exploited by Vichy propaganda to discredit resistance.[76]

So worried was *Chef national Maquis* Michel Brault about the growing reputation for lawlessness of the *maquis* that on 25 May 1943 he issued a *charte du maquisard*, a code of conduct that called on *maquisards* to respect private property, pay peasants for animals, and attack only Vichy services. *Maquisards* were also encouraged to wear some emblem – armbands, uniforms, crests – to identify them as legal combatants. But Brault's was an uphill struggle. Not only were *maquisards* too focused on survival to adhere to some London-imposed code of conduct, but also some criminals adopted a *maquis* cover to enrich themselves, especially around Marseilles, the Southern Alps, and the Dordogne, as did gangs of youths too young for STO. Some legitimate *maquis* went rogue, pillaging farms, even raping, especially if they contained a high percentage of *Osttruppen* deserters. In the Massif Central, *maquis* leader Georges Guingouin, known as "le Tito Limousin," was tried after the war for setting up his own military tribunal that carried out forty executions. In November 1943, Brault's successor, Georges Rebattent, tried to reign in these "rebel *maquis*," promising to courtmartial criminals. But denunciations of *maquis* conduct also revealed fractures in the resistance between communist and non-communist elements.[77]

So, while refusal to answer the STO call-up did not necessarily offer a direct path to resistance, it certainly created a potential recruitment pool for "*résistance-organisation*" through the *maquis*, although it more often translated into "*résistance sans organisation*." Resistance groups served as intermediaries between the *maquis* and the Allies to organize, supply, clothe, and arm this spontaneous civilian mobilization. But the high degree of variation in the organization and arming of different *maquis* groups, which were constantly evolving, reforming, and shifting location, makes a standard definition of the *maquis* elusive (Figure 4.2). Unlike *résistance-organisation*, members of the *maquis* did not take on an assumed identity. Small groups of STO refugees huddled in primitive shelters, often sick with scabies and boils. Most of these *maquis* camps were unsustainable simply because they lacked food, and because they frequently met hostility from the local inhabitants, for whom they constituted a threat. The young men spent the day playing cards, talking, scrounging, or stealing food from local farmers or shopkeepers. Periodic raids by the police, the gendarmes or *la Milice* carried little threat initially, especially as *la Milice* was unarmed until January 1944. However, the situation worsened with D-Day, as many more young men fled into the *maquis*, and an estimated 12,000 of 40,000 gendarmes defected to the resistance, sometimes after being captured. In desperation, Joseph Darnand launched Plan MO (*maintien de*

Figure 4.2 French *maquis* encampment 1944. Although highly romanticized, and often filmed in staged military poses, many *maquisards* lived in primitive encampments, fighting sickness, forced to steal to survive, and in fear of raids by the GMR, *la Milice*, or *Osttruppen*. (Photo by Art Media/Print Collector/Getty Images)

l'ordre) after D-Day, concentrating gendarme brigades in the major towns. But this concentration, combined with defections, drained large areas of police presence, especially in the Massif Central and the Alpes.[78] This left repression largely to German military units, sometimes formed from the estimated 1.5 million Soviet POWs who volunteered to serve in the Wehrmacht. Organized as *Osttruppen* or *Ostbataillone*, these former Red Army soldiers with a reputation for brutality might kill, incarcerate, or scatter *maquisards*.[79] "Therefore, the *maquis* was constituted of small groups of individuals, sometimes collected in larger 'camps,' sometimes extremely dispersed, who survived thanks to the aid of local populations, because neither resistance organizations, nor *la France libre*, nor later the Allies covered all of their needs," writes Balu.[80]

Nor were local *maquis* leaders idle, but rather they vigorously promoted their assemblies as a popular mobilization of France's shadow army. From the spring of 1943, Henri Romans-Petit, chief of the *Maquis de l'Ain*, began to organize his refugee population into sixty-man camps. But these large numbers attracted the attention of Vichy and of the occupation authorities, who moved to break them up. So, camps had to become smaller and peripatetic. In April 1943, at Frenay's suggestion, the MUR had established a "*Service national Maquis*" headed by Brault. A wounded and decorated Great War veteran, after 1918 Brault had become an international lawyer, who had lived in China, spoke excellent English, and formed many contacts in the UK and the United States. A reserve captain in the air force, Brault had funneled intelligence through the US military attaché at Vichy, before his network was betrayed and broken up, with Brault narrowly escaping capture. He was subsequently enlisted by Frenay to head *Combat*'s intelligence service, where, from the middle of April 1943, he was tasked with evaluating the dimensions of the STO phenomenon. Brault's reports were forwarded to London with pleas for assistance, in the process introducing the term "*maquis*" into the Allied military lexicon.[81]

As chief of *le Service national Maquis* in the autumn of 1943, Brault served as the key *maquis* information feed to the interface services represented in the British capital by OSS Major Paul Van der Stricht, Colonel Maurice Buckmaster and Lieutenant-colonel L. H. Dismore in the SOE, and Major André Manuel at the BCRA. Brault was among the first to call attention to the military potential offered by the *maquis* if London were able to provide arms and a military infrastructure. Brault's *rapport Jérôme* (Brault's resistance moniker) of February 1944 estimated that 30,000 *maquisards* stood mobilized for action, while another 120,000 "sedentary" recruits dispersed in farms, shelters, and camps for the winter stood ready to rally on D-Day. Nevertheless, while Brault was instrumental in updating London on the *maquis* phenomenon, he ticked too many negative boxes to earn a central place in the history of French resistance. For starters, his visceral anti-communism made him a controversial and unpopular figure in important sectors of the internal resistance. Second, Brault panned the "fortress *maquis*," like those developing spontaneously in le Vercors and Gilières, as too vulnerable, too costly to maintain, and militarily inactive, suggesting instead a reorganization based around twenty-five-man mobile platoons of *maquisards*. His insistence on command centralization, to regulate notoriously independent regional and departmental *maquis* leaders, was opposed by the MUR, which sought to decentralize into regional commands under its *comité directeur*. Finally, his adamant refusal to subordinate his *Service national Maquis* to the AS, which, along with the arrest of Moulin and Delestraint, basically gutted the AS of substance and helped further to isolate the *maquis* from the general resistance movement, accounts for the mixed reception accorded Brault when he arrived in London in February 1944.

Brault was admired chiefly for his foundational technical work on the *maquis* and his advocacy for the *maquis* to be integrated into Allied military plans. His honest message that *maquisards* were not yet battle-ready, but expended their energy merely struggling to survive, and that many French civilians had paid a high price for supporting them, did not fit a Gaullist narrative built around "heroic *maquisards*." Nor did it penetrate de Gaulle's Olympian indifference to popular suffering in the cause of French grandeur. Brault's solution that priority in the short run should be given to food, rather than arms drops, was even less appreciated, especially by the CNI director Emmanuel d'Astier. His insistence that the *maquis* was a national phenomenon, rather than simply prevalent in the Alpine southeast, put him at odds with Churchill's strategy to break into southern France via Italy rather than by means of an amphibious assault, as well as with many in the Gaullist camp, for whom the *maquis* was viewed as a ticket to political influence within the Alliance.[82]

Not surprisingly, Algiers and London were slower to detect and evaluate a spontaneous movement that had exploded outside the established resistance networks, because of sporadic contact with the mainland, skepticism over Brault's numbers, and the impediments to agent infiltration into France via Lysander in the winter months. Assessment was also delayed by bureaucratic constraints, namely the need to consult and coordinate between the BCRA, SOE, OSS, and regular planning staffs; and a lack of consensus on the value and organization of a civilian resistance; as well as by competing priorities that included the Tunisia campaign, the struggle with Giraud for preeminence in Algiers, and the occupation of Corsica. This delay caused friction, because the internal resistance was quick to accuse Algiers and London of indifference, especially as the French service of the BBC had been broadcasting appeals to boycott STO. So, tensions escalated as leaders of the *maquis*, backed by sections of the internal resistance, claimed that they were being deliberately ignored as a tactic to marginalize the internal resistance in favor of a claque of Gaullist *émigrés* and lightly laundered *Maréchalist* colonial mercenaries. This was a signal to the BCRA in London that the resistance required more vocal spokesmen, lest the already fissiparous and independent-minded groups go their own way and throw in their lot with the SOE or, like Frenay, the OSS, and hence slip the leash of BCRA oversight.

For their part, the interface services began to realize, with the approach of D-Day and the end of clandestine warfare, that the *maquis* had become their *raison d'être*. SOE headquarters at Baker Street enjoyed a well-merited reputation as "an eccentric club," a catch-all of civilian misfits, "among whose higher executives many displayed an enthusiasm [for irregular warfare] quite unrestrained by experience, some had political backgrounds which deserved rather closer scrutiny than they ever got, and a few could only charitably be described as nutcases."[83] Its research departments especially enjoyed a wide reputation for "sophomoric bright ideas and general eccentricity," for example inventing exploding horse turds "for placement on roads traveled by German military traffic." The SOE's Director of Operations from September 1943, Sir Colin Gubbins, was frequently caricatured, and most likely served as the model for Brigadier Ernest Pudding in Thomas Pynchon's post-war spoof novel *Gravity's Rainbow.* Although sometimes described as "a real Highland toughie," Gubbins had in fact been born in Tokyo and schooled at Cheltenham College. Highly decorated for bravery as an artillery officer in the Great War, he had acquired an interest in insurgency as an observer of the Russian Civil War in 1919, and during the Irish rebellion (1919–1921), so that, in 1940, he had been tasked with organizing Auxiliary Units of the Home Guard as an insurgent force should the Germans invade the British Isles. Fortunately for everyone, "Dad's Army" never had to meet that challenge, although some of Gubbins' more enthusiastic recruits did manage to annoy important generals such as Bernard Montgomery by mounting mock attacks, which in the pursuit of realism might incorporate hurling Molotov cocktails through opened French windows at division HQ. Indeed, the fear in the upper echelons of the British High Command and Government, was that, rather than "set Europe ablaze," SOE enthusiasts were more likely to incinerate Whitehall. This civilian amateurism and ad hoc character of SOE was encouraged from its founding in the wake of Dunkirk by Minister of Economic Warfare Hugh Dalton. Despite – or perhaps because of – his conventional Church of England upbringing, and Eton and King's College Cambridge education, Dalton was a Labour Member of Parliament (MP) and true radical who believed regular British officers too hidebound to embrace subversion and sabotage as a wartime mission, and too conservative to interact with the mainly anti-fascist resisters encountered abroad. However, SOE operative and post-war historian M. R. D. Foot described the SOE as more operationally than politically focused, while in Foot's opinion "Baker Street brigadier" Gubbins served as SOE's "mainspring." Hardly had Gubbins assumed his new post in 1943 than calls for SOE's dismantling were renewed, when it was realized that its operations in Holland had been thoroughly penetrated and turned by German counterintelligence. As D-Day neared, if "The Firm," or "The Racket," as its members aptly referred to their organization, failed to devise a strategy to meld clandestine war into conventional operations, they might as well transfer to the infantry.[84] In the event, the SOE's military mission was rescued in part by the Foreign Office, which argued that Allied abandonment of the *maquis* would be interpreted as a betrayal that might poison post-war Franco-Allied relations.[85] In this way, bureaucratic and diplomatic pressures, as well as pleas for support from hard-pressed *maquis* groups, rather than any obvious military utility linked to established doctrine or viable strategic vision, propelled the incorporation of the *maquis* into Allied plans.

Only gradually in the autumn of 1943 did the interface services become aware, through reports of its agents in France, of the scope of the STO crisis, and communicate this situation up the chain of command. The capture in June 1943 of Moulin and Delestraint, along with the AS archives, had thrown London into turmoil, at the very moment that an estimated 6,000–10,000 STO refugees had infiltrated France's Alpine regions, largely surviving on their own and occasionally clashing with Italian troops. By the autumn, the Vichy Prefect of the Haute-Savoie reported that a *maquis* numbering perhaps 1,600–2,000 men had become the source of a growing number of incidents. A joint SOE–BCRA mission – code-named Musc (Musk) – had been dispatched in September to take stock of the resistance in the Haute-Savoie, Savoie, and the Isère, where, on 11 November, eager to promote the military potential of his Maquis de l'Ain, Romans-Petit organized a parade of his initiates in Oyonnax, a town of 12,000 in the Ain department. Musc reported that 2,350 *maquisards* were mustered and ready for combat, although few were armed.[86] By December, the tireless campaign by Frenay and CNI director Emmanuel d'Astier found that even SHAEF regularly employed the term "*maquis*," after having jettisoned the communist preference for "partisans."[87]

The CFLN came to realize that blackmailing the Allies over their failure to support the *maquis* offered a more fruitful tactic than threatening to turn to Moscow. Also, that the ends of policy could be best served by mobilizing Allied public opinion. In this spirit, Emmanuel d'Astier organized a 15 November press conference to lambast Allied failure to supply arms to the *maquis* and for underestimating its military potential. Churchill subsequently met with d'Astier and praised his efforts in support of the *maquis*. SOE agent Wing Commander Forrest Yeo-Thomas' upbeat assessments of *maquis* potential were circulated among decision-makers.[88] When he transferred to Britain in early 1944, Brault brought a film of the Oyonnax parade to London, as well as other films of *maquis* activities, a selection of which the SOE previewed for Churchill. The Oyonnax film was not released for general distribution, and SOE professionals chuntered about the security risk taken by Romans-Petit. Nevertheless, the British press picked up on the image of French national resilience, to send a message that, like Tito's partisans in Yugoslavia, the *maquis* was "liberating" expansive zones in central and southeastern France at a time when discussions on arming the *maquis* had entered a critical stage.[89]

This campaign seemed to influence Churchill, who, after being reassured by Emmanuel d'Astier's responses to his questions seeking reassurance that "you French will not use the weapons we provide to shoot each other? And that you will follow strictly the orders of Eisenhower without question or considerations of a political nature?," on 27 January 1944 ordered the RAF "to help the French patriots." Thus 13,000 tons of weapons were to be showered on the *maquis*, in the hope that it would be "possible to bring about a situation in the whole area between the Lake of Geneva and the Mediterranean comparable to the situation in Yugoslavia." Henceforth, arming the French resistance became the RAF's second priority after the strategic bombing campaign. The goal was to arm 20,000 *maquisards* in February alone.[90]

Why Churchill, who had refused de Gaulle's March 1943 request to arm the resistance, suddenly reversed course has both a long- and a short-term explanation. Churchill had nurtured a fascination for insurgency ever since his war correspondent days covering the Second Anglo-Boer War. His post-Dunkirk directive to Dalton to "set Europe ablaze," though issued in desperation and out of a sense of weakness, spoke to the persistence of that faith. In the near term, he did not want to stand accused by Allied and French opinion of having abandoned the resistance, which both the Foreign Office and the SOE reminded him would be important for post-war Anglo-French relations, especially after the CFLN made it clear that they did not want to accept the responsibility of having failed to arm the *maquis*. He also wanted to ensure that the resistance would have a positive impact on D-Day, rather than contribute to confusion.[91]

But, more importantly, Churchill's romanticized vision of Alpine France as a sort of Gallic replica of Tito's Yugoslavia formed part of his ploy to waylay the American-sponsored Operation Anvil/Dragoon in favor of a transalpine invasion via Italy, to be smoothed by a resistance solidly established in France's southeast.[92] Churchill's scheme to assist the Alpine *maquis* was the spinoff of a basket of strategically fanciful stratagems that included invading Germany through the Ljubljana gap, as well as operations in the Eastern Mediterranean, which he had proposed at the Tehran and Cairo Conferences of November–December 1943.[93] "Alone against everyone, Churchill confused the *maquis* with the Alpes, and in his plans, considered [it] less a form of resistance than a place, thereby disinheriting the other *maquis de France*," concludes Balu.[94] Furthermore, Churchill had short-circuited the chain of command by insisting that the *maquis* be armed without specifying where the personnel, weapons, supplies, agents, and planes, already heavily committed in Greece and other Balkan regions, were to come from. The chronically understaffed BCRA sent eight agents to France each month in the first half of 1943, rising to fifteen by the end of the year, and twenty-four in early 1944. In January, only seven CFLN *délégués militaires*, vital to liaise with the *maquis*, had arrived for the twelve resistance regions. The SOE scrambled to send men from sections F and RF to France. But there were simply not enough Allied agents and radio operators to support the *maquis*. In this way, as in others, Churchill's January order to arm the French *maquis* set up a competition between Churchill and SHAEF and between the interface services/*comité maquis* and the regular staffs over where operations were to be expanded and which *maquis* were to be prioritized.[95]

Furthermore, the fact that the resistance was being armed before a strategy, much less a doctrine, had been evolved to employ them on D-Day simply added to the confusion. Churchill's argument that, unless the *maquis* were integrated into Allied plans, they would become a wild card on D-Day, at least forced a skeptical Chief of Staff (COS) to devise plans to arm and integrate them into operations.[96] From January 1944, prodded by Churchill, the UK and the United States gradually began to arm the resistance and integrate it into Allied invasion plans. But this process was hardly a smooth one. In fact, the unanticipated appearance of the *maquis* sparked considerable conflict among resistance groups and the Allies, which exposed fissures in the alliance over the financing, arming, and commanding of the resistance, as well as strategies to deploy it.[97]

Nor could Churchill's 27 January order be instantly implemented, because the matériel, arms, parachutes, and planes to deliver them had not been allocated, and the techniques to parachute arms had yet to be developed. Because France was considered a "minor ally" in a very cumbersome and complex Allied command system, an order given by the Prime Minister (PM) to the Allied Commander to support the *maquis* was likely to meander through SHAEF's hall of command mirrors that stretched between London and Algiers, ricochet off the various service chiefs, and trigger jurisdictional disputes between the CFLN, the "interface services," and the Combined Chiefs of Staff (CCS) in Washington as well as SHAEF, the Special Air Service (SAS), and Special Forces Headquarters (SFHQ) – and its Algiers spinoff the Special Project Operations Center (SPOC) which trained agents and directed operations in southern France – which ultimately had to sign off on arms deliveries.[98] Nor was this to reckon with the politically powerful bomber commands, who behaved like Medieval dukedoms, resisting any centralizing effort which limited their autonomy, especially if exerted by ground pounders in SHAEF, and remaining convinced that strategic bombing alone could break German morale and end the war *sans invasion*. Airmen argued that the risk of losing aircraft designed for high-altitude bombing missions, each with a highly trained seven-man crew, to enemy fighters or ground fire increased exponentially if they were required to fly at low altitude in daylight to parachute weapons. Furthermore, the air resources committed were disproportionate, given the marginal value of irregular operations to the outcome of the war. This argument also came at a time when bomber production had slowed due to industrial manpower shortages. In these conditions, the air forces became adept at playing corner-boy shell games with their bomber inventory to mystify an inquisitive SHAEF staff.[99]

Given the vagaries of weather, the imprecision of navigation, miscommunication, the difficulty of identifying landing zones, and an absence of trained reception crews on the ground, there was no guarantee that the arms and supplies would actually end up in the right hands. The SOE reckoned that half to two-thirds of their arms drops failed because no reception committee mustered on the ground to recoup them. A quarter to a third of drops were aborted because of climatic conditions. Even a successful drop often set off a footrace between the *maquis* and the Germans/GMR/*Milice* to retrieve them.[100] This especially became the case as summer approached in 1944, which brought shorter nights and hence reduced the possibility that a plane departing the UK or North Africa/Corsica could make a return run under cover of darkness, which was considered essential for survival. For this reason, the eighteen Halifax bombers of the RAF's Special Duty Squadron 624 were moved to Blida in February 1944. The expanded scope of the drops in early 1944 brought in pilots and crews, some American, who were less experienced in *maquis* support techniques of feints and low-altitude approaches to obtain a tighter drop pattern. They might make several earsplitting passes over the drop zone to make sure that they had the correct site, and then tended to release their parachutes from higher altitudes, which meant that containers might scatter over a 15-kilometer-long area.[101]

Le maquis required a high degree of organization to receive the warning signal on the BBC the night before, and then collect and store the items delivered, and eliminate all traces of the drop, before dawn. Upon impact, poorly secured containers might strew detonators, ammunition, medical supplies, or boots over a wide area. This required the participation of the local population and their mules, which opened them to fierce reprisals if the repressive services heard a Halifax making repeated passes over a remote French village at low altitude at 02:00, or discovered an arms cache in a barn or basement. Arms then had to be redistributed on the ground, which became another source of contention among the various resistance factions, especially the communists, for whom everything was political. The Constituent Assembly in Algiers soon rung with denunciations of the "external resistance" and the Western Allies who intentionally withheld arms from communist resistance groups. The fact that these communist accusations became more vociferous with the approach of D-Day forced Emmanuel d'Astier to pressure the British for more drops. Once Churchill had ordered the *maquis* to be armed, Washington had no choice but to follow suit. And, having decided to arm the *maquis*, planners were forced to integrate them into Allied invasion plans.[102]

In this way, the French were able to exploit Anglo-American rivalries, so that, from February, air drops to the *maquis* picked up pace as fourteen heavy bombers were assigned to supply them. Worried lest in the post-war period they might be accused of failing to help the resistance, which the communists were primed to do however many arms were dropped, in January 1944, the US Army Air Force (USAAF) dedicated six planes to deliveries in France, which by May had risen to thirty-two. In this way, the USAAF reported 2,237 containers delivered by the middle of February, of which 505 went to "the largest *maquis*," while it delivered 25 agents. However, many of these deliveries were explosives destined for SOE-directed sabotage operations because "in early 1944, SHAEF, like the Supreme Allied Command (CCS) remained skeptical of the real efficiency of the resistance," concludes Balu.[103]

Like many dimensions of the Second World War's air war, in early 1944, the techniques, tactics, and procedures of supplying the resistance had yet to catch up with the theory. Given the problems of communication and navigation, many of the deliveries turned out to be "blind drops" – that is, simply parachuting canisters over an area where the *maquis* was thought to be active. One OSS operative described a 4 March 1944 "blind drop" near Romans in the Isère as "criminal," because it set up a sprint to recuperate the weapons that was won hands down by the "Boches" – "90 per cent of the parachuted materiel was lost or seized by the enemy," reported one SOE major, a rather typical outcome of air-supplied resistance support on other fronts too.[104] Not only were Allied drops supplying the Germans, but also the population was subjected to "harsh reprisals," which also put the *maquis* at risk. If the locals failed to report an air drop, they might find their farms burned and animals slaughtered in reprisal.[105] In any case, contemporary best estimates were that 40 percent of arms deliveries were crowned with success but 10 percent fell into enemy hands, while 50 percent of the planes returned without delivering their loads. Nevertheless, the SOE estimated that, by D-Day, 20,000 resisters could be armed in France, 9,000 of them from French resistance organizations, while 11,000 belonged to SOE-organized groups. Such was the enthusiasm and competition among various agencies to implement Churchill's order that the goal was set at 33,000 armed resisters by D-Day.[106]

Yet, the reality on the ground was somewhat different. The drops contained a smorgasbord of weaponry, including Axis weapons captured in Tunisia and Italy. Many weapons arrived unassembled, with no directions included; and there were no instructors on the ground. But by far the most frequently dropped hardware was the Sten gun (Figure 4.3). Originally rushed into mass production after Dunkirk, ostensibly to arm the 1.5-million-man Home Guard, but also to increase the firepower of British infantrymen burdened with 0.303-inch bolt-action Lee-Enfield No. 4 rifles, the no-frills Sten was advertised as a "street fighting machine carbine" for close-quarter combat. Its main advantage was simplicity. Its cold, hammer-forged barrel could be stamped out with hard steel mandrels every ten seconds on production lines without the need for boring and rifling machines. Attach a bolt, a side-mounted magazine to facilitate prone firing, a recoil spring, and a trigger, *et voilà!* Requiring no sophisticated and scarce machine tools, the Sten gun's minimalism allowed resistance groups in Norway, Denmark, and Poland to fabricate their own unpatented knockoffs in clandestine workshops. Stens proved not only easy to produce, but also easy to disassemble, transport, and conceal. Like many British designs of the period, the Sten's aesthetic qualities drew unflattering

Figure 4.3 Members of the British ATS pack Sten guns, temperamental but robust and easy to produce, for delivery to resistance forces in Europe. (Photo © Hulton-Deutsch Collection/CORBIS/Corbis via Getty Images)

comparisons with devices used by plumbers to unblock toilets. But, at the equivalent of £2 a pop – seven times cheaper than its popular rival the Thompson M1928 sub-machinegun – the Sten's dual-purpose utility proved such a plus that 4.5 million were eventually produced. As Colonel-in-chief of the Home Guard, King George VI seldom appeared Sten-less in public. Even fourteen-year-old Princess Elizabeth and her ten-year-old sister Margaret practiced firing Stens on a range installed in Buckingham Palace, which must have caused a *frisson* at royal garden parties.

When the Sten became a general issue weapon in the British forces in the second half of 1941, early reviews included words like "inaccurate," "unreliable," even "dangerous," adjectives usually preceded by "bloody" or something worse. Its crude manufacture sent the message that the government was unwilling to spend much money arming the troops. On 27 May 1942, Jozef Gabčík's Sten inopportunely jammed when he attempted to assassinate

Reinhard Heydrich near Prague. "Jam" became among the more polite expletives voiced by Canadian troops who managed to survive the 19 August 1942, Dieppe "raid." The Sten also had an "unpredictable" hair trigger that, when inadvertently engaged, or when the Sten was dropped or received a knock causing the recoil spring to drive the bolt forward, blasted off the entire magazine. In the commendable spirit of British "fair play," the temperamental Sten posed a danger to the trigger puller, his fellow soldiers, and the enemy in almost equal measure.[107]

Grenades were popular in the *maquis* – both the Mills and the adaptable Gammon bombs – although again these had to be armed and were deadly to everyone unsheltered, including the thrower, at 25 meters. By the summer, the ever-popular bazooka made an appearance, but in numbers too small to shift the tide of battle. The weapon most in demand in the Alpine "*réduits maquisards*" was the 3-inch mortar. But none were dropped because the ammunition was unstable and liable to explode on impact, transforming a resupply mission into something indistinguishable from a bombing raid.[108] But these were all technical and tactical quibbles. The point was that parachutes created hope among the *maquisards*, while the arrival of SOE and BCRA agents and, from D-Day, Jedburgh teams and Operational Groups (OGs) broke their isolation and telegraphed the message that they remained in the thoughts, prayers, and, it was hoped, plans of the Allied general staffs.[109]

Plan Montagnards: A Strategic Vision for the *maquis*

If the *maquis* developed spontaneously and independently of "*résistance-organisation*," a vision for how to mobilize a *maquis* predated its actual manifestation. At the same time, special operations doctrine and tactics were also groping for ways to operationalize resistance. On the theoretical level, a French doctrine for *maquis* deployment might be traced to Pierre Dalloz, an architect, Grenoble native, and enthusiastic mountaineer. In March 1941, Dalloz had speculated with a friend over the le Vercors plateau's possibilities as a strategic redoubt. The idea had also occurred to General André Laffargue, Armistice Army commander in Grenoble, who had envisaged the huge limestone fortress that dominated the Isère valley to the south and west of Grenoble as an ideal withdrawal point to contest an Axis invasion of the *zone libre*. Those musings came to naught when, in November 1942, Laffargue had allowed his troops to be disarmed by Italians, no less, an event that so disgusted and disheartened Dalloz that he jotted down his ideas for the use of le Vercors as a base for guerrilla operations in a brief three-page treatise.

Dalloz's timing was impeccable. While not exactly a hotbed of resistance activity on the scale of, say, Lyon, Grenoble nonetheless was home to local resistance groups. In what became known as "the first Vercors," from the autumn of 1941, exiles from the *zone occupée* and Alsace-Moselle, as well as Jews, Poles, and other foreigners, had sought refuge among the villages, small farms, and forests that dotted the plateau's summit. In December 1942, Grenoble began to experience the leading edge of what would become the STO crisis. By February 1943, as *la relève* transitioned to STO, Grenoble had developed well-established networks to channel refugees up the funicular railway to Villard-de-Lans on the plateau's summit, then by bus to Pont-en-Royans, where a guide would lead them to one of several remote farms or forestry huts folded into the Gorges de la Bourne or les Petits Goulets. In autumn 1943, as German forces supplanted Italians in the Alpine regions of the former *zone libre*, increasing numbers of French and foreign Jews fleeing roundups trekked to le Vercors, to seek refuge in one of an increasing number of camps, some organized by *Francs-tireurs*.[110]

Meanwhile, in January 1943, Dalloz traveled to Lyon, where he delivered his plan to fortify le Vercors to Yves Farge, foreign affairs editor of *Le Progrès de Lyon*, who quickly passed it on to Jean Moulin.[111] On 10 February, a brief meeting was arranged at Bourg-en-Bresse between Dalloz and AS chief Delestraint, during which Dalloz delivered a more developed version of the paper that he had given to Farge, along with a map of le Vercors and a guidebook. Two days later, both Moulin and Delestraint flew back to London with Dalloz's plan. In this way, "*Plan Montagnards*," a name supplied by Delestraint, sometimes referred to as "*Plan Vidal*" – Delestraint's resistance handle – and approved by Moulin, to transform the le Vercors plateau into a "strongpoint" was born.[112]

The "redoubt" idea, not dissimilar in concept from Orde Wingate's contemporaneous tactical experiments behind Japanese lines in Burma, seemed practically contagious – in early 1943, Frenay had proposed creating parachute-supplied "mountain redoubts" in various regions of France, from which mobile bands of resisters numbering no more than thirty would launch guerrilla raids. This very vague operational aspiration, inspired by Alpine romanticism, was made concrete as STO dodgers congregated in "mountain strongholds," now transformed through the aspirations of resistance leaders into "*avant-postes*" of Liberation.[113] Subsequently, SOE agents not only endorsed Dalloz's concept, but did so enthusiastically, which might be explained by the fact that most were total military novices representing an organization whose agenda was to put irregular operations on the map of modern warfare. In May 1943, SOE agent and member of Union Mission I Henry Thackwaite endorsed le Vercors as a strategic redoubt from which an active *maquis* might block the Rhône valley, even though most of the *maquisards* he observed were barefoot and obviously in no physical shape to resist *la Milice*, much less the Wehrmacht. Three months later, SOE agent Francis Cammaerts looked in on le Vercors and departed enthusiastic about the strategic possibilities of *Plan Montagnards*, all anchored in best-case operational scenarios – among which were a rapid Allied advance from the Mediterranean coast and a drop of paratroop reinforcements on le Vercors within forty-eight hours. After the war, Cammaerts complained that "in the minds, particularly of French command in North Africa, it got twisted into a way of flying the flag – of acquiring a little panache, a little *gloire.*" Both Thackwaite and Cammaerts, it must be noted, were schoolmasters, not soldiers.[114] Nor had they done a thorough net assessment, which would have revealed that, while appearing remote, over the nineteenth century, le Vercors had become a favorite tourist destination, so that it was both accessible and crisscrossed by a web of roads. Water sources on the summit to sustain a large *maquis* were also scarce.[115]

In this way, *Plan Montagnards* became an inexorable first step toward the calamities at Glières, Mont Mouchet, and "the second Vercors," as well as smaller *maquis* misadventures elsewhere. Both *la France combattante* and the interface services had encouraged the growth of *le maquis* through BBC exhortations to defy STO, and through resistance channels. Despite skepticism from conventional soldiers and planners at SHAEF in 1943, no one save Brault sought to apply the brakes on the snowballing enthusiasm in London to harness the military possibilities of the *maquis*. In this way, political insecurity and eagerness overwhelmed military prudence, as Allied strategy fell hostage to French political objectives, Churchill's insurgent romanticism, the interface services' eagerness to define a mission to ensure their institutional survival, and Foreign Office apprehensions about Britain's post-war relationship with France. In these conditions, the Gaullists cleverly manipulated Anglo-American rivalry at the turn of the year to extract arms for the *maquis*. Meanwhile, to advance their own political agenda, the communists whined that they were being deliberately starved of armaments. Once this process of *maquis* mobilization, armament, and integration into Allied liberation plans was set in motion, there could be no "abandonment" of the *maquis* without, it was feared, creating a legend of betrayal that would cast a pall over post-war Anglo-French relations.[116] Hence, the "myth of the *maquis*" preceded – and primed – its mobilization.

In the wake of Torch, Dalloz became an *évadé de France*, reaching Algiers via the Pyrenees and Gibraltar on 25 November 1943, where he was disconcerted to discover that no institutional memory of *Plan Montagnards/Vidal* seemed to have survived the demise of Moulin and Delestraint, either in Algiers or in London.[117] However, he need not have worried, at least on an operational level, for, by this time, the idea of "*réduits maquisards*" (*maquis* redoubts) had assumed a life of its own, impelled in part by an undated 1943 paper, "Le rôle des guerillas dans l'opération d'ensemble contre le continent Européen," authored by Polytechnician and naval engineer Camille Rougeron, a near-contemporary of de Gaulle. Having wearied of trying to convince the French navy of its vulnerability to air attack, Rougeron transferred to the Air Ministry in the 1930s, before fleeing to Algiers in June 1940. Although he is remembered principally as a theoretician of air power, Rougeron's short meditation on the nature of guerrilla warfare, its advantages against a conventionally armed and organized adversary, and its application to France's situation under the occupation appears to have found its way into Giraud's hands, probably in early 1943. "The power of the guerrilla in modern warfare no longer requires proof," Rougeron asserted, citing "the inability of Axis forces to gain the upper hand in Russia as in the Balkans." (In fact, guerrillas were getting their arses kicked in both places!) In a rather curious conversion of a proponent for the mechanization of modern warfare into a Rousseauian romantic, Rougeron now argued that the guerrilla with his primitive resources merely required an appropriate terrain on which to act.[118]

Comparisons drawn between the French resistance and that in Eastern and Southeastern Europe were seldom to French advantage, a misperception anchored in bogus intelligence, but given credibility as a follow-on from the 1940 "decadence" verdict on the fragility of French popular will. Axis occupations applied racial and political stereotypes to justify exploitative, criminal, and even murderous policies toward civilians.[119] While racism was certainly a primary ingredient of these imperial holocausts, historian of the German military Isabel Hull argues that operational failure caused German forces to concentrate their frustrations against non-combatants – a common enough professional reflex hardly confined to Germany. Hull argues that Germany's political culture had been shaped by "a pervasive sense of national insecurity," which politicized the officer corps and made civil authority especially reluctant to constrain actions judged to be of "military necessity."[120] The racist legacy of the German army's imperial past was reinforced by its Eastern Front experience in the First World War, where, in the wake of the collapse of Russian forces in 1917, the takeaway became that "soft" occupations only served to encourage popular resistance.[121]

The view among many conventional German soldiers that irregular warfare was both dishonorable and unlawful, when fused with a contrived narrative of race war and communist conspiracy, offered a recipe for war crimes on a catastrophic scale in the Second World War. Allied governments and their military leaders increasingly integrated irregular warfare to augment and supplement conventional operations, in which resistance groups, organized as a patriotic *levée en masse*, launched a popular revolt in the enemy's rear. Thus, while circumstance, strategic opportunity, and bottom-up demand had served to rehabilitate irregular warfare in the eyes of Allied strategists, Nazi propaganda preached the illegitimacy of "*Volkskrieg*" and its departure from the norms of civilized combat and military custom. Given their history and ideology, German soldiers and their Nazi overlords saw popular insurgency as both illegal and morally intolerable, a tactic prosecuted by inferior races and

Bolsheviks that contravened the laws of war and so merited no legal protections. Conflict arising out of the coexistence of these two incompatible concepts unbolted the prospect of deportation, mutilation, murder and torture, hostage-taking, extra-legal executions, and collective reprisals as a central strategy of the "war of the shadows."[122]

Occupation, followed by the organization of the resistance and an upwelling of a *maquis*, placed non-combatant civilians smack in the bullseye of the battlefield. In the Western tradition, organized violence remained the preserve of the state. But what if the legal state had ceased to exist or fled into exile, and its on-site stand-in had been delegitimized in the eyes of much of the population through collaboration with the occupier? Furthermore, France's republican tradition of the *levée* required all citizens to mobilize for war. The laws of war meant to define the boundaries between legal combatant and non-combatant civilian collapsed in irregular warfare conditions. Initially, the German administration in France attempted to maintain a veneer of legality and apply a more targeted repression than in Eastern Europe for juridical, political, economic, and pragmatic reasons. However, the escalation of "judicial violence" in the wake of Hitler's June 1941 invasion of the USSR, which peaked in early 1944, the mobilization of "bellicist" societies reflected in the rhetoric of just-versus-unjust-war theory, and demands, especially by the communists, for "immediate action" combined to spark "national insurrection." These trends were juxtaposed with debates over military necessity and the limits of violence, all to create a culture of mayhem. This increasingly made German occupations in Eastern and Western Europe indistinguishable. The verdicts of Militärbefehlshaber in Frankreich (MBF, Commander of occupation forces in France) tribunals came to be seen as blind and arbitrary, justified solely by *Kriegsnotwendigkeit* (the needs of war). The alternative was to be handed over directly to the Sipo/SD, the security police under Himmler's trusted adjutant Reinhard Heydrich, who made even the MBF's kangaroo proceedings seem models of impartial jurisprudence.[123]

For the PCF, Tito had become the exemplar for "immediate action" through guerrilla warfare. By January 1944, Churchill, acting on faulty information and because it suited his strategic agenda, too, cited Yugoslavia as the model to be replicated by France's Alpine *maquis*.[124] The implication, of course, was that, within the insurgency category, the French failed to pull their weight. Yet drawing analogies between France and Eastern and Southeastern Europe had its limits, as Moulin and Delestraint explained when they passed through London from 14 February to 19 March 1943, at the very moment that the STO crisis in France had begun to accelerate. Although Delestraint claimed that the AS numbered 50,000 men in *zone nord* and 75,000 in *zone sud*, he explained to Chief of the Imperial General Staff (CIGS) Alan Brooke that geographical and political conditions did not favor the creation of large, self-sustaining military formations as in Yugoslavia. Delestraint's priority at the time was to create a network of small arms caches that could be accessed on D-Day. Brooke noted that arms drops would require 1,318 bomber sorties, using planes diverted from bombing runs over Germany, Italy, and the Romanian oilfields at Ploieşti, and tactical support missions in North Africa. Besides, there was also the question of how the Allies could sustain a shadow army of 40,000–50,000 men in France by supply through the air for an indefinite period. Churchill and the SOE were also torn between a desire to send cash and weapons, and fear that a premature uprising and subsequent massacre might ensue if so many impatient and inexperienced youths, led by communists whose priority was to end French *attentisme* and so divert Wehrmacht divisions from the Eastern Front, were armed.[125]

While Rougeron paid homage to the ongoing people's war in Eastern and Southeastern Europe, he nevertheless remained acutely aware of the costs paid by the civilian population. Rougeron's solution was to use guerrillas to create vast occupation-free zones where populations would be safe from reprisals: the "expansive areas of France . . . the Pyrenees, the Massif Central, the Jura, the Vosges, Corsica" offered propitious terrain for guerrilla operations (Map 4.1). He also mentions the Alps and even the forest of Fontainebleau as potential enclaves where the Axis presence was weak. "The unleashing of guerrillas would then be not a desperate act ending in the massacre of the French population, but . . . a true rescue operation, that the normal unfolding of an [Allied] landing would support."

For the visionary engineer, here is where technology kicked in. "Surprise is facilitated by the material at our disposal today. Parachutists, the landing even of aircraft on fields that we could seize, would permit the arrival in several hours of numbers needed in these regions where we enjoy Allied air superiority and where the occupation forces in the region have few resources, which assure an intervention with few losses." Of course, seizing airfields as a sort of "*tâche d'huile*" had already featured in several campaigns – Crete, Torch, and Tunisia among them.[126] Rougeron's vision called for a joint air–insurgent operation. Having seized an airhead with resistance coordination, a landing force could then mobilize, organize, arm, and lead the population to defend these remote insurgent enclaves, supported by air supply, and defended by anti-aircraft and anti-tank weapons, denying the occupiers these cleared zones. Rougeron claimed that, in this way, areas in Russia "liberated" by Soviet forces parachuted into the rear held out for weeks, even months, although the source for these assertions is unclear. The strategic effect would be increased if several operations were coordinated simultaneously. If such enclaves bordered the Spanish or Swiss frontiers, they could not be encircled. In any case, Rougeron concluded, what did France have to lose?[127]

Map 4.1 Principal Resistance zones 1944.

By 1944, the idea of coordinating an insurgent–air-power tandem to create "cleared zones" in the enemy rear, "redoubts" from which roving "flying columns" might harass enemy communications, sabotage, collect intelligence, identify targets for air attacks, and kill or kidnap enemy leaders, had worked its way into special operations doctrine, which emphasized their potential benefits, while minimizing their obvious disadvantages. "There are few examples of offensive action far removed from main force activity, that produced a good 'return,'" notes Andrew Hargreaves.[128] Nevertheless, in the wake of Torch, French officers and strategists looked to increase France's contribution to metropolitan liberation, while modernizing French forces. Innovative tactics, and "bottom-up adaptation," especially in the context of a "resistance movement," might also offer a force multiplier. While it would be an exaggeration to claim that France's "resistance" strategy was inspired by Rougeron, in its essential respects, Rougeron both summarized France's strategic options and, visionary engineer that he was, integrated the technological components that might contribute to the operationalization of his strategic vision. Given support, in Rougeron's formula, resistance could be made cost-effective: "One fights equally well, often better, with a bazooka, a grenade, or a trench knife than with a 50-ton tank," insisted a man who obviously had never tried to lob a grenade or wield a trench knife against a 50-ton tank.[129] In the post-war period, Rougeron became an enthusiastic promoter of special operations forces (SOF). He castigated "the repugnance of the professional soldier for the guerrilla," and made the bold strategic case that, because of the resistance experience in France and elsewhere in Europe, going forward the guerrilla had "become an integral part of modern war, in the same category as artillery preparation, strategic bombing, peace offensives or atomic destruction."[130]

Despite his prescience and keen strategic intuition, there were at least four things wrong with Rougeron's strategic analysis. First, his belief that extensive guerrilla zones could be created in France, regions where insurgents could defend themselves and where their supporting civilian population could be relatively secure, was naive, even morally ambiguous. In Yugoslavia, in Greece, and on the Eastern Front, the Germans lacked sufficient troops to crush the partisans. So, the objectives of their periodic anti-partisan sweeps were simply to clear lines of communication. Even in the alleged *maquis* citadel of le Vercors, as elsewhere in France's "*réduits maquis*," the Germans and Vichy's repressive forces continued to patrol actively in the spring and summer of 1944, inflicting brutal reprisals on civilians suspected of hiding STO *réfractaires* or weapons.

Second, the operational capabilities of the *maquis* were bound to be limited, even when they were "stiffened" by regular soldiers. Of roughly 11,000 French army officers in 1942 who were not in *Oflags*, around 4,000 gravitated to the internal resistance. To the uniformed French military, enlistment in the resistance held few attractions. Vichy's appeal had been based on a promise to maintain order. Combat out of uniform, where arms were not carried openly, and which required ambush and assassination, contravened the military ethic. These were the tactics of communists and the cowardly, not of honorable soldiers. Nor did the work of resistance networks focused on intelligence collection hold much appeal for officers, many of whom rationalized their *attentisme* with the argument that the Armistice Army's dissolution in November 1942 had not released them from their oath to the Marshal, a belief that also commanded a large following in the French civil service.[131]

But these attitudes began to shift in 1943 for several reasons, beginning with the fact that the BCRA saw recruiting officers as a means to gain influence in, and intelligence on, Vichy. Also, if upon Liberation resistance groups were to coalesce into "national insurrection," however defined, the *maquis* would need professional soldiers to augment its military proficiency. As early as in December 1942, Colonel Jean Vallette d'Osia, former commander of the 27ᵉ *Bataillon de Chasseurs Alpins* (BCA) at Annecy, was approached to take charge of the local *maquis* during a meeting of the Savoyard resistance, seconded by two other *chasseurs alpins* resisters, Théodose (Tom) Morel and Captain Maurice Anjot.[132] This set off a competition among resistance groups to enlist large numbers of recruits to augment their military potential and hence political clout.[133] There was also a growing fear that, if the BCRA did not place people within the three largest resistance organizations in the former *zone libre*, these groups would have no choice but to throw themselves into the arms of the SOE, which was already in contact with some of them, or to imitate Frenay's courtship with the affluent OSS.[134]

Not surprisingly, given France's history of fraught civil–military relations capped by military loyalty to Vichy, *maquisards* did not invariably welcome professional soldiers with open arms. While soldiers viewed resisters as undisciplined and far too political, many resisters believed that resistance groups should be populated by "citizen soldiers" representing the republican values of the *levée* – "It's with civilians that you make military men," future French President Sergeant François Mitterand is alleged to have believed.[135] Indeed, together with excessive numbers of refugees and the inability to seal off the plateau from German encroachment, friction between *maquisards* and professional soldiers who stepped forward to lead them was cited subsequently as one of the main causes of le Vercors' collapse in 1944.[136] *Maquisards* resented attempts by their professional mentors to replicate a barracks ambiance in these refugee camps, and even accused military officers of culling the parachute drops for chocolate, uniforms, and cash. When British Major Henry Thackwaite parachuted onto le Vercors plateau on the night of 5–6 January 1944, along with his United States Marine Corps (USMC) partner Peter Ortiz as part of the Union I mission, the two men discovered troops of nearly destitute, leaderless young men, many barefoot and shivering beneath a blanket shared between two or even among three *maquisards*, reduced to acts of brigandage to survive. But, he concluded, "the civilian soldiers [*maquis*] show more bite than the ex-officers of the Armistice Army," in whom the *maquisards* understandably had no confidence. "Many [former Armistice Army] officers . . . gave us the impression that all serious fighting can be left to the Allies."[137] Not surprisingly, France's civil–military divide transferred to le Vercors in 1944, when regular soldiers organized a mass in which the officers – resplendent in their dress uniforms – had a priest bless the arms and a standard, which featured a Bourbon *fleur-de-lis* rather than a cross of Lorraine, of the "reconstituted French army," while the penurious, hungry, ragged, and largely faithless *maquisards* looked on with mounting fury.[138]

For his part, in March 1944, BCRAL chief André Manuel in London believed that the infusion of former Armistice Army personnel into the resistance at least had helped refocus resistance groups in the *zone sud* on their military tasks.[139] Not surprisingly, communist FTP chief Charles Tillon complained that de Gaulle and the Allied high command sought to militarize the resistance so that "it could provide troops that could be directed according to classic military methods of command."[140] For their part, officers aimed to make the *maquis* quickly operational, and condemned resistance leaders who immobilized these STO refugees in "clandestine barracks." But this was simply one of many divisions within a resistance splintered along the lines of tactics, politics, and personality.[141]

A third weakness of Rougeron's analysis, was that resistance or irregular forces were most effective when adjuncts to conventional operations, as behind the Eastern Front, or after the Allied landings in France where they often performed useful roles for reconnaissance, guarding the flanks, tactical intelligence, perhaps sabotage or small ambushes. But the idea persisted that, as in Churchill's vision, a civilian resistance might "set Europe ablaze" and create innumerable obstacles for the Germans. Fourth, as Corsica had shown, and confirmed by the aftermath of liberation in Greece and Yugoslavia, Communist resistance movements nurtured their own political agendas.[142] Thus, as Tillon had charged, "setting France ablaze" hardly matched de Gaulle's agenda, which was to channel resistance into a narrow political and military framework. "Comparison helps weigh the achievements of the French Resistance," concludes Paxton. "Resistance movements had less military impact in France than in Yugoslavia or behind the lines in the Soviet Union, though probably more than in Italy. On a more positive note, power was transferred smoothly in France at the liberation, without the bitter conflicts that occurred in Yugoslavia, Belgium, and especially Greece. The feared civil war never took place."[143]

But that was later, and owed more to Stalin's intervention and resistance weakness, than to an absence of aspiration among some French communists to seize power. In early 1943, Rougeron's promotion of the "stronghold concept" coincided with the STO crisis, at an important turning point in the war when Torch appeared to unlock sweeping strategic possibilities in France. This combined several factors that included a desire by the Gaullists in AFN to get into the fight as expeditiously as possible through SOF as a vehicle to operationalize the burgeoning *maquis* phenomenon; the availability of new technologies such as the wireless, the airplane, and the parachute; a perception that Axis occupation forces were overextended and vulnerable to guerrilla strikes; and a desire of many of the French led by de Gaulle to contribute to their country's liberation. But what is clear is that, while it was a spontaneous phenomenon, the "*maquis* redoubt" also offered an evolving operational concept.

However, for the moment, while engaged in the emerging strategic opportunities of 1943, there was little the external resistance or the Allies could do to sustain a supposed army of 40,000–50,000 men in the Alps for an indeterminate period. Nor had the Western Allies concocted a strategy to operationalize the *maquis*. Conventional soldiers were skeptical of the military utility of a resistance improvised from often antagonistic groups of politicized amateurs. A premature uprising would shake up Allied planning for D-Day, redirect the focus away from the amphibious landing, bring pressure to divert limited resources, and result in unnecessary slaughter and recrimination. If the Germans decided to move against these "armed bastions," there was little the Allies could do to sustain and protect them. Nevertheless, the numbers of fugitives collecting in remote areas continued to swell in 1943. So, the Allies came under pressure to offer limited support.[144]

In the course of 1943, the concept of "*réduits maquisards*" crept into Allied planning. As envisioned by the BCRA and the Gaullist general staff, four large zones of resistance would be created in the Massif Central, the Pyrenees, the Alpes, and in the center-east (le Morvan, le Jura, and les Vosges).[145] From the French perspective, these *maquis* enclaves offered several advantages. On the psychological level, STO resisters denied moral ascendency to a powerful enemy and its Vichy minions, especially when France lacked the means to fight conventionally. The *maquis* expanded resistance in France, raised the status of the CFLN as a political actor, and in theory required the Allies to factor civilian resistance – and hence include the French – into Allied invasion planning. The downsides were also considerable, however, beginning with the moral dimension. While established resistance groups were invisible and their operations – intelligence gathering, propaganda, sabotage, escape, and evasion – clandestine, assemblies of young men in forests and on mountain tops offered obvious targets, as did the populations among whom they lived. The fact that the Communists might believe this a plus, because in their view a German/Vichy crackdown would radicalize the population and end *attentisme*, thus distracting Axis troops from the Eastern Front and possibly laying the foundation for a communist power grab on Liberation, offered a further reason to disqualify their counsel. An additional problem for Allied planners was that these "*réduits maquisards*" were too far from potential invasion beaches to work in tandem with conventional forces. Nor did Allied planners envision "*réduits maquisards*" as impregnable citadels, but rather, along with Rougeron, they regarded them as broader regions where *maquisards* might operate in small groups with relative impunity.[146]

In a three-nation meeting of the SOE, the OSS, and the BCRA held on 29 November 1943, under the title "*planning maquis*," the assumption was that the *maquis* would become "true military units, operating alone or reinforced by parachutists dropped on D-Day onto previously reconnoitered and secured drop-zones." Three types of *maquis* were envisaged: "strategic *maquis*," who would take guerrilla action to cut roads and railroads; "geographical *maquis*"– also called "fortress *maquis*" – who would block choke points through which occupation forces would be obliged to pass, like the Rhône Valley; and finally, "reserve *maquis*" – sometimes called "*centres mobilisateurs*" – who would secure drop zones to receive weapons and serve as "a sort of depot for the other two types of *maquis*," to assemble and train *maquisards*. But the concept outdistanced the practicalities in at least two ways: Brault cautioned that the *maquis*, even if concentrated, would not be able to go on the attack without a significant infusion of weapons, boots and clothing, and training, not to mention considerable assistance from conventional Allied forces, a realistic but politically unpopular assessment that caused him to be branded an "*attentiste*." A second problem was that "*centres mobilisateurs*" became a territorial objective in their own right when, with *Plan Caïman*, they became confused with "liberated zones" where the GPRF might establish its authority independently of the Anglo-Americans.[147]

The knock-on consequences from the decision for *Plan Montagnards* would lead to one of the great French polemics of the war, that was to mirror on the Western Front the controversy over the August 1944 Slovak National Uprising, and that of Warsaw earlier that month, both of which were brutally crushed while making no significant contribution to liberation. What role, exactly, were these "strongpoints" meant to perform? Bastions to be defended? Logistical centers? "Cleared zones," where an autonomous CFLN authority could be established? In Frenay's view, they offered bases from which guerrilla units "of no more than thirty men" could launch attacks against German communications. But the SHAEF planners believed it unrealistic that any "unconventional attrition" of German forces could be accomplished without the commitment of conventional forces, and argued that raids meant to "beat up" the Germans served merely to call attention to weak points in their defenses. The resistance lacked the leadership, tactics, arms, and experience to inflict meaningful attrition, a situation that fifteen three-man Jedburgh teams and nine OGs, and a handful of French paratroops and the *Bataillon de choc* imported on D-Day, were too diminutive to remedy. But the *maquis* myth had long since outdistanced such mundane tactical nit-picks. De Gaulle required "symbols of heroism," proof that the French people stood ready to abet their own liberation, evidence that the CFLN was not *attentiste* as the communists charged, and "cleared zones" in the Hexagon where the GPRF might establish its authority lest Roosevelt cook-up another Darlan deal.[148]

The imprecise function and ephemeral character of the "mountain redoubt" concept gave rise to skepticism, most notably at SHAEF. To scatter relatively scarce, highly trained but lightly armed paratroop or glider-borne units to defend *maquis* enclaves distant from main-force action, rather than concentrate them to support Overlord, diverted precious assets from a high-stakes invasion upon which the outcome of the war hinged. "Resistance," *maquis*, and special operations came to be seen as a ploy through which peripheral players – most notably the French and the interface services – might crowbar their way into the heart of Allied planning and stay politically and operationally relevant once Anglo-American armies were on the ground in France. Furthermore, Churchill and the Foreign Office sought to brandish the Alpine *maquis* to scupper the invasion of southern France, which the Prime Minister opposed. Conventional commanders quite rightly feared that these *maquis* enclaves created vulnerabilities by threatening to consume scarce resources just to sustain themselves, and would divert manpower and assets meant for Overlord and Anvil/Dragoon, or the strategic bombing campaign. The Americans in particular expected resistance activity to be tied directly to supporting conventional operations behind the front. However, little was done for almost a year for a number of reasons: ignorance of the scope of the *maquis* phenomenon; problems of cash; a dearth of planes, techniques, and resources to supply clusters of idle *maquisards* indefinitely; skepticism in the Allied high command about the military value of a *maquis*; the insecure status of the interface organizations in the military hierarchy; reluctance to launch premature resistance action; and a jealously guarded operational autonomy among leaders of resistance groups, which led to complaints from London and Algiers that resistance leaders ignored advice, refused to follow direction, or failed to cooperate. All of which meant that, only in early 1944, as D-Day loomed, were steps taken to operationalize resistance.[149]

In the course of 1943, the strategic context of resistance had shifted from being a substitute for invasion to mobilizing as a force to support D-Day. But how that was to happen was not entirely clear, especially as the SOE's view throughout most of 1942 had been that, unlike robust Balkan folk, the faint-hearted French were neither politically nor psychologically primed for insurrection. Only in the course of 1943 could information on the growing dimensions of the *maquis* phenomenon be gathered through agents in France and assessed, which helped to prompt Churchill's 27 January 1944 order to weaponize France's Alpine *maquis*. This helped to silence critics, but it did not necessarily facilitate the integration of the *maquis* into Allied planning. Many technical problems also remained: the decision to decentralize the resistance command structure as part of Plan Maquis had been taken from November 1943 largely as a security measure. But command decentralization also offered a mechanism to prevent the Gaullists from dominating military and political events through control of the resistance. From a tactical perspective, the argument was that those on the ground were better able to assess their situation than were the interface organizations or conventional soldiers in London or Algiers. So, the command philosophy behind Plan Maquis was that the *maquis* was to act as "autonomous units" under local resistance leaders, who had a relatively free hand once the decision to permit "immediate action" had been taken. London's grasp of conditions in *maquis* "strongholds" was imperfect. The prevailing assumption was that, in keeping with the operational concept, they were composed of independent thirty-man "mobile groups." No one in planning had any settled notion of what guerrillas were meant to do – attack airfields, blow up railway tracks, and generally operate as a "fifth column," which had become a ubiquitous but empty cliché since the Spanish Civil War. But, as EMFFI chief Koenig realized, no doctrine existed to mobilize the *maquis*, while many French officers nurtured a deep distrust of the resistance as a claque of communists and military postulants, a stereotype returned with interest by many *maquisards*.[150]

The goals of the two major actors were also different, even at cross purposes – the Gaullists sought to use the *maquis* to achieve political recognition and inclusion in Allied planning, while the Allies had a war to fight. On 16 May 1944, de Gaulle signed off on *Plan Caïman*, which laid out instructions for resistance in the southeast, the center-west, and Brittany. A second addendum to Caïman, which was produced after D-Day by General Billotte, designated an "air bridgehead" in the Massif Central, where French paratroops working in tandem with the resistance were to create a "liberated zone" independent of Allied operations. The goal was the political one that would allow the CFLN to establish its authority in the center of France and expand in *tâche d'huile* fashion. The primacy of the political objective for the Gaullists is cited as a reason why *Caïman* was so poorly conceived from a military standpoint.[151]

Balu argues that *Caïman* should be viewed not in isolation, but rather as one of a myriad of plans to engage the resistance to support D-Day, part of de Gaulle's larger goal to activate popular participation in the liberation, viewed as an essential pre-condition for the restoration of France's self-esteem and great power status. Plans to engage the resistance had been devised from April 1943: *Plan Vert* would look to enlist railway workers to disrupt the railroads; *Plan Violet* focused on the PTT to cut radio and telephone communications; and *Plan Tortue* sought to keep German reinforcements from reaching the main theaters, mainly by sabotaging railway switching capabilities. Other plans included *Plan Bleu* to destroy high-tension power lines, *Plan Rouge* to attack German supply depots, and *Plan Jaune* to target German munitions, while *Plan Noir* laid out a scheme for guerrilla activity. *Plan Montagnards/Vidal* remained on the books, although some wondered whether it were still operative.

Bloc Planning

A strong team was required to operationalize these plans. The November 1943 amalgamation of the Giraudist and Gaullist secret services into the DGSS had seemed to put soldiers back into the driver's seat. The *maquis* assumed an ever-larger role as it was folded into D-Day plans, with soldiers tasked with devising "an operational doctrine for the army behind the lines." This became the mission of "Bloc Planning" under Edmond Combaux, a forty-one-year-old Polytechnician and signals officer, who had fled over the Pyrenees after Vichy booted him out of the Armistice Army when his Masonic affiliation was exposed.[152] All of these plans had been carefully studied and revised by a group in Algiers called Bloc Planning, whose purpose was not to plan for an invasion, but to envision the various invasion scenarios in which the cadres of the AS might most usefully intervene. Bloc Planning's going-in assumption was that the invasion would trigger a race between the Allies and the Germans to move the most men and resources quickly toward the invasion zones, a competition that the resistance as the home team might influence by handicapping the occupier. Because Bloc Planning could only guess where an Allied invasion might come ashore, it envisioned a careful three-phase escalation of resistance activity by region which would aim in the first instance to impede the enemy's concentration of forces. A second phase, judged to last for between four and eight weeks, would see the resistance mobilize "behind the lines" to stymie German plans to transfer reinforcements from other sectors and theaters through guerrilla activity and attacks on lines of communication, while remaining "invisible." In this phase, resistance forces and their cadres were to assemble as "*maquis mobilisateurs*" in the Pyrenees, Massif Central, Vosges, Jura, and Alpes, where they would clear reception zones for parachuted matériel and reinforcements, create supply depots, train, and launch guerrilla operations of increasing scope. While London might designate the objectives of these missions, it would leave the planning details and execution to the men on the spot. Only in the third and final phase were resistance forces to appear on the battlefield. In the interim, Bloc Planning worked with the SOE to revise the various sabotage plans. However, when it was realized, in February 1944 (Map 4.2), that most of these plans had not yet been communicated to the resistance, or that the groups lacked the resources and capacity to execute them, the focus was shifted to refining *Plans Vert* and *Grenouille* against the railways, and *Tortue* that targeted Panzer divisions expected to utilize the highways. The other plans to attack German depots and command centers would be folded into guerrilla action in phase two, while the BCRA acknowledged that it lacked the resistance networks in the PTT to carry out *Plan Violet*, the sabotage of subterranean telephone cables. One task of the DMRs was to make certain that the various resistance groups retained the capacity to execute *Plans Vert* and *Tortue*. Bloc Planning's approach assumed that resistance activity was to take place over

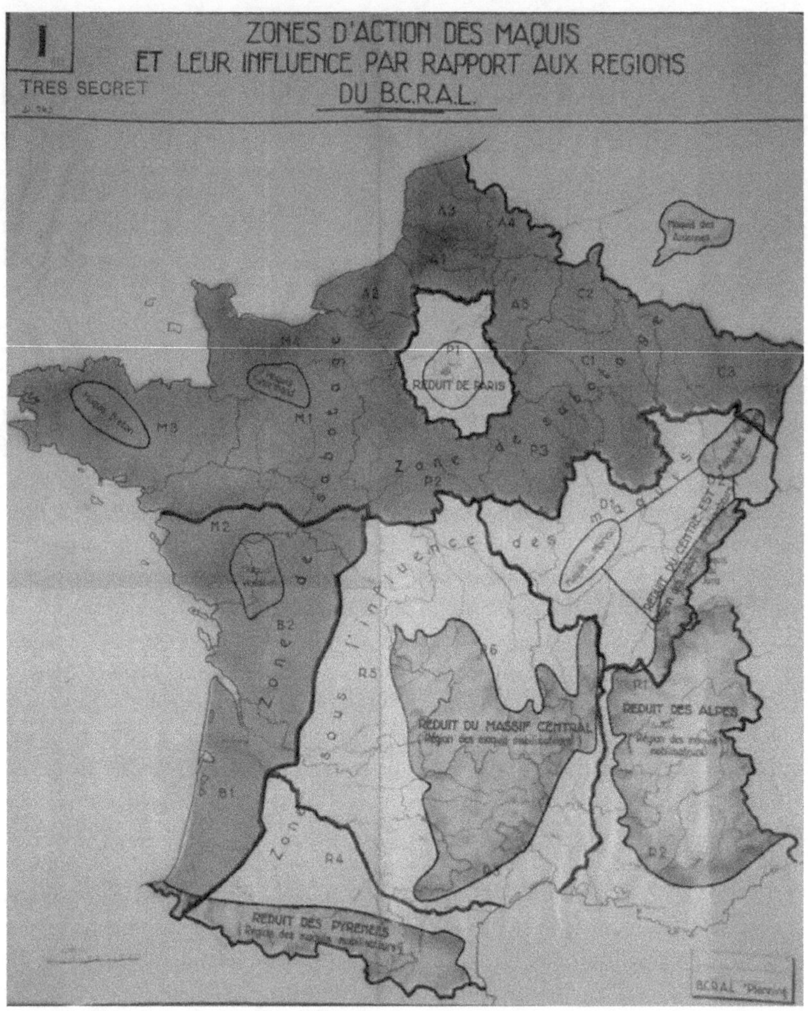

Map 4.2 The BCRAL (London) vision in February 1944 of the role to be played by the resistance in the liberation.

time, and gradually to gain in intensity as recruits were trained, weapons accumulated, and German possibilities for reprisal attrited. This shelved the notion of a single, spontaneous "national insurrection" on D-Day.[153]

There were at least three problems with *Caïman*. First, it showcased the competing priorities of de Gaulle, who looked to create a "liberated zone" in the Massif Central to establish CFLN/GPRF authority, and Churchill, who favored a Yugoslav-like Alpine enclave as a ploy to sabotage Anvil/Dragoon. De Gaulle sought to control political events in France so that any vacuum created by Vichy's collapse could be filled neither by a Communist power grab, as per Corsica, nor by the Allies through a Darlan deal/Giraud/Badoglio/Allied Military Government of Occupied Territories (AMGOT) scenario. With this goal in mind, he sought to limit the power of departmental liberation committees named by the CNR, which he feared would transform into Soviets on the Liberation to challenge the authority of prefects named by Algiers.[154] A second problem with *Caïman* was that it pitted the centralizing vision of planners in Algiers and London, who struggled to coordinate *maquis* action with the advance of Allied conventional forces, against the principle of command "decentralization." For Billotte, the coordination versus decentralization conundrum lay at the heart of *Caïman*, as he struggled simultaneously to convince the Allies to arm the *maquis* in the Massif Central, while incentivizing their commanders to coordinate their operations with the progress of an Allied invasion, so as to prevent a premature "national insurrection." London's view was that the *maquis* should operate with "prudence," becoming active only as Allied armies advanced out of their beachheads. But decentralization assumed that commanders on the ground were best positioned to determine the optimal moment to seize their strategic opportunities. So Billotte's instructions permitted resistance commanders in the south to launch "broad guerrilla operations ... over large regions" if regional chiefs ordered them and if the Allies advanced. The *maquis* was also to create "bastions" in the less accessible regions within which to mobilize and ready volunteers for action. De Gaulle's 16 May 1944 final directives to accompany *Caïman* sought to avoid "a general and reckless uprising," but did allow for "insurrection" in the Jura, the Dauphiné, and the Savoie.[155]

Needless to say, these contradictory directives created confusion – a third problem with *Caïman*, as indeed with all planning involving the *maquis*, that was to have considerable repercussions. *Caïman* was only one of multiple schemes that rolled down the planning conveyor belts of London and Algiers. Which plan was to receive priority, *Caïman* or *Montagnards/Vidal*? What authority specifically did local commanders have to order operations? And how were they to balance "prudence" with initiative, especially when news of D-Day excited impatience in *maquis* ranks to launch a "national insurrection"? The assumption in France was that, having been approved by someone in Algiers and London, or acquiesced to by the SOE agent on the ground because he felt powerless to oppose it, the "*réduits maquisards*" would only have to hold out for forty-eight hours before Allied reinforcements arrived, when in fact Allied air and paratroop support would be committed to the invasion beachheads, not to floating in to rescue *maquis* enclaves.[156]

Not surprisingly, Allied priority focused on the final adjustments to Overlord. The resistance, and especially the *maquis* in their redoubts distant from the main invasion sites, were very much an ancillary consideration for SHAEF planners. For these reasons, no lingering desire existed at the planning level to engage in yet another exhausting quarrel with the "excitable" and "politicized" French over what was seen by many conventional soldiers as a peripheral detail in a complex inventory of invasion priorities. The primary French objective was to deploy the *maquis* in ways that would limit potential Allied political initiatives in France and boost the case for Allied recognition of a French provisional government. A second goal was to substitute resistance sabotage for inaccurate and destructive Allied bombing, an ambition that found no traction in an air power-addicted Allied command that viewed the resistance at best as an unproven appurtenance that cluttered and confused the battlefield. But, as the *maquis* phenomenon swelled, it became too big to ignore without alienating French opinion or forfeiting the cooperation of *maquisards* on D-Day. This was the opinion of Michael Brault, when in a substantial January 1944 report, he insisted that, unless the *maquis* were supported, "The entire country will feel a profound bitterness which could turn against Algiers and the Anglo-Saxon Allies." This would have played into the hands of Vichy – already in his broadcasts, Vichy propagandist Henriot would read out a list of intercepted parachute drops, evidence he insisted, that the *maquis* were on their own. So, in this way, the French managed to pressure the SOE and Foreign Office into acting as their advocates with SHAEF, which also suited Churchill's political agenda insofar as the Alps were concerned, to have "*réduits maquisards*" approved as an accepted strategic concept almost through a process of attrition.[157] In fact, the French attitude toward the *maquis* was far more ambivalent.

Glières

Another reason why Rougeron's "*réduit maquisard* " concept might have received closer scrutiny was that *Plan Montagnards* botched its March 1944 debut at Glières, a 1,500-meter-high plateau 30 kilometers from Annecy. For Crémieux-Brilhac, Glières marked a "turning point in the clandestine war" by putting on display all of the "problems" faced by the resistance on the eve of D-Day: those of liaison with the Allied high command; tactical shortcomings ("how to fight a guerrilla war"); the limits of a "national insurrection" ("when to do it and in which form"); and constraints on how far the French nation was willing to participate in its own liberation.[158] However, rather than a "turning point," Glières simply provided a curtain raiser for the systemic crumple of "*réduits maquisards*" in the shadow of D-Day. All true, agrees Raphaële Balu, who nevertheless points out that the congregation of STO fugitives at Glières, as elsewhere in France, had been spontaneous and ad hoc. And while, at the time and subsequently, Glières seemed to offer a sinister portent of the signature July–August 1944 *maquis* disasters at Barcelonnette, Mont Mouchet, and le Vercors, in fact, it should be viewed in the context of a chain of roundups, executions, and indiscriminate massacres inflicted on many *maquis* and their civilian enablers and bystanders in the shadow of D-Day (Map 4.3). The magnitude of the mayhem offers a first reason why Glières has received a prominent place in French memory of the war. A second was Vichy's notorious role in the massacre. Finally, at the time and since, the *maquis* came to be linked with the Haute-Savoie, which gave a regional focus to *maquis* memory.[159]

Why the authorities both in London and in the resistance did not foresee the Glières catastrophe can only be explained by invoking a fragmented command, wishful thinking, a confusion of strategic concept, and an unshakable belief among *maquisards* that D-Day rescue was imminent. Since he had entered the government on 1 January 1944 as *Secrétaire Général au Maintien de l'Ordre*, replacing René Bosquet as head of the police, *Obersturmführer* Joseph Darnand had itched to enact a dramatic demonstration of the ruthless efficiency of Vichy's "militia state." A state of siege in the Haute-Savoie, declared on 24 January 1944, was accompanied by an infusion of gendarmes, *gardes mobiles*, the GMR, and around 1,000 *Francs-gardes*, the stormtroopers of *la Milice*, all under the command of Gendarme Colonel Georges Lelong headquartered in Annecy. Darnand also launched a campaign to recruit informers to infiltrate the *maquis*. Although the Germans were usually content to delegate containment of the *maquis* to the French police and *la Milice*, swelling assemblies of STO refugees indicated a serious erosion of public order in the Alpine east.[160] *Maquisards*, emboldened by the approach of Liberation, had begun to attack German customs officers, steal vehicles and explosives, and assassinate collaborators, and had even audaciously attacked a German convoy. Aware that the Allied invasion was only months – maybe weeks – away, the Germans criticized Vichy lethargy while they sought to drain this "festering abscess." In March 1944, Oberbefehlshaber West (OB West) Gerd von Rundstedt imported troops from Yugoslavia with anti-guerrilla experience into the Alpes, where they joined the panoply of German forces fused since June 1942 under the Höherer SS- und Polizeiführer (HSSPF). From February 1944, OB West launched a brutal campaign of repression behind a volley of decrees and extraordinary measures, propelled by a "*psychose du franc-tireur*," throughout France, but especially in the Alpes. Torture, summary executions, and random massacres of unarmed *maquisards* and unlucky civilians, carried out by French and German police, *la Milice*, which on 1 April was brought under direct German control, and the Wehrmacht, accounted for an estimated 10,000–15,000 deaths in the brief months around D-Day, of which Glières became emblematic.[161]

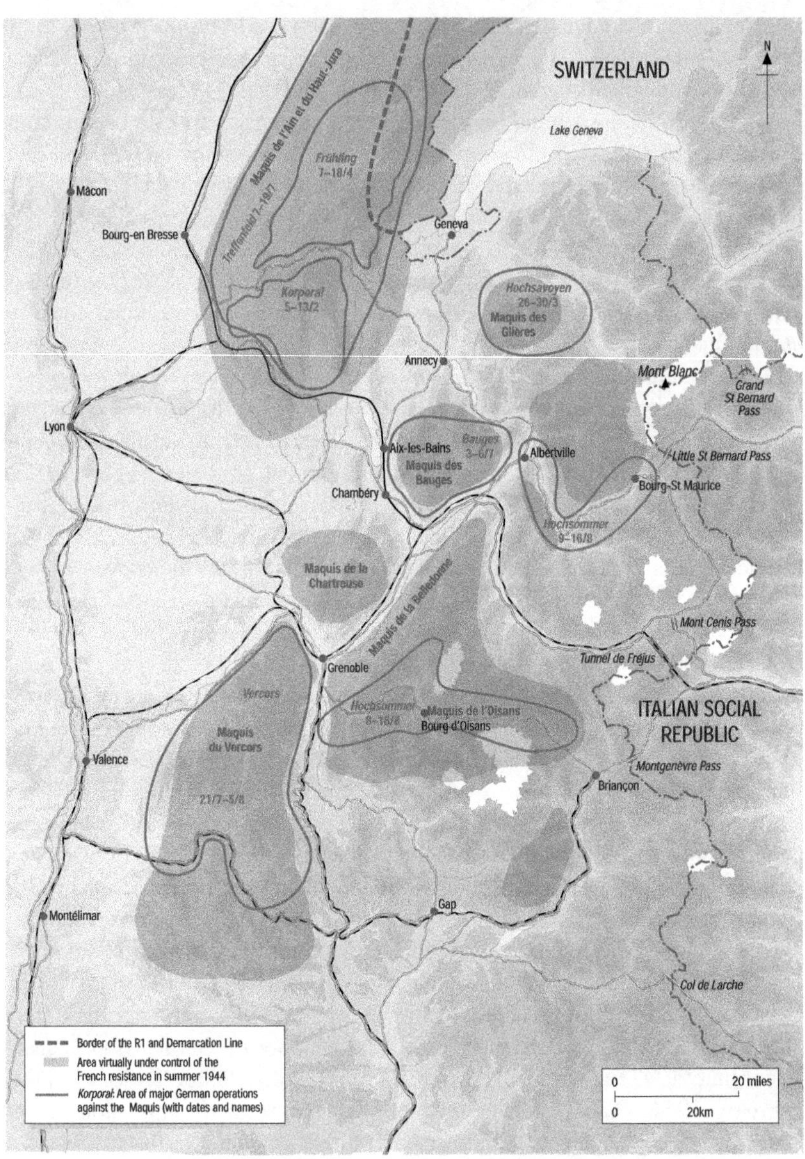

Map 4.3 Maquis in the R1 Sector and major German anti-partisan operations in 1944.

France's Alpine region fell within the bailiwick of the Kommando der Sicherheitspolizei und des SD (KdS) in Lyon, with sub-stations in Annecy, Grenoble, Chambéry, and other towns, which had a special 280-man commando made up of Abwehr, Gestapo, and regular German police who specialized in detecting and destroying resistance radio transmitters. Section IV (intelligence) commanded by Nikolaus "Klaus" Barbie ran a team of "false Jews" whose task was to ferret out and deport real ones. He also kept a stable of French snitches on his payroll, men and women recruited in bars and nightclubs, and from the Corsican mafia, who delivered up to 150 denunciations a day. Double agents infiltrated the *maquis* and resistance groups – it is reckoned that Section IV probably found the information that led to the arrest of Moulin at Caluire and Delestraint in Paris in June 1943 using turned former resisters. The Montluc prison at Lyon housed 9,000–10,000 people arrested over 2 years. An estimated 600 prisoners were executed on Barbie's watch, while 3,000 Jews were deported. Both the French police and the KdS directed operations using *la Milice*, under Francis André, an active member of the PPF and former Légion des volontaires français contre le bolchévisme (LVF) member who had served briefly on the Eastern Front. His partial facial paralysis earned André the unimaginative moniker "*Gueule tordue*" ("Twisted Mug"). Guided by the Sipo/SD, André led *Franc-garde* assassination squads to target Masons, Jews, communists, resisters, and anyone else who displeased them, such as Victor Basche, President of the League of the Rights of Man, whom they gunned down in January 1944.[162]

Intelligence meticulously collected through bribes, threats, Vichy aficionados, or in a spirit of personal revenge made the arrival of a German raid, often chaperoned by *la Milice* or French police, particularly terrifying. A CFLN report for March–April 1944 noted, under a subheading of "*Opérations de répression*," "When he arrives, the [German] officer always has in his possession: 1) the list of people to arrest. 2) the list of people to shoot on the spot. 3) the list of Jews residing in the area with orders to shoot the men and deport the women. 4) a usually very precise list of the shops having supplied the resistance. 5) the list of farms to burn for having sheltered the resisters."[163] L'Ain in particular suffered from deportations, hostage-taking, executions, including of the mayors of towns where the resistance was active, and farm burnings. From late 1943, the CFLN began to insist that resisters were legal soldiers in a "national army." But neither Vichy nor Berlin bought into that argument, pointing out that even the Allies had refused to extend diplomatic recognition to the CFLN. Nor were the Allies keen to press French demands lest the status of their own soldiers be placed in jeopardy. The attitude was that *maquisards* must face the same risks as captured agents from the interface services, also not covered by the laws of war, who were subject to "*Nacht und Nebel* " – that is, simply disappeared. Sometimes the terror was targeted, sometimes random, as when people might be shot or hanged in an action meant as a "warning."[164] The Germans and *la Milice* then might forbid the burial of those executed as further insult to the dead and their families. But, if a German soldier or member of *la Milice* died in action, elaborate funerals were organized, which the locals, including schoolchildren, might be compelled to attend, during which the criminality and violence of *le maquis* was denounced in a funeral harangue. While this spread fear and hatred of the Germans and *la Milice*, above all it demonstrated that, beyond assassinating a smidgin of collaborators and snitches, the *maquis* was powerless to protect the population. SOE agent Francis Cammaerts reported in March 1944 that the Germans were applying "reign of terror" methods perfected in Russia, that included "incinerated farms, firing squads and hangings. Those places where the resistance is active live in a state of siege. Everywhere else [there is] a ferocious attack against the '*maquis*' and those who support it. Road blocks are everywhere, which makes movement excessively difficult and dangerous." Arrests meant that "resistance in all of its forms has received a serious setback." Ironically, in his view, popular blame both among the French population and in the resistance, who dwelled in impatient expectation of D-Day, was laid on the Allies.[165]

As the result of Vichy's January declaration of a state of siege, road blocks and search parties dispatched by Vichy "*forces de l'ordre*" in the valleys drove around 120 fugitives out of the surrounding towns and villages into makeshift camps on the Glières Plateau. While *la Milice* terrorized the countryside, the resistance was joined by 56 Spanish Republicans, a handful of Italians, and even a few deserters from the German army, so that, by the end of January, an estimated 450–600 fugitives had collected on the plateau, or about one-third of the *maquisards* in the Haute-Savoie.[166] So, rather than a conscious strategy envisaged by Rougeron and *Plan Montagnards*, Glières witnessed a largely spontaneous gathering provoked in part by a desire to spare civilians at the mountain base from retaliation and by the expectation that they would be armed by the Allies. The instinct to assemble also emerged from a search for fellowship and comradery, as well as the requirement to secure a drop zone. This refugee *maquis* was taken in hand by "Tom" Morel – a 1937 Saint-Cyr graduate, *chasseur alpin*, former Armistice Army officer, and devout Christian who had enlisted in the AS. Morel's idea was to gather the fugitives in what he believed to be an easily defensible position until the Allies parachuted arms and – rumor had it – paratroop reinforcements, at which time they would transform into a mobile force to attack the enemy. In the meantime, Morel made a modest attempt to create a daily military routine at Glières, consisting of calisthenics, weapons and tactical training, long hikes, mounting guard on approach routes, saluting the colors, and carrying out camp chores, with perhaps a theatrical production in the evening. But the general word was that no action was to be launched before D-Day. So, mostly these fugitives shivered, coughed, and yawned through the winter of 1943–1944 in a posture of procrastination that made the *drôle de guerre* seem positively frenetic in comparison.

Neither the chief of the *maquis* of l'Ain and the Haute-Savoie, Henri Romans-Petit, nor Richard Heslop, the SOE agent who advised him, envisaged the Gilières "redoubt" as a strategic concept; they saw it simply as a drop zone for weapons to be distributed to resistance groups. That was also the view of SHAEF, for which "redoubts" were not to form before D-Day. Nor were they to become static positions. But theory discounted the realities on the ground where men gathered for shelter, defense, and community in the expectation that arms, reinforcements, and D-Day would activate them. In their own minds, they were hardly fugitives on the run, but rather soldiers in a vast coalition of Allied armies: "The morale of [resistance] fighters was linked to the realization that they were part of a powerful alliance that supported them," concludes Balu.[167] This view was reinforced by a media campaign spearheaded by the BBC and the *Times* of London that, in keeping both with Churchill's Yugoslav-inspired vision and with Gaullist aspirations, portrayed the resistance as creating vast "liberated zones" in southeastern France.

Colonel Lelong's dilatory siege of the plateau caused Darnand to take charge of repression, prompting a 3 February alert by Schumann on the BBC that an anti-*maquis* operation against Glières was imminent: "It's up to you, and you alone, to decide when and where to flee," while cautioning them against surrender. But two days later the "BCRA military delegation" composed of Paris jeweler turned BCRA agent Jean-Pierre Rosenthal (Cantinier) and *délégué militaire de R(égion)1* Maurice Bourgès-Maunoury, Polytechnician, artillery officer, and scion of a long line of Radical Party politicians who would himself become Prime Minister in 1957, insisted in multiple messages to London that they could hold out. So, the next day, Schumann encouraged Frenchmen to "rally to the *maquis*" and apply a "*dispositive de défense*," without indicating exactly what that meant. A confused 7 February meeting of special operations principals, which opened with Emmanuel d'Astier reading an urgent request from Glières for arms, concluded that the authority to order military action at Glières rested with SHAEF. The next day, Manuel ordered his agents in the Hautes-Alpes to clear drop zones to be indicated by bonfires at night, and to identify enemy assembly points that might be bombed. On the BBC, Schumann backtracked and urged the Glières *maquis* to split into small groups of guerrillas to harass the enemy.[168]

Emmanuel d'Astier's efforts bore fruit as the first of three parachute drops consisting of light arms and explosives occurred on the night of 14 February. While this energized young *maquisards* from across France, who saw themselves as "*l'avant-garde de l'armée de la Libération*," resources remained scarce, as whatever food could be secured in the valley had to be dragged up the mountainside on sleds. Unfortunately, dropping weapons also alerted Vichy and the Germans to the growing danger, while fixing the *maquis* on the Glières plateau, thus forfeiting the mobility and invisibility that Bloc Planning sought to preserve until D-Day. Nevertheless, with the CNR calling for the launching of "immediate action," Rosenthal insisted that Glières formed an "impenetrable citadel." A preliminary clash with the GMR occurred on 7 February, and two days later shots were exchanged with *la Milice*. On 12 February, a serious skirmish left four GMR dead, and three captured, whom Morel sent back to their lines.[169] On Radio Paris, Philippe Henriot fulminated that the situation was getting out of control, with shopkeepers robbed and killed and peasants attacked by the *maquisards*. In a mid-March meeting, Rosenthal managed to browbeat local resistance chiefs to insist that Glières could hold out. In the meantime, Morel organized his garrison into twelve platoons, each with its own sector and defense responsibilities linked to his HQ by runners, as well as a mobile force of twenty-five well-armed *maquisards*. For the moment, frozen in a defensive posture on their snowbound highland, they prepared to receive weapons drops and paratroop reinforcements.[170] On the night of 9–10 March, Morel was killed leading a raid on the Hôtel de France in the village of Entremont which had been requisitioned as a GMR barracks. Sixty GMR prisoners were led up the plateau. The largest parachute drop of arms occurred on the next night – seventeen four-motor bombers dropped ninety tons of material.[171]

So far, timid attacks by the GMR and *la Milice* on Glières had been easily repelled. Lelong tried unsuccessfully to negotiate with Captain Maurice Anjot, Saint-Cyrian, former Armistice Army officer, and member of the AS, who had volunteered to replace Morel. *La Milice* focused on "purging" villages they believed filled with resistance supporters by surrounding them, carrying out "*vérifications d'identité* " as a prelude to arrest, and finally setting fire to houses. A *Milice* tribunal set up in Annecy began to pronounce and carry out death sentences. On 20 March, *la Milice* launched a coordinated attack on the two roads leading to the top of the plateau, which was thwarted, as was a subsequent attack four days later. After the war, the communists accused the BCRA of sacrificing the Glières garrison by not ordering them to disperse as at Bir Hakeim. But, as Albertelli notes, London was in a dilemma – the British had begun to drop arms, so that they needed to maintain resistance teams to receive and distribute them. On the other hand, they did not want to encourage premature action on the basis of what Brault called the "chimerical" belief that the Glières *maquis* would be rescued by paratroops, or that their action would spark the "*insurrection nationale*." So, rather than order the *maquis* to disperse, London continued without success to pressure the RAF to bomb German troop concentrations, which the RAF insisted were too distant and too dispersed to offer a viable tactical target for high-altitude bombers. Too many impediments existed for London to direct the defense at Glières, especially as messages took six to eight days to decipher. As the Red Army reached the Polish frontier, hopes also rose that the Germans were on their last legs. For their part, the garrison continued to search the skies for paratroops, while flight would have meant abandoning their precious arms stocks to the enemy. Glières featured prominently in the "war of the air waves" between Henriot, who denounced the "red terrorists," and Radio Londres, on which Schuman glorified Glières as the opening act in "*l'insurrection nationale*," and proof of *maquis* vitality. In these conditions, Anjot concluded that evacuation had become "psychologically impossible."[172]

The inability of *la Milice* and the police to take Glières caused Generalleutnant Karl Pflaum to intervene. As a colonel, Pflaum had led Infanterie Regiment 19, one of the most prestigious commands in Bavarian service. However, his meteoric ascension nose-dived when he was relieved of his divisional command on the Eastern Front in January 1942, and transferred to command the 157th Reserve Division in France, considered a training unit for mostly young Bavarian recruits just out of basic training who, after six months, would transfer from the "reserve" to the field army. While health reasons had allegedly prompted Pflaum's reassignment, he was again to be relieved in August 1944 during the German retreat from France. Most probably, the fifty-four-year-old Pflaum was considered insufficiently ruthless for his counterinsurgency mission. A genial Francophile, who as a boy had spent time in France, Pflaum initially at least had opposed the radicalization of German counterinsurgency tactics that targeted civilians. Most of the cadres of the 157th Reserve Division were combat-experienced, often highly decorated officers and NCOs, who, because of wounds or other infirmities such as combat trauma, had been transferred from the field army to a training division. Nevertheless, Pflaum's division incorporated both an attached artillery regiment and an engineering battalion, and its infantry was equipped with an arsenal of heavy weapons. After D-Day, it would be reinforced by a *Panzergrenadier* (armored infantry) battalion, as well as airborne forces designed to land in the midst of the "*réduits maquisards*," with Luftwaffe tactical and logistical support. In September, it was reclassified as a "light infantry" or "Alpine" division. Otherwise, many of the German troops in the Alps were made up of older men assigned to territorial or security units. These were reinforced by *Osttruppen* or *Ostbataillone*, former Red Army soldiers, often poorly trained, prone to desertion, and considered third-class troops, but who quickly gained a reputation for brutality with the French, who often referred to them as "Mongols." German violence was often blamed on the Sipo/SD, whose personnel accompanied the Wehrmacht on anti-partisan operations to provide intelligence and interrogate "suspects." Meanwhile, fighting was outsourced to reserve divisions, *Ostbataillone*, *la Milice*, and the GMR (although these Vichy police formations proved so limp that the Germans used them only as backup after

Glières), and to French collaborators gathered in *8. Kompanie/Brandenberg Regiment 2*, a small detachment mustered for anti-partisan operations.[173] But counterinsurgency is a radicalizing experience, and soldiers who carry it out reason that the "*maquis*" could not exist without an easily targeted civilian base of support.

Guided by Gestapo intelligence, and accompanied by agents from the SD, *Jägdkommandos* ("hunting commandos") from the 157th Reserve Division combed the countryside in the Savoie, Haute-Savoie, and the Isère to ferret out and scatter "terrorists" and "bandits" in operations *Korporal* in February and *Frühling* (spring) in April. Those caught might be shot on the spot or turned over to the SD for interrogation. Failure to report a parachute drop resulted in confiscation or slaughter of livestock. "It shows that in the end the police and the German Gestapo are the soul of the operations against the French Resistance and that the Wehrmacht is merely the faithful executant and auxiliary," read a French summary of German anti-*maquis* operations compiled in December 1944. "This perhaps explains the curious contrast between the constant admonitions of the German command about sparing the innocent civilian population and the mutiple revolting acts of barbarism against the population carried out throughout the territory."[174] But the German dilemma was that, while they could not count on their French allies, they required *la Milice* and the GMR to stabilize an area, because as soon as their *Jädgerkommandos* departed, leaving a trail of smoke and carnage, the *maquis* returned. And this situation would only worsen with D-Day.[175]

Historian of the Wehrmacht Peter Lieb argues that the role of the Luftwaffe in suppressing the "*réduits maquisards*" has been underemphasized. While the German air force was only a shadow of its former self by 1944, it remained a scourge for the *maquis*. By late June 1944, the Luftwaffe had gathered sixty-seven planes into the *Geschwader Bongart* (Bongart Wing) to backstop counter-*maquis* operations. The fact that many aircraft were Italian Reggiane Re.2002 fighter bombers hardly mattered in a low-tech counterinsurgency campaign.[176] From 8 March, the Luftwaffe had reconnoitered, strafed, and bombed the Glières plateau. On 22–23 March, Pflaum shifted 6,000–7,000 of his soldiers from Grenoble to Glières. On 23 March, Anjot rejected a *Milice* demand to surrender. For the next two days, German artillery peppered the plateau with shells. On 26 March, Pflaum's division, wearing white camouflage and snowshoes, accompanied by mules carrying supplies, munitions, and mortars, attacked the plateau from the east, while 800 *Francs-gardes*, GMR members, and a Wehrmacht infantry company took up blocking positions along the potential escape routes. Realizing that it was folly for his 456 largely untrained *maquisards* to oppose a regular Wehrmacht division, Anjot ordered his command to scatter. Over the next 4 days, 210 *maquisards*, including Anjot, were killed, captured and executed, or deported. All of the arms delivered by the British in three parachute drops were seized. While *la Milice* and Henriot trumpeted Glières as a brilliant victory, by some accounts the storming of the Glières plateau had offered a rabbit hunt of fleeing *maquisards* – a Bulson in the snow. Crémieux-Brilhac disputed this assessment: the Germans reported violent clashes, while the Glières *maquis* had skirmished with the GMR and *Milice* for weeks, during which both sides experienced significant losses. "One cannot deny that, despite everything, there had been a true battle that cost the Resistance numerous deaths," he wrote in what one feels constituted a sort of apologia.[177]

While Radio Londres trumpeted Glières' patriotic sacrifice as a "victory of the spirit," the disaster served to reinforce Allied skepticism of the operational sustainability of *réduits maquisards*. But it is doubtful whether Glières caused the "interface organizations" seriously to reevaluate the "strategic redoubt" strategy, for several reasons, beginning with the fact that the basic ingredients that led to the calamity – notably the spontaneous congregation of STO refugees on high ground for comradery, defense, to receive arms drops, and to avoid reprisals against civilian populations – were difficult to manage from London, among young men impatient for Liberation. *Réduits maquisards* offered an important symbol of resistance, which discouraged a cold-blooded assessment of their tactical limitations, except by Brault, who had been sidelined for speaking candidly. It was also possible to argue that it had been the execution, rather than the basic concept of the *réduits maquisards*, that had failed at Glières. Even before Glières' fall, by late 1943, the Allies had concluded that *réduits maquisards* should not offer static concentrations of men but rather serve as temporary reception zones and bases from which raids could be launched. It was all well and good for London and Algiers to opine that the "*maquis mobilisateurs*" should adopt a posture of "semi-dispersion" over expansive, difficult-to-access terrain. "But it's difficult to see how these gatherings of men could be avoided," opines Balu, especially as "following Glières the strategists of *France libre* did not abandon the notion of the 'natural fortress' that protected the *maquisards*," at least from armored assaults.[178]

Encouraged by Churchill, the interface services became increasingly invested in the growing *maquis* as 1943 progressed, buoyed by optimism and best-case scenarios. Such was the case of BCRA liaison Rosenthal, who was subsequently faulted for the failure of the Glières *maquis* to disperse. But Rosenthal appears to have assumed, as did many, that the *maquisards* must resist only for forty-eight hours before they would be reinforced by paratroops, and that D-Day was imminent.[179] This misperception and miscommunication determined the static posture of several *réduits maquisards* in the wake of D-Day. A capacity for self-delusion and a dedication to the mission that overwhelmed caution was practically limitless in the civilianized interface services. The BCRA in London assumed that the *maquis* was far more tightly organized than it was: "nuclei containing one to three officers and fifteen to twenty NCOs" answering to senior authority. SOE agent Francis Cammaerts believed that Glières had fallen because the *maquisards* lacked heavy weapons and because Anjot had made the fatal error of ordering his men to disperse. He retained a "faith" that the *maquis* at le Vercors "would not make the same mistakes."[180]

Rather than shape a strategy based on the realistic limitations of the *maquis*, in the wake of Glières, the interface services and the CFLN instead looked to expand their role. BCRA operative Pierre Fourcaud, parachuted into the Haute-Savoie in February 1944, devised audacious plans for the *maquis* to occupy Alpine valleys, throw roadblocks across highways, attack German garrisons, and so on. This got pushback from EMFFI chief Pierre Koenig, who warned that Fourcaud's vision far exceeded *maquis* capacities, and violated the main takeaway of Glières – that going *mano a mano* with the Wehrmacht with a group of perhaps courageous and enthusiastic, but untrained and lightly armed, young men was invariably a losing proposition. But the BCRA and the EMFFI still seem to have believed that the *maquis* retained a capacity to liberate great swaths of France on their own, even if Glières reinforced opposition in the BCRAL (London) to "the principle of a national insurrection."[181]

"In the end, despite the emotion it caused in the Allied camp, the events at Glières perhaps modified strategies, but not their execution," concludes Balu. "Finally, they failed to envision how defensive positions could be transformed into traps, because these strategies were all now subordinated to D-Day, that would insure for the *maquis* a fate different from that of Glières." The assumption in the interface services and on the ground was that invading troops would advance quickly inland, and/or that "*maquis* redoubts" would be reinforced by paratroops and glider-borne heavy weapons. The BCRA's *déformation professionelle* caused it to envision D-Day as a rush by the regular armies to link up with the *maquis*. Unfortunately, D-Day planners conceptualized the process in reverse – a slow buildup of conventional forces behind the beaches for a number of weeks as "resistance" harassed enemy communications in the rear. The interface services failed to reconcile these conflicting concepts, possibly because they occupied the basement of the SHAEF pecking order, or because they hoped to receive many more resources once the invasion was launched. In any case, the prevailing view was that, confronted with an Allied invasion, the Germans would lack the forces and resolve to cover "these regions of difficult access for the German invader, and of easy defense for the French patriots." In which case, explained Captain Ferdinand Otto Miksche, a Czech officer assigned to de Gaulle's planning staff, "firm strongholds can be established – operational bases of lasting value for the organization of the French Resistance." The SOE's wishful thinking on 22 March predicted that the German occupation would be confined to the populated areas and main roads. Therefore, a phased uprising of *réduits maquisards* from D-Day would proliferate problems for German defenders. In this way, the anticipation that somehow D-Day would magically resolve the *maquis* dilemma of assisting Allied conventional forces while being marooned virtually defenseless deep behind enemy lines jelled into optimistic expectation. In the wake of Glières, such an analysis offered the triumph of boundless hope over bitter experience, but one that transferred to Romans-Petit and Albert Chambonnet, who believed that, if attacked, the *maquis* could carry out a successful static defense until rescue arrived.[182]

Conclusion

In the course of 1943, London and Algiers gradually became aware of the scope of the STO crisis, and of the proliferation of mountain redoubts formed spontaneously by STO refugees. While the Allied camp was keen to operationalize this *maquis*, everyone had different motives for doing so. The theoretical groundwork combined Dalloz's Alpine romanticism with Rougeron's belief that technology allied with insurgency could create "cleared zones" to replicate in France the imagined successes of partisans in Eastern and Southeastern Europe. This appealed to de Gaulle's desire to have the French participate in their own liberation, to restore French self-esteem and grandeur, capitalize on *maquis* "cleared zones" to establish the CFLN's political authority independently of the Anglo-American beachheads, and to deploy the resistance as a lever to force their inclusion into Allied planning for D-Day. The communists believed that the resistance could become the vanguard of a "national insurrection" that would end *attentisme*, assist the Red Army, and possibly offer a vector to seize power on Liberation. Churchill's support combined his affinity for guerrilla warfare with a desire to deploy France's Alpine *maquis* to undermine Anvil/Dragoon. The Foreign Office and the interface services argued that, unless the *maquis* were supported, the Allies would pay a high post-war price in French resentment. All of these considerations caused Allied planners to minimize the military limitations of the *maquis*, an individual and highly localized phenomenon, grouped around independent leaders who resisted inclusion into a hierarchical command structure and operational schema dictated by London and Algiers. An overestimation of resistance and *maquis* capabilities abounded, extrapolated from an optimistic, when not deliberately deceptive, reading of the Yugoslav example, to include the inviolability of "maquis redoubts" and the willingness and ability of Anglo-American conventional forces rapidly to reinforce them with arms drops and paratroops. The fate of the *maquis* at Glières should have served as a wake-up call. But too many players had too much vested in the *maquis* concept to submit their aspirations to a reality check. One result was that the alleged "betrayal" of the *maquis* by the Gaullists and the Allies became a focus of a polemical debate in the post-war years pursued principally by the communists, but also a theme in films and novels.[183]

5 "The Supreme Battle"

"The supreme battle has begun," Charles de Gaulle broadcast to his countrymen over the British Broadcasting Corporation (BBC) on 6 June. "It is of course the Battle of France, and the battle for France!" Liberation, a moment for which most French men and women had yearned for four years, was nevertheless anticipated with apprehension, not least because "the Battle of France," a binary battle between the forces of the Allies and those of Nazi Germany, threatened to transform the Hexagon into a combat zone.[1] However, many worried even more about the "battle for France," a non-binary conflict whose evolving contours were defined by a swelling *maquis* and increasingly assertive yet politically fragmented resistance movement armed and emboldened by the Allied interface services, which the Comité français de libération nationale (CFLN)/Gouvernement provisoire de la république française (GPRF) must strive to contain. Therefore, Liberation would play out on the dual levels of conventional and unconventional warfare, in all their partisan dimensions and legal ambiguities.

If anyone were cavalier about the prospects for destruction, the relatively limited but imprecise and highly lethal Allied bombing of selected targets in occupied France had resulted in an estimated 67,078 French civilian deaths. This figure amounted to about a third more than the number of Britons killed in the Blitz and lost to V-weapons combined, which has traditionally received much more attention in accounts of the war because it fit a narrative of British resolve.[2] Vichy's denunciations of Allied bombing were also in part an attempt to obscure inadequate French civil defense preparations, as well as its high degree of collaboration with Germany. However, the reality was that, from 1940, French ports that might serve as bases for an assault on Britain, or that hosted naval shipyards, U-boat pens, oil refineries, and ammunition factories were working for Berlin. Bomber Command had paid special attention to Saint-Nazaire, Lorient, Nantes, and Le Havre, which ranked them among those French towns hardest hit. In March 1942, a Royal Air Force (RAF) raid on the Renault works at Boulogne-Billancourt on the outskirts of Paris, which was known to be supplying trucks for the German forces, inaugurated a policy of attacking towns that hosted industries working for the Germans. Boulogne-Billancourt was revisited in September 1943. The Schneider-Creusot works that had produced the famous SOMUA S35 tank and which during the occupation pumped out armaments for Germany was also struck. On 17 October 1942, a raid by 94 RAF bombers killed 63, wounded 250, and damaged the factory. However, on 21 June 1943, a 3-hour raid by 500 US Army Air Force (USAAF) bombers killed 360 civilians and wounded another 600. Seventy percent of Le Creusot's houses were leveled, as well as the city hall and schools, leaving 10,000 people homeless. In the wake of this disaster, the Germans began deporting the workers, including the factory director, who failed to return at war's end, as well as the statue of the company's founder, Eugène Schneider, to Germany.[3]

While the French accepted the requirement to disrupt German war production, they puzzled over this seemingly wanton collateral destruction.[4] Rémy (Gilbert Renault) recounted his disappointment after having passed on intelligence about U-boats operating out of Bordeaux, only to witness many French civilians perish in subsequent Allied bombing. Because U-boat pens were indestructible, the best the bombers could do was to transform the neighborhoods of French workers who maintained the U-boats into rubble.[5] From February 1943, many Allied air raids began to prioritize communications as well as war production – the so-called "Transportation Plan." This meant that attacks on rail yards, usually located in populated areas, not only killed civilians, but also disrupted the coal supply, dropping electricity output to reduce industrial productivity. "The destruction of rail communications threw the German military machine into chaos on what turned out to be the eve of the Normandy landings," concludes Robert Gildea.[6] The prospect of liberation at the hands of the wantonly destructive and culturally inferior Americans was viewed by some French people as a deliberate ploy to reduce France's global standing, or even to destroy the values and refinements of French civilization.[7] But Vichy attempts to exploit the destructive effectives of Allied bombing for propaganda purposes did little to turn French opinion against the Allies. Nevertheless, if 1940 had been a defeat, the prospect of Liberation raised fears of destruction, humiliation, and further decline.[8]

The fraying of public order as Vichy's legitimacy crumbled offered a second reason for concern. "Resistance was not merely personally perilous," concludes Paxton. "It was also a step toward social revolution."[9] In many rural areas, the appearance of *maquisards* announced that the government was losing its grip as public confidence frayed. And if Vichy were clearly headed for the exit, who or what would take its place? The future of the resistance, its status and role in a liberated France, remained undefined. All resistance forces, including the *maquis*, were amalgamated in February 1944 into the *Forces françaises de l'intérieur* (FFI), under Pierre Koenig, named chief of the FFI General Staff in April. The État-major des Forces françaises de l'intérieur

(EMFFI) had three purposes. The first was to control and channel a politicized and largely inchoate resistance for the ends of French policy. Its second goal was to elevate France's political status from that of a "minor ally" into a major player, as became apparent on 3 June 1944 when the CFLN transformed itself into the GPRF, a diplomatic upgrade that blindsided both London and Washington.[10] Third, the FFI aimed to increase the CFLN/GPRF's military clout, as well as its political standing, through the amalgamation of resistance volunteers to balloon de Gaulle's hitherto diminutive conventional military forces.

In these conditions, many, including the Anglo-Americans, feared that liberation might fling open the door to disorder, perhaps even civil war, that could compromise the military campaign to defeat Germany. As Koenig would join the Supreme Headquarters Allied Expeditionary Force (SHAEF) staff as the coordinator for resistance action in France, Eisenhower would be obliged to fold the FFI into Allied campaign plans. But Roosevelt's refusal to recognize the CFLN/GPRF meant that, on the eve of Overlord, Eisenhower still had been given no clear policy guidance on the political future of France.[11] So, Overlord would be launched with no official Allied decision on who would govern France, or with whom Allied soldiers must deal on the ground, only a series of ad hoc and ultimately fragile arrangements worked out on the military level. Faced with this "dangerous" policy vacuum, Eisenhower informed the Combined Chiefs of Staff that his only option was to deal with the "Committee of National Liberation."[12] But, "incredibly enough," writes Michael Neiberg, Roosevelt "seemed to believe that the Americans could still find a way to rid themselves of de Gaulle," because, upon liberation, "other political forces would naturally emerge and give the Americans options other than the GPRF or AMGOT [Allied Military Government of Occupied Territories]." Indeed, the American President's obstinate and apparently irrational hostility to de Gaulle, in the face of overwhelming evidence that he "has become the symbol of deliverance to the French people," baffled both Eisenhower and Stimson, as much as it did senior British officials, who wondered whether the Americans had not made "a secret agreement with Pétain and/or Laval," through one of Murphy's shady contacts like Lemaigre-Dubreuil.[13] Indeed, A. J. Liebling's resistance sources speculated that Liberation would witness the imposition of a pre-war appeaser not directly tainted by the "'later excesses' of the Vichy regime" on France, someone like Georges Bonnet or Camillle Chautemps.[14]

As D-Day approached, the resistance offered a clutter of strategic options in search of a plan. The Western Allies, including the Gaullists, began to fear that a "national insurrection" might slip out of control, and so preferred to narrow the concept in an attempt to strike a balance between "military requirements and political calculations." The objective of "Bloc Planning" became to "eliminate the myth of D-Day" by refining and controlling resistance action.[15] While the Western Allies continued to believe that some degree of popular rebellion against Vichy and the occupation would accompany D-Day, their preference clearly was for French people to remain spectators as Koenig's FFI operated as a disciplined military force in support of a conventional invasion. The Foreign Office feared a cascade of popular insurrection that would not only result in slaughter, but also benefit the communists. But, beyond these fears, no one really knew how events would unfold once the ramps on the Higgins boats splashed down on the Normandy beaches.

"The 'national insurrection' was thus a complex and evolving notion that referred to diverse political and military cultures, even specifically for France in the period of the Second World War," writes Raphaële Balu. While the concept of insurrection did not disappear from British strategy, it became "increasingly intertwined with the *maquis* in that [national insurrection] was understood as an autonomous, militarized action, capable of spreading to entire regions." The intention became that the "national insurrection" could be channeled by the interface services and the resistance organizations, of which the *maquis* was a component, "upon whom were conferred the responsibility for directing the action of the 'masses.'" The principal role of the resistance was to slow the movement of enemy forces, declared a 26 January 1944 Allied strategy paper. "But together with this, every *maquis* district must be prepared when called upon . . . to foment and support the uprisings of the civilian population." This expressed perfectly Churchill's vision for the *maquis* in the Alpine southeast, but not that of de Gaulle, who, having been burned once by the communists in Corsica, envisaged "a circumscribed insurrection, supervised and militarized under Gaullist command," consisting of strikes and sabotage in the workplace, the seizing by citizens of symbols of authority such as prefectures and town halls, and guerrilla action by the *maquis*, that in the eyes of some should exceed in nature and scope the mere sabotage of rail lines and communications.[16]

The Gaullists realized that, whatever military control they might exercise through the Comité d'action en France (COMIDAC or COMAC), the EMFFI, and the *Délégués militaires régionaux* (DMRs), political control resided with the resistance groups, the most powerful of which was the communist-led Francs-Tireurs et Partisans (FTP), backed by the Conseil national de la résistance (CNR) and COMAC, who intended to direct resistance action from Paris. For the communists, "national insurrection" as the centerpiece of Liberation had become a dogma, so that the fate of Glières could be rationalized only as the result of abandonment by an "*attentiste*" Bureau central de renseignements et d'action (BCRA). "National insurrection," when linked with the "immediate action" demanded by the communists, thus threatened Gaullist ability to control events on the Liberation. The fear in London was that the Germans would attempt to incite a "national insurrection" to destroy the resistance before D-Day. In a worst-case scenario, "national insurrection" might lead to a civil war that would require Allied intervention, and the imposition of the feared, if imaginary, AMGOT.

The problem for London was that communist calls for "immediate action" merely echoed those of the resistance, and even of the BCRA, which argued for sabotage as a preferred form of "immediate action." Of course, one of the main objectives of resistance-sponsored sabotage was to convince the Anglo-Americans to cut back on bombing to preserve French lives and infrastructure, which they mostly refused to do.[17] Furthermore, the Allies argued that premature sabotage could be quickly repaired, as well as reveal critical weaknesses to the Germans, and so sabotage should be closely timed with D-Day. The short-term solution was to strike a compromise that, while paying lip service to citizen participation in the Liberation, nevertheless circumscribed it within a military framework. In reality, this cautious pre-invasion strategy was derailed by pressure from the field as well as Churchill's push for stepped up arms deliveries to the *maquis*. At a minimum, this would lead to a reprise of Glières. At its worst, it might spark civil war.[18]

While the *maquis* had emerged spontaneously, several players sought to operationalize it for their own ends. For the communists, the resistance and the *maquis* were to provide the tinder for a "national insurrection" meant to cleanse France of Vichy elements and reforge society along more "democratic" lines, while *en passant* paving the path to power for the Parti communiste français (PCF). Nor were the communists alone – in early 1944, Commissariat national à l'Intérieur (CNI) director Emmanuel d'Astier, too, "remained convinced of the requirement for an insurrectionary period" as a purgative to cleanse France of Vichy collaboration, and as a cathartic event in the Storming of the Bastille tradition to consecrate the GPRF by popular acclamation.[19] As argued in the previous chapter, the Gaullist investment in the resistance had several objectives: to establish de Gaulle's democratic bona fides; to increase his leverage in the Alliance and gain a foothold in Allied planning for the liberation; to expand his conventional armed forces through a *levée en masse*; and, through *Plan Caïman*, to establish a potential third bridgehead in the Massif Central, separate from Overlord and Anvil/Dragoon, that would allow the GPRF to establish its legitimacy independently of an Allied military presence. For different reasons, Churchill, the Foreign Office, and the interface services had strenuously promoted the *maquis* cause in Whitehall, Washington, and at SHAEF in London and Allied Forces Headquarters (AFHQ) in Algiers. Now, the Allies must cash in on that investment.

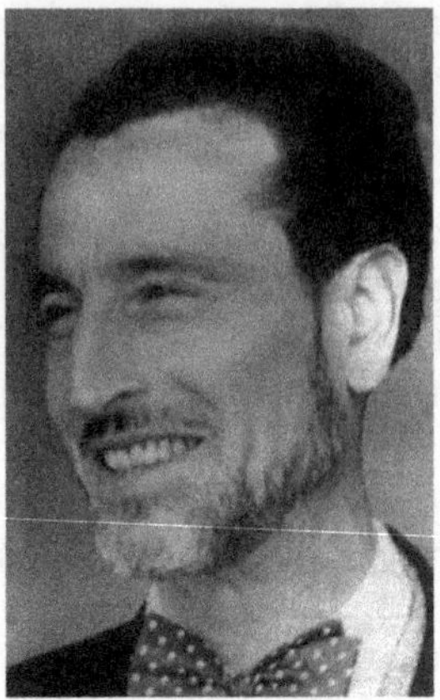

Figure 5.1 Emmanuel d'Astier de La Vigerie, Commissar national à l'Intérieur, later criticized as a principal purveyor of "resistentialist romanticism" who advocated for an "insurrectionary period" spearheaded by the FFI to speed Liberation, cleanse France of collaborators, and restore France's Republican purity. (Photo by Apic/Getty Images)

Planning for the Resistance

On 1 April 1944, de Gaulle insisted that "military action must now become the principal goal of the resistance." Emmanuel d'Astier (Figure 5.1) confirmed in May via clandestine courier that the CFLN expected "activism," and that orders would be given for arms to be distributed equitably according to the importance of the movements, "and not be determined by political considerations."[20] Indeed, to read de Gaulle's war memoirs, one would think that, by 6 June, the *maquis* practically had the Germans on the run, especially in the southeast: "Before the Allied armies set foot on our shore, the German was losing thousands of men," he recorded. "He is enveloped everywhere in an atmosphere of insecurity that undermines the morale of the troops and disorients his leaders." Through an avalanche of reports of resistance strikes, and of "cruel reprisals" carried out by the occupier, "one discerned to what degree the war in the interior had become effective."[21] That would have been news to the Germans. In fact, the SOE reproached the BCRA for being so preoccupied with establishing Gaullist political dominance that they neglected the military dimensions of liberation.[22] But, from the Gaullist viewpoint, the problem became how to mobilize the resistance on D-Day while avoiding civilian slaughter at the hands of the occupiers. Clearly, this required close coordination with Allied forces, a task complicated by at least two factors. First, the French were cut out of Allied planning. But while "the when and where" of Overlord and Anvil was not revealed to the French, Allied planners needed to be aware of French plans for the resistance/*maquis*/FFI. For this reason, and because the French were dependent on Allied arms and supplies, French plans for the *maquis* after D-Day were circulated within the Allied high command and folded into Allied calculations.

A second, and potentially more vexing, problem focused on coordination. Was the *maquis* to cooperate with regular forces as the British wanted, operate in its own sphere "behind the lines" as envisaged by the Americans, or spearhead a uniquely French political agenda, creating "*réduits maquisards*" and "*maquis mobilisateurs*" over which the GPRF could proclaim its sovereignty? But the French camp was far from united, as the CFLN, through the interface services, struggled to convince the Allies to arm the resistance as a means to leverage resistance participation to gain access to Allied planning in SHAEF (UK) and AFHQ (Algiers), while attempting through COMIDAC and Koenig's EMFFI to assert its political and tactical control over a collection of politicized resistance condottieri. Between January and April 1944, Bloc Planning shouldered the task of creating a doctrine for the utilization of "the army behind the lines." This group produced ten studies that sought to coordinate resistance action with the advances of Allied forces from D-Day, relying on the assumption that the Battle for France would require four to six months of combat. Therefore, in opposition to communist calls for a spontaneous and full-blown "national insurrection," Bloc Planning advocated a phased engagement to preserve the resistance, that initially prioritized sabotage of communications, and eventually of munitions and petrol depots, with the goal of closing down "the national economy."[23] In the meantime, "*maquis mobilisateurs*," supervised by cadres parachuted into France, would collect arms, organize resistance, and train reserves to carry out guerrilla action to assist the advance forces.[24]

An "Instruction" drawn up in March 1944 by General Secretary of the Comité de défense nationale (CDN) Colonel Pierre Billotte, and approved by de Gaulle on 5 April, insisted that, because of its "great weakness," the FFI must acknowledge the authority of COMIDAC in Algiers over resistance operations. "A general, reckless uprising" was to be avoided in favor of an operation that would be "controlled, progressive, and measured, and closely coordinated with conventional forces." De Gaulle's 5 April definition of "national insurrection" as a prolonged, phased, and controlled process predictably earned the denunciation of communist-dominated COMAC in Paris as "*attentiste*."[25] But the "Instruction" was also ambiguous, because it recommended that it might be possible "progressively to mature a general insurrection in the Dauphiné–Savoie–southern Jura," as Allied operations progressed, denying these departments to the enemy and forcing them to use the Rhône corridor, where they were constantly to be harassed. In the north, only Paris and its immediate suburbs might host a general insurrection, whose FFI must protect bridges and, at the appropriate moment, seize airfields for immediate use by the Allies.[26]

So, while everyone expected "military action" from the FFI from D-Day, the difference was that London sought a "controlled" escalation of FFI activity, coordinating insurgent action with geographical zones defined by the advance of Allied armies, and gradually building in scale as the Wehrmacht was attrited and pushed back. This phased approach reflected the message that Chief of the *Service national maquis* Michel Brault had delivered in London from early 1944, namely that the *maquis* was too diminutive, too poorly armed, and too inadequately trained to liberate great swaths of territory. The problem was that the FFI was treated by Bloc Planning and eventually the EMFFI as a regular, hierarchically organized military force, able to respond to concise orders.[27] The strong message of *maquis* weakness, reinforced by the experience of Glières, should have invited caution. But Brault's plain-spoken and pessimistic assessments of *maquis* capabilities and his criticism of the communists, who were ideologically committed to the concept of the *maquis* as the *avant garde* of national insurrection, turned the resistance against him. Emmanuel d'Astier, who boasted that 30,000 fully armed and trained *maquis* stood ready for action in the Alpes, undermined Brault's more realistic estimates. Brault's assessment that the *maquis* was incapable of defending "*réduits*" and that "*maquis mobilisateurs*" were a non-starter upset the strategies of the BCRA and deflated those who had bet their future on *Plans Montagnards/Vidal* and *Caïman*, as well as Churchill, who counted on an Alpine Yugoslavia to torpedo Anvil/Dragoon. Finally, de Gaulle distrusted Brault as a cosmopolitan Parisian brief far too cozy with "les Anglo-Saxons, " with whom he freely shared his measured assessments of *maquis* capabilities. As a result, Brault found his *Service national maquis* dismantled when Koenig's EMFFI was stood up in April 1944. He reverted to his rank as reserve captain in the Air Force, and a desk was found for him in the *commissariat à l'Air*, where he became a fervent advocate of S-phones so that the *maquis* on the ground could speak directly to pilots of Lysanders and Hudsons. But, on the cusp of D-Day, those clandestine days were over. Brault was eventually parachuted over Beauvais on the night of 6–7 June, no doubt to clear him out of the front office and consign him to historical oblivion.[28]

By D-Day, "the Resistance" had muscled its way into Allied calculations as the French contribution to the Liberation. Those who expressed reservations about "*réduits*," concepts blessed by such resistance luminaries as Frenay, Moulin, and Delestraint, were branded "*attentistes*," the scarlet letter of the internal resistance.[29] Optimism remained *l'attitude du jour et de rigeur*. Of course, in early 1944, the Allies were trying to play the hand they had been dealt. The spontaneous *maquis* phenomenon had placed a severe strains on a resistance edifice that had been laboriously negotiated in 1942–1943 by Moulin and Brossolette. For reasons of politics and prestige, de Gaulle had determined that the French people must partake in their own Liberation.[30] The resistance had acquired powerful spokesmen in leaders like Henry Frenay, Emmanuel d'Astier, and a claque of communists brought into the CFLN as a way to control them, as well as in the interface services, and – last but not least – the British Prime Minister. Even Eisenhower admitted that "we were depending on considerable assistance from the insurrectionists in France. They were known to be particularly numerous in the Britanny [sic] area and in the hills and mountains of southeast France. An open clash with De Gaulle [sic] on this matter would hurt us immeasurably and would result in bitter recrimination and unnecessary loss of life . . . We had already, with the consent of our governments, accepted De Gaulle's representative, General Koenig, as the commander of the French forces of the Interior, who was serving as a direct subordinate of mine in the Allied organization."[31]

Intelligence reports, some of them "wildly inaccurate," indicated that insurgent warfare had already proven its worth in the east.[32] Early failures, as at Glières, could be explained by invoking poor command decisions on the ground. The calculation was that, once the Allied invasion had been launched, the Germans would be too stretched to quell a prudent and phased FFI uprising. From the spring of 1943, the SOE had laid plans for guerrilla action on a vast scale, with the assistance of paratroop reinforcements dropped into *réduits maquisards*. In April 1944, the Citronnelle Mission parachuted into the Ardennes with the task of delineating drop zones for an airborne division as well as gliders carrying heavy weapons. *Plan Montagnards* looked to transform le Vercors into "an entry for airborne troops and material to attack the enemy rear." In fact, instead of skies filled with constellations of white billows in the slipstream of flotillas of C-47 Skytrains, or the swish and rattle of gliders importing heavy weapons, all the Allies could spare for the *maquis* from D-Day was a paltry fifteen three-man Jedburgh teams and nine OSS Operational Groups (OGs).[33]

On 16 May, de Gaulle issued an "instruction" that refined Billotte's earlier plan by designating more precise objectives, and emphasizing the chain of command to which the FFI were to respond. In his memoirs, de Gaulle explained that these initial goals focused on sabotage, both because the FFI lacked arms and because "the Allied command envisaged with a certain distrust the extension of guerrilla warfare."[34] But Crémieux-Brilhac insisted that the updated 16 May directive was influenced by an accelerating program of air drops which ought to give the FFI more punch, as well as the growing conviction in French ranks that a second landing would occur sooner rather than later on France's Mediterranean coast. Also attached to what Crémieux-Brilhac describes as the 16 May "operations order" was a twenty-page summary of *Plan Caïman*, which specified "decisive action" that targeted the liberation of "the southwest-center zone" and "the block Savoie–Dauphiné–southern Jura." Although it is not clear whether *Caïman* was included when the May "instruction" was communicated to the DMRs,[35] it had certainly circulated among Allied planners, whose jousts with *la France libre* since 1940 had sensitized them to the political agenda of Gaullist military proposals. Lieutenant General James Gammell immediately spotted the CFLN's inverted priorities and *Caïman*'s political dimensions: "This plan gives the impression that plan Overlord must support the French resistance, i.e. draw off enemy armor from the liberated zones, and not the inverse," reported Maitland Wilson's chief of staff (COS) on 2 June 1944. After noting that *Caïman* was far too ambitious for the resistance to carry out, he also cautioned that "One must be aware of *Plan Caïman*'s political implications, in that the French are visibly anxious to establish a liberated zone in which the government of the CFLN would be unchallenged. It is obvious that this objective is more of a concern to them than giving assistance to Overlord." Nevertheless, no doubt aware of Churchill's preferences, Gammell conceded that, once the major objectives of Overlord had been met, the Allies could make an effort to recreate "'Balkan conditions' in the south of France, leading to the liberation of entire zones. The objective will be to create a major diversion in the enemy rear." But, given the weakness of the *maquis*, and the fact that air support might not become available, the Allies insisted that "*réduits*" and "*maquis mobilisateurs*" be kept to a relatively few sites of modest geographical dimensions, which happened in any case due to lack of men and weapons.[36]

So, Franco-Allied negotiations determined that *Caïman*'s immediate priority was to be Brittany, and resistance activity must focus on the *zone nord* directly to support conventional operations. As a consequence, Béthouart declared the *zone nord* the "decisive" theater where sabotage operations would be prioritized. And yet, planners were aware that guerrilla activity might also develop in the center-southwest, while FFI in the south-southeast might be able to inhibit communications along the Rhône–Nîmes–Alès–Carcassonne–Toulouse axis. Region 1 – essentially the Alpine center-east – could witness the development of "*grandes guerrillas*." "However, one must not lose sight of the fact that these actions could develop spontaneously in certain parts of France at any moment, independently of our control – and in these circumstances, it will be necessary to support them as much as possible."[37]

On 21 May, Manuel messaged the *délégation générale clandestine* to "apply the brakes on a national insurrection." But the concept was too far advanced and had too many advocates to "brake" at short notice. COMAC had already announced in early May 1944 that it planned for the FFI to liberate zones *before* Allied armies arrived. Although the political agendas of COMAC and de Gaulle were at cross purposes, strategically speaking, in its two versions, *Caïman* also looked to liberate French zones of sovereignty beyond Allied control.[38] This did not differ appreciably from the intentions of the communists, who advocated "immediate action" in the pursuit of a "national insurrection." Bloc Planning simply sought to reformulate and redefine the "national insurrection" into a series of progressive local uprisings that ought to spare lives and advance a Gaullist, rather than a communist, ascendency as on Corsica.[39]

But a phased approach presented multiple challenges, beginning with the fact that it ran counter to the pre-liberation *Zeitgeist*, inspired in part by a vigorous BBC propaganda operation. But it was also enthusiastically promoted by CNI director Emmanuel d'Astier, scion of a truly unconventional family, who began his career as a naval officer and, after dabbling in various occupations that included song writer, a flit through the resistance, and a marriage to the daughter of the first Soviet ambassador to France, became a dedicated communist and recipient of the Lenin Prize, before subsequently denouncing communism. Nor, as Glières had demonstrated, did "immediate action" appear a theoretical concept to *maquisards*, who were the targets of a brutal campaign of repression spearheaded by *la Milice* and the *Groupe mobile de réserve* (GMR) in partnership with occupation forces. Billotte's "instruction" also failed to address the delicate question of how a strategy of phased engagement was to be calibrated over distance, through an ill-defined command structure peopled by resistance warlords, whose communications with the CFLN/GPRF hierarchy were at best intermittent. The FTP's adherence to the FFI's chain of command was purely hypothetical. The FFI technically fell under Koenig at EMFFI, which did not become fully operational until July 1944. According to the historian of the SOE M. R. D. Foot – himself an SAS intelligence officer parachuted into Brittany in August 1944, where he was severely beaten and left for dead by French peasants, before being captured and tortured by the Germans – nor was the EMFFI accorded much respect in SHAEF. Indeed, in Ike's headquarters (HQ), the EMFFI was viewed as a cosmetic command addendum that had been stood up for political reasons, commanded by a French "general" whose principal claim to fame was a skirmish in the Western Desert that most Allied officers had never heard of. Many of the BCRAL's old hands who actually had first-hand knowledge of the resistance, like Brault, who was cubbyholed in a back-office job with the air force, and even Passy, named Koenig's COS for the FFI, were sidelined. Complaints continued that the BCRA was being encumbered with "incompetent" superannuated majors and colonels, castoffs from depots and regiments, even "traitors" who, Gaullists insisted, should be made to sign loyalty oaths. Meanwhile, the amalgamation of Giraudists and Gaullists into the Direction générale des services spéciaux (DGSS) under Soustelle, an academic out of his league in intelligence work, in effect amounted to a hostile takeover by the Giraudist secret service, which destroyed any "esprit d'équipe." Infighting in the French intelligence services, as well as hostility to the BCRA among many resisters, caused the SOE, as well as Harold Macmillan, to conclude that the French were not interested in military cooperation but "only in the political future of France."[40] Meanwhile, urgent requests for arms and munitions from FFI networks languished unanswered, "in the day-to-day telephone and teleprinter chaos of EMFFI ... Many of the French were so deeply concerned with the political future of France that they found it hard to concentrate on their unfamiliar daily tasks," concluded Foot.[41]

Foot's evaluation of EMFFI's inefficiency may be too severe, but probably not – himself an officer in the post-war Royal Marines and Military Intelligence 6 (MI6), Paddy Ashdown too judged Koenig's EMFFI to have been "famously dysfunctional."[42] BCRA historian Sébastien Albertelli also describes the establishment of a "tripartite and with French predominance" EMFFI as "slow and chaotic," as Gaullist reservists were elbowed aside by "Giraudist" regulars, further roiling already politicized competition within French intelligence services.[43] It was unclear from whom EMFFI was to take orders, and to whom EMFFI should transmit orders, especially because it had to deal with two chains of command – AFHQ/Special Forces Headquarters (SFHQ) under Maitland Wilson in Algiers, which claimed to control southern France, and Ike's SHAEF in London for the north.[44] Hierarchically, while EMFFI fell under the SHAEF G3 (Operations), it had little input into operations. Among the "political and military" reasons for naming Koenig "commander of the French resistance" was Eisenhower's desire to prevent Churchill from meddling in resistance operations for his own nefarious ends through the SOE. For this reason, on 30 May, Eisenhower assigned authority over all SOE and OSS agents, 265 Jedburghs, 18 SAS missions, the 20 OGs, and 26 Inter-Allied Missions operating in France to Koenig.[45] This was regarded as a disaster in the SOE, one that transgressed the basically civilian character of covert operations and of the resistance networks in France. Not only did Koenig and his EMFFI staff lack special operations experience, but also, since Dakar in 1940, the French labored under the stigma of being an intelligence sieve, which further threatened the incorporation of SOE operations into Allied planning.[46] This caused the British to complain that Ike had demoted the SOE to a "logistical agency between the FFI and the War Office."[47] Passy took his demotion in this new scheme to act basically as a liaison officer between Koenig and the BCRAL badly. He quarreled so frequently with Koenig's new COS "Colonel Vernon" – real name Henri Ziegler, a thirty-eight-year-old Polytechnician and pilot who, until his eleventh-hour February 1944 defection, had worked in Vichy's air ministry – that in August Koenig parachuted the former BCRA chief into Brittany on what Manuel categorized as a "useless" mission.[48]

The complexity of EMFFI's organizational chart offered a tip-off that Koenig's job was largely "symbolic," and that in practice COMAC saw itself as a command division at least coequal with Algiers, with its own staff structure, one replicated on each regional level. One consequence of decentralization was that the EMFFI's "feeble pulse" actually strengthened the embrace of the communists over an internal resistance whose leadership was temperamentally and politically disinclined to execute orders from London in any case. Of course, the resistance was unified insofar as the goal of its members was Liberation. While Bloc Planning had evolved a three-phased intervention scheme for the FFI as Allied troops progressed from their bridgeheads, a large slice of the internal resistance and those who spontaneously would rally to it, impatient to participate in the long-anticipated liberation, was primed for a D-Day jumpstart.[49]

SHAEF expected the FFI to behave as a regular army, rather than respect its true nature as a loose aggregation of insurgent bands under very autonomous leaders. Koenig's ambition was to transform the FFI into a disciplined force, complete with courts martial to punish desertion and so on, while de Gaulle insisted in vain that they be treated by the Germans as regular combatants with Geneva protections. Of course, this suited a Gaullist political agenda that sought to strengthen the CFLN's control over communist elements in the resistance, swell France's direct military contribution to the Liberation, and sever contact between the FFI and the SOE/OSS. But the CFLN could never define the combatant status of the FFI, while Berlin would never acknowledge a motley of resisters and *Service du travail obligatoire* (STO) truants as legal combatants so long as Vichy remained France's legal government. Koenig's attempts to tighten control over his rebellious flock rekindled the old centralization versus decentralization debates of 1943, got pushback from the field, and annoyed the Allied interface services upon which the CFLN depended for resources and communications with the resistance. So, while the *maquisards* might see themselves as a *levée en masse*, lineal descendants of the patriotic "volunteers of the Year II," an imperial bias caused Algiers to view *maquisards* as a metropolitan version of *goumiers* – that is, tribal levies recruited on a contractual basis for non-conventional battlefield tasks, whose legal status remained vague and whose disciplinary parameters were rather elastic, except that *maquisards* had neither a contract nor a daily stipend. A 9 June 1944 ordinance thus categorized FFI as "partially assimilated" soldiers.[50] For their part, the Germans continued to denounce FFI actions as "gang or terrorist activities," so that they were under no obligation to accord prisoner of war (POW) status to captured FFI.[51]

A central point of Balu's thesis is that, rather than neglect or sacrifice the *maquis*/FFI as the communists later claimed, the Allies made every effort to fold the resistance and the *maquis*, amalgamated into the FFI, into operational planning for D-Day at all levels of the military hierarchy, the planning staffs, and the interface services. And, although this decision was taken in London and Algiers, that process was not a uniquely top-down one, but rather one that required an interaction and negotiations between emissaries, agents, missions, and resistance leaders on the ground to gain information about the *maquis* and transfer that knowledge back to London, and then to build a command infrastructure to mobilize and militarize it. "As the *maquis* melded into the FFI, their relations with *la France libre* and the Allies inscribed themselves more than ever in a dual context of the resistance and combined operations," writes Balu. "They continued to require a unique strategic approach, which was debated and refined during the first semester of 1944."[52]

Despite this, the charge that the Allies intentionally sacrificed the *maquis* became a core indictment of both communist and Vichy propaganda, one etched into French memory of the war. But, while both camps ardently promoted this myth of Allied betrayal, neither the communists nor Vichy propagandist and part-time *Milicien* Philippe Henriot had invented it. Rather, they deftly marketed for their own ends a widespread feeling of abandonment and neglect that gripped the *maquisards* as the highly anticipated invasion of the mainland stalled in the wake of Torch, repression intensified, and they faced a winter–spring of 1943–1944 as men stalked by *Sturmführer* Joseph Darnand's *milice* and the Germans, desperate for

Allied rescue. A 12 January 1944 report, probably written by Brault, who had newly arrived in London via Spain, informed the CFLN that, unless steps were taken to alleviate the "tragic" situation of the *maquisards*, "the entire country would feel a deep bitterness that could turn against Algiers and the Anglo-Saxon Allies," a warning repeated in other reports from the front.[53]

Churchill had kickstarted a program of *maquis* armament in the southeast on 27 January 1944. Eisenhower understood the importance of associating the French through the CFLN and the EMFFI with planning for the Liberation, as did British and US diplomats in the interest of future diplomatic relations with Paris. The entire point of the SOE – as well as the OSS, not to mention the BCRA – in Foot's view, had been to stimulate and structure "the French will to resist."[54] Of course, Allied planning mechanisms were cumbersome, multilayered, bureaucratic, and dispersed in multiple staffs scattered between SHAEF in London and AFHQ in Algiers. Their calculations were shaped by important logistical, strategic, political, and diplomatic constraints. For the RAF and the USAAF, dropping weapons to fugitives scattered in the French Alpes, Brittany, and the Massif Central figured near the bottom of their priority lists. Regular soldiers quite rightly and responsibly expressed skepticism about the military capabilities of the FFI and tried to reign in the expansion of "*réduits maquis*" mustering on battlefields imagined by Alpine romantics, communist ideologues, and Balkan mimics. Many Allied staff officers confronted by these schemes had actually been in combat against the Wehrmacht. And even if the Germans had dedicated only eight "– admittedly about the worst eight – of their sixty-odd divisions in France to hold down their rear areas while OVERLORD was going on,"[55] they could literally make mincemeat of the largely children's crusade, and their adult enablers, which defined the *maquis*. The ability of Allied – including French – planners to reduce the gaps between *maquis* concepts and actual capabilities was circumscribed by politics, ideology, ignorance, pride, and desperation. For probably the first time in modern warfare, the Allies were attempting to integrate an insurgent element into planning for regular operations. That this "national insurrection" would scar French memory of the war was in retrospect entirely foreseeable.[56]

Operationalizing "National Insurrection"

"With hindsight, one can ask if the key to the drama doesn't lie in the disproportion between political ambition and the military means?," Muracciole inquires of France's resistance effort.[57] On the eve of Overlord, Eisenhower and SHAEF planners envisaged a phased, coordinated FFI cooperation that would assist an Allied advance, although they were unsure how to control it. Eisenhower's preference was for the "passive resistance" of the French population. The CFLN's priority was to establish a government before a "settling of scores" could erupt. The Foreign Office feared that a popular insurrection would open the door to a communist power grab.[58] But, on the eve of D-Day, confusion reigned over whether resistance mobilization should be "general" or "phased," whether it should consist solely of sabotage or include "guerrilla warfare," and whether "redoubts" were sanctioned by Allied planners. This was largely as a result of a 21 May SHAEF meeting that decreed that all resistance groups throughout France, and not just in the north as originally planned, should "put their general guerrilla plan into effect." Koenig and Brigadier Eric Mockler-Ferryman, SOE's operations chief for Western Europe, agreed on 25 May to defer the decision on resistance mobilization to Eisenhower.[59]

As seen, the 26 May proclamation in Algiers of the GPRF, simply added another complication to D-Day planning. On 3 June, Mockler-Ferryman and his OSS equivalent Joe Haskell called on Bedell Smith, Eisenhower's COS, in Portsmouth to ask for a decision on resistance mobilization. At 04:00 on 4 June, Eisenhower opted for a "national insurrection," reasoning that the narrow margins for Overlord success required it. Had the Germans been confronted by resistance sabotage solely in the north, he reasoned, they would have realized that Overlord was not a diversion but the main attack, and so would concentrate their forces there. "If the cost Eisenhower had to pay to keep his enemy off-balance was the destruction of a few Resistance networks, then that was a price he was prepared to pay," concluded Ashworth, in a statement that reinforces the communist thesis of an intentional Allied sacrifice of the *maquis*.[60] Of course, Ike's green light for "national insurrection" upended phased resistance action meant better to align insurgency with the progress of conventional operations. But, in Balu's view, the onus for the military failure and subsequent slaughter of "national insurrection" may also be shared by the interface services. "In this inexplicable way," concludes Balu, Gubbins and Mockler-Ferryman of the SOE and David Bruce of the OSS, "who for several years had awaited their big show . . . perhaps instrumentalized" Eisenhower's insecurities. It is also possible that the Anglo-American interface services wanted to get in front of a resistance wave that they had concluded would surge in any case. Confronted by his American superior's last-minute decision, chief of the EMFFI Koenig had no choice but to acquiesce.[61]

In his memoirs, Eisenhower makes no mention of this last-minute intervention by the interface services, but expressly states that he wished to avoid an FFI "uprising and useless sacrifice at non-critical points." In the event, he actually triggered them. The launch of Overlord was accompanied by a swirl of last-minute tensions, events, and decisions – attempts to abort the drop of two airborne divisions on the Cotentin Peninsula; last-minute visits to troops poised to embark; refusing requests by Churchill to be allowed to accompany the invasion fleet; the weather upon which the date and time of Overlord's launch hinged; and de Gaulle's stubborn 4 June refusal to broadcast to the French people a script handed him by Eisenhower. Given this environment, it may be that the decision at 04:00 on 4 June to jettison five months of Bloc Planning and staff discussion about how to avoid an FFI massacre became a detail he failed to recollect.[62] Or it may have been, as Ashworth speculates, that invasion casualties were expected to be high in any case. So, the possibility of diverting even a few German forces to smother a "national insurrection" was viewed as a small price to pay.

In this reading, Eisenhower's volte-face sought to spread confusion about whether the Normandy beachhead was the main invasion site, or a diversion to draw in German troops for an amphibious Allied *Schwerpunkt* in the Pas de Calais. The resistance was considered a "bonus," and not critical to the success of the invasion. Therefore, the FFI might serve a greater purpose as a diversion. A problem with this speculation is that, strategically, Eisenhower's go ahead for a "national insurrection" made no sense. The primary Allied deception plan – Operation Fortitude South – had sought to make the Germans believe that the Allies had more troops in the UK than was actually the case. In this scenario, Normandy would be seen as an attempt to cause the Germans to commit their armored divisions, that then would be unavailable to counter the main invasion in the Pas de Calais. Calling for the activation of *réduits maquisards* in the south, therefore, did nothing to support the primary Allied deception plan. This thesis is reinforced by the fact that Eisenhower was actively guided – indeed, required – to take this decision by SOE and OSS representatives, who had a huge institutional, ideological, and personal investment in "national insurrection." Passy and Koenig were informed of this interface service coup at 17:30 on 5 June – that is, after the invasion fleet had sailed. Passy claimed that he protested. But the silence of de Gaulle and Koenig implied assent.[63] As a consequence, the BBC began to diffuse the 200 "personal messages" to the resistance from 21:15 on the night of 5 June. Potentially, this should have alerted the Germans that the invasion was approaching. And, indeed, the German Fifteenth Army, which occupied the Pas de Calais down to the river Dives just east of Caen, believed that these messages heralded an imminent assault. However, neither the Seventh Army occupying Brittany and the Cotentin Peninsula where the invasion force would land, nor the German naval authorities, nor the Oberkommando der Wehrmacht (OKW) West was convinced that increased radio traffic necessarily offered a cause for alarm. Therefore, the Allied landings achieved strategic surprise, despite the tip-off call for *l'insurrection nationale*.[64]

Ashdown insists that de Gaulle also bears some of the responsibility.[65] While the French leader's 6 June address over the BBC is regarded as among his greatest wartime orations, read as an operations order, it was also ambiguous. After announcing the initiation of "the supreme battle," de Gaulle ordered that,

"For the sons of France, wherever they may be, whoever they may be, the simple and sacred duty is to fight the enemy by all means available. The directives given by the French government . . . must be followed to the letter . . . It's a question of destroying the enemy, the enemy that crushes and soils the Fatherland, the detested and dishonored enemy . . . Behind the heavy clouds of our blood and our tears, the sunshine of our grandeur is reemerging."[66] True, Crémieux-Brilhac concedes. But de Gaulle's call to arms included numerous qualifiers, that also emphasized that the duty of the resistance was to persist: "Everyone must realize that the action of the armies will be difficult and long. Which means that the action of Resistance forces must last, then ramp up until the moment of the German defeat." De Gaulle's nuance was lost on most resistance leaders, many listening as his directives crackled into their clandestine hiding places through Axis jamming and background noise, who were surprised by a call for a "national insurrection," when they had been indoctrinated into the need for phased mobilization and prudent action. It seems that de Gaulle went along with the idea of a general uprising. "It is true that, the same day [6 June], I implored them on the contrary to fight with all the means in their power, following the orders given them by the French command," de Gaulle conceded in his memoirs. "But arms deliveries depended on the Allied command and remained limited. It is above all sabotage of the railways, the roads, the communications, the importance of which was critical, that was the concern of the 'combined chiefs of staff.'"[67] One consequence of the broadcasts was a *maquis* groundswell, as hitherto small, ad hoc FFI formations mushroomed with enthusiastic recruits itching to "liberate" their towns and villages and take the fight to the Germans. By 10 June, Koenig tried to slam on the brakes, proliferating secret telegrams that urged "Curb guerrilla activity. It is impossible for the moment to resupply arms and munitions in sufficient quantities. Break off contact everywhere possible to allow reorganization. Avoid large concentrations. Break into small, isolated groups."[68]

But the communist-controlled COMAC in Paris diffused a contrary message, one that echoed de Gaulle's accusation that the Western Allies plotted to hasten France's decline as a world power: "Only the National Insurrection, liberating the national soil as completely and as rapidly as possible, can avoid the devastation and slaughter of France by a more or less slow progression of Allied forces, so that she will be weakened for decades, and drop to the rank of a second-tier nation." And, in a blow to phased escalation, it proclaimed that "The National Insurrection cannot succeed without the masses . . . Insurrection can't be adjusted like a musical score." De Gaulle's 6 June broadcast had inadvertently reinforced the COMAC message. The result, in the view of Crémieux-Brilhac, "amidst the confusion of contradictory initiatives and divergent views, of rivalries and dramas of the time, was a polarized national memory over the success of the resistance . . . that retained the image of an intentional and successful national insurrection."[69]

The Collapse of the *réduits maquisards*

Despite the debate over who was responsible for the costly *maquis* uprising after D-Day – the last-minute green light given by Eisenhower in the early morning of 4 June; de Gaulle's inspiring call to arms that caused resisters to ignore its qualifiers; command confusion between Algiers and the EMFFI; the machinations of the interface services; or an ideological commitment to the "national insurrection" by resistance leaders led by the communists – in many respects "national insurrection" had been baked into French plans. The point of *Plans Montagnards/Vidal* and *Caïman*, after all, was to stimulate "Balkan conditions" in the south of France that could create chaos "behind enemy lines," lead to the pre-D-Day liberation of entire zones, and provide a foundation for the establishment of French sovereignty. National Defense COS Antoine Béthouart was among those who understood that, at a minimum without Allied air support, guerrilla action from *réduits maquisards* could not succeed – this seemed to be the most basic lesson from Glières.[70] But the self-assumed autonomy of the local leaders was the most salient characteristic of resistance, one reinforced by command decentralization, confusing organizational charts that were largely meaningless in the regions, and Bloc Planning schemas refined by Allied staffs in Algiers and London that, while perhaps prodigies of general staff housekeeping, ignored local conditions and failed to factor in popular expectations. The major mechanisms of control for the CFLN/GPRF ran through the DMRs and the radio. The counterweight was COMAC, that might encourage local leaders to interpret Koenig's directives broadly and seek to short-circuit the authority of the DMRs, who were resented as drive-by busybodies and, in any case, were thin on the ground. Resistance chiefs, continually forced to improvise, might use their SOE or OSS agents to radio for an arms delivery without going through "channels," so that the interface services became enablers, not just on the SHAEF level, but also for a string of local uprisings. De Gaulle's subsequent hostility to SOE agents on the ground, often decried as simply another example of the General's ungracious lack of appreciation for Allied assistance, in fact was bound up with his efforts to reign in independent-minded resistance chiefs who harbored their own political agendas *à la Corse*.

After Glières, Mont Mouchet in the Auvergne, at 6,000 men the largest of the "*grand maquis*," was the second significant "*réduit maquis*" to implode. This disaster was purely of local manufacture. In April 1944, Émile Coulaudon, a thirty-seven-year-old native of Clermont-Ferrand who had formed a successful resistance group in the Auvergne in 1943, decided, with the accord of SOE operatives, to call for a mobilization of the *maquis* in three "*réduits*" around Mont Mouchet (Zone R5 on Map 4.2). The 20 May mobilization call exceeded his wildest expectations, bringing in 5,000–6,000 volunteers. On 25 May and 9 June, the SOE team arranged for fifty tons of arms to be dropped. But, on 10 June, Brigadier Kurt von Jesser assembled a 4,000-man *Kampfgruppe* that included an *Ostbataillone* made up of Azerbaijanis and Volga Tartars, together with Sicherheitspolizei (Sipo)/Sicherheitsdienst (SD) and interrogation teams. This force, supported by *Stukas*, converged on Mont Mouchet. In the opening clash, 130 or so defenders were killed and the rest put to flight, initiating a predictably murderous clean-up operation that continued for most of the month.[71]

Such scenes were repeated on an almost industrial scale, especially in the Alpine southeast, and in central and southern France, where news of the D-Day landings had put the population, led by the communists, in a bold mood. At Grenoble, young men were urged to "get up to the [le Vercors] plateau." Barcelonnette, a small town 175 kilometers southwest of Grenoble, was seized from its German garrison by local *maquisards*, who promptly raised the tricolor over the town hall, and proclaimed their municipality a "Free Republic." Roman-Petit's *maquis* "liberated" Nantua and Oyonnax in l'Ain. Local resistance leaders, agents, and Jedburghs parachuted into France reported with practically paschal fervor that their regions "had risen," whereupon these reports were aggregated into exhilarated SOE communiques. And while it might appear as if the "national insurrection" had begun, in fact, these reports were often simply a reaction to the "crystallization" of opinion in the wake of D-Day, and a surge of volunteers for the *maquis*. Public opinion swung violently against the FFI once German reprisals began. In fact, on 20 June, the German High Command reported "no serious disturbances" in areas of "long-occupied France," meaning presumably the former *zone occupée*.[72]

Retribution was swift. Perhaps the most notorious and chilling murders were carried out by the *2. SS-Panzerdivision* "*Das Reich*," which was recuperating near Toulouse from three years of Eastern Front casualty-heavy combat that had included the winter battle for Moscow in 1941–1942, fighting in winter–spring 1943 around Kharkiv in Ukraine, and the Kursk offensive in the summer of 1943. Upon receiving news of the D-Day landings, the unit was ordered to head north for Normandy. After a major in the division was kidnapped and killed by a resistance group, the unit launched a retaliatory rampage, committing numerous atrocities, most notoriously at Tulle and Oradour-sur-Glane, where 642 inhabitants of both sexes and all ages were murdered, and the village was destroyed.[73] Of the ten largest massacres carried out by the Germans in the summer of 1944 in France, led by Oradour, nine were perpetuated by the *Schutzstaffel* (SS) or Sipo/SD. Peter Lieb argues that massacres usually required four pre-requisites: Nazi ideology; membership in an elite unit; experience on the Eastern Front; and involvement in anti-partisan operations.[74] One scholar has estimated that German forces carried out 6,800 massacres – defined as "summary executions and massacres of more than five persons" – in France between D-Day and November 1944.[75] Through these methods of savage reprisals both against *maquisards* and against the civilian population, the ephemeral "*République libre de Barcelonnette*" was back in German hands by the middle of June, forming, together with Glières and Mont Mouchet, "the third costly failure of the redoubt strategy," Ashdown calculated.[76]

Rape and "sexual mutilation" were also deployed by the Germans as an "*arme de guerre*." Many of the atrocities, including rape, are attributed to *Ostbataillonen*. Indeed, Balu wonders why, when scholars have chronicled the sexual violence inflicted by Allied armies, German rapes in France has been accorded so little historical attention.[77] Perhaps one reason is because the level of German retaliatory violence against the French population in reaction to *maquis* acts was so extreme and sustained that sexual violence became lost in the mix. Also, sexual violence went largely unpunished, even encouraged, in the German forces for institutional, legal, ideological, and systemic reasons. "Rape was viewed as a minor offense in line with the idealized notions masculinity nurtured in the almost exclusively male Wehrmacht and SS," writes Sabine Frühstück. The military priority was to maintain fighting strength, so that sexual violence was punished only if it threatened good order and discipline. Legally, the woman had to file a complaint, which seldom happened, or perhaps such complaints were seldom registered. Raping "non-Aryan" women of "inferior race" was not considered a crime, although French women had a better chance of success did those in the East. "Rape was also a form of aggression that structured the everyday life of the occupation," from sexual slavery in military brothels and concentration camps, to an interrogation technique regularly used by the Gestapo and Sipo/SD.[78]

Le Vercors

After Glières, followed by Mont Mouchet, the concept of "natural fortresses" that anchored *Plan Montagnards* lay in tatters, as did any hope envisioned in *Plan Caïman* for the Gaullists to slip into France through a "strategic redoubt" side door held ajar by the *maquis*. On 20 June, SHAEF began to receive requests to support le Vercors, which caused London to enquire why *maquisards* in the south were mobilizing. The SOE's Mockler-Ferryman blamed Algiers for secretly ordering the mobilization, a reasonable supposition given that, in May, Eugène Chavant, a local socialist politician who had been named the "*chef civil* " of the *maquis* of le Vercors, had traveled to Algiers to receive assurance from the Special Project Operations Center (SPOC) that 4,000 paratroopers stood poised to reinforce his "*réduit maquisard*." But the truth was that the French in Algiers had little clout in Maitland Wilson's AFHQ. This was in part because de Gaulle's view that cooperation with the Allies should never compromise French sovereignty meant that increasingly the French were not accepted fully as members of the Allied command team. Meanwhile,

Gaullist interest had increasingly focused on *Caïman* and the Massif Central, rather than on the southeast.[79]

To appropriate Robert Gildea's imagery, "The Vercors was a volcano waiting to erupt." With news of D-Day, an estimated 4,000 young men, including former Armistice Army and other veterans, had flocked to le Vercors, a plateau 45 kilometers long and 20 kilometers wide that towered over Grenoble. Southern France had been organized into six regions. The Alpine zone of R1 in which le Vercors was located was commanded by Marcel Descour, a cavalry officer who transferred his HQ to le Vercors, as did the head of zones R1 and R2, Colonel Henri Zeller. Before his departure to take charge of the FFI in the Isère, *chasseur alpin* Alain Le Ray had devised a defense scheme that divided le Vercors into five sectors, with the strongest defenses concentrated on Saint-Nizier, which blocked the main road from Grenoble. But, by some calculations, to be successful, Le Ray's defense plan for le Vercors required roughly 8,000 *maquisards* supplied with heavy weapons, and assumed a reinforcement of paratroops with accompanying air support.

Le Ray surrendered his command in May 1944 to thirty-nine-year-old Saint-Cyrian François Huet. Huet was a "Moroccan" to his fingertips – Spahi, Rif War veteran, and an ardently Catholic officer who took his inspiration from Lyautey's "rôle social de l'officier," which had made him a natural liaison between the Armistice Army and the *Chantiers de la jeunesse*. Huet had joined the Alliance network in 1943. But only in January 1944 did he duck underground after Vichy disbanded the *Compagnons de France*, of which Huet served as general secretary. With the assistance of 169 regular French officers and 317 NCOs, Huet set out to militarize his command, which self-branded as *l'Armée secrète du Vercors*. The various *maquis* camps were named for traditional French units – the *11e Régiment de cuirassiers*, the *14e battalion de Chasseurs alpins*, and so on, to generate a sense of discipline, hierarchy, and purpose in his spontaneous force. A remarkable film that captures the final weeks of *le maquis du Vercors* shows a pastoral if purposeful preparation shaped by military routine and ceremony.[80] However, by all accounts, Huet's *maquisards* chafed at his *Chantiers de la jeunesse*/Armistice Army barracks choreography that included obligatory saluting, standing rigidly in formation at regulation intervals, thumbs along trouser seams, and marching in step. Garrison rituals transgressed this civilian *levée* ambience, contravened informal *maquis* comradery, and further puffed up the pretentions of professional soldiers. Above all, Huet's parade ground practices seemed totally irrelevant to their survival.[81]

In the post-war period, the Allies were criticized for not having done more earlier for the resistance. From late June, fifteen men of OG "Justine" and seven, mainly British, soldiers from the SOE's Mission 'Eucalyptus' had floated onto le Vercors. Originally conceived as a US version of commandos and the Special Air Service (SAS), OGs evolved a "versatile mandate" to serve as "operational nuclei" to raise, train, support, and direct indigenous forces, but also to undertake *coup de main* missions. Their heavy weaponry was calculated to "stiffen" Jedburgh teams. Jedburghs were basically independent groups inspired by SOE Mission 101 and Orde Wingate's Gideon Force in Abyssinia in 1941, whose purpose was to arm and coordinate partisan movements. A demonstration of the concept during exercise "Spartan" in March 1943, before a multinational audience, gave rise to the idea of tri-national teams of two officers and a radio operator, one of whom was preferably a native of the occupied nation, who would make contact with the local resistance or with an existing SOE organization, to distribute arms, arrange wireless communications, designate drop zones, and organize reception committees for arms. But the appearance of OGs, "Jeds," and the SAS amplified the complaints of conventional soldiers, at least since the Western Desert campaign, about the proliferation of special operations forces (SOF) – often criticized as private armies, or "mobs for jobs" – with imprecise operational doctrine, carrying out vague and overlapping missions, and operating outside the chain of command, which might complicate operations rather than advance them. The SOF excused failure with the argument that conventional soldiers "misused" special ops, by assigning missions the SOF had not been configured to carry out. But, as Hargreaves notes, "misuse" requires a definition of proper roles. And, given the experimental, not to mention fantastical, nature of most SOF missions that were new, unique, improvised, or even harebrained, one never knew what configuration of forces was suitable until the mission had been attempted and the after-action assessment written. In any case, because SOF required a significant investment in men and resources, deployment was better than sitting in barracks, as was the case of the 1,800 French paratroopers who idled for weeks on the Trapani air base in Sicily as le Vercors was crushed, because no planes could be found to transport them to the fight.[82]

Lieb judges OG "Justine" to have been of "limited help" to *le maquis du Vercors*, because they were not professional soldiers – in fact, most SOF were simply volunteers from line units – and spoke little French. Nor were there enough of them to make a difference. But it was also possible that their advice – to limit recruitment and stick to guerrilla activity – was both impractical because it was impossible to staunch the influx of volunteers and also not welcomed by French professional soldiers, who were already committed to a "pitched battle" defense of the plateau. The British suspected that le Vercors had been ordered by the BCRA to apply *Plan Montagnards*, without alerting the Anglo-Americans. But, as the British in Algiers controlled the radio communications, how the French might have transmitted secret directives to the *maquis* remains unexplained. A third mission, called "Union II," floated in on 1 August with a new weapons drop, by which time the citizens of "*la république du Vercors*" had been killed or put to flight.[83]

On 16 June, Koenig reiterated his orders for phased action, perhaps in reaction to the news that the Germans had taken the village of Saint-Nizier, in the process penetrating the main *maquis* position blocking the road from Grenoble, and had established a foothold on the plateau.[84] But all that did was to provoke renewed requests from *maquis* chiefs for arms and reinforcements of paratroopers. As head of Allied mission in southeastern France, Francis Cammaerts backed their requests, because, along with the rest of le Vercors' hierarchy, he believed it too late for the *maquisards* to flee without dire consequences for them as well as for the local population. Rather than disperse into the forest as they should have done earlier, the conventional mindset of le Vercors' leadership called for the defense of the "*réduit maquisard*," in keeping with the spirit of *Plan Montagnards* and the assumed lesson of Glières.[85] But, with the Allied armies locked in a deadly battle in the Norman bocage, neither Cammaerts nor these *maquis* leaders had quite grasped the fundamental concept that resistance optimizes conventional forces, not vice versa.

However, because the special ops tail had come to wag the SHAEF dog, supporting the *maquis* had become a political rather than an operational priority. From 17 June, SHAEF public relations became worried that "the consequences of a massacre of thousands of men in the Maquis areas due to inadequate provision of suitable arms by the Allies would be very grave and would continue long after the war ... As regards armaments, there are undoubtedly enough machine guns, anti-tank guns of various types and field service rifles at the disposal of Britain and America for arming 100,000 or considerably more French guerrillas ... if the Allies meet this need they will earn ... deep gratitude ... if they fail they will never be forgiven."[86] Requests for new arms were not well timed. With little in the way of planes, Algiers seemed paralyzed by a dispute between Communist Air Commissioner Fernand Grenier, who wanted to support le Vercors, and Jacques Soustelle, the General Secretary of the National Defense Committee, who opposed it. De Gaulle eventually sided with Soustelle, provoking an explosive denunciation from Grenier of "the criminal policy of having the means of support but not using them when our brothers in France call for help."[87]

On 20 June, Churchill ordered Rondell Palmer, Third Earl of Selborne, who had been promoted in 1942 from his post as Director of Cement in the Ministry of Public Works to Minister of Economic Warfare, which by some quirk of bureaucratic configuration put him in charge of the SOE, to dispatch heavy weapons to support the *maquis* uprising in southeastern France. Churchill's personal assistant Desmond Morton delivered the same message to Bedell Smith. On 23 June, the "Eucalyptus" mission left Algiers for le Vercors. A "minor" weapons drop on 13–14 June was supplemented on the morning of 25 June with Operation Cadillac, a series of deliveries throughout the region, during

Figure 5.2 Arms and supplies for the *maquis* float to earth from the bomb bays of Eighth US Army Air Force B-17 Flying Fortresses (1944). (Photo by Photo12/UIG/Getty Images)

which 37 B-17 Flying Fortresses parachuted 420 containers onto the plateau. Three days later, another weapons drop – this one from Algiers – included the nineteen GIs of OG "Justine." On 30 June, Eisenhower prioritized weapons deliveries to the southeast, six days before he took the final decision to launch Anvil/Dragoon. On 14 July, guided by fires lit on the drop zones cleared on the plateau, 72 B-17s dropped 860 containers (Figure 5.2). Collecting them proved challenging, as Focke-Wulf Fw 190s strafed the drop zones and Heinkel bombers sprinkled incendiary bombs and *Chaplets* – canisters of grenades that exploded about 100 meters above the ground before scattering.[88]

Operation Cadillac transformed *l'Armée secrète du Vercors* into France's worst-kept secret, and energized the Germans to excise the Alpine abscess. The region fell under the authority of Generalleutnant Heinrich Niehoff,

Kommandant des Heeresgebiets Südfrankreich, a policeman by profession. Karl Pflaum, already mentioned above, who commanded the 157th Reserve Division, was considered professionally competent, but suffered from a bad heart. He was seconded by Oberst (Colonel) Franz Schwehr, the commander of the reserve *Gebirgsjäger* (Mountain Infantry) Regiment, who was physically robust, but an average officer suffering from what today would be called post-traumatic stress disorder (PTSD), which explained his assignment to a reserve unit. All were supported by a police hierarchy under SS-Gruppenführer Carl Oberg from the Höherer SS- und Polizeiführer (HSSPF), and an intelligence organization run by SS-Hauptsturmführer Klaus Barbie, head of the Kommando der Sicherheitspolizei und des SD (KdS) Lyon, whose brief was to suppress "enemies of the Reich."

From February 1944, orders for "the struggle against the gangs" began to resemble criminal orders from the East. The Germans could not concede lawful combatant status to *maquisards* without bringing into question Berlin's official recognition of the Vichy regime. In the East, the Germans created "dead zones" where the population was evacuated and villages destroyed, a technique applied in France at least partially at Glières and le Vercors. No *Einsatzgruppen* existed in France to murder Jews on the spot as in the East. The estimated 10,000–15,000 civilians, including resisters, executed in France, while barbaric and tragic, pale beside the half-million calculated to have perished on the Eastern Front. The Germans continued to view resistance in France as a military, rather than an ideological or "racial," problem. In Berlin's view, as *maquisards* were not protected under international law, they could be legally executed, and frequently were.[89]

War crimes were covered by a 3 February 1944 "edict" issued by Marshal Hugo Sperrle, deputy commander under the Oberbefehlshaber West (OB West). Similar orders were repeated on the division level, like the one of 23 February 1944, which instructed troops attacked on the march or in their cantonments to

> (a) Respond immediately with fire. If innocents are killed, that's regrettable, but it's the fault of the terrorists. (b) Immediately encircle the vicinity of the attack and arrest all the civilians who are in the environs without taking into account their situation or who they are. (c) Immediately set fire to the houses from which the shots were fired . . . To evaluate the conduct of a troop leader one will immediately judge his *decisiveness* and the *speed* of his reaction. Only weak and indecisive leaders will be severely punished, because that undermines the security of their command and respect for the German army. Because of the present situation, rigorous measures taken by leaders will in no circumstances become grounds for punishment.[90]

According to the historian Gäel Eismann, the German authorities did attempt to rein in the worst atrocities, especially when Vichy protested, which it did over the "Sperrle edict." This would seem to be confirmed by orders from Niehoff on

22 July, belatedly reiterated by Pflaum on the 29 July, reminding German commanders to stay vigilant for brutality against civilians, whose support was vital for the success of anti-resistance activity, especially by "troops from the East."[91] These directives were obviously issued after the fact. But, in any case, the "Sperrle edict" remained in force for the summer of 1944, absolving German commanders of responsibility for war crimes committed on their watch.[92]

The sheer brutality of German counterinsurgency tactics was often exemplified by the *Osttruppen*, who had been recruited among the 1.5 million Soviet POWs who, after being brutalized by the Soviet regime, volunteered to serve in the Wehrmacht, which from 1943 imported into France what Sean McKeekin calls the "self-reinforcing logic to this war of attrition on the eastern front."[93] In this way, the intractable nature of insurgency conflict created frustrations that quickly transformed "war among the people" into "war against the people." The frequently murderous nature of the anti-*maquis* campaign was augmented by the fact that France was sparsely garrisoned. With combat divisions concentrated near the beaches, the *Militärbefehlshaber* probably commanded no more than 95,000 occupation troops, including *Osttruppen* and *Ostlegionen*, who been distributed as garrison troops in many towns, where they guarded bridges, railways, and depots, manned flak batteries, and so on. Perhaps as few as 30,000 German troops were available for counterinsurgency operations for the entire country. From the end of 1943, they were mustered to attack resistance centers. In some cases, they might get assistance from armored forces recovering in France, like the 2. SS-Panzerdivision "Das Reich," or from the 157th Reserve Division classified as a training unit.

Vichy *forces de l'ordre*

The Germans were backstopped by the GMR and *la Milice*. Created in 1941, the GMR's original purpose was to provide "a supplemental force for public security" that prefects and local police commissioners in the *zone libre* could call upon to shore up a deteriorating public order. Named police secretary in April 1942, René Bosquet envisioned the GMR as a mechanism to bypass France's fragmented and multilayered police structure, wherein authority was shared among mayors, prefects, and the interior secretariat. Bosquet brought the GMR under his direct control through the *Direction des Groupes mobiles de reserve*, a post occupied from April 1943 by Saint-Cyr graduate Pierre Labarthe. Like Huntzinger, Dentz, and others, Labarthe's central role in the 1940 collapse at Bulson served only to enhance his professional bona fides at Vichy, which had transformed itself into a Hôtel des Invalides for vanquished soldiers and scuppered sailors.[94] Allowed to expand into the *zone occupée* from the end of 1942, Vichy could transmit orders to the GMR through the

"*Délégation du ministre de l'intérieur*" in Paris. Despite relatively high pay, in 1942, applications to join the GMR had plummeted, forcing a lowering of the recruiting age from twenty-three to eighteen. Even then, roughly 25 percent of applicants were rejected for political or physical reasons, which increasingly became a problem among malnourished French youth. Composed of Vichy loyalists, military veterans, and furloughed POWs, with a top-up of the devout, rather than police officers, in August 1944, the GMR numbered 11,294 inadequately trained personnel for public order tasks. Prefects complained that GMR interventions resembled combat operations, often launched without their knowledge or permission. The GMR seldom executed people out of hand or tortured as did their bitter rivals in *la Milice*. Nor did they play a major role in the Jewish round-ups other than holding back curious crowds. Corralling Jews was a task assigned mainly to specialized police groups, *la Milice*, the *Gestapo*, *Sipo/SD*, *Ordnungspolizei* (*Orpo*), or *Feldgendarmerie*. However, their operations against the resistance and round ups of STO dodgers, combined with the fact that they wore black uniforms, caused some to confuse the GMR with the SS. Darnand's *Milice* despised the relative restraint of the GMR, and branded them "*des tapettes*" (pansies).[95]

Like the GMR, *la Milice* also actively participated in the repression of the *réduits maquisards*. The abolition of the Armistice Army had prompted Vichy to appeal to Berlin for weapons to use against a swelling resistance. On 30 January 1943, with Pétain's blessing, Laval had created *la Milice*. At his 1945 trial, Laval claimed that Hitler's 19 December 1942 "ultimatum" to assemble a force to stop resistance attacks on Germans, or face the "Polandization" of France, had forced the stand-up of *la Milice*. But, according to Rassemblement national populaire (RNP) chief Marcel Déat, Hitler's "ultimatum" simply confirmed Laval's growing conviction that the French police were losing the battle against a mushrooming "*résistance-organisation*" and required the assistance of a "supplemental police force."[96] With Faustian resolve, in the wake of the Torch fiasco, Laval strove to authenticate Vichy's partnership in Hitler's "New Europe." France's sharpening civil war witnessed right-wing political parties increasingly reinventing themselves as "armed bands," bashing people who refused to accept their tracts, brandishing arms, and denouncing "traitors" to the *Sipo/SD*. Also, the police increasingly seemed to go wobbly in the face of resistance-induced sabotage and assassinations. In January 1942, Joseph Darnand had demanded that his *Service d'ordre légionnaire* (SOL) be designated as a "supplemental police force." In these circumstances, Laval feared that a union between the SOL and the extremist parties of the *zone nord* would dispute his power, and was justifiably suspicious of Darnand's ambitions to push Vichy closer to fascism by transforming *la Milice* into a combination political party, intelligence service, and on-call vigilante squad. The Germans, who also had a vote, preferred the creation of a single force that they could superintend, rather than encouraging a proliferation of militias sponsored by France's factious right-wing mafiosi whose unrestrained "counterterror" thuggery might provoke an even greater backlash against occupation.[97]

While *la Milice* formed "the army of the last quarter of an hour," it was hardly an aberration, but more a logical evolution of Pétain's decision to collaborate at Montoire. "Neutrality in the war, but a toughening in the maintenance of order," writes Burrin. "*La Milice* will carry out its work, with a thousand horrors, against their countrymen in the name of an obsessive respect for order."[98] A direct descendent of the Légion française des combattants (LFC) via the SOL, Darnand's *Milice* was modeled on the Nazi Party, and was meant to impose political order among a shriveling but increasingly cacophonous right-wing claque, while also serving as "a praetorian guard" for a "regime without an army."[99] The problem for *la Milice*, as it had been for the LFC and SOL, was that a party limited to political fanatics and hoodlums was invariably detested and shunned. But when it opened its ranks to expand its base, its identity and message became diluted. As an expression of Vichy's obsession with order, intelligence collection, and security became the organization's defining characteristics. Although *la Milice* technically answered to Laval, Darnand served as its operational commander from his headquarters in Vichy's Hôtel Moderne. Many viewed *la Milice* as a Gallic replication of the SS or the Sturmabteilung (SA), although it operated more like a "low caliber" French Gestapo, good at intimidation, torture, and assassination, but an organization that wilted when called upon to undertake serious combat. Indeed, one SAS soldier dropped into France after D-Day noted that "The *miliciens* guarding the rail lines are very afraid, and shoot all the time. They also carry out interval firing – one presumes that it's a signal that all is going well." They also press-ganged civilians into guarding the rail lines, "who are completely indifferent and often help to blow them up."[100]

Its mission was to infiltrate where the Germans could not go without attracting attention, to track down Jews, STO truants, and resisters. While the political element consisted of a general militia that enlisted people of all ages and both sexes, its *Franc-Garde* was a paramilitary unit made up of around 25,000 militants of more-or-less military age, perhaps 10,000 of whom were active and some of whom lived in barracks in the former *zone libre*. Although how many were deployable rather than mere card-carrying sympathizers is more difficult to judge.[101] Socially *la Milice* was a mixed bag, but included many factory and agricultural workers, or unemployed people, and even minor criminals and gangsters, convicted felons, and men who enlisted to escape STO, or for room and board and 6 francs 70 centimes an hour, supplemented by the opportunity to shake down local businesses, Jews, or Masons. "More generally, *la Milice* was made up of men strong on order, who set the greatest store by the legitimacy of Pétain and the French state and could not tolerate the rise of resistance on their territory, finding it far more unbearable than the presence of the Germans and even believing it to justify closer cooperation with the latter," asserts Burrin.[102] Darnand's ambitious vision included expanding his *Franc-Garde* to 40,000–50,000 men, establishing *la Milice* in the *zone nord*, absorbing the constellation of right-wing factions into a single political movement, and transforming the *Légion des volontaires français contre le bolchévisme* (LVF) into an expeditionary wing of *la Milice*. Most of this plan was not realized because Laval feared Darnand as a political rival, while German Ambassador Otto Abetz sought to keep the French divided. Other groups, such as the Parti populaire français (PPF), were forming their own militias in the *zone nord* with Berlin's blessing, most of them small, whose swaggering but rather pathetic parades elicited catcalls, insults, and derision from spectators. By the summer of 1943, Darnand had become so frustrated by Laval's obstruction, and by the fact that his unarmed militiamen were being assassinated at an alarming rate by the resistance, that he even considered defecting to Algiers. One tragedy for France was that circumstance forced him to wait until October 1945 before being court-martialed and shot, after being denied a pardon by de Gaulle.[103]

As the Senior SS and Police Commander in France, Carl Oberg rescued at least part of Darnand's project by agreeing in September 1943 to arm *la Milice* from captured Armistice Army stocks. In return, Darnand must swear unconditional loyalty to Hitler and agree to be mobilized for active service in the SS should his presence be required. He also worked with the SS to set up a French Waffen-SS unit by contributing 200–300 *Francs-Gardes*. In return, *la Milice* was allocated camps in 21 departments, where 600 *miliciens* were to be trained by SD officers. But Darnand proved an indifferent administrator, much more gifted at giving increasingly incendiary and ideological speeches at poorly attended rallies and spending long hours exchanging war stories over bottles of Beaujolais rather than putting his organization on a solid footing. Marcel Gombert, a sadist known as "the French Heydrich," was put in charge of *Milice* security and intelligence, which specialized in torture teams and assassinations carried out by a *Groupe spécial de sécurité* (GSS) of 200 fanaticized and depraved *miliciens*.[104]

With support for collaboration collapsing, Darnand's increasing desperation was reflected in the aggressive tactics of his militiamen. *Milice* headquarters became Denunciation Central, where anyone with a grudge or an outstanding debt could trigger a visit by a squad of *Francs-Gardes* who might accuse the victim of black marketeering, or of hiding STO escapees, followed by a ransacking of their property and arbitrary arrest. Restaurants and grocery shops became favorite shake-down targets. Recently bombed towns also found *miliciens* swarming like rats over the rubble in search of booty. Darnand ordered his men to take hostages from lists furnished by the collaborationist press. Taken to *Milice* headquarters, these unfortunates would be stripped and blindfolded before being tortured or their families threatened to get information, and might even undergo a mock execution. So, the resistance retaliated in kind, by sending them death threats, often in the form of small coffins, to amplify their sense of insecurity, before eventually assassinating them.[105]

Darnand urged his men to seize hostages and "meet blows with blows." With Oberg's approval, militiamen launched a campaign of counter-terror from the autumn of 1943, which combined "murderous violence" with "ideological frenzy." Jews, Masons, resistance sympathizers, and even prisoners seized from jails with Oberg's connivance were assassinated as reprisals for murders of militiamen. In Vichy's death spasm, *la Milice* created a "climate of fascist terror" by the summary executions of prominent left-wing figures such as Jean Zay and Georges Mandel, and Radical Party journalist Maurice Sarraut, among others.[106] By the turn of the year 1943–1944, Vichy was well on its way to becoming a *Milice* state. In January 1944, Vichy proclaimed Darnand secretary general for the Maintenance of Order. Backed by Oberg, *la Milice* expanded into the former *zone occupée*, extended its authority over the forces of order and the prison system, and began to infiltrate the administration. The numbers of militiamen swelled to what *la Milice* claimed to be between 26,000 and 30,000 men, roughly half of them *Francs-Gardes*, "dubious characters with criminal records, admirers of violence, brawlers in search of good pay and warlike adventures, a few 'daddy's boys' swept up in the movement, and hotheads who preferred the *Franc-Garde* to STO." These were reinforced by SS "auxiliaries" estimated at 9,000–10,000 "collaborationists, former voluntary workers in Germany, people in trouble with the law," including black marketeers, often supplied by right-wing political parties, whose job was to surveil, infiltrate the resistance, and snitch. In early 1944, Sauckel sought to create a special force to pursue STO evaders under the hallucinatory moniker "Action Group for Social Justice." *Milice* tribunals, created from 20 January 1944, were allowed to sentence suspects to death and carry out executions immediately without appeal. The *Milice*'s GSS inflicted "unimaginable" brutalities. Of course, the resistance hardly took this lying down, and repaid *la Milice* in their own coin, executing an estimated 4,000 collaborators, of whom perhaps 300 were militiamen. One of the largest executions was of seventy-six of ninety-eight militiamen who surrendered to *maquisards* at the Grand Bornand in the Haute-Savoie in August 1944. But, on the eve of liberation, control of *la Milice* made Darnand the most powerful man at Vichy after Laval.[107]

La Milice and the GMR became critical auxiliaries for the dwindling numbers of German troops available for tasks that consisted of "combing out" a village, detaining all males between seventeen and forty years of age for interrogation by the Sipo/SD, confiscating the cows of a farmer who failed to report a parachute drop, or burning a school, town hall, or barn used to house *maquisards*, operations that might be circumscribed only because a bona fide combat division had priority for scarce petrol.[108] In the Alpes, for instance, the Germans controlled only the principal towns and the major highways. In this context, the decision to defend *réduits maquisards* merely allowed the Germans and Vichy to concentrate their few available forces rather than having to scatter them to hunt down mobile bands of resisters. It also helps to explain why they attacked the population, which offered a stand-in target and a way to limit the recruitment and logistical support for a *maquis* phenomenon that seemed as ubiquitous as it was elusive. For instance, at le Vercors, any building used by the *maquis* was to be destroyed. German operational orders for 17 July directed that, "to prevent the resistance from again reoccupying le Vercors, one will leave in the farms only the minimum of cattle indispensable for the local population to feed themselves."[109]

The End of le Vercors

The Germans had auditioned their anti-*réduits maquisards* tactics at Glières: static troops would encircle the objective by blocking all roads and natural approaches. Then *Kampfgruppen* – battlegroups pieced together from infantry, artillery, and engineer units tailored to the objective, as well as Sipo/SD – would launch assaults. *Maquisards* attempting to flee would be scooped up by the blocking forces. The problem for the Germans was that they often lacked sufficient troops completely to seal off the objective, especially an expansive one like le Vercors. But for this operation, they massed 8,000–10,000 men, including an 800-man Panzergrenadier battalion as well as airborne troops in relatively large numbers (Map 5.1). Two disciplinary companies, equipped with small arms, light machineguns and mortars, were to be delivered by DFS 230 gliders to Vaissieux-en-Vercors, where the Germans speculated that the *maquis* headquarters was located (in fact, it was at Saint-Martin about 8 kilometers away). Although Vassieux had already been extensively damaged from the air, the calculation was that its capture would dislocate *maquis* command and control. In fact, Huet depended on runners and the telephone to convey orders and bring back information, a system that quickly broke down once the German attack began. The German plan was to reinforce their initial airborne wave with *Osttruppen* and *Brandenburgers* (Wehrmacht special forces) flown in from Valence. All summer the sixty-seven aircraft of the *Geschwader Bongart*, stationed at Chabeuil airfield near Valence, had been attacking *maquis* concentrations in the Alpes. Requests for Allied air attacks on Chabeuil went unanswered.[110]

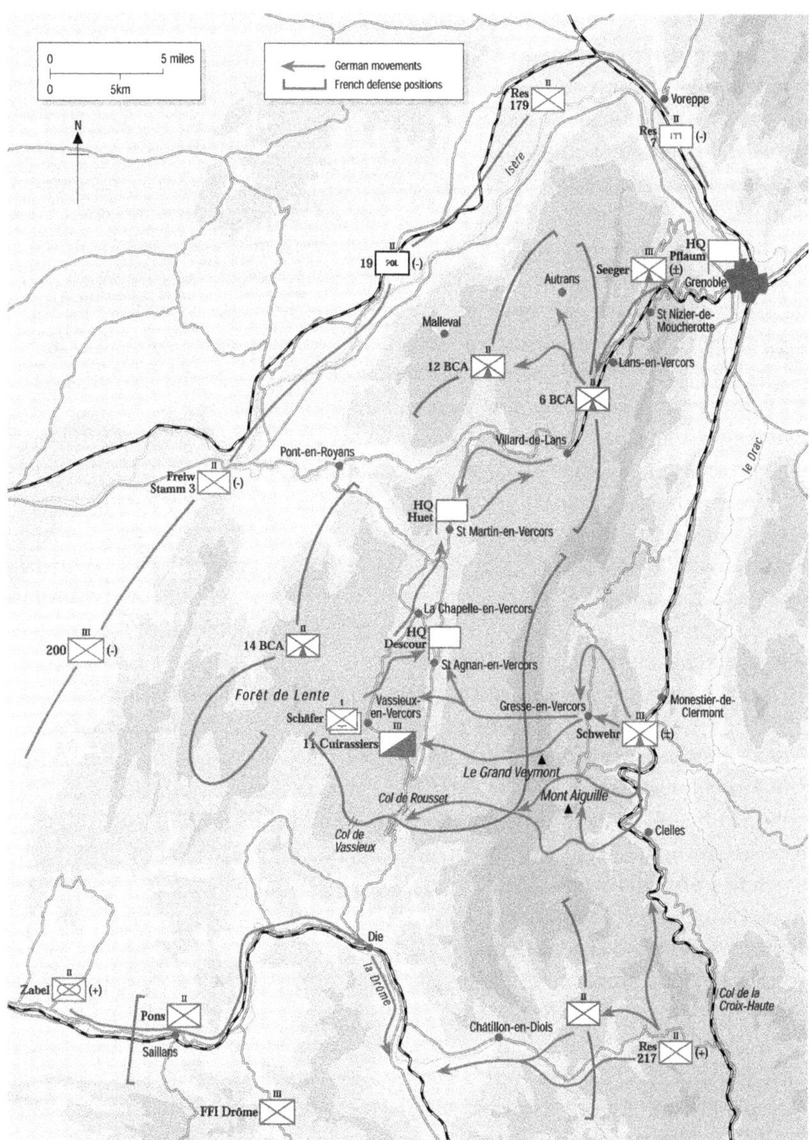

Map 5.1 The original German plan for the attack against the *maquis du Vercors*.

At 09:00 on 21 July 1944, *maquisards* working to complete an airstrip suddenly spied a flotilla of planes approaching from the south, which in their minds signaled another Allied weapon drop from Blida. But instead of canisters dropped with the signature red, white, and blue parachutes, the Heinkel He 111s unfastened their tow ropes, detaching gliders that drifted earthward at 60 degrees, before releasing a braking parachute 300 meters above the ground. They slipped silently to earth, rattling across the fields before detonating a retro-rocket to brake their taxiing. Then the section of men burst out of the side door, as the pilot flipped open the roof hatch and set up his 7.92 mm MG 15 on the fuselage to provide covering fire. This airborne landing in the middle of the defensive position, executed by gliders brought to Valence by road so as not to tip the German hand, offered the first tactical surprise of the day.[111] The *maquisards* at Vassieux, many caught sleeping in their beds, were quickly overwhelmed. When the second glider wave arrived in the late morning, it was greeted by machinegun fire, which caused two of the gliders to crash. However, with the Germans ensconced at Vassieux, the *maquisards* lacked the requisite heavy weapons and tactical expertise to eject them, despite repeated attacks over the next two days. In the event, all the Germans had accomplished by their air assault was to lock up around 200 troops inside Vassieux. But this did not stop them from massacring civilians at the direction of the Lyon Sipo/SD *Obersturmbannführer* Werner Knab.[112]

The second tactical surprise was that Huet had failed utterly to guard the passes on the steep eastern face of the plateau, calculating that the Germans would find them inaccessible and unsuitable for heavy weapons. In any case, with only 4,000 men, 1,000 of whom were not yet fully armed, Huet had little option. Pflaum realized this, and sent his *Gebirgsjäger* (mountain infantry) backed by light artillery through passes that were each guarded by only a handful of *maquisards*. The *Kampfgruppe* pushed up the slopes to the crest from various directions, backed by close air support of *Geschwader Bongart*. A hasty command meeting was called at 22:00 on the night of 21 July to consider Huet's proposal to disperse in small groups. A majority opposed this proposal: it was too late, because retreat would abandon the civilian inhabitants to savage German retribution, and because flight would be an admission that their sacrifices had been in vain.[113] By 22 July, the situation was serious for the *maquis*, but not entirely hopeless. There were still defensive positions where the FFI might make a stand, and the German advance into the plateau was more tentative than expected. However, on 23 July, more gliders landed, as some of the main French defenses collapsed. On this news, Huet and his staff fled, along with OG "Justine" and any surviving *maquisards*, toward the Forêt de Lente to the west of the plateau. For the next ten days, the Germans searched for refugee *maquisards*, while they casually murdered civilians, shot hostages, and put guards on le Vercors' few water sources, allegedly under the orders of Niehoff who sought to make sure that resistance would not reconstitute on the plateau. Survivors were not allowed to bury the bodies of the fallen: 639 *maquisards* had been killed, as well as 201 French civilians, while the Germans counted 65 men killed, 133 wounded, and 18 missing in action (MIA). Roughly 84 percent of the 4,000 *maquisards* had in fact escaped.[114]

The Legacy of le Vercors

The unsettling ambiguity of the Liberation for the internal resistance, in particular the *maquis*, was rooted in an acute and enduring sense of abandonment. Even before the war's end, this black legend of the betrayal of the *réduits maquisards* by the Allies and the external resistance became a focus of conspiracy theories and political conflict. The fact that, despite their preoccupation with Overlord, the Allies had done much to provision le Vercors with weapons, and that a vastly greater percentage of *maquisards* there had escaped than had *biffins* (grunts) in 1940, did nothing to lessen the bitterness. On the night of 20–21 July, Eugène Chavant, who had returned from Algiers on 7 June with assurances that le Vercors would be supported, messaged Algiers thus: "If no assistance, population and us will judge Algiers to be criminals and cowards. I repeat, criminals and cowards." The "national insurrection" meant that the experience of le Vercors had been replicated in small ways elsewhere, in the process, "traumatizing *maquisards* and civilians."[115] Even at the time, perceptive observers recognized that le Vercors had quickly become cloaked in a myth that locked special operations and resistance in an indissoluble embrace. An undated report, obviously written after August 1944, complained of an attempt by Henri d'Astier to create units of commandos to organize FFI units behind the lines: "We are in the presence of a case of 'Resistantialist Romanticism,' justified by events and circumstances: partial knowledge in Algiers [at a subordinate level but introduced into diverse political milieus] about the *maquis*, but profound ignorance about their daily existence, psychology etc . . . especially vis-à-vis le Vercors or le maquis de l'Ain."[116]

The "Resistentialist Romanticism" of the *maquis* was important to France's image. Of an estimated 200,000–350,000 young Frenchmen who refused to report for STO, perhaps a quarter joined a *maquis* or resistance group.[117] As part of the resistance, the *maquis* symbolized a thumping rejection of the 1940 defeat and the armistice, and served as an in-your-face plebiscite on Vichy collaboration. Unlike the Anglo-Americans, for whom the image of the liberation of France was that of conventional combat, with Omaha Beach as the centerpiece, regular French forces had played only a marginal role after 1940. "*Résistance-organisation*" may have comprised only a small percentage of the population. But its legitimacy came from the fact that, just like the soldiers of the Year II rallied to defend France when the regular army had faltered, French men and women were prepared to contribute to their own liberation at the side of the Allies, which is what de Gaulle required of them.[118] In this context, it was easy to conflate the *maquis* at Glières, Mont Mouchet, in the Ain and the Jura, and above all at le Vercors with a *levée en masse*. Romanticized by Maurice Schuman on the BBC as a sort of sylvan republic, "the *maquisards*, but above all their leaders, were viewed as true heroes who, in the middle of the occupation, lived in liberty."[119]

For that reason, in France's wartime memory, *maquisards* became "ironic heroes," innocents randomly selected by age and gender, whose flight from STO singled them out as exceptional, but who failed to triumph in the end. Instead, they were made to pay the price for a guilty society.[120] Their destruction was mustered to support two narratives, both promoted primarily but not exclusively by the communists: first, that the Anglo-Americans sought to reduce France to the level of a second-tier power; and second, that they conspired with the "external resistance" to allow the Germans to quash France's "national insurrection." Of course, this oversimplified a complex debate over what form "national insurrection" was to take: centralization versus decentralization of resistance command; the spontaneous origins and problems of operationalization of *réduits maquisards*; the relationship between conventional and unconventional war; when and how to muster resources to support the *maquis*, and so on.[121] Nevertheless, this mythical narrative of abandonment of these hapless victims coarsened in the Cold War, as communist propaganda flipped the script on the Warsaw insurrection to charge Anglo-American and Gaullist inaction for allowing German repression of the *maquis*. Even the history profession, led by Henri Michel, creator of the *Comité d'Histoire de la Deuxième Guerre Mondiale*, extolled the *maquis* as a symbol of a "national war," and echoed a wartime theme of the "rich Allies" betraying the "poor resistance."[122] Erased in this memorial scuffle, and in conformity with de Gaulle's propaganda priorities of the French people "liberating themselves," were the SOE, Allied arms drops, and teams of Jedburghs/OGs and SAS operatives.[123]

A third chapter in the "black legend" stemmed from fraught civil–*maquis* relations. Unlike the other two *maquis* legends, this one was more solidly anchored in fact. Relations between the resistance and the population quickly broke down in many areas at the Liberation, as resistance leaders occupied town halls, and the frustrations and resentments of four years of occupation erupted, as "September resisters" began to administer their own brand of feral justice. For their part, former *maquisards* regarded their treatment in the wake of liberation as a continuum of disrespect, when as many as 2,000 of them were jailed for "illegal requisitions" during the war. Above all, popular ambivalence toward the *maquisards* can be explained by the fact that they were more likely to be remembered for lawlessness, disorder, pillaging, and triggering harsh

German/Vichy retribution, for little strategic gain, than for their patriotic martyrdom. Estimates of FFI casualties vary – the Militärbefehlshaber in Frankreich (MBF) claimed to have killed 7,900 "terrorists" between 6 June and 4 July, which was before the suppression of le Vercors, 4,000 of them claimed by the 2nd SS Panzer Division Das Reich. These figures included civilians massacred in anti-partisan operations.[124] Balu hypothesizes that 10,000–13,700 FFI were killed in combat or summarily executed out of an estimated 120,000–192,000 active in the FFI, which would mean a casualty rate of 5–11 percent. German reprisals against civilians were particularly harsh after they reclaimed a village or town that had temporarily been "liberated" by the *maquis*. Peter Lieb believes that around 5,000 civilians were killed in reprisals for assisting the *maquis*, which may be on the low side, because 21,600 French people were deported to concentration camps between 6 June 1944 and the end of November.[125]

Myths often have a foundation in reality, no matter how tenuous. The intellectual foundations for "strategic redoubts" had their roots in Dalloz's Alpine romanticism and Rougeron's technocratically inspired quest to find a formula that would replicate in France the people's wars that Churchill and the SOE imagined to be raging in Eastern and Southeastern Europe in 1943–1944. These claims were bolstered by resistance leaders, Gaullists and communists foremost among them, eager to promote the image of resistance as a popular *levée* to underpin the CFLN/GPRF's legitimacy, act a referendum to discredit Vichy and the Occupation, and surge France's clout in the Alliance. Finally, Delestraint, echoed by the interface services eager to carve out an operational niche for themselves, confirmed the military soundness of a resistance strategy, which resulted in *Plan Montagnards/Vidal*. The spontaneous materialization in the course of 1943 of *réduits maquisards* confirmed their place in resistance strategy. But le Vercors and the debate over the "national insurrection" only served to illustrate how politicized Allied strategic decision-making regarding France had become by 1944. Politics were primordial in Koenig's plans, especially when, on 17 July, he gained control of all agents – French and Allied – operating in France. Although the EMFFI was technically under SHAEF, the Foreign Office suspected that Koenig's role would be to deploy the resistance to buttress a Gaullist power grab. For his part, de Gaulle anticipated that the liberation would result in local power vacuums in small liberated zones. The communists presented his biggest challenge, especially in Paris through COMAC, the FTP, and the *Milices patriotiques*, the shock troops of the CNR/FTP, which he feared would refuse to follow his orders.[126] But the Allied interface services were supplying the resources, and stoking the pretentions to power, of a motley of local actors and their followers primed to take advantage of the chaos of liberation for political and/or criminal ends. Therefore, by affirming his authority over the resistance, and all Allied agents and advisors serving with them through the EMFFI, de Gaulle sought to avoid a repetition of the Corsica shambles, this time on a national scale. With distrust within the resistance running high, when communist deputy in the Algiers Consultative Assembly André Marty learned of *Caïman*, he immediately objected that the plan's true purpose was to install a reactionary military and political clique in France's heartland.

But de Gaulle also wanted, through *Caïman*, to impose his authority on an international level. The *maquis* phenomenon attracted outside players who, for different reasons, tried to orient it to achieve their particular objectives: Eisenhower agreed to arm the *maquis* as a concession to force the British Prime Minister to acquiesce to Anvil, the invasion of southern France, which he never did. De Gaulle, via *Plan Caïman*, sought to use the *maquis* to create GPRF-dominated "liberated zones," while the "interface services" aimed to boost their lowly status in the military pecking order by carving out an important role in the Liberation for irregular warfare. For his part, de Gaulle interpreted the proliferation of Anglo-American "advisors," agents, OGs, and "Jeds" as a tactic to undermine the GPRF's authority. Eisenhower's refusal to support *Caïman* short-circuited Gaullist attempts to transform the *maquis* into a regular army.[127] Once the Germans abandoned France, the various intelligence and special operations forces simply cluttered the liberation landscape, proliferating armed and politicized vigilantes under often headstrong, self-appointed, and ambitious leaders, who, pumped with a sense of interface service-bestowed entitlement, had to be reined in by conventional soldiers through "*l'amalgame*" and the imposition of the apparatus of the French state.

If "strategic redoubts" served the political agendas of some resistance leaders, as well as of de Gaulle, Churchill, and the interface services, at its core, these STO refugees constituted a civil disobedience movement that proved difficult to operationalize for military purposes. While the Germans began to create *Jagdkommandos* from November 1942, the *maquis* and Vichy "*forces de l'ordre*" continued to spar, especially after Darnand was named *secrétaire général au Maintien de l'ordre* in January 1944. Ironically, it was the Allied decision, for political rather than military reasons, to militarize, mobilize, and arm the *maquis* as D-Day loomed that convinced the Germans to target these vulnerable "strategic redoubts." The interface services imagined the *maquis* as a French version of Tito's partisans, with the potential to become a trained army able to respond to orders from SHAEF. Many of the military leaders who appeared in the Alpes to lead them also planned and organized for "pitched battle," a form of warfare with which they were most familiar, but one beyond the capacities of their amateur forces, *sans* heavy weapons and air support.[128] In the end, distance, political proclivities, lack of a clear concept of operations, and a fluid and ill-defined command structure divided between Algiers and London, into which the "interface services" – not to mention

Churchill – imposed themselves, with their diverse political, national, and institutional agendas, meant that decision-making devolved to the local level.

Nor did the external resistance send a clear message. Gaullist political ambitions to create "liberated zones" *à la Plan Caïman* actually required *réduits maquisards*. But if, in the summer of 1944, the CFLN returned to "phased mobilization," neither Emmanuel d'Astier nor Georges Boris in the *commissariat à l'Intérieur*, not to mention COMAC in Paris, abandoned hope for a mythical "national insurrection," an aspiration stoked by the BBC. On 1 July, Koenig called for an open insurrection in Brittany, the Massif Central, and east of the Rhône, even though the breakout in Normandy as well as the Côte d'Azure landings were more than a month into the future. "If the contradictions of the GPRF were not alone responsible for the outcome at le Vercors, they contributed to it," insists Balu. So, the mythology of abandonment evolved in the shadow of the "tragedy of the *grand maquis*," the dispersions and reformations of smaller ones, in the tattered morale and profound sense of bitterness of the survivors, and not least among many civilians who felt that they had been the primary victims of *maquis* activism and flawed Allied operational experimentation.[129]

La Deuxième Division Blindée

On 3 June 1943, de Gaulle and Giraud had become "co-presidents" of the CFLN. Despite Larminat's best efforts to preserve the Gaullist forces under British command, officially the FFL had ceased to exist on 31 July 1943, having been "fused," in the vernacular of the day, with *l'armée d'Afrique* in AFN and *l'armée coloniale*, the lineal descendants of the *troupes de marine* in sub-Saharan Africa. This transition into a unitary French force did not seem at first glance to favor Leclerc's Force L because, while the Anfa accord of January 1943 had dangled the promise of three armored divisions in a modernized French order of battle, it had not factored in FFL mechanization. Stripped of its Chadian infantry, Force L's strength hovered at around 3,000 soldiers marooned in Tripolitania. Things began to perk up when in August 1943 the 2e DFL was integrated into the Anfa program and renamed the 2e *Division blindée* (armored division). But Leclerc's new command was neither yet a division nor was it armored. While able to assemble a scaffolding for one of the three armored regiments required for his division from his own resources, the 1ère DFL, which for the moment was quarantined by its British (rather than US) equipment, and destined to join the CEF in Italy in a few months' time, was decidedly uncooperative. Therefore, Leclerc must recruit among France's imperial soldiers and even attract marooned sailors, among whom Leclerc's reputation was toxic, to raise the other two armored regiments, as well as artillery, engineers, mechanics, medical and support services, and so on that the Americans insisted were integral to a modern force. Larminat noted that Leclerc possessed an "impetuous and violent temperament," that caused him to become "abrasive and rough in discussions, quarrelsome and aggressive." Nevertheless, "neither his social origins, nor his religious faith – which was deep – caused him to overlook reality. He was the freest spirit ever." In the event, the cavalryman approached *l'armée d'Afrique* as if he were breaking in a recalcitrant horse, a method that combined "patience, finesse. and tact" with "boldness and vigor."[130] After all, despite the rifts caused by 1940, the professional French officer corps was a brotherhood, united by bonds formed at Saint-Cyr, Saumur, and *l'École de guerre*, and on the staffs of influential generals. None of this ruled out sibling rivalries, of course. Nor did it hurt that he was de Gaulle's pet and fair-haired boy, except, of course, with Giraud, who, when Leclerc came calling in his search for recruits, figuratively speaking slammed the door in his face.

The forty-one-year-old Major General set up his headquarters in Temara, a seaside suburb of Rabat, where he began to recruit and build his division. Beyond the tight circle of his division staff, the unit that would come to symbolize Gaullism was as yet far from being a Gaullist unit. By temporarily suspending his confrontational style vis-à-vis Giraudists, and by emphasizing the obligation to make common cause against the occupation, Leclerc gradually managed, through a sequence of dinners, informal discussions, conferences, meetings, and *têtes-à-tête*, to cajole, inveigle, Shanghai, and even occasionally charm officers and recruits into enlisting in his crusade. By mixing and combining units, and by a measured distribution of the symbols of Gaullism – the Cross of Lorraine as his new division's crest, and the red *fouragère* – he would gradually fashion a divisional identity.

On 18 September 1943, CFLN co-presidents de Gaulle and Giraud had asked the Allies to include a French unit in their plans for the liberation of Paris. In November, de Gaulle had designated the 2e DB as his flagship, whose purpose would to undertake "a purely national and French mission, for example reestablishing authority in Paris." On 30 December 1943, Eisenhower agreed, recognizing the value of a French presence in Overlord, as well as eager to smooth French collaboration in Italy and Anvil. For logistical reasons, it was far easier to transport an infantry division to the UK and then across the Channel. But 60 percent of French infantrymen at this stage of the war were soldiers of color. The UK would not welcome French colonial troops, while de Gaulle, ever sensitive to optics, believed that images of Paris liberated by GIs, North Africans, and Senegalese would deflate France's already battered self-esteem and further tarnish its international standing. This made perfect sense to the Anglo-Americans, who commanded racially segregated armies. A modern, hard-hitting armored division would serve also as backdrop and *garde de corps* for de Gaulle's grand entry into the French capital, where his young protégé was designated as interim military governor. The unit was to be kept intact, not scattered in throwaway tactical detours and diversions. And Leclerc must remain in command. In the meantime, the 2e DB must also be "whitened," as its 4,000 Senegalese were dispatched to de Lattre's *Armée B*, with the result that only one-quarter of the 2e DB was made up colonial subjects.[131]

The Senegalese were replaced by combing the camps of *évadés de France* in Morocco, by enlisting Jews, Corsicans, volunteers from Saint-Pierre et Miquelon, and 150 Spanish Republicans, and in France he would top up with FFI, and even *Miliciens* and other collaborators eager to "launder" their pasts.[132] The result was that, unlike Brosset's solidly Gaullist 1ère DFL, politically speaking, the 2e DB was a mix and match of military refugees comprising twenty-two nationalities, led by the rump of the *Corps franc d'Afrique*, with its Freemasons and Spanish Republicans who had served in the 3rd Battalion of the CFA under former International Brigade volunteer Captain Joseph Putz. Refusing to enlist in "*l'armée de Giraud*," which had shunned them in Tunisia, many were incorporated into the 2e DB's 9th Company, which became known as *la nueve*, part of the 1,150 Spaniards who had served in the FFL and the *Corps franc d'Afrique*.[133] The Senegalese were replaced by a *Régiment de marche du Tchad*, with a cadre of the original FFL volunteers from the colonial army led by future French army commander Jacques Massu, as the ranks filled with *évadés* and *pieds noirs*. Tanks were distributed to the *501er Régiment de chars de combat* and the *1er Régiment de marche de spahis marocains*, which had also been magically "whitened." *L'armée d'Afrique* supplied some artillery and the *7e Chasseurs d'Afrique*, a unit which was quickly confiscated for the Italian campaign. Indeed, it required some hard politicking for Leclerc to prevent de Lattre from appropriating his "division" for *l'Armée B* designated for Operation Anvil/Dragoon.

To compensate for the loss of the *Chasseurs d'Afrique*, de Gaulle dispatched a unit of French marines, that included de Gaulle's son Philippe. Many of them, including the commander, naval Captain Raymond Maggiar, had been captured in Madagascar by the British and spent six months incarcerated in a POW pen with German U-boat crews. Others had fought the Axis in Tunisia. When the US Navy could find no boats for them to crew, they transferred to the army. Leclerc reluctantly enlisted them after Juin pointed out that, as many had gunnery experience, they might do well in American tank destroyers. Nevertheless, the abrasive Leclerc made it patently clear to Maggiar that "I didn't want you. I accepted you because General de Gaulle imposed you on me." This red-carpet embrace was sealed by denying the marines the privilege of wearing the division's red *fouragère* until they had proven themselves on the battlefield, but forcing these apostate Vichyites to paint the cross of Lorraine on their vehicles.[134] So, one ironic result was that the notoriously choleric cavalryman, portrayed by his hagiographers as a Gaullist thoroughbred bolted in a paddock of Giraudist mules, became a catalyst for military unity *malgré lui*, if hardly an apostle of reconciliation. Leclerc's technique was to apply political mix-and-match to forge a modern armored division built around three US-style "combat commands." Although the division was forced to integrate former Vichyites into the ranks, the 2ᵉ DB's command echelon remained unalloyed FFL.[135]

Unlike the unlucky Bacquier, when offered a choice by Koenig in the autumn of 1943 between assignment to Leclerc's 2ᵉ DB or to de Lattre's *Armée B*, American Florence Conrad, leader of the Rochambeau ambulance group, had jumped at the chance to secure "*le ticket pour les Champs-Élysées*."[136] Unfortunately, this complicated her task of recruiting female staff for the 2ᵉ DB's medical section. To predictably conservative *pied noir* objections to surrendering their daughters to the military was added the "animosity," "distrust," and "jealousy" provoked by the division's *France libre* stigma and its intrepid young leader about whom legends – or calumnies, depending on one's viewpoint – were already being spun. Competition for a limited supply of female "auxiliaries" – a term that many women found demeaning – was keen, and *Auxiliaires féminines de l'armée de terre* (AFAT) in Algiers proved predictably uncooperative. Rumor was rife: "you'll never leave," or "General Leclerc is caught between two stools," and so on, which caused some female volunteers to depart Morocco for Algiers.[137] Leclerc also shared command apprehensions about the presence of women in his division as a threat to good order and discipline, and agreed to accept them only on a trial basis. The Rochambelles were integrated into the 13th Medical Battalion and settled, uncomfortably, into military life on a rat-infested floating barracks in Rabat's Oued Bou Regreg. By day, they worked in the segregated wards of a makeshift hospital created in a former music college. Despite a lack of basic equipment – thermometers, syringes, pencils and charts, even bedsheets – they nursed *évadés*, who often arrived malnourished and malarial after months spent in a Spanish jail, while treating soldiers suffering the consequences of everything from car crashes to sexual promiscuity. But recruits trickled in – bored, patriotic, refugees from France marooned by war in Morocco. The female drivers practiced driving through dummy mine fields, evacuating the wounded, and arranging camouflage nets so that their ambulances would not cast shadows to alert German aircraft. Leclerc even stopped by for lunch with US Brigadier General Allen Kingman, whose team was to inspect the division's integration of US arms and equipment. The French had long since discovered that the quickest path to a declaration of combat readiness from Kingman was to give him a good lunch. Adding female company, some of them Americans, possibly accelerated Leclerc's accreditation.[138]

The wait for transport to the UK seemed interminable, interrupted only by Leclerc's attacks of malaria, or bouts of rage invariably accompanied by threats to resign. In late January, the division received its baptism of fire of sorts when it was mobilized to quell Istiqlal-organized pro-independence demonstrations in Rabat. In the middle of April, the 2e DB transferred to the UK, even though it was still seriously deficient in vehicles. The armor and artillery loaded on Landing Ships, Tank (LSTs) at Casablanca for Swansea and Liverpool. The Rochambelles joined the infantry for a dusty overland convoy to Oran, during which the nurses slept on stretchers in the back of their nineteen Dodge ambulances. The wait in Oran was filled with the usual diversions of military life – calisthenics, drill, first-aid courses delivered by the battalion doctor, potato peeling, and bridge. While awaiting transport, the unit's deputy commander, Suzanne "Toto" Torrès, began an affair with Lieutenant colonel Massu "that shocked some of the younger women in the group." Massu and Torrès eventually married in 1948 after she finalized her divorce from her Parisian lawyer husband.[139] The unit shipped for the UK from Mers-el-Kébir on 20 May aboard two requisitioned Cunard liners. Landed at Liverpool, they crossed a gray, rain-soaked Britain to Yorkshire, where Leclerc established his headquarters at Dalton Hall, a Georgian mansion in the East Riding, whose grounds had become festooned with large tents with duckboard floors to accommodate the men. The tracked vehicles were delivered by rail from Swansea.[140]

The unit had not yet "settled," and many political and personal tensions, as well as doubts about leadership in combat, persisted, which caused Leclerc to make some command changes. He soon discovered that a "political" division brought command headaches, when de Gaulle dispatched Pierre Billotte to lead one of the 2e DB's combat commands. This was a crisis of Leclerc's own making, after he had fired Colonel Michel Malaguti, with whom he had personal and doctrinal differences.[141] The son of Gaston Billotte, the late executor of the ill-fated Dyle–Breda Plan of May 1940, Pierre Billotte had been a tank commander in 1940. But, since escaping his *Oflag* to England via a Soviet prison in 1941, he had spent the last three years on de Gaulle's staff. Knowledgeable enough in the infantry support role of 1940-era Renault tanks, Billotte was unschooled in the evolving techniques of armored warfare. His only role, a mistrustful Leclerc surmised, was to serve as de Gaulle's snitch, a gnawing suspicion that triggered another of Leclerc's signature meltdowns.

In England, the Rochambelles ransacked the local stores and the Navy, Army and Air Force Institutes (NAAFI) for women's underwear, and everyone tried to adjust to US Army field rations. While the wax-covered cardboard boxes presented a marvel of culinary efficiency, there was little chance that the tinned ham, beans, crackers, chocolate, vitamins, toilet paper, and occasional condom inside would ever compete for a Michelin star, even in the al fresco category. In early June, George Patton, into whose Third Army the 2e DB was to be incorporated, appeared in his signature helmet, jodhpurs, and Mexican spurs to inspect the division, which he pronounced inadequately trained – inaccurate gunnery, combined with armored units that must be reorganized to prioritize speed. News of the 6 June invasion brought impatience to a fever pitch. But, following an exercise against the Polish 1st Armored Division, they had to endure more Patton-produced theater on 28 June, with an inspection which this time the 2^e DB passed with flying colors – ironically, Maggiar's marine infantry, dressed in US khaki topped with French sailors' red pompoms, snatched the laurels of the day. A pre-embarkation parade of the signature French unit in an Anglo-American Liberation cascade saw Koenig hand out regimental standards. Every soldier was presented with the divisional insignia – a gold cross of Lorraine etched on a blue background. For Leclerc, this meant that his division's combat worthiness and valor must redeem the shame of 1940, a fairly generalized sentiment in a revitalizing French army. For de Gaulle and the GPRF, as the standard bearer of France, the 2^e DB was designed and positioned to make a political statement. This was communicated to the volunteers whatever their political persuasion. One result of the selectivity of the personnel, combined with hyped expectation of unit performance in the glare of history, was that the percentage of psychological casualties in the 2^e DB during the course of the campaign to liberate France was only 0.3 percent, compared with between 5.2 and 14.4 percent among Third Army GIs with whom the 2^e DB served.[142] The problem for Patton and Eisenhower was that the 2^e DB had no manpower reserves to replace losses. As a symbolic "political" division, its combat utility was circumscribed, at least until Paris was liberated.[143] They need not have worried: according to Larminat, Leclerc was a master scrounger and persuasive recruiter. On-the-spot enlistments, combined with American supplies and local resources, meant that, by the war's end, the 2^e DB counted 2,000–3,000 personnel and 500 vehicles over regulation strength.[144]

As the month drew to a close, the division's 4,000 vehicles were directed south, tracked vehicles to Southampton, while wheeled vehicles made for Weymouth. Once they had arrived, they drove up ramps onto LSTs that had just returned from Normandy to disgorge crocodiles of German POWs. The men were stuffed into filthy Liberty ships as the division was lifted piecemeal to France. At 02:00 on the morning of 1 August 1944, one of those ships, the *Philip Thomas*, anchored off Utah Beach at the base of the Cotentin Peninsula after a tedious three-day crossing from England. In the darkness, everyone scrambled down the soggy rope mesh into lighters which slowly nosed toward the dark shore beneath tethered barrage balloons, swerving to avoid the shadowy hulks of destroyed landing craft. The LSTs carrying the division's vehicles beached to allow their cargos of tanks, trucks, and ambulances to plunge down the steep ramps, nose into the shallow surf, and race up the dunes as arm-pumping US beachmasters urged them to hustle, because behind stretched a steel horizon of ships waiting to offload, and return to the UK for more men and matériel to feed into the battle that raged among emerald Normand hedgerows. Once off the beach, they drove south toward Avranches, through a maze of narrow, twisting lanes lined with signs that warned of minefields, past shattered stone villages and families towing cartloads of salvaged belongings. The fields reeked with the bloated carcasses of dead cattle.

The 2^{e} DB had missed all the fun – from 24 July, Operation Cobra had launched an offensive that had carried Patton's Third Army through Avranches and into Brittany, in the process obliterating eight German divisions. By 6 August, the 2^{e} DB was encamped at Saint-James, south of Avranches, when they were hit by a Luftwaffe attack that killed 20 soldiers and wounded another 200, among them one of the Rochambelles, who had her legs shattered. This became the last straw for Rochambelle leader Florence Conrad. As the wounded shrieked and Senegalese stretcher-bearers shuttled bodies toward the medical tent, a clearly rattled Conrad surrendered command to Torrès.[145] In the meantime, Leclerc struggled to master the intricacies of maneuver in the bocage, where his tanks were obliged to align in etiolated columns along sunken roads between high hedges, which invited ambushes and flank attacks. And tank warfare tended to be casualty-heavy, because, while immune from small-arms fire, when punched by an 88 mm cannon or a *Panzerfaust*, his Shermans flamed like Molotov cocktails, incinerating their crews. But Leclerc's impatience proved contagious – in the 2^{e} DB, awaiting orders to advance constituted a court-martial offense, improvisation was mandatory, and indecision was sanctioned. Many a map-studying colonel was surprised to see a jeep speed into view with Leclerc upright in the passenger seat, thrusting his signature Malacca walking stick in his direction, and ordering *en avant!*

On 8 August, Billotte took charge of his combat command, as the division raced toward Le Mans. On 10 August, the 2^{e} DB went into action for the first time as part of Wade Hampton Haislip's XV Corps, whose task was to envelop Alençon, seize bridges over the Sarthe, and then move north to close the Falaise Gap. A man in a rush, Leclerc's agitated impetuosity often infuriated American commanders, who discovered that he treated division boundaries as a theoretical concept. His command echelon seldom knew where he was. Although Haislip was generally willing to indulge volatile "Frenchies," Leclerc taxed Haislip's patience when he ordered Billotte's tanks into Sées, where they succeeded only in creating a mammoth traffic jam when they became entangled with the 5th US Armored Division (AD). But Leclerc redeemed himself, in US eyes at least, when he made common cause with Patton to assign blame to Montgomery for failure to close the Falaise Pocket.[146]

News of the 15 August landings in Provence accelerated the unraveling of the German position. It also distanced the possibility of a resistance-led "national insurrection." On the very day that de Lattre set foot on the Côte d'Azure, Patton had ordered the 2^{e} DB to push toward Dreux. Patton's order produced a foreseeable resignation threat from the volcanic Leclerc, certain that he would be denied the liberation of Paris, an honor that he feared might even fall to his preening rival de Lattre. On 16 August, Patton's COS Major General Hugh Gaffey ordered Leclerc to detach part of his division to join the 90th US Infantry Division (ID) in an attack that aimed to close the Falaise Gap. Leclerc refused, both because he wanted to keep his division intact for the march on Paris and because he considered the plan poorly conceived and underresourced in infantry support. This set up a serious command confrontation with Patton, who lectured Leclerc that divisional commanders in the Third Army were not allowed a vote on when and where they were to fight. However, on 17 August, the American commander was informed that Leclerc's division would be transferred to Courtney Hodge's First Army, to position him to liberate Paris. This was a huge blow to the egotistical Patton, who smelled an Eisenhower maneuver to deny him the glory of Paris' liberation.[147] However, the ever wary de Gaulle, permanently on the *qui vive* for American treachery, guessed correctly that Eisenhower had no intention of sending Allied troops to liberate Paris. In de Gaulle's view, the real reason for the 2e DB's transfer to Hodges was to bring the division under the "tight surveillance" of Hodges' V Corps commander Major General Leonard Gerow and have it "held at Argentan as if one suspected that it would bolt for the Eiffel Tower."[148]

The "Bolt for the Eiffel Tower"

In retrospect, the liberation of the French capital offered a fitting finale to the Normandy campaign, one that gave it focus and purpose. After Paris, the Allied advance became mired in a muddle of missed opportunities that arguably prolonged the war for another nine months.[149] And while the liberation of Paris did not mark the end of the resistance's role in France's liberation, henceforth, the context of resistance participation would change. Paris proved a "particularly brilliant exception" to the rule, where the resistance actually played an active role in the liberation of the city. But its scope was limited by the fact that it was initiated by the communists, who did not entirely control their own resistance organization, the FTP, and by the fact that the BBC never broadcast "*consignes d'action*" to the Parisians as it had done to the resistance on D-Day.[150] The liberation of Paris stood in contrast to the 84 percent of other French cities that were liberated by the Allies, or where the Germans simply walked out. "We can therefore conclude that the national insurrection, at least in a form envisaged by a certain number of resisters, meaning the communists, was a failure," concludes Philippe Buton.[151]

Given Paris' political symbolism and importance as a command, communications, reinforcement, and supply hub for OB West during the Normandy campaign, Eisenhower's impulse to bypass it seems inconceivable. Hitler sought to lure the Allies into a costly street-by-street struggle to retake the capital. But, much to his disappointment, SHAEF planners had never intended to be drawn into a Stalingrad on the Seine. Nor, obviously, had many of Hitler's commanders. For, even though German troops were still fighting west of the city, by 19 August, OB West, Navy Group West, the Third Air Fleet, and the MBF had evacuated the French capital.[152]

On that day, too, a logistical crisis loomed for the Allies, as American armies reached Mantes and crossed the Seine the next day. Eisenhower realized too late that he should have focused on seizing Antwerp and the Scheldt, instead of surging Patton into a Breton cul-de-sac. The only harbor open to the Allies in August and September was Cherbourg, which had been cleared of mines and made fully operational only in August. Until then, supplies and reinforcements had to come from the UK via LSTs, that would founder on the Normandy sands, unload, and wait for high tide to lift off for another run. Logistically speaking, the sudden breakout at Avranches in early August switched the supply emphasis from ammunition to fuel and lubricants for a highly mechanized force. Nor did the Allied logistical services have time to establish forward supply dumps in conditions of a rapid and unexpected advance. This meant that 600–700 tons of supplies every 24 hours for each of 36 Allied divisions, which were advancing up to 75 miles a day, had to follow on the railways and roads repaired as they advanced, and pontoon bridges thrown across rivers. The Allies devised some imaginative logistical innovations, incuding the Red Ball Express and frontline fuel airlift, but these proved merely palliative. Understandably, in these conditions, the SHAEF Commander hesitated to shoulder the responsibility for feeding a city of 5 million inhabitants until more harbors and rail lines had been rehabilitated for the stockpiling of food. Eisenhower, Bradley, and Patton were also apprehensive that a street battle for Paris would devour troops and delay the Allied advance by weeks. There was also a fear of revolution among a starving population. Twenty-three civil affairs units readied to enter Paris.[153]

The argument might be made that the liberation of Paris and consolidation of de Gaulle's power may actually have contributed to the escape of German forces and the eventual hardening of German defenses, because 37 percent of US airlift tonnage meant to keep frontline troops supplied and moving forward had to be diverted to feed Paris, according to Ludewig, which actually worsened the Allied supply crisis. Nor did diverting Leclerc's 2ᵉ DB to Paris in defiance of orders from his frustrated minder Gerow help. In short, the logistical needs of the French capital combined with de Gaulle's requirement to consolidate his power "during critical moments … absorbed far too much attention, which was diverted from the really critical points along the front," insists Ludewig.[154] On the other hand, if the United States and the UK were conducting an international war, Eisenhower could not ignore the fact that, even as a "minor partner" of the Allied coalition, the GPRF also harbored national ambitions which centered on the consolidation of power in Paris. These sometimes conflicting interests had to be balanced. But the Allies' hand was forced by the actions of the Resistance.[155]

The solution to Eisenhower's dilemma was strategic, not logistical. In retrospect, what Eisenhower might have done was to curtail the advance into Brittany and the costly assault on Brest, bypass Paris, prioritize his left wing to seize Antwerp and the Scheldt, and thrust into the North German Plain as Montgomery advocated (see Map 5.2). In this case, Operation Market Garden – the attempt launched on 17 September to seize the Rhine bridges at Arnhem as a prelude to an offensive into the Ruhr – might have succeeded had it been carried out sooner, assuming that Montgomery would not have squandered his opportunities. Ultra informed Eisenhower that his window of advance was closing, as OB West commander Field Marshal Walter Model repositioned the 215,000 troops from two field armies and scattered garrisons that the Germans had managed to extract from France. But SHAEF's planners had envisaged a broad-front advance, which would complicate the accumulating of reserves and logistical prioritization to seize operational opportunities offered by a precipitous German retreat from France. Also, one of Eisenhower's command strengths was to maintain an equilibrium in a coalition composed of strong personalities with diverse and often conflicting national agendas. Therefore, his decision for a "broad front" advance, like that to liberate Paris, while politically risk-averse, failed to hasten the war's end.[156]

De Gaulle had prioritized the liberation of Paris as the prelude to establishing the GPRF's authority, short-circuiting possible attempts by former Vichyites or members of the resistance to seize power, and preempting possible civil war. Leclerc's 2[e] DB had been planted in Overlord precisely to preclude these potential outcomes. Although focused on the operational dimensions of the campaign, Leclerc's immediate superiors – most notably Gerow – had failed to grasp the political scope of his role. From this perspective, Eisenhower's inclination to bypass Paris predictably primed de Gaulle to imagine an American conspiracy to sabotage his consolidation of power.[157] Furthermore, there was the question of civilian resistance. The scattering of the *réduits maquisards* found both the Allies and de Gaulle accused of doing too little too late to rescue *maquisards*. If the resistance in Paris staged an uprising, what would be the Allies' reaction? The August 1944 insurrection of the Polish Home Army in Warsaw was on everyone's mind. Rather than support the Polish nationalists, Stalin halted his troops on the Vistula, allowing the Germans systematically to raise the Polish capital to the ground and massacre the resisters, an act that gave rise to a bitter post-war polemic.[158] In Paris, Warsaw's situation was reversed, in that the resistance, commanded by Spanish

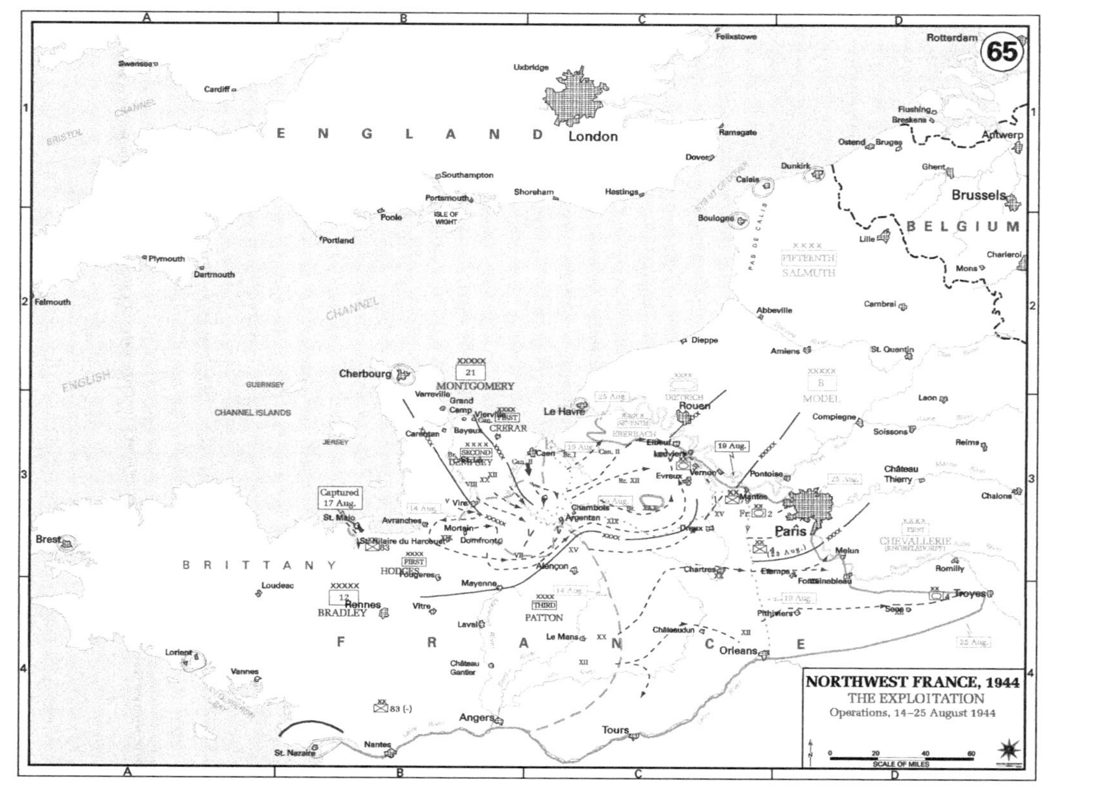

Map 5.2 Northwest France 1944.

Civil War veteran Henri Rol-Tanguy, was dominated by the communists and COMAC. These men were committed to national insurrection both as a political and as a military strategy, and treated de Gaulle's military delegate, former French Rugby international and future Prime Minister Jacques Chaban-Delmas, who was meant to keep a lid on the situation, as a mere messenger boy.

Events in Paris were moving rapidly as the American armies approached the city. On 10 August, the communist trades union federation, the Conféderation générale du travail (CGT), had called on railway workers to strike, a call soon honored as well by postal workers. The communists had celebrated 14 July 1944 with a call for a massive demonstration in Paris. When even the police, sensing the approaching reckoning and worried lest they be categorized as collaborators, put on civilian clothes and joined the strike on 15 August, von Klug ordered that they be disarmed. He also stuffed imprisoned resisters into boxcars bound for Germany. Increasingly, resisters assumed police functions in neighborhoods. In fact, although the communists in particular criticized the police for allowing Vichy to function, by 1943 at least three resistance groups were active in police ranks. The defection of the police proved important, if overly mythologized in the history of Paris' liberation, because it accelerated events. The strike of 15 August by the police, and their seizure of the Prefecture on the Île de la Cité four days later, convinced *délégué général du CFLN en zone occupée* Alexandre Parodi to support communist demands from 18 August for "immediate action," against the advice of military delegate Chaban-Delmas, and Algiers, whose messages were not getting through to Parodi.[159]

Although the German occupation of the Prefecture of Police caused panic, it was clear that the German troops were evacuating the city. By 17 August, US troops had reached Mantes, Fontainebleau, and Melun, and news of Anvil had bolstered spirits. They knew they were winning when even Radio Paris signed off the air, as its best-known surviving announcer, Jean-Hérold Paquis, packed up and fled east.[160] On 18 August, several town halls in the Paris suburbs were seized by the FTP in answer to Tillon's call for a general mobilization. The police strike also encouraged Rol-Tanguy to accelerate the insurrection. Probably 20,000–25,000 men were available for action in Paris, although Rol-Tanguy had only 600 weapons to distribute. But he was encouraged that 20,000 police, gendarmes, and *gardes mobiles* might also join in. The call for insurrection was formally endorsed that afternoon. Rol-Tanguy ordered placards posted for dawn on 19 August. Learning that the police had joined the insurrection, Leclerc sent them the following message: "hold firm, we're coming." The key to de Gaulle's consolidation of power was the fact that representatives of the GPRF occupied the ministries, in particular that of the Interior, which reduced the possibility of conflicting authority.[161]

On 19 August, fighting broke out in Paris as the FTP called for a *mobilisation générale*. Policemen seized the Prefecture at 07:00 and began to attack isolated

German posts in the city. Barricades were erected as FFI wearing armbands patrolled the streets in requisitioned automobiles and on bicycles. Arrondissement halls were occupied, Pétain's photos dislodged, and crosses of Lorraine painted on walls and buildings began to appear. In Algiers, the GPRF was disturbed by news of "looting" and disorder from Paris. Like Weygand in 1940, but with more justification, de Gaulle feared the political implications of an uprising that might replicate the Commune of 1871, with the communists seizing control of the city, provoking oceanic levels of German-sponsored bloodshed and inviting destruction *à la* Warsaw, or both. At 05:00 on 20 August, resisters seized the Hôtel de Ville. A fragile truce was negotiated through Swedish consul-general Raoul Nordling, whereby the Germans agreed not to evict resistance fighters from buildings they occupied, while resisters would not attack German troops evacuating the capital. Communist resisters, convinced that they were acting in accordance with Paris' revolutionary traditions, denounced the truce, which lasted barely a day. But it became clear that Allied armies would not reach Paris in time to avoid a potential reenactment of Warsaw. Nor would it be possible, given their limited armaments, for the resistance to liberate Paris before the Allies arrived. At the same time, von Choltitz threatened to meet any disorder with SS troops and Panzers, muscle that he clearly did not have.[162]

On 20 August, Hitler directed that Paris be defended "regardless of the city's destruction." "Rol" dispatched his chief of staff to Eisenhower's HQ to request a prompt intervention of regular forces. On that same day, de Gaulle, his mood more mistrustful and cantankerous than usual, departed Casablanca by air to land near Saint-Lô. He was informed by his staff about what seemed to be a brewing explosion in Paris. When briefed by Eisenhower at his HQ near Rennes on the disposition of Allied forces, de Gaulle was shocked that "no one was marching on Paris." He subsequently explained to the SHAEF Commander the dangers posed by a communist takeover of the French capital, and, speaking as head of the French government, requested that Leclerc be allowed to travel the 150 kilometers that separated Argentan and Paris. Eisenhower replied that he did not want to be drawn into a battle in the streets of Paris. But an ever suspicious de Gaulle believed Eisenhower's reluctance to enter Paris was motivated by a "supreme intrigue" instigated by Roosevelt, who had yet to extend official diplomatic recognition to the GPRF, but instead continued to criticize de Gaulle for appointing officials in liberated areas. Nevertheless, events on the ground had long made Roosevelt's hesitation to acknowledge the GPRF's sovereignty obsolete, and even he had admitted in July that the CFLN was the "working authority for civilian administration in the liberated areas of France."[163] For his part, for some days, Laval had schemed to recall the National Assembly of 1940, set up a government in Paris or a city in eastern France, and seek Allied recognition, a scenario that the

Allies were certainly aware of. Laval's plans were cut short when everyone at Vichy was abducted to southern Germany. In other liberated areas, de Gaulle's representatives were often being ignored by local and clerical notables, as well as by the Americans, who continued to transact business through Vichy legacies.[164]

On 21 August, fearing famine and anarchy in Paris, and finding it "intolerable" that the Germans continued to occupy the French capital, "when one had the means to chase him out," de Gaulle practically issued an ultimatum to Eisenhower to intervene, or else he would order Leclerc to do so. The urgency for regular troops to arrive in Paris was reinforced by Juin, in his capacity as National Chief of Staff, and by Koenig, who cautioned Eisenhower that, if he did not authorize Leclerc to march on Paris, he would go in any case.[165]

"My hand was forced by the action of the Free French forces inside Paris," Eisenhower records in his memoirs.

> Throughout France the Free French had been of inestimable value in the campaign. They were particularly active in Brittany, but on every portion of the front we secured help from them in a multitude of ways. Without their great assistance the liberation of France and the defeat of the enemy in western Europe would have consumed a much longer time and meant greater losses to ourselves. So, when the Free French forces inside the city staged their uprising it was necessary to move rapidly to their support. Information indicated that no great battle would take place and it was believed that the entry of one or two Allied divisions would accomplish the liberation of the city.[166]

In fact, by 22 August, when he received de Gaulle's letter, Eisenhower had concluded that the political risks of avoiding a Parisian stopover far exceeded the logistical benefits of bypassing the French capital, in part because of pressure from de Gaulle, but also because he did not want to leave a German-occupied capital in his rear. Events in the German camp also helped to convince the Allied Commander that seizing Paris would not overly delay his advance. Hitler continued to insist that the "decisive political significance" of Paris would force the Allies into a costly street battle, that would leave them occupying "a field of rubble."[167] However, the 20 July attempt on Hitler's life by Colonel Claus von Stauffenberg, combined with the breakout in Normandy, had produced considerable disarray in the German high command in France. The failure of the 20 July plot had resulted in the execution of MBF Carl-Heinrich von Stülpnagel, who under torture had implicated Erwin Rommel, which triggered Rommel's forced suicide. OB West commander Field Marshal Günther von Kluge, who had ordered a full-scale retreat on 16 August, was summoned to Berlin to explain himself. Convinced that Hitler was aware of his role in von Stauffenberg's plot, he committed suicide on 19 August, and was replaced at OB West by Walter Model.

For the fifty-year-old Dietrich von Choltitz, who had begun the Polish campaign in 1939 as a battalion commander in an ordinary infantry regiment, to have Hitler bestow upon him the title of Commanding General and Wehrmacht Commander of Greater Paris symbolized quite a remarkable wartime ascension, and something of a reversal of fortune. Choltitz had established a reputation for toughness on the Eastern Front, which in June had translated into command of the LXXXIV Corps before Avranches. Unfortunately for Choltitz, this is precisely where Patton hammered his breakthrough. Stripped of command by von Kluge, von Choltitz was out of work when Hitler summoned him to his "Wolf's Lair" at Rastenberg in East Prussia on 7 August 1944. Hitler's brief for von Choltitz was to maintain order in the French capital, deal with what the Germans euphemistically called "rear-echelon phenomena," and cull shirkers out of support formations to put them into the fighting line – a subject on which Hitler was an authority as he had successfully "shirked" his way through the Great War.[168] But von Choltitz's encounter with his shaking, ill, totally out of touch Commander in Chief, coming on top of his experience of breathtaking American firepower in Normandy, had undercut any residual faith in a German victory. Furthermore, he was unsure whether Paris should – or could – be defended. Most of the 20,000 fighting troops deployed west of the city were the remnants of the 352nd Infantry Division (ID), and other demoralized Falaise Pocket refugees. The garrison inside the city was made up of a handful of security battalions, reserve anti-aircraft units, and "Paris Alert Battalions" composed of clerical personnel – in all about 5,000 men. Only 18,000 of the 40,000 kilometers of French railway track remained usable in the wake of the invasion. The pre-war inventory of 6,000 locomotives and 300,000 freight wagons of the Société nationale des chemins de fer français (SNCF) had been reduced to 1,233 and 31,000, respectively.[169] This caused logistical problems for the Allies, but it also meant that the French *Ravitaillement général* had broken down, bringing Paris to the cusp of starvation. The initial "*attentisme*" of the population had been troubled by well-founded rumors that the Germans planned to deport every able bodied male to Germany as forced labor, which had ignited popular resistance. On 17 August, all Vichy offices in Paris as well as the German embassy had packed their bags and evacuated east. On 20 August, Laval and Pétain followed to Sigmaringen, putting paid to Laval's scheme to gain Allied recognition. The German commander organized a parade of all of his available troops in Paris as a show of force. His tactic was to buy time to defuse the situation until the German First Army either dispatched reinforcements or ordered him to abandon the city.

Faced with Hitler's 20 August directive to defend Paris "regardless of the city's destruction," von Choltitz reverted to long-established Wehrmacht protocols to seem to comply with Hitler's orders, while executing only those elements he deemed feasible. While Model was prepared to contemplate defending Paris from its western perimeter, he lacked the time and the numbers to make a last stand on the Place de la Concorde while carrying out "demolition of residential housing blocks, public executions," and so on as required by what was sardonically labeled in OB West the "Rubble Field Order." Instead, he ordered the establishment of "emergency reserve lines" north and east of the city, while informing the Wehrmacht operations staff that there were far too many bridges in Paris to destroy, and the order was militarily senseless in any case as the Allies had already crossed the Seine in several places. Von Choltitz concurred that a campaign of systematic bridge destruction in Paris would provoke a general revolt, which he sought to avoid because the police had been disarmed and were on strike, and he lacked the troops to contain it. So, he informed the German Supreme Command by telephone that he had given the order to destroy bridges, although there is no evidence that he had actually done so. Von Choltitz's tactics of playing for time by issuing threats to replicate the destruction of Warsaw rapidly lost effectiveness, as his reinforcements amounted to no more than a handful of haggard escapees from Normandy, while the food situation shifted from mere starvation to famine. After conferring with von Choltitz, on 23 August, Model informed Alfred Jodl, chief of operations at OKW, that there was no possibility of holding Paris with the derisory forces available, requesting that "these situation assessments be reported to the Führer clearly." This, of course, made no difference whatsoever.[170]

Ignoring orders from a powerless Gerow, the 2ᵉ DB struck out at 06:00 on 23 August in 400 vehicles, covering 120 miles in 15 hours. Bradley ungraciously complained that Leclerc's men ceased to party and "burned up their treads on the brick roads" only because they feared that the 4th US ID would liberate Paris ahead of them.[171] Model's hope was that at least Paris' outer defenses would hold long enough for him to extricate two retreating field armies west of Paris. By that time, in a flip of the concept of "*réduits stratégiques*," the FFI had taken control of Paris' streets, with pockets of Germans holed up in le Vercors-like strongpoints. But, by 21:00 on 24 August, the Spanish Republican refugees of *la nueve* had occupied Paris' Hôtel de Ville, which provoked a popular celebration.[172] At midnight, von Choltitz reported that French troops were camped on the Place de l'Étoile, as well as the Palais du Luxembourg, traditionally the seat of the French senate. "This was the moment when the internal and external resistance met physically for the first time," concludes Gildea.[173]

On 25 August, Leclerc's soldiers forced their way into von Choltitz's HQ at the Hôtel Meurice. After Nordling had convinced von Choltitz to capitulate, the German Governor was brought to the Prefecture of Police to sign the surrender document, along with Leclerc and "Colonel Rol, commandant les FFI de l'Île-de-France," on the logic that the resistance had participated in the liberation. Officers from von Choltitz's staff, accompanied by French officers, including Philippe de Gaulle in the company of a German major, fanned out over the city to order German troops to surrender. Everyone then adjourned to Leclerc's headquarters at the Gare Montparnasse to repeat the surrender ceremony in a more formal manner. Von Choltitz re-signed the order for his troops to surrender. Around 17:00, de Gaulle arrived (Figure 5.3). "I congratulated Leclerc," recorded de Gaulle. "What a stage on the road to his glory! I also congratulated Rol-Tanguy, whom I see at his side. It was in effect the action of the forces of the interior that had, in the course of the preceding days, chased the enemy from our streets, decimated and demoralized his troops, blocked his units in their fortified islands. Also, since the morning, groups of partisans, despite their very poor armament, courageously helped the regular troops in cleaning up the pockets of German resistance." Upon reading the surrender document, however, according to his memoirs de Gaulle saw that von Choltitz had actually surrendered to Rol-Tanguy. In de Gaulle's mind, this certified that Paris had been liberated by popular insurrection rather than by the tanks of the 2^e^ DB. He declared this "wording" to be "unacceptable." As the senior French officer present, it was Leclerc who should accept the German surrender. So, Rol-Tanguy's signature was crossed off. De Gaulle also read the proclamation issued by the CNR that morning, which claimed victory for "the French nation," giving credit neither to the French government nor to de Gaulle. "Leclerc immediately understood."[174] However, this set up the post-war memorial competition between the Fondation Leclerc and the Musée de la Résistance nationale over which man deserved greater credit for the liberation of Paris.[175]

In a meticulously choreographed itinerary meant to restore French unity and consign Vichy to a postscript in French history, de Gaulle left Montparnasse for the War Ministry on the rue Saint-Dominique, then to the Prefecture of Police, where de Gaulle pinned the *Légion d'honneur* on the police flag, as he praised "the courageous 'guardians' of the Parisian police [who] gave a fine example of patriotism and solidarity to the whole nation which was one of the main factors in the success of the battles for the liberation of the capital."[176] A ribbon was a small price to pay to memorialize the eleventh-hour "*insurrection des policiers*," putting Bosquet and his cops back on the right side of history to avert revolution, restore order, and guarantee institutional continuity.[177] In the process, 12,000 French Jews, whom in 1942 Bosquet and the French police had rounded up, incarcerated in the Vel' d'Hiv, and shipped off to their deaths in Germany were consigned to memorial oblivion and remain a source of political polemics into the modern era.[178] Having visited the two institutions of state, de Gaulle reluctantly agreed to Parodi's request that he meet the CNR at the Hôtel de Ville, where he delivered his "imaginary vision" of the Liberation of Paris:

> Paris! Paris outraged! Paris broken! Paris martyred! But Paris liberated! Liberated by itself, liberated by its people with the help of the armies of France, with the help and assistance of the whole of France, of that France which fights, of the only France, of the true France, of eternal France.

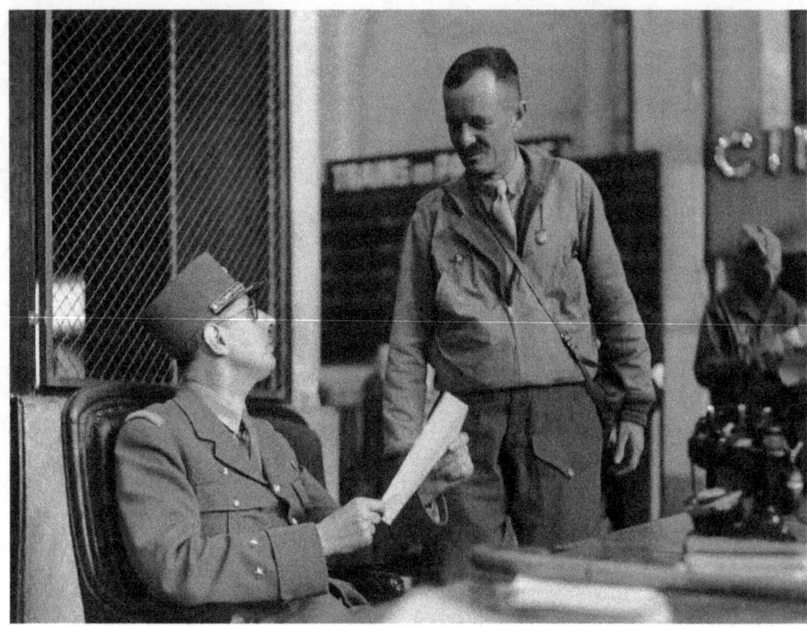

Figure 5.3 Arriving at Montparnasse station in Paris, de Gaulle realizes that von Choltitz has surrendered to Rol-Tanguy, not to Leclerc, the CFLN's official representative. Rol-Tanguy's signature was subsequently crossed off the document. (Photo by Keystone-France/Gamma-Keystone via Getty Images)

While de Gaulle's memorable and highly controversial address should not be conflated with history, it did convey its own irony. Although he did make a fleeting reference to "the support of our dear and admirable Allies," who were needed to expel the enemy from French soil, "De Gaulle certainly wanted Paris to be seen to liberate itself – but only at the moment the Allies arrived," concludes Julian Jackson.[179]

The myth of Paris' self-liberation was given an inadvertent boost by the "Anglo-Saxon" media, which had announced the liberation of Paris on 23 August, and by the Political Warfare Executive (PWE) which on the next day pronounced that "The manner of her liberation by the FFI gives thrilling proof that Paris, despite the oppression and hardship of a four year occupation by the enemy, had lost none of its *élan*."[180] The remainder of de Gaulle's visit to the Hôtel de Ville was totally in character. When Georges Bidault, President of the CNR, asked de Gaulle to proclaim the Fourth Republic, an appropriate request as both the Second and the Third Republic had been launched from the Hôtel de Ville, in 1848 and 1870, respectively, he was put firmly in his place: "The republic never ceased to exist," but had been incarnate in *la France libre*. "I am the president of the Government of the Republic. Why would I proclaim it?" This statement shocked and disappointed many, who believed that the republic had been abolished in 1940, and also sought reassurance of de Gaulle's democratic intentions. But Parodi and the CNR served as mere intermediaries. They were not "eternal France." After waving to the large crowd below from one of the windows of the Hôtel de Ville, de Gaulle returned to the Ministry of War, "leaving everyone dumbstruck."[181]

While de Gaulle's performance was calculated to find quick unity and evict Vichy from French history, it established a "fraught" relationship with the resistance. The assertion of Paris' self-liberation was an allegorical statement of French sovereignty, as well as an attempt to rehabilitate the French people by associating them with resistance and liberation. Pétain had been installed by a panicked parliament manipulated by a handful of traitors. The republic had persevered in *la France libre* and the CFLN, with de Gaulle as president. "*La France éternelle*" could admit neither divisions nor hesitations incompatible with de Gaulle's requirement for a continuity from 1914 of the *union sacrée*. With Paris "liberated by itself," 1940 disappeared, Vichy was sealed off in brackets, the Allies became invisible, and the nation was transubstantiated from "*attentiste*" to heroic. In this way, "resistentialism" – a national myth that inflated the importance and scope of resistance to the German occupation, eliminated *attentisme*, and restricted collaboration to a claque of criminals and traitors at Vichy – became the foundation for "the unitary myth" as symbolized by "the man of 18 June."[182] De Gaulle's glacial dismissal of the internal resistance, not only in Paris but repeated in his tour of the provinces, was meant "to signify that its role was now over and the State was to be restored." Not only did this signify that, in de Gaulle's view, the removal of Vichy and the occupation did not constitute a liberation, but rather a restoration, but also it set up a memorial competition between de Gaulle and a resistance that "resented de Gaulle's presumption that resistance had started with his speech of 18 June 1940. Most resisters had started by acting quite independently of de Gaulle – if indeed they had heard his speech at all. Some of them felt that the 'emigrés' of London had not shared their dangers."[183]

By the afternoon of Saturday 26 August, "no American troops were stationed in Paris," and Gerow's orders to Leclerc to participate in no ceremonies "would certainly not have been issued without instructions from higher authority." At de Gaulle's behest, various dignitaries from the internal and external resistance assembled at the Place de l'Étoile. After reviewing the *Régiment du Tchad*, whose soldiers stood erect in their vehicles, de Gaulle rekindled the flame on the tomb of the unknown soldier. He then descended the Champs-Élysées on foot, to the acclamations of the crowd. For the leader of *la France libre*, who had sought exile four years earlier, this event symbolized the reestablishment of a unified French community with "only one thought, one desire, one cry, differences vanish, individuals disappear." This ceremonial victory stroll down Paris' most iconic boulevard festooned with billowing tricolored banners was witnessed by perhaps the largest crowd ever to gather in France, many of whom had walked for hours into the center from outlying suburbs. Most had no idea what de Gaulle looked like, having only been offered Vichy caricatures of "ex-General de Gaulle" for four years. In a spectacle that evoked "the shadow of Bonaparte," "the selfless savior-healer in uniform" made his way down the Champs-Élysées to his *sacre* in Notre-Dame.[184] It also launched a fight for precedence, as representatives from the internal resistance – Bidault, Parodi, Le Troquer, and Chaban-Delmas – jostled to precede "the men from London" – Juin, d'Argenlieu, Leclerc, and Koenig. At 16:30 the party arrived at Notre-Dame. Paris' Cardinal Archbishop Monseigneur Suhard, who had presided over a mass for Pétain four months earlier, and had officiated at Henriot's funeral in the preceding month, had been invited to make alternative plans by "the new authorities." The mass was abbreviated by shots fired inside the Cathedral, an interruption which de Gaulle suspected was orchestrated by communist elements in COMAC, although there is no evidence to support that accusation.[185]

Unlike Warsaw, Paris had survived. The victory of the resistance, or at least the communist elements in it, had been only partial and fleeting. A Communist strategy to take power would have been based on three pillars: gain control of the internal resistance; make it independent of Algiers; and create a national insurrection.[186] While the communists had seized control of COMAC, and in the person of Rol-Tanguy commanded the FFI around Paris, only 4,000 of an estimated 20,000 resisters in the Paris region counted as communists, despite the best efforts of Rol-Tanguy to have more militants enlist. Chaban-Delmas had informed London on 11 August that the FTP lacked the numbers to control events in Paris. But "Chaban's" messages were often decoded several days later, so that Gaullist officials had no up-to-date grasp of events. De Gaulle feared that the series of strikes launched in Paris from 10 August might serve as a prelude to a communist-led insurrection. But the impediments to coordinating that were practically insurmountable. The chain of command and interactions among the various resistance groups and "*la milice patriotique*" (MP) – the armed wing of the PCF that had originally been formed to act in strikes and demonstrations during the occupation and to carry out political tasks on the Liberation, such as the arrest of collaborators – were complex and sometimes non-existent, especially as the MPs were confined largely to urban, industrialized areas.[187] The means of coordinating and arming the various groups were in the hands of the EMFFI and the Allies. Rol-Tanguy complained that he lacked money to finance his networks, arms to make them combat worthy, and explosives to carry out sabotage operations, nor did he receive clear orders. This was in part because Rol-Tanguy's DMR, Lieutenant-colonel Pierre Sonneville, a regular officer incensed that Rol-Tanguy called himself "colonel," saw it as his job to make sure that "Rol doesn't really command."[188]

Unlike on D-Day, the BBC sent no "personal messages" to Paris calling for "immediate action." The result was that the Liberation of Paris produced few casualties and minimal destruction, in large part because of the approach and intervention of Allied armies, an inducement to von Choltitz to make a deal that helped further to marginalize the communists, even had they agreed on the feasibility of "national insurrection." Pétain played his part by emphasizing the "neutrality" of France, sending emissaries to de Gaulle to assure the peaceful transition of power, whom de Gaulle rejected, and ordering his supporters to do nothing that could "provoke tragic reprisals."[189]

With no sense of irony, on 27 August, the head of the GPRF, who had stoked a fear of AMGOT to keep his supporters in line, visited Eisenhower to request that two US divisions be quartered in in the French capital "to use, as he said, as a show of force and to establish his position firmly." Paris may have "liberated itself," but obviously de Gaulle believed that he required US troops to shore up the authority of the GPRF. In the end, Eisenhower organized a march down the Champs-Élysées of two US divisions on the way to the front as de Gaulle and Omar Bradley stood side-by-side in the reviewing stand (Figure 5.4). "My memory flashed back almost two years, to Africa and our political problems of that time. There we had accepted the governmental organization already in existence and never during our entire stay had one of the French officials asked for Allied troops in order to establish or affirm his position as a local administrative authority. Here there seemed a touch of the sardonic in the picture of France's symbol of liberation having to ask for Allied forces to establish and maintain a similar position in the heart of the freed capital." While de Gaulle's praising of Paris for having "liberated itself" and US troops marching down the Champs-Élysées offer two indelible images of the Liberation, the link between them is seldom noted. Like de Gaulle, Eisenhower too worried about "partisan disunity in localities behind us" and "a threatening physical weakness in our communications zone, stretching from the French coast to the front, that did endanger our future offensive operations. The lifeblood of supply was running perilously thin throughout the forward extremities of the Army."[190] But, beyond his immediate operational concerns, Eisenhower had long advocated for Washington's diplomatic recognition of de Gaulle, fearing that, "'if France falls into the orbit of any other country (e.g. the USSR) the other countries of Europe will do the same,' and it would not 'be in our interest to have the continent of Europe dominated by any single power.'"[191] In fact, the fear of both SHAEF and Koenig of resistance-

Figure 5.4 Soldiers of the US 28th ID, on their way to the front, were diverted at de Gaulle's request to parade down the Champs-Élysées on 29 August 1944 to overawe "the French Resistance" and bolster the authority of the GPRF in the wake of Liberation. (Photo by –/AFP via Getty Images)

induced chaos in the rear persisted into the autumn and winter of 1944, which lent a particular urgency to the making of an *amalgame* incorporating the FFI into the regular French army.[192]

Conclusion

While the French longed for Liberation, they also feared its destructive and divisive potential, which had been foreshadowed in Allied bombing. Given that the conventional French forces were diminutive, de Gaulle counted on popular resistance to symbolize the participation of the French people in their own liberation. However, the fear that a "national insurrection" would cause great slaughter, and benefit the communists, caused planners to downgrade the concept. The STO crisis and the emergence of the *maquis* phenomenon seemed to offer political opportunities to various players. However, despite considerable Allied and resistance efforts to operationalize the *réduits maquisards*, they played at best a marginal role in the Liberation, while their destruction offered another "black legend" of betrayal, first by the Allies, to diminish France's international standing, and then by the Gaullists, who sought to avoid civil war, impose the French state, and deny political power to communists.

The liberation of Paris served as one of the Second World War's iconic moments, both as a milestone in the rollback of Nazi power and a consecration of France's republican resurrection. The fact that the city could self-liberate without an outbreak of civil disorder, and that de Gaulle's GPRF moved rapidly to assume the levers of national power, and limit the scope for local autonomy, was a credit to pre-invasion planning. Yet, by forcing a resistance that had consecrated, democratized, and legitimized him to step back into the ranks, de Gaulle opened himself to charges of adopting the myth of popular liberation while elbowing its leadership from power. But it also was a concession of realism by the communists, who were relatively weak and reluctant to initiate an overt power struggle with de Gaulle, especially while Germany remained in the war. The acclamation of de Gaulle removed any lingering reservations, even in Washington, that he was the legitimate leader of France. With the French state restored in its capital, de Gaulle disbanded the CNR after a perfunctory 27 August meeting at the rue Saint-Dominique. The next day, the COMAC and leading members of the FFI were dismissed in a similarly cursory manner, as de Gaulle announced the dissolution of the EMFFI. The resistance *levée* was closed down, the emergency over, and former FFI would henceforth fight Germans "amalgamated" as soldiers in the regular army, not serve the political ambitions of resistance leaders and communists facilitated by the interface services.[193]

6 Anvil/Dragoon

As a military endeavor, Operation Anvil – renamed Dragoon on 1 August 1944 – posed far fewer hazards than did Overlord. The option of simultaneous invasions of northern and southern France had been on the table since the Anfa (Casablanca) Conference of January 1943. The proposal for an invasion of France's Mediterranean coast emerged from the Trident Conference of May 1943, and was approved at Tehran (28 November–1 December 1943), but not without controversy. Although Trident had opted for an attack on Italy, the idea of invading southern France proved resilient. By late summer, the American Joint Chiefs had put their weight behind Anvil as a way to assist Overlord, by seizing the ports of Toulon and Marseille and advancing up the Rhône Valley. But, when this was proposed at the Quadrant Conference in August, the British pointed out that neither enough landing craft nor troops were available to carry out both Anvil and Overlord, while sustaining operations in Italy. By October, with Allied operations stalled on the peninsula, Eisenhower placed Anvil on indefinite hold.[1]

Indeed, the Americans came to see a shortage of landing craft, especially Landing Ships, Tank (LSTs), as a Churchill ploy to postpone Overlord, tentatively scheduled for 1 May 1944. The issue was forced in part by Stalin, who at Tehran bluntly declared all operations in the Mediterranean to be diversions, with the possible exception of an invasion of southern France, and insisted that Overlord be executed "certainly not later than 15 or 20 May." Stalin's promise to enter the war against Japan upon Germany's defeat allowed the "Second Cairo Conference" (2–7 December 1943) to recuperate and rationalize the use of amphibious craft.[2] But the stalemate at Anzio from January 1944 caused Churchill and his British Chiefs of Staff (COS) chorus to press for a land invasion of southern France smoothed by the Alpine *maquis*.

Given his hostility to Anvil, the Prime Minister's proposal to the Combined Chiefs of Staff (CCS), just after 6 June 1944, to advance to Vienna through Ljubljana hardly came as a surprise, as both Alexander and Maitland Wilson had already floated this trial balloon. Churchill's Ljubljana proposal was a desperation pitch, as his preference for prolonged operations in the Mediterranean and the Balkans had found no traction either at Tehran or subsequently in Cairo the preceding year.[3] It was also badly timed. The fall of Rome on 4 June, followed by the rapid Allied surge up the Italian peninsula, coincided with Operation Bagration, which by July had pushed Soviet lines 300 kilometers further west. Meanwhile, Overlord appeared stalled in the Norman hedgerows. Eisenhower vetoed Churchill's "adventures in Southeastern Europe," and instead insisted on the need to capture Marseilles and Toulon to support operations in France and distract German forces in Normandy. Last-ditch British proposals to maintain the momentum of the Allied advance in Italy into the Po Valley were scuttled on 2 July, when the CCS ordered a halt at the Pisa–Rimini line. On 5 July, Supreme Allied Commander Mediterranean (SACMED) Maitland Wilson informed Supreme Commander Allied Forces Headquarters Harold Alexander that his priority was to create a ten-division force for southern France. Incorrigible to the last, Churchill attempted to persuade Eisenhower to launch an assault in the Bay of Biscay, on the pretext that the French army that was to provide the bulk of the troops for Anvil was untested and incapable.[4]

The French also cast a vote affecting the debate's outcome. Having taken the decision to arm and equip up to eleven French divisions in January 1943, the Allies initially had been undecided how to deploy them. While French forces had turned in a game performance in Tunisia, a casualty rate there of over 20 percent was hardly sustainable. Both Roosevelt and Churchill had realized the advantages of associating the French army with the liberation of Europe. Juin and the *Corps expéditionnaire français* (CEF) had earned Anglo-American respect. Churchill's argument that French forces were unready for continental combat was recognized as a transparent ploy to sabotage Anvil. And in any case, having armed the French, given the shipping shortage, the only way to get them home was either by forcing a passage through Italy – an arduous and increasingly unlikely possibility – or via France's southern coast.[5]

Not content merely to serve in "secondary operations" like Italy, or insert a token division into Overlord, de Gaulle and the *Comité français de libération nationale* (CFLN)/*Gouvernement provisoire de la république française* (GPRF) sought to liberate France, a French army in the vanguard, with the goal of reestablishing the Republic, but also to referee the "national insurrection" and impose order in the wake of Liberation. A series of ordinances passed in the winter and spring of 1944 had created seventeen "regional commissaires" armed with exceptional powers "to take all measures necessary to assure the security of French and Allied armies, provide administration for the territory, to reestablish republican legality and satisfy the needs of the population." Shadow ministries prepped to supplant their Vichy counterparts, while the municipal councils of 1939 were to be reestablished. To give the resistance a voice, a "Liberation Committee" was to be created in each department from among members of resistance groups and political parties to advise the prefect. This transition was to be supervised by a "*commissaire national délégué en territoire libéré*," in this instance, the commissioner for war André Le Troqué.[6] But, in the end, it was the army that had to supply both the muscle behind this transition and the means to control the resistance. In the view of Claire Miot, de Gaulle envisioned "*une armée rassembleur*," a unifying force that would "amalgamate" *Forces françaises de l'intérieur* (FFI) volunteers into its ranks. "Amalgamation" became both an aspiration and a symbol that would simultaneously channel the "national insurrection" and integrate the resistance into the war, while providing a patriotic recruitment base to rejuvenate, rehabilitate, and sustain the French army in the war's final stages.[7]

With a capable French army operating on home soil, de Gaulle calculated that the Allies must treat France as an equal alliance partner, rely on GPRF cooperation, and accord it diplomatic recognition. The French had reluctantly agreed to dispatch the CEF to Italy, because to submit to Allied command priorities had been a condition of rearmament, and because the decision had been taken during the leadership struggle between de Gaulle and Giraud. There was also an argument to be made that a rearmed French army must become battle hardened and acclimatized to operating within the Allied command structure before it was launched into the Liberation. On 27 December 1943, Bedell Smith had informed de Gaulle that the CCS had agreed that all French forces, including those in Italy, would participate in an invasion of southern France as a unitary army with its own commander, while a symbolic division would be inserted into Overlord. However, this agreement hinged on the evolution of the campaign in Italy. Furthermore, the CCS refused to go further by agreeing to consult with the "French command" on those deployments as de Gaulle wished, because the French were considered too "turbulent" to be included in strategic decision-making.[8]

While it was agreed that the French army would provide the primary force for Anvil, everything hinged on the progress of operations in Italy. On 13 May 1944, Franklin Roosevelt had allowed Eisenhower to deal with de Gaulle on military matters, a de facto recognition of the CFLN. But, without a formal accord on the use of French troops, de Gaulle feared that French forces might remain sidelined in Italy as the Anglo-Americans invaded France. Over Churchill's protests, the availability of four French divisions freed for action by the success of Operation Diadem – the breakthrough at Monte Cassino – allowed Eisenhower to execute Anvil/Dragoon without impacting either Overlord or Italy, hence paving the way for an Anglo-American compromise.[9]

"The King of Attitude"

On 26 December 1943, Henri Giraud had officially designated Jean de Lattre de Tassigny to command the Second French army, thereby keeping a November promise by de Gaulle to name him to "an important operational command," a few days after de Lattre had officially "regularized" his situation with *la France combattante*. De Gaulle's offer followed a strong recommendation from Admiral/Father Thierry d'Argenlieu, who had vouched for the sincerity of de Lattre's eleventh-hour conversion to the Cross of Lorraine.[10] Although he held authority over practically all units in French North Africa (AFN), apart from two divisions initially designated for service in Italy, de Lattre believed that the infusion of a semblance of unity and purpose into his nascent command would constitute his biggest challenge. For starters, the Second French army, which in January 1944 was renamed *l'Armée B*, was a virtual command. Its disparate elements included a miscellany of "Senegalese" and North African units, *Forces françaises libres* (FFL), and *évadés de France*, in various stages of rearmament and training. Raoul Salan, who would command the *6ᵉ Régiment de tirailleurs sénégalais* (6ᵉ RTS) in *l'Armée B*, declared that by the end of 1943 the "fusion" had restored the army's "equilibrium," a statement that is rather belied by the tensions that he then proceeded to recount.[11]

All armies offer an aggregation of castes defined by arm, regiment, and rank, regulars and reservists, staff and line. Colonial armies further segregate into a juxtaposition of "race," which accentuates by skin color and usually religion a hierarchy of commanders and commanded. The preference was for "martial races," like Moroccan Berbers, whose rusticity habituated them to hardship, whose tribal values accustomed them to hierarchy and hence made them amenable to military discipline, and whose fear of dishonor for themselves and their families mandated battlefield courage. The military caste system defines power, certainly, but also prestige. Which caste is "dominant," which is more worthy of respect because of its armaments, experience, competence, political motivation, or alleged cultural characteristics? The truth was that, despite a "fusion" of Gaullists and "Giraudists," the architecture of caste in de Lattre's *Armée B* had hardened into a kaleidoscope of attitudes, resentments, allegiances, grudges, jealousies, and disciplinary approaches that would make it a force difficult to "grip." And, once in France, *l'Armée B* would be required to integrate into its ranks FFI Untouchables. During a preliminary visit to several units in his future command over the Christmas holidays of 1943, de Lattre discovered that the soldiers had been largely abandoned by their officers, leaving their cantonments neglected, with a "message" from Marshal Pétain still prominently displayed in one unit, all of which would require a "serious adjustment to get this army into a frame of mind to execute its incomparable mission."[12]

While officially the FFL had ceased to exist, its units, led by Diego Brosset's *1ère Division française libre* (1ère DFL), cleaved ferociously to their Gaullist character, branded by combat against Vichy forces at Dakar and in Syria, which hardened their sense of righteous ascendency. They regarded themselves as an apostate fraternity bonded by their rejection of Vichy and Giraud, with a casual front-line attitude to military courtesies, who resisted integration into *l'Armée d'Afrique*'s racialized norms. Whenever possible, they preferred to fill vacancies by promotion through the ranks, rather than accept transfers from outside the clan. For his part, the incorrigible General Joseph de Goislard de Monsabert disdained these Gaullists as "deserters" on parole. An unrepentant Giraudist, Monsabert believed that "the hero of Königstein" had been "sacrificed" and that a vengeful de Gaulle was determined to punish all those loyal to his former rival, while the simple truth was that de Gaulle was utterly dependent on the former Giraudists like Monsabert to command his army.[13]

Nor did it help de Lattre that Juin had poached the best staff officers, as well as many rearmed and trained units, for transfer to Italy to burnish the CEF's brilliant combat performance, even if it was tarnished by its post-Cassino misconduct. Although approved at Tehran, Anvil was still "hypothetical" in Juin's view, which gave him priority claim on French personnel. De Lattre's intrigues with General Béthouart, COS of National Defense, to have staff officers transferred from the CEF to *l'Armée B* further envenomed an already testy rivalry between the two generals. Juin complained to de Gaulle that de Lattre was putting out slanderous stories that the Germans had liberated him so he would transfer French material in North Africa to Rommel, and that in Italy he was profligate with the lives of his *tirailleurs*.[14] Given Juin's brilliant success in Italy, the announcement that de Lattre would command French forces in Anvil caught both *l'armée d'Afrique* and the Americans by surprise. War commissaire Le Troquer had opposed de Gaulle's choice of his Saint-Cyr senior de Lattre, while Juin was mortified by de Gaulle's seeming ingratitude. Mark Clark denounced "the scandalous manner in which Juin is treated," when he learned on 16 June of the transfer of two French divisions in Italy to Anvil.[15] Giraudists in *l'armée d'Afrique* had deeply resented what they saw as de Lattre's opportunistic defection to the Gaullist camp and held it against him for the rest of his life. The standard explanation for de Gaulle's decision to jump de Lattre over Juin was that the French leader realized that Juin's *pied noir* and Vichy antecedents made him unacceptable to the internal resistance.[16] A dissenting, if minority, opinion holds that de Gaulle saw no advantage in promoting a power rival in Juin who, through an accumulation of military triumphs, might be elevated in French martial mythology into another Foch, with a latent potential to become a Pétain.[17]

And certainly, as a "metropolitan" officer with a Boy Scout enthusiasm for "leadership schools" and similar character-building experiments, de Lattre seemed better suited to lead the "amalgamation" of FFI into *l'Armée B* on Liberation. But as a former Weygand protégé and pillar of the Armistice Army, de Lattre's political baggage wouldn't fit into a steamer trunk. Where Gaullists doubted the sincerity of de Lattre's jail-house conversion, *l'armée d'Afrique's* closet *Maréchalists* smelled rank opportunism. Indeed, de Lattre's eclectic politics followed those who might best fulfill his ambitions, careening from the extreme right in the 1930s, through Vichy to de Gaulle. In the post-war period, he would even flirt with the communists. At the same time, a distinctive if controversial command style made him a contentious choice to lead a composite army and preside over an FFI–*armée d'Afrique* shotgun marriage. If few in the French army remained oblivious to de Lattre, "*le général soleil*," as he was sometimes disparagingly known, was not universally popular, especially among holdovers from the CEF's "team Juin." Even the skeptical Gaullists such as Larminat and Brosset had been seduced by Juin's earthy competence. Polytechnicien and *évadé de France* Louis-Christian Michelet, who fought as a lieutenant in the 1ère DFL, remembered that "We were shattered because we swore by our spiritual father Juin! . . . We didn't take de Lattre seriously. His adventure of 27 November 1942, his escape from the Riom prison, all seemed a little suspicious." When de Lattre laid claim to Juin's chief of staff Marcel-Maurice Carpentier, a "pure product of *l'armée d'Afrique*," Carpentier appealed to de Gaulle for emancipation. Future General Bernard Saint-Hillier, COS in the 1ère DFL in early 1944, found de Lattre to be a "capricious, unpredictable, ignorant on many matters, quick-tempered, actor," but also irresistibly "charming" when he had a mind to be. Saint-Hillier's boss, Diego Brosset labeled de Lattre "the king of attitude."[18]

"The theatrical side of his character probably had something to do with his bisexual nature," conclude Antony Beevor and Artemis Cooper. It also shaped the attitude of his subordinates toward "that woman."[19] Even though he counted among de Lattre's defenders, the plain-spoken Monsabert acknowledged the "extraordinary 'feminine' qualities" of his boss, that included inconsistency and whimsicality, his desire "continually to change things, to follow his inspirations, the suggestions of the moment." This made him a difficult commander to fight under. He approached a problem with "preconceived ideas, each time with a fixed solution." However, pushback from his staff and subordinate commanders invariably provoked "heroic–comic scenes, when he pretends to be angry, and we lighten up with jokes. He laughs, and then agrees to follow our suggestions . . . It's a permanent spectacle in which he is the only actor, and he knows it." Less attractive was the feeling that de Lattre was two-faced, eager to praise his subordinates when it reflected well on him ("notably in front of foreign leaders"), but quick to throw them under a bus if confronted by criticism from his immediate superiors or public opinion.[20] Edgard de Larminat complained that de Lattre was disloyal, sending unfavorable reports about him to the War Ministry, and darkened his reputation with his American superior Jacob Devers, who, as a result, "saw me as an outlaw mired in the rear, incapable of fulfilling his mission, thus unworthy of all support."[21] But others found that, whatever his failings, de Lattre had charisma.[22] Indeed, de Lattre's flair for theatrics earned him the nickname "Sacha Guitry in uniform" – which was definitely not intended as a compliment, as the well-known French actor and dramatist was later incarcerated for collaboration, though criminal charges were dropped. His staff meetings were likened to the Théâtre Marigny, a popular playhouse in the Jardins des Champs-Élysées, because they invariably featured thespian harangues about the "absence of enthusiasm" followed by declamations about the requirement for *l'Armée B* to reflect "the new France that has given birth to the Resistance." While many regarded de Lattre's stand-up routines as tiresome and predictable, even puerile, others condemned them as a form of demagogy.[23]

De Lattre was definitely the star in his own show. His command style, summarized as "terrorize those you cannot convince," did not invariably endear him to subordinates, who both feared and flattered him. His staff struggled to rein in his luxurious tastes, only to find themselves denounced as "grocers," "notaries," or "accountants" by their profligate superior. *Le Monde* correspondent Jean Planchais spun de Lattre as fundamentally an educator, imbued with the paternalistic mission of his squirearchy class. Hence, his obsession with forming *écoles des cadres* to imbue youth with military and civic values. He believed that human factors were primordial in war – morale, imagination, speed, intuition, *coup d'œil.* Connoisseurs of command complained that de Lattre's glitz and emphasis on "zeal" substituted for the "meticulousness, patience, and judgement that one expected of a good manager. Material constraints that limited or stymied his grand visions irritated him." He ostracized Polytechnicians as too "systematic." Command was an intuitive art, one exemplified in the improvisations and *audace* of Rommel, von Manstein, Guderian, and Patton. His detractors, led by the firebrand Leclerc, complained that de Lattre, a failed cavalryman who had transferred to the infantry in the trenches of the Great War, was far too tentative a commander to have his name whispered in the same breath as those in this pantheon of martial chancers. For this reason, the flamboyant de Lattre held Eisenhower in mild disdain because the Supreme Headquarters Allied Expeditionary Force (SHAEF) Commander represented "the American way of war," with its emphasis on firepower and matériel, which de Lattre deemed unimaginative, perhaps because *l'Armée B* packed so little of either. Furthermore, in his view, plodding Ike's inclination to temporize, reconcile, and adhere to the plan rather than roll the battlefield dice and seize the initiative produced mistakes and missed opportunities.[24]

Whatever Juin's political baggage, at least he was a team player, one whose battle plan was well thought out and meticulously executed. Initially, some Americans had hoped that de Lattre might substitute for Giraud to counterbalance de Gaulle. But they quickly realized that this complicated personality was egotistical to the point of arrogance, a defect that he managed periodically to camouflage with a certain noblesse oblige and spasms of captivating charm.

Unlike Juin, who had dutifully submitted to Clark's command in Italy, de Lattre began to cavil as soon as he learned in March 1944 that he was to be yoked with US Seventh Army commander General Alexander Patch to serve in Jacob Devers' Sixth Army Group. The initial hope in the French camp was that Giraud would command Anvil. This was dashed on 9 March 1944, when Maitland Wilson made clear that Anvil was to be an American-led invasion. Never one to take a setback lying down, de Lattre sought to maximize French autonomy. Sixth Army Group had been created expressly to insert a command buffer between Eisenhower and the volatile Frenchman. Devers complained to Marshall that de Lattre was both "dangerous" and inexperienced. The American view was that the French contribution should be broken down into two corps, with Juin and Larminat taking charge of one each, and de Lattre acting as the liaison with the Allies. Even though the Office of Strategic Services (OSS) reported that de Lattre's appointment would not sit well in metropolitan France, the Americans recognized Juin's political handicaps and conceded that, in the end, it was up to the CFLN to decide who was to command French forces.[25]

L'Armée B

That the French would send an army, not an expeditionary corps, under a commander of their own choosing to liberate their country at least constituted a symbolic victory. But *l'Armée B* had been included for political reasons, in an operation whose on-again/off-again character had disjointed the planning cycle. The fact that it would be forced to submit to Allied direction on French territory was viewed as an insult. The situation that de Lattre had inherited in January 1944, if not calamitous, might have demoralized anyone lacking his irrepressible energy and optimism. But de Lattre's greatest challenge would be to transform this 150,000 man "army of empire" into "the army of liberation," which was not an easy task, given the glaring military deficiencies of *l'Armée B*: a heterogeneous, largely unmodernized "melting pot" of colonial mercenaries, with a sprinkle of former FFL and *évadé de France* idealists, resentful *pieds noirs*, press-ganged North African Muslims, and 15,000–20,000 sub-Saharan soldiers with their "childlike mentality" and debilitating superstitions, all short of training, equipment, and logistics. Appeals to women to occupy support roles had succeeded by Anvil in producing only 4,000 volunteers out of 48,000 females deemed eligible for service in AFN. Given the ephemeral nature of Anvil, training had not been prioritized. Many units that had not fought in Italy or in the lightning Elba audition lacked battle experience. In both places, French soldiers had acquired an unsavory reputation for violence against civilian populations. Such undisciplined and rapacious colonial customs could not be tolerated in France.[26]

The final 23 January 1944 accord between the CFLN and the Allied command had set *l'Armée B* at eight divisions – five infantry divisions and three armored divisions – combining 256,000 men. This, the Americans argued, offered the most balanced force to deploy in France. But the *2e Division blindée* (2e DB) under Leclerc was designated for Normandy. Four of the infantry divisions slated for *l'Armée B*, as well as the three *Groupements de tabors marocains* (GTMs), in all slightly over 100,000 men, were in Italy. This left de Lattre with the 1ère DB under General Jean Touzer du Vigier, the 5e DB under General Henri de Vernejoul, and, from April 1944, the *9e Division d'infanterie coloniale* (9e DIC) under General Joseph Magnan, as well as a sprinkle of commandos stationed in Corsica. De Lattre's aspirations for a fourth armored division crashed for lack of tanks and personnel. To build a balanced force, de Lattre was obliged to dissolve three infantry divisions, transforming some of them into combat engineers and transportation units. But this reshuffling of personnel could not give him more specialists; it just freed up more fighters. Above all, the uncertain status of Anvil caused a "nagging fear that the army would not go into combat," a dark cloud of demoralization that de Lattre sought to dispel by multiplying inspections and intensifying training.[27]

Not only had Italy deprived de Lattre of a stable staff and many of the French army's scarce specialists. But also, largely due to a shipping shortage, *l'Armée B* lacked trucks, artillery, and signals equipment. But the French were not blameless in this situation – they were late with their orders to the Joint Rearmament Committee and had diverted equipment to arm units not included in the Anfa program, such as *batallions de choc* and commandos. They flouted or found it impossible to meet US norms on the ratio of service to combatant units and delayed the creation of transport and maintenance battalions. Of 60,000 support troops needed, they had recruited only 12,000, which made them almost entirely dependent on US logistics and maintenance, and rather made a mockery of French pretentions to operational autonomy. In March 1944, the French acknowledged an inability to stand up the three military hospitals required by the Anfa plan. While *l'armée d'Afrique* and *l'armée coloniale* took pride in their rusticity, de Lattre was eager to promote a modern military image upon his arrival in France. The reality was that, beneath a façade of armored and mechanized infantry units meant to symbolize the renaissance of the French army, in which many of his white troops were concentrated, *l'Armée B* remained largely an ill-equipped and unbalanced force of colonial infantry. Many of its Africans soldiered in primitive, morale-destroying conditions, with no underwear and no American equipment.[28]

The four divisions that had endured the hecatomb of Italy had been bled white and exhausted. The breakout on the Garigliano followed by pursuit up the peninsula, while hailed as Juin's most brilliant tactical feat, had proven especially lethal: between 11 May and 4 July, 31 percent of infantrymen, 22 percent of tankers, 6 percent of artillerymen, and 11 percent of sappers in the CEF had become casualties. This percentage was even higher in the *3ᵉ Division d'infanterie algérienne* (3ᵉ DIA), which had lost 47 percent of its strength between May and July, including half of its officers.[29] Many survivors had contracted malaria and diarrhea. A lack of soap had led to shockingly poor hygiene. Although desertions of indigenous soldiers in Italy had increased, they were still manageable, although morale had slumped among soldiers not given leave in over a year, and who now faced the prospect of another protracted and lethal campaign. But, as fast as these decimated units were pulled out of line, de Lattre withdrew them to Naples, where they were rearmed and motorized, while replacements filled vacancies and specialists were given extra training.[30]

Nor did the soldiers receive much encouragement from home. While the official line was that AFN virtually quivered with patriotic anticipation at the prospect of liberating the metropole, this was impossible to verify, especially among indigenous troops whom the French command clearly regarded as expendable. The commitment of former FFL and *évadés de France* could not be in doubt. Professional officers who had missed out on Italy looked forward to burnishing their combat records. And, while prefects reported that Gaullism had gained adherents in Algeria, *pied noir* opinion remained deeply ambivalent, proud of the CEF's accomplishments in Italy, but "equivocal" about liberating the mainland. In right-wing circles, the prospect of liberation was greeted with "a reserve made up of skepticism, bad humor and almost regret." As a whole, the *pied noir* population felt that the CFLN took them for granted and failed to acknowledge AFN's sacrifices for the war effort. They approached Liberation in a spirit of duty rather than with a *union sacrée* fervor, concerned about France's condition in the wake of occupation, Vichy, and resistance. News of Overlord was greeted with joy, primarily because it raised hopes that war demands on AFN would now decrease. The army recorded 2,000 deserters or absent without leave (AWOL) soldiers, while another 18,000 cases were under investigation.[31]

While there was no evidence that indigenous nationalism had contaminated the contingent, the morale of Muslim soldiers was closely monitored. A prominent nationalist talking point was that, once the mainland had been liberated by Muslim soldiers, Paris would be obliged to concede independence to the Maghreb. To diffuse discontent, a 7 March 1944 ordinance opened most military and civilian posts in Algeria to Muslims, as well as new paths to citizenship for certain indigenous categories without their having to abandon their Muslim faith. Not surprisingly, this move was severely contested by *pied noirs*, who were already upset at being governed by a claque of CFLN carpetbaggers. Nor did these promises of reform appease Algerian nationalists, who had heard similar mellifluous assurances during the First World War, only to see them go unfulfilled. Around 10,000 Muslim conscripts had failed to report for service in Algeria, but it was unclear whether this was because many had migrated to find work, because of poor communications, or because of a political boycott. Even though – or perhaps because – the French had imprisoned Tunisian nationalist leader Habib Bourguiba, the German image in Tunisia remained positive. Enthusiasm for mobilization was virtually non-existent, while desertion in Tunisian units remained a problem. Early 1944 had witnessed nationalist unrest in Morocco, followed by many arrests. The feeling among colonial officials was that nationalism in the Maghreb was mainly an urban phenomenon that so far had failed to contaminate a largely bucolic soldiery.[32]

Operation Brassard

Operation Brassard, the capture of Elba (Map 6.1), carried out on 16–20 June by the mainly sub-Saharan soldiers of the 9[e] DIC, the 2[e] GTM, a regiment of engineers, and other odds and ends, all of which in total numbered 12,000 men

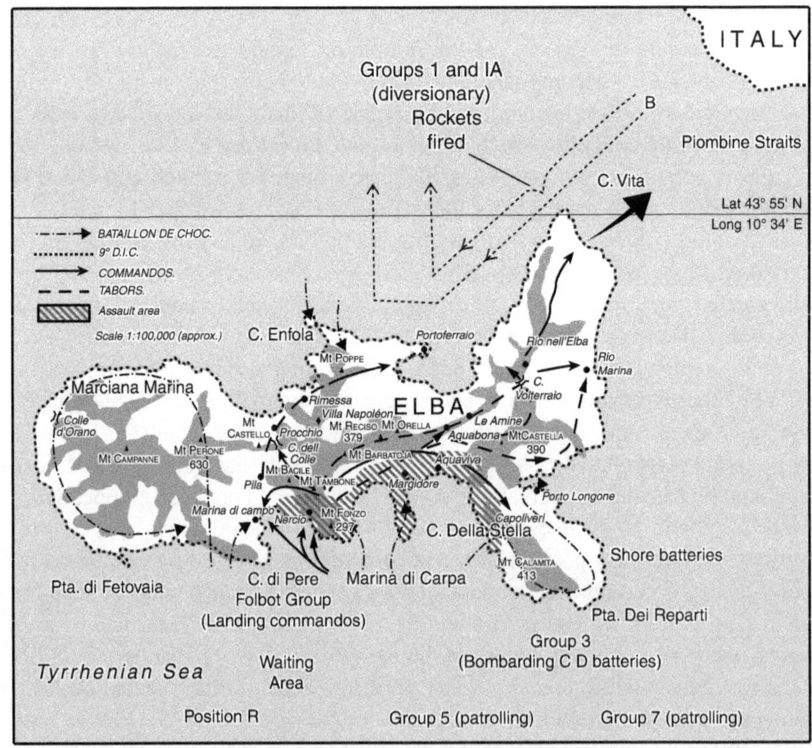

Map 6.1 The Elba campaign.

and 600 vehicles, gave de Lattre an opportunity to raise the profile of *l'Armée B* with the Anglo-Americans, and test his units' skills in maritime assault and staff work in a joint and combined environment (British maritime support with US air cover), in a terrain that resembled the south of France. Both operational commander General Henry Martin and 9ᵉ DIC chief Magnan cautioned that their troops were insufficiently trained to execute the mission. Nor was there any particular urgency to capture the island, whose strategic significance was marginal now that it had been bypassed by the breakthrough at Cassino. But de Lattre was keen to blood his troops. The large number of defensive works undertaken on the island seemed out of proportion to an intelligence-estimated small garrison. In fact, many of the 3,000 Germans and Italian Fascists manning the island's defenses were veterans of the Eastern Front. Five or six coastal batteries of 149 mm and 152 mm guns were buried in deep emplacements which made them largely invulnerable to air attack. Coastal artillery, combined with mines, was meant to keep an amphibious attack at bay. Virtually the only way to neutralize these batteries was to send in Gambiez's commandos. The garrison was well supplied with field guns, morale was high, and they fully expected an attack. At the last minute, plans for an assault by the *1er Régiment de Chasseurs Parachutistes* (1er RCP) were canceled due to a lack of aircraft. For this reason, the official casualty figures for Brassard of 178 killed in action (KIA), 80 missing in action (MIA), and around 700 wounded in 3 days of combat were probably understated.[33]

Furthermore, Italian carabinieri reported 191 rapes and 20 attempted rapes, carried out mostly by colonial soldiers, during Brassard. While the army blamed a lack of cadres required to supervise indigenous units, as in Italy these crimes seemed more a result of the negligence, tolerance, or powerlessness of the cadres rather than their absence. As in Italy, GTM Commander Guillaume deflected criticism from his *goumiers* onto the support services. In the end, only one *tirailleur* was given two years in jail for "attempted rape," according to Miot. But, in his memoirs, Raoul Salan, who, thanks to de Lattre's intervention, commanded the 6ᵉ RTS on Elba and in France, noted that, "Unfortunately, our Senegalese made several mistakes ... We quickly reasserted our control over the soldiers. But not before we had to shoot a Senegalese NCO [non-commissioned officer] and a *tirailleur* for rape."[34] However, the rapes in Elba, coming close on the heels of the much larger scandal in Italy, provided more than a minor footnote to the operation, because some began to question whether the soldiers of *l'Armée B* were disciplined enough to operate in France. André Diethelm, who had replaced Le Troquer as war commissioner, insisted that "It would be inconceivable in effect, that on territory that will be reconquered by our soldiers, they do not behave as liberators and that the civilian population, who suffered foreign occupation, could be forced to fear violence or excesses." When de Gaulle contemplated banning the GTM from participating in Anvil, de

Lattre, who planned to deploy 6,000 *goumiers* to scour the Massif des Maures behind Toulon, turned in a *Palme d'or* performance to change the French leader's mind. In the process, he denounced accusations of rape as "an orchestrated calumny by moralists."[35] Upon receiving de Lattre's assurance that no similar incidents would be repeated in France, and that his soldiers of color would be tightly controlled, de Gaulle relented. Strict orders were issued to the soldiers of *l'Armée B* on the eve of Anvil "to warn personnel that any act of violence committed in France, theft, rape, etc. will be immediately dealt with with the greatest severity, and that those caught in the act risk being shot on the spot."[36] Apparently, everyone got the message.

Nor did Brassard advance a decision on Anvil, as Churchill continued to scheme for Italy and Ljubljana. But the French carried on as if Anvil were a done deal and began withdrawing troops from the Italian front on 20 June. Only on 2 July was Maitland Wilson given the green light for Anvil, renamed Dragoon on 1 August, and scheduled for 15 August. The next day, de Gaulle signed the order transferring CEF divisions to *l'Armée B* as they were withdrawn from the front in Italy.

Dragoon

While Devers expressed optimism that coordination with the French was in place, only on 22 July was the composition of the French planning mission at Allied Forces Headquarters (AFHQ) in Algiers set. In the second half of July, less than a month before the operation was set to launch, Sixth Army Group was activated, and de Lattre assembled his staff at Naples to prepare the invasion. Although Dragoon was of small scale compared with Overlord, unlike in Normandy, the French would be well represented in the Riviera operation, and not just in ground forces. They also contributed 34 ships to the Dragoon armada, while the French air force supplied 250 planes in the expedition sent to bomb German air bases, lines of communication, and fortifications. The Allies were also increasingly attracted by the idea of working with the *maquis* in the Massif Central and the Alpes. In the first two weeks of August, five commandos and ten Jedburgh teams, as well as a dozen liaison officers, were dropped into the southern zone, to join those teams already deployed to stiffen what Wilson estimated to be 76,400 FFI in the region, although only a third were believed to be armed. The idea was that they would impede the arrival of German reinforcements, attack communications, and create diversions by generating an immense guerrilla zone in the German rear and attacking out of *réduits maquisards* in the Massif Central, Alpes, l'Ain, le Morvan, les Vosges, and the Pyrenees. Not only was it believed that they had the potential to cut the Rhône corridor, but also de Gaulle thought that the resistance could open the road from the invasion beaches to the interior via Digne–Grenoble–

Chambéry, while Eisenhower preferred that the FFI stick to sabotage operations. FFI activity was coordinated through État-major des Forces françaises de l'intérieur (EMFFI) chief Pierre Koenig and former *Vichysto-resistant* and French Air Force (FAF) General Gabriel Cochet, who was named "military delegate for southern operations" in April 1944. Cochet's brief was both to coordinate military operations of the resistance and to "deal with questions concerning the administration of liberated territories" – that is, insure the GPRF's sovereignty. Although Cochet was clearly an agent of the GPRF with a political mission, "it seems that he was kept in the dark about Allied preparations," concludes Miot, whose officers preferred to work directly with the FFI rather than detour through Cochet.[37]

The Germans were in a poor posture to defend France's south coast. The fourteen German divisions that Allied intelligence had identified in April–May south of a line running from Bordeaux to Lyon had gradually dwindled because of the demands of the Normandy front, and they had only partially been replaced. The German command was divided on the wisdom of defending the south of France. The position of von Rundstedt and Rommel since June had been that the German army lacked sufficient troops to cover both the Mediterranean and Channel coasts, and so should abandon the south and southwest to establish a defense line across central France. Despite Blaskowitz's insistence that he was short of men and weapons to hold the south of France, predictably Hitler ordered him to stand fast, a decision encouraged by Oberkommando der Wehrmacht's (OKW's) assessment, at the end of July 1944, that the Allied buildup in the Mediterranean targeted the Ligurian coast, with the goal of collapsing the German front in Italy. This misperception lingered, especially in the mind of Walter Warlimont, deputy chief of the Wehrmacht operations staff, even after Allied air attacks launched against German radar stations, Rhône bridges, and railroad installations and airfields in southern France had begun.[38]

Originally assigned the defense of Marseilles, the 244th Infantry Division (ID) found its responsibility extended to the mouth of the Rhône, while the 242nd ID defended Toulon. Both of these divisions contained significant numbers of Armenian and Azerbaijani *Ostbataillone*, whose combat potential was questionable, as well as convalescent and semi-disabled soldiers and officers no longer considered fit for front-line duty. In fact, Blaskowitz was in virtual despair over the combat-worthiness of his forces, which lacked motor transport, anti-tank weapons, and artillery, including coastal batteries – apart from a composite miscellany of captured guns, partially manned by Italian crews, so poorly sited that the batteries lacked overlapping fields of fire. Without long-range radios, Blaskowitz's communications relied on the French Postes, télégraphes et téléphones (PTT) whose lines ran through the "terrorist territory" of the Rhône Valley, and so were repeatedly cut.

Furthermore, German reactions were characterized by confusion, caused by the constant misdirection of Allied deception tactics and Hitler's micro-management of operations from his East Prussian "Wolf's Lair." Indeed, Hitler ordered a retreat only from 16 August once he had concluded that Operation Lüttich, his Mortain counterattack to seal off Patton's Normandy breakthrough, was a bust. As a result, the German command failed "to establish a defensive center of gravity" on the south coast. Newly appointed Chief of German army engineers Karl Sachs lacked the manpower and resources to rig fortifications along the coast of Brittany, the Gironde estuary, and southern France, with a command that was in the process of reorganization in August 1944. All Blaskowitz could do was deploy a thin defensive crust of second-tier, when not third-tier, troops along the coast, with no mobility and no depth.[39]

Therefore, not surprisingly, Allied intelligence assessed the Nineteenth Army's 7 infantry divisions assigned the task of defending 650 kilometers of France's Mediterranean coast from Italy to the Spanish border as "relatively low grade." The fact that these units had been stripped of most of their motorized anti-tank weapons for Normandy severely limited their ability to oppose the Allied landings. The 198th ID was the only infantry division there considered capable of offensive operations. The best unit in Blaskowitz's inventory was the 11th Panzer Division (PzD), which served as his mobile reserve. But even it had surrendered units and weapons for Normandy, so that its tank inventory was only at 60 percent of full strength. However, in the eyes of both the Allies and Blaskowitz, a "decisive" factor was that the 11th PzD's tanks were split by the Rhône, most of whose bridges had been destroyed by Allied air attack. This meant that repositioning the 11th PzD and 338th ID was reduced to slow ferrying operations. This, together with the absence of a corps reserve, undermined the ability of Blaskowitz to counterattack the Franco-American beachhead, even had the 11th PzD not been pulled left and right by a deluge of countermanding orders.

The Allies held a "crushing" superiority in air power, while there was little the Kriegsmarine could do to oppose an invasion fleet of 880 ships that included 5 battleships, 9 carriers, 24 cruisers, and 111 destroyers. But the eleven Franco-American divisions – three US infantry divisions, one US paratroop division, five French infantry divisions, and two French armored divisions – could only be introduced piecemeal over ten days, and might initially fight at a disadvantage. Army commanders de Lattre and Alexander Patch agreed that the French would be assigned "the lion's share" – Toulon and Marseilles – while three American divisions, as yet too weak to pursue retreating Germans up the Rhône Valley, would move inland via Aix-en-Provence toward Sisteron and Grenoble (Map 6.2).[40]

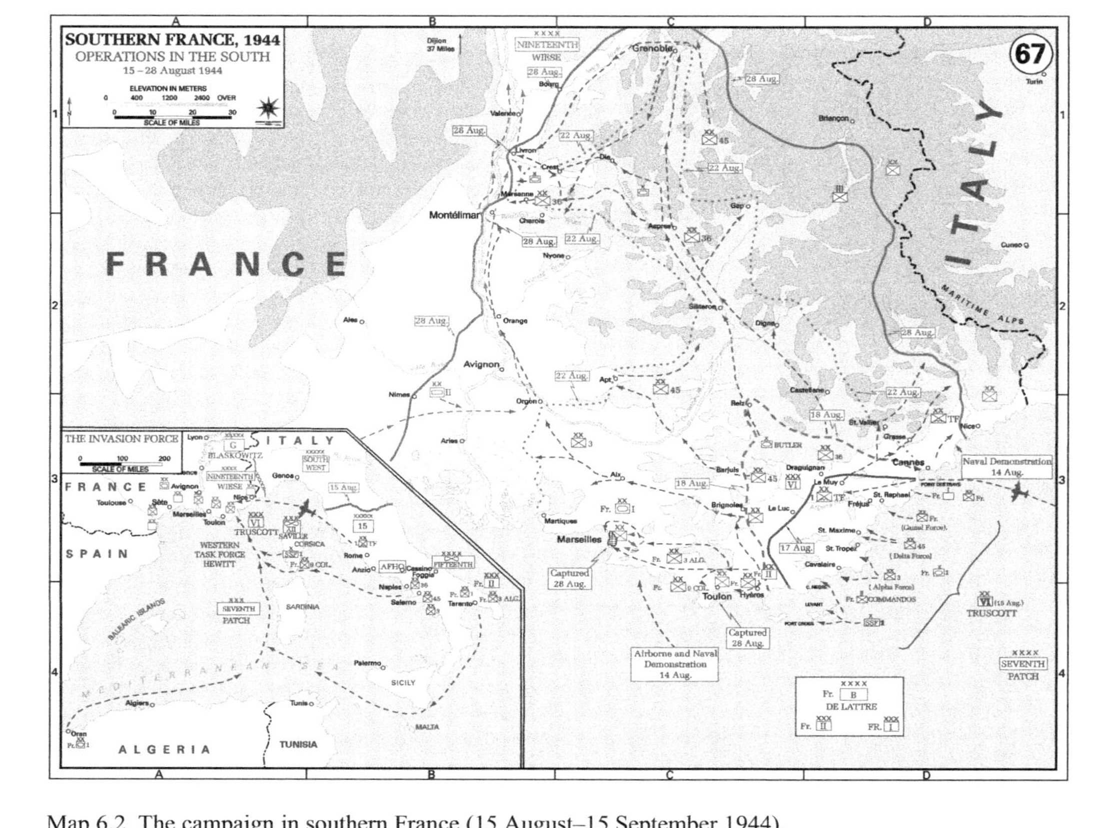

Map 6.2 The campaign in southern France (15 August–15 September 1944).

On the morning of 15 August, three US infantry divisions of VI Corps under Lucian Truscott splashed ashore along 70 kilometers of coast between Cavalaire and Agay, just to the east of Saint-Raphaël. During the night, 5,000 American, British, and Canadian paratroops and glider-borne forces had landed behind the beachhead with the mission of capturing the critical road juncture at Le Muy, to block any German reinforcements. Only three supply companies of the Wehrmacht's 242nd ID were available to counter them. French troops in this first amphibious assault wave included commandos, as at Elba tasked with silencing coastal batteries, and a combat command of the 1ère DB. As resistance-supplied intelligence had predicted, the German Nineteenth Army crowded the coast, but had little defense in depth. German units on the beaches around Saint-Tropez, many of them *Osttruppen*, had been thoroughly intimidated by the preparatory Allied artillery barrage and put up little resistance. Some even defected to the invaders. German coastal guns were silenced by air strikes. By the end of the day on 15 August, the Allies had landed 60,150 troops and 6,737 vehicles on three separate beachheads. The few casualties were concentrated in the paratroops and commandos.[41]

Besides, since 14 August, Blaskowitz's attention had been focused not on the Riviera, but north on the Loire, where the Americans threatened to cut off his line of retreat. On 16 August, as Blaskowitz's headquarters in Avignon began to burn classified documents, Hitler approved a Nineteenth Army withdrawal up the Rhône Valley with the 11th PzD acting as a rear guard. The 242nd ID and most of the 244th ID would remain behind to defend Toulon and Marseilles. Blaskowitz in Avignon did not receive that order until the morning of 18 August, which was passed on to Nineteenth Army that afternoon. Meanwhile, on 18 August, Allied intelligence deemed Luftwaffe activity "too insignificant for comment."[42] On 16 August, Hitler reiterated his orders, issued on 19 January 1944, for his troops to transform harbors on the Mediterranean and Atlantic coasts into *Festungen* (fortresses) to be defended to the last man. In the south, this meant Marseilles and Toulon, as the Germans were to abandon Sète on 20 August, as well as Saint-Jean-de-Luz, Biarritz, and Bayonne.

Wedged between the mountains and the sea, and garrisoned by an estimated 18,000 troops, Toulon was expected to present a particularly formidable objective, and might have done so, "had the Germans had more time and materiel" to fortify it. In the absence of the senior army general, command of the defense fell to Admiral Heinrich Ruhfus, who busied himself evacuating about 100,000 civilians, which left him little time to shore up his defenses. Eager to avoid seeing his army immobilized and shattered in a siege of two formidably defended "pockets" similar to those forming on the Atlantic coast, de Lattre, with the approval of Patch, decided to hasten his attack (Map 6.3). The French commander infiltrated Monsabert's 3e DIA through the mountains to encircle

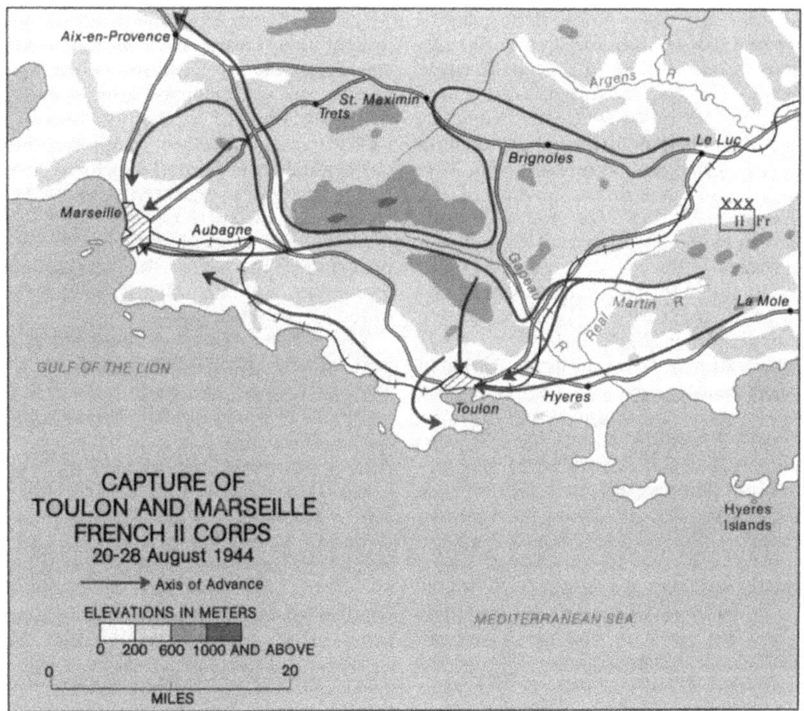

Map 6.3 The capture of Toulon and Marseilles by French II Corps, 20–28 August 1944.

Toulon from the north, where the defenses were "spotty and incomplete, in some cases no more than roadblocks," in part because the Germans lacked mines and explosives to strengthen those barriers. "If the Allies moved quickly," concluded the US official history, "the Germans would have difficulty putting up any effective resistance."[43]

When Salan was finally put ashore with one of his Senegalese battalions on 19 August north of Saint-Maxime, he found de Lattre with a small staff in an olive grove near Cogolin. After a brief interrogation, de Lattre announced: "Toulon awaits you."[44] From the hills, one could spy the rusting hulks of Darlan's High Seas Fleet. Magnan's 9ᵉ DIC, which included Salan's Senegalese, was to accomplish the third phase of de Lattre's plan, that consisted of the "final reduction" of Toulon's inner defenses, once the other divisions had invested the town and dismantled its outer defenses. The risk for de Lattre was that he was rushing his attack before all of his troops were ashore, but also, he hoped, before the Germans could solidify their emplacements.[45] By 26 August, after some hard street fighting, Toulon had been "liberated" by a combination of French troops and FFI. Only on 28 August, however, did Admiral Ruhfus surrender. De Lattre recorded 2,700 French casualties, but had captured a vital harbor, which the Allies had not expected to control until a month after the initial invasion, along with 17,000 German prisoners of war (POWs).[46] While French forces claimed that they had encountered considerable resistance, the US official history, extrapolating from French casualty figures, concluded that the Germans surrendered Toulon after taking only 1,000 casualties, "hardly a serious attempt to follow Hitler's orders to fight to the last man."[47] Suzanne Lefort-Rouquette's memory of liberated Toulon was that it reeked of dead horses.[48]

Surprised by the unexpectedly rapid fall of Toulon, de Lattre had not initially planned to take Marseilles "on the bounce." A sequence of suburbs threaded along the coast that contained a million people, Marseilles was garrisoned by 13,000 Kriegsmarine, Luftwaffe, and soldiers of the 244th ID. While the commander, Major General Hans Schaeffer, had established strong blocking positions along the four main approach roads, "time and lack of materiel" had worked against strongly fortifying the city's core. However, the rapid erosion of German resistance in Toulon, combined with a civilian uprising in Marseilles from 22 August, invited an acceleration of de Lattre's plan, so that the liberation of Toulon and that of Marseilles became simultaneous rather than sequential operations.[49]

Factionalized and disorganized by German arrests, resistance at Marseilles was not expected to participate significantly in the city's liberation. However, in May, Marseilles had witnessed civil protests over food shortages that spread to the suburbs, demonstrations further enflamed by news of the 6 June landings. Nevertheless, Dragoon found Marseilles' resistance, few in number and with limited arms, divided even as orders arrived from Algiers to "place the enemy in difficulty," because, with limited numbers and few arms, it was difficult to see how that directive might be executed. The first attacks on isolated German soldiers that were aimed to recuperate their weapons occurred on 18 August. By the following day, when the CGT called for a "general insurrectionary strike," walkouts had shuttered most of the factories and brought train travel to a halt. On 21 August, as the Vichy prefect defected to the resistance, barricades began to appear throughout the city. But, on 22 August, de Lattre suddenly halted the advance into Marseilles, according to the US Army's official history, because he lacked the numbers to secure the city, and it was known that the 11th PzD was concentrating at Aix-en-Provence.[50] But, in Monsabert's telling, de Lattre's real concern was that French troops would clash with communist resisters intent on seizing political power: "'If we enter Marseilles,' he said, 'it's the Revolution. Military necessity must therefore give way to political considerations.'" When Monsabert pointed out that he doubted that the Americans, eager to capture Marseilles' harbor, would see it that way,

"I was sent packing. 'It's purely a French problem!' Theoretically, yes. As a practical matter, no." In the instance, lingering in the suburbs on de Lattre's orders while the population begged him to enter the city struck Colonel Abel Felix André Chappuis, commander of the 7e RTA, as absurd. His regiment entered Marseilles on 23 August, "literally sucked into the city by the meridional crowds," according to de Lattre, and Monsabert insisted that he simply followed Chappuis into a city whose mood was deliriously festive rather than insurrectionary.[51] "Sometimes it's difficult for a leader to make his troops advance," de Lattre concluded philosophically. "But at other times, it's difficult to hold them back."[52]

By 10:00 on 23 August, Algerian troops were on the Canebière, Marseilles' central avenue, and moving toward the Vieux Port, reinforced by troops hastily extracted from Toulon. But Marseilles had to be cleared neighborhood by neighborhood. With Toulon secure by 26 August, de Lattre was able to shift his forces, including his heavy artillery, to Marseilles. The German garrison surrendered 2 days later, but not before inflicting 1,825 casualties on the French – the *goums* in particular suffered – and leaving Marseilles' harbor "an indescribable chaos of twisted ironwork, shattered concrete, and entangled cables." Seventy-five ships had been sunk in the heavily mined harbor, and 257 cranes had been sabotaged.[53] Within twelve days of landing, and at least a month ahead of the most favorable estimates, de Lattre had secured the major objectives, namely the two French harbors. He had also captured 37,000 German POWs.[54] The rapid Franco-American advance had been accelerated by Hitler's withdrawal order, which was generalized on 19 August. Nevertheless, the costs had been relatively high – 1,000 KIA and 3,500 WIA. Again, this may have been an underestimate, because Salan's 6e RTS alone took 587 casualties, or a sixth of its strength.[55]

Typically, de Lattre organized a victory parade, one delayed for an hour by the theatrically late arrival of the First Army Commander, who, smiling with the magnanimous benevolence of a Cardinal of the Church, shook hands with a swarm of Marseilles' "junk" resisters – while perhaps 700 FFI had mustered to see the Germans off, fully 10,000 turned out for the post-Liberation parade, records historian Jean-Paul Cointet.[56] "On la Canebière, the women were decked out in striking outfits, hair piled on top of their heads, very short dresses, high cork-wedge-heeled shoes, and faces that, after Italy, appeared to us outrageously made up," remembered André Beaufre, a battalion commander in Carpentier's *7e Régiment de tirailleurs marocains* (7e RTM). "Numerous FFI, imaginatively bedecked with arms and grenades, moved about, filling the cinemas and cafes, stopping people in the street and pointing weapons at them ... In fact, we walked in on the middle of a revolution."[57] For his part, as former commander of the Bohemian *corps franc d'Afrique* (CFA), Monsabert declared the "chaos" of Marseilles' liberation parade "*très sympathique*."[58] In Brosset's opinion, the victory procession offered a typically "capricious" *Armée B* performance, led by Magnan's 9e DIC, that contained Salan's Senegalese. "This division, still too young, march better than they fight, unlike mine." At least the crowd was enthusiastic, although "Vive de Gaulle!" acclamations were notably few.[59] However, the liberation of Marseilles touched off a command crisis at the summit of *l'Armée B*. The proximate cause was de Lattre's "excessive fear of the Commune" of 1871, a dread that permeated right-wing military circles generally, but which in this instance had caused de Lattre to hesitate to order troops into a "revolution" in Marseilles, whose well-deserved reputation as the "cesspool of the five continents" might engulf them. This brought to the surface political tensions and personal resentments among de Lattre's subordinates, who had been frustrated and factionalized by his flamboyant, but ultimately tentative and febrile, command style.[60]

Either some of the de Lattre's subordinates had failed to grasp that the clinching argument for Dragoon had been the logistical requirement to capture Toulon and Marseilles, or the caste tensions concealed in the fusion of French forces spilled into the open as soon as they set foot on the mainland. Infected with ingrained Gaullist mistrust of US motives, Brosset imagined Dragoon as an American ploy to lock down French forces in what had been expected to be lengthy and debilitating sieges of Toulon and Marseilles. Meanwhile, Truscott's VI Corps raced north to grab liberation glory. "Delattre [sic] claims to see all that, but has decided to accept anything and perhaps in fairness he had no choice." In fact, one of de Lattre's biographers insists that it was the commander of *l'Armée B* who had convinced Patch to allow him, rather than Truscott, to liberate the two port cities because he thought that they needed to be taken quickly.[61] Also, he probably lacked the mobility to shadow Blaskowitz's flight up the Rhône Valley. But, as with de Gaulle, dependence upon the Americans had spawned a suspicion in *l'Armée B* of American motives.

De Lattre's vertiginous leadership style also disconcerted his subordinates. When Leclerc threw a command tantrum, everyone was put on notice that the boss was seriously upset and corrective action was instantly required. However, de Lattre's staff could almost set their watches by their chief's practically hourly boil-overs. Increasingly, many began to suspect that his repetitive and increasingly tedious dramatic affect was calculated to mask an absence of knowledge and confidence. De Lattre made even a blue-blood Gaullist like Brosset nostalgic for the no-nonsense Juin, and desperately unhappy at being assigned to a "music hall army" led by a "clown." For this veteran of the Western Desert and the breakthrough at Cassino, being subordinate to de Lattre, whose recent campaign experience was limited to the 1940 débâcle and a three-day cameo on Elba, was like joining the Baby-Sitters Club. "No one has any confidence in de Lattre," he wrote in his diary on 21 August.

Figure 6.1 Jean de Lattre de Tassigny and Edgard de Larminat (center) en route to the Dragoon landings in Provence, 15 August 1944. No sooner had the two temperamental generals set foot on French soil than they squabbled over the conduct of operations. (Photo by Keystone-France/Gamma-Keystone via Getty Images)

"He reorganizes his command every 24 hours, gets excited about unverified intelligence reports, addresses problems only superficially, and like the Sun King thinks only of his glory" (Figure 6.1).[62]

De Lattre's command pirouettes at the gates of Marseilles had pushed the impulsive Larminat beyond the limits of tolerance. By 27 August, de Lattre's deputy was in open revolt against his boss, whom he accused of being a "megalomaniac," building a staff of former Vichyites, running a slipshod command, mismanaging his force, and allowing himself to be duped by the Americans into besieging the Mediterranean ports. While these accusations were mostly true, Larminat found precarious support among other senior officers reluctant to endorse his charges that de Lattre's maneuver on Toulon and Marseilles had been "disjointed," that his frequent absences to lead parades and bathe in the civic adulation of newly liberated towns had slackened operational control, and that his "capricious" leadership remained uninformed by a campaign concept. "Larminat is basically correct on the substance but wrong on the form," concluded Brosset. "To attack the concept of a maneuver that succeeded in accomplishing the mission is a mistake."[63] Off the record, Brosset informed Catroux, who had been assigned by de Gaulle to investigate the incident, that "[Larminat and de Lattre] are both mad, but de Lattre is a winner."[64] Nor was Catroux an entirely impartial adjudicator – in 1942, Catroux had noted that, while Larminat's subordinates praised him as "a man of action" who understood modern warfare, he failed to inspire loyalty, "because of his command style that is not always generous and humane." Six months later, in his annual officer evaluation of Larminat, Catroux confessed that, "while I've always esteemed the military talents of this officer, I can no longer excuse his character."[65] Above all, de Lattre had been de Gaulle's choice to lead the army and the invasion not because he was a systematic and careful commander, but because he belonged to no faction, was more or less acceptable to the internal resistance in a way that Juin was not, and embraced the logic of the amalgamation of the FFI with the regular army. De Lattre's view of Larminat, expressed in a subsequent 1946 inspection report after de Lattre had become army chief of staff, was that he was "without restraint and unshakable in his judgements as in his behavior, [which,] depending on the circumstances, can prove successful or dangerous."[66] For his part, Brosset had concluded that Larminat had become so "unstable, discontent, embittered, nervous in his command," as to be virtually "useless." Larminat's request to go over Catroux's head to appeal directly to de Gaulle was overruled by *Commissaire à la Guerre* since April 1944 André Diethelm, who instead relieved him and sent him back to Algiers. Following Catroux's report, which reflected unfavorably on both French generals, in October Larminat was reassigned to the comparatively inglorious role of supervising the siege of the "Atlantic pockets."[67] Monsabert was rewarded for his loyalty, or at least his quiescence, by being slipped into Larminat's corps command, while de Lattre's long-suffering chief of staff and former Juin protégé Carpentier inherited the 2ᵉ DIM.

The 700-Kilometer Pursuit

The obvious route opened to the 138,000 men of Wiese's Mediterranean garrison slated for evacuation was via the Rhône Valley, their rendezvous destination being designated as the area between Dijon and the Swiss frontier (Map 6.4). Fifty-one thousand soldiers of Army Task Group G were left behind to man fortresses and defensive perimeters on the Mediterranean coast. Yet, the Rhône Valley offered a hazardous evacuation route, especially the east bank, which was lined with mountains and cut by tributaries of the Durance, Drôme, and Isère Rivers. The N7 highway passed along the foot of le Vercors, made more dangerous because Karl Pflaum's 157th Reserve Division had already been withdrawn to the Italian frontier. To protect the N7 from resistance

Map 6.4 The German retreat from the Mediterranean and Atlantic coasts.

attacks, on 18 August, the Army Territorial Commands along the route were brought under Task Force G's operational control. But this force amounted to "very few security units and those had rather insignificant levels of combat readiness." The 11th PzD was to act as a fire brigade, covering the vulnerable eastern flank of the march column. In fact, neither the resistance threat expected in the Rhône Valley south of Lyon nor the popular insurrection that the German command had anticipated in the south of France ever materialized. German units retreated through the Massif Central to the west of the Rhône largely unmolested. "Not only did the FFI not delay in the least the retreat of the German units [from the south of France]," concludes Joachim Ludewig, "the French operations in the rear areas were for the most part meaningless."[68]

One of the most notable resistance actions in the south occurred on 16 August, when the FFI blew the bridge over the Drôme River at Loriol at the foot of le Vercors several miles north of Montélimar, which backed up the German Nineteenth Army's retreat along the N7 which paralleled the Rhône. The ensuing ten-day battle during 21–31 August was characterized by miscommunication between VI Corps commander Lucian Truscott and 36th US ID chief John Dalquist, who demonstrated a lack of urgency to cut off the German retreat up the N7. Above all, Dalquist failed to concentrate his forces to block the highway, which, combined with shortages of transportation, fuel, and ammunition, allowed most of Wiese's command to escape, either by fording the shallow Drôme or by finding alternative routes on the western bank of the river. Nevertheless, the German casualty rate was estimated at 20 percent.[69]

While Blaskowitz could breathe a sigh of relief as the Nineteenth Army filtered into Dijon, concern remained for the fate of Karl Sachs' LXIV Corps, in part because Blaskowitz could solidify his defensive position only after Sachs' troops had arrived. Roughly 220,000 Axis personnel were garrisoned in the Biarritz–Limoges–Toulouse triangle. While the resistance did not chase the Germans out of Toulouse, resistance-induced disorder there meant that retreating Germans avoided the town, a great inconvenience as Toulouse was a major transportation hub. On 22 August, 1,200 German troops at Saint-Gaudens surrendered, while others in the Pyrenees fled into Spain.[70] German troops in Bordeaux and its environs numbered 60,000. Headquartered in Poitiers, Sachs had received no more than a garbled retreat message from Kriegsmarine radio in Royan. He issued a withdrawal order on 19 August and began that evening to extract the garrisons along the Atlantic coast and the Gironde estuary. As at Toulon and Marseilles, Sachs was ordered to leave behind between 85,000 and 95,000 troops protected by 1,300 artillery pieces, many of heavy caliber, to garrison the "Atlantic pockets" in southwestern France, beginning in the south with the "*poche de Royan*" that straddled the entrance to the Gironde estuary (the Arvert peninsula and the Pointe de Grave).[71] Not only did this deny the Allies access to the port of Bordeaux, but also this *Festung* Gironde sheltered the radar and radio station near Soulac-sur-Mer, whose 300-mile operating radius could give warnings of Allied approaches by sea and air. Just to the north, 5,000 soldiers and around 2,000 workers were left behind to garrison La Rochelle, and its important U-boat base at La Pallice.[72]

By early August, rumors reached German garrisons on the Atlantic coast via soldiers returning from leave that the French front was collapsing. Forty-three-year-old German private August Hampel, stationed in Royan with a construction unit, watched as Allied planes attacked and sank two minesweepers in the Gironde estuary. "A few days later, Royan became like an anthill. Trucks filled with soldiers left the town, while others arrived in a disorganized ballet which seemed to make no sense," remembered Hampel. "You could read the almost tangible excitement that lit up the faces. It would have taken very little for all the streets, all the squares to have resounded with the cry: 'Every man for himself!'"

News reached them of the landings on the south coast as Brittany was overrun by American armor and swamped by a geyser of FFI. The French laborers Hampel regularly requisitioned for work gangs vanished. One of them attempted to persuade him to desert – which would be dishonorable, he insisted. But he also knew that Gestapo-recruited snitches were ubiquitous in the French work crews. So, it was dangerous to become too friendly with the locals.[73] Furthermore, as a father of four children, he was aware that the families of deserters faced retribution. French intelligence reported that "200–300 executions were carried out" among foreign troops at La Rochelle in August, affecting "Poles, Russians, Italians . . .," and that desertions among Poles at Royan ceased only when they were withdrawn from the front, and the command threatened to shoot three Poles for every Polish deserter.[74]

Orders came to destroy all records, followed by a call for volunteers to remain behind. Only one hand went up. So Hampel became one of six men in his unit designated as a stay-behind. But, when the order came at night to abandon the town, several of his army comrades tried to persuade him to join the exodus. His departure would not be noticed in the confusion. And besides, what was the point of defending Royan? Again, he refused, believing that the garrison would simply radio ahead to have him apprehended. And, with rumors rife of the massacre by Das Reich at Oradour, he feared that he might be murdered in revenge should he desert. Nevertheless, along with the other stay-behinds, he felt like a condemned man: "Buggered. We're buggered, that's what everyone is thinking. The only uncertainty: is it death, or only captivity that awaits us?" The six designated stay-behinds promptly became blind drunk.[75] Two-thirds of Sachs' 87,000 fleeing personnel were made up of a miscellany of 5,000 headquarters staff, 12,000 Luftwaffe, 15,000 Kriegsmarine, and odds and ends of Labor Service, railway workers, customs officers, and 2,000 female auxiliaries, who had requisitioned every available means of transportation – civilian automobiles, *gazogène* trucks, even horse-drawn carts – organized into three "march units" and directed via circuitous secondary routes north along the Atlantic coast that avoided the former *zone libre*, where the resistance was most active, through Poitier to the Sens–Dijon assembly point.[76] Given these complications, Sachs' LXIV Corps did not begin its retreat until 27 August, the last units setting out only on 30 August. As most of these units were sedentary garrison and administrative troops with poor cohesion and morale, already in the grip of a *sauve qui peut* (every man for himself) mentality, they might have been fairly easy pickings for even moderately organized FFI. Sachs' slow start upset Hitler, who relieved him on 3 September. However, no attempt was made either by the resistance or by Allied air power to obstruct bridges across the Garonne River at Bordeaux or on the Dordogne, which might have corralled considerable numbers of retreating Germans.[77]

In fact, the lack of reaction from the resistance can be traced to the German break-up of resistance networks in Bordeaux in 1943, which caused a cascade of arrests in the region. This had been followed in February 1944 by the arrest and suicide of *Délégué militaire régional* (DMR) Claude Bonnier, which also served to destabilize the resistance by triggering a succession dispute between Colonel Jean-Baptiste Morraglia, an air force officer supported by the *Comité d'action en France* (COMAC), British Major Roger Landes of the Special Operations Executive (SOE), and Charles Gaillard, who received his mandate in May through Gaullist channels. This quarrel opened a command path for two outsiders: forty-six-year-old Saint-Cyr graduate Lieutenant colonel Henri Adeline and fifty-six-year-old former NCO Joseph Druilhe, both of whom had been active in the Dordogne resistance. With the 22 August liberation of Bergerac, Adeline organized two columns of FFI to march on Bordeaux: one under the command of a Belgian officer, Georges Moressée, and the second under Druilhe, which entered Bordeaux on 28 August, twenty-four hours after the Germans had departed. On 2 September, Gaillard named Druilhe "Commanding General of the 18th Region," while Adeline was given operational control of the FFI, an authority that was eventually extended to include Royan and La Rochelle. The presence of the SOE proved disruptive, because at least one petitioner cited Roger Landes as the authority for his promotion to FFI general, and hence his rejection of Druilhe's authority. Similar disputes disorganized the resistance in the Charente and the Poitu, where several "Jeds" bolstered the autonomy of dissident groups of FFI. The *Commissaire de la République* in Poitiers created a *Région FFI B2* that corresponded to his administrative circumscription. He named a regular officer, Félix Chêne, to take charge. But, even though FFI leaders distributed power "in a more or less amiable fashion," this led to overlapping jurisdictions and a duplication of tasks among people who represented the multiple organizations and ministries in London, Paris, Algiers – the EMFFI, DMRs, BCRA, SOE, COMAC, and so on.[78]

Given the late date, with Paris already in Allied hands, the Germans realized that they would not able to extract all of their isolated garrisons in the Montluçon–Clermont-Ferrand area of the Massif Central. Surrounded by FFI, the German commander of Limoges was on the verge of surrender, before he was arrested by his own men, who then proceeded to organize a successful escape. Colonel Ernst von Bauer plowed his way north from Pau to Dijon with 10,000 men. The most significant surrender was that of 19,200 personnel of Sachs' rear *Marschgruppe Süd* under General Botho Elster (Figure 6.2). The resistance claimed credit for having bagged *Marschgruppe Süd*, which on 10 September signed a preliminary surrender agreement with Major General Robert Macon, commander of the 83rd US ID, at Issoudun. However, reluctant to disarm while surrounded by FFI, Elster's troops were allowed to retain their

Figure 6.2 General Botho Elster surrenders *Marschgruppe Süd* to Major General Robert Macon, commanding officer of the 83rd US ID, at Beaugency near Orleans on 10 September 1944, in the only action in which harassment by the resistance contributed to the capitulation of a German force. (Photo by Photo12/UIG/Getty Images)

weapons while they marched 120 kilometers to Beaugency on the Loire River near Orleans, where they formally capitulated to the Americans on 17 September. And while it is true that the groups in what the resistance designated Region 5 (R5) of central France had been brought into exceptionally close cooperation by the DMR Eugène Déchelette, in fact, the surrender of *Marschgruppe Süd* was precipitated by a combination of factors: the local *Organisation de résistance de l'armée* (ORA) and *Armée secrète* (AS) units in R5 were comprised of a large number of professional soldiers, Jeds and SOE operatives able to radio the coordinates of Elster's column for air strikes – indeed, the Americans ungraciously credited air strikes, not the resistance, with convincing Elster to surrender. The fact that the 83rd US ID was close by also speeded up the process, as it is unlikely that Elster would have placed his soldiers in the hands of resistance fighters.[79] Ludewig cites Elster's defeatism, which encouraged his misconception that his route of retreat through Châteauroux to Nevers, via Bruges to Dijon was "occupied by three regular French armies." Why Elster imagined that the French could muster three "armies" to block his flight may be explained in part by the atmosphere of "mass panic which had gripped many [German] units on the western front in September." This recalled the French army's 1940 implosion at Bulson, another example of what typically happens when unnerved, poorly trained, and badly led soldiers, psychologically primed to opt out of combat, become gripped by panic when they imagine an enemy much more powerful and proximate than is invariably the case. Elster's "defeatism" was further warranted by the fact that Blaskowitz had stripped *Marschgruppe Süd* of its screen of combat troops, mobile forces, and vehicles to shore up his stop line around Dijon. By 5 September, the Oberbefehlshaber West (OB West) congratulated itself that it had been able to extract the great bulk of its troops from southern and southwestern France, troops that were subsequently used to solidify German defenses in the Vosges mountains. OB West's war diary attributed the almost miraculous escape to the "outstanding performance of the troops and their clever and energetic leadership."[80]

But, as has been seen, with the possible exception of the 11th PzD, most of the retreating German troops were second-tier infantry divisions mixed with administrative and support troops, and Kriegsmarine and Luftwaffe personnel. The resistance had not been able to contain them. But, then, neither had the 36th US ID at Montélimar, which admittedly had to deal with the 11th PzD, but also packed considerably more firepower than did lightly armed and poorly coordinated FFI formations. Ludewig also places some of the blame on Eisenhower, who "forced the U.S. Third Army to stand down and do nothing" as the Germans made good their escape. Of course, from Eisenhower's perspective, this was simply one corner of a rapidly evolving front, and hardly the most critical one. As discussed above, the Allied breakout from Normandy had created a logistical crisis for two armies still dependent on the limited port capacities of Cherbourg and the artificial harbor at Arromanches. "When action is proceeding as rapidly as it did across France during the hectic days of late August and early September every commander from division upward becomes obsessed with the idea that with only a few more tons of supply he could rush right on and win the war," Eisenhower noted in his memoirs. His immediate focus was on capturing Antwerp, clearing the Low Country launch sites of the V-1 and V-2 rockets that were pummeling southern England, and linking up with Devers' Sixth Army Group coming up the Rhône Valley, whose operations until 15 September were still under Maitland Wilson's operational control. With Paris secure, at the end of August Bradley released Patton to link up with the US Seventh Army, a junction which occurred from 10 September at Epinal, by which time most German forces had escaped from their southern France cul-de-sac.[81]

That said, US Army evaluation characterized the leadership of Wiese and Blaskowitz as "confused and indecisive." The German defense of Toulon and Marseilles had been poorly prepared and executed, especially when compared with that of the "Atlantic pockets." German forces in Italy made no attempt to attack the open right flank of the Allied advance up the Rhône valley, in part because they lacked the transport to cross the Alpes and the airpower to support an attack once they arrived in France, and because they had their hands full dealing with Allied advances in Italy.[82] While the Dragoon landings had been successful, Allied forces in the south remained relatively weak and undersupplied. "Traversing France in this period was a real adventure," remembered Beaufre. "Most of the bridges had been destroyed and everywhere FFI guarded the crossings with whimsical unpredictability."[83] Ambulance driver Suzanne Lefort-Rouquette remembered that the advance up the Rhône valley was stalled by frequent and often prolonged halts due to a lack of petrol, during which her eight Senegalese stretcher-bearers were either "chattering like Cockatoos," or snoring in unison.[84] Nor was there any significant coordination between the Allied invaders and the FFI. While the German bolt from the Côte d'Azur and the Atlantic coast was largely successful, it was not because of a lack of aggressiveness of Allied commanders, including de Lattre, but due to a lack of vehicles, fuel, and troops in the pursuit. "The later stubborn German resistance in the Vosges by forces that were less well trained and equipped only underlined the poor initial performance of the *Nineteenth Army* in the Riviera campaign," concludes the US Army official history.[85] As a result, according to US estimates, 131,250 troops, or 40 percent of Army Group G's strength on 15 August, had been captured by Anglo-French forces, or interned themselves in Gironde fortresses. If one adds German casualties, estimates rise to 143,250, or 50 percent. Those German units that had survived their exhausting anabasis were disorganized and depleted of manpower and equipment. "And many of these 'effectives' were not experienced infantrymen at all, but a mixture of police, administrative, and logistical support, navy, and other fillers thrown into depleted units as cannon fodder." The 11th PzD had lost many of its tanks during 3–15 September, although these losses were quickly replaced from stocks in Germany.[86]

Although both French harbors had been severely damaged, Marseilles received its first liberty ship on 15 September, followed by Toulon on 20 September. Together, these Mediterranean ports were the transit points for 425,000 of 1,309,000 tons of US matériel dispatched to Europe. But, as was the case following the Normandy breakout, logistical problems also handcuffed the pace of pursuit in the south, in great part because, expecting a prolonged resistance as in Normandy, ammunition had been favored over vehicles and petrol in Dragoon load plans. Also, not anticipating a rapid liberation of Marseilles and Toulon, Patch had not factored de Lattre's *Armée B* into his pursuit, which condemned some French units to advance toward Avignon on foot. But some German units were not much better off, as the prioritization of the Eastern Front for personnel replacements, vehicles, spare parts, and fuel, not to mention the deterioration of French railways over four years of requisition, deferred maintenance, and Allied bombing as part of the "Transportation Plan," had severely restricted German mobility in France.[87] For instance, on 9 September, the 1st Foreign Legion Battalion bagged a marching column of 3,500 Germans with their officers in the vanguard near Autun. "I haven't seen that since Tunisia," Brosset recorded.[88] Furthermore, the Americans had got the jump on them, moving north while the French cleaned up Toulon and Marseilles, "thus the inconvenience of maintaining us beneath their deployment . . . a sort of trap," which de Lattre looked to break out of "to be the first in the race toward the essential objective, constituted by Alsace and the Rhine, passing through the intermediary objective of Lyon." The progress of *l'Armée B* was assisted by the fact that the axis of the American advance had bifurcated toward the east, liberating Grenoble on 22 August, and by the fact that de Lattre possessed an armored division – the 1ère DB.[89]

Political concerns remained paramount. De Lattre feared that his command might be shunted off into "unrewarding and defensive missions," such as guarding the Italian frontier,[90] or fragmented and diluted among US troops. To improve command and control, de Lattre divided his force into two corps – I Corps under Béthouart, who had been summoned from Italy, and II Corps under Monsabert, promoted from his command of the 3e DIA, which was now assumed by the GTM commander Guillaume.[91] The French priority was rather to liberate French cities and towns, especially those where the FTP and the *milices patriotiques*, a communist initiative to create a police force under the Conseil national de la résistance (CNR), had rushed to fill vacuums created by departing Germans and were in many places contesting the authority of the *comités départementaux de libération*. The liberation of Lyon was accorded special urgency by de Lattre both because of its symbolic importance and also because the Germans and *la Milice* were executing captured FFI, hostages, and Jews. Given the petrol shortage, only the tanks of the reconnaissance company of Brosset's 1ère DFL were able to enter Lyon on 3 September, along with several nearby FFI units, to reestablish order once the Germans had vacated the city, after having blown the bridges on the Saône and Rhône Rivers.[92]

De Lattre believed himself in a race with the US VI Corps to arrive at the Belfort Gap, the passage between the southern slopes of the Vosges mountains and the Swiss frontier, to cut off the retreating Nineteenth Army. "Alert to the threat," Wiese set up a series of blocking positions to buy time for his etiolated "march groups" to filter into the Belfort Gap. Logistical problems continued to slow the Allied pursuit both by Patton from the west and by Patch from the south. Following the symbolic meeting of a squadron of marines from the 1ère DFL and a platoon from the *1er Régiment de Marche de Spahis marocains* from Leclerc's 2e DB at Châtillon-sur-Seine on 12 September, on 19 September, de Lattre's *Armée B* became the *1ère Armée française*.[93]

Nevertheless, the bulk of German forces in the south and southwest had managed to flee. The good news for de Gaulle was that the evacuation had been so rapid that Gaullist administrators and the resistance had been able quickly to fill the ensuing vacuum of authority, leaving Allied civil affairs units outdistanced and in search of a mission. That did not invariably make for stable relations, however, especially in towns bypassed by Allied and French forces, such as Toulouse and elsewhere in the "Red South." In these circumstances, GPRF officials sometimes found their authority contested by groups – resistance or those claiming to be "*officiers* FFI" – who rushed to fill the power vacuums in prefectures and town halls. The communist Francs-Tireurs et Partisans (FTP) in particular saw it as their patriotic duty to settle scores with "traitors" by extra-judicial means.[94] As a result, the Liberation witnessed an explosion of vigilante behavior that persisted for weeks – even months – in some areas. The Allies monitored these developments closely, looking for two indications: first, whether disorder threatened Allied lines of communication; and second, whether there was evidence of a concerted communist conspiracy to seize power. While, on the whole, the Allies found that the FFI behaved responsibly, they remained concerned about the large numbers of weapons in the hands of people whose conduct was unpredictable, and that a shortage of food and fuel might spark popular disorder. The Allies were also worried by the presence of large numbers of refugees in some areas, such as *Osttruppen* deserters in Lorraine; and by the potential actions of Spanish Republicans, who made up between 8–10 percent of *maquisards* in the southwest, some of whom were conspiring to invade Spain. In these conditions the GPRF worried about its ability to extend its control over the country as the campaign in Alsace locked down many troops in the autumn.[95]

Resistance in Brittany

Resistance in Brittany following D-Day is often cited as especially effective in speeding the Allied advance (Map 6.5) and saving lives, for several reasons. Because Eisenhower sought to capture Breton ports, Special Forces Headquarters (SFHQ) had worked out a coherent plan to incorporate the FFI there into operations. For this reason, Brittany saw a large investment of Jedburgh and Special Air Service (SAS) teams to coordinate resistance groups to carry out sabotage operations, which proved very costly to the special operators. Proximity to the UK allowed weapons drops, which armed an estimated 18,000 Breton FFI by 1 August. The fact that resistance groups in Brittany (Figure 16.3) were overwhelmingly FTP minimized political rivalries that roiled FFI cooperation elsewhere. Combined operations allowed resisters to play important roles as local intelligence sources, guides, POW guards, and auxiliary forces to help advancing US troops, ambush retreating German columns, "mop up" pockets of bypassed German garrisons, and guard Third

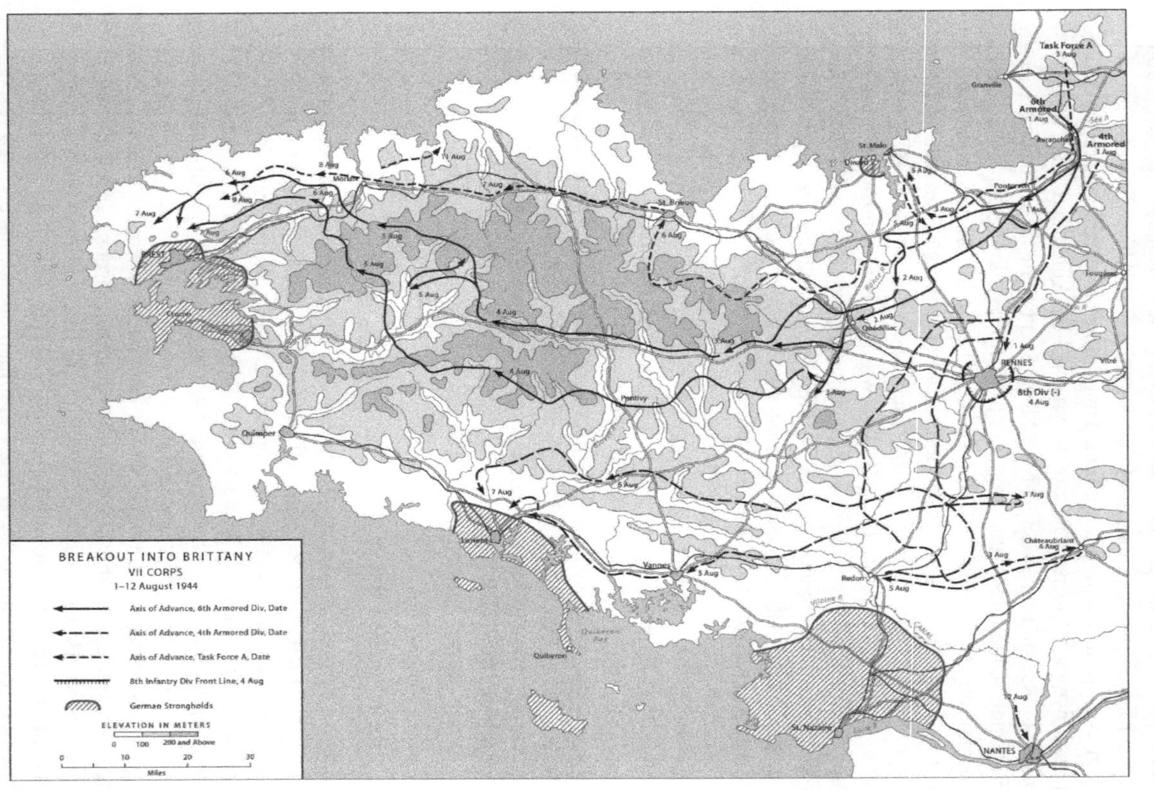

Map 6.5 The US advance into Brittany (1–12 August 1944).

Figure 6.3 *La Milice* rounds up resistance suspects, including women, in Ploërmel, Brittany in June 1944. (Photo by Keystone-France/Gamma-Keystone via Getty Images)

Army supply lines by ensuring that retreating Germans did not blow bridges and railways.[96]

Unlike *réduits maquisards* in the Alpes or the Massif Central, resistance in Brittany had organized into small mobile bands, which were most numerous in lower Brittany. But, as elsewhere, the Gestapo and Sipo/SD had cut great swaths in the resistance leadership from 1943, often guided by informers from the Parti national breton (Strollad Broadel Breizh, PNB) (Figure 6.3). The province was garrisoned by two German army corps, which since 6 June had been bled of an estimated three-quarters of their combat-worthy troops for Normandy, and had been under constant air attack. From 2 August, these soldiers fell under the control of General Wilhelm Fahrmbacher, who on 3 August was ordered to retreat into the Breton *Festungen* (fortresses), as per Hitler's 19 January 1944 directive. At 18:00 on that day, the British Broadcasting Corporation (BBC) had broadcast the message "*Le chapeau de Napoléon est-il encore à Perros-Guirec?*," the signal for a general uprising which brought several thousands of men into the resistance, perhaps three-quarters of whom were armed. On the night of 4–5 August, the Aloès mission arrived at Kérien, south of Guingamp, to take command of the Breton resistance. The most common resistance tactic was to attack Germans as they withdrew from their outlying garrisons. This often caused the Germans to shoot hostages, or to place them in the lead vehicles of their convoys; or led villagers to believe that they had been liberated, only to see the Wehrmacht return to exact bloody vengeance. But damage was limited by the fact that the Americans quickly liberated Brittany: by 4 August, Patton's Third Army had circumvented Rennes; by 5 August, American tanks had reached Vannes and Lorient; by 7 August, they were at the gates of Brest; and by 9 August, they had reached Nantes. Sometimes the tanks drove through villages already occupied by FFI. Because US armor often outran its infantry, the FFI were called upon to mop up; or tanks, artillery, and FFI might combine to coerce a pocket of stubborn Germans or *Osttruppen* to surrender. Two major battles occurred in Brittany: in the first the 86th US ID had to fight street by street, beginning on 7 August, to capture Saint-Malo from its garrison of 10,000–12,000 Germans, which finally surrendered 10 days later. Brest and its environs, into which 35,000 Germans had retreated, took from 7 August to 18 September to clear, in the process totally destroying the town, whose harbor was not put back into operation before the German surrender in May 1945.[97]

However, the general verdict, even for the relatively successful use of FFI in Brittany, was that the Allies had belatedly recognized the operational potential of the resistance. The "Jeds" were introduced only after D-Day, so that the entire effort offered a last-minute improvisation, often as the Germans had already begun to withdraw into their "Atlantic pockets" at Saint-Malo, Brest, Lorient, Saint-Nazaire, La Rochelle, and Royan. The staff of "Colonel Eono" – presumably Colonel Albert Éon, who, as part of the Aloès mission, was meant to coordinate resistance operations in Brittany with the help of four "Jeds," did not parachute in until 4–5 August, after the breakout at Avranches. The Americans reported that the delay was caused by the fact that "Colonel Eono is not parachutable" but required a glider landing, which delayed his arrival. Lack of communication with SFHQ and the EMFFI as well as command-and-control problems meant that, rather than a coordinated effort, resistance activity became a series of improvised local initiatives that smoothed a US advance that already had achieved an unstoppable momentum. And, of course, civilians suspected of cooperating with the resistance were shot by the Germans and their farms destroyed.[98] But, by 23 August, Éon and the Aloès mission had returned to the UK, complaining of chaos in Brittany caused by FFI leaders who insisted that they answered to COMAC, not London. The dissolution of FFI structures with the stand down of the EMFFI touched off local power struggles among resistance leaders, that favored the reemergence of the *naphtalards* – a derisive nickname for the "mothballed" soldiers of the Armistice Army, derived from a popular song, *Ça sent la naphtaline* ("That Smells of Mothballs"). Nor did things get any better from 27 August, when Koenig left London to become military governor of Paris and the FFI fell under General René Chouteau, who began to stand down his command from 23 September.

The bottom line is that Brittany was quickly liberated by US forces as the Germans scurried into their "Atlantic pockets." Patton's detour into Brittany constituted an unfortunate diversion of four US divisions numbering 80,000 troops, who might have been more usefully employed in an early break-in into Germany, although at the time the Allies believed that Breton ports would serve as vital supply bases.[99] While the FFI might play a useful role as auxiliaries to conventional forces, they had done virtually nothing to impede the German retreat, while bringing down retaliation on the civilian population. Also, relations between FFI and GIs in Brittany quickly degenerated into "unconcealed antagonism" over the friendly treatment of German POWs by the Americans. According to one US intelligence officer:

> FFI headquarters told me the following story: on June 6th, or thereabouts, the German commander of about 300 men had contacted the village authorities of which the present Captain of the FFI was one, saying that he would give his word of honor not to use any more force toward the French, providing he was allowed to remain unmolested until he could surrender to the American Army. From June 6th onwards, these 300 men had committed countless atrocities against French men and women. Photographs of some of the men who had committed these atrocities were available. When the village was liberated, the prisoners were taken away by the Americans and openly treated with consideration [Cigarettes, friendliness, etc., etc.]. The FFI were in no way consulted and their Captain who had accepted the German word was not allowed to deal with the German commander in the "proper" manner. [He had sworn to kill him and was forcibly restrained from doing so.] Neither the photographs nor the atrocity stories were asked for and there is a strong feeling that the criminals might not be brought to justice.[100]

The Atlantic Pockets

After the "disgrace" of Cherbourg, which was captured by the Americans at the end of June, commanders of the Atlantic *Festungen* were to be selected carefully.[101] On 19 January 1944, Hitler had declared that, in the event of an Allied landing, eleven ports between Holland and the Gironde estuary were to be transformed into *Festungen* that were to be held at all costs.[102] This was not an idea unique to the French front, but the replication of *Festungen* in Crete, on the Aegean islands, and at Pillau (now Baltiysk) in East Prussia. *Festungen* presented several advantages in Hitler's mind, beginning with the fact that they would become "breakwaters" for his Atlantic Wall.[103] Denying the Allies the use of French harbors would also confront the attackers with logistical conundrums. However, a priority in France for Hitler was to preserve the U-boat bases at Lorient, Saint-Nazaire and La Pallice/La Rochelle. Although the German U-boat campaign of 1943 had failed to staunch the arrival of Allied troops and supplies, and the surviving U-boats had been evacuated from France to Norway and the Baltic, the indestructible Todt Organization-built *U-Boot-Bunker* – reinforced concrete honeycombs that combined bases, dry docks, and resupply "garages" for U-boats – in the three French ports had survived repeated Allied bombing attacks unscathed. For this reason, and in keeping with his hope that an eleventh-hour "miracle weapon" might yet salvage the Third Reich, Hitler sought to preserve them to receive the new Typ XXI and Typ XXIII submarines then in the process of Kriegsmarine development. These were true submarines, much faster than old submersibles, with double hulls, and had snorkels that allowed the Typ XXI to stay submerged for up to three days. However, while production difficulties augmented by Allied bombing had delayed their development, the German leader remained convinced that they could turn the tide of the war. "If we lose the battlefield of France, we lose the base for the submarine war," he insisted. "We have to realize: the submarine war is launched from France."[104] But, on 17 August, when Hitler ordered a general retreat from France, the situation was chaotic and his decision last-minute, while German forces that had been chewed up in Normandy were simply not available. As a result, the Allied breakout from Normandy was followed by the capture of Le Havre, Calais, Boulogne, Saint-Malo, and Brest. This left the Germans holding Dunkirk, the Channel Islands, Lorient, Saint-Nazaire, La Rochelle, and Royan/Pointe de Grave at the mouth of the Gironde estuary that effectively closed down Bordeaux, whose port facilities had been severely damaged by the retreating Germans in any case. In August, the Germans sought to close off access to their *Festungen* to advancing American troops and FFI, which proved relatively easy because, by the middle of August the liberation of German-held ports in southern Brittany and southwestern France was no longer an Allied priority.

Nor does the term "pocket" appear in official correspondence until the middle of October, because until then the siege lines remained rather porous. August Hampel noted that peasants continued to bring produce into Royan into October, while electricity was furnished by the generating station at Saintes, 30 kilometers away "in enemy territory."[105] September witnessed sorties by the garrisons to expand their perimeters and destroy bridges to deny access, especially around Saint-Nazaire, while the French expected that, having finally liberated Brest on 19 September, the Americans would then turn south to Lorient and Saint-Nazaire. Unfortunately, the Germans had transformed Brest into a defensive labyrinth, which required a coordinated block-by-block assault that combined the efforts of engineers to demine and to blow down walls, chemical mortars and Churchill Crocodile tanks armed with flamethrowers to smoke the Germans out of their bunkers and tunnels, tank destroyers to provide direct fire support for assaulting infantry, and an arsenal of 0.50 caliber machineguns.[106] It was certainly an all-arms task well beyond the combat capabilities of the poorly armed and equipped, and largely untrained, FFI.

The slow, costly reconquest of Brest had taught Eisenhower that containment offered a more cost-effective strategy than assault, so that he proved unwilling to commit additional forces to take the "Atlantic pockets" (Map 6.6), especially as an opportunity to trap retreating German forces in the Falaise Pocket developed from early August. By the middle of September, the troops from Dragoon had linked up with those of Overlord, in the process liberating Dijon, Arras, and Nancy.[107] The Wehrmacht appeared to be on the ropes, and the logistical value of the Atlantic ports, even if they could be liberated without destroying the harbors, appeared negligible for the purposes of the war. Battle lines had shifted north and east, while the French rail system was too damaged or debilitated effectively to link rapidly advancing Allied troops to harbors well to the rear, whatever de Gaulle's priorities. Most important, from a logistical perspective, was the 4 September liberation of Antwerp, a major port much closer to the front lines than was distant Brittany. Realizing this, Hitler ordered his 15th Army to reinforce the islands of Walcheren, Vlissingen, and Zeeland. For this reason, the first convoy of ships arrived at the Belgian port only on 29 November, after Canadian and Polish troops had cleared the Scheldt in hard fighting, and the harbor and its approaches had been demined.[108] As a result, American forces in Brittany limited their action before Lorient and Saint-Nazaire to encirclement and reconnaissance-in-force probes.

From the German perspective, the *Festungen* strategy proved largely a failed experiment, as the "pockets" became traps, "where the decisive arms were shells, hunger, and time."[109] The Germans had written off two divisions at Saint-Malo alone, and marooned a further 92,000 soldiers in Brest, Lorient, and Saint-Nazaire. "The bottom line for Model was that, along with the 319th Infantry Division based in the Channel Islands, eight semi-well-trained and fully equipped major units had to be scratched." And while they were denying the Allies the use of these Atlantic harbors, they were not tying down significant Allied forces, but principally FFI.[110] Nevertheless, the rapid Allied advance had left blisters of *Festungen* in the Allied rear, the most formidable of which was undoubtedly Dunkirk, whose defenses stretched for 20 kilometers along the sea, with its 10,000-man garrison made up largely of troops who had escaped the Normandy débâcle, with 350 artillery pieces, and

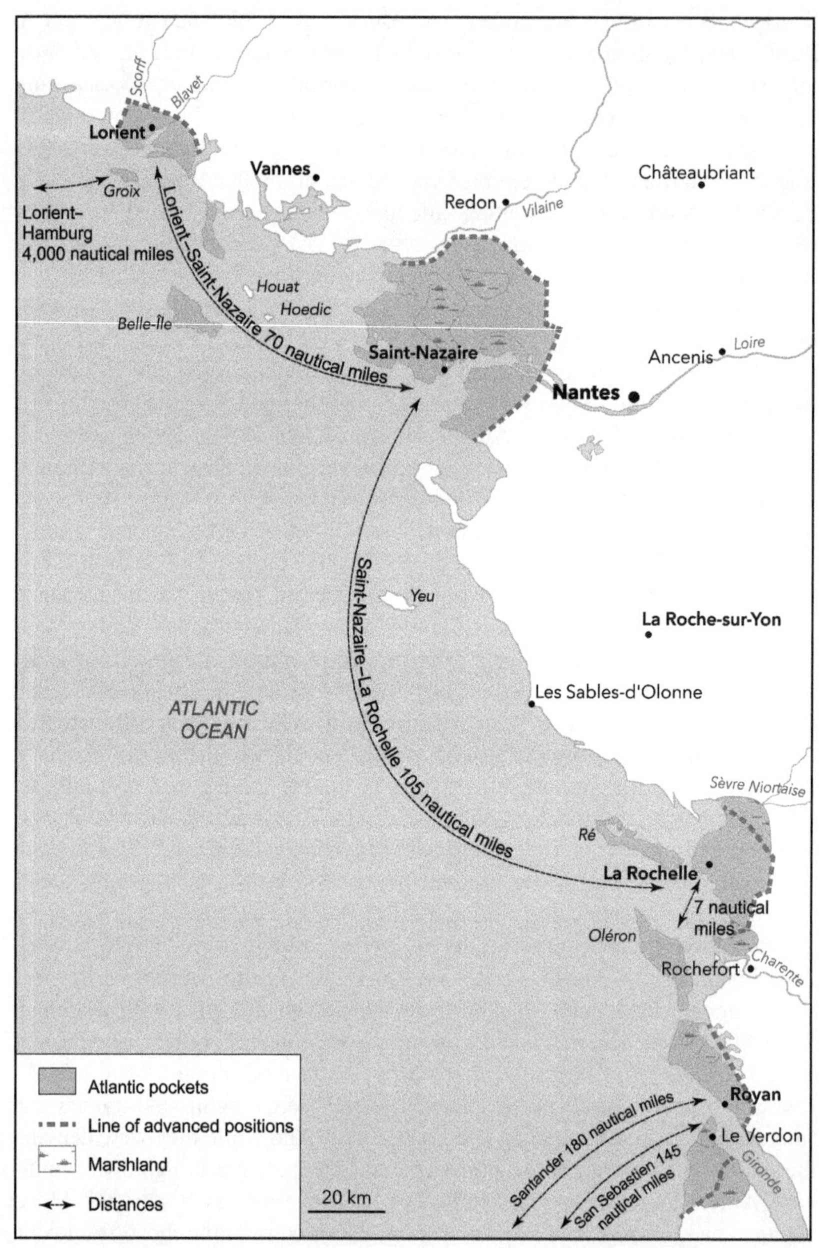

Map 6.6 The Atlantic pockets.

protected on the land side by pillboxes, anti-tank trenches, and flooded fields. After some initial attacks in September, the Canadian troops investing it were transferred to clear out the Scheldt, and the siege of Dunkirk was left largely to Czech troops and FFI.[111]

Southern Brittany and southwestern France were networked by a string of pockets stretching for almost 500 kilometers from Lorient in the north, through Saint-Nazaire, whose defense perimeter blocked the mouth of the Loire, and hence the river port of Nantes, to La Rochelle, and in the south Royan/Point de Grave astride the Gironde estuary. Lorient was protected by over 250 artillery pieces and a garrison estimated at 25,000 men – a mix of regular troops, *Osttruppen*, Kriegsmarine, and Luftwaffe personnel to man the *Flak* batteries, as well as Todt Organization workers, who constantly toiled to strengthen the defenses. Lorient's *Bunker* had space for forty U-boats. Thirty small surface craft assured liaison with Saint-Nazaire and the islands. While around 6,000 civilians had been evacuated,10,000 remained at Lorient in starvation conditions, as well as 5,000 more on the Quiberon peninsula and on the island of Groix. Because Lorient had such a small agricultural hinterland, fishermen were allowed to work, with many seizing the opportunity to carry refugees and escapees, while importing contraband.[112]

About 140 kilometers south of Lorient, Saint-Nazaire's *raison d'être* was a bunker able to shelter twenty U-boats. Commanded by Luftwaffe General Hans Junck, Saint-Nazaire counted 700 artillery pieces of all calibers. Its garrison was slightly larger than that of Lorient, but had a far larger area to defend, as Saint-Nazaire's hinterland stretched 50 kilometers into the littoral and covered both banks of the Loire estuary. Saint-Nazaire's extensive perimeter also enclosed 120,000 civilians, by far the largest civilian population of any of the "pockets," most of them refugees from the massive Allied bombings of Saint-Nazaire in 1942–1943 that had destroyed 85 percent of the port city and forced its population to flee to smaller towns such as Guérande and Pouliguen, or to the lowlands of the Pays de Retz south of the Loire. The Allies did not want civilians in the Atlantic pockets to become a battlefield encumbrance, while the Germans lacked the means to feed them, and distrusted them as spies. In this way, evacuations were calculated to disrupt French resistance and intelligence networks and provide a means for the Gestapo to recuperate their own agents. Farmers were forced to remain behind to produce food and maintain their herds, even in active combat zones.[113] As a result, negotiations saw six separate evacuations from Saint-Nazaire in September–October, and more convoys in January–February 1945, that removed an estimated 20,000 civilians. Although French intelligence had warned since November 1944 that Gestapo informants and other collaborators were being exfiltrated among the refugees, only in February 1945 did the prefect at Nantes began to monitor and arrest evacuees "*douteuses au point de vue national.*"[114]

For those "*empochés*" (pocketed) or "*pochards*" left behind, life became a daily struggle to find fuel for heating and cooking, if indeed they could find anything to cook – fishing was forbidden and the coast mined, the traditional industries that provided work were bombed out or closed for lack of raw material, so few salaries were paid, and the Germans requisitioned most of the food produced within the pocket. Transportation was limited to bicycles, even for sick and wounded. The Germans took a census of the remaining population. Every movement within the "pocket" required an *Ausweis* (pass). A resistance numbering around 2,000 eventually formed, its role principally to organize escape and evasion for Polish, Czech, or *Osttruppen* deserters, POWs, or downed aviators. They also provided intelligence to the Allies on German defenses, and circulated news among the population. As the Germans confiscated all radios, and there was no electricity in any case, bicycle-powered crystal sets appeared, as well as clandestine newssheets.[115]

This left a garrison of 25,000, which included 7,000 soldiers from the German XXV Corps, which had been cut off on the Brittany peninsula by the American breakout at Avranches, as well as disarmed Italian troops and *Osttruppen*, who were particularly ubiquitous in the German Seventh Army in Normandy and later at Royan and La Rochelle. French reports in November 1944 estimated the numbers of foreigners in Royan at 35 percent of the garrison, "with no devotion to the Reich ... and disposed to surrender."[116] *Osttruppen* were considered "*unsichere*" (unreliable), especially from September 1944, after 300 Ukranians under a Colonel Potiereyka deserted the 275th ID to join the *maquis*.[117] A Polish officer was attached to the Forces françaises de l'Ouest (FFO) to interrogate Polish deserters. For these reasons, German practice in the "pockets" was to post *Osttruppen* in locations from which it was difficult to desert, such as Belle-Île, Groix, or the Île de Ré, where many Poles were stationed, use them as labor troops, or integrate them in small groups into German units, which nonetheless contained up to 30 percent non-*Reichsdeutsche* – Poles, Czechs, Austrians, Italians, Georgians, Alsatians, Mosellans, and so on.[118]

La Rochelle encompassed the U-boat base at La Pallice, which by the autumn of 1944 berthed only surface boats, as well as an airfield behind a 40-kilometer defense perimeter, and a population of 16,000 civilians. Most importantly, it was home to a large Würzburg radar station that allowed the Germans to anticipate an attack far out to sea. The Île d'Oléron and the Île de Ré also fell under the authority of La Rochelle's commander, Rear Admiral Ernst Schirlitz. La Rochelle offered an atoll of Vichy allegiance in a sea of French liberation, with two collaborationist newspapers that continued to publish until the war's end, as well as an active contingent of *la Milice*, who served in German uniform and continued to track down resisters through house searches, and a radio-detection van. Schirlitz struck an agreement with the besiegers not to destroy the historic town in return for a French promise not to shell the garrison. No such agreement was struck for Royan and Pointe de Grave,[119] which incarcerated 20,000 French civilians as well as a German garrison of 10,000.[120] However, in the opinion of Hampel, most of the soldiers were "too old to serve effectively, only the technical arrangements compensated for the fear of the insufficiency of numbers." But those "technical arrangements" proved formidable enough to deter poorly equipped FFI – 300 guns and a solid air defense, as well as being shielded by natural obstacles, including the *marais* (marsh) *de la Seudre*. All roads into Royan were mined. *Panzerwerk* surveilled a no man's land beyond a line of demarcation along a 30-kilometer front. From October, the occupiers realized that the French were taking the siege seriously when the market suddenly contained no provisions, and the electricity was cut. The garrison rigged small generators from the antique locomotives that had operated a small coastal train. The chief engineer explained the defense plan, and ordered new trenches dug, a task executed by a polyglot 120-man work crew that spoke Spanish, Polish, Basque, and even German. Sailors installed cannon. But, according to Hempel, the garrison felt totally isolated and abandoned. Beside the odd patrol, there was little to do. By mutual agreement, there was no fighting at night. Increasingly "insolent" Allied planes occasionally dropped a bomb or two. By turn, the men in the garrison were allowed to radio message home.[121]

All in all, life inside the Atlantic pockets was not too uncomfortable for the German forces, especially when compared with the conditions of the FFI besiegers and French "*pochards*." Indeed, a "live and let live" attitude among combatants perfectly content to allow the outcome of the war to be decided on other fronts meant that combat in the Atlantic pockets combined the *Sitzkrieg* of 1939–1940 with the cattle-rustling raids of the Old West. Since many of the German personnel in the pockets were support troops, Kriegsmarine, and so on, the command set up basic training courses lasting four to six weeks, the culmination of which was to mount against one of the FFI outposts a raid whose objective was to inflict casualties and capture POWs.[122] The Saint-Nazaire perimeter especially encompassed an extensive agricultural hinterland. Elsewhere, the Germans paid high prices to farmers for produce, raided to bring in food and cattle and sharpen their tactical skills, or simply pillaged the civilian population. U-boats imported supplies, medicines, and mail, while La Rochelle ran an intermittent trade with Spain, from which the Germans imported fruit, olive oil, sardines, and chocolate. Each "pocket" had its own electricity generators, as well as windmills for water. Powerful radio stations kept them in touch with Berlin, while, until April 1945, weekly flights of Heinkel He 111s – designed in 1934 as a medium bomber but from 1943 downgraded to a transport aircraft – between Germany and the "pockets" parachuted in mail, French bank notes, medicine, and a few personnel. These flights also raised fears that the Germans would station air squadrons to give their "pockets" more offensive punch, although this never happened, in part because the airfields were in bad shape and lacked an infrastructure to support squadrons of aircraft.[123] Garrison morale was maintained through football matches, choral and theater groups, patrols, agricultural labor, the publication of newssheets such as *Die Gironde Festung* at Royan, and, of course, contact with French women. But discipline was strict, and the besieged soldiers worried about their families, and increasingly the consequences for them of impending defeat.[124]

When, in the middle of September 1944, the 94th US ID invested Lorient and Saint-Nazaire, they discovered porous and fluctuating perimeters occupied by poorly armed FFI. Algiers dispatched General Henri Borgnis-Desbordes to Lorient and Colonel Raymond Chomel to Saint-Nazaire to recruit and restructure the FFI units there in keeping with de Gaulle's 28 August directive that FFI groups were to disband, and their members must enlist individually in the army. From 18 August 1944, the FFI in Brittany were to be organized into the *19e Division d'infanterie* (19e DI) under Borgnis. Chomel commanded the FFI Loire-Inférieure. Both men experienced the same problems with recognition of FFI ranks and a widespread refusal to serve under former Armistice Army "*planqués*" (pen-pushers). Depending on the unit, 60–80 percent of the FFI were too young to have done their military service before 1940 and under 30 percent of them had been in an active *maquis*, while professional soldiers made up only 15–17 percent of their cadres. Ironically, some of the most militarily experienced among the besiegers were veterans of *la Milice* and the *Légion des volontaires français contre le bolchévisme* (LVF) eager to burnish their post-Liberation resistance resumés and probably avoid being lynched.[125] Roughly 12,000 enlistees were given a hasty military instruction at a Breton barracks in November–December, and then sent to the field as part of three newly raised divisions – the 1ère, 23e, and 25e DIs. By April 1945, 21,000 French troops besieged Lorient, while 17,000 invested Saint-Nazaire. From January 1945, 16,500 volunteers from the Sarthe, the Vendée, Loire-Inférieur, Indre-et-Loire, and Vienne were grouped in the 25e DI under Chomel, who had been promoted to general. This division was armed with German equipment that had been captured in the Falaise Pocket. However, while winter on France's Atlantic coast failed to replicate Alsace's Arctic conditions, casualties from sickness were especially high before La Rochelle/Royan, where winter weather rendered 8,000 men *hors de combat*, largely due to lack of shoes, warm clothing, and elementary hygiene. Another 20 percent of the FFI were sent home because they refused to sign an enlistment contract as required, or because they were physically unfit, too young, or represented a professional category required for national reconstruction, which included agriculture. The remainder fractured into "battalions" that fluctuated between 250 and 800 men, initially recruited principally from the hinterland of the pockets, but who were joined over the winter and spring by volunteers from Paris, the northeast, and even the Var on the Mediterranean coast, as the government directed reinforcements to beef up forces to attack Royan and open the Gironde estuary, as one of de Gaulle's priorities was to supply the southwest through the port of Bordeaux. From November 1944, some North African reinforcements meant for de Lattre's *1ère Armée* were diverted to the southwest, as well as sub-Saharan Africans, some of them POWs from 1940 liberated from *Frontstalags* in France and pressed into logistical and labor roles, to make up a contingent of 13,600 "colonials" by April 1945. Motorized infantry and even armored units equipped with recovered SOMUA S35 and B1bis tanks, as well as elements of Leclerc's 2e DB with more modern equipment, were deployed against Royan and La Rochelle. Spanish Republicans, as well as Belgians, Poles, Italians, and even former *Ostruppen* also served in French ranks.[126]

Meager rations, which featured a relative abundance of bad wine, were supplemented by rabbits and other furry prey ensnared between the lines, and shellfish scraped from the extensive marshes, all at the risk of mines and booby traps, which, along with German night raids and weather-related casualties, thinned the ranks. A dearth of rations also placed the besiegers in competition with civilian "*pochards*," who were periodically sent supply convoys, as well as with famished civilians in the hinterland.[127] On 1 January 1945, the 94th US ID was switched out for the 66th US ID, an inexperienced unit demoralized by the loss of 800 soldiers when a troop ship transporting part of the division to France had been torpedoed off Cherbourg in December 1944. Between them, the 66th US ID and the FFI manned a 150-kilometer front at Lorient and Saint-Nazaire, while, further south, Henri Adeline, a regular officer and Saint-Cyr graduate who had been responsible for the FFI in Dordogne, was put in command of the troops besieging the pockets at La Rochelle–Royan/Pointe de Grave. By March 1945, a steady process of the "regularization" of *maquis* formations around the "*poches*" would see them designated as the *détachement d'armées de l'Atlantique*.[128]

A week later on 14 October, de Gaulle tapped the "awkward but steadfastly loyal" Larminat, who had been unemployed since his August tiff with de Lattre, to organize the FFO with his headquarters at Cognac. As with de Lattre's *1ère Armée*, the FFO fell under the command of Devers' Sixth Army Group, which rather had its hands full on the other side of the country attempting to complete the liberation of Alsace and cross the Rhine.[129] In many respects, the Atlantic Front, with its ad hoc collection of FFI under the command of buccaneers and narcissists, offered a perfect fit for Larminat, who was fundamentally "an adventurer, non-conformist, in permanent rebellion with his milieu." Rather than transform his FFI *levée* into disciplined soldiers, he accepted them as they were, "representing the impetus of the people."[130] However, while Larminat praised the FFI as "essentially courageous, often to the point of temerity, devoted to the point of death ... very intelligent and agile, disciplined when they had leaders who themselves had a sense of command and discipline," their organization was chaotic: "The proliferation of staffs and the like was astonishing," he remembered. "In particular, '2e Bureaux' flourished with exuberance. Headquarters companies or personal *gardes du corps* had pride of place." Adeline had his name embroidered on the sleeves of his personal guard, an effeminate touch that earned him the nickname "Mademoiselle Adeline" among his FFI. The man named to command the siege of the Pointe de Grave – known to the oenophile French as "*la poche du Médoc*" – resistance "Colonel" Jean de Milleret, appropriately served only Grand Médoc in his mess. Many of the young FFI were armed "with a mediocre gun and a handful of bullets. Otherwise, there was no problem except that, poorly trained, badly armed, without competent cadres, they allowed themselves to be killed joyfully although not always usefully when the fellow opposite played the clown. The cadres were perfectly useless," in Larminat's opinion, because the pro-Vichy middle classes declined to step forward to lead FFI whom they viewed as communists. Because the besiegers lacked artillery, all they could do was sit in isolated posts and try to prevent German raiding parties from rustling cattle which farmers incautiously grazed too close to the siege lines. For instance, in October, a German raid on the village of Frossay on the south bank of the Loire netted 500–600 cattle. With their limited ammunition, lack of heavy weapons, and inadequate clothing – many were still wearing clogs during the winter – the FFI did not offer much of a deterrent. The French authorities often refused to pay them, so they lacked money to buy food, which reduced the besiegers of Saint-Nazaire and Lorient to begging from the Americans, while 27 October 1944 even witnessed a mutiny against their officers, which appears to have been quickly talked down. For this reason, on 30 October, Colonel Chomel asked Larminat for 1 million francs to pay his troops.[131] "The men have only one shirt, one pair of underpants," wrote the lieutenant-colonel commanding the *6e Régiment d'infanterie* (6e RI) besieging Rochefort in January 1945. Overcoats were lacking, and men wearing clogs had no socks. As a result, 18 percent of his strength was hospitalized. Without means to cook, they relied on civilians to prepare their soup.[132] Quite naturally, penurious FFI looked to the Americans, who were themselves already straining to support their troops in Belgium and Alsace, to supply them. And when provisions were not forthcoming in sufficient quantities, FFI, often encouraged by their communist cadres, simply raided US depots or even supply trains in the Morbihan and Côtes-du-Nord. These and other "regrettable incidents" between GIs and FFI, that included brawls and even brief firefights, contributed to an atmosphere of what many feared portended incipient civil war, especially in the south.[133]

The Strategic Value of the FFI

After the war, the *maquis*, along with the rest of the resistance, was presented as an operational triumph. Eisenhower is often quoted as saying that the French resistance was worth fifteen divisions.[134] What he writes in his memoirs is that, without the help of what he calls the "Free French," "The liberation of France and the defeat of the enemy in western Europe would have consumed a much longer time and meant greater losses to ourselves."[135] As Muracciole points out, fifteen divisions is more troops than Montgomery had at El Alamein, and about the number of Axis troops that surrendered at Stalingrad and at "Tunisgrad." The SOE quoted Maitland Wilson as saying that civilian resistance reduced Wehrmacht effectiveness in southern France by 40 percent, while the Seventh Army's commander, Alexander Patch, allegedly opined that resistance was worth four to five divisions at Anvil/Dragoon, which, if this were so, would equal more or less the strength of de Lattre's *Armée B*.[136] A July 1945 SHAEF report drawn up by Bedell Smith credited the SOE with "fostering the French will to resist, keeping the enemy's attention taut, sapping his confidence, disrupting his communications – especially telephone and rail, and forcing 'extensive and intricate detours' on his reinforcements 'at a critical time,' so that his troops reached the formal battlefield 'in a state of extreme disorganization and exhaustion.'" In this way, the FFI tied down what Foot calculated amounted to eight German divisions in counter-partisan operations.[137]

So, if resistance in France could inflict fifteen divisions' worth of damage at Overlord, and another four or five at Dragoon, it must have been a formidable force indeed! But, as Wieviorka notes, it would have been surprising if the resistance had proven militarily significant when the French had not been associated with invasion planning, so that "the Gaullist authorities were unable to send clear instructions to their troops."[138] In any case, even regular armies with recognized political leadership that set policy and strategic priorities, conveyed through an institutionalized chain of command, backed by professional cadres, schools that established doctrine and educated officers, training bases, technology, weapons, and an industrial and popular support base, took time and hard experience to acquire combat efficiency. It would have been unprecedented if a resistance, most of whose leaders had no or minimal military training, who were unable to prepare for armed combat given their clandestine existence and an eleventh-hour explosion of enthusiastic but often adolescent volunteers, even had they possessed sufficient arms and munitions, could have made a significant military impact. The purpose of "the French Resistance" for Roosevelt, the Gaullists, the interface services, Churchill, and the Foreign Office was political rather than military. While Roosevelt was probably determined to invade AFN in November 1942 with or without "resistance," the promise of widespread support for an Anglo-American invasion in AFN provided the "invitation" that allowed him to silence opponents of Operation Torch among the Chiefs of Staff and his cabinet. That said, Allied leaders struggled to find ways to operationalize resistance for military ends, which created a hot competition for influence among the diverse resistance groups within the interface services, and sharpened friction among Allied governments, especially as Churchill sought to invoke the *maquis* in southeastern France and Yugoslav partisans to derail Anvil/Dragoon. Many of the post-invasion senior testimonials were solicited by the interface services, led by the SOE, seeking to justify their institutional role in the war, while creating an operational and strategic niche for special operations going forward.[139]

A second purpose of resistance was memorial. Unlike de Gaulle's émigré army, an incidental and even divergent assembly of political and "racial" refugees, colonials, and aristocratic rebels against Vichy order, the internal resistance conformed to the "soil and frontiers" image of the "soldier peasant," memorialized by the 1916 defense of Verdun.[140] Like the Great War *poilus*, resisters and *maquisards* distilled and humanized the venerable narrative of France's martyrdom, because they reinforced or reiterated prevailing conceptions. And, while the embrace of resistance as a symbol of a national war and a refusal to accept the verdict of 1940 was perhaps necessary for French prestige, it distorts the military record. For the French, one irony of civilian resistance was the spectacular incongruence between war as anticipated and war as it unfolded, and the yawning chasm between the benefits of war, its moral ambiguities, and the immense suffering inflicted. On the other hand, one might argue that France's celebration of resistance reflected the romantic resilience in French popular culture of nineteenth-century concepts of the *levée en masse*, the *franc-tireur*, and the Commune. "Ironic heroes" became mythologized in a war without front lines, absent the absurdities and abuses of power inherent in military hierarchies, as well as a sort of refutation of the implosion in 1940 of French international prestige and power. Civilian resistance stood the notion of the "military hero" on its head – it was the admirals and generals at Vichy, Algiers, Tunis, Casablanca, Dakar, and Toulon who embodied collaboration and treachery, while the sacrificed "dead Gods" of the resistance Moulin and Brossolette underwent post-war "Panthéonisation." Nevertheless, if a resort to popular resistance in the shadow of the breakdown of military institutions restored moral content to an otherwise tragic parenthesis in French history, it also offered a cautionary lesson of how the *levée* might spin out of control to inflict its own capriciousness, cruelties, and injustice.[141]

As Wieviorka notes, resistance mythology also devalued in French popular memory the contribution of the Allies, without whom resistance in France could not have survived and expanded.[142] The Gaullist-promoted mythology of "*Paris libéré par lui-même*" also masked the fact that, without Churchill's initial political and public relations (PR) investment in *la France libre* from

1940, de Gaulle would never have become a household name. Without British support followed by that of the interface services, France's internal resistance would have never evolved beyond a *pléïade* of small, isolated groups without resources or even an ability to communicate. Resistance also created vulnerabilities – a distortion of strategic priorities and diversion of operational assets. Because the activities – even the mere presence – of resistance also put non-combatants at risk, its actions were morally ambiguous, especially in the hands of communists like "Colonel Fabien," who saw German retaliation, often in the form of the execution of a random selection of hapless hostages, as a tactic to radicalize the French population. No wonder resistance encountered equivocal, indifferent, or even hostile attitudes from a population who feared it as politicized, undisciplined, and factious, a haven for refugees and *Osttruppen* deserters with little to lose, directed by politically ambitious pistoleros. Many French civilians resented the *maquis*, because its members, or criminals purporting to be *maquisards*, often preyed on the population and because civilians fell victim to brutal reprisals invariably triggered by resistance/*maquis* presence. The high moral costs of resistance, often paid by society at large, were inescapable, as the massacres of civilians at Mont Mouchet, le Vercors, Oradour, and elsewhere confirmed. Outsized communist influence, real or imagined, on resistance caused many law-abiding citizens to fear it. Posturing "September resisters," "Fifi colonels," and misogynists, offspring of a "guilty society," invariably materialized upon the Liberation, young toughs looking to mete out "justice," seize town halls, and humiliate women. Given these conflicting visions, the resistance and *maquis* were quickly subsumed into a Cold War polemic, that reverberated in the French culture wars as the left blamed the Allies and Gaullists for failing to arm the *maquis levée en masse*, while the French right denounced "*Résistentialisme*" as a resurrection of the Terror of 1793 in which summary retaliation substituted for the guillotine.[143]

The mythology of the *maquisard* armed with a Sten defending his "*réduit strategique*" against assault by Germans and *la Milice*, or a patriotic railway worker derailing a train in René Clément's 1946 film *La Bataille du rail* (*The Battle of the Rails*), served several purposes: to provided romantic resistance images that recalled the patriotic fervor of the *levée* of August 1793, or the *franc-tireur* of 1870, and to offer vindication that, despite the débâcle of 1940, the Second World War generation was equal to its Great War predecessor.[144] The truth, however, was that "*attentisme*," not resistance, remained the dominant French attitude during the war, because, in the circumstances of occupation, resistance could only operate on the margins – clandestine newssheets and demonstrations, with the occasional act of sabotage or assassination.[145] Rather than an indictment of generational failure, *attentisme* offered a perfectly logical choice, as the risks of resistance were great, while the scope for action, and its potential to impact the course of the war, was marginal.

A second point to make is that special operations on their own proved incapable of producing strategic effect, which is why civilian resistance proved militarily most effective when working in tandem with conventional operations. Sabotage became "heroized" in the resistance press as a sort of FFI version of Bir Hakeim.[146] However, since the 1970s, when Alan Milward suggested that the impact of industrial sabotage in France was not only "insignificant," but also, "in terms of opportunity, one of the most costly of all of the war's strategies," historians have grown more skeptical about claims for the impact of resistance-led sabotage.[147] "Even calculating a disproportionate effect, how could one imagine that fifty-seven acts of industrial sabotage which caused serious damage in the Paris region could have massively disrupted production delivered to the Germans?," asks Sébastien Albertelli.[148]

Unfortunately, sabotage, like much of the residual tactical and operation potential of resistance in France, was further compromised by the collapse of plans for "phased mobilization" on D-Day. This left the execution of sabotage plans to local resistance groups, some of whom acted, while others did not – because of confusion about orders, because targets were too well guarded, or because they lacked means. Resistance groups might be broken up by arrests, or have their matériel confiscated before D-Day. While resourcefulness was valued, freelancing might prove detrimental to the mission: "On one occasion an agent took it on himself to make an attempt on a power station which was known to the local leader to be well guarded," read a September 1944 report on the value of resistance activity France from D-Day. "Not only did the attempt fail, but an 'anti-maquis drive' followed, which forced the local FFI to disperse for some weeks." The report noted that it was difficult to assess the value of sabotage between the D-Day landings on 6 June and the Normandy breakout from early August for a variety of reasons: reports of destruction were delayed, often piecemeal, without date or location, and could not be independently verified, except through POW interrogations. Albertelli argues that, while many railway workers were active in passing on information about railway traffic, sabotage of rail lines or rolling stock was rare, if for no other reason than because, utterly dependent on French railways for mobility and logistics, the German occupiers watched them like hawks, executing workers on the mere suspicion of sabotage. In any case, damaging locomotives and other railway infrastructure violated the *cheminot* culture.[149] The assessment concludes that roughly 50 percent of the railway targets specified in *Plan Vert* were taken out – possibly more – although "unquestionably" resistance demolitions only "complemented" air bombardment. The value of resistance activity, the report suggests, lay in its secondary effects – the diversion of up to 45,000 German railway personnel to operate French railways; forcing the Germans to use the roads, which expended valuable petrol, as well as the "bunching" of troops on the march, which made them more vulnerable to air attacks; and the diversion of six of seventeen divisions stationed south of the Loire to deal with the FFI, which was clearly a vast overestimate. "But it is the 2. SS Panzer Division which bears the most eloquent testimony to the fact that the F.F.I. were a force seriously to be reckoned with."[150] Unfortunately, while resistance attacks prodded the *Das Reich* division into its murderous rampage, and an SAS-directed air bombardment against trains on a siding at Châtellerault carrying the division's petrol reserves delayed the division's arrival at the front for two to three days, this made no difference to the outcome in Normandy. Because, even when the division arrived at its destination, it was held in reserve.[151] A more contemporary assessment holds that, by 1944, Berlin's prioritization of the Eastern Front for vehicles, personnel, and logistics, as well as requisitions and deferred maintenance especially of French railways, rather than bombing or resistance sabotage, had seriously attrited OB West's capacity to resist the Allied invasions of France.[152]

Elsewhere in France, *Plan Violet* temporarily cut off phone contacts between Amiens and Rouen, Rouen and Caen, and Trappes and Le Mans, but, for a variety of reasons, it was launched too late. A third problem was the wave of self-congratulation that swept over the EMFFI and the interface services in the aftermath of D-Day, which made it difficult to assess the strategic impact of resistance activity, in part because some of the targets hit were of limited value, because damage was quickly repaired, or the Germans found alternative solutions.[153] Funk concludes that "the *Maquis* brought substantial assistance to regular forces. Comments from Allied units . . . bear consistent witness to Resistance cooperation and aid, just as German statements reiterate the repugnance and fear that governed the occupiers' attitude toward the 'terrorists.'"[154] *Maquisards* covered the flanks of advancing US soldiers and harassed the German retreat, which began on 12 August in the north, and on 16 August in the southeast. They scoured the hills, brought in stray POWs, patrolled at night to bring in intelligence, and served as guides. Some US commanders were criticized for substituting FFI as regular infantry, especially when their tanks had outrun US infantry support.[155] At the same time, FFI also complained that they were assigned only minor tasks, such as guarding POWs. But even Funk conceded that much of the cooperation with FFI was improvised, because the Balkans and Greece were prioritized for arms deliveries, and Hitler's 16 August retreat order meant that many Operational Groups (OGs) and Jedburgh teams arrived just in time to observe the German exit. Nor did the FFI make a meaningful contribution to the critical liberation of Marseilles and Toulon by *l'Armée B*, beyond preventing some damage to the harbor.[156] In fact, it was de Lattre's fear of an FFI-led "revolution" in Marseilles that caused him to hesitate to advance until his subordinates forced his hand.[157] Benjamin Jones judges the escape of the bulk of the German Nineteenth Army from southwestern France to Dijon "disappointing when considering what the FFI might have done if organized more coherently and armed more effectively."[158] Yet how that "coherent" organization could have been realized is unclear, given the clandestine, spontaneous, and improvised nature of the *maquis*, and its lack of cadres and heavy weapons. To expect anything like military effectiveness out of a flash resistance sparked by news of D-Day would appear to strain credulity.

At least, the FFI were able to exact a measure of revenge on Pflaum's 157th Reserve Division. The surrender on 19 August to the FFI of 500 policemen of the SS-Polizei Regiment 19 at Annecy, part of the garrison responsible for so many of the deaths of Glières *maquisards*, signaled to the 157th Reserve Division at Grenoble that they were trapped between the Americans of Task Force Butler and the 36th US ID, advancing from the south, and FFI, in the north. On 21 August, the 157th Reserve Division withdrew from Grenoble toward three mountain passes that led to Italy. Several battalions surrendered to FFI and US forces, as Grenoble was liberated on 22 August. The 157th Reserve Division's retreat through the ambush-hedged Maurienne Valley that led to the Mont Cenis Pass was successful only because of the intervention of the 90th Panzergrenadier Division from Italy, and because German troops held the passes. But the fighting was bitter, and saw the execution of POWs on both sides, after news arrived that the Sipo/SD was executing prisoners in Lyon's Montluc Prison, and the Germans had murdered twenty-eight civilian hostages near the Little Saint Bernard Pass on 28 August. Pflaum was relieved of command for poor performance after he lost 2,000 soldiers. His division was rebranded as the *157. Gebirgs* (157th Mountain) Division, and in December 1944 assigned to the Apennine front.[159]

"It is nevertheless an exaggeration to say that the Resistance 'liberated' these portions of the territory," argues Muracciole, when in fact FFI simply moved into towns from which the Germans had departed, but which were not in the path of the Allied advance. "The maquis hardly bothered" the Germans, who, as in Yugoslavia, simply abandoned large tracts of territory judged by them to be "without strategic value."[160] So, in fact, the only places in which the resistance could assemble in relative security were those where the Germans declined to go. Of course, the SOE had an interest in putting positive spin on the performance of civilian resistance, as did de Lattre, one of whose primary responsibilities was to realize a successful *amalgame* of FFI units into his *1ère Armée*.[161] The Allies, who considered the resistance merely a bonus, were going to succeed with or without their aid.

For their part, the Germans never viewed resistance in France as a significant military threat. But the idea that it posed less of a menace than insurgencies in the East or in the Balkans because the French people lacked the rusticity, ethnic enmity, or ideological fanaticism found in less advanced regions, while exaggerated and inaccurate, accorded with a "decadence" narrative flowing from the French collapse of 1940. As was their practice when operating against Soviet or

Yugoslav partisans, the Germans deployed only reserve and training units, or contingents of foreign collaborators, to counterinsurgency operations in France, units unsuited to conventional military operations. This replicated German practice on the Eastern Front, where the partisan movement was significantly more militarized, and its movements more closely coordinated with the operations of regular forces, at least from 1943. Soviet partisans sabotaged railways and bridges because Soviet airpower was relatively weak. They also dispatched collaborators and collected intelligence on the location and movement of German units. The Red Army soldiers among them realized that it was foolhardy to confront the Wehrmacht head-on. But, even with a higher percentage of regular soldiers than in the FFI, partisan units in the East "did not actually damage German frontline operations in any meaningful way, or indeed draw substantial forces away from frontline duty for sustained periods of time, which was the Soviet intention," concludes Alexander Hill.[162]

This was somewhat surprising, as *Barbarossa* was never meant as a conventional military operation, but rather was a "war of extermination," complete with the "Hunger Plan" of 23 May 1941 that would mean that millions in the USSR must starve or leave for Siberia. A *Führererlaß* (Führer edict) authorized the killing of civilians who "attacked German soldiers," with "attack" liberally defined. *Politruks* (Political Commissars) and Communist Party officials were targeted for assassination in Hitler's Commissar Order of 6 June 1941, a measure meant to disaggregate military discipline and Moscow's control over the population. In 1941, 2,252 *Politruks* were shot by the Wehrmacht alone, a figure that does not include those assassinated by the Waffen-SS and *Einsatzgruppen*. One might conclude that extreme German violence would have served to swell partisan ranks. But, rather than resist, locals, especially in areas with largely non-Russian populations such as the Baltic states or Ukraine, who initially at least saw in *Barbarossa* a promise of liberation from Soviet tyranny, often cooperated with the invaders. Popular antisemitism also played a role, as Jews were well represented among the *Politruks*, in the People's Commissariat of Internal Affairs (NKVD), and in the Communist Party apparatus, which helped to transition the arrival of German forces into a vast pogrom, which found no shortage of local collaborators.[163]

McMeekin also insists that the vaunted reputation of Tito's Partisans in Yugoslavia, one that, in September 1943, caused Churchill to stiff royalist Draža Mihailović's Chetniks, was part of a deep conspiracy that saw military reports out of Cairo, as well as BBC broadcasts by Soviet spy Guy Burgess, minimizing Chetnik success. Meanwhile, in 1943, Churchill promoted Foreign Office Soviet expert and future conservative Member of Parliament (MP) Fitzroy Maclean to brigadier and dispatched him to head the SOE's mission to Tito's partisans with orders to send "positive" reports directly to the Prime Minister, who was keen to demonstrate his support to Stalin. The facts on the ground were that the Chetnik and Partisan movements spent as much time attacking each other as they did fighting the Axis enemy, with whom each group periodically negotiated ceasefires and POW exchanges. From June 1943, weapons drops to Tito's Partisans soon came to dwarf those airlifted to Mihailović, at a time when Chetnik attacks against Germans peaked in the wake of the September 1943 Italian surrender, but which the BBC credited to Tito's Partisans. "Maclean's evaluation was based only on fireside chats with Tito and his adjutants," McMeekin asserts. "He did not observe a single battle or sabotage operation during the three weeks he travelled with the partisans in Bosnia and Herzegovina before returning to Cairo . . . Tito had told him about partisan exploits, not anything Maclean had witnessed." Maclean passed on fantasy casualty ratio reports and vastly inflated Partisan numbers, while, "in reality, the Germans had easily defeated the partisans," inflicting significant casualties against minimal losses. "Maclean's wildly inaccurate report on Tito's partisans was bound and circulated in Cairo and forwarded to London . . . In politics as in history, it does not always matter who is right, but who gets their story in first," concludes McMeekin.[164]

If partisan units on all fronts registered only modest military success, it would have proven surprising indeed had a late blooming French *maquis*, assembled in remote Alpine regions or in the Massif Central and partially armed with hair-trigger Stens, led by self-appointed amateur chiefs, whose movements were not synchronized with regular formations, produced significant outcomes. A week after D-Day, OB West concluded that the level of sabotage activity had fallen short of anticipated. Nor did the "national insurrection" ever materialize. While the destruction of the bridge over the Drôme River at Loriol is often cited as an example of resistance effectiveness, Ludewig points to the many bridges that resistance fighters neglected to destroy, obstacles that might have seriously dislocated and delayed the German retreat from southwestern France. Bridge destruction at Loriol was less effective for two reasons. First, the Drôme was a shallow river, fordable in several places. Second, Wiese's Nineteenth Army outfought the Americans who attempted to cut them off at Montélimar and escaped. When confronted with German units in retreat, the resistance units simply got out of the way, a wise maneuver as they were totally outgunned. "The FFI's military effectiveness remained relatively minor, contrary to German fears. The FFI did, of course, create pockets of uncertainty along the German march routes, but they were not able to restrict the withdrawal in any significant manner," concludes Ludewig. General Botho Elster's surrender of his 28,000 soldiers to the 83rd US ID, on 10 September near Issoudun, constituted the "one and only quantifiable major victory of the FFI," whose contingent circumstances have already been discussed. Even though the resistance had considerable opportunities to block the German retreat, "Not only did the FFI not delay in the least the retreat of the German units, the French operations in the rear areas were for the most part meaningless ... The FFI units that had penetrated into the German assembly areas achieved relatively little. There were firefights and minor obstacles encountered here and there, such as the guerrillas turning the road signs the wrong way. The French population remained mostly quiet." And while resistance activity "did cause considerable time delays for units marching toward the front, they did not decisively influence the outcome of the Battle of Normandy ... Seen against the background of the primary battlefront, the effect of FFI operations amounted to little more than pinpricks."[165]

But even if one concedes that Eisenhower was being diplomatic about the resistance contribution to Overlord's success to spare French sensibilities, the behavior of the resistance continued to be a source of anxiety for Allied military leaders. Eisenhower's praise for the resistance was prefaced by the statement that "my hand was forced by the action of the Free French forces inside Paris," which was one factor that caused him to alter his plan to bypass the French capital and instead move to occupy it. The liberation had witnessed "as much a Franco-American conflict as an Allied–German struggle," wrote American historian Martin Blumenson. "The French secured almost all they wanted by convincing a reluctant, but in the end amenable, Allied command to do their bidding. The restoration of French dignity, implicit in the liberation, had come about largely through French efforts sustained by Allied complaisance."[166]

While Funk argued that the Allies might have done more to increase the military effectiveness of resistance in France, even he concedes that how far a "hypothetical" recognition of de Gaulle's government "in, say, February or March 1944," combined with an "unlikely" massive influx of arms and advisors, and "a unified military organization, more effective than the FFI structure headed by General Koenig," might have increased FFI effectiveness is merely speculative. Soviet partisans combined a higher degree of militarization with close coordination with regular operations, and still their military impact is judged to have been marginal. However, in the case of France, it begs the question of whether the role of the resistance/*maquis* was primarily a military one. For de Gaulle, resistance was meant to bestow democratic legality on *la France combattante*, delegitimize Vichy and Giraud, and underpin a myth of French self-liberation. Many in the resistance saw their movement as a force to revitalize France. However, as Wieviorka notes, resistance constituted an unprecedented, spontaneous phenomenon that emerged from civil society, which represented diverse political views and whose activities assumed multiple forms. De Gaulle's challenge was to channel a movement of which he had become the symbol, lest it derail his goal of reestablishing the French state. Because he prioritized political control rather than increasing the military impact of a paramilitary force in which he had little faith, rank-and-file resistance had to be directed into a conventional military system, to raise France's military profile while preempting the political projects of some of its more free-spirited leaders. In de Gaulle's view, importing foreign advisors in the form of Jedburgh teams, SOE operatives, or SAS commandos whose goal was to increase military efficiency threatened the restoration of the French state. The military value of the resistance on liberation was ephemeral, and its main advantages were propagandistic. Organizing resistance in France as a military force was largely uncharted territory both for the resisters themselves and for Allied military leaders, who were slow to recognize the scope of the *maquis* phenomenon, and had neither a doctrinal framework nor institutional mechanisms for coordinating regular and irregular operations. Nor were officers, even in France's "external resistance," aware of conditions inside France, or able to actualize the combat potential of civilian resistance.[167]

Comparisons between the relative weakness of resistance in France and more robust movements in Yugoslavia, in Greece, and in Italy from September 1943 were a subject of debate from at least 1943. But conditions in these three countries differed significantly from those in France. The Allies had no plans to invade Yugoslavia, while Churchill dispatched British troops to occupy Athens as guerrillas of the Greek People's Liberation Army (ELAS) moved to supplant the departing Germans from 12 October 1944. Arms to the Italian resistance could be directly linked to support for the front. The Allies believed that withholding arms from the *maquis* in France would prevent a premature mobilization and slaughter, which would not directly benefit the war effort.[168] As Overlord loomed, Allied priorities in arms deliveries switched to France. However, the military payoff of simply raining Sten guns and Mills bombs on *Service du travail obligatoire* (STO) refugees collected on mountaintops in the Alpes and the Massif Central proved disappointing, even counterproductive. In May 1944, the SOE had been authorized to stock 21,000 containers, on the calculation that 32 US and 22 British bombers could deliver 5,000 containers a month. In fact, according to Crémieux-Brilhac, 50,000 containers and 25,000 "units" were dropped to the FFI between July and the end of September 1944, as well as 7,500 containers flown in from AFN. The Americans set up a 400-man packing station in the UK to ready containers for several daylight supply operations, beginning with Zebra, which deployed 176 planes to deliver 2,109 containers and "units," followed by Cadillac on 14 July that saw 9 formations of 36 planes, each flying at 500 feet, drop 791 containers with 417 tons of weapons. Buick on 1 August massed 72 bombers to deliver 2,286 containers to l'Ain and Savoie. The drops were completed by Grassy on 9 September. These operations received breathless press reports, which portrayed them as an Anglo-American competition to arm the *maquis*. And, while these deliveries offered proof that the *maquis* had not been forgotten, on the ground, these drops scattered over vast areas often proved difficult to collect, let alone distribute. Furthermore, while Koenig boasted that the Anglo-Americans had flown in enough weapons to arm

425,000 FFI, in fact, the *maquis* was turning away volunteers because it lacked weapons and food, while many in the camps remained unarmed, which had a devastating effect on morale. But the Allies realized that the more arms they dropped, the more men would flock to the *maquis*, and the more resistance might become a public order burden rather than a military asset. So, while Allied strategy was hardly inflexible, and factored the *maquis* into planning, the *maquisards* nevertheless felt that they had been abandoned, a sentiment that became stamped onto wartime memory.[169]

Of course, these drops were targeted at areas with large concentrations of *maquisards*, or that were deemed critical to the success of Overlord, such as Brittany. Other areas that were too far from the front, or *maquis* located in areas where SOE agents had not ventured, might receive few arms. Funk's observation also begs the question of whether more arms would have made the *maquis* more effective. The influx of volunteers into the FFI following D-Day had overwhelmed desperately inadequate local command structures, as well as the SOE's ability to deliver weapons and supplies, not to mention train resistance fighters on their use. The FFI were severely short of cadres with military experience. In some cases, French regular officers and reservists might take charge. But, as has been seen, many *maquisards* distrusted the French military as "mothballed" Vichyites on "Armistice leave," and resisted their attempts to militarize them. In that case, it made little sense to arm a *maquis* which swelled into unwieldy, undisciplined aggregations of young men who congregated in remote areas where they invited German attack, but did little to facilitate the Anglo-American invasion. Much of the pressure to do so seems to have come from the Foreign Office and the Political Warfare Executive (PWE), concerned mainly about post-war Anglo-French relations, and the interface services, which were committed to a doctrine of irregular warfare and keen to carve out an operational niche for special ops.

To fill the command deficit, the Allies resorted to tactical experiments. The first tri-national Jedburgh teams parachuted in on the night of 5–6 June and continued to arrive throughout summer. The SAS, created in 1941 to raid behind enemy lines, had delivered mixed results in the Mediterranean theater. Montgomery's idea was that special operations forces (SOF) operating from mobile "strongholds" where supplies could be stored, located 75–100 miles behind the battlefront, could disrupt enemy command and control facilities and logistics with sabotage, small-scale raids, and support for guerrilla operations. But, as the *maquis* discovered at le Vercors and elsewhere, "strongholds" and "mobility" proved to be antithetical concepts. These "arms dumps" absorbed too many personnel and were vulnerable to discovery and destruction. This was the case most notably when, on 1 July 1944, an SAS camp near Poitiers was targeted by German security police, who detained and executed thirty-four SAS personnel, as well as a downed American pilot and several resisters.[170] "The

Jedburghs had been instructed to deploy, assess the capabilities of local groups, get arms to them, train them, and then at the appropriate time take manageable numbers into hit-and-run actions against carefully selected enemy targets," concludes Jones. "The SAS wished to do its operations immediately and was supplied out of airlift sortie allocations separate from the ones for the Jedburgh teams." The SAS undermined the "Jeds" in that they made the *maquis* "look impotent and illegitimate." Rather than having the SAS work in tandem with Jedburghs and local *maquis*, SAS "mayhem" served to alert the Germans and brought down reprisals on the local populations and attacks on *maquis* camps.[171]

During 6–22 June, 600 men reinforced the FFI, consisting of 559 from the SAS, to which French paratroops were attached, 9 tri-national Jedburgh teams numbering 27 men, and an OG of 15 men. The initial mission of the French in these SAS teams was to cut rail links, and secondarily to "provoke a large-scale revolt in Brittany." While the SAS might instruct French *maquis* in the use of weapons, mostly they valued their operational autonomy, consulting resistance groups occasionally to gather intelligence to facilitate raids with jeep-mounted mobile teams, in the spirit of Bagnold's Long-Range Desert Groups in the Western Desert. Once the breakout occurred in August and the front became more fluid, "jeeping" became more feasible, which made Operation Wallace–Hardy (27 July–19 September 1944) one of the SAS's more successful operations. "It has been proven again that jeeping is not only possible but easy when the enemy front is unstable," concluded Wallace–Hardy's commander Major Roy Farran.[172] In contrast, Jedburghs and OGs, like the SOE and OSS, were meant to liaise with and advise, but not to command, resistance groups. US OGs had an ambiguous status, because, although they were attached to the OSS, they were in fact volunteers from line units, usually with low linguistic skills and no special experience of working behind the lines. If they were captured, their fate rather depended on whether the local German commander elected to respect Geneva codes, or instead chose to carry out the OKW's 18 October 1942 "commando order," issued in the aftermath of the 19 August 1942 "Dieppe raid," which allowed German forces, Gestapo, or SD to kill commandos or saboteurs even if they had been captured in uniform. From 17 July 1944, all Allied troops, agents, missions, DMRs, *Commissaires de la République*, and so on – in total, probably between 3,000 and 3,500 men and a few women, the majority British – serving with or beside the FFI as advisers, trainers, saboteurs, radio operators, on information- and intelligence-gathering missions, or, in the case of the French, to impose operational and political discipline on an inchoate resistance, technically fell under Koenig's EMFFI. Initially at least, this concession to French sovereignty remained more political than operational.[173] In fact, EMFFI chief Koenig complained to Bedell Smith that Jeds were short-circuiting his command, and that some were staying on long after their military mission had been completed, behaving like "feudal lords" – a frequent reproach among Gaullists. These criticisms headlined a volley of French complaints in the autumn of 1944 about the failure of Allied troops to respect French sovereignty.[174]

A top-up of advisors did not automatically upgrade *maquisard* military proficiency, for several reasons. The historiography often draws the distinction between patriots, who joined the *maquis* to liberate France, and what the French called the "*faux maquis*," who essentially became outlaws. In fact, the *maquis* "movement" offered a sliding scale of motivations and actions. Many young men fled to Glières or le Vercors precisely because they sought a safe place to opt out of the war. Even those who rushed to join after D-Day discovered that, after three or four days of enthusiasm, monotony and hunger caused morale to plummet. They often had to prey on the local population for food and resources. For their part, some advisors were shocked by the FFI's lack of military preparation and informal discipline that slipped toward anarchy, even echoing Henriot's propaganda that many *maquisards* were simply "brigands" who terrorized and robbed local peasants, who melted away when attacked, and, as liberation spread, prioritized shaving the heads of horizontal collaborators over ejecting Germans from France. One Belgian SAS operative dropped near Le Mans wrote that "[The Résistance] is poorly organized . . . The majority were young people between 15 and 20 [years old], completely ignorant of how to hold and use their arms. Most showed great enthusiasm with the arrival of the Allies. But at night they became a great danger for us, shooting haphazardly without trying to verify the identity of who was before them." In this way, friendly fire from trigger-happy *maquis* became a battlefield hazard, especially for resupply parties. Koenig issued orders to the FFI to stop shooting at Allied paratroopers dropped to reinforce them.[175]

Nor was this military assistance invariably appreciated on the ground. Communists suspected that these Allied interlopers had been dispatched to checkmate their ambitious political agenda. De Gaulle resented their encroachment and believed them the avant-garde of the Allied Military Government of Occupied Territories (AMGOT), which is why he insisted that they be subordinated to Koenig and the EMFFI. The August arrival of *l'armée d'Afrique* via the Côte d'Azur obviated the need for the "interface services" and reinforced de Gaulle's "amalgamation" agenda. Many local resistance leaders complained bitterly that they had not been armed sufficiently. They could not fathom why Eisenhower and de Gaulle had called for uprisings on 5 June, only to have Koenig slam the brakes on "premature liberations" five days later. This set up a clash between the EMFFI and COMAC's clandestine Paris headquarters (HQ) under the strong-willed and doctrinaire Pierre Villon (a.k.a. Roger Ginsburger). Tension rose throughout July as Villon called for the Allies "to adapt their strategy to new situations created in the interior," by the extension and consolidation of liberated territories. He also demanded that command of the FFI pass to COMAC. But, in the end, Villon had to back down – the communists lacked the muscle outside of Paris to expand "national insurrection." "Until the breakthrough at Avranches . . . Koenig and his staff in London, [Alexandre] Parodi (*délégué général du GPRF en zone occupé*) and Chaban [Jacques Delmas] in Paris, would block all the attempts at strategic autonomy by the Resistance," wrote Crémieux-Brilhac.[176] "Despite their devotion, their courage, and their heavy losses, the French Resistances could not wipe away the immense catastrophe that was the 1940 defeat," concludes Muracciole. "The military contribution of the internal Resistance essentially consisted in the formation of escape and evasion networks, intelligence collection, and on occasion sabotage. The conventional military forces [FFL, then the army of liberation] participated in a common fight, which contributed in slowing Axis forces [Bir Hakeim, Kasserine], notched up some signature victories [Tunisia, Cassino, Provence], but only offered a modest contribution to the final victory. Keitel's terrible comment at [the surrender ceremony in] Berlin on 8 May 1945 ['What, the French too!'], [was] excessive and unfair. But the image of a France of resisters achieving its own liberation is largely the product of myth."[177]

One might argue that evaluating the resistance as does Murriciole by its operational results offers too narrow a criterion. For this reason, Wieviorka flips the question: in the circumstances of occupation, what could a resistance realistically accomplish? It collected and exfiltrated around 3,500 pilots downed in France and the Low Countries, and rescued crews of ships sunk in the Mediterranean. Resistance networks also published clandestine journals, organized demonstrations, provided intelligence, carried out sabotage, painted V signs on walls, and even on occasion carried out assassinations, which invited retaliation. But the principal role of the resistance networks was "political, psychological, and moral rather than military" – to manage the expectations of many young men and women who were fed up with the occupation and eager to fight, and permit "a minority to become actors in their history, by abandoning the morose limitations of *attentisme* or acquiescence."[178]

Conclusion

Even though Dragoon was a last-minute operation, the landings succeeded at relatively little cost largely because German forces on the south coast were depleted, and Hitler ordered them to evacuate. Unfortunately, neither the resistance nor the 36th US ID was able successfully to block the German evacuation. Controversy over the seizure of Toulon and Marseilles also revealed command tensions at the summit of *l'Armée B* that would simmer for the remainder of the war. Although the Anglo-Americans, through the interface services, made considerable efforts to arm resistance in France, its military contribution to liberation disappointed expectations. Various personalities and political factions in France, beginning with de Gaulle, attempted to exploit the resistance as a source of political legitimacy and/or personal ambition. Resistance became a measure of popular political commitment in the fight against Vichy and Nazism. In this respect, propaganda produced and broadcast by the BBC and published in resistance publications was important, but of limited value. While the BBC kept captive populations informed, and propaganda helped to discredit collaboration, inspire hope for liberation, and encourage certain forms of resistance, such as the rejection of STO, it succeeded neither in transforming resistance into a mass movement nor in triggering a national insurrection. As Wieviorka makes clear, the Germans were defeated by military force, not propaganda.[179]

Resistance also had a rehabilitative purpose in the Gaullist lexicon. The assertion that, apart from "a handful of wretches and dishonorable men," most French men and women supported it at least spiritually, as part of "*résistance-mouvement*," helped to burnish France's image after it had been tarnished by 1940, followed by Vichy collaboration. It also served to legitimize de Gaulle and Fighting France, which smoothed the transition of power from Vichy to the GPRF while dodging civil war, although that was probably never on the cards.[180] Resistance became a symbol of France's popular mobilization and republican renewal, which helped to rehabilitate France's status as a minor ally. But its memorial image is ambiguous and contested, for several reasons. First, de Gaulle and many veterans had sought to define resistance in military terms, which excluded acts of a civil, popular, and political nature like organizing strikes, distributing tracts, saving Jews, and so on. Second, by its frequently illegal and violent acts, the resistance also posed at least an indirect threat to the French population, which might therefore maintain an ambiguous – when not hostile – attitude toward it. Third, its political diversity, minority status, and the fact that "resistance" crowded out other victims of the war, such as Jews, STO forced laborers, and POWs, from France's wartime memory meant that its grip on French popular imagination loosened with the passing of de Gaulle in 1970. Beyond its negligible operational impact, historians find it difficult to calculate the influence of resistance activity, in part because intangible psychological and morale factors are impossible to quantify. France would have been liberated in any case without the resistance, but perhaps not on the same terms. Despite the momentary disorder, even anarchy, of the Liberation, ultimately resistance in France helped to smooth the transition from Vichy to the GPRF by shaping a French narrative of liberation.[181]

7 *L'amalgame*

In the wake of the 1940 defeat, France's military effort had devolved into a constellation of combatants in search of a structure. Vichy had envisaged the Armistice Army, nourished by the *Chantiers* and various "leadership schools," as a sort of papier mâché *Reichswehr* with the potential to underpin France's military renaissance, an ambition stymied by Axis constraints until it finally crashed in November 1942. At Anfa in January 1943, Giraud had acquiesced to an upgrade of a maximum of eleven French divisions, most of them to be carved out of *l'armée d'Afrique*, reinforced by the "fusion" with the FFL from July. But the manpower resources available in Africa were limited to largely illiterate indigenous recruits, which constrained military modernization and hence adaptability. From 1941, a web of resistance networks had begun to organize on the mainland, but the requirement for security kept them discreet and "*ultra minoritaire*." Of 11,000 officers present in France in November 1942, an estimated 4,000 had participated in some form in the internal resistance, while another 1,500 became *évadés de France*. The major manpower infusion into the internal resistance had come in the form of the *maquis*, as young men opted out of *la relève* from August 1942 and subsequently from *Service du travail obligatoire* (STO) imposed in the following year. The emergence of an internal resistance and especially the *maquis* had added an entirely new chapter to the history of the *levée en masse*. Liberated from its attachment to the professional army, the *levée* transitioned definitively from conventional to irregular warfare, adopting the "black legend" of the *franc-tireur* of 1870 and the Commune as its wartime persona. As a source of heroes who rejected the Vichy government's prescription of acquiescence to occupation and collaboration, Resistance in France offered a remedy for France's crisis of masculine confidence and national identity, although its contribution to France's liberation had been mainly symbolic.

Upon liberation, however, the *Gouvernement provisoire de la république française* (GPRF) sought to reassemble a "proper army," with the goal of reestablishing internal order, transitioning internal resisters and *maquisards* into regular soldiers, allocating France a starring role in the Third Reich's *coup de grâce* final act, and hence granting France more clout in the Alliance and a vote in Europe's post-war provisions.[1] Recourse to a *levée* was precluded by a lack of *matériel*, so officers envisaged a system of volunteers or selective enrolment anchored administratively on the fact that the 1939 mobilization order remained in effect. But only on 22 June 1944, was the possibility of incorporating the *Forces françaises de l'intérieur* (FFI) into the regular army either individually or as "specialist units" such as commandos or parachutists envisaged. On D-Day, the numbers of young men rallying to the resistance had exploded. On 6 July 1944, Béthouart had sent a request to the War Department in Washington for enough matériel to outfit three new French infantry divisions (IDs), one armored division (AD), and an airborne division, together with command and support units.[2]

Initially, at least, *l'amalgame* had self-sparked, undergoing what Claire Miot calls the "informal amalgamation."[3] During both Overlord and Dragoon, FFI volunteers had linked with French and American regular forces to supply intelligence and to serve as guides, prisoner-of-war (POW) guards, and even auxiliary infantry. In his race up the Rhône valley and toward the Swiss frontier, de Lattre had recourse to FFI because, due to petrol rationing, his infantry often failed to keep pace with the advance of his armored forces.[4] The Commander of the *2e Division blindé* (2e DB) also discovered in Normandy that he needed more specialists, to augment the number of infantrymen in his armored division, as well as to raise a road management company. Also, Leclerc was able to replace 630 soldier and 28 officer casualties lost in his race to Paris, by recruiting among a flood of Parisian volunteers.[5] On 8 September, he attached an FFI squadron to each of the three battalions in the *Régiment de marche du Tchad*, and, the following month, incorporated an FFI unit into his reconnaissance battalion, after the Americans had agreed to clothe and arm them.[6] By the end of the siege of Toulon, Colonel Raoul Salan's regiment had lost a sixth of its strength, and so he successfully opened his unit to the FFI replacements. As his Senegalese advanced north, he set up recruitment bureaus in Lyon and Grenoble: "We had lots of enlistments," he recorded.[7] In early November, recruiters from the *1ère Division française libre* (1ère DFL) brought in 500 volunteers from Rennes, and another 2,000 from the Ardennes. The *3e Division d'infanterie algérienne* (3e DIA) integrated 2,000 men from an ad hoc FFI assembly that called itself "*le régiment du Morvan*," although they lacked uniforms, while their weaponry resembled something lifted from museum displays.[8]

While, in the former *zone occupée*, volunteers came forward individually, Paris, the Alpes, and the southwest tended to produce organized FFI formations that participated in operations in Lorraine, Burgundy, and the Jura. On the Atlantic coast, resistance groups and volunteers besieged the "Atlantic pockets."[9] In the wake of liberation, some towns organized FFI "mobile columns" to march to the front, but also to defuse often tense local situations between armed FFI factions that threatened to erupt into violence in places like Toulouse, Limoges, or Montpellier.[10] Thus, on 1 September, a series of "mobile

Figure 7.1 "Colonel" Henri Rol-Tanguy (in beret) reviews volunteers for the French Forces of the Interior (FFI) at the Reuilly barracks, "the cradle of the new French army," in the 12th arrondissement of Paris, in October 1944. (Photo by Georges Melamed/AFP via Getty Images)

columns" formed in the south under the direction of Colonel Jean Schneider, who had been dispatched from Algiers to command and structure this tide of FFI enthusiasm as the *Groupement mobile sud-ouest*. Rushed north on trains, they became a factor in forcing the surrender of General Botho Elster's *Marschgruppe Süd* and in the liberation of Autun. In Paris, "Colonel Fabien," the resistance name of 25-year-old Pierre Georges, notorious or venerated, depending on one's viewpoint, for the 21 August 1941 assassination of Alfons Moser which had triggered a brutal cycle of assassinations and German reprisals, also organized a 3,000-strong *Groupement tactique de Lorraine* (GTL), better known as the "Paris Brigade" or the "Fabien Column."[11] On 27 August 1944, Koenig had asked Henri Rol-Tanguy (Figure 7.1), alias "Colonel Rol," to recruit a 900-man *Bataillon de marche* to accompany Allied armies and to "protect the civilian population." This initiative was backed up by the Parti communiste français (PCF), which for political reasons also wanted to keep FFI units intact, and not scatter them as per de Gaulle's orders as individual enlistees under the army's iron thumb.

Mont-Valérien, and especially the Reuilly barracks in the 12th arrondissement of Paris, declared the "cradle of the new French army," had become main recruitment centers even before the Liberation of Paris was complete. While "chaos reigned" at Reuilly, surviving records show enlistees as young – average age 20.5 years old – and overwhelmingly working class, but not especially communist. Men often enlisted in neighborhood or work groups. Poles, Spanish Republicans, and *Osttruppen* deserters were prominent. Many recruits were workers whose main motivation was to escape the drudgery of the factory floor and to "fight Nazis." On 30 August, "Colonel Fabien" took the title of Francs-Tireurs et Partisans (FTP) chief of staff for the Seine, Seine-et-Oise, and Seine-et-Marne. From 2 September 1944, buses covered with slogans – "*Vive la France*," "*Vive de Gaulle*," "*Mort aux Boches*," "*Tous à Berlin*," or V signs with a cross of Lorraine in the middle – departed Reuilly barracks as crowds applauded and sang *la Marseillaise* and *l'Internationale*. Most were still dressed in their civilian clothes, with perhaps a blouse from *la Milice* or a pair of gendarme trousers serving as a uniform. American units at Verdun gave them 1,200 pairs of boots out of pity. But many still lacked jackets when autumn temperatures began to drop. Most of the vehicles they managed to requisition were at the end of their utility, or sluggish *gazogène* trucks. They survived by sticking to US units. But, once withdrawn from the front and no longer an object of US largesse, they received neither pay nor rations. Unable to buy food, they were forced to hunt, fish with grenades, or simply steal to survive. Paris refused to release funds despite Fabien's repeated requests, citing the GTL's "undefined status." By the time that the GTL had transformed into the *151er Régiment d'infanterie* (151er RI), scurvy and other diseases associated with malnutrition had begun to appear. By the autumn, many were deserting the GTL to enlist in real units such as the 2e DB. "At least by enlisting with Leclerc . . . I was certain to be armed, paid, and given boots," one GTL deserter commented. Otherwise, it appeared to many that the government was intentionally neglecting FFI units because "they want to get us killed."[12]

But a lack of *matériel* proved only one of several problems the GPRF faced in creating a "proper army," and not necessarily the most important. As has been seen, the FFI were hardly a homogeneous group, but represented multiple identities. While the internal resistance and the *maquis* often recognized that they could benefit from "militarization," they instinctively distrusted what the French army represented. Officers compared *maquisards* and resisters to *goumiers*, who, while armed, were loosely commanded irregulars mobilized for tribal warfare in Morocco, whose status as legal combatants in "civilized" warfare was ambiguous. *Maquisards* were too young and most of their leaders too inexperienced to lead their men successfully in combat. Some groups were denounced as little more than "terrorist gangs" preying on the local population. Many of the 4,000 officers who volunteered for the resistance found senior positions occupied by civilians with self-conferred "fictitious" military ranks. Their authority might be bolstered by one of 1,800 operatives from one of the "interface services," or after D-Day a Jedburgh team or Operational Group (OG) who procured arms and supplies for "their" *maquis*. Nor was the GPRF always eager to strip resistance or *maquis* leaders of their rank, because at least it created a hierarchy which made them marginally easier to manage. One result became that French officers who volunteered for a resistance group might be assigned tasks in the organization normally performed by a non-commissioned officer (NCO).[13]

Koenig's ambition in imposing a regular military structure was to contain political factionalism in the resistance. However, liberation had set up a confrontation between the external resistance, which was anxious to resurrect France's military institutions, and an internal resistance, which sought to revivify citizenship through the *levée* – a theme especially emphasized by the PCF.[14] For the internal resistance, France's revitalization required a deep purge of former Vichy politicians and administrators, and "the necessity of creating a 'new' French army, of which they would form the nucleus."[15] The Fabien column aimed to demonstrate that FFI, organized and led by communists, were capable of fighting in conventional war conditions independently of the regular army. It was also a ploy to maneuver the communists into the forefront of liberation and demonstrate that the FFI should constitute the framework of the new army, not individual replacements frittered away to plug *armée d'Afrique* manpower shortfalls. On 12 September, the communist newspaper *L'Humanité* reported that "an FFI regiment 2,000 strong, in liaison with the Fifth American army [highly unlikely as the Fifth Army was in Italy], undertook forced marches to help to push the Germans back to the Luxembourg frontier . . . The FFI need their own statute . . . The responsible authorities must take a position, conferring with Comac [Comité d'action en France], on the FFI, the deserved title of the legal army!" These FFI "mobile columns," especially that of Fabien (Figure 7.2), symbolized a refusal by the FFI to "amalgamate" into the regular army, and a desire to maintain their FFI identity, juxtaposed with a revolutionary vision for an *armée nouvelle*, which amalgamation sought to quash.[16]

When Salan first encountered the "Paris Brigade" and its commander at Habsheim south of Mulhouse, he was amazed by their "motley matériel. There was every type of vehicle and artillery including Russian pieces. Their equipment was French model 1939–1940. Their French helmets seemed out of place with our American equipment and matériel. It took a lot of fortitude for these men to go to war in those conditions!" He also conceded that, whatever one thought of "Fabien's" politics, one had to admit that the man had charisma. "Young, alert, quick-witted, of average height, beneath his French helmet held in place with a chinstrap, his face adorned with thick eyebrows was that of a mystic. He exercised a lot of influence over his men and had never stopped

Figure 7.2 Pierre Georges, a.k.a. "Colonel Fabien," sought through resistance acts to provoke German retaliation to radicalize and mobilize the French population actively to resist the occupation. (Photo by Roger Viollet via Getty Images)

fighting the occupant in the ranks of the clandestine communist party ... 'Fabien' often came to dine in our mess at Blotzheim. His Parisian street wit made him very popular with us." Salan drew up some simple instructions and gave him some equipment for his training company. "Little by little, they were broken in and able to hold their own." Unfortunately, "Fabien," whose civilian trade was that of pipe fitter, insisted on dismantling a German mine in his command center – the predictable explosion killed Fabien as well as several on his staff. In the context of the amalgamation, this triggered conspiracy theories among FFI that "Fabien" had been assassinated.[17] However, not all regular soldiers celebrated Fabien's passing. "No more colonel!," Louis Bacquier's Corsican Adjutant chef Léonetti announced when he retailed a slightly garbled version of Fabien's demise. "But really, what are these amateurs thinking! War is not a kindergarten. Everyone knows that a mine is as delicate as an old maid. You can grope it, coddle it, cajole it." But not jump on it. "At least, it will create vacancies for promotion. But it's a pity – apparently, he was a good lad."[18]

This reunion of the external resistance and the homeland revealed tensions that helped to undercut *l'amalgame*, as independent FFI commanders like Schneider and Fabien proved reluctant to place themselves under the orders of regular soldiers. While, in his memoirs, de Lattre claims that he "thought it indispensable to preserve their name, their mystique, and the pride of their groups," FFI units were too heterogeneous, poorly armed, and ill-disciplined, and, perhaps most importantly, too politicized to provide a foundation for an "*amalgame*." The attitude of some of the resistance leaders toward the army ranged from cool to antagonistic, a suspicion stoked by the resistance press, which evoked memories of the 1940 débâcle, overwhelming military support for Vichy, and the imperial character of the *1ère Armée*. "In most of the departments the men do not have much desire to become part of the regular Army, unless that Army becomes predominately F.F.I. and is divorced as far as possible from the Army of 1939," read an autumn 1944 report on FFI in ten departments in the center and southeast.[19] A combination of praise lavished on the resistance as central to France's liberation and the purely "local perspective" of their wartime experience had served to convince many resistance leaders "of the excellence of the military system that circumstances allowed them to construct, and that they looked to substitute for the traditional system, considered out of date." In other words, de Gaulle's myth of French self-liberation served to reinforce the independent attitude of resistance leaders and made their submission to *l'amalgame* more problematic. Resistance aversion to the amalgamation was also buttressed in de Lattre's estimation by a sense of FFI inferiority vis-à-vis regular units, but also arose from an atavistic desire of resistance chiefs to keep their FFI units close to home to bolster their authority. Colonel Schneider sought to expand his "sovereignty ... with the same tendency to view his role *vis-à-vis* the Army command as feudal lords in the wars of the old monarchy." In fact, stigmatizing resistance leaders as "feudals," eager to reimagine the nobles' revolt of La Fronde (1648–1653) against monarchical centralization, allowed the GPRF to reclaim the "modernizing" goal of reestablishing state control and hence social order, and, through the resurrection of the regular army, France's great power prestige. In de Lattre's view, the FFI must fall under the command of a "regular" army which represented "traditional military virtues," equally proud of its professionalism, "its uniform, its discipline, and its strength." Above all, *l'amalgame* drew on the strengths of each group: the army desperately needed patriotic FFI manpower, while the FFI required professional leadership, discipline, and *métier*. The goal that de Lattre envisioned at this stage was "synthesis" or "harmony," a "mixing" or "organic amalgamation." But confusion over the status of FFI lingered well into the autumn, as officials tried to devise compromises, establish new structures that would lay a basis for *l'amalgame*, and because the army lacked the cadres, uniforms, arms, and equipment to incorporate and train FFI volunteers expeditiously in any case.[20]

Not surprisingly, de Gaulle, who had once embodied disobedience as a moral duty, now condemned it as a practical matter while praising it rhetorically. Clearly, yesterday's rebel, who now personified the French State, had concluded that the resistance could be made more militarily effective, and its potential for political disruption significantly diminished, if it were forced into uniform. Henceforth, France's clout in the Alliance – and its potential to gain an occupation zone in Germany – would be measured in active divisions, not conferred out of gratitude and admiration for an ill-disciplined, politicized, and sometimes manipulated coalition of *sans-culottes* organized and radicalized by communists and empowered by the interface services, who pranced around in liberated towns shaving women's heads. "In the last phase of the war, finally there would be more than fifteen French divisions in the line," de Gaulle wrote. "Taking account of the miseries of the present, that truly was all that was possible. Alas, for France that was little, relative to the past. 'Allah! Who will give me back my formidable army?'"[21] On 28 August, he announced the dissolution of the *État-major des Forces françaises de l'intérieur* (EMFFI), and that henceforth all FFI would be incorporated into the regular army on a volunteer basis. The *levée* was finished, the emergency over; henceforth, resistance was to be corralled, disciplined, and militarized.[22] By ordering resisters to enlist as individuals, de Gaulle could rebrand the French Resistance as a movement of "the nation as a whole,"[23] while the French army could at least recreate the illusion of a Republican *levée* in the final months of the war, "according to the proven and reassuring pre-war formulas, and not the adventure of a people's army."[24]

The position of the Resistance, especially the communist elements in it, was that it constituted a "people's army," in contrast to the "praetorians" of the professional army, which had been responsible in their eyes for the defeat of 1940 and the failure to defend the *zone libre* in November 1942. However, the communist goal of building "*une nouvelle armée populaire*" based on a revolutionary *levée en masse* appeared increasingly unrealistic, if not outright suicidal. De Gaulle did make rhetorical concessions to the *levée* when he spoke of "a new phase in the reconstruction of a new French army . . . thanks to the nation's most patriotic and active elements." But this modern "amalgamation" of the Resistance with the regular French army which recalled Year II of the Revolution would prove a stormy one, as one Resistance leader explained: "The disbanded army had discredited itself beyond belief. After losing the war, it set itself up in defeat by pompously espousing virtues that it never practiced. Then it let itself be surprised in bed in November [8 November 1942] when the fleet at Toulon theatrically scuttled itself."[25] For this reason, the auguries for a successful *amalgame* were inauspicious – while the PCF did not view the regular army as a homogeneous organization, the FFI and the renascent regular army were separated by the nature of their recruitment, by their political outlook, and by profound mutual distrust. Communist boss Jacques Duclos complained on 3 September 1944 that de Gaulle's "amalgamation" "rejects the reorganization of the French army as a people's army."[26] But what was the alternative? Plans to resurrect the French army on the foundation of a Resistance *levée* were a non-starter – while the Resistance contained some remarkable leaders, its formations were often composed of "cadres without troops, troops without cadres, soldiers without arms or arms without soldiers." Resistance groups were divided by personality, ideology, goals, and tactics.[27] Nor did many *maquisards* feel up to sparring a few more rounds against the Wehrmacht in the bitter winter of 1944–1945.[28]

However, the war was ongoing, French territory had yet to be completely liberated, and Germany remained battered but unbowed. The fear was that, unless an essentially colonial army topped up with French recruits, it would prove unable to align with the US-imposed organizational schema. Colonial subjects were thought to make good infantrymen but poor technical specialists, which explains why indigenous recruits made up 65 percent of the strength of the *4ᵉ Division marocaine de montagne* (4ᵉ DMM), but only 20 percent of the soldiers in the 5ᵉ DB. "*L'Armée B* is therefore an imperial army that employed the logic of recruitment and management inherited from the Third Republic and *France libre*," insists Miot. Contemporary critics complained that, beneath a glittering façade of armored and mechanized infantry divisions, the French army was a hollow force utterly dependent on the overstretched colonies for under-educated and poorly motivated manpower and on the Americans for technical, logistical, and fire support, and yet committed to preserving the colonial order. Their aspiration was that the invasion of France might change that.[29]

French units had to replace losses, which would only multiply throughout the winter and spring. A 23 September 1944 decree assimilated the FFI with the regular army. But all volunteers were required to enlist individually. The army conceded that many of these FFI units were like a family, with resisters very attached to their "seigneur," embracing a particular sense of equality and *esprit de corps* to which conventional officers must remain sensitive, which was seldom the case. FFI were also distrustful of *l'armée d'Afrique*, as well as the Armistice Army veterans, whom they denounced as "*Naphtalinés*" or "moth-balled soldiers," who besieged de Lattre and Leclerc, often brandishing "*certificats de résistance*" for which there was a buoyant black market. De Lattre acknowledged FFI particularisms and tried whenever possible to attach an FFI battalion to one of the regular army, as had been the practice in 1793–1794 to build Revolutionary demi-brigades. But the size and composition of FFI units varied so greatly that this was often impossible, while FFI chieftains with their self-conferred military ranks had to be dislodged so that regular officers could take charge.[30] Not surprisingly, this led to tensions, as FFI often regarded military regulations as mere suggestions, military courtesies as quaint medieval custom, and turning out smart on parade as a reactionary ceremonial, which rather somersaulted the notion of who was a "feudal" and who was "modern." Some had also picked up bad habits in the *maquis*, such as "requisitioning" whatever struck their fancy, a reflex prolonged by a paucity of *1ère Armée* logistics. But these negative traits might also be exaggerated by more tradition-bound officers skeptical of Fifi military potential, and suspicious of politicized resisters, whom they saw, not completely without reason, as a PCF Trojan horse to subborn the officer corps.[31] While, in the autumn of 1944, II Corps of the *1ère Armée* praised FFI "motivation," it also noted that these volunteers were "young, insufficiently trained . . . and often recruited in haste . . . The lack of discipline, training, and hence the behavior of these volunteers is every day more flagrant." They lacked equipment and vehicles and were unevenly armed. Muster rolls appeared to be entries, if not for a Prix Goncourt, at least for a runner-up Renaudot prize for fiction – leaders either inflated troop numbers to justify retention of their self-declared resistance rank, or were powerless to take an accurate census of FFI whose definition of "present for duty" remained elastic. Some FFI were clearly too young, and in poor physical shape, while many foreigners filled the ranks – most especially Ukrainians, Poles, Spanish, and Russians. Nor was their combat performance likely to improve, given the mediocre quality of their cadres, toward whom they displayed little deference in any case.[32] "One witnessed the flowering of a new military fauna," recorded Beaufre of *l'amalgame*, "in composite uniforms, coming from every background or popping up from the soil itself, which combined the 'mothballed' of the Armistice Army, the adventurers of London or Africa, and the resourceful with unverifiable antecedents, who participated in a proliferation of services whose functioning became inextricably tangled."[33]

For de Gaulle, the French army served both as a symbol of national unity and as a mechanism to achieve that national unity, "*une armée rassembleur*," around which France must reconstruct its battered pride, associate the French people with liberation and victory, and heal France's civil–military divide, while amplifying France's voice in the Alliance and its diplomatic influence in the post-war world. Now that a legitimate government ruled from Paris, an army factionalized among FFL diehards, imperial nostalgists, *évadés de France*, international refugees and deserters, and militants from the internal resistance must be welded into a unitary force under the government of the Republic. Of course, *l'amalgame* was simply the latest iteration of a process of French military reorganization that had begun in September 1939, cycled through the "fusion" of Gaullist and Giraudist elements from 1943, and the mobilization of a fissiparous North African contingent for Tunisia, Italy, and Dragoon, but this time applied on a metropolitan scale. The imposition of a traditional military system could channel resistance patriotism and *élan*, upgrade the army as a technical instrument to support government policy, restore the authority of the French state, and refocus public energy on the defeat of a common enemy.[34] By participating in the war effort, French youth would acquire a moral vigour linked to the exhilaration of victory, a pride that would supplant bitter memories of the suffering and humiliation of occupation, surmount partisan passions, and defuse the post-Liberation conflict that roiled many localities. At the same time, the army would benefit from a transfusion of "*l'esprit maquisard*," while the FFI would be prevented from devolving into "*grandes compagnies*" under warlord chieftains. Amalgamation would also transform FFI into lawful combatants.[35]

Eisenhower balked at standing up new French combat divisions, reiterating his need for pioneer and security units to repair French infrastructure. Furthermore, the man who is credited in the post-war period with saying that the French resistance was worth fifteen division expressed doubts about the military potential of these converted FFI units, as well as his reluctance to commit considerable resources to arm and support them logistically. In the wake of the German stampede to exit France, which initiated on 16 August, Berlin had seemed to be on its last legs. Eisenhower and Marshall had no interest in expanding a French army whose new divisions they believed would come into the line too late to deliver Hitler's death blow. Washington also declined to buy into the French argument that, unless they were brought under army-imposed control, the FFI might pose a threat to France's democratic order. As was frequently the case in Allied eyes, the French seemed consumed with their own anxieties and agendas to the detriment of the main goal – the defeat of Nazi Germany. De Lattre's superior, Jacob Devers, grew impatient with the "considerable confusion" caused by *l'amalgame* on Sixth Army Group's front.[36] Furthermore, to the chaos of the Liberation was added the fact that conscription registration had not been carried out during the occupation. With many young men in Germany or having fled into a *maquis*, Paris proved incapable of producing accurate numbers of potential conscripts upon which to base military expansion requests. In these circumstances, Washington was prepared only to complete the eleven-division Anfa program, by equipping three new infantry divisions.[37]

However, as autumn faded into winter, the problem had evolved from how to expand the French army to how to keep it combat worthy. While Eisenhower praised the "brilliant" performance of French forces in Italy and southern France, it was clear that "their efficiency rapidly fell off with the arrival of winter weather in late 1944."[38] The Anfa divisions that had fought through Italy and were now aligned along the Vosges front had been hollowed out. The Americans were especially concerned by the growing troop deficits in the 4e DMM, *9e Division d'infanterie coloniale* (9e DIC), and 5e DB, while even the 1ère DFL counted 1,000 vacancies in its ranks. This was especially alarming as the *1ère Armée* was short of specialists, which recourse to female recruitment had failed to repair. The *1ère Armée* required 20,000 replacements by January 1945, and 12,000 a month until the end of the war.[39] On 9 November, de Lattre confessed to Diethelm that the morale of his command had cratered. Harsh material conditions of service had played a large role, certainly. But the primary cause was the feeling among soldiers that, now that most of France had been liberated, the French population considered the war effectively over. Postal censorship revealed that soldiers were "fed up" that they continued to fight against a background of public "indifference," where "second-hand FFI or the many worthless elements in the rear prepare [according to them] a new France." Meanwhile, so harsh were combat conditions that many soldiers in Alsace began to doubt that they would survive the winter.[40] And they were not wrong.

Le Blanchiment or "*le premier amalgame*"

Without consulting Washington, the French took the initiative to reorganize their army. What became known as the "*Blanchiment*" (sometimes "*Blanchissement*"), or "Whitening," had several origins. Magnan, who commanded the 9ᵉ DIC, noted that some of his Senegalese had been mobilized since 1939, and had begun to manifest morale and discipline problems. Many in Brosset's 1ère DFL had seen combat since 1941 in Syria, the Western Desert, and Italy. The French army was as desperate for FFI replacements as de Gaulle was eager to enlist the French people in their own liberation. And while this was a major driver of the "whitening" process, the scope and mechanics of "*l'amalgame*" overwhelmed the GPRF that was only tentatively reestablished in Paris, as well as the *1ère Armée* that also had a war to fight. And, in some respects, the *blanchiment* merely generalized a process of recruiting replacements that had already begun in Toulon and Marseilles, where units like Salan's *6ᵉ Régiment de tirailleurs sénégalais* (6ᵉ RTS) had replaced losses among Africans with local volunteers.[41] Only on 1 October did de Gaulle inform Eisenhower and Devers, already alarmed by the ad hoc incorporation of FFI along the route of march whom they were expected to arm and feed, of his intention to trade out his Senegalese *tirailleurs* for FFI. However, in the autumn of 1944, the Americans tiresomely insisted on respecting Anfa's logistical limitations. In the face of US obstruction, it was decided literally to strip experienced sub-Saharan *tirailleurs* of their uniforms, arms, and equipment, and hand them over to Fifis.[42]

Another excuse for a mass switch-out of FFI for the roughly 20,700 Senegalese, concentrated principally in the 9ᵉ DIC and the 1ère DFL, came on 7 September from de Lattre. The commander of the *1ère Armée* believed that liberating France with Senegalese would send the wrong message, although North African Muslims seemed not to evoke similar qualms. Nevertheless, he was diplomatic enough to advance the traditional French military argument that sub-Saharan soldiers would find French winters too punishing – in fact, *everyone* would find the winter of 1944–1945 too punishing![43] But, beyond climatic concerns, colonial officials and officers were wary of allowing African soldiers to witness the disorders of the Liberation, and possibly establish relationships with French women that might subvert the imperial order.[44] The specter of rapes, which had blotted the CEF's copybook in Italy and that of the 9e DIC on Elba, also remained an ongoing concern, so that separate brothels – considered an antidote to rape – had been organized in France for soldiers of color.[45]

Concerns about the inability of Senegalese units to adapt to the Regimental Combat Team organization which stood at the center of US doctrine was also a factor. A mix of infantry, tanks, engineers, and artillery units, these teams emphasized flexibility, autonomy, and initiative, and required many specialists, which the Senegalese – as well as indigenous North African – units lacked. Received wisdom in the French army was that African units could be made maneuverable and adaptable only when at least a third of their troops were white. From the end of 1942, an attempt was made to upgrade Senegalese units destined for the 9e DIC and 1ère DFL. The Invasion Training Center at Arzew delivered instruction in urban combat, attacking villages and blockhouses, demining, the use of "Bangalore torpedoes," and the practice of amphibious assault in realistic conditions. But the 9e DIC lacked signals specialists and combat engineers, and the French were short of the personnel, time, and cash, or indeed the inclination, to identify and train them, which reduced the utility of Senegalese units, so that they were considered suitable only for basic infantry tasks. Most *tirailleurs* were illiterate and might speak only pidgin French. Many had never seen an airplane or a tank before they had been conscripted, nor were many even accustomed to wearing shoes. At the conclusion of the Elba campaign, the 6e DIC still lacked the adequate number of white cadres required to maximize its battlefield adaptability.[46] A final argument for *blanchiment* that was attractive to the GPRF was that it offered a mechanism to recuperate troops to form two divisions for the Far East, impressing the Vietnamese about the power of empire, while assuaging Allied skepticism of the military value of FFI.[47] So, for all of these reasons, Senegalese units were singled out as prime candidates for *blanchiment*.

As the lines congealed in Alsace, what Salan calls "the great relief" began, as FFI substituted for some of his Senegalese. "Little by little our recruiters sent us the boys . . . the men that we incorporated were young, between seventeen and nineteen . . . The Senegalese are large men, and the exchange of clothes is often comic." By 1 November, enough FFI replacements and volunteers had arrived so that Salan's 6e RTS could be rechristened the *6e Régiment d'infanterie coloniale* (6e RIC). Such a rebranding was applied to all Senegalese units in France.[48] Brosset took advantage of the 1ère DFL's passage through Lyon to top up with FFI to replace his African soldiers.[49] In November–December, a small tsunami of FFI replacements allowed the dispatch of 5,500 more sub-Saharan *tirailleurs* to the rear, so that, by January 1945, the *blanchiment* was considered complete. The number of Senegalese "*blanchis*" is usually rounded up to

20,000, although the Americans placed the number at 15,000, probably calculating that the French would inflate their ration strength.[50] In this way, 793 Africans continued to serve in the 1ère DFL, and another 1,742 in the 9e DIC, in support units, especially medical services.[51] In terms of military efficiency, the *blanchiment* made no sense, as Brosset confided to his diary on 10 October – in his opinion, de Lattre was foolish to switch out experienced Senegalese for FFI, who, absent intense training, would take "absurd losses," and be forced to confront a harsh winter on the Vosges summits with inadequate numbers and "defective weapons," which would most likely result in waves of desertion or require massive medical evacuations.[52] On 1 October, he complained that the process of incorporation was taking so long that many FFI simply took French leave. "In these conditions, the problems of the *blanchiment* are out of my hands." Nine days later, he told his commander that, "whitened, this division *will fall far below its previous quality*" (italics in the original). Neither the FFI officers nor the replacements were sufficiently trained, while promoting them over the heads of the more experienced professional cadres would spark resentment and crumple morale.[53] In practice, some of the FFI were thrown into the front lines on the Vosges with as little as four days' training against battle-hardened German units, which at least one French colonel qualified as "criminal."[54]

How the Senegalese felt about their swap out is largely unrecorded. Many were no doubt happy enough to escape a winter siege in Alsace. Brosset cautioned that the Senegalese should not be given the impression that "*blanchiment*" conveyed a lack of confidence, although some *tirailleurs* at least seemed insulted at being forced to hand over their weapons to men "who had been afraid" in 1940. Indeed, fear was widespread that the return of imperial witnesses to the 1940 débâcle and subsequent turmoil of state and society in France, followed by liberation-spawned disorder, would, combined with racist attitudes they had encountered in army ranks and from French society at large, menace imperial stability.[55] Most of all, Africans resented surrendering their uniforms and warm overcoats at the onset of winter. Their cadres stayed behind with the FFI, while the soldiers were sent to six hastily organized transit camps established along the Mediterranean coast to await repatriation, which was long delayed due to shipping shortages. They mixed in camps with African POWs from 1940, most of whom had spent the war laboring for the Todt Organization in France, and with diverse colonial subjects who, having escaped capture but unable to return home, had simply idled for four years in camps without news from their families. Without the officers and NCOs they had known since mobilization in 1943, incidents of indiscipline and even open mutiny among Senegalese formations in France multiplied. This growing disorder finally exploded in the 30 November 1944 mutiny and subsequent massacre of 35 and the wounding of another 100 repatriated *tirailleurs Sénégalais* at the Thiaroye camp outside of Dakar, Senegal.[56]

As usual with rebellions in colonial units, questions arose over whether they were sparked by discontent over conditions of service or by a growing sense of indigenous nationalism. The incident that triggered the Thiaroye explosion was a dispute over back pay owed the *tirailleurs Sénégalais*. But colonial officials saw pay issues as a mere pretext exploited by "non-qualified people" to stir up trouble among these "big children." Because the Thiaroye rebellion seems to have been caused by former POWs, not soldiers from the First Army's "whitened" units,[57] the colonial authorities blamed German propaganda, which they believed had influenced POWs during the war. Proximity to Black GIs was also cited. African Americans in US forces enjoyed the same pay and standard of living as white GIs, which helped to obscure the fact that they were clearly at the bottom of the military pecking order. However, this might have been less apparent to French colonial soldiers, who, ever since the first encounters at Torch, had been impressed by the weapons and equipment of US forces. Contact between Senegalese and African Americans intensified with Dragoon. Even though these encounters were inhibited by the language barrier, Africans noted that Black GIs exuded a "cheeky" self-confidence that would have been punished as impudence in a Senegalese. They also had cash, chocolate, and access to the cornucopia of the Post Exchange (PX). One of the threats made by Senegalese in November 1944 was that, "If you don't want to pay us, we are going to find the Americans and ask them to take over in Africa."[58]

In fact, the real problem of troops of color in France in the eyes of French officers like Brosset was that "prolonged contact with the French population," especially in the liberated cities, "has inculcated among the Blacks a spirit of entitlement." Furthermore, sensitive to the transgressions of some colonial soldiers in Italy and Elba, colonial soldiers in France had "crossed the colonial taboo" of contact with French women, "[which ... has developed [in Black soldiers] a contempt for the white race."[59] The influence of the "*marraines de guerre*" "of doubtful morals" was also cited as being particularly subversive. "War godmothers" was a practice initiated during the First World War when a female, perhaps just a schoolgirl, "adopted" a soldier at the front, wrote to him, and might even invite him into her home during leave periods. These women were accused of corrupting these *tirailleurs* both morally and politically through sexual relations and filling their heads with progressive notions of racial equality. But a sense of grievance among these African soldiers probably required stoking neither by white idealists nor by Senegalese "*évolués*." Sub-Saharan French colonies had been more intensely mobilized in the Second World War than during the Great War, both in 1939 and later by competing FFL and Vichy forces. An estimated 200,000 Africans had served in French ranks between 1939 and 1945, 15,000–16,000 of whom had become POWs in 1940. Another large number had escaped captivity but were subsequently suspended in a Vichy-imposed limbo, in camps in the *zone libre* in conditions that were by some accounts worse than in German-run *Frontstalags*.[60] *Tirailleurs sénégalais* were made to feel unwelcome in France at the Liberation, with de Lattre eager to remove African troops from the ranks of the *1ère Armée*. Their experience in the French military had helped to forge a collective consciousness that caused them to demand "equal rights for equal sacrifice," not attempt to capsize the colonial order.[61]

A Competition of Resistances

The expansion of the French army had been decided in the early autumn of 1944. The problem was how to go about it. FFI were seen as being very attached to their mates, their leaders, and their locale, an attitude that was underappreciated in the army.[62] The 9 June 1944 GPRF ordinance had declared FFI "an integral part of the French army." But, although the 1939 mobilization order remained in effect, the GPRF lacked the means to take a census of FFI or reestablish rosters of eligible conscripts. As has been seen, this had left individual units landed in Dragoon to set up their own recruiting offices as they moved north, a practice that had been common especially in Morocco and other under-administered corners of empire.[63] De Lattre's idea in November 1944 was gradually to transform FFI units into regular divisions as arms, specialists, and cadres became available.[64] However, he recognized that, at best, FFI offered only a small-unit esprit de corps, that did not necessarily transfer to larger units, so that it took practically the "spirit of a chemist" to attain the correct regional composition of personnel even when pairing battalions.[65] This occurred in part because flight from STO had transformed the resistance from an urban to a rural phenomenon, as city youth had often decamped to remote regions, especially the Alpes and the Massif Central, to join a *maquis*. FFI units had also continued to recruit at least until the end of September, and possibly beyond. In this way, for instance, an unknown percentage of the 2,000 men who made up the FFI "*régiment du Morvan*" integrated into the 3e DIA might not be from the Morvan. Nor did the army keep track of whether volunteers had previously been active in the resistance/ *maquis*, or were simply walk-ins, swept up in the patriotic enthusiasm of liberation, or perhaps looking to "whitewash" their occupation conduct.[66]

In early September, the GPRF had established a *19e Division d'infanterie* (19e DI) to group all the Breton FFI units besieging the Atlantic ports of Lorient and Saint-Nazaire. Likewise, a *1ère Division alpine* FFI had formed spontaneously to police the frontier with Italy, which in November was officially incorporated as the *27e Division d'infanterie alpine* (27e DIA). At the end of September, it was decided to standardize FFI organizations by transforming them into regular 800-man battalions based on the 18 military regions in France. In October, Larminat produced a plan for converting FFI units besieging the Atlantic pockets into regular formations, based on territorial recruitment.[67] In de Lattre's *1ère Armée*, Brigadier General Aimé Molle, a charismatic recipient of a Great War *croix de guerre*, who had further embellished his already considerable martial reputation as colonel of the *8e Régiment de tirailleurs marocains* (8e RTM) in the breakthrough on the Garigliano, was named de Lattre's adjutant to supervise the mechanics of the "amalgamation." But establishing an accurate tally of FFI was practically unachievable – FFI leaders often had no clue how many of their peripatetic combatants, who came and went as the mood struck them, they commanded. Piecing together a military administration and locating former Armistice Army cadres proved a protracted process. By the middle of October 1944, the War Ministry came up with a figure of 338,400 FFI, of whom 157,000 belonged to organized battalions, although recounts gave lower figures.[68]

In early September, de Lattre calculated that he had incorporated thirteen FFI battalions, most from the Alpes and the southwest, a number that rose to thirty battalions by the following month. Unfortunately, these "battalions" ranged from 300 to 1,200 men each.[69] FFI units mingled Frenchmen and foreigners, who legally were required to enlist in the Foreign Legion. Nor were they in good shape: the first 600 volunteers for the 2e DB were "in rags," to the point that Koenig's deputy, Brigadier General Roger Noiret, was ashamed to send them to the UK for training until the Americans could scrounge up some uniforms "to dress them decently."[70] Furthermore, most FFI were enlisted without even a cursory physical examination, which meant that some went straight from the recruiting depot into hospital.[71] The extreme youth of FFI recruits was a universal complaint. Since these recruits had not been broken into military service through a barracks routine that inculcated a reverence for – or terror of – hierarchy, FFI informality remained the rule, including addressing their sergeants with the familiar "*tu*" form and neglecting to salute superiors, a nonchalance that enraged martinets like Monsabert.[72] During an inspection tour of Salan's 6e RIC, the patrician de Lattre snapped at a recently incorporated FFI who casually proffered him a Gauloise: "Gentlemen, I didn't come here for chit-chat."[73]

It was hardly the first time that regular – especially *armée d'Afrique* – officers, accustomed to a highly racialized and punctual discipline, were appalled by what they considered to be slovenly – even disrespectful – metropolitan manners. The irony was that those – especially former FFL – who themselves had made unorthodox choices that they had often expressed in eccentricity of dress and more informal notions of discipline, now criticized the same reflexes among metropolitan recruits. Part of the explanation was that received wisdom in the military blamed a lack of discipline in the army for the collapse of 1940. First encounters with the FFL in 1943 had revealed a similar disciplinary ambience characterized by "proximity between soldiers and NCOs, absence of marks of respect, fraternity and a spirit of camaraderie." FFL military culture had been anchored in non-conformism, even disobedience, where enlistment was itself an act of rebellion of men for whom time spent in a military organization constituted a civic imposition rather than a vocation. So, FFL discipline was voluntary, not an acquired reflex or an expression of social or political conformity. Also, the FFL preference for casualness had been reinforced by service in the Western Desert, where a rustic setting combined with an emphasis on competence and courage in a combat environment made barracks routines and formalities superfluous, even counterproductive.[74] However, one should not exaggerate: Brosset's command philosophy held that discipline should be strict, although just and not arbitrary, while Leclerc was so tightly coiled that one might easily imagine him decapitating with his signature Malacca cane any FFI who casually offered him a Gitane Maïs.

But a basic question that underpinned *l'amalgame* was this one: "where does legitimate authority originate?" *L'armée d'Afrique* approached *l'amalgame* with a sense of professional superiority based on what its officers believed to be the requirement to keep soldiers of color – indeed, the entire colonial order – in line through routines of ritual, respect, and, when necessary, chastisement. In their minds, their stunning *tour de force* on the Garigliano had validated their methods. "This French army, reformed, armed, equipped, trained, is twenty times better than the immense Allied armies, who of course appreciate its quality, but don't accept us on an equal footing," Monsabert confided to his diary.[75] Italy had witnessed the revenge of French professional soldiers against the Germans primarily for 1940. But, also, they had struck a blow against the condescending Americans who, despite their numbers, lavish firepower, industrial scale logistics, and copious if insipid rations, in the French view were clueless about "the art of war." The Gaullists, too, were disdained as "adventurers" and renegades in uniform. And now they had to deal with the FFI, dressed in their blue overalls and berets that made them look like refugees from the Spanish Civil War *Retirada* of 1939 – which in fact some of them, led by Rol-Tanguy and "Colonel Fabien" were. And the ultimate insult: "female soldiers!"[76] An attitude widespread in the *1ère Armée* held that life in the *maquis* had been a lazy dawdle on a sun-drenched Alpine meadow or bird watching deep in a spruce forest, followed, once Allied armies appeared, by a frenzy of head shaving, pillage, and similarly lawless behavior, often carried out by "September resisters." "We rejected the armistice, and they refused to work [in Germany]," ran an unjust critique by former Gaullists *vis-à-vis* their new STO-shy *maquis* colleagues.[77] A languid informality, considered an endemic FFI character trait, would no longer be tolerated among new recruits. The FFI had to be taught to fight in articulated, all-arms formations, and to defend ground by organizing defenses (digging foxholes, stringing barbed wire, laying mine fields, sighting heavy weapons, coordinating air strikes, and so on). This required discipline, which began with a haircut, a uniform, and the strict enforcement of military courtesies and ritual. The problem was that, once in France, the American-organized and supervised training in AFN that had included feedback loops and adjustments based on combat observations was dismantled, as the French were now responsible for training their own troops. Each division was ordered to set up a regimental training center, where group instruction could be delivered to the FFI battalions assigned to it, to maintain their sense of identity and morale. Unfortunately, the French lacked the camps, arms, and matériel to do this efficiently, so that, for the remainder of the war, training for French units was largely ad hoc and abbreviated.[78]

Nor could the FFL and the FFI forgive those officers of *l'armée d'Afrique* and of the Armistice Army who had served Vichy. For them, the fact that military discipline had been invoked as a political tool to reinforce obedience to the Marshal discredited the very concept. While *l'armée d'Afrique* had redeemed itself at least militarily in Italy, for France the year and a half prior to liberation had driven AFN from the national consciousness, to be replaced by events on the Eastern Front, developments in Italy, and above all STO and ferocious internal repression. After the war, refugees, Jews, and dissidents interned in camps in AFN were never officially recognized as resisters.[79] Like the FFL, the FFI had rejected Vichy as illegitimate. Who deserved to be held in higher esteem, patriots who had made a commitment to live a clandestine existence despite considerable risks or officers who, despite technical competence acquired at Saint-Cyr and the *École de guerre*, had botched the battle in 1940 and subsequently served a collaborationist Marshal? And the latter now invaded France at the head of wild-eyed and lightly civilized imperial mercenaries with a reputation for committing sexual and other crimes against non-combatants. It would all come down to who was best able to perform well in combat.[80] While de Lattre remained upbeat about the *esprit de corps* of most FFI, in his view, rather than seek inspiration from the French army's past, those from Toulouse "held ambitions to embody *l'armée nouvelle*."[81] One of *l'amalgame*'s purposes was to dissolve these armed "fiefdoms" and warlords' militias. While many FFI seemed eager to fight, de Lattre at least realized that their morale was fragile and might implode at first contact with the Wehrmacht.

A further problem with integrating FFI into the regular army was what to do about self-conferred FFI ranks. A regular French infantry regiment counted 3 percent officers and 13 percent NCOs. Percentages in FFI units varied but could go as high as 13.5 percent officers and 20.7 percent NCOs. While these FFI cadres might include regular and reserve officers and NCOs, these men had not experienced conventional operations since 1940. Modern warfare developments, therefore, had passed them by. Meanwhile, the proliferation of FFI units, combined with rank inflation, "resulted in a plethora of officers with insufficient military knowledge," who were mostly idle because they occupied no function in a conventional unit and were too attached to their new rank even to step down a notch or two.[82] From October, various committees were created to ratify or adjust FFI ranks, a task facilitated by the fact that independent FFI command structures ceased to exist from the end of November.[83] FFI "officers" were dispatched for training to assess their suitability for command. On 10 March 1945, the lieutenant-colonel commanding the "*Centre de perfectionnement des officiers supérieurs FFI*," at Provins, reported that, of forty-nine senior FFI officers with ranks ranging from major to colonel sent for evaluation, twelve had been dismissed for "various reasons." Of the thirty-seven graduates, only one was considered capable of commanding a battalion, normally the job of a major or lieutenant colonel; five qualified as company commanders, effectively meaning the rank of captain; and one – Rol-Tanguy, who orchestrated the "self-liberation" of Paris and to whom Dietrich von Choltitz had technically surrendered – was pronounced capable of serving in a staff capacity. These seven officers would be dispatched to the *1ère Armée* for a month of on-the-job training. Of course, it would be tempting to interpret these demotions, exclusions, and negative fitness reports as a closing of ranks of the old-boy network in *l'armée d'Afrique* against FFI gatecrashers. But, from a conventional army perspective, organizing dead letter drops and outsmarting *la Milice* were not skills in high demand in Alsace in the winter of 1944–1945. While many of these novice FFI senior officers seemed to grasp tactical concepts in the classroom, they became "lost" in the field "when they had to act in conditions approaching the reality of combat." A dozen graduates would be assigned platoon command, effectively a lieutenant position, while eighteen would be sent to the front as NCOs. Nor, unfortunately, did the following class evince much more promise. Other schools complained that they had few qualified instructors, no instruction material, library, NCOs, or administrative staff, vehicles, or troops that the officers could direct as practice, which made the training "both artificial and superficial" according to one director.[84]

On 20 September, the GPRF offered FFI in liberated areas the choice of joining the army or demobilizing. From 23 September, all FFI were required to sign individual enlistment papers, which in theory gave the War Ministry control over their assignments. Eventually, the *1ère armée* had to incorporate 137,000 volunteers, which, along with the stand-up of other FFI-based units, would create logistical demands that would further exasperate the Americans.[85] But, in the short term and as a practical matter, allowances must be made for resistance particularism. One of the advantages of de Lattre's selection to command *l'Armée B* was that the amalgamation offered just the sort of project that fired his imagination and appealed to his deeply paternalistic attitudes rooted in social Catholicism and Hubert Lyautey's celebrated 1891 article "Du rôle social de l'officier."[86] While a division commander in the Armistice Army, de Lattre had promoted "*écoles des cadres*" as a device to cultivate patriotic commitment, develop the leadership potential of young Frenchmen, and promote national reconciliation around respect for hierarchy, order, and conservative values. No sooner had he arrived in AFN in December 1943 than he created an *école des cadres* at Douéra, an Algiers suburb, whose purpose was to lay a foundation for the unification of the French military. On 15 July, Larminat had written to de Lattre about the importance of enlisting young Frenchmen, "from a moral point of view, because this will allow us to discipline and incorporate those of good will, but [who are] sometimes disorderly ... By not integrating the partisans into our standard military system, we run the risk of seeing them divide according to independent formulas that could undermine public order." Before he sailed from Naples for Dragoon, de Lattre reminded his officers that the FFI were their brothers, that they must be treated with respect, and that they had no other desire but to join the ranks of the army.[87] It all rather replicated in tone patronizing Wehrmacht instructions about how to treat Alsatian and Mosellan *Volksdeutsche.*

But this nation-building project bumped up against several obstacles, not the least of which was its *l'armée d'Afrique* nucleus – a bastion of unreconstructed colonial conservatism and fidelity to National Revolution dogmas that exalted racial and cultural determinism and rejected republican "cosmopolitanism" represented by fifis, whom they scorned as a swarm of communist ragamuffins. And while the violence and disorder that they witnessed in the wake of Liberation was only fleeting, and certainly did not portend the onset of civil war as in Greece, it triggered confirmation bias. In his diary, even the stoutly Gaullist Brosset decried "All the drama of this terrible disorder. An extraordinarily amplified phenomenon of discordance between us, who for four years have dreamed of victory, and those who for four years have accepted to be the vanquished. An imprudent inflation of the resistance which, in fact, was exceptional. Atrocious cupidity of the peasants. Shameful fear of mobilization among most. Ingratitude toward the Allies. Criminal indulgence vis-à-vis the Germans."[88]

The rapidity with which de Gaulle reestablished the French state on liberation is regarded as one of his most deft accomplishments. But, for many French citizens, the "amalgamation" as envisaged by their new president begged the question of what the Liberation had been about. It meant the end of occupation and of Vichy, certainly – on that everyone could agree. But Liberation also symbolized an end to old ways of doing things, an *adieu* to people, institutions, and practices that had begot defeat, national disgrace, and occupation. Liberation implied renewal, not a historical rewrite amid a chorus of calls for an "appeasement of emotions" framed by exaggerated claims of the victimization of erstwhile Vichy supporters.[89] Defeat in 1940, followed by exile of a small Armistice Army to the *zone libre* and its dissolution in November 1942, had severed the links between the French people and their army. European cadres of *l'armée d'Afrique* failed to appreciate the roots of the indifference, even hostility, of their countrymen toward them, and became indignant that their sacrifices in Italy went unacknowledged. But, for many in the Metropole, "*l'armée d'Afrique* was considered as representing the old order having led to catastrophe," writes Miot.[90] An army of colonial mercenaries reinforced by their "mothballed" Armistice Army counterparts, the very men who had failed to defend the country, who *en masse* had sworn an oath to obey the Marshal, supervised the *Chantiers de la jeunesse* as disguised transit camps to STO, resisted Torch, acquiesced to the Axis occupation of Tunisia, and followed orders to surrender the *zone libre* without a fight and betray their weapons caches to the Germans rather than transfer them to the resistance, and then had the temerity to proclaim the High Seas Fleet scuttle an act of "resistance," before volunteering to shoot down Allied bombers, was now to provide the nucleus of de Gaulle's "*armée rassembleur*"!

Most FFI were not opposed to an *amalgame*. Regional FFI groups had begun to organize training like the four-week course laid on by the Aveyron FFI at Sévérac east of Rodez, where in October 1944 "rural youth" could be introduced to "a sort of military service. Good atmosphere, a military ambience. Lots of difficulties from a material and diplomatic point of view."[91] But some of their more radical leaders advanced a prima facie case that it was they, not discredited professional soldiers, who should inspire France's military makeover. In its original 1793 version, the *levée en masse* had been a product of political radicalism. And, in a highly mythologized analogy, the FFI identified themselves as the heirs of the *sans-culottes* of Year II, who had rallied to defend the Fatherland after the professional army had faltered. The communists especially advocated that "*épurations*" (purges) should lay the foundation for a Jaurèsian "*armée nouvelle*." However, more traditionalist elements led by de Gaulle would argue that a radical military makeover was antithetical both to the values and structure of French society and to the exigencies of modern warfare. In this view, *l'amalgame* was to be defined by its military requirements, not the political agendas of the more radical resistance elements. In this way, most of the resistance accepted the premise that the rejuvenation of the French military through the FFI must be guided by the requirements of war. The French needed professional specialists to staff their army, not political organizers and shadow conspirators who had self-promoted in a clandestine crusade.

In fact, while the communist presence in the FFI varied by region, their numbers were never overwhelming, even in Fabien's "Paris Brigade." Most volunteered for the regular army out of patriotism, not politics. But, predictably, *l'amalgame* resurrected the army command's fear of communist infiltration of the barracks, an obsession since the inter-war years that bordered on paranoia. Nor was the expansion process a smooth one – roughly 30 percent of volunteers counted as "wastage," among them farmers or shopkeepers who, during the long wait between enlistment and reporting, had to support themselves by returning to work. Miners, railway workers, teachers, and farmers vital for national recovery were exempted from military service. *L'amalgame* was also an affair of youth. Students needed to take their exams. Those too young for the army were sent home. Others might simply desert during the march to the front, concluding that, having joined a *maquis*, they had satisfied their civic obligation. Many became upset that their lack of arms and uniforms offered a sign of second-class status, and so might desert their FFI unit to enlist individually in a *1ère Armée* regiment or, as seen, the 2e DB. But, of course, the entire army lacked uniforms and equipment, not just the FFI. By the end of the year, if not before, the radical fringe of the resistance began to realize that they could not impose their concepts on the army.[92] Once the idea of *l'amalgame* became accepted, it had to be made to work. Nor had the behavior of professional soldiers entirely discredited them, especially after November 1942, when an estimated 1,500 officers and 10,000 NCOs had joined the *Organisation de résistance de l'Armée* (ORA), 1,000 associated with the *Armée secrète* (AS), and a further 600–700 enlisted in the FTP. A further 1,500 officers became *évadés de France*. In a spirit of patriotic indulgence, by this calculation roughly 42 percent of the 11,000 professional officers in France in 1942 might be counted as resisters. But the public perception was that, if the army had not been openly collaborationist, at the very least it had been composed of "half-hearted" patriots.[93]

Épuration

The notion of *épuration* (cleansing, purging, purifying), as a mechanism to break free of the past and a prelude to renewal, conveys pious aspirations. As a French political phenomenon, however, the concept dates from the French Revolution, when Abbé Sieyès called for "parasites" and impure elements to be eliminated from civic life as a requirement for national "regeneration." Denunciation was hailed as a civic virtue, and violence in the pursuit of popular justice aimed to intimidate the adversary and electrify public opinion. Therefore, from this perspective, "*les tontes*" and "settling of scores" on the Liberation might be viewed as historical reenactments in a contemporary setting. Nor was *épuration* limited to the left. Successive regimes in French history had consigned their predecessors' loyalists to emigration, whether foreign or internal. On the right, by the inter-war years, *épuration* had taken on a practically medical as well as a racial connotation, as in Céline's call for the purging of "impure" elements from society: "Disinfection! Cleaning! …

the Jews, Afro-Asian hybrids, quarter, half-negroes, and Near Easterners ... They should beat it."[94] *Épuration* was also viewed as an antidote for decadence, a perception that had become almost an obsession on the French right since the middle of the nineteenth century. Although, with some irony, in this case their theory was turned against them.

Historically, the French army and civil service had been subjected to drawdowns, and purges, both by the right and by the left.[95] Therefore, it is hardly surprising that, given a general view that 1940 had been a product of France's social and political malaise, combined with a requirement for judicial revenge and a conviction that "resistance" was to form the basis of France's post-war renewal and identity, *épuration* was high on the CFLN/GPRF agenda. But, in a nation shattered by defeat and occupation, the process of national "purification" was bound to be seen as piecemeal, slow, incomplete, unsatisfactory, or even unjust. *Épuration* had multiple agendas that traced their origins to the divisions of the 1930s, responsibilities for defeat, for the sabotage of the Republic, for Vichy's social subversion, shameful compromises, and violence against the French people, for Pétain's abuse of confidence, and for the outright treason of the extreme right. A combination of multiple agendas, a divided political culture, and as a practical matter that the French state had been compromised by collaboration meant that *épuration* was unlikely to lead to a renovation that would repair the divisions and encourage French men and women to put a divisive past behind them. *Épuration* was bound to be compromised, incomplete, even subverted, especially in a military that had a world war to finish, to be succeeded by wars of decolonization.

On 18 August 1943, Algiers had created a mechanism to investigate public officials and officers who might have, "by their acts, writings, or personal attitude, either favored the enterprises of the enemy, or undermined the action of the United Nations and French resisters or undermined constitutional institutions or fundamental public liberties." For the military, purges had begun in North Africa in October 1943 with the creation of a military tribunal that punished some of the more notorious collaborators. Pierre Pucheu became "the first in a long line of martyrs which right-wing anti-Gaullists would accumulate over the next forty years," that grew to include Air Force Colonel Sarton du Jonchay and Lieutenant-colonel Pierre Simon Cristofini, both associated with the *Phalange africaine* in Tunisia. These executions were viewed as the blood-price of de Gaulle's alliance with the communists that confirmed "an image of de Gaulle as sanguinary and vengeful."[96] Trials of senior officers that began in May 1944 in Algiers were pursued in Paris in the spring of 1945, which saw Admiral Derrien sentenced to life at hard labor for turning over Bizerte to the Germans, while Dentz and Esteva were condemned for treason for allowing Axis forces into Syria and Tunisia, respectively.[97] Hardly had Paris been liberated than, on 27 August 1944, a decree from the War Ministry excluded all officers who did not qualify as "resisters" – that meant all career officers not in the service of the GPRF, in Corsica, the empire, or the FFL should consider themselves "on extended leave" until they could justify their retention in writing. All promotions handed out by Vichy after 8 November 1942 were rescinded.[98] A three-man "purge committee" was created in September 1944. Composed of general officer representatives from the three services, it was to examine 12,000 files for the army, 2,300 for the French Air Force (FAF), and 3,200 for the navy, looking for collaboration with the occupier or "hostility to the resistance." "If the guidelines were strict, their application was less so," concludes Miot. By the end of November 1944, a review of 11,528 army officers had eliminated a mere 649, with another 260 files forwarded to the *commissaire à la Justice* for further scrutiny. But even this was too much. A lack of officers with technical expertise, many of whom had been incorporated into industry rather than the resistance, was deemed "*catastrophique*." But, in the middle of a war when the forces were expanding, and technical specialists were in short supply, only 841 officers were excluded from service, which included 79 from the air force and 104 from the navy.[99]

The resistance, especially the PCF, complained that the so-called "purge" had been laughable, effectively rewarding "*attentisme*," and threatened to create a Vichy "5th Column" in the rehabilitated army.[100] So, the true "*blanchiment*" of the French army became not simply the replacement of soldiers of color by FFI, but the way in which former Vichy loyalists were permitted to undergo a preliminary purge committee wash and rinse, followed by a steam clean of their records through an eleventh-hour baptism in the "Rhin et Danube" via Leclerc's 2e DB or de Lattre's *1ère Armée.* Although the scope of this political "*blanchiment*" must not be exaggerated, the spectacle of Vichy supporters and fellow travelers being embraced by the army offered evidence that French military culture rewarded comradery and conformity over true patriotism, which did little to heal the civil–military divide in France.[101]

On the surface, the population welcomed liberation with enthusiasm. Brosset attributed the series of carefully choreographed fêtes and parades through towns liberated by the *1ère Armée* to de Lattre's "truly puerile vanity," which spawned his craving to marinate in the adulation of the populace.[102] However, the larger purpose of these public celebrations was to rehabilitate the army's tarnished reputation in the eyes of the French population, as well as to banish bad press about rapes in Italy and heal the divisions between units for whom conflicting choices made at various times since 1940 remained a source of bitter recrimination and rivalry. The feared epidemic of rapes and pillage in France did not occur, and brothels were set up for soldiers of color so that they would not molest French women as they had females in Italy – although the idea that *bordels militaires de campagne* (BMCs) offered an antidote for sexual

Figure 7.3 "September" resisters in Marseilles. The ephemeral transit of *l'Armée B* through the "red south" left an unsettled political situation in its wake, so that government officials often struggled to impose their authority over bickering and self-empowered resistance leaders. (Photo by Roger Viollet via Getty Images)

violence against civilians allowed the command to shirk responsibility for sexual crimes committed against the women of their enemies, by transferring culpability onto the shoulders of their soldiers.[103] Military parades were also meant to signal that the government was back in control, although government officials often struggled to impose their authority over bickering and self-empowered resistance leaders in FFI-"liberated" towns such as Toulouse. In Lyon, mobs of bellowing "second-hand resisters" sheared the hair of women, lynched members of *la Milice*, careened through the streets shooting into the houses and apartments of "hypothetical adversaries," and eventually set fire to the general hospital to clear imaginary snipers from the roof. But, when Brosset sent out his soldiers to disarm them and reestablish order, local officials complained that the military was usurping civilian authority. In this way, the ephemeral transit of *l'Armée B* through the "red south" left an unsettled political situation in its wake (Figure 7.3).[104]

A 26 June 1944 GPRF ordinance had created courts in each department to judge crimes of collaboration, intelligence with the enemy, and "undermining national defense." But these attempts to channel the "settling of scores" into a legal setting had to contend with "*Milice* hunts" organized in places like the Haute-Savoie and the Massif Central where encounters between *Milice* and *maquis* during the war had turned homicidal. The head of the intelligence department of the Chambéry *Milice*, Paul Touvier, skulked into hiding, while, in Lyon, captured *miliciens* were beaten, a mere preliminary to the firing squad. Even if they managed to survive long enough to be dragged before one of many spontaneously proliferating tribunals, just to be wearing *la Milice*'s blue uniform often demanded a death sentence, even if no crime was charged, especially if the "judge" were an FTP appointee. Spectators in the packed courtrooms fast-tracked verdicts by vociferously demanding exemplary justice for traitors. Onlookers concluded that these "people's tribunals," where an "*atmosphère de sans-culotte*" reigned, offered reverential reenactments of their French Revolution precursors. "The debates are short," remembered one observer. "The fastidious reading of the interminable charges is dispensed with, and no witnesses are called: the witnesses are everyone in the room . . . As for the pleading, they reflect the atmosphere. They are short, which doesn't mean that they aren't eloquent. All the defense attorneys are appointed on the spot." In the spirit of Danton's urging, "Let us be terrible, so that the people will not have to be," the subsequent executions, all carried out in public, were equally festive. On 2 September 1944, in the shadow of le Vercors at Grenoble, the *maquis service d'ordre* had to fire into the air to prevent the crowd from lynching six *Francs-Gardes* from the *École des cadres* d'Uriage, before they could be officially executed. To give their last seconds dignity, some *miliciens* proclaimed their loyalty to Pétain with their last breath. Gradually, order was imposed, public executions were outlawed, and trials assumed a more regular pattern. This meant that prison sentences and even acquittals were handed down, none of which pleased the communists, who in many regions denounced the failure of the "purges." In some instances, they might break into prisons to execute *Francs-Gardes* considered inadequately punished, or in the Dordogne dynamite the property of former collaborators whom they believed had been treated too leniently by the tribunals.[105]

Soldiers from Africa, as well as GIs, were shocked by the bacchanalia of revenge and score settling that accompanied Liberation, as FFI pillaged the homes and shops of "collabos," and carried out extra-judicial purges of officials, even executions of militiamen in places like the Alpes.[106] Although often ugly, the violence that erupted in the Liberation requires some context. The occupation had required law breaking daily, which had undermined public order, and broken the bonds of civility between neighbors, who might denounce each other to the police or Gestapo, both services that cultivated informant networks. The State's monopoly on violence had slipped away as its agents acted in support of the occupying power, of an increasingly delegitimized Vichy regime, or in the name of "the Resistance," which opened the door to plenty of freelancers and criminal entrepreneurs in between. While the post-war generation would struggle to define the parameters of "resistance," collaboration, real or imagined, had been plain for all to see. Not surprisingly, the Liberation was a time for retaliation against those who had gained some illicit advantage during the Occupation. The fact that it was usually carried out by the FFI in a public space made it semi-legal.[107] An estimated 20,000 "*tontes*" ("shearings") were reported in 322 communes in France, beginning in 1943 and continuing through the summer of 1945.[108] These rituals required French women accused of fraternization with the occupier to be publicly humiliated – sometimes stripped to the waist and with swastikas painted on their backs, they had their head shorn in public places as "horizontal collaborators," in acts of symbolic justice for sexual relations with the enemy. Hair was targeted as emblematic of female sexuality and carnal transgression. The instances varied according to region, and in fact the phenomenon began even before liberation. In La Manche, "*les tontes*" began in the summer of 1944 and lasted for a year, not only in towns but also in small villages. At Carentan, market day following liberation saw a dozen women shorn and then driven around town for all to see. In Cherbourg, women were paraded through streets behind a man sitting on the cab of a truck beating a drum. Resisters decrying "slow justice" might organize posses of rubble-clearing workers to go in search of women who had been in relationships with Germans. In the months following liberation, idle young men might grab women on the street and cut their hair. At Villedieu, Robert Storez, head of the local resistance, ordered his men to "shave all the German chickens." Even the French cleaning woman at the *Kommandantur* joined the ranks of "*les tondues*." These public humiliations often attracted large crowds. Sometimes the police or locals intervened. But, once they had been humiliated, the women were released because they had violated no law.[109]

For historian Fabrice Virgili, the first point to make is that 1940 had traumatized French society, as it shattered the individual and collective social bonds, and accelerated a national identity crisis that had been in evidence since the 1930s. Confronted with a situation of absent POWs, STO, deportations, rationing, curfews, arrests, Allied bombardments, and collaboration, a population of women, children, and the old had struggled to survive. The occupation had been a dreary time. Imposing German time advanced dusk when curfews were imposed, and the blackout extinguished street lighting, forbade illuminated shop signs, and required that windows be curtained. Paradoxically, lights were kept on in cinemas during newsreels to discourage subversive commentary. Public dances and celebrations were also banned. But curfew did not apply to French women in the company of Germans or to those whose contacts had procured for them an *Ausweis*. These women had gone out, smoking, dining, and dancing with their German lovers while patriotic French people had remained confined in their homes, were imprisoned in *Stalags*, were stalked by the Gestapo, were deported to Germany, or fled into the *maquis*.[110] *La tondue* (the shorn woman) symbolized the retaliation of the cuckolds, meant to avenge a symbol of shame and restore French virility. But *la tondue* also served as a reminder of France's defeat. She joined the prostitute who solicited German soldiers as an exemplar of France's dishonor.[111]

"*Les tontes*" offered a ritual of purification that cleansed the community of these fallen women, that closed out the war and prefaced the relaunch of the reconstruction of the economy and the nation. They also were a form of popular pressure on the authorities to pursue an official purge of state institutions.[112] Liberation represented the revival of a republican tradition, the return of warrior heroism, identification with suffering, a rediscovered virility not totally extinguished by defeat and occupation.[113] But, for many, liberation was an ambiguous event, and not just for Vichy supporters. "Liberation had hardly been a triumphal march, a long, tranquil river flowing from victory to victory." Rather, it had been "a procession of dramas imprinted on local, regional, and national memory" of deportations, bombardments, massacres, martyrdom of villages, and repression as at Glières, le Vercors, and Oradour.[114] Nor did things suddenly get better on liberation. Food remained scarce. Essential items such as soap and sugar were virtually unobtainable. In places where fighting had been heavy, towns including Caen, Lisieux, Vire, Cherbourg, Brest, and Rouen had endured extensive damage. Among the ruins of Saint-Lô, 5,000 survivors lived in "deplorable conditions" in January 1945, in basements, garages, or a few intact rooms of houses that had otherwise been reduced to rubble. Unexploded ordnance was everywhere and might kill or maim the incautious. Most French POWs still had not been repatriated, and now communication with them was completely severed.[115]

For the French, liberation quickly veered into a humiliating, when not a dangerous, experience, as a German occupation was quickly replaced by an American one. GIs soon wore out their welcome – they requisitioned buildings, drove too fast, and threw away food when the French were starving. German POWs were given oranges and chocolate, and supplied with uniforms denied the FFI, while the French dressed in rags, and still put cardboard in their shoes because they lacked leather for new soles. American flags flew everywhere, symbolizing a loss of status for the French. Rapes, thefts, and other crimes carried out by American soldiers joined an explosion of prostitution that further soured relations and deepened French humiliation. Within a few days of its 27 June capture, its population reduced from 40,000 to 5,000 people, with a quarter of the town destroyed, the large number of prostitutes already working the streets of Cherbourg raised concerns in US medical services about an epidemic of syphilis.[116] In the wake of the Liberation, the French were anxious about the future of their country. The presence of African American GIs especially, who, being concentrated in construction, supply, and transportation units, were disproportionately in rear areas, was interpreted as a US attempt "to ruin France and make it an American colony." Prostitution and rape, for which Black GIs were most often accused, showcased France's decline in an adverse power relationship with the United States, even more so because of the lowly status of African American soldiers in the US military. French officials agreed: "The population fears black troops," gendarmes in La Manche reported.[117] "The body of the raped French woman symbolized a new world of French subservience," writes Mary Louise Roberts. Occupation by African American soldiers combined with rape as a metaphor for national degradation. "The black-soldier-as-rapist became a communal fantasy," as well as a symptom of deep anxiety. Rather than France being treated as a member of the victorious Alliance, France's status, despite liberation, remained that of a defeated country, more dependent on the United States for food and security, as French women sold their bodies to the new occupier for chocolate and cigarettes.[118] On 11 January 1945, Saint-Lô witnessed an anti-American demonstration during which shots were fired at GIs after police had registered thirty rapes allegedly committed by US troops.[119]

Life in Paris only slowly found a semblance of normalcy, as banks reopened, rubbish was collected, and the metro was put into working order, although buses (since many had been requisitioned by retreating Germans) remained scarce, and streets dug up for barricades were slowly repaired, although the Louvre remained shuttered. But not before 35,000 US supply, communication and transportation troops were quartered in Paris as part of the communication zone (COMZ). Civil Affairs requisitioned choice digs on the Place Vendôme, as Supreme Headquarters Allied Expeditionary Force (SHAEF) set up in its headquarters in Versailles. US troops occupied 300 hotels and the student residences of the *cité universitaire*. Another 11,000 rooms were requisitioned for GIs on leave, as were movie theaters, warehouses, hospitals, garages, and so on. Former collaborators, members of the *Légion des volontaires français contre le bolchévisme* (LVF) or *Parti populaire français* (PPF), some with criminal records, seemed to find no trouble being hired by the Americans, while German Jews employed as translators were excluded by Army counterintelligence as "enemy nationals." Placing Paris' 180 registered brothels off limits to American troops simply drove an estimated 68,000 freelance prostitutes onto the streets. French women conspicuously courted GIs to gain access to the PX for cigarettes and other items unobtainable in France. The winter of 1944–1945 proved bitterly cold, straining electricity and coal supplies. A lack of petrol, manpower, and horses to harvest crops plunged food stocks to below occupation levels and forced many restaurants to close. Although Eisenhower allocated 1,000 trucks for civilian food transport, and even flew in food from the UK as Le Havre had been severely damaged, Parisians seemed to subsist on

K-rations. While the French begrudged what seemed to them a cushy GI lifestyle, American soldiers resented what they saw as French ingratitude for their liberation, as expressed by price gouging and Parisian incivility.[120]

In these conditions, Virgili argues that collective acts of retribution against collaborators were essentially cathartic, a way to deescalate the tensions of war and occupation, and transition to peace, with diminishing violence exercised against the "enemy." Retribution also provided a distraction against shortages. Payback against collaborators allowed the population to participate in the Liberation, to reaffirm a common patriotic identity, "a founding act of a new time." The fact that these rituals were often carried out in front of the town hall or the *monument aux morts* meant that they were interpreted as an act of purification and reappropriation of political and public spaces, along with town halls, prefectures, and markets. Punishments offered an assertion of republican identity in the spirit of Revolutionary precedent that legitimized the accusers, as well as testimony to the intensity of France's traumatization. In Paris, Saint-Sulpice was a favorite shearing spot, as was *la gare de l'Est*, the gateway of deportation. "Horizontal collaboration" symbolized defeat, the forfeiture of national dignity, and, at its extremes, fears of the disappearance of the French nation. Whatever its military shortcomings, at least resistance had sought to reclaim virility and male attributes – valiance, courage, and glory. Men who fought in the shadows formed the first circle around *les tondues*, to punish female betrayal that had soiled the nation and insulted the French people through sexual treason. Shearings offered a ritual of cleansing, a necessary first step for France to make a new beginning through the recovery of its global rank and national honor.[121]

Les tontes were also meant to make the "purges" visible, especially as official justice seemed both lethargic and inexcusably lenient. At Saint-Lô, the Departmental Liberation Committee disbanded in the spring of 1945 to protest "purges" that amounted to "a farce to put the people to sleep." Courts were acquitting and "whitewashing" too many people – an entrepreneur who had made money building the Atlantic wall was treated as a leading citizen; a former collaborator was running for public office; a PPF militant was licensed to open a barbershop; nor was the irony lost on the public when a sub-prefect who had spent the war hunting down resisters officially opened the hunting season in Coutance. "Nothing surprises us," it was said in Avranches, "the Vichyites are still kings!"[122]

To outsiders, these collective acts of vengeance carried out in a carnival atmosphere seemed like a revival of archaic rituals, a refutation of modernity and reassertion of some primeval savagery. "*Les tontes*" appeared to be the work of "September resisters," *attentistes* who, now that the Germans had fled, belatedly emerged in berets and FFI armbands, careening through the streets while precariously balanced on the running boards of black Citroëns, to seek out, bully, and assault females. Rather than being punished as "*les poules aux Boches*" ("German chickens") and "*putins et collabos*" ("whores and collaborators"), the shorn women became pitied as victims of the very men whose sexual insecurity, deficit of masculinity, and lack of courage had been responsible for France's defeat and decline. GIs viewed this head shaving as "harsh," "indecent and vicious," as well as "unmanly." Although warned not to get involved, GIs often came to the aid of these women. But, like *l'armée d'Afrique*, rather than these acts being understood as products of the pent-up hostility of the occupation, this revenge lowered the respect for FFI "as failed men and frustrated cuckolds." "Male mourning over lost honor and power coincided with contact with American soldiers," and influenced GIs' attitudes to FFI, who were looked down upon as small-in-stature, volatile, undisciplined soldiers, who often failed to follow orders, drank too much wine, and were in the habit of shooting German POWs and looting German corpses, accusations that they vehemently denied. They were also shocked when "young hooligans" exacted ugly resistance vengeance on "*collabos*." GIs resented that they were doing most of the fighting to liberate a nation that could not defend itself, a nation that deployed colonial soldiers as cannon fodder, but depended on the United States for virtually everything. This resentment especially came to the fore when American troops were halted so that French units could scurry forward to "liberate" a city such as Paris, Metz, or Strasbourg. De Lattre's soldiers dressed in a mix and match of US and French uniforms, were armed with an array of weapons, many of them German recycles recuperated on the battlefield, rode in every conceivable vehicle "from Austins to buses," were paid even less than Tommies, were fed poor-quality rations, and were perennially short of tobacco. The FFI returned GI contempt with crude stereotypes of their own, by denouncing American soldiers as spoiled and oversupplied, and as lacking courage in battle, advancing only after artillery, tanks, and air strikes had taken care of the enemy, and in the process turned French cities and towns to rubble.[123]

"*Les tontes*," along with grossly inflated claims by conservatives that between 50,000 and 100,000 people had been executed by vengeful FFI during a "blood bath" of "unauthorized purges," became essential ingredients in the "black legend" of the Liberation that Vichy apologists advanced to cover their own monstrous crimes.[124] These women were being punished for carnal pleasures amidst the suffering of the occupation. In this reading, much like the rapes perpetrated by soldiers of the CEF in Italy, "*les tontes*" constituted an inglorious episode, defined by hatred, vengeance, and misogyny, that sullied the memory of the Resistance. Liberation violence allowed Vichy, too, to claim victimization, which challenged the Gaullist liberation narrative.[125] In fact, the situation looked much worse than it was. The official number calculated by the Justice Ministry was 9,870 executed on the Liberation, a number which later studies confirmed.[126] Nor were these all revenge or extra-legal killings. In fact, an estimated 20–30 percent of these killings occurred before 6 June 1944, and another 50–60 percent, which would include, for instance, the death of Vichy propagandist Philippe Henriot at the hands of resisters, happened between 6 June and the liberation of a particular department. Admiral Charles Platon, Vichy's colonial secretary, who had been airlifted to Bizerte in November 1942, to facilitate the German invasion of Tunisia, was captured by resistance fighters at his home in Pujols between Toulouse and Bordeaux in July 1944. Found guilty of "*intelligence avec l'ennemi* " – that is, "treason" – he was allowed to command his own firing squad on 28 August, as German forces streamed out of southwestern France and Allied forces from Dragoon closed in. So fully three-quarters of these deaths constituted "acts of war." However, more right-wing historians eager to demonstrate the vengefulness of the resistance denounced these figures as gross underestimates.[127]

That said, it is true that women were disproportionately singled out for punishment on the Liberation. Of 31,380 people interned in February 1945 for collaboration, 10,430 were women, and this does not include "*les tondues*." Most were held for having sexual relations with Germans or keeping a bar where German troops met prostitutes. In some areas in the *zone occupée*, up to 60 percent of those incarcerated were women, with even higher proportions in the Morbihan and the Marne. On their repatriation to France, the "*travailleuses volontaires d'Allemagne*" were treated as prostitutes – which many of them had been – to be subjected to medical examinations to prevent the spread of venereal disease. Many of these incarcerated women were acquitted by *chambres civiques* – local tribunals created in 1944 to examine crimes of collaboration – because they had broken no law. Others, however, were given quite stiff sentences of five to fifteen years of "*indiginité nationale*," a generalized penalty often imposed for acts that were not specifically crimes, like joining a collaborationist political party, but which barred them from political office, voting, or practicing certain professions or occupations for a defined period.[128]

Everyone mocked "September resisters." But the fact remained that only with D-Day did the resistance expand, because only with the Liberation could most act. This made the summer of 1944 the bloodiest period for resistance.[129] Virgili argues that the shearings were anodyne punishments for women who otherwise might have been killed by crowds who often shouted "*à-mort-à-mort* " – indeed, one study of twenty departments calculates that 20 percent of those killed during the liberation were women.[130] A more "black legend" interpretation rejects this "letting off steam" function of Liberation exuberance as unconvincing. A focus on "*collabos*" offered an excellent distraction in a period of shortages. It demonstrated the intensity of social traumatization, gave satisfaction to the accusers, and delegitimized Vichy, a first step in national recovery and renovation.[131]

While the Gaullists and the army worried that FFI excesses might portend civil war, popular violence in France failed to match the level of Greece and Yugoslavia. Nor did retribution against "*collabos*" equal that meted out by Stalin to returning *Osttruppen* and *Ostarbeiter*. For the Americans, in most cases the FFI proved helpful in restoring order. Fears of a communist-led civil war proved unfounded, in great part because, even in the "red south," socialists and radicals emerged to check communist power.[132] By refusing "*l'amalgame*," the communists might have launched a "strategy of rupture" on the 1917 model to seize power in the name of the FFI. On the surface, the situation looked propitious: the party had rehabilitated itself by its vanguard role in resistance. Popular opinion supported PCF calls for purges. By the end of September, the party had exploded from 60,000 to 205,323 members. The PCF was prominent in local liberation committees. Prefects' reports noted that the PCF seemed to be everywhere. The FTP counted around 200,000 resisters in its ranks. But, despite all this, the situation was not ripe to pursue a "strategy of rupture." By September, most of the FFI had concluded that refusal to integrate into the regular army was not a viable political alternative. The French population was acclaiming de Gaulle, not exiled communist leader Maurice Thorez. Most of the "new communists" who had joined the party were more nationalist than communist, while maybe only 10–25 percent of rank-and -file FTP were communists. The Communist Party had difficulty controlling "its mass organizations," which put a "national insurrection" beyond reach. While the PCF had seized power in some localities, this did not translate into national power, when *commissaires de la République* and prefects named by de Gaulle were already in place, along with *Missions militaires de liaison administrative* and military commanders of regions and military subdivisions. The country was swamped by Anglo-American soldiers. Even though fears that de Gaulle would seize personal power lingered, the PCF's solidarity with the USSR dictated that it follow Stalin's priority, which was to defeat Germany, not execute a Paris power-grab. But just because a PCF seizure of power was not on the cards on liberation, the party was not prepared to acquiesce to a reinstallation of the "bourgeois state."[133]

On the military front, the FFI organizations defied orders to cease enlistments and continued to compete with the regular army for recruits. And, when FFI units arrived at the front, they frequently refused to submit to military authority.[134] Not all commanders viewed the FFI as ideal recruits, beginning with Leclerc, who judged 10 percent of them "very good, courageous and true soldiers," and 20–25 percent "acceptable and will follow orders." The majority he qualified as "riffraff and frauds," who seemed determined to incite civil war.[135] Indeed, included in the plans for Dragoon was the post-invasion disarming of the resistance, a process that did not always go smoothly. "The population was jubilant, and gave us a triumphal welcome," 6e RTM Second lieutenant Louis Bacquier remembered of a small village in the hills behind Fréjus. "A patriotic banquet was organized. Waves of eloquence flowed. Young men decked out with machineguns, grenades hanging from their suspenders, oversaw security. At dessert, the captain thanked everyone. This day marked the definitive return of peace to the village. Arms were no longer necessary. Teams of *tirailleurs* peacefully collected them. Faces showed a little discomfort, but I don't recall the slightest incident. It was true that we offered an excellent outlet for the patriotic ardor of those present. We would enlist volunteers to continue the war. No living in barracks. Just on-the-job training at the pace of combat. Battle and women all the way to Berlin! There was not one – I truly mean not one – volunteer."[136]

On 8 October, Colonel Schneider was informed by *Commissaire à la guerre* Diethelm that his "mobile group" was disbanded, and his soldiers placed at the disposal of General de Lattre, an order that de Lattre had to reiterate to the stubborn colonel two weeks later. De Lattre's solution was to standardize what had been a process of commanders simply enlisting FFI volunteers on an individual basis. Each group of 500 FFI would be organized into a "reduced battalion," with each armored division instructed to incorporate four of them, each infantry division five, with others placed in the general reserve. But it was clear that the mechanics of amalgamation had been placed onto de Lattre's shoulders, and to a lesser extent those of Leclerc and their subordinate commanders, who also had a war to fight. A process of weeding out of the unfit, underaged, foreigners, those who refused to complete enlistment papers, and so on significantly decreased numbers. Utilization of FFI formations was also impacted by the problem of clothing, arming, and feeding them, as well as supplying new units with radios, artillery support, transportation, and other accouterments of modern warfare. Each division was ordered to set up a training regiment, while in October an *école des cadres* was created at Valdahon in the Doubs, followed by a second one at Rouffach in the Haut-Rhin in March 1945. But commanders continued to complain about uneven capabilities and a lack of standardization which made units of FFI provenance difficult to deploy. So, in the autumn of 1944, divisions were left basically to evolve their own philosophies and methods to incorporate FFI.[137] This would not prove easy, as Bacquier speculated when his by now battle-hardened Moroccan *tirailleurs* were dispatched to Mulhouse in early January 1945 to collect an FFI contingent:

> The men waited for two or three hours with their weapons. Train service had done its best but was not quite perfection . . . The train finally arrived: twenty freight cars full of scruffy men bellowing war songs. The cars were entirely covered with grotesque slogans written in chalk, imbecile boasts: "the avengers of the fatherland," "the volunteers of death," . . . They disembarked in a screeching scrum before the impassive and

disdainful *tirailleurs*. When they marched before us in silence and in an order more or less reestablished, I couldn't bring myself to present arms.[138]

As in many wars, a real *amalgame* occurred among the various factions at the front in solidarity against the indifference of the "rear." Some of those FFI who had volunteered to fight considered themselves "mugs" or "suckers," especially as the war pushed to France's periphery, while the rear seemed to be swamped with military bureaucrats and FFI driving automobiles, living in requisitioned houses, and eating well. On 7 March 1945, communist resister and member of the Defense Committee of the Consultative Assembly Maurice Kriegel-Valrimont reported that, while French forces posted a ration strength of more than 1 million soldiers, fewer than 250,000 were serving in the Atlantic pockets, the Alpine region, or in Alsace, where a high percentage of soldiers were North African Muslims. And, just as in Italy, the Mohammeds or Ahmeds, all known by their numbers, were killed before anyone had time to learn their names. The non-participation of French civilians in the war, even their seeming indifference, became a source of profound bitterness in the *1ère Armée*.[139] Bacquier's platoon, which had a theoretical strength of thirty-five, never numbered more than twenty, and might be down to fifteen after a couple of days of hard combat. "I never understood why," he wrote. "The rear was full of men in a state to fight. For mysterious reasons, they never appeared at the front."[140]

For those at the front, "shirkers" were most ostentatiously typified by *les zazous*, who, dressed in their high collars, long jackets that reached to their knees, drainpipe trousers and suede shoes, slouched along the Boul' Mich and the Champs-Élysées, or crowded into reopened Latin Quarter jazz clubs with their giggling platinum blond girlfriends.[141] Resistance denunciation of *les zazous* and PCF admonitions to enlist fell on deaf ears. Brosset became indignant that his FFL continued to fight for a nation of "vanquished," who seemed absorbed by "end of war worries." The French had not ceased to support the war – polls showed that only 8 percent favored a compromise peace. There was also an outpouring of public initiatives to get warm clothing to soldiers at the front and to take care of the wounded. But, even though the war continued into winter, "end of war worries" for the population were hardly inconsequential, as working men had witnessed a 40 percent fall in the purchasing power of their wages, food supplies and coal were scarce, and infant mortality was on the rise. Families who had a son at the front, or remained without news of their POW/STO fathers, husbands, brothers, and sons, deeply resented those who seemed to have tuned out the war, especially as the Western Front congealed into a winter stalemate. The December 1944 German offensive in the Ardennes momentarily provoked tremors of apprehension. But, overall, the country felt secure behind the screen of US infantry, tanks, and planes. While *l'armée d'Afrique* may have felt that they had erased the shame of 1940, and de Gaulle proclaimed Paris to have self-liberated, most of the country gave credit to Eisenhower and his GIs.[142] Increasing public detachment from the war was also in part an expression of a growing divide between the population and the "resistance." While respecting their clandestine contribution to victory, many remained apprehensive about the resistance-incited popular justice, political disorder, and even assassinations and banditry that persisted into the autumn, not to mention the claims of some of the more progressive elements to assume a vanguard political role in France's renewal, fears that reinforced support for de Gaulle's restoration of republican institutions and stability.[143]

If volunteers in France felt disgruntled, the popular sentiment in AFN was that they had shouldered the war's burden since November 1942. One of the purposes of *l'amalgame*, after all, was to "metropolitanize" mobilization. Conscription had been applied in AFN and Corsica – AFN would dispatch 24,706 more replacements to France between 15 February and 24 April 1945 – while, in France, the army was still relying on volunteers. Worries increased in AFN as death notices continued to arrive, along with rumors about deteriorating conditions at the front. De Lattre informed Diethelm that North African Muslims believed that they were being "abusively exploited by the Metropole," especially as the interval between the breakthrough on the Garigliano and the launch of Dragoon had been only a few short weeks. Now *tirailleurs* and *goumiers* faced grueling winter conditions with inadequate uniforms and equipment. Lack of shipping meant that a maximum of 200 *pied noirs* could be given home leave each month. But many Algerians and Moroccans had not been given leave for almost a year and a half. By some marvel of French administrative logic, they had seen their pay cut with the argument that, now that they were fighting "at home," they no longer qualified for overseas pay. This had left many families without resources. In December, *tirailleurs* were given a modest pay raise, but it was still inferior to the amount paid to white troops and utterly inadequate to support their families as inflation ballooned. A disappointing 1944 harvest in AFN had flooded many towns with destitute rural refugees. "If the French are open to certain arguments: duty, patriotism . . ., the natives are not," de Lattre warned. "The result is a feeling of lassitude that, if one is not careful, will cause them to lose their combativity and resilience." Seventeen percent of Tunisian Muslims who had been sent mobilization notices had failed to report by February 1945. And, while officials believed that nationalist propaganda had not yet impacted Muslim mobilization, especially as there had been no anti-conscription demonstrations, the dawning conclusion was that, although the colonial order remained intact, it had "seriously eroded."[144]

As 1944 closed out, the General Staff in Paris noted that, over the past year, some battalions that had been part of the CEF had seen a 100 percent turnover of officers, while others had experienced an 85–90 percent replacement rate.

On 19 December 1944, de Lattre's *1ère Armée* reported officer casualties of 30 percent for the Tabors and 4e DMM, 50 percent for the 2e DIM and 9e DIC, and 109.3 percent casualties for the 3e DIA, a division in which statistically every soldier had experienced at least one trip to the hospital since landing in southern France four months earlier. AFN had already given up 70 percent of its mobilizable Europeans, creating what was felt to be a potentially dangerous situation should political disorder erupt among the Muslim population. Around 20,000 Senegalese had been demobilized from the ranks of the First French Army. With a limited ability to carry out more than a partial mobilization in France, the only way to sustain and expand the army was to fall back on an immediately available reservoir of an estimated 40,000–45,000 FFI. But this was complicated by the fact that the French were dependent on American forces for equipment and supplies, which would be forthcoming only for French soldiers included on the Combined Chiefs of Staff (CCS)-approved "troop list."[145] Nor were the Americans fooled by French attempts to pad rosters and overstock supplies, which left the French to rely on parachuted Sten guns, captured or abandoned German equipment, and "*le système D*" (improvisation). While even the most hardbitten *armée d'Afrique* cadres admired the enthusiasm of these FFI, they also commented upon their youth, their lack of fitness, training, and discipline, and an absence of leadership. Furthermore, "*le système D*" effectively encompassed many unattractive *maquis* practices – notably "pillaging" – which rather sabotaged the cause of good order and discipline. To throw these volunteers wholesale into combat without adequate training invited massacre.[146]

Several things helped to soften US resistance to French military expansion, beginning with the fact that Berlin doggedly refused to throw in the towel. By the end of October, most of Belgium and Luxembourg had been liberated, as well as Aachen, the first Allied-occupied German city. But American forces had become embroiled in the Battle of the Hürtgen Forest on the German–Belgian frontier that would churn until December. Metz and Strasbourg would be liberated in November, but de Lattre's advance had stalled in southern Alsace. The Ardennes offensive launched by the Germans on 16 December merely served to reinforce the conclusion Eisenhower had reached at the end of October, namely that he would in fact need the 137,000 French replacements who were to be battleworthy by May 1945, especially as the American army "combed through our own organization to find men in the Services of Supply and elsewhere who could be retrained rapidly for employment in infantry formations," who were often replaced by Women's Army Corps (WAC) personnel.[147] French plans to rehabilitate their army also found support from the British, who were eager to stand up enough French divisions to assist in the occupation of Germany and Austria, in this way liberating British divisions to close out the war against the Japanese. After four months of negotiations with the Anglo-Americans, on 30 November 1944, the French war commissariat evolved a plan for the creation of eight new divisions, including one armored and one mountain division, to incorporate into a Second French Army. Seven more divisions were to be raised for the Alpes and to lay siege to the "Atlantic pockets," where they were known as the *Forces françaises de l'ouest* (FFO), with a further three divisions earmarked for the Far East, as well as forty regiments for internal security. But where all these men were to come from when de Lattre's *1ère Armée* with a strength of 241,000 men was short some 58,000 support troops was unclear.[148]

Historical assessments of *l'amalgame* are mixed. The French army gradually stood up divisions made up almost entirely of FFI. The 27e DIA recruited heavily from *maquis* from the Alpes, while the 19e DI had a high proportion of Bretons and others from the west. By the end of January 1945, 39,000 volunteers, an unknown percentage of whom were former FFI, were serving in the ranks of the *1ère Armée*, plus 12,000–15,000 men in the all-FFI 10e DI integrated into the critical Vosges front. The estimated 40,000 foreigners in FFI ranks also proved a conundrum. The GPRF was reluctant to enlist them, as legally foreigners were not allowed to serve in French units, a prohibition that had been effectively waived in the First World War by enlisting volunteers in the Foreign Legion, and promptly transferring them to a line unit. The government also feared that many were communists. But, given de Lattre's pressing need for recruits, in the absence of statistics, Miot speculates that "several thousand" Poles, Czechs, Spaniards, and Italians "probably" found their way into the ranks of the *1ère Armée*.[149] Bacquier certainly mentions incorporating *Osttruppen* deserters into his 2e RTM in Alsace.

FFI field-grade officers came to "complete their training" at the front, where they were taught tactical techniques and the functioning of modern weapons. *L'école des cadres d'Uriage* reopened on 25 September, the first of several schools where officers would perfect their training in two-week courses, during which it would be possible to standardize army norms and procedures, as well as socialize officers from varied backgrounds. Koenig established a War College at Fontainebleau for senior commanders. In this way, de Lattre's *1ère Armée* became an "*armée école*," where graduates of the *écoles des cadres* were sent for evaluation. Tension between the various factions of the army hardly evaporated, and many FFI remained deeply resentful of career soldiers, who reciprocated their antipathy with professional disdain. But, whatever his personal idiosyncracies and professional limitations, de Lattre's tact and enthusiasm played an important role in transforming the *1ère Armée* from an assortment of bands and factions into an organization that was at least groping for cohesion and uniformity in very challenging circumstances.[150]

Sigmaringen

While the *1ère Armée* was poised to conclude liberation and participate in the invasion of Germany, a similar *amalgame* ensued across the Rhine. Although Laval acknowledged that the LVF experiment was failing catastrophically, not only in the quantity and quality of recruits, but also in the political divisions and absence of military efficiency of the organization, he remained deeply committed to collaboration. Consequently, on 22 July 1943, he had waived nominal Vichy sovereignty to permit French citizens to volunteer "to fight bolshevism, outside of French territory, in units constituted by the German government to be grouped in a French unit" – the *SS-Sturmbrigade Frankreich* – with the proviso that it would not be deployed in France. The French propaganda secretariat under Paul Marion distributed recruitment posters, that invited young Frenchmen "to keep the West in existence and preserve the spiritual culture of France and Europe."[151] Unfortunately for them, French volunteers would soon learn that the reputation of the *Schutzstaffel* (SS, literally "Protective Echelon") for military elitism was totally unmerited. The SS, which was launched as an armed wing of the Nazi Party – as distinct from the Wehrmacht – was promoted by Himmler as "the people's grenadiers" to embrace and mobilize a Teutonic *levée en masse* and to maintain order at home. From 1940, Himmler looked to recruit Nordic races as a step to the creation of an imperial military force for an expanding German empire. At various stages in the war, the SS swelled to incorporate communities of *Volksdeutsche* in the Balkans and Eastern Europe and recruits from occupied populations. Because the Wehrmacht controlled conscription, they got first pick of recruits. But also, many Germans shunned the SS as a political service with a reputation like that of the SD for thuggish behavior. By 1943, as the Reich's manpower resources had become stretched, even "racially impure" recruits such as Walloons, French, and Spaniards were courted by the SS. In 1942, Himmler had used his political influence to acquire panzers and artillery to create and motorize SS field divisions, which the Wehrmacht to this point had vigorously and successfully opposed. But SS efficiency was compromised by the fact that its "Black Order" leadership was chosen for reasons of party loyalty, political connections, and "strong personality," rather than professional proficiency. Himmler's patronage guaranteed his SS underlings a ceaseless drizzle of medals and promotions. But political patronage and a parallel hierarchy also meant that the SS behaved more like a gang than a military organization, one in which division commanders under Himmler were allowed the autonomy and political cover to ignore orders they judged inconvenient.[152]

Units were assigned names that flattered the nationalism of their recruits and sought to impart a regional identity. But the Germans disdained French *laisser-aller* that in their view had contributed to France's 1940 implosion. According to LVF volunteer Pierre Rostaing, the French returned their contempt through small acts of disrespect or non-compliance that fell short of the level of a punishable offense, but rather demonstrated a Gallic independence of spirit. Much of this tension centered on the oath, a regular feature of life in the German forces. All French volunteers, whether LVF or SS, swore to serve Adolf Hitler "and the struggle against Bolshevism" as "loyal soldiers." Required to take an oath to serve Hitler at least three times during his service, Rostaing opined that, while most French volunteers were happy to fight Communists, they were less keen to swear allegiance to Hitler. So, while the men would raise their hands as required while a German officer read out the oath, they would not repeat it, and so claimed subsequently not to be bound by it. The same objections occurred when members of *la Milice* were later incorporated into the Charlemagne Division, to the point that *Milice* leader Joseph Darnand soothed the scruples of his *miliciens* by interpreting the pledge to serve Hitler as a military rather than a political commitment, although what that meant in practice was unclear.[153]

Around 20,000 French are reckoned to have served in the Waffen SS after Himmler took control of foreign volunteer units in the last two years of the war. While SS soldiers were meant to be a racial elite, their training became increasingly perfunctory as the war progressed. Having completed his baccalaureate exam in July 1942, André Bayle witnessed the German occupation of his native Marseilles in November. This triggered vivid childhood memories of the Berlin Olympics, and his first view of black-uniformed SS framed in a dazzling extravaganza of Swastikas and excited crowds, that had left an indelible impression. As a former Sea Scout, Bayle had imagined a career in the navy or merchant marine. But after the High Seas Fleet scuttle swept the maritime option off the table, he volunteered to work for the Todt Organization. Sent to Alsace, he enlisted in the SS, and, with 2,480 French volunteers who had arrived by December 1943, was tattooed with his blood group under his arm. Most of his fellow volunteers were just out of school and "sincere idealists." Training consisted mostly of sport and singing, with occasional visits to the rifle range where they shot at painted wooden heads – blue for French, khaki for English. Three times a month their penis was checked for venereal disease, and their anus for evidence of homosexuality. He returned to Paris on leave for Christmas 1943 in his SS uniform and claimed to have met with no hostility.[154]

Selected to become an NCO despite his youth, Bayle was sent to Poznań for a further eight-week training course, which proved much more arduous than had the earlier basic training, with an emphasis on squad tactics, firing, and night marches under the supervision of a Walloon whose orders issued in French were confusing for soldiers who had been trained to obey German commands. While it was becoming clear that they had enlisted in a forlorn cause, according to Bayle everyone was determined to honor their oath to Hitler and to build a new Europe. In fact, Bayle paints a rosy picture of SS training. The truth was that rapid expansion, heterogeneity, and language problems among those who, by March 1945, numbered 829,400, about half of whom were non-German, often saw NCOs plucked out of the police reserve, and junior officers elevated from the ranks through "battlefield promotions." This militated against unit cohesion and an ability to operate in a combined arms environment. *Waffenoberführer der SS* Edgar Puaud continued this tradition of "irregular promotions" in what was to become his Charlemagne Division, without ensuring that they had the perquisite qualifications or time in rank.[155] Many SS recruits whose training lasted a bare four weeks by war's end might not know how to fire their weapons, handle anti-tank guns, or drive their vehicles. One result was that the road discipline which had characterized the 1940 attack on France deteriorated sharply. These drawbacks did not become readily apparent until 1944, when the Waffen-SS ceased to be treated as the Wehrmacht's "strategic reserve" and moved into the front lines, which resulted in the rapid destruction of the SS Panzer Divisions. The SS attempted to maintain a fearsome reputation through bluff, by pursuit of the "dramatic act," and by cultivating a culture of violence that was frequently directed against defenseless civilians, as showcased at Oradour. But the war of attrition exposed the hollowness of the unit's reputation for battlefield ferocity, which lingers largely because of a mythology of heroism promoted by post-war Lost Cause romanticism.[156]

The LVF's finale came in the summer of 1944. On 22 June 1944, the Soviets had unleashed Operation Bagration in Belarus. To cover the German retreat across the Berezina River near Borisov, the LVF was ordered to hold the front along the Bobr River, a tributary of the Oder. Pierre Rostaing remembered the Soviet offensive arriving like the rumble of an earthquake on 26 June. Although reinforced by four Tiger tanks, the LVF had no anti-tank guns. While the Tigers knocked out a few Soviet T-34s, a shower of mortar shells rained down on the French position. The LVF managed to hold the line for a day. This constituted the LVF's most notable military action, as well as its curtain call. The LVF was withdrawn to the Danzig corridor where it was to amalgamate with other French refugees from *la Milice* into the SS.[157]

At the end of eight weeks of training, Bayle had been assigned to the artillery. However, as everyone's ambition was to become a *Panzergrenadier*, he feigned illness, which delayed his departure to the artillery school near Prague, and allowed him to join the *Französische SS-Freiwilligen Sturmbrigade*, which everyone called the *Sturmbrigade* or the *Brigade Frankreich* because it was easier to pronounce.[158] On 15 July 1944, they entrained for Galicia with their machineguns painted with nicknames – La Sardine, Bonne Chance, and

Monica – where on 10 August 1944, they had their baptism of fire as part of the Horst Wessel Division. For twenty-two days in August, they were engaged at Sanok, and subsequently in the forests of Tarnów. At the end of this "catastrophic" engagement, the *Brigade Frankreich* had been reduced to 170 soldiers fit for service.[159]

In June 1944, some, like Abetz and Doriot, had been eager to deploy the *Brigade Frankreich* against the Anglo-Americans. However, this had been vetoed by Laval and the Germans, with good cause – Rostaing recorded that, when news arrived of the Normandy invasion, the general hope was that *Sturmbrigade Frankreich* would be sent west so that many of its soldiers might desert to the Americans, as "an audacious way to get a pardon, they thought."[160] However, with the breakthrough on the Normandy front from late July 1944, followed by Dragoon on 15 August, and the liberation of Paris ten days later, the refugee flow turned east.

On 17 August 1944, as the Allied armies closed in on Paris, Joseph Darnand had ordered each *Milice* regional leader to evacuate his subordinates and their families to Germany. By then, some *miliciens* had already hit the road, joining improvised convoys of "requisitioned" vehicles heading east. In all, an estimated 10,000–15,000 French collaborators joined this strategic repositioning to Germany, which included around 6,000 militiamen led by 1,800 remnants of Darnand's *Francs-Gardes*, and perhaps 4,000 family members, as well as other right-wing refugees, mainly members of the PPF.[161] The convoys, joined by members of the PPF or Rassemblement national populaire (RNP) who feared for their lives, often had to fight off resistance ambushes, but found time to empty bank vaults and tobacco shops along their route of retreat. Patriot to the last, Darnand hoped to make a last stand at Belfort, "so as not to be dependent on the SS or the Wehrmacht," he explained at his post-war trial. But, after thoroughly pillaging Belfort, what can only be described as a rolling rabble of rightist refugees entered Alsace, where Darnand sought to raise deflated spirits by promising a reconquest of France. The cavalcade briefly lingered at the Natzweiler–Struthof death camp in the Vosges mountains, where thirty *milicien* deserters were shot. But, with the approach of Allied armies, on 21 September, this mongrel pack lurched into Germany. Most of the *miliciens* and their families were settled in Ulm. Pétain and Laval were installed in a supervised residence about 80 kilometers distant in Sigmaringen – a gingerbread château perched on a rock in the middle of the town, where, even in the castle's most remote bedrooms, the deafening chapel organ made sleep impossible during Mass. In this fantasy décor, the Marshal presided over a sham "governmental commission" recognized only by Berlin, Japan, and Mussolini's Republic of Salò. But, because the plan of Pétain and Laval to remain at Vichy and attempt to strike a "Darlan deal" with the Allies had been stymied by Hitler, they considered themselves prisoners and began to prepare their legal defense.[162]

At Ulm, militiamen and their families were given an ironic choice under the circumstances – "work or fight." That is, STO, an option that some had joined *la Milice* to avoid, or enlist in the SS. To encourage cooperation, Darnand was offered the plum position of "political animator" of a French SS brigade, the first installment on a French force that, it was promised, would expand to several divisions. At last, collaboration would be rewarded, "Kamerad" Darnand was assured. Thus, 2,500 *miliciens* were directed to Wildflecken to begin training, and, thereafter, to join a French unit to be named after either Jeanne d'Arc or Charlemagne. Five hundred, who were judged too old or too young for active service, were sent to Sigmaringen as Pétain's personal guard under Darnand's command. Two thousand militiamen along with their families were installed at Sießen, a camp 35 kilometers from Sigmaringen, where conditions were primitive, hunger and sickness endemic, and death, especially of young children, common. From there, apart from women with very young children, the Sießen inmates were assigned to various factories, where they would join other French forced laborers. Seven to eight hundred of the refugees, labeled "*les clochards de la milice*" because they were considered virtually useless, were transferred to a camp at Heuberg close to Sigmaringen.[163]

These military refugees were dispatched to train at Wildflecken, where they were incorporated into the two regiments of the 33rd Waffen-Grenadier SS Charlemagne Brigade. Rostaing recorded that *la Milice* marched into the Adolf-Hitler-Platz at Wildflecken in their blue uniforms and *berets basques* singing the *Madelon* and the *Marseillaise*. Although everyone was given black SS uniforms, the amalgamation was far from smooth: fights between former *Milice* who had elevated Darnand into a cult figure, SS, and LVF punctuated this merger of the LVF (Infantry Regiment 638), survivors of the *Brigade Frankreich*, the *4. Nationalsozialistisches Kraftfahrkorps (NSKK) Motorgruppe Luftwaffe* (a transport unit made up of 2,500 drivers and mechanics attached to the Luftwaffe from July 1942, which had seen service in the Balkans, Denmark, Hungary, and Romania), Kriegsmarine, and French workers for the Todt Organization – in all perhaps 7,500 men – into the Charlemagne Brigade in September 1944. "This was a difficult birth because it gave rise to political arguments that revealed the divergent viewpoints between the LVF and *la Milice* that opted above all for the Waffen-S.S." Members of the *Milice* and LVF balked at being commanded in German. LVF members insisted that incorporating them into the SS was a violation of the promise that they would serve in a French unit. According to Rostaing, those in the Kriegsmarine objected to being assimilated with "foot-sloggers," while many LVF members simply deserted or attempted to resign. The Third Reich was facing annihilation, and the French were quibbling over the fine print in their enlistment contracts! In fact, many had come to realize that what may have seemed in 1942 or 1943 to have been an idealistic or bold decision to enlist in the victorious German army had in fact channeled them into the Third Reich's death embrace.[164]

The arrival of *la Milice* especially had stirred factionalism as more French worms were added to a bucket already writhing with nationalists, anti-communist crusaders, "Europeans," messianic Christian redeemers, Nazi-inspired pagans, gangsters, pimps, and other bottom-feeders. Unfortunately for these French, even in the Third Reich's twilight, the Germans retained robust remedies for dealing with dissent – around 200 LVF members who refused to join the SS subsequently traded field gray for the stripped pajamas of the Natzweiler–Struthof concentration camp.[165] Training at the SS camp at Wildflecken was much tougher than "Jew hunts" or sacking eateries in Limoges or Lyon, especially on inadequate rations. This latest reiteration of this down-market army of Condé was sustained by the dream of reentering France in a conquering vanguard. As a down payment, an *Organisation technique* created "Spy Schools" under German direction, whose graduates were to infiltrate a "white *maquis*" into France to carry out executions, "purges, and the settling of scores," as well as supplying intelligence to the Germans. A few, mainly former PPF members, were sent to France, where most were quickly arrested, but not before they managed to execute some minor sabotage operations.[166]

Like the LVF, *miliciens* objected to being commanded in German and taking an oath to serve Hitler. While Rostaing insisted that the three-month training period, all carried out in German, was rigorous, in fact, because it was based on no uniform military procedures, every officer and NCO trainer basically applied his own methods. Even Rostaing admitted that there were never enough weapons, so that troops had to share their arms. Nor were they ever issued heavy weapons before departing for the front in February 1945. In fact, most were not even issued helmets or grenades, but were flung into combat with only a rifle and twenty cartridges. "Overall, the brigade had no idea how to fight against tanks, or cooperate with them," read a post-war evaluation. "Nor did they know how to protect themselves against air attack, as the men considered any air defense exercise to be a punishment."[167]

On 2 February 1945, the brigade was upgraded to a two-regiment Charlemagne Division. Although the Germans had scant confidence in Puaud, he was breveted *Oberführer* – literally "senior leader," an SS rank between colonel and brigadier – because, although a fanatical anti-communist, he was associated neither with Doriot nor with Darnand, and so was unlikely to "politicize" his force. In this way, Puaud became the "straw commander" behind whom *Brigadeführer* Gustav Krukenberg would effectively lead his "badly equipped, badly trained" brigade, which entered the line against the Russians at Hammerstein in Pomerania on 18 February 1945. "The shock was decisive: offloaded 800 meters from Russian tanks that shot at point-blank range, they suffered 75 percent losses." The survivors were reorganized and resumed their retreat. Puaud went missing after a 12 March engagement, which triggered more desertions. "While some men barricaded themselves in Kolberg, the others fled toward the center of Germany." About 1,200 survivors were regrouped into five companies by a Colonel Herscher. They marched and countermarched for most of April. As a final irony, a handful of French *Untermensch* survivors gathered in the ruins of the Berlin air ministry, ostensibly to protect Hitler's bunker, before finally surrendering on 30 April. Of 7,600 volunteers, perhaps 15–20 percent survived.[168]

Conclusion

As a mechanism of social control, *l'amalgame* might be considered a partial success, insofar as it formed part of a larger Gaullist strategy to reestablish a legal state and curtail the temporary anarchy of the Liberation. But many of the more politicized FFI simply declined to be integrated into de Lattre's *1ère Armée*, in order to remain politically active in Paris or Toulouse. *L'amalgame*'s military utility is more debatable. In one respect, the GPRF really had no choice – its exhausted Anfa divisions were desperate for replacements, while AFN manpower had already been mobilized beyond levels that were demographically sustainable or politically prudent. One goal of *l'amalgame*, and its corollary, the *blanchiment*, had been to transform an imperial army into a metropolitan one, through the conversion of FFI into conventional soldiers. But, insofar as it was a product of military necessity, *l'amalgame* lacked means. The American-directed training apparatus set up in AFN was dismantled after Dragoon, which meant that training for former FFI and volunteers was ad hoc and piecemeal, at the very moment when the *1ère Armée* was to face one of the most challenging campaigns of the war in Alsace. For regular soldiers, the biggest "*fantaisie*" of *l'amalgame* was the attempt to maintain FFI units as distinct organizations within a larger army framework.[169] In the chaos of Liberation, integrating complete FFI units seemed both administratively practical and politically expedient. But the experiment was completely abandoned by early 1945, as a second phase opened with the deployment in Alsace of the fully FFI 10e DI to relieve imperial troops and allow the *1ère Armée* to defend Strasbourg. For this reason, the entire process had witnessed a succession of compromises and ad hoc solutions concocted on the fly amid war and Liberation. Nor did Washington agreed to arm and equip French divisions beyond the troop limits set at Anfa, which set back de Gaulle's goal of creating a large army to increase France's clout in the Alliance, stake out an occupation zone in Germany, and position Paris to be a post-war player. Miot suggests that *l'amalgame* might be considered a "semi-failure," in part because it was never fully achieved in 1944.[170] It remained to be seen in the final campaign whether

France could field a real army, or *une armée en trompe l'œil.*[171] In the meantime, many of the Vichy loyalists were evacuated to Sigmaringen, accompanied by a rump of *Francs-Gardes* and their families. Few of the collaborators who were evacuated to Germany to be integrated into what became the Charlemagne Division survived.

8 Les Vosges

Many in France were prepared to savor the remainder of the war as an extended "afterword." While Brittany and the Basse Normandie were battered, and Alsace and the Atlantic pockets awaited liberation, the occupation had ended rapidly for the vast majority of the population. *L'amalgame* aimed to sustain the army and repair French civil–military relations, but also to enlist the French in their own liberation, disarm the resistance, curtail disorder, and resuscitate the State. Despite a stubborn Teutonic reluctance to accept the inevitable, the Allies seemed to have the situation well in hand. Many in France were eager to put the unpleasantness of the occupation behind them and get on with their lives. So, what remained at stake for France in the last winter of the war?

At a quarter of a million men organized by January 1945 into two armored and five infantry divisions, sixteen artillery groups (three of which were heavy artillery), six tank destroyer regiments, seven engineer/pioneer regiments, fourteen motor transport groups, ten muleteer companies, plus odds and ends of support units (quartermaster, fuel, transport) which logistically gave "a degree of self-sufficiency," Jean de Lattre de Tassigny's French First Army constituted only 11 percent of Eisenhower's seventy-one divisions.[1] Although the First Army was banished to the extreme right wing of a vast Anglo-American military array, from de Gaulle's perspective, the last months of the war could not be outsourced to the Anglo-Americans for a number of reasons, beginning with the fact that Alsace was symbolic territory to be reclaimed by French arms. There also remained a million French prisoners of war (POWs) in Germany, to which one must add several hundred thousand *Service du travail obligatoire* (STO) laborers, as well as political and "racial" deportees, to liberate. The traitors who had fled – willingly or not – with the retreating Germans to Sigmaringen, led by Pétain and many of his closest Vichy collaborators, as well as *Francs-Gardes* of *la Milice* and their families, where they joined volunteers grouped in the Charlemagne Division, had to be apprehended, repatriated, and judged.

Above all, in the wake of Liberation, the French army had to be reconstituted as a viable national force composed of citizen soldiers. This would offer a first step toward mending tattered French civil–military relations, resurrect a heroic narrative to expunge the dishonor of 1940 and the humiliation of occupation, restore French virility and self-respect, and inflict a measure of revenge on France's historic enemy. An active French presence in the Allied armies would recoup France's great power status, give Paris a place at the table in deciding the fate of post-war Germany, adjourn the chance of a last-minute "Darlan deal" with one of Hitler's henchmen, and hence help to restore France's leadership role in Europe. Paris sought an occupation zone in Germany and Austria, to participate fully in post-war institutions of European and international governance, to join the war against Japan, and to recover Indochina. For all these reasons, an exhausted and politically riven country had to muster its energies for a crowning effort.

The Vosges

The fighting in the Vosges in the winter of 1944–1945 is sometimes labeled "the Forgotten Campaign." However, in many respects, perhaps "the Forgettable Campaign" offers a more accurate descriptor, although it was hardly that for those forced to endure it. To speculate whether Alsace might have become an important front where different command decisions might have shortened the war by several months is to meander through merely one of several counterfactual conjectures. Nevertheless, because the Vosges ranked near the bottom of Eisenhower's list of strategic priorities, a few more "missed opportunity" episodes were added to a narrative that had stalked the Supreme Headquarters Allied Expeditionary Force (SHAEF) commander since Algiers in 1942. Depending on one's viewpoint, Eisenhower was toasted or disparaged for a practically slavish adherence to "the plan" – in this instance a broad front advance whose primary objective was to sweep up German forces west of the Rhine (Map 8.1).[2]

Yet, there were reasons – some objective, others perhaps less disinterested – why Ike defaulted to an agreed set of ground rules rather than spin off strategic decisions on the fly as opportunities beckoned. Primary among them was the fact that he led the military forces of a diverse coalition, led by strong personalities, each with his own political and personal objectives that surged to the fore as Germany's defeat loomed. Among the more subjective reasons for downgrading the Vosges front in Eisenhower's mind was that de Gaulle and the French had little clout in Allied decision-making. Consequently, the French leader would become even more assertive – if that were possible – in his demands to prioritize French interests. Second, Eisenhower put scant faith in the military capabilities of the French First Army, or in its mercurial and relatively inexperienced commander Jean de Lattre de Tassigny. Had de Gaulle named the highly respected Alphonse Juin rather than de Lattre to command the *1ère Armée*, then French counsels might have weighed more

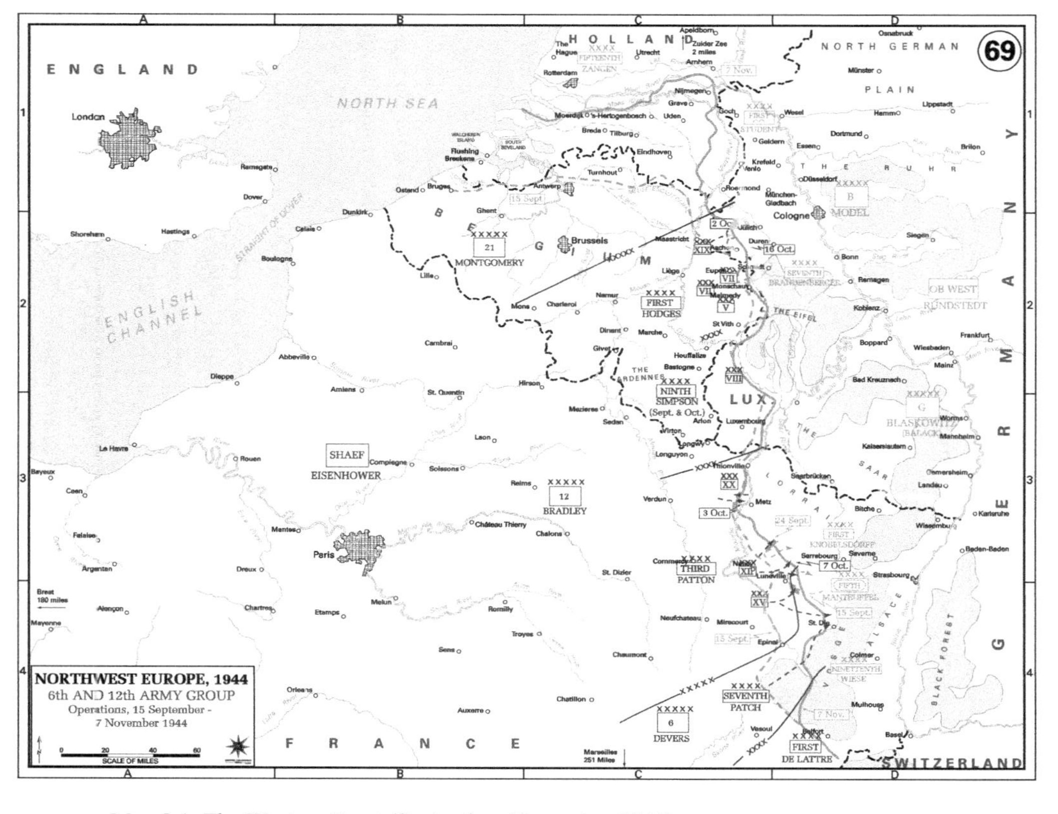

Map 8.1 The Western Front (September–November 1944).

heavily in Allied decision-making, but possibly not – the *1ère Armée* was not the *Corps expéditionnaire français* (CEF). And its mission was as much a political as a military one. Eisenhower opined to Marshall in January 1945 that French forces "are always a questionable asset," whose divisions had "low combat value."[3] There were probably many factors that contributed to Eisenhower's low assessment of French military potential, beginning with 1940, and reinforced by the antiquated armaments of *l'armée d'Afrique* in 1942–1943. Part of his problem might have been cultural skepticism of the cohesion and combat potential of a multiracial French force, in that the American army did not thrust African Americans into combat roles until forced to do so by manpower constraints toward the end of the war. The political dysfunction and infighting that Ike had witnessed between Gaullists and Giraudists in North Africa, a discordance repeated on multiple levels during the Liberation of France, reinforced a generalized opinion among the Allies that the French remained preoccupied with their divisive internal politics, rather than getting on with the war.

On the operational and tactical level, while Anfa had sought to upgrade the French army, it remained an unbalanced force. A lack of technical specialists had been a problem in North Africa, one that *l'armée d'Afrique*'s endemic antisemitism did little to rectify. Yet, it had also been a choice among the architects of French military renewal to favor combat over support troops in a bid "to restore national honor," one endorsed by patriotic recruits who had no desire to skulk as *planqués* in support units. Signals were in acceptable shape, but de Lattre's force was particularly short of combat engineers, supply, and fuel specialists. Lack of logistical capacity especially complicated the shell supply for the artillery – the largest logistical item by weight – because much of the First Army's artillery inventory was guns of First World War legacy or upgrades bequeathed by the Americans as they modernized the US arsenal. This would lead to clashes between de Lattre, who complained that the First Army was logistically shortchanged by Sixth Army Group, and the Americans, who countered that the French had failed to organize adequate logistical capacity to receive and distribute matériel. The First Army contained so few medical personnel that medical equipment earmarked for them was redirected to other Allied units. Obviously, this would impact morale.[4] A further contributor to Franco-American discord was de Gaulle's decision, for political and manpower reasons, to "amalgamate" *l'armée d'Afrique* with *Forces françaises de l'intérieur* (FFI) and other in-country volunteers to create a truly national army. While this decision made sense on political and manpower levels, it further hybridized the French army, which had to restructure while fighting, further compromising military proficiency – and hence Allied confidence in French operational and tactical effectiveness.

Fraught relations between Eisenhower and de Lattre's US superior – Sixth Army Group commander Jacob Devers, whom Ike mistrusted as a professional and personal rival – might also have impacted SHAEF's strategic priorities and downgraded the Vosges front. In fact, initially Eisenhower had preferred to send Alexander Patch's Seventh Army to Bradley's Twelfth Army Group. However, the inclusion of French forces in the Allied order of battle as an independent army, rather than distributed piecemeal within established US or British forces, required the creation of an American-dominated command echelon, lest de Gaulle insist on naming his own army group commander.[5] In the event, Eisenhower habitually prioritized the fronts, armies, and advice of Omar Bradley and the steroidal George Patton. He also needed to mollify Twenty-First Army Group, so as not to boost Bernard Montgomery's covert campaign to supplant him as SHAEF commander. Ike's requirement to mollify Montgomery was to spark an end-of-year crisis with de Gaulle over the defense of Strasbourg. Finally, a combination of challenging terrain, atrocious weather, and unanticipated German tenacity in the defense of what Berlin regarded as its *Oberrhein* province conspired in Eisenhower's mind to transform Alsace into an unpromising strategic venue.

On 15 September, Alexander Patch's Seventh Army and de Lattre's *1ère Armée*, folded into Devers' Sixth Army Group, had reached the Swiss frontier, and prepared to assault the Belfort Gap, which was believed to be lightly occupied by a jumble of broken Nineteenth Army units. However, that operation was suddenly halted, as control of Devers' command transitioned from Maitland Wilson's Mediterranean Allied Forces Headquarters (AFHQ) to that of Eisenhower at SHAEF. In the early autumn of 1944, Allied forces formed a huge arc, with Montgomery's Twenty-First Army Group consisting of the First Canadian and Second British Armies numbering five corps on the left flank, while the center was occupied by Bradley's Twelfth Army Group consisting of the First and Third US Armies, which combined seven corps. The US Ninth Army, still in Brittany, would join the Twelfth Army Group in October. The Allied right flank, held by Devers' single-corps Seventh Army and the two corps of de Lattre's *1ère Armée*, was, at this opening stage of the siege of Germany, by far the most "insignificant" of the three army groups, one barely eligible for the designation. Devers' request to bulk up his anemic command by transferring American units from Italy was denied by Wilson. Focused on clearing German forces from the Scheldt Estuary, to open Antwerp, and on penetrating the Ruhr, and blind to the potential of a hook through southern Germany, Eisenhower had no real operational task for Devers beyond "holding the flank," while destroying German forces manning defensive fortifications between the Sixth Army Group and the Rhine. In fact, the Sixth Army Group's *raison d'être* was to buffer Eisenhower, so that he would not need to deal directly with de Lattre, and by extension de Gaulle. This left Devers great latitude to evolve his own operational goals, especially as for the moment he benefited from an independent logistical chain stretching back to Toulon and Marseilles.[6]

However, by late September, Devers faced at least three problems. First, Sixth Army Group's sector included the Vosges Mountains, where the Germans were determined to make a stand. Second, as Eisenhower noted, the "efficiency" of one of the major components of his Sixth Army Group – de Lattre's *1ère Armée* – "rapidly fell off with the arrival of winter weather in late 1944."[7] But Truscott's VI Corps had also lost a step due to fatigue, almost 10,000 casualties, increasingly etiolated logistics that stretched back to the Mediterranean, "the hilly, often wooded ground that gave many advantages to the defense," and the onset of winter rains, which complicated ground operations and reduced the availability of air support.[8] Finally, relations between Eisenhower and Devers had been frayed since December 1942 by a series of clashes which had caused Eisenhower to conclude that the man who now had become his direct subordinate was a "lightweight in over his head." This launched a whispering campaign of character assassination against Devers in Eisenhower's inner circle, piloted by George Patton, who pronounced Devers ".22 caliber," a verdict retailed by Eisenhower's staff and some of his closest associates, including Bradley. While Devers' organizational talents and technician's eye for tank design had attracted the attention of George Marshall, he had acquired a reputation in the US Army as a know-it-all with strong opinions on strategy and especially on the tactical deployment of armored forces, but who was in fact a "rear area soldier" with limited combat experience. Nevertheless, Devers' uninhibited and often tactless criticism of his fellow senior commanders began to gain traction as strategic opportunities offered by the precipitous German retreat slipped away in the late summer and autumn. Logistical constraints that allegedly slackened the advance of the Anglo-American armies increasingly appeared to be an alibi for Eisenhower's absence of *coup d'œil*, his seeming inability to prioritize, his deference shown to the Bradley–Patton command tandem, and an overweening desire to placate Montgomery and Churchill. As a result, the campaign in the European Theater of Operations (ETO), which had optimistically been projected to end before Christmas 1944, lengthened into the bitter winter of 1944–1945.[9]

Although, since 6 June, the Germans had been hammered and disorganized in France, the US Army's official history does not judge this mid-September halt order in Alsace a squandered opportunity. Under the slogan "time against space," the Wehrmacht had quickly recovered its equilibrium, concentrating its best remaining troops in the West in the belief that Berlin could delay the Anglo-American–French advance until new weapons came on line, which would deliver tactical victories that would split the alliance. Although this was an unconvincing theory of victory as the Third Reich's clock was clearly running out, caught within the poles of "the Führer's apocalyptic vision of 'victory or annihilation'" in the autumn of 1944, "time against space" galvanized the resolve even of "many who did not see themselves as Nazis," writes Nicholas Stargardt. "As the ruthless logic of defending Germany at its borders took hold, there was a new murderousness in the air."[10] At only three corps, this new Franco-American Sixth Army Group was understrength, exhausted, and had suffered significant attrition in its sprint up the Rhône Valley. Furthermore, logistical problems, a lack of close air support, the challenging terrain of the Vosges mountains, and deteriorating weather would have complicated the exploitation of any breakthrough into southern Alsace even had it been possible. Nevertheless, the delay gave a banged-up German Nineteenth Army a breather. Wiese's actual troop numbers were unknown, probably even to him. But he was able to align something in the region of 55,000 troops, not all of them combat formations by any means, some rushed in from Norway, along a front stretching from Strasbourg to Belfort behind a defense line backed by some field artillery and about twenty-five tanks. On 21 September, Hitler replaced Army Group G commander Blaskowitz with Lieutenant General Hermann Balck.[11]

Eisenhower, Bradley, and Patton were focused on Metz, "the capital of the Maginot Line" surrounded by fortifications, the most powerful being Fort Driant. Metz was finally seized by the Americans on 22 November.[12] During this period, Devers had a relatively free hand to organize his 90-mile front, along the Vosges. A thickly wooded mountain chain with peaks rising to over 1,000 meters that measures about 70 miles from north to south and is 30–40 miles wide, the Vosges were far easier to bypass than to penetrate, especially from September when heavy rains gradually transitioned to snow. The Alsace plain that borders the Rhine and upon which are located the cities of Strasbourg, Colmar, and Mulhouse is best accessed via the Saverne Gap to the north of the mountains, or that of Belfort to the south. The only person who saw an opportunity in this apparent strategic sideshow in Alsace was de Lattre because, despite being on the periphery of the main action, at least he commanded his own sector in the Belfort Gap between the slopes of the southern Vosges and the Swiss frontier.[13]

Eager to attack before Weise could solidify his defenses, on 20 September, VI Corps commander Lucian Truscott launched his three divisions across the Moselle in a northeasterly direction along a minimalist road network through the Vosges with Strasbourg as his distant objective. Caught by surprise, the Germans allowed the Americans to establish lodgments on the right bank of the Moselle. But, by 25 September, Truscott's advance had slackened as it diffused into the narrow, wooded valleys of what are called the High Vosges, where Weise held the defensive advantage. Patton's drive on Metz had stalled for the

Figure 8.1 De Lattre with Sixth Army Group Commander Jacob Devers, I Corps commander Émile Béthouart, and II Corps commander Goislard de Monsabert, posed before the Lion of Belfort, November 1944. (Photo12/UIG/Getty Images)

moment, leaving the Saverne Gap and Strasbourg beyond firmly in German hands. Overextended fronts, the slow arrival of reinforcements for units that were seriously understrength following the fighting in Normandy and the chase across France, and logistical delays caused the Allied advance to stall at the onset of winter.[14] With his *1ère Armée* strung out along a 75-kilometer front, de Lattre (Figure 8.1) appealed directly to Devers over the head of Patch, whom de Lattre regarded as "not up to the rapid change of events," lamenting that he lacked adequate artillery support, munitions, and gasoline, all of which he complained were being allocated disproportionately to the Americans.

In de Lattre's telling, his protest had caused Devers to pull back on extending the length of de Lattre's front. Also, on 1 October, 65,000 gallons of gasoline, 53,000 rations, and 279 tons of ammunition purloined from US stocks materialized for French forces, with another 60,000 gallons of gasoline promised on 2 October, although, "in private, Seventh Army logisticians believed that French supply problems stemmed largely from inadequacies in their own supply services."[15]

But nothing seemed to mollify the temperamental French commander, who continued to criticize his US partners, superiors, and suppliers to the press. "I couldn't accept constantly and unexpectedly the idea of having a new boundary imposed on me," he wrote.[16] However, de Lattre's volcanic "tirades," which Devers judged to erupt at least twice a week, hardly raised his stock with his US superiors.[17] But, to be fair to de Lattre, he placed a distant second to George Patton, who may have skillfully and publicly deployed logistical alibis to mask command failures on multiple levels, and to force Eisenhower to increase Third Army's petrol allocation or face a public backlash for shortchanging America's most flamboyant and successful rival to Montgomery and Rommel. Nor was American command skullduggery, not to mention "leakage" into the black market, entirely absent from the politics of supply allocation.[18]

Furthermore, what Devers dismissed as just another of de Lattre's public tantrums may have been carefully timed to reinforce de Gaulle's running grievance about the Americans' "great frugality" toward France and French forces.[19] In October 1944, as Allied armies camped on Germany's doorstep and the war seemed to be drawing to a rapid finale, de Gaulle's fear was that the end of hostilities would leave France with only eight fully equipped divisions, insufficient, as Juin explained to Bedell Smith, to support France's imperial role, much less secure for France an occupation zone in Germany. The SHAEF response was that newly equipped French divisions would come into the line too late to participate in the war. Nor was equipping a post-war French army Washington's responsibility. Only on 3 January 1945, in the shadow of Berlin's Ardennes offensive and the subsequent Strasbourg crisis, which put paid to lingering hopes of an imminent German collapse, would the Combined Chiefs accept France's 30 November Plan for the formation of eight new divisions in excess of the Anfa schedule, including an armored division, as well as a considerable expansion of the French Air Force (FAF).[20] Meanwhile, in the short term, de Lattre's complaint does appear to have opened the logistical spigot – by March 1945, as the Allies prepared to complete the invasion of Germany, France in general and the *1ère Armée* in particular had benefited from significant deliveries of US supplies and equipment, as well as food and economic aid to French industry and infrastructure repair.[21]

The first operational take away for Devers from de Lattre's ostensible fit of pique, according to his biographers – one apparent since early 1943 – was that the French lacked not only service units, but also "experienced and trained administrative personnel," and so would require considerable US logistical assistance. Second, for a general whose command philosophy hitherto had been to allow his subordinates considerable freedom of action, Devers realized that he must coordinate detailed directives so as better to harmonize the US and French efforts. In the meantime, to assuage de Lattre's capacious self-esteem, on 16 October, Devers decorated him with the Legion of Merit, an award reserved for foreign military personnel, in a public ceremony at Besançon.[22]

In October, Monsabert had attempted to outflank the Belfort Gap to the north, an effort that ended in a casualty-heavy failure for II Corps, for which de Lattre blamed German resistance and the fact that his attacks were "in part disorganized by the sometimes tragic hesitation on our left flank caused by the successive changeover of American units." With his front overextended and his casualties so high that he was forced to throw poorly trained FFI into the fight, on 17 October, de Lattre called off his Vosges offensive.[23] However, October in the Vosges had offered Louis Bacquier his first experience of combat: driven at night from his encampment near Épinal, the immense convoy conveyed the battalion through sleeping villages to deposit them at dawn at the front – "this strange outlaw world where everything is permitted," where each tree concealed a booby trap, and where each soldier must "learn to recognize the subtle traces of the enemy in the undergrowth, the helmet of the lookout, too flat, too smooth for a plant-covered surface, the path barely indicated by repeated passages, and also to put a name and a caliber to these strange things that zing over our heads, and above all to guess, by the sound, their true destination." In his first action, a bullet shattered his belt buckle, leaving a huge bruise on his stomach, while a piece of shrapnel nicked his eyebrow, causing profuse bleeding but little other injury. For his *tirailleurs*, most of whom spoke a Tamazight dialect from the Central Atlas, this was proof that their commander possessed the *Baraka* (the benediction) – "The angel of death had brushed me with his wing and spared me." His tall Corsican Adjutant chef Léonetti agreed: "It's a fact, *mon lieutenant*, you're lucky. A platoon leader in the regiment survives on average three *barouds* [firefights]. Most of the new arrivals are killed immediately. They can't distinguish an incoming round from a discharge. And as they can't stay on the ground all the time, the poor things remain upright once too often. That's why we decorate them with the *croix de guerre* at the first opportunity. It's safer and the families are pleased. But those who survive, they've understood everything. You and I are immortal . . . well, almost."[24]

Despite grudging Allied advances, German reinforcements swelled the numbers of defenders facing the *1ère Armée* front to 52,000 backed by 25 artillery groups.[25] Nevertheless, from a logistical perspective, October had been far from wasted as French canals, roads, and railways were gradually brought back into commission, a petrol pipeline laid from the Mediterranean coast as far as Dijon, and a network of forward supply depots created, which allowed Sixth Army Group to reach a strength of eight US and seven French divisions by early November. Focused on the Ruhr, however, Eisenhower appears to have been "indifferent" to the offensive potential of Sixth Army Group. His aversion to his "rival" Devers, with whom he usually communicated through Bedell Smith or his operations (G3) officer Pinky Bull, combined with a lack of confidence in the French, might also have played a role. In any case, when orders went out for the November offensive, Sixth Army Group's role was to "protect the southern flank of the Central Group of Armies" and "to act aggressively with the object, initially, of overwhelming the enemy west of the Rhine and, later, in advancing into Germany." No date was specified for Devers' attacks to begin.[26]

By the time twenty-year-old Second Lieutenant Paul Fussell climbed down the cargo nets draped over the gunwales of the troopship *General Brooks*, anchored in the "monstrously damaged" Marseilles harbor, autumn was already well advanced. The next days were spent assembling crated trucks, jeeps, and weapons, marveling at the convenience of the ubiquitous *pissoirs* "right out on the sidewalk," and paying nocturnal visits to Marseilles' "bars and whorehouses." The trip up the Rhône Valley was festive, with "flowers thrown to us by lovely girls, the bottles of wine proffered by smiling and nodding old men, the cheers and applause, which we accepted as if we'd earned them." But, by the time his company, part of the US Seventh Army, entered the front line overlooking Saint-Dié-des-Vosges, the mood had shifted. Alsace offered a picturesque but primitive landscape of small villages and farms "set in the midst of steaming manure piles" inhabited by "the most impoverished people [who] slept with their animals to keep warm," wore wooden shoes, and exhibited "dubious loyalty to the Allied cause,"[27] or so they were informed by *Stars and Stripes*. Their superiors, too, warned them to remain alert to spies and fifth columnists, as many families had sons in the German army and daughters working on German farms and in armament factories.[28] Concluding that many Alsatians were Nazis, GIs showed no hesitation in evacuating villages *manu militari*. Nor could Alsatian and Mosellan deserters and POWs expect any sympathy from the Yanks. Pillage and robbery of the inhabitants by GIs was widespread. GIs on leave in Metz insisted on carrying their weapons because rumor held that German snipers lurked among the population.[29] In January 1945, the liaison officer of the 45th US Infantry Division (ID) decried the violence of the US Army's liberation of Alsace.[30]

The Gouvernement provisoire de la république (GPRF) became concerned that growing hostility to the Americans would undermine their legitimacy and spin off animosity toward the *1ère Armée*.[31] Since D-Day, the task of managing the civil–military interface had fallen to thirty-eight-year-old former diplomat François Coulet, de Gaulle's *commissaire* for inter-Allied relations, who, without adequate staff or interpreters, had struggled since D-Day to assert the GPRF's authority in a Liberation tumult in which Anglo-American commanders, former Vichy officials, and self-appointed FFI "liberation committees" all claimed to represent legal authority. In October, what must have by then been a frazzled Coulet requested that SHAEF please remind GIs that, even though most of the citizens of Alsace and Moselle spoke a German dialect, they were still French.[32] But even the French felt unsure of where the true loyalties of Alsatians lay. In 1939–1940, French soldiers had pillaged the homes of Alsatians evacuated to the rear, because they blamed them for the war. In Italy, Alsatians and Mosellans captured in German uniform were turned over to the French, who thoroughly interrogated them to determine their loyalties, and then integrated them into rear echelon positions, lest recapture by the Wehrmacht cause them to be executed for desertion. In France, however, the Americans did not separate out Alsatian and Mosellan POWs, which upset de Gaulle, who predictably saw it as a sovereignty issue. Only in January 1945 did the Americans began to turn over Alsatians and Mosellans to the French, who in any case lacked the ability to house and feed them properly. But the fact that the French claimed jurisdiction over Alsatian and Mosellan POWs did not mean that they welcomed them as brothers – in October 1944, the National Defense Committee proposed that Alsatians and Mosellans who had attained the rank of sergeant in the German forces, or who wore German decorations, should be interned in France or Afrique du Nord (AFN) and the process begun of stripping them of their French nationality. "Therefore, there was in practice no real distinction drawn between Alsatian POWs and Wehrmacht deserters" by the French army, concludes Claire Miot.[33]

In the field, the French often understood no better where they stood with their "Alsatian brothers" than did the Americans. For instance, in late November 1944, when Bacquier's truck became separated from his night convoy and lost in the Vosges,

> I told the driver to stop at the first house. I knocked violently on the door. I heard vague jabbering in German. "Open, for God's sake!" We shot the bolt off. "You can't speak French, for Pete's sake! I've been knocking for an hour." The man looked dazed. He lifted his lantern to my face repeating, "français ... français ...," then suddenly he turned toward the interior of the house and shouted: "Germaine, Germaine, it's the French!"; noise of footsteps, exclamations, the women appeared all speaking at once, crying, wanting to kiss me. "Where are we?" "At Henfligen, of course!" "And Waldighoffen? Where is that?" [that's where we were supposed to turn off.] "But you've come from there!" "And are there any French here?" "Of course not, you're the first; the Germans were here when we went to bed!" I jumped in the truck: "Turn around, fast!" Never has a maneuver been so rapidly executed. After a while, the driver asked: "So, what's happening?" "We just liberated a village, old boy. You can tell that to your friends!"[34]

The Belfort Gap

Devers created a joint planning staff that, on 15 October, laid out a scheme for the *1ère Armée* to attack toward Colmar through the High Vosges north of Belfort to draw in German reserves, so that the Seventh Army could advance further north. But de Lattre dissented, and on 27 October presented his own scenario, which called for a four-division punch into the Belfort Gap, an undulating plain that stretched from the Doubs River to the Rhine, to coincide with the Seventh Army's advance. In his memoirs, de Lattre claims that Devers immediately approved his plan, integrated it into his battle order, and attached extra artillery commanded by an American Brigadier to the *1ère Armée*.[35] However, preparations for this offensive were somersaulted when, on 25 October, Devers was informed that, without consulting either Devers or de Lattre, Eisenhower had approved de Gaulle's request that, by 11 November, two French divisions be diverted from the *1ère Armée* to the southwest of France to clear German "pockets" along the Gironde estuary. These two divisions represented 15 percent of the strength of Sixth Army Group and 25 percent of that of the *1ère Armée*. Predictably, this "disaster [that] surpassed my worst fears," that he qualified as nothing less than an "amputation,"[36] yet again tipped de Lattre "into a tirade," to the point that he demanded that the November offensive be canceled, which Devers lacked the authority to do. Instead, because Eisenhower had specified no start date for the Sixth Army Group's attack, Devers simply slow-rolled the departure of the two divisions. While Eisenhower is frequently lauded for his tact in navigating around de Gaulle's imperious *froideur*, Devers' biographers give equally high marks to the Sixth Army Group commander's serene management of the Vesuvian de Lattre. This was because Devers never allowed his personal exasperation with the Frenchman's volatility to stand in the way of a genuine respect for de Lattre's military talents, his fierce pride in the French army, his desire for success, and his "realistic" approach to combat. In any case, in Devers' opinion, de Lattre's ego was no more overblown than was that of Fifteenth Army Group commander Mark Clark.[37]

After learning that Patton and Bradley planned to launch their attack toward Metz between 13 and 15 November, Devers ordered plans to be laid for Sixth Army Group to crush Wiese's Nineteenth Army in a vice between US forces in the north and French from the south, between 13 and 18 November. The calculation was that, if de Lattre's attack were delayed by two to three days, the Germans would have by then shifted their reserves north to deal with the Americans. The *1ère Armée*'s attack would begin a day after that of the US Seventh Army, whose objective was Strasbourg. On 14 November, Monsabert's II Corps, composed of the 1ère DFL and the *3e Division d'infanterie algérienne* (3e DIA) launched a diversionary attack into the Vosges in the midst of a snowstorm.[38] In the north, on Seventh Army's front, as Leclerc's 2e DB captured Saverne, the northern portal to the Alsace plain, de Lattre launched his I Corps composed of the *2e Division d'infanterie marocaine* (2e DIM) and the *9e Division d'infanterie coloniale* (9e DIC), reinforced by US artillery as the snowstorm abated. The 2e DIM's attack caught the *338.*

Volksgrenadier Division by surprise, killing its commander General Hans Oschmann and allowing the French to capture important documents that pinpointed German dispositions and revealed that the Germans believed that the French were digging in for the winter. However, by the time the 9^{e} DIC, which had been heavily reinforced by FFI replacements during the *blanchiment*, launched its attack along the Doubs two hours later, not only had the Germans been alerted, but also snow had once again begun to fall. According to de Lattre, Wiese still believed the Vosges to be the main French objective, and that the 9^{e} DIC's push into the Belfort Gap was simply "a big *coup de main*."[39] In fact, German confusion had been reinforced by deception plans as well as the fact that German telephone communications had been cut by artillery bombardment. This produced a disagreement between the Nineteenth Army commander Wiese and Balck at Army Group G over French intentions, which resulted in the issuing of a cacophony of orders and counter-orders by their respective headquarters.[40]

On 16 November, de Lattre threw his tanks, which so far had mostly been held in reserve to exploit any breakthrough, into the offensive that "is everywhere decisive." Aided by two French armored divisions, the advance of Béthouart's I Corps gained momentum, led by the 9e DIC's progress along the Swiss frontier, in the process smashing the links of German positions that formed a defensive chain of villages and road junctions. Only on 25 November, after hard street-by-street combat, had Belfort been cleared and secured.[41] However, prior to this, on 19 November, the French had reached the banks of the Rhine, where they turned north to seize Mulhouse, but not before the 1ère DFL's commander Diego Brosset, ironically a champion swimmer, tragically drowned when his jeep toppled into a raging river.[42] On 23 November, as two US infantry divisions secured the Saverne Gap, the first elements of Leclerc's 2e DB penetrated Strasbourg (Figure 8.2), where, unlike in Paris some months earlier, Leclerc had no need to share the stage with police, FFI or the Americans. As promised, liberation found the Lion of Kufra "alone in the middle of the Place Kléber, saluting his division that arrives alone, to liberate the Alsatian capital." While the Germans continued to bombard the city from their side of the river, in a highly emotional speech to the Constituent Assembly meeting in the Palais du Luxembourg, de Gaulle announced the culmination of "one of the most brilliant episodes of military history."[43] With typical Gaullist hyperbole, he neglected to mention that, as with Paris, it was the US Army that had forced the Saverne Gap, allowing his hand-picked protégé to pluck the emblematic prize of Strasbourg. Nor, unlike at Kufra, were any Senegalese troops present to celebrate the fulfillment of his oath.

But the costs had been high. Bacquier recorded that, during the penetration of the Belfort Gap in November 1944, and in particular the fighting in the Bois de Trembles near Abbévillers.

Figure 8.2 In "one of the most brilliant episodes of military history," in de Gaulle's hyperbolic telling, the 2e DB liberated Strasbourg on 23 November 1944, thus fulfilling Leclerc's Oath of Kufra. (Photo by Roger Viollet via Getty Images)

. . . the list of casualties was terrifying. Half the platoon leaders and almost all the section chiefs, most of the veteran *tirailleurs* were dead or evacuated. The survivors counted the losses with a morose satisfaction, showing a pride in having been involved, once more, in a huge massacre . . . Abbévillers, ignoring the bloody aura that surrounded it, smiled joyously from all the open windows, from which the girls blew us kisses. The peasants from surrounding farms lined the road offering baskets full of apples. A little green, they left a bitter taste. The children, the old people did not grow tired watching the passage of the victorious army. I told myself, this must be what it means to be triumphant: march straight ahead, with confident steps, along a limitless road, while civilians brought offerings. I felt part of a different species, clothed in a dignity beyond me. We are liberators, those who protect; we're also the sacrificed. One was not surprised at being adored. We felt that everything was owed us. Night fell on a large open plain. Fires glowed on the horizon.[44]

Soldiers in the 1ère DFL complained that inadequate artillery support, the result of limitations placed on expenditure of munitions, had translated into high casualties: "If we already left 215 tombs in the cemetery at Villersexel [on the way to Belfort], it's because we didn't shoot enough [artillery] to open the way for the infantry or protect it adequately . . . when one refuses to fire or limits the consumption [of munitions], everyone knows it will come at the price of more wooden crosses."[45]

During 13–23 November, Sixth Army Group had reached the Rhine in two places, having penetrated both the Belfort Gap and the Saverne Gap to seize Mulhouse and Strasbourg. Plans were laid to bounce across the Rhine in front of Strasbourg. But SHAEF refused to supply airborne units to secure a bridgehead, or the bridging equipment required to cross the river. Instead, in a meeting at Vittel on 24 November, Eisenhower told Devers to halt all preparations for a Rhine crossing and to surrender two of his Seventh Army divisions to help Patton break the Siegfried Line, an order that Ike rescinded in the face of Devers' vigorous objections. Nevertheless, he was required to turn Seventh Army north to assist Patton's advance into the Saar basin. "Devers was also confident – mistakenly, as it turned out – that the First French Army, with the aid of one or two Seventh Army divisions would make short work of the Nineteenth Army in the Colmar Pocket . . . The Supreme Commander appeared extremely reluctant to capitalize on the Seventh Army's unexpectedly rapid breakthrough to Strasbourg and the Rhine, and he seemed to attach little or no significance to the concomitant First French Army drive through the Belfort Gap to the Rhine and the possible collapse of the Nineteenth Army," concluded the official US Army history.[46]

The official historians pronounced the SHAEF commander's failure to capitalize on the crashing of the "gaps" at Belfort and Saverne to allow Sixth Army Group to bridge the Rhine as "difficult to understand." If the SHAEF commander thought a Rhine crossing premature, he might at least have turned Patch south to combine with de Lattre to clear the Alsatian plain with the capture of Colmar. For this reason, the official historians concluded that "Eisenhower's later criticism of Dever's inability to eliminate the Colmar Pocket thus appears both unfair and unjustified."[47] Eisenhower's defense of his veto of a November Rhine crossing was that "I had gotten tired of dropping off troops to watch enemy garrisons in the rear areas, so I impressed upon Devers that to allow any Germans to remain west of the river in the upper Rhine plain, south of Strasbourg, would be certain to cause us later embarrassment." Presumably, this was a reference to the Atlantic pockets and the Alps, which were overwhelmingly besieged by FFI. Devers argued that "the French First Army . . . could easily take care of the remnants of the German Nineteenth Army still facing them in the Colmar area. In describing the situation to me he said, 'The German Nineteenth has ceased to exist as a tactical force.'" Eisenhower dismissed Devers' assessment of French capabilities as "overoptimistic . . . while he probably underrated the defensive power of German units when they set themselves stubbornly to hold a strong position."[48] Eisenhower and Bradley doubted that Sixth Army Group had the punch to cross and hold a lodgment on the Rhine's right bank in the face of what would most certainly have been a savage German riposte. It would also have exceeded Devers' 28 October mission order to protect Twelfth Army Group's right flank. Dever's argument was that the Germans were disoriented and had few troops to oppose a Rhine crossing.[49] At the very least, a Rhine crossing might have forced the Germans to adjourn preparations for their Christmas Ardennes Offensive. According to Devers' biographers, what the November offensive did illustrate was "Eisenhower's unwillingness to exploit unexpected success and his poor relationship with Devers" and probably, too, his lack of confidence in de Lattre and the *1ère Armée*.[50] The result, as Eisenhower conceded, was that the late autumn and winter would witness "the dirtiest kind of infantry slugging," which was to result in high losses in rifle platoons.[51]

The Burnhaupt Maneuver

De Lattre's breakthrough to Belfort, and then north along the left bank of the Rhine to Mulhouse, had left a U-shaped sack of German troops between Mulhouse–Altkirch and the Vosges. De Lattre's plan was to seal the mouth of the sack at Burnhaupt by attacking simultaneously west out of Mulhouse and east out of the Vosges (Map 8.2). In one respect, he had no choice, lest Wiese punch east where Béthouart's I Corps had formed a narrow and tenuous wedge along the Rhine to Mulhouse. De Lattre was aware that Wiese was reorganizing his divisions into a "*masse de manœuvre*" as a prelude to offensive action. Béthouart's forces on the eastern face of the "sack" launched several spoiling attacks on 21–22 November to counter German infiltration of their positions. Wiese's troops continued to attack aggressively the eastern flank of the French position around Mulhouse and Altkirch on 23–24 November with heavy machineguns and *Panzerfäuste*, with the clear intention of retaking Mulhouse. De Lattre requested Patch to turn the Seventh Army south from Strasbourg, in order definitively to clear the Alsatian plain of German forces. But Eisenhower's gaze was fixed on the Ruhr, so that he instead ordered Devers to reorientate Seventh Army north to cover Patton's flank for an attack on the Siegfried Line, abandoning de Lattre to deal solo with Wiese, "who had concentrated the majority of his forces at the bottom of the sack with the clear intention of breaking out, in the short run we had no choice but to close him up in the pocket."[52]

By 24 November, de Lattre had finalized his plan of attack, which had been made urgent by the scheduled 28 November transfer of two divisions to the Atlantic pockets. The Germans surprised de Lattre by abandoning some positions in the night of 24–25 November, but as usual leaving behind a thicket of booby traps and mines, which slowed the pursuit of Monsabert's II Corps. Sealing the top of the "sack" at Burnhaupt proved arduous, as the Germans had

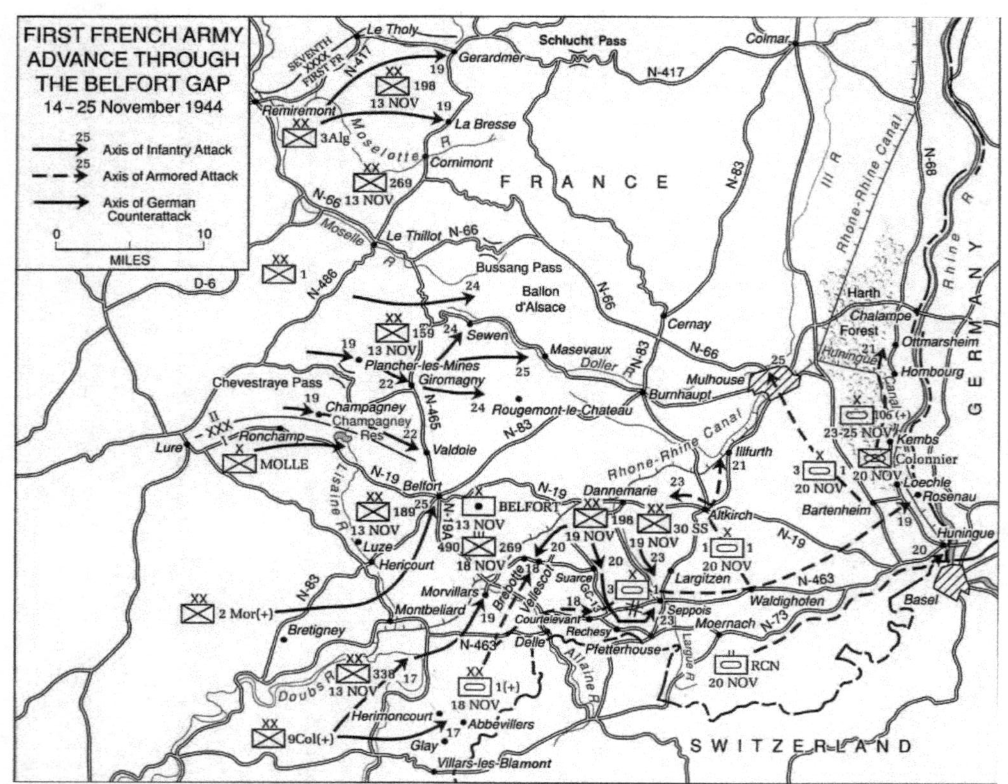

Map 8.2 The Burnhaupt maneuver (14–25 November 1944).

been reinforced with engineering troops and heavy panzers. By 27 November, it was clear to de Lattre that Wiese was gradually extracting his forces from the pocket to the north. The next day, de Lattre renewed his attacks. At 14:30 on 28 November, the I and II Corps met at Burnhaupt. De Lattre trumpeted the capture of 17,000 German POWs, and claimed to have inflicted a further 10,000 casualties, probably an overestimate. But most of Wiese's troops had escaped the trap, while the costs for the *1ère Armée* had been high: 1,300 killed in action (KIA), 4,500 wounded in action (WIA), 1,691 evacuated with frost-bite, and 2,824 evacuated because of sickness. Critical losses in tanks and equipment also had to be replaced.[53]

The Burnhaupt maneuver marked the finale of de Lattre's Belfort Gap offensive, regarded by many as among his most successful. In a brief two weeks, he had seized both Belfort and Mulhouse, and outflanked German positions on the Vosges, despite the relative combat inexperience of portions of his "whitened" divisions – particularly the 9e DIC and the 1ère DFL – many of whose volunteers were barely trained, as well as the previously untested 5e DB. However, the decision taken from Anfa to favor the creation of combat formations in the revitalized French army over administrative and support services also showcased the *1ère Armée*'s limitations, especially as, unlike Devers, de Lattre tightly micromanaged his subordinate commanders. This meant that, as his offensive broadened and his forces advanced, he lacked sufficient staff and a communications infrastructure to exert effective control over the battlespace, as well as ordnance, signals, engineers, and supply to maintain his forward momentum. This was a situation that he had inherited, rather than one he could control. While he could not have succeeded without American logistical and artillery support, he had also been done a disservice by Eisenhower, who failed to grasp opportunities on his Vosges front. Nor did the SHAEF commander prove particularly sensitive to French political objectives in Alsace, which was even more surprising, given "the spirit of understanding and loyalty that Eisenhower usually showed toward his French allies."[54] In this way, de Lattre's Belfort Gap gambit became a successful tactical offensive in search of a meaningful strategic objective. That strategic objective in Alsace was Strasbourg, whose liberation had been an honor provisionally earmarked for de Lattre, designed to match in symbolic importance Juin's part in the capture of Rome and Leclerc's liberation of Paris.[55] But two things prevented this. First, it required the *1ère Armée* to approach Strasbourg from the south, via Colmar. But Allied failure to finish off the Nineteenth Army allowed the swaggering Leclerc, buoyed by his "Oath of Kufra" pledge, to claim that golden prize by slipping the leash of Seventh Army restraint to capture Strasbourg from the west through the Saverne Gap. Without guidance from SHAEF, and forbidden to cross the Rhine, Devers could only assume/hope that the Germans would abandon the Alsatian plain and scuttle back across the river. That, alas, was not to be.[56]

The Colmar Pocket

Eisenhower mocked the failure of Devers and de Lattre to hound the Nineteenth Army out of Alsace. On 23 November, Leclerc had seized Strasbourg. This had offered a perfect opportunity to coordinate the attacks of de Lattre's two armored divisions, from the south, with that of Leclerc's 2e DB, only 60 kilometers to the north, to seize Colmar and trap the remaining German troops, which his *Deuxième Bureau* reported were weak and ill organized, west of the Rhine. Instead, to the utter astonishment of his generals, on 29 November, de Lattre had halted his advance on the Doller River, pulled his 5e DB into his army reserve, and ordered his infantry to assume a defensive posture. A furious Eisenhower demanded that de Lattre be relieved, a request refused by de Gaulle "for political reasons."[57]

The result was the formation of what became known as the Colmar Pocket (Map 8.3), a German blister 65 kilometers long and 50 kilometers deep, on the Rhine's left bank that lay between the French in the south and the Americans plus Leclerc in the north. This further nettled an already prickly command relationship, with Leclerc and 5^e^ DB commander Henri de Vernejoul joining a swelling chorus of de Lattre's detractors, who echoed complaints like those leveled by Larminat at Marseilles.[58] The charge sheet went something like this. The Germans were down to one division and were throwing policemen into the front lines. Instead of exploiting his momentum, de Lattre allowed the enemy to consolidate on the Masevaux–Mulhouse–Rhine line. Vernejoul offered two explanations for de Lattre's failure to liberate Colmar in late November 1944. The first was that he did not want "the man of Kufra" to affix Colmar to his lengthening list of battle honors. This accusation would further envenom an already rancorous rivalry between the two French generals, each supremely attentive to his image, that would erupt in the New Year. But this seems far-fetched, as Leclerc seized Strasbourg only on 23 November, and subsequently took at least two days to consolidate the city. So, he would not have been able to attack south until almost the end of November, whereas Vernejoul's orders were for 21 November.

A second and, in the French context, most damning charge was that de Lattre failed to use armored divisions imaginatively, because he remained mired in the tactical concepts of 1940, if not 1918.[59] Not for the first time, de Lattre's detractors whispered that his aristocratic demeanor and mastery of the dramatic arts in fact masked a lack of confidence, decisiveness, and grasp of modern warfare. De Lattre's initial excuses for his late November halt order were that his troops were worn out, he lacked munitions, the roads were in horrible shape, and

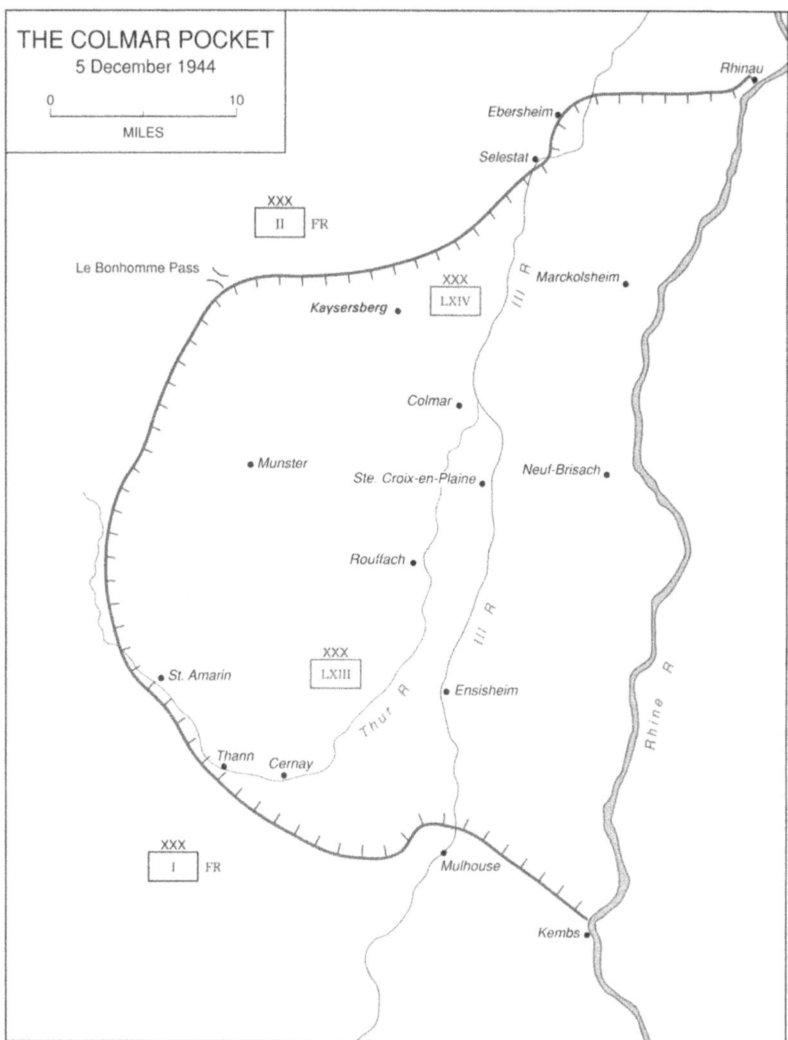

Map 8.3 The Colmar Pocket (December 1944).

he had to manage large numbers of German POWs.[60] Monsabert faulted a lack of replacements and artillery shells, which folded into the official justification for de Lattre's failure to advance north of Mulhouse after 21 November.[61] However, de Lattre's explanations seemed to evolve. For instance, in a 1947 address, he tried to pin the blame on his 1ère DB commander Jean Touzet du Vigier's "lack of intellectual discipline," claiming that he had hesitated to advance on 21 November until he could pull together the combat commands of his division and descend on the Alsace plain "like a Montgolfier." By 30 November, the Germans were counterattacking along the Doller, the Forest of Hardt was criss-crossed with German trenches which required a methodical infantry clean-out, and the German defenses were supported by artillery on the Rhine's right bank.[62] So, perhaps the Colmar Pocket was not so ripe for eradication on 21 November as Eisenhower believed.

In his history of the First Army, de Lattre writes that he would have needed Patch to turn south to catch the Germans in a pincer.[63] This explanation is advanced by one of de Lattre's biographers, who argues that the Colmar Pocket resulted from a series of Allied decisions taken in the wake of the 23 November liberation of Strasbourg, to redirect the US Seventh Army north to relieve pressure on Patton's stalled offensive in the Saar, rather than south, as de Lattre had requested, to clear the left bank of the Rhine. This produced a heated exchange between Eisenhower, Bradley, and Devers on the night of 24–25 November, when Eisenhower ordered Devers to abandon plans for a Rhine crossing at Rastatt north of Strasbourg, and instead surrender two of his divisions to Patton's Third Army. On the 25 November, Eisenhower and Bradley visited de Lattre, who effused in his history over the "expression of the warm congratulations ... for the successes of the 1st French Army since 14 November." In fact, "Nothing that Eisenhower saw in the southern sector of the 6th Army Group altered his decision" to reinforce Patton rather than cross the Rhine or to clear German forces from Alsace. The US Army official history categorizes Eisenhower's call as a "dubious decision," while Devers labeled it a "major error." At the very least, Eisenhower might have consulted his Ultra intercepts that would have confirmed Devers' assertion that the Germans in Alsace were disorganized and disoriented. "Had the Seventh Army begun crossing the Rhine in strength, the reserves that were later poured into the Colmar Pocket would have been needed elsewhere, and Hitler might have been more amenable to a general withdrawal back across the upper Rhine if the Reich heartland were under a more immediate threat," according to the official history's harsh judgement of the SHAEF commander. In fact, the decision, for political reasons, to occupy the Colmar Pocket ultimately favored the Allies, in that it soaked up German manpower that might have been more profitably deployed further north and in the Black Forest and on the West Wall. In the view of his critics, Eisenhower's decision reflected the SHAEF commander's unimaginative adherence to "the plan," his preference for attrition over maneuver, his deference to Bradley and Patton, or perhaps his concern about relations with the arrogant and headstrong Montgomery. It showcased his limited role for Devers' Sixth Army Group, as well as perhaps a lack of confidence in de Lattre's force. The result, in the view of some at least, was to highlight Eisenhower's characteristic failure to "reinforce success" by crossing the Rhine or grasp the operational opportunity to hasten what seemed to be the impending collapse of Wiese's Nineteenth Army by squeezing the Germans out of Alsace.[64] As a result, though it was gradually attrited, the Nineteenth Army remained upright and throwing punches until the final bell in May 1945. However, the inclination to blame de Lattre's ego, or his out-of-date operational concepts, for the persistence of the Colmar Pocket fit better into a narrative of a French command burdened with an outmoded battlefield vision, while split by personal and political rivalries.

Depending on one's viewpoint, either de Lattre or Eisenhower had once again handed breathing space to the Germans, as divisions were transferred between Allied armies and new operational boundaries set. "Like us, the Americans suffer from a battle that is not taken in hand," Monsabert complained at the end of October, "and it's a crisis of lost opportunities, which might rebound on us if the enemy recovers his capacity to counterattack. Two dogs attached by their tails that pull in different directions: that's how brother Truscott, commander of VI US Corps, describes Devers' failure and the action of two army chiefs, one American, the other French."[65] Hitler's plans to reinforce his troops in Alsace and build his reserves for an Ardennes offensive went forward without the interruption that a Rhine crossing might have created. It also meant that Devers' 2 December order to de Lattre to renew his offensive in Alsace could not be executed before 5 December.[66] On 26 November 1944, the surviving bits and pieces of Nineteenth Army were not in a strong position to defend the Colmar Pocket. Army Group G commander Hermann Balck had not been keen to maintain the remnants of eight divisions on the Rhine's west bank, and nothing in Ultra indicated that the Germans would make a stand around Colmar.[67] But, true to character, Hitler had vetoed a withdrawal. Devers' plan called for Leclerc's 2e DB, together with the 36th US ID under John Dahlquist, to attack the pocket from the north as part of Monsabert's II Corps, while the rest of de Lattre's force could attack from the south in the first two weeks of December. De Lattre was poorly placed to carry out that mission. The significant losses in men and equipment suffered in closing the sack at Burnhaupt were compounded by preparations for the transfer of two divisions to *Les forces françaises de l'ouest* (FFO), as well as logistical difficulties. But the Germans were not expected to fight to the knife to defend Colmar. On the contrary, at the time, de Lattre, like many others in the Allied camp, including Devers' military intelligence (G2), expected the Germans to retain troops in Alsace only long enough to prepare their defenses on the right bank of the Rhine. This proved to be a major miscalculation.[68]

Despite the transfer of two French divisions to the west, as well as high casualties, de Lattre was expected to hold a 200-kilometer front with what remained of his forces, in perilous conditions, as, with the onset of winter, the clothing situation for the French had become desperate. André Diethelm appealed to Eisenhower for equipment for 112,000 soldiers, 52,000 of whom were already serving with the *1ère Armée*. The French command allocated 72,000 French uniforms recovered from various depots for FFI units serving on the Atlantic coast, while 25,000 Canadian uniforms were shipped from Algiers for French soldiers in Alsace. But a further 105,000 FFI still needed uniforms and equipment, which could not easily be provided due to a lack of shipping and congestion in the ports. Furthermore, Eisenhower's willingness to help was not improved by the failure of the French command to provide labor troops to SHAEF to repair damaged infrastructure.[69]

Since landing on 15 August, the *1ère Armée* had suffered 27,000 combat casualties, including many of its professional *armée d'Afrique* cadres, and another 18,000 non-battle casualties – mainly frostbite and trench foot, caused when feet became wet from perspiration, or from crossing streams, which eventually resulted in extensive tissue damage. This caused soldiers first to hobble, and then to become too lame to walk. Shoepacks issued to GIs designed to keep feet dry were often distributed without liners, so that GIs would learn to carry extra socks, while drying wet socks by carrying them next to their body or lining their boots with strips of army blankets. In contrast, French soldiers seldom enjoyed the luxury of a change of socks and uniforms, much less of access to the laundry units that accompanied US forces. An inability to wash combined with the requirement often to sleep in barns meant that soldiers' uniforms were soon infested with fleas and lice. Not surprisingly, these conditions lowered morale and heightened "battle fatigue." The US Army found the best antidote to neuropsychiatric disorders to be frequent rotation of units for rest periods, a luxury that, because of insufficient French replacements, and the fact that FFI units were slow to become battle ready, de Lattre could ill afford. The Americans also discovered that units that had registered high casualties among company-level cadres – a recurring feature of the French experience – reported the highest rates of neuropsychiatric breakdown. The pressure increased for companies and platoons stationed in the Vosges, that were often isolated, operating with infrequent contact with higher echelons of command and only intermittent logistical support, which left them vulnerable to demoralization, possibly even surrender. The prioritization of combat over support units in the restructured French army had been intentional. And, while the Americans stepped in to supplement French logistical deficiencies somewhat, in the long run, the lack of support services added to the psychological burden of French-led soldiers.[70] Like everyone else – not least the Germans – the Americans, too, were scouring the bottom of their manpower barrel, so that Womens Army Corps personnel (WACs) replaced male soldiers in service units, 10,000 airmen were culled for transfer to ground forces, and African Americans hitherto confined to logistics and support were organized into combat units, while infantry divisions assembled in the United States were rushed to Europe without their artillery, trucks, and other heavy equipment, to be slotted into line units as individual replacements, sometimes without even having fired an M1 Garand rifle.[71]

Devers' growing confidence in de Lattre was reflected by the fact that, on 5 December, the Frenchman was given command of all units besieging the Colmar Pocket, including the 36th US ID, "one of the elite divisions of our Allies, commanded by a solid leader, with a sharp eye, with a reputation for toughness, loyalty, and a preference for maneuver warfare," de Lattre enthused.[72] Unfortunately, John Dahlquist failed to reciprocate de Lattre's high esteem, but instead complained that the Frenchman farmed out much of the fighting to his division. At a 6 December meeting with de Lattre, Devers objected that French batteries were firing almost three times as many shells per gun as were the Americans, and that he should emulate Patch's "more ruthless" control over ammunition expenditure.[73] Monsabert found American criticism unfair, in that, "aware of our success in Italy," they assigned tasks to the French in Alsace that they simply lacked the resources to carry out, and then accused the French of being combat shy, "because they have immense resources in men, and we don't."[74] Devers replaced the 36th with the 3rd US ID. But something else was going on beside simple attrition that had caused an inversion in the respective reputations of the combat power of the two armies. Monsabert noted that US combat performance in Alsace had improved by leaps and bounds over that in Italy, where, for instance, the 36th US ID had been "worthless." From a combat-effectiveness perspective, in Monsabert's view the French "mistake" was to have declared *l'amalgame* and to have purged many professional soldiers, rather than mobilize the Armistice Army.[75]

But the First Army's problems were structural – a dearth of cadres, doctrine, and matériel; a lack of feedback loops to inculcate "lessons learned" into training; heavy casualties that undermined "the effectiveness of primary group loyalty," increased psychiatric casualties, and disrupted adaptation of units to combat situations, and so on. In important ways, the stellar French combat performance in Italy had been enabled by an elaborate system of training bases, schools, and logistical centers that had been created in AFN from May 1943, under Brigadier General Alan F. Kingman's French Training Section (FTS).[76] However, upon arrival in France, in September, Patch requested that General Wilson transfer training responsibility to the French, in the four AFN training centers in the process of moving to southern France to train personnel recruited in France. But, in the conditions of *l'amalgame*, this system broke down – unlike in North Africa, where many trainees had prior military service and just needed familiarization with US-supplied weapons, in France FFI volunteers were often adolescent novices. By December 1944, SHAEF was admonishing the French better to prepare for combat replacements directed to the *1ère Armée*. The French reply was that the *1ère Armée*, which was responsible for giving basic training, lacked the personnel, resources, and equipment to rehabilitate old French training camps and create new ones, while the War Ministry had little capability to train specialists for engineers, signals, transportation, and anti-aircraft artillery (AAA). And, as was frequently the case with the French, logistics were an afterthought. In December, a plan was entertained – then abandoned – to send two divisions of FFI volunteers to the United States for training. The London War Office belatedly sent a contingent of instructors in March 1945 to train French recruits. But, in April, the new French divisions – the 1st, 10th, and 36th IDs – had neither been fully trained nor received their full complement of equipment.[77]

First French Army staff work, "although now improving, has never been up to standards in accuracy, timeliness and completeness as that of American units," Sixth Army Group complained in April 1945. This made it difficult to ascertain the scope of French losses and to know where to direct replacements and supplies.[78] Part of the problem was systemic, as after 1871 the French army, replicating the Prussian system, treated staff officers as the military equivalent of the Roman higher clergy, defined by their selectivity and *école supérieure de guerre* education, rather than as men doing a straightforward administrative job to which most competent line officers might be temporarily assigned. According to Marc Bloch's observations from 1940, French staff officers "lack[ed] imagination and [had] a tendency to take refuge from the urgency of fact in abstractions." They underestimated the fog and friction of war because many of them lacked command experience, so that they issued orders too late for units adequately to prepare to execute them. And yet, flag officers were reluctant to part with their staff, so that they were unable to get hands-on command experience.[79]

Also, *l'amalgame* overwhelmed the few professional officers not cooling their heels in an *Oflag* and imported FFI "officers" totally unschooled in the requirements of military bureaucratic housekeeping. Nor was discipline all it should have been. For instance, complaints were registered in the middle of April that a battalion of reinforcements from the *42e Régiment d'infanterie* (42e RI) destined for the *1ère Armée* had arrived at Verdun firing their weapons out of train windows. Once in town, they were accused of hunting wild boar with machineguns, "pillaging," and sleeping on guard, and their "exceptionally long hair" and disheveled appearance was deemed unsoldierly. Meanwhile, contrary to orders, their officers were frequenting dance halls, which had reopened on the Liberation. An inspection concluded that FFI "officers" were only "superficially trained" and failed to maintain discipline. Battalion records were a mess. "The 2nd Co did not have a record of punishments. It is evident that most of the cadres don't know how to apply a disciplinary measure," or enforce "the most elementary disciplinary regulations." One of the company commanders, incarcerated by the Americans after an incident in which a GI had died, threatened that his men would come with arms to force his release. The battalion commander had organized no training either for his cadres or for his soldiers, who were frequently absent without leave (AWOL), and followed orders as the mood took them. The commander's defense was that the army and the population were simply hostile to FFI and had exaggerated reports of their indiscipline. Officers had only been told in the middle of April that they were being demoted one rank below their FFI ranks, while since the middle of February they had paid for food for their men out of their own pockets, for which they had not been reimbursed. Some officers were threatening to leave, and many of their troops would no doubt follow suit. "As the leader goes, so go the troops," was the conclusion.[80] This battalion may have been atypical – its level of training and of discipline was so inadequate that it never made it into combat. But all such hastily raised units for an army whose professional cadres were in the front lines experienced the 42e RI's problems to varying degrees. And the unit's disciplinary problems continued into the summer, even after a professional colonel took command, because former FFI officers proved slow to apply regular army norms of discipline, which perhaps were not all that rigorous to begin with.[81] "The army of the Fourth Republic . . . was as sloppy as its soldiers looked," concluded historian of German denazification Constantine FitzGibbon. "And they looked very sloppy indeed in 1945 and 1946. The level of discipline was low compared to the American, and even more so to the British armies."[82]

Sixth Army Group's G2 initially believed that the Wehrmacht would withdraw to the German side of the Rhine, a logical deduction, as it reflected the preference expressed on 24 November of both Army Group G commander Hermann Balck and Oberbefehlshaber West (OB West) commander von Rundstedt. German command-and-control hung by a thread; indeed, contact with some of units in southern Alsace had been lost as the German command struggled to adjust to Allied advances.[83] Of course, such an assessment was totally to misread Hitler, whose default mode was to veto retreat requests, and who instead reinforced the Colmar Pocket. Although, by 29 November, Patch and Devers noted a definite stiffening of resistance north of Colmar, they dismissed it as temporary. The tip-off, however, came from reports that the 2e DB was capturing soldiers of the 106th Panzer Brigade. Only on 4 December was Sélestat cleared of its German defenders by elements of the 36th and 103rd US IDs, while the 2e DB skated past this infantry slog, with its goal the liberation of Colmar. On 6 December, the Germans launched a series of counterattacks that continued for a week. Although they failed to gain ground, they succeeded in disrupting the planned Franco-American offensives.[84]

On 15 December, Wiese was replaced by Lieutenant General Siegfried Rasp, and the Colmar Pocket – henceforth renamed by Berlin Army Group

Oberrhein – was brought under Himmler's direct command. While the former policeman's military qualifications were borderline, his ability to summon up reinforcements from Deutschland's shriveling manpower reserves went unchallenged, as did his Gestapo-enforced directives. Ten infantry divisions – some desperately understrength and topped up with administrative troops – were packed into a tenuous *Oberrhein* bridgehead. They were reinforced by two tank brigades composed of *Panzerkampfwagen V Panther* tanks, a 1943 design intended to exceed in lethality the Soviet T-34, and *Jagdpanther* tank hunters, put into production the following year, which, with their sloped armor and 88 mm gun, far outclassed any tank in the Allied inventory. The German line in the south of the pocket was anchored on the Hart Forest south of Mulhouse, while, in the west, the Wehrmacht controlled the approach passes through the High Vosges. The northern fringe of the *Oberrhein* was secured by an interlocking defense system that had turned every village and crossroads into a mine-laced strongpoint, with *Panzerfäuste* bristling beneath a canopy of heavy artillery.

So reinforced, the Colmar Pocket offered an objective that the *1ère Armée* was simply too anemic to overcome, even with the addition on 15 December of the 3rd US ID and with US logistical support, because the 241,000 men of the French First Army were short 58,000 support troops by US calculations.[85] De Lattre had lost too many irreplaceable cadres and technicians, his main colonial manpower reserve was over 1,500 kilometers away, and he had been required to transfer the 1ère DFL and the 1ère DB to besiege the Atlantic pockets. Meanwhile, whipping the FFI into battle-ready units with a largely novice leadership proved a glacial process. The order to dispatch two divisions to the west was suspended, although not before the 1ère DFL was halfway across France, which removed it temporarily from de Lattre's order of battle. Nor was the battle for the Colmar Pocket popular with French troops, especially as Leclerc had pipped them to the post symbolically with his liberation of Strasbourg: "We felt frustrated wasting our time with these obscure rearguard skirmishes while the other bastards swaggered in the conquered towns," complained Bacquier. The French even incorporated *Osttruppen* deserters into their defensive dispositions: "We made them understand that they were responsible for a hundred meters of front, that no one should break through, against which they would be fed three times daily and given generous drink," remembered Bacquier. "They had never had it so good. By 10 am, they were already drunk. But we quickly realized that they were marvelously trained. Never was a position so well guarded! Our Moroccans recognized it immediately. They learned a thing or two [from the *Osttruppen*] that their trainers had neglected to teach them."[86] Like the French units, the 36th US ID had been beaten up during its journey from the Côte d'Azur and was not at its fighting peak, while the momentum of Leclerc's 2e DB was broken by a waterlogged and canal- and mine-laced Alsatian plain.

Nevertheless, de Lattre's orders from Devers were to eliminate German forces in Alsace, which he intended to do from 5 December by simultaneously squeezing this Teutonic abscess from north and south. But, quite apart from the fact that the "tired and undersupplied First French Army"[87] had taken huge losses and was at the end of its tether, de Lattre's attack would be further complicated by atrocious weather that had brought winter floods. This would channel the Combat Commands along predictable and hence well-defended routes of advance, while the Germans could maneuver on interior lines. Bad weather also suspended air support, while that of the artillery would in some instances be restricted so as not to damage architectural treasures, for example the Gothic church at Thann.[88] Indeed, in Italy, Monsabert had gained a reputation as something of a historical preservationist for threatening to court martial any artillery officer who fired on a building that predated the eighteenth century.[89]

As with the Atlantic pockets, one option might have been simply to surround the "Colmar Pocket" with partially trained FFI and redeploy the *1ère Armée*'s more mobile units with those of Patton and Patch to attack in the Saar. This would have offered a mission better adapted to the capabilities of an army with an underdeveloped command-and-control system, cadres less experienced in inter-arm operations, and an inadequate logistical apparatus to sustain offensive operations. However, to have left occupied territory in Alsace may have opened the Allies to surprises. Such a course of action certainly would have put de Gaulle in a foul humor – never difficult to achieve – as the subsequent flutter over the defense of Strasbourg would confirm. The elimination of the Colmar Pocket was given a green light. This was to be de Lattre's show, as, apart from surrendering the 3rd US ID and the 2e DB to Monsabert's II Corps, Patch was required merely to give logistical support to the *1ère Armée*. But, to ensure success, Devers decided to allow de Lattre more time to position his troops.[90]

These factors, together with continuous artillery-backed German spoiling attacks that resulted in 5,800 more French casualties, when combined with over 4,000 cases of frostbite and sickness, blunted de Lattre's offensive. Serving in the medical battalion of the 9e DIC, Suzanne Lefort-Rouquette noted that troop morale plunged with the onset of worsening weather, which put pressure on the medical staff, who set up hospitals in abandoned houses and barns that offered little shelter from the snow and −20 °C temperatures. Each morning ten ambulances were dispatched over the frozen roads, while five were held in reserve to deal with emergencies. The wounded often had to be collected under artillery fire, while soldiers suffering from frozen feet were put in the command car with their feet covered. So many soldiers were wounded in the fighting in Alsace in the middle of November 1944, with everyone begging for a shot of morphine, that Lefort-Roquette's teams decided to prioritize those with head wounds. Rolling a young wounded soldier in a blanket and abandoning him no doubt to perish from blood loss, shock, and hypothermia, left them "with an atrocious feeling of guilt."[91] Traffic jams, especially on roads churned into "a magma of mud and snow, often mined," or in small villages where the narrow streets might be blocked by tanks or artillery pieces pulled by General Motors Truck Company (GMC) trucks, made it difficult to get the wounded back to the dressing stations, where, in any case, "We stepped over our poor dead reposing in their rigidity on stretchers that, by their number, blocked the entrance of the 6e RTM's [*6e Régiment de tirailleurs marocains*'] advanced dressing station." Not only were the drivers responsible for keeping their ambulances in running order, but also, at the end of the day, they had to cleanse them of the accumulation of mud, dried blood, cigarette butts, and used bandages, which was difficult to do when the water was frozen.[92]

By 12 December, Béthouart's I Corps had shot its bolt, and he asked de Lattre temporarily to suspend operations, while attacks from the north lacked the drive to advance more than a few kilometers.[93] The *1ère Armée*'s casualties for November represented 8.1 percent of strength, compared with 5 percent in the US Seventh Army, which reminded veterans of Italy. There were probably several reasons for this, some already mentioned, including the poor equipment, clothing, and minimal training of French replacements, and the fact that French divisions counted fewer men than did American units in the relatively safe logistical and support positions. But a further contributory factor was that French medical infrastructure had made little progress since Italy. While it was easier for the *Compagnies de ramassage* to evacuate casualties in Alsace than it had been in Italy's mountainous terrain, former FFI units that suffered up to 50 percent casualties lacked even basic medical equipment such as stretchers. Psychological casualties, who were especially high among French volunteers, continued to be treated as shirkers, discipline problems, or evidence of "Arab hysteria," while doctors were sanctioned for evacuating them.[94] "Both Eisenhower and Devers had underestimated the German ability to strengthen the bridgehead and overestimated de Lattre's ability to keep his basically colonial army moving against suddenly renewed and greatly strengthened German resistance," concludes the US Army's official history.[95]

On 18 December, Devers dispatched a stinging letter to de Lattre, reproaching him for his failure to act "with vigor and determination. I must avow that I am really dissatisfied with the results that you have obtained." He also told him that he expected all German troops in the Colmar Pocket to be dead, POWs, or back in the Fatherland by 1 January. Devers' letter was issued on the heels of a 16 December report written by de Lattre asking for a further reinforcement of two US IDs on his front. The French commander had also pointed out that morale in the *1ère Armée* had been tanked by the feeling that they had been "abandoned" by the French people. De Lattre understood that Devers' letter had been written under pressure from Eisenhower. In a come-to-Jesus meeting at Sixth Army Group HQ at Phalsbourg on 22 December, the day that Devers temporarily suspended the offensive against the Colmar Pocket, he and de Lattre discussed ways to upgrade what Devers saw as a trailing French performance, by incorporating FFI replacements and a top-up of artillery support. Eisenhower also reinforced Devers to eliminate a thorn in the side of the Allied disposition that had absorbed eight Franco-American divisions.[96]

"The Dreadful Vision of 1940": The Strasbourg Crisis

De Lattre's 16 December request for a reinforcement of two US IDs proved singularly ill-timed, on the day the Germans launched *Unternehmen Herbstnebel* (Operation Autumn Fog), heralded by an artillery barrage as massive as it was unexpected. The launch of the Ardennes offensive caused Eisenhower concern that Allied troops east of the Vosges might be "severely handled" either by a German thrust south toward Sarrebourg (Moselle) or by one north out of the Colmar Pocket.[97] On 26 December, Eisenhower told Devers that, in the event of a German attack, he was to "give ground slowly on his northern flank, even if he had to move completely back to the Vosges. The northern Alsatian plain was of no immediate value to us. I was at that time quite willing to withdraw on Devers' front, if necessary, all the way to the eastern edge of the Vosges."[98]

Thus, the stage was set for the Strasbourg crisis, which further strained Franco-American relations, roiled by the failure of Devers and de Lattre to eliminate the Colmar Pocket. The Strasbourg episode, despite its fleeting nature, also allowed de Gaulle the opportunity once again to reinforce his message of Gaullist self-reliance by emphasizing the serial American inability or unwillingness to respect French interests. Of course, Strasbourg was symbolic territory – the "capital" of Alsace, annexed by the Germans and liberated by *France libre*'s Gallic Guderian to honor his sacred Saharan oath. And now, after this carefully choreographed Gaullist *mise-en-scène*, the fitting sequel to the 2e DB's gatecrash of Paris to liberate the French capital, Eisenhower ordered Strasbourg and its Francophile population abandoned as if this sacrosanct outpost of the Hexagon were as insignificant as a rattlesnake-infested expanse of Kansas prairie. The Strasbourg crisis also took place against the background of the Ardennes offensive, so that Eisenhower's retreat order at least offered an operational logic. Nevertheless, the prospect of a German reoccupation of Strasbourg and the northern Alsatian plain raised the specter of the prolongation of the war, possibly even a resuscitation of German military fortunes, that put French nerves on edge. "The situation is not catastrophic, but for the country, it's agonizing," Monsabert noted in his diary on news of the

Ardennes attack. "I feel in my spirit and in my heart, in the middle of the dreadful vision of 1940."[99]

But, in truth, the French, like the Americans, seemed skeptical about the loyalties of a population whose liberation Gaullist propaganda had promoted as an emotive national rendezvous. Alsace-Lorraine had been idealized by *la France libre*, which had adopted the Cross of Lorraine as its symbol, while the "*Serment de Koufra*" declared the spire of Strasbourg cathedral to be the symbolic pinnacle of the liberation of the French people. However, the reality on the ground was less obvious. Loyalties in the frontier departments of Alsace-Moselle, already existing in linguistic and cultural limbo and pummeled by history, had been further scrambled by four years of occupation, Nazification, conscription, deportations, flight, and the fact that the province had become a bitterly contested battlefield for several months. At the very least, the war had depopulated the region – Strasbourg, for instance, had dropped from 220,000 inhabitants in 1939 to 90,000 by 1944 – and helped to create distrust between civilians and their liberators. GIs were not alone in regarding Alsatians with suspicion – North African troops, probably taking their cue from their French superiors, called them "*Boches*," and often held them at gunpoint. Despite harsh penalties ordered for pillage and rape from December 1944, these crimes continued in the provinces well into 1945. French liaison officers admitted that many Alsatians did not seem particularly joyful to be "liberated." They especially distrusted Alsatian women who became friendly with *tirailleurs*, speculated that any pro-French Alsatians had been eliminated during the occupation, and suspected that some acted as German spies.[100] Protestants, most numerous in the Bas-Rhin and already distrusted in France as the faithful adherents of a foreign religion and hence apostates of a "*catholicocentrique*" concept of French identity that shaped de Gaulle's world view, were viewed as pro-German. Nor was the Roman Church in Alsace perceived as a bastion of Francophilia after 1918, in the face of a secularizing French Republic and an aggressive promotion of the French language. Paris sought to avoid a repetition of the "triage commissions" which in 1918–1919 had expelled 110,000 "*Altdeusche*" to Germany, in the process creating the so-called "*malaise Alsacienne*," which had contributed to a spike of autonomist sentiment in the inter-war years. Nevertheless, hardly had Strasbourg been liberated than, in December 1944, the arrest of Alsatians for collaboration by *commissions d'épuration* (purge committees) run by the FFI or the Army began, so that the German capitulation in May 1945 found 3,320 Alsatians interned in the Bas-Rhin, while 1,327 were behind barbed wire in the Haut-Rhin. The conversion of marks into francs had wiped out the savings of many families, who were already anxious about sons and daughters in Germany, while war damage in Alsace was matched only by that behind the D-Day beaches in La Manche and the Calvados.[101]

Therefore, when the German counteroffensive was launched on 16 December, it is fair to say that, while Strasbourg may have been "liberated," it had yet to be secured. The Americans noted that hostility to French forces in Strasbourg remained high, and that several French officials had been assassinated – Leclerc's "sniper order," which decreed that "five German hostages would be shot" for every French soldier killed, was issued after two French soldiers had been killed by police.[102] The "sniper order" is remarkable for at least three reasons, beginning with the fact that it was unclear how these "hostages" were to be chosen. Leclerc's biographer claims that Leclerc selected his hostages from "the thousand German employees stranded in the town by the rush of the division and the dozens of arrested Gestapo agents." But who among them was German and who was French had yet to be determined. Leclerc's action is excused by "his devouring passion for France, boosted by the euphoria of having realized his dream, that of Kufra that seemed for many a utopia." Not surprisingly, the Germans threatened retaliation.[103] Second, the "sniper order" was the moral equivalent of the retaliation by the German occupiers against French citizens for resistance acts. Finally, Leclerc's order was illegal, as General "Iron Mike" O'Daniel discovered when his 3rd US ID relieved the 2e DB in Strasbourg on 26 November and announced that Leclerc's "sniper order" remained in effect. When this policy was reported by Paris newspapers, Devers immediately rescinded the Leclerc–O'Daniel "sniper order," and informed de Lattre and all his subordinate *1ère Armée* commanders that "no proclamations or notices . . . at variance with the provisions of international law," which prohibits summary executions, would be tolerated. But French-controlled newspapers in Strasbourg refused to publish Devers' recension, forcing O'Daniel to issue a press release. The result was that US troops garrisoned the city until January 1945, "to protect French officials."[104]

If French attitudes toward Alsatians were ambiguous, the Americans in Sixth Army Group were totally confounded. They, too, noticed that Alsatians did not seem to be grateful for Allied deliverance, especially those captured in German uniform, as Captain Force, liaison officer with the 45th US ID, reported in January 1945:

> Numerous Alsatians deserted the German Army. Certain left during the summer of 1944 and hid for months. I know of some who left the Russian front and crossed all of Germany when they learned of the American advance across France. These Alsatian deserters who were so impatiently awaiting their American liberators have been arrested by them. Great emotion was caused by these arrests. I have intervened but without success, the American authorities informing me that they were carrying out an order of the Commander-in-Chief, by virtue of which all foreigners [Russian, Poles, Alsatians, etc.] who had belonged to the Wehrmacht were to be arrested for interrogation and verification of their identity. Insofar as the Alsatians are concerned, a procedure of rapid verification of identity in collaboration with French officers should have been organized.

But Force, one of whose jobs was to designate mayors in Alsatian towns, conceded that local loyalties were often very difficult to determine: "There are too many intermingled questions of families, friendship or enmity. It is infinitely complex." While the French questioned whether the wholesale detention of Alsatians in German uniform by US troops violated the 25 August accords on sovereignty, they conceded that the French *securité militaire* was assisting the Americans in making these arrests. To add to the confusion, 30,000 German refugees were trapped in Alsace, while some German soldiers had shed their uniforms for civilian clothes but continued to resist.[105] While officially the French considered Alsatians as "victims," they too were inclined to toss noncommissioned officer (NCO) captives from Alsace-Moselle, or those captured wearing German combat decorations, straight into POW pens.[106]

The fact that Eisenhower's order to withdraw from Strasbourg was opposed by many of his subordinate American commanders, led by Devers, did little to puncture that myth. At the base of their disagreement was Eisenhower's desire to straighten his line, withdraw to a more defensible position, and create a tactical reserve, which even de Gaulle conceded made sense from a "strategic" perspective. However, Ultra revealed no credible German threat to justify that withdrawal. Devers believed that any German attack, should it come, would be directed west of the Vosges down the Saar Valley into Lorraine. In any case, in his view, Eisenhower had been spooked by the Ardennes attack. His order to withdraw from northern Alsace made no operational sense, as it would have surrendered the Rhine front, opened Monsabert's II Corps to attack from the north, placed the Saverne Gap in jeopardy, and simply obliged Sixth Army Group to reconquer hard-won territory.[107]

When, at a 27 December meeting in Paris between Eisenhower and Devers, Eisenhower reiterated his decision to relinquish the "no value" Alsatian plain, Devers was "shocked when he saw the extent of the withdrawal ... The position I give up is much stronger than the one to which I go," he wrote. He had also been in France long enough to realize that "giving up the town of Strasbourg is a political disaster to France." He was supported by Patch and the liaison officer, the former Massachusetts Senator Henry Cabot Lodge. Devers did not reveal the extent of Eisenhower's planned withdrawal to de Lattre, but merely told him to prepare to reinforce Seventh Army. At their 27 December meeting, Devers pointed out to his boss that the French would simply refuse to obey such a withdrawal order. But Eisenhower insisted that Devers must retreat 60 kilometers to the Vosges, despite the fact that there was no immediate threat to his position.[108] Patton complained that Ike's decision was "disgusting and could discredit the value of our army and undermine the confidence of our people."[109] In fact, Eisenhower's decision had been prompted by Montgomery, who believed that Devers and Patton should hold the hinge, while his Twenty-First Army Group pivoted across the Rhine through the Ruhr to Berlin. It was part of Montgomery's campaign to replace Eisenhower as SHAEF commander, an initiative that Marshall scotched on 30 December. At the same time, while incessantly complaining about Eisenhower's leadership, and although given command of all US troops in his sector, the British commander had been slow to attack the north shoulder of the Bulge. In fact, Juin's point to Bedell Smith was that, if Eisenhower's rationale for ordering a retreat to the Vosges was to create a strategic reserve, why did he not take the troops from Monty, who seemed to be hoarding an abundance of idle manpower?[110]

Devers slow-rolled Eisenhower's orders, resorting to an inventory of transparent delaying tactics that simply reinforced Ike's ingrained perception of Devers' "disloyalty." On 31 December, the Germans launched *Unternehmen Nordwind* (Operation North Wind, Map 8.4). A scaled-down version of their Ardennes Offensive, the purpose of *Nordwind* was to capture the Saverne Gap, isolate the US VI Corps in Strasbourg, link up with the Colmar Pocket, disrupt the rear of Patton's Third Army as it counterattacked into the Ardennes, and isolate de Lattre's *1ère Armée* south of the Vosges. As Devers had predicted, the major German thrust fell well west of Strasbourg along the Saar River valley. It made little progress against badly outnumbered but entrenched US forces, whose commanders made good use of Ultra intelligence to anticipate enemy movements and of interior lines to thwart German attacks, with a skill much superior to that of German commanders conducting similar defensive operations in the Vosges.[111] Rather than mount a simultaneous attack out of the Colmar Pocket at the rear of the Seventh Army, Himmler bided his time, in part because French aggressiveness helped to lock down his troops in defensive battles, but also because he nurtured his own plans. The retreat order brought relations between Devers and Eisenhower to a crisis, and forced Devers to promise that he would begin his withdrawal on the night of 1 January and have Sixth Army Group back to a Vosges line by 5 January. Soon after, however, Devers received a second phone call from Bedell Smith informing him that the French were determined to defend Strasbourg. In a move clearly calculated to force the Americans' hand, Juin had visited on the morning of 30 December, "to say that the French Government are prepared to accept a big sacrifice in order not to let STRAUSBOURG [sic] fall undamaged into enemy hands. They offer to put into the STRAUSBOURG area three F.F.I. Divisions. They are prepared, if necessary, to lose these Divisions in the defense of Strausbourg." These divisions, stationed in Toulouse, Rheims, and Limoges, were all armed with captured German equipment, "although of course short of artillery. General Juin says he controls sufficient stocks of ammunition for the job ... Are there any reasons, from your point of view, why we should not accept this French offer if the Sixth Army Group wish to do so?"[112] Of course, there were multiple reasons why Devers would refuse a reinforcement of roughly 45,000 semi-trained and poorly disciplined French infantrymen with their Fifi officers,

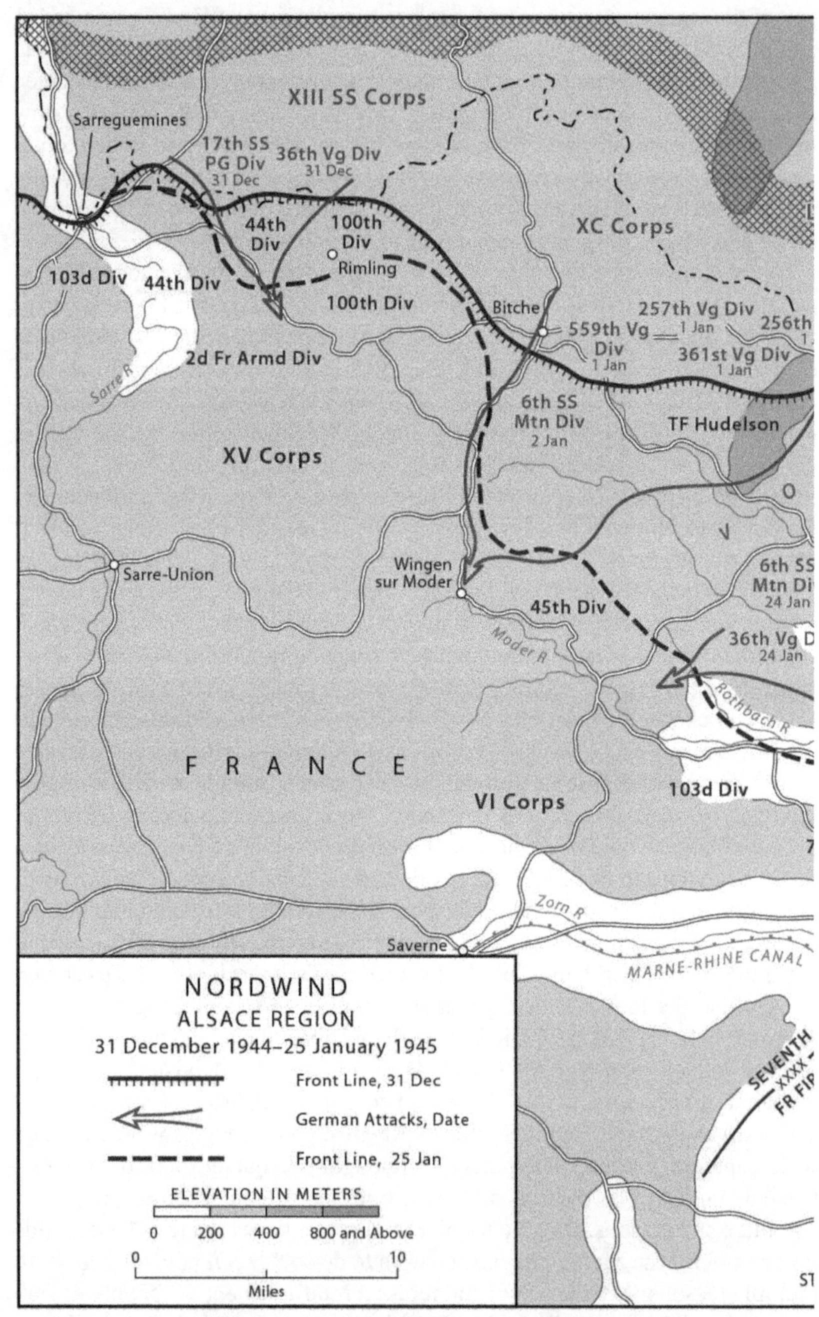

Map 8.4 Operation North Wind (31 December 1944–25 January 1945).

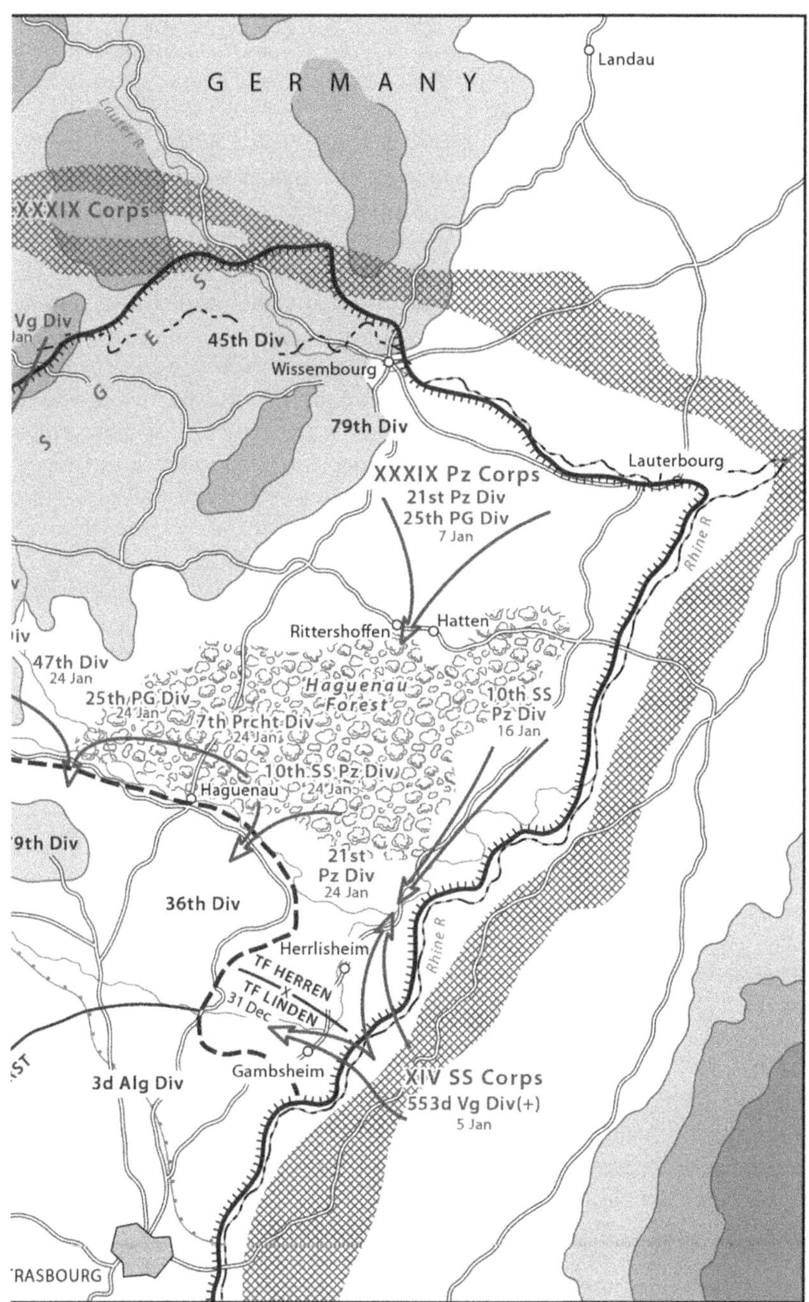

Landau
G E R M A N Y
Lauter R
XXXIX Corps
Vg Div
45th Div
Wissembourg
79th Div
Lauterbourg
XXXIX Pz Corps
21st Pz Div
25th PG Div
7 Jan
Rhine R
Rittershoffen
Hatten
47th Div
24 Jan
25th PG Div
24 Jan
Haguenau
Forest
7th Prcht Div
24 Jan
10th SS
Pz Div
16 Jan
10th SS Pz Div
24 Jan
Haguenau
9th Div
21st
Pz Div
24 Jan
36th Div
Herrlisheim
TF HERREN
X
TF LINDEN
31 Dec
Rhine R
Gambsheim
3d Alg Div
XIV SS Corps
553d Vg Div(+)
5 Jan
RASBOURG

Map 8.4 (cont.)

armed with German weapons, with no artillery, logistics, or probably communications to be "sacrificed" in some *Stalingrad-am-Rhein* Gaullist fantasy *Götterdämmerung*. No sooner had the offer been made than it seems to have been withdrawn.

That evening, de Gaulle's emissary, and designated military governor of Strasbourg, General du Vigier appeared at Sixth Army Group HQ with a personal letter from Juin requesting that Devers defend Alsace. Devers explained his retreat order to du Vigier and pointed out the phase lines on a map. He then put him on a plane to Paris, where du Vigier alerted Juin: "The Americans are buggering off!" The two men then informed de Gaulle, furious that Eisenhower had lacked the courtesy to forewarn him. The French leader ordered Juin to reiterate previous instructions to de Lattre that he was to defend Strasbourg, "if necessary, only with French forces."[113] He then wrote a polite letter to Eisenhower, explaining that, while he understood the operational logic of a withdrawal, "the French government obviously cannot allow Strasbourg to fall back into enemy hands without making . . . every possible effort to defend it." As the logic of the withdrawal was to build up Sixth Army Group reserves, he offered the 10^{e} DI to aid in Strasbourg's defense.[114]

In fact, in his memoirs de Gaulle claimed that, as early as 19 December, silence from SHAEF on renewing the attack on Colmar signaled that the Americans might indeed "*foutre le camp*," abandoning Strasbourg. During his Christmas tour of the front, he noted that Devers had transferred his headquarters from Phalsbourg to Vittel, 120 kilometers in the rear, while Patch's command post had retreated west from Saverne to Lunéville. By 28 December, de Gaulle was convinced that the Americans were preparing a withdrawal. Intelligence reports indicated an imminent German attack on the Saverne Gap.[115] But also, information began to reach the War Ministry in Paris, via French liaison officers, that the Seventh Army was beginning to mine roads and had already abandoned several villages in the Moder Valley. Nor did Juin have any confidence in Bedell Smith's denials when, on 28 December, he attempted to clarify rumors that Strasbourg was to be evacuated.[116] Alerted by du Vigier, on New Year's Day, de Gaulle had dispatched a letter to Eisenhower stating that the French army would defend Strasbourg. "De Gaulle's argument seemed to be based upon political considerations, founded more on emotion than on logic and common sense," Eisenhower recorded.[117] But Churchill blamed Eisenhower for having blindsided Juin and de Gaulle rather than coordinate with the GPRF. On 1 January, de Gaulle sent an appeal to both Churchill and Roosevelt asking for support.[118] He also copied de Lattre, warning him to be prepared to defend Strasbourg.[119]

The Ardennes offensive shook French faith in American protection and raised anxieties of a German resurgence. Strasbourg was gripped by panic as preparations for an American withdrawal became evident, despite Seventh

Army denials. Many civilians, including FFI and civil servants ordered to evacuate, fled by any means possible, crowding into unheated boxcars, in the process spreading alarm in Nancy and other towns already spooked by the appearance of Belgian refugees from the Ardennes, rumors of German parachutists masquerading as GIs, *Osttruppen* deserters and fugitives from *la milice* lurking in the forests, and FFI *bandes armées irregulaires* looking to settle scores. US civil affairs officers complained of a lack of cooperation from Paris, although Eisenhower had keep them in the dark about his evacuation plan. On the ground, however, French officials and American officers pitched in, commandeering empty ammunition trucks returning from the front to transport 2,000 evacuees a day to the far side of the Vosges, as Military Police (MPs) struggled to clear the roads of refugees.[120]

On the morning of 2 January, de Gaulle repeated his order to de Lattre to defend Strasbourg. On that day, de Lattre sent a passionate appeal to Devers, saying that the *1ère Armée* would defend the city from the south if only Patch could hold in place.[121] In a desperate move, de Lattre dispatched the 3e DIA to Strasbourg, while the FFI 10e ID slotted into their position on the Vosges. The 3e DIA was worn out, while Koenig believed the 10e ID, "from a material point of view, gives the impression of an absolutely depressing insufficiency."[122] While de Lattre confirmed that he would follow de Gaulle's order, he also expressed the hope that some sort of accord could be reached to save the solidarity of the Alliance and avoid a fate in which the 3e DIA would be condemned to "replicate Stalingrad alone" in the ruins of Strasbourg. "The act of disobedience in the middle of a battle poses a serious problem of conscience," de Lattre informed de Gaulle. An accord with SHAEF, "more would allow me, and I ask you urgently to consider it, to reconcile my duty as a French General toward my country, with the honor of my Army and toward you, my Political and military Leader, a duty that is primordial, with the discipline I owe, as a soldier, toward the Supreme Commander of Allied Armies among which the *1ère Armée française* plays a vital strategic role." De Lattre informed de Gaulle that he was entirely unable to pull any of his forces out of the line before 7 January, and that he would need an FFI division (presumably the 10e DI) as well as a US division to cover his left flank between Saverne and Brumath. Therefore, de Lattre's recommendation was that de Gaulle try to persuade the Americans to delay their withdrawal for as long as possible.[123] Not surprisingly, this earned the First Army's commander a stiff rebuke from his "Political and military Leader" obsessed with French sovereignty – "I little appreciated your last communication in which you seem to feel that the mission to defend Strasbourg, which was entrusted to your army in my letter of 1 January, is dependent on agreement by the Allied High Command." In fact, de Lattre's initial response to the Strasbourg crisis caused a furious de Gaulle to want "to sack [de Lattre] immediately."[124] In any case, on 3 January, de Lattre assured de Gaulle that, while the *1ère Armée* stood ready to defend Strasbourg, this would require a significant redeployment of troops that "could have repercussions for overall operations, [so] that it must be undertaken urgently, in coordination between the French government and the Allied Supreme command."[125]

In fact, de Lattre was probably saved by Eisenhower's change of heart. On 1 January, Devers had flown to Saverne to order Patch to fall back to the Vosges by 5 January. De Lattre wrote that he did not learn of this order, which would have meant the abandonment of Strasbourg and northern Alsace, until the late morning of 2 January, upon which he penned an emotional appeal to Devers with dramatic de Lattrean flourish to defend Strasbourg as "a symbol of French resistance and grandeur." But Devers reiterated his order by telegram at 21:47 that evening. De Lattre explained that the retreat order forced him to choose between obeying the Allied chain of command or his political boss de Gaulle, who categorically insisted that the interests of France took precedence over tactical concerns: "If the French government chose to confide its forces to a foreign commander, it is with the formal condition that their deployment will be in conformity with the national interest," de Gaulle recorded. "If that is not the case, [the leader] is duty bound to reassume command. That's what I decided to do, with even less hesitation as Allied headquarters had not judged it necessary to inform me of an action that touched France to the heart."[126]

On the night of 2–3 January, as the French took steps to evacuate civilians from Strasbourg and the Rhine plain, French COS Juin had explained to Bedell Smith the implications of an Allied abandonment of Strasbourg – certain German retaliation against the population, which the French could not allow to happen. On 3 January, the Mayor of Strasbourg sent a vigorous protest to de Gaulle about the "sacrifice" of the population by the "American command," demanding that his city be defended "by French troops."[127] Therefore, French forces would defend Strasbourg alone if need be, which could have severe implications for the Alliance, including the potential withdrawal of French forces from SHAEF command, a declaration that so infuriated Smith that he claimed: "If [Juin] had been an American, I'd have put my fist in his face."[128] Juin's report of his failed mission so disquieted de Gaulle that he threatened to make Strasbourg "a French Stalingrad," and to cut off the use of French harbors and railways if the Allies denied supplies to the French. De Lattre's plea to de Gaulle to find an accommodation with Eisenhower may have had some effect, because on 3 January de Gaulle wired de Lattre that he would indeed seek to have "SHAEF's decision to withdraw delayed for our purposes or modified as far as the 7th US Army is concerned. In any case, we cannot abandon Strasbourg without a fight."[129]

On the afternoon of 3 January, at de Gaulle's request, a meeting that included Churchill, Alan Brooke, Juin, Eisenhower, and Bedell Smith was convened at

Eisenhower's Versailles headquarters. Eisenhower began by setting out the exposed position of the Seventh Army, to which de Gaulle replied that, if he perhaps agreed with Eisenhower's operational logic, the abandonment of Alsace without a fight might lead to civil disorder and even the overthrow of the Republic. And that if Eisenhower persisted in his course of action, France would withdraw its forces from SHAEF command. At this point, Eisenhower lost his composure, and blamed the requirement to retreat on de Lattre's failure to eliminate the Colmar Pocket. He also lambasted the French failure to keep their combat divisions in fighting shape. As the two leaders traded heated threats, Churchill stood up and, pointing to the map, said "Strasbourg, this point."[130] While Churchill's meaning was unclear, at least it allowed Eisenhower to recover his self-control. Perhaps the American commander in chief realized that a French secession from SHAEF, following on the heels of his "personal embarrassment" over the Ardennes surprise, would not reflect well on his command tenure. On the contrary, it would unnecessarily complicate his task of defeating Germany.[131] After a few minutes of unruffled discussion, Eisenhower agreed to phone Devers and rescind his retreat order. De Gaulle insisted that Juin travel with Bedell Smith to Vittel to ensure that the order was received and executed. The two leaders also agreed to adjust the army boundaries so that Strasbourg fell within the *1ère Armée*'s zone of operations.[132] In his memoirs, de Gaulle claims that Eisenhower was won over by his compelling argument on the need to defend "sacred Alsace."[133] However, it appears that two factors combined to resolve the crisis. The first was Churchill's intervention, which de Gaulle never acknowledged, because he apparently assumed that Eisenhower had requested the presence of the British Prime Minister (PM) to bolster the case for withdrawal. The second was the fact that, by 3 January, *Nordwind* was contained, and the emergency had passed in any case.[134] In fact, Alan Brooke was surprised and a little disappointed that Eisenhower had ceded to de Gaulle's pressure, because he knew that it had been Montgomery, who refused to attack until he had recouped more troops from Devers' withdrawal to the Vosges, who had triggered Eisenhower's retreat order. On 5 January, the French formally took over the defense of Strasbourg.[135]

The Bombing of Royan

Not surprisingly, Eisenhower's containment strategy for the Atlantic pockets displeased de Gaulle, who on 18 September announced that he wanted "a French victory against the pockets … on the west coast."[136] In the larger scheme of the war, the occupied Atlantic harbors were not required for Allied logistics. Cleaning up German stay-behinds on the west coast of France would not hasten the end of the war. Evacuations had been organized to remove the most vulnerable civilian populations. Nor were the pockets "symbolic" territory, like Alsace-Moselle. Nevertheless, in what the US Army history calls a "wasteful" and "somewhat questionable effort . . . to boost the legitimacy of de Gaulle's provisional government,"[137] what was labeled Operation Independence looked to liberate the "southwestern fronts." De Gaulle gave priority to Royan, partly because it was the smallest pocket, whose garrison contained the largest number of non-German troops, and whose defenses were the weakest. But also, more importantly, the seizure of Royan would open the Gironde estuary to allow access to Bordeaux whose port was "relatively intact and whose utilization would greatly facilitate the resupplying of France. I pressed Eisenhower to procure the means for the French to reoccupy the German redoubts on the two banks of the Gironde. He was agreed in principle. It also fell to the French whose task was to lay siege – as a prelude to reoccupying – to the other Atlantic pockets: La Rochelle, Saint-Nazaire, Lorient."[138] Given de Gaulle's priorities, the besieging garrison for the southwest pockets grew to almost 35,000 troops by March–April 1945. To add muscle to the FFI-led siege, on 7 October 1944, the French leader had announced that the 1ère DFL and the 1ère DB would march west to reinforce the FFI, but a combination of delaying tactics by de Lattre and Devers, who were eager to eliminate the "Colmar Pocket," and the German offensives in Alsace meant that they would never arrive.[139]

A 10 December meeting at Cognac that included *Forces aériennes françaises libres* (FAFL) Brigadier General Édouard Corniglion-Molinier and the American General Ralph Royce of the First Tactical Air Force assigned to support Devers' Sixth Army Group discussed an assault on Royan. "One can predict that an attack on Royan could rapidly evolve in a favorable direction if it is undertaken with adequate means," the French *service de renseignement* had concluded in November 1944.[140] Different versions of the meeting subsequently surfaced. The basic agreement was that a ground assault on Royan would be preceded by an air bombardment. Royce came away with the idea that the central German defenses in Royan, that included the Fort du Chay, would be bombed, while Larminat insisted that the agreed-upon target was the Arvert Peninsula north of Royan. But mission evaluation in London appears to have been short-circuited as targeting prioritized Germany. The launch of the Ardennes offensive on 16 December, followed by *Nordwind*, once again prevented the planned transfer of the two *1ère Armée* divisions to the FFO, so that no troops were available to coordinate a ground attack with an air bombardment. Meanwhile, foul weather over Germany in early January caused Bomber Command in London to cast around for alternative objectives. Consequently, Royan was selected off a list of potential targets. But the Royal Air Force (RAF) failed to connect with the French liaison at Vittel, while a coded message sent to Larminat's headquarters at Cognac announcing

Figure 8.3 Because the 5 January 1945 bombing of Royan was not coordinated with a ground assault, it failed in its objective of opening the Gironde estuary to maritime traffic. (Photo by Roger Viollet via Getty Images)

the imminent bombing went unanswered. Nevertheless, even though, without a ground attack, the bombing of Royan would serve no strategic purpose, at this stage of the war Bomber Command ran on autopilot. The bombers took off in two waves from England after dark on 4 January and arrived over Royan in the early hours of 5 January (Figure 8.3).

August Hampel remembered the night of 4–5 January 1945 as being glacially cold. He was awakened by a low drone: "The sky lit up with red, yellow, and green glimmers, while in neat waves innumerable aircraft approached." He sprinted for the bunker. Three German soldiers arrived with their female companions. "They seemed thin, weary, withered . . . a few blotches of lipstick still clung to their lips. Their underclothes barely covered their tired breasts, any more than did a coat thrown over their shoulders at the last minute. So, here they are cast into the whirlwind of the war, these girls who, just a few years ago, walked obediently on Royan's boulevards next to their mothers who sought only to preserve their virginity." The soldiers were followed by a rush of civilians trying to gain access to the bunker, but who were prevented by the sergeant, who told them that there was not enough oxygen to sustain everyone.

Unfortunately, they had already seen "the whores standing in the corridor." "You were happy enough to make us construct the shelter for you," one screamed. "Now you leave us outside like beggars." But, at that moment, the earth began to shake, as the first wave of 217 Lancasters, preceded by 6 de Havilland Mosquitoes that launched flares to mark the target, arrived overhead, and the sergeant bolted the door with a large oak timber. Inside, the only light was a candle. But Hempel could see the three French women sitting on the floor clinging to each other, screaming as what sounded like a battering ram shook the bunker for fifteen minutes as bombs rained down on the center of Royan. When the noise stopped, the sergeant removed the timber and everyone filed outside into a black night, illuminated only by a few fires. Almost immediately, they began to hear cries for help. Huge craters pockmarked the town. As the garrison and townsfolk were picking through the debris looking for survivors, a second wave of 124 Lancasters arrived at 05:30. The soldiers rushed back into the bunker, and the sergeant replaced the timber. Once the second wave had passed, "everything was bathed in a strange yellow orange glow. Above the town, the sky was flecked with numerous purple sparks . . . Fires devoured any building still standing. A quick look showed that nothing had been spared. The woods looked as if they had been flattened by a hurricane of unimaginable strength. As far as one could see, the ground was pitted with craters. From time to time, a delayed action bomb exploded. I raised my eyes to a red sky. The smoke from the flames was asphyxiating. Our uniforms were covered with cinders." French civilians were nowhere to be seen. "German soldiers who had not made it to the bunkers, but had by some miracle survived at the bottom of a hole, were dazed. Their terror was evident in their eyes. In broken sentences, they described a continuous hail of monstrous projectiles, their fingers in their ears to spare their ear drums, and their amazement at still being alive . . . For a long time, we wandered like mindless automatons, mute and overwhelmed . . . Why didn't the enemy use the opportunity to attack the fortress? It would have been so easy, given our psychological state! The place would have fallen without a shot being fired."[141]

In all, 1,576 tons of explosives and 13 tons of incendiaries were dropped on Royan, destroying the historic heart of the city; 442 French civilians, two-thirds of them women, were killed. Only forty-seven Germans perished.[142] The German commander allowed a ten-day truce for the French to gather the casualties. Royce was relieved of his command. However, he was subsequently made commander of the *Légion d'honneur*. For their part, the Royanais blamed Larminat and Corniglion-Molinier. Although no one was punished, the principal culprit appears to have been Bomber Command in London, which was in the habit of prosecuting its own war irrespective of coordination with forces on the ground.[143]

The End of *Nordwind*

While the Allies' flutter over Strasbourg had passed, the Germans did not give up their attacks against French and American forces in Alsace, as Himmler attempted to retake Strasbourg from the south. The French reported that German "tactical groups" sought to infiltrate portions of the line not covered by artillery with a few hundred men behind tanks to create an opening in the front for penetration by larger armored formations. To counter, operations recommended immediate counterattacks using mobile artillery and tank destroyers.[144] Nevertheless, the German offensives in the Ardennes followed by *Nordwind* had run out of steam, as the Red Army closed on Berlin from the east. Without the benefit of surprise, orchestrated across a flat landscape nevertheless severed by numerous streams, rivers, and canals, by a high command fractured between OB West, Army Group G, Himmler's Army Group *Oberrhein*, and the First and Nineteenth Armies, with Hitler always casting the deciding vote, most German attacks were hastily planned, and lacked staying power. The dreaded German heavy tanks found it difficult to gain traction on the icy roads, while destroyed bridges, minefields, and high fuel consumption limited their mobility, and served to separate them from their infantry.

But this was not always apparent to the *1ère Armée* defenders, assigned a 240-kilometer front, against which a tide of *Jagdpanther* tank destroyers and Tiger tanks crashed across frozen fields, behind eruptions of artillery shells whose intimidating geysers left sooty circular footprints in the snow. Veteran units had absorbed significant casualties, which meant that the inventory of armored formations had been reduced by half, while infantry companies might number only thirty-five men.[145] Nor did mobilization seem to offer brighter prospects. After Koenig had inspected the fifteen indifferently armed and partially trained Parisian-raised FFI battalions of the 10e DI under Brigadier General Pierre Billotte, he reported on 11 December that, while morale was high, "from a matériel point of view, the units give the impression of wretched poverty: the lack of uniforms, of shoes, blankets, equipment, and matériel for training is such that one fears that, if this misery continues, it will demoralize the cadres, which have some good elements, and the rank-and-file, which is excellent."[146] Fully 56 percent of the 10e DI's officers had no prior military experience.[147] "The number of vehicles, mechanized engines, and collective arms necessary for combat can be considered as non-existent," reads the division's diary, presumably meaning that the 10e DI was reliant on horse-drawn transport and otherwise had little heavy weaponry. "The individual equipment is reduced to a single uniform per man." On 11 January, de Gaulle presented the division with its flag. On 20 January, they went into the line on the Vosges nonetheless, with neither automatic weapons nor radios, in temperatures as low as −28 °C.[148]

Fortunately, the German attacks ceased abruptly on the night of 25 January 1945, in part because Hitler was finally convinced that the defense of Berlin against the advancing Soviets had become more urgent than snatching the trophy of Strasbourg.[149] In the end, the Germans had little to show for an estimated 17,000 killed and wounded and 6,000 POWs. In all, the German offensives had cost 100,000 casualties, destroyed most of Germany's mobile reserves, undermined morale, and put the Soviets in a far better position to seize Vienna and Berlin.[150] Despite being relatively inexperienced, Sixth Army Group commanders and units had performed well, with the 2e DB earning plaudits as the best armored unit in Sixth Army Group.[151] For his part, de Lattre gave the prize to Garbay's 1ère DFL, which defended south of Strasbourg, and Guillaume's 3e DIA, which blocked the approaches to the north, with much assistance from US airpower and "*la fraternité d'armes franco-américaine*."[152]

Morale Crisis

Stalemate in Alsace brought tensions dangerously to the fore, both in the Alliance and within the French army. The Strasbourg crisis had highlighted that, as the war drew to a close, de Gaulle prioritized the defense of French political objectives over preserving harmony in an Allied coalition whose military leadership remained operationally focused. Second, military setbacks had rekindled rivalries at the summit of the French command, which fractured along old Gaullist–Vichy, colonial–metropolitan, and infantry–cavalry fault lines, accentuated by the arrival of FFI replacements, as well as those created by critics who censured de Lattre's personally flamboyant but operationally timorous command style. Eisenhower blamed de Lattre's 21 November halt order for having permitted the Colmar Pocket to form in the first place. Perhaps reacting to Devers' comment that *1ère Armée* seemed to have "an inferiority complex," Monsabert complained that the Americans asked the French to perform tasks beyond their ability to carry out, in part because of an "eternal lack of infantry," and then treated the French as if they were combat-shy.[153]

These tensions at the top of the hierarchy communicated downward. The stalemate in Alsace that stretched into the New Year eradicated hope for a rapid victory and accelerated a morale slide in the French forces that had been apparent at least since the Belfort Gap in October. French casualties had numbered over 10,000 troops for the month of December. Since Dragoon, almost a third of the soldiers in de Lattre's four infantry divisions had become casualties. Half of the French soldiers removed from the line because of frozen or trench foot in temperatures that reached −20 °C were permanently *hors de combat*.[154] The optimism that had sustained the rapid advance from the Mediterranean and the enthusiasm of early FFI volunteers now receded into bitterness felt by soldiers against a French population disengaged from the war, morale-busting combat conditions that seemed to replicate those of the Eastern Front, and the vain wait for replacements, which the GPRF lacked the means to mobilize, train, and equip on a significant scale. Alsace reminded CEF veterans of the winter stalemate before Cassino.[155] Many North African soldiers had not been given leave in two years and feared that their families could not survive on meager army allotments in a time of food shortages and rampant inflation in AFN. *Caïds* in Tunisia were also taxing the herds of *tirailleurs*. These complaints caused the 3e DIA to send officers to North Africa to investigate further assistance for the families of their *tirailleurs*. And, while the arrival of FFI replacements reassured them that the French at last were contributing to the fight, "their lack of order and discipline," combined with seeing so many French "tranquilly going about their business, and living with their families," leaving Muslims to lead the fight, had caused "acrimony."[156]

In fact, the French combat performance had been on a slide since 15 August 1944. But, to put this in context, as the war thrashed to its bloody conclusion, "ground armies in particular, staggered under the weight of losses and, like a punch-drunk boxer, found it harder to land the knockout punch the longer combat was sustained," writes Richard Overy. "Numerous examples of front-line panic are to be found among small units across all the battlefront."[157] Hardly had they landed in France than Brosset had complained that his division lacked European troops and required a top-up of FFI and *Chantiers* inmates. The only replacements that he received were North African Muslims, "who I am required to return to Nîmes," because he had no cadres to organize them. Throughout the autumn, he reported that his troops were furnished "no physical and moral" comforts to sustain morale – including shelter, alcohol, clothing, and mail – but were forced to live in the open in appalling weather.[158] And, while tensions between front and rear were hardly new in French wars, they intensified in the autumn and winter of 1944–1945 in the absence of a general mobilization *à la* 1914. How could one be surprised at the lack of solidarity among the French population, one officer in the 1ère DB asked in February 1945, "when there is no sense of solidarity in the army."[159] In the view of many soldiers, the French population, deaf to the principles at stake in the war, remained happy enough to be liberated, so long as they were not expected to bear any sacrifice – a grievance heard since Torch. "In this way, while tensions between front and rear made manifest in the winter of 1944–1945 were nothing new," concludes Miot, "nevertheless, the intensity of the division was striking."[160]

Indeed, since the early Third Republic, it had been said that France's "truly religious" love for its army was matched only by "the pathological fear that it harbors of having to serve in it,"[161] a phenomenon that operated in other leading countries, as well. Through the haze of his pietistic nationalism, even de Gaulle acknowledged that the French population had largely tuned out the war in Alsace, which he attributed to several factors: for most, liberation had meant the war's end; the continuing campaigns were viewed as an Allied affair, in which French forces, composed in great part of North African Muslims and other colonial levies, played a relatively marginal role; popular esteem for a French army already impugned for the bloodletting of 1914–1918 had plunged in the shadow of the 1940 defeat and the support of many professional officers for Vichy; and, finally, the fact that the course of the war, already deemed to have been effectively won, was no longer a preoccupation for politicians and the press.[162] Indeed, the government had helped to undermine mobilization in part by prioritizing the urgency of national reconstruction, a rebuilding that would extend beyond clearing the rubble, kickstarting the economy, and retaining a grip on an increasingly restive empire. Defeat and occupation had revealed too many political failings, required moral compromises, and tangled the boundaries between combatant and civilian, all of which would necessitate a painful reconstruction of a national psyche pommeled by a "plurality of ordeals."[163]

Grumbles about the detachment of the French population were intensified in the ranks by grievances about the poor combat conditions and logistical shortcomings. Abundantly supported and warmly clothed GIs highlighted a shocking *1ère Armée* penury. The French lacked everything, which sent a strong message that they were the least valued and most expendable members of the Alliance. A lack of combat experience, arms, and adequate clothing resulted in a high casualty rate, that further lowered morale and sabotaged the army's renaissance. Professionals complained that *l'amalgame* had overreached by incorporating for political reasons more troops than the French could possibly arm, train, supply, and lead. Consequently, soldiers had begun to pillage to survive. Furthermore, North African soldiers and former FFL had seen their pay cut because now they were "home" and no longer qualified for overseas pay.[164] Many had seen their friends and cadres thinned out since Italy. But, rather than promote Muslims, skin color and religion, rather than battlefield experience and command competence, justified the promotion of "mediocre" French cadres. The morale crisis even began to affect the redoubtable *goumiers*.[165] Monsabert complained that, while the Americans sent their wounded home, some of his *tirailleurs* had been returned to the front having been wounded up to three times:

> Our lack of men, of cadres means that our best units, like my dear 3e DIA, are no more than phantoms, even when we reinforce them – [men who] never trained because they are sent too soon [into combat]. They are condemned men – and they know it! What a mistake, this question of purges and FFI illusions, that prevented the mobilization and the recall of trained cadres of the armistice army. All the young blood, and even more motivated because it would have wanted to redeem itself, we're lacking, and this accumulates bitterness for the future.[166]

For an ever decreasing percentage of FFL veterans, a proliferation of "mothballed" senior officers in staff and service jobs, "whose service records between the years 1940 and 1944 our soldiers would be curious to know," combined with growing casualties to lower morale. Not only was the character of the 1ère DFL changing as the veterans of Bir Hakeim shriveled to a handful, but together with it evaporated the "confidence" of the soldiers in their leadership. The manifest fear was that the spirit of *la France libre*, which had been under threat since Torch, when North Africa was swamped by the Anglo-Americans, superseded by *l'armée d'Afrique*, and subverted by *l'amalgame*, would be submerged by the general indifference of the population to the army's sacrifice. One of the ironies of liberation was that the more its minority status became confirmed with losses, transfers, and *l'amalgame*, the more the FFL, who regarded themselves as the "pure" resistance, feared contamination and marginalization by a wave of last-minute domestic resisters with "feudal tendencies who considered their soldiers as their property: demands, intrigues, games between the diverse groups and command, all to keep their troops intact and inflate their numbers with no consideration for the general interests." Of course, this was mirror imaging to a degree, precisely because they reflected the criticisms that opponents had leveled against the Gaullists since 1940.[167]

But suspicion cut both ways. The point of *l'amalgame* was to metropolitanize mobilization and revivify the spirit of patriotism in an army that at its core was composed of professional soldiers and colonial mercenaries. But this process took time to gain traction, which played a major role in the erosion of morale. By the end of January, around 39,000 recent volunteers were fighting in the *1ère Armée*, with another 3,000 integrated into Leclerc's 2e DB, although the figures do not indicate whether volunteers were former FFI. The 10e DI, made up almost entirely of volunteers and former FFI, had joined the front. As late as December 1944, 90 percent of those mobilized were from AFN, with Corsica a distant second, because these were the only places where the French had current census records and conscription mechanisms in place. Death notices and reports of tough combat conditions in Alsace reinforced the conviction prevalent since Tunisia that North Africa continued to underpin the French war effort. For those on leave from the front, the rear seemed to abound with food- and jazz-addicted *zazous* and their frivolous girlfriends. "September resisters" battled for municipal power in many towns, especially ones in the southwest that had been bypassed by the liberating armies. Meanwhile, soldiers in Alsace starved; and in AFN "the natives lived in misery." While AFN squeezed out another 24,706 reinforcements for the front between 15 February and 24 April 1945, fully 17 percent of the contingent in Tunisia had failed to answer the call-up in February. But, in the absence of anti-conscription demonstrations, the military remained convinced that nationalist propaganda had failed to penetrate Muslim ranks. Nevertheless, the trend was worrying, even to the Americans alarmed since December by the yawning vacancies in the ranks of French divisions in Alsace.[168]

Many young Frenchmen had volunteered in the heady days of August–September, calculating that the Wehrmacht was on the ropes, and that they need only turn out for the victory parade. The reality was that, after four years of occupation, most were suffering the effects of severe malnourishment and were therefore desperately unfit, as the front hardened and a particularly harsh arctic winter settled on the Vosges. Nor did the army have enough weapons and warm clothing for them. While the French army in AFN had been responsible for the basic instruction of its soldiers, with Dragoon, the Americans no longer trained French troops on weapons systems and in specialist skills. In early January 1945, a training camp was set up at Valdahon, southeast of Besançon, where an estimated 5,000 volunteers were taught the rudiments of soldiering. On 22 February 1945, de Lattre created one of his signature *écoles des cadres* at Rouffach near Colmar, where former FFI would be put through a five-week training course. But the program received bad reviews for its "disorganization" and attempts to "fanaticize" recruits rather than inculcate the basics of soldiering. The result was that the initiation for *1ère Armée* recruits proved perfunctory.[169] A chronic manpower shortage meant that units soon complained of replacements sent straight from hospital, men often barely recovered from their wounds or frozen feet, or with inadequate military skills, which failed to augment the fighting quality of units. Desperately needed technical specialists were often exempted from conscription in the interest of national recovery, as were fathers, former POWs, those from Alsace-Moselle, and workers in vital industries including mines and agriculture, as well as categories of civil servants. Those with a record of "anti-national acts" were also banned. One million POWs still languished in Germany, while the conscript classes of 1940–1942 had been hollowed out by *la relève* and STO. Others were exempt for economic reasons. Confusion, rumor, lack of records, or even of a functioning government on the local level also played a role in determining who was called up. And even then, the army lacked a structure to incorporate them, so that many never left home. For these reasons, only a "partial mobilization" was applied to the class of 1943, which, after generous exemptions, created a deep sense of injustice among those required to serve.[170] Thus, in the absence of a systematic program of conscription in the metropole, *l'amalgame* had failed to realize the fusion of the regular army with the *levée en masse*, and hence it did not bridge France's civil–military chasm.

Significant losses combined with *l'amalgame* had also disrupted the functioning of *armée d'Afrique* units, where discipline and combat performance were anchored in the personal relationship established between European officers and NCOs and Muslim soldiers. By 15 January 1945, the *1ère Armée* listed 8,568 KIA/missing in action (MIA), with 26,625 WIA, to which almost 2,000 FFI casualties were added.[171] A fusion of French metropolitan volunteers and Muslims dislocated *l'armée d'Afrique*'s racialized military culture. French volunteers became disheartened when regular officers and NCOs showered them with condescension, a contempt returned with interest by FFI distrustful of "*l'armée prétorianne*" or "the army of 50,000 colonialists commanded by Vichyite officers." Many former FFI felt that "their stripes [had been] usurped" by professional soldiers, and that they were simply being deployed as cannon fodder. Fed into combat with as little as a week's training, many had not even fired their weapons. Once at the front, they were ordered to attack across fields laced with *Schü-Minen*, without the support of mortars or heavy machineguns. Nor had they been prepared psychologically and morally to endure German artillery barrages, so incidents of shell shock became common.[172]

The chief of the *1ère Armée*'s liaison mission, Lieutenant-colonel du Souzy, reported that Devers had expressed his disappointment with the performance of de Lattre's organization. *Deuxième Bureau* reports arrived late and lacked precision. The 2e DB "especially" came in for criticism, as did the *4e Division marocaine de montagne* (4e DMM). In Devers' view, Leclerc had withdrawn from a perfectly defensible position and failed to attack the German troops in the northern sector of the pocket, who were clearly on the defensive.[173] Speaking for the 1ère DFL, on 28 January 1945, General Pierre Garbay explained that, since 7 January, in the space of 3 weeks, his division had taken around 2,700 casualties, of which 2,200 were due to enemy action, the rest mainly frozen feet, a condition which required at least a month in hospital before a soldier was fit for action – in February 1945, 859 convalescent soldiers were returned to duty in the 1ère DFL against only 359 fresh replacements. The good news for Garbay was that – amazingly – his MIA rate was under 1 percent. If this figure is accurate, it indicates that, despite the harsh conditions of combat, his soldiers were neither surrendering nor seizing the opportunity to desert. But, as French statistics made no distinction between KIA and MIA, it is impossible to know. And, while this may have been true for the 1ère DFL, Miot found that an increasing number of soldiers simulated illness, took French leave, refused guard duty, or even engaged in self-mutilation. Little of this shows up in the court-martial records because the tradition in *l'armée d'Afrique* was summary justice. A resort to the judge advocate was considered a blot on an officer's record.[174] In any case, to commit a soldier to the justice system was to give him precisely what he sought – escape from combat.

The bad news was that three-quarters of the frozen feet constituted a perfectly avoidable casualty category had the division issued adequate footwear. In any case, with insufficient numbers of infantry, Garbay's 1ère DFL was reduced simply to defending conquered ground:

> Since the 23rd [January 1945], the men are in the front lines in the snow, attacking and counterattacking without a respite, with no relief possible. No unit has more than 100 men in its infantry companies, while some battalions like the 2e BLE [Foreign Legion Battalion] for example have no more than 35 men in each of their companies [normally numbering around 180–200 men]. The survivors are exhausted and at the end of their endurance, especially the young recruits and the North African *tirailleurs*. The 7 battalions in the attack sector are all engaged and not available for further offensive action. The seizure of Elsenheim and Ohnenheim, as well as securing these two positions, requires two additional battalions, which I don't have.[175]

As the Americans had noted, without a tradition of a strong NCO corps, the French depended on their officers to motivate the troops. Although an "African" only by adoption, "after my third or fourth skirmish, I took myself for a veteran and showed a paternalist solicitude toward the *boujadis* [new recruits] sent in profusion to replace losses in the last offensives," wrote Bacquier. "One quickly grew up at the front. I followed closely the trends that imposed themselves in the battalion: I attacked without a weapon, without a helmet, with a cane, a pipe between my teeth [which I broke naturally], with a top hat [that one of my jokers had liberated from the ruins of a house], and always with butter-colored gloves that Aomar handed to me solemnly a minute before the assault, as I ordered 'prepare to attack.' It made the *tirailleurs* laugh as they fixed bayonets: 'the officer's putting his gloves on. The shit's gonna hit the fan.'" Eventually, after observing "my fantasies with amused tolerance," his company commander brought down the curtain on his theatrics: "*Mon cher* Bacquier, stop behaving like an idiot and wear your helmet. Otherwise, I'm gonna kick your arse!"[176] But a system that put officers in the lead translated into high officer casualties, which invariably impacted performance. A confidential report issued by the *État-major de la défense nationale* (EMDN, General Staff of National Defense) at the end of 1944 noted that in some battalions all the officers had become casualties, while others had reported 85–90 percent casualty rates among officers. Sickness had also taken a toll. In the middle of December 1944, de Lattre reported that, since the beginning of Anvil, 30 percent of the *tabors* (*goumiers*) and the 4e DMM, 50 percent of the 2e DIM and the 9e DIC, and 109.3 percent of the 3e DIA had become casualties. An undated report, probably drawn up in February–March 1945, for the 3e DIA put officer casualties since Dragoon at 132, which would have been roughly a 20 percent casualty rate, while the troops had suffered 4,393 casualties, meaning a rate of around 30 percent.[177] De Lattre desperately needed reinforcements, but they were slow to arrive from AFN, hence, his need to incorporate 44,000 FFI into the *1ère Armée* by the end of January, as well as make the 10e DI available for combat, if not combat-ready.[178]

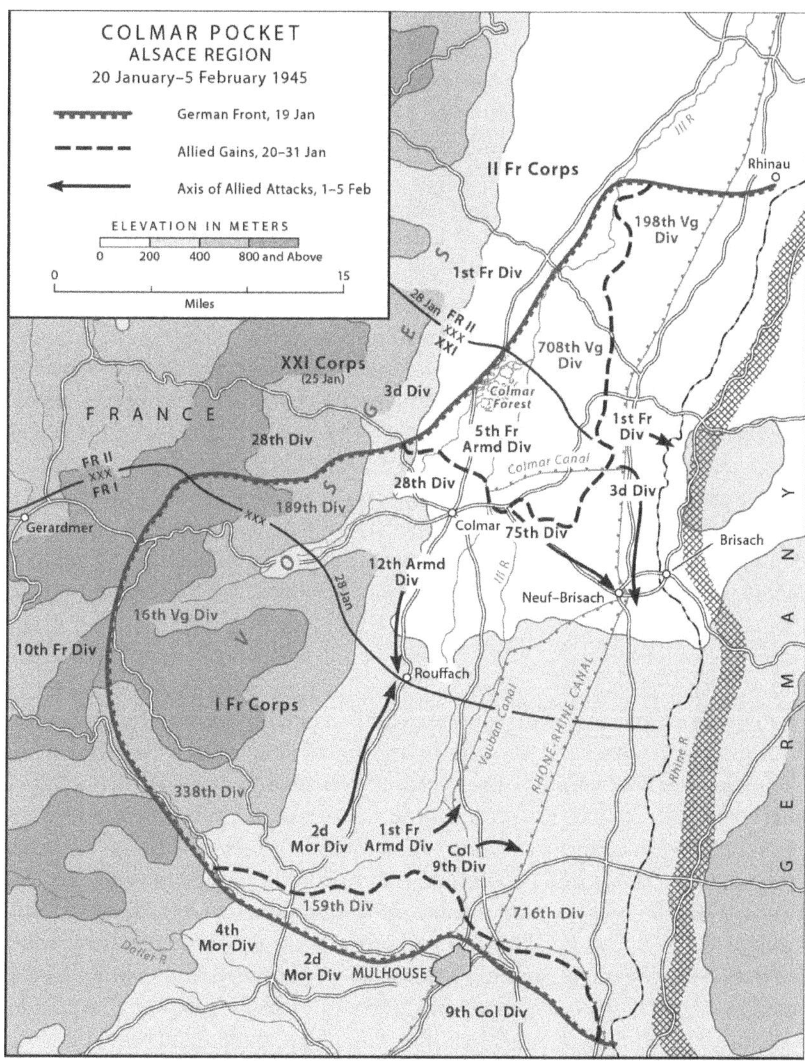

Map 8.5 Elimination of the Colmar Pocket (20 January–5 February 1945).

"Operation Cheerful": The Elimination of the Colmar Pocket

With the danger of *Nordwind* behind him, Eisenhower refocused his attention on the Colmar Pocket (Map 8.5), which, he confessed, "had always irritated me and I determined that it was to be crushed without delay."[179] In effect, the pocket created a 50-mile gap in Allied lines along the Rhine. For the French, the complete liberation of Alsace, together with that of the Atlantic pockets, had become "a major national interest" of enormous symbolic and moral importance.[180] Even as *Nordwind* continued to blow like a force 8 gale, Devers and de Lattre met at Vittel on 11 January to discuss the elimination of the pocket, estimated to contain two German corps, combining eight under-strength infantry divisions, and a tank brigade that assembled perhaps sixty-five tanks as well as assault guns. German tanks were able to disable Sherman tanks and US tank destroyers at 2,400 meters, while the American machines had to approach within 500 meters of the German engines to have a chance with a 76.2 mm hollow-charge round, of which the *1ère Armée* had very few.[181] While the Germans counted numerous artillery pieces, shells were rationed. The requirement to spread troops to support a formidable defensive web of villages and crossroads left the German defenders few reserves to mount anything other than local counterattacks. The key to "strangle" the German defense would be a fuel pipeline, the two intact Rhine bridges, and numerous ferries that assured the logistical links – and evacuation routes – to Germany. These would constitute the primary objectives of an Allied offensive which, in de Lattre's plan, would see simultaneous attacks from both north and south of the pocket converging on Neuf-Brisach on the Rhine and thus cutting off the German escape routes.[182] On the other hand, numerous rivers, streams, and canals, as well as forests, Colmar's urban landscape, and the remnants of 1914 fortifications, as well as Maginot Line strongpoints, offered the Germans formidable defensive positions protected by minefields, and served as launch-pads for counterattacks. All of this, in de Lattre's imagination, transformed the Alsatian plain into "an immense necropolis covered by the snow with a thick sheet of death." While Devers liked de Lattre's plan, he did not believe the French strong enough to execute it, and appealed to Bedell Smith for more troops, a request that brought a promise of Frank Milburn's four-division XXI Corps to Devers, who would also count in his inventory the French 5ᵉ DB, Leclerc's 2ᵉ DB, and the 12th US Armored Division (AD). De Lattre would have an overwhelming superiority in tanks and artillery, and could also call upon sixty battalions of replacements, forty of them FFI. However, de Lattre categorized his force as "solid but tired." In his estimation, the best unit in his inventory was "Iron Mike" O'Daniel's 3rd US ID.[183]

By 14 January, Sixth Army Group staff had prepared "Operation Cheerful," with I Corps attacking north to draw in German reserves, followed two days later by a II Corps offensive directed to the south, to be reinforced by the 28th US ID, a unit that had been mauled in the Ardennes and was considered useful only for defensive operations, and 10th US AD, together with the crack 3rd US ID. Devers' concern was to launch the offensive before a thaw would turn the frozen fields of Alsace into a quagmire. In any case, the many streams, rivers, and canals that crisscrossed the Alsatian plain would strain scarce bridging equipment. The fighting during *Nordwind* had exhausted stocks of ammunition and petrol, while a lack of spare parts sidelined many vehicles awaiting repair. "Personally, I would have waited another 24 hours," de Lattre remembered, mainly to pre-position his supply depots and bring more vehicles into the line – "G3 [operations] proposes, but G4 [logistics] disposes." But the 28th US ID would revert to SHAEF control on 27 January, while the Americans needed the French to provide a diversion for *Nordwind.* A forward supply depot was quickly established at Schirmeck, linked to the rear by rail, while plans were laid for vehicle repair and medical stations to be sited along the routes of advance. But nothing could be allowed to move in advance, so as not to give away the plans for the attack. However, sub-zero temperatures had frozen petrol barges on the canals and temporarily disabled pumping stations along the pipeline. Snow had also backed up rail traffic to Marseilles, which meant that de Lattre would attack with only a 24-hour stockpile of fuel.[184]

On 20 January, covered by a deception operation like that which had preceded the Belfort Gap push, I Corps attacked with Béthouart's two Moroccan divisions (the 4e DMM and 2e DIM) in the lead, backed by a sudden barrage unleashed by 102 artillery batteries. Assaulted in a glacial blizzard, the Germans, who did not expect an Allied offensive while they were still preoccupied with *Nordwind*, were caught by surprise. But the effect of the attack was blunted by appalling weather, that ruled out air support and hampered communications with the rear.[185] Heavy snow prevented even the mules, let alone the vehicles, from accompanying the advance. From the evening of 21 January, de Lattre realized that his attack was in trouble, and toured his frontline commanders to urge them to action.[186] By 27 January, Devers had become concerned that the French were making little progress, while expending large quantities of ammunition, and concluded that they would require assistance. "Only the stubbornness of their own officers and the assistance of the Americans finally gave them the edge," concluded the US Army's official history.[187]

The artillery rightly had been the French army's pride at least since Napoleon. However, it was not simply a question of reacquiring an inventory of tubes, which the French did through a heterogeneity of types and calibers from US and British donations, stocks in AFN, and guns captured or abandoned by the enemy on the battlefield, which complicated and restricted the ammunition supply. It was necessary also to acquire the communication, observation, displacement, and coordination equipment and habits to operationalize indirect fire support. As it was, the ability of the French to field eight new artillery regiments by 8 May 1945 was a tribute to their energy and improvisation.[188] However, the result was that there would be no repeat of the Garigliano on the Rhine. With Operation Cheerful seemingly in stalemate, on 25 January, General Frank Milburn's XXI Corps, consisting of three infantry divisions and one armored division, came under de Lattre's command, although logistically the Americans continued to support it. This was a Godsend, because it gave de Lattre a wealth of artillery ammunition, which he hitherto lacked – on 29 January, the 3rd US ID alone fired 16,438 rounds in 3 hours, as GIs began to cross the Colmar canal in pneumatic boats. On the same day, Berlin abolished Army Group *Oberrhein* and reassigned Himmler to the Eastern Front – not as far "east" as it once was – an indication that the Colmar Pocket was no longer considered vital to the German defenses. On the night of 28–29 January, Hitler permitted a partial withdrawal from the northern zone of the pocket. Yet only on 30 January, as the full weight of the XXI US Corps began to be felt, did it occur to the Germans that the Allies sought to cut off their retreat at Neuf-Brisach, so that they stepped up the pace of withdrawal from the Vosges to protect their escape hatch.[189]

Yet, no operation seemed complete without another flareup at the top of the French command. On 6 December, Devers had transferred Leclerc's 2e DB to the *1ère Armée*'s authority. With de Gaulle in Moscow, Leclerc appealed to Devers and Diethelm to return the 2e DB to Patch's Seventh Army, with the argument that, while he regarded the divisions in the *1ère Armée* as being individually good, "as a whole it works poorly." In his view, the 2e DB was much more effective within the US system, especially as the *1ère Armée*'s logistical organization was backward and parsimonious. Diethelm had subsequently written to Devers that Leclerc's assignment to de Lattre's command could only be temporary. Leclerc's initiative earned an admonishment from de Gaulle, vexed that his protégé would appeal to an American general to escape French authority. Leclerc was also rebuffed by his patron when he insisted that the 2e DB was needed in towns "contaminated" by the resistance to "reassure the honest French population" that a communist takeover would not succeed. "You tell General Leclerc that the internal order in France is my concern and not his," de Gaulle informed one of Leclerc's subordinates, Paul de Langlade. On 20 January, Devers dispatched the 2e DB to the *1ère Armée* to liquidate the Colmar Pocket. However, on 29 January, Leclerc refused to follow an order from II Corps' commander Monsabert to attack into wooded terrain unless he was given "an American division in support." Monsabert replied that, in that case, he should ask Devers for an American division, which is precisely what he did – bypassing de Lattre, Leclerc appealed directly to Devers at Vittel. Monsabert's attack order was canceled.

On 1 February, de Lattre called in all his division commanders to coordinate the final attack on the Colmar Pocket, at the end of which Leclerc demanded to be sent back to Seventh Army. De Lattre exploded with rage, accusing Leclerc of not being a team player, of "bad comradeship" and "crazy pride." De Lattre cleared the room, and the two men had ten minutes alone. One rumor emerged that they almost came to blows. However, Devers found it particularly intriguing that Leclerc did not want to be part of his own army. Monsabert's explanation was that Leclerc, who in normal circumstances would have been a squadron (battalion) commander at his age, simply behaved like de Gaulle's spoiled darling: "Oh how wonderful, rapid promotion."[190] In its essential respects, however, a crusading mentality in the service of a holy mission encapsulated the attitude of a Gaullist firebrand who sought to humiliate and delegitimize the French army by contrasting its collaboration, institutional paralysis, lack of dynamism, and contempt for innovation with Gaullist actions. When Devers raised the subject of Leclerc's indiscipline with de Lattre, the First Army's commander simply threw up his hands and said that he could not control his division commander, which in Devers' mind spoke volumes about the politicization of the French army and its dysfunctional command climate. Leclerc was a knight in the service of de Gaulle, with no intention of submitting to the egotistical caprices of a "Vichy general." None of this raised Leclerc's stock with the commander of Sixth Army Group, who did not view him as a "sound soldier . . . [Leclerc] goes places with his division when he has open spaces, but when he gets up against real competition and things do not move rapidly, he fails." For Devers, Leclerc was both too politicized and a whiner, always complaining about a lack of artillery support, the inadequacy of his infantry, and the poor state of his equipment, when, in Devers' view, Leclerc had plenty of equipment – all he needed to do was to deploy it properly. Devers remarked that, in the US Army, Leclerc would at the least have been relieved of command, while Zhukov no doubt would have slapped him against a wall and shot him. But disciplining de Gaulle's volatile young acolyte was beyond the power even of France's senior army commander.[191] In February 1945, Leclerc was swapped out with the 1ère DB and sent west. Thus, like Eisenhower in North Africa and Normandy, Devers had to fight two wars in Alsace, one against the Germans, the other while trying to referee *1ère Armée*'s tempestuous command climate.[192] All of this was predictable, according to Bacquier's experienced Adjutant chef: "Léonetti concluded, sententiously, 'Cavalrymen, they're arseholes.' There's nothing to add."[193]

One reason for persistent indiscipline in the French army's senior ranks was that, while primed to behave in an overbearing manner with foreign leaders and senior military commanders when he believed French interests required it, de Gaulle "hated dealing with the quarrels of subordinates," and so failed to gavel his squabbling underlings to order. This may seem surprising, as the French leader believed that his main bargaining counter with the Allies lay in France's military contribution to the war. Yet, his attempts to calm the bickering among his senior commanders were usually limited to citing to them one of his favorite aphorisms: "all that is exaggerated is pointless," advice that he seldom applied to himself. To which Leclerc's puckish reply was that exaggeration exemplified the very soul of the Gaullist project, as did a refusal to follow the orders of a politically compromised hierarchy.[194]

In fact, beyond the incompatible personalities of the two French generals lay their conflicting concepts of the use of armor. Leclerc's complaint was that de Lattre treated his armored divisions as clearing houses for tanks and reservoirs of support for the infantry as in 1940, rather than as mobile, hard-hitting divisions capable of independent initiative.[195] In de Gaulle's vision, the 2^e^ DB had been conceived originally to symbolize a revitalized and modernized French army, and as a vanguard to seize objectives of symbolic national value, such as Paris, Baccarat, and Strasbourg. Furthermore, upon landing in Normandy, the 2^e^ DB was integrated into the Third Army commanded by George Patton, a cavalryman who shared Leclerc's "go for broke" mentality and his view of the value of massed armor to knock over and encircle the enemy, and to exploit breakthroughs by disrupting the enemy's command and control. For this reason, Leclerc argued that the impact of the 2e DB doubled when under US direction. The January 1945 transfer of the 2e DB to support Monsabert's corps meant that they would be "sausaged" with the infantry, as the 1ère and 5e DBs habitually were, that they would lack the logistical support they received as part of the US Army, and that they would probably be assigned operational objectives of secondary magnitude. The attacks that ran from 23 January to 10 February were made worse by two factors. First, Monsabert's infantry units were topped up with poorly trained FFI who had scant notion of how to coordinate infantry–armor attacks, which allegedly caused a plethora of friendly fire incidents. The second problem was that the general thrust of de Lattre's offensive meant that the tanks continually encountered river barriers that broke their momentum. In the eyes of his critics, de Lattre's utilization of armored forces in Alsace was "on the margins of doctrinal orthodoxy."[196]

Colmar fell on 2 February, while on the next day the north side of the pocket began to crumble. "The exploitation phase was about to begin," reads the French after-action report.[197] On 3 February, de Gaulle intervened to transfer the 2^e^ DB to the US XV Corps in Lorraine. But advances were made treacherous by infestations of plastic mines and systematic German counterattacks. The French I Corps and the US XXI Corps rendezvoused at Rouffach at the foot of the Vosges on 5 February. Neuf-Brisach fell the next day, as the Germans struggled to transfer troops and equipment to the east bank of the Rhine. But formal permission from Hitler to withdraw from the Colmar Pocket was received by Nineteenth Army only on the afternoon of 8 February, by which time the Colmar Pocket had been reduced to a wedge seven miles long and two miles wide along the Rhine. By 9 February, Alsace had become *Reichsdeutschefrei*. On 11 February, Leclerc was promoted "*grand officier de la Légion d'honneur*."[198]

The Allies had bagged 16,438 German POWs in the Colmar Pocket, with an estimated 22,000 German soldiers killed or wounded. "Certainly, no more than 400 to 500 combat effectives from each of the eight [German] divisions [in the Colmar Pocket] managed to escape across the Rhine," in the process abandoning most of their equipment, concludes the official US Army history. De Lattre reported 2,137 KIA and 11,253 WIA, the price paid to bag 20,000 German POWs.[199] French casualty figures must be taken as approximations for several reasons, beginning with the fact that, in Sixth Army Group, the Americans and French shared many of the same casualty and evacuation stations. It may have been that many French casualties were simply not recovered, and therefore not counted, as the French lacked an adequate number of ambulances and medical personnel, even stretchers.[200] Nor, according to Bacquier, did French units invariably report casualties, at least not immediately:

[Adjutant chef] Léonetti knew all the tricks that assured the comfort and survival of professional NCOs in the field. And he shared them with me: "Never declare all your casualties at once. In any case, the parents in the Berber mountains, in Corsica or Brittany are in no hurry to learn that their son is dead. And it's also useful to have a small list of casualties available when some staff idiot wants to order you to undertake a useless suicide mission. Or send out a patrol to see what the enemy is up to: 'Patrol encountered sustained and heavy fire: one killed, and two slightly wounded . . . And can we have some air support?' It's amazing what you can make a *tirailleur* who's been dead for two days say."[201]

Devers recognized that the "winter battles" had hammered the French, whose army would need "refitting and retraining before it would be ready for major offensive action."[202] For instance, Salan recorded that, of the 3,200 men in his 6ᵉ RIC who had landed at Toulon, 635 had been killed and 1,659 wounded by the end of the Alsace campaign, a casualty rate of 71 percent.[203] Increasingly, barely trained FFI had to serve as replacements for more experienced colonial infantry in an attacking role, which required more training in small-unit tactics, and coordinating attacks with infantry, artillery, and armor.[204] By the end of January 1945, de Lattre reported the *1ère Armée*'s strength as 295,000 men. Infantry losses were especially heavy, running at 12.5 percent, leaving infantry companies at 60–65 percent of establishment strength.[205]

In his history, de Lattre celebrates the liberation of Colmar as the culmination of First Army unity. The truth was that, despite the dire battles in Alsace, the *1ère Armée* had failed to craft an identity.[206] In addition to the usual complaints about de Lattre's "archaic" tactical approaches, de Lattre and Juin factions reproached each other for their profligacy with the lives of their men, which at least one of de Lattre's biographers declares unfair.[207] On the other hand, the explosive Leclerc found few regular officers willing to join his unit. Former FFI and volunteers resented the attitude of superiority, when not the expressions of contempt, of both factions. Nor was the American camp free of dissension. On 8 March 1945, Devers was promoted to full general over the demurral of the SHAEF commander, who persisted in holding Devers responsible for the Colmar Pocket. This made the Sixth Army Group's commander the second-highest-ranking American officer in Europe after Eisenhower.[208]

Conclusion

One of de Gaulle's great successes in the Second World War was to allow France to punch above its weight in the Alliance. However, the French army struggled to match in military proficiency de Gaulle's lofty aspirations for French power and influence. The Vosges campaign proved yet another punishing test for a French army constantly required to reinvent itself under fire. With its professional cadres seriously attrited in Tunisia, in Italy, and in the march from the Mediterranean coast, distant from its North African base, utterly dependent on the Americans for supplies, the command echelon riven by rivalries of a political, doctrinal, and personal nature, the poorly equipped First French Army was forced to endure a bitter campaign in the harshest of winter conditions, while simultaneously "amalgamating" clusters of poorly trained and disciplined FFI and volunteers. While the reconquest of Alsace and that of the "Atlantic pockets" were symbolically important for de Gaulle and the French, they were low priorities for the SHAEF commander, whose mission for Sixth Army Group was to "hold the flank" while advances were to be made further north. Eisenhower's personal rivalry with Jacob Devers, combined with a lack of confidence in the volatile de Lattre and a rebuilding French army, possibly caused him to "miss opportunities" for an early crossing of the Rhine in late November 1944 and the disruption of the German Ardennes offensive, which caught him by surprise on 16 December. While Eisenhower blamed Devers' and de Lattre's timorousness and lack of mastery of armored warfare for the persistence of the Colmar Pocket, and pressured Sixth Army Group to eliminate it, he constantly diverted resources which might have allowed them to do so to Patton. Tensions between de Gaulle's political agenda and Eisenhower's operational focus, apparent since Algiers in 1942, exploded with the Strasbourg crisis of January 1945, which was successfully resolved only after Churchill's intervention. However, the Allied failure to clarify the French role in the post-war occupation of Germany created conditions for further misunderstandings between Eisenhower and the French during the culminating invasion of Germany.

9 Rhine and Danube

The role for France in the invasion of Germany was viewed by de Gaulle as critical for the future of France and of Europe, so that the termination of the war was bound to spin off new clashes between the French leader and the Allies, especially the Americans. By early March, de Gaulle was aware that Bradley and Montgomery were poised to cross the Rhine. And he wanted to make sure that the *1ère Armée* was in the vanguard of their advance, to "conquer towns, fields, and trophies, and receive, along with the allies, the surrender of the defeated," de Gaulle wrote. "This was a condition dictated by a concern about prestige, certainly." But he was also determined that "we would have a zone on German soil, [so that] Germany's future could not be decided without us. Otherwise, our right to victory would remain at the discretion of others. In short, I understood that we cross the Rhine and also stake out a French front as soon as possible in the southern German states."[1]

The reason de Gaulle claimed that he had to force the hand of the Allies on the battlefield was that the issue of a French occupation zone in Germany remained in abeyance.[2] In fact, the occupation of post-war Germany, and of Europe generally, had become an Allied preoccupation at least since 1943, that had impacted Allied operations.[3] Fearing that the Americans might bolt from Europe as in 1919, and because Britain needed France to share the burden of the coming occupation of Germany, Churchill advocated for a French occupation zone. Nevertheless, the British Prime Minister was leery of being drawn by de Gaulle into a confrontation with Washington over the carve-up of Germany, especially as the French President's program called for the creation of independent states in the Rhineland and the Ruhr. Nor did it help that occupation zone discussions coincided with Franco-British tensions over Syria, where the British army intervened after French forces had shelled Damascus, an act that angered and humiliated de Gaulle, persuaded that London sought to supplant France in the Middle East.[4] Stalin's view was that France had failed to accrue enough equity in Hitler's defeat to merit a zone. But, if the Western Allies cared to carve out an occupation zone for Paris, it would have to come out of territory allocated to the British and Americans. In early January 1945, the Allies had conceded France's right to participate in Germany's surrender and to be allocated an occupation sector in Berlin. And, although French ambassador to the

UK René Massigli feared being "excluded from [Berlin's] elegant neighborhoods and the ministries," by February, he was optimistic that the Americans would cede Baden and Hesse-Darmstadt to the French, while the British would surrender the Saarland and the Palatinate from their zone.[5]

So, the bottom line is that de Gaulle's claim in his memoirs that he had to force the Allies' hand on the battlefield of Germany was disingenuous to a point. Even though the French leader had been excluded from Yalta at Roosevelt's insistence, at least the American President had conceded the principle of a French occupation zone. A seat on the European Advisory Commission (EAC) guaranteed that France would play a role in the "control machinery" of post-war German governance. France had been penciled in for a fifth seat on the future United Nations (UN) Security Council. So, the results of Yalta could be seen as "very satisfactory" for France, although de Gaulle's anger over Syria, and a desire to claim credit for France's liberation and recovery of great power status, made de Gaulle loath to acknowledge Churchill's backing, as anything that elevated Great Britain in French memory recalled the humiliation of Dunkirk, Mers-el-Kébir, Dakar, and Vichy.[6] What Paris lacked was any firm guarantees on paper, because these details were not finalized until after the four zones were officially delineated on 5 June 1945. The Gaullist view was that Washington had never accorded France the respect that it deserved.[7] As de Gaulle had explained to US Ambassador to France Jefferson Caffery in early 1945, "the USA has done an enormous number of very helpful things for us . . . but you always seem to do it under pressure and grudgingly." Therefore, he decided to apply a little pressure.[8] "In the final analysis, in 1944–1945, the German question was intimately linked in the mind of the Chief of Government to that of *grandeur*," concludes Claire Miot. The French army would provide de Gaulle's crowbar to insert Paris into the negotiations over the future of Germany. Unfortunately, the behavior of the army did little to contribute to French prestige, but rather replicated in Germany the actions that had led to recriminations being leveled against it in Italy.[9]

De Gaulle fully expected to have the support of the French people for his policy of defiance of his Allies, especially of the Americans. The need for France to have a say in Germany's future was popular across the political spectrum in France. The halcyon dawn of Liberation had given way to a mood of sullen impatience. With the British army transported across France's northern frontier, a ubiquitous American presence from Cherbourg and Le Havre to Alsace, and from Marseilles up the Rhône Valley had internalized negative images that each country held of the other.[10] The spectacle of de Gaulle acting independently against an American tendency "to treat the French like children" could only boost his standing at home. An occupation zone was viewed as the *sine qua non* of France's post-war status, constituting a barrier against German resurgence, as well as providing a test of de Gaulle's leadership. Allied treatment of the resistance in Belgium and Greece was viewed as a bad augury. The French press bitterly criticized French exclusion from Yalta and feared that France might not recover its Pacific territories that had been seized by Allied forces. It was against this background of increasing bitterness, blame, and anti-Americanism in France that the dénouement of the war in Europe played out.[11]

Agreement on the final allocation of occupation zones had not been forthcoming in part because the Allies viewed de Gaulle's desire to create a separate Westphalian state along both banks of the Rhine, running from Cologne to Lake Constance, as a non-starter. The French leader, together with his foreign minister Georges Bidault, believed that failure to fragment the Reich had been the great security blunder of Versailles. Access to the economic resources of the Saar, Württemberg, and the Palatinate would also jumpstart French economic recovery.[12] Operation Eclipse, originally prepared in November 1944, aimed to defeat the German forces, disarm and impose order in Germany, and settle Allied forces into zones of occupation.[13] However, in April 1945, as Eclipse was about to kick off, the future occupation zones remained undefined. De Gaulle was assured that the French would be allocated the occupation of Württemberg. But this seemed not to be reflected in the Eclipse plan. The final offensive, as Eisenhower envisaged it, called for Montgomery's Twenty-First Army Group to advance northeast toward Bremen and Jutland but, much to Montgomery's disappointment, not to cross the Elbe. Bang went the British Field Marshal's dream of entering Berlin atop the turret of a tank. He was also forced to restore the Ninth US Army to Bradley's Twelfth Army Group. Montgomery's job became to protect Bradley's left flank, while Twelfth Army Group thrust across central Germany toward Leipzig. Sixth Army Group's role was to cover Bradley's right flank, clean out the Black Forest, and drive southeast toward Nuremberg–Regensburg–Lenz. American estimates put German forces at roughly 22,000 infantrymen, which should offer a mere speedbump for the 600,000 men in Sixth Army Group.

Operation Eclipse

De Lattre's *1ère Armée* set to invade Germany (Map 9.1) consisted of two corps combining three armored and four infantry divisions, for a total of 280,000 men, two-thirds of whom, thanks to *l'amalgame*, were now "whitened" troops.[14] Unfortunately, Sixth Army Group protested that some were fit only for occupation duties and should never have been included in the order of battle.[15] The French role in this scenario was for one corps to clear the right bank of the Rhine, including the Black Forest, to the Swiss frontier, while the other corps was to capture Karlsruhe and Pforzheim and then move toward Stuttgart, as operations evolved.[16] The objectives of Eisenhower and de Gaulle were not necessarily compatible, as, "by April 1945 . . . an independent French

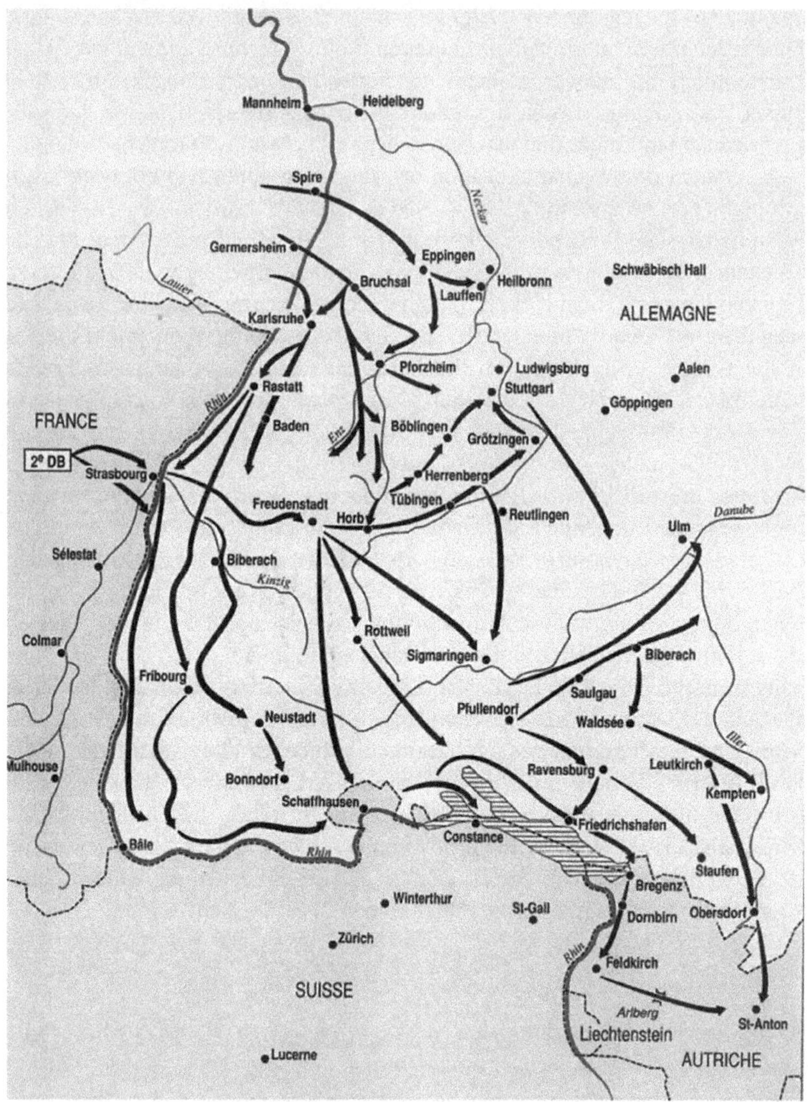

Map 9.1 The French First Army's advance into Germany, 1945.

regime emerged with clear political objectives of its own, and a surprising tendency to withhold cooperation with the Allies if French interests might be compromised."[17] Eisenhower was prepared to allow the French to administer all the territory they conquered, which tentatively was designated in Sixth

Army Group's amended version of Operation Eclipse as "Karlsruhe, Stuttgart, Bruschal."[18] To remove doubts that the French were capable of governing this territory, by April they had assembled a corps of 500 civil affairs officers, a sort of French knock-off of the Allied Military Government of Occupied Territories (AMGOT), under the ubiquitous General Louis Koeltz.[19] The elimination of the Colmar Pocket had shortened the French front along the Rhine, and had allowed de Lattre to dispatch two divisions to western France. The problem, as de Gaulle saw it, was that de Lattre's role in Eclipse was to be largely defensive, freeing up Patch's Seventh Army to make the bulk of the conquests in southern Germany and Austria. Only one French division was designated to cross the Rhine at Brisach, before proceeding to occupy a corridor between the Rhine and the Black Forest, excluding Karlsruhe. And de Lattre feared that American civil affairs units stood ready to preempt the French arrival by establishing their own administrations there. This hardly accorded with de Gaulle's vision of a *1ère Armée* juggernaut "conquering towns, fields, and trophies, and receiving, along with the allies, the surrender of the defeated." De Gaulle's problem was one of numbers: on 8 May 1945, the French army officially numbered 1.3 million men. Unfortunately, not all were under arms and in uniform. In effect, the French army counted only "eight true combat divisions," or under 3 percent of Allied forces, quite a relegation from 1918 when French soldiers made up 37 percent of the forces of the victorious Allies.[20]

In de Gaulle's view, because French interests, as well as French forces, had been marginalized by the Allies, the *Gouvernement provisoire de la république française* (GPRF) was under no obligation to abide by arrangements concluded in France's absence. This had been the story of Allied–French relations in the war: the less the French were told about Allied intentions and plans, the more de Gaulle felt empowered to gift the Allies with multiple Gallic *faits accomplis*. Therefore, at de Gaulle's direction, de Lattre would be required to regard Devers' command directives as elastic – even as mere suggestions. De Gaulle eyed Stuttgart, Ulm, and Sigmaringen, as well as an occupation zone in Austria, as trophies to be seized by French forces.[21]

In preparation for the invasion of Germany, Sixth Army Group built up its logistics, and trained new *Forces françaises de l'intérieur* (FFI) recruits in the basics of map reading, small arms, and squad- and platoon-level tactics.[22] But, from 23 February, rumors reached de Gaulle that French armored divisions were being stripped of their bridging equipment. In a 4 March meeting, de Lattre also informed de Gaulle that he had been allocated insufficient ammunition to tackle German positions in the Black Forest. But he suggested that, if he were to advance further north toward Speyer, he could loop through Pforzheim and take Stuttgart from the north. On 5 March, Patton's forces crossed the Moselle. On 9 March, Bradley seized a bridgehead at Remagen. As Seventh Army's attack, begun on 15 March, progressed into what the Americans called the "Saar–Palatinate," Monsabert's II Corps under Seventh Army's control moved north along the west bank of the Rhine, which opened more possibilities for a Rhine crossing, which de Gaulle ardently desired, around Karlsruhe, or perhaps further north closer to Stuttgart. The first French soldiers to enter Germany were the *7e Régiment de tirailleurs tunisiens* (7e RTT), as part of the Seventh Army. By 22 March, German resistance west of the Rhine had ceased. The Allies had bagged 90,000 German prisoners of war (POWs), while Patton crossed the Rhine near Oppenheim. Seventh Army breached the Rhine in two places near Worms on 26 March. On 27 March, the *1ère Armée* was directed to regroup at Germersheim. On 29 March, de Gaulle wired de Lattre to cross the Rhine, "even if the Americans are not willing, and you have to cross on boats. It is an issue of high national interests. Karlsruhe and Stuttgart await you, even if they don't want you."[23] Elements of the French II Corps began to cross the Rhine on 30 March. By 2 April, French engineers had erected bridges at Speyer and Germersheim. By 4 April, 130,000 French troops were on the Rhine's right bank and had seized Karlsruhe.[24]

De Gaulle interpreted the diminished French role in Eclipse as yet another act of Anglo-American bad faith.[25] From this point, the relationship between Devers and de Lattre would be seriously roiled by a series of misunderstandings, beginning with de Lattre's own "partisan order," similar to that issued by Leclerc at Strasbourg, which promised that any German soldier who refused to surrender by a certain date would be treated as a partisan, "without regard to his clothing, open carriage of arms or other circumstances." Likewise, any German soldier discovered in civilian clothes would be treated as a spy. Devers ordered him to rescind both directives.[26]

Although the Germans seemed to be on their last legs, they still managed on occasion to put up stiff resistance, and some towns, such as Würzburg, had to be cleared street by street. From 15 April, Eisenhower shifted Devers' focus southeast toward Bavaria and western Austria to preempt the establishment of an Alpine redoubt. Devers' goal was to encircle what was left of the German Nineteenth Army in Stuttgart. This required de Lattre to clear the Rhine's right bank, including the Black Forest, in a holding operation, while the US IV Corps moved to block the Nineteenth Army's retreat from Stuttgart. But, on 15 April, de Gaulle had ordered de Lattre to enter Stuttgart before the VI Corps had taken up its blocking position, despite Devers' repeated orders to halt his advance. "Today still, I apologize to General Devers for having, for once, exceeded my orders. But I don't think that he's ever held a grudge, given the results," de Lattre insisted in his history of the *1ère Armée* history.[27] In fact, Devers did hold it against de Lattre for jumping the gun, for not only did it take Monsabert's II Corps three days to clear Stuttgart, in the process repeating many of the transgressions of which the French army had been guilty in Italy, but also much of what was left of the Nineteenth Army managed to escape toward the southeast. Eisenhower informed de Lattre "that I could no longer count with certainty on the operational use of any French forces they might be contemplating equipping in the future. This threat of possible curtailment of equipment for French forces proved effective, and the French finally complied."[28] Harry Truman, who had assumed the US Presidency on the 12 April 1945 death of Roosevelt, also sent an angry wire to de Gaulle threatening to cut the French out of the Supreme Headquarters Allied Expeditionary Force (SHAEF) command. "One result of the mini-crisis over the city was to poison his relations with a new President who harboured none of the anti-Gaullist animus of his predecessor," writes Julian Jackson.[29] In the immediate aftermath of conquest, to avoid further friction, Devers had withdrawn US troops from Stuttgart. De Gaulle shrugged off objections from both Eisenhower and Truman that the French seizure of Stuttgart had violated the Anfa agreement and mobilized the French diplomatic corps to support his position. Eisenhower later conceded that occupation zones were an issue to be decided by the various governments following Germany's surrender. But, until then, "the French remain in Stuttgart."[30]

Encouraged by de Gaulle, who in his single-minded pursuit of a French occupation zone was keen that his forces preempt the Americans, French troops pinballed over southern Germany and into Austria, ignoring operational boundaries, and occupying cities and towns as directed by de Gaulle.[31] Early April had seen the French seized Karlsruhe, Freiburg im Breisgau, and eventually Stuttgart, often being forced to overcome pockets of fierce German resistance. But elsewhere, as at Baden-Baden, the populations often intervened to prevent last-ditch defenses of the town and so avoid destruction. Nevertheless, the arrival of the French at Baden-Baden was initially terrifying: "The first days . . . were like all occupations: search the houses, arrest the men, rape the women, requisition arms, cameras, pillage the stores," recounted one resident. "After several days . . . the children were the first to come out onto the streets. It was exotic because the Moroccans roasted their sheep on spits in Baden-Baden's beautiful parks. At that point, everything returned to order."[32] The French were also accused of using excessive force in the name of Lex Oradour (the Law of Oradour), most notably when on 18 April they burned Freudenstadt, a spa town in the Black Forest whose hotels had been converted into hospitals. Major Christian de la Croix de Castries, the man who nine years later would achieve notoriety for surrendering Dien Bien Phu to the Viet Minh, called in a heavy artillery barrage, followed by bombs and incendiary grenades, when a summons to surrender went unanswered.[33]

De Lattre ordered Béthouart to capture Sigmaringen and arrest everyone. However, by the time French forces entered Sigmaringen on 22 April, most former Vichy officials had decamped, leaving behind only a handful of *Francs-Gardes*. Andreas W., a Wehrmacht corporal allegedly on leave, reported that most inhabitants had taken refuge in their cellars when, "around ten in the morning, the arrival of tanks broke the silence. I came out of my hiding place to see what was going on. The French had put the mayor on one of the tanks, in case there were snipers on the roofs. In the night, the battle recommenced, but the German troops didn't stick around. The townspeople had a terrible time putting out the fires given that the French had arrested the firemen. The next day the Moroccans were replaced by the '*bataillons de choc*,' who must have been from the Resistance, communists, and immediately the reign of terror began. The French loyal to Pétain passed a few bad moments with those guys. I think that they shot anyone who was armed."[34] The GPRF's orders were that any Frenchman in German uniform captured was to be sent to France for trial, although Leclerc is reported to have summarily executed a dozen or so members of the *Légion des volontaires français contre le bolchévisme* (LVF) in German uniform turned over by the Americans.[35]

Despite an almost resistance-free, victorious promenade through southern Germany and Austria, the command climate within the First Army's leadership discouraged teamwork and cooperation. This became the case especially after 11 April, the date that de Lattre relieved the *2e Division d'infanterie du Maroc* (2e DIM) commander General Marcel Carpentier. Carpentier's alleged sin was to have marched straight into Karlsruhe, hence upending the artistry of de Lattre's planned envelopment that had been meticulously explained beforehand to reporters. While de Lattre complained of the 2e DIM commander's "lack of intellectual discipline," the fact that Carpentier had served as Juin's Chief of Staff (COS) in Italy was lost on no one. "You have to have worked, fought in the atmosphere of the *1ère Armée* to understand its current mentality," one officer complained. "General de Lattre is – and I repeat – hated. He is a hypersensitive satrap. You have to love him and have his name always on your lips. For him, it's all about personalities . . . Apart from a few units that enjoy special privileges, from top to bottom, the army is fed up . . . It's whimsy at its most odious, a regime of terror. You have to accept it or resign. I made my choice a long time ago."[36]

On 29 April, the *5e Division blindé* (5e DB) and the *4e Division marocaine de montagne* (4e DMM) crossed into Austria, while the *1ère Division française libre* (1ère DFL) entered the southern Alps. Rushed in from Royan, Leclerc's 2e DB crossed the Danube on 29 April and occupied Berchtesgaden on 4 May. US forces cut off de Lattre's attempt to seize the Alpine pass at Landeck and enter Italy.[37] On 4–8 May, US forces liberated French very important persons (VIPs) including Daladier, Reynaud, Gamelin, and Weygand, who had been incarcerated at Itter Castle in the Austrian Tyrol.[38] However, de Gaulle ordered de Lattre to arrest any French internees who had served Vichy, "in particular General Weygand, whatever your personal sentiments in his regard." Perhaps it gave de Gaulle some perverse pleasure to force de Lattre take his "old boss" into custody. On 5 May, when Devers accepted the surrender of the Nineteenth Army in southern Germany and Austria near Harr, de Lattre was not invited. When Alfred Jodl signed the unconditional surrender of German forces in the West at Eisenhower's headquarters at Reims on 7 May, no French flag decorated the room and the French representative, General François Sevez, like his Soviet counterpart, was present only as a witness. On 8 May, at de Gaulle's insistence, de Lattre represented France in Berlin. However, the arrival of the French delegation took organizers by surprise: no French flag decorated the hall of a former military academy where the signing was to take place. When he spied the French delegation, an American brigadier general tactlessly shouted "And why not China?" When Field Marshal Keitel saw de Lattre sitting at the table with Zhukov, Sir Arthur William Tedder, and Carl Spaatz, he grumbled "Ah, the French are also here. It only lacked that!" Despite de Gaulle's insistence that the French be a signatory to the Berlin surrender, only Marshal Zhukov and Air Chief Marshal Arthur Tedder, Eisenhower's deputy at SHAEF, were designated as signatories. The American representative, US Army Air Force (USAAF) General Carl Spaatz, and de Lattre signed only as witnesses.[39]

The Elimination of the Atlantic Pockets

With the Colmar Pocket eliminated and the defeat of Germany imminent, "the spirit of least resistance might perhaps counsel us to remain passive on this front," wrote de Gaulle, "for the fruits would fall by themselves when the Reich capitulated. But in war, the habit of the least effort always carries the risk of being costly . . . In any case, I refused to admit that German units could remain intact on French soil until the end and taunt us from behind their ramparts."[40] By March 1945, the French had put together a series of operations to eliminate the Royan pocket. Operation *Vénérable* grouped 23,000 assailants, including 10,000 men from Leclerc's 2e DB imported from Alsace, together with both air and sea support, and a US artillery brigade. *Vénérable* was launched on 14 April behind 100 planes that dropped 8,300 tons of bombs and, within 24 hours, the French occupied the ruins of Royan. Two days later, Royan *Festungskommandant* Rear Admiral Hans Michahelles surrendered at the Royan suburb of Pontaillac. This success was quickly followed by Operation *Jupiter*, which saw the seizure of the Île d'Oléron in an amphibious operation on 30 April–1 May. In all, de Gaulle claimed 1,000 Germans killed, with 12,000 made POWs, including Admiral Michahelles.[41]

On 12 April, Admiral Ernst Schirlitz at La Rochelle had been informed that the truce between the two sides meant to preserve the historic city had been suspended on Larminat's orders. The French attack, launched on the same day as *Jupiter*, met little opposition from the garrison. On 5 May, Schirlitz pledged

Figure 9.1 Major Adalbert Engelken, COS for Major General Hans Junck, commander of the German garrison at Saint-Nazaire, gives a final *Sieg Heil!* on 9 May 1945, as he prepares to surrender to the 66th US ID two days later, making the Saint-Nazaire garrison the last major German force to surrender. (AFP via Getty Images)

not to order the destruction of the port facilities. The next day, Admiral Dönitz announced that the battles in the West were no longer useful. On 7 May, German troops were confined to barracks, and the next day, French forces entered the town. Around 2,600 troops on the Île de Ré, including Italian marines as well as many Poles, surrendered on 9 May. Captured with them was François Sidos, the head of *la Milice* in La Rochelle, as well as his wife and two sons, as he prepared to flee to Spain in a fishing trawler. Sidos was tried and shot the following year. Sidos' two sons, both *Francs-Gardes*, were also given prison sentences. After their release, they formed a group called *Jeune nation*, which would become active in the 1960s in support of *Algérie française*. German POWs were put to work demining the beaches and approaches of the Gironde estuary.[42] On 9 May, Dunkirk surrendered, followed two days later by Saint-Nazaire, the last town in Europe to be liberated, when General Hans Junck signed the surrender at Bouvron, a non-descript village at the limit of the "pocket" (Figure 9.1). While Junck saluted General Kramer, the commander of the 66th US Infantry Division (ID), he refused to salute FFI "General" Chomel.[43]

"The Russians of the West"

The French had laid the groundwork for the invasion of Germany with the September 1944 publication of a soldier's guide whose goal was "to reestablish the prestige of France in Germany, because it's through force – that is, through the French army – that the German people will accept the reality of their defeat, and the belief in the reestablishment of our power." Every French soldier was "to consider himself as a representative responsible for French prestige." But the question of who had been responsible for the war was never resolved: was it only a criminal elite, or was the German population complicit in the crimes of the regime? Propaganda outlining German atrocities was distributed to the troops, as well as warnings that the character of the German people had been shaped by the "German mentality and National Socialism." While the French command anticipated that the German population would prove "apathetic," soldiers should be alert to the "servility and deceit" of a nation that considered itself to be racially superior. "In Germany, the enemy is everywhere . . . the man like the woman, and even the child . . . Always remember that you are in enemy territory." The mission of the French soldier was to represent the superiority of French civilization while displaying "the attitude of the victor," which included a show of "distant scorn" for a defeated population with whom they were not allowed to fraternize. Officers were told to allow no violence that might encourage popular resistance.[44] But the message conveyed by the high command was one of "disdain" for the "duplicitous" Germans. If Germans complained, they were to be reminded of Oradour, the deportations of French citizens, and the concentration camps. In the French view, German civilians shared in the collective guilt of the Nazi regime. On 7 April, the *1ère Armée* liberated a concentration camp at Klein-Glattbach, containing "650 persons . . . priests, scientists, officers, engineers, doctors, principally from Western nations," many infected with typhus. "Some died upon reaching Speyer hospital, over a hundred could not be moved at all and were placed in requisitioned quarters to finish in peace the few days still allotted to them. The camp was well up to the usual Nazi standards."[45] And when Germans invariably replied "We didn't know," they merely reinforced official French propaganda that the Germans were "hypocrites."[46]

This rather ambiguous message, combined with memories of defeat and occupation among the soldiers of the *1ère Armée*, whose heterogeneous composition, clan rivalries, and pent-up animosities did not augur well for the maintenance of discipline.[47] Furthermore, given the track record of the *Corps expéditionnaire français* (CEF) in Italy, it should have come as no surprise when reports soon reached Devers about extreme disorder in the wake of the French advance, including numerous rapes. Devers dispatched the 100th US ID and civil affairs units to Stuttgart to impose order and stop violence against civilians, which the Americans declared to be "shocking," although some GIs too stood accused of rape.[48] The Sixth Army Group's commander subsequently opined that reports of French misbehavior in Stuttgart were true "but greatly exaggerated" and that, apart from significant looting, there had been *only* 1,500–2,000 rapes, although the Office of Strategic Services (OSS) reported this number to be an underestimate by at least two-thirds. He admonished de Lattre to discipline his troops, but the French commander refused to evacuate the city on de Gaulle's orders and declared the accusations a calumny designed to tarnish his brilliant victory.[49]

Nevertheless, from the moment that French forces entered Germany, de Lattre too began to receive reports of pillage and rapes, which he feared might be used to deny France an occupation zone, and so issued orders for it to stop, but obviously to no avail. Of 222 French soldiers tried for rape or attempted rape in the invasion of Germany, 200 were colonial soldiers.[50] The blame often fell on Moroccans, particularly on *goumiers*, whose behavior was explained as "the law of their tribe." But it is equally clear that French soldiers were also at fault, "particularly the commandos, who set a deplorable example for our men and our cadres." FFI were also blamed. The French were sometimes astonished to find that on occasion French POWs from 1940 intervened to protect the German population and asked French soldiers to stay and guard a village lest the *Schutzstaffel* (SS) returned to retaliate. "For me, it was a real shock," declared a French sergeant. "There was no such thing as good Germans."[51]

Overall, Liberation was a terrifying time for French POWs, whose "bomb shelter" in their camp or factory under attack by Allied planes might be no more than a slit trench. From January 1945, the exodus toward the west began. For Michel de Cazote, the first indication of impending catastrophe came from January 1945, as long lines of refugees moved west along the road that crossed the sinister Silesian plain beyond the barbed wire of his *Offizierslager* (*Oflag*) (Figure 9.2). "All the treasured possessions of the fleeing families, including many of their farm animals, could be seen fastened more or less precariously on the big wagons, not forgetting the bedding and mattress, almost never left behind." Most of the French officers began fashioning small handcarts to pull their possessions. As the low thunder of battle over the eastern horizon became louder and more ominous, the POWs were divided into groups of 500, and set out west guarded by Wehrmacht, but also by regular police and even a contingent of Hungarian SS, who were soon directed elsewhere, leaving a guard escort of men too old or infirm for combat. At night, they were locked up in a village church or school. By day they merged with a western migration of displaced Germans, political prisoners, POWs, and *Ostarbeiter*.[52] Guarded by German soldiers, POWs might be surrounded and trapped by Soviet troops, who made no distinction between Wehrmacht and POWs. Some French POWs

Figure 9.2 The US Ninth Army's commander and the French Commandant take the salute at a march-past of 4,000 French officers liberated from an *Oflag* at Soest in Westphalia, on 13 April 1945. (Photo by Fred Ramage/Keystone/ Getty Images)

had taken up residence with German women who needed protection from Soviet troops, frequently drunk and primed to trigger their signature Pistolet-pulemyot Shpagina-41 (PPSh-41) sub-machineguns with round magazines at the slightest provocation.[53]

One view is that French soldierly violence against the German population replicated the "*tontes*" and other acts of revenge carried out by "FFI" in France, expressions of aggrieved French masculinity, intended to surmount the humiliations of 1940 and the exactions and brutality of the occupation, and as a reaction against the discovery of concentration camps. However, "absurd rumors" reported by the German press of the rape of German women by Africans gained credence because it represented a revival of "the black shame" of the French occupation of the Rhineland after 1918 – Nazi propaganda had denounced the *1ère Armée* as a mongrel force, "a cluster of terrorists and Negroes," as a device to firm up German resistance to the Allied invasion. But the French fear was that the resurfacing of rape accusations, which earned

French soldiers the nickname of "the Russians of the West," undermined de Gaulle's case for a French zone of occupation.[54]

Miot concludes that "the sexual crimes committed by the French army [in Germany] are therefore massive," although, as in Italy, impossible to assess in scope because of underreporting.[55] De Lattre blamed French-induced disorder on "the deficiencies of captains and lieutenants," who lacked authority over their subordinates. Others noted that the *1ère Armée* was desperately short of cadres, which perhaps explains why the Americans complained that French officers and non-commissioned officers (NCOs) were virtually invisible in French-occupied towns. Nor were French-led security patrols much in evidence. However, as in Italy, the ambiguous attitude of the military hierarchy became a precursor of violence against the enemy population. Complaints of French misconduct were rebuffed as "hypocritical," given the crimes committed during the German occupation of France. Guidance from the military chain of command was unclear, even contradictory, and as in Italy failed definitively to put an end to rumors that a tacit *carte blanche* was in effect for pillage and even rape. Silence conveyed a message of tolerance. As in Italy, soldiers' misconduct and violence were also excused as a *repos du guerrier*, a "psychological compensation" for the survivors of a long and difficult campaign, and not just in the French army. De Lattre allowed the soldiers to take what they needed from the population. The feeling was that colonial soldiers had been promised that, if they refrained from pillage and rape in France, the rules would be relaxed in Germany, where the women, although white, were still the enemy. Of course, violence in the French zone failed to measure up to that in the Soviet sector, but the trauma was significant nonetheless, provoking "hysteria" and suicides.[56]

Men of military age were rounded up, incarcerated, and mistreated, some even executed. So vengeful were many French soldiers that they admitted to even being tempted to open fire on the swarms of German refugees on the road.[57] The fear, of course, was that a German resistance might emerge: "A great many German soldiers are still at large, dressed in civilian clothes, on both banks of the Rhine; caches of carefully wrapped and protected arms and supplies have been found . . . " the 5th Bureau reported on 1 May. "In view of eventual action against the *maquis* of the Black Forest or elsewhere, notices have been posted setting a date and time limit for the surrender of all isolated enemy troops; the population is informed that persons found to have aided all such in avoiding capture shall be tried before a military court and may be liable to capital punishment."[58] Deficiencies of French logistics meant that many units simply had to requisition – or pillage – to survive, although in many cases stolen items – including cameras, slippers, linen, jewelry, and even accordions – were hardly required for survival. For French soldiers, the German population seemed to have plenty of food, and to live well in comparison with France. German women might be forced to cook for soldiers or wash their uniforms. None was safe from sexual assault. "As in Italy, collective rapes were common," insists Miot. German women were particularly vulnerable in a society stripped of most menfolk. One woman remembered the French arrival in Lichtental, a small village south of Baden-Baden, after the *Volkssturm* had unsuccessfully attempted to defend the town: "For several days, the French pillaged everything they saw. The number of rapes in the region was very high. When the Moroccans came through the door, the drama truly commenced. We were alone with my mother and my sister. She was fourteen, me sixteen . . . ."[59] As in Italy, the tactic was to gain admittance to a house on the pretext of looking for weapons, cameras, or binoculars (forbidden items), deserters, or war criminals, and then proceed to rape the women, often at gunpoint in the presence of their husbands, mothers, and children, who, if they tried to intervene, might be shot. Many families remained for days in their basements out of fear, while women sought refuge in convents or churches. Between the entrance into Germany in the middle of March and the German surrender on 8 May, 222 French soldiers were tried for rape, only 10 percent of whom were white. This was basically the number arrested for rape in Italy, although there were far more French troops in Germany than had been the case in Italy. Possibly another twenty or so were summarily executed. From the moment it entered Germany to the surrender, Seventh Army tried seventy-seven soldiers for rape, of whom twenty-four were acquitted, eight were hanged, and three shot.

But prosecutions represented barely the tip of the iceberg. Women often declined to report a rape, out of shame or fear of reprisals – one 2 July 1945 OSS report speculated that 5,000–6,000 rapes had gone unreported in Stuttgart. Skeptical officers might fail to register a complaint, insisting that "Nazi women . . . were determined to lodge false claims of rape," perhaps to extort cash.[60] Those who did report a rape might find that the accused would merely insist that he had been misidentified, that the sexual act had been consensual or invited by provocative behavior, that the woman had been trading sex for food, or that "she seemed to enjoy it," thereby inviting a dismissal of the charge or at least a reduced sentence. Unit mobility, a lack of investigative resources in combat units, or a desire to protect their hard-to-replace combatants from what many believed to be overly severe penalties for the rape of enemy women might lead to deliberate sabotage of an investigation. The fact that courts martial were left in the hands of line officers without judicial training, ignorant of or reluctant to apply the law, made conviction for rape problematic. And, while the blame usually fell on "Moroccans," others pointed that Gaullist "terrorists" represented by poorly disciplined FFI and commandos were also active in this criminal enterprise. "While fearing that this violence would discredit the French army in the international arena, the military hierarchy did little to control it," concludes Miot. Hospitals in Stuttgart, Karlsruhe, Freudenstadt, Ulm, and other towns occupied by the French were besieged by women who had been raped or who were demanding an abortion. The population of Karlsruhe breathed a sigh of relief when French troops were switched out for Americans.[61]

Even small, rural villages might record as many as 200 rapes. When Bacquier was approached by a German woman in the small village who claimed to have been raped and robbed, he lined up his company. "She recognized none," he wrote.

> If truth be told, that wasn't surprising. Each unit contains a few louts who learned to commit their crimes on the territory of neighboring units where there was less risk of being identified. To finish up, I paid her the money that had been robbed on the spot. The preceding week, we had captured the van of a Wehrmacht paymaster and I was weighed down with marks. She was more or less reassured … The other affair was less pleasant … One morning, Silberman informed me that number 422 requested a change of company. The request was unexpected, even insulting. I called in number 422, told him that I was happy to be rid of him, and forwarded his records to the battalion. A few hours later, a peasant from a neighboring farm came into the command post to complain that his ten-year-old son had been raped by a *tirailleur*, then strangled and thrown into the river. Fortunately, the cold water revived the child, who ran home panic-stricken, soaking wet, unable to speak, and crying. The father demanded justice. It didn't take a genius to make the link between 422's recent request and the crime. He confessed almost immediately. I tore off the military insignia from his uniform, ripped off his corporal's stripes and handed my revolver to the boy's father: "He's yours. Do what you want. I guarantee on my honor as an officer that there will be no repercussions. We'll just list him as a deserter." The captain was present but didn't say a word. I later thought that he wasn't averse to killing two birds with one stone. The man stood there, my revolver in his hand. He was trembling. Finally, he gave me back my weapon. I locked up the prisoner in a storage room guarded by a sentinel, and on the spot wrote a detailed report for the court martial. I asked for the maximum penalty. As I was transferred to France three weeks later, I never learned the fate of number 422. I hope that he croaked.[62]

But Bacquier's attitude may have been atypical, in part because "422" was not only a criminal, but also an ill-disciplined soldier whom he had already threatened to execute for refusing to obey orders in combat. French civil affairs officers were sometimes appalled by the lack of control exercised by combat officers over their troops.[63] Nevertheless, while everyone was paralyzed with fear when confronted by "Arabs," Germans near Baden-Baden considered themselves lucky compared with the news they heard coming out of the East, where freed Russian and Polish POWs often joined in the mayhem.[64] American historian of the Russian zone in Germany Norman Naimark concludes that rapes by "Moroccans" in Germany were second only to the mass rapes, estimated at as many as 2 million, carried out by Soviet soldiers in eastern Germany that continued into 1947.[65]

German POWs

In the view of some Germans, the French invasion was unnecessarily violent, especially as the French zone quickly gained a reputation as the toughest zone in Germany, even more so than that administered by the Soviets, where the "Law of Oradour" was applied, vigilantism was exercised by the occupiers, and another former SS man floating face down in the Danube raised little notice. An internment camp run by an officer who, it was said, had lost his family in the deportation, was established at Hüfingen near the Swiss border. Hufingen saw former German soldiers executed for attempting to escape, while a high "accident" rate among the inmates eventually led to his reassignment.[66] In fact, concerns about ill-treatment of Axis POWs by the French had been raised since July–August 1943 in AFN by British and Americans who feared that these accusations would rebound against Anglo-American war captives. However, wartime complaints by the Germans lodged through Switzerland about the treatment of their POWs had been met by accusations that the Axis powers sought to utilize POWs for propaganda purposes, that at best French treatment was entirely appropriate given mistreatment of French POWs by the Axis powers, or by stony silence. The "whitening" of French units in the autumn of 1944 saw some colonial soldiers converted to POW guards, which allegedly led to an increase in abuse. "However, by February 1945, when the Red Army had liberated many Allied POWs in the East and the end of the war was in sight, the Allied leadership had no hesitation in surrendering complete control to the French, irrespective of what this might mean for German POWs," concludes Bob Moore.[67]

At the end of the war, France held 63,000 German POWs captured in Tunisia in 1943, and another 237,000 corralled in France and Germany in 1944–1945. The Germans became very upset when the French appropriated 740,000 POWs out of American camps. Some of these POWs had been captured in North Africa, sent to the United States, and then liberated after the war to return to Germany, only to be plucked out of transit stockades by the French at ports such as Le Havre. The British shipped over 25,000 German POWs to French camps. "Conservative estimates" put the number of German POW deaths in French hands at 16,500 in 1945 alone.[68] By the summer of 1945, over 2,000 Axis POWs forced into demining in France died each month, as the French press demanded that German POWs be made to clean up the mess that they had created (Figure 9.3). This brought complaints from Washington that French treatment of German POWs violated the Geneva Convention. In fact, in the five months following the German surrender, 17,773 German POWs officially perished in French custody.[69] Overall, fully 2.6 percent of German POWs in French custody died, compared with 0.1 percent of Germans held by the United States, and 0.3 percent of those

Figure 9.3 German POWs demining the Mediterranean coast in July 1945. "Conservative estimates" put the number of German POW deaths in French hands at 16,500 in 1945 alone, with demining being a factor. (Photo by –/AFP via Getty Images)

held by the British. Of course, this paled beside the 35.8 percent of Axis POWs who perished in Soviet custody,[70] retaliation in part for the treatment of the 3.5 million Soviet POWs, over half of whom died in German detention.[71] Nor did the parade of deportees returning to France in debilitated health produce a wave of popular sympathy for German POWs. Not surprisingly, the French were totally unsympathetic to German complaints. But the good news for the Germans was that the French desire for revenge was not matched by their vigilance, so that escape to Germany became fairly routine for those with a mind to do so. On the other hand, 20 percent of German POWs held in France elected to settle there as "free laborers" after official incarceration ended in December 1948.[72]

Repatriation

Repatriation required roughly 1 million French POWs, 650,000 French labor conscripts, 76,000 surviving French Jewish deportees, and 60,000 French political deportees, convicted criminals, and hostages held in Germany to be identified and collected. Many of these were cleared in the massive repatriations of French and Soviet citizens in the summer and autumn of 1945. But, by the end of September 1945, an estimated 200,000–300,000 remained classified as "missing," mostly from Alsace-Moselle, but also *Service du travail obligatoire* (STO) conscripts on whom Vichy had collected little data.[73] Tens of thousands of displaced persons, often Poles, Ukrainians, and those from the Baltic states reluctant to be shipped back east, encumbered the zone and weighed on the budget. When ordered by the French to work or face imprisonment, many were left with no choice but to return to the very jobs that they had held as forced laborers, often under the same Nazi foremen.[74]

Paris was particularly keen to prosecute French collaborators, members of *la Milice*, and the Waffen-SS. Authorities had to sort through French refugees who had "lost their papers," probably somewhere on the Eastern Front, deportees, POWs, some of whom had "transformed" to civilian worker status, "*emigrés de Sigmaringen*," who claimed to be STO laborers, and the occasional German who masqueraded as a *malgré-nous*. Most repatriated POWs were happy to be sent home, even if this was "colored by sadness" about the death of loved ones, the large degree of destruction in battle zones, rampant inflation, "the egotistical mentality" of the population, and the fact that many collaborators had retained their administrative positions in France. Nor had absence necessarily made the heart grow fonder – wives left in France may have found other male protectors or even been forced into prostitution to survive, while French POWs, too, may have found a niche in German society – for instance, the *Renseignements généraux de la Manche* noted in 1945 that some returned POWs complained that they had been repatriated against their will and expressed "a certain nostalgia for the country"[Germany], which suggested that "they had some sentimental attachments there." Divorces, rare in France in the 1930s, multiplied in 1946–1947.[75]

But other French refugees in Germany might be in no hurry to be repatriated because "it wasn't always good to return to the village too soon. For militiamen or the SS, it could be bad ... I remember several cases that stuck me then: a second lieutenant who had done service in the Wehrmacht, militiamen who had an honorable war with us ... women who volunteered to become nurses after whoring for the Germans ... There was a little of everything. The soldiers of the *armée d'Afrique* weren't particularly interested in those French. It was rather the fellows who came from the resistance who wanted to see justice done, as they said back then." One had to distinguish between Wehrmacht and SS, and ferret out war criminals, who might mingle among German POWs or the masses of displaced persons (DPs). The search for war criminals was handed over to the *Organe de recherche des criminels de guerre* (ORCG), established on 1 December 1944 under the *Direction générale des études et recherches* (DGER), the successor intelligence service to the *Bureau central de renseignements et d'action* (BCRA)/*Direction générale des services spéciaux* (DGSS). Theirs was an exacting task as numerous networks emerged to spirit Nazi and French criminals through Italy and Spain to the Middle East or South America, often with ecclesiastical complicity. Eventually, almost 5,000 were arrested by the French, some 3,150 of whom were tried in Germany, whereas another 1,500 were sent to France, while others were turned over to other countries for prosecution. Otto Abetz was found skulking in Baden under the name of Laumann and sent to Paris, where he was given twenty years in prison, before being amnestied in 1954. General Otto von Stülpnagel was also arrested and sent to Paris, where he hanged himself in the Cherche Midi prison in 1948. The wife and daughter of the Alsace Gauleiter Robert Wagner were detained by the French and paraded through the streets of Strasbourg, before Madame Wagner allegedly was sent to a Paris brothel frequented by North Africans, where rumor had it that she committed suicide. Wagner gave himself up to the Americans, who promptly turned him over to the French, who in August 1946 put him before a firing squad at Fort Ney in Strasbourg, along with three of his closest collaborators.[76]

One of the quandaries for the *1ère Armée* was what to do with the estimated 12,000 French combat troops serving in the German army by the summer of 1944, often accompanied by their families, supported by 10,000 uniformed auxiliaries.[77] Bayle recorded that 30 French women whose average age was around 20 were assigned to his Waffen-SS unit as nurses, part of the estimated 70,000 French women, not including those from Alsace-Moselle, conscripted to work in Germany, or who volunteered in some capacity there during the war.[78] French volunteers served in other capacities, for instance supporting V-1 missile sites in the Pas-de-Calais in 1944, and providing a logistics company for the 21st Panzer Division. Four thousand sailors and dockers worked for the Kriegsmarine. From a German perspective, probably the most useful role was played by the approximately 10,000 French collaborators who worked directly for the Abwehr, Gestapo, and Sicherheitspolizei (Sipo)/Sicherheitsdienst (SD), plus three times that number of informers and auxiliaries in German service. Various French formations such as *la Milice*, the *Groupe mobile de réserve* (GMR), and the police also had cooperated closely with the Germans in their fight against internal resistance.[79]

The LVF and its spinoffs eventually gathered into the *Division Charlemagne* stood as a monument to the failure of Vichy collaboration, and the schisms and ideological incoherence of the French right. Sending volunteers into the German forces had not offered a path to the resurrection of a French army as Vichy had originally hoped. Nor had it managed to help France's military reputation recover from the mortal blow suffered in 1940. Abetting the "Franco-German campaign against the Russians" was one of the main charges laid against Pétain that ultimately led to his condemnation for "treasonous collaboration with Germany, a power at war with France, with a view to advancing the undertakings of the enemy." The fact that Laval had "notably encouraged and supported the formation of a French contingent in German uniform to fight alongside Germany against Russia" was found by the court to merit his death sentence.[80]

Veterans of German service who did survive might expect something less than a warm homecoming. Bayle left Tambov by train on 10 December 1945. Given rations by the Americans when they entered West Berlin, the French gradually abandoned the train so that by the time it reached Valenciennes on 21 January 1946, only about 100 former POWs, a mix of SS and *malgré-nous*, were left. A "repatriation officer" took their names and then walked away. Three soiled posters indicated directions to Mulhouse, Colmar, and Strasbourg for the "Alsacos." Eventually, after having been informed of their arrival by the Société nationale des chemins de fer français (SNCF), an NCO, looking very annoyed, arrived and led them to the police station, where they were given a meal and interrogated. When Bayle admitted that he had volunteered for the SS in accordance with a 1943 Vichy law, he was informed that that law had been abrogated and that the abrogation applied retroactively. Then he was locked in a cell. After a week, he was taken before an examining magistrate to be charged with "bearing arms against France." He was subsequently confined to a dormitory in the company of black marketers, Gestapo auxiliaries, and other collaborators, where they were visited at least twice weekly by Foreign Legion recruiters who suggested that five years in the Legion would "thereby erase our mistake." When he finally came up for trial on 13 March 1946, the judge dismissed the charge because he had been a minor at the time of enlistment, but reminded him that, when he turned twenty, he would be required to report for military service.[81]

Bayle's fate was typical. The courts tended toward indulgence, as many of the volunteers, like Bayle and Guy Sajer,[82] had been minors at their time of enlistment. The spirit of vengeance which had characterized the Liberation had gradually subsided. Even before the amnesties of 1951 and 1953, most volunteers for the German army in French custody had been freed. Rostaing spent three years in jail before he was released in 1949. But only the 1951 amnesty restored his full civil rights and allowed him to collect his military pension. However, French society tended to be less forgiving. Many former SS and LVF members could not get jobs, or, like Bayle, might be fired once an SS past was discovered by his employer. Christian de La Mazière, whose public relations (PR) firm frequently catapulted him into the presence of French film stars such as Juliette Gréco, Dalida, and Brigitte Bardot, was outed when interviewed about his fleeting stint in the *Division Charlemagne* for the 1972 Marcel Ophüls film *Le Chagrin et la Pitié* and was forced to reinvent himself as a journalist. Some published their memoirs to "put the past behind me," to justify their actions, to honor dead comrades, and to memorialize what they portrayed, in a new Cold War context, as a heroic, anti-communist community of which they had been pioneers.[83]

The ignominious end of the *Division Charlemagne* has already been recounted. But Joseph Darnand avoided that fate – on 12 March, he fled Sigmaringen to Italy with *la Milice*'s "treasury," hoping to board the clerical-facilitated underground railway to South America. On 25 June, he was arrested by the British and turned over to French *sécurité militaire*, who managed to recover the funds that Darnand had stashed in an Italian monastery. He was incarcerated in Fresnes and tried on 3 October 1945 in Paris, for "treasonous collaboration with Germany . . . with the view of favoring the enterprises of this power against France." Darnand's trial lasted barely five hours. Like many other accused, he claimed to have played a "double game." *La Milice* answered to Laval and the Prefects, he insisted. As "general secretary for the maintenance of order," he had been obliged to act against the resistance, which had "assassinated entire families." *La Milice* had been overwhelmed by the task assigned them. But he accepted responsibility for their excesses. The prosecution insisted that Darnand's exemplary military record did not excuse "four years of treason," nor the murderous conduct of militiamen under his command. His defense presented him as "naive," a patriot, a "*condottiere*," and a victim of his loyalty to Pétain, who had been the true author of collaboration with the armistice and the handshake with Hitler at Montoire. The jurors were urged not to vote for a death sentence that later generations would repudiate. But they deliberated for less than fifteen minutes before finding Darnand guilty. De Gaulle refused a pardon, so that Darnand died before the firing squad on 10 October 1945 at the Fort de Châtillon.[84]

The French Occupation of Germany

June 1945 began with a crisis sparked by de Gaulle's order to General Paul-André Doyen to seize the Val d'Aosta, a Francophone territory on the Italian frontier. Already piqued by Stuttgart, in this instance, Truman refused to back down when faced with de Gaulle's high-handed Italian land snatch. Juin was sent to Caserta to broker a deal with Allied military leaders, where he admitted that no one in the government had supported de Gaulle's action. The French President was forced to withdraw French troops back over the border on 8 June, because he did not want to quarrel with Washington at a moment when he was also at loggerheads with London over British intervention in Syria. Nevertheless, he protested "a taste for hegemony that the United States willingly displays and that I have not failed to point out on each occasion."[85]

Nor did de Gaulle's strategy of "blackmail" necessarily deliver at the negotiating table where German occupation zones were divvied up

(Map 9.2). De Gaulle spends at least two-and-a-half pages in his memoirs memorializing his preemptive occupation of Stuttgart under the noses of the Americans, a stunt to force the Allies to define a French occupation zone, after which he surrendered it to the Americans when the occupation zones were finalized in June.[86] The *zone d'occupation française* (ZOF) was a compromise between what de Gaulle had laid out in his 12 August 1944 plan – basically the two banks of the Rhine from the Swiss frontier to Cologne – with an expanded northern section, and some of the positions occupied by the French army at the war's end. De Gaulle's ambitions to occupy Cologne were dashed when Churchill insisted on retaining a city that the British had occupied in 1919. The Americans also came away with Stuttgart, Kassel, Frankfurt, and Karlsruhe. France was allocated the Saarland, the Palatinate, and a significant part of the Rhineland, as well as parts of Baden and Württemberg, thus splitting the two provinces. It also occupied a sliver of Bavaria which allowed access to the French zone in Austria. An American corridor essentially separated the ZOF into two separate zones. Apart from the Saarland, whose status had not been defined, and Paris' demands for control of mines in the Ruhr, the French zone was composed principally of agricultural areas, comprising 6 million inhabitants or 9.6 percent of the German population. The ZOF also contained four second-tier towns: Mainz, Saarbrücken, Ludwigshafen, and Freiburg im Breisgau, and its chief administrative center at Baden-Baden. This result occurred because, despite de Gaulle's attempts at military preemption, the Allies calculated that, given limited French troops and resources, that was about as many Germans as Paris could effectively govern.[87] Therefore, the message sent by the allocation of occupation zones was that France was "a solid second," a power that had entered the occupation through the backdoor.[88] The good news was that, compared with the other sectors, the French sector had sustained minimal war damage. But its recovery was jeopardized by the extensive war reparations that France exacted as revenge for the "enormous loot . . . from our factories and laboratories," and by the retention in France of hundreds of thousands of German POWs, whose labor was badly needed for German reconstruction. In the view of the Military Governor of the US zone of occupation, General Lucius Clay, French exactions merely passed the burden of occupation costs in Germany onto the United States and Great Britain.[89]

Eager to remain in Germany as Military Governor of the French zone and commander in chief of the French occupation force, on 11 June, de Lattre met with de Gaulle to put his case. But the French leader remained non-committal. De Gaulle sent a more emphatic message to de Lattre on 18 June 1945, when, far from riding a horse down the Champs-Élysées at the head of the "*défilé de la Victoire*," as had Foch in 1919, the "national celebration of victory" found de Lattre placed on the third row of the reviewing stand behind the members of the government and the Sultan of Morocco. Insulted, he stormed away from this

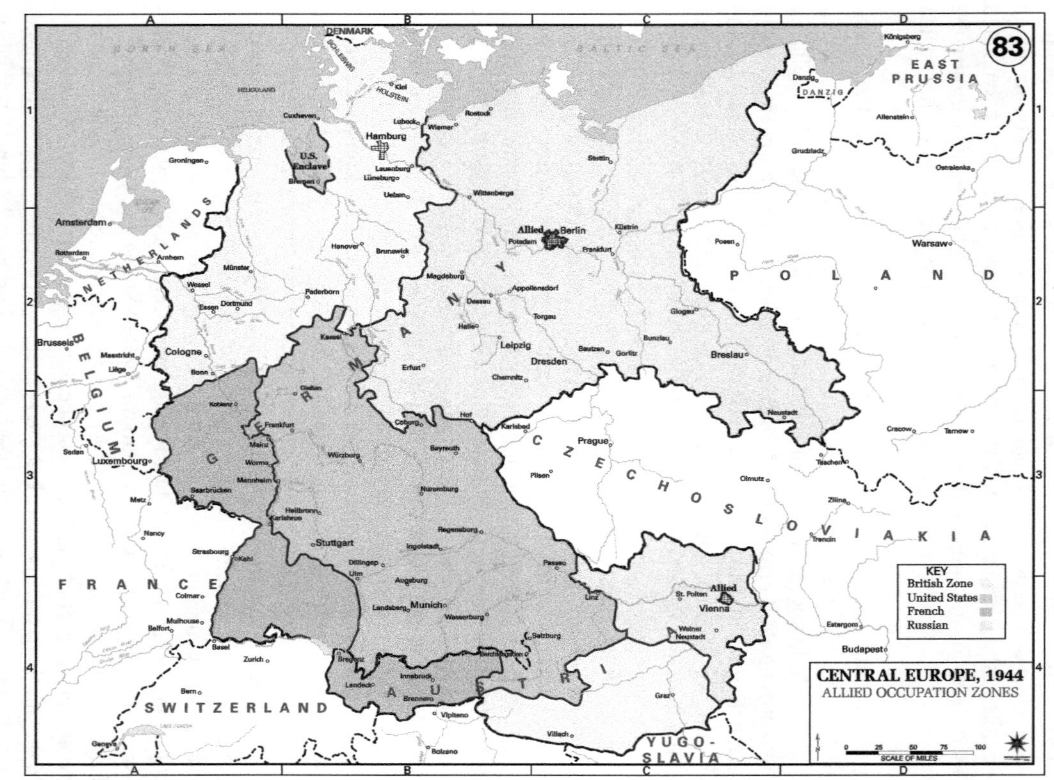

Map 9.2 Occupation zones in Germany and Austria.

celebration of "the man of destiny." Moulin and Leclerc would form the two pillars of Gaullist-fashioned "resistentialist" memory. Moulin had given *la France combattante* democratic legitimacy, in the process helping to scupper Roosevelt's attempt to impose Giraud on the French, by uniting the resistance in the *zone libre* behind de Gaulle. But the internal resistance could not expunge the memory of 1940. Much to de Lattre's displeasure, that responsibility would fall to the 2e DB led by Philippe Leclerc.

De Gaulle held no fewer than five victory parades in three months during the spring and summer of 1945, which American officers at SHAEF found tiresome and over the top, considering France's modest contribution to Hitler's demise. French civilians groused that de Gaulle's parades wasted precious quantities of hard-to-come-by petrol.[90] French soldiers questioned the iconography of these celebrations. Despite the fact that it featured fully 50,000 French soldiers, the 18 June 1945 Paris victory parade, which conflated "resistance" with "*le geste Gaulliste*," created more losers than winners.[91] The purpose of the celebration of 18 June was to legitimize an action taken by "the squatter on the banks of the Thames," who in fact could claim no basis in legality, beyond de Gaulle's conviction that taking up arms in defense of France constituted in itself a self-legitimizing act.[92] This 18 June parade followed the traditional route from the Arc de Triomphe to the Place de la Concorde to erase the humiliation of the German victory march along the same route roughly five years earlier. The march-past was "presented" to the President of the Republic by Pierre Koenig as Military Governor of Paris, while the featured 2e DB was led by de Lattre's young nemesis Leclerc. Who better to represent France's renaissance than the man – and the unit – whose August 1944 liberation of Paris reunited an insurgent people with their renascent army, and whose planting of the tricolor on Hitler's "Eagle's Nest" at Obersalzberg avenged that of the swastika flag on the Place de la Concorde?

Erect in the turret of his Sherman "Tailly" at the head of his now legendary division, "the star" Leclerc embodied the "bright young knight" aglow with Gaullist virtue, a Bayard, *le chevalier sans peur et sans reproche*, "who had kept faith with his sovereign." Leclerc de Hauteclocque symbolized by his very name a ceasefire between aristocracy and Republic that flattered France's national self-image. A Napoleonic marshal reincarnated "in the swiftness of an exceptional destiny," Leclerc had spurned defeat, and instead walked and cycled the length of France to reach Lisbon and London, in the process twice escaping German captivity. Of course, Leclerc would not have existed without de Gaulle. But what a contrast with de Lattre, twelve years his senior and "stained with the compromises of an overlong existence"! "*Le Général Soleil*" was defined by "his extraordinary feminine qualities," his volatility, tantrums, thirst for flattery, and capriciousness, all of which tested the patience of those who fought under his command.[93] Meanwhile, France's young Apollo had surged out of the Sahara, as he explained to de Gaulle, to lead a "crusade . . . of all sorts of people of diverse origins, grouped behind the leaders who raised the standard of Holy War."[94] He had liberated Paris as the bells of Notre Dame reverberated across the fabled French capital. As André Martel noted, Paris may have been "liberated by its own people," but Parisians did not like anonymous heroes.[95] By November 1944, when Leclerc erupted through the Saverne Gap to recoup Strasbourg, the African soldiers who had actualized his "Oath of Kufra" had been "whitened" out of French memory.

Leclerc was first to arrive at the Place de l'Étoile on 18 June at the head of his 2e DB, where, assailed by photographers, he dismounted for a symbolic stride around the tomb of the unknown soldier. His division then rolled like slow thunder down Paris' most iconic boulevard. "The names of the battles in which they distinguished themselves were written on their tanks," remembered 1ère DFL veteran Bernard Lucas. "We were stupefied to discover the name Bir Hakeim. That gave us an opportunity to have words with them, because no member of the Free French Brigade remembers having seen them in that part of the desert." *Évadée de France* Yves Gras, who fought with the 1ère DFL in Italy and France and later became the division's historian, found the entire concept of the parade "bizarre," when his combat-hardened division that had suffered the crucible of the Western Desert and the baptism of the Garigliano was expected almost to "rush" down the Champs-Élysées, paired in the parade with a neophyte FFI unit that had not heard a shot fired in anger. The 1ère DFL felt the popular adulation accorded the rival 2e DB in this Gaullist-impresarioed *fête* treated Leclerc as if he had commanded a victorious army, rather than a mere division that habitually fought as part of the American army.[96] It also downgraded the importance of the victories of the 1ère DFL at Bir Hakeim, on the Garigliano, in Provence, and in Alsace. In fact, "*les grognards de l'honneur*" of the 1ère DFL had been shouldered out of Overlord by Leclerc, missed out on the symbolic liberations of Paris and Strasbourg, seen their cadres stripped away for *l'amalgame*, been progressively swallowed up by *l'armée d'Afrique*, and been diluted with brash and undisciplined FFI in a failed experiment to recreate *l'armée de Valmy*, all while suffering 5,000 combat casualties since Dragoon. Their supreme misfortune had been the loss of their legendary commander Diego Brosset in a freak road accident. The irony was that de Gaulle's 18 June *mise-en-scène* treated his original initiates as discards, rather than as the archetypal "resistance" of a triumphant crusade. "In many respects, therefore, the end of the war was for the Free French of the *1re Division français libre* a time of self-renunciation," writes Guillaume Piketty.[97] The 18 June "*défilé de la Victoire*" also offered a mere glimpse of the *1ère Armée* in the form of units from Monsabert's corps. But so packed was the parade that, by the time the *1ère Armée* troops reached the Place de la

Concorde, the reviewing stand had emptied and the crowds, saturated by the seemingly interminable march-past, had thinned.[98]

Unlike the 1919 Paris victory celebration, the 18 June 1945 "parade of the victorious armies" also coldshouldered the armies of the Allies. Although all of the equipment and uniforms, including the planes that overflew Paris in a Cross of Lorraine formation, had been supplied by the Anglo-Americans, Britain's ambassador to Paris Duff Cooper complained that there was neither a British nor an American flag in sight.[99] This was not quite accurate, as de Gaulle apparently had ordered Koenig to dissolve the Hadfield–Spears Ambulance Corps after they paraded with French and Union flags, a badly timed initiative, as not only had de Gaulle and Spears had a bitter falling out, but also he and the British were a loggerheads over Syria in May–June 1945. Despite its lengthy and often heroic service, Hadfield–Spears was petulantly denied a unit citation by de Gaulle.[100] In some respects, France was not unique, as all nations fashioned their memory of the Second World War in national terms.[101] But de Gaulle's subsequent boycott of commemorations of the Normandy and Côte d'Azur landings on the pretext that France had been treated as a "doormat" by Allied leaders, was singular, because it would have showcased the fact that his elevation of resistance into a war for national salvation had been inconsistent with the means at his disposal.[102]

On 18 June 1945, de Gaulle's purpose was to present the image of "a resistant France realizing its own liberation." Any acknowledgement of Allied help would have spoiled the party, as would a reminder that many foreigners had filled the ranks of "the French Resistance." How could this celebration of a resistance *levée* meant to sanctify and legitimize the republic take place if many in the resistance were not citizens, but foreigners, Jews, and radicals who escaped political control? The lesson of the First World War was that victory depended on keeping populations united. By June 1945, de Gaulle had won his "war among the people," and so no longer felt the need to intimidate the internal resistance by parading US troops down the Champs-Élysées as he had in the wake of the Liberation. Resistance "feudals" had been separated from their interface services enablers, while a "polycentric" FFI had now been either disarmed and sent home or "amalgamated" into the ranks of the regular army. Thorez had returned from Moscow in November 1944 with the message from Stalin for his communist brethren that, for the moment, the priority was to defeat Hitler, not spark revolution in France. The *gardes civiques*, successor organization to the *milices patriotiques*, had been disbanded following a meeting of the Central Committee of the Parti communiste français (PCF) at Ivry on 21–23 January 1945. Although some militants proved reluctant to surrender their weapons, mindful of what had happened to the communist attempt to seize power in Greece, Thorez had declared that "Public security must be assured by the regular forces of the police organized for this task. The *gardes civiques*, and generally all the irregular armed groups constituted for this purpose must no longer be maintained." The word was official: France's resistance *levée en masse* would not transition into another Commune, much less an October Revolution.[103]

Some leaders of the internal resistance complained that, by turning 18 June into a celebration of *la France libre*, "the head of the Free French confiscated the Resistance's capital of sacrifice, suffering, and dignity amassed by the obscure soldiers of the night."[104] Resistance in France had jumpstarted without de Gaulle, and many deeply resented that an *émigré* who had not shared their dangers commemorated victory with a military parade. But de Gaulle's goal had always been to reestablish the State and rehabilitate the French army. Therefore, he had required the resistance to authenticate his democratic bona fides by unifying under his leadership, while they expected through his sponsorship to position the resistance to play the central role in the regeneration of French democracy. Once de Gaulle's position had been legitimized in the eyes of the French people and the Allies, it became inevitable that he would no longer require resistance consent, or even cooperation.[105] This explains why he behaved with such Olympian *hauteur* toward resistance leaders at the Liberation. Thus domesticated, an insurgency that, because of its clandestine nature and dispersion had presented a fractured and even inchoate phenomenon, drawing in a spectrum of volunteers and assuming many forms, could now safely be mustered as "a moral and individual reaction" against defeat, occupation, and Vichy collaboration. De Gaulle's Liberation *mise-en-scène* fused the resistance groups while "Gaullifying" them, to present a mirror reflecting "a heroic vision of the French people." De Gaulle lent a face, a voice, and a vision to resistance which had grown up outside of Gaullism, and that in some corners had even been hostile to it. Nor would this heroic vision of a unified wartime resistance long survive de Gaulle's 1970 disappearance.[106]

The so-called "*Vichysto-résistants*" continued to argue that, through the Armistice which preserved the Empire and the fleet, spared France total occupation, and kept North Africa Axis-free, followed by the National Revolution, and its spinoffs such as the *Chantiers de la jeunesse*, *écoles des cadres*, secret arms caches, and so on, the Marshal had been plotting *la revanche*. When, after November 1942, that argument became unsustainable, some former Pétainists sought refuge in *Giraudisme*, a sort of proto-resistance that "provided a bridge for Petainists who wished to detach themselves from Vichy without needing to renounce their political convictions."[107] However, its Vichy antecedents and American sponsorship rendered *Giraudisme* insufficiently national. This "Pétainism by other means" was too institutionally anchored in *l'armée d'Afrique* and the settler population of French North Africa (AFN), lacked a unifying narrative, and excluded too many categories of dissent to serve as a halfway house between Pétain and de Gaulle. It should have been no surprise, then, that by virtue of its rejection of democratic principles, *Giraudisme* folded in the face of de Gaulle's robustly Jacobin assault, behind a resistance vanguard whose following was motivated by a vision of a heroic, patriotic, and democratic mobilization for war by the nation, in defense of the idea of humanity and democracy embodied by *La France éternelle*.[108] But, in reality, while couched in the language of total war, Vichy and *la France libre* had been engaged in a proxy conflict, one that aligned *la Milice*, the police, the GMR, Gestapo, Sipo/SD, a few German reserve divisions, and *Osttruppen* against resistance networks of various political hues, the *maquis*, the interface services, Jeds and Operational Groups (OGs). The problem is that proxies bring their own political agendas and strategic objectives to the battle. For this reason, de Gaulle required Allied armies on the ground to shape the outcome.

De Gaulle's parades and his canonization of the resistance myth were meant to heal a society traumatized by defeat, occupation, and deportation. The message of 18 June 1945 was that, far from being a minority phenomenon with no basis in legitimacy and of marginal military benefit, 18 June 1940 had mobilized the French people in a collective struggle whose victorious outcome was being celebrated on the Champs-Élysées five years on. This offered a palliative narrative, as insurrection in the service of liberation had been encoded into French memory since the Revolution. But, to be legitimate, resistance had to evince democratic aspirations contained within a Republican framework. Whereas in the popular imagination towns rebelled in acts of self-deliverance, in reality this seldom happened, and rightly so because, without arms, the townsfolk would have been slaughtered to no purpose.[109]

Part of the problem was that Liberation witnessed the juxtaposition of two myths. The first was that of self-liberation through the resistance embodied in de Gaulle's 18 June 1940 call for France to continue the war, which he marketed as the inception of resistance, culminating in the 25 August 1944 declaration of "*Paris libéré par lui-même*." The second myth was salvation of France through its global empire. Dragoon followed by *l'amalgame* witnessed the collision of these two competitive and ultimately incompatible myths, which de Lattre's leadership and the cauldron of combat proved unable to reconcile. "Myths are mythical stories assured credibility by their popular origins," writes Marianne Colonna.[110] The Francs-Tireurs et Partisans (FTP)/PCF embraced the "myth of general mobilization" to advance the interests of their party, just as de Gaulle promoted the "myth of the insurrection" to devalue the role of the Allies. And, because the French people were primed to believe in the power of popular revolt in the service of the people's cause, and because crowds gathered in the streets as Allied armies approached and German forces began to retreat, it seemed inconceivable that popular insurrection as a prelude to liberation seldom occurred. But the FFI did emerge as a real if factionalized force, whose "soldiers" often backed rival politicians who occupied town halls and prefectures to challenge the sovereignty of the state, and so had to be reined in.[111]

But if de Gaulle's celebration of France's self-emancipation through a resistance *levée* consigned Allied armies to the margins of the Gaullist narrative, so too this reframing devalued the *1ère Armée* as a major protagonist in France's Liberation saga. De Gaulle's celebrated 25 August 1944 praise for Paris' self-liberation consigned the French army to a tidying-up role in the aftermath of a popular liberation of France's major cities and towns.[112] As bitterly as *la France libre* and Vichy had quarreled, their supporters shared a mutual sense of grievance against Allies who had abandoned France at Dunkirk, and then proceeded to bomb French cities, spurn its resisters, withhold arms from its valiant soldiers, snatch its colonies, mount a gratuitously destructive invasion, menace France with AMGOT, threaten to sacrifice Strasbourg on spurious operational grounds, and treat French citizens as if they were Africans. SHAEF then had the temerity to invade Paris, requisitioning hundreds of hotels and offices for its bloated staffs, while establishing the French capital as the headquarters of a burgeoning black market in cigarettes, gasoline, and army rations.[113] De Gaulle's serial post-Liberation parades were mean to redress this *Gaullisme noir* narrative, to showcase the survival and triumph of "eternal France" in a systemic and morally cosmic conflict. Through a Gaullist-orchestrated campaign of redemption, France had reemerged energized and united. The "imagined revolutionary act" became a shared belief, a requirement for social cohesion in a nation emasculated by defeat and dishonored by its errors and hesitations, as well as by their consequences, as the return of deportees created a social malaise. Error is redeemed by revolt. Through its courage and sacrifice, resistance had reclaimed French virility and bestowed legitimacy on a restored State.[114] The trouble was, "de Gaulle was no less aware that the Resistance had been a minority, but was ready to overlook this truth in the interest of restoring political unity and national self-respect," writes Julian Jackson. "For the Resistance, whose objectives were as much moral as political, French renewal could not be built on a lie: an ethical vision of the Resistance competed with Gaullist *realpolitik*."[115]

The resistance myth also converged with the requirement of political parties to associate with the resistance heritage to ensure the credibility of their claims to represent the people's interests, to gain political leverage through shared popular perceptions. Reconstruction and the renaissance of the republican ideal required the creation of a collective memory, as was vigorously promoted by de Gaulle and the PCF in their various ceremonies designed to assure the French people that they had been courageous, and that France had been "*libéré par son peuple*." It also showcased the glorious role of their leaders. Within the general myth, various groups develop sub-myths – for example, that the success of

Torch hung by a thread, until it was rescued by the initiative of a clutch of Jewish resisters in Algiers, whereas, in fact, Roosevelt was determined to invade AFN with or without a resistance "invitation," with a force that was "too big to fail." Another example is the belief that the "*réduits maquisards*" could never have been so easily dispersed by a motley of GMR, *Milice*, *Osttruppen*, and Reserve Divisions without Allied/Gaullist complicity and indifference. Any contradiction within the sub-group becomes sacrilege leading to excommunication, because the acts of heroes validate the nation while also revivifying it, evoking sacred sentiments that underpin national identity. De Gaulle's message on 18 June 1945 was that the salvation of the French people had been secured by their national uprising. The French leader was brilliant in his deployment of hyperbole, both to put his exasperated Allies on the defensive and to create a sense of French pride, unity, and national communion. Failures and black moments are dismissed as aberrations – "a handful of wretches" at Vichy who betrayed the national trust and must be exorcised by a collective insurrection. "Resistance is a moral act, and the sacrifice required assumes the appearance of redemption." In this way, France could celebrate Liberation and excuse its lapses as an inevitable product of human frailty.[116]

When de Lattre complained about the underrepresentation of his "Rhine and Danube" contingents in the June 1945 "*défilé de la victoire*," he was told that 18 June was not meant as a *1ère Armée* coronation. Yet, de Gaulle's attempt barely a month later, on 14 July, to showcase both *1ère Armée* and the Parisian FFI also competed with a rival "civilian" parade, so that the reviewing stand, which de Gaulle shared this time with the Bey of Tunis, was set up at the Place de la Bastille. Motorized troops and infantry marched via different routes, while the Gaullists organized a by-invitation-only ceremony at Mont-Valérien, appropriated as a *France libre lieu de mémoire* (place of memory) to honor an elect of *compagnons de la libération* – like every cult, Gaullism conjured its constellation of martyrs. Consequently, 14 July met with indifference and even resentment in the *1ère Armée*, where many felt that FFI and "the shirkers in Paris" had been the honorees.[117]

De Gaulle's dilemma was that, while his celebration of France's self-liberation might rehabilitate popular self-esteem, France's grandeur and global standing could not be restored and maintained without empire, which had become a rapidly wasting asset. De Gaulle's relationship with *l'armée d'Afrique*/*1ère Armée*, never affectionate, was further strained by a feeling that, at best, its officer corps and settler political base remained incorrigibly *Giraudiste*, when not out-of-the-closet *Maréchaliste*. Gaullist veneration of the internal resistance and the 2e DB had nudged the French army to the margins of French consciousness. The French population refused to buy into a narrative whereby *l'armée d'Afrique*'s breakthrough on the Garigliano and the *1ère Armée*'s collapse of the Colmar Pocket had erased the shame of 1940.

L'amalgame had come too late and had fallen far short of a *levée* to alter the culture of the French military, that if anything had become more colonialized, more isolated from a French population that continued to assign blame for 1940 and Vichy to professional soldiers, and to credit the Allies and the internal resistance for Liberation. Their victories were stained by the crimes of their soldiers, while, despite laurels harvested on the battlefield, they remained a sort of *Vichysto-patriotic* fraternity and bastion of imperial pride and parochialism. This rejection and lack of popular gratitude was poorly received by French soldiers, who had been indoctrinated in the myth of imperial liberation and whose sins – such as they were – had been cleansed on the Garigliano.[118] As an *évadé de France* and by now a grizzled *1ère Armée* veteran of Dragoon, Alsace, and Germany, Bacquier labeled the 14 July 1945 Paris parade as the "grotesque apotheosis" of his military career:

> For all reasonable people, the war ended in August 1944, and Paris, "liberated by itself," rested on its wartime laurels by reading the communiqués over breakfast . . . The biggest concern was food supplies. Since the armistice in Europe, ongoing operations were considered in the realm of folklore. "Okinawa, where's that? Do you think that they will accept the [ration] ticket for fats in July?" . . . There was also the victory parade. Preceded by the ram in green and red harness, the band with its shining brass, the regiments of Africa climbed toward the Arc de Triomphe. They had not liberated Paris or Strasbourg; they had not conquered Hitler's last lair. But from Tunisia to Arlberg, by way of Italy, Alsace, and Baden, they suffered. Many of their companions fell along the way. "Corporal Lahcen ben Mohammed, 2e RTM, died for France," and the Gonzalez's, Lopez's, Santinis and how many others? They were proud but tired. And who brings up the rear, but the *service d'ordre* of the Paris police, happy with their handsome red *fourragère* (of the *Légion d'honneur*) so quickly won, the people cheered them. And what did the good people of Paris shout at their victorious army? They shouted "*Vive les Hindous!*," "*Vive les bicots!*," and I even heard – I swear it – "*Vive les bougnoules!* " [both racist terms for North African Muslims] . . . The balance sheet was straightforward: luckier than most of my comrades, I had survived unscathed. But I felt strangely empty. The country for which I had fought disappointed me. It was the era of grand speeches and smart parades. A brilliant magician persuaded the French that they were still a great country and that they were not dishonored. But I had no time for these heroes who shaved women's heads and spat on prisoners. I didn't like these policemen who had moved in the space of a few weeks and with no apparent soul-searching from the hunt for resisters to [the status] of colleagues, nor this administration that "forgot" having been Vichyite. The same judges who condemned resisters presided over the trials of Marshal Pétain or Pierre Laval. And the girls who had for five years slept with Germans were found in the arms of American soldiers bedecked with dollars and chewing gum.[119]

All soldiers had a difficult readjustment to civilian life. But France's wartime experience of occupation and exile was so divisive, its "victory" so tenuous and contingent, that it created more than the usual gulfs of incomprehension between fighters and non-combatants. This meant that, like Bacquier, many veterans of the 1ère DFL brought to Paris to celebrate the victory also felt discomfited and out of place: "I'd had enough of the loudmouths who surrounded us, who hadn't done anything," Alexis le Gall remembered. "I had nothing in common with them. We weren't from the same world." When Louis Leclerc was confronted with "what we see in civilian life, the chaos, inertia, filth, war profiteers, traitors, the government's powerlessness or incompetence, the political skullduggery," he wondered what his companions had died for.[120]

Ironically, the *Forces françaises libres* fared little better in France's post-war memory sweepstakes, marginalized by de Gaulle's emphasis on the primacy of the internal resistance in France's liberation. De Gaulle's mythologizing of "the French Resistance" offered an update of the First World War narrative that attributed France's deliverance at Verdun in 1916 to the stolid tenacity of its peasant soldiers – "*les braves gars*." France was defined by soil and frontiers. The FFL had sparked from outside of both. They were always a small and disparate group, a skim of adventurers, foreigners, and colonials, who skirmished mostly in remote *théâtres d'opérations extérieurs* (TOEs). The FFL arrived in France as outsiders, innocent of the realities of Occupation. As with *l'armée d'Afrique*, their "homecoming," in a land which many had never visited, often came as a shock: "We heard talk about Liberation committees ... *Gardes Patriotiques* ... *Groupes Francs* ... *Gardes Civiques Républicaines*," remembered Casablanca native Solange Cuvillier, transported in Dragoon with the 6e RTM. "We got lost in these multiple designations ... Politics? Naively I was unaware of the harmful connotation this term could hold."[121] "Except for a few insiders, the words FFI, concentration camps, resistance, didn't cross the Mediterranean," remembered Suzanne Lefort-Rouquette, serving with the 9e DIC's medical battalion.[122] As Muracciole notes, the FFL's outsider status paradoxically acquired a negative connotation, as their wartime activism by default cast aspersion on a French people who, rather like the legions of French POWs of 1940, the deputies who had voted "full powers" to Pétain, or those who departed to Germany as STO laborers, had yielded to "legality" in the shadow of defeat and acquiesced to occupation. They had allowed themselves to be seduced by Pétain, and had drifted into *attentisme* when not collaboration. *La France libre* conjured the sense of duty and sacrifice of Corneille's *Le Cid*, the unflinching patriotism of Jeanne d'Arc, or the steadfast fidelity of the aristocratic *émigrés* of Condé, not the civic spirit and peasant fortitude that underpinned France's Republican traditions. FFL veterans were liberating a country they had venerated for four years, but which they no longer recognized. They were shocked by the French population's nonchalance, when not indifference to the war, and its hedonism. Many became upset by displays of noxious misogyny by "September resisters," who sought to reclaim their manhood and failure to defend the country by humiliating women, and by the "weak combat motivation, military amateurism, politicization, and inflated ranks" of FFI *poseurs* whom they were forced to "amalgamate" into their units. Ingratitude also figured among their grumbles – given a meal, an ill-fitting suit, and a metro or train ticket at the war's end, they were "liberated."[123]

"A captain, probably of Vichy origins, received me in a very administrative manner," remembered Bernard Lucas of the 1ère DFL. "I was entitled to a small severance bonus and a voucher good for a suit. I also had two months to decide whether I wanted to enlist in the army. After five years with my brothers in arms, I found myself unceremoniously returned to civilian life . . . Once our goal had been achieved, I had no desire to remain in uniform. I wasn't a soldier at heart."[124] Those with a mind to do so could apply to the colonial ministry, where they would be given preference for employment as administrators in some central African agglomeration of mud huts with corrugated iron roofs that stank of excrement and rotting refuse.[125]

Women who had volunteered for service felt particularly aggrieved. After having been decorated for bravery at Bir Hakeim, and piloting an ambulance at Monte Cassino, Susan Travers had been taken on as a truck driver for Dragoon, a huge demotion in status as, unlike nurturing ambulance crews, who rescued the wounded, "Merlinettes," who operated radios, or Mad Cat's elegant administrative staff, female truck drivers had the status of – well, truck drivers. By September, she found herself backing artillery pieces into the front lines in Alsace. Her messmates in the 1ère DFL were "disillusioned with all the infighting with the Vichyists," reluctant to pursue a military career in Indochina, and so fled the army in droves at war's end. Although Koenig no longer played her Pygmalion, the army had been her life for the past six years. Alternatives were scarce. At the war's end, Paris remained a drab military camp, with army vehicles on every street and frequent checkpoints. Shops were shut or their display windows taped and empty. Phones worked intermittently, while she could almost set her watch by the power cuts. The Foreign Legion was desperate for recruits, so she signed enlistment papers that made no mention of gender.[126]

Cuvillier had been left embittered by the way France treated female volunteers who, like male soldiers, had endured countless hardships. She was particularly offended by de Lattre's farewell speech thanking the nurses for their service, despite "*certaines critiques*." De Lattre's tactlessness simply confirmed "the perception of malaise throughout my entire career in the French army, spent in a perpetual misogyny that does not honor this 'French spirit' characterized by an uncommon pettiness." In her view, these women volunteers should have at least been made NCOs. But, rather than look out for their "physical and moral welfare," the military and political authorities just "released them in the wild after they had given so much." In fact, of all armies most in need of female personnel to fill vital non-combat roles, the French army was the least structured, both administratively and psychologically, to incorporate them. Quite apart from conservative social and even legal norms that treated French women as minors, and not simply in AFN, the French army viewed females in uniform as subversives. Women threated the "military masculinity" that all armies generate as a bonding principle, of which martial race theory serves as a sub-set. "Military masculinities" are strengthened so long as women are reduced to clichés – as mothers, wives, widows, or prostitutes. While, in other Allied armies, the Second World War, or Great Patriotic War in Soviet terminology, worked to transform gender relationships in the military, this process in France had been a tentative one at best. This happened in part because, after 1940, winning the war was outsourced to the Allies, so that the *levée* was limited to semi-organized, clandestine, and irregular forces, where women did have more of a presence. In military circles, the 1940 collapse was interpreted as the result of a generational deficit of masculinity, a feminization of French culture and society. This was apparent in Vichy's near-frantic attempts to toughen up French youth through the *Chantiers* and *écoles des cadres*. In Italy, during Liberation, and in Germany, French masculinity might be recovered by tolerating, when not tacitly encouraging, the rape of enemy women, or the "*tontes*" of "horizontal collaborators," real and imagined. The enlistment of women in the French army was viewed as a wartime emergency measure that had run its course. At the war's end, women were not offered reserve status as were men, and, in January 1946, all women who declined to volunteer for Indochina were separated from service. In February, Cuvillier was handed 1,000 francs ($8.40), a second-class train ticket from Lyon to Paris, and, presumably in lieu of a demob suit, an army blanket "that could be useful under the Paris bridges."[127]

The return to civilian life for veterans was not necessarily a relief. Those who had been students were forced to retake their exams. Without any organization to help them to reintegrate into French society, FFL veterans found that POWs and deportees were given employment preference, where otherwise they also encountered prejudice both from the PCF and from former Vichy supporters, and even from many other French civilians, shamefully aware that they had merely prioritized survival during the war. De Gaulle's annual 18 June rituals at Mont-Valérien, which was transformed into a mausoleum of resistance martyrdom, or the 19 December 1964 *panthéonisation* of Jean Moulin, aimed to reinforce the Gaullist discourse of national unity around the resistance myth. Moulin was, in Malraux's words, "the face of France," who represented both Republican meritocracy and the incarnation of all martyred resisters. Malraux's speech emphasized the "people of the night," synthesized into the symbol of France's organic unity.[128] But this simply further marginalized FFL *émigrés*, as did the fact that the broad *Gaullisme de guerre*, centered on a patriotic rejection of the armistice and collaboration, was superseded in the post-war years by the appearance of a right-wing Gaullist political party. While 2e DB veterans basked in Leclerc's reflected glory, the rest of the FFL shifted to the marginalia of France's wartime memory.[129]

Germany

Despite his allegedly feminine intuition, in Germany, the chronically self-absorbed de Lattre failed to pick up on this fluid post-war ambiance. In defiance of war-torn Europe's austerity, he established his headquarters in Lindau, a chocolate-box town spectacularly situated on the shores of Lake Constance with views across the water to the snow-capped Swiss Alps. Cuvillier recalled the immense joy that erupted when the 6ᵉ RTM reached the shores of Lake Constance. "We screamed, we cried, we hugged." Unfortunately, for the women in her ambulance section, "Our existence changed dramatically," she wrote. "Equal in the face of danger, we would never more be so in peacetime. The military hierarchy implacably reasserted its privileges."[130] De Lattre predictably transformed the French zone into a perpetual pageant, with himself as master of ceremonies. At Lindau, he lavishly entertained a continuous cortège of visiting dignitaries. Military parades became the quintessential feature of the French zone, because they were purportedly required to deliver a psychological shock and hoist French prestige for a German population de Lattre believed particularly receptive to martial spectacle. As one of de Lattre's subordinates explained, de Lattre's serial ceremonials were meant to demonstrate that the French, too, could "conceive big ideas, to carry out huge schemes, to achieve the beautiful, but by means where man, the individual, was not crushed by the mass but raised up."[131] But, as many suspected, de Lattrean flamboyance also sought to veil the poverty of French means and distract from the political pandemonium that had gripped post-Liberation Paris. And it is unlikely that the Germans saw these rituals as anything but compensatory displays to revive France's convalescent reputation and mask de Lattre's maladministration. Cuvillier's nurses, who had spent the winter in Alsace treating wounds and frozen feet, were now confronted with an explosion of *les maladies du régiment*.[132]

Ever the showman, de Lattre invited Devers, together with 15 US generals and 200 American officers most closely associated with the *1ère Armée*, to a review of French troops. Two thousand *tirailleurs* lined Devers' route as his boat docked along the shore of Lake Constance. An extravagant going away party had been organized in a park where the trees were strung with lights and officers sipped champagne and munched *canapés* as an orchestra played and a choir sang "heroic songs."[133] De Lattre had his villa at Lindau landscaped, and imported artists from the Villa Médicis, the French Academy in Rome, to decorate it as well as other buildings. The Paris Opera arrived to give performances. He set up summer camps on the shores of the lake and in the Black Forest for French schoolchildren.[134] A similar extravagance occurred on 20 May 1945, when the 2e DMI at Obersdorf in Bavaria hosted a luncheon for de Gaulle, in the company of de Lattre, Béthouart, Monsabert, and the 2e DMI's commander, François de Linarès (the replacement for Carpentier, who had been relieved in the wake of his unimaginative frontal assault on Stuttgart). The feast began with four *tirailleurs* in full dress uniform entering the mess carrying a *gigue de Brocard grand veneur* on a flower-covered litter, the main course in an elaborate seven-course feast accompanied by *premier cru* Chablis, Bordeaux, Burgundies, Champagne, and liqueurs. To express his displeasure at this carnival of gluttony, de Gaulle ate quickly, and exited the mess before the assembled officers could gobble down their first course, obliging everyone to follow him out. For Parisian resistance commander Lieutenant colonel Henri Rol-Tanguy, who had joined the *151er Régiment d'infanterie* (151er RI), which was created out of Fabien's *Groupe tactique de Lorraine* in January 1945 and attached to the 2e DMI, respect for military etiquette had its limits. While Rol may have been a communist, he was loathe to let this bourgeois feast go to waste – after a suitable interval, he led his table into the mess through a side entrance to polish off de Lattre's venison.[135]

Unfortunately for "the most photographed general in history," the occupied population declined to be dazzled by de Lattre's pathological pageantry, but instead quietly mocked the French presence under "*Der ungekrönte König*" ("the uncrowned king"), comparing his administration to a chef's quest to earn a Michelin star: "Take a handful of French, put them in American uniform, put them on a tank, also provided by the Americans, wait until they oblige their Moroccans and Senegalese to march behind the tank, and you would learn how the French resolved the question of . . . *la grande nation*." The Germans deeply resented French pretentions, and vexatious rules like obliging German men to tip their hats every time they passed a French flag. Germans were especially apprehensive when *la Sûrété* set up shop in Strasbourg and began to search for German war criminals. De Gaulle quickly concluded that he needed to bring down the curtain on de Lattre's "Rhine and Danube" roadshow, which constituted an affront to war-traumatized and famished France, especially as the extravagance of France's Proconsul gave the impression that the government was powerless to rein him. Indeed, some wondered whether de Lattre were not preparing a military coup, suspicions that, to be fair, would also trail his successor Koenig and the French military generally.[136]

From a German perspective, not only was de Lattre insufferably vain, but also, as his military subordinates had learned, "he consciously rejected the virtues of meticulousness, patience, caution that characterize good administrators. Material contingencies that limit or slowed all great visions irritated him." His principal strengths, at least in his own mind, were his intuition, his charm, and his ability to innovate. He despised administrative tasks, planning, and technology, surrounding himself with sycophants who flattered and humored him, while mocking him behind his back.[137] Following the German capitulation, officials of the French military government, the *Administration militaire forces armées* (AMFA), began to arrive from Paris, administrators who, in de Lattre's opinion, were "improvised and little qualified," so that they could be safely ignored by military officers, with de Lattre's encouragement. In any case, "government directives were rare," de Lattre recorded. "In three months, despite my requests, I received nothing on the general policy to follow in Germany nor on the organization to create." Because he claimed that Paris permitted no initiatives, de Lattre established no policies of his own, leaving military governors in the five ZOF "regions" with a free hand to act.[138] But there was much work to be done.

De Lattre's extravagant lifestyle, his excessive requisitioning of German labor and resources, and the profligate use of precious gasoline in the ZOF seemed to many in Paris to have turned the French occupation zone into (another) de Lattre vanity project, which undermined the Allied goal of the democratic recalibration of the German psyche. At the same time, the occupation army had to transfer units, guard frontiers, and regulate a traumatized and apathetic German population, while beginning to demobilize its own soldiers. It remained unclear whether French policy was to rehabilitate the Germans or punish them, as one part of the army sought to create radio programs to indoctrinate Germans, while the other part busily confiscated German radios. Officers proved too ready to arrest the wrong people on the basis of denunciations of vengeful former Nazis. It's no wonder that de Lattre found it much easier to "improvise and hold military parades."[139]

Press stories about de Lattre's unrestrained lifestyle, as well as that of the *1ère Armée* gorging on the carcass of a defeated Germany, soon reached the *Ministère des armées* – well-nourished officers living in Baden's luxury hotels and sumptuous villas, with unlimited supplies of American cigarettes, being chauffeured about the ZOF by female auxiliaries, which simply added to disgust over 1940 and military support for Vichy. Meanwhile, conditions in Paris were so austere that the Americans began to transfer US soldiers and headquarters, which had often simply replaced Germans in requisitioned building and hotels, out of Paris in an attempt to reduce the American footprint, free up space, crack down on a thriving black market in US military supplies, and assuage France's anti-American ambience. In Germany, frustration increased among French soldiers exasperated by de Lattre's "*politique de prestige*," deepening the feeling that the army's sacrifices were not appreciated within the Hexagon. On 24 July, de Lattre was informed that the *1ère Armée* was henceforth dissolved, to be replaced by something to be known as "Occupation Troops in Germany." De Lattre was to be named the French Army's Inspector General, ironically the same position that Giraud had indignantly refused in April 1944. Although fully aware that de

Gaulle had declared him redundant, de Lattre, unlike Giraud, actually accepted a title that came with neither an office nor a staff. Nevertheless, flamboyantly memorable to the end, de Lattre's finale characteristically consisted of appearing three hours late for a 4 August stand-down review in his honor at Kehl. He then crossed the Bailey bridge rigged by French engineers on the pilings of the destroyed stone structure that had spanned the Rhine to Strasbourg.[140]

Effectively unemployed, cast into "semi-disgrace" by de Gaulle for his proconsular immoderation at Lindau, de Lattre was free to consecrate much of his time to his "Association Rhin et Danube," created on 4 October to act both as a fraternal organization and as a "lobby" to promote the memory of the *1ère Armée* within the ranks of the army and of French society in general, and to begin work on his *Histoire de la première armée française*, which would appear in 1949. The "memory" of the *1ère Armée* was progressively hijacked by a reactionary fringe keen to fold *l'armée d'Afrique* into the broader theme of "resistance" and to associate it with the cause of *l'Indo* and *Algérie française*. But, after the French military rebellion of 1958 in Algeria, "*la mémoire militaro-conservatrice*" fell from fashion.[141] Unemployed and looking to rebrand, the mercurial de Lattre began to read left-wing authors and flirt with the communists, who it was rumored had promised him the War Ministry once they gained power and agreed to pay his significant debts. While all this seemed highly improbable, the rumors raised suspicions in SHAEF, which was becoming increasingly reluctant to share intelligence with him.[142] De Lattre's prospects took an upturn, however, when the new government voted into office on 29 November 1945 named him COS of the French army. However, just as he thought that he had been handed the power to reconstitute France's military, de Gaulle split the defense ministry to prevent the communists from dominating it, while de Lattre's old rival Juin was named COS of National Defense.

De Lattre's tenure as Army COS during 1945–1947 was hobbled predictably by his unconventional leadership style, which both irked subordinates and led to confrontations with superiors. In June 1947, de Lattre's new favorite *bête noir*, former Nuremberg deputy prosecutor and War Minister Paul Coste-Floret, engineered de Lattre's "promotion" into Gamelin's former portfolio of Vice-President of the *conseil supérieur de la guerre*, now largely gutted of any substantive powers, and dispatched him on a triumphal tour of those Latin American nations seemingly unaware that the Axis had lost the war, which had become havens for many of Europe's war criminal escapees.[143]

Indochina

The embrace of the imperial myth expressed a commitment of "a diminished nation . . . to cling on to the main source of influence left to her."[144] Wartime conditions in the colonies, or how imperial mobilization and military service had shaped an evolution of colonial mentalities, went unacknowledged in Paris. The 8 May 1945 Sétif uprising, if reported at all, was characterized by the press as a minor incident provoked by "Hitlerite agents." Other colonial disturbances at the end of the war, demands for equal treatment with whites among the *évolués* of French West Africa (AOF), nationalist agitation in Morocco and Tunisia, petitions to the UN by Malagasy separatists, anti-colonial propaganda, and the renunciation of Trusteeship by the San Francisco Conference, which put the French empire on notice, began to creep into the French press in the summer of 1946. By 1947, some French at least had begun to view the colonies as "*une mauvaise affaire.*" However, official opinion, haunted by the specter of a new war while embracing the colonies as France's strategic hinterland, trailed this emerging popular epiphany. Rather than search out new symbols of modern power, many cited France's "numerous subjects and the surface area of the empire" as measures of France's enduring global relevance.[145]

Nowhere did the application of de Gaulle's concept of French grandeur through empire prove more out of date and tragically consequential than in Indochina. France's "balcony on the Pacific" had been a quirk of nineteenth-century peripheral imperialism. "An artificial creation of the colonial administration," French Indochina offered a constellation of territories cobbled together with different statutes, whose managerial principle was "divide and rule." Too distant for France adequately to defend, especially in the shadow of a rising regional power like Japan, it was too brittle to survive a surge of Vietnamese nationalism, whose primary demand was the independence of the "three Kys" of Cochinchina, Annam, and Tonkin. If Gaullist "imperial rhetoric had made no impression on North African opinion," it carried even less credibility in Indochina, where "French colonial rule seemed administratively hollow and morally bankrupt," conclude Thomas and Toye, especially in the wake of the Great Depression, which had hit Indochina hard. Indeed, even de Gaulle likened French Indochina to a "crippled ship" drifting on a storm-tossed sea.[146]

Recalled after having failed to convince Washington to rearm the desperately understrength Indochina garrison, Governor General in Indochina Georges Catroux had been replaced on 25 June 1940 by the Commander of French Naval Forces in the Far East, Vice-Admiral Jean Decoux. Reserved, distant, radiating all the cordiality of a barnacle, Decoux was blessed with an unshakable sense of duty. Like other maritime collaborationists, post-war Decoux portrayed himself as a courageous custodian of French interests who, despite his isolation, made minimal concessions to unremitting Japanese ultimatums that kept the tricolor flying over Indochina until 9 March 1945. Alas, rather than a hapless victim of Japanese bullying, in true French navy fashion, Decoux proved an accredited Anglophobe and fervid acolyte of Vichy's "National Revolution." His meritorious conduct in Vichy eyes began with an obligatory purge of Jews and Freemasons from the colonial administration and navy command, forcing survivors to enlist in a *Légion des combattants et des volontaires de la Révolution nationale*. Gaullist mutineers condemned to the brig by Decoux included Pierre Boulle, future author of *The Bridge over the River Kwai*. However, when Decoux, invoking his title of High Commissioner for the Pacific, proposed a joint Franco-Japanese naval expedition to snatch New Caledonia from the Gaullists, even Vichy drew the line. But, in their tropical quarantine, Indochina's expatriot community entrusted Decoux with the mediation of Japanese demands, while protracting imperial stability and planter privilege.[147]

But events quickly went downhill for Decoux. Encouraged by Japan, Thailand asserted claims to frontier provinces in Cambodia and Thailand, which led to a brief Franco-Thai War in January 1941. When the French scored a naval victory over the Thai squadron off Ko Chang island on 17 January 1941, the Japanese intervened to force Vichy to sign a peace treaty in May that ceded territory to Thailand, the first of serial concessions in Indochina and Syria that found Washington fretful that "Vichy looked more and more like an active Axis partner," writes Michael Neiberg.[148] Washington's view was buttressed in July 1941 when Governor General Decoux signed a military protocol which ceded military bases in Indochina to Japan, while obligating Vichy to made a "common defense" with Japan to defend Indochina from outside attack. "In this way, Indochina became the only European colony occupied by Japan before the outbreak of the war in the Pacific, transforming it into a launch pad for their subsequent conquests," concludes Thomas Vaisset.[149] Aware of French weakness exposed by the Thailand débâcle, indigenous communities that included religious and ethnic minorities, bandits in remote regions, but above all communists in Cochinchina, who launched an insurrection in November 1940, moved to assert their independence. Decoux attempted to waylay discontent by embarking on a vast infrastructure project to improve harbors, build roads, and expand irrigation for agriculture, as well as establish 4,000 schools. "Folkloric" celebrations ostensibly crafted to honor Indochinese culture joined administrative reforms meant to create a façade of democratic consultation. Unfortunately from France's perspective, the first reinforced the nationalist message, while the second bolstered the authority of Indochinese notables, while projecting an image for Decoux of Confucian nobility, wisdom, and compassion.

Like the Germans in France, by 1943 the Japanese were disinclined to reward compliant Vichy behavior in Indochina, where the occupiers continued to expand their garrison and network of informers, while plundering Indochina's rice, corn, rubber, and minerals, requisitions that sparked rampant inflation and created food shortages that escalated to outright famine in Tonkin. The next year, as the noose of America's island-hopping campaign tightened –

US submarines nosed around the shores of the home islands, and bombs rained on Japanese cities – Tokyo's situation transitioned from merely critical to desperate. The installation of the CFLN in Paris in August delegitimized Decoux. With all communication severed with the Metropole, Decoux's attempts to make clandestine contact through Chungking (Chongqing), where a Gaullist military mission had been installed since January 1942, and Algiers were rebuffed by de Gaulle, who declined to absolve Decoux's "complaisant passivity" toward Japan's Indochina occupation. Furthermore, while still co-president of the CFLN, de Gaulle had begun to lay the foundation for France's Indochinese homecoming, plans that did not include Decoux. Unfortunately, attempts to create a "French resistance" in Indochina foundered on distance, Chiang Kai-shek's hostility, the Maréchalist loyalities of the expat community, and the torpor of an isolated, sedentary, overwhelmingly indigenous colonial garrison, whose anemic combat qualities made the FFI look like Rommel's Afrika Korps in comparison. Furthermore, Vietnam's patriotic space was increasingly occupied by Nguyen Ai Quoc, better known as Ho Chi Minh, who had crossed from China into Vietnam in the spring of 1941. By the winter of 1944, Ho's Viet Minh had swelled into a force that could not be ignored.

As 1944 drew to a close, indications that Indochina's sultry wartime idle was drawing to a close were manifest. US forces began their invasion of the Philippines on 20 October, causing Tokyo to switch out their avuncular ambassador to Indochina for a hardliner close to the military. Strategic wisdom in Tokyo held that, once Manila fell, the Americans would assault Indochina. This caused the Japanese to transfer two divisions from China and one from Burma into Vietnam to reinforce the Japanese Thirty-Eighth Army headquartered in Saigon, with reinforcements aligned along the Chinese border. Rumors and warnings from Chinese intelligence that the Japanese were preparing a coup against the roughly 60,000-strong French-led garrison in Indochina, 12,000 of whom were Europeans, had been circulating for some time – indeed, the Japanese staff had finalized plans to decapitate the French administration and install Ngo Dinh Diem as leader, a course of action approved by Japan's Supreme Council on 1 February. Indeed, any Vietnamese rickshaw driver, house boy, or opium den attendant seemed privy to the "secret." Yet Decoux downplayed warnings, as did many in the French military, cocooned in the belief that Vichy "neutrality," together with the proximity of US forces in the Philippines, would shield Indochina from a Japanese takeover, when in fact the opposite was true. Contingency plans were drawn up, but ignored, as the Japanese poured reinforcements into Indochina. De Gaulle foresaw that, from Japan's perspective, once Vichy vanished, Decoux enjoyed neither diplomatic cover nor even the *raison d'être* that he relieved Japan of the burden of administering Indochina. Furthermore, Tokyo had received assurances that Moscow would not intervene to assist its French "ally."[150]

On 9 March 1945, the Japanese unleashed Operation *Meigō Sakusen* (Bright Moon), which saw the arrest of most French administrators and senior military officers, some of them after being invited to dinner or a reception by their Japanese interlocutors. Resistance by the French garrison was cut short by surprise and a lack of ammunition. In less than twenty-four hours, the Japanese wrapped up eighty years of French presence in Indochina.[151] De Gaulle's choice for High Commissioner in Indochina in 1945, Admiral Thierry d'Argenlieu, likened the "apathy," "lack of combativity," and absence of any "sense of honor" displayed by France's Indochina garrison in March 1945 to the humiliation of 1940.[152] Others have suggested French Indochina's fate paralleled that of Singapore in February 1942.[153] An absence of will, leadership, and military preparation, as well as a failure to anticipate enemy action, meant that, in the space of 24 hours, *Meigō Sakusen* had corralled 15,000 French POWs and killed another 4,000, while around 5,000 had fled across Indochina's northern frontier, where they were interned. The strategic success of *Meigō Sakusen* offered a third vindication, along with 1940 and Torch, in the space of one short war of Clausewitz's prediction that surprise can be "*outstandingly* successful" only when its objective – in this case Decoux – demonstrates "sheer inactivity and lack of energy."[154] Around 30,000 French citizens – plantation owners, colonial civil servants, and merchants – were interned. Indigenous populations greeted the Japanese takeover with a collective shrug, while many French-led colonial troops simply dispersed to their villages.

The Minister of the Economy and Finance René Pleven predictably excused indigenous indifference with the flawed but inescapable analogy of Indochina as France's Asian "Alsace-Lorraine," where the population allegedly was torn between its love of France and its regional culture and requirement to kowtow to a powerful Japanese neighbor.[155] "For me, the final Japanese aggression was beyond a doubt," de Gaulle remembered. "I therefore wanted our troops to fight, despite the fact that their situation would have been hopeless."[156] Unfortunately, *Meigō Sakusen* elicited no Bir Hakeim response from Vichy's marooned administrators and soldiers, who had lost face during the Japanese occupation. As all too frequently in the past, de Gaulle blamed the Americans for refusing to arm and transport a French expeditionary force to the Far East, although spare military resources at hand to reclaim Indochina were meagre to say the least. On 18 September 1943, de Gaulle and Giraud had sent a memorandum to the "Big Three" proposing the participation of French forces in the "liberation" of Indochina, much to the consternation of Roosevelt, who did not "want to get mixed up ... in any effort toward the liberation of Indo-China from the Japanese" or to arm any French project to do so while the liberation of Europe was still pending.[157] The *Comité de défense nationale* had passed a statute creating a *Corps expéditionnaire français d'Extrême-Orient*

(CEFEO) on 4 October 1943 to participate in the war against Japan. But finding soldiers for what was originally conceived as two brigades recruited in Madagascar and sub-Saharan Africa proved problematic.[158]

For de Gaulle, France had to participate in Japan's defeat to reclaim its global status. Yet, by April 1945, the CEFEO was expected to number only 8,500 second-tier troops, hardly enough to turn the tide in Indochina, even if they could reach the Far East by March, while French forces strained to liberate the Atlantic pockets and prepared to invade and occupy Germany.[159] Most of the 5,000 surviving French troops who had fled Indochina had been interned in China. At Japanese insistence, Vietnamese Emperor Bao Dai nullified the treaty of protectorate with France, as did the sovereigns of Cambodia and Laos. Indigenous civil servants were maintained in place. General Tsuchihashi, commander of the Thirty-Eighth Japanese Army, replaced Decoux as governor general. Pro-Japanese nationalists rallied to the new regime, as did religious minorities and provincial mandarins. But Indochina slid slowly toward anarchy as the famine worsened.[160] Therefore, the end of the war found Paris virtually bereft of means to reassert French presence in Indochina.[161]

Furthermore, French negotiations to have a CEFEO included in Allied plans for the Pacific war had been episodic and uncoordinated between French representatives in London and Washington. In January 1945, Washington had accepted the principle of a French naval task force to participate in the war against Japan. Unimpressed by the way the French had allowed the Japanese to push them around in Indochina, Roosevelt was not keen to reestablish the French presence there and did not agree to include a French ground force, which initiated a strong lobbying and PR effort by the French for "the right to fight Japan," and promises to create a kinder, gentler French colonial order. Thus, American opposition and French weakness required the French to return to Indochina under British cover.[162]

De Gaulle's fixation on the restoration of French grandeur through empire required him to support "resistance" in Indochina. Unfortunately, the real resistance in Indochina was that of the Viet Minh led by Ho Chi Minh and armed by the OSS. But the colonial ministry bombarded the French public with praise for "Franco-Indochinese solidarity" and lauded "the Franco-Vietnamese resistance to the Japanese coup [of March 1945]," a narrative echoed by the French press. The Viet Minh formed an inconsequential footnote. *Meigō Sakusen* had allegedly forced French policy toward Indochina out of its "disastrous inertia." De Gaulle's 24 March 1945 "governmental declaration" that proposed a federal structure for Indochina was hailed as an enlightened liberalization of imperial policy in the spirit of Brazzaville, that accorded significant autonomy to Indochina's five – not three – political entities through various consultative groups within the framework of a French community. But, on closer inspection, the 24 March declaration seemed hasty, improvised, infused with of imprecise and ambiguous language about "consultation with the qualified organs of Indochina," and unacceptable to the nationalists because it maintained Vietnam's division into the "three Kys" (Tonkin, Annam, and Cochin China) while the French governor general had the last word.[163]

Even though Roosevelt had seconded Stalin's proposal at Tehran that France should not be permitted to reoccupy Indochina after the war,[164] no sooner had the Germans surrendered in May than Paris again insisted that Washington equip the CEFEO. One of the main stumbling blocks became the "Stuttgart incident." Juin assured Leahy that such behavior would not be repeated in the Pacific, a promise called into question by the June 1945 Val d'Aosta crisis, not to mention recent memories of the Christmas Eve 1941 seizure of Saint-Pierre et Miquelon which still rankled in Washington as a Monroe Doctrine trespass.[165] In July, the French returned to Washington, promising to raise a CEFEO of 62,000 men, "all volunteers and all white." On 19 July, the Combined Chiefs of Staff (CCS) agreed to underwrite a French expeditionary force if certain conditions were met. But, in any case, shipping would not become available until the spring of 1946.[166]

In the middle of August 1945, Tokyo unsportingly surrendered, leaving de Gaulle's outdated policy glaringly exposed. The subsequent power vacuum in Vietnam was filled in part by Ho Chi Minh and the Viet Minh, who on 2 September declared Vietnam to be a unified, independent republic. So, it is quite likely that, without de Gaulle, France's role in Indochina might have elided into history, Vietnamese unity and independence would have been recognized as a *fait acompli* in September 1945, and much of the three decades of turmoil that subsequently rocked Southeast Asia might have been avoided. Those Gaullists who knew Indochina best – Henri Laurentie, who had organized the Brazzaville Conference, and Georges Catroux, the pre-war governor of Indochina – had understood that de Gaulle's 24 March declaration was already passé.[167] The French were also caught flatfooted when they learned that the Potsdam Conference had cleaved Vietnam along the 16th parallel, the north to be occupied by the Chinese while the south was to become a British zone.[168] The GPRF scrambled desperately to improvise, ordering Leclerc, d'Argenlieu, and the CEFEO to Indochina as soon as possible. On 17 August, all French troops in the Far East were placed under Leclerc's command. Despite opposition from Washington, Mountbatten in South East Asia Command (SEAC) facilitated the French return. Nevertheless, the French had lost the race to control the political structures in Vietnam, which, between the Japanese surrender in August and the arrival of the first French forces in Cochin China in October, were occupied by the Viet Minh, with the complicity of the Chinese in the north.[169]

Volunteers for the CEFEO were scarce. Leclerc, chosen to lead the reconquest of this distant corner of empire, held sub-Saharan African soldiers in low esteem. A Moroccan tabor had mutinied in May 1945 at the mere rumor that they were to be sent to Indochina, while the 15,000 or so Vietnamese in France seemed, to Salan at least, to have been thoroughly infected by nationalism.[170] French soldiers keen to fight Japan evinced little enthusiasm to enlist in a crusade for imperial restoration. Even few in the 2e DB proved eager to shadow their charismatic commander into a Southeast Asian morass. German POWs appear to have been a fruitful source of recruitment for the Foreign Legion, which made up 8 percent of French strength during the Indochina War.[171] The government organized a massive advertising campaign to draw in volunteers, lowered the recruitment age to nineteen, and even scoured the prisons, so that legitimate volunteers, at least 25 percent of whom had an FFI past, served alongside rapists, those incarcerated for self-inflicted wounds, militiamen, LVF members, *Division Charlemagne* survivors, black marketeers, and other castoffs who sought an *Indo* hideaway. "It is this divided army, weakly renewed and democratized, that commits to fight the wars of decolonization," writes Miot.[172]

De Gaulle's decision to reassert the French presence in Indochina was poorly timed. With both Washington and Chungking hostile to a French return to Southeast Asia, and with the Viet Minh surging into the vacuum left by the Japanese surrender, the prognosis for Paris' reoccupation of its "Balcony on the Pacific" appeared unpromising.[173] The empire was in crisis; France was economically prostrate; popular enthusiasm to reclaim Indochina was low; the army lacked the muscle and the navy the reach to transport, land, and sustain an expeditionary force; and, finally, the makeup of the French Republic had not yet been determined, so that the mechanisms of government policy and of civil–military control were not yet firmly fixed at the end of a war that had confronted France with a latent crisis of civil–military relations. A tenuous solidarity forged between army and nation in the Liberation quickly atomized with the German surrender. *L'armée d'Afrique* was desperately out of touch with France; the Resistance, with de Gaulle's assistance, claimed to have liberated the country; of all groups, the PCF attempted to market its "*resistentialisme*" by branding itself as the "party of the Resistance" and the "party of the executed." A rapid return of pre-war governmental instability, combined with bad blood left over from the Occupation, enflamed partisanship.[174] Nor was France able to launch a major imperial *reconquista* while simultaneously purging, downsizing, restructuring, and "renewing" its military forces. The inelasticity of the Gaullist imperial vision, one actively pursued by the Rassemblement du Peuple Français (RPF) in the post-war period, combined with fractured civil–military relations fatally to weaken the Fourth Republic and hamstring the ability of France's proconsuls in Indochina to realize viable concessions in the context of a political and military situation careening toward catastrophe.[175]

In 1945, the prospect for a successful compromise between France and the various Indochinese factions was torpedoed when de Gaulle confided France's return to Southeast Asia to a dysfunctional command team. Many imagined that the job of High Commissioner would go to Henri Laurentie, the Director of Political Affairs in the Colonial Ministry, or, given the turmoil in Indochina, to a military man. Unsurprisingly perhaps, de Gaulle delegated the mission "to return Indo-China to the fold of Christian civilization" to his two most anachronistic and intractable disciples. Appointed High Commissioner in 1945, monk/Admiral Thierry d'Argenlieu, alleged with due deference to Peter Abelard to possess "the most brilliant mind of the Twelfth Century," was yoked to the impetuous Leclerc, inexperienced in political affairs, to lead the CEFEO.[176] Although both men were "Gaullists of the First Hour," it proved a particularly schismatic consortium, and vintage de Gaulle, whose management technique called for "stoking the rivalries" of his inner circle.[177] In Indochina, this command mechanism would produce calamitous consequences.

The classic narrative was that France's Indochinese reentry combined two mismatched personalities, holding incompatible visions for Indochina's future. Beneath his oleaginous clerical façade, d'Argenlieu was rigidly doctrinaire, while it was the eternal "Colonel of Hussars" Leclerc who proved the more politically flexible, because he realized that, thanks to his Nationalist Chinese shield, Ho Chi Minh had been able to solidify his position north of the 16th parallel. So, the received version is that d'Argenlieu's inflexibility sabotaged a potential compromise in Indochina, which Leclerc realized was vital. "De Gaulle the decolonizer was far in the future where Indochina and the Levant were concerned," concludes Julian Jackson.[178]

D'Argenlieu's biographer Thomas Vaisset unpacks this chronicle as, at the very least, incomplete, a lionization of de Gaulle's young protégé in the wake of Leclerc's tragic early death in a 1947 plane crash, by his subordinate Raoul Salan and by journalist/historian Jean Lacouture and Philippe Devillers, Leclerc's press attaché in 1945.[179] Unfortunately, the d'Argenlieu–Leclerc relationship (Figure 9.4) was almost immediately curdled by issues of personality, service rivalry, and policy. The only thing that held them in harness was their shared fealty to de Gaulle.[180]

On 20 September 1945, General Douglas Gracey allowed the first contingent of French troops to land in Saigon, to establish a 30-kilometer defense perimeter around the capital of Cochin China. Almost immediately, Leclerc set his staff to plan a landing north of the 16th parallel as a prelude for the reconquest of Northern Annam and Tonkin, occupied by 180,000 Chinese troops, beneath whose protective umbrella the Viet Minh formed a government on 19 November, with which in December d'Argenlieu felt that he had no choice but to negotiate. "In December 1945, the Admiral was one of the few people in Saigon who was willing to use the term 'independence,'" writes Vaisset. On

Figure 9.4 Leclerc greets the new High Commissioner for Indochina, Admiral Georges Thierry d'Argenlieu, at Saigon airport on 30 October 1945, as Douglas Gracey, the facilitator of France's Indochina homecoming, looks on approvingly. (Photo by Keystone-France/Gamma-Keystone via Getty Images)

14 December, de Gaulle agreed to unify Vietnam and give it "independence" within the Indochinese Federation and the French Union under Vietnam's former emperor, Prince Vinh San, if certain conditions were met. But fast-moving events sabotaged this evolving political compromise: the death of Vinh San in December 1945; de Gaulle's abrupt resignation as President of the Republic on 20 January 1946, which "orphaned" d'Argenlieu; the evolution of France's China policy; Leclerc's inflexible operational timetable to "catch the tides" for an invasion north of the 16th parallel; and, finally, the inexperience, lack of coordination, and even mutual antipathy that divided France's Indochina command duo.[181]

The Franco-Chinese accord, signed 28 February 1946, aimed to speed Chinese departure from Indochina. But, eager to secure his southern border in preparation for his showdown with Mao's communists, Chiang insisted that Chinese troops would not leave Indochina until Paris signed an agreement with the Viet Minh. Leclerc had to be cautious until he could build up his troop strength, calculated to number 53,750 by 16 March.[182] The accords of 6 March 1946, negotiated under Leclerc's authority by Salan, and signed by Jean Sainteny and Ho Chi Minh, consisted of two documents: a "preliminary agreement" and an "annex," which laid out the military aspects negotiated principally by Salan, which, when the conditions became known in Paris, were regarded as a disaster. This was a direct result of de Gaulle's January 1946 resignation, which had left Indochina policy both rigid and rudderless. With de Gaulle's departure, d'Argenlieu was required to report to the new Minister of Overseas France, the socialist Marius Moutet, who, in February 1946, offloaded Indochina affairs on to an inter-ministerial committee. D'Argenlieu's reputation for intransigence comes from this moment, because he wanted to take no initiatives without de Gaulle's approval. At the same time, Leclerc's reputation for flexibility came from his willingness to make further concessions to China to convince Chiang to withdraw his troops from the north. Leclerc's "flexibility" was driven by purely operational considerations – the tides would become favorable for large ships to sail up the Red River to Haiphong, the port of Hanoi 30 kilometers from the sea, in early March, to launch Operation Bentré – the French reoccupation of the North. D'Argenlieu's fear was that Leclerc was so intent on launching his invasion of Tonkin that he was willing to risk war with China. For its part, Chungking insisted that it would remain in Vietnam until the French had finalized a settlement with the Democratic Republic of Vietnam.

In the end, the 6 March accords were full of language so imprecise and ambiguous that d'Argenlieu accused his subordinates, especially Salan, who had been responsible for negotiating the "military accords," of disloyalty. The French negotiators had agreed to a unified Vietnam and conceded to Ho Chi Minh the right to set the numbers of French troops to be stationed in Vietnam and the location of their garrisons. But the real surprise was hidden in the "annex," negotiated by Salan, which obliged the French progressively to withdraw all troops from the Indochinese peninsula by 1951. When Paris learned of the conditions of the annex, the various ministries concerned were outraged, and demanded Salan's recall, which was blocked by d'Argenlieu. The result was that Paris immediately looked for ways to sabotage this "Indochinese Munich," while maintaining the 6 March accord as purely "decorative." The smoldering antipathy between d'Argenlieu and Leclerc burst into flame. D'Argenlieu eventually managed to arrange for Leclerc's reassignment, citing his "*nervosisme et l'instabilité d'humeur*," which at least delivered a tactical victory in Indochina's "*guerre des chefs*." But it proved a Pyrrhic one, as, in February 1947, d'Argenlieu was recalled to Paris for "consultations," and never returned to Indochina. Unhappy in retirement, de Gaulle continued to wonder, as the Cold War took shape and the PCF surged at the polls, while his sacrosanct French state seemed unequal to France's post-war challenges, who would save France if it forfeited its empire? He was livid that "we allow Ho Chi Minh to mock us in our own country – as little by little the empire disaggregates." In the end, a strategy of placing his acolytes in key slots to protect French interests and allow him to influence policy from the wings – d'Argenlieu in

Indochina, Leclerc as Inspector General in AFN, while Koenig supervised Germany – was quickly overtaken by events.[183]

Conclusion

The war for the *1ère Armée* ended more with a whimper than a bang. While Sixth Army Group had succeeded in eliminating the Colmar Pocket, morale in the *1ère Armée* at the end of a tough winter campaign was low, especially as soldiers felt that the French population had disengaged from the war. Operation Cheerful saw the French army invading Germany as part of the Sixth Army Group, directed by de Gaulle to seize objectives to force the Allies to designate a ZOF, which they had already conceded in principle. As had been the case in Italy following the breakthrough on the Garigliano in 1944, the defeat and occupation of Germany witnessed violence inflicted on the civilian population, which earned French soldiers the unflattering nickname of the "Russians of the West." De Gaulle's post-Liberation victory celebrations sought to shrink the role of the Allies and the *1ère Armée*, while celebrating that of the resistance and Leclerc's 2e DB. None of this served to repair French civil–military relations, which had been badly damaged by the war, or to acknowledge the role played by the empire in France's liberation, all of which stored up future tensions. Incorrigible to the last, de Lattre settled into an extravagant lifestyle at his headquarters in Lindau, which flouted the conditions of post-war austerity and caused de Gaulle to recall him to France.

Committed to the retention of empire as a symbol of French *grandeur*, de Gaulle insisted that France reclaim its Indochinese "balcony on the Pacific." However, the fact that the French colonial infrastructure had been obliterated by the Japanese, allowing Ho Chi Minh's Viet Minh, with Chinese complicity, to fill Vietnam's political vacuum, would have made it difficult in the best of circumstances for a debilitated France to reassert its sovereignty in Southeast Asia. France's return to its far-away colony was hobbled by an absence of a viable policy for Indochina, a situation exacerbated by political instability in Paris following de Gaulle's precipitous January 1946 resignation, a defective command tandem in Saigon that yoked two headstrong commanders in d'Argenlieu and Leclerc, each with different priorities, and political concessions made by France's negotiators led by Salan under pressure from Leclerc to catch the tides to launch Operation Bentré – the reoccupation of Vietnam north of the 16th parallel.

10 Conclusion

1940: "A Verdict on France?"

Hardly was the ink dry on the 1940 armistice than debate erupted over whether the Fall of France signaled an across-the-board collapse of French government and society within a brittle alliance system, or whether German tactical skill had partnered with operational surprise to snowball into strategic catastrophe. Among the first out of the gate and certainly the most influential was Marc Bloch's *Strange Defeat*.[1] Penned in "a white heat of rage" in the weeks immediately following the débâcle, Bloch's extended essay was part Jean Jaurès and part Clausewitz, while anticipating S. L. A. Marshall's post-war treatises on the behavior of soldiers under fire.[2] Whatever the deep-seated causes of France's defeat, the proximate cause in Bloch's view was the "utter incompetence of the high command," a gerontocracy incapable of thinking in terms of a "new war. In other words, the German victory was, essentially, a triumph of intellect."[3]

Much of Bloch's critique might have been lifted straight from Jaurès' ground-breaking 1911 call for a remaking of the French army to reflect the republican ideal of the citizen in uniform as a corrective to militarism.[4] Jaurès' message had been that many in the French population had lost faith in the utility of armed force, a subversive sentiment that posed an existential threat to the professional army, who had viewed the introduction of two-year service in 1905 as "an affront," the Republic's humiliating payback for the military commanders who had persecuted Dreyfus, emboldened by bogeymen in the guise of Jews, Freemasons, and socialist pacifists, to whom might be added "les Anglo-Saxons," whose alleged objective had always been to shrink French *grandeur*. This reinforced doubts in the professional military class about the staying power of democracy, or the capacity of French citizens to understand the core professional mission of national defense, the eternal hierarchy of the battlefield, and the science of war mastered only by a cloistered *breveté* elect. The army had required certainty in the swirl of Clausewitz's theory that counterpoised political purpose and reason, the interplay of chance amid genius versus friction, and the centrality in warfare of anger, violence, hatred, and enmity. For professional soldiers, if the Republic failed to provide "reason," and the French people – wary of war and distrustful of military leadership – lacked passion, how could a small staff elite reduce "chance and probability" through doctrine, the only dimension of warfare in a democracy that theorists might control?

The result was that, in the run-up to two world wars, French doctrine was shaped by three factors: fraught civil–military relations; comparative French weakness, which required a credible alliance offset; and the strategic quandary of Belgian neutrality. Before 1914, France had witnessed the twin phenomena of the industrialization of war, which favored large-scale combat operations, and its corollary of battlefield dominance by defensive firepower, which was confirmed at the turn of the century in South Africa and Manchuria. This threatened to transform inter-state conflict into wars of attrition as predicted by Ivan Bloch, which would disadvantage a lightly industrialized and less populated France in a competition with Germany.[5] The French staff solution had been to prioritize strategies of preemption, with an emphasis on the decisive nature of the "first battles," combined with the tactical offensive, whose rationale was anchored in a fantasy dominance of Gallic morale over Teutonic matériel. An absence of political guidance beyond a prohibition on violating Belgian neutrality, it may be argued, negatively impacted the formulation of strategy, because it complicated the establishment of clear, attainable, goals and consequently left the military without guidance to define objectives and the level of the effort required to achieve them.

As a result, in 1914–1918, "the mass army, 'army of the French people'" had corroborated Jaurès' prescience, in the view of French historian Olivier Cosson:

> The entry into war of the French army's professional cadres is today associated with failed plans, useless and cruel sacrifices, with a seemingly total lack of preparation and . . . a suicidal posture. The conduct of the war that followed is etched in national memory in the form of a tactical doggedness that seemed to flow from the intellectual depravation inherited from a prolonged pre-war synonymous with social isolation, routine, and the most culpable negligence. The resentments incubated toward a society grown soft during these years of peace formed the opening arguments of a vengeful "caste" eager for combat, with a sovereign disdain for the human, social and political consequences.[6]

In Marc Bloch's view, defeat in 1940 demonstrated that not much had changed in thirty years. The disastrous consequences of political detachment which had parented military make-believe had served only to validate Jaurès' assertions in 1911 that strategy and tactics must no longer dwell in a politics-free zone dominated by military technicians. Relative French weakness in the European state system, combined with a reckless profligacy of professional soldiers with the lives of their citizen combatants in 1914–1918, meant that theory, experience, a generalized loss of faith in the utility of military force in the wake of Germany's resurgence under Hitler, and the requirements of civilian control combined to dictate France's defensive posture in 1939–1940 corseted by the Maginot Line. The result was that, while France's political, economic, and psychological stakes in war were cast as being total, the decision to engage state and society in a mass army via total war was circumscribed in indoctrination and strategy.

As in France, Germans viewed the Second World War through the lens of the First. This allowed Goebbels to "mine" historic German fears of "encirclement" by hostile powers orchestrated by imperialist Great Britain in support of a "defensive" war. Preexisting feelings, even among non-Nazis, that Germans "needed to be redeemed from the sin of revolution and self-inflicted defeat" of 1918 translated into an "intergenerational responsibility" for sons to accomplish their fathers' unfinished task. These sentiments were socialized by high levels of popular participation in Nazi organizations, backed by police and domestic intelligence services dedicated to squelching dissent with brutal, arbitrary, and visible tactics, and legitimized and sustained by Hitler's seemingly effortless early victories.[7]

France's battlefield collapse, culminating in the Bordeaux crisis, revealed that, rather than represent "*la force morale de la nation*," as reflected in republican values, the French military had offered asylum to political reactionaries stratified into a constellation of cliques committed to scholastic military science. An inter-mixing of corporate hierarchies produced by a combination of *concours et cooptation* and political connections merely served further to fragment the French military command, muddle coherent planning, and hinder the development of a realistic strategic vision. The High Command proved a risk-averse collection of "elderly men, weighed down with honors and spoiled by a lifetime of office work and easy success," who distrusted the very soldiers they had been tasked to lead, but at the same time hesitated to impose discipline. In this way, France's army had devolved into a cumbersome machine guided by leaders whose mental "flabbiness" rendered them unable to adjust to war's dynamic character.[8] Behind a Maginot Line meant to serve as a constraint on the proclivity of French professional soldiers to view war as a moral competition in which combatants were expended as collateral to reaffirm the inviolability of the national community, the French army was meant to serve as a deterrent. In this imagined scenario, size was confused with quality – "We'll win because we're stronger," or "the mouthful is too large!" France wasn't Poland, *quand même*!

As Marc Bloch asserted, the fall of France in 1940 offers a case study in a failure of supreme command. The ability to act effectively at any level requires a commitment to the mission and an understanding of its political purpose. French leaders on the political and military level failed to question their optimistic assumptions about the inviolability of Allied defenses, and instead trusted their armed forces to deliver. French propaganda stubbornly repeated themes of French inviolability, which failed to prepare a population already skeptical about the utility of military force for the psychological shock of battlefield reverses. Indeed, an inability accurately to assess the combat morale of their own soldiers was part of the pathology of the system.

An army's will to fight is difficult to predict, especially when strategic miscalculation was amplified by the French military's struggle with the fog and friction of complex maneuver warfare. The outcome of battle is governed by qualitative and human factors. French doctrine underestimated the importance of delegated authority and local initiative. A rigidly hierarchical command structure proved unable to absorb and adapt to information from the ground and, crucially, did not enable French units to respond rapidly to changing circumstances. Technology was incorporated into existing "controlled battle" doctrine, rather than imagine, as did de Gaulle and other soldiers and military theorists, how armor and aircraft might accelerate the pace of combat to achieve operational, and even strategic, results.[9] In May–June 1940, it was the Germans who had sharper tactics, brought together by command structures, from the highest political level to the lower field commanders, which achieved a stunning victory. In 1940, German tank commanders discovered that "the French tanks were easy to shoot up from the side because they were 'slow and especially sluggish when turning . . . The enemy tanks behave [as if] leaderless, aimless, badly commanded, tactically inferior, and try to get away quickly.'" In the view of their German opponents, the tactical ineptitude of the French army in 1940 was matched only by the "poor combat morale" of its soldiers.[10] Indeed, Lieutenant Gaston Vuchot had divined that his sliver of morale-challenged Pyrenean conscripts and reservists lacked the small-group cohesion to put up much of a fight. Nor had the army done much to engender professional pride and institutional unity, against a background of Phoney War-induced societal disengagement. The Germans may have been lucky, and their victory "contingent." But their "luck" was fostered by the coherence of a tactical and operational system that emphasized intelligence which accurately identified French strategic weaknesses and Gamelin's likely response to *Fall Gelb* (Case Yellow). This was abetted by *Auftragstaktik*, which encouraged responsive battlefield adjustments, active air support, and a robust logistical system that, unlike that of the French, which collapsed in retreat, continued to function despite the demands of a lightning advance.

While the quality and maintenance of arms and equipment, the motivation and expertise of soldiers trained to use it, and the resilience of logistical systems are important, above all, military power depends on effective command. And that includes both a country's political leaders, who act as supreme commanders, and officers seeking to achieve their operational goals on the battlefield. Command should encourage subordinates to take the initiative to deal with the circumstances at hand; commanders should trust those close to the action to make the vital decisions, yet be ready to step in if events go awry. Inflexible command systems can lead to excessive caution, a fixation on certain tactics even when they prove unsuitable. Faced with orders they dislike or distrust, subordinates may seek alternatives to outright disobedience. They can procrastinate, follow orders half-heartedly, or interpret them in a way that better fits the situation that confronts them. French command philosophy in 1940 was far too hierarchical. The rapidity and relentlessness of the German advance disadvantaged Allied generals who were locked into their managerial mindset, and hence proved unable to replenish troops or remedy the failings exhibited in the opening phase of the war. As a result, French retreats degenerated into a succession of *sauve qui peut!* events, most spectacularly at Bulson. As retreat, confusion, and German air power increasingly collapsed French logistics and denied French soldiers access to the equipment and supplies they needed to fight on, the absence of mutual trust between senior and junior levels of command was exposed. France had never developed a forceful non-commissioned officer (NCO) corps that ensured the basic requirements of an army on the move, from equipment maintenance to maintaining fighting trim. After the Maginot Line had been outflanked and the French front ruptured at Sedan, operational solutions such as *colmatage* ("plugging the gap") and Weygand's "hedgehogs" on the Aisne – whose primary purpose in any case was to preempt a Breton Redoubt – rapidly collapsed, command-and-control structure imploded, and soldiers became leaderless and confused, simply concluding, as did Bloch, that continued resistance would only get them killed to no purpose.

However, whatever the faults of the French command – and they were multiple in Bloch's view, from poor intelligence to inadequate troop training, via out-of-touch staff work – as a member of the *Annales* School, whose mantra was "*histoire totale*," not surprisingly, Bloch quickly ballooned his indictment to implicate French politics and society. Among the factors that culminated in defeat, Bloch impeached a French education system, in which he was a prestigious senior participant, that had failed to impart moral and ethical values to its pupils; a press often "secretly enslaved to unavowed and, often, squalid interests," some of which were foreign; trades unions captivated by inflated wage claims and becoming "tangled up in the political game," in the process forgetting that their workers were as much soldiers as were the men in uniform at the front; industrialists obsessed by "petty profit"; a political system that dispensed military deferments as if unsold tickets to a third-division football match; the "irritating and crude optimism" of government propaganda that failed to define war goals and forfeited credibility, serving only to make Frenchmen skeptical of the official line, which further delegitimized the regime; an "ideology of international pacifism" on the left which devalued patriotism, and "intellectual lethargy" and defeatism on the right which sabotaged resistance; mayors quick to surrender their towns rather than see them damaged; and so on. All of this was capped by a parliamentary regime whose "monstrously swollen assemblies" became "chaotic" and "too often favored intrigue at the cost of intelligence and true loyalty."[11] A dysfunctional political system may limp along in normal times, as technocrats moderated the impact of institutional friction as regime resilience ebbed away. How would decision-makers who had flourished in this defective environment behave when the chips were down? The difference between France and Britain would be stark.

However, the raw immediacy, rage, and promiscuous scope of Bloch's indictment also served to disqualify it "as a history of the defeat." Rather, historians, primed to treat "the evidence of experience" as a primary rather than a secondary source, cautioned rightly that Bloch must be read "as the testimony of a participant-observer."[12] Likewise, Pertinax's unflattering rapportage on the high personages and collusions of the late Third Republic might be dismissed as café tattle fossilized into testimony.[13] Nevertheless, French diplomatic historian Jean-Baptiste Duroselle packaged Bloch's *j'accuse* for posterity as *la décadence*. In Duroselle's telling, a dysfunctional government structure, populated by venal, incompetent, and/or corrupt players, bore witness to "an extraordinary incapacity of the French people to submit to governance, a stupefying inability to reform, whether it be social, or fiscal, or economic, even constitutional ... Without invoking the doubtful concept of 'national character,' one can conclude that there existed, in the inability of France in the 30s to avoid disaster, a collective responsibility, where the government classes, by definition, played the principal role."[14] Like Bloch, Duroselle enjoyed home-field advantage, in that the "decadence" label stuck on the late Third Republic merely updated an analytical framework crafted for Marie Antoinette, Louis-Napoleon Bonaparte, and other *fin du régime* stumbles in French history at least since 1789, a theme replicated in the Gaullist narrative of France's past as recurring cycles of decline, defeat, and renewal summoned from the soil of France by a charismatic leader.[15]

Nor, in the course of the war, did France evolve a redemptive national narrative that came to define the heroic communal sacrifice generated in Britain, the United States, and the Soviet Union.[16] On the contrary, if anything, liberation found the class and political fault lines, not to mention the civil–military divide, laid bare in France in 1940, to have been calcified by defeat and occupation, seemingly bringing France to the brink of civil war. As Susan Perlman convincingly argues, the post-war period institutionalized Washington's anti-Gaullist attitude. Much of Washington's diplomatic and intelligence community viewed post-liberation France as weak, unreliable, and "wreathed in communist intrigue." This was in part because, while the myth of widespread popular resistance to the occupation may have affirmed

Gaullist legitimacy, the prevalent attitude had been *attentiste*, while, when not outright collaborationists, official France had been staffed by men who were at best reluctant Giraudists. These were the conservatives who had helped to poison Leahy's mind against de Gaulle, and whom "Vichyite" Robert Murphy had assiduously courted in North Africa. But Murphy was no outlier – this mindset was sustained into the post-war period by US Ambassador to France Jefferson Caffrey, who viewed the French as "irrational" and "temperamental," plagued by "post-Liberation neuroses." H. Freeman Matthews, former first secretary at the US Embassy in Vichy and a bitter critic of de Gaulle, became the State Department's post-war chief European affairs expert. American officers, such as Czarist émigré Robert Solberg, who had hobnobbed with Vichy attachés in wartime Madrid and Lisbon, or had worked with *l'armée d'Afrique* after Torch and who went on to fill US intelligence and attaché ranks, assimilated the view of their French interlocutors that democracy in France means "the forty-hour work week, atheism and revolution," because they, too, saw FDR's New Deal as a giant step toward socialism. These French conservatives continued to insist to their US contacts in 1945–1946 that the French Communist Party, in conjunction with its Kremlin enablers and imperial offshoots, was plotting seizures of power both in France and in the colonies. And while this information was overly alarmist and served the political ends of French conservatives, it was given credibility not only by the solidifying Cold War, but also by "the shocking French collapse ... in 1940, a contentious wartime relationship between Franklin Roosevelt and Charles de Gaulle, and fear of a communist France after the war. American perceptions of French weakness drove US officials to feminize France and view it as emotional and unstable, in need of more masculine oversight," concludes Perlman.[17] Meanwhile, the myth of the "clean Wehrmacht" which had fought a valiant campaign against Bolshevik "Mongols" in the East gained creedence in conservative circles in Washington, to the point that some Republican politicians denounced the prosecution of white men at Nuremberg as judicial overreach and downright "un-American."[18]

Given the critical nature of historical discourse, what one might categorize as the Bloch–Duroselle "decadence" interpretation of France's 1940 collapse has been poked, prodded, and catechized by subsequent generations of historians, an evolution that has been meticulously chronicled elsewhere.[19] Meanwhile, the allure of "*histoire totale*" wilted with the increasing specialization and sophistication of sub-fields of historical study, including that of military history, that the *Annales* School had scorned as fact-focused *histoire événementuelle*. The interpretation of the Fall of France as a failed "test of national vitality" which merited in full the reprimand delivered by Vichy defeatists, Gaullist scolds, and leaders of the France's internal resistance lost its allure as subsequent generations less ensnared in the passion, humiliation, and consequences of those events engaged in a more dispassionate analysis of the defeat. "Structural factors," political divisions, and legitimate differences over France's strategic options became factored into the mix.[20] While concord is far from having been achieved in the historical congregation, gradually the focus on 1940 as "a military event and not as an expression of national decline,"[21] has gained ascendency. This process was eased no doubt by the fact that the Bloch–Duroselle moral indictment of French politics and society of the 1930s echoed in part Vichy's attempt to place "democracy" in the dock at Riom in February–March 1942, and hence could be canceled as a "narrative with political uses." Clearly, for many revisionists, the French army's second collapse at Sedan in seventy years, followed by Vichy's flailing response to Torch two years later, demonstrated that the French high command and their cultural-pessimist staff officers, beset by the class conflict of the epoch, deployed military theory wrongly and so failed to adapt to the changing face of war. In this way, the failures of the Republic were quarantined as just "one piece of the puzzle, and not the most important one at that."[22] War creates its own dynamic, operates by its own rules, and plays out in the realm of "chance" and "uncertainty." In May–June 1940, the Germans had rolled the dice and scored a "strange victory," which blindsided even them. This self-proclaimed "miracle" became part of the myth whose origins can be traced to a post-war collusion between Guderian and Sir Basil Liddell Hart to promote their pre-war prescience about the revolutionary nature of tank warfare, followed by a required whitewash of the Wehrmacht's war crimes as the price of the Bundeswehr's integration into the North Atlantic Treaty Organization (NATO).[23] As a "narrative with political uses," contingency did not merely allow a refutation of "decadence," while redeeming the republican principles which underpin assertions of French exceptionalism. Contingency also rebuts the infantilizing Gaullist "great man" – or "great woman" in the case of Joan of Arc – rendering of French history, whereby querulous Gauls must at suitable intervals of national peril be gripped by a forceful and far-sighted French Führer. Or, to refute an argument of Jaurèsian inspiration via the French Revolution prominent among more left-wing elements of the internal resistance, contingency also torpedoes the claim that only a patriotic *levée en masse* could revitalize moribund French institutions, beginning with its army.

In this way, the revisionist interpretation of 1940 evolved from the declinist vision that France in the 1930s had lost the sense of cooperation, community, and trust that underwrite the "art" of self-government, to view the French military merely as having botched once again the mission of national defense. In other words, 1940 had showcased a military episode that combined doctrinal rigidity with strategic blunder in the context of "the disintegration of a flimsy western alliance," topped by a right-wing coup against the Republic. Gamelin was "branded as 'the man who lost the Battle of France.'"[24] Ultimately, betrayal by a coterie of generals, politicians, and senior officials, not "decadence," or French moral decline, had scuttled the Republic. Had French armies balked Case Yellow, as they had the Schlieffen Plan in 1914, a scenario "not beyond the realm of possibility, the Republic would have held too."[25] In this revisionist scenario, a June 1940 misfire of French exceptionalism in the shadow of the heroic Great War *union sacrée* is explained by a stab-in-the-back storyline, that somewhat ironically clones Germany's "November criminals" *Dolchstoßlegende* "big lie" of 1918.

If "decadence" did not foreordain France's fall, then it becomes possible to imagine other, more favorable outcomes for France, contingent events upgraded into counterfactual scenarios that might have assured the survival of a resilient Republic – oppose Hitler's dismemberment of Czechoslovakia at Munich in 1938; keep Giraud's Seventh Army at Reims; do not promote Pétain to deputy prime minister; expel the doom-monger Weygand from cabinet meetings; retreat to a Breton redoubt and/or North Africa and fight on; and so on.[26] Like most myths that conjure events that did not transpire, these speculations contain a kernel of plausibility – while the Anglo-French armies and their commanders were certainly surprised, outmaneuvered, and outfought, *Fall Gelb* was also fortunate to have succeeded without the usual "fog and friction" that accompanies most daring military plans. Defeatists at Bordeaux outwitted advocates for continued resistance. Unfortunately, while plausible, none of the alternative imaginings suggested above actually came to pass. At their core, the assertion that France's defeat resulted from battlefield bad luck that triggered Bordeaux treachery in the shadow of Belgian capitulation and British flight seeks to assuage France's humiliated pride while redeeming the Republic, and so provides its own "narrative with political uses."

If, as revisionists correctly argue, decadence offers an imprecise and inadequate framework to explain France's defeat, what does "military event" mean? What constitutes it? What are its contours and boundaries? How does one disconnect "one piece of the puzzle" from the others, and prioritize the "most important"? Can military malfunction in the form of devastating strategic decisions, obsolete doctrine, inept generalship, inadequate weaponry, or poor training, lack of discipline, and miserable morale be isolated from the context of a regime, and a people, who maintain, regulate, finance, and direct the armed forces? If all victorious armies are alike, every defeated army is vanquished in its own way. As an apostle of "*histoire totale*," Marc Bloch might have rejected the concept of a "military event" as "*histoire événementielle* … surface disturbances," having only proximate explanatory power within the "vital cohesion of any historical event or society."[27] While Bloch was clear that *Strange Defeat* was to be read "not as history," but rather as the "testimony of a participant-observer," in his view, France's army merely refracted the nation's systemic shortcomings that encompassed intellectual mediocrity, social ossification, economic stagnation, and political dysfunction.[28] "Our War College and General Staff are not the only institutions in France which have preserved the mentality of the oxcart in the age of the automobile," Bloch charged.[29] By way of comparison, while *Unternehmen Barbarossa*, the June 1941 German attack launched against the Soviet Union, certainly had a military dimension, its devastating success can be traced to Stalin's misjudgment, reinforced by the totalitarian nature of the Soviet system, which prized political loyalty over military professionalism, whose mediocrity was exposed by Barbarossa. (Some have seen these regime-induced shortcomings replicated in Vladimir Putin's faltering assault on Ukraine.)[30] "The history of war, I came to realize … was the study of entire societies," concluded the late Michael Howard of his initiation as a military historian. "Only by studying their cultures could one come to understand what it was that they fought about and why they fought in the way they did. Further, the fact that they did so fight had a reciprocal impact on their social structure … I would certainly not claim to have invented the concept of 'War and Society,' but I think I did something to popularize it."[31]

A generalized antipathy, born of a common resentment of political meddling in what soldiers saw as their autonomous operational field, at least provides a degree of consistency in French civil–military relations over the long term. It also drew on a conviction common among professional soldiers and sailors, who saw themselves as the last bastion of Christian civilization in face of what they considered to be France's – and Europe's – moral decay as exemplified by metastasizing communism. In this view, the political left had deployed "civilian control" to weaken the army's operational capacity, and hence reduce the government's resolve to deal effectively with both internal and external threats to national defense. The idea of the armed forces as the only useful tool to protect and expand French civilization was hardly a new one, and formed the bedrock of France's *mission civilisatrice*, on prominent display in the writings of Hubert Lyautey on the French army's social and colonial vocations, as well as Paul Chack for the navy. This "civilizing mission," combined with the fact that France alone was too anemic to uphold the European order, which was imperiled by Germany's recurring bid for European hegemony, also helps to explain the quest for a rationalist framework of analysis for the military, which translated into the appeal of inflexible doctrines and a quest for operational formulas. These swung wildly from *offensive à outrance* in 1914, to static defense in 1940, whose ruptures were to be repaired by *colmatage*, via de Gaulle's *Vers l'armée de métier* tank army. When these defense formulas faltered, responsibility for defeat could be transferred to the Republic's political leadership and their combat-shy constituents who congested army ranks.

As Patrick Finney perceptively notes, while Vichy's purpose at Riom was to "concretise this anathematisation of the Third Republic" by embracing the myth of foreordained overthrow, ironically, that aborted trial sparked the Republic's rehabilitation. But this recalibration from decadence to contingency was slow to take hold for a variety of reasons: the post-war autopsy perpetuated pre-war sentiment and obviated the need for public soul-searching; because a popular acknowledgment of the Third Republic's dysfunction assimilated a familiar "death and resurrection" narrative deployed to legitimize successive French regimes; and because, whatever France's pre-war failings, they had been redeemed by de Gaulle's resistance myth and recovery of "French exceptionalism" and grandeur, which buttress French identity.[32]

Imagining revisionist scenarios that result in the Republic's survival offers enticing counterfactuals, even if fixated largely on the operational/tactical level. However, as Richard Evans cautions, counterfactuals must not be confused with the more important aspect of contingency seen not by persons in the present but by figures in the past. Military campaigns certainly obey their own Clausewitzian dynamic of genius, chance, and friction. But viewing France's defeat in 1940 principally as a matter of contingency and bad luck invites one to discount the context in which strategic decisions were made, that included the fragility and limitations of France's foreign policy options, the glaring structural weaknesses of Republican governance, oversight of its military forces, and the precarious state of French civil–military relations so apparent to contemporaries. "Because strategic decision making is a fusionist process that involves a variety of groups and individuals, it has been suggested that military incompetence 'is no longer the sole property of generals, but results from the combined efforts of inept strategists, in and out of uniform,'" concluded political scientist Amos Perlmutter.[33] It also rationalizes the strategic and operational successes of the opponent as "strange" or "miraculous," however repugnant on a moral plane Hitler's Germany and the Wehrmacht, Waffen-SS, and Luftwaffe surely were. It treats decision-makers as free-floating agents, while downplaying the constraints on their choices. It posits "a *parallel* history that shadows the history that actually happened but reverses it at every step. Causation is thrown out the window and there is no attempt to consider how one change in the pattern of events might have affected others." Much of it comes down to "arbitrary speculation" about what might have happened had a momentous decision not been made, that slithers over into "wishful thinking." In this way, the motives of contingent/counterfactual speculation are "fundamentally presentist" – not only "what if," but "if only."[34] In fact, this fascination with a kind of fairy land or science fiction past may have its place in popular culture that finds the truth too boring and the search for cause and effect too tedious, but it explains little about what actually happened in the past without the conceit and arrogance of hindsight. Counterfactualism becomes a peculiarity of popular history that speaks to the anxieties of decline via the cult of the past and nostalgia. "The past was never just the past," concludes the novelist Julian Barnes. "It was what made the present able to live with itself."[35]

De Gaulle shouldered the burden of confronting the consequences of 1940, which were to knock France from its global pinnacle and reduce it to bystander – when not victim – status within the greater world conflagration. And, even for him, explanations for France's 1940 implosion oscillated between "moral collapse" and "accident," "decadence" and "contingency," depending on his interlocutor.[36] The fact that historians are to be found at both extremes, as well as along the spectrum in between, "has more to do with one's perspective on history and its driving forces than with the evidence as it presents itself," concludes Talbot Imlay.[37] But, taking a cue from Bloch, the post-mortem on 1940 originally focused on the "systemic" political, diplomatic, economic, and intellectual constraints under which French decision-makers labored.[38]

While it is certainly true that military organizations generate their own distinct cultures, these are invariably linked to their political and social context, which determines the selection of the high command, the structure of the forces, funding, length of service time, disciplinary norms, even operational and tactical deployment, and order of battle. Central to this generalized problem in the epoch and ever since is the contentious place of the general staff in the entities of the national cabinet, the high command, war ministries, parliament, and other branches of government, economy, and society. As has been seen, distrust of strong, unified military leadership, baked into the Republican mindset since 18 Brumaire of Year VIII (9 November 1799), had been reinforced by the Boulanger and Dreyfus episodes in the 1880s and the turn of the century. One consequence was that the war and defense ministries were characterized by administrative overlap, petty intrigues, and a proliferation of bureaus and study groups whose role in producing a coherent vision of defense remained ad hoc and undefined. While surely not limited to France in this time, how this phenomenon worked there deserves close analysis. The corporate culture at the summit of the French military determined that, while senior officers groused in the mess about *la Troisième*, they carefully cultivated influential politicians – indeed, had they not done so, they would never have arrived at senior rank. This weakened Gamelin's command authority among his military peers, who viewed his elevation to commander in chief in the wake of the formidable Weygand as a quirk of parliamentary roulette, and attributed his longevity to Daladier's stubborn sponsorship. The labels of "right" or "left" were assigned in a French political context according to an officer's religious habits, offensive or defensive preferences, and source of political patronage. Like any bureaucracy, arms and services defended their interests and promoted their most articulate and talented officers to advocate for them in arenas in state and society beyond the walls of the general staff.

One of the weaknesses of "decadence," was that the metrics which defined it were flawed. From its inception, the generational failure of 1940 was contrasted unfavorably with 1914's popular resilience. The myth of 1914 – that French men and women had greeted the outbreak of the Great War with an outburst of patriotic enthusiasm and a desire to defend democracy against Europe's autocratic regimes – has undergone its own historical revision. In the aftermath of 1940, the dogma that the French had marched steadfastly to war in 1914, and doggedly persisted through unimaginable crucibles like Verdun and the Chemin des Dames was considered history, not memory, a more-or-less post-modern invention. "Many people joined the crowds precisely because they felt that history was being made," Hew Strachan writes of the demonstrations of public approbation that accompanied declarations of war in 1914. "Indeed, historians told them that this was the case." The outbreak of war in 1914 marked the frontier between a sun-dappled "long nineteenth century" and its transformation literally overnight into its mud-streaked, murderous successor, and so required some sort of popular coronation. "But the historian's knowledge of what is to come, not only in the war itself but also in the rest of the twentieth century, can make any analysis of the sentiments of 1914 mawkish and maudlin."[39]

In truth, a moralist technique of construing communal crises as evidence of ethical and societal decline, to be regenerated in the character-building crucible of war, while perhaps espoused in some conservative intellectual circles, was seldom embraced on the popular level. Larger cities witnessed boastful if brittle patriotic jamborees that celebrated the reconciliation of France's social and political divisions in an *union sacrée*, as well as anti-war demonstrations. However, the overall reaction to the 1914 declaration of war in *la France profonde* had been rather one of surprise, stupor, silence, even sadness, that war had broken out at all, and that the populations of Europe seemed fatalistically to embrace it rather than reject war as a catastrophic malfunction of international relations.[40] Soldiers displayed detached insouciance, "while in the crowded streets, people embraced, shook hands with a spontaneous cordiality, a few women cried with emotion," one witness recounted. "We chat, discuss thoughtfully, with a calm that indicates resolution."[41] "France did not want war; France was attacked; we will do our duty," is how Elizabeth Greenhalgh characterizes the population's attitude to the outbreak of war in 1914.[42] "Passive acceptance" by a population for whom "*faire son régiment*" had become both a social ritual and a civic duty and legal obligation, not a matter of enthusiasm, categorized the advent of war in 1914, as in 1940. The survival of the Third Republic in 1914 had been a close-run thing, a "strange victory" in its own right.

Contingency and counterfactual legends and myths in their day suggested that, with minor adjustments, Schlieffen's *Aufmarsch* too would have succeeded – a historical syndrome of wounded professional military pride which says much about civil–military relations in Weimar Germany versus the shape of conflict in the years 1914–1915. Gazing into the kaleidoscope of war had blinded French military leaders to its realities. They responded with *l'offensive à outrance*, not a rational doctrine but "*une sorte d'attaque à tout va*," anchored in a "metaphysical" concept of combat that conjoined tactics and strategy which had captured the *Zeitgeist* of the pre-1914 *École de guerre*. Consequently, "enemy firepower disarticulated often instantaneously units advancing in the open, provoking retreat, confusion, even panic, as well as horrifying losses."[43] The French army forfeited much territory amid the carnage. Events might easily have cartwheeled into defeat as they did in 1940. But according to Jean-Jacques Becker, the difference in outcomes can be explained by "*ces forces morales*" that ultimately derailed the Schlieffen Plan and also rationalize "the totally unforeseen duration of the conflict."[44] In doing so, Becker rather directly echoes Clausewitz, who emphasizes the shared responsibility of national resilience, which coalesces when society as a whole takes ownership of national defense.[45]

But, if the contemporary historiography of 1940 has gradually migrated through various states of decadence and constraint toward "contingency," the view that revisionism has gone too far persists, especially but not only in France, where some scholars refused to absolve the Third Republic's leadership for France's "lack of material and moral preparation."[46] This idea may have arisen because the "decadence" verdict long persisted in popular memory, in part because it combined a familiar explanation, with the power of Bloch's scorching indictment, and a conservative/Gaullist provenance. France's 1940 "collapse in rout and ruin"[47] crowned an almost inexorable downward trajectory of French power and influence characterized since Waterloo in 1815 by cycles of revolution that triggered regime change.[48] It offered a profound national humiliation with catastrophic consequences, one that fixed an indelible image of a nation in decline, paralyzed by its divisions, whose politicians proved incapable of acting with speed and purpose, but instead blindly eschewed salvation as the nation stumbled tragically toward defeat and occupation.[49] De Gaulle's attempt to relegate 1940 to an ephemeral episode in France's Thirty Years' War with Germany, which concluded in triumph, was joined by mitigating popular alibis that France's fall was also an Allied defeat. Even so, the historical indictment includes a failure to grasp diplomatic opportunities in the 1930s, if not earlier, to contain Nazi Germany; rejuvenate France's professional military class quarantined in resentment and groupthink; revise outdated military doctrine and restructure to create hard-hitting armored divisions; and resurrect its "glorious air force" of 1914–1918 to support the French army's strategic mission, rather than allow it to decline into obsolescence. Above all, France needed to reconcile the functional conditions of operational armed forces with the liberal principles of a democratic constitutional state.[50] These failures, the argument continues, flowed from the "moral culture" with which each nation attempted to adjust to "the imperatives of a totalizing war."[51] Depending on one's viewpoint, French political culture of the 1930s was inexorably shaped by ideological polarization, popular trauma over Great War sacrifices, the Third Republic's institutional dysfunctionality, and the failure of France's risk-adverse and complacent national leadership, locked into their political games, to pay attention to the basics of government: economic development, rearmament, the challenges of diplomacy, and the operational conundrums of coalition building in the face of German resurgence. Clearly, the question of whether these shortcomings rose to the level of a "moral failure" or whether they can be attributed to "structural" constraints or legitimate political differences divides historians, as it did contemporaries.[52]

Defeatism offered the most salient characteristic of French "decadence," being manifested in the 13 May 1940 panic of the largely Parisian reservists of the *55e* and *71ère* *Divisions d'infanterie* (55e and 71ère DIs) at Bulson near Sedan, the gateway to France's northern frontier. This two-division stampede buckled the French front and kindled a military meltdown that an antiquated leadership guided by a doctrine of "methodical battle" and "*colmatage*" proved powerless to staunch. Bloch insists that soldier panics, more generalized than the signature flight at Bulson, were invariably triggered by orders to retreat, even when no Germans were in view.[53] Fleeing soldiers joined a southward refugee tsunami, topped off by the British exodus at Dunkirk and Saint-Nazaire and the 10 June 1940 fall of Paris, confirming the urgency of an armistice. These events of May–June 1940, punctuated by the long lines of French POWs marching to captivity in Germany, seemed to substantiate an absence of national "will." France's defeat was memorialized by a Gaullist indictment of betrayal by a claque of defeatists, collaborators, and opportunists assembled at Vichy under Philippe Pétain. France was liberated and renewed by a heroic resistance that surged first in exile, and subsequently within the country.

Indeed, a prime incentive for the revisionist emphasis on contingency is that it rejects Vichy's "decadence" verdict, while downgrading France's 1940 defeat from a national disgrace to a "military misfortune" triggered by cascading institutional malfunction.[54] Misfortune anchored in contingency also sidesteps a stumble through the French culture wars of the 1930s within the ideological division of Europe itself. There were several contingent aspects that help to explain the different outcomes in 1914 and 1940, the main one being the sheer magnitude in 1940 of surprise on all levels – strategic, operational, tactical, and technological – which paralyzed the French response. Clausewitz viewed surprise as a "tactical device" whose primary benefit was to shake enemy morale. "By its very nature [surprise] can rarely be *outstandingly* successful," especially "the more it approaches the higher levels of policy ... unless, of course, we confuse them with instances of states being ill-prepared for war because of sheer inactivity and lack of energy . . . For the side that can benefit from the psychological effects of surprise, the worse the situation is, the better it may turn out; while the enemy finds himself incapable of making coherent decisions. This holds true not only for senior commanders, but for everyone involved; for one particular feature of surprise is that it loosens the bonds of cohesion, and individual action can easily become significant."[55]

This shock was due to the speed of the German advance, the Wehrmacht's unexpected focus on Sedan, and the absence, unlike in 1914, of any distracting offensive against Germany out of the East. Among the many shortcomings that contributed to defeat in 1940 was that the French operational and tactical system was simply not designed to remain functional during an unexpected and precipitous retreat – among the most difficult of any maneuver and the greatest burden to the imponderables of morale, discipline, and command and control. Dependent on telephones for communications, the French army progressively forfeited its wire, and rapidly collapsed into congregations of leaderless platoons.

In the process, French soldiers lost confidence in their leadership, and surrendered both psychologically and physically, encouraged by German soldiers who assured them that the war was over, and that they would soon go home. This phenomenon can be explained in part by the fact that citizens surrender much of their autonomy when they join a military organization, and feel helpless, especially when a system whose purpose is to impose order seriously malfunctions on the strategic and operational level. After all, SNAFU and FUBAR are not French expressions, but are from the US military lexicon of the Second World War. Legend has it that Stalin, too, was thrown into the depths of despair by news of the fall of Paris, because, according to Khrushchev, the Soviet dictator realized that, coming on the heels of the Red Army's embarrassing performance in Finland, it meant "that now Hitler was sure to beat our brains in."[56] Nevertheless, the fact that 1.8 million French soldiers – or roughly 80 percent of the French troops serving on the northern front in 1940 – became POWs at least proves that French soldiers had agency. While an anti-republican senior military leadership and their civilian enablers may have delivered the Third Republic's *coup de grâce*, France's 1940 exit from the war was initiated at the squad level in the face of German tactical and operational superiority despite what was often brutal combat.[57]

If, by 1944, the Gaullist storyline of a heroic self-liberation via "the French Resistance" had shouldered *attentisme* and collaboration into the touch lines of France's wartime memory, the collapse of 1940 as "a ready acceptance of the lottery of fate" became more difficult to amend.[58] During the Phoney War, Sartre had discovered that France's citizen soldiers "weren't sustained by any patriotic or ideological ideal. They didn't like Hitlerism, but they weren't wild about democracy either – and they didn't give a bugger about Poland."[59] In late

May 1940, three weeks before Pétain's infamous 17 June address announcing his intention to seek an armistice, de Gaulle for one found it deeply humiliating to discover that many French soldiers simply stood by the roadside and allowed their arms to be smashed by advancing Germans, who did not "have time to take you prisoner." Too many simply awaited the armistice, and then obediently filed into POW cages as a prelude to extradition to Germany, where most would spend the next four-and-a-half years.[60] Indeed, France's roughly 1.8 million POWs have often been mustered to support the decadence thesis, because mass surrenders might offer an insight into the mental state of the French nation.

French soldiers certainly were not the only combatants to experience morale problems.[61] British censors in the Western Desert in 1942 "understood morale to relate to the soldiers' attitudes on topics such as the competence of the high command and progress of the war," concludes Steven O'Connor.[62] In 1946, Montgomery defined soldierly morale as "endurance and courage in supporting fatigue and danger . . . the quality which makes men go forward in attack and hold their ground in defence." How a military institution instils morale and unit cohesion among its soldiers has always concerned military commanders, at least since the time of Machiavelli. With the rise of modern national armies in the nineteenth century, morale became a subject of study in France with Charles Ardant du Picq.[63] Morale had several components, beginning with a belief in the cause which the troops have been mobilized to defend and its expression in command, but also resting in the soldier's discipline, obedience, and welfare. Second, the troops should have confidence in their doctrine and armaments, and in the ability of their commanders to deploy them in such a way as to create tactical advantage on the battlefield. Training offered an important component in morale, as did confidence in company-level command and leadership.[64] André Beaufre lamented that the Norwegian campaign had simply served to advertise an "out-of-date" Franco-British military system: "no modern equipment, no ack-ack, no decisive bombing policy, no drive in the troops – except the very best – and no incisive command."[65] This was especially the case when French forces were compared with a Wehrmacht which, via the Reichswehr, had paid significant attention to excellence of command and to which was added Nazi ideology via the paramilitary training of the Hitler Youth or the Sturmabteilung (SA) and Schutzstaffel (SS). Paul Fussell believed that, for 90 percent of his company, part of the US Seventh Army in Alsace in 1944–1945, a refusal to surrender or flee had nothing to do with ideology, war goals, or even training. Rather, it was about "maintaining our self-respect, protecting our manly image from the contempt of our fellows. By persisting without complaint, we were saving our families from disgrace. We were maintaining our honor by fulfilling an implied contract. We were not letting the others down," even though "all of us desperately wanted to be removed from danger, but we now sensed that the war would not end in a few days and that only death or wounds would be likely to grant us our respite. We kept on. There was nothing else we could do." Most frustrating and incomprehensible for Fussell's companions, not to mention the Allied high command and subsequent generations of historians, was why German soldiers continued ferociously to resist, although they had clearly lost the war. Their opponents were often adolescents and old men, and – unlike the cruelly exquisite summer of 1940 – they were forced to endure the punishing conditions of combat in the harsh winter of 1944–1945. Part of the answer is that "to act out the 'final battle' now which they believed should have been fought in 1918," had become an "*idée fixe*" in a large segment of the German population and armed forces.[66]

Mobilizing the economic and military resources of the state to fight is the norm. It requires enhanced coordination between ministries to reorganize and redirect industry, natural resources, transportation, and communications to military benefit, as well as to provide the needs of the population in times of war. This requires investments in arms procurement, in improved conditions of service in the armed forces and defense industry, and in command-and-control systems.[67] It engages domestic and foreign affairs alike. It defines politics as belligerence and belligerence as politics, embracing jingoism to justify militant patriotism. To justify going to war over the invasion of Poland, Paris and London needed to state strong reasons for war against a Nazi enemy to frame the conflict, state clear objectives, and enlist active public buy-in. This was because mobilization not only depletes the economic resources of the State, but also drains the psychological resilience of the people, especially when, in the case of France in 1939, it was improvised with minimal competence by an army clearly ill-equipped to receive the spur-of-the-moment deluge of reservists and conscripts, on a pretext rationalized by an unconvincing propaganda campaign, and complicated by contradictory criteria that only increased confusion and resentment of *planqués* and those excused by professional deferments. In these conditions, transforming Frenchmen into motivated, competent, and effective soldiers proved a challenge.

If, as is sometimes suggested, a new historical consensus is emerging which views Allied pre-war policy as a strategy of deterrence and containment to buy time for rearmament, "rather than supporting the tired myths about appeasement," there is little evidence of this in French pre-war policy.[68] In France, the Phoney War was something less than war that failed to define objectives, let alone craft a convincing message to explain what the war was about, or why the stakes were so high, beyond an ironic assertion that "we'll win because we're the stronger." "*Sitzkrieg*" offered a vacuous military mission with no political direction or convincing "theory of victory" beyond seeking to produce a "negative stalemate" – some version of a scenario in which Berlin, realizing that France was inviolate, and gradually weakened by economic blockade, peripheral operations, and popular impatience, would simply throw in the towel. But, as both British and German propagandists were to discover in the middle years of the Second World War, stagnation and stalemate resulted "in the feeling of entrenchment, uncertainty and war-weariness on the part of the population." It discouraged strong emotions brought to the surface by casualties and proportional sacrifices on the home front. Mobilization in 1939 seems to have provided cover for those seeking to freeze conflict with Germany. Girardoux's propaganda shop presented Germans as a cultured people, an extension of European civilization temporarily deceived by an evil regime that mobilization in France and Great Britain, combined with economic blockade, would force to denazify.[69]

This meant that, in its opening months, France's war was prosecuted in a strategic and propaganda vacuum. This was in part because, as Hew Strachan and Ruth Harris have argued, governments are reluctant to mobilize volatile public opinion in strategic debate. This was particularly true in interwar France, where living memory of the trench slaughter of 1914–1918, combined with the rapid reconstruction of German power since 1935, had rightly left the population skeptical of the utility of military force. "The propagandist is a man who analyses an already existing stream," observed Aldous Huxley. "In a land where there is no water, he digs in vain."[70] The problems of confiding strategy formulation to a cluster of specialists, however, are several, beginning with the fact that it may make governments strategically "risk averse." But, above all, failure to make strategy formulation part of a public dialogue creates a "democratic deficit . . . that merely multiplies the risk that the country will be exposed when the crisis deepens, and the public is alerted to what is being done in its name." It basically removes one of the "the triumvirate of actors – the people, the armed forces and the government." While, as in all battles, probability and chance play a role in the outcome, in a Clausewitzian sense, France's approach to war divorced "passions and policy," two essential components of an energetic and robust strategy.

One may certainly concede that, on the strategic and operational level, a defensive posture calculated over time to attrit the Axis and transform Germany's initial operational and tactical advantages into wasting assets made sense, even though, according to Imlay, by the outbreak of war, many in France had ceased to believe in it, while the Nazi–Soviet Pact rendered it moot. But, as Strachan and Harris note, "Whether that strategy is successful or not depends on the war itself, not on the strategy's unilateral merits."[71] Battle is not about applying a fixed methodology to the inert matter of war. War requires the creative interaction of two or more opponents. It creates its own milieu. Doctrine merely offers a guide, an initial game plan. War requires its participants to anticipate the unexpected. Commanders require a sense of moral purpose and conscientiousness, a capacity for building trust among allies and subordinates, an aptitude for seeing complex situations clearly, an instinct for maintaining the initiative, and the perception, imagination, and *coup d'œil* to respond nimbly to changing or unexpected conditions. Their troops must have confidence in their leaders' ability to deliver victory and be made aware of the dire consequences of defeat for them, their families, and the nation. May–June 1940 offered a clash between an active German initiator, who seized the strategic initiative, and a reactive French high command that never managed to reclaim it. In the name of caution, the Third Republic's strategists, both military and political, denied the contingency of human affairs.

France's political leaders failed to consider how the Wehrmacht might take advantage of France's flawed military system of semi-trained reservists encased in Maginot Line concrete, strategically overextended in forward deployed positions on the "Dyle–Breda Line," or hunkered down on the Meuse in half-completed bunkers, behind inadequate minefields. Nor were they likely to get much help from an unresponsive artillery *poste central de tir* (PCT) support system designed for static front warfare, combined with the French Air Force's (FAF's) "long war" prioritization of plane preservation over providing air cover for troops on the ground. Meanwhile, aging generals, members of a fragmented command arrangement, ensconced in châteaux well to the rear, proved unable to respond to a cascading strategic catastrophe. This happened for several reasons, beginning with the fact that French intelligence proved unable to divine German intentions, the axis of the German offensive, its development, or the numbers of troops engaged, especially of German armored divisions. In this way, no intelligence was forthcoming to challenge the assumption reached by the staffs of Gamelin and Georges on 8 April 1940 that Belgium, not the Ardennes, would be the focus of the German attack.[72] And even had French intelligence chief Colonel Louis Rivet dropped a copy of *Fall Gelb* on Gamelin's desk, it would likely have made little difference, because, according to French historian Olivier Forcade, "While intelligence provided periodic strategic alerts, the 'deciders' were generally willing to utilize intelligence only when they were psychologically and intellectually, if not politically disposed to accept its significance."[73] By the time that the German breakthrough on the Meuse had diverted the French general staff's focus from Belgium, it was too late to adjust. This was because French command and control, largely dependent on antiquated field telephones, had begun to unravel, as French forces forfeited their wire in retreat. Of course, one must not overstate the coherence of the German approach, as the so-called "Blitzkrieg legend" intended to do. In many respects, the Germans got lucky. *Fall Gelb* resembled a "special military operation" far from sufficient to overwhelm the Allied coalition, drive the UK from the continent, and occupy France, much less maintain a war of attrition, had the Allied armies stitched together any sustained resistance. But, both in France and in Great Britain, operations unfolded within a broader framework of a brittle alliance and tenuous political consensus. Much as Jaurès had argued in 1911, "societal ownership itself underpins resilience . . . a shared responsibility."[74]

In this way, the Phoney War menaced like a downpour that refused to burst. *Sitzkrieg* not only lulled many Frenchmen and women into believing that the German attack would never come, because "the mouthful is too large," but also raised doubts about France's unity, resolve, and even ability to confront Nazi Germany.[75] Unlike in Great Britain, Daladier made no attempt to enlist working class buy-in for a long-war strategy, but rather seemed more intent on punishing French workers for their strikes during the Popular Front. While the official logic of *Sitzkrieg* sought to weaken Germany through peripheral action and blockade, "by always attempting to fight the war elsewhere, Gamelin in effect made it impossible to fight at all," concludes Nicole Jordan.[76] Nor did the Phoney War find much buy-in among soldiers mobilized seemingly for naught. Of course, the morale of all soldiers plummets when they are left to molder with no clear mission. For Richard Bennaïm as for Marc Bloch, the "recollection of the disorganization of the French army defeated in advance, and of its soldiers whose disastrous morale was equal to their equipment," was "engraved" on his memory:

> Memories of incompetent generals and most of the French officers whose arrogance was matched only by their spinelessness, and the memory also of their panic during bombardments. Memories of the horrors of captivity, but paradoxically not of the majority of Germans, whom I found for the most part organized, humane, and who detested the war as much as did I. Memories also of the waste of these years of prison for millions of young soldiers who, like me, were deprived of our youth. Memories of my hatred for the cult of Pétain by the immense majority of French. Pétain whom age does not exempt from contempt – certainly, one of the greatest criminals of all time. Memories of the insult of having lost my entire identity upon returning to Algeria. Memories of typhus. Memories of the height of cruelty in the French concentration camps in Algeria. I have no good memories of that war, except the immense joy of the American landing in North Africa.[77]

While one can certainly understand and sympathize with Bennaïm's bitter verdict on the war, memory offers limited explanatory power. To be sure, military professionals in France and Germany struggled to retain their social prestige and political power while adapting to the changing face of twentieth-century warfare.[78] Contingency may have gone against France in 1940. But "even contingencies took place within the broader context of a problematic military plan and lack of effective coordination with England in preparing for and executing the battle," writes Sara Fishman.[79] As the late Peter Paret noted, war takes place in the context of "social and political change, of technological transformation, and of repeated adjustments to the ways men become soldiers and fight . . . [of] changes in the type of government that controls and employs this power . . . The reasons men become soldiers and the ways their societies view war are at the core of the matter."[80] Nor could the "contingency" of the French defeat sidestep the impact of French military culture and civil–military relations. In the view of France's Third Republic, the officer corps composed a "functional elite," a class of civil servant with their *grandes écoles* to prepare them to train and lead citizen soldiers in the context of the *levée en masse*. However, this republican managerial mindset was at odds with the conservative ideology and mental orthodoxy of senior officers from Lyautey to Weygand, for whom the French army embodied the institutional foundation, patriotic expression, and moral destiny of the nation. On a doctrinal level, these clashes played out most publicly in differences over the relative value of defensive versus offensive warfare, debates that took place behind a façade of the implications of technological innovation for the conscript army of a democratic republic.[81] The scale of this evolution in warfare in turn required for integral or total war the dominance of the modern industrial manager together with the working class in the trade unions just as much as raising an air service or building independent echelons of armored vehicles. For Charles de Gaulle and his cult of the high-tech professional soldier in fighting machines, the *levée en masse* lay like a dead hand on the French army and nation, because it underpinned a defensive reflex whose concrete manifestation was the Maginot Line, itself a monument to pervasive French pacifism which nurtured diplomatic inertia and devalued military professionalism.[82] The *levée* stifled operational and tactical innovation, constricted the intellectual horizons of French officers, and hence constrained the strategic and operational options of the French high command – a highly partisan collection of elderly gentlemen who lacked the curiosity, cutting-edge expertise, and energy to integrate technology effectively into their operational and tactical echelons and maneuver, the intellectual flexibility to anticipate and react to strategic surprise, and the mental toughness to manage setbacks on the battlefield or in command.[83]

So, far from being "contingent," 1940 appears more like an ideologically driven disaster spawned by deep political and social divisions, capped by toxic French civil–military relations and strategic inertia. While *Strange Defeat* may be relegated to "testimony," Bloch's prescient view was that 1940 represented an "intellectual defeat," because the French high command was prepared to fight war only as they imagined it would unfold. But, in fairness, their expectations were shared by French society at large.[84] Nor did de Gaulle's avant-garde vision of targeted armored warfare directed by professional soldiers offer a marketable formula to allow Paris to manage France's inter-war security challenges. Given the French military's misgivings over the lack of adequate political guidance and their smoldering antipathy toward politicians, not surprisingly, when assumptions of German collapse quickly crumpled after 10 May 1940, soldiers stepped in to seize control of policy in Bordeaux that the politicians seemed too divided, insecure, inept, or clueless of reality to define.

So, rather than buy time for rearmament, the French wasted the strategic breather of the *drôle de guerre*. As a result, French soldiers remained undertrained, and acquired scant knowledge about the latest weapons of war in combined operations – tanks, anti-tank guns, and mines, artillery and anti-aircraft artillery, and modern communications. Logistics were pre-modern while tactical concepts, like methods of communication and mission-type orders, remained mired in the trenches of the Great War. By the outbreak of hostilities, the FAF was rebuilding after almost two decades of neglect. But the French failed to give airpower the priority it received in Great Britain, Germany, or the United States, for instance. Nevertheless, although French reconnaissance aircraft and bombers were slow and vulnerable, the air force included some excellent fighters, which nevertheless were too few or poorly deployed, in part because they lacked a radar-vectored system of air defense to guide them. Aircraft were also held back from the front in keeping with a "long war" strategy. In Clausewitz's scenario, speed and surprise should have given the Germans only a momentary tactical lift before "the friction of the whole machine" kicked in. The only cases of "momentous surprises" that came to his mind were "Saxony in 1756 and Russia in 1812." But these frailties of airpower gone wrong combined with other French inadequacies to allow the Germans to cartwheel operational surprise on the classical offensive into "catastrophic failure."[85]

Before 1914, many complained that military authority had been hobbled by politics, which had undermined discipline, and that French military culture rewarded staff positions over field command. The French army in 1914 lacked training and armaments, and had been led by a largely ill-educated and intellectually incurious officer corps fundamentally at odds with the Republican institutions and outlook of the country.[86] It entered the Great War in an "*anarchie doctrinale complète*," according to Dimitry Queloz, deficient in logistics and firepower, and strategically guided by the suicidal Plan XVII.[87] The events of 1914 witnessed an exodus of the population from Belgium and northern France, as well as the second-highest annual casualty rate of the war after a mere four months of combat, one that far outstripped 1940's losses.[88] Indeed, Julian Jackson flips the question, which should not focus on how contingency propelled France to defeat in 1940, but rather, given its significant comparative disadvantages vis-à-vis Germany, how had Paris ever managed to emerge on the winning side in 1918?[89] Only frantic improvisation and the diversion of German divisions to the Russian front had combined to produce the just-in-time "miracle of the Marne" on 5–12 September 1914. French commander in chief General Joseph Joffre relieved 162 French generals in the first 5 months of the war, including 2 army commanders, although probably for the wrong reasons.[90]

The panic of French reserve divisions at Bulson on 13 May 1940 is taken as the signature illustration of the combat-shy French soldier. However, Bloch indicates that, rather than being an exception, Bulson simply offered the visible tip of an iceberg of chain French soldier panics. The sudden appearance of Germans in unexpected places was particularly disorienting, and resulted in "certain breakdowns, which cannot, I fear, be denied . . . Unfortunately, the inevitable withdrawal of the front assumed, only too often, the character of a headlong flight, which, in some instances, developed even before the enemy had attacked," and that implicated senior officers.[91] But soldier panics, especially in the early phases of the war, were hardly exceptional and affected all armies, including that of France in 1914, as panic gripped many French units, causing the War Ministry on 1 September 1914 to authorize death sentences without court martial, a "punitive and repressive discipline" whose effectives proved "positive."[92] But not entirely, because, by the opening months of 1915, officers reported that many French soldiers were refusing orders to attack.[93] The thesis of Leonard V. Smith's important study of the French 5^e^ DI in the First World War is that willingness to follow orders in the trenches evolved into a process of negotiation between commanders and their troops, and that soldiers imposed limits on their combat participation despite the threat of draconian punishments.[94]

S. L. A. Marshall argued that "non-participation" in battle was a common phenomenon among GIs, which he attributed to the loneliness and sense of isolation of the battlefield, where dispersion was necessary for survival, but which required tight cooperation for the execution of complex all-arms maneuvers. Because Bulson was not an exceptional event in warfare, it does not by itself offer evidence of French "decadence."[95] What made Bulson critical and emblematic was its strategic consequences. Because of its catastrophic dimensions, it became difficult to separate the French defeat from accusations of a failure of French masculinity as a national or generational phenomenon. The fact that many of the panicked soldiers at Bulson were Parisians allegedly made soft by city life and defeatist by communist propaganda offered a sort of inverse martial race alibi. On the tactical and operational level, that the French army and ultimately the Third Republic unraveled inexorably in the face of a practically routine and easily anticipated tactical setback can be explained as a breakdown of "command and control," which became the focus of *La commission d'enquête sur les repliements suspects*. An account of May–June 1940 offers a cascade of poor decisions by Allied commanders, beginning with the Dyle–Breda Plan and its consequences. Nevertheless, it is difficult to escape the conclusion that the Fall of France was more than a mere chronicle of bad luck and contingency. The "Blitzkrieg" may have been improvised.[96] Unfortunately, the German attack of

10 May 1940 laid bare the fragility of France's political–military interface. "Military history ... can be illuminating in itself, but also needs to be situated in a larger economic and cultural context," writes Richard J. Evans, in an echo of Marc Bloch.[97] As Jaurès had envisioned, a defensive strategy bolstered by the Maginot Line operated as a mechanism of civilian control, meant to short-circuit the "military adventure" on prominent display in murderous Great War offensives. At the same time, it was at odds with the Dyle–Breda Plan, which committed the French army to an "encounter battle" in the Low Countries, which, from a doctrinal perspective alone, it was ill-equipped to fight.[98]

Revisionists rightly insist on viewing France's collapse within an Allied context, while often neglecting to slot the revival of France's republican traditions within a global war framework. If, in the 1930s, Paris and London had failed to pursue a Soviet alliance with vigor, the implosion of the Soviet front in the summer of 1941 also had systemic and ideological origins, of which contingency was a mere spinoff. "Stalin was too blinkered by his ideological preconceptions to allow the Soviet Union to play other than a passive role in dealings with the west in the summer of 1939," concludes Ian Kershaw. In the Soviet system, "toadying, at all levels, was endemic. The Politburo kowtowed. The military were generally no different and, when voicing reservations, were browbeaten into submission." Stalin congratulated himself on the Nazi–Soviet Pact, which he saw "as a great Soviet diplomatic coup. But in practice it worked more in favour of Germany." By 1941, "[Stalin's] preference for non-provocation over deterrence was another fateful choice ... As it was, the frontier defences were hopelessly stretched, divisions badly deployed, fortifications incomplete."[99] Sean McMeekin agrees: "Far from wishing to forestall a European war between Germany and the Western powers, Stalin's aim was to ensure that it would break out," he writes, precisely because he wanted the capitalist powers to destroy each other.[100]

Hitler's awareness of US military weakness and that popular isolationism hamstrung Roosevelt's options combined with his contempt for America's mongrel racial composition to reduce the United States to "near irrelevance in German policy formation," according to Kershaw. Hitler remained convinced that, by the time Washington found the resolve to react to his aggression, Germany would have defeated France, Britain, and the Soviet Union to control the European continent. Nor was he alone in his evaluation of US popular resolve – news of Barbarossa caused US Secretary of State Henry Stimson to wonder in July 1941 whether "[the United States] has it in itself to meet such an emergency. Whether we are really powerful enough and sincere enough and devoted enough to meet the Germans is getting to be more and more of a real problem." In these conditions, the real miscalculation of the Axis powers was aggressively to threaten US interests, which triggered rearmament and support for a beleaguered Britain, and then declare war on Washington. But isolationists formed a minority in the United States, albeit a boisterous one, and found no allies in the administration, where "there was unanimity behind the need urgently to rearm and build up American defences." Even had Germany not declared war on the United States in the aftermath of Pearl Harbor, "by the autumn of 1941, the most obvious outcome, whether through formal declaration or not, was war in the near future against both Japan and Germany," concludes Kershaw.[101]

Julian Jackson insists that British morale during the Phoney War was as delicate as that of the French. Churchill's position when he assumed power on 10 May 1940 was no more secure than was that of French Premier Paul Reynaud. Some British leaders, led by Foreign Minister Lord Halifax, were prepared to ask Hitler for terms following Dunkirk in June 1940. Indeed, we are told that, in the dark aftermath of the Fall of France, Churchill himself might have been willing to consider some sort of accommodation with a triumphant Hitler once he had proven that Britain could not be defeated. "The difference between Halifax and Churchill was therefore not as stark as might be imagined," Julian Jackson contends.[102] Philip Nord agrees that, despite some initial setbacks, France's rearmament was far from meager. Its leader on the outbreak of war, Premier Édouard Daladier, if not "first-class," was at least "capable … and public opinion stood behind him … Daladier was ready to take the fight to Hitler in a way Chamberlain never was."[103] Peter Jackson, too, cautions that this assessment of France as "the sick man of Europe" was in part a legacy of stereotypes and prejudices prevalent within the British establishment, which viewed the French as sectarian, quarrelsome, mercurial, and hence unreliable, a view that suffused early scholarship of the war.[104] That the disharmonies and pretentions of the various French factions in the aftermath of the 1940 Fall of France did little to amend that pre-war impression might help to explain its post-war persistence.

But this was precisely the assessment of Churchill, Halifax, and the Foreign Office at the time, as well as many historians. After March 1938, Churchill began to doubt France's ability to resurrect a 1914-style *union sacrée*. The fault, he believed, lay with French politicians who had exacerbated the divisions in French public opinion and thus undermined national cohesion. In this way, the British shift to the American "special relationship" received its impetus before the Fall of France, not because of it.[105] So, in this view, France really was an outlier. While Philippe Garraud warns against personalizing France's defeat, he finds Daladier too wrapped up in his parliamentary maneuvers and his rivalry with Reynaud "to consecrate much attention to the military institution as such or to its internal functioning." And while he credits Gamelin with the "partial modernization" of French forces, his responsibility for questionable strategic decisions, failure to reform doctrine, the absence of reserves on the Sedan front, incapacity to coordinate operations with the

Belgians, and his delegation of operations in 1940 to subordinates not up to the task is judged "very heavy, even overwhelming."[106] Neither Daladier nor Gamelin was especially attentive to intelligence reports on the evolution of German capabilities and plans, which further undermines the argument that French strategy aimed to "buy time" to better organize for war.[107]

Julian Jackson notes that the political cultures of France and Britain differed in fundamental ways – French political and ideological conflicts ran deeper and were more personalized. In a crisis, this offered insurmountable stumbling blocks to national unity. "If in Britain, public opinion was irrelevant to the crucial decision of May 1940,"[108] defeat, confusion, demoralization, and lack of national direction had devastated popular morale in France, which found no Churchill in the context of the Battle of Britain to rally the nation. The British army may not have performed stoutly in May–June 1940. But, from a Tommy's perspective, fighting for Britain was not the same thing as fighting for France. If the French and Belgian soldiers were unwilling to defend their own countries, why should the British do it for them?[109]

France's riven political culture also made it more difficult for dedicated Republicans to unite against Pétain and Weygand to oppose an armistice. The era of strong political leadership had given way to "system politicians" of the late Third Republic. Daladier had put his protégé Gamelin in place and never questioned his decision to move the strategic reserve to Breda, even when other senior commanders objected. He succumbed to a pointless peripheral operation, which eventually metamorphosed into the Narvik expedition, to appease those in his coalition who continued to view the USSR as France's principal challenge, and to bolster the British alliance. When the breakthrough at Sedan confirmed Reynaud's lack of confidence in Daladier's protégé Gamelin, the French Premier recalled Weygand and Pétain, which proved a fatal mistake. But while this chapter in France's fall might be dismissed as a "contingent circumstance," it was a product of an insecure politician with a scant political following, elevated into the premiership by a political elite divided over the wisdom of war, suspicious of their British allies, acutely conscious of France's relative weakness, and who saw Reynaud as an easy mark precisely because he was backed by no major political party.

While Churchill's impact on British popular morale remains difficult to assess with precision, Reynaud remained politically isolated and possessed all the charisma of an organ grinder's monkey.[110] The result, as Imlay points out, was that, "by May 1940, no obvious majority existed in France for continuing the war."[111] British resolve to fight on was solidified by the survival of the British army at Dunkirk, and by the realization – even by Halifax – that Hitler's terms were likely to prove "harmful to [Britain's] independence" and initiate the unraveling of the Empire.[112] The French leadership was capable of arriving at identical conclusions, and those who evacuated on the *Massilia* obviously had. The fact that resistance failed to spring forth from this rubble of Republican refugees, but rather was spearheaded by a maverick temporary brigadier, was perhaps surprising. But it was also foreseeable that resistance must emerge from outside the traditional institutions of state discredited by defeat. Riven by tribal hatreds and separated into cults of provincial loyalty and clientele networks, habituated to maneuvering within the parliamentary system, the Third Republic's leadership lacked the resilience, the vision, and the reflex to fill the leadership void created by national catastrophe. On the extremes of the French political spectrum, provincial patriotism and cosmopolitan treachery were two sides of the same coin. Fear of another Commune made French military leaders, led by Weygand, reluctant to evacuate the army to a Breton redoubt or to North Africa. In this way, too many French leaders proved willing to entrust their country to Hitler's magnanimity in a way that even Halifax never was.

Insofar as "taking the fight to Hitler" was concerned, in the view of Martin Alexander, Daladier embodied all that was dysfunctional about Third Republic war planning, a system in which power was diffused and political responsibility shirked. In this view, Daladier's accomplishments were limited to the appointment of Raoul Dautry as armaments minister, and displacing Bonnet at the Quay. Otherwise, his energies were dissipated in combating the intrigues of appeasers such as Chautemps, Laval, and Flandin, who were supported by Pétain, and placating the press, rather than stripping down the executive and focusing it on the war. Daladier's biographer concedes that he became immersed in day-to-day trivia and "found it difficult to see the bigger picture."[113] This was perhaps because, overwhelmed by his multiple responsibilities as premier, defense minister, and foreign minister, he retreated behind a barricade of advisors, assistants, and junior ministers, quickly gaining a reputation as indecisive, not in command of his multiple portfolios, and reliant on the opinions of others. Unfortunately, Daladier's "lack of resoluteness" and "congenital weakness" typified the leadership of the late Third Republic, a giant void ruled by unwieldy cabinets incapable of taking decisive action as the strong personalities of an earlier era ceded power to party machine politicians. Rather than a demonstration of resolve, Daladier's late outsourcing of the Armaments Ministry to the "technician" Dautry offered an admission that the politicians were incapable of effectively leading and managing France's war mobilization.[114] In early September 1939, it was Daladier who was dragging his feet now that Chamberlain seemed resolved – at last – to confront Hitler. For this reason, *Sitzkrieg* as a component of a "long war" strategy was attractive to Daladier and Gamelin precisely because it aimed to defeat Germany *without* the requirement for combat. In the opinion of Alexander, it was Gamelin who forced the decision for war over Poland in September 1939, precisely because he had sensed a decision-making vacuum at the highest reaches of the French state. But he had no intention of initiating battle.[115]

Nord's argument is that France's defeat was hardly exceptional, because no other countries "were any better prepared for Hitler's attacks, nor did any of them perform better on the battlefield in the war's early stages [the Battle of Britain apart]. In fact, they had all bet on France to do the heavy lifting."[116] While certainly true to a point, inter-Allied comparisons have limited utility in this context. "Great Britain in 1939 was ill-prepared for the exigencies of war, partly because the British Empire had wagered on the preservation of peace, and partly because British leaders found it difficult in a democracy to deploy effective mobilization tools, such as a propaganda ministry or agencies of surveillance," writes Jochen Hellbeck. "France's defeat and Churchill's simultaneous appointment as prime minister changed this. Churchill's embrace of dire realism proved highly effective for mobilization purposes. How he and others portrayed the plight of Britain 'fighting it alone' catalysed feelings of strength and determination that resonated with much of Britain's population."[117] Imlay argues that Churchill was named Prime Minister (PM) precisely because Britain's political class had jettisoned "limited liability." Unlike the French Section française de l'internationale ouvrière (SFIO), the Labour Party was not divided by pacifism and infected with anti-militarism, while, for the Tories, "defeating Germany remained the priority."[118]

"When the Republic's record is scrutinized in comparative perspective, what it did manage to accomplish doesn't look so meager after all," Nord insists.[119] Garrard agrees that "the army of 1940 was no longer the army of 1918, even that of the end of the 1920s . . . but had undergone a real modernization in the 1930s, above all in equipment." The problem in Garrard's view was that technical upgrades did not go far enough. Nor were they matched by doctrinal evolution, which willfully ignored advances in motorization, armored warfare, and airpower, which left the army mired in a remaindered "methodical battle" doctrine. This reflected a popular French obsession with "security," which bred inertia and *attentisme* both in diplomacy and in civil–military relations.[120] This requires revisionists to define a selective approach to 1940. Stanley Hoffman noted that the humiliation and shame of 1940 understandably encouraged a pointillist revisionist counternarrative that accentuates highlights of war preparation, technological upgrades, martial success, and personal courage precisely in an attempt to separate the defeat from a "verdict on France" – notably the brilliance of the Maginot Line that protected France's northeastern frontier and conserved French manpower, and "not one of its major fortresses was captured in the fighting."[121] Unfortunately, this anecdotal focus on parochial episodes of small-group courage in the tradition of Alphonse de Neuville's *La dernière cartouche*, meant to proclaim that the French spirit endured unbroken even in defeat, offers a post-1870 recycle that requires others to elucidate the dysfunction of French politics, the obsolescence, mental flaccidity, and ineptitude of the high command, the confusion, anguish, and humiliation of French soldiers, and the martyrdom of the nation.[122] With the benefits of hindsight, however, it was Dautry's industrial mobilization; de Gaulle's counterattacks in late May–early June; an improvised if ephemeral resistance of "Weygand's hedgehogs" on the Somme and Aisne in early June; and the symbolic defense of the Cadets at Saumur, *pour l'honneur*, that appear contingent, not the sweeping "strange victory" of German arms.[123] So, perhaps this upgrades *Strange Defeat* from testimony into "history" after all?

Nevertheless, the attempt to normalize French martial performance in 1940 with claims that no one did any better carries its own air of desperation. The revisionist agenda has its roots in Riom. The goal of highlighting France's fleeting and localized military successes in 1940 is to emphasize that not everything had gone disastrously, that at its core French society remained solid and its soldiers fought courageously despite bad command decisions which opened the army to surprise and collapse. If the fog and friction that enveloped the French high command is factored out, then perhaps France might have avoided defeat and preserved its dignity as in 1914. This special-pleading approach has its own "presentist" political agenda, is one-dimensional, and slithers perilously into the counterfactual "if only" fantasy. Above all, it fails to ask some basic questions. For instance, what if the Maginot Line was more of a benefit to the Wehrmacht than to France, because it diverted defense funds from what might have been more profitably invested in military modernization, such as modern communications, a new generation of artillery, army motorization, air force upgrades, and logistics, all of which were severely lacking in 1940? It is certainly possible to argue that the lack of reserves at Sedan had less to do with Gamelin's decision in the spring of 1940 to shift Giraud's Seventh Army from Reims to Breda than with the fact that the Maginot line, combined with the threat of a German attack through Switzerland, effectively sidelined 45 percent of French divisions from the battle for France. The Maginot Line, combined with the Dyle–Breda Plan, diverted the bulk of French forces to the wings, opening the Ardennes to a *Schwerpunkt*. Indeed, Karl-Heinz Frieser concluded that "Protecting the Maginot Line had almost become an end in itself," because the inviolability of French territory was imbedded in French strategic culture.[124]

In fact, Philip Bankwitz argued that the Maginot Line was the result of a civilian initiative that had a political rather than a military agenda – deal with constituent pressures to protect vulnerable northern industrial areas that had been overrun in 1914 certainly, and secure Alsace-Moselle, an irredentist territory of tenuous political loyalty. It also acted as a brake on a repeat of the 1914 offensives, which had caused so much suffering. But, ultimately, the Maginot Line substituted a carapace of concrete for a well-armed and equipped force of "cover" troops to protect mobilization, with the objective of securing military buy-in for the one-year service that passed into law in 1928.[125] For this reason, Nord's claim that "the Maginot Line itself was still standing at the end;

not one of its major fortresses was captured in the fighting, and in this sense the line did what it was supposed to do" is misleading, inaccurate, and ultimately hollow.[126] First, Garraud questions the logic of maintaining forty French divisions in an around the Maginot Line during the entire month of May 1940, when there were only nineteen German divisions opposite. And this was even after it had become clear that the main thrust of the German offensive was through the Ardennes, where the Germans had massed their best divisions, including seven *Panzerdivisionen*, against the seam between two second-tier French armies whose reserves were too far away to ride – or rather walk – to the rescue.[127] Second, most of the Maginot Line's garrison surrendered, like an estimated 50 percent of French troops, without firing a shot, which obviated the need to attack it. But where the Germans did choose to attack, the Maginot Line proved to be remarkably vulnerable, for several reasons, beginning with the fact that concrete fortresses demonstrated the lesson learned at Douamont in 1916, repeated at Eben-Emael in May 1940, that fixed defenses required defending from without as well as within. Once French "interval troops" were belatedly withdrawn by Weygand on 13 June 1940, the Maginot Line's myriad of vulnerabilities became exposed.

A pointillist recitation of other Third Republic "accomplishments" also appears in retrospect to fall short of national salvation had all the fragments come together, rather than shatter at Bulson. While de Gaulle's proposal to mass tanks to attack the flanks of *Fall Gelb*'s tactical overstretch in late May–early June 1940 may have been obvious, it was unlikely to be operationalized by a risk-averse Weygand saddled with "methodical battle" doctrine and château generalship. Unfortunately, the results at Montcornet, Crécy, and Abbeville, while perhaps enjoying (in the case of Abbeville) modest tactical success, served only to reveal how ill-prepared from a doctrinal and matériel perspective French forces were to execute an "encounter battle." In the end, these three failed skirmishes, plucked from the shambles of national collapse, were embellished to boost the Gaullist myth of tactical and operational prescience to complement that of his strategic foresight. But improvised armored divisions hardly support a plausible counterfactual "if only" scenario. And, rather than showcase the "ferocious" resistance of French forces, Weygand's ephemeral "hedgehogs" on the Somme and Aisne in June simply offered a thumping demonstration, after barely three weeks of combat, of the French army's limitations in weaponry, logistics, communications, tactical skill, and will. Furthermore, the political agenda of Weygand's "hedgehogs" was to short-circuit calls for a Breton redoubt and thus, in his paranoia, abandon France to a communist-inspired Commune, which speaks volumes about the state of French civil–military relations. Were the cadets of Saumur simply a romanticized survival of a cavalry "*bataille pour l'honneur*," a public relations (PR) reprise, predictable in the shadow of defeat, of the courageous futility of the cuirassiers at Reichshoffen in 1870?[128] In this way, the history of war offers an uninterrupted process of mythmaking, especially when one needs to explain the "defeats," even "pyrrhic victories," that interrupt the narrative of national exceptionalism and invoke anxieties of decline. The mirror of war becomes warped through myth and legend, and softened by the nostalgia that all of the belligerent societies continue to conjure to adjust to the traumas of the Second World War.

Why did Daladier, "eager to take the war to Hitler in a way that Chamberlain never was," not institute military upgrades during his long tenure in the ministries of war and defense, quell the factionalism in the French high command, veto the Dyle–Breda Plan, retire Gamelin, create more armored divisions, and so on? As Minister of Armaments, Raoul Dautry did what he could amidst "disappointing production figures, dwindling financial resources, and the sharpening perception of a disgruntled workforce," without much help from Daladier.[129] This suggests that French strategy wasted more time than it "bought." And, while a lack of preparation for war was hardly a uniquely French problem, as Bloch realized, Dautry's position should have been created much earlier – not on 20 September 1939![130] In a vacuum of centralized planning – yet another Daladier legacy – Dautry inherited an antiquated industrial infrastructure, constricted by a "notorious insufficiency" of coal and raw materials, as well as financial constraints. He had to compete with the military for precious manpower, especially technical specialists.[131] Industrial mobilization went for naught because, as de Gaulle predicted, it merely reinforced an antiquated concept of war rather than serving to reconceptualize, reengineer, and modernize French defense. "Ultimately, the operational doctrine of 'methodical battle,' as such, is less relevant than the 'structural' and organizational conditions in which it was implemented, that considerably worsened its effects, and which originated in an ideology of the defensive supported by a broad military and political consensus," concludes Garraud.[132]

Nor, had the Republic managed miraculously to survive Hitler's May–June 1940 onslaught by keeping the Seventh Army at Reims, or via another counterfactual scenario, would Daladier's market-based approach to armaments production and manpower allocation likely have proven able to sustain a long war. Furthermore, the pre-war preference on the right to launch peripheral operations against the Soviet Union might have resurfaced, with disastrous consequences.[133] If the French navy chose at a stroke to write itself out of the history of the Second World War, not in the throes of defeat like the German High Seas Fleet at Scapa Flow in June 1919, but while it retained the ability to make a contribution to the war's outcome and maintain France's influence and prestige at least as a regional power, this hardly constituted a "military event." Rather, it resulted from an attitude, a mentality, and an anti-Allied political agenda that scuppered Clausewitz's "war is politics" axiom at the bottom of Toulon harbor. What was the value of expending French treasure and economic energy building an air force that would be preserved well to the rear to conform to a "long war" strategy? Planes, tanks, lorries, and small arms would simply be surrendered to the occupier in 1940, or by Darlan's Paris Protocols of May 1941, with the remainders swept up in the Armistice Army and Air Force garage-sale giveaway post-November 1942. Torch proved that the FAF's "long war" plane-preservation policy remained in effect as the commander in chief of the North African *armée de l'air* General Mendigal ordered his pilots to seek safety in the Algerian outback rather than oppose the Axis arrival in Tunisia. Given the French military's generally equivocal Second World War performance, it is hardly surprising that post-war French memory fixated on skirmishes like Bir Hakeim and André Malraux's "people of the night."[134]

The alibi that no military performed any better in the war's early stages falls short of being convincing. The Royal Navy virtually destroyed the Kriegsmarine surface fleet off Norway in May 1940, thus effectively eliminating the threat of a seaborne invasion of the British Isles. The RAF's victory in the Battle of Britain demonstrated that even the appeasement-minded Chamberlain had realized the importance of investing in radar, anti-aircraft artillery, modern fighters, and a coordinated command system. While on paper the Red Army looked formidable, "the shocking part was that [Stalin's] vaunted war machine . . . proved so brittle when it was finally put to the test against a first-rate military opponent," writes Sean McMeekin. "The terrible truth, which dawned on Stalin in that first week of war, was that his soldiers either did not know how to or did not want to fight."[135] Like the French in 1940, the Red Army's soldiers the following year seemed to suffer from an asymmetry of motivation. Nevertheless, despite Stalin's purges, combined with ignoring intelligence warnings of Hitler's impending attack, and poorly positioning his divisions, the Red Army halted the Wehrmacht short of Leningrad and Moscow in December 1941, and went on to develop into a formidable tank army. Indeed, in Moscow, "The Great Patriotic War" was memorialized as a victory for the Soviet system, a testament to the devotion of Soviet peoples to their homeland, and a vindication of the 1917 Revolution.[136] The United States absorbed early setbacks both at sea and on land, found better commanders, developed more effective training techniques, and evolved tactically and operationally to wear down and eventually defeat the Wehrmacht on the Western Front.[137] In this view, "structural factors" alone cannot explain France's collapse, but reasons must also be sought in "the lack of confidence and resolve [Imlay] identifies among civilian and military leaders."[138]

"[France's battlefield failings] were the result of flawed, indeed blundering, decision-making on the part of the nation's military leadership," Nord opines. "It was the army command that lost the Battle of France, not civilian error or a disinclination to fight, let alone faults, real or imagined, in French society as a whole."[139] One can certainly agree with Nord that French generalship hardly sparkled with operational and tactical brilliance in 1940. Rather, the French army's operational methods and equipment – especially in communications, artillery, ground mobility, and logistics – were designed for static front warfare in keeping with the evolution of the theory of the *levée en masse* and the lessons of the Great War. When this was balked by the German offensive, French commanders were stripped of many of the tools they required to manage the battle. While airpower was not a decisive element in France's defeat, the FAF's deficiencies virtually ceded the skies to the Luftwaffe, which made good use of them, especially to deny aerial reconnaissance to French commanders and so open them to surprise, blunt artillery support, attack divisional headquarters, further disrupting French command and control, and sow panic and disorder in the French army's largely horse-drawn supply columns. The opportunity was there for the FAF to reciprocate, but it mostly failed to do so.

The problem is how does one separate out "civilian error or a disinclination to fight" from "flawed, indeed blundering, decision-making on the part of the nation's military leadership"? If Montgomery argued that bad generals get the soldiers they deserve, this was because the British discovered in North Africa – not to mention Singapore – in 1942, that, when their soldiers perceived that the enemy commanded better leadership, more effective weaponry, and superior tactical and operational skill, the number of "MIA," desertions, and psychological casualties compared with soldiers killed in action (KIA) skyrocketed.[140] If the defeat of 1940 can be blamed on contingency and poor command performance, one must ask how France came to select the generals it did, and why were they were permitted to make such disastrous strategic and doctrinal choices? Apart from approving the Dyle–Breda Plan, the other major knock against Daladier and Gamelin was that they allowed a coterie of anti-republican generals and admirals – Pétain, Weygand, Coulson, Huntzinger, FAF General Betrand Pujo, Darlan, Georges, the list is virtually endless – to coagulate in senior command positions. "Gamelin's real failure," writes Alexander, "was in transforming or sufficiently remodeling the ideology of the French military caste. The measure of his lack of success was the refusal of the officers, especially the generals, to stay shoulder-to-shoulder with the regime in France's hour of supreme crisis ... [in] an ethos of complete military–civil integration ... The republican–military compromise ... had always been a fragile thing, ever since the earliest days of the *Troisième*, seventy years before."[141] Battlefield reversals exposed the Third Republic's systemic civil–military fault line.

Because French senior officers drew a distinction between loyalty to France and loyalty to its government, slotting the French military's performance in 1940 into an Allied context has its limitations. The *levée en masse* had made war "the business of the people." "The Second World War was a war of 'bellicist' societies," declare Geyer and Tooze. For this reason, "soldiering and war-making cannot be separated out from the moral economies that inform them wittingly and unwittingly and the Second World War as mortal combat between mutually exclusive war projects," which requires the historian to explore "society and culture as forces of war" through the "moral economy of war and peace."[142] This army–society interface was reflected in the fact that France was a republic with a long-established tradition of civilian control of the military through mostly civilianized defense-related ministries and a myriad of parliamentary committees and study groups. From 1934, de Gaulle actively lobbied deputies to adopt his defense proposals laid out in *Vers l'armée de métier.* He was ultimately unsuccessful, but he did generate public discussion of the issue of mechanization in a very high-profile way. Maurice Gamelin was selected to succeed the abrasive Weygand in January 1935 precisely because he was viewed by the politicians as safely "republican." Likewise, many of the imperial governors who opted to sabotage attempts to fight on and save the Republic from the empire in June 1940 were Popular Front appointees, some of whom, like Moroccan Resident General Charles Noguès, had deep personal ties to one of the giants of the Third Republic.[143] Certainly, colonial governments required hierarchy and stability to maintain their authority over increasingly restive indigenous populations. Economic and security interests, as well as opportunity, also helped to decide whether a colony defected to the Gaullists or remained loyal to Vichy. Civilian fingerprints were all over French defense choices brought into play in 1939: Raymond Poincaré, André Maginot, and Georges Leygues are credited with restructuring the navy and nurturing the career of French naval chief Admiral François Darlan, who was allowed to run the navy through his *Amis de Darlan* (ADD) clientele network, precisely because he had powerful parliamentary backing. Pierre Cot and Guy La Chambre directed the air force from its inception in 1935; this was topped by Daladier's domination of the Defense Ministry from 1935, not to mention the input of parliamentary committees and study groups. The military leadership of the army and air force was particularly weak, allowing civilians an outsized influence on defense choices made by those services. While Bloch blamed "our ministers and our assemblies" for France's lack of war preparation, he added "Not, it is true, that the High Command did much to help."[144] And, of course, the *levée en masse* provided the consensus civil–military theoretical framework for French defense that, along with pacifism and anti-militarism, inspired, for better or worse, the Maginot Line and France's defensive "long war" strategy that imploded with breathtaking speed.[145]

In the furtherance of his contingency argument, Nord especially blames Gamelin's decision to pluck Giraud's Seventh Army from the general reserve and send it into Holland, "leaving the front stripped of reserves in what proved to be the decisive sector." "Giraud's army, initially stationed near Reims, was made up of some of France's 'most mobile and modern units.' Imagine such a force available for a counterattack against Germany's charge across the Meuse," Nord teases.[146] Unfortunately, "imagining" the Republic's survival anchored on such a fragile "if only" scenario would most probably have not saved France, because, as Martin Alexander points out, two-thirds of Giraud's infantry were "without motor transport and unable to move faster than the heavily laden *poilu* could march" in 1914. The divisions that composed the Seventh Army had "massive gaps" in important weaponry such as anti-tank guns and anti-aircraft artillery. Like most of the rest of the army, the Seventh Army had spent the winter pouring concrete, not training for an encounter battle with the Wehrmacht.[147] In May 1940, the Seventh Army was also commanded by Henri Giraud, certainly among the most impetuous and retrograde of France's constellation of incapable generals. The shortcomings of French defense were numerous, and included Gamelin's lack of strategic awareness; the compartmentalization of intelligence and operational planning and evaluation, a defect more characteristic of Axis Second World War militaries;[148] the decision to surge into Belgium, which had been telegraphed to the Germans in January, a strategic choice endorsed by both French and British political leaders; the lock-down of thirty-six to forty French divisions in and around the Maginot Line; the systemic shortcomings of French command and control that progressively crumpled in the chaos of retreat; a lack of motorization; artillery that lacked mobility, range, and timely fire-direction techniques; poor design, tactics, and deployment of air cover both offensively and defensively; château generalship; a lack of initiative baked into a hierarchical command system; repeated and uncorrected mistakes on the operational and tactical levels; logistical breakdown; and so on. None of these defects would have been mitigated simply by a decision to maintain the Seventh Army in reserve at Reims in the hopes of a repeat of the "Miracle of the Marne." In theory, of course, history-altering alternative options existed. However, events worked out like they did for a reason. In Kershaw's view, "a rich variety of imaginary 'what if' scenarios" of the sort offered by counterfactualists boil down to "a harmless but pointless diversion from the real question of what happened and why."[149]

If one is making contingent comparisons, it is certainly possible to argue that the great Allied wartime leaders – Churchill, Roosevelt, and even Stalin after he recovered from his 1941 disaster, not to mention Clemenceau in 1917 – imposed their strategic vision on their military commanders, not vice versa. If the Breda variant of the Dyle Plan was so operationally unsound that even Gamelin's senior commanders dissented, then why did the political leadership not intervene to stop it? Part of the answer is that the Dyle–Breda Plan was considered essential in solidifying the Western Alliance. Another part, as Philip Bankwitz pointed out in his important 1967 book, was that the military acted with a great degree of independence from political constraints in France, especially in the 1930s era of "system politicians." Nor were French military commanders free-floating agents who made bad decisions simply because they were arrogant or foolish. They operated in a political and social context and based their doctrine, with its defensive mindset and avoidance of "encounter battles," on such factors as economic weakness, demographics, and what they saw as a loss of faith in the utility of military force in a population bled white in 1914–1918, after reality had collapsed the edifice of military theory and organization based on the moral ascendency of *l'offensive à outrance*.

1940 offered a re-run of the previous conflict, in which cultural-pessimist French officers beset by the class conflict of the epoch deployed military theory incorrectly to adapt to the changing face of war. And, when that failed, they became obsessed with the survival of the professional army and its *esprit militaire*, which they believed under threat from the democratizing *levée en masse*. These factors spoke volumes about the fragile state of French civil–military relations in the inter-war years. For these reasons, in Bankwitz's view, the fall of France showcased civil–military collaboration, in that politicians abdicated their responsibility to exercise broad policy direction over the military, while professional soldiers resisted change that they believed would trigger civilian interference. As a result, the military command succumbed to a paralyzing sense of inferiority vis-à-vis Germany, which the Dyle–Breda Plan was meant to minimize, in the process diminishing the "passions of the people" dimensions of the Clausewitzian triangle.[150]

On one level, Hervé Drévillion is certainly correct to claim that "defeat has its own actors that do not dissolve into the collective identity of a nation or a social group."[151] But isolating the military defeat of 1940 from its political context is a slippery proposition. Armies and societies intersect on multiple levels – in their ideologies, politics, personnel, strategies, and choice of doctrine, armaments programs, and budgets, operational methods and tactics, leadership, recruitment, mentality, and morale. French politicians and soldiers may not have been "decadent," whatever that means. But, as Robert Young suggests, many certainly appear to have been "ambivalent" – about the republic, about the war, about the enemy, about the resolve of their own soldiers, about the willingness of the French people and imperial subjects to support a "long war" strategy, and about the place of France in an ideologically divided Europe. For Bloch, as for so many others, too many French politicians defined governing as an activity that fell somewhere between sport, cabaret, and clan combat, as the nation persevered on the fading imperial vapors of French "exceptionalism." To suggest, as do some revisionists, that the accusation that France was "decadent" suggests *ergo* that Germany was dynamic is to pose a false dichotomy.[152] Explanations for France's defeat are often overdetermined. For Karl-Heinz Frieser, "the fighting power of the German Wehrmacht was not based on the dynamism of National Socialism but rather primarily on the kind of efficiency that is purely inherent in the [German] military system." Although improvised, Blitzkrieg typified the Oberkommando der Wehrmacht's (OKW's) operational approach, which traced its origins to Frederick the Great, and was simply more dynamic, better integrated technology, and was anchored in the realization that Germany was too weak and geographically exposed to win on defense. Aerial reconnaissance, twelve times the number of radios in the French army, and *Stoßtruppe-Taktik* evolved and mechanized from 1917 combined with "mission-based orders" to allow German troops to adapt to a rapidly evolving battlefront. As a consequence, the Allied armies were surprised, encircled, and rapidly disarticulated.[153]

In this way, systemic frailty in France's military organization evolved as the spinoff of a civil–military partnership, a collaboration that framed the contingency that played out on the battlefield in 1940. Likewise, the decision to request an armistice and its overwhelming acceptance by the French military and population required more than a fortuitous constellation of defeatists who usurped the crisis produced by a military setback and an unprecedented refugee flow to execute a *coup d'état*. At the very least, a sense of moral purpose, "a determination to win through," the judgement or aptitude to see complex situations clearly, and the ability to respond nimbly to changing or unexpected conditions were lacking at the highest levels of French command. None of these systemic inadequacies would have been repaired by keeping the Seventh Army at Reims. Jean-Pierre Azéma concludes that defeat was greeted by popular "ambivalence" – Jean Bruller, who would later stake out a literary reputation under the pseudonym Vercors, wondered whether defeat at the hands of seemingly all-powerful Germany had not been fortuitous, in that it had swept away France's "glorification of a beneficial mediocrity."[154] Unfortunately, the French military's profound sense of inferiority vis-à-vis Germany was transferred to Vichy to underpin collaboration.

In this respect, the counterfactualists have a point – continuing the war from North Africa was technically possible in June 1940, precisely because Hitler was a strategic incompetent, Germany lacked industrial planning, the "profoundly pathological" Nazi state was evolving toward a semi-feudal model, the German armed forces were absorbing unsustainable losses, and in its empire and its Allies, and given the strategic landscape, France commanded the resources and strategic depth to continue the struggle with an excellent chance of success.[155] The problem for Germany was that what came to be labeled *Blitzkrieg,* like *Stoßtruppe-Taktik* in 1917, proved to be tactics for tactics sake, untethered from a rational policy and strategy. But to realize that in the debris of France's 1940 débâcle required strategic foresight and political will, and no one of sufficient authority in France was capable of rousing popular resolve in

June 1940 or motivated to do so. In the end, "if," "should," and "might" are not history, but speculation anchored in nostalgia and the neurosis of decline.[156]

"Fighting quality is intertwined with an even more abstract quality, perhaps best described as 'will,'" writes Andrew Buchanan.

> This intangible element combines top-level political and military leadership with broader moral factors, including popular political commitment, nationalism, resilience, and fear of defeat. The determination of the Soviet people to fight on in the face of the stunning defeats suffered during *Barbarossa* demonstrated collective will, as did the willingness of the British people to face large-scale bombing after the disaster at Dunkirk. Will is easily mythologized and packaged as national exceptionalism, but that does not mean that it should be discounted. The effects of its absence – in France in 1940, British-ruled Southeast Asia in 1942, and Italy in 1943 – all underscore its significance. Nor, of course, was will unique to the allies. In Germany, popular determination to continue fighting was stoked by anti-Semitic propaganda after the intensification of Allied 'terror bombing' in summer 1943, and in both Japan and Germany the war was sustained long after defeat had become inevitable. The outcome of World War II was determined by the complex *interplay* between economic determinism and contingent factors that included fighting quality and will.[157]

Redeeming France

In sum, a premise of this book is the unfashionably seditious one that the demise of *la Troisième* was more than a historical hiccup during which France's resilient republican tradition suffered a fleeting four-year sabbatical. All wars are ironic, Paul Fussell famously declared in his classic *The Great War and Modern Memory*. None were more so than the European phase of the Second World War, which began as an attempt by London and Paris to guarantee Poland's sovereignty, but in six short weeks in May–June 1940 somersaulted into France's humiliation and occupation and Britain's ejection from the Continent.[158] De Gaulle and those aboard the *Massilia* believed, in June 1940, that France might still use space to buy time by playing its colonial card – after all, the rationale for imperial expansion had been to give France strategic and demographic depth. However, a further irony was that this option was preempted by defeatists on the French right. Most French generals and admirals, civil servants, and colonial officials ditched democracy with indecorous haste, amidst an atmosphere of public confusion and apathy, underpinned by a loss of faith in the utility of military force. As Robert Paxton noted, Vichy's survival depended on an Axis victory, an irony which official Washington failed to grasp. The foundation for collaboration with Hitler's New Order was laid at the 24 October 1940 meeting between Pétain and the German leader at Montoire. Drawing inspiration from threadbare dictators Franco and Salazar, Vichy's "National Revolution" evolved into an emotional dependency among many soldiers and sailors who felt betrayed by the Republic and by its unpatriotic citizenry. For much of the French military surviving outside of *Oflags*, unwavering loyalty to the Marshal became an act of contrition sanctified by sword and altar as the path to national salvation. Eager to heighten French influence and reconstruct French military power, Vichy allowed Berlin to define the ends and means of the war. A pantomime "Armistice Army" was joined by military volunteers who eventually coalesced into the SS Charlemagne Division as part of a strategy to reconstitute French military capacity in the shadow of Axis occupation. Meanwhile, with Vichy acquiescence, conscripts from Alsace-Moselle also made a significant, if mostly involuntary, contribution to the Axis war effort. Isolating Jews as a prelude to detention and deportation offered a modest *prix d'entrée* to Hitler's New Europe, one compatible with the French right's historic prejudices and Catholic-centric construct of French identity.

November 1942 was an important moment in France's transition from defeat to liberation, one in which Vichy and the French fleet snubbed redemption, hence substantiating the conviction reached in Washington and elsewhere after 1940 that France no longer numbered among the great powers. The role of *l'armée d'Afrique* to defend AFN "against whomever" was exposed as directed against the Allies, because, as the November 1942 surrender of Tunisia proved, the will to deny AFN to the Axis was weak at Vichy. And, in the absence of a firm signal from above, and in the circumstances of an evolving international environment, officers at every level hedged their bets. Only on 19 November 1942, when French troops opened fire on Axis soldiers at Medjez-el-Bab, 60 kilometers west of Tunis, did the "official" French army reenter the war in the Allied camp.[159] Nevertheless, French loyalty to the Allies seemed ambivalent. *L'armée d'Afrique* rallied to Giraud and the Anglo-Americans because, impotent, fearful, and vulnerable, its leadership obsessed with imperial stability, they sought to save themselves through military upgrades, not embark on a crusade to liberalize the empire and rescue French democracy. For this reason, they continued to reinforce a dark racism and the anti-liberal opinions entrenched in AFN's settler population, as war crumbled the status quo of France and its empire. Eisenhower's dilemma was that his job was to win the war, not referee French political disputes, which were both ideologically profound and personality-driven. Nevertheless, French politics would continue to impact Allied operations and Alliance relationships. Even after November 1942, along with its *pied noir* political base, nostalgia for the Marshal and the cult of "*Sa Majesté le soldat*" lingered on AFN's colonial frontier. De Gaulle's view was that the Americans posed the greatest challenge to France's international standing, when, in fact, imperial irredentism germinated among his own soldiers and their political base in AFN, one reflected among Vichy hardliners. Indeed, in his important essay, Julian Jackson insists that anti-Gaullism remained deep and visceral into the post-war era especially on the French right, but also among Republicans and communists distrustful of de Gaulle's dictatorial tendencies. However, this *contre mémoire* coalition was too fragmented and at cross purposes, "too built around a stock of myths and wishful thinking," to upend de Gaulle's redemptive death-and-resurrection wartime narrative.[160]

Vichy's attempt to rebuild French military power through collaboration had misfired, as, after November 1942, the Armistice Army, never intended to do battle, was disbanded, while what remained of the FAF transitioned into an air defense unit dedicated to shooting down Allied planes. But the main impulse for Vichy's unpopularity – not to be confused with nostalgia for the Third Republic – came with the mobilization of France's economy to support Germany's war effort, a policy that included labor conscription. *La relève* was negotiated between Laval and Fritz Sauckel in June 1942, followed by *Service du travail obligatoire* (STO) in February 1943. STO, combined with the cumulative effects of starvation, made it obvious that Vichy merely facilitated the German pillage of France's finances, economy, and manpower, on the phantom pretext of recuperating French prisoners of war (POWs) from 1940 and accreting Vichy influence in Hitler's Europe. Like other Axis-occupied countries, France was lashed to the mast of the Reich's war effort, contributing to the massive population flows that further globalized the war. Of the 7.6 million workers and POWs employed in German industry, 16.5 percent were French, part of a "hierarchy of slavery that by 1942 at the latest dictated the daily life in many German industries," which meant that France supplied the third-largest national contingent after the Soviets and Poles.[161] Of course, this merely mirrored the patterns of forced labor and conscription imposed in the colonial world.

These events accelerated the resurrection of *le franc-tireur,* a further irony as this was the very phenomenon which conservatives had sought to preclude by signing the armistice. Meanwhile, AFN lurched toward separation as the Hexagon endured a vigorous intensification and radicalization of the National Revolution, one punctuated by scarcity, the black market, denunciations, detentions, executions, and intensifying violence. In keeping with the conservative ideology that motivated Vichy, repression was represented as a response to pleas for protection from a French population besieged by lawlessness. The criminalization of resistance to collaboration further radicalized Vichy policy and hence flung open the door to the Shoah and to dirty war via counterinsurgency and other less savory dimensions of "special warfare." The Gestapo and other branches of the German security services served as backstops, and Berlin might dispatch the odd "reserve" division or *Osttruppen* contingent when the *maquis* menace swelled to threatening proportions in 1944. However, the main burden of resistance suppression devolved onto an ad hoc panoply of paramilitary experiments and police organizations designed to bolster the coercive power of the Vichy state, including the *Légion des volontaires français contre le bolchévisme* (LVF), *la Milice*, and the *Groupe mobile de réserve* (GMR). These were recruited among right-wing fanatics, sadists, criminals, opportunists, and young men grasping at an STO deferment, deploying all means legal and illegal to cleanse a "defeatist" population.

From 1941, France's main resistance groups had begun to emerge from outside traditional republican institutions, and begrudged the resuscitation of the Third Republic's political parties within the context of the *Comité français de libération nationale* (CFLN) as an unmerited recompense for their pre-war mismanagement and venality, and evidence of a plot to sabotage French renewal as embodied in resistance. Meanwhile, the man who came to represent France's rejection of the armistice and Vichy collaboration initially refused to embrace a republican restoration as his political goal. *L'amalgame* of 1944 failed to "republicanize" an army, not to mention a navy, steeped in an authoritarian and imperial ethos. The result was that France's republican traditions resuscitated their legitimacy "beyond the boundaries of the national state," within the context of a globalized alliance of anti-fascist nations that adopted Washington's nomenclature of "World War II," rather than de Gaulle's framing of France's "Thirty Years' War" against Germany. In short, France's republican restoration becomes "de-exceptionalized" within a wider historical and political context of subaltern and colonized actors engaged in globalized conflict.[162]

However, the tension persists between the macro dynamic of "World War II" and the requirement for a redemptive national narrative, *de rigueur* for many wartime societies for whom, in Sartre's words, "the myth of the hero and the military leader's infallibility, is indispensable to a nation's health, even though it's condemned by reason."[163] If historians have found "decadence" elusive in a French context, "resistance" is equally ambiguous, and not just in France.[164] While the French population may have longed for liberation, in the circumstances of occupation and collaboration, *résistance-organisation* remained of necessity small, fragmented, politicized, and infiltrated, all of which made a decision to join its "shadow war" inside France both intensely personal and practically suicidal. Those few French soldiers who had reached the UK had first to surmount a paralyzing sense of "stupefaction," "astonishment," and "despondency," not to mention "humiliation" in the wake of France's precipitous 1940 collapse. Many soldiers were disgusted with the attitudes they had encountered on the battlefield, irked by the incompetence, fatalism, and passivity of their superiors, and enraged by an armistice signed in their view with indecent haste by a cabal of cowards and reactionaries who feared revolution from their population more than occupation by a fanaticized enemy.[165] For imperial exiles from the metropolitan battlefield, the stunning rapidity of

France's collapse and the docility with which many French soldiers allowed themselves to be disarmed and marched off into captivity seemed incomprehensible. However, a refusal to accept defeat, armistice, and national humiliation, choosing instead to enter into resistance, was initially the reflex of a small minority, for whom it required great determination, imagination, daring, and a leap of faith to leave everything behind to enlist at the side of a British people whose image in France as detached, condescending, cold, insincere and nationalistic, as well as perfidious, had become steel-clad by Dunkirk, Mers-el-Kébir, and Dakar.

The resistance, no matter how broadly defined, was not a continuation of a fighting spirit exhibited in 1940 by soldiers in de Gaulle's improvised 4e DB, by "Weygand's hedgehogs," or by the cadets of Saumur. Nor was it sparked by nostalgia for the Republic. Rather, resistance was the companion to the *Chantiers de la jeunesse*, *les écoles des cadres*, and so on, in that it offered a reaction to an overwhelming feeling of national humiliation that flowed from a flaccid military performance in 1940, a widespread popular acceptance – even relief – at news of the armistice, and mortification at the accumulating indignities, privations, and injustices of a Vichy-enabled occupation.[166]

The revisionist view of 1940 as "a military event and not as an expression of national decline,"[167] an ambiguous concept that at the very least seeks in part to align France's wartime narrative with that of other victorious Allied nations, as a sequence of setback, mobilization, and national sacrifice ultimately rewarded by victory. Deserted by its British ally at Dunkirk, knifed in the back by defeatists in Bordeaux, an initially confused and disoriented French people gradually coalesced in resistance to triumph at the Liberation. This narrative's purpose is to relegate 1940 to one of the war's early ephemeral episodes, along with Poland, Dunkirk, Barbarossa, Pearl Harbor, Corregidor, Singapore, and the Kasserine Pass. Yet, this familiar linear storyline ignores the fact that, after June 1940, France's response to defeat shattered into a constellation of refusal that included *la France libre*'s band of "*émigrés stipendié de l'étranger*" ("émigrés bribed from abroad"), eventually affiliated with spontaneously generated internal resistance groups whose political philosophies spanned the spectrum, and imperfectly militarized *maquisards* on the lam from STO. Despite Gaullist declarations in 1944 about "*Paris libéré par lui-même*," resistance in France idled in a sort of fretful *attentisme*, never developing into a Great Patriotic War, nor could it in the shadow of German occupation and Vichy repression. "Resistance" broadly defined has been dismissed as inconsequential to the war's outcome – it was "*ultra minoritaire*," while France was liberated by Allied armies, not by a resistance *levée*. Olivier Wieviorka has formulated the category of "*résistance-mouvement*," to suggest that popular support for a rejection of fascism, and those Frenchmen who collaborated with it, extended beyond the schematic organization charts and skeletal strata of *résistance-organisation*. In Malraux's imagery, these "parachutists already on station," who for reasons of security and limited scope for action must remain discreet, nonetheless embodied the aspirations of the French people for Liberation.

Yet, the importance of resistance lay less in its military impact than in what it represented, which was, above all, an aspiration. If the ability of the French people to "resist" in the debris trail of their shattered army was limited, the symbolic importance for France of popular resistance, "as a political and moral statement," was immense. This was multiplied by the fact that "the French Resistance" is now viewed by historians as a sub-set of popular opposition to an Axis "imperial nexus" launched in 1931, which has globalized a panoply of regional conflicts into the Second World War.[168] In this way, "Resistance in France" situated the latest outbreak of a smoldering civil war sparked by the French Revolution into an international context.

A globalized view of the "long Second World War" subsumes the "contingency" of 1940, as well as the resiliency of France's republican institutions, into a less triumphalist revisionist narrative. Even though a "huge chasm ... separated America's words from its actions," Roosevelt's "Atlantic Charter" constituted a direct attack on the empire, and hence on France's global reach and cultural prominence.[169] Torch, a controversial strategic decision which shaped the course of the war in Europe, as well as the post-war period, was also impacted by "resistance." If the promise that a significant "resistance" in AFN stood ready to ease an Anglo-American invasion was largely a figment of Robert Murphy's cooked intelligence reports, the resisters nevertheless supplied Roosevelt with the "actionable intelligence" to overcome the skepticism of his Secretaries of War and State and service chiefs.[170] Yet, in the final analysis, for geostrategic and political reasons, Roosevelt was determined to execute Torch in the face of high-level opposition.[171] It is also a good bet that, despite its operational and tactical novelty – or perhaps because of it – Torch was too overwhelming to fail against an under-armed, scattered, and surprised *armée d'Afrique*. According to the archives, the high command in AFN feared that many of its soldiers had been infected by Gaullism. The odds for success were also strengthened by the policy confusion and strategic misdirection of "defence against whomever," the intentional scrambling of the French chain of command in the wake of Weygand's departure, and a desire for *la revanche* among rank-and-file French soldiers that made their commanders unsure that they would follow orders to resist the Anglo-Americans. Accepted wisdom among the Vichy French in the autumn of 1942 was that amphibious operations remained an unproven tactical concept, especially on a scale that would challenge Vichy control of AFN. This certainty underpinned received wisdom that the war had reached a "stalemate," which had the potential to enhance Vichy's influence as a mediator. Thus, while Robert's claim that the mainly young Jews of Géo Gras guaranteed the success of Torch in Algiers invites skepticism, they certainly represented the vanguard of a trend that contributed to change the strategic direction of the war, and to how the Second World War is memorialized in France and elsewhere.

"Resistance" also offered a military tactic that institutionalized, for better or worse, a new branch of warfare in the form of "special operations," promoted by the interface services to mobilize, militarize, and operationalize popular dissent as a strategic weapon of war. Resistance interpreted as a rejection of the armistice allowed de Gaulle to consign Vichy collaboration to a memorial footnote. Its glorification also aimed to mobilize popular passions seemingly lacking in 1940, to reenergize the war in the context of the Clausewitzian trinity, and to legitimize *la France libre* as a bona fide democratic expression of the French people that replicated the *levée* of 1793. While the military impact of *résistance-organisation* may have been marginal, as the visible incarnation of *résistance-mouvement*, it affirmed that, spiritually, the French people had deserted neither the Republic nor the Allied cause.

Unfortunately, resistance also had its limitations, beginning with the fact that longing for liberation did not necessarily correlate with supporting "*résistance-organisation*," much less the *maquis*, which was more often seen as a threat to law-abiding folk and public order. For French conservatives, France always appeared to be a country balanced on the cusp of calamity. The challenge for a traditionalist like de Gaulle was to contain the fractures of the population within a customary, statist political framework that circumscribed radicalized political projects and spared France the civil wars, regional conflicts, and wars of national liberation that percolated in the backwash of Axis defeat. While "the French Resistance" was necessary to authenticate *la France combattante*/the *Gouvernement provisoire de la république française* (GPRF) as a democratic expression of the French people, as so often in history when French national unity and state authority had been challenged by religious heretics, "federalists," and communards, resistance "feudals" threatened de Gaulle's plans to rebuild the state and the army to reassert France's European and global influence. Furthermore, the international dimensions of "resistance in France," combined with a lack of resources, invited outside intervention into French internal politics from indigenous nationalists besotted with Atlantic Charter illusions, Moscow-directed operatives, agents of the Anglo-American interface services, and the threat of "Allied Military Government of Occupied Territories" ("AMGOT"), and from competing Allied political visions for the organization of post-war Europe. For this reason, in de Gaulle's view, "the 'volcanic' arrival of the American-led world system announced at Bretton Woods, Hiroshima and San Francisco"[172] posed a greater threat to France's political stability and global position than did a ramshackle Vichy administration buttressed by unsustainable Axis ascendency.

In this respect, Vichy and *la France libre* shared the commonality of coupling France's fate with that of a foreign power, while masquerading as a uniquely national vector. A globalized perspective would view the revival of France's republican tradition as less bound up with the enthusiasm of French elites including de Gaulle for "democracy." The French Republic's measure of its global influence was anchored in great part in an "autarkic–imperial" model of empire that mimicked in its economic exploitation and racial apartheid that of the Axis. Republican restoration was "constructed under the aegis of American predominance ... crafted to promote a broad new middle-class meritocracy while heading off more radical alternatives," concludes Andrew Buchanan. "This zeal for democracy dovetailed with the explicit abandonment of revolutionary goals by Communist parties across Europe and the adoption instead of reform-minded 'national roads' to socialism."[173]

Going forward, gatekeepers of collective memory running from the Vichy right, through the Gaullists, to the communist left determined who and what was to be remembered under the capricious rubric of "resistance." Torch gave the "resistance myth" a huge lift, that allowed it to underpin a liberation narrative embraced by multiple actors – "resistance" in the cause of France's resurrection formed the bedrock of de Gaulle's legitimacy; it democratized the crusade of the Western Allies against Nazism; it supplied an "invitation" to invade, essentially handing the Allies a political mandate; it empowered the interface services to operationalize the "parachutists" already "in place." The downsides of "resistance" were multiple, however, beginning with its questionable military utility, which seemed calculated to enhance the status of the "interface services" in the military hierarchy, largely impervious to the moral repercussions of resistance action that rebounded on non-combatant populations. "Resistance" also elevated the prestige and power of resistance "feudals," which threatened civil war and the integrity of the state. The cut-and-dried Stalinists of the Parti communiste français (PCF) took their marching orders from Moscow, not from the GPRF or Koenig's *État-major des Forces françaises de l'intérieur* (EMFFI). Hence, de Gaulle's eagerness on the Liberation to demobilize resisters, or get them into uniform, and so end the Second World War with the Liberation of France and the defeat of Germany, rather than allow "resistance" to transition into local power grabs, or even escalate into civil war as in Greece and the Balkans. The myth of "*Paris, libéré par lui-même*," accompanied by the *blanchiment* of 1944, was confected in part to minimize the pivotal role of Allies and Africans in France's resistance and liberation, and to mask the fact that the "post-war" era found France in a weak position to oversee an empire where wartime mobilization had transformed mentalities. Meanwhile, a settler population in the Maghreb sought to bank its role as waystation of France's liberation, to entrench settler apartheid in France's sub-imperial citadel. In the end, France's post-war purges proved so tepid precisely because disagreements between Vichy and *France libre* hinged on tactics and personalities, not on fundamental structural differences or diametrically opposed philosophical visions of France's place in Europe and the world.

But the problem going into the post-war years remained how to explain 1940, as contingency or moral failure? Viewed as a moral indictment of the Republic's elite and the "apathy" and "incapacity" of the population, defeat forfeited France's claim to great power status, at least in the view of Roosevelt and Stalin. Military weakness at the Liberation threatened to cut Paris out of an occupation zone in Germany, seen as vital to French interests and European stability going forward. Ultimately, like Vichy, de Gaulle was forced to acknowledge France's deficit of moral leadership and second-tier status under a hegemonic power in a new world order. As Buchanan argues, "globalizing" the Second World War also forces one to consider the "globalization of the post-war," including the 1947 Truman Doctrine bolstered by the Marshall Plan, which ultimately propelled Paris, albeit reluctantly, to accede to decolonization, German rearmament, NATO, and the European Union.[174] But a reassuring story about a glorious past that embraces grandeur, republican democracy, and self-liberation, one that streamlines historical explanation with scapegoats and counterfactual contingencies, even if invented in part, will frequently eclipse a pathway to an unpredictable future fraught with hazards. The fact that Gaullism, like Vichy, constituted a "revolt against the future" testified to the anxieties faced by post-war France, which has impacted its wartime historiography.

Despite this evolution accelerated by the Second World War, to which must be added Vichy's complicity in the Shoah, the so-called "values" of Vichy's National Revolution continued to command a following, as did its promise of "modernization" and efficiency, although the two programs were competitive, not complementary. Nor did popular infatuation with Vichy's anti-Republican symbol Philippe Pétain wane with the Liberation. As Julie Le Gac has noted, one irony of 1944 was that the Liberation of France was spearheaded by *l'armée d'Afrique*, a coerced convert to the Allied cause. Its leadership remained convinced that Pétain had restored its honor, by reallocating responsibility for 1940 onto the Republic. *L'armée d'Afrique*'s fealty to Vichy had to be severed by an Allied invasion, the Anfa agreement, "fusion" with *la France libre*, participation by the *Corps expéditionnaire français* (CEF) in the Italian campaign, and "*l'amalgame*" with *Forces françaises de l'intérieur* (FFI) posturing as a scaled-down *levée en masse*. Rather than demonstrate the resiliency of France's republican institutions, this shotgun wedlock of the professional army and the *levée* miscarried and rekindled historic French civil–military tensions that were to burst forth in France's post-1945 wars of colonial independence.[175]

Hardly had the war ended than mythologies proliferated. Accused in 1945 of collaboration, Vichy's Navy Minister Admiral Jean-Marie Abrial complained that, had he been in Algiers in November 1942 rather than in Toulon, he might have ended the war as a decorated *compagnon de la libération,* rather than incarcerated in Fresnes prison. In other words, whether a French soldier or sailor ended up in the dock on the Liberation, marching down the Champs-Élysées in one of de Gaulle's serial "victory parades," or repatriated with the stigma of having sat out the war in an *Oflag* or lived a relatively cushy existence on a German farm was simply the luck of the draw. Resistance, like collaboration, was "contingent," a theme advanced in Louis Malle's 1974 film *Lacombe, Lucien*. And yet, the decision to join the resistance, whether internal or external, was a journey, in which location constituted only one "contingency," and not necessarily the most essential one. Nor did a desire to restore the republic top the list of incentives. Some, like d'Hautcloque, d'Argenlieu, Dewavrin, Muselier, or Roman Kacew grabbed the first opportunity to exit France and enlist in the external resistance. Yet, most of the French sailors and soldiers marooned in England in June 1940 demanded to be repatriated, and, in general, the British were relieved to see the back of them. As one of their superiors, Antoine Béthouart insisted that duty required him to escort his troops home, not to join de Gaulle's crusade to liberate France, which was surely the higher responsibility. Nor was Béthouart the only French soldier to postpone his decision to rebel and invest his faith in Pétain. The *Forces navales françaises libres* (FNFL) were cobbled together mainly from Breton fishermen and merchant mariners, not French sailors. Not one air force general volunteered for *la France libre* in 1940. Regular officers viewed de Gaulle as "*antipathique*," although by 1942 even those like Martial Valin, a lieutenant colonel air attaché to Brazil in 1940, who created the *Forces aériennes françaises libres* (FAFL), and Catroux agreed that this unconventional and much reviled, yet courageous and prescient leader, had become irreplaceable. The leader of *la France libre* envisioned both the FNFL and the FAFL "essentially as a propaganda vehicle."[176] Not all soldiers in French Equatorial Africa opted for *la France libre*. A critical factor in that colony, as well as in French enclaves in India, seemed to be economic dependence on Great Britain. The attitude of the Governor Félix Éboué also empowered those who chose to resist in French Equatorial Africa. But where imperial governors opted for Vichy, as in AOF, AFN, and the Levant, aspiring resisters such as Larminat or Kacew were forced to devise more imaginative escape plans.

To opt at some point over the next few years to resist required one to discard Vichy's consoling alibis for defeat. Abandoning Vichy-imposed conformity was difficult for officers, for whom the pledge of political loyalty to the Marshal enforced by Weygand was viewed as an ethical obligation that substituted for "the individual conscience of a free citizen." Vichy embodied the military conception of order and hierarchy. Pétain was one of them. Allegiance to the Marshal was sentimental as much as self-interested. Convinced that Vichy's chief was anti-German, following him became the patriotic obligation, which in their own minds made them part of what Nord calls "the resistance understood in the broadest terms," if not part of France's pro-republican "moral reawakening," insofar as it existed.[177] Above all, Pétain had shifted responsibility for defeat onto the shoulders of the Republic's "reign of impure politics." For these reasons, they surrendered to a totalitarian, anti-Republican process that required a loyalty oath as evidence of allegiance, servility, and, in Huntzinger's view, "*attachement total* " to the person of the Marshal. But occupation, Vichy's deepening collaboration with the Axis, and France's smoldering civil war demanded individual choices based on values. The message from Nuremburg would be that military obedience was conditional, subject to conscience and law. Torch forced French officers to square their obligation to obey with their patriotic duty.[178] But, beyond these considerations of character, culture, and politics – rejection of the armistice, loyalty to the ideals of "eternal France," honoring one's "oath to the Marshal," service solidarity, and so on – always in the back of the minds of colonial commanders was dread of civil war between whites, that would shatter racial solidarity and compromise imperial authority. Any repetition of Dakar in 1940 must be avoided at all costs, even if it meant acceding apprehensively to Torch.[179]

The evolution of the war also played a role in the decision to resist, as the prospects for an Axis victory transitioned from inevitable, through "stalemate" – largely an illusion to sustain Vichy's quest for relevance and survival through reveries of a French-brokered Allied–Axis peace or a just-in-time "Laval deal" – toward improbable, save for some miracle. The war grew in intensity, the occupation tightened, famine loomed, and Allied bombs rained down on France, eliminating the ephemeral shards of French autonomy. Nevertheless, to resist required one to abandon family and social milieu, or, like de Lattre, to defy the orders of Vichy's rump army. Those who opted for the external resistance enlisted as refugee combatants in the ranks of a foreign service. Their first task was to learn English. Those inside France adapted to unfamiliar forms of clandestine warfare, in which former officers must accept subordinate roles beneath politicized and pretentious civilians who required them to carry out acts that slithered over into versions of terrorism. In any case, for military men to resist required them to cast off traditional conventions of obedience and discipline, to break with hierarchy and order, to fuel France's dreaded civil war. Each soldier's decision was highly personal, and grew from hostility to Vichy, to Germans or Italians, family tradition, perhaps a religious motivation, but invariably a sense of deep humiliation at France's defeat. Whoever opted to resist put himself or herself and his or her family in danger, risked confrontation with former comrades and classmates, and defied political authority, while reaffirming his or her identity and reclaiming his or her autonomy.[180]

One might, like Louis Bacquier and around 20,000 others eager "to fight in the open," attempt to escape France's vast prison by crossing the Pyrenees. But this took money, contacts, initiative, courage, and stamina. Failure might mean instant deportation to Germany, while "success" translated into weeks if not months spent in a Spanish jail, followed by a rebuke for having "defied the Marshal" by serving "the man of the English," the warmonger who divides the French, the "stateless" anti-patriot.[181] Nor did all *évadés* hanker to join France's military effort, like many in the *maquis* who sought to opt out of war and flee STO, but who became combatants *malgré eux*. Therefore, to frame France's war as a saga of a ballooning "French Resistance" that gradually overwhelmed the Occupation and the "handful of wretches" in Vichy, and allowed France to be "liberated by itself, liberated by its people with the cooperation of the armies of France, with the support and the cooperation of all of France. That is the France that fights. That is the only France, the true France, eternal France," was as misleading as it was moving. But it did align France's wartime saga with a Second World War Allied narrative of the gradual mobilization of the popular will, manpower, and resources within conventional and unconventional military institutions to achieve victory over the forces of fascism. It also conformed to de Gaulle's "Thirty Years' War" storyline, that 1939–1945 simply witnessed the Great War's Franco-German encore, with the *union sacrée* firmly in place, and "The French Resistance" substituting for a Verdun not only *sans* Pétain, but also against him. For French men and women, as well as foreigners trapped on French soil, all disoriented by defeat, surviving under an increasingly oppressive occupation, and muddled by Pétain's "shield of France" spin that conflated collaboration with patriotism, redemption, and the only path to recover French POWs, war, defeat, and occupation offered a constellation of unpalatable and dangerous choices. But, rather than exhibiting a linear progression from defeat to victory, France's wartime theme splinters into a chronicle of compromise, digression, ambiguity, prevarication, confusion, *attentisme*, and guilt, which a narrative of heroic resistance – which certainly coexisted – was meant to assuage.

The French army's margin of maneuver to put initial setbacks behind it, reorganize and recover military proficiency, as France had done after the 1914 Battle of the Marne, or Great Britain, the USSR, and the United States did in the Second World War, was constrained. The *Forces françaises libres* (FFL) were barely a blip on the screen of the British forces operating in Abyssinia, Syria, and the Western Desert. But their actions there at least advertised that French forces had not abandoned the fight, in contrast to an inactive Armistice Army, which offered a first step in the legitimization of *la France libre*. Italian POWs captured in those actions served as a counterpoint to the acquiescence to defeat of French POWs of 1940. While the 1940 armistice threatened to treat French who continued to fight as *francs-tireurs*, in effect, captured FFL were assimilated by the Axis as captured British troops, and so accorded legal combatant status even by the enemy.[182] While highly symbolic for the purposes of Gaullist propaganda, initially Bir Hakeim struggled to find a niche in the war's heroic narrative, because it was neither a victory, nor did it constitute an important turning point in the history of the war, such as Midway, El Alamein, Stalingrad, or "Tunisgrad." Indeed, because Koenig and Amilakvari appeared to have abandoned the battlefield with their chauffeur Susan Travers in a confusion of retreat, initially Bir Hakeim looked more like a case for *la Commission d'enquête sur les repliements suspects* formed to investigate officer conduct in the 1940 débâcle. In the short term, Bir Hakeim was marketed as a rejection of Laval's "hope for a German victory," so that some resistance groups adopted the name. Only in the 1950s, however, did Bir Hakeim become sacralized as the counterpoint to 1940 and collaboration.[183]

An MIA rate of around 20 percent during the Tunisia Campaign (November 1942–May 1943) bore testimony to the fact that *l'armée d'Afrique* consisted of an ill-armed colonial constabulary of largely unenthusiastic indigenous recruits, untutored in modern warfare.[184] The true resurrection of the French army via its offshore subsidiaries could only initiate with the Anfa agreement of 24 January 1943, that committed the Americans to provide equipment for a French army of up to 250,000 men, organized in three armored and eight motorized infantry divisions, as well as a significant air force.[185] Anfa lashed a resuscitated French army – modestly bolstered by the "fusion" of Giraudist and Gaullist contingents at the end of the Tunisian campaign in May 1943, and the creation of the CFLN in Algiers the following month – to an American technological, operational, and logistical model. Yet, French adaptation and innovation would be circumscribed by AFN's lack of an industrialized infrastructure, by the limitations imposed by the relatively small and diverse population of assimilated Algerian Jews and literate European settlers with an often anemic sense of "Frenchness," resentful at the sacrifices that AFN had again been called on to make, and by the mere dribble of *évadés de France*. The understandable desire to prioritize combat over support units, combined with an uneducated, often illiterate, and conspicuously indifferent indigenous population from which to coerce recruits, limited the scope of this Anfa-promised modernization and expansion of French forces. American arms inserted into US tactical and operational concepts required *l'armée d'Afrique* to adapt to a US-led training program, supervised by Brigadier General Alan Kingman's French Training Section under the overall authority of the Joint Rearmament Commission.

In many respects, while combat in the mountains of central Italy proved highly demoralizing for British and American troops, the terrain was tailor-made for the CEF, which, by the late spring of 1944, had grown to a four-division, US-trained and -equipped colonial infantry force under its *français d'Algérie* commander Alphonse Juin. Roosevelt's Anfa investment certainly paid off at Monte Cassino. Juin's breakthrough on the Garigliano River was artful, courageous, and strategically important, in that it allowed the capture of Rome, a necessary prelude to the redemption of the American President's much-criticized Italian policy, in many respects a sequel to Washington's "Vichy gamble," and further his goal of turning the Mediterranean into an American lake.[186] It also freed up naval assets tied down at Anzio for Anvil/Dragoon. Nevertheless, Cassino did not completely rehabilitate the French army because "the recognition of the military value of the CEF by the Americans would not truly upset the pecking order," concludes Le Gac. "Honors and congratulations lauded the role played by French troops, but they remained nothing more than a corps subordinate to Fifth Army command."[187] Furthermore, the CEF's battlefield success suffered the shame of its post-breakthrough delinquencies.

While Anfa lashed a rehabilitating French army to Anglo-American strategic priorities, despite his complaints, the outcome was hardly a negative one for de Gaulle. Anfa delivered a modernized military force which provided a visible French presence in the Liberation and allowed de Gaulle to reestablish his sacrosanct French state, expel Allied interface services operatives, and hence bridle the "feudals" of the internal resistance. Given the paucity of conventional forces available to France after 1940, much attention was given to the role of unconventional French forces. As discussed, resistance in France, which slowly emerged following the defeat, ballooned into a fugitive *maquis* with the imposition of *la rélève* in 1942 followed the next year by STO. The coalescence of *réduits maquisards* offered an important political statement, as well as evidence of a robust determination to resist Vichy collaboration among some young Frenchmen. But, of necessity, the *maquis* offered a minority phenomenon amid German and Vichy-driven repression. Nor did the Allies become aware of the scope of the *maquis* until late 1943, when it attracted attention in large part because the Foreign Office feared that Allied failure to support these STO absconders would result in diplomatic recrimination after the Liberation. Competition between the Office of Strategic Services (OSS) and the Special Operations Executive (SOE) to militarize the *maquis*, as had been done with resistance groups in Greece and the Balkans, also inflated the importance of the interface services. The problem in France was that the Allies could come up with no effective strategy to operationalize these extremely localized pockets of untrained, largely leaderless young men, beyond proliferating Sten guns and, from D-Day, parachuting "Jeds" and Operational Groups (OGs) to "advise" them. Nor were these "maquis redoubts" large or stable enough to transform into sovereign atolls from which to expand the GPRF's political authority in

France independently of the Allies. Consequently, the *maquis* played only a marginal military role in the liberation and was easily dispersed amidst the destruction, round-ups, and deportation of the surrounding civilian population, who of necessity viewed this fugitive mobilization more as a menace than as a patriotic *levée*. And, to be fair to the French, resistance to the Axis enjoyed only a marginal military impact on all fronts, except perhaps as a vehicle to catapult communists into power after the Second World War in Yugoslavia, Indochina, and China.

Nevertheless, several factors combined to exaggerate the contribution of resistance-led sabotage or intelligence gathering in France, that included the desire by interface services alumni to promote the value of special operations, laudatory statements solicited from Eisenhower and other Allied military leaders, issued no doubt with the best of intentions to raise French self-esteem, and a Gaullist-promoted mythology which sought to present the French people as the catalysts of their own emancipation. Nevertheless, as compensatory myths, the resistance offered a dramatic if inadequate redemption for 1940, as did Leclerc's highly symbolic 2^{e} DB-led liberation of Paris and Strasbourg. Resistance also sustained the liberation narrative central to the Allied "crusade."

With Dragoon in August 1944, France's military contribution to the war was upgraded from an expeditionary corps to a full army. However, to the surprise and consternation of the Anglo-Americans, de Gaulle sidelined the man who was undoubtedly his best general in favor of Jean de Lattre de Tassigny to lead the French army's invasion of mainland France. The traditional narrative maintains that Juin had been too compromised by his links to Vichy and his equivocal response to Torch to be acceptable to the resistance, and hence oversee an *armée d'Afrique*–FFI *amalgame*. However, de Lattre combined his own political baggage with a mercurial temperament that alienated many of his subordinates while exasperating his American minders, who found him at once unsystematic, temperamental, operationally cautious, and on the trailing edge of modern warfare developments. For these reasons, de Lattre proved a contentious choice to lead a politically and professionally factionalized force in what became one of the war's most difficult, if overlooked, close-out campaigns. To be fair to de Lattre, he faced many impediments, among them a dependency on US logistics; a fitful supply of mostly young, poorly trained replacements; the requirement simultaneously to oversee *l'amalgame* while fighting a war; a lack of organic air power and artillery support; and appalling weather, not to mention an insubordinate division commander in Leclerc. All of this meant that Sixth Army Group commander Jacob Devers had constantly to shield de Lattre from Eisenhower's growing wrath with a faltering French performance in the Colmar Pocket, by infusing the *1ère Armée* with US manpower, firepower, and logistics. Also, creating a technical apparatus around a basically infantry force proved challenging, and prolonged French dependency on American support. This positioned de Lattre uncomfortably between de Gaulle's imperious demands that he direct his army to achieve French political objectives at Strasbourg and Stuttgart and his position within an Allied military command that furnished direction as well as firepower and logistical support to keep the *1ère Armée* combat-worthy.

Of course, de Lattre promoted the *1ère Armée* gate-crash into southern France, followed by the Belfort Gap, the siege of the "pockets" at Colmar and on the Atlantic coast, and the invasion of Germany as evidence of the French army's true resurrection and significant contribution to Allied victory. Proportionally, he took fewer KIA/MIA casualties than had Juin in Italy – 5.33 percent compared with the CEF's 8.15 percent. He also took a smaller percentage of KIA/MIA than did Patch's Seventh US Army, which reported 8.64 percent. But his contribution was strategically less significant than had been Juin's breakthrough at Cassino, in admittedly unpropitious conditions.[188] This, together with *l'amalgame*, a call for volunteers carried out in improvised circumstances by a reorganizing state that lacked the administrative ability to implement conscription, stymied the creation of a coherent and adequately trained, armed, and supplied force. It also short-circuited any sense of civil–military solidarity, leaving the army with the feeling that it was fighting the war of liberation for a population detached from and indifferent to the suffering of its soldiers.

A comparison between French and Allied military performances in the war is further complicated by the fact that the French POWs of 1940 number among the casualties of de Gaulle's memorial effort to consign both the defeat of 1940 and Vichy to an epigrammatic parenthesis in France's long and glorious history.[189] Together with Jews and those mobilized for STO, POWs failed to carve a niche in Gaullist wartime memory. There is a memorial case to be made for POWs as part of a resistance in the context of escape, creation of false papers, and eventually acts of sabotage in conjunction with STO in the war industries into which many were conscripted. However, no French equivalent of the "Colditz myth" with its "lasting stereotype of the British prisoner in German hands as an ingenious, brave and skillful officer, fixated with taunting the enemy ['goon baiting'] and escaping," emerged. This was in great part because de Gaulle associated POWs with the French army's crumbling in May–June 1940, and so regarded being taken prisoner as shameful – indeed, British POWs also viewed their French campmates as acquiescent to their fate, probably in the hope that docility combined with devotion to the Marshal might merit release.[190] POWs were viewed at least initially as Vichy loyalists, because Pétain justified his policy of collaboration in large part to secure their liberation, and publicized efforts like *la relève* of 1942 and Vichy's paltry efforts to help POW families and prohibit divorce of POW spouses. When escaped POW Sergeant François Mitterand, who in 1943 had been awarded a *Francisque* by Vichy, tried to create a category of "*PDG* [*Prisonnier de guerre*, POW] *résistants*," de Gaulle sardonically suggested that his time might be better spent organizing hairdressers.[191] Unlike the "Colditz myth," which gripped Great Britain by the 1970s, a popular stereotype in France was that, having failed to defend the nation in 1940, French POWs had spent a cushy war in farms and villages nestled in the arms of German women whose husbands and fathers were away at the front. Only in 1992, during Mitterand's second presidential term, was his *Mouvement national des prisonnier de guerre et des déportés* (MNPGD) recognized as "a combatant unit in the French resistance from 22 March 1944 until the Liberation," a belated Greatest POW Generation tribute.[192]

Drawdown, Purges, and Amnesties

De Gaulle's global power ambitions immediately collided with the reality of the French military drawdown, which saw the strength of the armed forces progressively cut by parliament from 1.3 million in May 1945 to under 0.5 million by March 1946. Furthermore, this reduction in force occurred in the context of two controversies: first, cleansing the French military of men closely associated with Vichy; and second, the fight over the "homologation" of FFI ranks in a "revivified" French army. Both challenged the Gaullist myth of a universal resistance of the French people, and the transformation and renewal of France and its armed forces through war, resistance, and *l'amalgame*.

Although "Vichy was never put on trial" became conventional wisdom at the time, in fact, the French *épuration* offered a vigorous, if uneven and occasionally unjust reckoning.[193] Men who had served at the top of the Vichy forces were judged before a *Haute cours de justice*.[194] Their defense invariably was that they had merely followed orders in serving the legal regime at Vichy, while the man that Vichy had always referred to as "ex-General de Gaulle" had made war with a mercenary band of renegades, deserters, and dragooned colonial subjects.[195] Echoing generations of Frenchmen, Paxton questioned the mythology of the French military's apolitical tradition of *la grande muette* (the great mute), noting all sorts of ways during the Third Republic in which generals and admirals intervened in the political arena to influence policy, directly through their actions, by exerting professional pressure through various policy-formulation mechanisms, or acting through pro-military deputies, themselves often former soldiers, to influence defense policy. "Military discipline in France had always had its limits of tolerance," he wrote. Therefore, Vichy was simply the culmination of a long tradition of politicization and quasi-obedience of the French military to the State which stretched back to the nineteenth century, especially in the empire, which soldiers and sailors had conquered, administered, and policed. The thrust of Gaullist propaganda throughout the war was that Vichy was an illegal regime buttressed by an enemy power. In this way, war in France, and war for France, became "moral debate about what is right and wrong, what makes peoples and nations proud and what sullies their honour. This is the cultural reality of the Second World War as a peoples' war."[196] In these conditions, legality ultimately came down to moral choice.

A second phase of the drawdown, known as the "*dégagement des cadres*," initiated, from 3 November 1945, a process made urgent by France's debilitated economy and the phaseout of US and British military support. Given the meager financial incentives for retirement, very few volunteers stepped forward. The decision about who would remain in the ranks was further complicated – even embittered – by the need to balance the requirements of professionalism with a "renewal" of the forces through an infusion of new blood. Unlike the conscripts of 1940, or most of the professionals of *l'armée d'Afrique*, who had not experienced occupation, former FFI knew exactly what they had been fighting for.[197] While some officers who had been too close to Vichy were let go, this reduction in force, driven more by economic and financial rather than juridical or political motives, saw former FFI demoted in favor of *naphtalards* (Vichy's "mothballed soldiers"), who might have done little more than supervise charcoal making at a *Chantier de la jeunesse* or escort an STO contingent to Germany. In the National Assembly, the PCF led the charge against an obvious sabotage of army renewal, while many former FFI linked their demotion or "release" to the perpetuation into the post-war period of a "mothballed" Armistice Army. But, with the military firmly in control of *La Commission supérieure des FFI*, the officer corps of the three services quickly dropped from 36,000 to 22,500, which meant the elimination of 12,000 officers in the army, and 1,200 each in the navy and air force, by the end of 1946.[198]

The amnesty of 6 August 1953, which eliminated all administrative sanctions for collaboration, as well as rearmament in the context of the Cold War and the wars in Indochina and Algeria, witnessed a return to active service for some "purged" officers. Nevertheless, Claire Miot rejects the notion that the drawdown was designed specifically to cull former FFI from army ranks. At least some resistance activity was a criterion for retention, and 6,000 officers who had played no role in resistance were returned to civvy street to open opportunities for younger officers.[199] So, while the drawdown was not intended to recreate the Armistice Army, Paxton argued that, beneath a smokescreen of "renewal," this was precisely what happened. All the generals on the French army list of December 1946 had been in the regular army before 1939, while only nine of the army's 259 colonels had not been pre-war professionals. "A closer look reveals a direct line of descent from the Armistice Army to the postwar French army," concluded Paxton. "A revolution in personnel notwithstanding, it was still Armistice Army veterans who ran the French Army through the liberation period, through the Fourth Republic, and into the Fifth."[200]

Also working against "renewal" was the Gaullist myth, embraced by the political class and much of the population, that Vichy had represented an incongruity, a fleeting intermission in France's Republican tradition.[201] While the purges after 1944–1945 were meant to be "democratic," they spawned the black legend in the army of a "*communo-resistantialiste*"-triggered drawdown. Communists complained that this post-war reduction in force simply confirmed a pattern, along with *l'amalgame*, the insistence on individual enlistments in 1944–1945, and a refusal to "ratify" FFI ranks, amounting to the army's attempt to reconstitute France's reactionary military establishment.[202] The left mirror-imaged the high retention of pre-war cadres as a "*vichysto-militaire*" sabotage of the French military's democratic military makeover. But the bottom line was that the "*dégagement des cadres*" sought to retain technicians and staff officers, and gendarmes, who were in short supply, and purge aging or poorly rated officers.[203] These purges were the most significant since 1815. Nevertheless, the government's policy of homologation, purge, and drawdown produced only a limited renewal among officers and NCOs, especially in the navy and FAF, where "professionalism" was prized above "democratization." Furthermore, from 1949, an escalating war in Indochina and the need to integrate French forces into the Atlantic alliance joined the 1953 amnesty to witness a significant return of purged officers.[204] None of these trends offered a foundation for a French civil–military relations remodel.

For republicans, loyalty to the principles of the National Revolution on the right may well have represented a "minoritarian current,"[205] of which the French military constituted a reactionary rump. For the anti-Gaullists, however, Vichy represented the "crystallizing of national sentiment," while a robust "catholico-traditionalist counter-model" rendezvoused in the military with France's imperial ideology. This transformed de Gaulle into "the last battleground of the *guerres franco-françaises* in which, for more than two hundred years, the French have fought over the legacy of the Revolution."[206] This means that, while Vichy may have encapsulated a "vision of the vanquished," it was hardly a "parenthesis" in France's republican ascendency. The National Revolution consecrated a "concurrent legitimacy" opposed to the universalist republican secularism which had been designed to unite France's heterogeneous society. This helps to explain Pétain's ambiguous legacy, especially in the armed forces, whose attitudes "fostered institutional instability."

Even before 1951, when the onset of the Cold War allowed the General Staff to eliminate many former FFI officers with the claim that they were communists, wartime resisters like Henri Rol-Tanguy bumped up against a steel ceiling in an army that often refused to assign command positions to former FFI, and so denied them the essential criteria for promotion. Most former FFI officers could expect to age out as captains.[207] Of course, not everyone who left the army did so for political reasons: in 1945, some had remained in service because it offered a modest paycheck in hard times and resigned as soon as the job market improved. Others had no desire to fight in Indochina. Rather than "renew" and democratize the French officer corps as many resisters had desired, the post-war years reinforced the phenomenon of auto-recruitment, as the military increasingly enrolled the sons of military men – almost 50 percent at Saint-Cyr by the time of the Algerian war.[208] In the end, few officers were purged. Most departures were a result of the reduction in force, while the FFI criterion might be expansively interpreted to reintegrate regular officers through the back door.[209]

Nor were some of Vichy's most egregious supporters held accountable for their acts. Governor General of Indochina Admiral Jean Decoux had collaborated extensively with the Japanese and, despite numerous warnings, had been caught totally unaware by the Japanese coup of 9 March 1945 –another tactical surprise which, defying Clausewitzian norms, together with 1940 and Torch, cascaded into a catastrophic French defeat. For his part, Weygand had actively pushed for an armistice in June 1940, subsequently rejected all entreaties from Leahy and Murphy to tip AFN into the Allied camp, and had imposed the notorious "oath" to the Marshal on officers. Nevertheless, the high court gave both men a pass because they had "saved" the empire.[210] Elsewhere, long trials terminated in unreadable legalese, when not unfathomable verdicts, amnesties, cancellations of condemnations, dismissals, and so on. There was a brisk traffic in faux *attestations de résistance*, with the PCF-dominated *Conseil national de la résistance* among the most prolific purveyors, while the going rate for a *Légion d'honneur* – a decoration that weighed heavily in the accused's favor – was 1,500,000 francs ($12,500 or £3,125), so it was worth taking out a loan when the alternative might be a three-year sentence to Fresnes or La Santé. Some of France's biggest black marketeers in November 1945 were in uniform, especially in occupied Germany, where the army's power to "requisition" and resell went practically unchecked.[211]

France's purge trials and hearings also revealed "resistance" to be a fluid concept, when so many accused claimed to be resisters in collaborators' clothing. Resistance became defined as having an "anti-German attitude." So, doing nothing directly to help the Germans qualified as resistance for someone like Weygand. Former Vichy officials cited German mistrust and hostility toward the Vichy regime, their suspicions that *la Milice* was unreliable or inefficient, or that the LVF had been simply a collection of military misfits, unemployable cranks, and gullible adolescents in search of adventure, to puff their resistance credentials. "'An anti-German attitude,' henceforth terribly *en vogue*, [became] the corollary of the double game," writes Vergez-Chaignon. Vichy presented itself, in the words of the Secretary of State of the Vichy Navy Rear Admiral Gabriel Auphan, as the "legal resistance." No one wanted to govern France during the Occupation, went their argument. By accepting their "duty" to defend France, Vichy officials and military men had shouldered a "sacrifice." Compromises were perhaps made, but they had been beneficial in the long run because they served French interests. Vichy's "resistance" to German demands took the form of prevarications, delays, and obfuscation, which had preserved French sovereignty and saved French lives. A well-orchestrated right-wing campaign led by people like Pierre Laval's son-in-law René de Chambrun, who gathered testimonials of "resistance" acts by Vichy officers and officials allegedly endorsed by the American embassy and high Allied officials such as Eisenhower and Omar Bradley, sought to rehabilitate collaborators.[212] Meanwhile Gaullist dissidents, "deserters" like Thorez, and communist "terrorists" like "Colonels" Fabien and Rol had "played to the public" with dangerous and counterproductive actions. This "legal resistance" storyline played well in a population for whom "resistance" and especially the *maquis* conjured memories of untethered young terrorists and communist hooligans who pillaged, robbed, and above all brought down retaliation on the heads of innocent civilians. Indeed, exaggerated claims in the press of thousands of executions as the result of an *épuration sauvage* in the immediate wake of the liberation, repeated by some historians, as well as the internment of 126,000 suspects for collaboration between September 1944 and April 1945 in the same camps that before had housed resisters and STO evaders, the majority of whom were released without being charged, inclined courts toward leniency. Also, the fact that three-quarters of the magistrates now adjudicating cases of "collaboration" had spent the previous four years judging resistance "crimes" might also have nudged them toward clemency. "The most severely punished were the unimportant and the poor," concluded Jean-Pierre Rioux, although 90 percent of those tried for "military collaboration" were convicted. And if the Gaullists continued to insist that Vichy was an illegal regime, on what grounds was *la France libre* recognized as legitimate, beyond asserting a tenuous spiritual kinship with Joan of Arc? Nor was the government-in-waiting eager to upset the Allies with "illegal punishments" that might suggest that score settling took precedence over a commitment to public order and winning the war.[213]

Faithful to Vichy's "Shield of France" defense, which stubbornly persists in French political discourse,[214] Fernand de Brinon, one of the main architects of Franco-German collaboration, was marketed by his defense as "*un bon traître*," who used his connections to soften German demands. When he was not organizing Jewish "*rafles*" like his emblematic July 1942 Vel d'Hiv rodeo, apparently *Sécretaire général de la Police* Bousquet issued discreet tip-offs about anti-*maquis* sweeps, saving resisters from arrest and certain death, or intervened to spring captives from jail. Actions in favor of the resistance or the Allies played well with the *Haut cour de justice*, and Bosquet dealt that card like the consummate political gambler he was.[215] The concept of "legal resistance" allowed the FAF to reintegrate several hundred officers *à titre FFI*, when in fact they had never stopped obeying orders from Vichy.[216] For Jean-Pierre Rioux, *épuration* theater diffused popular discontent over "the shortages, the black market, and a daily life of humiliation and hardship for which no end was in sight."[217] But judicial forbearance sent a strong memorial signal to 1940 veteran, former POW, and "Algerian" Richard Bennaïm: "Us Jews, if we would like to live in peace and prosperity in the middle of French people, must henceforth accept that our difference only expresses itself quietly, among ourselves, and in a quasi-culpability."[218]

So, while *épuration* was meant to ensure that France would not slip back into its old ways, it transformed into a perplexing and divisive – rather than restorative – process, "revolutionary justice without the Revolution,"[219] a feeling not helped by the onset of amnesties, the first of which, in April 1946, pardoned crimes committed by the Resistance. A major purpose of amnesty was to separate Vichy, increasingly marketed as a regime that had sought to modernize and stabilize French society along technocratic and traditionalist lines, from the sin of collaboration. And, if Nazis occasionally infiltrated Vichy, communist vigilantes, toughs, and criminals featured prominently in the internal resistance. After all, de Gaulle had allied with communists to oust Giraud and execute Pucheu, and even introduced communist ministers into the GPRF, thereby, in the minds of the right, creating a moral equivalence between collaboration and resistance.[220]

The Cold War opened the door to a right-wing redemption, in the wake of cathartic but unpopular and hence limited purges. Vichy alumni protested their political persecution and dedicated themselves to setting the record straight. In this way, Vichy's Lost Cause mythology sought to convert a shameful betrayal of France and her people into a celebration of courage, honor, patriotism, and strategic foresight. The blame for 1940 appeared to be widely shared, not just a "military event," but one rooted in political and diplomatic muddle, "decadence," and defeatism. Besides, in retrospect, "Liberation" was tinged with ambiguity – estimates of French people killed by Allied bombing of France hovered between 48,000 and 70,000, while another 40,000 French workers perished in the Allied bombing of Germany. In the French view, the Anglo-American invasion had been unnecessarily destructive, especially in Normandy and Alsace, killing an unknown number of French civilians, destroying infrastructure, and leaving many homeless.[221] Above all, despite de Gaulle's Herculean efforts, the post-war global profile of France, a world power in 1939, had shrunk. In these conditions, 1940 seemed to be ancient history, which few proved eager to revisit. One of the motivations for the barrage of amnesties issued during 1946–1953 was to restore the republican synthesis, to homogenize and reconcile France's past in the name of national reconciliation and civil peace, in the context of the wars of decolonization, and in the interests of Franco-German reconciliation within the European Economic Community. It replicated the German *Schlußstrich* (drawing of a line under the past) in the interest of European unity and Cold War solidarity, while effacing German war crimes, "a similar amnesia as a prerequisite for a reformulation of memory."[222] It also allowed Paris to reclaim "French exceptionalism" and "Republican distinctiveness," and to reconcile the Republic's universalist principles with *raison d'état*. But these post-war amnesties also reinserted erstwhile Vichy supporters into the political arena.[223] All this served as a dress rehearsal for a post-1962 replay, when partisans of *l'Algérie française* and the Organisation armée secrète (OAS) claimed to be authentic heirs of de Gaulle and the wartime resistance to earn a slate-clearing salvo of exonerations for crimes and treason in the wake of the War for Algerian Independence. In this way, the "lapses of the nation" were simply ignored in the pursuit of republican stability, to reconcile the "two Frances" and surmount a national identity crisis laid bare by war and occupation in order to allow France to recover the values vital to the functioning of democracy and keep it open to the wider world.[224]

In 1947 there were amnesties for those from Alsace-Moselle and those under twenty-one years of age who had served in the German forces voluntarily or as conscripts. These categories were expanded in 1949, but not before the formation in 1948 of a "Committee for the Liberation of Marshal Pétain," a martyr cult in which his lawyer Jacques Isorni played the spirited impresario, with Weygand as a prominent sacristan. In 1948, the Mouvement Républicain Populaire (MRP), a Christian Democratic refuge for recovering Vichyites, and the Gaullist Rassemblement du Peuple Français (RPF) had also agreed to work toward a partial amnesty. This was opposed by the SFIO, who argued for amnesties on a case-by-case basis, while the PCF puffed its Central Committee as praetorians for popular justice via inflexible *épuration*. When, on 5 January 1951, a general amnesty was declared for those sentenced to 15 years of "national indignity" and who had already served 3 years in prison, fewer than 4,000 of an original 40,000 accused collaborators remained behind bars.[225] Others might request personal amnesties. With the resistance legacy under serious attack, the general impression began to take hold that *épuration* had been sabotaged by judicial leniency and a lack of political will, so that amnesty became a focus of the 1951 electoral campaign. Pétain's death in July 1951, at the age of ninety-five, triggered a robust movement for his posthumous canonization that culminated in 1973, when Vichy diehards kidnapped his coffin with the intention of reburial at Douamont, in an unsuccessful attempt to expunge collaboration from Pétain's legacy. On 6 August 1953, the French parliament passed a general amnesty, which also abolished the penalty of "national degradation." By then, only 1,500 remained in jail for crimes of collaboration.[226] And, although the preamble of the 1953 "Grand Amnesty" praised the French Resistance, symbolically, "with it evaporated the dreams of a unified Resistance resulting in a regenerated republic." The next year, amnesties for Oradour murders confirmed the general feeling that "no real justice was possible while the population as a whole refused to submit to a searching self-examination." This was in part because no one could – or would – actually define the criminal dimensions of "collaboration," or "the nature of the links between the Collaboration and the National Revolution."[227] Other liberated Western European nations had punished collaboration far more severely than had France.[228] "It's a senile France led by an old man that made the cowardly choice not to choose, to acquiesce to disaster, to collaborate with horror," constituted Bennaïm's bitter verdict.[229]

Yet, France's post-war balance sheet was not entirely negative. For instance, in the armed forces, Jean-François Muracciole contends that, had Paxton extended his timeline into the 1960s and 1970s, he would have discovered that many former FFL pursued brilliant military careers, especially in the army, where they were most numerous. In his view, the 6,300 FFL officers, roughly a third of whom were professional soldiers, sailors, or airmen, had formed a sort of Gaullist Reichswehr in the ranks of the post-war French military. Seventy percent of the 5,750 who had survived the war were drawn from a "social" but also a "cultural" elite, which included France's *grandes écoles* – for instance, Koenig was the only FFL "*grand chef*" who was not a Saint-Cyr graduate. While 86 percent of FFL soldiers returned to civilian life after 1945, 80 percent of FFL officers remained in the forces. Despite complaints that FFL were last in line behind the despised POWs, "Vichy shirkers," and FFI "*pistoleros de village*," "obviously, belonging to the FFL did not damage careers as was often claimed in memoirs," concludes Muracciole. Furthermore, for those with political inclinations, a *France libre* resumé flung open doors to the highest reaches of politics and the civil service, especially from 1958 when the Gaullist old-boy network was mobilized to staff the Fifth Republic.[230]

Nevertheless, the Vichy legacy proved tenacious, as the onset of the Cold War further tarnished the resistance patriotism of the PCF, "the party of a foreign power," and with it the goals of *épuration*, while allowing the right to rehabilitate not only Vichy, but also those who had fought the Red Army in German uniform, as prescient Cold War pioneers. The Armistice had been the correct strategy, their argument went, because it preserved France and opened AFN for Torch. Collaboration had simply been a cover for Vichy's "legal resistance." Echoing many in the Allied camp, they charged that de Gaulle focused more on seizing power in France than on fighting the Germans. Allied armies would have liberated France with or without a French resistance. In contrast, the Liberation and its aftermath had been a profoundly lawless time that had further polarized the French people. And how, exactly, had de Gaulle's stiff-necked pursuit of French *grandeur* improved France's post-war status? "The anti-Gaullist critique is not entirely without validity," concludes Julian Jackson. "There were patriots at Vichy; in the long run the armistice probably did serve the interests of the Allies [even if this was certainly not the intention of its signatories]; the Resistance, whatever its moral importance, made no significant difference to the conduct of the war; it is arguable that France's position in the world would have been no different after 1945 if de Gaulle had never existed; de Gaulle's nationalism was in some respects anachronistic; and the Gaullist myth about the war delayed France's coming to terms with the past."[231]

From a globalist perspective, France's colonial wars offered aftershocks of what de Gaulle had attempted to define as France's "Thirty Years' War" with Germany. The May 1954 defeat at Dien Bien Phu reminded people of 1940, although it more closely paralleled the fate of le Vercors and other *maquis* redoubts, and further compromised the French army's precarious rehabilitation. True to form, the high command deflected blame for their Indochina débâcle onto the prevarications of the Fourth Republic's politicians and the indifference, decadence, and hedonism of their constituents – as a sequel to 1940, democracy now expedited France's imperial twilight. The War for Algerian Independence (1954–1962) resurrected political cleavages inherited from Vichy, but with some former Gaullists stung by their leader's betrayal of *l'Algérie française*.[232] "The eerie and ironic echoes of 1940 – an ageing hero emerging from retirement and requesting full powers to reform the constitution – were only too evident" in the 1958 collapse of the Fourth Republic.[233] In this way, a ruthless separation of the present from a "past that is still with us," that has permitted subsequent generations of historians to weigh Bloch's *Strange Defeat* as a crime-scene deposition influenced by emotion, or Duroselle's *Décadence* as a generational reaction too impressionistic to be entered into the record as historical "evidence," struck an emerging post-war school of interpretation at least as artificial and exclusionary.[234] By drawing a line between past and present, *épuration* had ignored the Shoah, and Vichy's role in the "final solution," first by isolating the Jewish community in France, "a technique indispensable to genocide," as a prelude to assisting the Germans in deporting them.[235] It had left too many criminals like Bosquet free to pursue virtuoso post-war careers, all of which seemed to show that judicial process had been incomplete, complaisant, and blind. Meanwhile, the post-Liberation "*tontes*," trials, and summary executions, whose numbers were vastly exaggerated by Vichy apologists, tarnished the Liberation as "a disdainful and profoundly unjust time."[236]

A final impediment to France's full reckoning with its Vichy past was a lack of access to French archives, a deficit of transparency whose motives, as Marc Bloch noted, are "seldom respectable."[237] Robert Paxton's books on the Armistice Army and Vichy France, as well as Eberhard Jäckel's pathbreaking 1966 *Frankreich in Hitlers Europa*, were based largely on German sources.[238] Not surprisingly, the French navy in particular pulled in the gangplank and cast off when outsiders attempted to investigate its wartime conduct. Complaints were filed against only ten naval officers, an extraordinarily low number given the high degree of the navy's politicization, its self-image as a bulwark against "materialist individualism," and its outsized influence at Vichy. In what French naval historian Jean-Baptiste Bruneau calls a "fairly typical" case, the minister of the colonies had demanded that Rear Admiral Pierre-Michel Rouyer be "severely punished" for "arbitrary arrests, and [disseminating] anti-French propaganda on Guadeloupean radio," not to mention the fact that he had been the French commander of Lorient, the largest U-boat base on France's Atlantic coast. However, investigators discovered that Rouyer's file was virtually empty, so that prosecution would require a meticulous reconstruction of his crimes, a process that the naval minister was disinclined to assist. In any case, Rouyer was allowed to retire with impunity. Of those whose prosecution was recommended, only one, Admiral Georges Robert, celebrated as "the Shield of the Antilles," and the "implacable zealot of the National Revolution," was committed for court martial. Under Robert's authority as High Commissioner, opponents of the "navy state" were tortured, even raped. When he was removed in July 1943, Robert had taken the precaution of destroying all High Commission archives under the pretext that he did not want them to fall into American hands. The brief of the investigating commission was to focus narrowly on maritime and command issues. Many potential witnesses were not called, and some officers refused to testify, in part because the navy did not want to advertise divisions in the officer corps. Robert shifted blame for excesses of internal repression onto subordinates, while justifying his measures as necessary to prevent Washington from seizing the French Antilles. Condemned to ten years' hard labor, Robert was amnestied in 1954, his pension and *Légion d'honneur* restored. Other compromised senior officers retired to avoid prosecution, saw their promotions merely delayed, or were condemned to a six-month sabbatical suspension with no further penalties. Meanwhile, scholars who attempted to investigate the conduct of the navy in the Second World War found access to the archives blocked by Auphan, Hervé Cras, and the chief of the historical section between 1953–1965, Captain René Caroff.[239]

De Gaulle's Legacy

As de Gaulle's latest biographer has noted, beyond his commitment to national grandeur, "If de Gaulle had frequently said of the war that it was a great revolution he seems not to have grasped the full dimensions of that revolution for the international position of France, the future of her Empire or of her relationship with Germany." For this reason, "Gaullism was doctrinally a blank sheet upon which some of the Free French and some resisters hoped to write their own script."[240] *Gaullisme de guerre* had been defined by a rejection of the 1940 armistice and of Vichy. André Malraux famously likened Gaullism to "a metro stop at rush hour." People hopped on and off, depending on at what stage of the war or post-war period the Gaullist train glided into their station. At its core, Gaullism embodied national independence anchored in "a certain idea of France," the predominance of French national interests over ideology, the significance of the State, "resistance to a common enemy," and the centrality of French culture to the development of European and world civilization.[241] In wartime, de Gaulle's tactic had been to present himself as France's shield against catastrophe. Most of the threats, real or imagined, as he presented them came not from the Axis, whose defeat was only a matter of time, but from the soon-to-be-victorious Anglo-Americans: feared British land grabs in Syria and Madagascar; clashes with Washington over the Free French occupation of Saint-Pierre et Miquelon; the Atlantic Charter as an ideological assault on the imperial foundations of French grandeur; the imposition of Giraud or AMGOT; the surrendering of Strasbourg; and the prevention of France from acquiring an occupation zone in Germany, taking up a seat on the United Nations (UN) Security Council, and reoccupying Indochina punctuated his *Gaullisme noir* narrative. But, despite the fact that he led a minority exile crusade and commanded a largely symbolic military force, he managed frequently to outmaneuver both Churchill and Roosevelt, qualifying him perhaps as the most adept politician in the Second World War. De Gaulle's tactic was to "create an event ... to force himself on the attention of those who wanted to ignore him" and, through his show of intransigence, "to regain the moral high ground he ought to have lost ... Behaving like a great power was Gaulle's way of becoming one."[242] One can certainly argue that France and its empire would have ended up more or less in the same place in 1945 with or without de Gaulle. The British had no plans to absorb Madagascar or Syria, nor the Americans to end French rule in North Africa. They simply wanted to prevent Vichy from allowing the Axis to use them as bases. But London was keen that France share the burden of Germany's occupation. Washington failed to live up to its Atlantic Charter rhetoric either in AFN or Indochina, in large part because Washington's wartime policy prioritized enticing France back into the war.[243] AMGOT was reserved for enemy states like Italy and Germany, not France.

On 20 January 1946, de Gaulle abruptly resigned, ostensibly to protest the Assembly's 20 percent defense budget cut.[244] On one hand, de Gaulle's departure might be rationalized with the argument that he had fulfilled his mission – civil war had been averted on liberation and his sacrosanct French State restored. De Gaulle's intransigence had been rewarded with France integrated into a tetrarchy of victorious powers, with its ZOF in Germany and a seat on the UN Security Council, while upholding a wobbly but more or less intact empire. Eighty percent of French people polled believed that France had been restored to its former Great Power status. On the other hand, it is possible that, through resignation, de Gaulle sought to create another crisis, which would have produced a parliamentary cave-in on the question of a constitution that conveyed strong presidential prerogatives.[245] However, had that been his intention, it failed. The catastrophe that he had predicted did not happen – at least, not immediately. "The 'system' had held out," as Julian Jackson notes.[246] On the other hand, while it counted its successes, most notably the *trente glorieuses* of France's post-war prosperity, the Fourth Republic proved ill-structured to manage two wartime Gaullist legacies: that of imperial grandeur and that of civil–military relations, that *l'amalgame* with its goal of creating *l'armée rassembleur* had failed to repair. Post-war, Gaullism hardened into the partisan carapace of the anti-parliamentary RPF, which "struck a chord with the nostalgic Pétainists while alienating the left with whom de Gaulle had been allied since the Liberation," writes Julian Jackson. "Some of the early Gaullists dropped out and even opposed their former leader." But others, especially those too young to have served in the war, felt that, through attending boisterous RPF rallies, "they were living a surrogate Resistance."[247] In essential respects, 1954 and 1962 would offer a 1940 *déjà-vu*, with professional soldiers quick to pin defeat on the "apathy of the nation," fostered by unpatriotic French schoolmasters and, as Bloch had charged in 1940, a parade of "spineless" French governments at the head of a "swollen" and "chaotic" National Assembly.[248]

But the promise of Gaullism – indeed the pledge that de Gaulle had given in a 24 March 1942 British Broadcasting Corporation (BBC) oration – had been that, liberated, France would bc governed by a new elite:

> Thus, from the crucible where seethes the pain and fury of the French nation, we watch as little by little a new elite emerges, a combat elite. We watch as men appear and organize, men who go forward without retreating, without second thoughts, with no questions asked. And in the actions of those men, as in their eyes, we see the glimmer of the first signs of a French renewal. It is on that audacious elite that henceforth depends the destiny of our country.[249]

Combat had transported resisters from the periphery of Vichy humiliation and rebellion to the epicenter of victorious Gaullism, as symbolized by Leclerc's bounding liberation of Paris and Strasbourg. FFL volunteers had left everything behind, embraced as their own their leader's iconoclastic temperament and fling with destiny, and crossed the desert both literally and figuratively to grasp the prize of Liberation and immortality. De Gaulle's émigré army was not the same as the internal "elite of the shadows"; it was more diverse, more democratic, and included many foreigners, part of a broader European "community of suffering and of combat." While the resistance exemplified in its energy and courage a rejection of "decadence," as Olivier Wieviorka points out, it also embodied at least two further characteristics. First, it had been "*ultra-minoritaire*." Second, the resistance not only emerged spontaneously outside of formal republican institutions – the army, the administration, the political parties and unions, and the Church – but also exemplified a direct rejection of them. Rather than reveal a nostalgia for the Republic, "[the resisters] revealed above all the vitality of a society that knew literally how to invent the terms and modes of a combat, without having any historical precedents to draw upon."[250] In fact, in its essence, the resistance ethic was a reaction to the failure – both institutional and moral – of Republican institutions to rise to the challenge of Nazi aggression, and a manifestation of a desire for a renewal and rebirth of French democracy shorn of the baggage of discredited forms of governance. The overwhelming sentiment on both right and left was that the nation must regenerate itself from within, that salvation was to be found in France's sacred soil, not imported by Charles XI in the baggage trains of the Allies. This helps to explain why Pétain remained popular – at least, more popular than the regime he headed – even as the French prayed for liberation.[251] This added a moral dimension to resistance and Liberation that rejected the quasi-corrupt habits of *la Troisième*'s "Republic of pals." And, while the French public may have embraced "resistance broadly speaking" as a concept, many viewed resisters and *maquisards* at best as a nuisance, and at worst as a rowdy rabble of foreigners, communists, and juvenile delinquents, not an avant-garde of French renewal.

That the republic would be restored by Charles de Gaulle, a man of authoritarian temperament, was somewhat ironic. Initially, de Gaulle represented a refusal to accept the armistice, not a determination to restore the Republic. As Robert Belot observes, he was a solitary man who stood outside of any political tradition. He also became "one of the most reviled men in French history."[252] Both left and right accused him of seeking to establish a personal dictatorship. Republican restoration came about in part because democracy was a prerequisite imposed by de Gaulle's Anglo-American sponsors, in part because the restoration of the state and democratic life was his ambition, and in part through an interaction between de Gaulle and the "feudal powers" of the internal resistance. Resistance did not seek a republican restoration because political realism was not its strength. While composed of diverse, even antagonistic elements, "resistance in France" saw itself as representing a new moral way to practice politics outside of the old republican institutions. Ironically, perhaps, for the man for whom the Battle of Agincourt seemed as if it had been fought only yesterday, upon Liberation, de Gaulle insisted upon republican continuity as a device to delegitimize Vichy. The Resistance had no ambition to democratize in the old style, to proselytize their faith and convert large numbers, for to do so would forfeit their elite status. Presenting himself as the bulwark between salvation and catastrophe, de Gaulle wielded the phantom cudgel of AMGOT to force the internal resistance to fall into line behind a republican restoration or run the risk of a recycled American-imposed Darlan deal. Some resisters viewed the creation of the Fourth Republic in 1945 as a betrayal of their ideals.[253]

Resistance offered a phenomenon sparked within civil society, an articulation of citizenship as well as a pan-European rejection of fascism. De Gaulle became a symbol behind which an inchoate resistance could federate, acquire legitimacy through patriotism and resources by association with the Allied cause, and expand modestly within the constraints of occupation and collaboration. De Gaulle also imported political party representation into the Conseil national de la résistance (CNR), which caused tensions with some resistance groups, for whom the parties symbolized division, decadence, and defeat.[254] But, in doing so, he restored French democracy and debate, both of which had been suppressed by Vichy, relegitimized the political parties, and assured a smooth transition of power on liberation that avoided civil war and strife of the sort that afflicted Greece and the Balkans. The military accomplishments of the resistance were limited, and necessarily so in the straitjacket of occupation. De Gaulle's declaration of "*Paris libéré par lui-même*" imported marginal resistance players into the center of France's liberation narrative. Inevitably, the transition of resisters into politicians was hardly more successful than their conversion into soldiers. *L'amalgame* failed to infuse the army with a new spirit – it came too late, was too peripheral, too politized, and too amateurish to be regarded by career soldiers as anything other than an assault on their professional prerogatives and expertise, an insult to their patriotism and sacrifice, and a subversion of imperial ascendancy. Nor could this eleventh-hour "fifi" *levée* expunge the shame of 1940, despite the suffering during the winter campaign in Alsace or the siege of the Atlantic pockets. Resisters did what they could in straightened circumstances, even if was just to decorate *monuments aux morts* with flowers, paint a Cross of Lorraine on a wall, or decline to report for STO in Germany. The Resistance certainly spun off its heroes, Moulin and Brossolette emblematic among them, as well as many anonymous men, women, and foreign refugees whose honorable and courageous actions undertaken out of patriotism and civic duty offered a rejection of Vichy and the occupation, for which many paid with their lives. But to view them solely through a heroic lens, even in the service of national pride, threatens to turn them into two-dimensional characters, measure the resistance only in terms of its accomplishments, and strip the past of its audacities, ruthlessness, anxieties, fears, and doubts.[255]

Nor did de Gaulle and resistance manage to transform the French political landscape, so that France's Fourth Republic quickly metamorphosed into its predecessor's *Doppelgänger.* "If political culture little disposed the elected to resist, the resistance culture did not foster political engagement," wrote Robert Belot. "The attempt to 'resistentialize' politics quickly showed itself to be illusory once it became clear that the long-dreamed-of Fourth Republic reestablished the old partisan rules and resuscitated the party spirit."[256] On a practical level, resistance organizations offered little preparation on how to conduct debates, write bills, and pass legislation through political deal-making, while the politicians quickly rebounded with blueprints for nationalization, social security, and "le Plan," ideas and aspirations resurrected from the 1930s Popular Front and Roosevelt's New Deal that laid a foundation for *les trente glorieuses* of post-war French economic resurgence. On a broader institutional and psychological level, de Gaulle's argument had been that Vichy was an illegal regime, and the Republic had never ceased to exist, so that Liberation had restored continuity. France needed "renewal" and "republican order," not resistance-generated "revolution." De Gaulle's obsession with the restoration of the State, combined with the need for technicians to restore the economy, stabilize the franc, get the trains running, redistribute coal, administer the colonies, and rebuild the military meant that liberated France witnessed a resurgence of a traditional party structure accompanied by administrative continuity. So, on one level, one could argue that the impact of de Gaulle on the renewal of French politics and institutions, including the army, was limited at best. Democracy's homecoming witnessed a return of division and weakness. The failure of *épuration* served to showcase Resistance impotence, while the PCF's annexation of Resistance martyrdom as the self-affirmed "*parti des fusillés*" quarantined the resistance legacy on the extreme left of France's political spectrum, tainted its moral authority, and confirmed that resistance would not transition to revolution in a France eager to rebuild the State, recover national dignity, reconstruct the country, and transition to normalcy. De Gaulle realized that, once Liberation had been achieved, the resistance had to fade away, discarded like men who had served their purpose and must be either jettisoned or heroized in death – Muselier, Monclar, Moulin, Brossolette, Juin, Leclerc, and de Lattre, among others. "The resistance lost the battle of the Liberation," because, while de Gaulle might praise it as a concept which democratized, republicanized, and legitimated Gaullism, while boosting the morale and cohesion of the nation, as a movement he conspired to keep it out of power because it had been dominated by the communists, who actually had a party. This gave rise to the charge that de Gaulle had "betrayed" the Resistance.[257]

Another view was that the resistance had failed to provide "a model for a new society," because "resistance" was an ill-defined concept: "A multitude of individuals, living multiple resistance experiences, engaged in various acts, at different times, but which creates . . . a consciousness of an identity greater than the sum of their individuality."[258] Those who claimed the resistance mantle were a heterogeneous collection of men and women of diverse political views. Many of the French retained at best an ambiguous view of "resistance." In de Gaulle's binary narrative, the French people had crystallized into a resistance, against a handful of collaborationist traitors. But the contours of this battle had been more complex. The Germans added a further destabilizing influence in an already polarized France. No one knew in advance who would remain in charge, although, in the first two years of the war, those who predicted Axis defeat seemed fantasists. Even in November 1942, officials in Vichy and Algiers seemed to believe that "stalemate" characterized the war's most likely outcome. Not surprisingly, for reasons of ideology or opportunism, some elements in France were drawn toward the occupiers. Most people worried about security, the survival of their families, and the fate of POWs or STO conscripts in Germany. They might participate in the experiments initiated, or at least inspired, by defeat – *Chantiers de la jeunesse*, *écoles des cadres*, *la Milice*, the LVF, the GMR, even *la relève* and STO, and so on – all of which gave the impression of cooperation and support for Vichy. But these choices were personal and the question of who cooperated and who refused was often linked to one's circumstances, values, family dynamics, and the hyper-local nature of French politics.

Following the 1972 publication of Robert Paxton's *Vichy France*, which laid bare the regime's craven quest for collaboration, Vichy and resistance were branded as antithetical concepts. However, two decades later, historians in France formulated the term "*Vichysto-résistant*" to describe "those who were definitely resisters . . . although anti-German, initially loyally serving the Vichy regime, to the point of being ready to prepare *la revanche*." Following Torch, many *Vichysto-résistants* evolved into Giraudists, a designation used by both Gaullists and communists. Once it became clear by mid 1943 that the Axis defeat was simply a matter of time, the impetus for collaboration ebbed, except for those too deeply implicated, or who lacked the deftness of a René Bousquet or François Mitterand to distance themselves in timely fashion from a doomed regime. Nevertheless, some self-described "*vichyssoise* anti-Nazis" continued to profess admiration for the Marshal and the xenophobic, anti-communist, antisemitic, anti-democratic ideals of the National Revolution, nested in "resistance" in the forms of the Alliance network, Paillole's *Service de sécurité militaire*, the "*camouflage du matériel*," *Organisation de résistance de l'armée,* infiltration of the Vichy police and the administration, and so on.[259]

The question became: who best laid claim to legitimacy on Liberation? The answer was not immediately obvious, as 1940 had scrambled the notion of "legitimacy" in France. Resistance was defined as refusing to accept the defeat. At what point did one's "refusal" kick in – 1940? Torch? Stalingrad/ "Tunisgrad"? When one received one's notice to report for STO and bolted for the *maquis*? When Allied armies kicked in the door of occupied France? Not only was "resistance" an imprecise neologism. It was a permeable concept, one which allowed its actors to slip between the legal and the clandestine worlds, and back again, be both anti-German and Anglophobe, Vichyite and resister. *Résistance-mouvement* had been mirrored by *attentisme*, perhaps better categorized as *collaboration passive*. By transforming "resistance" into the consummate "double game," *Vichysto-résistants* might surmount the contradictions of collaboration.[260] But, beyond the imprecise definition, by projecting themselves as a pure and homogeneous elite of wartime activists, a "moral statement," post-war former resistance leaders set themselves as ethically superior to what they denounced as a largely "*attentiste*" French society and so separated, when not alienated, themselves from it. Yet, if the resistance had played a more active role in the political reconstruction of France, it would have revealed its divisions and forfeited its self-conferred aura of a unified expression of the French people and would have become banal. "The mindset of the State could not be reconciled with the mystical approach of the resisters." In the end, the resistance proved to be no more unified post-war than it had been during the fight. Its failure as a transformative movement was inevitable and, as de Gaulle realized, even a requirement for the restoration of the State and of French democracy.[261]

But if the Resistance settled into France's post-war mythology, de Gaulle, too, gradually slipped into his solitude. The ascent of de Gaulle and of Gaullism rated a place among the war's most remarkable chronicles – an unprecedented phenomenon born in the wake of defeat and beyond any formal political tradition, led by an introverted military loner, whose ambiguity was such that it had to be defined initially by those who rejected him. But this "*gaullisme historique*," a "national gathering welded together in resistance," did not renew France any more than did the internal resistance. Instead, it transitioned into a "*gaullisme d'opposition*" which contributed in many ways to the failure and eventual collapse of the Fourth Republic.[262] Civilians found Gaullism too military, while soldiers, unable to identify it as right or left and conscious of de Gaulle's maverick reputation, thought it too political. But the soldiers were about to discover that all wars are political. The Allies found de Gaulle's conviction, purloined from his reading of history, that France was "*la Grande Nation* … whose calling is to be strong, outreaching … indispensable to the world" infuriatingly pretentious and hollow in the wake of the dual "disgraces" of 1940 and Vichy collaboration. Together with French people on the left and right, they feared, as did Roosevelt, that de Gaulle harbored dictatorial ambitions. And in fact, for all the ballyhoo about the resiliency of France's republican traditions, the GPRF functioned:

Essentially as a dictatorship by consent. There were no formal limitations on de Gaulle's authority except those which he himself voluntarily accepted. The cabinet was hand-picked by de Gaulle and was responsible to him alone; he in turn was accountable only to the people. But his responsibility was totally without sanctions, and presumably the people could only exercise their powers by an uprising or a threat thereof.

He felt no need to consult political parties on his cabinet nominations. He treated the Consultative Assembly as an embellishment required by democracy, much like a saber or a *croix de guerre* for a soldier, whose votes were merely advisory and whose powers were circumscribed, even as its membership ballooned after it arrived in Paris. And when the deputies complained, in an ironic echo of Roosevelt, de Gaulle explained he would take their opinions into account only after they had been returned as representatives by popular vote.[263] Because Gaullism defied classic political definition, much of the resistance held aloof, when they did not oppose de Gaulle outright. Despite all, "*Gaullisme de guerre*" federated a heterogeneous "coalition of refusal" gathered into *La France combattante*. As de Gaulle had first disarmed resistance groups before subsuming them into "the emollient tutelage of Gaullism," so the political parties which he had self-legitimated increasingly asserted their independence.[264]

However, while the politicians eased de Gaulle toward the exit, and myths reinforced in ceremonies and parades might prolong illusions, France could not escape the realities of the war's consequences. The trauma of defeat, combined with the widespread conviction that France had been "saved by the empire," clashed with countervailing forces that could not long be ignored. The active intervention of the United States in 1941 transformed de Gaulle's parochial "Thirty Years' War" with Germany into the Second World War, a multifaceted, global conflict. Torch had threatened to reduce *la France combattante* to one of the Second World War's fading footnotes. By November 1942, the Gaullists had managed only to subvert a few colonies in sub-Saharan Africa and the Pacific, along with Saint-Pierre et Miquelon, places that most French people could not locate on a map. The most significant military contribution of *la France combattante* to the war so far had been Bir Hakeim, a courageous stand by a fistful of French-led soldiers who refused to surrender when British "boxes" at Gazala were throwing in the towel. However, a combination of Laval's assumption of the Vichy premiership in April 1942, which strengthened collaboration, together with Eisenhower's Darlan deal, followed by the elevation of the hapless Henri Giraud as the figurehead for France's rearmament and return to the Allied fold, flung open the door for a Gaullist rebound. Although he frequently denounced American actions toward France, in fact, de Gaulle owed Roosevelt a debt of gratitude because he profited from Washington's missteps, as well as from Roosevelt's Anfa decision to rearm a French military. From Eisenhower's perspective, the Darlan deal may have made operational sense in that it provided the "cover" for *l'armée d'Afrique* to suspend resistance. But it also raised the specter of Roosevelt dictating the political outcome in liberated France, a view reinforced by the Armistice signed with Badoglio and King Victor Emmanuel in Italy the following September. Unsubstantiated fear lingered in Washington that the Darlan gaffe might also encourage the ever-suspicious Stalin to cut a similar agreement, if not with Hitler, then at least with one of his henchmen, hence the "unconditional surrender" declaration at Anfa.[265]

De Gaulle's moving 11 November 1942 Albert Hall speech had called for French unity. Axis occupation of the "*zone libre*," Pétain's refusal to flee to AFN, the scuttling of the High Seas Fleet at Toulon, and the disbandment of the Armistice Army removed all pretense that Pétain was anything but *Der Führer*'s hand-puppet. Resisters in France may have harbored doubts about de Gaulle. But Giraud's blunders and congenital cluelessness, his inability to cash out on Anfa rearmament, the victory in Tunisia, and the liberation of Corsica to his political benefit, his lack of democratic principles, the maintenance of concentration camps in the North African desert and delay in reinstating the Crémieux law that guaranteed citizenship for Algeria's Jews quickly alienated Allied opinion, and convinced the resistance movements warily to turn to de Gaulle. It became impossible politically to organize a "French Resistance" independent of the head of *la France combattante*, although, much to de Gaulle's annoyance, resisters often turned to the British SOE and the American OSS for resources, and foreign refugees or Wehrmacht deserters for recruits. For the internal resistance, the choice between Giraud and the imaginary threat of AMGOT, on the one hand, and de Gaulle on the other was clear cut.[266] Moulin and Brossolette plied occupied France to prod and cajole resistance "feudals" into declarations of fealty to their London liege. From January 1943, a "parade of political personalities" was lifted by Lysander to London to genuflect before France's emerging pretender and pledge the support of their parties, trade unions and resistance groups to his crusade.[267]

The 20 May 1943 victory parade in Tunis had been calculated from a French perspective to reverse Dunkirk, intimidate the Arabs, and announce the return of the French army to the war. But all it did was to advertise the disparities between Allied capabilities and France's meager means. In other words, the war had been radicalized through Nazi notions of racialized "total war," and Allied – especially American – rhetorical commitment to the Four Freedoms and the Atlantic Charter. Even in France, de Gaulle's calls for a *levée en masse* of "the French Resistance" enabled by the interface services had raised expectations of political renewal, even revolutionary change in France. In these conditions, it should be no surprise, then, that attitudes within the empire had begun to shift, which meant that many among France's imperial subjects, wise to patriotic evocations of French grandeur, proved unwilling to submit to the *status quo ante*. An identical phenomenon occurred in the British Empire, where a globalized war became very divisive in Canada and South Africa, both of which contained significant minority populations with bitter memories of their coerced annexation. "Unequal, class-conscious societies breed disengaged and under-motivated citizen soldiers," concludes Jonathan Fennell, speaking of the British and Commonwealth soldiers of the Second World War. "It was the British Imperial system, of which its armed forces were just one part, that was to blame for the loss of Britain's place in the world."[268]

Second, in some cases, most especially in Indochina, the international community would intervene so that France was no longer granted a decision-making monopoly there. The Brazzaville conference of January 1944 had suggested that de Gaulle and the CFLN sought to lay a foundation for the post-war modernization and transformation of the relationship between France and its empire. While the Gaullists lauded the "liberal" spirit of Brazzaville, the conference mounted a Gaullist deception operation largely to neutralize Roosevelt's Atlantic Charter and deescalate imperial expectations, that "laid bare the innate conservatism of the politicians and imperial administrations involved."[269] The dilemma, for the conservative de Gaulle, was that "sovereignty," "self-government," and "citizenship" were concepts that exceeded the parameters of France's "civilizing mission." As Julian Jackson records, speaking of Algeria in the 1950s, de Gaulle was "the prince of equivocation," who "never believed in integration, nor did he welcome it." Rather, he was a "racist" convinced that the introduction into the mainland of large numbers of Muslims would shatter "the republican consensus."[270] The only reform on offer at Brazzaville was a smidgeon of internal autonomy for African territories and a French-directed restructuring. Otherwise, under the palliative presidency of René Pleven, the conference produced only a blather of democratic banalities.[271]

De Gaulle's blind spot was failure to acknowledge the huge changes that the war had brought to the empire. World war had left the French empire simmering, as it had that of Great Britain, "a pale shadow of its former self. The cohesion of its constituent parts had been badly damaged."[272] While, to a point, de Gaulle understood the requirement to reform the empire to ensure its survival, given that AFN had provided the springboard for the liberation of France, reforms in Algeria had been limited to giving citizenship to 65,000 Algerian Muslims in March 1944. This was barely three times more than the 1936 Blum–Viollette legislation had proposed, in the wake of a war that had seen a significant mobilization of North African Muslims and had demanded significant economic sacrifices of France's imperial subjects.[273] Besides, the alacrity with which the Vichy French had stripped citizenship from Algerian Jews sent a strong message to Algerian Muslims that the quest for French nationality promised a merely ephemeral prize. A tentative outreach to the Viet Minh had been attempted from February 1945 on the cusp of the Japanese coup of 9 March 1945 in Indochina. Ho Chi Minh had even offered to join a French-led resistance against the Japanese. But this proposition was declined, because it would have obliged Paris to extend official recognition to the Vietnamese resistance, and would have set a bad precedent for Algeria, at a moment when the example of Philippine independence was rippling through the colonial world.[274]

While de Gaulle dominates the history of wartime France, it is difficult to define his longer-term impact. He was certainly a brilliant political tactician and conjurer of imagery. His "resistentialist" myth had been enabled by the "unifier" Jean Moulin, a legendary figure whose courage and political skill temporarily repaired the shortcomings and divisions of resistance in the *zone libre* to challenge Roosevelt's contention that de Gaulle lacked a democratic mandate. De Gaulle's maneuvering allowed France at least to become a player on the margins of the Grand Alliance, with the accoutrements of Great Power status. This was the result of a Gaullist vision of France's historical role imposed on the Allies rather than a reflection of France's actual military power and influence in the world. To succeed, the requirement was to present the Resistance neither as a minority phenomenon nor as a local manifestation of a global rebellion against Axis ideology and occupation, but rather as a militarily decisive and politically legitimizing *levée* of the French people in the cause of Liberation. Resistance became the foundation upon which France's post-war national identity was to be reconstructed and the shame of 1940 erased. The counternarratives of the anti-Gaullists, both political and generational, had surprisingly little impact. The result was that "de Gaulle triumphed over his enemies, and contemporary France is more modelled in his image than theirs."[275]

La zone d'occupation française (ZOF)

One irony of the Second World War was that it had created few bonds of unity among the Western Allies, for at least three reasons, beginning with the fact that 1940 had confirmed the growing credence in London that, going forward, a special relationship with the United States must form the bedrock of British security. Second, London and Paris had real conflicts of interest, most especially in the Levant, but also toward the nascent development of a European community. And, finally, the towering personalities of the three Western leaders served as an impediment to the formation of special relationships. This had been especially true of de Gaulle, who deeply resented the condescension with which "*les Anglo-Saxons*" had treated France. This was reinforced by lingering popular bitterness over the roughly 60,000 French people killed by Allied bombing of France, and what was viewed as a needlessly destructive liberation.[276] These trends provided an opening in

Figure 10.1 French General Marie-Pierre Koenig, hero of Bir Hakeim, Commander in Chief of French Forces of the Interior, Governor of Paris, and CCFA. (Photo by Hulton Archive/Getty Images

Paris to end decades of Franco-German rivalry, although this would not happen immediately.

De Lattre's exit from Germany saw Pierre Koenig named *Commandant en chef français en Allemagne* (CCFA), a post created on 15 June 1945 (Figure 10.1). De Lattre snubbed "The Old Rabbit" as his undeserving replacement, barely more qualified than "an FFI general." Koenig's symbolic skirmish at Bir Hakeim begged comparison with de Lattre's liberation of Toulon and Marseilles, his sprint up the Rhône Valley via the Belfort Gap, excision of the Colmar Pocket, and vault over the Rhine to storm the posterns of the Third Reich. Koenig lacked *panache*, and in the thespian de Lattre's estimation seemed to view drama as something one paid to see at *la Comédie française*, rather than as a critical command attribute.[277]

Occupation duty was hardly new to the forty-seven-year-old Koenig, who had served in the French administration of the Ruhr following the First World War. Not surprisingly, he pronounced the situation inherited from de Lattre a "shambles."[278] Furthermore, Koenig was expected to administer Germany on a shoestring budget amid a post-war drawdown.[279] Unable any longer to pillage, and with a black market largely stocked from pilfered US supplies, especially gasoline, the quality of occupation life plummeted. Dressed in captured German uniforms, *tirailleurs* had been parked behind barbed wire in camps such as Sélestrat in Alsace or Sainte-Marthe near Marseilles, to await transportation to North Africa. "Rather than send them home, proud and decorated, bearing the glory of the metropole, one returns them disguised as *clochards*," fulminated de Lattre.[280] Forced now to suffer the tedium of barracks life, resentful soldiers concluded that Germans were eating much better than they were, as their officers transferred to AFN, Madagascar, Indochina, or retired. Having survived the horrors of the Colmar Pocket, volunteers clamored to be liberated so that they could, in the words of decorated *France libre* airman Roman Kacew, "disappear forever in the fraternal mass of four-horsepower Renaults, paid holidays, *cafés-crèmes*, and the boycotting of elections."[281] Industries vital for national reconstruction were prioritized for demobilization, beginning with farmers and miners, and those from AFN. One predictable spin-off of the inexplicable delays in the release of volunteers and FFI was "an uncontrollable surge in desertions, men failing to return from leave, and all manner of misdemeanors."[282] A dysfunctional occupation bureaucracy, balkanized among separate ministries in Paris, that applied an outmoded and confused French policy toward Germany, hardly put Koenig in an ideal position to succeed.[283]

De Gaulle's policy toward the defeated Germany, driven by the kindred objectives of *grandeur* and revenge, while *en passant* "reeducating" Germans to assume a constructive role in Europe's political system, was as rooted in the past as his imperial vision. Like the preservation of empire, the ZOF was meant to send the message of France's resurrection as a world power.[284] But the initial problem with the German occupation in a French political context was that it brought a focus on two issues that lingered in post-Liberation France: poor civil–military relations; and the failure of *épuration*, for which Baden-Baden, the "capital" of the ZOF, became the showcase. Excluded from the Potsdam Conference in July 1945, Paris did everything in its power to sabotage Potsdam's promise, thereby retarding Germany's recovery. Largely due to French objections in the Allied Control Council, Germany was denied a central administration and permission to field national political parties, resurrect a central postal system, create a transportation and communications network, and be treated as a single economic unit. Instead, each zone was meant to be virtually self-sufficient. De Gaulle also continued to demand that the Rhineland be separated from Germany, and that the Ruhr be "internationalized."[285]

Raymond Aron, among others, argued that the division of Germany into zones had solved France's "German problem," while the emerging Cold War had anchored West Germany firmly in the camp of the West. Indeed, the Cold War context of reconstruction reconciled some on the right, both in France and in Germany, to the "European project" as a perpetuation of a Vichy–Third Reich grand vision, stripped of its racism and updated behind a now obligatory democratic façade.[286] American High Commissioner in Germany General Lucius Clay insisted that the Western powers should rehabilitate German prosperity, not burden it with exactions. Nevertheless, General Louis Koeltz, last seen as head of XIX Corps in Algiers in November 1942, and subsequently commander of the "*détachement d'armée française*" in Tunisia before being shunted into retirement, was recalled to represent France on the Allied Control Commission in Berlin, where predictably he vetoed any measure that might hint at West German rehabilitation. This only began to change from 1948 with the arrival of Robert Schuman at the Quai d'Orsay and Alain Poher as *Commissaire général aux Affaires allemandes et autrichiennes*. Like French policy toward Indochina, that toward Germany was slow to evolve, in part because Germany remained one of the few places outside of Africa where Paris could continue to play a great power role. But, by 1948, Paris had begun publicly to abandon the "convenient myth" of the German threat and acknowledge the requirement for German rehabilitation.[287]

From the summer of 1945, Baden-Baden, an elegant aristocratic oasis in the heart of the Black Forest, miraculously preserved in a landscape of ruins, became home to the French "*Kommandantur*" and ZOF capital. The resemblance between Vichy and Baden-Baden went beyond a Gallic affinity to set up shop in spa towns, which was lost on no one. The criticisms of the ZOF were three: first, that Baden-Baden had become a sanctuary for former Vichy apparatchiks and collaborators: second, that the army and military government lived an extravagant lifestyle in Germany, while French people at home coped with post-war shortages and austerity; and, finally, that a bloated French administration in the ZOF was desperately ill-organized, bureaucratic, and fell short of its rehabilitative role. In a perverse way, the congregation of former servants of Vichy in the ZOF bore testimony to the success of the purge. *Commissions d'épuration* (purge committees), which were mandated in most ministries on 27 June 1944, had handed out around 12,000 sanctions, of varying degrees of severity, to French civil servants for their occupation behavior. However, eager to stabilize the country, repair the infrastructure, and jumpstart the economy, de Gaulle had been willing to overlook conduct that had not been too egregiously criminal by allowing compromised prefects, policemen, military officers, and personnel from the ministries of finance and the economy to "do their purgatory in Germany." While senior administrative positions in the ZOF were monopolized by men with impeccable resistance records, lower down, many of the "assimilated officers" exiled to Germany were "barely laundered." It was even said that war criminals turned up with bogus orders that allowed them to hide out in the ZOF's sprawling bureaucracy, fueling jokes that the distance between Vichy and Baden-Baden was not as great as one imagined. "One meets the Pétainist who woke up one bright morning in September 1944 a convinced Gaullist, the French bureaucrat for whom the (political) climate has taken away none of his absurdity, the organizer convinced of the importance of his mission, and the communist who a year ago fought in the *maquis* and who today occupies one of the most important posts in the military government," the Zurich newspaper *Die Woche* wrote on 19 October 1945. "Baden-Baden offers a faithful image of today's France." In December 1945, the French Assembly commissioned a study chaired by Salomon Grumbach, a Jewish Alsatian, SFIO activist, and resister, who reported that some sectors of the ZOF administration had become an asylum for former collaborators, where up to 80 percent of the functionaries were Vichy holdovers. Even though the definition of "collaboration" was as imprecise as that of "resistance," this led to the April 1946 recall of thirteen senior officials in the ZOF.[288] Criticism of the Vichy character of the ZOF extended to the army, from which, critics complained, Minister of War André Diethelm had purged former FFI in favor of professional officers. By early 1946, the left-wing press protested that the Armistice Army had been resurrected in the ZOF. But the collaboration issue gradually faded, pushed from public debate in part by the worsening war in Indochina.[289]

Backdrop for a "French Vaudeville," a theatrical décor with so many jeeps, military trucks, and official and police cars that a one-way traffic system had to be devised for the town, Baden-Baden hosted the sumptuous exile of former Vichy expats. A bureaucracy known as the "*Corps des assimilés pour les territoires occupés*" employed 44,000 French civilians who swamped the local population of 35,000. These French functionaries were assigned a military rank – 1,300 of them from captain to general – and dressed in "*uniformes de fantaisie*," ostensibly to bolster their authority and to encourage regimented Germans to follow orders. Even secretaries who could type with one finger were given a rank. Persuaded that they had now become real officers, some newly "commissioned" functionaries rushed to the co-op in Strasbourg, a mere 60 kilometers away, to purchase jodhpurs and even a riding crop. Not surprisingly, this martial pantomime enraged real French officers, while it left the Germans slightly bemused, although this ersatz militarization of French civil servants merely plagiarized the German practice in occupied France. Multiple versions of a gag that each morning a lion emerged from the Black Forest to devour one of the 800 French "colonels," and no one even noticed, circulated among the occupied population.[290]

The problem was that these "colonels" brought their families with them. And because "family" was an elastic concept in the ZOF, soon a cavalcade of wives, mothers, grandmothers, aunts, daughters, distant cousins, and mistresses arrived in the baggage trains of the "victorious *1ère Armée*." In December 1946, the London *Times* reported that 40,000 "wives and relatives" had accompanied an unusually large number of French administrators.[291] As at Vichy, most of the hotels had been commandeered as offices, so that the female dependents squabbled over scarce lodgings, maids, cooks, cars, chauffeurs, and other trappings of bureaucratic status, while taking the waters, or tumbling into debt playing roulette in the casinos. As in the military, the concept of hierarchy translated into social precedence. Wives referred to their husbands as "le Colonel" or "le Commandant," behaved arrogantly toward the "les Boches," participated in the black market, and advertised on the back page of the heavily censored local newspapers for furs and jewelry that hard-up Germans might be eager to sell, or which had been pillaged from Jewish homes. "Officers" escorted their ostentatiously attired companions to the racetrack, or to Baden-Baden's non-stop balls and receptions. The Germans commented that, while the married women behaved like *parvenues*, the single ones were brazenly venal, and wondered whether these were not some of the same French women who had slept with German soldiers during the occupation? No one except the Alsatians bothered to speak German, in part because Germans had become Baden-Baden's most endangered species. The latest French films were shown at local cinemas, shops accepted French ration coupons, newsstands and reading rooms stocked the latest Parisian magazines, and soon film stars and minor royalty popped in on what the Americans dubbed "Merry Baden" and "the headquarters of *l'occupation Mondaine*." So active was the social life that soon Czechs, Poles, Belgians, Dutch, and other military missions established a presence, to the point that the Kurhaus (Assembly Rooms) soon filled with men wearing highly decorated uniforms that no one could identify.[292]

In retirement, de Gaulle grew exasperated with the failure of his countrymen to embrace the global profile he had rescued for France. For instance, in April 1946, he complained to his personal secretary Claude Mauriac, son of the author François Mauriac, that he had led the Gauls to the Rhine, where all they could do was party and complain. "Do you think that a single Frenchmen is surprised and overjoyed?," he asked Mauriac rhetorically. "Don't imagine it! What they see, and what causes them to produce shouts of indignation, it's an AFAT [*auxiliaire féminine de l'armée de terre*] in uniform, or one too many colonels. I gave them back Hanoi – and that wasn't easy. But the only thing they care about is that someone kicked the arse of a socialist journalist. I kept Syria, where French influence has radiated for a thousand years. But no one cares. And as soon as I turn my back, the government gives away the Rhine, Indochina, and Syria."[293]

Not surprisingly, the French elicited no more respect from the German population than they had from Stalin: "[The French] were arrogant, but my father, who had fought in Normandy and in the Ardennes, told us that he had never encountered a French soldier on the battlefield. From that moment, we let them swagger about, because, for us Germans, the invasion had begun in Normandy and that is where we had lost the war in the West. We never spoke of the battles in the south of France." For this reason, the image of the French in

Germany remained that of the soldier of 1940. The French realized that they were making fools of themselves, but reasoned that at least it made up for the indignities of the Occupation and that "there was a war on," even in 1948![294]

Soldiers generally showed no interest in participating in Germany's rehabilitation, only in being soldiers. So, the army became merely "window dressing" for the ZOF, which was probably just as well, because holdovers from *l'armée d'Afrique* especially were criticized for their "colonial mentality," while metropolitan officers sought a posting in Baden-Baden because they deemed France to have become "too red." But a primary reason to remain in Germany was to enjoy a standard of living far above that allowed the military in France, a situation which officers attributed to a lack of "gratitude" of the French population for the army's role in the Liberation. French resentment of military high life in Germany further widened the civil–military divide. One-third of France's supply of gasoline and tires was said to be used by the military in their interminable parades. Soldiers were also at the center of a thriving black market that transported goods across the Rhine. A combination of these criticisms, budget constraints, and the demands of the war in Indochina saw the French garrison in Germany shrink from nearly 1 million men at the war's conclusion, to 75,000 by May 1947, to 53,000 a year later.[295]

The effectiveness of the administration of the ZOF also came in for criticism. The centralization of the French administration was at odds with the decentralization Paris insisted on imposing on the Germans. It was also judged to be overstaffed and inefficient. In fact, such was the overlap and duplication of responsibilities that half of the French administrators assigned to the ZOF were reckoned to administer the other half.[296] The ZOF's dysfunctionality began at Paris' "General Commissariat for German and Austrian Affairs," which was meant to coordinate occupation policy across the government. Paris gradually evolved a more flexible policy for Germany. But everything had to be approved by commander in chief Koenig. The Germans found Koenig competent but "cold," by turn difficult and distant, mistrustful of a people against whom he had fought for four years. Koenig also was in perpetual conflict with his civilian counterpart, the thirty-eight-year-old lawyer and mining engineer Émile Laffon, an SFIO activist and resistance companion of Brossolette, who was dispatched in August 1945 to act as civil governor of the French zone. In a repeat of the d'Argenlieu–Leclerc rancor in Indochina, this ill-defined "dual authority" did not ease relations between Laffon, who answered to the Ministry of the Interior, and Koenig, who until December 1946 reported directly to the President of the GPRF.[297] Koenig's seriatim quarrel with Laffon terminated only when Koenig unceremoniously abolished Laffon's post in November 1947. But their disputes set the tone for French administrators and soldiers, who clashed endlessly over prerogatives and responsibilities in an occupation authority whose structure and even purpose were only vaguely defined.[298]

Meanwhile, the army acted independently of either man. Hettier de Boislambert complained that the army behaved like a plague of locusts – for example, its relentless requisitions included half the wine production of Rhineland-Palatinate in 1948 – while the ZOF administration applied a program of cultural and political education designed to reintegrate Germany into Europe's political mainstream.[299] As in AFN from 1942, the French exported their quarrels to Germany, not only the Vichy–resistance divide, but also their "Alsatian problem." Political competition between PCF, SFIO, and MRP appointees also roiled the ZOF, and might result in the sabotage of policies made in Paris if they ran counter to party or personal interests. And political appointees crossed swords with the economists and technicians who cocooned Koenig, men often seconded to the ZOF by banks or industries which maintained business interests there. Finally, in the opinion of some, this left the French administration of Germany in the hands of several thousand "hopeless functionaries, sociopolitical cretins . . . really very numerous." The French were criticized for their reluctance to relinquish political power to the Germans to the same degree as did the Americans, whose oversight of the American sector resembled Balzac's rapidly shrinking *peau de chagrin*.[300]

"The French were not loved by the Germans in their zone," concludes Constantine FitzGibbon. "They were hardly even respected. But they were surprisingly successful."[301] That this was so was somewhat surprising, as most Germans believed that they had fought a legitimate and heroic war of self-defense, pretended that they had been totally unaware of the Holocaust while simultaneously opining that wartime Allied bombing represented "the revenge of World Jewry," and embraced the theme of Germans as victims – indeed, an August 1947 poll found that 55 percent of Germans "endorsed the proposition that National Socialism had been 'a good idea carried out badly carried out' . . . Austria followed an even shorter route to transforming its citizens from perpetrators into victims."[302] The ZOF did post some achievements, most notably in education, a particular French emphasis which reinforced Germany's democratization, process of self-examination, and assumption of moral responsibility for the war, and which served as a foundation for reconciliation.[303] It also contributed to French economic recovery through exploitation of German resources, purchasing German products at high discounts, maintaining German POWs in France until January 1949 as a form of reparations, and keeping the German standard of living low. Another dimension of French success was perhaps to be found in a uniquely Gallic combination of intellectual liberalism with administrative corruption, which telegraphed that the French were much more mindful of the compromises one had to make under an authoritarian regime, and less willing than were the Americans, through their much-resented *Fragebogen* – interminable questionnaires about German attitudes to wartime events – to make hard and fast judgments about moral choice. The downside was that the French were viewed as lax enforcers of denazification, so that fugitives in the American or British zones might slip into the ZOF to avoid prosecution and even find employment.[304] The rebuttal was that the judicial basis of denazification was "presumptive guilt," and that the task executed by inexperienced junior officers combined naiveté with cluelessness about how German wartime society had functioned.[305] The three zones were fused on 9 April 1949, as West Germany was to be given autonomy compatible with the requirements of Allied occupation. On 8 May, legislation was passed that created the Bundesrepublik, the Federal German state. Koenig stepped down as High Commissioner, to be replaced by former French ambassador to Berlin in the 1930s André François-Poncet. A final irony was that a war that had begun as "a crisis of global stability" saw the situation in the French colonies deteriorate daily, while, in a new post-war world polarized between the United States and the Soviet Union, France and the Federal Republic of Germany discovered a convergence of national interests. By 21 September 1949 when the ZOF closed its doors, the French and Germans, with their town twining, cultural and educational exchanges, participation in NATO, soon-to-be European Coal and Steel Community, and so on, were finding it increasingly difficult to recall what their Thirty Years' War had been about.[306]

Notes

PREFACE

1. Marc Bloch, *Strange Defeat: A Statement of Evidence Written in 1940* (New York: W. W. Norton & Company, 1968), 137.
2. Michael S. Neiberg, *When France Fell: The Vichy Crisis and the Fate of the Anglo-American Alliance* (Cambridge, MA: Harvard University Press, 2021), 4.
3. Neiberg, *When France Fell*, 16, 8.
4. John Lamberton Harper argues that American policy was confused by different visions of Europe's and France's future world role. John Lamberton Harper, *American Visions of Europe: Franklin D. Roosevelt, George F. Kennan, and Dean G. Acheson* (New York: Cambridge University Press, 1994); Hilary Footitt and John Simmonds, *France 1943–1945* (Leicester: Leicester University Press, 1988), xxii.

CHAPTER I

1. General Jean Delmas, "Synthèses des travaux du colloque," in Fondation pour les études de défense nationale, Institut d'histoire des conflits contemporains, Service historique de l'Armée de terre, Service historique de la Marine, and Service historique de l'Armée de l'air, *Les armées française pendant la seconde guerre mondiale 1939–1945* (Paris: École nationale supérieure de techniques avancées, 1986), 448.
2. Robin Leconte, "Face au débarquement allié de novembre 1942: La Division de Marche de Constantine, entre obeisance et résistances aux ordres," in Claire Miot, Guillaume Piketty, and Thomas Vaisset (eds.), *Militaires en résistances en France et en Europe* (Villeneuve d'Ascq: Presses universitaires du Septentrion, 2020), 72.
3. Leconte, "Face au débarquement allié de novembre 1942," 71.
4. Maréchal Alphonse Pierre Juin, *Mémoires*, tome 1, *Alger, Tunis, Rome* (Paris: Fayard, 1959), 117–119.
5. SHD-GR, 1P 35, 30 January 1942, "Instruction personnelle et secrète: Pour le commandant supérieur des troupes de Tunisie pour la défense de Tunisie en cas d'aggression de l'Axe par surprise." "The goal of an Axis attack on Tunisia, launched from Sicily and the south of Italy and possibly Tripolitania, would be the conquest of the naval and air bases to *preempt British action* [italics in original] and to insure more secure communications with its forces in Tripolitania. In all likelihood, it would proceed by surprise, suddenly confronting us with a fait accompli, and forcing us willingly or by obliging us to come to terms with it, by taking advantage of our initial lack of means."
6. Philippe Burrin, *France under the Germans: Collaboration and Compromise* (New York: The New Press, 1996 [French edition 1993]), 161–163.
7. In December 1941, Juin had informed Darlan that the cadres and soldiers of *l'armée d'Afrique* "are anti-German and anti-Italian and their consciences would be certainly troubled if they were forced to fight at the side of Germans and Italians on our own territory." Marcel Spivak and Armand Leoni, *Les forces françaises dans la lutte contre l'Axe en Afrique*, tome II, *La campagne de Tunisie, 1942–1943* (Vincennes: Ministère de la Defense, État-major de l'armée de terre, Service historique, 1985), 70 (henceforth *La campagne de Tunisie, 1942–1943*).
8. Michael S. Neiberg, *When France Fell: The Vichy Crisis and the Fate of the Anglo-American Alliance* (Cambridge, MA: Harvard University Press, 2021), 188, 190.

9. Spivak and Leoni, *La campagne de Tunisie, 1942–1943*, Chapter IV explains the tortuous French command system in AFN.
10. Leconte, "Face au débarquement allié de novembre 1942," 72–74.
11. For inventories allowed by the Axis control commissions, see Spivak and Leoni, *La campagne de Tunisie, 1942–1943*, 30–34.
12. Stanley P. Hirshon, *General Patton: A Soldier's Life* (New York: Harper Collins, 2002), 349.
13. Leconte, "Face au débarquement allié de novembre 1942," 73–74. A native of Mulhouse and 1911 Saint-Cyr graduate, Jacob Schwartz was a wounded Great War veteran captured while defending the Maginot Line in 1940. Released by the Germans, he had been posted by Vichy to Sétif. He subsequently served under de Lattre during the liberation, and finished his career a major general. A road has been named after him, see http://museedelaresistanceenligne.org/media9562-Rue-du-GA.
14. Jean Lapouge, *De Sétif à Marseille, par Cassino: Carnet de guerre de Jean Lapouge, sous-lieutenant au 7e RTA. Campagnes de Tunisie, Italie et Provence, 1942–1944* (Parçay-sur-Vienne: Éditions Anovi, 2007), 11–14, 35–39.
15. Leconte, "Face au débarquement allié de novembre 1942," 68, 70.
16. Spivak and Leoni, *La campagne de Tunisie, 1942–1943*, 63.
17. Spivak and Leoni speculate that German cognizance of Weygand's defense plan might have precipitated his 19 November 1941 recall at Berlin's insistence. Spivak and Leoni, *La campagne de Tunisie, 1942–1943*, 55–56.
18. One of the purposes of Darlan's presence in Algiers in November 1942 had been to pep up imperial soldiers to resist the Anglo-Americans when the time came. Bernard Costagliola, *Darlan: La collaboration à tout prix* (Paris: CNRS Éditions, 2015), 240.
19. To this calculation must be added the fact that Vichy was not at war with "les Anglo-Saxons," while conflict with the Axis temporarily idled in an armistice time-out. Spivak and Leoni, *La campagne de Tunisie, 1942–1943*, 57–58.
20. Julie Le Gac, *Vaincre sans gloire: Le corps expéditionnaire français en Italie (novembre 1942–juillet 1944)* (Paris: Les Belles Lettres/Ministère de la défense-DMPA, 2013), 320–322.
21. "An adversary coming from the east can enter Tunisia, either by sea, and more easily in the north, via the harbors of Bizerte and Tunis, which give access to the ancient route along the Medjerda leading to Algeria, or through Tripolitania from which he can easily reach, and by a good road, the steppe by passing the bottleneck of Mareth between the sea and the massif of Matmata. This bottleneck crossed, he can go north by the coastal route to Tunis, or turn west to enter into Algeria via Tébessa, thanks to another route, built just before the war, linking Gabès to Tébessa. The sea access in the north can be blocked by the defense of the ports of Tunis and Bizerte. But Tunis, which only offers a bad harbor, is in reality difficult to defend. In case of a surprise attack, it has always seemed preferable to cover communications with Algeria, by holding Bizerte on the one hand and the Dorsal on the other." Spivak and Leoni, *La campagne de Tunisie, 1943–1943*, 58.
22. Spivak and Leoni, *La campagne de Tunisie, 1942–1943*, 63–66.
23. Jean-Christophe Notin, *Maréchal Juin* (Paris: Tallandier, 2015), 145. A further argument for skepticism is that Rommel had yet to achieve the battlefield fame during the Battle of Gazala in the summer of 1942 that would make the "Desert Fox" a household name and transform him into something of a cult figure, especially in British memory of the Desert War. See Patrick Major, "'Our Friend Rommel': The *Wehrmacht* as 'Worthy Enemy' in Postwar British Popular Culture," *German History*, 26/4 (2008), 520–535. See also Joseph Campo, "Desert Fox or Hitler Favorite? Myths and Memories of Erwin Rommel: 1941–1970," Ph.D. Thesis, University of California, Santa Barbara, 2019.
24. France lacked the manpower, matériel, and logistics to defend southern Tunisia without a significant easing of restrictions imposed by the armistice, as well as direct German assistance. At a minimum, cooperation would require complete freedom for Vichy to use its navy and air force in the western Mediterranean, the liberation of French prisoners of war (POWs) required to staff indigenous units, a supply of petrol, and German air cover for maritime transports. Costagliola, *Darlan*, 202–203; Spivak and Leoni, *La campagne de Tunisie, 1943–1943*, 66 and Annex 11, 385–386.
25. André Martel, "Preface," in Spivak and Leoni, *La campagne de Tunisie, 1942–1943*, 2.
26. Juin, *Mémoires*, tome 1, 35–36. Spivak and Leoni put the Italian population at 175,000, which appears to be an overestimate. Spivak and Leoni, *La campagne de Tunisie, 1942–1943*, 59.
27. Chantal Metzger, *Le Maghreb dans la guerre 1939–1945* (Paris: Armand Colin, 2018), 245–255; Le Gac, *Vaincre sans gloire*, 108–114; Spivak and Leoni, *La campagne de Tunisie, 1942–1943*, 59–60.
28. Notin, *Maréchal Juin*, 131–136, 143–146. Spivak and Leoni suggest that differences between Juin and de Lattre over the defense of Tunisia "were probably the reason [de Lattre] was recalled to France." Spivak and Leoni, *La campagne de Tunisie, 1943–1943*, 60.

29. Spivak and Leoni, *La campagne de Tunisie, 1942–1943*, 56, 67.
30. Notin, *Maréchal Juin*, 143; Spivak and Leoni, *La campagne de Tunisie, 1942–1943*, 67–69.
31. Juin, *Mémoires*, tome 1, 53, 57.
32. On 2 May 1942, Laval issued a directive that defense priorities should focus on Madagascar, Djibouti, the French West Indies, Morocco, Oranie (western Algeria), and French West Africa (AOF). Darlan's assumption was that Tunisia would be attacked by the Allies. Spivak and Leoni, *La campagne de Tunisie, 1943–1943*, 69–70 and Annex 12, 389–395.
33. Bizerte would be Derrien's responsibility, while CSTT Barré was to defend northern Tunisia, gather resources, and gain time to put Bizerte's defenses in order, blocking approaches from the south. He had also to hold the Béja–Téboursouk region to allow reinforcements from Algeria to arrive. Spivak and Leoni, *La campagne de Tunisie, 1942–1943*, Annex 13, 396–400.
34. Costagliola, *Darlan*, 236, 238, 240; Spivak and Leoni, *La campagne de Tunisie, 1943–1943*, 56, 70.
35. Leconte, "Face au débarquement allié de novembre 1942," 72; Costagliola, *Darlan*, 257.
36. Jean Delmas, "Preface," in Spivak and Leoni, *La campagne de Tunisie, 1942–1943*, 2.
37. Vincent P. O'Hara, *Torch: North Africa and the Allied Path to Victory* (Annapolis: Naval Institute Press, 2015), 50, 62.
38. The groupement de Bizerte consisted of two battalions of colonial infantry (marines), a battalion of the *régiment mixte de zouaves et tirailleurs*, a group of horse-drawn artillery, and a mounted cavalry squadron from the Bey's personal guard. Some of the artillery at Sousse and Sfax also was manned by army personnel.
39. René Pierre Eugène Caroff, *Les débarquements alliés en afrique du nord (novembre 1942)*, second edition (Vincennes: Service historique de la marine, 1987), 249–250.
40. Rudolf Rahn, *Un diplomat dans la tourmente* (Paris: France Empire, 1980), 249, cited in Metzger, Le *Maghreb dans la guerre*, 183. See also Robert O. Paxton, *Parades and Politics at Vichy: The French Officer Corps under Marshal Pétain* (Princeton: Princeton University Press, 1966), 370.
41. Jacques Belle, *L'Opération* Torch *et la Tunisie: De Casablanca à Tunis et au-delà (novembre 1942–septembre 1943)* (Paris: Economica, 2011), 139–140.
42. Notin, *Maréchal Juin*, 263; Martel, "Preface," 2; Leconte, "Face au débarquement allié de novembre 1942," 80–81.
43. Paxton, *Parades and Politics at Vichy*, 369.
44. A "danger" alert was also issued for Oran at 17:56 on 6 November. Spivak and Leoni, *La campagne de Tunisie, 1943–1943*, 74–75.
45. "Take disposition to block Bizerte by sinking commercial ships if threats seem likely. I suggest the *Divona.* Don't hesitate if necessary to render the harbor unutilizable." This effort was only partially successful when the two cargo ships that were to be scuttled were instead carried by the currents and settled in the outer harbor, leaving free a 200-meter passage into the Lac de Bizerte to Ferryville and the French naval arsenal. Caroff, *Les débarquements alliés en afrique du nord*, 253; Spivak and Leoni, *La campagne de Tunisie, 1942–1943*, 75.
46. SHD-GR, 5P 2, "Ordre général du 8 novembre 1942 aux troupes de Tunisie" signed by Barré. Presumably Juin issued this order before he was sequestered by the plotters in Algiers in the early hours of 8 November. Douglas Porch, *Defeat and Division: France at War, 1939–1942* (Cambridge: Cambridge University Press, 2022), 525; Caroff, *Les débarquements alliés en afrique du nord*, 255–256; Spivak and Leoni, *La campagne de Tunisie, 1942–1943*, 76.
47. Caroff, *Les débarquements alliés en afrique du nord*, 253–255.
48. These officers were on their way by 16:15. Spivak and Leoni, *La campagne de Tunisie, 1942–1943*, 77–78; SHD-GR, 5P 2, "Rapport présenté par la commission special d'enquête de Tunisie" (henceforth Viard report), 30. Created in August and registered on 10 September 1943, the committee included an admiral, two generals, two law professors (one of whom was Dean of the Algiers law school Viard, who was also a member of the resistance group Combat), an appeals court judge, and a deputy.
49. Derrien was also copied in on this order. Caroff, *Les débarquements alliés en afrique du nord*, 256–257; Spivak and Leoni, *La campagne de Tunisie, 1942–1943*, 79.
50. Leconte, "Face au débarquement allié de novembre 1942," 73.
51. Leconte, "Face au débarquement allié de novembre 1942," 78.
52. This message was also sent to Derrien in Bizerte and Moreau in Algiers. Spivak and Leoni, *La campagne de Tunisie, 1942–1943*, 103; Caroff, *Les débarquements alliés en afrique du nord*, 257.
53. Leconte, "Face au débarquement allié de novembre 1942," 74.
54. Caroff, *Les débarquements alliés en afrique du nord*, 257–258.
55. Leconte, "Face au débarquement allié de novembre 1942," 75.

56. Frédéric Harymbat, *Les Européens d'Afrique du Nord dans les armées de la libération française (1942–1945)* (Paris: Éditions L'Harmattan, 2014), 50; Caroff, *Les débarquements alliés en afrique du nord*, 255–256; Spivak and Leoni, *La campagne de Tunisie, 1942–1943*, 79–80.
57. SHD-GR, 2H 228, "Récit des combats de Medjez-el-Bab du 19 novembre 1942," 3. This account was written in 1946, and states that, because the Allies could not have arrived in sufficient force before 20 November, a combination of retreat while negotiating offered the only viable French option, whereas, on 9 November, French troops were still in fact preparing to repel an Allied invasion. For their parts, both Noguès and Esteva had opposed giving the Luftwaffe permission to land in Tunisia. Darlan was not categorically opposed, but sought first to gain concessions from Germany. Nevertheless, he seems to have been keen on 8 November to have the Luftwaffe attack Allied ships off Algiers. Costagliola, *Darlan*, 243.
58. Spivak and Leoni, *La campagne de Tunisie, 1942–1943*, 81–82. One ship was scuttled at Bizerte, leaving a 125-meter passage that could be blocked by scuttling another ship if need be. Two ships were scuttled at Tunis, which left it open only to small craft, as was Sfax. Caroff, *Les débarquements alliés en afrique du nord*, 259.
59. Leconte, "Face au débarquement allié de novembre 1942," 78.
60. "If Germany helps us, it will be necessary to modify the armistice that permits us to recover our capabilities," asserts a "Quick analysis of the situation" issued at 13:00 on 9 November by the 4th Maritime Division in Algiers destined for Pétain and Auphan. Spivak and Leoni, *La campagne de Tunisie, 1942–1943*, 81; Paxton, *Parades and Politics at Vichy*, 361.
61. Belle, *L'Opération* Torch *et la Tunisie*, 131.
62. Caroff, *Les débarquements alliés en afrique du nord*, 258–259; Spivak and Leoni, *La campagne de Tunisie, 1942–1943*, 80.
63. Which of course was nonsense, because the 3rd S-Boot Flotilla whose dispatch from Sicily was announced on 8 November would convey Italian soldiers with German specialists. Spivak and Leoni, *La campagne de Tunisie, 1942–1943*, 79; SHD-GR, 5P 2, Viard report, 31; Caroff, *Les débarquements alliés en afrique du nord*, 258–259.
64. SHD-GR, 2H 228, "Récit des combats de Medjez-el-Bab du 19 novembre 1942," 1.
65. Caroff, *Les débarquements alliés en afrique du nord*, 259.
66. SHD-GR, 5P 2, Viard report, 31.
67. Caroff, *Les débarquements alliés en afrique du nord*, 260–261.
68. Spivak and Leoni, *La campagne de Tunisie, 1942–1943*, 103; Caroff, *Les débarquements alliés en afrique du nord*, 260.
69. Notin, *Maréchal Juin*, 208. This was presumably because only on 10 June was Juin officially reinstated by Darlan as commander in chief of French forces in North Africa under Darlan's authority. Caroff, *Les débarquements alliés en afrique du nord*, 260. Spivak and Leoni note that Juin's telephone message only told Barré not to send his troops or air forces to within 50 kilometers of Algiers. Spivak and Leoni, *La campagne de Tunisie 1942–1943*, 85.
70. The next morning, orders arrived from Bridoux ordering Barré to "take necessary measures to avoid any mixing of French and German troops. Regroup on terrain of your choice, but in no case abandon Tunisian territory. Inform resident general." This retreat seems only to have begun on the morning of 11 November, to a line Béja–Medjez-el-Bab–Téboursouk. Spivak and Leoni, *La campagne de Tunisie, 1942–1943*, 86–87, 105, 109. Caroff writes that Derrien had received the order to avoid contact with the arriving Germans and "regroup" elsewhere on the previous night. Caroff, *Les débarquements alliés en afrique du nord*, 261.
71. Spivak and Leoni, *La campagne de Tunisie, 1942–1943*, 87; Caroff, *Les débarquements alliés en afrique du nord*, 261.
72. Caroff, *Les débarquements alliés en afrique du nord*, 260–263.
73. Spivak and Leoni, *La campagne de Tunisie, 1942–1943*, 88.
74. SHD 5P 2, Viard report, 32–33.
75. Spivak and Leoni, *La campagne de Tunisie, 1942–1943*, 89–91.
76. SHD 5P 2, Viard report, 33–34; Spivak and Leoni, *La campagne de Tunisie, 1942–1943*, 91–92.
77. Spivak and Leoni, *La campagne de Tunisie, 1942–1943*, 91–92, 95; Notin, *Maréchal Juin*, 209.
78. Spivak and Leoni, *La campagne de Tunisie, 1942–1943*, 91–92, 95.
79. Spivak and Leoni, *La campagne de Tunisie, 1942–1943*, 93–94.
80. Spivak and Leoni, *La campagne de Tunisie, 1942–1943*, 112.
81. SHD-GR, 5P 2, Viard report, 34.
82. SHD-GR, 5P 2, Viard report, 39–54.
83. Notin, *Maréchal Juin*, 212–213; SHD 5P 2, Viard report, 55.
84. SHD-GR, 5P 2, Viard report, 26.

85. SHD-GR, 5P 2, Viard report, 27, 35–38, 67.
86. Spivak and Leoni, *La campagne du Tunisie, 1942–1943*, 115.
87. Derrien told his subordinates that the Axis was now the enemy, but for the moment not to fire on Axis aircraft, only ships. This order provoked a protest from Esteva and Vichy, forcing Derrien to withdraw it and revert to a policy of neutrality. Caroff, *Les débarquements alliés en afrique du nord*, 264–266, 268.
88. "In fact," read the archivist's note, "General Barré believed that he must modify the connection between events in Tunisia between 9 and 18 November 1942 . . . General Barré clearly seeks as much as possible to avoid his responsibilities during this period of hesitation." Cited in Leconte, "Face au débarquement allié de novembre 1942," 81.
89. Notin, *Maréchal Juin*, 241.
90. David Rolf, *The Bloody Road to Tunis: Destruction of the Axis Forces in North Africa: November 1942–May 1943* (London: Greenhill Books, 2001), 83.
91. On this confusion of orders and counter-orders, see Notin, *Maréchal Juin*, 193–227. For Allied suspicions of French resolve, see Marcel Vigneras, *Rearming the French* (Washington, D.C.: Center of Military History, United States Army, 1989), 33–34.
92. SHD-GR, 5P 2, Viard report, 56–57, 68.
93. Leconte, "Face au débarquement allié de novembre 1942," 80.
94. Juin complained that his orders were misunderstood, and that command confusion reigned in Tunis, which was truthful at least, as the surprise appearance of GIs on the beaches of Morocco and Algeria had thrown the French command into a total funk. He also accused the Viard Commission of launching a witch-hunt. Juin insisted that, as Darlan was in command, and then was replaced by Noguès, it was not his place to order Barré to resist the Germans. Notin, *Maréchal Juin*, 212–213, 308–310.
95. Juin's desire to withdraw to the Dorsal had been based on the premise of a British assault, either through the Mareth Line or directly against Bizerte and Tunis. In November 1942, the menace came from the Axis, who had practically no amphibious assault capability. Therefore, they were reliant on seizing harbors and airfields. All Juin need do was order Barré to hold the airfields and Bizerte long enough for the British First Army, that was disembarking at Bône, to cover the less than 250 kilometers to Bizerte. Rather, on 11 November, Juin told Barré to "*foutez le camp*" from Tunisia.
96. Georges Elgozy, *La vérité sur mon Corps Franc d'Afrique 1942–1943* (Monaco: Éditions du Rocher, 1985), 190.
97. Caroff, *Les débarquements alliés en afrique du nord*, 266–267.
98. Caroff, *Les débarquements alliés en afrique du nord*, 267.
99. SHD-GR, 5P 2, Viard report, 24.
100. Caroff, *Les débarquements alliés en afrique du nord*, 293.
101. Christine Levisse-Touzé, *L'Afrique du Nord dans la guerre 1939–1945* (Paris: Albin Michel, 1998), 272–273.
102. SHD-GR, 5P 2, Viard report, 25.
103. Spivak and Leoni, *La campagne de Tunisie, 1942–1943*, 110; Caroff, *Les débarquements alliés en afrique du nord*, 267–273.
104. Belle, *L'Opération* Torch *et la Tunisie*, 160–164; Robert S. Ehlers Jr. *The Mediterranean Air War: Airpower and Allied Victory in World War II* (Lawrence: University Press of Kansas, 2015), 252–255.
105. Belle, *L'Opération* Torch *et la Tunisie*, 162–164.
106. Guillaume Denglos, *Juin: Le Maréchal africain* (Paris: Belin, 2018), 157–159, 176–177, 388–389.
107. The Private Papers of Albert Rupert, Imperial War Museum Documents 15593, "Tunisian Campaign (November 1942–March 1943)."
108. Spivak and Leoni, *La campagne de Tunisie, 1942–1943*, 115. The Germans later claimed that the French had been the first to open fire, which produced a log jam of orders from Vichy and Tunis for Barré to cease fire and "join German forces." Caroff, *Les débarquements alliés en afrique du nord*, 279–281; Paxton, *Parades and Politics at Vichy*, 370–371.
109. The Private Papers of Albert Rupert, 7–15; SHD-GR, 2H 228, "Récit des combats de Medjez-el-Bab du 19 novembre 1942"; Spivak and Leoni list five killed, twenty-six wounded, two POWs and nine missing. Spivak and Leoni, *La campagne de Tunisie, 1942–1943*, 114–119.
110. Caroff, *Les débarquements alliés en afrique du nord*, 283–284, 298.
111. Caroff, *Les débarquements alliés en afrique du nord*, 282.
112. The German takeover of the Bizerte arsenal also netted three torpedo boats, three naval launches, one destroyer, one tanker, nine submarines, two mine sweepers, and three freighters, as well as tugs and some smaller craft. Caroff, *Les débarquements alliés en afrique du nord*, 281–290; Charles de Gaulle, *Discours et messages*, tome 1, *Pendant la guerre: Juin 1940–janvier 1946* (Paris: Plon, 1970), 244. Quoted in Thomas Vasset and Philippe Vial, "Toulon 27 novembre 1942. Rien qu'une défaite, ou plus qu'une défaite?," 4

(unpublished manuscript); SHD-GR, 2H 194, General (Georges) Barré, "Renseignements sur la région de Ferryville–Bizerte," 8 December 1942; Harold Callender, "Derrien on Trial at Secret Session," *New York Times*, 11 May 1944, www.nytimes.com/1944/05/11/archives/derrien-on-trial-at-secret-session-defense-protests-that-admiral.html.

113. Gabriel Paul Auphan and Jacques Mordel, *The French Navy in World War II* (Annapolis: United States Naval Institute Press, 1959), 267–270. Auphan had been Vichy *Chef d'état-major des forces maritimes* or basically Chief of Naval Operations (CNO)/First Sea Lord, and from April 1942 *Secrétaire d'État à la Marine* and a Weygand protégé who was condemned for collaboration after the war. Mordel was the pseudonym of the military doctor Hervé Cras, who gained a considerable post-war reputation as a naval historian. Harold Callender, "Derrien Gets Life in Algiers Trial," *New York Times*, 13 May 1944, www.nytimes.com/1944/05/13/archives/derrien-gets-life-in-algiers-trial-guilty-of-failure-to-scuttle.html.
114. Charles de Gaulle, *Mémoires de guerre*, tome 2, *L'Unité 1942–1944* (Paris: Plon, 1994), 332.
115. Belle, *L'Opération* Torch *et la Tunisie*, 140–150; Spivak and Leoni, *La campagne de Tunisie, 1942–1943*, 110–111; Levisse-Touzé, *L'Afrique du Nord dans la guerre*, 273; Callender, "Derrien on Trial at Secret Session."
116. Costagliola, *Darlan*, 258; Caroff, *Les débarquements alliés en afrique du nord*, 293.
117. This was probably because, on 29 November, Derrien had complained that he had received no instructions from the Admiralty in Vichy for fifteen days. The next day, Auphan told him "The orders haven't changed: resist Anglo-Saxon aggression; don't act against Axis forces." Caroff, *Les débarquements alliés en afrique du nord*, 266–282.
118. SHD-GR, 2H 194.
119. Paxton, *Parades and Politics at Vichy*, 370.
120. Belle, *L'Opération* Torch *et la Tunisie*, 131, 140–150; Spivak and Leoni, *La campagne de Tunisie, 1942–1943*, 110; Caroff, *Les débarquements alliés en afrique du nord*, 274; SHD 5P 2, Viard report, 25.
121. Caroff, *Les débarquements alliés en afrique du nord*, 275–277, 281.
122. Callender, "Derrien Gets Life in Algiers Trial." In fact, Derrien, who was by then totally blind, was released from prison in 1946 and died days later in a Constantine hospital.
123. F. W. Deakin, *The Brutal Friendship: Mussolini, Hitler and the Fall of Italian Fascism* (New York: Harper and Row, 1962), 282.
124. John Gooch, *Mussolini's War: Fascist Italy from Triumph to Collapse 1935–1943* (London: Penguin, 2020), 353–354.
125. Horst Boog, Werner Rahn, Reinhard Stumpf, and Bernd Wegner, *Germany and the Second World War*, vol. 6, *The Global War: Widening of the Conflict into a World War and the Shift of the Initiative, 1941–1943* (Oxford: Clarendon, 2001), 794, 813.
126. These included Hitler's decision to declare war on Poland in September 1939; the invasion of Norway, where he sacrificed much of his surface fleet that would have been vital if he planned to invade the UK; the decision to engage in the Mediterranean, a theater in which his forces were poorly configured to fight; Barbarossa, the invasion of the USSR; the declaration of war on the United States; and the failure to take Malta. Jacques Sapir, Frank Stora, and Loïc Mahé, *1940: Et si la France avait continué la guerre . . .* (Paris: Tallandier, 2010), 35–36.
127. Simon Ball, "The Mediterranean and North Africa, 1940–1944," in John Ferris and Evan Mawdsley (eds.), *The Second World War*, volume I, *Fighting the War* (Cambridge: Cambridge University Press, 2015), 381.
128. Sean McMeekin, *Stalin's War: A New History of World War II* (New York: Basic Books, 2021), 458–459.
129. Gooch, *Mussolini's War*, 363. Hitler did carry out some tactical withdrawals on the Eastern front that freed up reserves to retake Kharkov and Belgorod on the upper Donets in March. McMeekin, *Stalin's War*, 458.
130. Levisse-Touzé, *L'Afrique du Nord dans la guerre*, 271–272.
131. Ball, "The Mediterranean and North Africa," 388.
132. Gooch, *Mussolini's War*, 354–355.
133. Denis Mack Smith, *Mussolini* (New York: Knopf, 1986), 277, 287–290; Deakin, *The Brutal Friendship*, 145, 147; Albert Kesselring, *Kesselring: A Soldier's Record* (New York: William Morrow, 1954), 174.
134. I. S. O. Playfair, *The Mediterranean and the Middle East*, vol. IV, *The Destruction of the Axis Forces in Africa* (London: HMSO, 1954), 171, 239; Richard J. Overy, *The Air War, 1939–1945* (New York: Stein and Day, 1980), 44–45; Ehlers, Jr., *The Mediterranean Air War*, 254.
135. Rolf, *The Bloody Road to Tunis*, 87.
136. Unlike the Allies, the Axis never organized an integrated air command for the Mediterranean, so that these German transport losses became yet another source of discord between Berlin and Rome. Rolf, *The Bloody Road to Tunis*, 88–89.

137. Axis forces received only 60,000 to 70,000 tons of supplies a month, half what they needed to sustain offensive operations. Playfair, *The Mediterranean and the Middle East*, vol. IV, 189–190, 240–241, 274, 289; Mack Smith, *Mussolini*, 282.
138. Bastian Matteo Scianna, "Rommel Almighty? Italian Assessments of the 'Desert Fox' during and after the Second World War," *The Journal of Military History*, 83/1 (January 2018), 131–145.
139. F. H. Hinsley, *British Intelligence in the Second World War: Its Influence on Strategy and Operations* (New York: Cambridge University Press, 1981), vol. II, 576–577; B. H. Liddell Hart, *The Rommel Papers* (New York: Harcourt, Brace, 1953), 404; Rolf, *The Bloody Road to Tunis*, 53–54; Alan Moorehead, *The Desert War: The North African Campaign 1940–1943* (London and New York: Penguin, 2001), 516, 594.
140. Moorehead, *The Desert War*, 482.
141. Rolf, *The Bloody Road to Tunis*, 74.
142. Carlo D'Este, *Eisenhower: A Soldier's Life* (New York: Henry Holt, 2002), 406; Stephen E. Ambrose, *The Supreme Commander: The War Years of Dwight D. Eisenhower* (New York: Doubleday, 1970), 161–163; Stephen E. Ambrose, *Eisenhower: Soldier, General of the Army, President Elect, 1890–1952* (New York: Simon & Schuster, 1983), 220–221; Matthew Jones, *Britain, the United States, and the Mediterranean War, 1942–44* (New York: St. Martin's Press, 1996), 49–53.
143. Rolf, *The Bloody Road to Tunis*, 33, 41, 67, 226. In 1944, Montgomery would relieve Anderson of command of the Second British army in Overlord, and replace him with General Miles Dempsey. Bernard Montgomery, *The Memoirs of Field Marshal Montgomery* (London: Collins, 1958), 143, 151, 240–241, 522; Nigel Hamilton, *Master of the Battlefield: Monty's War Years, 1942–1944* (New York: McGraw-Hill, 1983), 378–379; Nigel Hamilton, *Monty: The Making of a General, 1887–1942* (New York: McGraw-Hill, 1981), 173.
144. Hinsley, *British Intelligence in the Second World War*, vol. II, 574; Playfair, *The Mediterranean and the Middle East*, vol. IV, 182–183, 189–190.
145. The following are the phases of the Tunisia campaign proposed by Pierre Lesouef, "La crise de novembre 1942 en Afrique française du nord et la campagne de Tunisie," in Fondation pour les études de défense nationale, Institut d'histoire des conflits contemporains, Service historique de l'Armée de terre, Service historique de la Marine, and Service historique de l'Armée de l'air, *Les armées française pendant la seconde guerre mondiale 1939–1945* (Paris: École nationale supérieure de techniques avancées, 1986), pp. 305–315, 310. Other authors propose slightly different but more or less congruent dates.
146. Vigneras, *Rearming the French* (Washington, D.C.: Center of Military History, 1989), 24.
147. The closest Allied airfield to the front was at Tébessa, 60 miles away. While its dirt landing strip was often put out of commission by the winter rains, an overlay of perforated steel matting called Marston Mat on dirt runways made airfields like Tébessa serviceable in the wet Tunisian winter. Ehlers, *The Mediterranean Air War*, 259–263, 267, 270–271; Richard Overy, *Blood and Ruins: The Last Imperial War* (London: Viking, 2022), 457.
148. Rolf, *The Bloody Road to Tunis*, 64–65.
149. Spivak and Leoni, *La campagne de Tunisie, 1942–1943*, 157–159, 205–206.
150. Harry C. Butcher, *My Three Years with Eisenhower: The Personal Diary of Captain Harry C. Butcher, USNR. Naval Aide to General Eisenhower, 1942 to 1945* (London and Toronto: William Heinemann, 1946), 202.
151. Caroff, *Les débarquements alliés en afrique du nord*, 71–74.
152. Belle, *L'Opération* Torch *et la Tunisie*, 121; Spivak and Leoni, *La campagne de Tunisie, 1942–1943*, 139.
153. Butcher, *My Three Years with Eisenhower*, 210.
154. Butcher, *My Three Years with Eisenhower*, 192.
155. Notin, *Maréchal Juin*, 237.
156. Spivak and Leoni, *La campagne de Tunisie, 1942–1943*, 147–148.
157. First Army resistance at Lille in 1940 is credited with allowing 100,000 men to escape at Dunkirk.
158. SHD-GR, 5P 50, 21 November 1942. The crews of French tanks were ordered to paint tricolors on their sides, rear, and front.
159. Lesouef, "La crise de novembre 1942 en Afrique française du nord et la campagne du Tunisie," 311; Vigneras, *Rearming the French*, 24.
160. Belle, *L'Opération* Torch *et la Tunisie*, 115–120.
161. Butcher, *My Three Years with Eisenhower*, 203.
162. Ambrose, *The Supreme Commander*, 171. The French troops included the Armée d'Afrique (63,000 men), consisting of the following units: the Division de marche de Constantine (DMC), commanded by General Welvert (who was killed on 10 April 1943 and replaced by Schwartz); the Division de marche d'Alger (DMA), under General Conne; the Division de marche d'Oran (DMO), under General Boisseau; the Division de marche du Maroc (DMM), under General Mathenet; the 1re Brigade légère mécanique

(1re BLM), under General Le Couteulx de Caumont; and the Corps franc d'Afrique (CFA), under General de Montsabert.

163. Robert O. Paxton, *Vichy France: Old Guard and New Order, 1940–1944* (London: Barrie & Jenkins, 1972), 282.
164. Harymbat, *Les Européens d'Afrique du Nord dans les armées de la libération française*, 47.
165. Le Gac, *Vaincre sans gloire*, 129–131.
166. SHD-GR, 5P 51 "Rapport résumant la mise sur pied de l'armée d'ALG dans la 19e région à la suite des événements des 8–10 novembre," 30 November 1942; 5P 52, Bulletin du renseignement no. 3, 26 November 1942; Le Gac, *Vaincre sans gloire*, 105–108.
167. Le Gac, *Vaincre sans gloire*, 130.
168. Richard Bennaïm, *Le Journal du soldat juif* (Lormont: Le Bord de L'Eau, 2017), 171.
169. Romain Durand, *De Giraud à de Gaulle: Les Corps francs d'Afrique* (Paris: Éditions L'Harmattan, 1999), 47–49; Robert Dallek, *Franklin D. Roosevelt and American Foreign Policy, 1932–1945* (Oxford: Oxford University Press, 1995), 366; SHD-GR, 5P 50, 10 February 1943.
170. Tarbé de Saint-Hardouin to foreign relations; Rigault to political and internal affairs; and Henri d'Astier to intelligence and military security; while Lemaigre-Dubreuil was dispatched on a mission to Washington with Béthouart to hammer out the details of French rearmament.
171. The *Chantiers de la jeunesse* were work camps for twenty-year-old males created by Vichy in lieu of military service. See Porch, *Defeat and Division*, 299–305.
172. Durand, *De Giraud à de Gaulle*, 27–29.
173. Levisse-Touzé, *L'Afrique du Nord dans la guerre*, 268–271, 276–277.
174. Harold Macmillan, *War Diaries: Politics and War in the Mediterranean January 1943–May 1945* (London: Macmillan, 1984), 45.
175. Butcher, *My Three Years with Eisenhower*, 212.
176. Général André Beaufre, *Mémoires 1920–1940–1945* (Paris: Presses de la Cité, 1965), 298, 277.
177. Spivak and Leoni, *La campagne de Tunisie, 1942–1943*, 207 and Introduction.
178. Levisse-Touzé, *L'Afrique du Nord dans la guerre*, 264–268.
179. Durand, *De Giraud à de Gaulle*, 71.
180. Moorehead, *The Desert War*, 529.
181. Lapouge, *De Sétif à Marseille, par Cassino*, 37–39.
182. Durand, *De Giraud à de Gaulle*, 27.
183. Butcher, *My Three Years with Eisenhower*, 192–193.
184. Moorehead, *The Desert War*, 481–482.
185. Paxton, *Vichy France*, 282–284.
186. Among the Vichy refugees was arch appeaser turned advocate for Franco-German collaboration Pierre-Étienne Flandin. There was also the "flabby and unpleasing" and "far from subtle" Marcel Peyrouton, once Vichy interior minister, named to replace the unacceptable Châtel as governor general of Algeria. Another former Vichy interior minister, Pierre Picheu, reached Algiers through Spain, as did Maurice Couve de Murville, a high official in the Vichy finance ministry and future French Prime Minister. Military men included defeated generals such as Alphonse Georges, who was recruited to bolster Giraud's brains-trust. Paxton, *Vichy France*, 104; Butcher, *My Three Years with Eisenhower*, 214; Moorehead, *The Desert War*, 481–482.
187. Lapouge, *De Sétif à Marseille, par Cassino*, 39–45.
188. Lapouge, *De Sétif à Marseille, par Cassino*, 46.
189. Lapouge, *De Sétif à Marseille, par Cassino*, 46ff.
190. Juin, *Mémoires*, tome 1, 128–132.
191. Lapouge, *De Sétif à Marseille, par Cassino*, 51.
192. The Private Papers of Albert Rupert, 16–17.
193. Lapouge, *De Sétif à Marseille, par Cassino*, 53–54, 61.
194. Juin, *Mémoires*, tome 1, 134–135.
195. Spivak and Leoni, *La campagne de Tunisie, 1942–1943*, 153, 157–158.
196. Juin, *Mémoires*, tome 1, 136–141.
197. Lapouge, *De Sétif à Marseille, par Cassino*, 50–56.
198. SHD-GR, 2H 228 TUNISIA "Récit de guerre du Captaine X . . . Commandant la 9e compagnie du Régiment de Tirailleurs Tunisiens," 14 March 1943.
199. Durand, *De Giraud à de Gaulle*, 143.
200. "Operation Satin," planned on Eisenhower's initiative during 6–11 January 1934, was canceled during the Anfa conference. Spivak and Leoni, *La campagne de Tunisie, 1942–1943*, 207.
201. Juin, *Mémoires*, tome 1, 138–139; Notin, *Maréchal Juin*, 235–237.

202. Spivak and Leoni, *La campagne de Tunisie, 1942–1943*, 166–170.
203. The Private Papers of Albert Rupert, 22–30.
204. Lesouef, "La crise de novembre 1942 en Afrique française du nord et la campagne de Tunisie," 311.
205. Butcher, *My Three Years with Eisenhower*, 211; Spivak and Leoni, *La campagne de Tunisie, 1942–1943*, 159; Vigneras, *Rearming the French*, 60.
206. Moorehead, *The Desert War*, 511–513.
207. Lapouge, *De Sétif à Marseille, par Cassino*, 63–75.
208. R. L. DiNardo, *Germany's Panzer Arm* (Westport: Greenwood Press, 1997), 107.
209. "Rapport de Général de Division Mathenet Commandant 1e Division de marche du Maroc sur les operations des 18, 19, 20 janvier 1943," 3 February 1943, SHD-GR, 11P 3; Spivak and Leoni, *La campagne de Tunisie, 1942–1943*, 192–202; Juin, *Mémoires*, tome 1, 146–151; Rolf, *The Bloody Road to Tunis*, 77–80.
210. Butcher, *My Three Years with Eisenhower*, 212.
211. Butcher, *My Three Years with Eisenhower*, 212.
212. Rolf, *The Bloody Road to Tunis*, 83–84.
213. Spivak and Leoni, *La campagne de Tunisie, 1942–1943*, 202.
214. The French XIX Corps under Koeltz became the *Corps d'armée français* (CAF) on 1 February that integrated a 16,000-strong *groupement français* under General Maurice Mathenet built around the *Division de marche du Maroc*, and from 10 March that of Constantine. The 1st US Infantry Division (ID) under Terry Allen, reinforced by elements of the *Division de marche d'Alger* under Colonel Pierre Conne, much of which was sent back into Algeria to be reequipped in February, was also attached to the CAF. SHD-GR, 5P 19, 11 February 1943.
215. Moorehouse, *The Desert War*, 530.
216. Notin, *Maréchal Juin*, 238–240; Juin, *Mémoires*, tome 1, 151–153; Spivak and Leoni, *La campagne de Tunisie, 1942–1943*, 237–239.
217. Butcher, *My Three Years with Eisenhower*, 226.
218. Axis troops in Tunisia required 140,000 tons of supplies every month, which was beyond Italian capabilities. The Italians alternated fast and slow convoys on regular schedules tracked by the RAF. The Italian merchant marine counted only six large tankers in its depleted inventory. This totally inadequate effort was supplemented by 440 Luftwaffe transport aircraft. By February, the Axis estimated Allied air strength at 2,769 planes, to 837 Luftwaffe and 100 Italian. The Axis lacked enough planes to maintain air superiority over their Tunisian bridgehead, support the Mareth line, protect convoys from Naples and North African ports, and accompany night bombing missions against Algerian harbors. Meanwhile, the Allies had set air priorities – first, gain air superiority by bombing Axis airfields, and then concentrate on the Axis convoys. Coastal areas were divided into fighter sectors with early warning radar. Allied convoys remained outside of Ju 88 air range during the day, while German bomber crews lacked the night bombing skills to damage Algerian harbors, and instead became easy prey for Allied fighters. U-boats were harassed by anti-submarine warfare (ASW) patrols, while having no air reconnaissance to help them locate ship targets. On 30 January, Admiral Erich Raeder resigned in protest over Hitler's refusal to take the Mediterranean theater more seriously. Ehlers, *The Mediterranean Air War*, 276–278.
219. Juin, *Mémoires*, tome 1, 153.
220. According to the French official history, Fredendall, Koeltz, and Welvert knew that the attack was coming. They simply believed that its objective was further north at Pichon. Spivak and Leoni, *La campagne de Tunisie, 1942–1943*, 220–226, 235. For the American role in the action, see Rolf, *The Bloody Road to Tunis*, 78–79.
221. Juin, *Mémoires*, tome 1, 154.
222. Lida Mayo, *The Ordnance Department: On Beachhead and Battlefront* (Washington, D.C.: Center of Military History, United States Army, 1966), 135–136.
223. Spivak and Leoni, *La campagne de Tunisie, 1942–1943*, 230, 240; Juin, *Mémoires*, tome 1, 15; Butcher, *My Three Years with Eisenhower*, 227.
224. Mayo, *The Ordnance Department*, 135–136.
225. Butcher, *My Three Years with Eisenhower*, 229.
226. Juin, *Mémoires*, tome 1, 155–156.
227. Ehlers, *The Mediterranean Air War*, 279.
228. Juin, *Mémoires*, tome 1, 156–159.
229. Butcher, *My Three Years with Eisenhower*, 229, 231.
230. Rolf, *The Bloody Road to Tunis*, 127–143.
231. Lapouge, *De Sétif à Marseille, par Cassino*, 76–84.
232. Durand, *De Giraud à de Gaulle*, 44–46.
233. Durand, *De Giraud à de Gaulle*, 24–25.

234. Général Joseph Goislard de Monsabert, *Notes de guerre* (Hélette: Éditions Jean Curutchet, 1999), 83, 85, 118.
235. SHD-GR, 11P 257, 1 and 3 December 1942; de Monsabert, *Notes de guerre*, 93.
236. SHD-GR, 5P 18, "Projet d'organisation des corps francs d'Afrique."
237. SHD-GR, 5P 18, "Fiche pour le chef d'état major."
238. SHD-GR, 11P 257, Ordre no. 2, 25 November 1942; Durand, *De Giraud à de Gaulle*, 27–32.
239. SHD-GR, 11P 257, 6 January 1943 letter from Prioux about recruiting those eligible for the call-up including reservists; 8 July 1943 letter complaining of recruitment of Foreign Legionnaires in Oran. And Noguès' letter cited below.
240. SHD-GR, 11P 257, 21 December 1942, 12 and 16 January 1943. A letter of 21 March 1943 from Giraud forbade Colonel Magnan to enlist forty interned Spaniards, reminding him that he was allowed to recruit in work camps but not internment camps.
241. SHD-GR, 11P 257, 23 December 1942 and 4 February 1943.
242. Quoted in Harymbat, *Les Européens d'Afrique du Nord dans les armées de la libération française*, 61.
243. Noguès objected that the CFA had recruited 200 Muslims in Marrakech, some of whom were reservists, and eligible for mobilization in regular *tirailleur* units or as *goumiers*. He seemed especially upset that these Muslims were attracted away from regular units by the generous recruitment bonus paid by the CFA. SHD-GR, 11P 257, two letters dated 6 February 1943. Also coded message "From Gustave to Nestor," 1 January 1943.
244. SHD-GR, 11P 257, 19 December 1942 and 23 January 1943.
245. Jean-François Muracciole, *Les Français libres: L'autre Résistance* (Paris: Tallandier, 2009), 156.
246. SHD-GR, 11P 257, Juin letter of 17 January 1943. On sailors, see Monsabert's letter of 16 December 1942 and Giraud's 20 December refusal. There was a long correspondence of "section féminine" letters of 21 March and late May–early June 1943. Georges Elgozy, *La vérité sur mon Corps Franc d'Afrique*, 71, 73, 82, 88–89.
247. A. J. Liebling, "Quest for Mollie," in A. J. Liebling, *World War II Writings: The Road Back to Paris. Mollie and Other War Pieces, Uncollected War Journalism. Normandy Revisited* (New York: Literary Classics of the United States, 2008).
248. De Monsabert, *Notes de guerre*, 116.
249. Spivak and Leoni, *La campagne de Tunisie, 1942–1943*, 311.
250. Elgozy, *La vérité sur mon Corps Franc d'Afrique*, 118.
251. De Monsabert, *Notes de guerre*, 103, 107.
252. Durand, *De Giraud à de Gaulle*, 74, 83–86.
253. SHD-GR, 11P 257, 12 and 21 January, and 9 April 1943.
254. Liebling, "Quest for Mollie," 573.
255. Durand, *De Giraud à de Gaulle*, 47, 63–64, 69–70, 183.
256. Rolf, *The Bloody Road to Tunis*, 76.
257. Rolf, *The Bloody Road to Tunis*, 157.
258. SHD-GR, 11P 257, Monsabert's letter of 16 January 1943 requesting trainers from the British army; Durand, *De Giraud à de Gaulle*, 120–121, 196–200; Elgozy, *La vérité sur mon Corps Franc d'Afrique*, 96–97.
259. Spivak and Leoni, *La campagne de Tunisie, 1942–1943*, 312–314; Durand, *De Giraud à de Gaulle*, 95–107, 117.
260. The NAAFI were organized in 1921 to run canteens, messes, bars, and shops for armed forces personnel.
261. Durand, *De Giraud à de Gaulle*, 43–45, 49–78, 127, 161, 163.
262. "Note au sujet des cadres coloniaux fournis au Corps Francs," 9 April 1943. See also SHD-GR, 11P 257, 12 and 21 January, and 9 April 1943.
263. Durand, *De Giraud à de Gaulle*, 117–118, 124, 165; Elgozy, *La vérité sur mon Corps Franc d'Afrique*, 90, 95–96.
264. Rolf, *The Bloody Road to Tunis*, 122.
265. Notin, *Maréchal Juin*, 243.
266. Juin, *Mémoires*, tome 1, 160.
267. SHD-GR, 11P 3, Circular no. 3, "Sur l'entrainement," 8 March 1943. This appears to be a translation of a general Allied circular that went out from the XIX Corps on 15 March.
268. SHD-GR, 11P 3, "Mémoire concernant les opérations recentes sur le front tunisien. Résumé d'une communication récente de l'État-Major Américain."
269. SHD-GR, 228, Tunisia, 10 March 1943, "Note sur l'Instruction no. 17."
270. Montgomery, *The Memoirs of Field Marshal Montgomery*, 151.
271. SHD-GR, 5P 49, 8 March 1943.

272. SHD-GR, 5P 39, Lorber report, 12–13.
273. Nigel Hamilton, *Master of the Battlefield: Monty's War Years, 1942–1944* (New York: McGraw-Hill, 1983), 163.
274. Colonel Christodoulos Tsigantes had graduated from the French staff college in the 1930s, but fled into the Foreign Legion after being given a life sentence following his participation in an unsuccessful March 1935 military putsch. Jean-Noël Vincent, *Les forces françaises dans la lutte contre l'Axe en Afrique*, tome I, *Les forces françaises libres en Afrique 1940–1943* (Vincennes: Ministère de la défense, État-major de l'armée de terre, Service historique, 1983), 319–321; SHD-GR, 4P 13, "France combattante. Commissariat national à la guerre; État major – 3ème bureau. Annexe 1 à Tableaux d'Effectifs," 8 February 1943.
275. André Martel, *Leclerc: Le soldat et la politique* (Paris: Albin Michel, 1998), 194–197; Vincent, *Les forces françaises dans la lutte contre l'Axe en Afrique*, tome I, 323–324.
276. Quoting the *Chicago Daily News*, Butcher, *Three Years with Eisenhower*, 249.
277. Chantal Metzger, *L'empire colonial français dans la stratégie du troisième Reich (1936–1945)* (Paris: Direction des Archives, Ministère des Affaires étrangères; Brussels, Peter Lang, 2002), vol. I, 614–664, 686.
278. Alan J. Levine, *The War against Rommel's Supply Lines, 1942–1943* (Westport and London: Praeger, 1999), 180–181; Rolf, *The Bloody Road to Tunis*, 230.
279. Butcher, *My Three Years with Eisenhower*, 242; Jean Monnet, *Mémoires* (Paris: Fayard, 1976), 223, cited in Metzger, *Le Maghreb dans la guerre*, 236.
280. Metzger, *Le Maghreb dans la guerre*, 195–210.
281. Belkacem Recham, *Les Musulmans algériens dans l'armée française (1919–1945)* (Paris: Éditions L'Harmattan, 1996), 233.
282. Lapouge, *De Sétif à Marseille, par Cassino*, 84–92.
283. Durand, *De Giraud à de Gaulle*, 126.
284. Martel, *Leclerc*, 184–190.
285. Jean-Christophe Notin, *Leclerc: Le croisé de la France libre* (Paris: Perrin, 2015), 86–99; Martel, *Leclerc*, 200–202.
286. Spivak and Leoni, *La campagne de Tunisie, 1942–1943*, 245–262; Juin, *Mémoires*, tome 1, 164–165.
287. Stanley Sandler, *"Cease Resistance: It's Good For You": A History of U.S. Army Combat Psychological Operations* (self-published, 1999), 54.
288. Butcher, *My Three Years with Eisenhower*, 243.
289. Butcher, *My Three Years with Eisenhower*, 249.
290. Juin, *Mémoires*, tome 1, 169.
291. Butcher, *My Three Years with Eisenhower*, 249.
292. Moorehead, *The Desert War*, 579.
293. Ehlers, *The Mediterranean Air War*, 282–283.
294. Rolf, *The Bloody Road to Tunis*, 246–247.
295. Elgozy, *La vérité sur mon Corps franc d'Afrique*, 168.
296. Rolf, *The Bloody Road to Tunis*, 270.
297. Rolf, *The Bloody Road to Tunis*, 248–250; Elgozy, *La vérité sur mon Corps franc d'Afrique*, 117–118, 168–174.
298. Playfair, *The Mediterranean and the Middle East*, vol. IV, 443.
299. Moorehead, *The Desert War*, 617.
300. SHD-GR, 11P 257, Ordre no. 65 bis.
301. Ehlers, *The Mediterranean Air War*, 285.
302. Caleb Milne, *"I Dream of the Day . . .": Letters from Caleb Milne. Africa, 1942–1943* (Woodstock, NY: privately published, 1944), 120.
303. Pierre Giolitto, *Volontaires français sous l'uniform allemand* (Paris: Tempus Perrin, 2007), 305; Levisse-Touzé, *L'Afrique du Nord dans la guerre*, 336–337. Three of the forty-three captured soldiers were from Alsace-Lorraine and may have been impressed into service with the German forces. SHD-GR, 5P 18, 27 April 1943. For captured Muslims, some of whom were NCOs in the French forces, see SHD-GR, 5P 18, "Rapport," 21 July 1943.
304. Spivak and Leoni, *La campagne de Tunisie, 1942–1943*, 279, 285–286, 321–325; Juin, *Mémoires*, tome 1, 170–171; Durand, *De Giraud à de Gaulle*, 127–141.
305. Moorehead, *The Desert War*, 618–621; Rolf, *The Bloody Road to Tunis*, 274–275; Omar Bradley, *A Soldier's Story* (New York: Random House, 1999), 109–110. For POWs, see SHD 5P 35, 16 October and 4 December 1943.
306. Butcher, *My Three Years with Eisenhower*, 267.
307. Butcher, *My Three Years with Eisenhower*, 254, 262.
308. De Monsabert, *Notes de guerre*, 122.

309. De Monsabert, *Notes de guerre*, 107, 116, 124–125.
310. Notin, *Maréchal Juin*, 301.
311. Louis Xueref, "Mémoires d'outre-mer. 1942–1943 (Autour de la campagne de Tunisie). Souvenirs d'une tranche de vie," http://tunisie-france.pagesperso-orange.fr/souvenirs_souvenirs.htm.
312. Durand, *De Giraud à de Gaulle*, 76; SHD-GR, 2H 194. Barré report 2 April 1943, p. 5.
313. Metzger, *L'empire colonial français dans la stratégie du troisième Reich*, 682–685.
314. SHD-GR, 2H 194, Barré report, 2 April 1943; Le Gac, *Vaincre sans gloire*, 108–114, 135.
315. Fred Kupferman, *Le Procès de Vichy – Pucheu, Pétain, Laval* (Paris: Éditions Complexe, 2006), 81.
316. Charles de Gaulle, *Mémoires de guerre*, tome III, *Le salut, 1944–1946* (Paris: Plon, 1959), 130.
317. Notin, *Maréchal Juin*, 247.
318. Butcher, *My Three Years with Eisenhower*, 164.
319. Julian Jackson, "General de Gaulle and His Enemies: Anti-Gaullism in France since 1940," *Transactions of the Royal Historical Society*, 9 (1999), 55.
320. Butcher, *My Three Years with Eisenhower*, 261.
321. Ehlers, *The Mediterranean Air War*, 286–288.
322. Chantal Metzger, *L'empire colonial français dans la stratégie du troisième Reich*, vol. I, 685–686.
323. Rolf, *The Bloody Road to Tunis*, 285.
324. SHD-GR, 7P 81, "Fiche au sujet des pertes de l'armée française," 10 May 1945. The high percentage of MIA to KIA would seem to suggest that many French-led troops became POWs. In which case, the official figures would more likely correspond to Belle's figures of 7,000 recovered POWs at the end of the campaign. Or it may be that many Muslim troops simply deserted or allowed themselves to be taken prisoner. This is especially striking, as the same document lists only 996 MIA, 791 of whom were "indigènes," for the *Corps expéditionnaire français* (CEF) that numbered over 100,000 men in the subsequent Italian campaign. Belle estimates that the 2,156 KIA and 10,276 wounded, plus 7,000 POWs who were recouped, were similar to US casualties. Belle, *L'Opération* Torch *et la Tunisie*, 215.
325. Vigneras, *Rearming the French*, 58, citing a post-war French study. A 16 June report estimated that 195 officers and 8,000 NCOs and soldiers had been killed. "Réponse à note No. 1102/4 du 15/06/43." A 23 November 1943 report lists 351 officers and 9,497 killed since 8 November 1943. These would include losses in the Torch, Tunisia, Sicily, and Corsica campaigns. But as the number of French killed in the other campaigns was comparatively minor, the vast majority of these deaths would have occurred in Tunisia. SHD-GR, 5P 19, "Renseignements hebdomadaires destinés au Q.C. des forces alliées."
326. SHD GR, 7P 81, 4 May 1945; Spivak and Leoni, *La campagne de Tunisie, 1942–1943*, 351. Recham offers the figure of 5,187 killed, of whom 3,458 were Muslims, and 7,442 wounded, of whom 4,900 were Muslims. Recham, *Les Musulmans algériens dans l'armée française*, 242. Another estimate of French KIA in Tunisia, excluding the Free French, was 2,300. Lt. Col. P. Santini, "Étude statistique sur les pertes au cours de la guerre 1939–1945," *Revue du Corps de Santé Militaire*, 10/1 (March 1954), quoted in Vigneras, *Rearming the French*, 403.
327. Juin, *Mémoires*, tome 1, 172–173.

CHAPTER 2

1. Harold Macmillan, *War Diaries: Politics and War in the Mediterranean January 1943–May 1945* (London: Macmillan, 1984), 88.
2. Harry C. Butcher, *My Three Years with Eisenhower: The Personal Diary of Captain Harry C. Butcher, USNR. Naval Aide to General Eisenhower, 1942 to 1945* (London and Toronto: William Heinemann, 1946), 263.
3. Stephen E. Ambrose, *Supreme Commander. The War Years of Dwight D. Eisenhower* (New York: Random House, 1970), 73.
4. Omar Bradley, *A Soldier's Story* (New York: Henry Holt, 1951), 109.
5. Macmillan, *War Diaries*, 89.
6. Macmillan, *War Diaries*, 88–92.
7. Butcher, *My Three Years with Eisenhower*, 264.
8. Bradley, *A Soldier's Story*, 109.
9. Butcher, *My Three Years with Eisenhower*, 264.
10. Macmillan, *War Diaries*, 89.
11. Erwin Fuchs, "May You Live in Interesting Times. Part II. The Foreign Legion Years 1939–1944," unpublished diary originally written in Hungarian. This portion seems to have been translated into English in 1992 and is in the author's possession. From pp. 169–170.

12. Romain Durand, *De Giraud à de Gaulle: Les Corps francs d'Afrique* (Paris: Éditions L'Harmattan, 1999), 143–144, 154.
13. André Martel, *Leclerc: Le soldat et la politique* (Paris: Albin Michel, 1998), 209.
14. As de Gaulle was about to depart London for Algiers on 4 April, he received a request from Eisenhower asking him to delay his arrival while the great battle for Tunisia was in progress. This left de Gaulle furious with the American Supreme Commander, when, in fact, the person behind the request was Catroux, who feared that, if de Gaulle appeared before an agreement had been worked out with Giraud, an explosion would ensue, whose result might be catastrophic for the reunion of the French camp. Jean-Louis Crémieux-Brilhac, *La France libre: De l'appel du 18 juin à la libération* (Paris: Gallimard, 2013), tome 1, 613
15. Jean-Christophe Notin, *Maréchal Juin* (Paris: Tallandier, 2015), 251; Martel, *Leclerc*, 203–209.
16. Marcel Vigneras, *Rearming the French* (Washington, D.C.: Center of Military History, United States Army, 1989), 404.
17. Robert Belot, *Aux frontières de la liberté: Vichy–Madrid–Alger–Londres. S'évader de la France sous l'Occupation* (Paris: Fayard, 1998), 543.
18. Chantal Metzger, *Le Maghreb dans la guerre 1939–1945* (Paris: Armand Colin, 2018), 256–258, 279–281.
19. Pierre Billotte, *Trente ans d'humour avec de Gaulle* (Paris: Éditions Mengès, 1978), 78.
20. Michael S. Neiberg, *When France Fell: The Vichy Crisis and the Fate of the Anglo-American Alliance* (Cambridge, MA: Harvard University Press, 2021), 216.
21. David Rolf, *The Bloody Road to Tunis: Destruction of the Axis Forces in North Africa: November 1942–May 1943* (London: Greenhill Books, 2001), 288–289.
22. Stalin did prefer to stay in telephone contact with his commanders at Stalingrad. Nevertheless, "the idea that Stalin did not place a high priority on meeting him did not occur to Roosevelt." Sean McMeekin, *Stalin's War: A New History of World War II* (New York: Basic Books, 2021), 438, 456.
23. Phillips Payson O'Brien, *The Second Most Powerful Man in the World: The Life of Admiral William D. Leahy, Roosevelt's Chief of Staff* (New York: Dutton, 2019), 203.
24. In June 1943, 30 percent of Axis troops could not be employed against the USSR, because they were tied down by fighting elsewhere, or by the threat of Allied invasion of Southern and Western Europe, a percentage that would inch closer to parity in the course of the year, as Hitler was forced to redeploy his forces to counter the invasion of Italy, replace the Italians in Greece and the Balkans, and reinforce his Atlantic Wall. In contrast, Moscow's neutrality pact with Japan and Stalin's refusal to aid Chiang left the Asia–Pacific theater largely the responsibility of the United States, which also supplied massive Lend–Lease aid to Moscow and, along with the UK, sustained an ever-growing strategic bombing campaign against Germany. McMeekin, *Stalin's War*, 467.
25. Andrew Buchanan, *American Grand Strategy in the Mediterranean during World War II* (Cambridge: Cambridge University Press, 2014), 86–87, 108.
26. Neiberg, *When France Fell*, 197.
27. Quoted in Julie Le Gac, *Vaincre sans gloire: Le corps expéditionnaire français en Italie (novembre 1942–juillet 1944)* (Paris: Les Belles Lettres/Ministère de la défense-DMPA, 2013), 23.
28. Le Gac, *Vaincre sans gloire*, 184–185.
29. Vigneras, *Rearming the French*, 24–34, 404.
30. Neiberg, *When France Fell*, 182, 205, 216, 218.
31. Buchanan, *American Grand Strategy in the Mediterranean during World War II*, 7–8, 87.
32. Jean Monnet, *Memoirs* (Garden City, NY: Doubleday & Company, 1978), 185. According to Robert Murphy, Monnet's appointment came over the objections of Secretary of State Cordell Hull, who pointed out that Monnet was a closet Gaullist who ended up promoting de Gaulle, not Giraud. Robert Murphy, *Diplomat among Warriors* (London: Collins, 1964), 223–234.
33. Julian Jackson, *De Gaulle* (Cambridge, MA: Harvard University Press, 2018), 251.
34. Jackson, *De Gaulle*, 252.
35. Murphy, *Diplomat among Warriors*, 213; André Martel argued that Giraud defended French sovereignty and with Murphy laid the basis for Lend Lease to be applied to France. André Martel (ed.), *Histoire militaire de la France*, tome 4, *De 1940 à nos jours* (Paris: Presses universitaires de France, 1994), 27.
36. Jean-Louis Crémieux-Brilhac, *La France libre: De l'appel du 18 juin à la libération* (Paris: Gallimard, 2013), tome 1, 582–583.
37. Jackson, *De Gaulle*, 254.
38. Charles de Gaulle, *Mémoires de guerre*, tome 2, *L'Unité, 1942–1944* (Paris: Plon, 1994), 343–344. Murphy wrote that de Gaulle was rebuffed by Giraud because at the time he was a suspect in Darlan's assassination, and because Giraud wanted to do nothing to jeopardize rearmament. Murphy, *Diplomat among Warriors*, 213.
39. Eventually published as Henri Giraud, *Mes évasions* (Paris: Juillard, 1946).

40. In his memoirs, de Gaulle states that he felt insulted that his scheduled post-Christmas visit to Washington had been canceled in the aftermath of Darlan's assassination, with the excuse that the American President had "prior engagements." Now it was Churchill who was inviting him to Morocco, not Roosevelt, with a view "to organize an interview between you and Giraud in discrete circumstances in favorable conditions." In fact, Eden had told him that the meeting was "to draw up common plans," to which *la France combattante* was obviously not to be a party. Instead, de Gaulle was to appear in Casablanca not as the legitimate representative of France, but as Churchill's protégé. He agreed to go, he says, only after the *Comité national* urged him that *la France combattante* must have a voice. De Gaulle, *Mémoires de guerre*, tome 2, 344–358; Jean Lacouture, *De Gaulle*, tome 1, *Le Rebelle 1890–1944* (Paris: Éditions du Seuil, 1984), 634.
41. On 17 January 1943, Eden had issued an "invitation" to de Gaulle to appear at Anfa. Initially, de Gaulle, who preferred to meet with Giraud discretely, had declined, and only changed his mind at the insistence of the Comité national français and high-level British pressure. Christine Levisse-Touzé, "Anfa," in François Broche, Georges Caïtucoli, and Jean-François Muracciole (eds.), *Dictionnaire de la France Libre* (Paris: Robert Laffont, 2010), 55–56.
42. Alan Moorehead, *The Desert War: The North African Campaign*, (London: Penguin, 2001), 540.
43. Général André Beaufre, *Mémoires 1920–1940–1945* (Paris: Presses de la Cité, 1965), 415.
44. Murphy, *Diplomat among Warriors*, 213–214, 220. In fact, Roosevelt had outraged the French of all persuasions, and alarmed the British, by hosting a dinner for the Sultan of Morocco during which independence and post-war economic relationships were discussed. Lacouture, *De Gaulle*, tome 1, 635.
45. McMeekin, *Stalin's War*, 440.
46. Robert Dallek, *Franklin D. Roosevelt and American Foreign Policy, 1932–1945* (New York and Oxford: Oxford University Press, 1995), 374, 376 note 18.
47. McMeekin, *Stalin's War*, 441, 453, 502.
48. Neiberg, *When France Fell*, 226, 233.
49. Jackson, *De Gaulle*, 307; Neiberg, *When France Fell*, 199.
50. Neiberg, *When France Fell*, 224, 232–233.
51. Neiberg, *When France Fell*, 217–218.
52. De Gaulle, *Mémoires de guerre*, tome 2, 352. De Gaulle was perhaps unaware that William Leahy "hated" him, an attitude that he communicated to the President. O'Brien, *The Second Most Powerful Man in the World*, 231.
53. This was the observation that John Maynard Keynes had made of Clemenceau at the Versailles Conference. John Maynard Keynes, *The Economic Consequences of the Peace* (New York: Harcourt, Brace and Howe, 1920), 38.
54. Neiberg, *When France Fell*, 220–221, 231.
55. Eric T. Jennings, *Free French Africa in World War II: The African Resistance* (Cambridge: Cambridge University Press, 2015), 45.
56. Neiberg, *When France Fell*, 61.
57. Lacouture, *De Gaulle*, tome 1, 638–639.
58. Jackson, *De Gaulle*, 256.
59. Muracciole subtracts "sovereignty forces" and imperial police. Jean-François Muracciole, *Les Français libres: L'autre Résistance* (Paris: Tallandier, 2009), 34–35.
60. Muracciole, *Les Français libres*, 34–37.
61. Martel, *Leclerc*, 205; Le Gac, *Vaincre sans gloire*, 147.
62. Lacouture, *De Gaulle*, tome 1, 676.
63. Many respected members of the French diaspora, such as Alexis Léger, former General Secretary of the Quai d'Orsay who fled to Washington in 1940 and commanded Roosevelt's ear in French affairs, or French Jewish intellectual Raymond Aron, worried, as did others, that de Gaulle aspired to dictatorial powers. When Daniel Mayer, founder of the *Comité d'action socialiste*, met de Gaulle in April 1943, he was "stunned" by a "long diatribe against *les Anglo-Saxons*," which Mayer worried hinted at de Gaulle's fascism. The "myth of BCRA-Gestapo," fanned by de Gaulle's detractors, had also been retailed by the US embassy in London in an attempt to discredit *la France libre* in the eyes of its British patrons. Robert Belot, *La Résistance sans de Gaulle* (Paris: Fayard, 2006), 521–533.
64. Macmillan, *War Diaries*, 122, 124.
65. Muracciole, *Les Français libres*, 143–144.
66. De Gaulle had dispatched Air Force General François d'Astier de la Vignerie on an official mission to gauge the possibilities of establishing a Gaullist presence in AFN in the aftermath of Torch. However, his contacts with René Capitant, the Algiers chief of the resistance network Combat, as well as with his brother Henri d'Astier and the Comte de Paris, caused Darlan and Giraud to prevail upon Eisenhower to force François

d'Astier to return to London. Sébastien Albertelli, *Les Services secrets du Général de Gaulle: Le BCRA 1940–1944* (Paris: Perrin, 2009), 246–250.

67. Vigneras, *Rearming the French*, 78.
68. Neiberg, *When France Fell*, 233.
69. Neiberg, *When France Fell*, 197.
70. Albertelli, *Les Services secrets du Général de Gaulle*, 252.
71. Albertelli, *Les Services secrets du Général de Gaulle*, 249–253.
72. Henri Giraud, *Un seul but – la victoire: Alger 1942–1944* (Paris: Juillard, 1949), 285, quoted in Belot, *La Résistance sans de Gaulle*, 336. Prior to "fusion" with former Vichy intelligence in AFN in October 1943, the BCRA in London was divided into "military" and "non-military" sections, an artificial division that Pierre Brossolette had convinced de Gaulle to abandon, in the process demonstrating how the French leader's view of intelligence had evolved, while Giraud clearly retained a limited view of intelligence as a source of military information. Sébastien Laurent, "Les guerres des services spéciaux en Afrique du Nord (novembre 1942–novembre 1944)," in Général Louis Rivet, *Carnets du chef des services secrets 1936–1944*, eds. Olivier Forcade and Sébastian Laurent (Paris: Nouveau Monde Éditions, 2010), 555.
73. Crémieux-Brilhac, *La France libre*, tome 1, 684–685.
74. Belot, *La Résistance sans de Gaulle*, 335–341.
75. Macmillan, *War Diaries*, 124, 150.
76. Crémieux-Brilhac, *La France libre*, tome 1, 687–695.
77. Le Gac, *Vaincre sans gloire*, 138.
78. Le Gac, *Vaincre sans gloire*, 185.
79. George F. Howe, *Northwest Africa: Seizing the Initiative in the West* (Washington, D.C.: Center of Military History, United States Army, 1993), 361.
80. Vigneras, *Rearming the French*, 80 and note.
81. Martel, *Leclerc*, 185.
82. Le Gac, *Vaincre sans gloire*, 147–154.
83. Martel, *Leclerc*, 203–206.
84. SHD-GR, 7P 111, Note-Circulaire 15 June 1943.
85. Neiberg, *When France Fell*, 226.
86. Martel, *Leclerc*, 211.
87. Martel, *Leclerc*, 210; Muracciole, *Les Français libres*, 240.
88. SHD-GR, 11P 257.
89. Frédéric Harymbat, *Les Européens d'Afrique du Nord dans les armées de la libération française (1942–1945)* (Paris: Éditions L'Harmattan, 2014), 123.
90. Durand, *De Giraud à de Gaulle*, 165–168.
91. Guillaume Piketty, *Français en résistance: Carnet de guerre, correspondances, journaux personnels* (Paris: Robert Laffont, 2009), 275–276.
92. The 9th Company of the 3rd Battalion of the *Régiment de Marche du Tchad*. Durand, *De Giraud à de Gaulle*, 190.
93. SHD-GR, 7P 59. "Declarations de Pierre Croissant, Sergent Chef au Corps Franc d'Afrique, recueillies par le Juge d'Instruction le 1e juillet 1943."
94. Durand, *De Giraud à de Gaulle*, 173; Muracciole, *Les Français libres*, 28–29, 156.
95. Harymbat, *Les Européens d'Afrique du Nord*, 123, 124, 127–128; Le Gac, *Vaincre sans gloire*, 155–158.
96. Crémieux-Brilhac, *La France libre*, tome 1, 637; Julian Jackson says 2,750. Jackson, *De Gaulle*, 268.
97. Muracciole, *Les Français libres*, 159.
98. Piketty, *Français en résistance*, 319, 321; Durand, *De Giraud à de Gaulle*, 175.
99. SHD-GR, 12P 91, "Rapport de Colonel Commandant le 6e Régiment de Chasseurs d'Afrique," 4 June 1943.
100. Durand, *De Giraud à de Gaulle*, 165; Muracciole, *Les Français libres*, 209, 211, 232.
101. Durand, *De Giraud à de Gaulle*, 168.
102. SHD-GR, 20P 18, 20 May 1943 and 11P 257.
103. Vigneras, *Rearming the French*, 113.
104. Durand, *De Giraud à de Gaulle*, 173, 196–197.
105. Of course, directing Jews and political refugees into "service units" like the pioneer corps was a way to deny them military status and hence claims to French nationality. Vigneras, *Rearming the French*, 106.
106. Louis Bacquier, *Aïwah: Au combat avec les Marocains. Souvenirs d'un officier de tirailleurs 1942–1945* (Paris: Éditions Laville, 2012), 92–93.
107. Durand, *De Giraud à de Gaulle*, 166.

108. Julian Jackson, "General de Gaulle and His Enemies: Anti-Gaullism in France since 1940," *Transactions of the Royal Historical Society*, 9 (1999), 44, 49, 53.
109. Piketty, *Français en résistance*, 332.
110. Muracciole, *Les Français libres*, 157–159, 161, 172–179, 186–187, 190–199, 362; Crémieux-Brilhac, *La France libre*, tome 1, 654–657; Martel, *Leclerc*, 210.
111. Durand, *De Giraud à de Gaulle*, 198.
112. Piketty, *Français en résistance*, 295–298.
113. Muracciole, *Les Français libres*, 235–237, 361–363; Le Gac, *Vaincre sans gloire*, 157.
114. Quoted in Morgane Barey, "Obéir et commander en périod de crise. Les élèves officiers dans la seconde guerre mondiale," unpublished paper kindly communicated by the author, 13–14, 17; Le Gac, *Vaincre sans gloire*, 143–146.
115. Harymbat, *Les Européens d'Afrique du Nord*, 130; Le Gac, *Vaincre sans gloire*, 146.
116. Durand, *De Giraud à de Gaulle*, 199–200; Le Gac, *Vaincre sans gloire*, 119–120.
117. "Tapers and Tadpoles" is a reference to the two political hacks in Benjamin Disraeli's 1844 novel *Coningsby; or, The New Generation*. Macmillan, *War Diaries*, 154.
118. See, for instance, Philippe de Gaulle's description of de Gaulle's family life in Algiers, in Jackson, *De Gaulle*, 282.
119. Lacouture, *De Gaulle*, tome 1, 671.
120. François Broche, Georges Caïtucoli, and Jean-François Muracciole (eds.), *Dictionnaire de la France Libre* (Paris: Robert Lafont, 2010), 316–317.
121. Lacouture, *De Gaulle*, tome 1, 676. Carlo D'Este points out that Eisenhower became one of de Gaulle's greatest advocates with FDR. Carlo D'Este, *Eisenhower: A Soldier's Life* (New York: Henry Holt, 2002), 418–419.
122. Crémieux-Brilhac, *La France Libre*, tome 2, 833–837.
123. Renée Poznanski, *Propagandes et persécutions: La Résistance et le "problème juif" 1940–1944* (Paris: Fayard, 2008), 396–397.
124. Macmillan, *War Diaries*, 127.
125. De Gaulle, *Mémoires de guerre*, tome 2, 388–389; Jackson, *De Gaulle*, 284.
126. Macmillan, *War Diaries*, 118.
127. Lacouture, *De Gaulle*, tome 1, 673–675; de Gaulle, *Mémoires de guerre*, tome 2, 389.
128. Neiberg, *When France Fell*, 229.
129. Vigneras, *Rearming the French*, 78–81; Crémieux-Brilhac, *La France Libre*, tome 2, 830–847; Jackson, *De Gaulle*, 275–276.
130. Vigneras, *Rearming the French*, 81.
131. De Gaulle, *Mémoires de guerre*, tome 2, 392.
132. Captain Harry C. Butcher, *My Three Years with Eisenhower*, 286.
133. Robert Belot, *Aux frontières de la liberté*, 655.
134. Lacouture, *De Gaulle*, tome 1, 684–685.
135. Jackson, *De Gaulle*, 279. In Giraud's absence, the CFLN, whose "commissariats" were ensconced in the classrooms and dormitories of Algiers' Lycée Fromentin, met twice weekly to tackle the myriad of political, diplomatic, and imperial issues in preparation for Liberation. To prepare for and facilitate these debates, Louis Joxe was appointed general secretary and given a staff. René Cassin headed a "judicial committee." An embryonic "council of state" was constituted, as well as a "military committee" with Billotte as secretary. Massigli headed foreign affairs, while the uncompromising Gaullist Gaston Palewski served as the General's chief of staff. This organization was designed to give a central direction to the administration of AFN to supplant and contrast with Vichy's "chronic improvisation." In this way, de Gaulle sought to reestablish a foundation of French governance and authority. De Gaulle, *Mémoires de guerre*, tome 2, 393–395.
136. Jackson, *De Gaulle*, 284–286.
137. Le Gac, *Vaincre sans gloire*, 134.
138. Pétain's portraits were first ordered taken down in AFN on 25 May, and this order was reiterated by the CFLN on 12 October 1943. Le Gac, *Vaincre sans gloire*, 126.
139. Belot, *Aux frontières de la liberté*, 656; de Gaulle, *Mémoires de guerre*, tome 2, 402–403.
140. Lacouture, *De Gaulle*, tome 1, 676, 681; de Gaulle, *Mémoires de guerre*, tome 2, 393; Neiberg, *When France Fell*, 229–232.
141. Suzanne Lefort-Rouquette, *Des Ambulancières dans les combats de la Libération: Avec les soldats de la 9e Division d'infanterie coloniale* (Paris: Éditions L'Harmattan, 2005), 38.
142. Moorehead, *The Desert War*, 482–483.

143. Raoul Salan, *Mémoires*, tome 1, *Fin d'un empire: "Le sens d'un engagement," juin 1899–septembre 1946* (Paris: Presses de la Cité, 1970), 109.
144. Harymbat, *Les Européens d'Afrique du Nord dans les armées de la libération française*, 54, 77.
145. Rolf, *The Bloody Road to Tunis*, 284–285; Louis Xueref, "Mémoires d'outre-mer. 1942–1943 (Autour de la campagne de Tunisie). Souvenirs d'une tranche de vie," http://tunisie-france.pagesperso-orange.fr/souvenirs_souvenirs.htm.
146. Omar Bradley, *A Soldier's Story*, 110.
147. Medical services calculated that a prostitute might service up to six Gis an hour, fifty to sixty in an eight-hour shift. Ebbe Curtiss Hoff, *Preventative Medicine in World War II*, volume viii, *Civil Affairs/Military Government Public Health Activities* (Washington, D.C.: Office of the Surgeon General, Department of the Army, 1976), 258–259, 267–287. The numerous brothels were only superficially monitored by French health officials, perhaps because they were understandably reluctant to tangle with the Corsican mafia that ran them. Richard Bennaïm, *Le Journal du soldat juif* (Lormont: Le Bord de l'Eau, 2017), 22.
148. De Gaulle, *Mémoires de guerre*, tome 2, 404; Crémieux-Brilhac, *La France libre*, tome 2, 851–852.
149. Neiberg, *When France Fell*, 229.
150. Jackson, *De Gaulle*, 285.
151. This was done in part through the efforts of Admiral Harold Stark, former US Navy Chief of Naval Operations (CNO) and from March 1942 Commander of US Naval Forces Europe. Crémieux-Brilhac, *La France libre*, tome 2, 848–849.
152. Le Gac, *Vaincre sans gloire*, 187–189.
153. Vigneras, *Rearming the French*, 86; Lacouture, *De Gaulle*, tome 1, 677; de Gaulle, *Mémoires de guerre*, tome 2, 405.
154. Lacouture, *De Gaulle*, tome 1, 677–678.
155. Macmillan, *War Diaries*, 261–262, 409–410; Neiberg, *When France Fell*, 215.
156. Piketty, *Français en résistance*, 339.
157. "As a practical matter, this translates into difficulties in feeding the troops, mediocre rations, irrational collective distribution that complicates the situation of detached units, that you have to account for in a modern army. I anticipate a lack of munitions allocated for training, lack of training facilities, lack of petrol. Another problem, replacing matériel." Piketty, *Français en résistance*, 312, 332.
158. Julie Le Gac provides a long discussion of the attitudes of *l'armée d'Afrique*. Le Gac, *Vaincre sans gloire*, 119–146. Frédéric Harymbat remarks that there was little enthusiasm for Gaullism in the *Corps expéditionnaire français* in Italy. Harymbat, *Les Européens d'Afrique du Nord dans les armées de la libération française*, 174.
159. French statistics for Tunisia are unreliable, both because of army disorganization and also because the CFA was technically part of the British First Army. Other units fought with the Americans at the end of the campaign. One estimate places French casualties in Tunisia at 9,600, or 24 percent of the force of 40,000 soldiers actually committed to combat. Vigneras, *Rearming the French*, 58, 403 note lists 2,300 "deaths" in Tunisia.
160. Fuchs, "May You Live in Interesting Times," 190, 206–208.
161. Le Gac, *Vaincre sans gloire*, 95–101.
162. SHD-GR, 5P 18, "Le rearmament français," 21 November 1943.
163. Jay Winter, "Cultural Divergences in Patterns of Remembering the Great War in Britain and France," in Robert Tombs and Emile Chabal (eds.), *Britain and France in Two World Wars: Truth, Myth and Memory* (London: Bloomsbury, 2013), 172.
164. Vigneras, *Rearming the French*, 131.
165. See Vigneras, *Rearming the French*, 38 for the text of the Anfa agreement.
166. It was only fair, as the French had largely armed the American Expeditionary Force when it arrived in France in 1917. Second, French rearmament honored the promise made by Clark to Mast at their Cherchell meeting in preparation for Torch. Third, using French troops would free up or supplement American manpower for other theaters and other tasks. Finally, American industrial production was hitting its stride, and seemed capable of furnishing the arms and equipment required.
167. O'Brien, *The Second Most Powerful Man in the World*, 268.
168. Vigneras, *Rearming the French*, 24–27, 33.
169. Army Chief of Staff (COS) George Marshall could find only 25,000 tons per month to dedicate to French rearmament, a rate that promised that the Third Reich would long be dead and buried before the French military reached critical mass. Giraud accused the Americans of having no intention of equipping French forces to participate in the liberation of France, which spurred Eisenhower to message Marshall for prompt action to get 100,000 tons of equipment to AFN, and to create a schedule for future deliveries. Giraud also offered up 246,000 tons of French shipping to the Allied pool. But much of it was in need of repair, and the

few dry docks in AFN were refitting Allied ships. In July, only 18,000 tons of French shipping was available. Vigneras, *Rearming the French*, 31, 33–44, 74–77.

170. Vigneras, *Rearming the French*, 63–69.
171. *Le système débrouille*, or, in more vulgar language, *démerde*, means to improvise, to sort things out.
172. Vigneras, *Rearming the French*, 59–60, 68–69, 71–72, 77.
173. Fuchs, "May You Live in Interesting Times," 201.
174. Vigneras, *Rearming the French*, 100–101.
175. Piketty, *Français en résistance*, 320.
176. The agreement was that the Americans would provide B rations for the *Corps expéditionnaire français* (CEF) – basically tinned, preserved food – but that the French would supply supplemental products more common in the North African diet, such as dried vegetables, fruit, lentils, sardines, flour, macaroni, and coffee, as well as cooking oil, brandy, and wine. But no sooner had the CEF arrived in Italy than it began to submit orders to the US Quartermaster Corps for flour, macaroni, fruit juice, canned fruit, and other items. While the French blamed bad harvests, US officials complained that the French were not living up to their agreement, and that food cultivation and distribution programs "had not been pursued with sufficient energy." But the French faced many problems in AFN: lack of petrol for the harvesting and transport of food products, a lack of canneries and packaging and storing facilities, especially for perishable foodstuffs, as well as a lack of shipping, especially refrigerator ships for meat. Therefore, they were forced to send live sheep to Italy, or purchase them in country. However, this contravened Allied policy, because the destruction of the Italian merchant marine combined with the arrival of two Allied armies in September 1943 to collapse Italy's already precarious food situation. The result was that CEF rations were insufficient in quality and in nutritive elements, as well as in sugar and fats. Muslim troops in the CEF were malnourished, in part because their set ration was less than that for American and French soldiers. But the monotony of the food and its lack of nutritive elements, of butter or margarine, resulted in a loss of appetite. In June 1944, the US Army assumed responsibility for feeding the CEF, as French forces were preparing for Operation Dragoon, the invasion of southern France. Vigneras, *Rearming the French*, 254–258; Le Gac, *Vaincre sans gloire*, 242–245.
177. SHD-GR, 5P 18, "Le réarmament français," 23 November 1943.
178. Le Gac, *Vaincre sans gloire*, 505–506.
179. Le Gac, *Vaincre sans gloire*, 85–96.
180. Fuchs, "May You Live in Interesting Times," 210–214.
181. Le Gac, *Vaincre sans gloire*, 506, 56, 84–95.
182. Le Gac, *Vaincre sans gloire*, 67.
183. German records did not distinguish initially between "Senegalese" and North African Muslims. Some sub-Saharan Africans were brutally murdered outright. But the Germans rapidly realized their propaganda and labor value. In December 1941, 10,000 North African Muslim POWs were released as a gesture meant to improve Germany's image. Raffael Scheck, *French Colonial Soldiers in German Captivity during World War II* (New York: Cambridge University Press, 2014), 27, 29.
184. Le Gac, *Vaincre sans gloire*, 69.
185. Of *l'armée d'Afrique*'s corps of 1,655 officers in April 1943, only 96 were Muslims, while only 1,582 of 7,133 NCOs were Muslims. Already the army command had begun to pay the price for failing to assign Muslims to the technical arms or expanding promotion possibilities. Belkacem Recham, *Les Musulmans algériens dans l'armée française (1919–1945)* (Paris: Éditions L'Harmattan, 1996), 233.
186. "That few Negro officers were capable and efficient was as widely believed," reads the US Army's official history of African American units in the Second World War. And, unlike the North African – especially Moroccan – units that were looked upon as a combat elite, most white American officers viewed assignment to command Negro troops, who were used mainly as service and support units, as a sign of low confidence in their leadership abilities. Ulysses Lee, *The Employment of Negro Troops* (Washington, D.C.: Center of Military History, United States Army, 1965), 231.
187. Ferhat Abbas et al., "10 février 1943, Le Manifest du peuple algérien," https://texturesdutemps.hypotheses.org/1458.
188. Harymbat, *Les Européens d'Afrique du Nord dans les armées de la libération française*, 138–140.
189. Many settler farmers had moved to the cities, in part to escape "the drip drip" of rural violence. As the settler population became urbanized, personal contacts between Europeans and Muslims diminished, as Muslim nationalists increasingly monopolized a hitherto shared "Algerian" identity. Martin Evans, *Algeria: France's Undeclared War* (Oxford: Oxford University Press, 2012), 92.
190. Le Gac, *Vaincre sans gloire*, 101–108.
191. Harymbat, *Les Européens d'Afrique du Nord dans les armées de la libération française*, 137–138.
192. Le Gac, *Vaincre sans gloire*, 108.

193. For instance, a *tirailleur* second class was paid 31–36 francs a day, against 16 francs for a day laborer or shepherd in Morocco. A recent enlistee was often sent on leave to his douar in uniform and with his recruitment bonus to attract other volunteers. *Goumiers*, technically tribal militia, were paid only 20 francs a day, and so might attract a less desirable recruit, even men who volunteered to escape prison. In keeping with tradition, *goumier* discipline was less strict, while pillage to augment their meager pay was tolerated. Quite apart from the lure of adventure and the uniform, army veterans and their families also might secure a degree of immunity from abuse by tribal leaders, because they could appeal to French Arab bureau officers if they encountered a difficulty.
194. Le Gac, *Vaincre sans gloire*, 70–81, 85–86.
195. Bacquier, *Aïwah*, 116–117.
196. Recham, *Les Musulmans algériens dans l'armée française*, 235.
197. Levisse-Touzé writes that Algerian Muslims alone furnished 172,749 combatants in the Great War, against 120,000 to 150,000 during 1943–1945. "Given a population growth [of 5 to 7 million inhabitants], the effort in 1943–1945 would be a third less." Christine Levisse-Touzé, *L'Afrique du Nord dans la guerre 1939–1945* (Paris: Albin Michel, 1998), 366. However, how many of the 170,000 Algerians called up in 1939 are reflected in these numbers is unclear.
198. SHD-GR, 7P 167; Keith E. Eiler, *Mobilizing America: Robert P. Patterson and the War Effort, 1940–1945* (Ithaca, NY: Cornell University Press, 1997).
199. The 1ère DFL was renamed the *1ère Division motorisé d'infanterie* (1ère DMI), although most continued to refer to it as the 1ère DFL.
200. In 1939–1940, 450,000 indigenous troops had been mobilized. Recham, *Les Musulmans algériens dans l'armée française*, 236–241.
201. Vigneras, *Rearming the French*, 104.
202. Recham, *Les Musulmans algériens dans l'armée française*, 236–237.
203. Vigneras, *Rearming the French*, 106–111, 114.
204. Vigneras, *Rearming the French*, 106.
205. Vigneras, *Rearming the French*, 58, 104, 106–111, 113, 123–129, 147; J. Vernet, *Le réarmament et la réorganization de l'armée de terre française (1943–1946)* (Vincennes: Ministère de la défense, État-major de l'armée de terre, Service historique, 1980), 24.
206. First reports came from German POWs who had escaped from the camp at Bouârfa, Morocco, where they had been switched out for Jews and Spanish Republicans forced by the Vichy regime to work in the magnesium mines, and who accused Senegalese guards of depriving prisoners of rations, and inflicting beatings and "punishment exercises." The implication of the German complaint was that Bouârfa was simply the tip of the iceberg, reported by German escapees who had presumably been able to reach the Spanish zone of Morocco. Italian POWs, hated for having "stabbed France in the back" in 1940, were allegedly the object of multiple barbarisms. After September 1943, when the Italians officially became Allied "co-belligerents," the Americans and British were eager to cultivate Italian cooperation on the Peninsula. By the autumn of 1943, escapes by Italian POWs from French control to the Americans had "reached epidemic proportions." At issue was the fact that, while de facto members of the Alliance, the French– *la France libre* or later the CFLN – had no official diplomatic status. For this reason, neither the Swiss nor the Spaniards would agree to act as the "protecting power" for German POWs under Geneva auspices. Nor could the Anglo-Americans make official approaches, not least because they did not want to acknowledge and hence be implicated in French mistreatment of Axis POWs. Unofficial approaches through the French military were rebuffed with observations that Axis POWs were practically pampered by the Anglo-Americans. Also, the French had every reason to feel aggrieved by Allied concern for Axis POWs. Reports had surfaced in 1941 that Axis troops were executing FFL soldiers captured in the Western Desert on the pretext that they were not legal combatants, a justification that would be invoked to murder resistance fighters in occupied France. The issue in the summer of 1943 was whether the Anglo-Americans could simply hand over Axis POWs to the French, or even employ troops from a non-recognized power to guard – and possibly mistreat – Axis POWs. More importantly, the Anglo-Americans feared that mistreatment by the French of Axis POWs would invite retaliation against Allied POWs in German custody. They wanted to know why the French were mistreating Axis POWs – was it due to hatred and revenge; a need to demean Axis POWs to enhance French status in the eyes of the indigenous population; or more structural problems that stemmed from the fact that the French neither would nor could properly supervise the POW guards; or was it because living standards were so low in AFN that the French lacked the resources to insure that POWs received minimal rations and base-line living standards? The high number of Italian escapes to the Americans was attributable to the fact that many were employed in agricultural labor with minimal supervision. Bob Moore, "Unruly Allies: British Problems with French Treatment of Axis Prisoners of War, 1943–1945," *War in History*, 7/2 (April 2000), 180–187.

207. The French air inventory in November 1942 had included 700 Dewoitine D.520 fighters, underperforming Bloch MB.150 fighters, Lioré-et-Olivier torpedo bombers, and Potez transport and observation planes, with a smattering of American Glenn Martin 167 medium bombers. Vigneras, *Rearming the French*, 195–196.
208. Vigneras, *Rearming the French*, 198–212.
209. On the state of the Alexandria and West Indies squadrons, see Philippe Masson, *La marine française et la guerre 1939–1945*, (Paris: Tallandier, 1991), 405–409, 412; Jean-Baptiste Bruneau, *La Marine de Vichy aux Antilles juin 1940-juillet 1943*, (Paris: Les Indes Savantes, 2014), 28; Vigneras, *Rearming the French*, 214–225.
210. Fuchs, "May You Live in Interesting Times," 160.
211. Vigneras, *Rearming the French*, 230–240.
212. Général Joseph Goislard de Monsabert, *Notes de Guerre* (Hélette: Éditions Jean Curutchet, 1999), 391–392.
213. Fuchs, "May You Live in Interesting Times," 204.
214. Le Gac, *Vaincre sans gloire*, 198–200, 209–211.
215. Alphonse Juin, *Mémoires*, tome 1, *Alger, Tunis, Rome* (Paris: Fayard, 1959), 227.
216. Le Gac, *Vaincre sans gloire*, 200–209.
217. Juin, *Mémoirs*, tome 1, 227.
218. Général André Lanquetot, *1943–1944: Un Hiver dans les Abruzzes. Le 8ᵉ Régiment de tirailleurs marocains et le 3ᵉ Groupe du 63ᵉ Régiment d'artillerie d'Afrique* (Vincennes: Service historique de l'armée de terre, 1991), 24–30.
219. Bacquier, *Aïwah*, 100–101.
220. Vigneras, *Rearming the French*, 89–90, 231–239.
221. SHD-GR, 2P 21 has several partial lists of officers, and above all students in military establishments, who were "présumés passés à la dissidence" following news of Torch.
222. Bacquier, *Aïwah*, 51–59.
223. Bacquier, *Aïwah*, 60–61, 29.
224. Eric Alary, *La Ligne de démarcation* (Paris: Perrin, 2003), 94–113, 277–284.
225. Belot, *Aux frontières de la liberté*, 77.
226. Alary, *La Ligne de démarcation*, 119–146.
227. On 1 December 1943, Algiers listed 287 officers and 3,468 NCO and soldier *évadés* for the army, 57 officers and 1,195 enlisted men for the air force, and 48 officers and 524 enlisted men for the navy, making a total of 5,879. SHD GR, 5P 20.
228. Bacquier, *Aïwah*, 179.
229. SHD-GR, 5P 20, "Rapport addressé par le Lieutenant Michon aux ambassades des États-Unis et de Grande Bretagne, à la Mission Française et au Président de la Croix Rouge."
230. Bacquier, *Aïwah*, 71–75.
231. On Spanish policy during the war, see Paul Preston, "Spain. Betting on a Nazi Victory," in Richard J. B. Bosworth and Joseph A. Maiolo, *The Cambridge History of the Second World War*, volume II, *Politics and Ideology* (Cambridge: Cambridge University Press, 2015), 324–348.
232. SHD-GR, 5P 20, reports of 3, 7, and 20 April, 19 May 1943; numbers 161 and 173; 21 June 1943.
233. Belot, *Aux frontières de la liberté*, 76–80, 660–664; Muracciole, *Les Français libres*, 65, 141, 152–153; SHD-GR, 6P 18, "Note sur la réception en A.F.N. des évadés de France," probably October 1943.
234. The order to reveal to the occupier secret arms caches that officers and NCOs had assembled, at great risk, demonstrated that "*l'armée de la revanche*" had been a deception and the camouflage of weapons had never been part of official Vichy policy. Vichy betrayal was further demonstrated by the requirement that all former officers report to the German military command on a monthly basis. On 15 December, officers were forced to sign a humiliating letter that made "the French officer corps collectively responsible for the attitude of each of its members." Belot, *La résistance sans de Gaulle*, 253–254.
235. SHD-GR, 5P 20, 26 April, 4 May, 24 August.
236. The names of only thirty-eight junior officers are attached. SHD-GR, 5P 20, 13 May 1943. For Mendigal's complaint, see 12 June 1943; and for Berger, see 22 June 1943.
237. SHD-GR, 6P 18, "Note sur la réception en A.F.N. des évadés de France."
238. Bacquier, *Aïwah*, 91.
239. Belot, *Aux frontières de la liberté*, 660; Jean Planchais, *Une histoire politique de l'armée*, tome 2, *1940–1967: De de Gaulle à de Gaulle* (Paris: Éditions du Seuil, 1967), 48.
240. SHD-GR, 5P 20, June 1943.
241. SHD-GR, 6P 18, "Note sur la réception en A.F.N. des évadés de France."
242. Bacquier, *Aïwah*, 93, 95–96.
243. Belot, *Aux frontières de la liberté*, 558–559.

244. Le Gac, *Vaincre sans gloire*, 195.
245. Joanna Bourke, *An Intimate History of Killing* (London: Granta, 1999), 30.
246. See, for instance, John Lynn, *Women, Armies and Warfare in Early Modern Europe* (Cambridge: Cambridge University Press, 2008).
247. Élodie Jauneau, "La feminisation de l'armée française pendant les guerres (1938–1962): Enjeux et réalités d'un processus irreversible," Thèse du doctorat, Université Paris Diderot (Paris 7), 2011, 15–37.
248. These issues are discussed by Gregory A. Daddis, "Mansplaining Vietnam: Male Veterans and America's Popular Image of the Vietnam War," *The Journal of Military History*, 82/1 (January 2018), 181–207.
249. Luc Capdevila, François Rouquet, Fabrice Virgili, and Danièle Voldman, *Sexes, genre et guerres (France, 1914–1945)* (Paris: Payot, 2010), 50–51, 67–71; Jauneau, *La feminisation de l'armée française*, 49–51.
250. Jean-François Dominé, *Les Femmes au combat: L'arme féminine de la France pendant la Seconde Guerre mondiale* (Vincennes: Service historique de la défense, 2008), 23; Susan Travers, *Tomorrow to Be Brave* (London: Corgi Press, 2001), 57–63.
251. Muracciole, *Les Français libres*, 47.
252. Jauneau, *La feminisation de l'armée française*, 80–81.
253. This appears to have required an "engagement à titre civil," which was done at the prefecture.
254. Capdevila et al., *Sexes, genre et guerres*, 56–57, 77–79. Four female pilots were "requisitioned" in a "volunteer status" by the FAF, see Dominé, *Les Femmes au combat*, 25.
255. Julie Le Gac, "L''étrange défaite' du divorce? (1940–1946)," *Vingtième Siècle. Revue d'histoire*, 2005/4, no. 88 (2005), 49–62.
256. Capdevila et al., *Sexes, genre et guerres*, 97–102, 139–140; Luc Capdevila, "L'identité masculine et les fatigues de la guerre (1914–1945)," *Vingtième Siècle. Revue d'histoire*, 2003/3, no. 75 (2003), 97–108, note 15, www.cairn.info/revue-vingtieme-siecle-revue-d-histoire-2002-3-page-97.htm; Nina Barbier, *Malgré-elles: Les Alsaciennes et Mosellanes incorporées de force dans la machine de guerre nazi* (Paris: Tallandier, 2018).
257. SHD-GR, 7P 73, "Instruction portant réglement des formations militaires féminines auxiliaires," 9 February 1944.
258. In fact, the initiative for a Corps féminin appears to have come from Muselier. The CVF replaced the "Corps féminin," a name that invariably made it the subject of jokes. British female organizations included the ATS for the army, the Women's Auxiliary Air Force (WAAF), the Women's Royal Navy Service (WRNS), and the Land Girls for agricultural work. Dominé, *Les Femmes au combat*, 27–31; Élodie Jauneau, "Des femmes dans la France combattante pendant la deuxième guerre mondiale: Le corps des volontaires françaises et le groupe Rochambeau," *Genre et Histoire*, 3 (Autumn 2008), https://journals.openedition.org/genrehistoire/373.
259. Frédéric Pineau, *Femmes en guerre, 1940–1946* (Antony: ETAI, 2013), 15–27.
260. Travers, *Tomorrow to Be Brave*, 79–85. Dominé notes that volunteers had to be French, which might explain why these women simply walked away from their contract. Although this explanation appears unlikely as the FFL contained many foreigners as soldiers. Dominé, *Les Femmes au combat*, 32.
261. Pineau, *Femmes en guerre*, 44–45.
262. Le Gac, *Vaincre sans gloire*, 62, 371; Pineau, *Femmes en guerre*, 43; Harymbat, *Les Européens d'Afrique du Nord dans les armées de la libération française*, 87.
263. SHD-GR, 7P 73, 9 February 1944 has a list.
264. The purpose was not to teach women to become soldiers, but to instruct them in appropriate Vichy-era subjects, including the role of women in the nation, the importance of family, and the psychology of command. Together with biographies of France's great colonizers, they were to acquire a top-of-the-waves familiarity with the war of 1914–1918, complemented with lots of physical training (PT), an introduction to explosives, and driver education. SHD-GR, 7P 73, "Stage des 'chefs' feminins."
265. SHD-GR, 7P 73, "Fiche au sujet du personnel féminin des formations auxiliaires de l'armée de terre," 8 January 1944.
266. SHD-GR, 7P 73, "Décret du 11 janvier 1944 portant création de formations militaires féminines auxiliaires"; Luc Capdevila, "La mobilisation des femmes dans la France combattante (1940–1945)," *Clio. Histoire, femmes et sociétés*, 12/2000 (2000), unpaginated, https://journals.openedition.org/clio/187, 5th page.
267. SHD-GR, 7P 73, "Effectifs A.F.A.T.," 25 January 1945. Capdevila et al. estimate that 14,000 women served during the war in various armed service formations. Capdevila et al., *Sexes, genre et guerres*, 107; Raphaële Balu, "Les maquis de France, la France libre et les Alliés (1943–1945): Retrouver la coopération," Thèse du doctorat, Université de Caen Normandie, 2018, tome II, 835–838.
268. Muracciole, *Les Français libres*, 48–49.
269. Capdevila, "La mobilisation des femmes dans la France combattante," 5.

270. Jauneau, *La feminisation de l'armée française*, 114–115; Le Gac, *Vaincre sans gloire*, 372.
271. In France, service to the state was officially linked to the citizen *levée*, not to gender, which made French women eligible for the *Médaille militaire* created in 1852. From the First World War, both men and women might be awarded the *Croix de guerre*. In April 1944, members of the resistance were classified as FFI, which gave them a military status. During the war, *la France libre* declared the resistance eligible for the prestigious *Ordre de la Libération* and the *Médaille de la Résistance*, 65,295 of which were eventually awarded, 4,000 of them to women. Only 6 women numbered among the 1,059 *compagnons de la Libération*. Balu, "Les maquis de France, la France libre et les Alliés," tome II, 864–867.
272. Jauneau, "Des femmes dans la France combattante pendant la deuxième guerre mondiale." A 9 February 1944 "instruction" does accord women temporary ranks from "auxiliaire" to major. SHD-GR, 7P 73, 9 February 1944.
273. Suzanne Massu, *Quand j'étais Rochambelle* (Paris: Grasset, 1969), 73, 109.
274. SHD-GR, 7P 73, 12 February 1944.
275. SHD-GR, 7P 73, 1 October 1943; Le Gac, *Vaincre sans gloire*, 371.
276. SHD-GR, 7P 73, Colonel Truchet letter, July 1944.
277. Le Gac, *Vaincre sans gloire*, 58–64, 117; Capdevila, "L'identité masculine et les fatigues de la guerre," Muracciole, *Les Français libres*, 45.
278. Balu, "Les maquis de France, la France libre et les Alliés," tome II, 817, 825, 869; Muracciole, *Les Français libres*, 45–46.
279. Jauneau, *La feminisation de l'armée française*, 110.
280. Quite apart from the breach of contract, "a number of parents of nurses did not hide that they had encouraged their child to sign a contract with the Expeditionary Corps only in the certainty that they would be part of a Red Cross team and under the direct and moral authority of a known team leader." SHD-GR, 7P 73, 18 November 1943.
281. On 24 March 1943, Jean Rolland, a teacher in a Casablanca *lycée*, wrote an indignant letter to explain that he had withdrawn his daughter from the *Corps féminin* of the CFA. In his view, the main motivation for enlistment of "a very diverse" group of women" was "sexual adventure and need of money, often both ... One of these women, whose mores would have honored classical Lesbos, was scratched by her lover in the middle of the hospital ward." His daughter had been allowed by her officers to visit the American encampments, while their French instructors had taken advantage of them. The final indignity was that she had been assigned to a "dissident formation." SHD-GR, 11P 257, 24 March 1943. Claire Miot, "Combattantes sans combattre? Le cas des ambulancières dans la première armée française (1944–1945)," *Revue historique des armées*, 272 (2013), 25–35.
282. Lanquetot, *1943–1944: Un Hiver dans les Abruzzes*, 144.
283. Jacques Schmitt, *Journal d'un officier de tirailleurs 1944* (Paris: Bernard Giovannangeli Éditeur, 1944), 44.
284. Harymbat, *Les Européens d'Afrique du Nord dans les armées de la libération française*, 86.
285. Quoted in Lynne Olson, *Last Hope Island: Britain, Occupied Europe, and the Brotherhood That Helped Turn the Tide of War* (New York: Random House, 2017), 111.
286. Jauneau, *La feminisation de l'armée française*, 110; Lefort-Rouquette, *Des Ambulancières dans les combats de la Libération*, 34.
287. Massu, *Quand j'étais Rochambelle*, 72–73.
288. SHD-GR, 7P 73, "Le recrutement au Maroc."
289. Solange Cuvillier, *Tribulations d'une femme dans l'armée française, ou le patriotisme écorché* (Paris: Éditions Lettres du Monde, 1991), 14–21. For a more upbeat description, see SHD-GR, 7P 73, "École de formation des conductrices sanitaires du Maroc à Casablanca."
290. SHD-GR, 7P 73, "Le recrutement au Maroc."
291. SHD-GR, 7P 73, 10 May 1944.
292. SHD-GR, 7P 73, "Le recrutement au Maroc." SANA had been founded in Algiers in July 1941 by veterans of the SSAs. Jean-Jacques Monsuez, "Les sections sanitaires automobiles féminines," *Revue historique des armées*, 247 (2007), 98–113, https://journals.openedition.org/rha/2033; SHD-GR, 7P 73, Catroux to commander in chief, 16 September 1943.
293. Massu, *Quand j'étais Rochambelle*, 70, 72. Madame Catroux's nickname was obviously lifted from Alexandre Dumas' 1845 novel of that title based on the life of Marguerite de Valois.
294. Vigneras, *Rearming the French*, 259.
295. Travers, *Tomorrow to Be Brave*, 174–175.
296. Cuvillier, *Tribulations d'une femme dans l'armée française*, 19.
297. Massu, *Quand j'étais Rochambelle*, 121.
298. SHD-GR, 7P 73, Catroux to commander in chief, 16 September 1943; 20 September 1943.
299. Massu, *Quand j'étais Rochambelle*, 116.

300. Piketty, *Français en résistance*, 343.
301. Le Gac, *Vaincre sans gloire*, 372.
302. Lanquetot, *1943–1944: Un Hiver dans les Abruzzes*, 145.
303. Le Gac, *Vaincre sans gloire*, 371.
304. SHD-GR, 7P 73, 28 November 1943.
305. SHD-GR, 7P 73, "Le recrutement au Maroc."
306. Piketty, *Français en résistance*, 307; Travers, *Tomorrow to Be Brave*, 140–141, 159, 255–259, 272–273; Macmillan, *War Diaries*, 74.
307. Lefort-Rouquette, *Des Ambulancières dans les combats de la Libération*, 24–35.
308. Lanquetot, *1943–1944: Un Hiver dans les Abruzzes*, 144.
309. Lefort-Rouquette, *Des Ambulancières dans les combats de la Libération*, 67.
310. Vigneras, *Rearming the French*, 258–260.
311. Plans were made to direct two-fifths of female conscripts each to the army and FAF, while one-fifth of them were to go to the navy. Pineau, *Femmes en guerre*, 44.
312. The rank assigned to a female volunteer was to be decided after they had passed through "*l'école des cadres de l'AFAT*." Women were also offered the option to stay at home in the "reserve." Miot, "Sortir l'armée des ombres. Soldats de l'Empire, combattants de la Libération, armée de la Nation: La Première armée française, du débarquement en Provence à la capitulation allemande (1944–1945)," Thèse du doctorat, Université Paris-Saclay, 2016, 290–293.
313. As in France, most females serving with the Red Army were in medical units, in communications, or drivers. But Soviet females also served in rifle regiments, even as snipers, while an estimated 10 percent of members of partisan units were female. "Rape was, as might be expected, not unusual," writes Alexander Hill. But nor was it uncommon for some Red Army females to use sexual relations to gain preferment, becoming known as "Mobile Field Wives," usually of senior officers, which "offered protection from other predatory men." Alexander Hill, *The Red Army and the Second World War* (Cambridge: Cambridge University Press, 2019), 324–330.
314. Dominé, *Les Femmes au combat*, 47–50.
315. Roughly 350,000 American women served, in the WACs, or as army nurses, or in one of the other service organizations for women. The number of British female soldiers peaked in 1943 at 470,700, or 9.39 percent of the British armed forces, although some estimates put the total number at around 600,000 British women. Beate Fieseler, M. Michaela Hampf, and Jutta Schwarzkopf, "Gendering Combat: Military Women's Status in Britain, the United States, and the Soviet Union during the Second World War," *Women's Studies International Forum*, 47 (2014), 115–126; Jeremy Crang, "'Come into the Army, Maud': Women, Military Conscription, and the Markham Inquiry," *Defence Studies*, 8 (2008), 381–395. Soviet women in uniform accounted for 800,000, or 3 percent of uniformed Soviet forces. Their numbers peaked at 473,074 in 1944, according to Fieseler et al. Soviet women also appear to have performed a variety of combat roles as snipers, pilots, and so on, and did not merely serve as female auxiliaries in support functions. The Wehrmacht incorporated 500,000 female volunteer uniformed auxiliaries, with similar numbers in air defense, plus 400,000 nurses. Karen Hagemann, "Mobilizing Women for War: The History, Historiography, and Memory of German Women's War Service in Two World Wars," *Journal of Military History*, 75/4 (2011), 1055–1094. Of the estimated 600,000 who served with Tito's army in Yugoslavia, 100,000 were women. Barbara Jancar, "Women in the Yugoslav National Liberation Movement: An Overview," *Studies in Comparative Communism*, 14/2 (1981), 143–164. For comparative numbers, see also D'Ann Campbell, "Women in Combat: The World War II Experience in the United States, Great Britain, Germany, and the Soviet Union," *Journal of Military History*, 57/2 (April 1993), 301–323. For this reason, Capdevila et al. note that France was far behind other countries in the numbers of women integrated into the armed forces. Capdevila et al., *Sexes, genre et guerres*, 107–108.

CHAPTER 3

1. Maréchal Alphonse Pierre Juin, *Mémoires*, tome 1, *Alger, Tunis, Rome* (Paris: Fayard, 1959), 228–229.
2. John Gooch, *Mussolini's War: Fascist Italy from Triumph to Collapse 1935–1943* (London: Penguin, 2020), 350, 401–403.
3. Andrew Buchanan, *American Grand Strategy in the Mediterranean during World War II* (Cambridge: Cambridge University Press, 2014), 109–118.
4. Buchanan, *American Grand Strategy in the Mediterranean during World War II*, 128–132.
5. René Massigli was advised by Macmillan and Murphy only an hour before Eisenhower's 8 September announcement, on the grounds of secrecy. Julie Le Gac, *Vaincre sans gloire: Le corps expéditionnaire*

français en Italie (novembre 1942–juillet 1944) (Paris: Les Belles Lettres/Ministère de la défense-DMPA, 2013), 251–257.

6. Hélène Chaubin, *La Corse à l'épreuve de la guerre 1939–1943* (Paris: Vendémiaire Éditions, 2012), 163. A 23 March 1943 report concluded that the conquest of Corsica must hopscotch from Sicily or Sardinia to have any chance of success, especially because it would have to piggyback on Allied air power and landing craft, although where the French could find and equip the soldiers during an ongoing campaign in Tunisia remained to be determined. In any case, French forces could not be prepared to invade Corsica – "the first metropolitan department" – before the summer of 1943. All was mere speculation so long as Algiers and the Gaullists in London remained uninformed of Allied plans for "Sicily–Sardinia–Corsica." And, after conquest, a garrison of 50,000 men would be required to discourage an Axis counter-invasion. SHD-GR, "Étude sur l'opération Corse," 23 March 1943.
7. Karine Varley, "Defending Sovereignty without Collaboration: Vichy and the Italian Fascist Threats of 1940–1942," *French History*, 33/3 (2019), 432.
8. Chaubin, *La Corse à l'épreuve de la guerre 1939–1943*, 151–157.
9. Chaubin, *La Corse à l'épreuve de la guerre 1939–1943*, 158–160.
10. Raphaële Balu, "Les maquis de France, la France libre et les Alliés (1943–1945): Retrouver la coopération," Thèse du doctorat, Université de Caen Normandie, 2018, 256–260. On Roger de Saule, see http://museedelaresistanceenligne.org/media3454-Roger-de-Saule.
11. After reading law at the University of Paris, Scamaroni followed his father into the prefectoral corps. Although his elevated civil service status would have exempted him, he insisted on being mobilized into the infantry in 1939. However, growing impatient with *drôle de guerre* lethargy, he volunteered for the air force, where he was made an observer. Although wounded in an action that won him the *croix de guerre*, Scamaroni managed to manufacture false orders that took him to Saint-Jean-de-Luz, where, on 21 June 1940, he boarded a ship for England. Once in London, Scamaroni enlisted among the "Gaullists of the first hour." Captured at Dakar during Operation Menace, he was shifted from prisons in Africa and Algiers to Clermont-Ferrand, where he benefited from Pétain's clemency, and was offered a modest job at Vichy's Ministry of Supply, where he proceeded to create a resistance group called Copernic. However, with the Gestapo hot on his trail, in January 1942, the BCRA spirited Scamaroni to Britain. Sébastien Albertelli, *Les Services secrets du Général de Gaulle: Le BCRA 1940–1944* (Paris: Perrin, 2009), 260–261.
12. Chaubin, *La Corse à l'épreuve de la guerre 1939–1943*, 172–173, 200.
13. Balu, "Les maquis de France, la France libre et les Alliés," 256.
14. Balu, "Les maquis de France, la France libre et les Alliés," 306–307.
15. SHD-GR, 5P 41, "Concernant la Corse," 12 January 1943; "Étude sur l'opération Corse," 23 March 1943; "Note sur l'opération Corse No. 2," 26 March 1943; "Instruction personnelle et secrète No. 3," 4 June 1943.
16. SHD-GR, 5P 41, "Réunion de 20 juin 1942 à 10 heures à la direction des S[ervices].S[péciaux]."
17. Chaubin estimates that no more than 605 Corsicans actively collaborated with the Italians. Chaubin, *La Corse à l'épreuve de la guerre 1939–1943*, 178, 247–249.
18. Chaubin, *La Corse à l'épreuve de la guerre 1939–1943*, 172–184, 187.
19. Chaubin, *La Corse à l'épreuve de la guerre 1939–1943*, 196–197.
20. SHD-GR, 5P 41, 15 August 1943.
21. Chaubin, *La Corse à l'épreuve de la guerre 1939–1943*, 198–200; Philippe Buton, *Les lendemains qui déchantent: Le Parti communiste français à la Libération* (Paris: Presses de la Fondation Nationale des Sciences Politiques, 1993), 27–34.
22. SHD-GR, 5P 41, "La campagne de Corse, 11 septembre–4 octobre 1943," 1.
23. Chaubin, *La Corse à l'épreuve de la guerre 1939–1943*, 200–201; SHD-GR, 5P 41, "La Campagne de Corse, 11 septembre–4 octobre 1943.
24. Buton, *Les lendemains qui déchantent*, 28–29.
25. Karine Varley, "'Laboratory of Liberation.' Lessons for France from the Liberation of Corsica," https://francehistory.wordpress.com/2014/05/31/laboratory-of-liberation-lessons-for-france-from-the-liberation-of-corsica.
26. Albertelli, *Les Services secrets du Général de Gaulle*, 348–350; Jean-Louis Crémieux-Brilhac, *La France libre: De l'appel du 18 juin à la libération* (Paris: Gallimard, 2013), tome 2, 861.
27. SHD-GR, 7P 166, 10 September 1943.
28. Balu, "Les maquis de France, la France libre et les Alliés," 306.
29. SHD-GR, 5P 41, "Compte Rendu de liaison prise par le Lieutenant colonel Baillif auprès du Brigadier Général Sugden," 13 September 1943.
30. SHD-GR, 5P 41, "La campagne de Corse 11 septembre–4 octobre 1943," 2–4.
31. SHD-GR, 5P 41, "La campagne de Corse 11 septembre–4 octobre 1943," 8.

32. SHD-GR, 5P 41, "La campagne de Corse 11 septembre–4 octobre 1943," 13–16; 18 June 1943; 15 August 1943.
33. Julian Jackson, *De Gaulle* (Cambridge, MA: Harvard University Press, 2018), 297.
34. SHD-GR, 5P 41, "Note sur l'instruction," 4 December 1943; "La campagne de Corse 11 septembre–4 octobre 1943."
35. Arthur Layton Funk, "Les Américains et les britanniques dans la libération de la Corse," *Guerres mondiales et conflits contemporaines*, 174 (1994), 7; Chaubin, *La Corse à l'épreuve de la guerre 1939–1943*, 214.
36. SHD-GR, 5P 41, "Compte-rendu des liaison en Corse," 18 October 1943.
37. Charles de Gaulle, *Mémoires de guerre*, tome 2, *L'Unité, 1942–1944* (Paris: Plon, 1994), 412–413.
38. De Gaulle, *Mémoires de guerre*, tome 2, 414–418.
39. Jackson, *De Gaulle*, 297.
40. Balu, "Les maquis de France, la France libre et les Alliés," 258, 654.
41. De Gaulle, *Mémoires de guerre*, tome 2, 418.
42. Balu, "Les maquis de France, la France libre et les Alliés," 679.
43. Crémieux-Brilhac, *La France libre*, tome 2, 862–864.
44. Jean Lacouture, *De Gaulle*, tome 1, *Le Rebelle 1890–1944* (Paris: Éditions du Seuil, 1984), 688–689. Quoting Macmillan, Michael S. Neiberg insists that, by 1944, even Georges "had turned on him." Michael S. Neiberg, *When France Fell: The Vichy Crisis and the Fate of the Anglo-American Alliance* (Cambridge, MA: Harvard University Press, 2021), 231.
45. Marcel Vigneras, *Rearming the French* (Washington, D.C.: Center of Military History, United States Army, 1989), 98, 100–101; Jackson, *De Gaulle*, 277, 297–298.
46. Vigneras, *Rearming the French*, 118, 152, 155.
47. Jackson, *De Gaulle*, 276–277.
48. Albertelli, *Les Services secrets du Général de Gaulle*, 82–84.
49. Hilary Footitt and John Simmonds, *France 1943–1945* (Leicester: Leicester University Press, 1988), 44–50.
50. SHD-GR, 5P 41, "Compte-rendu des liaisons en Corse," 18 October 1943.
51. Balu, "Les maquis de France, la France libre et les Alliés," 317.
52. It also included the commissaires of war, the interior, finance, and Giraud until April 1944, as well as the directeur général des services secrets du CFLN, Jacques Soustelle. Albertelli, *Les Services secrets du Général de Gaulle*, 350.
53. Gambiez's reported that his *Bataillon de choc* took 75 killed in action (KIA), 239 wounded, and 12 missing in action (MIA). German wounded were estimated at between 400 and 600, with 351 POWs. Another 270 Germans died in air operations, with an estimated 2,000 lost at sea. Balu, "Les maquis de France, la France libre et les Alliés," 310.
54. SHD-GR, 5P 41, "Compte-rendu des liaisons en Corse," 18 October 1943.
55. SHD-GR, 5P 41, "L'opération de Corse," 24 September 1943; "Compte-rendu succinct de l'action des patriotes corses pendant les opérations militaires du 8 septembre au 5 octobre 1943 du commandant Colonna d'Istria," 8 October 1943.
56. Chaubin warns that the list may be incomplete. Chaubin, *La Corse à l'épreuve de la guerre 1939–1943*, 263–264.
57. In fact, Tito's Partisans enjoyed little popular support, and carried out great cruelties. Sean McMeekin, *Stalin's War: A New History of World War II* (New York: Basic Books, 2021), Chapter 27.
58. Balu, "Les maquis de France, la France libre et les Alliés," 312–313, 317–318, 326–327.
59. McMeekin, *Stalin's War*, 467.
60. Sidney Mathews argues that Allied strategy exaggerated the value of Rome, and instead should have focused on destroying German forces. However, Fifth Army commander Mark Clark viewed the capture of Rome as evidence of US success in Italy. He did not want to share the prize with the British Eighth Army, but instead wanted to seize Rome because he knew that Overlord would soon take the spotlight away from Italy. Sidney Mathews, "General Clark's Decision to Drive on Rome," in Kent Roberts Greenfield (ed.), *Command Decisions* (Washington, D.C.: Center of Military History, 1990), 358. Rome's liberation would also free up naval assets that were being used to supply the Anzio beachhead. These were required for Operation Anvil, the invasion of southern France. Andrew Buchanan argues that Rome's capture was vital for political reasons, because it would precipitate the resignation of Badoglio and the king, and the transfer of power to Sforza and more democratic elements, which was central to Roosevelt's project to democratize Western Europe. Buchanan, *American Grand Strategy in the Mediterranean during World War II*, 140–143.
61. Carlo D'Este, *Eisenhower: A Soldier's Life* (New York: Henry Holt, 2002), 531.
62. Mark Clark, *Calculated Risk* (New York: Harpers, 1950), 348.
63. Juin, *Mémoires*, tome 1, 223.

64. Le Gac, *Vaincre sans gloire*, 35–39.
65. Le Gac, *Vaincre sans gloire*, 177–179.
66. Le Gac, *Vaincre sans gloire*, 182, 188–189.
67. Le Gac, *Vaincre sans gloire*, 184–185.
68. Jean-Christophe Notin, *La Campagne d'Italie 1943–1945: Les victoires oubliées de la France* (Paris: Perrin, 2007), 38.
69. Robert Merle, *Ahmed ben Bella* (Paris: Gallimard, 1965), 41–42.
70. Général André Lanquetot, *1943–1944: Un Hiver dans les Abruzzes. Le 8e Régiment de tirailleurs marocains et le 3e Groupe du 63e Régiment d'artillerie d'Afrique* (Vincennes: Service historique de l'armée de terre, 1991), 14.
71. Merle, *Ahmed ben Bella*, 42–45.
72. Notin, *La Campagne d'Italie 1943–1945*, 38. Christine Levisse-Touzé estimates that, during 1943–1945, AFN furnished between 200,000 and 250,000 soldiers, 120,000 to 150,000 of whom came from Algeria. Muslims were slightly more numerous than the 176,000 French. Christine Levisse-Touzé, *L'Afrique du Nord dans la guerre 1939–1945* (Paris: Albin Michel, 1998), 366.
73. Vigneras, *Rearming the French*, 343.
74. "French Operations," 1–6, National Archives and Records Administration (henceforth NARA), Record Group (henceforth RG) 407, Box 1777.
75. Notin, *La Campagne d'Italie 1943–1945*, 36–37, 192–193; André Martel, "La libération et la victoire: 'Quoi? Les Français aussi?,'" in André Martel (ed.), *Histoire Militaire de la France*, tome 4, *De 1940 à nos jours* (Paris: Presses universitaires de France, 1994), 199.
76. Juin, *Mémoires*, tome 1, 247–248; Notin, *La Campagne d'Italie 1943–1945*, 192.
77. NARA, RG 407, Box 1778. "*Goum*" is a French corruption of "*gûm*" or "*qawm*" in classical Arabic that means tribe or "people." From the inception of the French conquest of Morocco in 1908, tribal leaders who sided with the French were compelled to provide light cavalry to assist in the conquest and policing of Morocco, a process formalized in the French army from 1913 following a rebellion of Sharifian troops in Fez in 1911. Four "goums" were grouped into "tabors" – from the Turkish "*tabur*" – meaning a battalion of roughly 900 men. These units assisted the French in the conquest and stabilization of Morocco through 1934. In the Second World War, 4 *Groupements de tabors marocains* (GTM), each containing 3 tabors and a *Groupement de commandement et d'engin* (GCE), with sections of mules, pioneers, mortars, and anti-tank weapons, numbering 3,000 men, were organized into a brigade called the *Groupement des goums marocains*, first under General Augustin Guillaume and subsequently under Colonel Émile Hogard. Paul Gaujac, *Le Corps expéditionnaire français en Italie* (Paris: Histoire et Collections, 2003), 33.
78. "Report of Operations of the Unit Attached to the VII American Army for the Invasion of Sicily," NARA, RG 407, Box 1778; "La Composition du 1er groupement du I^{e} Corps de Débarquement," 6 October 1943, NARA, RG 407, Box 1779; Notin, *La Campagne d'Italie 1943–1945*, 107–108; Edward L. Bimberg, *The Moroccan Goums: Tribal Warriors in a Modern War* (Westport and London: Greenwood Press, 1999), xiii. For the performance of the *goums* in Sicily, see Lieutenant-Colonel Georges Boulle, *Le Corps expéditionnaire français en Italie (1943–1944)*, tome 1, *La campagne d'hiver* (Paris: Imprimerie Nationale, 1971), 16–19.
79. Peter Schrijvers, *The Crash of Ruin: American Combat Soldiers in Europe during WWII* (New York: New York University Press, 1998), 47–48.
80. "Juin '40" appears to be a reference to a song of Pacific island volunteers. "Juin '40. La France est à terre. Présent répondront les volontaires."
81. Le Gac, *Vaincre sans gloire*, 189–195.
82. De Gaulle, *Mémoires de guerre*, tome 2; cited by Notin, *La Campagne d'Italie 1943–1945*, 193.
83. Martel, "La libération et la victoire," 201.
84. SHD-GR, 5P 44, Mission française auprès de la Ve Armée US, "Étude sur le système defensive allemande à l'est de Rome (à la date du 2 décembre 1943)," 3 December 1943, pp. 5–6, 8.
85. SHD-GR, 5P 44, "Étude sur le système defensive allemande à l'est de Rome," 11–15.
86. NARA RG 407, Box 1779, 6 October 1943.
87. Juin, *Mémoires*, tome 1, 246–248; Notin, *La Campagne d'Italie 1943–1945*, 104; Le Gac, *Vaincre sans gloire*, 235–236. On French ranks, see www.legifrance.gouv.fr/codes/id/LEGISCTA000006166973.
88. Lanquetot, *1943–1944: Un Hiver dans les Abruzzes*, 43–44, 52.
89. Yves Gras, *La 1ère D.F.L.: Les Français libres au combat* (Paris: Presses de la Cité, 1983), 293.
90. Lanquetot, *1943–1944: Un Hiver dans les Abruzzes*, 44.
91. Lanquetot, *1943–1944: Un Hiver dans les Abruzzes*, 49.
92. Lanquetot, *1943–1944: Un Hiver dans les Abruzzes*, 63–71.
93. Lanquetot, *1943–1944: Un Hiver dans les Abruzzes*, 52.

94. Lanquetot, *1943–1944: Un Hiver dans les Abruzzes*, 61.
95. SHD-GR, 5P 44, "Sommaire d'une conference à la Ve Armée U.S. (15 novembre 1943)," 2 December 1943.
96. "French Operations," 6, NARA, 407/1777.
97. According to the US report, the attack scheduled for 14 December was postponed for two days until the tabors could be in position. NARA, RG 407, Box 1777, 9.
98. "The fighting on Mount Pantano continued all that day and the next and by morning of 18 December despite intense enemy mortar and artillery fire, all four knobs of the mountain were occupied, through the 5th RTM sustained 253 casualties." NARA, RG 407, Box 1777, 10. Lanquetot, *1943–1944: Un Hiver dans les Abruzzes*, 63; Le Gac, *Vaincre sans gloire*, 237–241.
99. Lanquetot, *1943–1944: Un Hiver dans les Abruzzes*, 59.
100. NARA, RG 407, Box 1777, 13–14; Le Gac, *Vaincre sans gloire*, 241.
101. Of these, 14 officers and 128 soldiers were KIA. Le Gac, *Vaincre sans gloire*, 240. German General Ringel, whose 5th Mountain Division forfeited the Mainarde, blamed poorly sited defenses and a lack of tenacity of the Austrian troops who composed the bulk of his force for his defeat. Others complained that reserves were hastily thrown into battle without their indispensable complement of pack animals. Lanquetot agreed to a point, noting that "effectively we could arrive close to their positions without too much trouble; but the lack of visibility also favored us." Surprise, too, played a role, as many of the mines surrounding the blockhouses had not been primed. Nevertheless, he testified that German artillery and mortar fire was very accurate, and the fact that they captured only sixty-four POWs testified to the tough resistance put up by the defenders. Lanquetot, *1943–1944: Un Hiver dans les Abruzzes*, 75–94. For a succinct report on the action, see NARA, RG 407, Box 1777, 14–16.
102. Juin, *Mémoires*, tome 1, 252–253; Lanquetot, *1943–1944: Un Hiver dans les Abruzzes*, 90.
103. Merle, *Ahmed ben Bella*, 54.
104. Jean Lapouge, *De Sétif à Marseille, par Cassino: Carnet de guerre de Jean Lapouge, sous-lieutenant au 7e RTA. Campagnes de Tunisie, Italie et Provence, 1942–1944* (Parçay-sur-Vienne: Éditions Anovi, 2007), 179.
105. Lanquetot, *1943–1944: Un Hiver dans les Abruzzes*, 137.
106. Lanquetot, *1943–1944: Un Hiver dans les Abruzzes*, 137–138.
107. Juin, *Mémoires*, tome 1, 208, 241–242.
108. The military tribunal focused on the conduct of Esteva (Tunisia), General Bergeret (Syria), Michelier (Casablanca), Derrien (Bizerte), Peyrouton (Algeria), and Boisson (French West Africa, AOF) as well as former ministers Flandin and Pucheu. François Rouquet and Fabrice Virgili, *Les françaises, les français et l'épuration (1940 à nos jours)*, (Paris: Gallimard, 2018), 74–87; Cremieux-Brilhac, *La France libre*, tome 2, 914–923. On the fate of Muslim collaborators in Tunisia, see "French Policy towards Arabs, Jews and Italians in Tunisia," December 1943, OSS, Research and Analysis Branch, NARA RG 334, E 315, NWC Lib, Box 895, cited in Rick Atkinson, *An Army at Dawn: The War in North Africa, 1942–1943* (New York: Henry Holt & Co., 2002).
109. Piketty, *Français en résistance*, 344.
110. Le Gac, *Vaincre sans gloire*, 193–195, 262–263.
111. Le Gac, *Vaincre sans gloire*, 358–368.
112. Macmillan, *War Diaries*, 382. For a description of the Pucheu trial, see Rouquet and Virgili, *Les françaises, les français et l'épuration*, 77–83.
113. Le Gac, *Vaincre sans gloire*, 133–134, 159–177; Crémieux-Brilhac, *La France libre*, tome 2, 914–923.
114. Lapouge, *De Sétif à Marseille, par Cassino*, 124–127.
115. Peter Caddick-Adams, *Monte Cassino: Ten Armies in Hell* (London: Arrow Books, 2013), 51–54.
116. Jonathan Fennell, *Fighting the People's War: The British and Commonwealth Armies and the Second World War* (Cambridge: Cambridge University Press, 2019), 398, 412–413; I. S. O. Playfair, *The Mediterranean and the Middle East*, vol. v, *The Campaign in Sicily 1943 and the Campaign in Italy 3rd September 1943 to 31st March 1944* (London: HMSO, 1973), 597; Le Gac, *Vaincre sans gloire*, 312; Schrijvers, *The Crash of Ruin*, 38–41.
117. Between October 1943 and September 1944, 16,892 British soldiers deserted, over 3,000 from the Eighth Army, catapulting the British desertion rate to the top of the Allied league table. By February 1944, 25 Eighth Army deserters were being arrested daily in Naples, 1,400 of whom were court martialed for desertion between 1 July 1943 and 30 June 1944. Most do not seem to have been psychiatric casualties, according to Le Gac. Desertions also seem to have been high among American soldiers, 72 percent of whom were subsequently categorized as neuropsychological casualties. Caddick-Adams, *Monte Cassino*, 88–89; Le Gac, *Vaincre sans gloire*, 132–133.
118. Robert Katz, *The Battle for Rome: The Germans, the Allies, the Partisans, and the Pope. September 1943–June 1944* (New York: Simon & Schuster, 2003), 139; Dominique Graham and Shelford Bidwell, *Tug of*

War: The Battle for Italy, 1943–1945 (New York: St. Martin's Press, 1986), 127–129; Playfair, *The Mediterranean and the Middle East*, vol. v, 579–581, 589, 771–774; Martin Blumenson, "General Lucas at Anzio," in Kent Roberts Greenfield (ed.), *Command Decisions* (Washington, D.C.: Center of Military History, 1990), 327; Carlo D'Este, *World War II in the Mediterranean, 1942–1945* (Chapel Hill, NC, Algonquin Books, 1990), 131–132.

119. Each regimental combat team was authorized a mule company of 300 animals, or 10 mules per company or equivalent formation. A regimental combat team was a basic infantry regiment augmented with various support formations like tanks, artillery, engineers, signals, and so on. SHD-GR, 5P 44, "Remarques faites entre le 25 novembre et le 5 décembre 1943," 9 December 1943.
120. "Étude sur le combat en montagne du 3e bureau du CEF," 15 April 1944, SHD 10P 58. Quoted in Le Gac, *Vaincre sans gloire*, 274.
121. Caddick-Adams, *Monte Cassino*, 36.
122. The huge effort at assembling mules worked out at only 30 mules per 800-man battalion, according to Lanquetot. This meant that heavy weapons such as anti-tank guns and machineguns had to be left at the foot of the mountains, as logistics prioritized ammunition. Lanquetot, *1943–1944: Un Hiver dans les Abruzzes*, 44. Furthermore, mules panicked under fire, as did their handlers, who rushed for cover. Once quiet had returned, surviving mules had to be reassembled, and their shed loads had to be collected and repacked. Lapouge, *De Sétif à Marseille, par Cassino*, 121–122.
123. Ernest F. Fisher, Jr., *Cassino to the Alps* (Washington, D.C.: Government Printing Office, 1977), 17.
124. Le Gac, *Vaincre sans gloire*, 272–280.
125. Merle, *Ahmed ben Bella*, 45–48.
126. Lapouge, *De Sétif à Marseille, par Cassino*, 175.
127. SHD-GR, 5P 44, "Remarques faites entre le 25 novembre et le 5 décembre 1943," 9 December 1943.
128. John Ehrman, *Grand Strategy*, volume v, *August 1943–September 1944* (London: HMSO, 1956), 60.
129. Lapouge, *De Sétif à Marseille, par Cassino*, 122.
130. "French Action and Pertinent Orders – Rapido–Cassino Operations," NARA, RG 407, Box 1622.
131. NARA RG 407, Box 1777, 31.
132. Merle, *Ahmed ben Bella*, 49–55.
133. NARA RG 407, Box 1777, 33; Le Gac, *Vaincre sans gloire*, 265.
134. Boulle, *Le Corps expéditionnaire français en Italie (1943–1944)*, tome 1, 128.
135. Lapouge, *De Sétif à Marseille, par Cassino*, 142.
136. Lapouge, *De Sétif à Marseille, par Cassino*, 145.
137. Winston Churchill, *The Second World War*, volume 5, *Closing the Ring* (New York: Houghton Mifflin, 1951), 432.
138. "Operations Report. The Action on Belvedere," 16 February 1944. NARA, RG 407, Box 1622; "The Battle for the Belvedere," NARA RG 407, Box 1622.
139. SHD-GR, 10P 56, 26 January, 8 and 13 February 1944; Le Gac, *Vaincre sans gloire*, 248–251.
140. Albert Kesselring, *The Memoirs of Field Marshal Kesselring* (New York: William Kimber & Co., 1953), 230, 233.
141. Lapouge, *De Sétif à Marseille, par Cassino*, 132–162.
142. Le Gac, *Vaincre sans gloire*, 369–370.
143. Clark, *Calculated Risk*, 269.
144. Graham and Bidwell, *Tug of War*, 148–49; John Ellis, *Cassino: The Hollow Victory. The Battle for Rome, January–June 1944* (New York: McGraw-Hill, 1984), Chapter 5.
145. See Bidwell and Graham, *Tug of War*, Chapter 10.
146. Playfair, *The Mediterranean and the Middle East*, vol. v, 593, 603; Bimberg, *The Moroccan Goums*, 68.
147. "French Operations," 37. NARA 407/1777.
148. SHD-GR, 5P 44, "La situation en Italie," 1 February 1944.
149. NARA, RG 407, Box 1777, 44.
150. Between 12 January and 2 April 1944, the CEF lost 1,566 dead and 5,497 wounded, or over 2 percent of its strength daily, a percentage that might rise to over 4 percent during periods of intense combat, such as from 12 January and 4 February 1944. According to French medical statistics, 64.4 percent of CEF losses were due to artillery fire or grenades, 7.5 percent of casualties were caused by mines, and 25.9 percent were killed or wounded by rifles or machineguns, a figure that reached 34 percent among the *goums*. So, while mines were most feared, artillery was by far the biggest killer. Days spent at high altitudes in wet uniforms and boots meant that, by 30 March, 1,733 soldiers had been evacuated because of trench foot, or 12 percent of casualties overall, a rate that surged to 30.3 percent during a bout of particularly bad weather during 11–17 February. Juin calculated that each of his two divisions of 15,000 men registered an average daily loss of 90 men, noting that one Frenchman died for every two natives. European junior officers, who accounted for

3.9 percent of strength in the infantry, were particularly hard hit, accounting for 5.2 percent of the KIA. Le Gac, *Vaincre sans gloire*, 272–285. "A patrol of the 7e RTA, sent to Mont Molino, was caught in an ambush," read a 9 January 1944 report. "An officer and 7 men did not return. 4 men survived, of whom three are wounded." SHD-GR, 5P 44, "Rapport du 3ème Bureau No. 6," 9 January 1944.

151. SHD-GR, 5P 44, "Rapport sur les opérations du C.E.F du 19 au 21 mars 1944," 22 March 1944.
152. SHD-GR, 7P 167, "Témoignages d'un fantasin," 7 June 1944.
153. Merle, *Ahmed ben Bella*, 55.
154. Lapouge, *De Sétif à Marseille, par Cassino*, 123, 256.
155. Only twenty-four men were convicted of abandoning their post in the presence of the enemy, seventeen of whom were accorded extenuating circumstances, and three had their death sentences commuted. Seventeen were court martialed for desertion in the face of the enemy, eight of whom were allowed "extenuating circumstances." Le Gac, *Vaincre sans gloire*, 243–246, 286–307, 281–285, 341–342, Annex 15, 535.
156. Le Gac, *Vaincre sans gloire*, 128.
157. Le Gac, *Vaincre sans gloire*, 101–102, 119–127.
158. Le Gac, *Vaincre sans gloire*, 128–143, 325–327.
159. Le Gac, *Vaincre sans gloire*, 286–307. For the view in the British army, see Caddick-Adams, *Monte Cassino*, 87, 91.
160. Quoted in Paul Fussell, *Doing Battle: The Making of a Skeptic* (Boston, New York, Toronto, and London: Little, Brown and Company, 1996), 175. The same was the case for American bomber crews, who were notorious for following rituals prompted by superstition, that included good luck charms or specific articles of clothing, taking mascots aloft, listing their thirteenth mission as 12½ or 12A, and so on, as coping mechanisms. S. P. MacKenzie, *Flying against Fate: Superstition and Allied Aircrews in World War II* (Lawrence: University of Kansas Press, 2018). For submariners, see Richard Overy, *Blood and Ruins: The Last Imperial War, 1931–1945* (London: Viking, 2022), 750.
161. For the "binary trap," see Paul Fussell, *The Great War and Modern Memory* (New York and London: Oxford University Press, 1975), 100. On courage, see Fussell, *Doing Battle*, 110, 120, 137–138.
162. Le Gac, *Vaincre sans gloire*, 303–305, 313, 337, 340; Overy, *Blood and Ruins*, 727–751.
163. Lapouge, *De Sétif à Marseille, par Cassino*, 163, 166–167.
164. Lapouge, *De Sétif à Marseille, par Cassino*, 173–174.
165. Le Gac, *Vaincre sans gloire*, 331, 343–355.
166. Solange Cuvillier, *Tribulations d'une femme dans l'armée française, ou le patriotisme écorché* (Paris: Éditions Lettres du Monde, 1991), 41–42, 45–46.
167. Macmillan, *War Diary*, 211; Varley, "Defending Sovereignty without Collaboration," 422–447.
168. Buchanan, *American Grand Strategy in the Mediterranean during World War II*, 116–118.
169. Buchanan, *American Grand Strategy in the Mediterranean during World War II*, 135, 182; Le Gac, *Vaincre sans gloire*, 254–261.
170. SHD-GR, 5P 44, "Rapport sur les opérations du C.E.F. du 19 au 21 mars 1944," 22 March 1944.
171. Le Gac, *Vaincre sans gloire*, 322.
172. Montgomery grumbled that the Mediterranean had become a vast car park for troops and supplies, and a diversion of scarce Landing Ships, Tank (LSTs) that might otherwise reinforce Overlord. Churchill questioned whether Roosevelt and Eisenhower were manipulating the LST shortage as a tactic to veto his calls for Eastern Mediterranean operations. Buchanan, *American Grand Strategy in the Mediterranean during World War II*, 167.
173. The Wehrmacht had 150 divisions on the Eastern Front, while 144 divisions were deployed in the West. Nor does this factor in the enormous amount of Lend–Lease aid pouring into the Soviet Union. McMeekin, *Stalin's War*, 518–519.
174. McMeekin, *Stalin's War*, 497–498.
175. Le Gac, *Vaincre sans gloire*, 317–318. In February 1944, the American President had informed the king that he must abdicate in favor of the crown prince. On 10 April, the king reluctantly agreed, after which Count Sforza, Palmiro Togliatti, and other members of the Italian "National Liberation Committee" (Comitato di Liberazione Nazionale, CLN) joined the cabinet and accepted the "long terms" of the armistice. Buchanan, *American Grand Strategy in the Mediterranean during World War II*, 136–146, 150, 165–174.
176. According to Juin's biographer Bernard Pujo, the Allies, miffed that the 4e DMM was in Corsica without the permission of the Chief of Staff (COS), were in no hurry to transport them to Italy. Bernard Pujo, *Juin, Maréchal de France* (Paris: Albin Michel, 1988), 178.
177. The 1ère DFL was officially called the *1ère Division motorisée d'infanterie*, and then the *1ère Division de marche d'infanterie*. But its membership and most historians persisted in calling it the DFL. Le Gac, *Vaincre sans gloire*, 321–322.
178. Notin, *La Campagne d'Italie 1943–1945*, 262.

179. In January 1944, Juin expressed his preference to de Gaulle for the 1ère DFL, fearing that the 9e DIC, composed in the main of "Senegalese," would not adapt well to Italy's frigid mountains – indeed "weather" had become the usual French excuse for rejecting Black troops who fit poorly into French martial race theory. "They probably couldn't arrive before the end of February or early March," he wrote to de Gaulle. "They would hardly be operational before this period because of their Blacks. In March, it will be possible to use them, taking certain precautions." Gras, *La 1ère D.F.L.*, 256–257.
180. Mechanics to service the division's 200 vehicles were grouped in the squadron of light tanks and three squadrons of scout cars, and an augmented transportation section, as well as heavy-equipment operators and ordnance specialists for an engineer battalion. Three signals companies required radio operators, not a French strength at the best of times, as well as heavy-weapons specialists proficient in anti-tank arms, mortars, and heavy machineguns. SHD-GR, 7P 167, "Témoignages d'un fantasin," 7 June 1944.
181. Piketty, *Français en résistance*, 338.
182. "The New Sector," 19–23. NARA, RG 407, Box 1777.
183. Le Gac, *Vaincre sans gloire*, 367.
184. Fisher, *Cassino to the Alps*, 24. André Martel puts the number of French troops at 112,000. Martel, "La libération et la victoire," 199–201. The difference may be that the French included US artillery, armor, and logistical troops attached to the CEF in their numbers. Or it may be that the French simply inflated their ration strength for logistical purposes.
185. Le Gac, *Vaincre sans gloire*, 381–382.
186. Le Gac, *Vaincre sans gloire*, 373.
187. Juin, *Mémoires*, tome 1, 290.
188. "The New Sector," 4. NARA, RG 407, Box 1777.
189. Alphonse Juin, *La campagne d'Italie* (Paris: Éditions Guy Victor, 1962), 97.
190. Juin, *Mémoires*, tome 1, 297–299; Notin, *La Campagne d'Italie 1943–1945*, 404–405.
191. "The New Sector," 5–9. NARA, RG 407, Box 1777.
192. Bidwell and Graham, *Tug of War*, 309–310.
193. "The New Sector," 11–18. NARA, RG 407, Box 1777.
194. Notin, *La Campagne d'Italie 1943–1945*, 389, 406, 408–412; Graham and Bidwell, *Tug of War*, 156–158, 309.
195. "Interview with General Marcel Carpentier," Rabat, 3 December 1948, NARA 407/1787.
196. Buchanan, *American Grand Strategy in the Mediterranean during World War II*, 152–154, 163.
197. The problem, as Ben Bella had noted, was that replacements were barely trained, because, under the Anfa agreement, all arms and equipment were earmarked for established units, not for allocation to training centers. Nor was there any procedure for replacing destroyed, lost, or stolen equipment. "Interview with General Marcel Carpentier," Rabat, 3 December 1948, NARA 407/1787.
198. Lapouge, *De Sétif à Marseille, par Cassino*, 198–199.
199. Juin, *La campagne d'Italie*, 97.
200. Le Gac, *Vaincre sans gloire*, 381; "The Advance on Rome of the Fifth Army, under the Command of Lieutenant General Mark W. Clark," NARA, RG 407, Box 1622, 15.
201. "Étude sur le combat en montagne," NARA, RG 407, Box 1784.
202. "Étude sur le combat en montagne. L'Offensive," 15 April 1944. NARA, RG 407, Box 1784; SHD-GR, 10P 56, 15 April 1944; Le Gac, *Vaincre sans gloire*, 374–383.
203. Piketty, *Français en résistance*, 359–360.
204. "The Advance on Rome of the Fifth Army, under the Command of Lieutenant General Mark W. Clark," NARA, RG 407, Box 1622, 15; "The CEF Drive to the West," unpaginated. NARA, RG 407, Box 1777.
205. "The Advance on Rome of the Fifth Army, under the Command of Lieutenant General Mark W. Clark," NARA, RG 407, Box 1622, 17.
206. Piketty, *Français en résistance*, 360.
207. Fisher, *Cassino to the Alps*, 91.
208. "The CEF Drive to the West," unpaginated. NARA, RG 407, Box 1777.
209. "The CEF Drive to the West," unpaginated. NARA, RG 407, Box 1777.
210. Cuvillier, *Tribulations d'une femme dans l'armée française*, 34, 36.
211. Cuvillier, *Tribulations d'une femme dans l'armée française*, 34–35, 53.
212. Suzanne Lefort-Rouquette, *Des Ambulancières dans les combats de la Libération: Avec les soldats de la 9e Division d'infanterie coloniale* (Paris: Éditions L'Harmattan, 2005), 67.
213. Cuvillier, *Tribulations d'une femme dans l'armée française*, 36–37.
214. Cuvillier, *Tribulations d'une femme dans l'armée française*, 49.
215. "The CEF Drive to the West," unpaginated. NARA, RG 407, Box 1777.
216. Piketty, *Français en résistance*, 360–361.

217. Playfair, *The Mediterranean and the Middle East*, vol. v, 624.
218. Fisher, *Cassino to the Alps*, 91. There is an extensive account of the CEF's participation in the breakthrough at Cassino in NARA, RG 407, Box 1777. See also Graham and Bidwell, *Tug of War*, 297–344. A detailed description of the French advance can also be found in Le Gac, *Vaincre sans gloire*, Chapter VIII. The Allies calculated the German losses as "1st Fallschirmjaeger [Paratroop] Division, the 90th and 15th Panzer Grenadier [sic] Divisions destroyed; Kampfgruppe Nagel [131st Infantry Regiment (IR)] completely scattered; 26th Panzer Grenadier Division severely depleted." "May Offensive 19–25 May," 1–13, NARA, RG 407, Box 1777.
219. Buchanan, *American Grand Strategy in the Mediterranean during World War II*, 154–155.
220. "May Offensive 19–25 May," 19–24. NARA, RG 407, Box 1777.
221. "French Operations," 53, NARA, Record Group 407, Box 1777.
222. Le Gac, *Vaincre sans gloire*, 379–392.
223. Le Gac, *Vaincre sans gloire*, 398–402.
224. Buchanan, *American Grand Strategy in the Mediterranean during World War II*, 171; Robert Dallek, *Franklin Roosevelt and American Foreign Policy, 1932–1945* (New York and Oxford: Oxford University Press, 1995), 456; Claire Miot, "Sortir l'armée des ombres. Soldats de l'Empire, combattants de la Libération, armée de la Nation: La Première armée française, du débarquement en Provence à la capitulation allemande (1944–1945)," Thèse du doctorat, Université Paris-Saclay, 2016, 54–58, 69–70.
225. Le Gac, *Vaincre sans gloire*, 402–416.
226. SHD-GR, 10P 10, CEF, 1e Bureau statistics, which are higher than figures produced in Martel, "La libération et la victoire," 201. See also Le Gac, *Vaincre sans gloire*, 395, 505. A 5 June report listed 91 officers and 1,433 men killed during 11–29 May, 201 officers and 6,315 men wounded, with 8 officers and 389 men MIA. SHD-GR, 7P 167, "Rapport du Lt-Colonel Frandon sur sa mission auprès du C.E.F.," 5 June 1944. Other estimates that aggregate Italy, Corsica, and Elba put French losses at 6,255 KIA (of whom 4,234 were "indigènes), 23,500 wounded in action (WIA, of whom 17,000 were "indigènes"), and 996 MIA (of whom 791 were "indigènes"). "Fiche au sujet des pertes de l'armée française," 10 May 1945, SHD 7P 81.
227. Overall, the 15th Army Group lost 7.3 percent of its strength between 1 April and 4 June 1944, of which 7,771 were KIAs. US casualties numbered 7.8 percent of strength, while British casualties amounted to 4.8 percent of strength. Le Gac, *Vaincre sans gloire*, 395.
228. SHD-GR, 7P 167, "Rapport du Lt-Colonel Frandon sur sa mission auprès du C.E.F.," 5 June 1944.
229. SHD-GR, 7P 167, "Témoignages d'un fantassin," 7 June 1944.
230. Ivan Cadeau, *De Lattre* (Paris: Perrin, 2017), 164–165, 293.
231. Miot, "Sortir l'armée des ombres," 738.
232. Le Gac, *Vaincre sans gloire*, 395–397.
233. Le Gac, *Vaincre sans gloire*, 464.
234. Le Gac, *Vaincre sans gloire*, 432–436.
235. Cuvillier, *Tribulations d'une femme dans l'armée française*, 45–46.
236. Le Gac, *Vaincre sans gloire*, 436–437, 444.
237. Le Gac, *Vaincre sans gloire*, 453, 465–466.
238. SHD-GR, 11P 42, "Note du service du Général Juin," 24 May 1944. Quoted in Le Gac, *Vaincre sans gloire*, 420.
239. Notin, *La Campagne d'Italie 1943–1944*, 642–648.
240. Le Gac, *Vaincre sans gloire*, 422, 426.
241. Le Gac, *Vaincre sans gloire*, 423, 466.
242. By 10 July, 53 cases of murder, 82 of rape, and 288 of pillage had been assigned courts martial. In all, 207 CEF soldiers were tried for rape, of whom 19 percent were acquitted, but 55 percent were accorded "mitigating circumstances" by military judges, which meant that only 60 were condemned to hard labor and 3 condemned to death, 2 of whom had their sentences commuted. Le Gac, *Vaincre sans gloire*, 458–461, 464.
243. Le Gac, *Vaincre sans gloire*, 436–440. For percentages of CEF soldiers convicted by court martial by nationality, see Le Gac, *Vaincre sans gloire*, 444.
244. Le Gac, *Vaincre sans gloire*, 432, 443.
245. Notin, *La Campagne d'Italie 1943–1944*, 518.
246. Le Gac, *Vaincre sans gloire*, 428.
247. It has been calculated that 23,479 Italian civilians, including women and children, were murdered by the Germans and their Italian Fascist allies between 1943 and 1945, mainly executed as suspected partisans or as collective punishments in retaliation for partisan attacks, for refusal to evacuate villages in the front line, or for some other misdemeanor. Overy, *Blood and Ruins*, 784, 790, 794, 809, 811.

248. The Italian War Ministry estimated that between 8 September 1943 and the war's end in 1945, 1,159 rapes and 391 attempted rapes had been carried out on Italian women, 88 percent of them in May–June 1944. Seventy percent of the assaults had occurred in Latium, the province that included Cassino and Rome, and 20 percent in Tuscany, that encompassed Siena. The CEF's own judicial records revealed that 84 percent of soldiers tried for sexual assault in Italy committed their crimes in May, June, and July 1944. Le Gac, *Vaincre sans gloire*, 433–434.
249. Julie Le Gac, "Comportement des troupes françaises en Italie," in François Broche, Georges Caïtucoli, and Jean-François Muracciole (eds.), *Dictionnaire de la France Libre* (Paris: Robert Laffont, 2010), 351.
250. Jacques Gachet, one of only two personnel assigned by the French to evaluate Italian allegations, reported on 3 June 1947 as follows: "One can evidently be surprised that the quasi-totality of women from selected villages could be victims ... without consent. Initially I shared this doubt. But, after having studied hundreds of files, after having interrogated the priests, the doctors, and the mayors, after the numerous assertions of many of these women or their relatives, I feel confident in saying, without fear of error, that, even if we find ourselves confronted by a certain number of false declarations or exaggerations, we are permitted to estimate that 80 percent of these complaints are legitimate. I can also say that, for the same reasons, the scope of the problem is underestimated, either because the victims wish to avoid that a request for indemnity would alert a husband or a father, or because, out of modesty, they do not wish to call attention to events of which they were the victims. To be surprised by the number of women violated in a village is to ignore how these events transpired. It is through the worst acts of violence, of extreme brutality that escalated to murder, that these Moroccans, who worked in gangs, could overcome the resistance of these tough and resilient girls of the Apennines. There were obviously rapes ... by mutual consent, the victims of which don't hesitate to exaggerate the loss of their virginity. But these charges are easily corroborated not only by the aforementioned mayors and priests who have pointed them out, but also by other women who are reluctant to see their names alongside that of the village prostitute." Le Gac, *Vaincre sans gloire*, 446–447, 485–486.
251. Miot, "Sortir l'armée des ombres," 17.
252. Mary Louise Roberts, *What Soldiers Do: Sex and the American GI in World War II France* (Chicago: University of Chicago Press, 2013).
253. Norman M. Naimark, *The Russians in Germany: A History of the Soviet Zone of Occupation, 1945–1949* (Cambridge, MA: Harvard University Press, 1995), 133.
254. Miot, "Sortir l'armée des ombres," 640–642, 655. While Miot is writing about French conduct toward Germans in 1945, many of the same attitudes applied in 1943 and 1944 in Italy.
255. Lapouge, *De Sétif à Marseille, par Cassino*, 222–223.
256. Le Gac, *Vaincre sans gloire*, 436–440.
257. Le Gac, "Comportement des troupes françaises en Italie," 351.
258. Le Gac, *Vaincre sans gloire*, 451–457, 462–463.
259. Julie Le Gac, "'Le mal napolitain': Les Alliés et la prostitution à Naples (1943–1944)," *Genre et Histoire*, 15 (Autumn 2014–Spring 2015), https://journals.openedition.org/genrehistoire/2154; Madeline Morris, "By Force of Arms: Rape, War, and Military Culture," *Duke Law Journal*, 45/4 (February 1996), 711, https://scholarship.law.duke.edu/dlj/vol45/iss4/1.
260. Lapouge, *De Sétif à Marseille, par Cassino*, 116–117.
261. Miot, "Sortir l'armée des ombres," 650.
262. Le Gac, *Vaincre sans gloire*, 451.
263. Le Gac, *Vaincre sans gloire*, 465.
264. William Gallois, *A History of Violence in the Early Algerian Colony* (London: Palgrave Macmillan, 2013), https://archive.org/stream/WilliamGalloisAuth.AHistoryOfViolenceInTheEarlyAlgerianColony/William+Gallois+auth.+A+History+of+Violence+in+the+Early+Algerian+Colony_djvu.txt.
265. Le Gac, *Vaincre sans gloire*, 444.
266. Miot, "Sortir l'armée des ombres," 630.
267. Numbers of actual rapes are impossible to verify because of underreporting and so on. Also, the French authorities in Italy simply dismissed complaints against *goumiers*, while the French treasury later made collective, rather than individual, payments to the inhabitants of certain towns or villages. Commanders also excused European soldiers accused of rape for having been "misled" by their Muslim comrades. Also, the 156 French soldiers convicted of rape in Italy were simply listed by their birthplace, that did not indicate whether they were of European or indigenous origin. Nevertheless, Le Gac calculates that 56 percent of those convicted were French. Le Gac, *Vaincre sans gloire*, 444.
268. Notin, *La Campagne d'Italie 1943–1944*, 650.

269. Le Gac, *Vaincre sans gloire*, 450. These issues are discussed in relation to the attitudes of US soldiers to the liberation of France by Roberts, *What Soldiers Do*.
270. See, for instance, Jean-Christophe Notin, *Maréchal Juin* (Paris: Tallandier, 2015), 343 and note, in which he accuses Le Gac of "des affirmations totalement subjectives." Le Gac, *Vaincre sans gloire*, 427–429.
271. Notin, *La Campagne d'Italie 1943–1944*, 644.
272. Miot, "Sortir l'armée des ombres," 611.
273. Le Gac, *Vaincre sans gloire*, 469.
274. In the short term, however, the French victory did not benefit the Italian community in Tunisia, already the object of reprisals in the wake of the Tunisia campaign, which included the expulsion of those who had served in the Italian armed forces and expropriation of their property. The privileged status of Italians in Tunisia by virtue of the 1896 treaty was revoked by a 22 June 1944 CFLN ordinance. Le Gac, *Vaincre sans gloire*, 471–472.

CHAPTER 4

1. Louis Bacquier, *Aïwah: Au combat avec les Marocains. Souvenirs d'un officier de tirailleurs 1942–1945* (Paris: Éditions Laville, 2012), 32.
2. Sébastien Albertelli, *Atlas de la France Libre: De Gaulle et la France Libre, une aventure politique* (Paris: Éditions Autrement, 2010), 60.
3. Julian Jackson, "General de Gaulle and His Enemies: Anti-Gaullism in France since 1940," *Transactions of the Royal Historical Society*, 9 (1999), 51.
4. Robert O. Paxton, "The Truth about the Resistance," *New York Review of Books* (2016), www.nybooks.com/articles/2016/02/25/truth-about-french-resistance.
5. There was no tidy divide between popular and military resistance behind the Eastern Front, where many soldiers had been left behind by the retreat of 1941, where the NKVD security services took an active role in organizing partisan bands, whose activities might be closely coordinated with conventional operations. Nor did the Germans distinguish between the partisan movement and the civilian population during anti-partisan operations. Alexander Hill, *The Red Army and the Second World War* (Cambridge: Cambridge University Press, 2017), 270–286. Nevertheless, partisan movements were less successful in Ukraine, where a combination of treeless steppe, aerial reconnaissance, mobile columns, and "violent hostility to the Soviet regime going back to 1918" meant that, "despite repeated efforts on the Soviet side, their partisans could find no footing." Adam Tooze, "The War of the Villages. The Interwar Agrarian Crisis and the Second World War," in Michael Geyer and Adam Tooze (eds.), *The Cambridge History of World War II*, volume III, *Total War: Economy, Society, and Culture* (Cambridge: Cambridge University Press, 2015), 398.
6. Jean-François Muracciole, "La France a contribué à la victoire des Alliés," in Jean Lopez and Olivier Wieviorka (eds.), *Les mythes de la seconde guerre mondiale* (Paris: Perrin, 2015), 340–342.
7. Olivier Wieviorka, *Histoire de la Résistance 1940–1945* (Paris: Perrin, 2013), 15–16.
8. Robert Belot, *La Résistance sans de Gaulle* (Paris: Fayard, 2006), 12.
9. Belot, *La Résistance sans de Gaulle*, 13.
10. Fabrice Grenard, *Maquis noirs et faux maquis 1943–1947* (Paris: Vendémaire, 2011), 14–22.
11. On *l'affaire Suisse*, see Raphaële Balu, "Les maquis de France, la France libre et les Alliés (1943–1945): Retrouver la coopération," Thèse du doctorat, Université de Caen Normandie, 2018, 122–137.
12. Olivier Wieviorka, *Normandy: The Landings to the Liberation of Paris* (Cambridge, MA: Harvard University Press, 2008), 337–338; Robert Gildea, *Fighters in the Shadows. A New History of the French Resistance*, (Cambridge, MA: Harvard University Press, 2015), 62–65, 127, 137–141.
13. Indeed, in one notorious incident, a painter from the Côte d'Azure named André Girard almost succeeded in convincing the British SOE to supply arms and cash to what he alleged was his "Carte" resistance network that numbered 50,000 men. The hoax was discovered only at the end of 1942. But the SOE's momentary gullibility in the shadow of Torch had been brought about by an eagerness to create a resistance organization independent of de Gaulle. Julian Jackson, *De Gaulle* (Cambridge, MA: Harvard University Press, 2018), 233.
14. Guillaume Piketty, *Pierre Brossolette: Un héro de la résistance* (Paris: Éditions Odile Jacob, 1998), 180.
15. Piketty, *Pierre Brossolette*, 152–176.
16. Piketty, *Pierre Brossolette*, 180–183.
17. Sébastien Laurent, "Les guerres des services spéciaux en Afrique du Nord (novembre 1942–novembre 1944)," in Général Louis Rivet, *Carnets du chef des services secrets 1936–1944*, eds. Olivier Forcade and Sébastian Laurent (Paris: Nouveau Monde Éditions, 2010), 555.
18. Piketty, *Pierre Brossolette*, 183–189.

19. Charles de Gaulle, *Mémoires de guerre*, tome 1, *L'Appel 1940–1942* (Paris: Plon, 1959), 245.
20. Reorganization saw the DGSS placed under Gaullist Jacques Soustelle. Passy was named to head a "*direction technique*" tasked with coordinating intelligence, counterintelligence, and "action" with the BCRAA (BCRA Algiers) under André Pélabon and the BCRAL (BCRA London) under André Manuel. Sébastien Albertelli, *Les Services secrets du Général de Gaulle: Le BCRA, 1940–1944* (Paris: Perrin, 2009), 127, 510–523. See also a discussion of the "fusion" of the intelligence services in Laurent, "Les guerres des service spéciaux en Afrique du Nord." For a shorter synopsis, see François Broche, Georges Caïtucoli, and Jean-François Muracciole (eds.), *Dictionnaire de la France Libre* (Paris: Robert Laffont, 2010), 454–456.
21. Jean-Louis Crémieux-Brilhac, *La France libre: De l'appel du 18 juin à la libération* (Paris: Gallimard, 2013), tome 2, 1071–1091; Laurent, "Les guerres des services spéciaux en Afrique du Nord," 564.
22. Wieviorka, *Histoire de la Résistance 1940–1945*, 272–274.
23. Albertelli, *Les Services secrets du Général de Gaulle*, 131–135.
24. Albertelli, *Les Services secrets du Général de Gaulle*, 135–139. Jean Moulin's mission to unify resistance groups in the former *zone libre* in 1943 fell under the CNI's direction, while Brousselette's in the *zone nord* was run by the BCRA. Guillaume Piketty, "La Mission Arquebuse–Brumaire," www.charles-de-gaulle.org/wp-content/uploads/2017/10/La-mission-Arquebuse-Brumaire.pdf.
25. Piketty, *Pierre Brossolette*, 187–194, 211; Albertelli, *Les Services secrets du Général de Gaulle*, 128–129, 143–145.
26. Albertelli, *Les Services secrets du Général de Gaulle*, 146–150.
27. Hugh Verity, *We Landed by Moonlight: Secret RAF Landings in France, 1940–1944* (Manchester: AirData Publications Limited, 1995), 11–22, 39.
28. Verity, *We Landed by Moonlight*, 75–86.
29. Piketty, *Pierre Brossolette*, 178, 187, 218; Jackson, *De Gaulle*, 225–229, 258. De Gaulle was again admonished by André Philip in 1943 and Michel Debré in 1948 about his dismissive attitude to subordinates. He was particularly cruel toward Jacques Soustelle, who, despite his early support and eventually assuming direction of the DGSS and post-war direction of de Gaulle's political party, the Rassemblement du peuple français (RPF), was never made a *compagnon de la Libération*, whereas André Malraux, who was more closely associated with the communists, whom de Gaulle met only in August 1945, was initiated into this Olympus of resistance deities. Jackson, *De Gaulle*, 406–409.
30. Wieviorka, *Histoire de la Résistance 1940–1945*, 240–258.
31. Gildea, *Fighters in the Shadows*, 129; Sébastien Albertelli, "The British, Free French, and Resistance," in Robert Tombs and Emile Chabal (eds.), *Britain and France in Two World Wars: Truth, Myth, and Memory* (London and New York: Bloomsbury, 2013), 124; Guillaume Piketty, "Le Conseil National de la résistance," in François Broche, Georges Caïtucoli, and Jean-François Muracciole (eds.), *Dictionnaire de la France Libre* (Paris: Robert Laffont, 2010), 363–365.
32. Arquebuse–Brumaire, fabricated from the codenames for Passy and Brossolette, respectively, had at least three objectives. First, compile an inventory of all groups – resistance, unions, political parties, even religious associations – that might take part in a "national insurrection" on the liberation. Second, convince them to compartmentalize political from military activity, and, for Passy, detach intelligence collection from "military action." Finally, create a framework for a "steering committee," which would take the form of a *Comité de coordination de la zone nord* (CCZN), to replicate Moulin's effort in the south. Piketty, *Pierre Brossolette*, 212, 241, 244–248, 250, 344; Wieviorka, *Histoire de la Résistance 1940–1945*, 307. Already a *compagnon de la libération*, Brossolette was named to the committee of the *Médaille de la Résistance française*, and decorated with the *croix de la Libération*. He became the obvious candidate to step into Moulin's shoes after June 1943. The problem was that the resistance had not warmed to Brossolette's ideas of centralization and inclusion of politicians in representative bodies. He was also criticized for ceding too much influence in resistance structures to the communists. He had clashed violently with Moulin, who saw Brossolette's creation of the CCZN as undercutting his project to unify the resistance movements throughout France under a single authority, a quarrel that roiled the BCRA. Although Passy was a close ally of Brossolette, André Manuel, now head of the intelligence section of the BCRA, counted among Brossolette's multiple detractors. Piketty, *Pierre Brossolette*, 301–304; Piketty, "La Mission Arquebuse–Brumaire"; Jackson, *De Gaulle*, 261–262.
33. Wieviorka, *Histoire de la Résistance 1940–1945*, 299, 311.
34. Although the pre-war prefect of Lyon, Émile Bollaert, replaced Moulin as *délégué général* in September, he was regarded by Passy as "a bit senile," and a poor fit because of his total ignorance of the resistance. Following Bollaert's arrest and deportation, Georges Bidault became *délégué général*. Although a Christian Democrat, Bidault allowed the communists further to strengthen their independence and influence over strategy. Gildea, *Fighters in the Shadows*, 288–289. Nor did Passy allow them much independence.

Guillaume Piketty, "Pierre Brossolette (1903–1944)," in François Broche, Georges Caïtucoli, and Jean-François Muracciole (eds.), *Dictionnaire de la France Libre* (Paris: Robert Laffont, 2010), 216–219.

35. Wieviorka, *Histoire de la Résistance 1940–1945*, 285–286; Jean-Pierre Azéma, "Des résistances à la Résistance," in Jean-Pierre Azéma and François Bédarida (eds.), *La France des années noires*, tome 2, *De l'Occupation à la Libération* (Paris: Éditions du Seuil, 1993), 260–263.
36. Wieviorka, *Histoire de la Résistance 1940–1945*, 287–291.
37. Balu, "Les maquis de France, la France libre et les Alliés," 262–266.
38. Balu, "Les maquis de France, la France libre et les Alliés," 81.
39. Wieviorka, *Histoire de la Résistance 1940–1945*, 327–334.
40. Quoted in Balu, "Les maquis de France, la France libre et les Alliés," 237.
41. By the time more accurate reports arrived, the impression had set in that, despite significant British arms drops, Mihailović was "not doing enough." In any case, McMeekin concludes that Maclean only told Churchill what the Prime Minister, eager to cut off Mihailović and so have something to offer Stalin at Teheran, wanted to hear: "Tito and Stalin could hardly believe their luck." Sean McMeekin, *Stalin's War: A New History of World War II* (New York: Basic Books, 2021), 483–484.
42. Balu, "Les maquis de France, la France libre et les Alliés," 244–246, 251–253, 674.
43. The DGSS was created out of the fusion of the Gaullist BCRA and the "Giraudist" SR. While the process had begun in November 1943, it was resisted by both services, and culminated only in April 1944, when Gaullist Jacques Soustelle was confirmed as chief. Nevertheless, former "Giraudists" continued to dominate the DGSS. Sébastien Albertelli, "Direction générale des services spéciaux," in François Broche, Georges Caïtucoli, and Jean-François Muracciole (eds.), *Dictionnaire de la France libre* (Paris: Robert Laffont, 2010), 454–456.
44. Marianne Colonna, "Mythologies de la libération: Propagande et résistance," in Yves Jeanclos (ed.), *La France et les soldats d'infortune au XXe siècle* (Strasbourg: Economica, 2003), 232–233.
45. Steve Weiss, "The Resistance as Part of Anglo-American Planning for the Liberation of Northwestern Europe," in Jacqueline Sainclivier and Christian Bougeard (eds.), *La Résistance et les français: Enjeux stratégiquee et environment social* (Rennes: Presses universitaires de Rennes, 1995), 53–66, https://books.openedition.org/pur/16351?lang=en.
46. Albertelli, *Les Services secrets du Général de Gaulle*, 510–511.
47. Jackson, *De Gaulle*, 261.
48. Balu, "Les maquis de France, la France libre et les Alliés," 262–274, 658; Albertelli, *Les Services secrets du Général de Gaulle*, 450–453; Jackson, *De Gaulle*, 262.
49. Crémieux-Brilhac, *La France libre*, tome 1, 1097–1102.
50. The Chef der Militärbefehlshaber, General Otto von Stülpnagel, whose headquarters were in Paris' Hôtel Majestic, was head of the military administration of the *zone occupée*. Although subordinate to the Oberkommando der Wehrmacht (OKW), he commanded no combat troops in France. Many of the Reich's ministries were represented in France by German civil servants. Although they wore uniforms with special badges and had been assigned a military rank, they answered to their various ministries, not to the army. Franco-German military and political relations relating to the 1940 Armistice fell under the purview of the Armistice Commission, the *Waffenstillstandskommission* (*Wako*) in Wiesbaden. A separate delegation dealt with economic questions. The departments of the Nord and the Pas-de-Calais were controlled from Brussels, while Alsace and Moselle fell under the authority of the Gauleiters of Baden and the Palatinate, Robert Wagner and Josef Bürckel. From November 1942, the former *zone libre* fell under Oberbefehlshaber West in Lyon, a situation that encouraged confusion and competition with the *Militärbefehlshaber*. As ambassador to France, but not accredited to Vichy, where Germany was represented by a consul, Otto Abetz's actual prerogatives were unclear. His initiatives were often purely personal ones, which brought him into frequent conflict with the army. Disputes were arbitrated by Hitler, who paid only intermittent attention to French affairs. The presence in France of the *Schutzstaffel* (SS), the security service the *Sicherheitsdienst* (SD), and the German police grew from 1942. In February 1942, Stülpnagel resigned in protest over the killing of French hostages, which he believed counterproductive, to be replaced by his cousin Karl Heinrich von Stülpnagel. Eager to impose a clear separation of political and security issues, in March 1942, Karl Heinrich imported Carl-Albrecht Oberg as *Höherer SS- und Polizeiführer*, who introduced into France many of the repressive policies that had been pioneered in the East. Public order, including "racial" persecution and suppression of the resistance, was increasingly imposed by the army and the SS. The voracious labor demands of Albert Speer's Ministry of Armaments were pressed by Commissioner of Manpower Fritz Sauckel. The German railways organized deportations with the cooperation of the Société nationale des chemins de fer français (SNCF), while Herman Göring's agents turned over Paris looking for "Aryanized" Jewish firms. And so on. Rainer Hudemann, "The Army as an Occupying Power: The German Army in 1940–1944, the French Army in 1945–1949," in Klaus-

Jürgen Müller (ed.), *The Military in Politics and Society in France and Germany in the Twentieth Century* (Oxford and Washington, D.C.: Berg, 1995), 141–146.

51. Alya Aglan, "'Wie Gott in Frankreich'? Les Allemands en France, 1940–1948," in Alya Aglan and Robert Frank (eds.), *1937–1947: La guerre-monde,* tome II (Paris: Gallimard, 2015), 1808–1812; Wieviorka, *Histoire de la Résistance 1940–1945*, 211.
52. Philippe Burrin, *France under the Germans: Collaboration and Compromise* (New York: The New Press, 1996 [French edition 1993]), 132.
53. Jean Estèbe, *Toulouse 1940–1944* (Paris: Perrin, 1996), 316, 318; Peter Lieb and Robert O. Paxton, "Maintenir l'ordre en France occupée. Combien de divisions?," *Vingtième Siècle. Revue d'histoire*, 2011/4, no. 112 (2011), 115–126.
54. Burrin, *France under the Germans*, 143–144, 166–167.
55. Rolf-Dieter Müller, *Hitler's Wehrmacht, 1935–1945* (Lexington: University Press of Kentucky, 2016), 36. Other estimates give higher figures.
56. Wieviorka, *Histoire de la Résistance 1940–1945*, 209.
57. This was because *la relève* fell heavily on skilled and older workers, rather than peasants and the young. Robert Gildea, *Marianne in Chains: In Search of the German Occupation of France 1940–45* (London: Macmillan, 2002), 281.
58. Gertrude Stein, "Tired of Winter Tired of War," in Anne Matthews, Nancy Caldwell Sorel, and Rodger J. Spiller (compilers), *Reporting World War II*, Part One: *American Journalism 1938–1944* (New York: The Library of America, 1995), 774–775.
59. In 1942, the productivity of a French worker in Germany was reckoned to be 85–88 percent that of a German worker, significantly above the average for Russians and Poles. Richard Overy, *Blood and Ruins: The Last Imperial War, 1931–1945* (London: Viking, 2022), 428.
60. H. Roderick Kedward, "STO et Maquis," in Jean-Pierre Azéma and François Bédarida (eds.), *La France des années noires*, tome 1, *De la défaite à Vichy* (Paris: Éditions du Seuil, 1993), 274–281; Gildea, *Marianne in Chains*, 277–290, 307; Wieviorka, *Histoire de la Résistance 1940–1945*, 439.
61. Philippe Buton, "La France atomisée," in Jean-Pierre Azéma and François Bédarida (eds.), *La France des années noires*, tome 2, *De l'Occupation à la Libération* (Paris: Éditions du Seuil, 1993), 380–381.
62. According to Burrin, while the Church never sought German protection, it had rejected the Popular Front's secularizing values. It also benefited from state-funded parochial schools under Vichy. While the Church did not endorse collaboration publicly, individual bishops did, and the Church supported it indirectly by denouncing Gaullists and the resistance, supporting *la relève*, offering a celebratory mass for the Légion des volontaires français contre le bolchévisme (LVF) and individual LVF members killed in the East, officiating at funerals of collaborators and *la Milice*, and so on. Anti-communism constituted the principal point of convergence between Nazism and the Church – for instance, Bishops Suhard and Baudrillart in Paris wanted to declare public approval of Unternehmen (Operation) Barbarossa. By the summer of 1942, bishops had begun to realize that public opinion had turned against Vichy and that Pétain's credibility and prestige had cratered. But this did not cause them to scale back their loyalty to the Marshal – in May 1943, the Church recommended "submission" to STO and remained silent on Nazi and Vichy crimes such as the execution of hostages, deportations, and the persecution of Jews. They stayed silent even when it became obvious that the Axis' days were numbered, because they clung to the hope of a compromise peace that would keep order and insure a peaceful transition at the Liberation. Burrin, *France under the Germans*, 81, 217–227. On missionary work, see Gildea, *Marianne in Chains*, 382.
63. Gildea, *Marianne in Chains*, 296; Robert O. Paxton, *Vichy France: Old Guard and New Order, 1940–1944* (London: Barrie & Jenkins, 1972), 369; Patrice Arnaud, *Les STO: Histoire des français requis en Allemagne nazi 1942–1945* (Paris: CNRS Éditions, 2014), 14.
64. Because his demands conflicted with the Todt Organization's requirement for workers in France, and because some German officials undermined his call-up by taking bribes, often from French industrialists trying to secure their work force, Sauckel conceded that 100,000 of the 350,000 could work in France.
65. In May 1944, 5.6 million foreigners were employed in German factories, or 21 percent of the industrial workforce. Julian Jackson, *France: The Dark Years 1940–1944* (New York: Oxford University Press, 2003), 234; Paxton, *Vichy France*, 369.
66. It was in this 22 June 1942 speech that Laval famously declared "je souhaite la victoire de l'Allemagne." Burrin, *France under the Germans*, 151–153. On repatriations, see Patrice Arnaud, *Les STO*, 46, 443–452.
67. Grenard, *Maquis noirs et faux maquis 1943–1947*, 34–35.
68. Stein, "Tired of Winter Tired of War," 764–765.
69. Gildea, *Marianne in Chains*, 286.
70. H. R. Kedward, *In Search of the Maquis: Rural Resistance in Southern France 1942–1944* (Oxford: Oxford University Press, 1993), 29–30, 35.

71. Arnaud, *Les STO*, 45–53; Wieviorka, *Histoire de la Résistance 1940–1945*, 497.
72. Colonna, "Mythologies de la libération," 228.
73. Grenard, *Maquis noirs et faux maquis 1943–1947*, 29.
74. Gildea, *Marianne in Chains*, 316.
75. According to the BCRA, the regions with the highest numbers of STO "*réfractaires*" were the Haute-Savoie and la Corrèze. Others with high numbers included the Savoie, the Ardennes, the Limousin, and Brittany. Cited in François Boulet, "Deux montagne-maquis exemplaires dans la France occupée (1943–1944): La montagne limousine et la Haute-Savoie," in Vincent Brousse and Philippe Grandcoing (eds.), *Un siècle militant: Engagement(s), resistance(s), et memoire(s) au XX*[e] *siècle en Limousin* (Limoges: Presses universitaires de Limoges, 2005), 45. But STO dodging was common throughout the country, so that "those who actually left on trains for Germany were only a minority of those called up." Gildea, *Marianne in Chains*, 287.
76. Balu, "Les maquis de France, la France libre et les Alliés," 50–52, 68–72.
77. Grenard, *Maquis noirs et faux maquis 1943–1947*, 35–38, 68–77, 110, 129–157.
78. Grenard, *Maquis noirs et faux maquis 1943–1947*, 28–30.
79. McMeekin, *Stalin's War*, 321.
80. Balu, "Les maquis de France, la France libre et les Alliés," 68.
81. Robert W. Duvall, "Maquis," in Spencer C. Tucker (ed.), *The Definitive Encyclopedia of World War II* (Santa Barbara and Denver: ABC-CLIO, 2016), vol. III, 1077.
82. Balu, "Les maquis de France, la France libre et les Alliés," 208–209, 360, 390–413; Gilles Vergnon, "Maquis mobilisateur" and François Marcot, "Michel Brault," in François Broche, Georges Caïtucoli, and Jean-François Muracciole (eds.), *Dictionnaire de la France Libre* (Paris: Robert Lafont, 2010), 941.
83. Osbert Lancaster, "Zhto, Zhto, KKE!," *Times Literary Supplement*, No. 3290 (18 March 1965), 205.
84. Paul Fussell, *The Great War and Modern Memory* (New York and London: Oxford University Press, 1975), 328–329; Peter Wilkinson and Joan Bright Astley, *Gubbins & SOE* (London: Leo Cooper, 1993), 71, 75–76; M. R. D. Foot, *SOE in France* (London: HMSO, 1966), 18.
85. Balu, "Les maquis de France, la France libre et les Alliés," 348.
86. Balu, "Les maquis de France, la France libre et les Alliés," 541. The British argument was that a general arming of the resistance was inefficient, required too many air assets, and was potentially dangerous. Arming the resistance also became emmeshed in the debate over the decentralization of the resistance organization. While decentralization made sense as a security measure, it would make the resistance more difficult to coordinate operationally, while politically facilitating British or communist domination of some resistance networks. Albertelli, *Les Services secrets du Général de Gaulle*, 364–365, 426, 436–441.
87. Balu, "Les maquis de France, la France libre et les Alliés," 58–61, 98, 183–187.
88. Crémieux-Brilhac, *La France libre*, tome 2, 1138–1143; Paddy Ashdown, cited in Balu, "Les maquis de France, la France libre et les Alliés," 370–373.
89. On the 9 February broadcast of "*Les Français parlent aux Français*," Schumann evoked *le défilé d'Oyonnax*, at the very moment that arming *maquis* groups was being discussed. Three days later, the *Times* spoke of pressure put upon the *maquis* at Glières, a 1,450-meter-high plateau in the Hautes-Alpes, with a follow-up article on 16 February. *Combat* released a special edition dedicated to "*le défilé d'Oyonnax*," praising the *maquis* for exerting its control over a town of 12,000. On 28 February, the *Evening Standard* published an article on "The Men of the Maquis," complete with lists of trains derailed, pylons blown up, and so on. Balu, "Les maquis de France, la France libre et les Alliés," 362–365, 526.
90. Paddy Ashdown, *The Cruel Victory: The French Resistance, D-Day and the Battle for Vercors 1944* (London: William Collins, 2014), 90–93; Balu, "Les maquis de France, la France libre et les Alliés," 373.
91. Balu, "Les maquis de France, la France libre et les Alliés," 348–349.
92. Balu, "Les maquis de France, la France libre et les Alliés," 370–375.
93. Maurice Matloff, "The ANVIL Decision: Crossroads of Strategy," in Kent Roberts Greenfield (ed.), *Command Decisions* (Washington, D.C.: Center of Military History, United States Army, 1960), 383–400, https://history.army.mil/books/70-7_16.htm; Andrew Buchanan, *American Grand Strategy in the Mediterranean during World War II* (Cambridge: Cambridge University Press, 2014), 171.
94. Balu, "Les maquis de France, la France libre et les Alliés," 624.
95. In December 1943, the British counted 140 men in Greece, of whom 79 were officers; 20 in Albania, of whom 9 were officers; and 100 in Yugoslavia, of whom 50 were officers, split between Mihailović and Tito. Churchill's order to arm the French came at a time when Balkan partisans had assumed a new importance in Allied planning as the campaign in Italy became bogged down. In January 1944, Passy could arm only around 4,000 men in France. Despite the post-January 1944 ramp-up of tonnage of arms and equipment sent to France, Yugoslavia received 16,000 tons, while France was in second position with 11,000 tons. Balu, "Les maquis de France, la France libre et les Alliés," 253–254, 370–375, 487–496, 635–637.

96. This would fall initially to the *Comité maquis* or Maquis Committee, which met from March 1944 under Lord Selborne and included representatives from the "interface organizations," namely the SOE, OSS, and BCRA, as well as the RAF. But, because its parameters were ill-defined, its status being merely consultative, and because it lacked SHAEF buy-in, the committee focused mainly and successfully on increasing arms deliveries to the *maquis* in Alpine France, which Churchill had prioritized, and on inserting agents. Balu, "Les maquis de France, la France libre et les Alliés," 350, 365–366, 370–371, 379–388, 603.
97. Balu, "Les maquis de France, la France libre et les Alliés," 23–25, 46, 83, 86, 95–97.
98. And finally, there was the État-major des Forces françaises de l'intérieur (EMFFI), stood up by de Gaulle on the eve of D-Day under Koenig, the operational purpose of which no one at SHAEF could initially decipher. In fact, its political purpose was to control the internal Resistance. For this reason, the EMFFI was not fully integrated into SHAEF before August 1944. Nor was the writ of Koenig's authority clear, as Eisenhower had been forbidden by Roosevelt to deal with an entity created by the self-proclaimed but as yet officially unacknowledged Gouvernement provisoire de la république française (GPRF). Ashdown, *The Cruel Victory*, 146–147; Balu, "Les maquis de France, la France libre et les Alliés," 220–222, 432–449, 454–457, 489.
99. Balu, "Les maquis de France, la France libre et les Alliés," 371–372, 579.
100. Wieviorka, *Histoire de la Résistance*, 339.
101. Ashdown, *The Cruel Victory*, 126–127.
102. Balu, "Les maquis de France, la France libre et les Alliés," 355–359, 427–430.
103. Balu, "Les maquis de France, la France libre et les Alliés," 376–378, 385–388, 450–451.
104. Richard Overy cites similar difficulties in air supply to the Polish resistance in 1944. Overy, *Blood and Ruins*, 701.
105. Balu, "Les maquis de France, la France libre et les Alliés," 532.
106. Balu, "Les maquis de France, la France libre et les Alliés," 179–180. According to Overy, between 1943 and 1945, the RAF dropped 9,455 tons of supplies to resistance groups in France, roughly half the amount dropped to Yugoslav partisans. Overy, *Blood and Ruins*, 706.
107. Some of these problems had been corrected by 1944 in the Sten Mk V. Chris McNab, "Cheap Shot: How the Sten Gun Saved Britain," *HistoryNet* (Autumn 2019), www.historynet.com/cheap-shot-how-the-sten-gun-saved-britain.htm.
108. Ashdown, *The Cruel Victory*, 116–117, 127, 129–130.
109. Balu, "Les maquis de France, la France libre et les Alliés," 237.
110. Jean-William Dereymez, "Vercors," in François Broche, Georges Caïtucoli, and Jean-François Muracciole (eds.), *Dictionnaire de la France Libre* (Paris: Robert Lafont, 2010), 1458–1459.
111. Upon the Liberation, Farge would become one of seventeen civilian *Commissaires de la République* appointed by de Gaulle to oversee the transition of power from Vichy to the CFLN/GPRF.
112. Ashdown, *The Cruel Victory*, 20–55; Olivier Wieviorka, *Histoire de la Résistance 1940–1945* (Paris: Perrin, 2013), 390; Gilles Vergnon, "Pierre Dalloz," http://museedelaresistanceenligne.org/media966-Pierre-Dalloz.
113. Wieviorka, *Histoire de la Résistance 1940–1945*, 216–217.
114. Ashdown, *The Cruel Victory*, 95, 370.
115. Dereymez, "Vercors," 1459.
116. Balu, "Les maquis de France, la France libre et les Alliés," 290–294, 339–340.
117. Ashdown, *The Cruel Victory*, 88–89.
118. Camille Rougeron, "Le rôle des guerillas dans l'opération d'ensemble contre le continent Européen," SHD-GR, 7P 167. The paper, that offers a short treatise on the value of the resistance, is undated but stamped "vu par le général," presumably Giraud. As Rougeron mentions that the Italians are still in the war and that Corsica offered a promising venue for insurgent operations, the paper was obviously written prior to September 1943. On Rougeron, see Claude d'Abzac-Epezy, "La pensée militaire de Camille Rougeron: Innovations et marginalité," *Revue française de science politique*, 54/5 (2004), 761–779, www.cairn.info/article.php?ID_ARTICLE=RFSP_545_0761.
119. The 1863 Lieber Codes developed during the American Civil War had been subsequently adopted by the Prussian Army. These, and the laws of war set out at The Hague in 1900, permitted militias, volunteer corps, and even spontaneous risings to defend against invasion so long as they assumed a form that closely resembled that of regular armies. Once an invasion phase is complete, and so long as the population does not resist beyond the point of capitulation, the invader settles into occupation, which assumes a return to quasi-normalcy and legality. Occupied populations trade non-resistance for safety. Civilians were to be treated well so long as they behaved. However, the military commander decided upon the standard of behavior required for military order. "He may expel, transfer, imprison, or fine the revolted citizens who refuse to pledge themselves anew as citizens obedient to the law and loyal to the government." Also permitted was

property destruction, starvation, and hostage-taking. Lawmakers meeting at The Hague in 1907 forbade the killing of surrendered enemy combatants and attacks against or bombardment of undefended towns or habitations, and ruled that inhabitants of occupied territories could not be forced to fight against their own country. They also forbade collective punishments. Sibylle Scheipers, *Unlawful Combatants: A Genealogy of the Irregular Fighter* (Oxford: Oxford University Press, 2015), 82–83. A horror of the *franc-tireur*, imbedded in German military culture since 1870, became reinforced by turn-of-the-twentieth-century colonial conquests, viewed by some as a rehearsal for genocide in all imperial armies, but especially that of Germany. See, for instance, Douglas Porch, *Counterinsurgency: Exposing the Myths of the New Way of War* (Cambridge: Cambridge University Press, 2013); Patricia Owens, *Counterinsurgency and the Rise of the Social* (Cambridge: Cambridge University Press, 2013).

120. The campaign against the Herero (1904–1907) had featured extermination camps as well as a tactic of driving tribes into the desert, where they perished from thirst. The winning tactic against the Maji Maji (1905–1907) proved to be a deliberately induced famine in which an estimated 300,000 Africans died. Elizabeth Hull, *Absolute Destruction: Military Culture and the Practices of War in Imperial Germany* (Ithaca, NY, and London: Cornell University Press, 2005), 191.
121. Unpublished lecture by Jonathon Gumz, Oxford University, 3 November 2014.
122. Scheipers, *Unlawful Combatants*, 143–144.
123. Michael Geyer and Adam Tooze, "Introduction to Part III," in Michael Geyer and Adam Tooze (eds.), *The Cambridge History of World War II*, volume III, *Total War: Economy, Society, and Culture* (Cambridge: Cambridge University Press, 2015), 416; Gaël Eismann, "L'escalade d'une repression à visage legal. Les pratiques judiciaires des tribunaux du Militärbefehlshaber in Frankreich, 1940–1944," in Gaël Eismann and Stefan Martens, *Occupation et repression militaire allemandes: La politique de "maintien de l'ordre" en Europe occupée, 1939–1945* (Paris: Éditions Autrement, 2007), 163–165.
124. Balu, "Les maquis de France, la France libre et les Alliés," 258–260.
125. Albertelli, *Les Services secrets du Général de Gaulle*, 292–294.
126. The Germans had begun their May 1941 invasion of Crete, and of course Tunis in November of the following year, by expanding out of airfields, while the Allies had also prioritized airfields in Torch.
127. Rougeron, "Le rôle des guerillas dans l'opération d'ensemble contre le continent Européen," SHD-GR, 7P 167.
128. Andrew L. Hargreaves, *Special Operations in World War II: British and American Irregular Warfare* (Norman: University of Oklahoma Press, 2013), 79–80, 208.
129. D'Abzac-Epezy, "La pensée militaire de Camille Rougeron."
130. Camille Rougeron, "La guerilla (I)," *Revue de Défense Nationale*, 3/43 (1947), 579–596; Camille Rougeron, "La guerilla (II)," *Revue de Défense Nationale*, 3/43 (1947), 758–777. Cited in Élie Tenenbaum, "Une odyssée subversive: La circulation des savoirs stratégiques irréguliers en Occident (France, Grande-Bretagne, États-Unis) de 1944 à 1972," Thèse du doctorat, Paris, Institut d'études politiques, 2015, 112–113, 137. See also Élie Tenenbaum, *Partisans et centurions: Une histoire de la guerre irrégulaire au XXe siècle* (Paris: Perrin, 2018).
131. No more than 2–3 percent of civil servants forsook their Vichy loyalties, Paxton calculates, about the same percentage as in the general population. Paxton, *Vichy France*, 285.
132. Balu, "Les maquis de France, la France libre et les Alliés," 78.
133. Colonna, "Mythologies de la libération," 228.
134. Guillaume Piketty, "Héros de la France libre – héros de la Résistance," *Revue de la France Libre*, no. 285 (1994), www.france-libre.net/sacrifice-brossolette.
135. François Hollande, "Putin Cannot Be Seduced. He Respects Force," *Financial Times*, 9 June 2023, www.ft.com/content/797390a5-aced-4c20-b6d7-6bd2a26f9e5a.
136. Dereymez, "Vercors," 1460.
137. Ashdown, *The Cruel Victory*, 94–95.
138. Ashdown, *The Cruel Victory*, 217–218, 241. For a rather burnished view of life in the maquis, see "Mystères d'archives 1944 dans le maquis du Vercors," https://www.youtube.com/watch?v=zoq7QREIgB8.
139. Albertelli, *Les Services secrets du Général de Gaulle*, 470.
140. Sébastien Albertelli, "Le BCRA et la résistance des militaires (1942–1944)," in Jean-William Dereymez (ed.), *Les militaires dans la résistance: Ain – Dauphiné – Savoie 1940–1944* (Avon-les-Roches: Éditions Anovi, 2010), 413–414.
141. Of those officers who joined the resistance, fully 760 were captured, of whom 360, including 27 generals, died in deportation. Christian Bachelier, "La Nouvelle armée française," in Jean-Pierre Azéma and François Bédarida (eds.), *La France des années noires*, tome 2, *De l'Occupation à la Libération* (Paris: Éditions du Seuil, 1993), 227; Jean-Pierre Azéma, "Des résistances à la Résistance," in Jean-Pierre Azéma

and François Bédarida (eds.), *La France des années noires*, tome 2, *De l'Occupation à la Libération* (Paris: Éditions du Seuil, 1993), 258.
142. Hargreaves, *Special Operations in World War II*, 218–226.
143. Paxton, "The Truth about the Resistance."
144. Wieviorka, *Histoire de la Résistance 1940–1945*, 218–224.
145. Balu, "Les maquis de France, la France libre et les Alliés," 613.
146. Balu, "Les maquis de France, la France libre et les Alliés," 654–659; Robert Gildea, "Resistance, Reprisals, and Community in Occupied France," *Transactions of the Royal Historical Society*, 13 (2003), 163–185.
147. Balu, "Les maquis de France, la France libre et les Alliés," 289, 399–401; Vergnon, "Maquis mobilisateur," 941.
148. Hargreaves, *Special Operations in World War II*, 221, 230; Balu, "Les maquis de France, la France libre et les Alliés," 666–668; Vergnon, "Maquis mobilisateur," 940.
149. Albertelli, *Les Services secrets du Général de Gaulle*, 294–299.
150. Balu, "Les maquis de France, la France libre et les Alliés," 145–146, 246, 263, 267, 297, 1210–1211.
151. Ashdown, *The Cruel Victory*, 152, 374–375; Balu, "Les maquis de France, la France libre et les Alliés," 656.
152. Albertelli, *Les Services secrets du Général de Gaulle*, 393.
153. Albertelli, *Les Services secrets du Général de Gaulle*, 464–469; Jean-Louis Crémieux-Brilhac, "Une stratégie militaire pour la Résistance: Le Bloc Planning et l'insurrection nationale," *Espoir*, no. 139 (2004), www.charles-de-gaulle.org/wp-content/uploads/2017/10/Une-strategie-militaire-pour-la-Resistance.pdf.
154. Balu, "Les maquis de France, la France libre et les Alliés," 288–289; Piketty, "La Mission Arquebuse–Brumaire"; Piketty, *Pierre Brossolette*, 201–212; Wieviorka, *Histoire de la Résistance 1940–1945*, 276–279, 315–317, 338–341, 361–365; Crémieux-Brilhac, *La France libre*, tome 2, 1073; Robert Belot, "État-major des forces françaises de l'intérieur de Londres," in François Broche, Georges Caïtucoli, and Jean-François Muracciole (eds.), *Dictionnaire de la France Libre* (Paris: Robert Lafont, 2010), 549–550; Ashdown, *The Cruel Victory*, 153.
155. Crémieux-Brilhac, "Une stratégie militaire pour la Résistance"; Balu, "Les maquis de France, la France libre et les Alliés," 657–658.
156. Balu, "Les maquis de France, la France libre et les Alliés," 659.
157. Balu, "Les maquis de France, la France libre et les Alliés," 295–300, 576–578, 663; Crémieux-Brilhac, *La France libre*, tome 2, 1150–1151; Ashdown, *The Cruel Victory*, 153.
158. Jean-Louis Crémieux-Brilhac, "Les Glières," *Vingtième Siècle. Revue d'histoire*, no. 45 (January–March 1995), 55.
159. Balu, "Les maquis de France, la France libre et les Alliés," 602–603.
160. Balu, "Les maquis de France, la France libre et les Alliés," 538.
161. Balu, "Les maquis de France, la France libre et les Alliés," 545–554.
162. Philippe Valode and Gérard Chauvy, *La Gestapo française* (Paris: Éditions Acropole, 2018), 300–314, 323–325.
163. Balu, "Les maquis de France, la France libre et les Alliés," 555–558.
164. Balu, "Les maquis de France, la France libre et les Alliés," 458–468.
165. Balu, "Les maquis de France, la France libre et les Alliés," 555–573
166. Balu, "Les maquis de France, la France libre et les Alliés," 604.
167. Balu, "Les maquis de France, la France libre et les Alliés," 1212.
168. Balu, "Les maquis de France, la France libre et les Alliés," 349; Albertelli, *Les Services secrets du Général de Gaulle*, 448–449.
169. Crémieux-Brilhac, "Les Glières," 61.
170. Crémieux-Brilhac, "Les Glières," 60; Crémieux-Brilhac, *La France libre*, tome 2, 1188; Balu, "Les maquis de France, la France libre et les Alliés," 608–610.
171. Crémieux-Brilhac, "Les Glières," 62.
172. Crémieux-Brilhac, "Les Glières," 63–64; Crémieux-Brilhac, "Jeux et enjeux d'Algier," in Jean-Pierre Azéma and François Bédarida (eds.), *La France des années noires*, tome 2, *De l'Occupation à la Libération* (Paris: Éditions du Seuil, 1993), 213–214; Albertelli, *Les Services secrets du Général de Gaulle*, 449–450.
173. Peter Lieb, *Vercors 1944: Resistance in the French Alps*, (London: Osprey, 2012), 12–22, 87.
174. The report was prepared from captured German documents, written in terse operational language, and is admittedly incomplete. "Synthèse de diverses opérations allemandes contre la Résistance Françaises éffectuées en Savoie, Haute-Savoie et Isère entre le 29 mars 1944 et le 8 août par le 157e Division de Réserve," 8 December 1944, SHD-GR, 7P 133.
175. Lieb, *Vercors 1944*, 10.

176. Lieb, *Vercors 1944*, 21.
177. Wieviorka, *Histoire de la Résistance 1940–1945*, 346–353; Crémieux-Brilhac, *La France libre*, tome 2, 1171–1193. Giolitto puts the number of maquisards killed at between 145 and 180, most executed in cold blood by the *Milice*, or deported. Pierre Giolitto, *Histoire de la milice* (Paris: Librairie Académique Perrin, 1997), 439–440. Crémieux-Brilhac says that 149 maquisards were killed, see Crémieux-Brilhac, "Les Glières," 65. See also Jean-Louis Crémieux-Brilhac, "La bataille des Glières et la 'guerre psychologique,'" in Jean-Louis Crémieux-Brilhac, *De Gaulle, la République et la France Libre, 1940–1945* (Paris: Perrin, 2014), 334–335.
178. Balu, "Les maquis de France, la France libre et les Alliés," 612–614.
179. Indeed, Stein recorded that rumors persisted in her small village of an Allied invasion in January 1944, "Tired of Winter Tired of War," 767.
180. Ashdown, *The Cruel Victory*, 140.
181. Albertelli, *Les Services secrets du Général de Gaulle*, 450.
182. Balu, "Les maquis de France, la France libre et les Alliés," 615–620; Ashdown, *The Cruel Victory*, 122–123, 371.
183. Gilles Vergnon, "Vercors: Polémiques d'après guerre," in François Broche, Georges Caïtucoli, and Jean-François Muracciole (eds.), *Dictionnaire de la France Libre* (Paris: Robert Lafont, 2010), 1461–1462.

CHAPTER 5

1. Général de Gaulle, "Discours radiodiffusé, Londres, 6 juin 1944," www.charles-de-gaulle.org/wp-content/uploads/2017/11/Discours-radiodiffuse.pdf.
2. The British lost 43,000 killed in the Blitz, and 6,000 to V-weapons. Helen Cleary, "V-weapons Attack Britain," www.bbc.co.uk/history/worldwars/wwtwo/ff7_vweapons.shtml.
3. Jean-Louis Beaucarnot, *Les Schneider: Une dynastie* (Paris: Hachette, 1986), 220–229.
4. Jean-Pierre Azéma and Olivier Wieviorka, *Vichy 1940–1944* (Paris: Perrin, 2004), 218.
5. Robert Gildea, *Marianne in Chains: Daily Life in the Heart of France during the German Occupation* (New York: Henry Holt, 2002), 291–295.
6. Gildea, *Marianne in Chains*, 298.
7. Tony Judt, *Past Imperfect: French Intellectuals 1944–56* (Berkeley: University of California Press, 1997).
8. Philippe Burrin, *France under the Germans: Collaboration and Compromise* (New York: The New Press, 1996 [French edition 1993]), 450; Jean-Charles Foucrier, *La stratégie de la destruction: Bombardements alliés en France, 1944* (Paris: Vendémaire, 2017), 192, 195.
9. Robert O. Paxton, *Vichy France: Old Guard and New Order, 1940–1944* (London: Barrie & Jenkins, 1972), 285–287.
10. The announcement was hardly a surprise, as the Consultative Assembly had voted for the change on 16 May. Nevertheless, if Churchill found the title change premature and presumptuous, for Roosevelt, it was unacceptable. Hilary Footitt and John Simmonds, *France 1943–1945* (Leicester: Leicester University Press, 1988), 65.
11. The issues addressed by the sub-committees of the War and State Departments were legal and financial questions, displaced persons, economic, and security. Talks between SHAEF and Koenig had centered on the role of the resistance. Footitt and Simmonds, *France 1943–1945*, 19–21, 26–29.
12. Footitt and Simmonds, *France 1943–1945*, 29. Phillips O'Brien reports that on 22 January 1944, Leahy noted in his diary that he had approved the request of Assistant Secretary of War John McCloy to allow liberated areas of France to be administered by the CFLN. *The Second Most Powerful Man in the World. The Life of Admiral William D. Leahy, Roosevelt's Chief of Staff*, (New York: Dutton, 2019), 268.
13. The Office of Strategic Services (OSS) suspected that Lemaigre-Dubreuil had used his advanced knowledge of Torch to help bankers spirit millions of francs out of French North Africa (AFN) in turn for a cut of the profits. Michael S. Neiberg, *When France Fell: The Vichy Crisis and the Fate of the Anglo-American Alliance* (Cambridge, MA: Harvard University Press, 2021), 234–235.
14. A. J. Liebling, "Notes from Kidnap House," in Samuel Hynes, Anne Matthews, Nancy Caldwell Sorel, and Robert J. Spiller (compilers), *Reporting World War II*, Part Two: *American Journalism 1944–1946* (New York: The Library of America, 1995), 83.
15. Sébastien Albertelli, *Les Services secrets du Général de Gaulle: Le BCRA 1940–1944* (Paris: Perrin, 2009), 446.
16. Raphaële Balu, "Les maquis de France, la France libre et les Alliés (1943–1945): Retrouver la coopération," Thèse du doctorat, Université de Caen Normandie, 2018, tome I, 674, 677–679, 685; Albertelli, *Les Services secrets du Général de Gaulle*, 447.

17. RAF attacks on trains, which greatly upset French opinion, were suspended between December 1943 and March 1944 as an experiment to see whether Special Operations Executive (SOE)-directed sabotage of locomotives could be as effective, which it was not. Other sabotage attacks carried out by teams trained in the UK included the attack on the dam at Port-Bernalin on 8–9 November 1943 that cut the canal joining the Seine to the Rhône for three months. Various attacks on factories making war material ensued. The most lucrative and easily destroyed targets proved to be electricity pylons. Albertelli, *Les Services secrets du Général de Gaulle*, 453–456.
18. Balu, "Les maquis de France, la France libre et les Alliés," tome I, 674–686; Albertelli, *Les Services secrets du Général de Gaulle*, 449, 451.
19. Albertelli, *Les Services secrets du Général de Gaulle*, 446.
20. Jean-Louis Crémieux-Brilhac, "Une stratégie militaire pour la Résistance: Le Bloc Planning et l'insurrection nationale," *Espoir*, no. 139 (2004), www.charles-de-gaulle.org/wp-content/uploads/2017/10/Une-strategie-militaire-pour-la-Resistance.pdf.
21. Charles de Gaulle, *Mémoires de guerre*, tome 2, *L'Unité* (Paris: Plon, 1994), 552.
22. Albertelli, *Les Services secrets du Général de Gaulle*, 460.
23. Albertelli, *Les Services secrets du Général de Gaulle*, 393–394.
24. Gilles Vergnon, "Maquis Mobilisateurs," in François Broche, Georges Caïtucoli, and Jean-François Muracciole (eds.), *Dictionnaire de la France Libre* (Paris: Robert Lafont, 2010), 940–942.
25. "Instruction concernant l'emploi de la Résistance sur le plan militaire au cours des opérations de libération de la métropole." Jean-Louis Crémieux-Brilhac, "Bloc Planning," in François Broche, Georges Caïtucoli, and Jean-François Muracciole (eds.), *Dictionnaire de la France Libre* (Paris: Robert Laffont, 2010), 165–166.
26. Crémieux-Brilhac, "Une stratégie militaire pour la Résistance"; Balu, "Les maquis de France, la France libre et les Alliés," tome I, 657.
27. Balu, "Les maquis de France, la France libre et les Alliés," tome I, 657.
28. Balu, "Les maquis de France, la France libre et les Alliés," tome I, 360, 390–413.
29. Paddy Ashdown, *The Cruel Victory: The French Resistance, D-Day and the Battle for the Vercors 1944* (London: William Collins, 2014), 183–184.
30. Resistance participation in the Liberation also forced an entrée into Allied planning, and staked a claim on Allied logistics, offered as a means to manipulate the competition between the SOE/Foreign Office and the OSS for influence over the resistance. Resistance sabotage also gave the French an argument to limit Allied bombing. Balu, "Les maquis de France, la France libre et les Alliés," tome I, 340, 390, 660–663.
31. Dwight D. Eisenhower, *Crusade in Europe* (Garden City, NY: Doubleday & Company Inc., 1950), 248.
32. Sean McMeekin makes the point that early British reports simply passed inflated claims for the military success of Tito's Partisans directly to Churchill, and speculates that more measured evaluations were slow to be deciphered and/or were held up by Soviet agents in Whitehall. Sean McMeekin, *Stalin's War: A New History of World War II* (New York: Basic Books, 2021), 482–483.
33. Ashdown, *The Cruel Victory*, 221; Balu, "Les maquis de France, la France libre et les Alliés," tome I, 665. Benjamin F. Jones gives different figures. Benjamin F. Jones, *Eisenhower's Guerrillas: The Jedburghs, the Maquis, and the Liberation of France* (Oxford: Oxford University Press, 2016), 236.
34. De Gaulle, *Mémoires de guerre*, tome 2, 552.
35. Crémieux-Brilhac states that it is unclear whether, or how much of, *Plan Caïman* was revealed to the resistance. Crémieux-Brilhac, "Une stratégie militaire pour la Résistance."
36. Balu, "Les maquis de France, la France libre et les Alliés," tome I, 668–670.
37. Balu, "Les maquis de France, la France libre et les Alliés," tome I, 670–673.
38. Albertelli, *Les Services secrets du Général de Gaulle*, 465; Balu, "Les maquis de France, la France libre et les Alliés," tome I, 653.
39. Crémieux-Brilhac, "Une stratégie militaire pour la Résistance"; Balu, "Les maquis de France, la France libre et les Alliés," tome I, 658–659.
40. Albertelli, *Les Services secrets du Général de Gaulle*, 385, 398–407; Douglas Porch, *The French Secret Services: A History of French Intelligence from the Dreyfus Affair to the Gulf War* (New York: Farrar, Straus, Giroux, 1995), Chapter 9.
41. M. R. D. Foot, *SOE in France* (London: HMSO, 1966), 360–361, 384–385. F section ran the "circuits" or networks in France. The RF section was the liaison with the BCRA.
42. Ashdown, *The Cruel Victory*, 372.
43. Albertelli, *Les Services secrets du Général de Gaulle*, 399, 404–405.
44. Ashdown, *The Cruel Victory*, 372.
45. Jones, *Eisenhower's Guerrillas*, 271, 280.
46. Peter Wilkinson and Joan Bright Astley, *Gubbins & SOE* (London: Leo Cooper, 1993), 195.

47. Balu, "Les maquis de France, la France libre et les Alliés," tome I, 436–449.
48. Albertelli, *Les Services secrets du Général de Gaulle*, 406–407. Ziegler would stake out a brilliant post-war career with Air France, where he played a leading role in the development of the supersonic airliner Concorde.
49. Balu, "Les maquis de France, la France libre et les Alliés," tome I, 435, 480–485, 489.
50. Balu, "Les maquis de France, la France libre et les Alliés," tome I, 472–485.
51. Joachim Ludewig, *Rückzug: The German Retreat from France, 1944* (Lexington: University Press of Kentucky, 2012), 27.
52. Balu, "Les maquis de France, la France libre et les Alliés," tome I, 537.
53. Balu, "Les maquis de France, la France libre et les Alliés," tome I, 574–578.
54. Foot, *SOE in France*, 442.
55. Foot, *SOE in France*, 441.
56. Balu, "Les maquis de France, la France libre et les Alliés," tome I, 696.
57. Jean-François Muracciole, "La France a contribué à la victoire des Alliés," in Jean Lopez and Olivier Wieviorka (eds,), *Les mythes de la seconde guerre mondiale* (Paris: Perrin, 2015), 343.
58. Balu, "Les maquis de France, la France libre et les Alliés," tome I, 688–694.
59. Ashdown, *The Cruel Victory*, 153–155, 371.
60. Ashdown, *The Cruel Victory*, 162.
61. Balu, "Les maquis de France, la France libre et les Alliés," tome I, 694–695.
62. Eisenhower, *Crusade in Europe*, 246–252.
63. Albertelli, *Les Services secrets du Général de Gaulle*, 494–495.
64. The BBC "personal messages" were rejected as an indicator because increased BBC activity and alert messages in the past had not been followed by an invasion, because the Germans believed the weather too bad for the Allies to attempt a landing, and because several Seventh Army senior commanders, including Rommel, were away from their posts on the night of 5–6 June. F. H. Hinsley, *British Intelligence in the Second World War: Its Influence on Strategy and Operations* (New York: Cambridge University Press, 1988), vol. III, Part II, 126–127.
65. Ashdown, *The Cruel Victory*, 372.
66. De Gaulle, "Discours radiodiffusé."
67. De Gaulle, *Mémoires de guerre*, tome 2, 552–553.
68. Crémieux-Brilhac, "Une stratégie militaire pour la Résistance."
69. Crémieux-Brilhac, "Une stratégie militaire pour la Résistance."
70. Balu, "Les maquis de France, la France libre et les Alliés," tome I, 669–670.
71. Balu, "Les maquis de France, la France libre et les Alliés," tome II, 808–811; Robert Gildea, "Resistance, Reprisals, and Community in Occupied France," *Transactions of the Royal Historical Society*, 13 (2003), 163–185; Peter Lieb and Robert O. Paxton, "Maintenir l'ordre en France occupée. Combien de divisions?," *Vingtième Siècle. Revue d'histoire*, 2011/4, no. 112 (2011), 115–126.
72. Balu, "Les maquis de France, la France libre et les Alliés," tome II, 803–805; Ludewig, *Rückzug*, 29.
73. Max Hastings, *Das Reich: The March of the 2nd SS Panzer Division through France, June 1944* (Saint Paul, MN: Zenith Press, 2013).
74. Killing of women and children occurred at Oradour, Maillé, Marsoulas, Bagnères-de-Bigorre, Buchères, Vassieux, and Gouesnou. But deportation was the more usual punishment for French women. Peter Lieb, "Wehrmacht, Waffen-SS et Sipo/SD: La répression allemande en France 1943–1944," in *La répression en France à l'été 1944*, Actes du colloque organisé par la Foundation de la Résistance et la ville de Saint-Amand-Montrond, Saint-Amand-Montrond le mercredi 8 juin 2005, pp. 12–14, www.fondationresistance.org/documents/ee/Doc00004-002.pdf.
75. Hélène Guillon, "Exécutions sommaires et massacres," in Michel Daeffler, Jean-Luc Leleu, Françoise Passera, and Jean Quellien (eds.), *La France pendant la Seconde Guerre mondiale: Atlas historique* (Paris: Fayard, 2010), pp. 212–213. Cited in Balu, "Les maquis de France, la France libre et les Alliés," tome II, 888.
76. Ashdown, *The Cruel Victory*, 174, 193.
77. Balu, "Les maquis de France, la France libre et les Alliés," tome II, 886–887. Fabrice Virgili found eighty-six cases of rape committed by the German army in Brittany alone, and emphasized the systematic use of sexual violence against members of the resistance from 1943. Fabrice Virgili, "Les viols commis par l'armée allemande en France (1940–1944)," *Vingtième siècle. Revue d'histoire*, 2016/2, no. 130 (2016), 104, 111, cited in Julie S. Torrie, *German Soldiers and the Occupation of France* (Cambridge: Cambridge University Press, 2018), 84–85.

78. Sabine Frühstück, "Sexuality and Sexual Violence," in Michael Geyer and Adam Tooze (eds.), *The Cambridge History of the Second World War*, volume III, *Total War: Economy, Society and Culture* (Cambridge: Cambridge University Press, 2015), 440–441.
79. Ashdown, *The Cruel Victory*, 156–157, 227, 244. Named *Délégué militaire pour les opérations de zone sud* (DMOS), French Air Force (FAF) Brigadier General Gabriel Cochet was the military liaison officer with the Allies for FFI operations, and also had responsibility for liberated French territories. Cochet's position was recognized in AFHQ only in July 1944. As a *Vichysto-résistant* and late convert to de Gaulle, Cochet was never fully trusted by the Gaullists. Although he technically served under Koenig's EMFFI, the fact that he continued to go straight to AFHQ, in great part because he could only communicate with the resistance through Allied radio links, displeased de Gaulle, who gave him a letter of reprimand after Maitland Wilson named Cochet and Koenig to command the FFI. Balu, "Les maquis de France, la France libre et les Alliés," tome II, 914.
80. According to the commentator, a team was sent by the Paris *Comité de la libération du cinema français* to film le Vercors. "Mystères d'archives 1944 dans le maquis du Vercors," www.youtube.com/watch?v=zoq7QREIgB8%26t=1393s.
81. Ashdown, *The Cruel Victory*, 241; Robert Gildea, *Fighters in the Shadows: A New History of the French Resistance* (Cambridge, MA: Harvard University Press, 2015), 354–355.
82. Andrew L. Hargreaves, *Special Operations in World War II: British and American Irregular Warfare* (Norman: University of Oklahoma Press, 2013), 71, 82–84, 179–180, 201–202; Ashdown, *The Cruel Victory*, 221.
83. Peter Lieb, *Vercors 1944: Resistance in the French Alps* (London: Osprey, 2012), 24–26; Balu, "Les maquis de France, la France libre et les Alliés," tome II," 812. The commentator in "Mystères d'archives 1944 dans le maquis du Vercors," which shows the maquisards being trained in weaponry and tactics by an American officer, possibly Captain Vernon G. Hoppers, notes that only one member of the group spoke French.
84. Gildea, *Fighters in the Shadows*, 354–355.
85. Ashdown, *The Cruel Victory*, 373.
86. Ashdown, *The Cruel Victory*, 219, 239, 228.
87. De Gaulle had rejected Grenier's plan as "insufficiently detailed." Ashdown, *The Cruel Victory*, 229. Gildea speculates that de Gaulle's veto of Grenier's plan came because "it may be that he wanted to put pressure on the Allies to commit, given that the French themselves had very little air potential," or that he wanted Billotte to command. Gildea, *Fighters in the Shadows*, 357–358.
88. Ashdown, *The Cruel Victory*, 241, 244–245, 270–271; Balu, "Les maquis de France, la France libre et les Alliés," tome II," 904–905; Gildea, *Fighters in the Shadows*, 357–358.
89. On numbers, see Balu, "Les maquis de France, la France libre et les Alliés," tome I, 554; Lieb, "Wehrmacht, Waffen-SS et Sipo/SD," 15–17. "Will be considered as a *franc-tireur* and as such condemned to death, he who, without wearing obvious insignia prescribed by international law that permit recognition as a member of an enemy army, carry or possess arms or other means of combat with the intention of utilizing them against the German army or an allied army or to kill a member of those armies, or he who carries out acts that, according to the customs of war, cannot be undertaken except by those members of the uniformed army. Also the sentence can order the confiscation of the property of the *franc-tireur*." SHD-GR, 7P 133, "Juridiction allemande," undated, but refers to legislation in 1940 and 1941.
90. SHD-GR, 7P 133, "Lutte contre les terroristes," 23 February 1944.
91. Lieb, *Vercors 1944*, 31; Gaël Eismann, *Hôtel Majestic: Ordre et sécurité en France occupée (1940–1944)* (Paris: Tallandier, 2010), 467–468; SHD-GR, 7P 133, "Combat contre les bandes terroristes; Précautions à prendre pour épargner la population civile," 22 and 29 July 1944.
92. Lieb, "Wehrmacht, Waffen-SS et Sipo/SD."
93. McMeekin, *Stalin's War*, 321.
94. Despite the fact that his command had been at the center of the controversy over the French collapse at Bulson in May 1940, Labarthe had been released from his *Oflag*, promoted to colonel, and named to oversee the GMR with the rank of brigadier general. For Labarthe's role at Bulson, see Robert A. Doughty, *The Breaking Point: Sedan and the Fall of France, 1940* (Mechanicsburg, PA: Stackpole Books, 1990), Chapter 8.
95. Yves Mathieu, *Policiers perdus: Les GMR dans la Seconde Guerre mondiale* (Toulouse: self-published, 2009), 50–71, 101–115, 130, 136, 177–180, 389.
96. Pierre Giolitto, *Histoire de la milice* (Paris: Librairie Académique Perrin, 1997), 130–131.
97. Giolitto, *Histoire de la milice*, 132–134; Philippe Burin, "La Guerre Franco-Française: Vers Sigmaringen," in Jean-Pierre Azéma and François Bédarida (eds.), *La France des années noires*, tome 2, *De l'Occupation à la Libération* (Paris: Éditions du Seuil, 1993), 34–40.
98. Burin, "La Guerre Franco-Française," 39.

99. Burrin, *France under the Germans*, 439.
100. Balu, "Les maquis de France, la France libre et les Alliés," tome II, 870.
101. Giotto estimates the number of militiamen at 10,000–15,000, of whom 3,000–4,000 were *Francs-Gardes*. Giolitto, *Histoire de la milice*, 152.
102. Burrin, *France under the Germans*, 440.
103. In June 1944, Abetz estimated that 2,000 French supporters of the occupation had been assassinated, including 300 *miliciens*. Burin, "La Guerre Franco-Française," 33.
104. Giolitto, *Histoire de la milice*, 215–218.
105. Giolitto, *Histoire de la milice*, 236–284.
106. Burrin, *France under the Germans*, 445–447, 451–452.
107. Burrin, *France under the Germans*, 448–455; Giolitto, *Histoire de la milice*, 161–218.
108. See, for instance, SHD-GR, 7P 133, "Synthèse de diverses opérations allemandes contre la Résistance Française effectuées en Savoie, Haute-Savoie et Isère entre le 29 mars 1944 et le 9 août 1944 par la 157e Division de Réserve," 8 December 1944, p. 12.
109. Lieb and Paxton, "Maintenir l'ordre en France occupée"; SHD-GR, 7P 133, "Synthèse de diverses opérations allemandes," p. 17.
110. Lieb, *Vercors 1944*, 11–14, 27.
111. Huet had been warned of the possibility of an airborne assault, but he had assumed it might target his HQ at Saint-Martin, and so had done nothing to prepare Vaissieux-en-Vercors to defend against it. Ashdown, *The Cruel Victory*, 289–290.
112. Lieb, "Wehrmacht, Waffen-SS et Sipo/SD," 12–13.
113. Ashdown, *The Cruel Victory*, 310–311; Balu, "Les maquis de France, la France libre et les Alliés," tome II," 963–967.
114. Lieb, *Vercors 1944*, 35–71.
115. Balu, "Les maquis de France, la France libre et les Alliés," tome II, 946–947; Olivier Wieviorka, *Histoire de la Résistance 1940–1945* (Paris: Perrin, 2013), 392–395.
116. SHD-GR, 12P 92, "Le détachement spécial de commandos de France," undated, probably September 1944.
117. Wieviorka, *Histoire de la Résistance 1940–1945*, 214.
118. Balu, "Les maquis de France, la France libre et les Alliés," tome II, 712.
119. François Marcot, "Maquis" in François Broche, Georges Caïtucoli, and Jean-François Muracciole (eds.), *Dictionnaire de la France Libre* (Paris: Robert Laffont, 2010), 938.
120. This interpretation is inspired by Leonard V. Smith, "Paul Fussell's *The Great War and Modern Memory*: Twenty-Five Years Later," *History and Theory*, 40/2 (May 2001), 258.
121. Marcot, "Maquis," 940. See also note 81 above.
122. For instance, an 18 August 1944 meeting in Brittany with the SHAEF G3 to ascertain resistance needs had been "carried on in a friendly atmosphere until [lieutenant] Colonel Rouvier [Inspector General of the FFI] delivered a provocative address accusing the Allies of treating the French Forces of the Interior shabbily, and of not being prepared to recompense them adequately for the work they were doing for the Allied cause. In order to make sure that his interest in the welfare of the French Forces of the Interior should be understood by all, the Colonel delivered his address in French." "Special Report on Resistance Operations in Brittany," undated, SHAEF G3 Division. NARA, RG 331, Entry 30A, Box 145.
123. And this view seemed to be bolstered as the OSS transitioned into the Central Intelligence Agency (CIA), with four former OSS agents serving as early directors – Allan Dulles (1953–1961), Richard Helms (1966–1973), William Colby (1973–1976), and William Casey (1981–1987) – while the Jedburghs became the inspiration for the Green Berets. Balu, "Les maquis de France, la France libre et les Alliés," tome II, 1176–1177, 1188, 1199–1201.
124. Lieb, "Wehrmacht, Waffen-SS et Sipo/SD," 15.
125. Wieviorka, *Histoire de la résistance 1940–1945*, 455–456. Balu favors the lower figure of 10,000 because not all FFI were maquisards, and not all of those deported were being punished for assisting the maquis. But the Gestapo and the Sipo/SD often used anti-*maquis* operations as an opportunity to round up Jews. Balu, "Les maquis de France, la France libre et les Alliés," tome II, 1039–1040.
126. Georges Vidal, "Milices patriotique," in François Broche, Georges Caïtucoli, and Jean-François Muracciole (eds.), *Dictionnaire de la France Libre* (Paris: Robert Laffont, 2010), 1000–1001.
127. Balu, "Les maquis de France, la France libre et les Alliés," tome II, 900, 915–928.
128. Lieb, *Vercors 1944*, 34.
129. Balu, "Les maquis de France, la France libre et les Alliés," tome II, 934–945, 1044.
130. Edgard de Larminat, *Chroniques irrévérencieuses* (Paris: Plon, 1962), 208.
131. Jean-Christophe Notin, *Leclerc: Le croisé de la France libre* (Paris: Perrin, 2015), 109–110; André Martel, "La libération et la victoire: 'Quoi? Les Français aussi?,'" in André Martel (ed.), *Histoire Militaire de la*

France, tome 4, *De 1940 à nos jours* (Paris: Presses universitaires de France, 1994), 122; Olivier Wieviorka, *Normandy: The Landings to the Liberation of Paris* (Cambridge, MA: Harvard University Press, 2008), 314–315.

132. Jérôme Maubec, "Diversité de l'amalgame des combattants de la 2e division blindée française (2e DB)," paper delivered at "E Pluribus Unum? Pluralité et identité des Français libres," Musée de l'armée, Paris, 27–28 November 2019.
133. Diego Gaspar Celaya, "Portrait d'oubliés. L'engagement des Espagnols dans les Forces françaises libres, 1940–1945," *Revue historique des armées*, 265 (2011), 46–55, https://journals.openedition.org/rha/7345.
134. Notin, *Leclerc*, 101–113; Anthony Clayton, *Three Marshals of France: Leadership after Trauma* (London: Brassey's, 1992), 53; William Mortimer Moore, *The Life of Philippe Leclerc, de Gaulle's Greatest General* (Philadelphia and Newbury: Casemate, 2011), 224–225.
135. A list of units that joined the 2e DB can be found in Martel, "La libération et la victoire," 121.
136. Ellen Hampton, *Women of Valor: The Rochambelles on the WWII Front* (New York: Palgrave Macmillan, 2006), 27; Notin, *Leclerc*, 106–108.
137. Suzanne Massu, *Quand j'étais Rochambelle* (Paris: Grasset, 1969), 72–73.
138. Hampton, *Women of Valor*, 29–31.
139. Hampton, *Women of Valor*, 44.
140. Moore, *The Life of Philippe Leclerc*, 230–231.
141. Moore, *The Life of Philippe Leclerc*, 243–245.
142. Of course, it could be that Leclerc simply refused to countenance psychological casualties. Wieviorka, *Normandy*, 269–270.
143. Notin, *Leclerc*, 111–119, 124.
144. Larminat, *Chroniques irrévérencieuses*, 215.
145. Massu, *Quand j'étais Rochambelle*, 129–133; Hampton, *Women of Valor*, 59–61.
146. Notin, *Leclerc*, 124–137.
147. Carlo D'Este, *Patton: A Genius for War* (New York: Harper Collins, 1995), 639; Notin, *Leclerc*, 136–139.
148. De Gaulle, *Mémoires de guerre*, tome 2, 569.
149. This argument is developed by David P. Colley, *The Folly of Generals: How Eisenhower's Broad Front Strategy Lengthened World War II* (Philadelphia and Oxford: Casemate, 2020).
150. Wieviorka, *Histoire de la Résistance 1940–1945*, 401, 407; Olivier Wieviorka, *Une histoire de la résistance en Europe occidentale* (Paris: Perrin, 2017), 394.
151. Of 212 towns studied by Philippe Buton, only 2 percent witnessed full-blown insurrections, while 13 percent saw partial insurrections. Fully 84 percent "were offered their liberation." Philippe Buton, *Les lendemains qui déchantent: Le Parti communiste français à la Libération* (Paris: Presses de la Foundation Nationale des Sciences Politiques, 1993), 104–106.
152. Ludewig, *Rückzug*, 131–133.
153. Footitt and Simmonds, *France 1943–1945*, 115–117.
154. Ludewig, *Rückzug*, 151–152.
155. Wieviorka, *Une histoire de la résistance en Europe occidentale*, 15; Footitt and Simmonds, *France 1943–1945*, 117.
156. Eisenhower, *Crusade in Europe*, 290–291; Ludewig, *Rückzug*, 147–152, 288–292. These issues are also addressed by Colley, *The Folly of Generals*, throughout the book, but especially Chapter 22 on reserves.
157. De Gaulle, *Mémoires de guerre*, tome 2, 562–563.
158. American historian of the Eastern Front in the Second World War David Glantz supported the contentions of Soviet historians that, "political considerations aside," operational factors explained the failure of Soviet forces to aid the Warsaw uprising. David M. Glantz, "The Soviet–German War: Myths and Realities. A Survey Essay" (2001), https://tigerprints.clemson.edu/cgi/viewcontent.cgi?article=1216&context=sti_pubs, 83–84. For his part, Sean McMeekin insists that Stalin's decision not to rescue the Warsaw uprising, nor allow the Allies to resupply it, was entirely political. "What Stalin did not want to do was to help the Polish Home Army liberate Warsaw," he concludes. McMeekin, *Stalin's War*, 565.
159. Julian Jackson, *De Gaulle* (Cambridge, MA: Harvard University Press, 2018), 325.
160. Roger Bourderon, *Rol-Tanguy: Des Brigades internationales à la libération de Paris* (Paris: Tallandier, 2013), 372.
161. Footitt and Simmonds, *France 1943–1945*, 135.
162. Ludewig, *Rückzug*, 137–142; Gildea, *Fighters in the Shadows*, 395–401.
163. Footitt and Simmonds, *France 1943–1945*, 87, 93, 186.
164. On Laval's plan, see NARA, RG 331, Entry 12, Box 107, 14 August 1944; Gildea, *Fighters in the Shadows*, 383–384.

165. Carlo D'Este, *Eisenhower: A Soldier's Life* (New York: Henry Holt, 2002), 574–575; Notin, *Leclerc*, 141; Wieviorka, *Histoire de la Résistance 1940–1945*, 402–403; de Gaulle, *Mémoires de guerre*, tome 2, 569–572.
166. Eisenhower, *Crusade in Europe*, 296.
167. Ludewig, *Rückzug*, 133.
168. Thomas Weber, *Hitler's First War: Adolf Hitler, the Men of the List Regiment, and the First World War* (Oxford: Oxford University Press, 2010).
169. Footitt and Simmonds, *France 1943–1945*, 152, 216.
170. Ludewig, *Rückzug*, 142–146.
171. Wieviorka, *Normandy*, 353–354.
172. Celaya, "Portrait d'oubliés," 7–8.
173. Gildea, *Fighters in the Shadows*, 402–403.
174. Notin, *Leclerc*, 149–153; de Gaulle, *Mémoires de guerre*, tome 2, 577–578
175. Gildea, *Fighters in the Shadows*, 477–478. During the initial surrender signing in the billiard room of the Prefecture, Rol had insisted that he sign the document, a request supported by Chaban-Delmas, to which Leclerc acquiesced. According to Antony Beevor and Artemis Cooper, the fact that Rol's signature was affixed above that of Leclerc was the result of "confusion." De Gaulle's objection came from the fact that Rol "had no official position in the provisional government or its armed forces." Antony Beevor and Artemis Cooper, *Paris after the Liberation: 1944–1949* (London: Penguin, 1994), 48–49. But Rol did command the FFI in Paris, which was technically integrated into the French armed forces through Koenig's EMFFI.
176. Gildea, *Fighters in the Shadows*, 395; Simon Kitson, "The Police in the Liberation of Paris," in H. R. Kedward and Nancy Wood, *The Liberation of France: Image and Event*, (Washington, D.C. and Oxford: Berge, 1995), 48–50.
177. Policemen had begun to "enter into clandestinity" on 8 August, went on strike from 15 August, and joined the "insurrection" on 19 August. Christian Chevalier, *Été 1944: L'insurrection des policiers Paris* (Paris: Vendémiaire, 2014).
178. See, for instance, Laurent Joly, *La falsification de l'histoire: Éric Zemmour, l'extrême droite, Vichy et les juifs* (Paris: Éditions Grasset, 2022).
179. "Paris! Paris outragé! Paris brisé! Paris martyrisé! Mais Paris libéré! Libéré par lui-même, libéré par son peuple avec le concours des armées de la France, avec l'appui et le concours de la France tout entière, de la France qui se bat, de la seule France, de la vraie France, de la France éternelle." Jackson, *De Gaulle*, 325.
180. Footitt and Simmonds, *France 1943–1945*, 147.
181. Jackson, *De Gaulle*, 325–327.
182. Henry Rousso, *The Vichy Syndrome: History and Memory in France since 1944* (Cambridge, MA: Harvard University Press, 1991), 16–18; Georges Kantin and Gilles Manceron, *Les échos de la mémoire: Tabous et enseignement de la Seconde Guerre mondiale* (Paris: Le Monde Éditions, 1991), 34–39.
183. Julian Jackson, "General de Gaulle and His Enemies: Anti-Gaullism in France since 1940," *Transactions of the Royal Historical Society*, 9 (1999), 46–47.
184. Simon Schama, "The Art of Outrage," *Financial Times Weekend*, 5–6 September 2020, 14, www.ft.com /content/32c11f2f-ac09-4160-8fd3-cd3b24de6ccb.
185. Gildea, *Fighters in the Shadows*, 404–405; de Gaulle, *Mémoires de guerre*, tome 2, 582–587; Jackson, *De Gaulle*, 327–329.
186. Buton, *Les lendemains qui déchantent*, 81.
187. The MP answered to the "alternative Resistance institutions, the CDLs [Comités départmentals de libération] and the CNR. The FN, the trades unions and the PCF were the most enthusiastic and active supporters of the group." Footitt and Simmonds, *France 1943–1945*, 160.
188. Bourderon, *Rol-Tanguy*, 304–308, 313, 321–324.
189. Wieviorka, *Histoire de la Résistance 1940–1945*, 404–409.
190. Eisenhower, *Crusade in Europe*, 297–298, 320.
191. Mark A. Stoler, *Allies and Adversaries: The Joint Chiefs of Staff, the Grand Alliance, and U.S. Strategy in World War II* (Chapel Hill and London: The University of North Carolina Press, 2000), 214.
192. Footitt and Simmonds, *France 1943–1945*, 178–179.
193. Footitt and Simmonds, *France 1943–1945*, 104, 106, 150–151; Jackson, *De Gaulle*, 330–331.

CHAPTER 6

1. Jeffrey J. Clarke and Robert Ross Smith, *Riviera to the Rhine* (Washington, D.C.: Center of Military History, United States Army, 1993), 7–11, https://history.army.mil/html/books/007/7-10-1/CMH_Pub_7-10-1.pdf.
2. Stalin's pledge allowed the Anglo-Americans to cancel Operation Buccaneer in the Bay of Bengal, which had nominally been designed to support Chiang Kai-shek. Admiral Ernest King also pledged to direct all new US production of landing craft to Europe rather than the Pacific. This would free up enough amphibious craft to support at a minimum a two-division Anvil assault. In the end, Cairo decided that the assault shipping in the Mediterranean and the UK would be considered as part of a "pool," so that planners could optimize the strength of each assault, rather than apply "arbitrary and unrealistic" limits on commanders. Richard M. Leighton, "Overlord versus the Mediterranean at the Cairo–Tehran Conferences," in Kent Roberts Greenfield (ed.), *Command Decisions* (Washington, D.C.: Center of Military History, United States Army, 1990), 255–285.
3. Sean McMeekin, *Stalin's War: A New History of World War II* (New York: Basic Books, 2021), Chapter 28.
4. Clarke and Smith, *Riviera to the Rhine*, 12–22; F. H. Hinsley, *British Intelligence in the Second World War: Its Influence on Strategy and Operations* (New York: Cambridge University Press, 1988), vol. III, Part II, 316–319.
5. Julie Le Gac, *Vaincre sans gloire: Le corps expéditionnaire français en Italie (novembre 1942–juillet 1944)* (Paris: Les Belles Lettres/Ministère de la défense-DMPA, 2013), 39.
6. Charles de Gaulle, *Mémoires de guerre*, tome 2, *L'Unité (1942–1944)* (Paris: Plon, 1994), 448.
7. Claire Miot, "Sortir l'armée des ombres. Soldats de l'Empire, combattants de la Libération, armée de la Nation: La Première armée française, du débarquement en Provence à la capitulation allemande (1944–1945)," Thèse du doctorat, Université Paris-Saclay, 2016, 738.
8. Jean-Louis Crémieux-Brilhac, *La France Libre: De l'appel du 18 juin à la Libération* (Paris: Gaillmard, 2013), tome 2, 945–949; Le Gac, *Vaincre sans gloire*, 41–42.
9. Miot, "Sortir l'armée des ombres," 36–70.
10. On the basis of conversations during the de Lattre's London interlude between his September 1943 escape from France and his 20 December arrival in Algiers.
11. Raoul Salan, *Mémoires*, tome 1, *Fin d'un empire*: "*Le sens d'un engagement," juin 1899–september 1946* (Paris: Presses de la Cité, 1970), 107.
12. Jean de Lattre de Tassigny, *Histoire de la première armée française: Rhin et Danube* (Paris: Presses de la Cité, 1971), 26.
13. Jean-François Muracciole, *Les Français libres: L'autre Résistance* (Paris: Tallandier, 2009), 236; Miot, "Sortir l'armée des ombres," 94–97.
14. Ivan Cadeau, *De Lattre* (Paris: Perrin, 2017), 156–165.
15. Le Gac, *Vaincre sans gloire*, 408.
16. Miot, "Sortir l'armée des ombres," 72; Jean-Christophe Notin, *Maréchal Juin* (Paris: Tallandier, 2015), 340–341.
17. Not only had Juin and de Gaulle been close since their days at Saint-Cyr and remained on a "*tu*" basis, but also, despite the fact that in 1960 the two men fell out over the issue of Algerian independence, Juin was no putschist. I thank Guillaume Denglos for this observation.
18. Guillaume Piketty, *Français en résistance: Carnet de guerre, correspondances, journaux personnels* (Paris: Robert Laffont, 2009), 345.
19. Anthony Beevor and Artemis Cooper, *Paris after the Liberation: 1944–1949* (London: Penguin, 1994), 221–222l.
20. Général Joseph Goislard de Monsabert, *Notes de Guerre* (Hélette: Éditions Jean Curutchet, 1999), 305–307, 323.
21. Edgard de Larminat, *Chroniques irrévérencieuses* (Paris: Plon, 1962), 259.
22. Miot, "Sortir l'armée des ombres," 98–99.
23. Jean Planchais, *Une histoire politique de l'armée*, tome 2, *1940–1967: De de Gaulle à de Gaulle* (Paris: Éditions du Seuil, 1967), 151–156.
24. Planchais, *Une histoire politique de l'armée*, tome 2, 65–67; Cadeau, *De Lattre*, 169–170.
25. Miot, "Sortir l'armée des ombres," 77–81; de Lattre, *Histoire de la première armée française*, 35–36.
26. Cadeau, *De Lattre*, 165–167; Miot, "Sortir l'armée des ombres," 83–89, 107–110.
27. De Lattre, *Histoire de la première armée française*, 30–31.
28. Miot, "Sortir l'armée des ombres," 118, 125–129.
29. Le Gac, *Vaincre sans gloire*, 409.

30. De Lattre, *Histoire de la première armée française*, 64.
31. Miot, "Sortir l'armée des ombres," 142–146.
32. Miot, "Sortir l'armée des ombres," 147–154.
33. Miot, "Sortir l'armée des ombres," 131–135; de Lattre, *Histoire de la première armée française*, 37–50 gives slightly different casualty figures. Raoul Salan lists 207 KIA, including 14 officers, 636 WIA, and 51 missing. Salan, *Mémoires*, tome 1, 120.
34. Salan, *Mémoires*, tome 1, 120
35. De Lattre, *Histoire de la première armée française*, 62–63. Cited in Miot, "Sortir l'armée des ombres," 141.
36. Miot, "Sortir l'armée des ombres," 136–141.
37. Miot, "Sortir l'armée des ombres," 163, 166, 174–180.
38. The Allies also heavily bombed the Lugurian coast. Joachim Ludewig, *Rückzug: The German Retreat from France, 1944* (Lexington: University Press of Kentucky, 2012), 47–49.
39. Ludewig, *Rückzug*, 50–52, 55–56, 58–60.
40. De Lattre, *Histoire de la première armée française*, 55–57, 61; Ludewig, *Rückzug*, 65.
41. Cadeau, *De Lattre*, 172–173; Ludewig, *Rückzug*, 68–73; Miot, "Sortir l'armée des ombres," 197.
42. Ludewig, *Rückzug*, 57, 60–62, 77, 79, 82; Hinsley, *British Intelligence in the Second World War*, vol. III, Part II, 273–275, 289.
43. De Lattre, *Histoire de la première armée française*, 61, 77–83; Clarke and Smith, *Riviera to the Rhine*, 138; Ludewig, *Rückzug*, 80.
44. Salan, *Mémoires*, tome 1, 125.
45. De Lattre, *Histoire de la première armée française*, 84–85; Arthur Layton Funk, *Hidden Ally: The French Resistance, Special Operations, and the Landings in Southern France, 1944* (Westport: Greenwood Press, 1992), 213.
46. De Lattre, *Histoire de la première armée française*, 104–105.
47. Clarke and Smith, *Riviera to the Rhine*, 140.
48. Suzanne Lefort-Rouquette, *Des Ambulancières dans les combats de la Libération: Avec les soldats de la 9e Division d'infanterie coloniale* (Paris: Éditions L'Harmattan, 2005), 84.
49. Clarke and Smith, *Riviera to the Rhine*, 140.
50. Clarke and Smith write that de Lattre's orders not to enter the city were "flexible." Clarke and Smith, *Riviera to the Rhine*, 141–142.
51. De Monsabert, *Notes de Guerre*, 275–276.
52. De Lattre, *Histoire de la première armée française*, 114.
53. Funk, *Hidden Ally*, 214–215.
54. On the liberation of Marseilles, see de Lattre, *Histoire de la première armée française*, 107–128; SHD-GR, 10P 70, "Journal de Marche Armée B," 69.
55. Salan, *Mémoires*, tome 1, 130. Clarke and Smith list 1,825 French casualties in Marseilles and 11,000 German POWs. Clarke and Smith, *Riviera to the Rhine*, 142.
56. Marianne Colonna, "Mythologies de la libération: Propagande et résistance," in Yves Jeanclos (ed.), *La France et les soldats d'infortune au XXe siècle* (Strasbourg: Economica, 2003), 230; Jean-Paul Cointet, *Expier Vichy: L'Épuration en France 1943–1958* (Paris: Perrin, 2008), 89.
57. Général André Beaufre, *Mémoires 1920–1940–1945* (Paris: Presses de la Cité, 1965), 480.
58. De Monsabert, *Notes de Guerre*, 281.
59. Piketty, *Français en résistance*, 389.
60. Miot, "Sortir l'armée des ombres," 205–206; Cadeau, *De Lattre*, 178–181. "The cesspool of five continents" is taken from Victor Serge, *Last Times* (New York: New York Review Books, 2022), 688.
61. Bernard Destremau, *De Lattre* (Paris: Flammarion, 1999), 351.
62. Piketty, *Français en résistance*, 380–381, 385.
63. Piketty, *Français en résistance*, 393.
64. Destremau, *De Lattre*, 357.
65. SHD-GR, 13YD 1529, Dossier du Général de Larminat, notes particulières et successives, 20 December 1942; 14 July 1943. For Juin's opinion, 20 July 1944.
66. SHD-GR, 13YD 1529, Dossier du Général de Larminat, notes particulières et successives, 15 December 1946.
67. Piketty, *Français en résistance*, 380, 385, 387–388; Miot, "Sortir l'armée des ombres," 198–200.
68. Ludewig, *Rückzug*, 115–117.
69. Clarke and Smith, *Riviera to the Rhine*, 144–170; Ludewig, *Rückzug*, 176–180.
70. Jean Estèbe, *Toulouse 1940–1944* (Paris: Perrin, 1996), 283–284.
71. Rémy Desquesnes, *Les poches de résistance allemandes: Août 1944–mai 1945* (Rennes: Éditions ouest-France, 2013), 17. French intelligence estimated the combined strength of German garrisons in the Atlantic pockets at 85,000 men. "Synthèse de renseignements sur l'ennemi," 15 February 1945," SHD-GR, 7P 151,

p. 4; "Synthèse de renseignements sur la situation des Allemands dans le secteur de Lorient," 1945, SHD-GR, 7P 151.

72. Éric Kocher-Marbœuf, "Entre guerre quasi totale et guerre quasi correct. Destins croisés des poches du Sud-Ouest," in Michel Catala (ed.), *Les poches de l'Atlantique 1944–1945: Le dernier acte de la Seconde Guerre mondiale en France* (Rennes: Presses universitaires de Rennes, 2019), 52–53, 56.
73. August Hampel, *J'occupais Royan 1943–1945* (Rioux-Martin: Le Croît Vif, 2011), 54–55.
74. SHD-GR, 7P 151, "Rapport N° 59. Renseignements sur la région de Royan," 20 novembre 1944, p. 2. As these reports were based mainly on interviews with civilians fleeing the "pockets," they were influenced by rumor and exaggeration.
75. Hampel, *J'occupais Royan 1943–1945*, 153–170.
76. Ludewig, *Rückzug*, 108–109.
77. Ludewig, *Rückzug*, 117–120.
78. Stéphane Weiss, *Les forces françaises de l'Ouest: Forces françaises oubliées? 1944–1945* (Paris: Les Indes Savantes, 2019), 27–29.
79. Benjamin F. Jones, *Eisenhower's Guerrillas: The Jedburghs, the Maquis, and the Liberation of France* (Oxford: Oxford University Press, 2016), 231–234, 274.
80. Nicholas Stargardt, *The German War: A Nation under Arms, 1939–1945. Citizens and Soldiers* (New York: Basic Books, 2015), 461; Ludewig, *Rückzug*, 181–184.
81. Dwight D. Eisenhower, *Crusade in Europe* (Garden City, NY: Doubleday, 1950), 292–295.
82. Clarke and Smith, *Riviera to the Rhine*, 580.
83. Beaufre, *Mémoires*, 486.
84. Lefort-Rouquette, *Des Ambulancières dans les combats de la Libération*, 84–85.
85. Clarke and Smith, *Riviera to the Rhine*, 563 (emphasis in the original).
86. Clarke and Smith, *Riviera to the Rhine*, 198. Wieviorka estimates that 209,000 of 320,000 German troops escaped from the south. Olivier Wieviorka, *Normandy: The Landings to the Liberation of Paris* (Cambridge, MA: Harvard University Press, 2008), 292.
87. Lack of mobility also partially explains why the 11th PzD was still in the south, and had not been sent north to contain the Normandy beachhead. Jean-Charles Foucrier, *La stratégie de la destruction: Bombardements alliés en France, 1944* (Paris: Vendémaire, 2017), 340–341, 348.
88. Piketty, *Français en résistance*, 394.
89. De Lattre, *Histoire de la première armée française*, 130–131.
90. Miot, "Sortir l'armée des ombres," 209.
91. De Lattre, *Histoire de la première armée française*, 136–137.
92. Piketty, *Français en résistance*, 391–392; de Lattre, *Histoire de la première armée française*, 141–144. The *milice patriotique* had been set up by the CNR on 15 March 1944 to serve as a police force under the Liberation Committees. But, in the confused circumstances of the Liberation, who was eligible to belong to it, its actual powers as opposed to those of the police, and to whose authority it answered became unclear. At the end of October 1944, the CNR ordered all civilian groups to surrender their weapons to the police. In January 1945, Thorez ordered all "irregular armed groups" under Parti communiste français (PCF) control to disband. Jean-Pierre Rioux, *The Fourth Republic, 1944–1958* (Cambridge: Cambridge University Press, 1987), 47–48. On the *milice patriotique*, see www.ffi33.org/cnr/milices/cnr4.htm.
93. De Lattre, *Histoire de la première armée française*, 172–173, 179.
94. Fabrice Grenard, *Maquis noirs et faux maquis 1943–1947* (Paris: Vendémaire, 2011), 120–122.
95. Hilary Footitt and John Simmonds, *France 1943–1945* (New York: Holmes & Meier, 1988), 108, 163–174. On 19 October 1944, 3,500 Spanish *maquisards* attacked the Spanish frontier, but were easily turned back by 45,000 Franquists. Nevertheless, several groups of Spanish guerrillas persisted until the summer of 1945 in Hérault and Ariège, waiting to attack Spain. Grenard, *Maquis noirs et faux maquis 1943–1947*, 120–122, 159–160. See also Diego Gaspar Celaya, "De l'oubli, des mythes, de l'histoire. Histoire et mémoire des volontaires espagnols dans la Résistance française," *Historiografías*, 12 (July–December 2016), 70–86.
96. Jones, *Eisenhower's Guerrillas*, 276.
97. Christian Bougeard, "La libération de la Bretagne. Plans, moyens, résultats (été 1944)," in Catala (ed.), *Les poches de l'Atlantique 1944–1945*, 26–34. For a description of the fighting in Brest, see SHD-GR, 7P 156, "Deuxième groupe d'armée. Expérience de combat," 9 October 1944, "Combat dans les rues de Brest."
98. Elliott J. Rosner, "The Jedburghs: Combat Operations in the Finisterre Region of Brittany, France from July–September, 1944," Master's Thesis, U.S. Army Command and General Staff College, Fort Leavenworth, Kansas, 1990, 103–117, https://apps.dtic.mil/dtic/tr/fulltext/u2/b148370.pdf. See also "Special Report on Resistance Operations in Brittany," a series of local bulletins collected on 10 November 1945, NARA RG 331, Entry 30A, Box 145.

99. David P. Colley, *The Folly of Generals: How Eisenhower's Broad Front Strategy Lengthened World War II* (Philadelphia and Oxford: Casemate, 2020), 198.
100. "Two Day Visit to Finistere," Major F. A. Chamier, Chief Intelligence Officer, 23 September 1944, NARA RG 0498, Entry UD578, Box 3908.
101. Ludewig, *Rückzug*, 37, 55.
102. The initial list had included IJmuiden, Hoek van Holland, Dunkirk, Boulogne, Le Havre, Cherbourg, Saint-Malo, Brest, Lorient, Saint-Nazaire, and Royan. The Channel Islands, La Rochelle, Marseilles, and Toulon were later added to the list. Ludewig, *Rückzug*, 37.
103. Rémy Desquesnes, *Les poches de résistance allemandes: Août 1944–mai 1945* (Rennes: Éditions ouest-France, 2013), 3.
104. Jean-Baptiste Blain, "Les trois bases de sous-marins allemands de Lorient, Saint-Nazaire et La Pallice au cœur des poches," in Catala (ed.), *Les poches de l'Atlantique 1944–1945*, 71–77.
105. Hampel, *J'occupais Royan 1943–1945*, 185, 194–195.
106. SHD-GR, 7P 156, "Deuxième groupe d'armée. Expérience de combat," 9 and 11 October 1944, "Combat dans les rues de Brest."
107. Ludewig, *Rückzug*, 99; Jacqueline Sainclivier, "Les poches de Lorient et Saint-Nazaire. Siège et incertitudes," in Catala (ed.), *Les poches de l'Atlantique 1944–1945*, 36–41.
108. Desquesnes, *Les poches de résistance allemandes*, 14–15.
109. Jean-Claude Catherine, "Les civils dans le piège de la poche de Lorient," in Catala (ed.), *Les poches de l'Atlantique 1944–1945*, 143–144.
110. Ludewig, *Rückzug*, 96; Éric Kocher-Marbœuf, "Entre guerre quasi totale et guerre quasi correcte. Destins croisés des poches du Sud-Ouest," in Catala (ed.), *Les poches de l'Atlantique 1944–1945*, 51.
111. Desquesnes, *Les poches de résistance allemandes*, 17–21.
112. Desquesnes, *Les poches de résistance allemandes*, 21–25; Catherine, "Les civils dans le piège de la poche de Lorient," 148–154.
113. SHD-GR, 7P 151, "Rapport N° 59. Renseignements sur la région de Royan," 20 November 1944, p. 4.
114. Marc Bergère, "Les poches de l'Atlantique et le processus d'épuration. Le cas de la poche de Saint-Nazaire," in Catala (ed.), *Les poches de l'Atlantique 1944–1945*, 230–231.
115. Sainclivier, "Les poches de Lorient et Saint-Nazaire," 42–43; Sicard, "Le quotidien des civils empochés de la région de Saint-Nazaire," 127–138.
116. SHD-GR, 7P 151, "Rapport N° 59. Renseignements sur la région de Royan," 20 November 1944.
117. Desquesnes, *Les poches de résistance allemandes*, 25–30.
118. Numbers of *Osttruppen* in France in 1944 are difficult to verify, but estimates run from 70,000 to 200,000. Frédéric Dessberg, "Les troupes de l'Est dans les poches de l'Atlantique," in Catala (ed.), *Les poches de l'Atlantique 1944–1945*, 191–193, 196, 200–201.
119. Kocher-Marbœuf, "Entre guerre quasi totale et guerre quasi correcte," 62–63.
120. Desquesnes, *Les poches de résistance allemandes*, 25–36. The French estimated the garrison at 11,000. SHD-GR, 7P 151, "Rapport N° 59. Renseignements sur la région de Royan," 20 November 1944.
121. Hampel, *J'occupais Royan 1943–1945*, 173–178, 182, 194–198.
122. Undated document. NARA, RG 331, Entry 30C, Box 190.
123. For the inadequacy of Royan's airfield, see SHD-GR, 7P 151, "Rapport N° 59. Renseignements sur la région de Royan," 20 November 1944, p. 3.
124. Desquesnes, *Les poches de résistance allemandes*, 97–98; Sainclivier, "Les poches de Loirent et Saint-Nazaire,"45; Kocher-Marbœuf, "Entre guerre quasi totale et guerre quasi correcte," 60–61; Jérôme de Lespinois, "L'enjeu aérien des poches. Entre stratégie et politique militaires," in Catala (ed.), *Les poches de l'Atlantique 1944–1945*, 107.
125. Stéphane Weiss, "Quotidien et moral des combattants volontaires des sièges de la Pointe de Grave, de Royan et de La Rochelle en 1944–1945," *Écrits d'Ouest*, no. 19 (2011), 128–129.
126. Stéphane Weiss, "'Venus de partout.' Des combattants français aux multiples provenances," in Catala (ed.), *Les poches de l'Atlantique 1944–1945*, 156–161, 167–171.
127. Weiss, "Quotidien et moral des combattants volontaires des sièges de la Pointe de Grave, de Royan et de La Rochelle en 1944–1945," 137.
128. Desquesnes, *Les poches de résistance allemandes*, 38–51; Christine Levisse-Touzé, "Le Général de Gaulle et le front de l'Atlantique et de la mer du nord," in Catala (ed.), *Les poches de l'Atlantique 1944–1945*, 101; Stéphane Weiss, "La régularisation des formations combattantes FFI engagés lors des sièges de la Pointe de Grave, de Royan et de La Rochelle en 1944–1945," *Écrits d'Ouest*, no, 20 (2012), 177.
129. Desquesnes, *Les poches de résistance allemandes*, 7–9, 52, 80.
130. Planchais, *Une histoire politique de l'armée*, tome 2, 78.

131. Larminat, *Chroniques irrévérencieuses*, 265–279. For the cattle raid and lack of pay, see SHD-GR, 10P 452, "Renseignements recueillis au sujet de la situation F.F.I. dans la région Sud de la Loire – Paimbœuf, Pornic et St Nazaire," 8 November 1944; Chomel to Commander of FFO, 30 October 1944.
132. SHD-GR, 12P 4, Report, 6e RI, 22 and 25 January 1945.
133. Robert Lynn Fuller, *After D-Day: The U.S. Army Encounters the French* (Baton Rouge: Louisiana State University Press, 2021), 162–165.
134. Jean-François Muracciole, "La France a contribué à la victoire des Alliés," in Jean Lopez and Olivier Wieviorka, *Les Mythes de la seconde guerre mondiale* (Paris: Perrin, 2015), 329.
135. Eisenhower, *Crusade in Europe*, 296.
136. Muracciole, "La France a contribué à la victoire des Alliés," 329–330; M. R. D. Foot, *SOE in France* (London: HMSO, 1966), 442; Andrew L. Hargreaves, *Special Operations in World War II: British and American Irregular Warfare* (Norman: University of Oklahoma Press, 2013), 420.
137. Foot, *SOE in France*, 442.
138. Olivier Wieviorka, *Histoire de la Résistance 1940–1945* (Paris: Perrin, 2013), 394–398.
139. For a history of special operations, see Douglas Porch, *Counterinsurgency: Exposing the Myths of the New Way of War* (Cambridge: Cambridge University Press, 2013).
140. Muracciole, *Les Français libres*, 362.
141. Leonard V. Smith quoting Paul Fussell. Leonard V. Smith, "Paul Fussell's *The Great War and Modern Memory*: Twenty-Five Years Later," *History and Theory*, 40/2 (May 2001), 242, 246–247.
142. Olivier Wieviorka, *Une histoire de la résistance en Europe occidentale* (Paris: Perrin, 2017), 402.
143. Raphaële Balu, "Les maquis de France, la France libre et les Alliés (1943–1945): Retrouver la coopération," Thèse du doctorat, Université de Caen Normandie, 2018, tome II, 1179–1185; Robert Gildea, *Fighters in the Shadows: A New History of the French Resistance* (Cambridge, MA: Harvard University Press, 2015), 447–448; Grenard, *Maquis noirs et faux maquis 1943–1947*, 165–168
144. Hargreaves, *Special Operations in World War II*, 234–235. In fact, originally *La Bataille du rail* had been commissioned as a documentary on railway workers during the occupation. But, upon the Liberation, the *Conseil National de la Résistance* asked the director René Clément to make it about resistance in the Société nationale des chemins de fer français (SNCF) that merged "left-wing collectivism and populist nationalism," to demonstrate how railwaymen had created "'a chain of solidarity' amongst themselves." One goal of the film, which became wildly popular following its January 1946 release, was to rehabilitate the company and its workers by "showing involvement in sabotages and strikes, especially in the Liberation," when in fact resistance among railwaymen had been "more scattered, circumstantial, and individual than it was organized or violent," and the company had been deeply involved in collaboration. In 1964, Hollywood promoted a knockoff entitled *The Train* starring Bert Lancaster, which predictably had "far more explosions and special effects." Ludivine Broch, *Ordinary Workers, Vichy and the Holocaust: French Railwaymen and the Second World War* (Cambridge: Cambridge University Press, 2016), 8, 223–229.
145. Matthew Cobb, *The Resistance. The French Fight against the Nazis*, (London, New York: Pocket Books, 2009), 4; Wieviorka, *Une histoire de la résistance en Europe occidentale*, 396.
146. I thank Guy Krivopissko for this observation.
147. Alan Milward, "The Economic and Strategic Effectiveness of Resistance," in Stephen Hawes and Ralph White (eds.), *Resistance in Europe, 1939–1945* (London: Viking, 1975), 196, cited in Wieviorka, *Une histoire de la résistance en Europe occidentale*, 394.
148. Sébastien Albertelli, *Histoire du sabotage: De la CGT à la Résistance* (Paris: Perrin, 2016), 381, cited in Wieviorka, *Une histoire de la résistance en Europe occidentale*, 394.
149. Sébastien Albertelli, "Les cheminots, fers de lance de la Résistance française et acteurs majeurs de la Libération," in Lopez and Wieviorka (eds.), *Les mythes de la seconde guerre mondiale*, 117–127.
150. Major C. K. Benda, Royal Artillery, "French Resistance. 6th June 1944–31st July 1944," 7 September 1944. NARA, RG 331, Entry 30A, Box 147.
151. Hargreaves, *Special Operations in World War II*, 210; Max Hastings, *Das Reich: The March of the 2nd SS Panzer Division through France* (Saint Paul, MN: Zenith Press, 2013), 189, 199. Resistance-generated human intelligence (HUMINT) passed up the chain to the Theater Intelligence Section through Jedburgh, SAS, and SOE teams, often via carrier pigeon, was combined with radio intercepts and photo reconnaissance to create tactical target dossiers (TTDs) to locate and bomb German petrol and munitions distribution points, that were usually concealed in forests. While the destruction of these logistical distribution points played an important role in weakening German defenses in Normandy, so did other factors such as the destruction of roads and railways through air bombardment, and a lack of vehicles for distribution. David Capps-Tunwell, David G. Passmore, and Stephan Harrison, "An Evaluation of Allied Intelligence in the Tactical Bombing of German Supply Depots during the Normandy Campaign, 1944," *The Journal of Military History*, 84/3 (July 2020), 829–833.

152. Foucrier, *La stratégie de la destruction*, 339–341, 348.
153. Albertelli, *Les Services secrets du Général de Gaulle*, 497–499.
154. Funk, *Hidden Ally*, 253.
155. Headquarters Allied Information Service, undated. NARA, RG 0498, Entry UD578, Box 3909.
156. Funk, *Hidden Ally*, 213–215.
157. Cadeau also suggests that de Lattre hesitated to become bogged down securing Marseilles while Lucian Truscott raced northward. Cadeau, *De Lattre*, 178–181.
158. Jones, *Eisenhower's Guerrillas*, 236.
159. Peter Lieb, *Vercors 1944: Resistance in the French Alps*, (London: Osprey, 2012), 84–87.
160. Muracciole, "La France a contribué à la victoire des Alliés," 343–347.
161. Miot, "Sortir l'armée des ombres," 202.
162. Alexander Hill, *The Red Army and the Second World War* (Cambridge: Cambridge University Press, 2017), 280–281.
163. McMeekin, *Stalin's War*, 306–307.
164. McMeekin, *Stalin's War*, Chapter 27 "Operation Tito."
165. Ludewig, *Rückzug*, 29, 116–119, 181, 286.
166. Martin Blumenson, *Breakout and Pursuit* (Washington, D.C.: US Government Printing Office, 1961), 628.
167. Funk argues that 26,581 tons of arms and supplies were sent to the three countries between 1943 and 1945, while southern France received only 2,878 tons. Funk, *Hidden Ally*, 257–258.
168. Balu, "Les maquis de France, la France libre et les Alliés," tome II, 897, 899.
169. Containers weighed 150 kilos, whereas "units," which the French called "colis" or packages, weighed 45–50 kilos. Crémieux-Brilhac, *La France libre*, tome 2, 1235, note 29; Balu, "Les maquis de France, la France libre et les Alliés," tome II, 678–680, 758–767.
170. Hargreaves, *Special Operations in World War II*, 79–80.
171. Jones, *Eisenhower's Guerrillas*, 279–280.
172. "2nd SAS Jeep Elements in France," undated. NARA RG 331, Entry 30A, Box 146.
173. Balu, "Les maquis de France, la France libre et les Alliés," tome II, 771–784; Crémieux-Brilhac, *La France libre*, tome 2, 1238–1239.
174. Footitt and Simmonds, *France 1943–1945*, 86, 175.
175. Balu, "Les maquis de France, la France libre et les Alliés," tome II," 785–787, 877–878, 940.
176. Crémieux-Brilhac, *La France libre*, tome 2, 1240–1245.
177. Muracciole, "La France a contribué à la victoire des Alliés," 350.
178. Wieviorka, *Histoire de la résistance*, 394; Wieviorka, *Une histoire de la résistance en Europe occidentale*, 395–396.
179. Wieviorka, *Une histoire de la résistance en Europe occidentale*, 394.
180. Wieviorka, *Histoire de la résistance*, 498; Balu, "Les maquis de France, la France libre et les Alliés," tome II, 1038–1043.
181. Wieviorka discusses many of these issues in Wieviorka, *Histoire de la résistance*, Chapter 18. See also Wieviorka, *Une histoire de la résistance en Europe occidentale*, 396.

CHAPTER 7

1. Raphaële Balu, "Militaires en résistance et maquisards de France: Les identités combattantes à l'épreuve de la Seconde Guerre mondiale," in Claire Miot, Guillaume Piketty, and Thomas Vaisset (eds.), *Militaires en résistances en France et en Europe* (Villeneuve d'Ascq: Presses universitaires du Septentrion, 2020), 140.
2. Claire Miot, "Sortir l'armée des ombres. Soldats de l'Empire, combattants de la Libération, armée de la Nation: La Première armée française, du débarquement en Provence à la capitulation allemande (1944–1945)," Thèse du doctorat, Université Paris-Saclay, 2016, 239. A 19 August 1943 law envisaged allowing voluntary enlistments in France to fill vacancies. On 16 March 1944, a "partial mobilization" was envisaged to supplement volunteers. A 5 June instruction allowed the *2ᵉ Division blindé* (2ᵉ DB) to fill its ranks with volunteers in liberated territory. Lieutenant colonel Roger Michalon, "L'amalgame F.F.I.–1ère Armée et 2ème D.B.," in Comité d'histoire de la Seconde Guerre mondiale, *La Libération de la France: Actes du Colloque international d'histoire de la 2ème guerre mondiale, 28–31 octobre 1974* (Vincennes: Ministère de la Défense, État-major de l'armée de terre, Service historique), 8–9.
3. Miot, "Sortir l'armée des ombres," 243.
4. Michalon, "L'amalgame F.F.I.–1ère Armée et 2ème D.B.," 29.
5. Philibert de Loisy, *1944, les FFI deviennent soldats: L'amalgame: de la résistance à l'armée régulière* (Paris: Histoire & Collections, 2014), 51–52.

6. Michalon, "L'amalgame F.F.I.–1ère Armée et 2ème D.B.," 28.
7. Raoul Salan, *Mémoires*, tome 1, *Fin d'un empire: "Le sens d'un engagement," juin 1899–septembre 1946* (Paris: Presses de la Cité, 1970), 133.
8. Ivan Cadeau, *De Lattre* (Paris: Perrin, 2017), 199.
9. Jean de Lattre de Tassigny, *Histoire de la première armée française: Rhin et Danube* (Paris: Presses de la Cité, 1971), 200.
10. J. Vernet, *Le réarmament et la réorganization de l'armée de terre française (1943–1946)* (Vincennes: Ministère de la défense, État-major de l'armée de terre, Service historique, 1980), 70–71.
11. Robert Gildea, *Fighters in the Shadows: A New History of the French Resistance* (Cambridge, MA: Harvard University Press, 2015), 405–406, 415; de Lattre, *Histoire de la première armée française*, 200–201.
12. Michel Pigenet, *Les "Fabiens" des barricades au front (septembre 1944–mai 1945)* (Paris: Éditions L'Harmattan, 1995), 7, 15, 17, 24–25, 80–94, 109–110, 131–132, 137–145.
13. Balu, "Militaires en résistance et maquisards de France," 142–145.
14. Balu, "Militaires en résistance et maquisards de France," 142.
15. Hilary Footitt and John Simmonds, *France 1943–1945* (Leicester: Leicester University Press, 1988), 156.
16. Philippe Buton, *Les lendemains qui déchantent: Le Parti communiste français à la Libération* (Paris: Presses de la Fondation Nationale des Sciences Politiques, 1993), 120–121.
17. Salan, *Mémoires*, tome 1, 138–140.
18. Louis Bacquier, *Aïwah: Au combat avec les Marocains. Souvenirs d'un officier de tirailleurs 1942–1945* (Paris: Éditions Laville, 2012), 143.
19. S.W. France. Elements of Military Regions XVI, XVII, XVIII, undated, probably November 1944. NARA RG 331, Entry 12, Box 110.
20. De Lattre, *Histoire de la première armée française*, 189–193, 198; Michalon, "L'amalgame F.F.I.–1ère Armée et 2ème D.B.," 30–31.
21. Charles de Gaulle, *Mémoires de guerre*, tome III, *Le salut, 1944–1948* (Paris: Plon, 1984), 730.
22. Julian Jackson, *De Gaulle* (Cambridge, MA: Harvard University Press, 2018), 330–331.
23. Henry Rousso, *The Vichy Syndrome: History and Memory in France since 1944*, (Cambridge, MA: Harvard University Press, 1991), 71.
24. André Martel, "La Libération et la Victoire. 'Quoi? Les français aussi!,'" in André Martel (ed.), *Histoire militaire de la France*, tome 4, *De 1940 à nos jours* (Paris: Presses universitaires de France, 1994), 234. See also "Political Developments in France and Their Effect on Military Operations," Joint Intelligence Council, Supreme Headquarters Allied Expeditionary Force (SHAEF), 1 January 1945. NARA, RG 331, Entry 2, Box 109.
25. Colonel Augustin de Dainville, *L'ORA: La Résistance de l'armée* (Paris-Limoges: Lavauzelle, 1974), 117, quoted in Christian Bachelier, "La Nouvelle armée française," in Jean-Pierre Azéma and François Bédarida (eds.), *La France des années noires* (Paris: Éditions du Seuil, 1993), tome II, 227.
26. Bachelier, "La Nouvelle armée française," 232. According to Yves Roucaute, the PCF divided the army into various categories. One group consisted of those coming from the internal resistance, and the Gaullists, which the PCF viewed as "allies." The most reactionary element was "*le clan des africains*," followed by Vichy loyalists, both of which they considered "enemies." Another group was made up of military bureaucrats, who rallied to the Allies only once assured that the war was won. Finally, there were returned POWs, who were "technically confused" because their notions of discipline and loyalty to Pétain had been "upended." Yves Roucaute, *Le PCF et l'armée* (Paris: Presses universitaires de France, 1983), 24–25.
27. Bachelier, "La Nouvelle armée française," 228, 235.
28. Martel, "La Libération et la victoire," 205–210, 234. Numbers are elusive, but Martel reckons that, of a pool of 300,000 FFI on the liberation, approximately 190,000 joined the regular forces from August 1944. Buton calculates FFI numbers at 200,000, meaning that 40 percent joined the army. Philippe Buton, "La France atomisée," in Jean-Pierre Azéma and François Bédarida (eds.), *La France des années noires*, tome 2, *De l'Occupation à la Libération* (Paris: Éditions du Seuil, 1993), 421. Communists in the FTP were the least likely to enlist, making up only 10 percent of FFI enlistees, although they did constitute the 151st Infantry Regiment under their leader "Colonel Fabien." Resistance detachments were more likely to be sent intact to the *Détachement d'armée des Alpes* or to lay siege to Atlantic ports retained by the Germans after August 1944. See Rémy Desquesnes, *Les Poches de résistance allemandes: Août 1944–mai 1945* (Rennes: Éditions Ouest-France, 2013). An estimated 137,000 men were sent to man General Jean de Lattre de Tassigny's First French Army, although not all remained. Those who did signed "individual enlistments," with many sent to basic training centers before "whitening" units such as the 1ère DFL or the *9e Division d'infanterie colonial* (9e DIC). "Individual enlistments" might also serve as a mechanism to conceal a Vichy-compromised past, which may have been the case for future French President Valérie

Giscard d'Estaing. Olivier Wieviorka, *Divided Memory: French Recollections of World War II from the Liberation to the Present* (Stanford, CA: Stanford University Press, 2012), 120.

29. Miot, "Sortir l'armée des ombres," 122–124.
30. Jean Planchais, *Une histoire politique de l'armée*, tome 2, *1940–1967* (Paris: Éditions du Seuil, 1967), 82–83, 90.
31. Michalon, "L'amalgame F.F.I.–1ère Armée et 2ème D.B.," 22; Roucaute, *Le PCF et l'armée*, 25.
32. Vernet, *Le rearmament et la reorganization de l'armée de terre française*, 30–34.
33. Général André Beaufre, *Mémoires 1920–1940–1945* (Paris: Presses de la Cité, 1965), 486–487.
34. Pigenet, *Les "Fabiens" des barricades au front*, 57.
35. André Kaspi, *La Libération de la France, juin 1944–janvier 1946* (Paris: Perrin, 2004), 96.
36. Miot, "Sortir l'armée des ombres," 312–316.
37. Vernet, *Le réarmament et la réorganization de l'armée de terre française*, 56–57; Marcel Vigneras, *Rearming the French* (Washington, D.C.: Center of Military History, United States Army, 1989), 323–324.
38. Dwight D. Eisenhower, *Crusade in Europe* (Garden City, NY: Doubleday & Company, 1950), 414.
39. Miot, "Sortir l'armée des ombres," 491–492.
40. Cadeau, *De Lattre*, 192–193.
41. Salan, *Mémoires*, tome 1, 132.
42. Claire Miot, "La retrait des tirailleurs sénégalais de la première armée française en 1944. Hérésie stratégique, bricolage politique ou conservatisme coloniale?," *Vingtième siècle. Revue d'histoire*, no. 125 (2015), 85–86.
43. Miot, "Sortir l'armée des ombres," 321–322, 324.
44. De Loisy, *1944, les FFI deviennent soldats*, 73.
45. Julien Fargettas, *Les Tirailleurs sénégalais: Les soldats noirs entre légendes et réalités 1939–1945* (Paris: Tallandier, 2012), 111–112.
46. Fargettas, *Les Tirailleurs sénégalais*, 191–193, 196–197.
47. Miot, "Sortir l'armée des ombres," 323–325; Miot, "La retrait des tirailleurs sénégalais de la première armée française en 1944," 78.
48. Salan, *Mémoires*, tome 1, 132–133.
49. Miot, "Sortir l'armée des ombres," 133.
50. Miot, "La retrait des tirailleurs sénégalais de la première armée française en 1944," 80.
51. Miot, "Sortir l'armée des ombres," 318–319.
52. Guillaume Piketty, *Français en résistance: Carnet de guerre, correspondances, journaux personnels* (Paris: Robert Laffont, 2009), 403.
53. SHD-GR, 111P 7, Brosset to de Lattre, 1 and 9 October 1944.
54. Miot, "La retrait des tirailleurs sénégalais de la première armée française en 1944," 80–81.
55. Matsunuma Miho, "La politique du gouvernement de Vichy vis-à-vis des militaires coloniaux rapatriables," *Outre-Mers*, 97/362–363 (2009), 240, www.persee.fr/doc/outre_1631-0438_2009_num_96_362_4391.
56. Fargettas, *Les Tirailleurs sénégalais*, 258, 261–294. The massacre at Thiaroye was memoralized in Ousmane Sembène's 1988 film *Camp de Thiaroye*, which, despite its highly fictionalized plot, struck a nerve in both France and Senegal because it exposed the depths of racial prejudice among the Allies, and the exploitation of Africans within the French colonial system and the French army, as well as recalled the French army's dependence on American support in 1943–1945. As a consequence, it was banned for a decade in both France and Senegal.
57. There had been a rebellion among demobilized First Army soldiers at Hyères in November 1944, which at least seems to have reflected the conditions of the "whitening," in particular the taking away of their uniforms, but also the sluggishness of repatriation. But incidents of desertion or indiscipline outside of these collective protests were few, possibly because an African wandering around France was hardly invisible. Miot, "La retrait des tirailleurs sénégalais de la première armée française en 1944," 84.
58. Fargettas, *Les Tirailleurs sénégalais*, 174–176. The Army Exchange Service had been created in June 1941, to set up stores on military posts to supply troops with consumer items not normally provided by the government at reasonable prices.
59. Miot, "La retrait des tirailleurs sénégalais de la première armée française en 1944," 83.
60. Matsunuma, "La politique du gouvernement de Vichy vis-à-vis des militaires coloniaux rapatriables," 227–240.
61. Myron Echenberg, *Les tirailleurs sénégalais en Afrique occidentale française (1857–1960)* (Paris and Dakar: Karthala et Crepos, 2009), 175–181, 184; Fargettas, *Les Tirailleurs sénégalais*, 294.
62. Michalon, "L'amalgame F.F.I.–1ère Armée et 2ème D.B.," 21.
63. Miot, "Sortir l'armée des ombres," 241.
64. Michalon, "L'amalgame F.F.I.–1ère Armée et 2ème D.B.," 40–43.

65. De Lattre, *Histoire de la première armée française*, 207, 211.
66. Cadeau, *De Lattre*, 199.
67. Vernet, *Le réarmament et la réorganization de l'armée de terre française*, 71–72.
68. This was probably an underestimate, because it did not include FFI already serving with de Lattre or 20,000 FFI in the Alpes. Nor had Marseilles turned in any figures. A recount in December gave a reduced figure of 239,500, as some FFI had simply returned home. An estimated 60,000 had joined the siege of the Atlantic pockets, a figure that rose to 76,000 by the middle of January 1945, although other sources believed numbers of 40,000–45,000 to be more accurate. Miot, "Sortir l'armée des ombres," 274–277.
69. De Lattre, *Histoire de la première armée française*, 194–195, 202.
70. Michalon, "L'amalgame F.F.I.–1ère Armée et 2ème D.B.," 27.
71. Michalon, "L'amalgame F.F.I.–1ère Armée et 2ème D.B.," 18.
72. Miot, "Sortir l'armée des ombres," 330–331.
73. "Messieurs, je ne suis pas venu ici pour faire salon avec vous." Salan, *Mémoires*, tome 1, 140.
74. Jean-François Muracciole, *Les Français libres: L'autre Résistance* (Paris: Tallandier, 2009), 235–236.
75. Général Joseph Goislard de Monsabert, *Notes de Guerre* (Hélette: Éditions Jean Curutchet, 1999), 186.
76. Planchais, *Une histoire politique de l'armée*, tome 2, 57, 86.
77. Claire Miot, "La concurrence des résistances. Maquisards et Français libres à la libération," paper delivered at "E Pluribus Unum? Pluralité et identité des Français libres," Musée de l'armée, Paris, 27–28 November 2019.
78. Miot, "Sortir l'armée des ombres," 330–334; Vigneras, *Rearming the French*, 238–240.
79. I thank Guy Krivopissko for this observation.
80. Miot, "Sortir l'armée des ombres," 328–329.
81. De Lattre, *Histoire de la première armée française*, 196.
82. Michalon, "L'amalgame F.F.I.–1ère Armée et 2ème D.B.," 17–21.
83. Vernet, *Le réarmament et la réorganization de l'armée de terre française*, 73.
84. SHD-GR, 7P 195, Compte rendu, 10 and 13 May 1945; Centre d'instruction de Pougues, 6 and 12 February 1945.
85. De Lattre, *Histoire de la première armée française*, 203.
86. Hubert Lyautey, "Du rôle social de l'officier," *Revue des deux mondes*, 3e période, tome 104 (1891), 443–459.
87. Kaspi, *La Libération de la France*, 96–97.
88. Piketty, *Français en résistance*, 408.
89. Laurent Joly, *La falsification de l'Histoire: Éric Zemmour, l'extrême droite, Vichy et les juifs* (Paris: Éditions Grasset, 2022), 58–59.
90. Miot, "Sortir l'armée des ombres," 259, 739.
91. SHD-GR, 7P 195, 15 October 1944, "Centre d'instruction de Sévérac des FFI de l'Aveyron."
92. Buton, *Les lendemains qui déchantent*, 184.
93. Miot, "Sortir l'armée des ombres," 237–238, 254–258, 263–264, 301–304, 370–375.
94. "Désinfection! Nettoyage! . . . des Juifs, hybrids afro-asiatiques, quart, demi-negres et proches orientaux . . . Ils doivent foutre le camp." Bénédicte Vergez-Chaignon, *Histoire de l'épuration* (Paris: Larousse, 2010), 27.
95. The most draconian army purge was that after 1815. But numbers of professional soldiers had also been severely curtailed during 1920–1923, not to mention "Armistice leave" after 1940 and the abolition of the Armistice Army in November 1942 at German insistence. From 1938, prefects had been instructed to expel undesirable foreigners. The next year, Spanish Republican refugees were interned. Vichy, of course, carried out its own purges, beginning with a 10 September 1940 order expelling civil servants thought "unsuited to collaborate in the establishment of the New Order." Among the eighty-nine members of the prefectoral corps who had been cut loose was Jean Moulin. "Masons, Jews, left-wing politicians and union leaders," as well as journalists, lost their jobs, while Gaullists and communists were arrested. Vergez-Chaignon, *Histoire de l'épuration*, 9–43.
96. Julian Jackson, "General de Gaulle and His Enemies: Anti-Gaullism in France since 1940," *Transactions of the Royal Historical Society*, 9 (1999), 49.
97. Claude d'Abzac-Epezy, "Épuration et renovation de l'armée," in Marc Olivier Baruch (ed.), *Une poignée de misérables: L'épuration de la société française après la Seconde Guerre mondiale* (Paris: Fayard, 2003), 436–437.
98. D'Abzac-Epezy, "Épuration et renovation de l'armée," 438.
99. Claude d'Abzac-Epezy, "Épuration, dégagements, exclusions. Les réductions d'éffectifs dans l'armée française (1940–1947)," *Vingtième Siècle. Revue d'histoire*, 59 (1998), 69–70; François Rouquet and

Fabrice Virgili, *Les françaises, les français, et l'épuration (1940 à nos jours)* (Paris: Gallimard, 2018), 215–216.

100. Miot, "Sortir l'armée des ombres," 265–269.
101. Miot, "Sortir l'armée des ombres," 739.
102. Piketty, *Français en résistance*, 396.
103. Miot, "Sortir l'armée des ombres," 219–221.
104. Miot, "Sortir l'armée des ombres," 222–223, 228; Yves Gras, *La 1ère D.F.L.: Les Français libres au combat* (Paris: Presses de la Cité, 1983), 336.
105. Pierre Giolitto, *Histoire de la milice* (Paris: Librairie Académique Perrin, 1997), 500–508; Miot, "Sortir l'armée des ombres," 230.
106. Marc Bergère, *L'Épuration en France* (Paris: Que sais-je?, 2018), 21.
107. Tony Judt, *Postwar: A History of Europe since 1945*, (New York: Penguin, 2006), 39, 42; Bergère, *L'Épuration en France*, 13.
108. François Rouquet, *Une Épuration ordinaire (1944–1949): Petits et grands collaborateurs de l'administration française* (Paris: CNRS Éditions, 2011), 47.
109. Michel Boivin, *1939–1945: Les Manchois dans la tourmente de la Seconde Guerre mondiale*, tome 6, *Les lendemains de la libération: Nouveaux pouvoirs, épuration et renaisssances* (Marigny: Éditions Eurocibles, 2004), 49–51.
110. Fabrice Virgili, *La France "virile": Des femmes tondues à la Libération* (Paris: Payot, 2000), 284–286, 293–296.
111. Mary Louise Roberts, *What Soldiers Do: Sex and the American GI in World War II France* (Chicago: University of Chicago Press, 2013), 79–83, 132; Bergère, *L'Épuration en France*, 17–18.
112. Rouquet and Virgili, *Les françaises, les français et l'épuration*, 599; Bergère, *L'Épuration en France*, 19.
113. Virgili, *La France "virile,"* 281.
114. Kaspi, *La Libération de la France*, 495–496.
115. Boivin, *1939–1945*, 93–125, 140.
116. Ebbe Curtiss Hoff, *Preventive Medicine in World War II*, volume VIII, *Civil Affairs/Military Government Public Health Activities* (Washington, D.C.: Office of the Surgeon General, Department of the Army, 1976), 433–434.
117. Boivin, *1939–1945*, 122.
118. Roberts, *What Soldiers Do*, 247–251.
119. Jérémie Halais, *Saint-Lô et son canton dans la tourmente de la seconde guerre mondiale 1939–1945* (Saint-Lô: Société d'archéologie et d'histoire de la Manche, 2007), 110.
120. Robert Lynn Fuller, *After D-Day: The U.S. Army Encounters the French* (Baton Rouge: Louisiana State University Press, 2021), 219–241.
121. Virgili, *La France "virile,"* 10, 292, 308–311; Rouquet, *Une Épuration ordinaire*, 22–23, 47–49.
122. Boivin, *1939–1945*, 80–81.
123. Roberts, *What Soldiers Do*, 88, 94–100; Peter Schrijvers, *The Crash of Ruin: American Combat Soldiers in Europe during World War II* (New York: New York University Press, 1998), 41–49.
124. Bergère, *L'Épuration en France*, 108.
125. Virgili, *La France "virile,"* 11–13, 297–299.
126. Vergez-Chaignon, *Histoire de l'épuration*, 568.
127. Rouquet, *Une Épuration ordinaire*, 20–21; Kaspi, *La Libération de la France*, 197–190.
128. Vergez-Chaignon, *Histoire de l'épuration*, 162–163.
129. Wieviorka, *Histoire de la résistance*, 115.
130. Bergère, *L'Épuration en France*, 71.
131. Rouquet, *Une Épuration ordinaire*, 22–23.
132. Miot, "Sortir l'armée des ombres," 230–232.
133. Buton, *Les lendemains qui déchantent*, 123–131.
134. Miot, "Sortir l'armée des ombres," 222.
135. Jean-Christophe Notin, *Leclerc: Le Croisé de la France libre* (Paris: Perrin, 2015), 157.
136. Bacquier, *Aïwah*, 107.
137. Michalon, "L'amalgame F.F.I.–1ère Armée et 2ème D.B.," 34–39.
138. Bacquier, *Aïwah*, 143.
139. Planchais, *Une histoire politique de l'armée*, tome 2, 85, 87.
140. Bacquier, *Aïwah*, 115–116.
141. Initiated as a vogueish youthful spoof of character-building components of Vichy conformity such as Joseph de La Porte du Theil's *Chantiers de la jeunesse* or Dunoyer de Segonzac's *écoles de cadres*, after May 1942, some *zazous* even dared sport yellow stars with "Zazou" or "Swing" scribbled across them.

Alan Riding, *And the Show Went On: Cultural Life in Nazi-Occupied Paris* (New York: Vintage Books, 2021), 102.
142. Planchais, *Une histoire politique de l'armée*, tome 2, 88; Miot, "Sortir l'armée des ombres," 472–481.
143. Buton, *Les lendemains qui déchantent*, 179–180. Jean-Pierre Rioux points out that disorder persisted mainly in rural areas where resistance and maquis groups had been most active – the north and west, the Massif Central, Aquitaine, Toulouse and the Rhône valley, the Alpes, the Jura, the Côte d'Or, and the Yonne. Jean-Pierre Rioux, *The Fourth Republic, 1944–1958* (Cambridge: Cambridge University Press, 1987), 30–31.
144. Cadeau, *De Lattre*, 194–195; Miot, "Sortir l'armée des ombres," 482–490.
145. In fact, US calculations were that de Lattre needed 58,000 support troops. Vigneras, *Rearming the French*, 337.
146. Michalon, "L'amalgame F.F.I.–1ère Armée, 2ème D.B.," 1–5.
147. Eisenhower, *Crusade in Europe*, 333.
148. The Far East program envisaged finding over 60,000 soldiers which the French did not have to stand up new divisions. Vernet, *Le réarmament et la réorganization de l'armée de terre française,* 65–68; Vigneras, *Rearming the French*, 335; Miot, "Sortir l'armée des ombres," 316–317.
149. Miot, "Sortir l'armée des ombres," 279–280, 282–290.
150. Miot, "Sortir l'armée des ombres," 335–341, 442–447; Cadeau, *de Lattre*, 201–202.
151. J. G. Shields, "Charlemagne's Crusaders. French Collaborators in Arms," *French Cultural Studies*, 18/1 (February 2007), 92–93; Giolitto, *Histoire de la milice*, 174.
152. Chris Bishop, *Hitler's Foreign Divisions: Foreign Volunteers in the Waffen-SS 1940–1945* (Staplehurst: Spellmount, 2005), 9–23.
153. Pierre Rostaing, *Le Prix d'un serment, 1941–1945: Des plaines de Russie à l'enfer de Berlin* (Paris: La Table Ronde, 1975), 33–34, 39–40. On early amalgamation of LVF and *la Milice*, see "Französische Brigade der S.S. Charlemagne," 19 January 1945; on reluctance to take oaths both among former LVF and among *miliciens*, see "La Division Charlemagne," undated, but clearly written after the defeat. SHD-GR, 7P 133; Pierre Giolitto, *Histoire de la milice*, 194.
154. André Bayle, *De Marseille à Novossibirsk* (Sausset-les-Pins: self-published, 1992), 12–13, 18, 20–21, 55–57, 63–64; Shields, "Charlemagne's Crusaders," 93.
155. Secretaire d'état de la défense à Monsieur le Secretaire général de la Légion des volontaires français contre le Bolchévisme, 23 February 1944, SHD-GR, 2P 14.
156. Jean-Luc Leleu, *La Waffen-SS: Soldats politiques en guerre* (Paris: Perrin, 2007), 809–822. See also Ronald Smelser and Edward J. Davies II, *The Myth of the Eastern Front: The Nazi–Soviet War in American Popular Culture* (Cambridge: Cambridge University Press, 2008).
157. Rostaing, *Le Prix d'un serment*, 133–141; "La Division Charlemagne," undated, SHD-GR, 7P 133.
158. Bayle, *De Marseille à Novossibirsk*, 77–79.
159. Bayle, *De Marseille à Novossibirsk*, 69–94. Shields says the unit was reduced to 140 men. Shields, "Charlemagne's Crusaders," 93–94.
160. Rostaing, *Le Prix d'un serment*, 145.
161. Philippe Burin, "La Guerre Franco-Française: Vers Sigmaringen," in Jean-Pierre Azéma and François Bédarida (eds.), *La France des années noires*, tome 2, *De l'Occupation à la Libération* (Paris: Éditions du Seuil, 1993), 42.
162. Giolitto, *Histoire de la milice*, 465–474; Burin, "La Guerre Franco-Française: Vers Sigmaringen," 43; Michèle Cointet, *La milice française* (Paris: Fayard, 2013), 305–307. On the discomfort of the castle, see Marie Vassiltchikov, *Berlin Diaries, 1940–1945* (New York: Vintage Books, 1988), 67.
163. Giolitto, *Histoire de la milice*, 474–480.
164. "La Division Charlemagne," undated, SHD-GR, 7P 133.
165. Rostaing, *Le Prix d'un serment*, 145–147; Shields, "Charlemagne's Crusaders," 94; "Französische Brigade der S.S. Charlemagne," 19 January 1946; "Marche d'un engagé volontaire de la LVF" and "La Brigade Charlemagne," SHD-GR, 7P 133.
166. Olivier Pigorneau, *Maquis blancs: La "résistance" des collabos, 1944–1945* (Paris: Konfident, 2022).
167. Rostaing, *Le Prix d'un serment*, 149–157; "La Brigade Charlemagne," SHD-GR, 7P 133.
168. Giolitto, *Histoire de la milice*, 486–495; Bishop, *Hitler's Foreign Divisions*, 178; Leleu, *La Waffen-SS*, 432; Philippe Burrin, *France under the Germans: Collaboration and Compromise* (New York: The New Press, 1996 [French edition 1993]), 455. This action is described in "Französische Brigade der S.S. Charlemagne," 19 January 1946, pp. 4–5, and "La Brigade Charlemagne," SHD-GR, 7P 133. See also Cointet, *La milice française*, 242–244.
169. Michalon, "L'amalgame F.F.I.–1ère Armée, 2ème D.B.," 23.
170. Miot, "Sortir l'armée des ombres," 376–377.
171. Muracciole, "La France a contribué à la victoire des Alliés," 348.

CHAPTER 8

1. Colonel John J. Neal, "The Shared Burden. United States–French Coalition Operations in the European Theater of World War II," Master's Thesis, School of Advanced Studies, U.S. Army Command and Staff College, Fort Leavenworth, KS, 2013, 19–20.
2. For potential war-shortening scenarios in the autumn/winter of 1944, see David P. Colley, *The Folly of Generals: How Eisenhower's Broad Front Strategy Lengthened World War II* (Philadelphia and Oxford: Casemate, 2020).
3. Eisenhower to Marshall, 15 January 1945. SHAEF Cable log-out (January 1945), (1)–(4) Box 26, Walter Bedell Smith collection, Dwight D. Eisenhower Presidential Library, quoted in Neal, "The Shared Burden," 13.
4. Neal, "The Shared Burden," 18, 20–23.
5. Jeffrey J. Clarke and Robert Ross Smith, *Riviera to the Rhine* (Washington, D.C.: Center of Military History, United States Army, 1993), 226.
6. Clarke and Smith, *Riviera to the Rhine*, 226, 229–230.
7. Dwight D. Eisenhower, *Crusade in Europe* (Garden City, NY: Doubleday & Company, 1950), 414.
8. Clarke and Smith, *Riviera to the Rhine*, 196–197, 292.
9. The origins of the Eisenhower–Devers *malentendu* began in 1943 when Marshall had dispatched Devers to North Africa to lead an "armored team" evaluation of American tank performance. Devers' arrival had caught Eisenhower at a vulnerable moment, in the wake of what many regarded as his mishandling of the Torch landings, followed by the much criticized "Darlan Deal" and what was viewed as an entirely avoidable campaign in Tunisia, whose early setbacks burnished the reputation neither of Ike nor of the US Army. Rumor held that, beneath the false flag of a technical study, Devers' true mission was to file a negative report on Eisenhower's leadership that would provide Marshall with the documentation needed to fire him. In the end, nothing in Devers' report was critical of either Eisenhower or Patton. However, the two American generals had again clashed in the summer of 1943, over the transfer of heavy bombers from the ETO, for which Devers was responsible, to support Eisenhower in the Mediterranean. While inter-theater disputes over air resources were common, especially at this relatively early stage of the Allied buildup, this particular disagreement had spiraled upward to Marshall and the British Chief of Staff (COS), who ultimately sided with Devers. James Scott Wheeler and Rick Atkinson, *Jacob L. Devers: A General's Life* (Lexington: University Press of Kentucky, 2015), 186, 189–190, 192–193, 225–226. According to David P. Colley, Eisenhower's negative opinion of Devers was widely shared in the upper echelons of SHAEF. Colley, *The Folly of Generals*, Chapter 17.
10. Nicholas Stargardt, *The German War: A Nation under Arms, 1939–1945. Citizens and Soldiers* (New York: Basic Books, 2015), 464, 483.
11. Clarke and Smith, *Riviera to the Rhine*, 193–198, 238.
12. Although the Germans continued to occupy its most powerful fortification, Fort Driant, for another three weeks. Carlo D'Este, *Patton: A Genius for War* (New York: Harper Collins, 1996), 667–669. David P. Colley questions the rationalization of the failure to capture Metz earlier, usually put down to a lack of gasoline to propel Patton's Third Army forward, as at best incomplete. Contributing factors including Eisenhower's inability to prioritize, Patton's failure to concentrate his forces, and stiffening German resistance. Colley, *The Folly of Generals*, Chapter 24.
13. Clarke and Smith, *Riviera to the Rhine*, 231.
14. Clarke and Smith, *Riviera to the Rhine*, 250–254.
15. On Truscott's crossing of the Moselle and advance into the Vosges, see Clarke and Smith, *Riviera to the Rhine*, Chapter 13. De Lattre asserted that, between 20 and 28 September, Seventh US Army's three divisions had received 2,102 tons of supplies per day, while the *1ère Armée*'s five divisions had received a daily delivery of only 968 tons. Jean de Lattre de Tassigny, *Histoire de la première armée française: Rhin et Danube* (Paris: Presses de la Cité, 1971), 217–223, 228–229; Wheeler and Atkinson, *Jacob L. Devers*, 332.
16. De Lattre, *Histoire de la première armée française*, 231.
17. De Lattre's most memorable and perhaps unfortunate outburst occurred on 8 October during a visit by George Marshall to Monsabert's II Corps headquarters (HQ) at Luxeuil, 18 miles northeast of Belfort, when de Lattre launched into an invective, denouncing Patch and once again complaining that the American supply chain shortchanged the *1ère Armée*. In his history, de Lattre recounts making a request to Marshall for more supplies, one that "surprised" the US Army COS, who had not expected it, but promised to remedy the shortfall. De Lattre, *Histoire de la première armée française*, 228. Monsabert and Devers remembered the incident differently: the French general categorized de Lattre's address to Marshall as a "very violent,

honest and clear diatribe . . . about the French army's situation in the battle." Général Joseph Goislard de Monsabert, *Notes de Guerre* (Hélette: Éditions Jean Curutchet, 1999), 300. A frequent audience for de Lattre's serial diatribes, Devers was a little more philosophical: "[de Lattre] goes into these tirades at least twice a week, at which times he seems to lose his balance," he noted in his diary. While Marshall proved the very model of restraint, caught by surprise and unaccustomed to de Lattre's serial melodramas, the US Army COS declined to be amused. Devers had a stiff letter delivered to Henry Cabot Lodge Jr., who had resigned his seat as senator for Massachusetts to see active service, and because of his proficiency in French had been named to de Lattre's staff: ". . . unwarranted criticism by General de Lattre and his assistants, including Major [former US Ambassador to France William] Bullitt, shall cease," Devers ordered. He reminded Lodge that "the method of supply and maintenance" was regulated by the Joint Rearmament Program, as de Lattre's staff was well aware. Lodge was ordered to stand up a liaison section "to work with and monitor the French army." Apparently, the memories of de Lattre's tantrum and ingratitude had so irritated Marshall that, several years later, he was to veto de Lattre's nomination as North Atlantic Treaty Organization (NATO) ground forces commander. The official US Army history concedes that more efficient US Army staff work as well as familiarity with US logistical organization gave the Americans a supply advantage. Clarke and Smith, *Riviera to the Rhine*, 301.

18. Colley, *The Folly of Generals*, Chapter 24.
19. Charles de Gaulle, *Mémoires de guerre*, tome III, *Le salut, 1944–1946* (Paris: Plon, 1994), 735.
20. Jean Lacouture, *De Gaulle: The Ruler 1945–1970* (New York: W. W. Norton, 1993), 32–33.
21. Five billion francs worth of tanks and tracked vehicles, 1,100 planes, 260,000 small arms and machineguns, "several thousand" artillery pieces with ammunition, 65,000 motor vehicles, uniforms for 300,000 combat troops, over a million and a half barrels of gasoline, oil, and so on; 31 million rations by 31 December 1944. For the *Forces françaises de l'intérieur* (FFI), the Allies had supplied 337,000 items of clothing and 362,000 items of equipment. US Army engineers had helped to repair French roads, bridges, utilities, and communications. There was Lend–Lease aid of imported raw materials to get French factories into production, the United States sent agricultural experts, and so on. First French Army units were allowed the same 7 percent monthly replacement of uniforms as were US troops. A further 57,000 uniform "sets" were given for French female soldiers. The Royal Air Force (RAF) had been critical in standing up the *Forces aériennes françaises libres* (FAFL), an effort taken over by the Americans after Torch both for the FAF and for the navy. US Navy yards also refitted for the French four cruisers, four destroyers, and eight submarines, as well as destroyer escorts, tankers, and auxiliary vessels, and the "carrier" *Béarn*. The United States spent 9 million dollars to upgrade the *Richelieu*, the equivalent of $167,922,883 in 2023. Significant efforts had been made by US forces to feed Paris and to import drugs, coal, and so on. Several thousand trucks and other vehicles were turned over to the French to transport civilian food and other products. Above all, the US military imported all but 2 percent of its food needs, so that it would not burden the French food supply. "Allied Aid to France," 2 March 1945. NARA, RG 0498, Entry UD578, Box 3904.
22. Wheeler and Atkinson, *Jacob L. Devers*, 343–344, 346–348.
23. De Lattre, *Histoire de la première armée française*, 230, 236–239.
24. Louis Bacquier, *Aïwah: Au combat avec les marocains. Souvenirs d'un officier de tirailleurs 1942–1945* (Paris: Éditions Laville, 2012), 109, 111.
25. De Lattre, *Histoire de la première armée française*, 241. Artillery groups were developed from 1942 to give more flexibility to the allocation of artillery support, devolving it mainly to the corps level. Major Russell A. Weathersby, "The Field Artillery Group in Support of Corps and Field Army, 1942–1953," Master of Arts, Command and General Staff College, Fort Leavenworth, Kansas, 1965.
26. Wheeler and Atkinson, *Jacob L. Devers*, 354–355.
27. Paul Fussell, *Doing Battle: The Making of a Skeptic* (Boston, New York, Toronto, and London: Little, Brown and Company, 1996), 1, 103–104.
28. Peter Schrijvers, *The Crash of Ruin: American Combat Soldiers in Europe during World War II* (New York: New York University Press, 1998), 127.
29. Claire Miot, "Sortir l'armée des ombres. Soldats de l'Empire, combattants de la Libération, armée de la Nation: La Première armée française, du débarquement en Provence à la capitulation allemande (1944–1945)," Thèse du doctorat, Université Paris-Saclay, 2016, 536–539.
30. "Abuses were numerous and serious, principally in the canton of Niederbronn. Pillage, destruction of property, threats and ill treatment, drunkenness, abuses of all kinds . . . Acts of pillage are most often committed immediately after the liberation of a city. The inhabitants are hiding in cellars; the soldiers take advantage of that fact to search through belongings and empty the wine cellars. With a shot of the rifle they blow the locks apart and plunder the houses. The drunkenness which follows is responsible for numerous examples of ill treatment and threats, and the Military Police do not seem to act with the desirable

forcefulness. As for unit commanders, too often they close their eyes." Captain Force, Administrative Liaison Officer, 45th Infantry Division, "General Report of the Last Six Weeks" (24 November 1944 to 8 January 1945), undated, SHD-GR, 8P 21.

31. Miot, "Sortir l'armée des ombres," 540–545.
32. NARA, RG 331, Entry 12, Box 109, 27 October 1944. On Coulet's tribulations, see Robert Lynn Fuller, *After D-Day: The U.S. Army Encounters the French* (Baton Rouge: Louisiana State University Press, 2021), 94–109.
33. Miot, "Sortir l'armée des ombres," 543.
34. Bacquier, *Aïwah*, 124.
35. De Lattre's logic was that, with German forces massed in the Vosges, the Belfort Gap was considered a "quiet front." Nor would he be forced to worry about his right flank, anchored on the Swiss frontier. De Lattre, *Histoire de la première armée française*, 250.
36. This was an evolution of an earlier request to send French divisions – the *1ère Division blindé* (1ère DB) and *1ère Division française libre* (1ère DFL) – to insure order in the face of FFI-seeded turbulence in Toulouse and Paris. De Lattre, *Histoire de la première armée française*, 253.
37. Wheeler and Atkinson, *Jacob L. Devers*, 357–358.
38. "Compte rendu des opérations menés par la 2ème DIM pour la prise de Belfort," 15 February 1945, SHD-GR, 7P 166.
39. De Lattre, *Histoire de la première armée française*, 264–267.
40. Clarke and Smith, *Riviera to the Rhine*, 413–414.
41. "Compte rendu des opérations menés par la 2ème DIM pour la prise de Belfort," 15 February 1945, SHD-GR, 7P 166; de Lattre, *Histoire de la première armée française*, 269–282; Clarke and Smith, *Riviera to the Rhine*, 420.
42. "The General wanted to overtake a truck already on the bridge. He suddenly found himself confronted by a large hole, previously occupied by a large bomb placed there by the Germans to blow up the road. He slammed on the brakes. The brakes were not working properly, as the driver had warned the General when he took [the jeep] . . . The vehicle, which was speeding, flipped over the parapet of the bridge and fell into the river . . . Stunned, the General lost consciousness and didn't try to free himself. He died asphyxiated by the immersion." "Rapport du Colonel Garbay commandant P.I. la 1ère D.F.L. sur la mort du Général Brosset," 23 novembre 1944, SHD-GR, 13YD 566.
43. André Martel, *Leclerc: Le soldat et la politique* (Paris: Albin Michel, 1998), 495; Jean-Christophe Notin, *Leclerc: Le Croisé de la France libre* (Paris: Perrin, 2015), 166–168; Lacouture, *De Gaulle*, 34.
44. Bacquier, *Aïwah*, 118.
45. "Synthèse des rapport sur le moral de la troupe," Forces françaises libres, 1ère Division, 10 October 1944. SHD-GR, 11P 10.
46. Clarke and Smith, *Riviera to the Rhine*, 439–442; Wheeler and Atkinson, *Jacob L. Devers*, 357–366, 372.
47. Clarke and Smith, *Riviera to the Rhine*, 563–564.
48. Eisenhower, *Crusade in Europe*, 331–332.
49. Clarke and Smith, *Riviera to the Rhine*, 443–445.
50. Wheeler and Atkinson, *Jacob L. Devers*, 366–368.
51. Eisenhower, *Crusade in Europe*, 332–333.
52. De Lattre, *Histoire de la première armée française*, 298–310.
53. De Lattre, *Histoire de la première armée française*, 311–325. The Germans claimed the total losses to have been "in excess of 10,000." Clarke and Smith, *Riviera to the Rhine*, 430, footnote 30.
54. Lacouture, *De Gaulle*, 36.
55. Julian Jackson, *De Gaulle* (Cambridge, MA: Harvard University Press, 2018), 355–356.
56. Clarke and Smith, *Riviera to the Rhine*, 431–432.
57. Miot, "Sortir l'armée des ombres," 462; Michel Pesquer, "L'emploi des blindés français sur le front occidental d'août 1944 à mai 1945," Thèse du doctorat, Université de Lorraine, 2018, 522.
58. Henri de Vernejoul and Armand Durlewanger, *Autopsie d'une Victoire morte* (Colmar: Saep, 1970), cited in Ivan Cadeau, *De Lattre* (Paris: Perrin, 2017), 205.
59. Cadeau, *De Lattre*, 205–206; Miot, "Sortir l'armée des ombres," 388–389, 465–467.
60. Pesquer, "L'emploi des blindés français sur le front occidental d'août 1944 à mai 1945," 523–524.
61. Monsabert, *Notes de Guerre*, 302. "The First French Army saw its élan slowed, and then stopped by all sorts of material difficulties, the extreme fatigue of the troops engaged, for four months, in merciless non-stop combat, and the extreme overextension of its lines of communication." "Rapport sur les opérations de la 1ère Armée française. La bataille d'Alsace et la Victoire de Colmar (20 janvier–9 février 45)," SHD-GR, 11P 191.

62. "Note relative à la bataille de la trouée de Belfort [novembre 44] et résumant un exposé fait par le Général de Lattre le 21 septembre 1947." See also "Compte rendu d'opérations. Journée du 30 novembre 1944" and "Directive particulière pour le 1re corps d'armée," 2 December 1944. SHD-GR, 11P 190.
63. De Lattre, *Histoire de la première armée française*, 309.
64. Clarke and Smith, *Riviera to the Rhine*, 437, 439–440, 442–444, 564; de Lattre, *Histoire de la première armée française*, 314.
65. Monsabert, *Notes de Guerre*, 303
66. Clarke and Smith, *Riviera to the Rhine*, 445.
67. Clarke and Smith, *Riviera to the Rhine*, 580.
68. Wheeler and Atkinson, *Jacob L. Devers*, 369, 374–379; Clarke and Smith, *Riviera to the Rhine*, 453–454; Miot, "Sortir l'armée des ombres," 389.
69. Marcel Vigneras, *Rearming the French* (Washington, D.C.: Center of Military History, 1989), 325–326.
70. Wheeler and Atkinson, *Jacob L. Devers*, 378–379; Clarke and Smith, *Riviera to the Rhine*, 291–292, 567–569; Colley, *The Folly of Generals*, 207.
71. Eisenhower, *Crusade in Europe*, 333–334; Colley, *The Folly of Generals*, 194.
72. De Lattre, *Histoire de la première armée française*, 326.
73. Sixty-two shells per gun for the French, versus twenty-four for the Americans. "Report on Conference with General de Lattre," Headquarters Sixth Army Group, 6 December 1944. NARA, RG 331, Entry 240D, Box 10. In February 1945, de Lattre dispatched his corps artillery officers to Seventh Army "to gain experience in U.S. Artillery Tactics and Techniques upon which U.S. weapons and ammunition supply are based," 26 February 1945.
74. Monsabert, *Notes de Guerre*, 323–324.
75. Monsabert, *Notes de Guerre*, 324.
76. Kingman's officers advised French units on maintenance, storage, and deployment of US equipment, and then inspected those divisions to ascertain their combat readiness. By November 1943, the French had organized basic training centers (*centres d'instruction*) in North Africa that gave a three-month training for new recruits, who were then sent to one of around forty *centres d'organisation*, where they received company-level training, and to which US instructors were detailed if requested. A number of officer training schools were also created. French soldiers were also admitted to US schools created in North Africa by the air force and airborne forces, as well as others that taught mechanics, ordnance, and so on. But training was hindered to a degree by the language barrier, lack of instruction manuals in French, and a dearth of weapons and ammunition. US observers were also attached to French divisions in Italy to observe and incorporate lessons learned into training. Three US-sponsored training centers were eventually created in Italy to train replacements for the CEF. Selected personnel were sent to the United States for signals, artillery ranging, Bailey Bridge School, ordnance, flight schools, and so on. In June 1944, the Americans turned over their training camp in Oran, with a capacity to train 8,000–10,000 recruits in preparation for Anvil, to be inspected by Patch. Vigneras, *Rearming the French*, 230–239.
77. Vigneras, *Rearming the French*, 388–390.
78. Headquarters Sixth Army Group, Chief of Staff, 27 April 1945. NARA RG 331, Entry 240D, Box 10.
79. Marc Bloch, *Strange Defeat: A Statement of Evidence Written in 1940* (New York: W. W. Norton & Company, 1968), 34–35.
80. "Note relative à l'Inspection passé par le Lieutenant-Colonel – Commandant le Régiment au 2e Bataillon les 10–11 à 12 Avril." 16 April 1945. SHD-GR, 12P 10.
81. Colonel Breveté Mouzel to Governor General of Paris personnel bureau, 26 July 1945. SHD-GR, 12P 10.
82. Constantine FitzGibbon, *Denazification* (New York: W. W. Norton & Co., 1969), 106.
83. Clarke and Smith, *Riviera to the Rhine*, 434–436.
84. Clarke and Smith, *Riviera to the Rhine*, 457–459; de Lattre, *Histoire de la première armée française*, 332–334.
85. Wheeler and Atkinson, *Jacob L. Devers*, 382.
86. Bacquier, *Aïwah*, 124, 133.
87. Clarke and Smith, *Riviera to the Rhine*, 459.
88. De Lattre, *Histoire de la première armée française*, 327–328.
89. Jacques le Groignec, *Pétain et les Allemands* (Paris: Nouvelles Éditions Latines, 1997), 40.
90. Clarke and Smith, *Riviera to the Rhine*, 463–464, 556.
91. Suzanne Lefort-Rouquette, *Des Ambulancières dans les combats de la Libération: Avec les soldats de la 9e Division d'infanterie coloniale* (Paris: Éditions L'Harmattan, 2005), 127.
92. Lefort-Rouquette, *Des Ambulancières dans les combats de la Libération*, 85–107; Solange Cuvillier, *Tribulations d'une femme dans l'armée française, ou le patriotisme écorché* (Paris: Éditions Lettres du Monde, 1991), 63.

93. De Lattre, *Histoire de la première armée française*, 328–332.
94. Miot, "Sortir l'armée des ombres," 395–409.
95. Clarke and Smith, *Riviera to the Rhine*, 463.
96. Wheeler and Atkinson, *Jacob L. Devers*, 382–385; de Lattre, *Histoire de la première armée française*, 337–339, 341–342.
97. SHD-GR, 11P 190, 6th Army Group to 1st French Army, 2 January 1945.
98. Eisenhower, *Crusade in Europe*, 352.
99. Monsabert, *Notes de Guerre*, 314.
100. Miot, "Sortir l'armée des ombres," 556–575.
101. Miot, "Sortir l'armée des ombres," 519–522, 558–564, 574–575.
102. Martel, *Leclerc*, 308.
103. Notin, *Leclerc*, 168–169.
104. Wheeler and Atkinson, *Jacob L. Devers*, 376–377.
105. Captain Force, Administrative Liaison Officer, 45th Infantry Division, "General Report of the Last Six Weeks [24 November 1944 to 8 January 1945]," undated; "Rapport sur l'activité de la M.M.L.A. auprès du 6ème Groupe d'Armées du 1er janvier au 1er fevrier 1945," 8 February 1945; Panafieu, chef de la M.M.L.A., 25 December 1944, SHD-GR, 8P 21.
106. Miot, "Sortir l'armée des ombres," 543–544.
107. Clarke and Smith, *Riviera to the Rhine*, 495–496, 503–504, 511; de Lattre, *Histoire de la première armée française*, 351; Franklin L. Gurley, "Politique contre stratégie: La défense de Strasbourg en décembre 1944," *Guerres mondiales et conflits contemporains*, no. 166 (April 1992), 100–101.
108. Gurley, "Politique contre stratégie," 93.
109. Gurley, "Politique contre stratégie," 95.
110. Gurley, "Politique contre stratégie," 94; Wheeler and Atkinson, *Jacob L. Devers*, 390–391.
111. Clarke and Smith, *Riviera to the Rhine*, 564–565.
112. J. F. M. Whitley, 30 December 1944. NARA RG 331, Entry 30C, Box 190.
113. Gurley, "Politique contre stratégie," 99–102.
114. SHD-GR, 11P 190, De Gaulle to Eisenhower, 1 January 1945.
115. De Gaulle, *Mémoires de guerre*, tome III, 740–741.
116. Gurley, "Politique contre stratégie," 104–105.
117. Eisenhower, *Crusade in Europe*, 363.
118. Gurley, "Politique contre stratégie," 103.
119. SHD-GR, 11P 190, De Gaulle to de Lattre, 1 January 1945.
120. Fuller, *After D-Day*, 205–206, 216–218.
121. De Lattre to Devers, 2 January 1945, NARA, RG 319, Entry A1 145A, Box 4.
122. Miot, "Sortir l'armée des ombres," 458.
123. SHD-GR, 11P 190, De Lattre to de Gaulle, 3 January 1945.
124. De Gaulle, *Mémoires de guerre*, tome III, 743; de Lattre, *Histoire de la première armée française*, 347–353; Miot, "Sortir l'armée des ombres," 458; Gurley, "Politique contre stratégie," 106–107.
125. SHD-GR, 11P 190, De Lattre to de Gaulle, 3 January 1945.
126. De Gaulle, *Mémoires de guerre*, tome III, 739.
127. SHD-GR, 11P 190, Charles Frey, Mayor of Strasbourg, to de Gaulle, 3 January 1945.
128. Gurley, "Politique contre stratégie," 106.
129. SHD-GR, 11P 190, De Gaulle to de Lattre, 3 January 1945; Jackson, *De Gaulle*, 356.
130. Wheeler and Atkinson, *Jacob L. Devers*, 393.
131. "Perhaps he realized that his intransigence was at least partly due to his distrust and dislike of Devers, who had advocated defending Alsace." Wheeler and Atkinson, *Jacob L. Devers*, 394.
132. Gurley, "Politique contre stratégie," 110.
133. De Gaulle, *Mémoires de guerre*, tome III, 744–745.
134. Clarke and Smith, *Riviera to the Rhine*, 511–512; Jackson, *De Gaulle*, 356–357; de Lattre, *Histoire de la première armée française*, 356.
135. SHD-GR, 11P 190, De Lattre to de Gaulle, 3 January 1945; Gurley, "Politique contre stratégie," 111–112.
136. Rémy Desquesnes, *Les poches de résistance allemandes: Août 1944–mai 1945* (Rennes: Éditions ouest-France, 2013), 80.
137. Clarke and Smith, *Riviera to the Rhine*, 579.
138. De Gaulle, *Mémoires de guerre*, tome III, 729.
139. Éric Kocher-Marbœuf, "Entre guerre quasi totale et guerre quasi correcte," in Michel Catala (ed.), *Les poches de l'Atlantique 1944–1945: Le dernier acte de la Seconde Guerre mondiale en France* (Rennes: Presses universitaires de Rennes, 2019), 55.

140. SHD-GR, 7P 151, "Rapport N° 59. Renseignements sur la région de Royan," 20 November 1944, p. 4.
141. August Hampel, *J'occupais Royan 1943–1945* (Rioux-Martin: Le Croît Vif, 2011), 252–261.
142. Kocher-Marbœuf, "Entre guerre quasi totale et guerre quasi correcte," 63–64
143. Kocher-Marbœuf, "Entre guerre quasi totale et guerre quasi correcte," 64–65; de Jérôme de Lespinois, "L'enjeu aérien des poches. Entre stratégie et politique militaires," in Catala (ed.), *Les poches de l'Atlantique 1944–1945*, 114.
144. SHD-GR, 11P 190, "Note pour le chef du 3e bureau de la première armée française," 4 January 1945.
145. The 4e DMM was in reserve, as well as *goumiers*, parachute infantry, and commandos. Eventually, de Lattre would have the 2e DB and the 28th US ID added to his order of battle. SHD-GR, 11P 191, "Rapport sur les opérations de la 1ère Armée Française. La Bataille d'Alsace et la Victoire de Colmar (20 janvier–9 févier 45)," undated, p. 3.
146. SHD-GR, 11P 164, Koenig to War Minister, 11 December 1944.
147. Of the division's 722 officers listed in March 1945, 115 were professional soldiers, while another 20 professional officers held FFI ranks; 106 officers were reservists, with another 74 reservists "*homologué*" – that is, "accredited" – as FFI, presumably so that they could retain their higher resistance rank. SHD-GR, 11P 164, "Journal de marche et opérations de la 10ème D.I."
148. SHD-GR, 11P 164, "Resurrection," p. 2, undated.
149. Gurley, "Politique contre stratégie," 113.
150. Mary Kathryn Barbier, "The War in the West, 1943–1945," in John Ferris and Evan Mawdsley, *The Cambridge History of the Second World War*, volume 1, *Fighting the War* (Cambridge: Cambridge University Press, 2015), 413.
151. Clarke and Smith, *Riviera to the Rhine*, 527–532. Wheeler and Atkinson estimate 23,000 German casualties against 25,924 for the Seventh US and First French Armies, as well as 47,688 non-battle casualties for the two armies. Wheeler and Atkinson, *Jacob L. Devers*, 398.
152. De Lattre, *Histoire de la première armée française*, 367–368, 371, 376, 379.
153. Monsabert, *Notes de Guerre*, 323.
154. Around 80 percent of GIs evacuated for this infirmity eventually returned to combat. Miot, "Sortir l'armée des ombres," 398–402.
155. Miot, "Sortir l'armée des ombres," 381–384, 393.
156. SHD-GR 11P 61, 3e DIA, "Rapport Technique A.M.M.," 29 December 1944 and 20 and 26 January 1945.
157. Richard Overy, *Blood and Ruins: The Last Imperial War, 1931–1945* (London: Viking, 2021), 740.
158. SHD-GR, 111 P7, Brosset to de Lattre, 7 September, 10 October, and 14 November 1944.
159. Miot, "Sortir l'armée des ombres," 517.
160. Miot, "Sortir l'armée des ombres," 449.
161. Bertrand Joly, "Le souvenir de 1870 et la place de la Revanche," in Stéphane Audoin-Rouzeau and Jean-Jacques Becker (eds.), *Encyclopédie de la Grande Guerre 1914–1918: Histoire et culture* (Paris: Bayard, 2004), 113–114.
162. De Gaulle, *Mémoires de guerre*, tome III, 735–736.
163. Olivier Wieviorka, *Divided Memory: French Recollections of World War II from the Liberation to the Present* (Stanford, CA: Stanford University Press, 2012), 6; Miot, "Sortir l'armée des ombres," 518.
164. SHD-GR, 111 P10, "Rapport sur le moral de la 1ère Brigade F.L.," 8 October 1944.
165. Miot, "Sortir l'armée des ombres," 412–416.
166. Monsabert, *Notes de Guerre*, 324.
167. SHD-GR, 11P 10, "Rapport sur le moral de la 1ère Brigade F.L.," 8 October 1944, and "Synthèse des rapports sur le moral de la troupe," 10 October 1944.
168. Miot, "Sortir l'armée des ombres," 481–491.
169. Miot, "Sortir l'armée des ombres," 513–515.
170. Miot, "Sortir l'armée des ombres," 500–517.
171. SHD-GR, 1P 191, "Instruction personnelle et secrète No. 8 pour le Commandant du Secteur des Vosges centrales," 18 January 1945.
172. Miot, "Sortir l'armée des ombres," 278–279, 349, 361, 366–367, 445–447, 472–475, 499.
173. SHD-GR, 11P 191, De Souzy to de Lattre, 29 January 1945.
174. Also, there was always a strong chance that a court martial would find a verdict of "extenuating circumstances" – the result in 63 percent of cases tracked by Miot – or that harsh sentences would be reduced on appeal. Only 7 percent of those convicted for desertion in the face of the enemy were given death sentences, few of which were carried out. In any case, despite the feeling that they were being used as cannon fodder, few colonial soldiers deserted, perhaps because they concluded that they would not get far. Miot, "Sortir l'armée des ombres," 420–425, 433.

175. Only 118 officers, NCOs, and soldiers reported as "missing," all Europeans, in a division that counted more than 12,000 men. SHD-GR, 111 P7, "1re Division française libre," 28 January 1945.
176. Bacquier, *Aïwah*, 112.
177. SHD-GR, 11P 51. Unit strength is not given, nor are casualties specified as dead, wounded, or missing, nor whether they were returned to action. These figures are based on a calculation for 645 officers and 14,600 men per division.
178. J. Vernet, *Le rearmament et la reorganization de l'armée de terre française (1943–1946)* (Vincennes: Ministère de la Défense, État-major de l'armée de terre, Service historique, 1980), 24; Miot, "Sortir l'armée des ombres," 279.
179. Eisenhower, *Crusade in Europe*, 363.
180. De Lattre, *Histoire de la première armée française*, 381–382.
181. SHD-GR, 11P 191, "Rapport sur les opérations de la 1ère Armée Française. La Bataille d'Alsace et la Victoire de Colmar (20 janvier–9 févier 45)," undated, 12.
182. SHD-GR, 11P 191, "Rapport sur les opérations de la 1ère Armée Française. La Bataille d'Alsace et la Victoire de Colmar (20 janvier–9 févier 45)," undated, 5–6.
183. De Lattre, *Histoire de la première armée française*, 384–385.
184. Clarke and Smith, *Riviera to the Rhine*, 533–539; de Lattre, *Histoire de la première armée française*, 382–383, 389–392.
185. SHD-GR, 11P 191, "Rapport sur les opérations de la 1ère Armée Française. La Bataille d'Alsace et la Victoire de Colmar (20 janvier–9 févier 45)," undated, 15–18.
186. De Lattre, *Histoire de la première armée française*, 393–402.
187. Clarke and Smith, *Riviera to the Rhine*, 547, 552. De Lattre writes that, on 25 January, Devers agreed to give him Milburn's XXI Corps. De Lattre, *Histoire de la première armée française*, 411.
188. Stéphane Weiss, "Recréer une artillerie française en 1945: La part belle à la recuperation," *Révue historique des armées*, 274 (2014), 95–107.
189. Clarke and Smith, *Riviera to the Rhine*, 547–550; Eisenhower, *Crusade in Europe*, 374.
190. Monsabert, *Notes de Guerre*, 330, 345.
191. Martel, *Leclerc*, 314–326; Cadeau, *De Lattre*, 209–211; Destremau, *De Lattre*, 418; Wheeler and Atkinson, *Jacob L. Devers*, 382–385.
192. Clarke and Smith, *Riviera to the Rhine*, 486–489.
193. Bacquier, *Aïwah*, 117.
194. Jackson, *De Gaulle*, 355.
195. "The armored units attached to the *1ère Armée* were therefore often employed in dispersed order, so that opportunities for division commanders to direct their units as they saw fit were rare," writes Michel Pesquer. "It was the same for the commanders of tank destroyers [dedicated anti-tank vehicles]. All commanders of these types of unit were accustomed to dispersing them among the different sectors," which forfeited the shock value of massed armor. Michel Pesquer, "L'emploi des blindés français sur le front occidental d'août 1944 à mai 1945," Thèse du doctorat, Université de Lorraine, 2018), 502, 515–516.
196. Only in the final stages of the closing of the Falaise Pocket, when it covered the flank of the 90th US ID, was the 2e DB briefly used for infantry support. Pesquer, "L'emploi des blindés français," 502–503, 509–512, 517–518, 526–527, 531.
197. SHD-GR, 11P 191, "Rapport sur les opérations de la 1ère Armée Française. La Bataille d'Alsace et la Victoire de Colmar (20 janvier–9 févier 45)," undated, 24.
198. Clarke and Smith, *Riviera to the Rhine*, 556–560; SHD-GR, 11P 191, "Rapport sur les opérations de la 1ère Armée Française. La Bataille d'Alsace et la Victoire de Colmar (20 janvier–9 févier 45)," undated, 13; Martel, *Leclerc*, 326.
199. The Americans estimated French casualties at around 16,000 in the Colmar Pocket. Clarke and Smith, *Riviera to the Rhine*, 556–557; de Lattre, *Histoire de la première armée française*, 456–457.
200. Lefort-Rouquette, *Des Ambulancières dans les combats de la Libération*, 127.
201. Bacquier, *Aïwah*, 113.
202. Wheeler and Atkinson, *Jacob L. Devers*, 401–405.
203. Raoul Salan, *Mémoires: Fin d'un empire*, tome 1, *"Le sens d'un engagement," juin 1899–septembre 1946* (Paris: Presses de la Cité, 1970), 147.
204. Clarke and Smith, *Riviera to the Rhine*, 551–552.
205. De Lattre, *Histoire de la première armée française*, 457.
206. Jean-François Muracciole, *Les Français libres: L'autre Résistance* (Paris: Tallandier, 2009), 282–283.
207. Cadeau, *De Lattre*, 295
208. Wheeler and Atkinson, *Jacob L. Devers*, 387–399; Clarke and Smith, *Riviera to the Rhine*, 556.

CHAPTER 9

1. Charles de Gaulle, *Mémoires de guerre*, tome III, *Le salut, 1944–1946* (Paris: Plon, 1959), 748.
2. The Moscow Conference of October–November 1943, had decided that post-war Germany would be divided into occupation zones. A European Advisory Commission (EAC) under the foreign ministers of the three major Allies (Eden, Hull, and Molotov) was created at the Moscow Conference to study post-war political problems and make recommendations, including the conditions of capitulation and future occupation zones. Despite repeated requests to be included, France was not admitted to the EAC until after the formal recognition of the *Gouvernement provisoire de la république française* (GPRF) on 23 October 1944, by which time three zones of occupation had been tentatively agreed upon. Only on 11 November did the French representative, René Massigli, attend his first EAC meeting. De Gaulle had lobbied Churchill in November 1944 over France's need for an occupation zone as a military barrier, as well as Stalin during his December 1944 visit to Moscow, only to find both leaders evasive. While, in his January 1945 State of the Union address, Roosevelt had acknowledged that French interests must be accommodated in the occupation of Germany, he had failed to back Churchill's proposal, at Yalta in February 1945, that France be allocated an occupation zone. In fact, in May 1945, de Gaulle complained to US Ambassador Jefferson Cafferty that Washington appeared to have written off France since 1940. Irwin M. Wall, *The United States and the Making of Postwar France, 1945–1954* (Cambridge: Cambridge University Press, 1991), 33.
3. The question of occupation zones was bound up with visions for a post-war world and planning for the size of post-war forces. But what becomes clear, from the perspective of the American Joint Chiefs of Staff (JCS) at least, is that French interests received little consideration. Mark A. Stoler, *Allies and Adversaries: The Joint Chiefs of Staff, the Grand Alliance, and U.S. Strategy in World War II* (Chapel Hill and London: The University of North Carolina Press, 2000).
4. Wall, *The United States and the Making of Postwar France*, 32–34; Robert Frank, "The Second World War through French and British Eyes," in Robert Tombs and Emile Chabal (eds.), *Britain and France in Two World Wars: Truth, Myth and Memory* (London: Bloomsbury, 2013), 187–189; Martin Thomas and Richard Toye, *Arguing about Empire: Imperial Rhetoric in Britain and France, 1882–1956* (Oxford: Oxford University Press, 2017), 189–190.
5. Claire Miot, "Sortir l'armée des ombres. Soldats de l'Empire, combattants de la Libération, armée de la Nation: La Première armée française, du débarquement en Provence à la capitulation allemande (1944–1945)," Thèse du doctorat, Université Paris-Saclay, 2016, 587–588; Hilary Footitt and John Simmonds, *France 1943–1945* (Leicester: Leicester University Press, 1988), 205–206, 210.
6. Miot, "Sortir l'armée des ombres," 581–583, 589–592; Frank, "The Second World War through French and British Eyes," 186–190.
7. Thomas and Toye, *Arguing about Empire*, 181.
8. Footitt and Simmonds, *France 1943–1945*, 207–208.
9. Miot, "Sortir l'armée des ombres," 589–590.
10. Wall, *The United States and the Making of Postwar France*, 111–112; Mary Louise Roberts, *What Soldiers Do: Sex and the American GI in World War II France* (Chicago: University of Chicago Press, 2013), 16; Hilary Footitt, *War and Liberation in France: Living with the Liberators* (New York: Palgrave Macmillan, 2004), 179.
11. Footitt and Simmonds, *France 1943–1945*, 205, 208–215, Wall, *The United States and the Making of Postwar France*, 37.
12. Miot, "Sortir l'armée des ombres," 584–588.
13. Earl Ziemke, *The U.S. Army in the Occupation of Germany*, Part I (Grandview Heights, OH: Bibliogov, 2013), 163–165.
14. Miot, "Sortir l'armée des ombres," 632.
15. "Directive concerning instruction and training of units of all branches of the First French Army," 24 February 1945. NARA RG 331, Entry 240D, Box 10; "Status of the 1st and 14th French Infantry Divisions," 1 May 1945. NARA RG 331, Entry 240D, Box 10.
16. James Scott Wheeler and Rick Atkinson, *Jacob L. Devers: A General's Life* (Lexington: University Press of Kentucky, 2015), 409.
17. Footitt and Simmonds, *France 1943–1945*, 228.
18. Miot, "Sortir l'armée des ombres," 592–593, 605.
19. Of Alsatian origin, Koeltz had spent the Great War in staff positions, briefly served as military attaché to Berlin in 1930, and before had been responsible for translating German doctrine for the *Deuxième Bureau*. He had been the very man dispatched in June 1940 to North Africa to carry Weygand's message to Moroccan Resident General Noguès that, should he choose to fight on, he must expect no help from the

Metropole. His subsequent job at Vichy had been to enforce the conditions of the 1940 Armistice. As 19e Corps commander in North Africa in November 1942, Koeltz had ordered an "energetic" resistance to the Anglo-American invasion, which unsurprisingly had pitched him into (temporary) retirement upon the "fusion" of Gaullists with *l'armée d'Afrique* in September 1943. Robert Paxton, *Parades and Politics at Vichy: The French Officer Corps under Marshal Pétain* (Princeton: Princeton University Press, 1966), 26–27, 148, 348, 361.

20. Jean-François Muracciole, "La France a contribué à la Victoire des Alliés," in Jean Lopez and Olivier Wieviorka (eds.), *Les mythes de la seconde guerre mondiale* (Paris: Perrin, 2015), 348.
21. Miot, "Sortir l'armée des ombres," 592–593, 605; Footitt and Simmonds, *France 1943–1945*, 228.
22. Jeffrey J. Clarke and Robert Ross Smith, *Riviera to the Rhine* (Washington, D.C.: Center of Military History, United States Army, 1993), 558–560.
23. De Gaulle, *Mémoires de guerre*, tome III, 751–752; SHD-GR, 11P 191, "Traduction d'un télégram chiffré," 29 March at 13:50.
24. Wheeler and Atkinson, *Jacob L. Devers*, 412–417.
25. "Now, in the spirit of the Allied command, obviously shaped by Washington, it was the American forces who must take over almost all the action in this final phase of the struggle," de Gaulle wrote. "As for the French, one tried at first to confine them to the left bank of the Rhine. As they managed, however, to find the means to cross the river, one will try to make sure they advance as little as possible. It goes without saying that in the very moment when the possibilities expanded, we were not going to accept such a diminished role." De Gaulle, *Memoires de Guerre*, tome III, 763–764.
26. Wheeler and Atkinson, *Jacob L. Devers*, 416–417.
27. Jean de Lattre de Tassigny, *Histoire de la première armée française: Rhin et Danube* (Paris: Presse de la Cité, 1971), 522–523. On Stuttgart, see de Gaulle, *Mémoires de guerre*, tome III, 764–765; Miot, "Sortir l'armée des ombres," 607.
28. Dwight D. Eisenhower, *Crusade in Europe* (Garden City, NY: Doubleday & Company, 1950), 413.
29. Julian Jackson, *De Gaulle* (Cambridge, MA: Harvard University Press, 2018), 358.
30. Wheeler and Atkinson, *Jacob L. Devers*, 421–423; de Gaulle, *Mémoires de guerre*, tome III, 766–767. In fact, de Gaulle may have had little interest in Stuttgart *per se*, but saw it as a bargaining chip to exchange against something he coveted – Cologne, for example. And, in the short term at least, the incident caught Marshall's attention, who suggested that Baden be given to the French, together with Württemburg and Sigmaringen. But negotiations for the final zones reopened only after Germany's surrender. Miot, "Sortir l'armée des ombres," 606–608.
31. De Gaulle, *Mémoires de guerre*, tome III, 765.
32. Marc Hillel, *L'occupation française en Allemagne 1945–1949* (Paris: Balland, 1983), 61.
33. Hillel, *L'occupation française en Allemagne 1945–1949*, 126–130.
34. Hillel, *L'occupation française en Allemagne 1945–1949*, 59–60.
35. Jean-Christophe Notin, *Leclerc: Le croisé de la France libre* (Paris: Perrin, 2015), 330–333.
36. De Lattre also accused Carpentier of having taken too many casualties during his Rhine crossing, although the crossing had been forced by de Lattre at de Gaulle's urging without a proper reconnaissance. Ivan Cadeau, *De Lattre* (Paris: Perrin, 2017), 226. On the French command climate, see also Henri Navarre, *Le Temps des vérités* (Paris: Plon, 1979), 177–180.
37. Wheeler and Atkinson, *Jacob L. Devers*, 426–427.
38. Recounted by Édouard Daladier, *Prison Journal 1940–1945* (Boulder, San Francisco, and Oxford: Westview Press, 1995), 337–341.
39. De Lattre, *Histoire de la première armée française*, 592–595. Technically, Eisenhower should have signed the document. But, as he outranked Zhukov, his deputy Tedder signed for the Western Allies. The Soviets insisted that, as the French, like the Americans, served under SHAEF, they did not qualify as signatories, but counted only as observers.
40. De Gaulle, *Mémoires de guerre*, tome III, 754.
41. De Gaulle, *Mémoires de guerre*, tome III, 755–756.
42. Éric Kocher-Marbœuf, "Entre guerre quasi totale et guerre quasi correct. Destins croisés des poches du Sud-Ouest," in Michel Catala (ed.), *Les poches de l'Atlantique 1944–1945: Le dernier acte de la Seconde Guerre mondiale en France* (Rennes: Presses universitaires de Rennes, 2019), 66–68.
43. SHD-GR, 10P 452, 11 May 1945, 55.
44. Hillel, *L'occupation française en Allemagne 1945–1949*, 69–79.
45. 5e bureau, Headquarters 1ère Armée, 1 May 1945. NARA, RG 0498, Entry UD578, Box 3905.
46. Miot, "Sortir l'armée des ombres," 638–640.

47. Of a *1ère Armée* strength of 279,331 officers and men in March 1945, 186,620 or two-thirds were French. The rest were North Africans, especially Algerians and Moroccans, and "colonials." Miot, "Sortir l'armée des ombres," 632.
48. R. M. Douglas, "Neither Apathetic nor Empathetic: Investigating and Prosecuting the Rape of German Civilians by U.S. Servicemen in 1945," *The Journal of Military History*, 87/2 (2023), 404–437.
49. Wheeler and Atkinson, *Jacob L. Devers*, 422.
50. Miot, "Sortir l'armée des ombres," 632.
51. Hillel, *L'occupation française en Allemagne 1945–1949*, 107–110, 124.
52. Michel de Cazote, "Oflag Adventure," Hoover Institution, 171.
53. Yves Durand, *Prisonniers de guerre dans les Stalags, les Oflags et les Kommandos, 1939–1945* (Paris: Hachette, 1994), 267–276, 282.
54. As in Italy, the scope of rapes by French colonial troops was difficult to assess with accuracy because accusations were often not believed, difficult to document because they were underreported, and so underestimated, or underinvestigated. Those most eager to publicize rapes by troops of color might also have a broader agenda. For instance, following a fact-finding mission in Europe, Mississippi Senator James Eastland informed the US Senate that 2,000–2,500 German women, "Christians from good families," had been raped by "Senegalese" – although there were few Senegalese left in the 1ère Armée. The Senator's goal was to limit the deployment of African-American troops, who were also often accused of sexual assault in Italy and Normandy, to occupation duty. Miot, "Sortir l'armée des ombres," 609, 629; Hillel, *L'occupation française en Allemagne 1945–1949*, 38. Rainer Hudemann argued in 1995 that the "supposed cruelty [of African soldiers that] Nazi propaganda had focused on so efficiently . . . assimilated by people who mixed up rumors of the days before and after the beginning of the occupation," combined with "absurd" stories of mass rapes carried out by African troops in Stuttgart, often retailed uncritically by "the Anglo-Saxon press," meant "that even today it is sometimes difficult to distinguish [. . .] what really happened in the zone when these troops marched in." Rainer Hundemann, "The Army as an Occupying Power: The German Army in 1940–1944, the French Army in 1945–1949," in Klaus-Jürgen Müller (ed.), *The Military in Politics and Society in France and Germany in the Twentieth Century* (Oxford and Washington, D.C.: Berg, 1995), 149.
55. Miot, "Sortir l'armée des ombres," 622.
56. Miot, "Sortir l'armée des ombres," 634–653.
57. Hillel, *L'occupation française en Allemagne 1945–1949*, 124.
58. 1 May 1945, NARA, RG 0498, Entry UD578, Box 3905.
59. Hillel, *L'occupation française en Allemagne 1945–1949*, 85.
60. Douglas, "Neither Apathetic nor Empathetic," 414.
61. Miot, "Sortir l'armée des ombres," 615–625, 630–631, 644, 655; Douglas, "Neither Apathetic nor Empathetic," 425.
62. Louis Bacquier, *Aïwah: Au combat avec les marocains. Souvenirs d'un officier de tirailleurs 1942–1945* (Paris: Éditions Laville, 2012), 152–153.
63. Bacquier had been coached by his father, a professional officer, how to handle challenges to the authority of young officers, which might come from corporals and NCOs: "Above all, don't hesitate, don't debate." And if one must threaten violence, be prepared to carry it out. Bacquier, *Aïwah*, 130; Miot, "Sortir l'armée des ombres," 645–648, 650–651.
64. Hillel, *L'occupation française en Allemagne 1945–1949*, 86, 96.
65. Norman M. Naimark, *The Russians in Germany: A History of the Soviet Zone of Occupation, 1945–1949* (Cambridge, MA: Harvard University Press, 1995), 107; Miot, "Sortir l'armée des ombres," 624.
66. Hillel, *L'occupation française en Allemagne 1945–1949*, 235.
67. Bob Moore, "Unruly Allies: British Problems with French Treatment of Axis Prisoners of War 1943–1945," *War in History*, 7/2 (April 2000), 197.
68. Richard Bessel, "Death and Survival in the Second World War," in Michael Geyer and Adam Tooze (eds.), *The Cambridge History of World War II*, volume III, *Total War: Economy, Society, and Culture* (Cambridge: Cambridge University Press, 2015), 264.
69. Use in demining offers one explanation for the relatively high death rate of German POWs in French custody. Those captured by the FFI might have been killed out of hand. Inadequate rations was another factor. The French excuse was that some were already sick when they surrendered. Moore, "Unruly Allies," 196–197; Claude d'Abzac-Epezy, "La France face au rapatriement des prisonniers de guerre allemands," *Guerre mondiales et conflits contemporains*, 2009/1, no. 233 (2009), 96.
70. Moore, "Unruly Allies," 182. France held 870,000 German POWs on 15 October 1945. D'Abzac-Epezy, "La France face au rapatriement des prisonniers de guerre allemands," 97.
71. Estimated at 57 or 58 percent. See Ronald Smelser and Edward J. Davies II, *The Myth of the Eastern Front: The Nazi–Soviet War in American Popular Culture* (Cambridge: Cambridge University Press, 2008), 243;

Klaus-Jürgen Müller, *The Army, Politics and Society in Germany, 1933–45: Studies in the Army's Relation to Nazism* (Manchester: Manchester University Press, 1987), 7.

72. French mistreatment of Axis POWs had been an issue since Tunisia in 1943. Moore, "Unruly Allies," 180–198. In the summer of 1945, the French took over the administration of US-run POW camps located in France. They also aspired to take 1,300,000 German POWs in US-administered camps in Germany, but lacked the resources to do so when many French people were surviving on 1,500 calories a day, and malnutrition was a factor in the deaths of an estimated 25,000 French children in 1945–1946. An estimated 120,000–150,000 POWs considered too debilitated to work were returned to the Americans or repatriated to Germany. "Work commandos" of former Axis POWs – Romanians, Hungarians, Austrians, and Italians, as well as Germans – were organized for demining, rubble clearing, and reconstruction. Private employers were also invited to take POW laborers, 81,000 of whom escaped back to Germany before all POWs were released in December 1948. Around 137,000 of the 657,000 POWs in France at the end of 1946 chose free laborer status. Claude d'Abzac-Epezy, "L'armée française et les prisonniers de guerre de l'Axe," in Natalie Genet-Rouffiac (ed.), *Les prisonniers de guerre aux personnes capturées* (Paris: Service de la Défense, 2010), 39–54; Hillel, *L'occupation française en Allemagne 1945–1949*, 98–103.
73. Laure Humbert, "French Politics of Relief and International Aid: France, UNRRA and Rescue of European Displaced Persons in Postwar Germany, 1945–47," *Journal of Contemporary History*, 51/3 (July 2016), 616, 624–626.
74. Humbert, "French Politics of Relief and International Aid," 616, 626, 630–631.
75. Michel Boivin, *1939–1945: Les Manchois dans la tourmente de la Seconde Guerre mondiale*, tome 6, *Les lendemains de la libération: Nouveaux pouvoirs, épuration et renaisssances* (Marigny: Éditions Eurocibles, 2004), 134–135. Estimates of the divorce rate in the immediate post-war years run between 7.76 and 10 percent. There is no way of knowing how many of these were POWs. See also Julie Le Gac, "L''étrange défaite' du divorce? (1940–1946)," *Vingtième Siècle. Revue d'histoire*, 2005/4, no. 88 (2005), 49–62. In her novel *Le Confident*, Hélène Grémillon's main character recounts "On ne pense jamais à ces femmes qui ont vu leur mari partir à la guerre avec le plus grand soulagement, elles existaient pourtant, et j'en fus." Hélène Grémillon, *Le Confident* (Paris: Plon, 2010), 222.
76. Hillel, *L'occupation française en Allemagne 1945–1949*, 135, 234–238; France. Archives nationales. Archives du service de recherche de crimes de guerre (1841–1949), https://francearchives.fr/en/facomponent/8b5bd094c3f67205fbd461c9b105a79491e8a0d1.
77. Philippe Burrin, *France under the Germans: Collaboration and Compromise* (New York: The New Press, 1996 [French edition 1993]), 436.
78. André Bayle, *De Marseille à Novossibirsk* (Sausset-les-Pins: self-published, 1992), 91; Luc Capdevila, François Rouquet, Fabrice Virgili, and Danièle Voldman, *Sexes, genre et guerres (France, 1914–1945)* (Paris: Payot, 2010), 97–102, 139–140; Luc Capdevila, "L'identité masculine et les fatigues de la guerre (1914–1945)," *Vingtième Siècle. Revue d'histoire*, 2003/3, no. 75 (2003), 97–108, note 15, www.cairn.info/revue-vingtieme-siecle-revue-d-histoire-2002-3-page-97.htm; Nina Barbier, *Malgré-elles: Les Alsaciennes et Mosellanes incorporées de force dans la machine de guerre nazi* (Paris: Tallandier, 2018).
79. Chris Bishop, *Hitler's Foreign Divisions: Foreign Volunteers in the Waffen-SS 1940–1945* (Staplehurst: Spellmount, 2005), 40.
80. J. G. Shields, "Charlemagne's Crusaders. French Collaborators in Arms," *French Cultural Studies*, 18/1 (February 2007), 102–103.
81. Bayle, *De Marseille à Novossibirsk*, 205–210.
82. Guy Sajer, *Le soldat oublié* (Paris: Robert Laffont, 1967).
83. Philippe Carrard, *The French Who Fought for Hitler* (Cambridge: Cambridge University Press, 2010), 159–166, 178–183; Bayle, *De Marseille à Novossibirsk*, 217. La Mazière had already served two years in prison at the end of the war after his attempt to pass himself off as an STO laborer was unmasked. He had been pardoned by French President Vincent Auriol in 1948.
84. Pierre Giolitto, *Histoire de la milice* (Paris: Librairie Académique Perrin, 1997), 480–499, 509–535; Michèle Cointet, *La milice française* (Paris: Fayard, 2013), 223–249.
85. Julian Jackson, *De Gaulle* (Cambridge, MA: Harvard University Press, 2018), 358; de Gaulle, *Mémoires de guerre*, tome III, 776–779.
86. De Gaulle, *Mémoires de guerre*, tome III, 764–767. See "The Ambassador in France (Cafferty) to the Secretary of State," 28 April 1945, in Office of the Historian, *Foreign Relations of the United States: Diplomatic Papers, 1945, Europe*, vol. IV, https://history.state.gov/historicaldocuments/frus1945v04/d664.
87. Hillel, *L'occupation française en Allemagne 1945–1949*, 153–157.
88. Miot, "Sortir l'armée des ombres," 664.
89. De Lattre, *Histoire de la première armée française*, 609; Jean Edward Smith, *Lucius D. Clay: An American Life* (New York: Henry Holt, 1990), 429. While the French were blamed for food shortages in their zone, in

fact, much of the problem was caused by the breakdown of the artificial Nazi war economy that depended on requisitions from abroad. Nor was the situation helped when Clay withheld US grain in an attempt to pressure Paris to liberalize its occupation policies. Müller, *The Military in Politics and Society in France and Germany*, 154–155.

90. Antony Beevor and Artemis Cooper, *Paris after the Liberation* (London: Penguin, 1994), 128.
91. Miot, "Sortir l'armée des ombres, 741.
92. Jackson, *De Gaulle*, 151.
93. General Joseph Goislard de Monsabert, *Notes de Guerre* (Hélette: Éditions Jean Curutchet, 1999), 305–306.
94. Quoted in Michel Pesquer, "L'emploi des blindés français sur le front occidental d'août 1944 à mai 1945," Thèse du doctorat, Université de Lorraine, 2018, 469.
95. André Martel, *Leclerc: Le soldat et la politique* (Paris: Albin Michel, 1998), 11–14, 492–495.
96. Général Yves Gras, "18 juin 1945. Le défilé de la victoire," 5, 13, 22, http://ekladata.com/kdhGQ1qYOiI RpJvO1UgGm5QiYJs/1eredfl-n-51-8-Mai-18-Juin-1945-La-France-Libre-fete-sa-Victoire.pdf.
97. Guillaume Piketty, "Français libre à l'épreuve de la libération," *Revue historique des armées*, 245 (2006), 27–35.
98. De Lattre, *Histoire de la première armée française*, 611.
99. Beevor and Cooper, *Paris after the Liberation*, 128.
100. Gras, "18 juin 1945. Le défilé de la victoire," 24. In fact, the presence of the Hadfield–Spears Ambulance Unit had been a source of tension since Syria in 1941 between Mary Spears and Madame Catroux. I thank Laure Humbert for this information, https://colonialandtransnationalintimacies.com/2021/03/05/gender-humanitarianism-and-soft-power.
101. Henry Rousso, *The Vichy Syndrome: History and Memory in France since 1944* (Cambridge, MA: Harvard University Press, 1991), 301.
102. https://actu.fr/normandie/bayeux_14047/la-question-pas-bete-mais-faisait-charles-gaulle-6-juin-1944_24 378078.html. His 1964 inauguration of the monument to North African soldiers on Mont Faron above Toulon was overshadowed by an unsuccessful Organisation armée secrète (OAS) attempt to assassinate him.
103. Philippe Buton, *Les lendemains qui déchantent: Le Parti communiste français à la Libération* (Paris: Presses de la Foundation Nationale des Sciences Politiques, 1993), 183–184; Yves Roucaute, *Le PCF et l'armée* (Paris: Presses universitaires de France, 1983), 20.
104. The complaint was that of François Mitterand, quoted in Julian Jackson, "General de Gaulle and His Enemies: Anti-Gaullism in France since 1940," *Transactions of the Royal Historical Society*, 9 (1999), 63.
105. Jackson, "General de Gaulle and His Enemies," 46; Robert Belot, *La Résistance sans de Gaulle* (Paris: Fayard, 2006), 647.
106. Olivier Wieviorka, *Histoire de la résistance, 1940–1945* (Paris: Perrin, 2013), 489.
107. Julian Jackson, "General de Gaulle and His Enemies," 48–49.
108. Belot, *La Résistance sans de Gaulle*, 11–13, 642–644.
109. Of 212 towns studied by Philippe Buton, only 2 percent witnessed insurrections, while 13 percent saw partial insurrections. Fully 84 percent "were offered their liberation." Buton, *Les lendemains qui déchantent*, 104–106.
110. Marianne Colonna, "Mythologies de la libération: Propagande et résistance," in Yves Jeanclos (ed.), *La France et les soldats d'infortune au XXe siècle* (Strasbourg: Economica, 2003), 232–236.
111. Buton, *Les lendemains qui déchantent*, 105–106.
112. See, in particular, Lucian Truscott, *Command Missions: A Personal Story* (New York: Dutton, 1954), 423, cited in Miot, "Sortir l'armée des ombres," 206–207.
113. SHAEF's staff took over 25 hotels, while its vast supply services, known as the communication zone (COMZ), requisitioned 300 hotels. David P. Colley, *The Folly of Generals: How Eisenhower's Broad Front Strategy Lengthened World War II* (Philadelphia and Oxford: Casemate, 2020), 188.
114. Fabrice Virgili, *La France "virile." Des femmes tondues à la libération* (Paris: Payot, 2000), 309.
115. Jackson, "General de Gaulle and His Enemies," 46–47.
116. Colonna, "Mythologies de la libération: Propagande et résistance," 232–238; Marc Olivier Baruch (ed.), *Une poignée de misérables: L'épuration de la société française après la Seconde Guerre mondiale* (Paris: Fayard, 2003).
117. Miot, "Sortir l'armée des ombres," 666–671.
118. Miot, "Sortir l'armée des ombres," 737–740. See also Guillaume Piketty, "From the Capitoline Hill to the Tarpeian Rock? Free French Coming Out of War," *European Review of History*, 25/2 (2018), 354–373.
119. Bacquier, *Aïwah*, 159
120. Gras, "18 juin 1945. Le défilé de la victoire," 13, 22.

121. Solange Cuvillier, *Tribulations d'une femme dans l'armée française, ou le patriotisme écorché* (Paris: Éditions Lettres du Monde, 1991), 58.
122. Suzanne Lefort-Rouquette, *Des Ambulancières dans les combats de la Libération: Avec les soldats de la 9e Division d'infanterie coloniale* (Paris: Éditions L'Harmattan, 2005), 114.
123. Jean-François Muracciole, *Les Français libres: L'autre Résistance* (Paris: Tallandier, 2009), 297–302.
124. Yves Gras, "8 Mai et 18 juin. La France Libre fête sa Victoire," 22, http://ekladata.com/kdhGQ1qYOiIRpJvO1UgGm5QiYJs/1eredfl-n-51-8-Mai-18-Juin-1945-La-France-Libre-fete-sa-Victoire.pdf.
125. Miot, "Sortir l'armée des ombres," 690.
126. Susan Travers, *Tomorrow to Be Brave* (London: Corgi Press, 2001), 298–303.
127. Cuvillier, *Tribulations d'une femme dans l'armée française*, 72–73, 77; Miot, "Sortir l'armée des ombres," 690–692. On the view that "war is parasitic on gender relations of power," see Patricia Owen's review of Tarak Barkawi's *Soldiers of Empire*, www.chathamhouse.org/sites/default/files/images/ia/INTA93_6_09_Review forum.pdf.
128. Rousso, *The Vichy Syndrome*, 90; "Discours prononcé pour le transfer des cendres du Jean Moulin au Panthéon, 19 décembre 1964," https://mjp.univ-perp.fr/textes/malraux19121964.htm.
129. Muracciole, *Les Français libres*, 352, 362–363.
130. Cuvillier, *Tribulations d'une femme dans l'armée française*, 68–71.
131. Frank Roy Willis, *The French in Germany 1945–1949* (Stanford: Stanford University Press, 1962), 75.
132. Cuvillier, *Tribulations d'une femme dans l'armée française*, 71.
133. Hillel, *L'occupation française en Allemagne 1945–1949*, 143–144.
134. Willis, *The French in Germany 1945–1949*, 75–76.
135. Roger Bourderon, *Rol-Tanguy: Des Brigades internationales à la libération de Paris* (Paris: Tallandier, 2013), 532–533.
136. Willis, *The French in Germany 1945–1949*, 76–79.
137. Jean Planchais, *Une histoire politique de l'armée*, tome 2, *1940–1967: De de Gaulle à de Gaulle* (Paris: Éditions du Seuil, 1967), 151, 154.
138. De Lattre, *Histoire de la première armée française*, 608.
139. Hillel, *L'occupation française en Allemagne 1945–1949*, 158–162, 169–173, 385.
140. Ivan Cadeau, *De Lattre* (Paris: Perrin, 2017), 235–237; Willis, *The French in Germany 1945–1949*, 82–83.
141. Miot, "Sortir l'armée des ombres," 741.
142. Beevor and Cooper, *Paris after the Liberation*, 221–223.
143. Cadeau, *De Lattre*, 237–243, 256–267.
144. Jackson, "General de Gaulle and His Enemies," 56.
145. Charles-Robert Ageron, "La survivance d'un mythe. La puissance par l'Empire colonial (1944–1947)," in René Girault and Robert Frank, *La puissance française en question! 1945–1949* (Paris: Publications de la Sorbonne, 1988), 34–49.
146. Thomas and Toye, *Arguing about Empire*, 191.
147. Philippe Franchini, *Les Guerres d'Indochine*, tome 1, *Des origines de la presence française à l'engrenage du conflit international* (Paris: Éditions Pygmalion, 1988), 157.
148. Michael Neiberg, *When France Fell: The Vichy Crisis and the Fate of the Anglo-American Alliance* (Cambridge, MA: Harvard University Press, 2021), 131.
149. Thomas Vaisset, *L'Amiral d'Argenlieu: Le moine-soldat du gaullisme* (Paris: Belin, 2017), 342. The Darlan–Kato accord of July 1941 allowed Japan to station forces throughout Indochina in the interest of "communal defense." Franchini, *Les Guerres d'Indochine*, tome 1, 156.
150. On the evolution of the situation in Vietnam, see Franchini, *Les Guerres d'Indochine*, tome 1, 169–183; Vaisset, *L'Amiral d'Argenlieu*, 340–344; Frédéric Turpin, *De Gaulle, les gaullistes et l'Indochine* (Paris: Les Indes Savantes, 2005), 87–89.
151. Franchini, *Les Guerres d'Indochine*, tome 1, 183–188.
152. Vaisset, *L'Amiral d'Argenlieu*, 348–349.
153. Jonathan Fennell, *Fighting the People's War: The British and Commonwealth Armies and the Second World War* (Cambridge: Cambridge University Press, 2019), 206–208, 692.
154. Michael Howard and Peter Paret (eds.), *Carl von Clausewitz: On War* (Princeton: Princeton University Press, 1989), 198, 200.
155. Turpin, *De Gaulle, les gaullistes et l'Indochine*, 46.
156. De Gaulle, *Mémoires de guerre*, tome III, 760.
157. Marcel Vigneras, *Rearming the French* (Washington, D.C.: Center of Military History, United States Army, 1989), 394.
158. Vigneras, *Rearming the French*, 392–393.

159. De Gaulle, *Mémoires de guerre*, tome III, 762. Nor, de Gaulle charged, did USAAF planes in China rush to the aid of the French, which was not entirely true, as the Fourteenth Air Force did carry out a few bombing runs and supply drops in support of fleeing French troops. Turpin, *De Gaulle, les gaullistes et l'Indochine*, 87. Sending airborne troops constituted an unfeasible option, because French paratroops were divided between regiments with British equipment and others that had been equipped to American specifications. Ministère de l'Air, 26 December 1944. NARA, RG 331, Entry 30C, Box 19D. In any case, training had not begun, while equipment was "practically non-existent except for some training equipment and small arms for the CLI [*corps léger d'intervention*]." Present Status of the French Far Eastern Expeditionary Force (FEFEG), 20 December 1944. NARA, RG 331, Entry 30C, Box 190. The purpose of this elite commando, notionally set at 500 men, was to be parachuted to reinforce a resistance, in the spirit of the *maquis* of le Vercors or Glières. Turpin, *De Gaulle, les gaullistes et l'Indochine*, 65.
160. Franchini, *Les guerres d'Indochine*, tome 1, 189–192.
161. Turpin, *De Gaulle, les gaullistes et l'Indochine*, 90–93, 131.
162. As early as 1942, Roosevelt had expressed a disinclination "to give back to France all her colonies," and advocated putting Indochina, New Caledonia, and Dakar under international trusteeship. Mark A. Stoler, *Allies and Adversaries: The Joint Chiefs of Staff, the Grand Alliance, and U.S. Strategy in World War II* (Chapel Hill and London: The University of North Carolina Press, 2000), 162, 168, 201, 307 (note 43). Wedemeyer barred French troops from the China theater. Eden and Mountbatten facilitated the French return by allowing the French to create a mission to South East Asia Command (SEAC) in October 1944. Turpin, *De Gaulle, les gaullistes et l'Indochine*, 67–71, 92–99.
163. Turpin, *De Gaulle, les gaullistes et l'Indochine*, 79–82; Jackson, *De Gaulle*, 362.
164. Sean McMeekin, *Stalin's War: A New History of World War II* (New York: Basic Books, 2021), 497.
165. On 18 December 1944, Chief of the French Naval Mission in Washington Vice-Admiral R. Fenard had assured the CCS "that whatever French Forces the Combined Chiefs of Staff would agree to use against Japan would be employed in such a way as the Combined Chiefs of Staff think fit." NARA, RG 331, Entry 30C, Box 190.
166. Vigneras, *Rearming the French*, 396–399.
167. Henri Lerner, *Catroux* (Paris: Albin Michel, 1990), 293.
168. One of the myths is that, in December 1945, de Gaulle was prepared to accept Indochinese independence under Prince Vinh San, the boy emperor who had ruled Annam during 1907–1916 as Emperor Duy Tan before being deposed and exiled by the French, but who had subsequently served in the *Forces navales françaises libres* (FNFL) during the war and participated as a major in the invasion and occupation of Germany. On 14 December 1945, de Gaulle met with Vinh San, and promised to reinstall him as the Emperor of Annam. Unfortunately, Vinh San's death in an air crash in central Africa subverted this scenario. But this counterfactual has no foundation in reality. "Independence" for de Gaulle was a relative term, that at its most democratic might mean the "interdependence" of colonial possessions under a French Union. How could de Gaulle have abandoned France's "balcony on the Pacific" at the very moment that he was trying to reestablish France's international stature? For their part, Indochinese nationalists, including the Viet Minh, had no intention of wasting the opportunity for Liberation. France would envisage negotiations only if it could not impose its will in Indochina through military means. Turpin, *De Gaulle, les gaullistes et l'Indochine*, 12–13, 109–112.
169. Turpin, *De Gaulle, les gaullistes et l'Indochine*, 94–96, 114–118, 123.
170. Salan, *Mémoires*, tome 1, 155–156.
171. Douglas Porch, *The French Foreign Legion: A Complete History of the Legendary Fighting Force* (New York: Harper Collins, 1991), 530–533.
172. Miot, "Sortir l'armée des ombres," 727–734.
173. Thomas and Toye, *Arguing about Empire*, 182.
174. Planchais, *Une histoire politique de l'armée*, tome 2, 75, 86; Belot, *La Résistance sans de Gaulle*, 635.
175. Turpin, *De Gaulle, les gaullistes et l'Indochine*, 570–573.
176. Philip Delves Broughton, "How Empire Ended," review of Bayly and Harper, *Forgotten Wars*, *Wall Street Journal*, 9 August 2007, www.wsj.com/articles/SB118662122851692478?mod=trending_now_video_4.
177. Jackson, *De Gaulle*, 411.
178. Jackson, *De Gaulle*, 360–363.
179. Philippe Devillers and Jean Lacouture, *End of a War: Indochina 1954* (New York: Prager, 1969).
180. Vaisset, *L'Amiral d'Argenlieu*, 350–357, 368–373.
181. Vaisset, *L'Amiral d'Argenlieu*, 376–381, 392–395.
182. Turpin, *De Gaulle, les gaullistes et l'Indochine*, 123, 175–189.
183. Vaisset, *L'Amiral d'Argenlieu*, 404–425. The texts of the accords can be found in Salan, *Mémoires*, tome 1, 330–332; Turpin, *De Gaulle, les gaullistes et l'Indochine*, 231, 234, 255, 299.

CHAPTER 10

1. Among other early analyses, see Charles Micaud, *The French Right and Nazi Germany, 1933–1939* (Durham: Duke University Press, 1943).
2. Samuel Lyman Atwood Marshall, *Men against Fire: The Problem of Battle Command in Future War* (New York: William Morrow, 1947).
3. Marc Bloch, *Strange Defeat: A Statement of Evidence Written in 1940* (New York: W. W. Norton & Company, 1968), x, 25, 36.
4. Jean Jaurès, *L'Armée nouvelle: L'organisation socialiste de la France* (Paris: Publications Jules Rouff, 1911).
5. Jean de Bloch, *The Future of War in Its Technical, Political, and Political Relations* (Boston: The Peace Foundation, 1914), www.armyupress.army.mil/Portals/7/combat-studies-institute/csi-books/Future-of-War.pdf.
6. Olivier Cosson, *Préparer la Grande Guerre: L'armée française et la guerre russo-japonaise (1899–1914)* (Paris: Les Indes Savantes, 2013), 10, 333.
7. Nicholas Stargardt, *The German War: A Nation under Arms, 1939–1945. Citizens and Soldiers* (New York: Basic Books, 2015), 9, 12, 16–17, 32.
8. Bloch, *Strange Defeat*, 89–94.
9. Robert A. Doughty, *The Breaking Point: Sedan and the Fall of France, 1940* (Mechanicsburg, PA: Stackpole Books, 1990), 27–30.
10. Patrick Wright, *Tank: The Progress of a Monstrous War Machine* (London: Faber and Faber, 2000), 273–275.
11. These indictments can be found in Chapter 3, "A Frenchman Examines His Conscience," of Bloch, *Strange Defeat*.
12. Peter Jackson, "Post-war Politics and the Historiography of French Strategy and Diplomacy before the Second World War," *History Compass*, 4/5 (2006), 873. The charge is somewhat ironic, as the knock on the *Annales* School was that its approach downgraded political and military history as *événementielle*. Emmanuel Droit and Franz Reichherzer, "La fin de l'histoire du temps présent telle que nous l'avons connue. Plaidoyer franco-allemand pour l'abandon d'une singularité historique," *Vingtième Siècle. Revue d'histoire* 2013/2, no. 118 (2013), 127.
13. Pertinax (André Géraud), *The Grave Diggers of France: Gamelin, Daladier, Reynaud, Pétain, and Laval. Military Defeat, Armistice, Counterrevolution* (Garden City, NY: Doubleday, Dorian, & Company, 1942).
14. Jean-Baptiste Duroselle, *Politique étrangère de la France: La décadence, 1932–1939* (Paris: Imprimerie nationale, 1979), 15, 20.
15. Peter Jackson, "Post-war Politics and the Historiography of French Strategy and Diplomacy before the Second World War," 875, 884.
16. The United States "good war" narrative is well known. For the Russo/Soviet mythology of the Great Patriotic War, see Jonathan Brunstedt, *The Soviet Myth of World War II: Patriotic Memory and the Russian Question in the USSR* (Cambridge: Cambridge University Press, 2021).
17. Susan McCall Perlman, *Contesting France: Intelligence and US Foreign Policy in the Early Cold War* (Cambridge: Cambridge University Press, 2023), 6, 9–13, 52, 197.
18. No such objections were raised over the Tokyo War Crimes Tribunal, which saw the execution of Tojo and six Japanese generals. Meanwhile, the US Army's "Operational History Section," otherwise known as the "Fritz Halder Group," inadvertently became the forum where the German High Comand could solidify their reputations for tactical and operational brilliance, offload defeat onto Hitler's "amateurism," and deny knowledge of the criminal dimensions of the war in the East, in which they had been active protagonists. Ronald Smelser and Edward J. Davies II, *The Myth of the Eastern Front: The Nazi–Soviet War in American Popular Culture* (Cambridge: Cambridge University Press, 2008), 54–63 and Chapter 3.
19. Quite apart from the Peter Jackson article cited above, see also Richard Carswell, *The Fall of France in the Second World War: History and Memory* (London: Palgrave Macmillan, 2019). Patrick Finney offers a very complete analysis of the multiple phases of historical interpretations of 1940 through the first decade of this century. Patrick Finney, *Remembering the Road to World War II: International History, National Identity, Collective Memory* (London: Routledge, 2011), Chapter 4.
20. P. Jackson, "Post-war Politics and the Historiography of French Strategy and Diplomacy before the Second World War," 887.
21. Philip Nord, *France 1940: Defending the Republic* (New Haven: Yale University Press, 2015), 165.
22. Nord, *France 1940*, 154–155.
23. John J. Mearsheimer, *Liddell Hart and the Weight of History* (Ithaca, NY: Cornell University Press, 1988), 188–191. For a more balanced view of the intellectual origins of the German Panzer arm, see Ian Ona

Johnson, "Ernst Volckheim, Heinz Guderian, and the Origins of German Armored Doctrine," *The Journal of Military History*, 87/1 (January 2023), 145–168. Smelser and Davies deal with the Cold War remake of the Wehrmacht's reputation in Smelser and Davies, *The Myth of the Eastern Front,* especially Chapters 3–6.

24. Martin S. Alexander, *The Republic in Danger: General Maurice Gamelin and the Politics of French Defence, 1933–1940* (Cambridge: Cambridge University Press, 1992), 378.
25. Nord, *France 1940*, 150–151.
26. For Ian Kershaw, going to war over Czechoslovakia, either in 1938 or the following year, would have made "an armed triumph of German might . . . a distinct possibility." Ian Kershaw, *Fateful Choices: Ten Decisions That Changed the World, 1940–1941* (New York: Penguin, 2007), 19. For arguments that France should have fought on from North Africa in June 1940, see Jacques Sapir, Frank Stora, and Loïc Mahé, *1940: Et si la France avait continué la guerre . . .* (Paris: Tallandier, 2010).
27. According to H. R. Trevor-Roper, the *Annales* "total history" approach "sought to recreate the totality of a society, past or present, to understand its delicate mechanism and yet to see it, not as a machine, but as a living organism with a dynamic of its own, distinct from the mere sum of its parts . . . circumstances are not themselves simple: they are not merely physical nor merely temporal; they are a complex of forces which is not easily disentangled because each of them acts and reacts on the others . . . The historians of the *Annales* school respect the organic nature of societies." H. R. Trevor-Roper, "Fernand Braudel, the *Annales*, and the Mediterranean," *The Journal of Modern History*, 44/4 (December 1972), 469–470.
28. Jean-Pierre Azéma, *1940: L'année noire* (Paris: Fayard, 2010), 436–37; Julian Jackson, *The Fall of France: The Nazi Invasion of 1940* (Oxford: Oxford University Press, 2003), 187.
29. Marc Bloch, *The Historian's Craft* (New York: Alfred A. Knopf, 1963), 70–71.
30. While, in 1941, the Red Army had plenty of tanks and troops, it lacked effective logistics. The longer-term impact of Stalin's pre-war purges of 28,000 Soviet officers is a subject of debate, especially as some of the purged officers were reinstated after Barbarossa. But the purges hit field-grade officers especially hard, while they also shut down debates over strategy, leaving Stalin as the sole custodian. Stalin remained convinced that Hitler would not attack so long as Britain remained undefeated, and distrusted intelligence reports that challenged this assumption. Nor was he keen to take any action that might provoke a German attack. Kershaw, *Fateful Choices*, 260, 268–276, 280–286. See also Bruce W. Menning and Jonathan House, "Soviet Strategy," in John Ferris and Evan Mawdsley (eds.), *The Cambridge History of the Second World War*, volume I: *Fighting the War* (Cambridge: Cambridge University Press, 2015), 213–244. For Soviet specialist Mikhail Tsypkin, professionalism was downgraded in a Russian military culture that believed that space and mass compensated for the relative backwardness of the Russian military. Furthermore, "Fear of Stalin, who did not want to confront the dangers inherent in his policy toward Germany, deterred the military from undertaking a sober analysis," concludes Tsypkin. "As a result, they failed to understand the nature of blitzkrieg and the fateful consequences of being surprised at the beginning of hostilities." Mikhail Tsypkin, "The Soviet Military Culture and the Legacy of the Second World War," in Frank Biess and Robert G. Moeller (eds.), *Histories of the Aftermath: The Legacies of the Second World War in Europe* (New York and Oxford: Berghahn, 2010), 275. For parallels with more contemporary events, see Lawrence Freedman, "Why War Fails: Russia's Invasion of Ukraine and the Limits of Military Power," *Foreign Affairs* (July/August 2022), www.foreignaffairs.com/articles/russian-federation/2022-06-14/ukraine-war-russia-why-fails.
31. Michael Howard, *Captain Professor: A Life in War and Peace* (London and New York: Continuum, 2006), 145. One criticism of the "War and Society" approach is that it is often more about societies than war, a rather curious charge to lay against Howard, who wrote a notable history of the Franco-Prussian War, not to mention a seminal study of Clausewitz. See also Eliot A. Cohen and John Gooch, *Military Misfortunes: The Anatomy of Failure in War* (New York and London: The Free Press, 1990), 39.
32. Finney, *Remembering the Road to World War II*, 154, 161, 170–171, 179.
33. Cohen and Gooch, *Military Misfortunes*, 24, quoting Amos Perlmutter, "Military Incompetence and Failure: A Historical Comparative and Analytical Evaluation," *Journal of Strategic Studies*, 1/2 (September 1978), 121, fn 51.
34. Richard J. Evans, *Altered Past: Counterfactuals in History* (London: Little Brown, 2014), 88–89, 145, 149, 176.
35. Julian Barnes, *England, England* (New York: Vintage Books, 1996), 6.
36. Julian Jackson, *De Gaulle* (Cambridge, MA: Harvard University Press, 2018), 368.
37. Talbot C. Imlay, *Facing the Second World War: Strategy, Politics, and Economics in Britain and France, 1938–1940* (Oxford: Oxford University Press, 2003), 355.
38. See, for instance, Carswell, *The Fall of France in the Second World War.* Patrick Finney offers a very complete analysis of the multiple phases of historical interpretations of 1940 through the first decade of this century. Finney, *Remembering the Road to World War II*, Chapter 4.

39. Hew Strachan, *The First World War*, volume 1, *To Arms* (Oxford: Oxford University Press, 2001), 103–104.
40. Strachan, *The First World War*, volume 1, 110.
41. Pierre Miquel, *La Grande guerre* (Paris: Fayard, 1983), 19.
42. Elizabeth Greenhalgh, *The French Army and the First World War* (Cambridge: Cambridge University Press, 2014), 30. "Stupefaction," followed by "indignation and a determination to fight to defend the country," is how Jean-Jacques Becker described the mood in the French countryside where half the population lived in 1914. Jean-Jacques Becker, "Entrées en guerre," in Stéphane Audoin-Rouzeau and Jean-Jacques Becker (eds.), *Encyclopédie de la Grande Guerre 1914–1918: Histoire et culture* (Paris: Bayard, 2004), 200.
43. Jean-Jacques Becker, "Prévisions des états-majors et effondrement des plans," in Audoin-Rouzeau and Becker (eds.), *Encyclopédie de la Grande Guerre 1914–1918*, 245; Frédéric Guelton, "Les armées," in Audoin-Rouzeau and Becker, *Encyclopédie de la Grande Guerre 1914–1918*, 225–226; Strachan, *The First World War*, volume 1, 191.
44. Becker, "Prévisions des états-majors et effondrement des plans," 246.
45. These issues are discussed in Hew Strachan and Ruth Harris, *The Utility of Military Force and Public Understanding in Today's Britain* (Santa Monica and Cambridge: RAND Corporation, 2020), 6–9, 24.
46. Carswell, *The Fall of France in the Second World War*, 251–252; Imlay, *Facing the Second World War.* "What [Imlay] has done, although he does not recognize it, is to give new life to decadent France." Michael Jabara Carley, review of Imlay's *Facing the Second World War, Canadian Journal of History*, 39/3 (December 2004), 603.
47. Winston S. Churchill, *The Second World War*, volume 2, *Their Finest Hour* (Boston: Houghton Mifflin Company, 1949), 4.
48. The left also blamed capitalists and their parliamentary allies for sabotaging rearmament out of a desire to seek revenge on the Popular Front. See Sara Fishman's review of Carswell's *The Fall of France in the Second World War, H-France Review*, 20/64 (April 2020), https://h-france.net/vol20reviews/vol20no64fishman.pdf; Carswell, *The Fall of France in the Second World War*, 259, 262.
49. Guillaume Piketty, "Souffances et ambiguïtes de la défaite," *Hypothèses* 2008/1, no. 11 (2008), 341–348.
50. Alexander, *The Republic in Danger*, 11.
51. Michael Geyer and Adam Tooze, "Introduction to Part III," in Michael Geyer and Adam Tooze (eds.), *The Cambridge History of World War II*, volume III, *Total War: Economy, Society, and Culture* (Cambridge: Cambridge University Press, 2015), 418.
52. See the differences on this point between Julian Jackson and Peter Jackson. Jackson, "Post-war Politics and the Historiography of French Strategy and Diplomacy before the Second World War," 887–888.
53. Bloch, *Strange* Defeat, 105, 107.
54. Cohen and Gooch, *Military Misfortunes*, Chapter 8.
55. Howard and Paret (eds.), *Carl von Clausewitz*, 198–201.
56. Kershaw, *Fateful Choices*, 260.
57. Calculated on the basis of 2,240,000 French soldiers serving on the northern front. Carswell discusses the various opinions on French willingness to fight, at what point in the battle French soldiers seemed to give up – Bulson, Dunkirk, the collapse of Weygand's "hedgehogs," the fall of Paris, the relationship between the civilian exodus and army decomposition, Pétain's 17 June announcement that he would seek an armistice, and so on – and its impact on the decision to sue for an armistice. Carswell, *The Fall of France in the Second World War*, 243–247. As a point of comparison, according to Nicolas Aubin, of 11 million conscripts who served in the American forces during the war, only 53,000 – or 0.48 percent – became POWs, "the lowest number among the belligerents." Nicolas Aubin, "Le soldat américain ne sait pas se battre," in Jean Lopez and Olivier Wieviorka (eds.), *Les mythes de la seconde guerre mondiale* (Paris: Perrin, 2015), 267. Unfortunately, Aubin gives no reference for this assertion. Other estimates, based on post-war requests for indemnification, put US POWs at slightly under 130,000 – 97,000 held by Germany, while 27,000 (not counting Filipino troops under US command) were held by Japan – out of an estimated 16.1 million US service personnel in the Second World War (this is a high estimate as most sources calculate that 12.1 million served in US forces in the Second World War). "US Prisoners of War and Civilian American Citizens Captured and Interned by Japan in World War II," Congressional Research Service Report for Congress, 17 December 2002, www.history.navy.mil/research/library/online-reading-room/title-list-alphabetically/u/us-prisoners-war-civilian-american-citizens-captured.html#:~:text=Summary.
58. "The mathematics of chance are based upon a fiction," wrote Marc Bloch. "From the outset, they postulate impartial conditions in all possible cases: a specific cause favoring a certain outcome in advance would be like a foreign body in the calculation ... in the criticism of evidence, almost all the dice are loaded. For extremely delicate human elements constantly intervene to tip the balance toward a preferred solution." Marc Bloch, *The Historian's Craft* (New York: Alfred A. Knopf, 1963), 78, 126.

59. Jean-Paul Sartre, *The War Diaries of Jean-Paul Sartre: November 1939/March 1940* (New York: Pantheon Books, 1984), 225.
60. Charles de Gaulle, *Mémoires de guerre*, tome I, *L'Appel 1940–1942* (Paris: Plon, 1954), 39.
61. Probably the closest equivalent of the Fall of France in terms of surrenders, albeit on a smaller scale, was the 1942 British Malaya campaign, when, of 139,000 British campaign losses, 94 percent were men taken as POWs. A large number of them were Indian colonial soldiers, between a third and a half of whom subsequently volunteered to fight for the Japanese in the Indian National Army. In this context, the fact that the French colonial army experienced morale problems that on occasion erupted in protests was hardly unique to France. British soldiers expressed their demoralization in the Western Desert in the summer of 1942, through a rise in the percentage of missing in action (MIA) in the British army's casualty statistics. And while the Australian and New Zealand Army Corps (ANZAC) soldiers were considered among the most valiant troops on the Allied side in the North Africa campaign, by 1943, their morale had seriously eroded, to the point that a large number sent on furlough to New Zealand mutinied rather than return to the mountain combat of Italy against an entrenched German defense. Like the First French Army in the winter of 1944–1945, the perception that New Zealand society seemed to have detached itself completely from the war, while many men at home had managed to secure jobs that entitled them to military deferments with good pay, demoralized troops on furlough. And speaking of Italy, the British army experienced 13,000 desertions and soldiers absent without leave (AWOL) in the Mediterranean theater between July 1943 and the end of the war, almost the strength of an infantry division. Jonathan Fennell, *Fighting the People's War: The British and Commonwealth Armies and the Second World War* (Cambridge: Cambridge University Press, 2019), 204–208, 379–390, 568.
62. Steven O'Connor, "Fighting a Coalition War: The Experience of the Free French Soldier in the British 8th Army," in Claire Miot, Guillaume Piketty, and Thomas Vaisset, *Militaires en résistances en France et en Europe* (Villeneuve d'Ascq: Presses universitaires du Septentrion, 2020), 153.
63. Charles Ardent du Picq, *Études sur le combat: Combat antique et modern* (London: Forgotten Books, 2018).
64. Fennell, *Fighting the People's War*, 684, 707–8.
65. Général André Beaufre, *1940: The Fall of France* (New York: Alfred A. Knopf, 1968), 175.
66. Paul Fussell, *Doing Battle: The Making of a Skeptic* (Boston, New York, Toronto, and London: Little Brown and Company, 1996), 124–125. Despite the Allied landings in France and setbacks on the Eastern Front, Eisenhower was informed that German POWs continued to express confidence in a German victory. Among the explanations for dogged German resistance was a widespread belief that "new weapons" would miraculously save Germany, fears that Asiatic hordes would be whipped into a frenzy by "Jewish commissars," and arguments that the Anglo-Americans, their reservoirs of men and matériel rapidly diminishing, could be convinced to strike a separate peace. Stargardt, *The German War*, 458, 461, 464, 470, 472, 478, 483–84, 523.
67. Andrew Monaghan, *Russian State Mobilization: Moving the Country onto a War Footing* (London: Chatham House, The Royal Institute of International Affairs, 2016), www.chathamhouse.org/2016/05/russian-state-mobilization-moving-country-war-footing.
68. John T. Kuehn review of Richard Overy, *Blood and Ruins: The Last Imperial War, 1939–1945, The Journal of Military History*, 87/1 (January 2023), 234.
69. Jo Fox, *Film Propaganda in Britain and Nazi Germany: World War II Cinema* (Oxford and New York: Berg, 2007), 309, 315.
70. Fox, *Film Propaganda in Britain and Nazi Germany*, 315.
71. Strachan and Harris, *The Utility of Military Force and Public Understanding in Today's Britain*, 17.
72. Olivier Forcade, "Le temps de la guerre et du désastre (septembre 1939–juillet 1940)," in Général Louis Rivet, *Carnets du chef des services secrets 1936–1944* (Paris: Nouveau Monde Éditions, 2010), 282. The rejection of the attack through the Ardennes had been in response to the March 1940 criticism by Pierre Taittinger that the Ardennes were inadequately defended. "Basically, General Georges always viewed intelligence through the prism of the school hypothesis … of an invasion via Belgium. Most French generals did not believe that the Ardennes constituted a threat, even though staff exercises had affirmed the validity of this possibility," concludes Forcade, "Le temps de la guerre et du désastre," 288–289. Forcade also notes that French intelligence in 1940 suffered from multiple handicaps, beginning with the fact that it was a military sub-specialty, many of whose members, like Louis Rivet, had been promoted through the ranks and so were not graduates of Saint-Cyr, much less the prestigious École supérieure de guerre, and so lacked status in the military hierarchy. The influence of intelligence had been further eroded by the high number of alerts sent out over the winter, which had not been followed by a German attack, encouraging the view that intelligence was easily "intoxicated" by German agents, and hence its reports must be taken with a grain of salt. Intelligence sources were often limited: in 1940, air reconnaissance was at

best intermittent, and had failed to detect German concentrations in the Ardennes on 9–10 May. Only from 11 May was the German buildup in the Ardennes detected. Signals intelligence was handicapped by a dearth of intercept stations, and the German change of its coding system (Enigma) on 1 May, that both blinded and overwhelmed French and Polish codebreakers in May–June. The extreme dispersion and fragmentation of the French command not only delayed the coordination and dissemination of information and hence French reaction time, but also muddled the message, as it created competing *Deuxième Bureaux* who were not always disseminating the same analysis to the various army commands, in part because French intelligence in 1940 had no system to centralize and cross-check intelligence from various sources. Henri Navarre's post-war claim that French intelligence had detected the German thrust through the Ardennes on 11 May may possibly be true, concludes Forcade. But there is no indication in the archives that this was reported up the chain of command. Forcade, "Le temps de la guerre et du désastre," 282–303. Many of these points are made by Douglas Porch, *The French Secret Services: A History of French Intelligence from the Dreyfus Affair to the Gulf War* (New York: Farrar, Straus, Giroux, 1995), Chapter 7.

73. Olivier Forcade, "Le temps des choix et des épreuves du renseignement français (1936–1939)," in Rivet (ed.), *Carnets du chef des services secrets 1936–1944*, 46.
74. Strachan and Harris, *The Utility of Military Force and Public Understanding in Today's Britain*, 6–28.
75. Imlay, *Facing the Second World War*, 364.
76. Nicole Jordan, *The Popular Front and Central Europe: The Dilemmas of French Impotence, 1918–1940* (Cambridge: Cambridge University Press, 1992), 301, quoted in Finney, *Remembering the Road to World War II*, 175.
77. Richard Bennaïm, *Le Journal du soldat juif* (Lormont: Le Bord de l'Eau, 2017), 231.
78. Klaus-Jürgen Müller, "The Military, Politics and Society in France and Germany" in Klaus-Jürgen Müller (ed.), *The Military in Politics and Society in France and Germany in the Twentieth Century* (Oxford and Washington, D.C.: Berg, 1995), 1–41, esp. 3.
79. Fishman's review of Carswell's *The Fall of France in the Second World War*.
80. Peter Paret, *Imagined Battles: Reflections of War in European Art* (Chapel Hill and London: University of North Carolina Press, 1997), 111–112.
81. Müller, "The Military, Politics and Society in France and Germany," 5, 7, 10.
82. Élisabeth du Réau, *Édouard Daladier 1884–1970* (Paris: Fayard, 1993), 286; Philippe Garraud, "L'idéologie de la 'defensive' et ses effets stratégiques: Le rôle de la dimension cognitive dans la défaite de 1940," *Revue française de science politique*, 54, no. 2004/5 (2004), 781–810, www.cairn.info/revue-francaise-de-science-politique-2004-5-page-781.htm.
83. Alexander, *The Republic in Danger*, 402.
84. Garraud, "L'idéologie de la 'defensive' et ses effets stratégiques."
85. Neither the Royal Air Force (RAF) nor the FAF was configured for ground support or for attacking Luftwaffe airfields and logistics in 1940. "The result was an air element that was inflexible and decentralized, a situation made worse by the primitive state of French communications." Richard Overy, *Blood and Ruins: The Last Imperial War, 1931–1945* (London: Viking, 2021), 453; Cohen and Gooch, *Military Misfortunes*, Chapter 8. Clausewitz also mentions Napoleon's 1800 crossing of the Alps, after which Austria "surrendered its entire theater of operations." Howard and Paret (eds.), *Carl von Clausewitz*, 198, 200.
86. The army had witnessed serious incidents of collective indiscipline – even mutiny – in 1907 when Clemenceau had directed the 17[e] RI to break strikes, and again in 1913 with the introduction of the three-year service law. In 1912, the French army counted almost 80,000 deserters or *insoumises*, while regimental life was characterized by smaller acts of soldierly defiance and indiscipline. The annual October departure of the contingent from the Gare de l'Est offered a raucous festival of anti-military protests as conscripts bellowed *l'Internationale* and the *Carmagnole*. Douglas Porch, *The March to the Marne: The French Army 1871–1914* (Cambridge: Cambridge University Press, 1981), Chapter 7, 188, 250–252.
87. Dimitry Queloz, *De la manœuvre napoléonienne à l'offensive à outrance: La tactique générale de l'armée française 1871–1914* (Paris: Economica, 2009), 502–508; Porch, *The March to the Marne*, 246–254.
88. France lost 301,000 men between September and the end of December 1914, compared with 349,000 men in the 12 months of 1915, the war's most casualty-heavy year. For a breakdown of French casualties, see Guy Pedroncini (ed.), *Histoire militaire de la France*, tome 3, *De 1871 à 1940* (Paris: Presses universitaires de France, 1992), 288–291. French casualties in 1940 are reckoned to have been 20–30 percent of that number.
89. Jackson, *The Fall of France*, 213.
90. Pierre Rocolle, *L'hécatombe des généraux* (Paris: Lavauzelle, 1980). French historian of the First World War Olivier Cosson argues that Joffre's *limogeages* did not target those who failed to break through or who led their troops to destruction, but rather those who showed lack of determination, who hesitated to attack to

the last man, which had been the "lesson" of the Russo-Japanese War. This was because he saw *l'offensive à outrance* as the basis of the French army's *esprit de corps*, and identity, one compatible with the sacrifices demanded by modern war. Cosson, *Préparer la Grande Guerre*, 337. A counterargument is that the test of combat forced Joffre to replace officers considered too old or who had failed in combat, often with those who had been passed over for senior command in peacetime because their republican loyalties had been considered suspect. Strachan, *The First World War*, volume 1, 226–227.

91. Bloch, *Strange Defeat,* 47, 107.
92. Strachan, *The First World War*, volume 1, 224–225.
93. Pedroncini (ed.), *Histoire militaire de la France*, tome 3, 162–163.
94. Leonard V. Smith, *Between Mutiny and Obedience: The French Fifth Infantry Division in World War I* (Princeton: Princeton University Press, 1994).
95. These issues are discussed in Anthony King, *The Combat Soldier: Infantry Tactics and Cohesion in the Twentieth and Twenty-First Centuries* (Oxford: Oxford University Press, 2013), 60–79.
96. Jackson, *The Fall of France*, 215.
97. Richard J. Evans, *The Third Reich in Memory and History* (Oxford: Oxford University Press, 2015), x.
98. Garraud, "L'idéologie de la 'defensive' et ses effets stratégiques."
99. Kershaw, *Fateful Choices*, 293, 296.
100. Sean McMeekin, *Stalin's War: A New History of World War II* (New York: Basic Books, 2021), 83.
101. Hitler's declaration of war was logical, as he knew he would have to confront the United States sooner or later. Nor were there any institutional constraints on his decision. Kershaw, *Fateful Choices*, 304, 385–394, 475–476.
102. Jackson, *The Fall of France*, 200–208.
103. Nord, *France 1940*, 52, 55.
104. Jackson, "Post-war Politics and the Historiography of French Strategy and Diplomacy before the Second World War," 875–877.
105. Antoine Capet, "Churchill's View of France & the French on the Eve of War," paper delivered at "Britain and France in World War II," Conference at the British Ambassador's Residence, Paris, 16 October 2015.
106. Garraud argues that the reluctance of Daladier to question the inner workings of the military was part of the civil–military tradeoff as the result of the Dreyfus affair, namely that civilians and soldiers would respect institutional boundaries. Garraud, "L'idéologie de la 'defensive' et ses effets stratégiques."
107. Gamelin consulted his intelligence chief Louis Rivet for information to rebut various press articles. In general, French politicians had no direct access to foreign intelligence, which was the quasi-monopoly of the army. Olivier Forcade suggests that it was also possible that Gamelin filtered intelligence sent up to his political superiors. For his part, Daladier seem to have been incurious as to German intentions. He held only five formal meetings with Rivet between 1936 and April 1940, one of which, in March 1940, was a phone conversation to glean information on the contacts of Flandin, Laval, and Piétri in Switzerland. Rivet, *Carnets du chef des services secrets 1936–1944*, 44–45, 286.
108. Kershaw, *Fateful Choices*, 479.
109. Strachan and Harris, *The Utility of Military Force and Public Understanding in Today's Britain*, 5.
110. Jackson, *The Fall of France*, 210–211.
111. Imlay, *Facing the Second World War*, 360.
112. Kershaw also notes that Stalin's choice to remain in the Kremlin in December 1941, "with the spearhead of the Wehrmacht on the outskirts of Moscow," steadied nerves in Russia and "dissipated" panic. Kershaw, *Fateful Choices*, 46–49, 290.
113. Du Réau, *Daladier*, 381.
114. Bloch makes the general point about the politicians' "spineless" capitulation to "technicians." Bloch, *Strange Defeat*, 157. While the Fall of France exposed the United States' lack of military preparedness, unlike Daladier, the "sobering lesson" of the experience of 1917–1918 for those in charge of mobilization in Washington was that "the cherished mechanisms of the free market were unsuited to total war." On the contrary, a free-market approach encouraged profiteering that sent prices soaring, and created bottlenecks paralyzing important sections of industry that unbalanced production. The result was delivery delays, shocking waste, stressed railways and ports, and civilian needs left uncatered for. Keith E. Eiler, Mobilizing America: Robert Patterson and the War Effort, 1940–1945 (Ithaca, NY: Cornell University Press, 1997).
115. Du Réau, *Daladier*, 367–368; Alexander, *The Republic in Danger*, 385–390.
116. Nord, *France 1940*, 155.
117. Jochen Hellbeck, "Battles for Morale: An Entangled History of Total War in Europe, 1939–1945," in Geyer and Tooze (eds.), *Total War: Economy, Society, and Culture*, 359.
118. Imlay, *Facing the Second World War*, 360; Garraud, "L'idéologie de la 'defensive' et ses effets stratégiques."

119. Nord, *France 1940*, 154.
120. Garraud, "L'idéologie de la 'defensive' et ses effets stratégiques."
121. Nord, *France 1940*, 65–66.
122. Ian Germani, *Dying for France: Experiencing and Representing the Soldier's Death, 1500–2000* (Montreal: McGill-Queen's University Press, 2023), 230, 234.
123. Stanley Hoffmann, "Le Trauma de 1940," in Jean-Pierre Azéma and François Bédarida (eds.), *La France des années noires*, tome 1, *De la défaite à Vichy* (Paris: Éditions du Seuil, 1993), 133, 137.
124. Karl-Heinz Frieser, *The Blitzkrieg Legend: The 1940 Campaign in the West* (Annapolis: Naval Institute Press, 2005), 247–251.
125. Philip Bankwitz, *Maxime Weygand and Civil–Military Relations in Modern France* (Cambridge, MA: Harvard University Press, 1967), 44.
126. Nord, *France 1940*, 66.
127. Garraud counts forty divisions made up of the Third, Fourth, Fifth, and Eighth French Armies guarding the Maginot Line or poised to seal off an attack through Switzerland, not counting the *Armée des Alpes*. These remained in place throughout the month of May, even after it became evident that the main German thrust was through the Ardennes. Garraud, "L'idéologie de la 'defensive' et ses effets stratégiques."
128. Gérard Saint-Martin argues that, in fact, this episode was overblown, mainly by the German press, because the enemy was the *Kavallerie Division*, so that it could be featured as an old-style "*combat d'honneur*." But the real significance, according to Saint-Martin, was that the "*cadets de Saumur*" – mainly young reserve "*aspirants*" or officer candidates – offered one of the few French examples in 1940 of a combined arms attack, and that those involved later went on to apply its principles in Tunisia in 1943 and during the invasion of southern France in 1944. Gérard Saint-Martin, *L'arme blindée française*, tome 2, *1940–1945: Dans le fracas des batailles* (Paris: Economica, 2000), 39–43.
129. Imlay, *Facing the Second World War*, 243, 285–286.
130. Bloch, *Strange Defeat*, 157.
131. Du Réau, *Daladier*, 381–383, 442–443.
132. Garraud, "L'idéologie de la 'defensive' et ses effets stratégiques."
133. "With the military front in the West stabilized," speculates Imlay, "A prolonged war would probably have fueled this process of (strategic) radicalization with the result that the Allies would have attacked the Soviet Union [the Baku project], thereby forcing together the Germans and Soviets with potentially dire consequences for the course of the war. At the same time, it [is] also likely that the intense pressure of active warfare would have reinforced, rather than diminished, the unfavourable forces at work in the domestic-political and political-economic dimensions in France. The counter-factual proposed, in short, might very well have proved disastrous not only for France and Britain but also for Europe and the world in general." Imlay, *Facing the Second World War*, 363.
134. André Malraux, "Discours prononcé pour le transfert des cendres de Jean Moulin au Panthéon, 19 décembre 1964," https://mjp.univ-perp.fr/textes/malraux19121964.htm.
135. McMeekin, *Stalin's War*, 296.
136. Norman M. Naimark "The Persistence of 'the Postwar': Germany and Poland," in Biess and Moeller (eds.) *Histories of the Aftermath*, 15.
137. Aubin, "Le soldat américain ne sait pas se battre."
138. Jackson, "Post-war Politics and the Historiography of French Strategy and Diplomacy before the Second World War," 887.
139. Nord, *France 1940*, 86.
140. In 1942, the British in North Africa registered 1,700 KIA and 57,0000 MIA. Overy, *Blood and Ruins*, 730.
141. Alexander, *The Republic in Danger*, 399.
142. Geyer and Tooze, "Introduction to Part III," 417.
143. Noguès was the son-in-law of Théophile Delcassé, foreign minister at the turn of the twentieth century and architect of the Entente cordiale with Great Britain.
144. Bloch, *Strange Defeat*, 157.
145. Garraud, "L'idéologie de la 'defensive' et ses effets stratégiques."
146. Nord, *France 1940*, 85.
147. Alexander, *The Republic in Danger*, 367–368.
148. Overy attributes this mainly to inter-service rivalry and reluctance to integrate civilians into Axis intelligence organizations. Nevertheless, the integration of intelligence at all levels into operational planning, and whether it is believed by those tasked with decision-making, impacted all military organizations. Intelligence was most impactful in naval warfare, where the German and Japanese navies remained unaware that their codes and signals were being read. Overy, *Blood and Ruins*, 500–501, 509–510.

149. Kershaw, *Fateful Choices*, 471.
150. Bankwitz, *Maxime Weygand and Civil–Military Relations in Modern France*, 156–158, 165–167; Overy, *Blood and Ruins*, 520–521.
151. Hervé Drévillon, "La défaite comme symptôme," *Hypothèses*, 2008/1, no. 11 (2008), 283–295, www.cairn.info/revue-hypotheses-2008-1-page-283.htm.
152. While the modernization of the German military in 1940 may have been superficial and limited, and Germany's industrial preparation for total war precarious, German society was psychologically primed for total war by a "negative mobilization" of Germans disoriented "by the nation's recent rather precipitous industrialization and commercialization" and resentment over Versailles. This "negative mobilization" was reinforced by Nazi propaganda that insisted that Hitler had "saved" Germany from the chaos of Weimar and restored German greatness through militarization and antisemitism. Together, this strengthened "the commitment of thousands upon thousands of Germans to fight for Hitler, Germany, and the ideal of a 'Master Race,'" all reinforced by "avalanching wartime threats to physical and mental well-being." Geoffrey Cocks, "Hors de combat. Mobilization and Immobilization in Total War," in Geyer and Tooze (eds.), *The Cambridge History of World War II*, volume III, *Total War: Economy, Society, and Culture*, 368.
153. Frieser, *The Blitzkrieg Legend*, 330–337.
154. Jean-Pierre Azéma, *1940: L'année noir* (Paris: Fayard, 2010), 436–437.
155. Sapir et al., *1940: Et si la France avait continué la guerre . . .*, 35.
156. While admittedly meaning to be provocative, Ian Kershaw lists neither the Dyle–Breda Plan nor a refusal of France to sign the Armistice with Germany in June 1940 as among the potential "fateful choices" of 1940–1941 that determined the course of the war. Kershaw, *Fateful Choices*.
157. Buchannan, *World War II in Global Perspective*, 204.
158. Paul Fussell, *The Great War and Modern Memory* (New York and London: Oxford University Press, 1975), 8.
159. Robin Leconte, "Face au débarquemnt allié de novembre 1942: La Division de marche de Constantine, entre obéissance et résistances aux ordres," in Claire Miot, Guillaume Piketty, and Thomas Vaisset (eds.), *Militaires en résistances en France et en Europe* (Villeneuve d'Ascq: Presses universitaires du Septentrion, 2020), 68.
160. Julian Jackson, "General de Gaulle and His Enemies: Anti-Gaullism in France since 1940," *Transactions of the Royal Historical Society*, 9 (1999), 64.
161. It is unclear whether this number includes conscripts from Alsace-Moselle or French industries working for Germany. Rüdiger Hachtmann, "The War of the Cities. Industrial Labouring Forces," in Geyer and Tooze (eds.), *The Cambridge History of World War II*, volume III, 312.
162. Andrew Buchanan, "Globalizing the Second World War," *Past & Present*, 258/1 (2023), 246–281.
163. Sartre, *The War Diaries of Jean-Paul Sartre*, 291.
164. Overy, *Blood and Ruins*, 681–695.
165. Bloch, *The Historian's Craft*, 172.
166. Olivier Wieviorka, *Histoire de la Résistance 1940–1945* (Paris: Perrin, 2013), 119.
167. Nord, *France 1940*, 165.
168. Daniel Hedinger, "The Imperial Nexus: The Second World War and the Axis in Global Perspective," *Journal of Global History*, 12/2 (2017), 184–205.
169. Michael S. Neiberg, *When France Fell: The Vichy Crisis and the Fate of the Anglo-American Alliance* (Cambridge, MA: Harvard University Press, 2021), 197.
170. Andrew Buchanan, *American Grand Strategy in the Mediterranean during World War II* (Cambridge: Cambridge University Press, 2014), 41–43; Overy, *Blood and Ruins*, 715.
171. FDR feared that Vichy would allow a German takeover of AFN, as they had allowed the Japanese encroachment in Indochina, and of the French fleet, and so sought to preempt. Neiberg, *When France Fell*, 169.
172. Buchanan, "Globalizing the Second World War," 247.
173. Buchanan, "Globalizing the Second World War," 261.
174. Buchanan, "Globalizing the Second World War." See also Maryliz Racine, "Le 'danger allemand.' L'évolution de la perception des members du Ministère des affairs étrangères françaises envers la menace allemande (1945–1954)," Mémoire de Maîtrise, Université Laval, Quebec, Canada, 2013.
175. Julie Le Gac, *Vaincre sans gloire: Le corps expéditionnaire français en Italie (novembre 1942–juillet 1944)* (Paris: Les Belles Lettres/Ministère de la défense-DMPA, 2013), 119.
176. Jean-Charles Foucrier, "Les FAFL: Création et exploitation d'une arme politique" and Thomas Vaisset, "Les FNFL de 1940 à 1942: Recrute, armer, combattre," presentations delivered at the conference "Bir Hakeim et les premiers combats de la France libre 1940–1942," Château de Vincennes, 1 June 2022.
177. Nord, *France 1940*, 164–165. This rather replicates Wieviorka's evocation of "*résistance-mouvement*."

178. Robert Belot, *La Résistance sans de Gaulle* (Paris: Fayard, 2006), 258–261.
179. Quoted in Géraud Létung, "'Une armée de clochards.' Sentiment de déclassement et fabrique d'une identité collective chez les Français libres du Tchad (1940–1943)," paper delivered at Colloque sur la France libre, Paris, November 2019. Also in Géraud Létung, *Mirages d'une rébellion: Être Français libre au Tchad (1940–1943)* (Paris: Sciences Po, 2019).
180. Guillaume Piketty, "Conclusion. Pour une histoire sensible des militaires en résistances," in Claire Miot, Guillaume Piketty, and Thomas Vaisset (eds.), *Militaires en résistances en France et en Europe* (Villeneuve d'Ascq: Presses universitaires du Septentrion, 2020), 248–253.
181. Belot, *La Résistance sans de Gaulle*, 92–96.
182. Robin Leconte, "Les combats des FFL en Erythrée mettrent en scène le succès des armes pour rallier Djibouti (janvier–juin 1941)" and Alain Alexandra, "À la recherche des FFL disparus: La sous-série AC 23P," presented at the conference Bir Hakeim et les premiers combats de la France libre 1940–1942, Château de Vincennes, 1 June 2022.
183. Bir Hakeim's symbolic importance was also dramatized because it occurred in the context of the withdrawal of Australian troops from the Western Desert in the wake of the fall of Singapore. Géraud Létang, "Entre les mines. Tenir la position de Bir Hakeim (février–jullet 1942)," presented at the conference Bir Hakeim et les premiers combats de la France libre 1940–1942, Château de Vincennes, 1 June 2022. On 18 June 1949, the existing Viaduct de Passy was rebaptized Pont du Bir Hakeim in a ceremony attended by de Gaulle, Larminat, Koenig, and Thierry d'Argenlieu. In 1955, it became associated with the monument to the 1ère DFL located nearby on the Quai de Branly as a Gaullist *lieu de mémoire*.
184. Claire Miot, "Sortir l'armée des ombres. Soldats de l'Empire, combattants de la Libération, armée de la Nation: La Première armée française, du débarquement en Provence à la capitulation allemande (1944–1945)," Thèse du doctorat, Université Paris-Saclay, 2016, 737.
185. Marcel Vigneras, *Rearming the French* (Washington, D.C.: Center of Military History, United States Army, 1989), 37–38.
186. Buchanan, *American Grand Strategy in the Mediterranean during World War II*, 154–157.
187. Julie Le Gac, "Le corps expéditionnaire français et l'armée américaine en Italie (1943–1944): Une alliance asymétrique," *Revue historique des armées*, 258/210 (2010), 57–66, https://journals.openedition.org/rha/6923.
188. And while Leclerc accused de Lattre of sacrificing his men, the 2e DB had a KIA/MIA rate of 14.2 percent between Utah Beach and Berchtesgaden. However, this obscures the fact that certain *1ère Armée* units took debilitatingly high casualties. For instance, the 6e RTM lost 2,529 men between Dragoon and the end of hostilities, 1,000 fewer than in Italy. Furthermore, in Alsace, 40,000 soldiers had been evacuated with frostbite, testimony to the terrible climatic conditions, but also to logistical problems and no doubt inattention by the command. Three-quarters of the 1ère DFL's combat deaths in the war occurred between its entry into Italy in April 1944 and the end of the war a year later. The 2e DIM lost over 9,000 men in each of the campaigns in Italy and France. Miot, "Sortir l'armée des ombres," 737–738.
189. Eric Conan and Henry Rousso, *Vichy, un passé qui ne passe pas* (Paris: Fayard, 1994), 21–22, 214.
190. Joan Beaumont review of S. P. MacKenzie, *The Colditz Myth: British and Commonwealth Prisoners of War in Nazi Germany* (Oxford: Oxford University Press, 2004), in Joan Beaumont, "Review Article: Prisoners of War in the Second World War," *Journal of Contemporary History*, 42/3 (2007), 539.
191. Jackson, "General de Gaulle and His Enemies," 64.
192. Conan and Rousso, *Vichy, un passé qui ne passe pas*, 172–183.
193. Intellectuals and journalists were especially targeted, because their words could be used against them in court, while economic collaboration was more difficult to ferret out. Conan and Rousso, *Vichy, un passé qui ne passe pas*, 16.
194. These included Generals Weygand, Colson, Bergeret, Bridoux, Delmotte, Dentz, Jannekeyn, Laure, Noguès, de la Porte du Theil, and Pujo. Admirals Abrial, Auphan, de Laborde, Michelier, and Marquis were also sent for trial. Robert Paxton, *Parades and Politics at Vichy: The French Officer Corps under Marshal Pétain* (Princeton: Princeton University Press, 1966), 410–411.
195. Jackson, "General de Gaulle and His Enemies," 48.
196. Geyer and Tooze, "Introduction to Part III," 418.
197. Robert Gildea, *Fighters in the Shadows: A New History of the French Resistance* (Cambridge, MA: Harvard University Press, 2015), 414.
198. A 23 April 1945 defense ministry directive had stipulated that FFI were to be incorporated into their pre-war active or reserve rank. FFI promoted in the war could have their rank recognized "only in exceptional cases of brilliant acts at the front." As a further incentive to retire, FFI who resigned would be allowed to keep their wartime rank "*à l'honorariat*," with the appropriate pension.

199. Miot, "Sortir l'armée des ombres," 701–711; François Rouquet and Fabrice Virgili, *Les françaises, les français, et l'épuration (1940 à nos jours)* (Paris: Gallimard, 2018), 216–217.
200. Paxton, *Parades and Politics at Vichy*, 412; Miot, "Sortir l'armée des ombres," 714.
201. Conan and Rousso, *Vichy, un passé qui ne passe pas*, 19; Nord, *France 1940*, 165.
202. On the other hand, the communists were hoist on their own petard, because the steep cutbacks in personnel were in part the result of a post-war parliamentary campaign led by the PCF to cut the military budget. Yves Roucaute, *Le PCF et l'armée* (Paris: Presses universitaires de France, 1983), 24–25, 33.
203. As a point of comparison, of 400,000 railway workers, under 2 percent were purged for collaboration on the Liberation, despite the mobilization of French railways in the German war effort, including transporting Jews and political deportees to death camps in Germany in inhumane conditions. This was partly due to interventions by influential people to quash indictments. But, above all, France required technicians to rebuild the railways. Ludivine Broch, *Ordinary Workers, Vichy and the Holocaust: French Railwaymen and the Second World War* (Cambridge: Cambridge University Press, 2016), 208–209.
204. D'Abzac-Epezy, "Épuration, dégagements, exclusions," 74; D'Abzac-Epezy, "Épuration et renovation de l'armée," 463–464.
205. Nord, *France 1940*, 164.
206. Jackson, "General de Gaulle and His Enemies: Anti-Gaullism in France since 1940," 43.
207. Miot, "Sortir l'armée des ombres," 714.
208. In July 1946, the War Ministry claimed that 12,183 of 34,025 officers had joined since 1940, which made for a renewal of one-third of the officer crops, and that 11,000 of them had seen service in the resistance. In total 25,242 officers were "*homologués*" – that is, their resistance ranks were recognized, but one-half of them, roughly 13,200, were accredited as reserve rather than active officers, and 7,000 were former NCOs who had been commissioned because of their resistance action. Among FAF officers who saw active service during 1942–1944, which would have meant mostly in anti-aircraft artillery shooting at Allied aircraft, the retention rate was 93 percent. So, a very small minority of officers were actually new. Miot, "Sortir l'armée des ombres," 712–716. For Saint-Cyr, see Raoul Girardet, *La crise militaire française 1945–1962: Aspects sociologiques et idéologiques* (Paris: Armand Colin, 1964), 46.
209. The French army purged 658 officers, 12,679 were let go in the reduction in force, and 604 voluntarily resigned; 3,585 FFI were integrated, along with 1,134 new officers. Only 28 officers were "purged" in the FAF, which lost 892 officers to the drawdown, while 620 voluntarily resigned, and 225 were integrated "*à titre FFI*," although, as has been seen above, these may have been professional officers as well, while 267 "others" were integrated. In the French navy, only 50 officers were purged, 808 left in the reduction in force, and 440 others voluntarily separated from service, while 34 FFI and 257 others were integrated into service. D'Abzac-Epezy, "Épuration et renovation de l'armée," 461.
210. Weygand was brought before a High Court of Justice in 1945, and summoned to appear before various parliamentary committees tasked with looking into the causes of defeat. The prosecution case against him was poorly prepared, while responsibility for various decisions taken in June 1940 or under Vichy could not be pinned exclusively on him. His opposition to the Paris Protocols also played in his favor. Charges against him were finally dismissed on 6 May 1948. Anthony Clayton, *General Maxime Weygand 1867–1967: Fortune and Misfortune* (Bloomington: Indiana University Press, 2015), 134–138.
211. D'Abzac-Epezy, "Épuration et renovation de l'armée," 454–455; Bénédicte Vergez-Chaignon, *Histoire de l'épuration* (Paris: Larousse, 2010), 507–511.
212. "Temoignage no. 409" and "Déclaration concernant Colonel Bouvet," 5 May 1973, Chambrun papers, Box 8, Hoover Institution. See also "Mémoire remise à la Commission d'instruction près la haute cour de justice. Procedure introduite au subjet du Général Weygand. Déposition du Général de Brigade de Périer des troupes colonials," undated. SHD-GR, 1P 89.
213. Hilary Footitt and John Simmonds, *France 1943–1945* (New York: Holmes & Meier, 1988), 242–243. Many of the accused were incarcerated at Schirmeck (Bas-Rhin) and La Noé (Haute-Garonne). Jean-Pierre Rioux, *The Fourth Republic, 1944–1958* (Cambridge: Cambridge University Press, 1987), 33–36.
214. See, for instance, Laurent Joly, *La falsification de l'histoire: Éric Zemmour, l'extrême droite, Vichy et les juifs* (Paris: Grasset, 2022).
215. Vergez-Chaignon, *Histoire de l'épuration*, 512, 517–519.
216. D'Abzac-Epezy, "Épuration et renovation de l'armée," 454.
217. Rioux, *The Fourth Republic*, 41.
218. Bennaïm, *Le journal du soldat juif*, 232.
219. Peter Novick, *L'épuration française 1944–1949* (Paris: Éditions Balland, 1985), 299.
220. Henry Rousso, *The Vichy Syndrome: History and Memory in France since 1944* (Cambridge, MA: Harvard University Press, 1991), 29–32, 302; Jackson, "General de Gaulle and His Enemies," 49.

221. Robert Lynn Fuller cites the figure of 250,000 French civilians killed during the course of the war as "the best most recent guess." Robert Lynn Fuller, *After D-Day: The U.S. Army Encounters the French* (Baton Rouge: Louisiana State University Press, 2021), 246–248.
222. Ronald Smelser and Edward J. Davies II, *The Myth of the Eastern Front: The Nazi–Soviet War in American Popular Culture* (Cambridge: Cambridge University Press, 2008), 55.
223. Finney, *Remembering the Road to World War II*, 247.
224. Conan and Rousso, *Vichy, un passé qui ne passe pas*, 21. Amnesties in the wake of the Algerian War were issued in 1962, 1964, 1966, and 1968. In 1982, President Mitterand pardoned Raoul Salan and seven other rebellious generals of that war. Dimitri Nicolaïdis, "La nation, les crimes et la mémoire," in Dimitri Nicolaïdis, *Oublier nos crimes: L'amnestie national: Une specificité française* (Paris: Autrement, 2002), 10–20. See also Joly, *La falsification de l'histoire*, 25–26.
225. Novick, *L'épuration française*, 297.
226. Novick, *L'épuration française*, 297.
227. Vergez-Chaignon, *Histoire de l'épuration*, 564–568; Rousso, *The Vichy Syndrome*, 55–58; Rioux, *The Fourth French Republic*, 41.
228. Novick, *L'épuration française*, 296.
229. Bennaïm, *Le journal du soldat juif*, 231–232.
230. The FFL comprises those who had served between 18 June 1940 and the "fusion" of the FFL with *l'armée d'Afrique* on 31 July 1943. In the post-war period, the FFL produced 2 Marshals of France (Leclerc and Koenig), 83 generals, 22 admirals, and 300 colonels or navy captains. Muracciole notes that, given the fact that many FFL officers were drawn from a social elite, they probably would have succeeded in any case, especially in the post-war economic prosperity of *les trentes glorieuses*. No one has done a comparative study of the post-war careers of officers from the *1ère Armée*, for instance, nor is it clear whether the careers of former FFL were accelerated by de Gaulle's return to power in 1958, or whether the fact that so many former FFL were highly placed in government, the military, and politics eased the advent of the Fifth Republic. Jean-François Muracciole, "Le devenir des officier français libres après la guerre," in Claire Miot, Guillaume Piketty, and Thomas Vaisset (eds.), *Militaires en résistances en France et en Europe* (Villeneuve d'Ascq: Presses universitaires du Septentrion, 2020), 184–198.
231. Jackson, "General de Gaulle and His Enemies," 50–52, 64.
232. Rousso, *The Vichy Syndrome*, 60, 69–75.
233. Jackson, "General de Gaulle and His Enemies," 54.
234. This school of historians introduced the concept of adding to the historical record oral archives harvested from "living witnesses" that led to the rehabilitation of *Strange Defeat.* Their argument was that history should participate in debates about the present, and that to exclude "testimony" constituted a form of "historical censorship." Droit and Reichherzer, "La fin de l'histoire du temps présent telle que nous l'avons connue," 126–27, 136.
235. Joly answers the alibi that Vichy mostly deported foreign Jews, in an effort to save French ones, by insisting that cleansing France of Jews was never a priority for the Third Reich, which was more concerned from 1943 with stabilizing France to better mobilize French manpower for STO, and stamping out growing resistance and *maquis* movements in the context of preparing for the inevitable Allied invasion. Joly, *La falsification de l'histoire*, 81, 97.
236. Vergez-Chaignon, *Histoire de l'épuration*, 570.
237. Bloch, *The Historian's Craft*, 75.
238. See Paxton's "Bibliographical Note," in Robert O. Paxton, *Vichy France: Old Guard and New Order 1940–1944* (London: Barrie & Jenkins, 1972). Both Paxton and Jäckel also benefited from Joseph Billig's pioneering work that destroyed the "Vichy shield" argument. Joseph Billig, *Le Commissariat Général aux Questions Juives (1941–1944)*, tome III (Paris: Éditions du Centre, 1960); Joly, *La falsification de l'histoire*, 88–89.
239. Jean-Baptiste Bruneau, *La Marine de Vichy aux Antilles juin 1940–juillet 1943* (Paris: Les Indes Savantes, 2014), 10, 183–191, 196, 200, 228–229.
240. Julian Jackson, *De Gaulle* (Cambridge, MA: Harvard University Press, 2018), 366, 369.
241. Frédéric Turpin, *De Gaulle, les gaullistes et l'Indochine* (Paris: Les Indes Savantes, 2005), 13.
242. Jackson, *De Gaulle*, 207–208.
243. Historians argue about whether Roosevelt ever believed in "the right of all peoples to choose the form of government under which they will live." In any case, evidence suggests that the State Department viewed the British Empire as the problem, and so gave assurances both to Vichy and to the French National Committee in London, "to maintain the integrity of the French empire." Martin Thomas and Richard Toye, *Arguing about Empire: Imperial Rhetoric in Britain and France, 1882–1956* (Oxford: Oxford University Press, 2017), 179–180.

244. Jackson, *De Gaulle*, 379–387.
245. All of which emphasizes Imlay's point that how France's republic would function, not, as Nord suggests, whether it would endure, was the central point of contention among France's various political factions. Talbot Imlay's review of Nord's *France 1940, H-France Review*, 16/38 (March 2016), 3–4.
246. Jackson, *De Gaulle*, 406.
247. Jackson, "General de Gaulle and His Enemies," 53; Jackson, *De Gaulle*, 415.
248. General André Beaufre, *1940: The Fall of France* (New York: Alfred A. Knopf, 1968), 60–61; Bloch, *Strange Defeat*, 157.
249. Cited in Létung, "Une armée de clochards."
250. Wieviorka, *Histoire de la Résistance 1940–1945*, 101.
251. Belot, *La Résistance sans de Gaulle*, 90–91.
252. Belot, *La Résistance sans de Gaulle*, 646; Jackson, "General de Gaulle and His Enemies," 43.
253. Belot, *La Résistance sans de Gaulle*, 623–624, 633–639, 647; Jean-Louis Crémieux-Brilhac, *La France libre*, tome 1, *De l'appel du 18 juin à la libération* (Paris: Gallimard, 2001), 48.
254. Guillaume Piketty, "Conseil national de la résistance," in François Broche, Georges Caïtucoli, and Jean-François Muracciole (eds.), *Dictionnaire de la France Libre* (Paris: Robert Laffont, 2010), 363–365.
255. Wieviorka, *Histoire de la Résistance 1940–1945*, 497–500.
256. Belot, *La Résistance sans de Gaulle*, 622.
257. Belot, *La Résistance sans de Gaulle*, 627; Rioux, *The Fourth Republic*, 39, 49.
258. Johanna Barasz, "De Vichy à la Résistance: Les vichysto-résistants 1940–1944," *Guerres mondiales et conflits contemporains*, 2011/2, no. 242 (2011), 27–50, www.cairn.info/revue-guerres-mondiales-et-conflits-contemporains-2011-2-page-27.htm#no14.
259. Jean-Paul Azéma is credited with evolving the term *Vichysto-résistant*. Barasz, "De Vichy à la Résistance." In the post-war period, many of the main actors in France's 1940 débâcle wrote what were called "mémoires de 'couverture'" to divest themselves of blame, which made it more difficult to discover the truth. Rivet, *Carnets du chef*, 285.
260. Barasz, "De Vichy à la Résistance."
261. Belot, *La Résistance sans de Gaulle*, 626–639.
262. Turpin, *De Gaulle, les gaullistes et l'Indochine*, 14.
263. Quoted in Footitt and Simmonds, *France 1943–1945*, 245–247.
264. Belot, *La Résistance sans de Gaulle*, 646; André Kaspi, *La Libération de la France, juin 1944–janvier 1946* (Paris: Perrin, 2004), 225, 627.
265. While Roosevelt believed that a demand for unconditional surrender would be an "impetus to the Russian morale," by showing that the Western Allies intended to crush the Third Reich, according to Sean McMeekin, Stalin instead viewed FDR's declaration as a substitute for the failure of the Western Allies to open a true "second front" in 1943. Meanwhile Stalin was attempting unsuccessfully to negotiate his own separate peace with Hitler, a campaign which failed because of Hitler, not Stalin. McMeekin, *Stalin's War*, 441–442.
266. Belot, *La Résistance sans de Gaulle*, 335, 646.
267. Guillaume Piketty, "La France combattante au cœur du maelstrom," in Nicole Cohen-Addad, Aïssa Kadri, and Tramor Quemeneur (eds.), *8 novembre 1942: Résistance et Débarquement allié en Afrique du Nord. Dynamiques historiques, politiques, et socio-culturelles* (Vulaines-sur-Seine: Éditions du Croquant, 2021).
268. Jonathan Fennell, *Fighting the People's War: The British and Commonwealth Armies and the Second World War* (Cambridge: Cambridge University Press, 2019), 698.
269. Thomas and Toye, *Arguing about Empire*, 190–191.
270. Jackson, *De Gaulle*, 510–512.
271. Turpin, *De Gaulle, les gaullistes et l'Indochine*, 75–77.
272. Fennell, *Fighting the People's War*, 692.
273. Jackson, *De Gaulle*, 360–361.
274. Turpin, *De Gaulle, les gaullistes et l'Indochine*, 79–82.
275. Jackson, "General de Gaulle and His Enemies," 62, 64.
276. Final conclusions of the Conference on Britain and France in World War II, held at the British Ambassador's Residence, Paris, 16 October 2015.
277. Cadeau, *de Lattre*, 235.
278. Miot, "Sortir l'armée des ombres," 672.
279. On 12 May, Washington announced that French rearmament was complete, and, on 2 September, Lend–Lease was interrupted. On 8 November, all British military aid to France ceased, at a time when France needed to occupy Germany and Austria, defend the colonies, recreate the home army, and stand up a professional "intervention force" to reoccupy Indochina. Miot, "Sortir l'armée des ombres," 698–700.
280. Cadeau, *de Lattre*, 238.
281. Romain Gary, *La promesse de l'aube* (Paris: Gallimard, 1980), 194.
282. Marc Hillel, *L'occupation française en Allemagne 1945–1949* (Paris: Balland, 1983), 181.

283. Miot, "Sortir l'armée des ombres," 674–680.
284. Hillel, *L'occupation française en Allemagne 1945–1949*, 132.
285. John Gimbel, *The American Occupation of Germany: Politics and the Military, 1945–1949* (Stanford: Stanford University Press, 1968), 16–18; Jean Edward Smith, *Lucius D. Clay: An American Life* (New York: Henry Holt, 1990), 342–346; Miot, "Sortir l'armée des ombres," 661–664; Jackson, *De Gaulle*, 382.
286. Peter Schöttler, "Trois formes de collaboration: L'Europe et la réconciliation franco-allemande – à travers la carrière de Gustav Krukenberg, chef de la 'Division Charlemagne,'" *Allemagne d'aujourd'hui*, 2014/1, no. 207 (2014), 246, www.cairn.info/revue-allemagne-d-aujourd-hui-2014-1-page-225.htm.
287. Hillel, *L'occupation française en Allemagne 1945–1949*, 215, 230–231; Jackson, *De Gaulle*, 364–367, 412. Michael Creswell and Marc Trachtenberg argue that official French realization that Germany needed to be reintegrated into Western Europe as a buffer against the Soviet Union began at least in early 1947. But, in public, officials maintained their opposition in order to avoid a "civil war" with the PCF and blowback from the Gaullist right. Paris also feared that a unified Germany might come to be dominated by Moscow. Nor, initially, were London and Washington all that keen on recreating a centralized West German state. The push for centralization came principally from Lucius Clay. Michael Creswell and Marc Trachtenberg, "France and the German Question, 1945–1955," *Journal of Cold War Studies*, 5/3 (Summer 2003), 8–14. An outlying interpretation that French soldiers maintained an Orientalized view of Germany that required rehabilitation through the application of "civilizing" colonial methods based on Hubert Lyautey's *Du Rôle colonial de l'armée*, published in 1900, can be found in Drew Flanagan, "La juste sévérité: Pacifier la zone française en Allemagne occupée, 1945–1949," in James Connolly, Emmanuel Debruyne, Élise Julien, and Matthias Meirlaen (eds.), *En territoire ennemi: Expériences d'occupation, transferts, héritages (1914–1949)* (Villeneuve d'Ascq: Presses universitaires du Septentrion, 2018), 205–216.
288. Hillel, *L'occupation française en Allemagne 1945–1949*, 169, 175–178, 186; Klaus-Jürgen Müller, *The Military in Politics and Society in France and Germany in the Twentieth Century* (Oxford and Washington, D.C.: Berg, 1995), 151.
289. Frank Roy Willis, *The French in Germany, 1945–1949* (Stanford: Stanford University Press, 1962), 83–86.
290. Hillel, *L'occupation française en Allemagne 1945–1949*, 10–12, 26, 186, 191–192.
291. The ZOF counted an administrative density of 18 French administrators per 10,000 Germans, compared with 10 British administrators per 10,000 Germans, while the Americans furnished only 3 administrators per 10,000 locals. Willis, *The French in Germany*, 88.
292. Hillel, *L'occupation française en Allemagne 1945–1949*, 182–192.
293. Claude Mauriac, *Un autre de Gaulle: Journal, 1944–1954* (Paris: Hachette, 1971), 183, quoted in Turpin, *De Gaulle, les gaullistes et l'Indochine*, 232.
294. Hillel, *L'occupation française en Allemagne 1945–1949*, 87, 192–195.
295. Willis, *The French in Germany*, 85–88.
296. Müller, *The Military in Politics and Society in France and Germany in the Twentieth Century*, 155.
297. Hillel, *L'occupation française en Allemagne 1945–1949*, 162–165, 179.
298. Müller, *The Military in Politics and Society in France and Germany*, 154.
299. Willis, *The French in Germany*, 89–91; Müller, *The Military in Politics and Society in France and Germany*, 155.
300. Hillel, *L'occupation française en Allemagne 1945–1949*, 179. By June 1946, US oversight on the local level was reduced to two-man security detachments ordered to observe German government but to intervene only in outright emergencies. Earl F. Ziemke, "Improvising Stability and Change in Postwar Germany," in Robert Wolfe (ed.), *Americans as Proconsuls: United States Military Government in Germany and Japan, 1944–1952*, (Carbondale and Edwardsville, IL: Southern Illinois University Press, 1977), 65. For an example of the rapid drawdown of US occupation, see John Gimbel, *A German Community under American Occupation: Marburg 1945–1952* (Stanford: Stanford University Press, 1961), 31.
301. Constantine FitzGibbon, *Denazification* (New York: W. W. Norton & Co., 1969), 107.
302. Stargardt, *The German War*, 563–565.
303. Willis, *The French in Germany*, 149–152.
304. Richard Davenport-Hines (ed.), *Letters from Oxford: Hugh Trevor-Roper to Bernard Berenson* (London: Phoenix, 2007), 21–22; Willis, *The French in Germany*, 161.
305. Gimbel, *A German Community under American Occupation*, 204–205.
306. Hillel, *L'occupation française en Allemagne 1945–1949*, 167–174, 179–180, 388; Overy, *Blood and Ruins*, xiii.

Bibliography

Archival Sources

Service Historique de la Défense, Château de Vincennes

GR-N: Troisième République
Direction et services du ministre. Gouvernement de Paris – GR 9 N.

GR-P: Deuxième guerre mondiale (1940–1946)
Vichy: instance de défense nationale – GR 1P
Vichy: cabinet du ministre et organismes en dependant directement – GR 2P
Vichy: état-major de l'armée puis organe liquidateur de l'armée – GR 3P
Londres: état-major du Gal de Gaulle et commissariat national à la guerre – GR 4P
Alger: état-major particulier du Gal Giraud, état-major du Gal Juin – GR 5P
Alger puis Paris: état-major général de guerre puis état-major de l'armée – GR 7P
Alger puis Paris: missions de liaison auprès des alliés – GR 8P
Armées et corps d'armée – GR 10P
Divisions et brigades – GR 11P
Petites unités – GR 12P
Commission d'enquêtes sur les repliements suspects de 1940 – GR 14P
Généraux de division et de brigade – GR 13 YD

SHD-GR, oral archives
Colonel Dominique Magnant GR 3 K 12–1, Planches 6, 7
Crémieux-Brilhac GR 3 K 32–1, Planche 2
Colonel André Perrin GR 3 K 39 1 (Planches 6, 7)

Hoover Institution, Stanford University
René de Chambrun Papers, 1919–1946
Cazotte, Michel de, "Oflag Adventure." Unpublished manuscript, edited by Louis Denis de Cazotte, summer 1997
Papers of Paul Van der Stricht (OSS section chief "Western Europe" 1943–1944)

National Archives and Records Administration (NARA) Washington, D.C.
Record Group (RG) 165, Records of the War Department:
Entry 77, Box 861 service de renseignements; 862 conditions in occupied France; 863 Allied bombing and French morale; 865, Armistice Army, armée d'Afrique, conditions in North Africa, etc.; 866 la Milice, SOL, LVF; 869 Conditions of Armistice; 873 French tactical doctrine, organization, materiel 1930s; 925 Fighting French 1942, Box 926– 927 general French matters, occupation zone in Germany, etc.
RG 218, Records of the Joint Chiefs of Staff:
Box 54–58 relations with Vichy, Fighting France, etc.
RG 319, Free French Army World War II:
Entry A1 145A, Boxes 1–48
RG 331, Records of Allied Operational and Occupation Headquarters World War II:
Entry 2, Box 109
Entry 3C, Box 190
Entry 30, Box 192, 193, 194, 195

Entry 30A, Box 145, 147 French Resistance
Entry 30C, Box 186 Operation Wallace–Hardy, 189 resistance in Brittany, 190 Poches Atlantiques, 196–197 First French Army
Entry 240A, Box 1
Entry 240D, Boxes 8, 9, 10, 31, 206
Entry 272, Box 110 French air force
RG 407, The Adjutant General's Office: World War II Operational Report:
Entry 427, Box 1622 French Action, Rapido–Cassino Operations January–February 1944; Box 1777, 1783, 1784 French Operations Italy, 1786 Training lessons from the Tunisian Campaign; 1787–1791 Italy
RG 0498, French Army Military Government:
Entry UD578, Box 3904, 3905, 3908

National Archives Kew Gardens

FO 660: Foreign Office and War Cabinet: Offices of Various Political Representatives

Second World War

16 Political situation: France. 1943 July 18 – Dec. 20.
188 French Army: re-entry into active operations against German Forces. Parts I and II. 1943 Nov. 19–1944 Mar. 12.
253 Army: French. Parts I and II. 1944 September 26–1945 January 4.
FO 892 Armaments for the Free French Forces 1
FO 1055/10 Reports on various visits to the Free French forces at Camberley 1941–1943

CAB 106: War Cabinet and Cabinet Office: Historical Section

361

HW 40: Government Communications Headquarters (GCHQ)

137 Reports revealing enemy successes against French Army high grade communications and related correspondence 1942 Jun. 12–1945 Apr. 02. L11 (A).
138 Reports revealing enemy successes against French Army high grade communications and related correspondence 1943 Oct. 21–1945 Apr. 05. L11 (B).

WO 204: War Office, Armed Forces, Judge Advocate General, and Related Bodies

1917 French Forces: operations 1944 Mar.–May
ADM 199/614
Free French Forces 1941–1943

Saint-Antony's College, Oxford University

Middle East Library, Speers Collection:
GB165-0269, Box 1A-B-C, Box 2

Films

"DIE GESCHICHTE DER FRANZÖSISCHEN BESATZUNGSZONE=1985 (Bayerischer Rundfunk 13.09.1986)," www.youtube.com/watch?v=3i6Y7LiXjos&t=382s.
Gago, Malgosha and Sulik, Boleslaw, *Les ombres de Casablanca* (Paris: Arte, 2009).
"Mystères d'archives 1944 dans le maquis du Vercors," www.youtube.com/watch?v=zoq7QREIgB8&t=1393s.
Sembène, Ousmane, *Camp de Thiaroye* (Enaproc, Fimi Domirev, and Films Kajoor, 1988).

Books, Theses, and Documents

Abbas, Ferhat et al., "10 février 1943, Le Manifest du peuple algérien," https://texturesdutemps.hypotheses.org/1458.
Abzac-Epezy, Claude d', *L'Armée de l'air des années noires, Vichy 1940–1944* (Paris: Economica, 1998).
Adamthwaite, Anthony, *France and the Coming of the Second World War 1936–1939* (London: Frank Cass, 1977).
Adelman, Jonathan R., *Hitler and His Allies in World War II* (New York: Routledge, 2007).
Agarossi, Elena, *A Nation Collapses: The Italian Surrender of September 1943* (Cambridge: Cambridge University Press, 2000).
Aglan, Alya and Frank, Robert (eds.), *1937–1947: La guerre-monde*, vol. II (Paris: Gallimard, 2015
Alary, Eric, *La Ligne de démarcation* (Paris: Perrin, 2003).
Albertelli, Sébastien, *Les Services secrets du Général de Gaulle: Le BCRA 1940–1944* (Paris: Perrin, 2009).
Albertelli, Sébastien, *Atlas de la France Libre: De Gaulle et la France Libre, une aventure politique* (Paris: Éditions Autrement, 2010).
Albertelli, Sébastien, *Histoire du sabotage: De la CGT à la Résistance* (Paris: Perrin, 2016).
Alexander, Martin S., *The Republic in Danger: General Maurice Gamelin and the Politics of French Defence, 1933–1940* (Cambridge: Cambridge University Press, 1992).
Ambrose, Stephen E., *Eisenhower: Soldier, General of the Army, President Elect, 1890–1952* (New York: Simon & Schuster, 1983).
Ambrose, Stephen E., *The Supreme Commander: The War Years of Dwight D. Eisenhower* (Jackson: The University Press of Mississippi, 1999),
Andrew, Christopher, *Her Majesty's Secret Service: The Making of the British Intelligence Community* (New York: Viking, 1985).
Andrew, Christopher and Noakes, Jeremy, *Intelligence and International Relations, 1900–1945* (Liverpool: Liverpool University Press, 1987).
Ardent du Picq, Charles, *Études sur le combat: Combat antique et modern* (London: Forgotten Books, 2018).
Army Service Forces, *Legal Work of the War Department. 1 July 1940–31 March 1945. A History of the Judge Advocate General's Department* (Washington, D.C.: Office of the Judge Advocate General, no date), www.loc.gov/rr/frd/Military_Law/pdf/Legal-Work_War-Department.pdf.
Arnaud, Patrice, *Les STO: Histoire des français requis en Allemagne nazi 1942–1945* (Paris: CNRS Éditions, 2014).
Ashdown, Paddy, *The Cruel Victory: The French Resistance, D-Day and the Battle for Vercors 1944* (London: William Collins, 2014).
Atkinson, Rick, *An Army at Dawn: The War in North Africa, 1942–1943* (New York: Henry Holt & Co., 2002).
Audoin-Rouzeau, Stéphane and Becker, Jean-Jacques (eds.), *Encyclopédie de la Grande Guerre 1914–1918: Histoire et culture* (Paris: Bayard, 2004)
Auphan, Gabriel Paul and Mordel, Jacques, *The French Navy in World War II* (Annapolis: United States Naval Institute Press, 1959).
Azéma, Jean-Pierre, *From Munich to the Liberation 1938–1944* (Cambridge: Cambridge University Press, 1984).
Azéma, Jean-Pierre, *Jean Moulin: Le politique, le rebelle, le résistant* (Paris: Perrin, 2003).
Azéma, Jean-Pierre, *1940: L'année noir* (Paris: Fayard, 2010).
Azéma, Jean-Pierre and Bédarida, François (eds.), *La France des années noires*, 2 volumes (Paris: Éditions du Seuil, 1993).
Azéma, Jean-Pierre and Wieviorka, Olivier, *Vichy 1940–1944* (Paris: Perrin, 2004).
Bacquier, Louis, *Aïwah: Au combat avec les Marocains. Souvenirs d'un officier de tirailleurs 1942–1945* (Paris: Éditions Laville, 2012).
Balu, Raphaële, "Les maquis de France, la France libre et les Alliés (1943–1945): Retrouver la coopération," Thèse du doctorat, Université de Caen Normandie, 2018.
Bancel, Nicolas, Denis, Daniel, and Fates, Youssef, *De l'Indochine à l'Algérie: La jeunesse en mouvements des deux côtés du miroir colonial 1940–1962* (Paris: Éditions la Découvert, 2003).
Bankwitz, Philip, *Maxime Weygand and Civil–Military Relations in Modern France* (Cambridge, MA: Harvard University Press, 1967).
Barbier, Nina, *Malgré-elles: Les Alsaciennes et Mosellanes incorporées de force dans la machine de guerre nazi* (Paris: Tallandier, 2018),
Barjot, Pierre, *Le Débarquement du 8 novembre 1942 en Afrique du Nord* (Paris: J. de Gigord, Éditeur: 1946).
Baruch, Marc Olivier, *Servir l'État français: L'administration en France de 1940 à 1944* (Paris: Fayard, 1997).

Baruch, Marc Olivier, *Une poignée de misérables: L'épuration de la société française après la Seconde Guerre mondiale* (Paris: Fayard, 2003).

Bauer, Alain and Dachez, Roger, *Nouvelle histoire des francs-maçons en France: Des origines à nos jours* (Paris: Tallandier, 2018).

Bayle, André, *De Marseille à Novossibirsk* (Sausset-les-Pins: self-published, 1992). Republished in 2008 as *Des Jeux Olympiques à la Waffen-SS* (Chevaigne: Éditions du Lore, 2008).

Bayly, Christopher and Harper, Tim, *Forgotten Wars: Freedom and Revolution in Southeast Asia* (Cambridge, MA: The Belknap Press of Harvard University Press, 2007).

Beaufre, Général André, *Mémoires 1920–1940–1945* (Paris: Presses de la Cité, 1965).

Beaufre, General André, *1940: The Fall of France* (New York: Knopf, 1968).

Beauvoir, Simone de (ed.), *Quiet Moments in a War: The Letters of Jean-Paul Sartre to Simone de Beauvoir (1940–1963)* (New York: Scribners, 1993).

Beevor, Antony and Cooper, Artemis, *Paris after the Liberation: 1944–1949* (London: Penguin, 1994).

Belle, Jacques, *L'Opération* Torch *et la Tunisie: De Casablanca à Tunis et au-delà (novembre 1942–septembre 1943)* (Paris: Economica, 2011).

Belot, Robert, *Aux frontières de la liberté: Vichy–Madrid–Alger–Londres: S'évader de la France sous l'Occupation* (Paris: Fayard, 1998).

Belot, Robert, *La Résistance sans de Gaulle* (Paris: Fayard, 2006).

Benbassa, Esther and Attias, Jean-Christophe, *Dictionnaire de Civilisation juive* (Paris: Larousse, 1997).

Bene, Krisztián, *La collaboration militaire française dans la Second Guerre mondiale* (Talmont St Hilaire: Éditions-Codex, 2012).

Bennaïm, Richard, *Le Journal du soldat juif* (Lormont: Le Bord de l'Eau, 2017).

Bergère, Marc, *L'Épuration en France* (Paris: Que sais-je?, 2018).

Berlière, Jean-Marc, and Chabrun, Laurent, *Les Policiers français sous l'occupation* (Paris: Perrin, 2001).

Béthouart, Antoine, *Cinq années d'espérance: Mémoires de guerre 1939–1945* (Paris: Plon, 1968).

Bezy, Jean, *Le S.R. Air* (Paris: Éditions France-Empire, 1979).

Biess, Frank and Moeller, Robert G., *Histories of the Aftermath: The Legacies of the Second World War in Europe* (New York and Oxford: Berghahn, 2010).

Billig, Joseph, *Le Commissariat Général aux Questions Juives (1941–1944)*, tome III (Paris: Éditions du Centre, 1960).

Billotte, Pierre, *Le Temps des armes* (Paris: Plon, 1972).

Billotte, Pierre, *Trente ans d'humour avec de Gaulle* (Paris: Éditions Mengès, 1978).

Bimberg, Edward L., *The Moroccan Goums: Tribal Warriors in a Modern War* (Westport and London: Greenwood Press, 1999).

Bishop, Chris, *Hitler's Foreign Divisions: Foreign Volunteers in the Waffen-SS 1940–1945* (Staplehurst: Spellmount, 2005).

Blanning, T. C. W., *The Culture of Power and the Power of Culture: Old Regime Europe 1660–1789* (Oxford: Oxford University Press, 2002).

Bloch, Jean-Richard, *De la France trahie à la France en armes: Commentaires à Radio Moscou, 1941–1944* (Paris: Éditions Sociales, 1949).

Bloch, Marc, *The Historian's Craft* (New York: Alfred A. Knopf, 1963).

Bloch, Marc, *Strange Defeat: A Statement of Evidence Written in 1940* (New York: W. W. Norton & Company, 1968).

Blumenson, Martin, *Breakout and Pursuit* (Washington, D.C.: US Government Printing Office, 1961).

Boissieu, Alain de, *Pour combattre avec de Gaulle: Souvenirs 1940–1946* (Paris: Plon, 1981).

Boivin, Michel, *1939–1945: Les Manchois dans la tourmente de la Seconde Guerre mondiale*, 6 volumes (Marigny: Éditions Eurocibles, 2004).

Bonichon, Philippe, Gény, Pierre, and Nemo, Jean, *Présences françaises outre-mer (XVIe–XXIe siècles)*, tome 1, *Histoire: Périodes et continents* (Paris: Karthala, 2012).

Boog, Horst, Rahn, Werner, Stumpf, Reinhard, and Wegner, Bernd, *Germany and the Second World War*, vol. 6, *The Global War: Widening of the Conflict into a World War and the Shift of the Initiative, 1941–1943* (Oxford: Oxford University Press, 2001).

Boris, Jean-Mathieu, *Combattant de la France Libre* (Paris: Perrin, 2012).

Bosworth, Richard J. B., and Maiolo, Joseph A., *The Cambridge History of the Second World War*, volume II, *Politics and Ideology* (Cambridge: Cambridge University Press, 2015).

Bouchinet-Serreulles, Claude, *Nous étions faits pour être libres: La résistance avec De Gaulle et Jean Moulin* (Paris: Grasset, 2000).

Boulle, Lieutenant-Colonel Georges, *Le Corps expéditionnaire français en Italie (1943–1944)*, tome 1, *La campagne d'hiver* (Paris: Imprimerie Nationale, 1971).

Bourderon, Roger, *Rol-Tanguy: Des Brigades internationales à la libération de Paris* (Paris: Tallandier, 2013).
Bourke, Joanna, *An Intimate History of Killing* (London: Granta, 1999).
Boyce, Robert and Maiolo, Joseph A. (eds.), *The Origins of World War II* (London: Palgrave Macmillan, 2003).
Bradley, Omar, *A Soldier's Story* (New York: Henry Holt, 1951).
Brignon, Jean et. al., *Histoire du Maroc* (Paris: Hatier, 1967).
Broch, Ludivine, *Ordinary Workers, Vichy and the Holocaust: French Railwaymen and the Second World War* (Cambridge: Cambridge University Press, 2016).
Broche, François, Caïtucoli, Georges, and Muracciole, Jean-François (eds.), *Dictionnaire de la France Libre* (Paris: Robert Lafont, 2010).
Broche, François, Caïtucoli, Georges, Muracciole, Jean-François, and Gallo, Max, *La France au combat: De l'appel du 18 juin à la victoire* (Paris: Perrin, 2007).
Brousse, Vincent and Grandcoing, Philippe, *Un siècle militant: Engagement(s), resistance(s), et memoire(s) au XXe siècle en Limousin* (Limoges: Presses universitaires de Limoges, 2005).
Brown, Frederick, *The Embrace of Unreason: France, 1914–1940* (New York: Knopf, 2014).
Bruneau, Jean-Baptiste, *La Marine de Vichy aux Antilles juin 1940–juillet 1943* (Paris: Les Indes Savantes, 2014).
Brunstedt, Jonathan, *The Soviet Myth of World War II: Patriotic Memory and the Russian Question in the USSR* (Cambridge: Cambridge University Press, 2021).
Buchanan, Andrew, *American Grand Strategy in the Mediterranean during World War II* (Cambridge: Cambridge University Press, 2014).
Buchanan, Andrew, *World War II in Global Perspective, 1931–1953: A Short History* (London: Wiley-Blackwell, 2019).
Burdick, Charles B., *Germany's Military Strategy and Spain in World War II* (Syracuse: Syracuse University Press, 1968).
Burrin, Philippe, *France under the Germans: Collaboration and Compromise* (New York: The New Press, 1996 [French edition 1993]).
Butcher, Harry C., *My Three Years with Eisenhower: The Personal Diary of Captain Harry C. Butcher, USNR. Naval Aide to General Eisenhower, 1942 to 1945* (London and Toronto: William Heinemann, 1946).
Buton, Philippe, *Les lendemains qui déchantent: Le Parti communiste français à la Libération* (Paris: Presses de la Fondation Nationale des Sciences Politiques, 1993).
Caddick-Adams, Peter, *Monte Cassino: Ten Armies in Hell* (London: Arrow Books, 2013).
Cadeau, Ivan, *De Lattre* (Paris: Perrin, 2017).
Campo, Joseph, "Desert Fox or Hitler Favorite? Myths and Memories of Erwin Rommel: 1941–1970," Ph.D. Thesis, University of California, Santa Barbara, 2019.
Cantier, Jacques, *L'Algérie sous le régime de Vichy* (Paris: Éditions Odile Jacob, 2002).
Capdevila, Luc, Rouquet, François, Virgili, Fabrice, and Voldman, Danièle, *Sexes, genre et guerres (France, 1914–1945)* (Paris: Payot, 2010).
Caroff, René Pierre Eugène, *Les débarquements alliés en afrique du nord (novembre 1942)*, second edition (Vincennes: Service historique de la marine, 1987).
Carrard, Philippe, *The French Who Fought for Hitler* (Cambridge: Cambridge University Press, 2010).
Carswell, Richard, *The Fall of France in the Second World War: History and Memory* (London: Palgrave Macmillan, 2019).
Catala, Michel (ed.), *Les poches de l'Atlantique 1944–1945: Le dernier acte de la Seconde Guerre mondiale en France* (Rennes: Presses universitaires de Rennes, 2019).
Cazals, Claude, *La Gendarmerie sous l'occupation* (Paris: Les Éditions La Musse, 1995).
Chaubin, Hélène, *La Corse à l'épreuve de la guerre 1939–1943* (Paris: Vendémiaire, 2012).
Chevalier, Christian, *Été 1944: L'insurrection des policiers de Paris* (Paris, Vendémiaire, 2014).
Churchill, Winston S., *The Second World War*, 6 volumes (Boston: Houghton Mifflin Company, 1951).
Ciano, Galeazzo, *Ciano's Diary 1937–1943* (London: Enigma Books, 2002).
Clark, Mark W., *Calculated Risk* (New York: Harper, 1950).
Clarke, Jeffrey J. and Smith, Robert Ross, *Riviera to the Rhine* (Washington, D.C.: Center of Military History, United States Army, 1993), https://history.army.mil/html/books/007/7-10-1/CMH_Pub_7-10-1.pdf.
Clayton, Anthony, *Three Marshals of France: Leadership after Trauma* (London: Brassey's, 1992),
Clayton, Anthony, *General Maxime Weygand 1867–1967: Fortune and Misfortune* (Bloomington: Indiana University Press, 2015).
Cochet, François, *Les soldats de la drôle de guerre: Septembre 1939–mai 1940* (Paris: Hachette Littératures, 2004).
Cohen, Eliot A. and Gooch, John, *Military Misfortunes: The Anatomy of Failure in War* (New York and London: The Free Press, 1990).

Cointet, Jean-Paul, *Expier Vichy: L'Épuration en France 1943–1958* (Paris: Perrin, 2008).

Cointet, Michèle, *Nouvelle histoire de Vichy* (Paris: Fayard, 2011).

Cointet, Michèle, *La milice française* (Paris: Fayard, 2013).

Colley, David P., *The Folly of Generals: How Eisenhower's Broad Front Strategy Lengthened World War II* (Philadelphia and Oxford: Casemate, 2020).

Colton, Joel, *Léon Blum: Humanist in Politics* (New York: Alfred A. Knopf, 1966).

Conan, Eric and Rousso, Henry, *Vichy, un passé qui ne passe pas* (Paris: Fayard, 1994).

Cornil-Frerrot, Sylvain and Oulmont, Philippe (eds.), *Les Français libres et le monde: Actes du colloque international au musée de l'Armée 22 et 23 novembre 2013* (Paris: Nouveau Monde Éditions, 2015).

Cosson, Olivier, *Préparer la Grande Guerre: L'armée française et la guerre russo-japonaise (1899–1914)* (Paris: Les Indes Savantes, 2013).

Costagliola, Bernard, *La Marine de Vichy: Blocus et collaboration* (Paris: Tallandier, 2009).

Costagliola, Bernard, *Darlan: La collaboration à tout prix* (Paris: CNRS Éditions, 2015).

Coutau-Bégarie, Hervé and Huan, Claude, *Darlan* (Paris: Fayard, 1989).

Crémieux-Brilhac, Jean-Louis, *Les français de l'an 40*, 3 volumes (Paris: Gallimard, 1990).

Crémieux-Brilhac, Jean-Louis, *La France libre*, 2 volumes (Paris: Gallimard, 2013).

Crémieux-Brilhac, Jean-Louis, *De Gaulle, la République et la France libre, 1940–1945* (Paris: Perrin, 2014).

Crémieux-Brilhac, Jean-Louis, *L'étrange victoire: De la défense de la République à la libération de la France* (Paris: Gaillimard, 2016).

Cuvillier, Solange, *Tribulations d'une femme dans l'armée française, ou le patriotisme écorché* (Paris: Éditions Lettres du Monde, 1991).

Dard, Olivier, Bour, Julie, Gueit-Montchal, Lydiane, and Richard, Gilles (eds.), *Louis Jacquinot, un indépendant en politique* (Paris: Presses de l'université Paris-Sorbonne, 2013).

Daeffler, Michel, Leleu, Jean-Luc, Passera, Françoise, and Quellien, Jean (eds.), *La France pendant la seconde guerre mondiale: Atlas historique* (Paris: Fayard, 2010).

Daix, Pierre, *Braudel* (Paris: Flammarion, 1995).

Daladier, Édouard, *Prison Journal 1940–1945* (Boulder, San Francisco, and Oxford: Westview Press, 1995).

Dallek, Robert, *Franklin D. Roosevelt and American Foreign Policy, 1932–1945* (New York and Oxford: Oxford University Press, 1995).

Davenport-Hines, Richard (ed.), *Letters from Oxford: Hugh Trevor-Roper to Bernard Berenson* (London: Phoenix, 2007).

Davis, Kenneth S., *FDR: The War President, 1940–1943: A History* (New York: Random House, 2000).

Deakin, F. W. *The Brutal Friendship: Mussolini, Hitler and the Fall of Italian Fascism* (New York: Harper and Row, 1962).

Dear, I. C. B. and Foot, M. R. D., *The Oxford Companion to World War II* (Oxford: Oxford University Press, 1995).

de Bloch, Jean, *The Future of War in Its Technical, Political, and Political Relations* (Boston: The Peace Foundation, 1914), www.armyupress.army.mil/Portals/7/combat-studies-institute/csi-books/Future-of-War.pdf.

de Dainville, Colonel Augustin, *L'ORA: La Résistance de l'armée* (Paris-Limoges: Lavauzelle, 1974).

de Gaulle, Charles, *Vers l'armée de métier* (Paris: Berger-Levrault, 1944).

de Gaulle, Charles, *Discours et messages*, tome 1, *Pendant la guerre: Juin 1940–janvier 1946* (Paris: Plon, 1970).

de Gaulle, Charles, *Mémoires de guerre*, 3 volumes (Paris: Plon, 1984).

Delperrie de Bayac, J. *Histoire de la Milice 1918–1945* (Paris: Fayard, 1969).

Denglos, Guillaume, *Juin: Le Maréchal africain* (Paris: Belin, 2018).

Dereymez, Jean-William (ed.), *Les militaires dans la résistance: Ain – Dauphiné – Savoie 1940–1944* (Avon-les-Roches: Éditions Anovi, 2010).

Desquesnes, Rémy, *Les poches de résistance allemandes: Août 1944–mai 1945* (Rennes: Éditions ouest-France, 2013).

D'Este, Carlo *World War II in the Mediterranean, 1942–1945* (Chapel Hill: Algonquin Books, 1990).

D'Este, Carlo, *Patton: A Genius for War* (New York: Harper Collins, 1995).

D'Este, Carlo, *Eisenhower: A Soldier's Life* (New York: Henry Holt, 2002).

Destremau, Bernard, *De Lattre* (Paris: Flammarion, 1999).

Devillers, Philippe and Lacouture, Jean, *End of a War: Indochina 1954* (New York: Prager, 1969).

Diamond, Hanna, *Fleeing Hitler: France 1940* (Oxford: Oxford University Press, 2007).

DiNardo, R. L., *Germany's Panzer Arm* (Westport: Greenwood Press, 1997).

Dominé, Jean-François, *Les Femmes au combat: L'arme féminine de la France pendant la Seconde Guerre mondiale* (Vincennes: Service historique de la défense, 2008).

Doughty, Robert A., *The Seeds of Disaster: The Development of French Army Doctrine 1919–1939* (Hamden: Archon Books, 1985).
Doughty, Robert A., *The Breaking Point: Sedan and the Fall of France, 1940* (Mechanicsburg, PA: Stackpole Books, 1990).
Dubief, Henri, *Le déclin de la IIIe République 1929–1938* (Paris: Éditions du Seuil, 1976).
Durand, Romain, *De Giraud à de Gaulle: Les Corps francs d'Afrique* (Paris: Éditions L'Harmattan, 1999).
Durand, Yves, *Prisonniers de guerre dans les Stalags, les Oflags et les Kommandos, 1939–1945* (Paris: Hachette, 1994).
Duroselle, Jean-Baptiste, *Politique étrangère de la France: La décadence, 1932–1939* (Paris: Imprimerie nationale, 1979).
Dutailly, Lieutenant-colonel Henry, *Les Problèmes de l'armée de terre française (1935–1939)* (Paris: Imprimerie nationale, 1980).
Echenberg, Myron, *Les tirailleurs sénégalais en Afrique occidentale française (1857–1960)* (Paris and Dakar: Karthala et Crepos, 2009).
Egremont, Max, *Under Two Flags: The Life of Major-General Sir Edward Spears* (London: Weidenfeld & Nicolson, 1997).
Ehlers, Robert S. Jr. *The Mediterranean Air War: Airpower and Allied Victory in World War II* (Lawrence: University Press of Kansas, 2015).
Ehrman, John, *Grand Strategy*, volume V, *August 1943–September 1944* (London: HMSO, 1956).
Eiler, Keith E., *Mobilizing America: Robert P. Patterson and the War Effort, 1940–1945* (Ithaca, NY: Cornell University Press, 1997).
Eisenbeth, Maurice, *Les Juifs de l'Afrique du Nord: Démographique et onomastique*. (Algiers: Imprimerie du Lycée, 1936).
Eisenhower, Dwight D., *Crusade in Europe* (Garden City, NY: Doubleday & Company Inc., 1950).
Eisenhower, Dwight David, *The Papers of Dwight David Eisenhower: The War Years* (Baltimore: Johns Hopkins University Press, 1970).
Eismann, Gaël, *Hôtel Majestic: Ordre et sécurité en France occupée (1940–1944)* (Paris: Tallandier, 2010).
Eismann, Gaël and Martens, Stefan, *Occupation et repression militaire allemandes: La politique de "maintien de l'ordre" en Europe occupée, 1939–1945* (Paris: Éditions Autrement, 2007).
Elgozy, Georges, *La vérité sur mon Corps Franc d'Afrique 1942–1943* (Monaco: Éditions du Rocher, 1985).
Ellis, John, *Cassino: The Hollow Victory. The Battle for Rome, January–June 1944* (New York: McGraw-Hill, 1984).
Ellis, John, *Brute Force: Allied Strategy and Tactics in the Second World War* (London: Viking, 1990).
Estèbe, Jean, *Toulouse 1940–1944* (Paris: Perrin, 1996).
État-Major de l'Armée de terre, Service Historique, *Guerre 1939–1945: Les grandes unités françaises. Historiques succincts* (Paris: Imprimerie nationale, 1970).
Evans, Martin, *Algeria: France's Undeclared War* (Oxford: Oxford University Press, 2012).
Evans, Richard J., *Altered Past: Counterfactuals in History* (London: Little Brown, 2014).
Evans, Richard J., *The Third Reich in Memory and History* (Oxford: Oxford University Press, 2015).
Facon, Patrick, *L'Armée de l'air dans la tourmente: La bataille de France, 1939–1940* (Paris: Economia, 2005).
Fargettas, Julien, *Les Tirailleurs sénégalais: Les soldats noirs entre légendes et réalités 1939–1945* (Paris: Tallandier, 2012).
Faron, Olivier, *Les chantiers de jeunesse: Avoir 20 ans sous Pétain* (Paris: Grasset, 2011).
Fennell, Jonathan, *Combat and Morale in the North African Campaign: The Eighth Army and the Path to El Alamein* (Cambridge: Cambridge University Press, 2011).
Fennell, Jonathan, *Fighting the People's War: The British and Commonwealth Armies and the Second World War* (Cambridge: Cambridge University Press, 2019).
Ferris, John and Mawdsley, Evan (eds.), *The Cambridge History of the Second World War* (Cambridge: Cambridge University Press, 2015).
Finney, Patrick (ed.), *The Origins of the Second World War* (London: Arnold Press, 1997).
Finney, Patrick, *Remembering the Road to World War II: International History, National Identity, Collective Memory* (London: Routledge, 2011).
Fisher, Ernest F. Jr., *Cassino to the Alps* (Washington, D.C.: Government Printing Office, 1977).
Fishman, Sarah, *We Will Wait: Wives of French Prisoners of War, 1940–1945* (New Haven and London: Yale University Press, 1990).
FitzGibbon, Constantine, *Denazification* (New York: W. W. Norton & Co., 1969).
Fleming, Thomas, *The New Dealer's War: F.D.R. and the War within World War II* (New York: Basic Books, 2001).
Florentin, Eddy, *Quand les Alliés bombardaient la France 1940–1945* (Paris: Perrin, 2008).

Fondation pour les études de défense nationale, Institut d'histoire des conflits contemporains, Service historique de l'Armée de terre, Service historique de la Marine, and Service historique de l'Armée de l'air, *Les armées française pendant la seconde guerre mondiale 1939–1945* (Paris: École nationale supérieure de techniques avancées, 1986).

Fonvieille-Alquier, François, *The French and the Phoney War 1939–1940* (London: Tom Stacey, 1973).

Foot, M. R. D., *SOE in France* (London: HMSO, 1966).

Foot, Michael, *Aneurin Bevan: A Biography I. 1887–1945* (London: MacGibbon & Lee, 1962).

Footitt, Hilary, *War and Liberation in France: Living with the Liberators* (New York: Palgrave Macmillan, 2004).

Footitt, Hilary and Simmonds, John, *France 1943–1945* (Leicester: Leicester University Press, 1988).

Foucrier, Jean-Charles, *La stratégie de la destruction: Bombardements alliés en France, 1944* (Paris: Vendémaire, 2017).

Fox, Jo, *Film Propaganda in Britain and Nazi Germany: World War II Cinema* (Oxford and New York: Berg, 2007).

Franchini, Philippe, *Les Guerres d'Indochine*, tome 1, *Des origines de la presence française à l'engrenage du conflit international* (Paris: Éditions Pygmalion, 1988).

Frankenstein, Robert, *Le Prix du réarmament français 1935–1939* (Paris: Publications de la Sorbonne, 1982).

French, David, *Raising Churchill's Army: The British Army and the War against Germany 1919–1945* (New York: Oxford University Press, 2000).

Frieser, Karl-Heinz, *The Blitzkrieg Legend: The 1940 Campaign in the West* (Annapolis: Naval Institute Press, 2005).

Fuchs, Erwin, "May You Live in Interesting Times. Part II. The Foreign Legion Years 1939–1944," unpublished diary in possession of the author, originally written in Hungarian and translated into English in 1992.

Fuller, Robert Lynn, *After D-Day: The U.S. Army Encounters the French* (Baton Rouge: Louisiana State University Press, 2021).

Funk, Arthur Layton, *The Politics of Torch: The Allied Landings and the Algiers Putsch, 1942* (Lawrence: University Press of Kansas, 1974).

Funk, Arthur Layton, *Hidden Ally: The French Resistance, Special Operations, and the Landings in Southern France, 1944* (Westport: Greenwood Press, 1992).

Fussell, Paul, *The Great War and Modern Memory* (New York and London: Oxford University Press, 1975).

Fussell, Paul, *Doing Battle: The Making of a Skeptic* (Boston, New York, Toronto, and London: Little, Brown and Company, 1996).

Gallois, William, *A History of Violence in the Early Algerian Colony* (London: Palgrave Macmillan, 2013), https://archive.org/stream/WilliamGalloisAuth.AHistoryOfViolenceInTheEarlyAlgerianColony/William+Gallois+auth.+A+History+of+Violence+in+the+Early+Algerian+Colony_djvu.txt.

Gamelin, General Maurice, *Servir: Les Armées françaises de 1940* (Paris: Plon, 1946).

Gary, Romain, *La promesse de l'aube* (Paris: Gallimard, 1980).

Gaujac, Paul, *Le Corps expéditionnaire français en Italie* (Paris: Histoire et Collections, 2003).

Gaunson, A. B., *The Anglo-French Clash in Lebanon and Syria, 1940–1945* (London: Macmillan, 1987).

Gayme, Evelyne, *Les Prisonniers de guerre français: Enjeux militaires et stratégiques (1914–1918 et 1940–1945)* (Paris: Economica, 2010).

Genet-Rouffiac, Natalie (ed.), *Les prisonniers de guerre aux personnes capturées* (Paris: Service de la Défense, 2010).

Germani, Ian, *Dying for France: Experiencing and Representing the Soldier's Death, 1500–2000* (Montreal: McGill-Queen's University Press, 2023).

Geyer, Michael and Tooze, Adam (eds.), *The Cambridge History of World War II*, volume III, *Total War: Economy, Society, and Culture* (Cambridge: Cambridge University Press, 2015).

Gildea, Robert, *Marianne in Chains: In Search of the German Occupation of France 1940–45* (London: Macmillan, 2002).

Gildea, Robert, *Fighters in the Shadows: A New History of the French Resistance* (Cambridge, MA: Harvard University Press, 2015).

Gimbel, John, *A German Community under American Occupation: Marburg 1945–1952* (Stanford: Stanford University Press, 1961).

Gimbel, John, *The American Occupation of Germany: Politics and the Military, 1945–1949* (Stanford: Stanford University Press, 1968).

Giolitto, Pierre, *Histoire de la milice* (Paris: Librairie Académique Perrin, 1997).

Giolitto, Pierre, *Volontaires français sous l'uniform allemand* (Paris: Tempus Perrin, 2007).

Girardet, Raoul, *La crise militaire française 1945–1962: Aspects sociologiques et idéologiques* (Paris: Armand Colin, 1964).

Giraud, Henri, *Mes évasions* (Paris: Juillard, 1946).

Giraud, Henri, *Un seul but – la victoire: Alger 1942–1944* (Paris: Juillard, 1949).
Girault, René and Frank, Robert, *La puissance française en question! 1945–1949* (Paris: Publications de la Sorbonne, 1988).
Gooch, John, *Mussolini's War: Fascist Italy from Triumph to Collapse 1935–1943* (London: Penguin, 2020).
Graham, Dominique and Bidwell, Shelford, *Tug of War: The Battle for Italy, 1943–1945* (New York: St. Martin's Press, 1986).
Gras, Yves, *La 1ère D.F.L.: Les Français libres au combat* (Paris: Presses de la Cité, 1983).
Greenfield, Kent Roberts (ed.), *Command Decisions* (Washington, D.C.: Center of Military History, 1990).
Greenhalgh, Elizabeth, *The French Army and the First World War* (Cambridge: Cambridge University Press, 2014).
Grenard, Fabrice, *Maquis noirs et faux maquis 1943–1947* (Paris: Vendémaire, 2011).
Halais, Jérémie, *Saint-Lô et son canton dans la tourmente de la seconde guerre mondiale 1939–1945* (Saint-Lô: Société d'archéologie et d'histoire de la Manche, 2007).
Hallion, Richard, *Strike from the Sky* (Washington, D.C.: Smithsonian Institution Press, 1989).
Hamilton, Nigel, *Monty: The Making of a General, 1887–1942* (New York: McGraw-Hill, 1981).
Hamilton, Nigel, *Master of the Battlefield: Monty's War Years, 1942–1944* (New York: McGraw-Hill, 1983).
Hamilton, Nigel, *The Mantle of Command: FDR at War, 1941–1942* (New York and Boston: Mariner Books, 2015).
Hampel, August, *J'occupais Royan 1943–1945* (Rioux-Martin: Le Croît Vif, 2011).
Hampton, Ellen, *Women of Valor: The Rochambelles on the WWII Front* (New York: Palgrave Macmillan, 2006).
Hargreaves, Andrew L., *Special Operations in World War II: British and American Irregular Warfare* (Norman: University of Oklahoma Press, 2013).
Harper, Glyn, *The Battle for North Africa: El Alamein and the Turning Point for World War II* (Bloomington: Indiana University Press, 2017).
Harper, John Lamberton, *American Visions of Europe: Franklin D. Roosevelt, George F. Kennan, and Dean G. Acheson* (Cambridge: Cambridge University Press, 1996).
Harymbat, Frédéric, *Les Européens d'Afrique du Nord dans les armées de la libération française (1942–1945)* (Paris: Éditions L'Harmattan, 2014).
Hastings, Max, *Finest Years: Churchill as Warlord 1940–45* (London: Harper Press, 2009).
Hastings, Max, *Das Reich: The March of the 2nd SS Panzer Division through France, June 1944* (Saint Paul, MN: Zenith Press, 2013).
Hawes, Stephen and White, Ralph (eds.), *Resistance in Europe, 1939–1945* (London: Viking, 1975).
Hazareesingh, Sudhir, *In the Shadow of the General: Modern France and the Myth of de Gaulle* (Oxford: Oxford University Press, 2012).
Hettier de Boislambert, Claude, *Les fers de l'espoir* (Paris: Plon, 1978).
Higham, Robin, *Two Roads to War: The French and British Air Arms from Versailles to Dunkirk* (Annapolis: Naval Institute Press, 2012).
Hill, Alexander, *The Red Army and the Second World War* (Cambridge: Cambridge University Press, 2019).
Hillel, Marc, *L'occupation française en Allemagne 1945–1949* (Paris: Balland, 1983).
Hinsley, F. H., *British Intelligence in the Second World War: Its Influence on Strategy and Operations*, 5 volumes (New York: Cambridge University Press, 1981).
Hirshon, Stanley P., *General Patton: A Soldier's Life* (New York: Harper Collins, 2002).
Hitchcock, William I., *Liberation: The Bitter Road to Freedom, Europe 1944–1945* (London: Faber and Faber, 2009).
Hoff, Ebbe Curtiss, *Preventative Medicine in World War II*, volume VIII, *Civil Affairs/Military Government Public Health Activities* (Washington, D.C.: Office of the Surgeon General, Department of the Army, 1976).
Horne, Alistair, *To Lose a Battle: France 1940* (London: Penguin, 1982).
Howard, Michael, *Grand Strategy*, volume IV, *August 1942–September 1943* (London: HMSO, 1970).
Howard, Michael, *Captain Professor: A Life in War and Peace* (London and New York: Continuum, 2006).
Howard, Michael and Paret, Peter (eds.), *Carl von Clausewitz: On War* (Princeton: Princeton University Press, 1989).
Howe, George F., *United States Army in World War II: The Mediterranean Theater of Operations, Northwest Africa. Seizing the Initiative in the West* (Washington, D.C.: Center of Military History, 1991).
Hucker, Daniel, *Public Opinion and the End of Appeasement in Britain and France* (Farnham: Ashgate, 2011).
Hull, Cordell, *Memoirs*, 2 volumes (New York: Macmillan, 1948).
Hull, Elizabeth, *Absolute Destruction: Military Culture and the Practices of War in Imperial Germany* (Ithaca, NY and London: Cornell University Press, 2005).
Hynes, Samuel, Matthews, Anne, Caldwell Sorel, Nancy, and Spiller, Rodger J. (compilers), *Reporting World War II*, Part Two: *American Journalism 1944–1946* (New York: The Library of America, 1995).

Imlay, Talbot C., *Facing the Second World War: Strategy, Politics, and Economics in Britain and France, 1938–1940* (Oxford: Oxford University Press, 2003).

Jackson, Julian, *The Popular Front in France: Defending Democracy, 1934–1938* (Cambridge: Cambridge University Press, 1988).

Jackson, Julian, *France: The Dark Years 1940–1944* (New York: Oxford University Press, 2003).

Jackson, Julian, *The Fall of France: The Nazi Invasion of 1940* (Oxford: Oxford University Press, 2003).

Jackson, Julian, *A Certain Idea of France: The Life of Charles de Gaulle* (Cambridge, MA: Harvard University Press, 2018).

Jackson, Julian, *De Gaulle* (Cambridge, MA: Harvard University Press, 2018).

Jackson, Peter, *France and the Nazi Menace: Intelligence and Policy Making 1933–1939* (Oxford: Oxford University Press, 2000).

Jähner, Harald, *Aftermath: Life in the Fallout of the Third Reich* (New York: Vintage Books, 2023).

Jauneau, Élodie, "La feminisation de l'armée française pendant les guerres (1938–1962): Enjeux et réalités d'un processus irreversible," Thèse du doctorat, Université Paris Diderot (Paris 7), 2011.

Jaurès, Jean, *L'Armée nouvelle: L'organisation socialiste de la France* (Paris: Publications Jules Rouff, 1911).

Jeanclos, Yves (ed.), *La France et les soldats d'infortune au XXe siècle* (Strasbourg: Economica, 2003).

Jennings, Eric, *La France libre fut africaine* (Paris: Perrin, 2014).

Jennings, Eric T., *Free French Africa in World War II: The African Resistance* (Cambridge: Cambridge University Press, 2015).

Joly, Laurent, *La falsification de l'Histoire: Éric Zemmour, l'extrême droite, Vichy et les juifs* (Paris: Éditions Grasset, 2022).

Jones, Benjamin F., *Eisenhower's Guerrillas: The Jedburghs, the Maquis, and the Liberation of France* (Oxford: Oxford University Press, 2016).

Jones, Matthew, *Britain, the United States and the Mediterranean War* (New York: St. Martin's Press, 1996).

Jordan, Nicole, *The Popular Front and Central Europe: The Dilemmas of French Impotence, 1918–1940* (Cambridge: Cambridge University Press, 1992).

Judge Advocate General, *Digest of Opinions of the Branch of the Judge Advocate General with the European Theater of Operations*, no date, volume II, 435–480, www.loc.gov/rr/frd/Military_Law/pdf/ETO-Index-Digest-Vol-II.pdf.

Judt, Tony, *Past Imperfect: French Intellectuals 1944–56* (Berkeley: University of California Press, 1997).

Judt, Tony, *Postwar: A History of Europe since 1945* (New York: Penguin, 2005).

Juin, Alphonse, *La campagne d'Italie* (Paris: Éditions Guy Victor, 1962).

Juin, Maréchal Alphonse Pierre, *Mémoires*, tome 1, *Alger, Tunis, Rome* (Paris: Fayard, 1959).

Kably, Mohammed, *Histoire du Maroc: Réactualisation et synthèse* (Rabat: Édition de l'Insitut Royal, 2012).

Kaiser, David E., *Economic Diplomacy and the Origins of the Second World War: Germany, Britain, France, and Eastern Europe, 1930–1939* (Princeton: Princeton University Press, 1980).

Kaiser, David E., *No End Save Victory: How FDR Led the Nation into War* (New York: Basic Books, 2014).

Kantin, Georges and Manceron, Gilles, *Les échos de la mémoire: Tabous et enseignement de la Seconde Guerre mondiale* (Paris: Le Monde Éditions, 1991).

Kaspi, André, *La Libération de la France, juin 1944–janvier 1946* (Paris: Perrin, 2004)

Katz, Robert, *The Battle for Rome: The Germans, the Allies, the Partisans, and the Pope. September 1943–June 1944* (New York: Simon & Schuster, 2003).

Kedward, H. R., *Resistance in Vichy France: A Study of Ideas and Motivation in the Southern Zone 1940–1942* (Oxford: Oxford University Press, 1978).

Kedward, H. R., *In Search of the Maquis: Rural Resistance in Southern France 1942–1944* (Oxford: Oxford University Press, 1993).

Kedward, H. R. and Wood, Nancy, *The Liberation of France: Image and Event* (Washington, D.C. and Oxford: Berge, 1995).

Kennett, Lee, *G.I.: The American Soldier in World War II* (New York: Scribner, 1987).

Kersaudy, François, *Churchill and de Gaulle* (London: Collins, 1981).

Kershaw, Ian, *Fateful Choices: Ten Decisions That Changed the World, 1940–1941* (New York: Penguin, 2007).

Kesselring, Albert, *The Memoirs of Field Marshal Kesselring* (New York: William Kimber & Co., 1953).

Kesselring, Albert, *Kesselring: A Soldier's Record* (New York: William Morrow, 1954).

Kiesling, Eugenia C., *Arming against Hitler: France & the Limits of Military Power* (Lawrence: University Press of Kansas, 1996).

King, Anthony, *The Combat Soldier: Infantry Tactics and Cohesion in the Twentieth and Twenty-First Centuries* (Oxford: Oxford University Press, 2013).

Kirshner, Jonathan, *Appeasing Bankers: Financial Caution on the Road to War* (Princeton and Oxford: Princeton University Press, 2007).

Kiszely, Sir John, *Anatomy of a Campaign: The British Fiasco in Norway, 1940* (Cambridge: Cambridge University Press, 2017).

Kitson, Simon, *Vichy et la chasse aux espions Nazis, 1940–1942: Complexités de la politique de collaboration* (Paris: Éditions Autrement, 2005).

Knapp, Andrew, *Les français sous les bombes alliées, 1940–1945* (Paris: Tallandier, 2014).

Kundahl, George G., *The Riviera at War: World War II on the Côte d'Azure* (London and New York: I. B. Tauris, 2017).

Kupferman, Fred, *Le Procès de Vichy – Pucheu, Pétain, Laval* (Paris: Éditions Complexe, 2006).

Lacouture, Jean, *De Gaulle*, tome 1, *Le Rebelle 1890–1944* (Paris: Éditions du Seuil, 1984).

Lacouture, Jean, *De Gaulle: The Ruler 1945–1970* (New York: W. W. Norton, 1993).

Lahaie, Olivier, *Guerre des services spéciaux en Afrique du Nord 1941–1944: Les mémoires du general Jean Chrétien ancient chef du contre-esponnage à Alger* (Paris: Histoire & Collections, 2015).

Lanquetot, Général André, *1943–1944: Un Hiver dans les Abruzzes. Le 8e Régiment de tirailleurs marocains et le 3e Groupe du 63e Régiment d'artillerie d'Afrique* (Vincennes: Service historique de l'armée de terre, 1990).

Lapouge, Jean, *De Sétif à Marseille, par Cassino: Carnet de guerre de Jean Lapouge, sous-lieutenant au 7e RTA. Campagnes de Tunisie, Italie et Provence, 1942–1944* (Parçay-sur-Vienne: Éditions Anovi, 2007).

Larminat, Edgard de, *Chroniques irrévérencieuses* (Paris: Plon, 1962).

Lattre de Tassigny, Jean de, *Histoire de la première armée française: Rhin et Danube* (Paris: Presses de la Cité, 1971).

Laub, Thomas, *After the Fall: German Policy in Occupied France, 1940–1944* (Oxford: Oxford University Press, 2013).

Lauterpacht, Sir Hersch, *Recognition in International Law* (Cambridge: Cambridge University Press, 1947).

Leahy, William D., *I Was There: The Personal Story of the Chief of Staff to Presidents Roosevelt and Truman Based on His Notes and Diaries Made at the Time* (London: Victor Gollancz, 1950).

Leconte, Robin, "Comprendre la défaite. La commission d'enquête sur les repliements suspects 1940–1944," Mémoire de Master 2, Université Paris I Panthéon-Sorbonne – UFR Histoire Centre d'histoire sociale du XXe siècle, 2013.

Lee, Ulysses, *The Employment of Negro Troops* (Washington, D.C.: Center of Military History, United States Army, 1965).

Lefèvre, Eric and Mabire, Jean, *La Légion perdue face aux partisans 1942* (Paris: Jacques Grancher, 1995).

Lefort-Rouquette, Suzanne, *Des Ambulancières dans les combats de la Libération: Avec les soldats de la 9e Division d'infanterie coloniale* (Paris: Éditions L'Harmattan, 2005).

Le Gac, Julie, *Vaincre sans gloire: Le corps expéditionnaire français en Italie (novembre 1942–juillet 1944)* (Paris: Les Belles Lettres/Ministère de la défense-DMPA, 2013).

le Groignec, Jacques, *Pétain et les Allemands* (Paris: Nouvelles Éditions Latines, 1997).

Leleu, Jean-Luc, *La Waffen-SS: Soldats politiques en guerre* (Paris: Perrin, 2007).

Lerner, Henri, *Catroux* (Paris: Albin Michel, 1990).

Létung, Géraud, *Mirages d'une rébellion: Être Français libre au Tchad (1940–1943)* (Paris: Sciences Po, 2019).

Levendel, Issac, *Not Germans Alone: A Son's Search for the Truth of Vichy* (Chicago: Northwestern University Press, 2001).

Levine, Alan J., *The War against Rommel's Supply Lines, 1942–1943* (Westport and London: Praeger, 1999).

Levisse-Touzé, Christine, *L'Afrique du Nord dans la guerre 1939–1945* (Paris: Albin Michel, 1998).

Levisse-Touzé, Christine (ed.), *La Campagne de 1940* (Paris: Tallandier, 2001).

Liebling, A. J., *World War II Writings: The Road Back to Paris. Mollie and Other War Pieces, Uncollected War Journalism. Normandy Revisited* (New York: Literary Classics of the United States, 2008).

Litsky, Elliott Burton, "The Murphy–Weygand Agreement: The United States and French North Africa (1940–1942)," Ph.D. Thesis, Fordham University, 1986.

Liddell Hart, B. H., *The Rommel Papers* (New York: Harcourt, Brace, 1953).

Lieb, Peter, *Vercors 1944: Resistance in the French Alps* (London: Osprey, 2012).

Loisy, Philibert de, *1944, les FFI deviennent soldats: L'amalgame: de la résistance à l'armée régulière* (Paris: Histoire & Collections, 2014).

Lopez, Jean and Wieviorka, Olivier (eds.), *Les mythes de la seconde guerre mondiale* (Paris: Perrin, 2015).

Ludewig, Joachim, *Rückzug: The German Retreat from France, 1944* (Lexington: University Press of Kentucky, 2012).

Lugan, Bernard, *Histoire du Maroc des origines à nos jours* (Paris: Critérion, 1992).

Lukes, Igor and Goldstein, Erik (eds.), *The Munich Crisis, 1938: Prelude to World War II* (London and Portland: Frank Cass, 1999).

Lynn, John, *Women, Armies and Warfare in Early Modern Europe* (Cambridge: Cambridge University Press, 2008).

Mabon, Armelle, *Prisonniers de guerre "indigènes": Visages oubliés de la France occupée* (Paris: Éditions La Découverte, 2010).
Mack Smith, Denis, *Mussolini* (New York: Knopf, 1986).
MacKenzie, S. P. *The Colditz Phenomenon* (Oxford: Oxford University Press, 2006).
MacKenzie, S. P., *Flying against Fate: Superstition and Allied Aircrews in World War II* (Lawrence: University of Kansas Press, 2018).
Macleod, Roderick and Kelly, Denis (eds.), *The Ironside Diaries, 1937–1940* (London: Constable, 1962).
Macmillan, Harold, *War Diaries: Politics and War in the Mediterranean January 1943–May 1945* (London: Macmillan, 1984).
MacVane, John, *War and Diplomacy in North Africa* (London: Robert Hale, 1944).
Maier, Klaus A., Rohde, Horst, Stegemann, Bernd, and Umbrett, Hans, *Germany and the Second World War*, volume II, *Germany's Initial Conquests in Europe* (Oxford: Clarendon Press, 1991).
Marcus, Sheldon, *Father Coughlin: The Tumultuous Life of the Priest of the Little Flower* (Boston: Little, Brown and Co., 1972).
Marrus, Michael R. and Paxton, Robert O., *Vichy France and the Jews* (New York: Basic Books, 1981).
Marshall, S. L. A., *Men against Fire: The Problem of Battle Command in Future War* (New York: William Morrow, 1947).
Martel, André (ed.), *Histoire militaire de la France*, tome 4, *De 1940 à nos jours* (Paris: Presses universitaires de France, 1994).
Martel, André, *Leclerc: Le soldat et la politique* (Paris: Albin Michel, 1998).
Masson, Philippe, *La marine française et la guerre 1939–1945* (Paris: Tallandier, 1991).
Massu, Suzanne, *Quand j'étais Rochambelle* (Paris: Grasset, 1969).
Mathieu, Yves, *Policiers perdus: Les GMR dans la Seconde Guerre mondiale* (Toulouse: self-published, 2009).
Matthews, Anne, Caldwell Sorel, Nancy, and Spiller, Rodger J. (compilers), *Reporting World War II*, Part One: *American Journalism 1938–1944* (New York: The Library of America, 1995).
Mauraic, Claude, *Un autre de Gaulle: Journal, 1944–1954* (Paris: Hachette, 1971).
May, Ernest R., *Strange Victory: Hitler's Conquest of France* (New York: Hill and Wang, 2000).
Mayers, David, *FDR's Ambassadors and the Diplomacy of Crisis: From the Rise of Hitler to the End of World War II* (Cambridge: Cambridge University Press, 2012).
Mayo, Lida, *The Ordnance Department: On Beachhead and Battlefront* (Washington, D.C.: Center of Military History, United States Army, 1966).
Mazière, Christian de la, *Ashes of Honour* (London: Allan Wingate, 1975).
Mazower, Mark, *Inside Hitler's Greece: The Experience of Occupation, 1941–1944* (New Haven: Yale University Press, 1993).
Mazower, Mark, *Dark Continent: Europe's Twentieth Century* (New York: Vintage Books, 1998).
McMeekin, Sean, *Stalin's War: A New History of World War II* (New York: Basic Books, 2021).
Mearsheimer, John J., *Liddell Hart and the Weight of History* (Ithaca, NY: Cornell University Press, 1988).
Melton, George F., *From Versailles to Mers el-Kébir: The Promise of Anglo-French Naval Cooperation, 1919–1940* (Annapolis: Naval Institute Press. 2015).
Merle, Robert, *Ahmed ben Bella* (Paris: Gallimard, 1965).
Metzger, Chantal, *L'empire colonial français dans la stratégie du troisième Reich (1936–1945)*, 2 volumes (Paris: Direction des Archives, Ministère des Affaires étrangères; Brussels: Peter Lang, 2002).
Metzger, Chantal, *Le Maghreb dans la guerre 1939–1945* (Paris: Armand Colin, 2018).
Micaud, Charles, *The French Right and Nazi Germany, 1933–1939* (Durham: Duke University Press, 1943).
Milne, Caleb, *"I Dream of the Day . . .": Letters from Caleb Milne. Africa, 1942–1943* (Woodstock, NY: privately published, 1944).
Miot, Claire, "Sortir l'armée des ombres. Soldats de l'Empire, combattants de la Libération, armée de la Nation: La Première armée française, du débarquement en Provence à la capitulation allemande (1944–1945)," Thèse du doctorat, Université Paris-Saclay, 2016.
Miot, Claire, *La première armée française* (Paris: Perrin, 2021).
Miot, Claire, Piketty, Guillaume, and Vaisset, Thomas (eds.), *Militaires en résistances en France et en Europe* (Villeneuve d'Ascq: Presses universitaires du Septentrion, 2020).
Miquel, Pierre, *La Grande guerre* (Paris: Fayard, 1983).
Monnet, Jean, *Mémoires* (Paris: Fayard, 1976).
Monnet, Jean, *Memoirs* (Garden City, NY: Doubleday & Company, 1978).
Monsabert, Général Joseph Goislard de, *Notes de Guerre* (Hélette: Éditions Jean Curutchet, 1999).
Montagnon, Pierre, *Dictionnaire de la colonisation française* (Paris: Pygmalion/Flammarion, 2010).
Montgomery, Bernard, *The Memoirs of Field Marshal Montgomery* (London: Collins, 1958).

Moore, William Mortimer, *The Life of Philippe Leclerc, de Gaulle's Greatest General* (Philadelphia and Newbury: Casemate, 2011).

Moorehead, Alan, *The Desert War: The North African Campaign 1940–1943* (London and New York: Penguin, 2001).

Moran, Charles, *The Landings in North Africa, November 1942* (Washington, D.C.: Naval Historical Center, 1992).

Moran, Daniel and Waldron, Arthur (eds.), *The People in Arms: Military Myth and National Mobilization since the French Revolution* (Cambridge: Cambridge University Press, 2003).

Morrison, Samuel Elliot, *History of U.S. Naval Operations in World War II*, volume 2, *Operations in North African Waters* (Boston: Little Brown, 1950).

Mouré, Kenneth and Alexander, Martin (eds.), *Crisis and Renewal in France, 1918–1962* (New York: Berghahn Books, 2002).

Müller, Klaus-Jürgen, *The Army, Politics and Society in Germany, 1933–45: Studies in the Army's Relation to Nazism* (Manchester: Manchester University Press, 1987).

Müller, Klaus-Jürgen (ed.), *The Military in Politics and Society in France and Germany in the Twentieth Century* (Oxford and Washington, D.C.: Berg, 1995).

Müller, Rolf-Dieter, *Hitler's Wehrmacht, 1935–1945* (Lexington: University Press of Kentucky, 2016).

Muracciole, Jean-François, *Les Français libres: L'autre Résistance* (Paris: Tallandier, 2009).

Murphy, Robert, *Diplomat among Warriors* (London: Collins, 1964).

Mysyrowicz, Ladislas, *Autopsie d'une défaite: Origines de l'effondrement militaire française de 1940* (Lausanne: L'Age d'homme, 1973).

Naimark, Norman M., *The Russians in Germany: A History of the Soviet Zone of Occupation, 1945–1949* (Cambridge, MA: Harvard University Press, 1995).

Navarre, Henri, *Le Temps des vérités* (Paris: Plon, 1979).

Neal, Colonel John J., "The Shared Burden. United States–French Coalition Operations in the European Theater of World War II," Master's Thesis, School of Advanced Studies, U.S. Army Command and Staff College, Fort Leavenworth, KS, 2013.

Neiberg, Michael S., *When France Fell: The Vichy Crisis and the Fate of the Anglo-American Alliance* (Cambridge, MA: Harvard University Press, 2021).

Némirovsky, Irène, *Suite Française* (Paris: Éditions Denoël, 2004).

Nicolaïdis, Dimitri, *Oublier nos crimes: L'amnestie national: Une specificité française* (Paris: Autrement, 2002).

Nicolson, Harold, *Diaries and Letters, 1939–1945* (London, Collins, 1967).

Noguères, Henri, *Histoire de la résistance en France*, 10 volumes (Paris: Laffont, 1969).

Noguères, Henri, *La vie quotidienne des résistants de l'Armistice à la Libération* (Paris: Hachette, 1984).

Nora, Pierre and Charles-André Julien, *Les français d'Algérie* (Chantenay: Julliard, 1961).

Nord, Philip, *France 1940: Defending the Republic* (New Haven: Yale University Press, 2015).

Notin, Jean-Christophe, *La Campagne d'Italie 1943–1945: Les victoires oubliées de la France* (Paris: Perrin, 2007).

Notin, Jean-Christophe, *Leclerc: Le croisé de la France libre* (Paris: Perrin, 2015).

Notin, Jean-Christophe, *Maréchal Juin* (Paris: Tallandier, 2015).

Novick, Peter, *L'épuration française 1944–1949* (Paris: Éditions Balland, 1985).

O'Brien, Phillips Payson, *The Second Most Powerful Man in the World: The Life of Admiral William D. Leahy, Roosevelt's Chief of Staff* (New York: Dutton, 2019).

Office of the Historian, *Foreign Relations of the United States: Diplomatic Papers, 1945, Europe*, vol. IV, https://history.state.gov/historicaldocuments/frus1945v04/d664.

O'Hara, Vincent P., *Torch: North Africa and the Allied Path to Victory* (Annapolis: Naval Institute Press, 2015).

Olson, Lynne, *Last Hope Island: Britain, Occupied Europe, and the Brotherhood That Helped Turn the Tide of War* (New York: Random House, 2017).

Overy, Richard, *Blood and Ruins: The Last Imperial War, 1931–1945* (London: Viking, 2022).

Overy, Richard J., *The Air War, 1939–1945* (New York: Stein and Day, 1980).

Owens, Patricia, *Counterinsurgency and the Rise of the Social* (Cambridge: Cambridge University Press, 2013).

Paret, Peter, *French Irregular Warfare from Indochina to Algeria: An Analysis of a Political and Military Doctrine* (New York: Praeger, 1964).

Paret, Peter, *Imagined Battles: Reflections of War in European Art* (Chapel Hill and London: University of North Carolina Press, 1997).

Passera, Françoise and Quellien, Jean, *Les normands dans la guerre: Le temps des épreuves 1939–1945* (Paris: Tallandier, 2021).

Passy, Colonel, *Souvenirs*, 2 volumes (Monte Carlo: Raoul Solar, 1947).

Pathé, Anne-Marie and Théofilakis, Fabien, *La Captivité de guerre au XXe siècle: Des Archives, des histoires, des mémoires* (Paris: Armand Colin, 2012).

Paxton, Robert O., *Parades and Politics at Vichy: The French Officer Corps under Marshal Pétain* (Princeton: Princeton University Press, 1966).

Paxton, Robert O., *Vichy France: Old Guard and New Order, 1940–1944* (London: Barrie & Jenkins, 1972).

Paxton, Robert O., *L'armée de Vichy: Le corps des officiers français 1940–1944* (Paris: Tallandier, 2004).

Payne, Stanley G., *Franco and Hitler: Spain, Germany, and World War II* (New Haven and London: Yale University Press, 2008).

Péan, Pierre, *Le mystérieux Docteur Martin* (Paris: Fayard, 1993).

Péan, Pierre, *Une jeunesse française: François Mitterand, 1934–1947* (Paris: Fayard, 1994).

Pedroncini, Guy (ed.), *Histoire militaire de la France*, tome 3, *De 1871 à 1940* (Paris: Presses universitaires de France, 1992).

Pellissier, Pierre, *De Lattre* (Paris: Perrin, 1998).

Perlman, Susan McCall, *Contesting France: Intelligence and US Foreign Policy in the Early Cold War* (Cambridge: Cambridge University Press, 2023).

Pertinax (André Géraud), *The Gravediggers of France: Gamelin, Daladier, Reynaud, Pétain, and Laval. Military Defeat, Armistice, Counterrevolution* (Garden City, NY: Doubleday, Doran & Company, 1944).

Pesquer, Michel, "L'emploi des blindés français sur le front occidental d'août 1944 à mai 1945," Thèse du doctorat, Université de Lorraine, 2018.

Pigenet, Michel, *Les "Fabiens" des barricades au front (septembre 1944–mai 1945)* (Paris: Éditions L'Harmattan, 1995).

Pigorneau, Olivier, *Maquis blancs: La "résistance" des collabos, 1944–1945* (Paris: Konfident, 2022).

Piketty, Guillaume, *Pierre Brossolette: Un héros de la résistance* (Paris: Éditions Odile Jacob, 1998).

Piketty, Guillaume, *Français en résistance: Carnet de guerre, correspondances, journaux personnels* (Paris: Robert Laffont, 2009).

Pineau, Frédéric, *Femmes en guerre, 1940–1946* (Antony: ETAI, 2013).

Pitt, Barry, *The Crucible of War: Auchinleck's Command. The Definitive History of the Desert War*, vol. 2 (London: Cassell, 2001).

Planchais, Jean, *Une histoire politique de l'armée*, tome 2, *1940–1967: De de Gaulle à de Gaulle* (Paris: Éditions du Seuil, 1967).

Playfair, I. S. O., *The Mediterranean and the Middle East*, 5 volumes (London: HMSO, 1954).

Porch, Douglas, *Army and Revolution: The French Army 1815–1848* (London: Routledge and Kegan Paul, 1974).

Porch, Douglas, *The March to the Marne: The French Army 1871–1914* (Cambridge: Cambridge University Press, 1981).

Porch, Douglas, *The French Foreign Legion: A Complete History of the Legendary Fighting Force* (New York: Harper Collins, 1991).

Porch, Douglas, *The French Secret Services: A History of French Intelligence from the Dreyfus Affair to the Gulf War* (New York: Farrar, Straus, Giroux, 1995).

Porch, Douglas, *The French Secret Services from the Dreyfus Affair to the Gulf War* (Oxford: Oxford University Press, 1997).

Porch, Douglas, *Path to Victory: The Mediterranean Theater in World War II* (New York: Farrar, Straus, Giroux, 2004).

Porch, Douglas, *Counterinsurgency: Exposing the Myths of the New Way of War* (Cambridge: Cambridge University Press, 2013).

Porch, Douglas, *Defeat and Division: France at War, 1939–1942* (Cambridge: Cambridge University Press, 2022).

Post, Gaines Jr., *Dilemmas of Appeasement: British Deterrence and Defense 1934–1937* (Ithaca, NY and London: Cornell University Press, 1993).

Poznanski, Renée, *Propagandes et persécutions: La Résistance et le "problème juif" 1940–1944* (Paris: Fayard, 2008).

Pujo, Bernard, *Juin, Maréchal de France* (Paris: Albin Michel, 1988).

Queloz, Dimitry, *De la manœuvre napoléonienne à l'offensive à outrance: La tactique générale de l'armée française 1871–1914* (Paris: Economica, 2009).

Rahn, Rudolf, *Un diplomat dans la tourmente* (Paris: France Empire, 1980).

Réau, Élisabeth du, *Édouard Daladier 1884–1970* (Paris: Fayard, 1993).

Recham, Belkacem, *Les Musulmans algériens dans l'armée française (1919–1945)* (Paris: Éditions L'Harmattan, 1996).

Reynaud, Paul, *Mémoires*, tome II, *Envers et contre tous: 7 mars 1936–16 juin 1940* (Paris: Flammarion, 1963).

Riding, Alan, *And the Show Went On: Cultural Life in Nazi-Occupied Paris* (New York: Vintage Books, 2021).

Riedweg, Eugène, *Les "malgré nous": Histoire de l'incorporation de force des Alsaciens-Mosellans dans l'armée allemande* (Strasbourg: La Nuée Bleue, 2008).

Rigoulot, Pierre, *L'Alsace-Lorraine pendant la guerre 1939–1945* (Paris: Presses universitaires de France, 1997).

Rioux, Jean-Pierre, *The Fourth Republic, 1944–1958* (Cambridge: Cambridge University Press, 1987).

Rivet, Général Louis, *Carnets du chef des services secrets 1936–1944*, eds. Olivier Forcade and Sébastian Laurent (Paris: Nouveau Monde, 2010).

Roberts, Mary *Louise Civilization without Sexes: Reconstructing Gender in Postwar France 1917–1927* (Chicago: University of Chicago Press, 1994).

Roberts, Mary Louise, *What Soldiers Do: Sex and the American GI in World War II France* (Chicago: University of Chicago Press, 2013).

Roberts, Sophie B., *Citizenship and Antisemitism in French Colonial Algeria, 1870–1962* (Cambridge and New York: Cambridge University Press, 2018).

Robertson, Charles L., *When Roosevelt Planned to Govern France* (Amherst and Boston: University of Massachusetts Press, 2011).

Rocolle, Pierre, *L'hécatombe des généraux* (Paris: Lavauzelle, 1980).

Rolf, David, *The Bloody Road to Tunis: Destruction of the Axis Forces in North Africa: November 1942–May 1943* (London: Greenhill Books and Pennsylvania Stackpole Books, 2001).

Rosner, Elliott J., "The Jedburghs. Combat Operations in the Finisterre Region of Brittany, France from July-September, 1944," Master's Thesis, U.S. Army Command and Staff College, Fort Leavenworth, Kansas, 1990, https://apps.dtic.mil/dtic/tr/fulltext/u2/b148370.pdf.

Rostaing, Pierre, *Le Prix d'un serment, 1941–1945: Des plaines de Russie à l'enfer de Berlin* (Paris: La Table Ronde, 1975).

Roucaute, Yves, *Le PCF et l'armée* (Paris: Presses universitaires de France, 1983).

Rouquet, François, *Une Épuration ordinaire (1944–1949): Petits et grands collaborateurs de l'administration française* (Paris: CNRS Éditions, 2011).

Rouquet, François and Virgili, Fabrice, *Les françaises, les français et l'épuration (1940 à nos jours)* (Paris: Gallimard, 2018).

Rousso, Henry, *The Vichy Syndrome: History and Memory in France since 1944* (Cambridge, MA: Harvard University Press, 1991).

Sadoul, Georges, *Journal de Guerre (2 septembre 1939–20 juillet 1940)* (Paris: Éditions L'Harmattan, 1994).

Sainclivier, Jacqueline and Bougeard, Christian, *La Résistance et les Français* (Rennes: Presses Universitaire de Rennes, 1995), https://books.openedition.org/pur/16338.

Saint-Martin, Gérard, *L'arme blindée française*, tome 2, *1940–1945: Dans le fracas des batailles* (Paris: Economica, 2000).

Sajer, Guy, *Le soldat oublié* (Paris: Robert Laffont, 1967).

Salan, Raoul, *Mémoires*, tome 1, *Fin d'un empire: "Le sens d'un engagement," juin 1899–septembre 1946* (Paris: Presses de la Cité, 1970).

Sandler, Stanley, *Glad to See Them Come and Sorry to See Them Go: A History of the U.S. Army Tactical Civil Affairs/Military Government, 1775–1991* (self-published, 1994).

Sandler, Stanley, *"Cease Resistance: It's Good For You": A History of U.S. Army Combat Psychological Operations* (self-published, 1999).

Sapir, Jacques, Stora, Frank and Mahé, Loïc, *1940: Et si la France avait continué la guerre . . .* (Paris: Tallandier, 2010).

Sartre, Jean-Paul, *The War Diaries of Jean-Paul Sartre: November 1939/March 1940* (New York: Pantheon Books, 1984).

Scheck, Raffael, *French Colonial Soldiers in German Captivity during World War II* (Cambridge: Cambridge University Press, 2014).

Scheipers, Sibylle, *Unlawful Combatants: A Genealogy of the Irregular Fighter* (Oxford: Oxford University Press, 2015).

Schiavon, Max, *Le général Alphonse Georges: Un destin inachevé* (Parçay-sur-Vienne: Éditions Anovi, 2009).

Schmitt, Jacques, *Journal d'un officier de tirailleurs 1944* (Paris: Bernard Giovannangeli Éditeur, 1944).

Schreier, Joshua, *Arabs of the Jewish Faith: The Civilizing Mission in Colonial Algeria* (New Brunswick: Rutgers University Press, 2010).

Schrijvers, Peter, *The Crash of Ruin: American Combat Soldiers in Europe during WWII* (New York: New York University Press, 1998).

Servent, Pierre, *Le mythe Pétain: Verdun ou les tranchées de la mémoire* (Paris: CNRS Éditions, 2014).

Shneyer, Aron, *Pariahs among Pariahs: Soviet-Jewish POWs in German Captivity, 1941–1945* (Jerusalem: Yad Vashem, 2016).

Simonet, Stéphane, *Les poches de l'Atlantique: Les batailles oubliées de la Libération. Janvier 1944–mai 1945* (Paris: Tallandier, 2015).

Singer, Barnett, *Maxime Weygand: A Biography of the French General in Two World Wars* (Jefferson and London: McFarland & Company, 2008).

Smelser, Ronald and Davies, Edward J., II, *The Myth of the Eastern Front: The Nazi–Soviet War in American Popular Culture* (Cambridge: Cambridge University Press, 2008).

Smith, Jean Edward, *Lucius D. Clay: An American Life* (New York: Henry Holt, 1990).

Smith, Leonard V., *Between Mutiny and Obedience: The French Fifth Infantry Division in World War I* (Princeton: Princeton University Press, 1994).

Snyder, Timothy, *Bloodlands: Europe between Hitler and Stalin* (New York: Basic Books, 2010).

Soustelle, Jacques, *Envers et contre tout: Souvenirs et documents sur la France Libre*, tome 2, *D'Alger à Paris, 1942–1944* (Paris: Robert Laffont, 1950).

Spears, Sir Edward, Assignment to Catastrophe, *volume II, The Fall of France* (New York: A. A. Wyn, 1955).

Spears, Sir Edward, *Fulfillment of a Mission: The Spears Mission to Syria and Lebanon 1941–1944* (London: Leo Cooper, 1977).

Spivak, Marcel and Leoni, Armand, *Les forces françaises dans la lutte contre l'Axe en Afrique*, tome II, *La campagne de Tunisie, 1942–1943* (Vincennes: Service historique de l'armée de terre, 1985).

Stargardt, Nicholas, *The German War: A Nation under Arms, 1939–1945. Citizens and Soldiers* (New York: Basic Books, 2015).

Stoler, Mark A., *Allies and Adversaries: The Joint Chiefs of Staff, the Grand Alliance, and U.S. Strategy in World War II* (Chapel Hill and London: The University of North Carolina Press, 2000).

Stora, Benjamin, *Histoire de l'Algérie coloniale (1830–1954)* (Paris: Éditions La Découverte, 2004).

Strachan, Hew, *The First World War*, volume 1, *To Arms* (Oxford: Oxford University Press, 2001).

Strachan, Hew and Harris, Ruth, *The Utility of Military Force and Public Understanding in Today's Britain* (Santa Monica and Cambridge: RAND Corporation, 2020).

Surkis, Judith, *Sexing the Citizen: Morality and Masculinity in France, 1870–1920* (Ithaca, NY: Cornell University Press, 2011).

Tenenbaum, Élie, "Une odyssée subversive: La circulation des savoirs stratégiques irréguliers en Occident (France, Grande-Bretagne, États-Unis) de 1944 à 1972," Thèse du doctorat, Paris, Institut d'études politiques, 2015.

Tenenbaum, Elie, *Partisans et centurions: Une histoire de la guerre irrégulière au XXe siècle* (Paris: Perrin, 2018).

Thomas, Martin, *The French Empire at war, 1940–1945* (Manchester: University of Manchester Press, 2007).

Thomas, Martin and Toye, Richard, *Arguing about Empire: Imperial Rhetoric in Britain and France, 1882–1956* (Oxford: Oxford University Press, 2017).

Thorne, Christopher, *The Approach of War 1938–39* (New York: St. Martin's Press, 1967).

Tombs, Robert and Chabal, Emile (eds.), *Britain and France in Two World Wars: Truth, Myth and Memory* (London: Bloomsbury, 2013).

Torrie, Julie S., *German Soldiers and the Occupation of France* (Cambridge: Cambridge University Press, 2018).

Toye, Richard, *The Roar of the Lion: The Untold Story of Churchill's World War II Speeches* (Oxford: Oxford University Press, 2013).

Travers, Susan, *Tomorrow to Be Brave* (London: Corgi Press, 2001).

Truscott, Lucian, *Command Missions: A Personal Story* (New York: Dutton, 1954).

Tucker, Spencer C. (ed.), *The Definitive Encyclopedia of World War II* (Santa Barbara and Denver: ABC-CLIO, 2016).

Turpin, Frédéric, *De Gaulle, les gaullistes et l'Indochine* (Paris: Les Indes Savantes, 2005).

United States, Department of State, *Peace and War: United States Foreign Policy, 1931–1941* (Washington, D. C.: U.S., Government Printing Office, 1943).

Vaisset, Thomas, *L'Amiral d'Argenlieu: Le moine-soldat du gaullisme* (Paris: Belin, 2017).

Valode, Philippe and Chauvy, Gérard, *La Gestapo française* (Paris: Acropole, 2018).

Vassiltchikov, Marie, *Berlin Diaries, 1940–1945* (New York: Vintage Books, 1988).

Vergez-Chaignon, Bénédicte, *Histoire de l'épuration* (Paris: Larousse, 2010).

Vergez-Chaignon, Bénédicte, *Pétain* (Paris, Perrin, 2014).

Vergnon, Gilles, *Le Vercors: Histoire et mémoir d'un maquis* (Paris: Les éditions de l'Atelier/Éditions Ouvrières, 2002).

Verity, Hugh, *We Landed by Moonlight: Secret RAF Landings in France, 1940–1944* (Manchester: AirData Publications Limited, 1995).

Vernejoul, Henri de and Durlewanger, Armand, *Autopsie d'une Victoire morte* (Colmar: Saep, 1970).

Vernet, J., *Le réarmament et la réorganization de l'armée de terre française (1943–1946)* (Vincennes: Ministère de la défense, État-major de l'armée de terre, Service historique, 1980).
Vigneras, Marcel, *Rearming the French* (Washington, D.C.: Center of Military History, 1989).
Vincent, Jean-Noël, *Les forces françaises dans la lutte contre l'Axe en Afrique*, tome I, *Les forces françaises libres en Afrique 1940–1943* (Vincennes: Service historique de l'armée de terre, 1983).
Vinen, Richard, *France, 1934–1970* (New York: St. Martin's Press, 1996).
Vinen, Richard, *The Unfree French* (New Haven: Yale University Press, 2007).
Virgili, Fabrice, *La France "virile": Des femmes tondues à la Libération* (Paris: Payot, 2000).
Wall, Irwin M., *The United States and the Making of Postwar France, 1945–1954* (Cambridge: Cambridge University Press, 1991).
Weathersby, Major Russell A., "The Field Artillery Group in Support of Corps and Field Army, 1942–1953," Master of Arts, Command and General Staff College, Fort Leavenworth, Kansas, 1965.
Weber, Eugen, *The Hollow Years: France in the 1930s* (New York: W. W. Norton, 1994).
Weber, Thomas, *Hitler's First War: Adolf Hitler, the Men of the List Regiment, and the First World War* (Oxford: Oxford University Press, 2010).
Weiss, Stéphan, *Les forces françaises de l'Ouest: Forces françaises oubliées? 1944–1945* (Paris: Les Indes Savantes, 2019).
Weygand, Maxime, *Mémoires*, tome III, *Rappelé au service* (Paris: Flammarion, 1950).
Wheeler, James Scott and Atkinson, Rick, *Jacob L. Devers: A General's Life* (Lexington: University Press of Kentucky, 2015).
Wieviorka, Annette, *The Era of the Witness* (Ithaca, NY: Cornell University Press, 2006).
Wieviorka, Olivier, *Une Certaine idée de la Résistance: Défense de France 1940–1949*, (Paris: Éditions du Seuil, 1995).
Wieviorka, Olivier, *Normandy: The Landings to the Liberation of Paris* (Cambridge, MA: Harvard University Press, 2008).
Wieviorka, Olivier, *Divided Memory: French Recollections of World War II from the Liberation to the Present* (Stanford, CA: Stanford University Press, 2012).
Wieviorka, Olivier, *Histoire de la Résistance 1940–1945* (Paris: Perrin, 2013).
Wieviorka, Olivier, *Une histoire de la résistance en Europe occidentale* (Paris: Perrin, 2017).
Wilkinson, Peter and Bright Astley, Joan, *Gubbins & SOE* (London: Leo Cooper, 1993).
Willis, Frank Roy, *The French in Germany 1945–1949* (Stanford: Stanford University Press, 1962).
Wright, Patrick, *Tank: The Progress of a Monstrous War Machine* (London: Faber and Faber, 2000).
Young, Robert J., *In Command of France: French Foreign Policy and Military Planning, 1933–1940* (Cambridge, MA: Harvard University Press, 1978).
Young, Robert J., *France and the Origins of the Second World War* (New York: St. Martin's Press, 1996).
Zahner, Armand, *Le Soldat Honteux: J'était un "Malgré-Nous"* (Mulhouse: Éditions Salvator, 1972).
Ziemke, Earl, The *U.S. Army in the Occupation of Germany*, Part I (Grandview Heights: Bibliogov, 2013).
Zeldin, Theodore, *France 1848–1945*, 2 volumes (Oxford: Oxford University Press, 1977).

Articles

Abzac-Epezy, Claude d', "Épuration, dégagements, exclusions. Les réductions d'éffectifs dans l'armée française (1940–1947)," *Vingtième Siècle. Revue d'histoire*, 59 (1998), 62–75.
Abzac-Epezy, Claude d', "La pensée militaire de Camille Rougeron: Innovations et marginalité," *Revue française de science politique*, 54/5 (2004), 761–779, www.cairn.info/article.php?ID_ARTICLE=RFSP_545_0761.
Abzac-Epezy, Claude d', "La France face au rapatriement des prisonniers de guerre allemands," *Guerre mondiales et conflits contemporains*, 2009/1, no. 233 (2009), 93–108.
Abzac-Epezy, Claude d', "L'armée française et les prisonniers de guerre de l'Axe," in Natalie Genet-Rouffiac (ed.), *Les prisonniers de guerre aux personnes capturées* (Paris: Service de la Défense, 2010), pp. 39–54.
Ageron, Charles-Robert, "La Survivance d'un mythe: La puissance par l'empire colonial (1944–1947)," *Revue française d'Histoire d'Outre-Mer*, LXXII no. 269 (1985), 387–403.
Albertelli, Sébastien, "The British, Free French, and Resistance," in Tombs, Roberts and Chabal, Emile (eds.), *Britain and France in Two World Wars: Truth, Myth, and Memory* (London and New York: Bloomsbury, 2013), pp. 119–136.
Alexander, Martin, "After Dunkirk: The French Army's Performance against 'Case Red,' 25 May to 25 June 1940," *War in History*, 14/2 (2007), 219–264.

Aouate, Yves-Claude, "La place de l'Algérie dans le projet antijuif de Vichy,"*Revue française d'histoire d'outre-mer*, 80/301 (1993), 599–613.

Barasz, Johanna, "De Vichy à la Résistance: Les vichysto-résistants 1940–1944," *Guerres mondiales et conflits contemporains*, 2011/2, no. 242 (2011), 27–50, www.cairn.info/revue-guerres-mondiales-et-conflits-contemporains-2011-2-page-27.htm#no14.

Baris, Tommaso, "Le corps expéditionnaire français en Italie. Violence des 'libérateurs' durant l'été 1944," *Vingtième Siècle. Revue d'histoire*, 93 (January–March 2007), 47–61.

Bédarida, François, "L'histoire de la résistance. Lectures de hiers, chantiers de demain," *Vingtième Siècle. Revue d'histoire*, 1986/11 (1986), 75–90.

Boudot, François, "Aspects de l'histoire de la captivité," *L'Actualité de l'histoire*, no. 10 (January 1955), 22–35.

Boudot, François, "Pour une histoire de la captivité: Souvenirs de qualité," *Annales. Economies, Sociétés, Civilisations*, 12e année, no. 1, 1957, 132–140.

Bruneau, Jean-Baptiste and Vaisset, Thomas, "Déchirements, déclassment et relèvement (1939–1945)," in Philippe Vial (ed.), "L'histoire d'une révolution. La Marine depuis 1870," *Études marines*, no. 4 (March 2013), 82–104.

Buchanan, Andrew, "Globalizing the Second World War," *Past & Present*, 258/1 (2023), 246–281.

Burgess, Greg, "The Repatriation of Soviet Prisoners and Displaced Persons in the Auvergne after the Second World War," 169–181, https://h-france.net/rude/wp-content/uploads/2017/08/vol7_Burgess.pdf.

Burgess, Greg, "Remaking Asylum in Post-War France, 1944–52." *Journal of Contemporary History* 46/3 (2014), 556–576.

Callender, Harold, "Derrien on Trial at Secret Session," *New York Times*, 11 May 1944, www.nytimes.com/1944/05/11/archives/derrien-on-trial-at-secret-session-defense-protests-that-admiral.html.

Callender, Harold, "Derrien Gets Life in Algiers Trial," *New York Times*, 13 May 1944, www.nytimes.com/1944/05/13/archives/derrien-gets-life-in-algiers-trial-guilty-of-failure-to-scuttle.html.

Campbell, D'Ann, "Women in Combat: The World War II Experience in the United States, Great Britain, Germany, and the Soviet Union," *Journal of Military History*, 57/2 (April 1993), 301–323.

Capdevila, Luc, "La mobilisation des femmes dans la France combattante (1940–1945)," *Clio. Histoire, femmes et sociétés*, 12/2000 (2000), unpaginated, https://journals.openedition.org/clio/187.

Capdevila, Luc, "The Quest for Masculinity in a Defeated France, 1940–1945," *Contemporary European History*, 10/3, (November 2001), 423–445.

Capdevila, Luc, "L'identité masculine et les fatigues de la guerre (1914–1945)," *Vingtième Siècle. Revue d'histoire*, 2003/3, no. 75 (2003), 97–108, www.cairn.info/revue-vingtieme-siecle-revue-d-histoire-2002-3-page-97.htm.

Capps-Tunwell, David, Passmore, David G, and Harrison, Stephan, "An Evaluation of Allied Intelligence in the Tactical Bombing of German Supply Depots during the Normandy Campaign, 1944," *The Journal of Military History*, 84/3 (July 2020), 825–842.

Celaya, Diego Gaspar, "Portrait d'oubliés. L'engagement des Espagnols dans les Forces françaises libres, 1940–1945," *Revue historique des armées*, 265 (2011), 46–55, https://journals.openedition.org/rha/7345.

Celaya, Diego Gaspar, "De l'oubli, des mythes, de l'histoire. Histoire et mémoire des volontaires espagnols dans Résistance française." *Historiografías*, 12 (July–December 2016), 70–86.

Chin, Rachel, "After the Fall. British Strategy and the Preservation of the Franco-British Alliance in 1940," *Journal of Contemporary History*, 55/2 (2019), 1–19, https://journals.sagepub.com/doi/abs/10.1177/0022009419846951.

Crang, Jeremy, "'Come into the Army, Maud': Women, Military Conscription, and the Markham Inquiry," *Defence Studies*, 8 (2008), 381–395.

Crémieux-Brilhac, Jean-Louis, "Les Glières," *Vingtième Siècle. Revue d'histoire*, no. 45 (January–March 1995), 54–66.

Crémieux-Brilhac, Jean-Louis, "Une stratégie militaire pour la Résistance: Le Bloc Planning et l'insurrection nationale," *Espoir*, no. 139 (2004), www.charles-de-gaulle.org/wp-content/uploads/2017/10/Une-strategie-militaire-pour-la-Resistance.pdf.

Creswell, Michael and Marc Trachtenberg, Marc, "France and the German Question, 1945–1955," *Journal of Cold War Studies*, 5/3 (Summer 2003), 8–14.

Daddis, Gregory A., "Mansplaining Vietnam: Male Veterans and America's Popular Image of the Vietnam War," *The Journal of Military History*, 82/1 (January 2018), 181–207.

Davies, A. Tegla, *Friends Ambulance Unit: The Hadfield–Spears Hospital Unit* (London: George Allen and Unwin, 1947).

Delmas, General Jean, "Synthèses des travaux du colloque," in Fondation pour les études de défense nationale, Institut d'histoire des conflits contemporains, Service historique de l'Armée de terre, Service historique de la

Marine, and Service historique de l'Armée de l'air, *Les armées française pendant la seconde guerre mondiale 1939–1945* (Paris: École nationale supérieure de techniques avancées, 1986).
Douglas, R. M., "Neither Apathetic nor Empathetic: Investigating and Prosecuting the Rape of German Civilians by U.S. Servicemen in 1945," *The Journal of Military History*, 87/2 (2023), 404–437.
Droit, Emmanuel and Reichherzer, Franz, "La fin de l'histoire du temps présent telle que nous l'avons connue. Plaidoyer franco-allemand pour l'abandon d'une singularité historique," *Vingtième Siècle. Revue d'histoire*, 2013/2, no. 118 (2013), 121–145.
Eismann, Gaël, "Maintenir l'ordre. Le MBF et la sécurité locale en France occupée," *Vingtième siècle. Revue d'histoire*, no. 98 (April–June 2008), 125–139, www.cairn.info/revue-vingtieme-siecle-revue-d-histoire-2008-2-page-125.htm.
Fauroux, Camille, "'Souvenirs d'une petite amie en captivité': Ouvrières françaises et prisonniers de guerre à Berlin entre 1940 et 1945," *Guerres mondiales et conflicts contemporains* (April–June 2019), 27–46.
Fieseler, Beate, Hampf, M. Michaela, and Schwarzkopf, Jutta, "Gendering combat: Military women's status in Britain, the United States, and the Soviet Union during the Second World War," *Women's Studies International Forum*, 47 (2014), 115–126.
Fishman, Sarah, "Grand Delusions: The Unintended Consequences of Vichy France's Prisoner of War Propaganda," *Journal of Contemporary History*, 26/2 (April 1991), 229–254.
Fitzpatrick, Sheila, "The Motherland Calls: "Soft" Repatriation of Soviet Citizens from Europe, 1945–1953," *The Journal of Modern History* 90/2 (June 2018), 323–350.
Flanagan, Drew, "La juste sévérité: Pacifier la zone française en Allemagne occupée, 1945–1949," in Connolly, James, Debruyne, Emmanuel, Julien, Élise, and Meirlaen, Matthias (eds.), *En territoire ennemi: Expériences d'occupation, transferts, héritages (1914–1949)* (Villeneuve d'Ascq: Presses universitaires du Septentrion, 2018), pp. 205–216.
Freedman, Lawrence, "Why War Fails. Russia's Invasion of Ukraine and the Limits of Military Power," *Foreign Affairs* (July–August 2022), www.foreignaffairs.com/articles/russian-federation/2022-06-14/ukraine-war-russia-why-fails.
Funk, Arthur Layton, "Les Américains et les britanniques dans la libération de la Corse," *Guerres mondiales et conflits contemporaines*, 174 (1994), 7–21.
Garraud, Philippe, "L'idéologie de la 'defensive' et ses effets stratégiques: Le rôle de la dimension cognitive dans la défaite de 1940," *Revue française de science politique*, 54, no. 2004/5 (2004), 781–810, www.cairn.info/revue-francaise-de-science-politique-2004-5-page-781.htm.
Gildea, Robert, "Resistance, Reprisals, and Community in Occupied France," *Transactions of the Royal Historical Society*, 13 (2003), 163–185.
Gras, Général Yves, "18 juin 1945. Le défilé de la victoire," http://ekladata.com/kdhGQ1qYOiIRpJvO1UgGm5QiYJs/1eredfl-n-51-8-Mai-18-Juin-1945-La-France-Libre-fete-sa-Victoire.pdf.
Gurley, Franklin L., "Politique contre stratégie: La défense de Strasbourg en décembre 1944," *Guerres mondiales et conflits contemporains*, no. 166 (April 1992), 89–114.
Hagemann, Karen, "Mobilizing Women for War: The History, Historiography, and Memory of German Women's War Service in Two World Wars," *Journal of Military History*, 75/4 (2011), 1055–1094.
Handel, Michael, "Intelligence and the Problem of Strategic Surprise," *The Journal of Strategic Studies*, 7/3 (September 1984), 229–281.
Hedinger, Daniel, "The Imperial Nexus: The Second World War and the Axis in Global Perspective," *Journal of Global History*, 12/2 (2017), 184–205.
Hofstadter, Richard, "The Paranoid Style of American Politics," *Harper's Magazine* (November 1964), 77–86.
Humbert, Laure, "French Politics of Relief and International Aid: France, UNRRA and Rescue of European Displaced Persons in Postwar Germany, 1945–47," *Journal of Contemporary History*, 51/3 (July 2016), 606–634.
Hundemann, Rainer, "The Army as an Occupying Power: The German Army in 1940–1944, the French Army in 1945–1949," in Müller, Klaus-Jürgen (ed.), *The Military in Politics and Society in France and Germany in the Twentieth Century* (Oxford and Washington, D.C.: Berg, 1995), 139–163.
Jackson, Julian, "General de Gaulle and His Enemies: Anti-Gaullism in France since 1940," *Transactions of the Royal Historical Society*, 9 (1999), 43–65.
Jackson, Peter, "Post-war Politics and the Historiography of French Strategy and Diplomacy before the Second World War," *History Compass*, 4/5 (2006), 870–905.
Jancar, Barbara, "Women in the Yugoslav National Liberation Movement: An Overview," *Studies in Comparative Communism*, 14/2 (1981), 143–164.
Jauneau, Élodie, "Des femmes dans la France combattante pendant la deuxième guerre mondiale: Le corps des volontaires françaises et le groupe Rochambeau," *Genre et Histoire*, 3 (Autumn 2008), https://journals.openedition.org/genrehistoire/373.

Johnson, Ian Ona, "Ernst Volckheim, Heinz Guderian, and the Origins of German Armored Doctrine," *The Journal of Military History*, 87/1 (January 2023), 145–168.

Jones, Edgar and Wessely, Simon, "British Prisoners-of-War: From Resilience to Psychological Vulnerability: Reality or Perception," *Twentieth Century British History*, 21/2 (2010), 163–183.

Lambauer, Barbara, "Un engagement pour l'Europe allemande: La collaboration," in Aglan, Alya and Frank, Robert (eds.), *1937–1947: La guerre-monde* (Paris: Gallimard/Folio, 2015), pp. 1109–1178.

Leconte, Robin, "Face au débarquement allié de novembre 1942: La Division de Marche de Constantine, entre obéissance et résistances aux ordres," in Miot, Claire, Piketty, Guillaume, and Vaisset, Thomas (eds.), *Militaires en résistances en France et en Europe* (Villeneuve d'Ascq: Presses universitaires du Septentrion, 2020), pp. 67–82.

Leconte, Robin, "The Commission d'enquête sur les repliements suspects and the 'Flight' of General Picard in May 1940," *Guerres mondiales et conflits contemporains*, 280/4 (4 October 2020), 27–45.

Le Gac, Julie, "L''étrange défaite' du divorce? (1940–1946)," *Vingtième Siècle. Revue d'histoire* 2005/4, no. 88 (2005), 49–62.

Le Gac, Julie, "Le corps expéditionnaire français et l'armée américaine en Italie (1943–1944): Une alliance asymétrique," *Revue historique des armées*, 258/210 (2010), 57–66, https://journals.openedition.org/rha/6923.

Le Gac, Julie, "'Le mal napolitain': Les Alliés et la prostitution à Naples (1943–1944)," *Genre et Histoire*, 15 (Autumn 2014–Spring 2015), https://journals.openedition.org/genrehistoire/2154.

Lesouef, Pierre, "La crise de novembre 1942 en Afrique française du nord et la campagne du Tunisie," in Fondation pour les études de défense nationale, Institut d'histoire des conflits contemporains, Service historique de l'Armée de terre, Service historique de la Marine, and Service historique de l'Armée de l'air, *Les armées française pendant la seconde guerre mondiale 1939–1945* (Paris: École nationale supérieure de techniques avancées, 1986), pp. 305–315.

Lieb, Peter, "Wehrmacht, Waffen-SS et Sipo/SD: La répression allemande en France 1943–1944," in *La répression en France à l'été 1944*, Actes du colloque organisé par la Foundation de la Résistance et la ville de Saint-Amand-Montrond, Saint-Amand-Montrond le mercredi 8 juin 2005, www.fondationresistance.org/documents/ee/Doc00004-002.pdf.

Lieb, Peter and Paxton, Robert O., "Maintenir l'ordre en France occupée. Combien de divisions?," *Vingtième Siècle. Revue d'histoire*, 2011/4, no. 112 (2011), 115–126.

Lily, J. and Le Roy, François, "L'armée américaine et les violes en France: Juin 1944–mai 1945," *Vingtième Siècle. Revue d'histoire*, 2002/3, no. 75 (2002), 109–121.

Lyautey, Hubert, "Du rôle social de l'officier," *Revue des deux mondes*, 3e période, 104 (1891), 443–459.

Major, Patrick, "'Our Friend Rommel': The *Wehrmacht* as 'Worthy Enemy' in Postwar British Popular Culture," *German History*, 26/4 (2008), 520–535.

Matloff, Maurice, "The ANVIL Decision: Crossroads of Strategy," in Roberts Greenfield, Kent (ed.), *Command Decisions* (Washington, D.C.: Center of Military History, United States Army, 1960), pp. 383–400, https://history.army.mil/books/70-7_16.htm.

Matsunuma Miho, "La politique du gouvernement de Vichy vis-à-vis des militaires coloniaux rapatriables," *Outre-Mers*, 97/362–363 (2009), 227–240, www.persee.fr/doc/outre_1631-0438_2009_num_96_362_4391.

McNab, Chris, "Cheap Shot: How the Sten Gun Saved Britain," *HistoryNet* (Autumn 2019), www.historynet.com/cheap-shot-how-the-sten-gun-saved-britain.htm.

Michalon, Lieutenant-colonel Roger, "L'amalgame F.F.I.–1ère Armée et 2ème D.B.," in Comité d'histoire de la Seconde Guerre mondiale, *La Libération de la France: Actes du Colloque international d'histoire de la 2ème guerre mondiale, 28–31 octobre 1974* (Paris: Ministère de la guerre, État-major de l'armée de terre, Service historique, 1974), pp. 1–55.

Miot, Claire, "Combattantes sans combattre? Le cas des ambulancières dans la première armée française (1944–1945)," *Revue historique des armées* 272 (2013), 25–35.

Miot, Claire, "La retrait des tirailleurs sénégalais de la première armée française en 1944. Hérésie stratégique, bricolage politique ou conservatisme coloniale?," *Vingtième siècle. Revue d'histoire*, no. 125 (2015), 77–89.

Monsuez, Jean-Jacques, "Les sections sanitaires automobiles féminines," *Revue historique des armées*, 247 (2007), 98–113, https://journals.openedition.org/rha/2033.

Moore, Bob, "Unruly Allies: British Problems with French Treatment of Axis Prisoners of War 1943–1945," *War in History*, 7/2 (April 2000), 180–198.

Morley, Neville, "Decadence as a Theory of History," *New Literary History*, 35/4 (Autumn 2004), 573–585.

Morris, Madeline, "By Force of Arms: Rape, War, and Military Culture," *Duke Law Journal*, 45/4 (February 1996), 651–781, https://scholarship.law.duke.edu/dlj/vol45/iss4/1.

Moullec, Gaël, "Alliés ou ennemis? Le GUPVI-NKVD, le Komintern et les 'Malgré-nous.' Le destin des prisonniers de guerre français en URSS (1942–1955)," *Cahiers du Monde russe*, 42/2–4 (April–December 2001), 667–678.

Muracciole, Jean-François, "La France a contribué à la victoire des Alliés," in Lopez, Jean and Wieviorka, Olivier (eds,), *Les mythes de la seconde guerre mondiale* (Paris: Perrin, 2015), pp. 329–352.

Nord, Philip, "Vichy et les survivances: Les Compagnons de France," *Revue d'histoire moderne et contemporaine*, 2012/4, no. 59 (2012), 125–163.

Nye, Robert A., "Neurasthenia and the Culture of Sport in Belle Epoque France," *Journal of Contemporary History*, 17/1 (January 1982), 51–68.

Offen, Karen, "Depopulation, Nationalism, and Feminism in Fin-de-Siècle France, *The American Historical Review*, 89/3 (June 1984), 648–676.

O'Hara, Vincent, "Operation Torch November 1942," in *Revue algérienne de prospective & d'études stratégiques* (2017), pp. 27–54.

Oliel, Jacob, "Les camps de Vichy en Afrique du Nord (1940–1944)," *Revue d'histoire de la Shoah*, 2013/1, no. 198 (2013), 227–244.

Patch, John, "Fortuitous Endeavor. Intelligence and Deception in Operation TORCH," *Naval War College Review*, 61/4 (Autumn 2008), 73–97.

Paxton, Robert O., "The Truth about the Resistance," *New York Review of Books* (2016), www.nybooks.com /articles/2016/02/25/truth-about-french-resistance.

Piketty, Guillaume, "Héros de la France libre – héros de la Résistance," *Revue de la France Libre*, no. 285 (1994), www.france-libre.net/sacrifice-brossolette.

Piketty, Guillaume, "Français libre à l'épreuve de la libération," *Revue historique des armées*, 245 (2006), 27–35.

Piketty, Guillaume, "Souffances et ambiguïtes de la défaite," *Hypothèses* 2008/1, no. 11 (2008), 341–348.

Piketty, Guillaume, "La Mission Arquebuse–Brumaire," www.charles-de-gaulle.org/wp-content/uploads/2017/10/La-mission-Arquebuse-Brumaire.pdf.

Piketty, Guillaume, "From the Capitoline Hill to the Tarpeian Rock? Free French Coming out of War," *European Review of History*, 25/2 (2018), 354–373.

Preston, Paul, "Spain. Betting on a Nazi Victory," in Richard J. B. Bosworth and Joseph A. Maiolo, *The Cambridge History of the Second World War*, volume II, *Politics and Ideology* (Cambridge: Cambridge University Press, 2015), 324–348.

Racine, Maryliz, "Le 'danger allemand.' L'évolution de la perception des members du Ministère des affairs étrangères françaises envers la menace allemande (1945–1954)," Mémoire de Maîtrise, Université Laval, Quebec, Canada, 2013.

Regnault, Jean-Marc and Kurtovich, Ismet, "Les ralliements du Pacifique en 1940. Entre legend gaulliste, enjeux stratégiques mondiaux et rivalités Londres/Vichy," *Revue d'histoire modern et contemporaine*, 2002/4, no. 49 (2002), 71–90.

Roberts, Sophie, "Jews, Vichy, and the Algiers Insurrection of 1942," *Holocaust Studies: A Journal of Culture and History*, 12/3 (Winter 2006), 63–88.

Sanders, Paul, "Anatomie d'une implantation SS – Helmut Knochen et la police nazie en France, 1940–1944," *Revue d'histoire de la Shoah*, 165 (January–April 1999), 111–145.

Schöttler, Peter, "Trois formes de collaboration: L'Europe et la réconciliation franco-allemande – à travers la carrière de Gustav Krukenberg, chef de la 'Division Charlemagne,'" *Allemagne d'aujourd'hui*, 2014/1, no. 207 (2014), 225–246, www.cairn.info/revue-allemagne-d-aujourd-hui-2014-1-page-225.htm.

Scianna, Bastian Matteo, "Rommel Almighty? Italian Assessments of the 'Desert Fox' during and after the Second World War," *The Journal of Military History*, 83/1 (January 2018), 125–145.

Shields, J. G., "Charlemagne's Crusaders. French Collaborators in Arms," *French Cultural Studies*, 18/1 (February 2007), 83–105.

Smith, Leonard V., "Paul Fussell's *The Great War and Modern Memory*: Twenty-Five Years Later," *History and Theory*, 40/2 (May 2001), 241–260.

Soucy, Robert J., "The Nature of Fascism in France," *Journal of Contemporary History*, 1/1 (1966), 27–55.

Storer, Mrs. Bellamy and Storer, Maria Longworth, "The Decadence of France," *The North American Review*, 191/651 (February 1910), 168–184.

Strachan, Hew, "Strategy and Democracy," *Survival*, 62/2 (2020), 51–82.

Taguieff, Pierre-André, "L'invention du 'complot Judéo-Maçonnique.' Avatars d'un mythe apocalyptique moderne," *Revue d'Histoire de la Shoah*, 2013/1, no. 98 (2013), 23–97.

Tenenbaum, Elie, "French Exception or Western Variation? A Historical Look at the French Irregular Way of War," *Journal of Strategic Studies*, 40/4 (2017), 554–576.

Thomas, Martin, "After Mers-el-Kebir: The Armed Neutrality of the Vichy Navy," *English Historical Review*, 112/447 (June 1997), 643–670.

Thomas, Martin, "France and the Czechoslovakian Crisis," *Diplomacy and Statecraft*, 10 (1999), 122–159.

Thomas, Martin, "The Vichy Government and French Colonial Prisoners of War, 1940–1944," *French Historical Studies*, 25/4 (Fall 2002), 657–692.

Trevor-Roper, H. R., "Fernand Braudel, the *Annales,* and the Mediterranean," *The Journal of Modern History*, 44/4 (December 1972), 468–479.

Varley, Karine, "'Laboratory of Liberation.' Lessons for France from the Liberation of Corsica," https://francehistory.wordpress.com/2014/05/31/laboratory-of-liberation-lessons-for-france-from-the-liberation-of-corsica.

Varley, Karine, "Defending Sovereignty without Collaboration: Vichy and the Italian Fascist Threats of 1940–1942," *French History*, 33/3 (2019), 422–443.

Vial, Philippe (ed.), "L'histoire d'une revolution. La Marine depuis 1870," *Études marines*, no. 4 (March 2013).

Virgili, Fabrice, "Les viols commis par l'armée allemande en France (1940–1944)," *Vingtième siècle. Revue d'histoire*, 2016/2, no. 130 (2016),103–120.

Weber, Eugen, "Gymnastics and Sports in *fin de siècle* France: Opium of the Classes?," *American Historical Review*, 76/1 (February 1971), 70–98.

Weber, Eugen, "France's Downfall," *The Atlantic* (October 2001), www.theatlantic.com/magazine/archive/2001/10/frances-downfall/302317.

Weiss, Stéphane, "Quotidien et moral des combattants volontaires des sièges de la Pointe de Grave, de Royan et de La Rochelle en 1944–1945," *Écrits d'Ouest*, no. 19 (2011), 127–146.

Weiss, Stéphane, "La régularisation des formations combattantes FFI engagés lors des sièges de la Pointe de Grave, de Royan et de La Rochelle en 1944–1945," *Écrits d'Ouest*, no. 20 (2012), 175–192.

Weiss, Stéphane, "Recréer une artillerie française en 1945: La part belle à la recuperation," *Révue historique des armées*, 274 (2014), 95–107.

Winter, Jay, "Cultural Divergences in Patterns of Remembering the Great War in Britain and France," in Robert Tombs and Emile Chabal (eds.), *Britain and France in Two World Wars: Truth, Myth and Memory* (London: Bloomsbury, 2013), pp. 161–178.

Wood, Elisabeth, "Rape as a Practice of War: Toward a Typology of Political Violence," *Politics & Society* 46/4 (2018), 523–537.

Xueref, Louis, "Mémoires d'outre-mer. 1942–1943 (Autour de la campagne de Tunisie). Souvenirs d'une tranche de vie," http://tunisie-france.pagesperso-orange.fr/souvenirs_souvenirs.htm.

Ziemke, Earl F. "Improvising Stability and Change in Postwar Germany," in Wolfe, Robert (ed.), *Americans as Proconsuls: United States Military Government in Germany and Japan, 1944–1952* (Carbondale and Edwardsville, IL: Southern Illinois University Press, 1977).

Index

Page numbers in *italics* refer to illustrations